ENGLISH HISTORICAL DOCUMENTS

General Editor
DAVID C. DOUGLAS
M.A., F.B.A.

ENGLISH HISTORICAL DOCUMENTS

General Editor: DAVID C. DOUGLAS, M.A., F.B.A.

The following is a complete list of volumes in preparation; those marked * are already published

GENERAL PREFACE

ENGLISH HISTORICAL DOCUMENTS is a work designed to meet a present need. Its purpose is to make generally accessible a wide selection of the fundamental sources of English history.

During the past half-century there has been an immense accumulation of historical material, but only a fraction of this has been made readily available to the majority of those who teach or who study history. The transcendent importance of the original authorities is recognized, but direct approach to them remains difficult, and even some of the basic texts (which are frequently quoted) are hard to consult. A gulf has thus opened between the work of the specialist scholar and those students, both at schools and universities, who best can profit by his labours. Historical studies tend too often today to consist of a commentary on documents which are not included in the available books; and, in the absence of any representative and accessible collection of the sources, the formation of opinion proceeds without that direct study of the evidence which alone can give validity to historical judgment. Correspondingly, the reading public outside schools and universities, has no adequate means of checking, by reference to the evidence itself, tendentious or partial interpretations of the past.

The editors of these volumes consider that this situation now calls for a remedy. They have striven to supply one by providing what they hope can be regarded as an authoritative work in primary reference.

An enterprise of this nature could only be effective if planned on a large scale. In scope and content, therefore, these volumes differ materially from the conventional "source-books" which usually contain only a restricted number of selected extracts. Here, within much wider limits, each editor has sought to produce a comprehensive *corpus* of evidence relating generally to the period with which he deals. His aim, in each case, has been to present the material with scholarly accuracy, and without bias. Editorial comment has thus been directed in the main towards making the evidence intelligible, and not to drawing conclusions from it. Full account has been taken of modern textual criticism to compile a reliable collection of authentic testimony, but the reader has in general been left to pass his own judgment upon this, and to appraise for himself the value of current historical verdicts. For this reason, everything in this work has been presented in such a manner as to be comprehensible by readers of English, and critical bibliographies have been added to assist further investigation.

The decision to display the texts (where necessary) in an English translation was thus dictated by the general purpose of this work. A translated text can, of course, never be a complete substitute for the original. But those who, today, can utilize a document in Anglo-Saxon, Latin or Old French are few, and are decreasing in number. This is certainly to be regretted. Nevertheless, there seems no adequate reason why the majority of those interested in English history should be arbitrarily deprived of the opportunity to consult the basic sources of their study. In this work, therefore, there is nothing that cannot be used by those who can only read English. At the same time, in every case where a translation appears, a reference is given to the place where the text in its original language may be found. In like manner, spelling and punctuation have been adapted to modern usage in all texts prior to 1714. After that date, all documents are in their original form.

The editors of these volumes are fully aware of the magnitude of the undertaking to which they have addressed themselves. They are conscious of the hazards of selecting from the inexhaustible store of historical material. They realize also the difficulties involved in editing so large a mass of very varied texts in accordance with the exigent demands of modern scholarship. They believe, however, that the essential prerequisite for the healthy development of English historical studies is wider acquaintance with the original authorities for English history. And they are content that their work should be judged by the degree to which they have succeeded in promoting this object.

DAVID DOUGLAS

VOLUME I

ENGLISH HISTORICAL DOCUMENTS
c. 500 — 1042

ENGLISH
HISTORICAL DOCUMENTS

c. 500–1042

Edited by

DOROTHY WHITELOCK

M.A., Litt.D., F.S.A.

Vice-Principal of St. Hilda's College, Oxford

1968

OXFORD UNIVERSITY PRESS

New York

First published 1955
Reprinted 1961 and 1968
Printed in East Germany
1.3

ACKNOWLEDGEMENTS

MY prime obligation is to Sir Frank Stenton, who has given his encouragement to the work since its inception and has generously bestowed his time on the discussion of innumerable problems and on help with the proofs. He has also allowed the map at the end of his *Anglo-Saxon England* to be used as the basis of the one at the front of this volume. At the time of writing these acknowledgements, it is uncertain which of the two, this volume or his book, *The Latin Charters of the Anglo-Saxon Period* (Clarendon Press, Oxford), will first appear; but he has kindly allowed me to read his proofs, and thus to have the relief of knowing that we are in essential agreement on Anglo-Saxon diplomatic.

It would be impossible to mention all the scholars who have given inspiration and help to a work carried on over several years. My special thanks are due to Dr. Eleanor S. Duckett, who has placed her knowledge of Medieval Latin at my disposal; to Mr. H. P. R. Finberg, who has given invaluable help with the difficult problem of setting out the text of the Anglo-Saxon Chronicle and has frequently made useful suggestions on other matters; to Professor I. Ll. Foster for his help with Nennius; to Mr. J. M. Wallace-Hadrill for information on the continental sources; and to Mr. N. R. Ker for answering my frequent palaeographical queries. A heavy claim has been made on the time and knowledge of my colleagues Miss Beryl Smalley and Miss Kathleen Major, concerning all types of problems as they arose. In addition, useful information has been supplied by Professor Bruce Dickins, Mr. Bertram Colgrave, Dr. Kenneth Sisam, Professor R. R. Darlington, Dr. Florence Harmer, Sir Edmund Craster, Mrs. M. J. Gelling, and Mr. Richard Vaughan. To all of these I offer my sincere thanks, and also to the officials and assistants of the Bodleian Library and of the Department of Manuscripts in the British Museum for much valuable service.

Moreover, I am indebted to some scholars for permission to use their translations: namely to Mr. Alistair Campbell in respect of No. 28; to Miss Margaret Ashdown in respect of Nos. 10, 12, 13 and 15; to Mr. Bertram Colgrave in respect of No. 154. I wish also to thank the Council of the Royal Historical Society for their permission in respect of No. 28, the Cambridge University Press in respect of Nos. 10, 12, 13, 15 and 154, as well as for permission to reprint here my own translations of Nos. 116, 121, 125, 126, 130 and part of 212, and the Clarendon Press, Oxford, for allowing the use of the map from Sir Frank Stenton's *Anglo-Saxon England*. Penguin Books Ltd. has kindly permitted me to re-use many scattered quotations used as illustration in my *Beginnings of English Society*, and I reprint No. 47 by the courtesy of the *English Historical Review*. All other translations are new, except that that of Bede's *Ecclesiastical History* is in some measure based on that of J. A. Giles, and that quotations from the Vulgate are usually given in the Douai version.

DOROTHY WHITELOCK

Oxford
7 August 1954

NOTE ON DATES
AND THE
SPELLING OF PROPER NAMES

Where there is a discrepancy of one year in the dating of an event in different parts of this volume, this is because of the practice of various records of using different systems of commencing the year, *e.g.* at 24 September or at Christmas. There is no certain instance in this volume of the commencement at the Annunciation.

As Anglo-Saxon personal names occur in a multiplicity of forms, varying with the date and locality of the document, and also with scribal preferences, their spelling presents great difficulty and consistency is impossible. The system here used is to give the name elements in the same form throughout, except in the case of names still in use or of those where some other spelling has become accepted and familiar by long use. The spelling in the few texts where a previously printed translation has been used has been altered into agreement with this system.

LIST OF ABBREVIATIONS

Æthelweard. *Chronicorum Libri Quatuor.* (See p. 129.)

Attenborough. *The Laws of the Earliest English Kings*, ed. F. L. Attenborough (Cambridge, 1922).

Birch. *Cartularium Saxonicum*, ed. W. de G. Birch (London, 1885–1893).

Brit. Mus. Facs. *Facsimiles of Ancient Charters in the British Museum*, ed. E. A. Bond (London, 1873–1878).

Chronicle. The Anglo-Saxon Chronicle.

Dümmler. *Alcuini Epistolae*, ed. E. Dümmler (*Mon. Germ. Hist., Epist. Karol. Aevi*, II, 1895).

Earle. *A Hand-Book to the Land-Charters and other Saxonic Documents*, ed. J. Earle (Oxford, 1888).

Emerton. E. Emerton, *The Letters of St. Boniface* (Columbia University Records of Civilization, 1940).

Florence. *Florentii Wigorniensis Monachi Chronicon ex Chronicis*, ed. B. Thorpe (London, 1848).

Haddan and Stubbs. *Councils and Ecclesiastical Documents*, ed. A. W. Haddan and W. Stubbs (Oxford, 1871).

Harmer. *Select English Historical Documents of the Ninth and Tenth Centuries*, ed. F. E. Harmer (Cambridge, 1914).

Jónson, F. *Den norsk-islandske Skjaldedigtning* (Copenhagen, 1908–1915).

Kemble. *Codex Diplomaticus Aevi Saxonici*, ed. J. M. Kemble (London, 1839–1848).

Kock. *Den norsk-isländska Skaldediktningen*, ed. E. A. Kock (Lund, 1946).

Kylie. E. Kylie, *The English Correspondence of Saint Boniface* (London, 1911).

Liebermann. *Die Gesetze der Angelsachsen*, ed. F. Liebermann (Halle, 1903–1916).

Ord. Surv. Facs. Ordnance Survey, *Facsimiles of Anglo-Saxon Manuscripts*, ed. W. B. Sanders (Southampton, 1878–1884).

Robertson. *The Laws of the Kings of England from Edmund to Henry I*, ed. A. J. Robertson (Cambridge, 1925).

Select Essays in Anglo-Saxon Law. Four essays, by H. Adams, H. C. Lodge, E. Young, and J. L. Laughlin, with an appendix of *Select Cases in Anglo-Saxon Law* (Boston, 1876).

Simeon. *Symeonis Monachi Historia Regum*, ed. T. Arnold (*Symeonis Monachi Opera Omnia*, II, 1885).

Tangl. *S. Bonifatii et Lullii Epistolae*, ed. M. Tangl (*Mon. Germ. Hist., Epist. Selectae*, I, 1916).

Thorpe. *Ancient Laws and Institutes of England*, ed. B. Thorpe (London, 1840).

Thorpe, *Diplomatarium. Diplomatarium Anglicum Aevi Saxonicum*, ed. B. Thorpe (London, 1865).

Vigfusson and Powell. *Corpus Poeticum Boreale*, ed. Gudbrand Vigfusson and F. York Powell (Oxford, 1883).

Whitelock. *Anglo-Saxon Wills*, ed. D. Whitelock (Cambridge, 1930).

Psalms are referred to by the numbering in the Vulgate.

CONTENTS

PART II. CHARTERS AND LAWS

A. THE LAWS

B. THE CHARTERS

INTRODUCTION

INTRODUCTION

(i) THE PERIOD

THIS volume contains most of the principal sources for English history from the time of the settlement of Germanic tribes in Britain until the accession of Edward the Confessor. It is a period of over five and a half centuries, and it saw the conversion of the English to Christianity, the union of England from a number of small kingdoms into a single monarchy, the long struggles against viking attack and the eventual absorption of a large Scandinavian population, and the development of an advanced culture which influenced western and northern Europe. While it could easily be divided into political periods, these would not fit other aspects of its history. In many ways English society remained remarkably stable and it is often possible to illustrate a particular institution or manner of thought from documents of widely different dates.

It is not practical to place the documents in strictly chronological order, since some are concerned with several periods, while rigid division by subject matter is impossible, for almost any document may contain evidence on many different aspects of history. Instead, the material is arranged in three divisions: chronicles and other works historical in intent; laws and charters; ecclesiastical documents, with which, since learning and Church history are inextricably interwoven, such literary remains are included as do not more naturally fall under the first head. This division is somewhat arbitrary, for some law-codes are almost entirely concerned with ecclesiastical matters, and the charter was in origin an ecclesiastical instrument, but it has practical convenience. The chief problem was the placing of Bede's *Ecclesiastical History*, for this is hardly less important for the political history of the early period than is the Chronicle for later times. It may seem illogical to divorce it from this and from the Northumbrian annals which form a continuation to Bede's work; but it is equally difficult to separate it from ecclesiastical biographies, and, since it is only incidentally, and not as part of its intent, that it affords information on other than ecclesiastical affairs, it is placed in Part III. With this exception, it would be true to say that Part I is most important for political history, Part II for administration and social life, Part III for the history of the Church, of education and of scholarship; but in fact, no full account can be written on any of these topics without using material from all three parts of the volume.

(ii) THE SOURCES

The documents in this volume consist of the more important of the contemporary sources for Anglo-Saxon history up to 1042, together with passages from post-Conquest writers who had access to contemporary materials which have not come down to us.

The two outstanding authorities, in significance as well as in bulk, are the Anglo-Saxon Chronicle and Bede's *Ecclesiastical History*. The first is given complete up to 1042, except for some additions made at Canterbury and Peterborough after the Conquest which are of no importance for pre-Conquest history; the great length of the second makes it impossible to print it here in full, but very large extracts are given, with indications of the content of omitted passages. Between them, these two works include a large proportion of the consecutive narrative of Anglo-Saxon history; but each has its limitations. Bede in writing a history of the Church did not set out to trace the history of the various kingdoms. Much can be learnt by reassembling his scattered statements, especially as concerns Northumbria; he was less well informed on events in other kingdoms, though it is not always safe to assume his ignorance when he omits to mention matters with no direct bearing on his subject. The value of the Chronicle varies in different periods. During all its earlier portion its entries can be tantalizingly brief. Sometimes, where we have other evidence for comparison, we can tell how much may lie behind a simple entry: the statement in 664 "and Colman went with his companions to his own land", is all we should have learnt from the Chronicle of the important Synod of Whitby;[1] equally momentous events may lie behind brief references to which we have no key. It may tell us that certain kings fought at a given place, but not the result of the battle; and there are stretches of some length when the Alfredian compiler could find little material. After becoming a full contemporary record for the Danish wars of Alfred and his son Edward, it is again very barren for the mid tenth century, and the excellent account of the reign of Ethelred the Unready is followed by a few scrappy annals for that of Cnut. During its Alfredian section its interests are predominantly West Saxon, and quite important events in the Midlands and North find no mention. Some of the omissions in the original chronicle were later remedied in individual manuscripts, but these additions have not the authority of a contemporary record.

The picture obtainable from these two major sources can be supplemented by other narrative sources, by Saints' Lives, of which the most useful are those which supply evidence for periods where the Chronicle is barren; by Asser's Life of King Alfred; and by the annals and other materials embedded in the work of post-Conquest authors. Some light is shed by references to English

[1] No. 1, p. 153. Cf. No. 151, pp. 639–642; No. 154, pp. 692 f.

affairs in foreign sources, Celtic, continental and Scandinavian, or by incidental statements or implications in sources that are not narrative, in laws, charters, letters and homilies. There are periods and areas when the course of events can be ascertained only by piecing together such incidental scraps of information. Many documents which supply information of this kind are included in this volume, but it has naturally not been possible to include all; my aim has been to supply a representative selection of the various types of record, and to refer in the introductions to important information not included in the chosen texts.

What can be assembled from the texts here given forms a framework into which evidence of other kinds may be fitted. No student of Anglo-Saxon history can rest content with contemporary written materials alone. This is true of political and ecclesiastical history, but still more so of economic and social history, where much of the evidence must be drawn from records of post-Conquest date. As Professor Douglas rightly says, "Domesday Book is a description of the England of Edward the Confessor almost as much as of the England of William I",[1] and many of the institutions and conditions it describes had arisen long before Edward's accession. Surveys and charters of the twelfth century and later may illumine pre-Conquest conditions: e.g. the peculiar features of land-holding in East Anglia probably date from the viking settlement, but we learn of them only in post-Conquest records.

Moreover, the statements in written documents, whether contemporary or later, are not the only sources for Anglo-Saxon history. They can be supplemented by archaeological remains, by coins, by place-names, by linguistic data, by studying the movement of manuscripts, the various influences on handwriting, or the spread of art motifs.

In conclusion, a word must be said on the question of survival. Bede's work and the Chronicle have come down in several manuscripts, because they were much read; but many documents have survived in one manuscript alone – or even only in an early printed text – and often the survival is not to be ascribed to their intrinsic value, but to a fortunate chance, or series of chances. No record had any chance of survival which did not reach ecclesiastical keeping, and hence it is dangerous to infer from the great preponderance of documents of ecclesiastical interest that secular records were rare. Moreover the muniments of some churches had better chances of survival than others. The burning of York minster in William's reign has much to do with the paucity of records from this area. Because of the danger of false assumptions based on the chance survival of records, I have been at pains in the separate introductions to indicate the relation of what survives to what may reasonably be assumed to have been lost.

There are some subjects on which it is impossible, even after pooling all sources of information, to give anything like a full account. The material for

[1] Vol. II, p. 10.

the reign of Offa is inadequate, there is a dearth of documents for the North after the Viking Age, and accounts of King Edgar are mainly one-sided and biased. In the following pages particular attention has been given to what can be gathered from the scanty evidence for such periods.

(iii) THE ENGLISH CONQUEST AND SETTLEMENT

There is little written evidence to allow us to date the English invasions and trace their course with any precision. English traditions were not put into writing until generations later, continental writers show little knowledge of events in Britain, and the only nearly contemporary British writer whose work has survived, Gildas, who wrote just before 547, was not writing history, but a tirade against the sins and excesses of the British kings of his day. Yet, in spite of its lack of precise detail, of names and of dates, his work is of great importance,[1] and not least in that the parts concerned with the English invasion were included by Bede in his *Ecclesiastical History*, and hence coloured the views of all later Anglo-Saxon writers regarding their early history. They accepted at their face-value his outpourings on the sins of the Britons, and were willing enough to regard their own ancestors, the invaders, as the instrument of an avenging God. Thus Bede, in his famous chapter on the invasion,[2] compares it to the destruction of Jerusalem by the Chaldeans; Alcuin writes of "the country which God conceded by his free gift to our forefathers"[3] and sometimes refers to Gildas and to the fate of the Britons when calling his contemporaries to reform; and Archbishop Wulfstan in 1014 borrows and translates one of these passages for the same purpose, stating that God "finally allowed the army of the English to conquer their land and to destroy the host of the Britons entirely".[4] The pride the English took in their achievement can be seen at the end of the poem on the battle of *Brunanburh*.[5] It is ironic that one effect of Gildas's book was to offer to English writers an argument to justify excesses against the Britons.

Gildas is the oldest authority for the landing of the newcomers as allies. Bede, and others after him, identified the leaders of this party with Hengest and Horsa, and the Chronicle can add a few details of their battles, presumably from Kentish tradition.[6] The use by Gildas of an English word for the three ships (*kyulis*) in which they came shows that he was not unaware of English as well as British traditions. As to the date of this event, all that one can learn from Gildas is that he placed it some time after an ineffectual appeal for help had been sent to Aetius during his third consulate (446). When Bede places the arrival in the joint reign of Marcian and Valentinian, which he dates 449–456, he may be using some other source, possibly a regnal list of the kings of Kent. This date is repeated in his chronological summary under the year 449, and

---

[1] The part of Gildas's work which deals with the English invasion can be read in No. 151, pp. 590–595.
[2] No. 151, pp. 593–595. [3] No. 202. [4] No. 240. [5] No. 1, p. 201. [6] No. 1, p. 143.

hence this is the year from which later Anglo-Saxon writers calculate the passage of time since the coming of the English.[1] Little significance need be attached to variant dating in Nennius, for his date 428, which occurs more than once in his work, is probably attributable to the influence of the Life of St. Germanus, which refers to a battle against the Saxons and Picts during Germanus's first visit to Britain in 429, and it is usually held that the Saxons concerned are a raiding band rather than settlers in Britain. The date 375,[2] given by Nennius in another place, and also added to genealogical material in a Corpus manuscript,[3] is impossibly early, and doubtless derived by both authorities from a common blundered source. The divergent dating in two Gaulish chroniclers, however, requires more serious attention: one, which goes no further than 452, says that Britain "was brought into the power of the Saxons" in the nineteenth year of Theodosius (i.e. 441–442); the other, which extends to 511, makes a similar claim for the sixteenth year of Theodosius.[4] Such strong wording can hardly refer to the peaceful settlement of three boatloads of allies; it could refer to the results of the subsequent revolt, which spread "from the eastern to the western sea".[5] Hence, if these are contemporary writers, we must either reject the letter to Aetius, or assume that Gildas mistook its occasion, and that the barbarians mentioned in it are the English, not the Picts and Scots. But the fact that these chronicles break off in 452 and 511 respectively is not overwhelming evidence that they were written soon after these dates; and the author of the Life of St. Germanus, writing about 480, mentions a second visit of the saint to Britain, about 447, without any reference to their subjection to the Saxons. Though the evidence of written documents is not clear enough to fix a precise date, they cannot be used to prove the traditional date far wrong.

Of Bede's other additions to Gildas's account, the threefold division of the invaders into Angles, Saxons and Jutes has the appearance of genuine tradition.[6] It is supported by the names West, East, Middle and South Saxons and East and Middle Angles, but Bede was not merely theorizing from such names, which would not have told him that the Mercians and Northumbrians were Angles, the people of Kent, the Isle of Wight and part of Hampshire, Jutes. The correctness of this allotment is borne out by the descent of the kings of Mercia from kings who reigned in continental Angel, while the memory of Jutes in Hampshire survived long enough for Florence of Worcester to say that the New Forest was called *Ytene* [7] by the English. Yet the documents in this volume

---

[1] In other parts of his work Bede avoids precise dating. He puts the coming of the English about 150 years before Augustine's mission, about 180 years before 627, about 285 years before 731 (No. 151, pp. 618, 682 f.). Though these are round figures only, they suggest that Bede did not think of the first settlement as much later than 449, for he would surely have used 280, not 285, if he thought it could be placed a year or two after 450. [2] Literally, 349 after the Passion.

[3] C.C.C.C., MS. 183. See H. M. Chadwick, *The Origin of the English Nation*, p. 41.

[4] These texts are edited in *Mon. Germ. Hist.*, *Auct. Antiq.*, IX, pp. 660 f. [5] No. 151, p. 594.

[6] *ibid.* [7] *i.e.* 'of the Jutes'. See *Chronicon ex Chronicis*, ed. Thorpe, II, pp. 44 f.

include several instances which show that Bede's distinction was not much observed. Celtic authors speak of the Germanic inhabitants of Britain as Saxons: thus Nennius speaks of Saxon robbers, referring to the Northumbrians,[1] and Adamnan uses the term *Saxonia* to include Anglian territory.[2] Anglo-Latin writers sometimes follow this usage: Abbot Hwætberht of Wearmouth in his letter to Pope Gregory II,[3] Eddi in his Life of Wilfrid,[4] Felix in his Life of Guthlac,[5] and Alcuin in his Life of Willibrord,[6] all use 'Saxon' to include, or even specifically apply to, the people of Northumbria, who are Angles according to Bede's division, and Boniface says Willibrord, a Northumbrian, was of Saxon race.[7] On the other hand Gregory I addressed Ethelbert of Kent as king of the Angles,[8] and Bede himself says that Eorcenberht of Kent was "the first of the kings of the Angles" to order the destruction of idols,[9] though the kings of Kent were of Jutish origin. In fact, it is abundantly clear from the title of Bede's work and from numerous passages in it that his term 'the Angles' can be used to include all the Germanic settlers in Britain. Nor is it only Bede, a Northumbrian and therefore an Angle, who so uses it. The West Saxon Boniface addresses a letter "to all God-fearing catholics in common, sprung from the stock and race of the Angles", and refers to himself as "a native of that same race".[10] Some of his other letters show that he, like Bede, uses Angles to cover the nation as a whole.[11] So does Archbishop Cuthbert[12] and Abbot Cuthbert of Wearmouth[13] and many others, and when later we get vernacular writings, we find that *Angelcynn* 'Angle-race' is the normal term for the whole race, and English the name of its language, even in the terminology of the West Saxon king Alfred.[14] It seems clear that original tribal differences had little significance by the early eighth century.

Men were far more conscious of their common Germanic origin. Bede refers to this again when speaking of Egbert's desire to convert heathen races in Germany,[15] and Boniface's appeal to all the English to further the conversion of the continental Saxons, since they were "of one blood and one bone" with them,[16] called forth a letter from Torhthelm, bishop of Leicester, in which he refers to the pagan Saxons as "our people".[17] The Anglo-Saxon poem called *Widsith*, with its lists of rulers and heroes of ancient German tribes, and the

---

[1] No. 2, p. 236.   [2] No. 153.   [3] No. 155, p. 705.   [4] No. 154, p. 694.
[5] No. 156, p. 711. But he also uses "language of the Angles" to describe the vernacular (ed. Birch, p. 11), and "nation of the Angles" when it is by no means certain that he is making any distinction between it and 'the Saxon Race' (see p. 711 n. 3).   [6] No. 157.
[7] See Levison, *England and the Continent*, p. 92.   [8] No. 151, p. 603.   [9] No. 151, p. 628.   [10] No. 174.
[11] Nos. 171, 177, 178. When it is used in this sense, I have translated it in accordance with general practice 'English', reserving 'Angles' for references to this separate tribe.
[12] No. 183.   [13] No. 185.
[14] No. 226. The combination which eventually became "Anglo-Saxon" rose on the Continent to distinguish the Saxons in Britain from those of Germany. It is used in No. 191, the report of the legates, and in Asser (No. 7, p. 264). See further Levison, *England and the Continent*, p. 92, n. Later it was sometimes used in England, *e.g.* in the regnal styles of tenth-century kings (see Nos. 100, 103, 105). See further Stevenson's *Asser*, pp. 148f.
[15] No. 151, p. 671.   [16] No. 174.   [17] Tangl, No. 47.

allusions to such persons and their exploits in *Beowulf* and *Deor*, reveal the close interest taken by the Anglo-Saxons of Christian times in the stories of other Germanic peoples, although only fragments survive of narrative poems on these heroic legends.[1] No doubt the consciousness of common origin was kept alive among the Germanic tribes settled in Britain by their nearness to Celtic peoples speaking a different language. The frequency of intermarriage between royal families may have helped. And this sense of kinship may have been one factor in the ready acceptance by the various English kingdoms of the idea of a single Church for them all, an idea which in its turn must have deepened any pre-existing feeling of unity.

The problems relating to the history of these tribes on the Continent cannot be entered into here. It is enough to say that there is supporting evidence for Bede's location of the Angles in *Angulus*, a name which survives in the modern Angeln in Holstein, but that the Saxons in the fifth century were a more maritime people than the Old Saxons of Bede's day, and archæological evidence shows them penetrating into the coastlands of Frisian territory from the fourth century. Procopius, writing in the middle of the sixth century in Constantinople, had learnt, presumably from a Frankish embassy, that Britain was inhabited by Angles, Frisians and Britons, and this suggests either that his informants failed to distinguish between two closely related peoples, or that the term Saxons was a name covering a confederacy, in which Frisians were included. The greatest difficulty in accepting Bede's statements in full is, however, with regard to the Jutes, for, while Bede implies that they dwelt north of the Angles, the evidence of archaeological remains in the parts of England in which Bede says they settled, and of the structure of Kentish society as ascertainable in later times, seems to connect them rather with the Rhineland than with Jutland. This has led to the opinion that Bede was misled by an accidental resemblance in names to locate in Jutland a rather mysterious people occasionally mentioned in continental sources along with the Saxons. Between the Anglian and Saxon districts of England, however, there are no discernible differences in social structure, while such archaeological differences as date from the period of settlement suggest a more complicated picture than the broad lines of Bede's account.[2]

To the tradition of the settlement of Kent under the leadership of Hengest and Horsa, the Chronicle added some entries about the origin of Wessex and Sussex.[3] The memory of chieftains who lived long before the keeping of written records can only have been preserved in genealogies and verse accounts of their exploits; and it would be absurd to expect precise dating of incidents whose

---

[1] A fragment of a poem, known as *Finnsburg*, which dealt with a story briefly treated in *Beowulf*; two fragments, *Waldere*, of a story which is the theme of a tenth-century Latin poem by Ekkehard of St. Gall; and possibly an obscure fragment once thought to be a riddle, now known as *Wulf and Eadwacer*.

[2] See authorities cited on pp. 102 f.   [3] No. 1, pp. 143-145.

memory was preserved in this way. Nor should we expect such accounts to be complete or free from bias. Only the more stirring events were likely to be celebrated in song, and the poet would naturally emphasize the part played by his own ancestors or those of his patron. Thus we should not be unduly disturbed by the apparent discrepancy between the Chronicle's account of the beginnings of Wessex by invasions from the south coast and archaeological evidence showing earlier settlements in the valley of the upper Thames, even if the tradition of penetration from the south coast had not the support of a group of early place-names in South Berkshire.[1] It is not surprising that the West Saxon chronicler should know only of the traditions of how the ancestors of his royal house came to Britain. Another difficulty in reconciling our sources, the discrepancy between Gildas's claim, that after the battle of *Mons Badonicus* (about 500) the Britons had a respite from foreign war, and the absence of any such period of peace in the Chronicle, is removed if, as Sir Frank Stenton suggests, we reject the Chronicle's dating of West Saxon successes in 514 and the following years, which appear to be merely a variant tradition of the landing of Cerdic and Cynric entered under 495, and their battles between that year and 508.[2] Gildas's claim that the invaders had received a setback is confirmed by Procopius, who speaks of large-scale migrations of Angles and Frisians as well as of Britons to Frankish territory about this time, while a tradition of the continental Saxons that their ancestors came from the Angles of Britain seems to enshrine a memory of a migration from Britain at a time when further advance there was blocked.[3]

Bede, who did not regard it as relevant to his theme to set out all he knew of events in heathen days, mentions in passing two of the persons who figure in the early part of the Chronicle, Ælle of Sussex and Ceawlin of Wessex, as the first two holders of an overlordship over all the provinces south of the Humber.[4] Of the origins of Northumbria he tells us nothing except that Ida, the founder of the royal family of the Bernicians, began to reign in 547.[5] A little can be added from Celtic sources. A poem called the *Gododdin*[6] shows how exposed Northumbria was to attack before Æthelfrith's victory at *Degsastan*.[7] Nennius may have derived the information he adds to the genealogies, information which shows that the English in Bernicia had little more than a precarious hold on the coast of Bernicia, from sources of a similar type.[8]

There is no written evidence at all for the settlement of a large part of England, so that we are entirely dependent on archaeology and place-names. Neither allows precise dates to be given, and further evidence may be brought to light to cause existing views to be modified. At any rate archaeological remains show that in the heathen period the English controlled the country as

---

[1] See F. M. Stenton, *Trans. Royal Hist. Soc.*, 4th Series, XXII, pp. 17f.
[2] *Anglo-Saxon England*, pp. 20–23.   [3] *ibid.*, pp. 4–8.   [4] No. 151, p. 610.
[5] No. 151, p. 683.   [6] See p. 117.   [7] No. 151, p. 605.   [8] No. 2.

far west as Wiltshire, Somerset, and the extreme east of Dorset in the South, and as far as the lower Severn, Staffordshire and Derbyshire in the Midlands. They were thickly settled in East Yorkshire and the plain of York, whereas remains are rare in Northumberland and Durham. Remains are earliest and most abundant in the coastal zones from Southampton Water to the Wash, in the great river basins, *i.e.* the middle reaches of the Nene, with its tributary the Soar, and of the Ouse with its tributaries the Cam and the Lark, the upper Thames and the south bank of the lower Thames, and in East Yorkshire. Place-names with heathen associations, or with elements which do not occur in districts of late settlement, are found in much the same area, though the correspondence is not exact. There are several early names in parts of Essex where no archaeological remains have as yet come to light, whereas some areas with early archaeological remains have few early names.

The expansion of the English settlements at the expense of the British inhabitants continued into historic times, and is sometimes mentioned in our records, though the whole story can never be discovered. The Chronicle notes certain landmarks in the south-western advance of the West Saxons: in 658 they are victorious in Somerset, in 682 Centwine "put the Britons to flight as far as the sea", in 710 Ine, with Nunna of Sussex, fought against King Geraint, whom from other sources we know to have been king of *Dumnonia*, the British kingdom which gave its name to Devon.[1] But we should not have known that already before 690 part of Devon was in English hands if Willibald's Life of St. Boniface had not told us of Boniface's entry into a monastery at Exeter about that time;[2] nor does the Chronicle mention an English defeat at the River Hayle in Cornwall recorded in annal 722 in the *Annales Cambriae*. The Chronicle tells of Cuthred's battles against the Britons in 743 and 753, and in the annal for 757 says Cynewulf often fought with great battles against them, but it does not say with what results.[3] Nor is it possible to gather the completeness of Egbert's conquest from the bare references to his harrying of Cornwall in 815 and his battle at Galford in 825.[4] This can be seen from Dunstan's statement that after subduing the West Welsh he gave a tenth of the land to the Church.[5]

The lower Severn valley seems first to have been opened by the West Saxon victory at Dyrham in 577,[6] though this territory, whose inhabitants became known as the Hwicce, became later subject to Mercia. In modern Herefordshire an English tribe called the *Magonsæte* was in possession by the mid seventh century at latest,[7] and in Shropshire there was a people called the "Wrekin-dwellers", mentioned in the Tribal Hidage, a document compiled

---

[1] No. 1, p. 158.
[2] Ed. Levison, p. 6. Note also that No. 69 shows a West Saxon king granting land at Crediton in 739.
[3] No. 1, p. 162.   [4] No. 1, pp. 170 f.   [5] No. 229.   [6] No. 1, p. 146.
[7] See F. M. Stenton, *Anglo-Saxon England*, pp. 46 f.

in Mercia in the time of one of the great overlords of the late seventh or the eighth century. But Offa's Dyke is more important than documentary evidence in showing the extent of English control on the borders of Wales in the eighth century.

Similarly, written sources have only occasional references to the expansion of the Northumbrians to the north and west. No great advance could be made until after the union of Bernicia and Deira allowed Æthelfrith to fight along with the combined forces of the two kingdoms.[1] The westward expansion from the plain of York was at first prevented by the British kingdom of Elmet, in the West Riding, whose conquest Nennius ascribes to the reign of Edwin,[2] but place-names of early form in Cumberland and Lancashire suggest that the Bernicians had begun to press through the Tyne gap by the end of the sixth century. A nunnery had been established at Carlisle by 685, the city was in the charge of an English reeve,[3] and Bede refers to a monastery by the River Dacre,[4] and to a hermit on an island in Derwentwater.[5] Anglian settlements spread also to the Scottish side of the Solway, and in about 731 an English see was established at Whithorn in Galloway. Eadberht of Northumbria added Kyle to his dominions in 750.[6] On the east, Northumbrian territory stretched as far as the Forth, where there was a monastery at Abercorn which was made the seat of a bishopric for the Picts during the short time they were under English rule.[7] If Nennius's *Iudeu* is correctly identified as Inveresk, Northumbria extended to the Forth already in the reign of Oswiu.[8] Lothian was ceded to Scotland in the tenth century,[9] and the lands north of the Solway, and even Cumberland, were again part of the British kingdom of Strathclyde by that time.[10]

(iv) THE HEPTARCHY

When historians speak of the Heptarchy, they have in mind the seven kingdoms of Kent, Sussex, Wessex, Essex, East Anglia, Mercia and Northumbria. Until late in the sixth century, however, and for brief periods later, Northumbria consisted of the separate kingdoms of Bernicia and Deira, and Lindsey once had a royal house of its own. Genealogies of the royal families survive for all these kingdoms,[11] except Sussex, and all trace their descent to Woden, with the exception of the kings of Essex, who considered themselves

---

[1] See No. 151, p. 605.   [2] No. 2, p. 237.   [3] *Two Lives of St. Cuthbert*, ed. Colgrave, pp. 122, 242.
[4] No. 151, p. 669, n. 3.   [5] No. 151, p. 669, n. 2.   [6] No. 5.   [7] No. 151, p. 666.
[8] No. 2, p. 237.   [9] No. 4, p. 258.   [10] No. 1, p. 203 ; No. 4, p. 257.
[11] These occur in collections, *e.g.* Nennius (ed. Mommsen, pp. 202–205, ed. Petrie, pp. 74f., ed. Lot, pp. 197–200; see No. 2), Brit. Mus. Cott. Vespas. B. vi, a Mercian work of the early ninth century, akin to the source used by Nennius, containing all except the Saxon genealogies (H. Sweet, *Oldest English Texts*, pp. 169–171); Brit. Mus. Addit. MS. 23211, a late ninth-century fragment of the East and West Saxon genealogies (*ibid.*, p. 179); the ninth-century C.C.C.C., MS. 183; and in the appendix to Florence of Worcester (ed. Thorpe, I, pp. 247–257). They are also scattered in various places in the Chronicle, *e.g.* Preface to ‘A’ and entries for 449, 547, 552, 560, 597, 626, 757, 855.

descended from Seaxneat, a god who is mentioned in a document concerning the continental Saxons. Some of the other peoples who made up the kingdom of the Mercians, the Middle Angles, the Hwicce, and the *Magonsæte*, may once have had kings of their own.

During long periods all the kingdoms south of the Humber recognized a common overlord. Bede, who calls this overlordship an *imperium*, first mentions it when speaking of Ethelbert of Kent.[1] In a later passage[2] he attributes this authority to the earlier kings Ælle of Sussex and Ceawlin of Wessex, though the kind of control exercised by these leaders over the small disconnected English settlements of the age of conquest must have differed from that of the overlords of later times. After Ethelbert this power passed to Rædwald of East Anglia and then to the three Northumbrian kings Edwin, Oswald and Oswiu. Bede's statement receives confirmation from Adamnan, who calls Oswald *imperator* of the whole of Britain.[3] Bede carries his list no further, though the terms in which he refers to Æthelbald of Mercia later on[4] show that he too held this position by 731, and from other evidence we can see that Wulfhere of Mercia had it in the latter part of his reign, which ended in 674. The compiler of the Chronicle, when he copied Bede's list, merely tacked on the name of Egbert of Wessex, ignoring the great Mercian kings, even Offa.[5] It is from a charter of Æthelbald, where he describes himself both as *rex Britanniae* and "king not only of the Mercians but also of all the provinces which are called by the general name 'South English' ",[6] that we get clear evidence what was implied by the term *Bretwalda* 'ruler of Britain' which the chronicler uses.

Some conception of an overlord's power can be gathered from the fact that Augustine was able under the patronage of Ethelbert to meet the members of the British Church in safety on the border between two heathen nations at the other side of England;[7] from the attendance of subordinate kings at the overlord's court, where sometimes in early days they learnt to accept the religion of the overlord;[8] from the association of Oswald of Northumbria with Cynegils of Wessex in the granting of Dorchester as a West Saxon see;[9] and from the overlord's confirmation or attestation of grants of land made by his vassal kings.[10] The most striking claim is made by Offa, who revoked a grant made by Egbert of Kent without his permission, referring to Egbert as 'his thegn'.[11] Kings of Mercia hold synods which deal with the ecclesiastical affairs of the country without any other kingdom being represented among the lay element.

---

[1] No. 151, p. 597.   [2] No. 151, p. 610.   [3] No. 153.   [4] No. 151, p. 682.
[5] No. 1, p. 171.   [6] No. 67.   [7] No. 151, p. 607.
[8] Note, for example, the visits of Rædwald to Ethelbert of Kent, of Sigebert of Essex to Oswiu of Northumbria, of Æthelwealh of Sussex to Wulfhere of Mercia (No. 151, pp. 619, 635, 654), and of Cynewulf of Wessex and Ealdfrith of Lindsey to Offa of Mercia (Birch, Nos. 208, 262).
[9] No. 151, p. 627.   [10] *e.g.* Nos. 59, 62, 76.   [11] No. 80.

The full story of the warfare by which such authority was established and maintained, as well as of the frequent conflicts between neighbouring kingdoms, often leading to the transfer of debatable border territories, is lost beyond recovery, and much of what is known is obtained from incidental references. It is, however, not difficult to get from Bede a consecutive picture of the political history of Northumbria, beginning with the successful reign of Æthelfrith, who, with the combined forces of Deira and Bernicia, defeated both the Scots and the Welsh. His death and the succession of his Deiran rival Edwin in 616, the latter's slaying by Penda and Cadwallon in 632, the restoration of the Bernician royal house under Oswald in 633, his death in battle against Penda in 641, the recovery of power by Oswiu, by the murder of Oswine of Deira in 651 and the defeat and slaying of Penda in 654, the successful revolt three years later which put Wulfhere of Mercia on the throne, Ecgfrith's defeat by Ethelred of Mercia in 678, the expedition he sent against Ireland and his disastrous invasion of Pictish territory in 685–all these are told in almost due sequence; but Bede tells of Penda's siege of Bamburgh only in relating a miracle,[1] and it is only incidentally that we learn that Deira had sub-kings after the murder of Oswine; first Oswald's son Œthelwald,[2] then Oswiu's son Alhfrith, who, after playing a prominent part until 664, disappears.[3] Beyond Bede's inclusion of him among Oswiu's adversaries,[4] nothing is known of his fate. After Ecgfrith's death in 685, Bede speaks of the prosperous reign of Aldfrith over a reduced kingdom,[5] but mentions little more than the bare accession of his successors Osred, Cenred and Osric. Ceolfrith, who was reigning when Bede wrote, is depicted in the letter to Egbert as willing to further reform in the Church;[6] after being driven out and then restored, he eventually retired into a monastery.[7] The chronological summary at the end of Bede's history adds a few events not mentioned in the work itself, the most important being the battle of the 'prefect' Brihtfrith against the Picts in 711; but it is from Irish sources that this is shown to have been an English victory.[8] It presumably stemmed further advance of the Picts. This explains why Bede could speak of peace in that quarter in 731.[9] Bede's account of Northumbrian history can be supplemented from other sources. Nennius tells of Edwin's conquest of the kingdom of Elmet;[10] Eddi of Ecgfrith's victory over the Picts between 671 and 673, and over Wulfhere of Mercia before 674, and also of the disputed succession on Aldfrith's death.[11] Aldfrith is the scholarly king with whom Aldhelm corresponded.[12] We learn of the vicious character and misrule of his son Osred in one of Boniface's letters[13] and in a ninth-century poem.[14]

---

[1] No. 151, p. 631.　　[2] No. 151, p. 636, n. 2.　　[3] No. 151, pp. 634–644.　　[4] No. 151, p. 630.
[5] No. 151, p. 666.　　[6] No. 170, p. 739.　　　　　[7] No. 151, p. 685; No. 3, pp. 239 f.
[8] *Annals of Tigernach* (*Rev. Celtique*, XVII, p. 222).　　　　　　　　　　　　[9] No. 151, p. 682
[10] No. 2, p. 237.　　[11] No. 154.　　　　[12] See p. 575.　　[13] No. 177.
[14] *Carmen Æthelwulfi* (*Symeonis Monachi Opera Omnia*, ed. Arnold, I, p. 268).

Names not now current......<u>Wodnesbeorg</u>

KYLE

Abercorn✸   Dunbar

NORTH
BERNICIA

Lindisfarne
Bamburgh
Yeavering

Whithorn✸   Carlisle   Hexham   R. Tyne   Jarrow
                                              Wearmouth

UMBRIA

R. Tees   Whitby

Catterick

Ripon   York

R. Ribble   Leeds
          ELMET

LINDSEY

Chester   MERCIA   R. Idle   R. Trent   Lincoln

OFFA'S DYKE
WREOCEN
SÆTE   Lichfield   Repton   MIDDLE   R. Welland   Elmham
       Tamworth   Leicester   R. Nene   EAST
                    A   ANGLIA   GYRWE   Ely   ANGLIA   Dunwich
Worcester   N   R. Ouse   Rendlesham
MAGONSÆTE   C   I
Hereford   A
           HWICCE   Cirencester   Thame   ESSEX
                    R. Thames   Dorchester   MIDDLESEX   Bradwell-on-Sea
                    Bensington   London   Tilbury
           Bath   ASHDOWN   Rochester   Canterbury
R. Parret   Wodnesbeorg   Otford   KENT
                    X
Somerton   S   Winchester   SUSSEX
Crediton   Exe   Sherborne   MEON-   HASTINGS
R. Tamar   W   Exeter   WARE   Selsey

CORNWALL

Scale of Miles
0   10   20   40   60   80   100

2. ENGLAND AT THE TIME OF THE HEPTARCHY

Mercia on this map denotes the original kingdom of the Mercians, not its later extension.

Bede, who had greeted his accession with enthusiasm,[1] is reticent about him, but he paints a clear picture of many of the kings of Northumbria. We are much worse off for the period after Bede, but yet, throughout the eighth century, an outline of events is obtainable from the northern annals,[2] and with the help of other sources we can get an occasional glimpse of some of the personalities concerned.

Eadberht Eating, who succeeded Ceolwulf in 737, was a strong king, and one who maintained contact with the world outside, for he received letters and gifts from Pippin of the Franks.[3] He fought against the Picts in 740 and added Kyle to his dominions in 750.[4] In 756, in alliance with the Picts, he marched on Dunbarton and forced the Britons to come to terms, though his army met with disaster nine days later.[5] He was not afraid to take strong action even against ecclesiastics, imprisoning Bishop Cynewulf of Lindisfarne and besieging his church until a rival, Aldfrith's son Offa, was dragged from it;[6] while in 757 Pope Paul I remonstrates with him for taking three monasteries from an abbot and giving them to a layman, the 'patrician' Moll.[7] Yet it is probable that in this action he was merely following Bede's advice about the suppression of false monasteries,[8] and his behaviour at Lindisfarne may have been occasioned by conspiracy against him. For he was certainly not regarded as hostile to the Church. Alcuin,[9] and later on Simeon of Durham,[10] looked back on his reign as a golden age. Very soon after receiving the papal reprimand he resigned his throne in 758 and became a cleric at York, where his brother Egbert had held the see since 732. His son and successor Oswulf was killed by his own household in the course of the year, and for the rest of the century Northumbria was greatly disturbed by civil war between men who claimed to descend from the royal house and noblemen raised to the throne.

The first of these, Æthelwold, had another name, Moll, so may be identical with the noble to whom Eadberht had given the above-mentioned monasteries. He was driven out after a reign of six years (759–765), and a reputed descendant of the royal house, Alhred, succeeded.[11] In his reign both Aluberht and Willehad were sent officially from Northumbria to the missions abroad,[12] and a letter from him and his wife to Boniface's successor Lul is extant, which shows that he was in contact with Charles the Great.[13] Alcuin's first meeting with this monarch probably belongs to this time also.[14] It may be that Alhred proved a more devout than efficient ruler; the only recorded secular incident of his reign is the burning of Catterick by the 'tyrant' Earnred.[15] He was deposed by the general consent of the people in 774, and the son of Æthelwold

---

[1] *Bedas metrische Vita Sancti Cuthberti*, ed. W. Jaager, p. 100.
[2] Nos. 3, 5, and northern entries in No. 1. See pp. 118 f.
[3] *Symeonis Monachi Opera Omnia*, ed. Arnold, I, pp. 47–49.   [4] No. 5.   [5] No. 3, p. 241.   [6] *ibid.*
[7] No. 184.   [8] No. 170, pp. 740–743.   [9] Poem on the Saints of York, lines 1247–1286.
[10] *Op. cit., loc. cit.*   [11] No. 3, p. 242.   [12] See p. 88.
[13] No. 187.   [14] See p. 89.   [15] No. 3, p. 243.

Moll, Ethelred, was made king,[1] only to be expelled about five years later in favour of a grandson of Eadberht Eating, Ælfwold, "a just and pious king".[2] Once again, we hear only of one secular event, and that an act of violence, when two ealdormen burnt his 'patrician' Bearn.[3] But Ælfwold was the king who received the papal legates in 786,[4] and held a synod the following year.[5] The decrees of the legates are witnessed by, among others, the 'patrician' Sicga, signing "with serene mind"; the same man led a conspiracy and slew Ælfwold in 788; many saw a miraculous light over the place where he was slain, and a church was built there in his memory.[6] Contemporaries would regard Sicga's death by his own hand in 793 as a divine retribution.[7] Alcuin says that from the time of King Ælfwold there was a decline in morals in Northumbria.[8] After his son Osred had reigned for a year, the deposed Ethelred was invited back.[9] Since his earlier reign had seen his treacherous slaughter of four ealdormen,[10] it is difficult to see why Alcuin, who expresses his disappointment with him in 790,[11] should have expected better things. The annals continue to relate only violent and treacherous acts on his part.[12] Nevertheless, he received the notice of Charles the Great,[13] and Offa gave his daughter in marriage to him.[14] Alcuin addresses him in 793 as "his most beloved lord",[15] and regards his murder in 796 as "most sad news".[16] He speaks with approval of Torhtmund, who avenged his murder in 799.[17] Thus it is possible that Ethelred, cruel and unscrupulous as he was in dealing with those who threatened his position on the throne, had some qualities as a ruler.

The 'patrician' Osbald, made king by one faction, held the throne less than a month,[18] and received a stern letter from Alcuin, who suspects him of complicity in Ethelred's murder and accuses him and his kinsfolk of shedding the blood of kings, princes and people.[19] Alcuin wrote also to Eardwulf, a nobleman who was made king after Osbald, admonishing him to rule well, remembering the punishment of his predecessors.[20] He reminds him of his preservation, a remark which is explained by Simeon's recording of an incident in Ethelred's reign, when Eardwulf, led out to execution at Ripon, was found alive in the church the following night.[21] But Alcuin was again disappointed; he confides to a Mercian ealdorman in 797 his fears that God will deprive Eardwulf of his kingdom for his dismissal of his wife and public taking of a concubine;[22] in 801 he comforts Archbishop Eanbald, who has incurred the king's enmity, reminding him how other kings perished who were opposed to the Church.[23] And in truth, Eardwulf did not sit securely on his throne. He defeated a conspiracy in 798, and had Alhmund, whom some said to be King Alhred's son, put to death

[1] No. 3, pp. 243 f.   [2] No. 3, p. 244.   [3] No. 3, p. 245.   [4] No. 191.   [5] No. 3, p. 246.
[6] ibid.   [7] No. 3, p. 247.   [8] No. 193.   [9] No. 3, p. 246.   [10] No. 3, p. 244.
[11] A letter to the abbot of Corbie, Dümmler, No. 9.   [12] No. 3, pp. 246 f.   [13] Nos. 197 f.
[14] No. 3, p. 247.   [15] No. 193.   [16] No. 198.   [17] No. 206; cf. No. 3, p. 250.
[18] No. 3, p. 248.   [19] No. 200.   [20] No. 199.   [21] No. 3, p. 246.   [22] No. 202.   [23] No. 207.

in 800,[1] and in 801 he went to war against Cenwulf of Mercia, who was harbouring his enemies.[2] Alcuin suspected Archbishop Eanbald of sheltering the king's enemies.[3]

At this point Simeon's use of the northern annals ceases, but the 'D' and 'E' versions of the Chronicle record that Eardwulf was expelled, dating it 806. This is their last entry from this early set of annals, but fortunately continental sources come to our aid, for the *Annals of the Frankish Kingdom* tell how Eardwulf sought the help of Charles the Great and then went to Rome, and was escorted back to Northumbria by envoys both of Charles and of the pope.[4] The evidence of Alcuin's letters fails us just about the same time as that of the northern annals, and little is known of Northumbrian history in the ninth century. The succession of kings and the length of their reigns is given in Simeon's *History of the Church of Durham*,[5] and, with some differences, in Roger of Wendover;[6] neither of these authorities knows of Eardwulf's restoration, but they allow a two-year reign to Ælfwold, who had driven him out. Afterwards, the kingdom continues in Eardwulf's line, his son and grandson succeeding, the only recorded break being in 844, when a certain Rædwulf seized the throne but was killed fighting the vikings in the same year;[7] Ethelred, Eardwulf's grandson, was restored and was succeeded about 848 or 849 by the Osbert whom the Chronicle mentions as the king who had recently been deposed when the Danes reached York in 866.[8] Apart from the submission of the Northumbrians in 829 to Egbert at Dore, mentioned both in the Chronicle and by Roger of Wendover,[9] nothing further can be discovered of political events in Northumbria in the pre-Viking period.

The sources for Mercian history are inferior. In as far as it touched on Northumbrian affairs, the early history of this kingdom can be studied in Bede, but much of the process of expansion and conquest which turned a small people in the basin of the upper Trent and its tributaries into a great Midland power is hidden from our sight. They controlled the Middle Angles by 653;[10] nothing suggests that this was a recent development. The Hwicce, in the valley of the lower Severn, presumably submitted to them after Penda's victory at Cirencester in 628,[11] and the other peoples along the Welsh border can hardly have maintained independence after that time. Lindsey was long debatable territory; it belonged to Northumbria in Edwin's reign, and in part of Oswald's, who was regarded as a foreign conqueror,[12] and it changed hands with all the vicissitudes of war between Northumbria and Mercia. Thus Wulfhere had it between

---

[1] No. 3, p. 250.   [2] *ibid.*   [3] Nos. 207f.
[4] No. 21. Two papal letters deal with the same subject, see p. 572.
[5] *Symeonis Monachi Opera Omnia*, ed. Arnold, I, pp. 52f.   [6] No. 4.   [7] No. 4, p. 256.   [8] No. 1, p. 176.
[9] Roger makes Egbert harry Northumbria, whereas the Chronicle only takes him to the frontier.
Cf. No. 1, p. 171, with No. 4, p. 255.
[10] No. 151, p. 684.   [11] No. 1, p. 150.   [12] No. 151, pp. 620, 629.

669 and 672, for it formed part of the Mercian diocese then,[1] but Ecgfrith had recovered it by 674.[2] It finally reverted to Mercia after the Battle of the Trent in 678.[3] We should never have suspected that it had kings of its own all this time, if their genealogy had not been preserved, allowing the identification of its latest name with a king who witnesses a charter of Offa.[4]

The Mercian control of Middle Anglia brought them into direct contact with the East Angles. This people never again secured power outside its own territories after the time of Rædwald.[5] Penda killed their king, Ecgric,[6] and later he killed his successor, Anna, who had given asylum to Cenwealh of Wessex when he was driven from his kingdom by Penda.[7] It was as a vassal king that Æthelhere, Anna's brother and successor, accompanied Penda to the battle of the Winwæd, where he was slain.[8] In view of the very incidental nature of these references in Bede, it would be rash to assume that we have the whole history of the relations between these two nations. Later kings of the East Angles are rarely more than names to us: Ealdwulf, who lived on into Bede's lifetime, is mentioned as remembering Rædwald's temple;[9] and Ælfwold, who died in 749, wrote a letter to Boniface,[10] and Felix dedicated his Life of Guthlac to him;[11] but of the dealings of this nation with its neighbours we hear nothing until Offa had King Ethelbert executed in 794.

The reign of Wulfhere (657–674) was an important one in the history of the growth of Mercian power. By about 664 the kings of Essex are said to be subject to him,[12] and a little later we find him selling the see of London to Wine,[13] though London had previously been an East Saxon town.[14] Mercian kings never lost their hold on London. Wulfhere also extended his control south of the Thames, where West Saxon power had been spreading, not only to the west, at the expense of the Britons, but also against eastern neighbours. They had fought against Ethelbert of Kent in 568, driving him into Kent;[15] and against Sussex in 607.[16] In 616 they won a victory over the East Saxons.[17] But the West Saxons met with reverses later. According to Bede, Cenwealh of Wessex suffered serious losses from his enemies after Wessex was left bishopless by Wine's departure.[18] Wulfhere harried as far as Ashdown in 661,[19] and by the end of his reign he was in possession of the West Saxon territory north of the Thames, for he had a residence at Thame.[20] At that time he was overlord of Surrey, which may at one time have belonged to Wessex, though Egbert of Kent had it at some period of his reign (664–673).[21] After Cenwealh's death (672), Wessex was probably weakened by internal troubles, for there must have been some basis for Bede's belief that it was governed only by sub-kings for ten years,[22]

[1] No. 151, p. 649.   [2] No. 151, p. 654.   [3] ibid.
[4] See F. M. Stenton, "Lindsey and its Kings", Essays in History presented to R. L. Poole, 1927.
[5] No. 151, pp. 610, 616.   [6] No. 151, p. 633.   [7] ibid.   [8] No. 151, p. 637.   [9] No. 151, p. 619.
[10] Tangl, No. 81; Kylie, pp. 152f.   [11] See p. 708.   [12] No. 151, p. 645.   [13] No. 151, p. 628.
[14] No. 151, p. 609.   [15] No. 1, p. 146.   [16] No. 1, p. 148.   [17] No. 151, p. 611.
[18] No. 151, p. 628.   [19] No. 1, p. 153.   [20] No. 54.   [21] ibid.   [22] No. 151, p. 653.

though this cannot be accepted as the whole truth, since it is contradicted not only by the Chronicle's record of the succession of Seaxburh, Æscwine and Centwine in this period,[1] but also by Eddi's reference to the last of these kings,[2] and more strikingly by Aldhelm's description of him as a powerful king who "duly ruled the *imperium* of the Saxons" and won three great battles.[3] Wulfhere seized the Isle of Wight and the mainland opposite to it, giving them to his godson Æthelwealh of Sussex,[4] obviously in order to put a barrier in the way of West Saxon expansion eastwards. Wulfhere's reign ended in disaster, for he was heavily defeated when he attacked Northumbria,[5] but when at the height of his power he must have been a Bretwalda.

His successor Ethelred (674–704) retained some of his gains. He was able to dispose of land in Middlesex,[6] and a Mercian see was placed at Dorchester-on-Thames for the lands north of the Thames which had once been West Saxon.[7] By his victory at the Trent he recovered Lindsey and removed any threat from Northumbria.[8] He raided Kent in 676,[9] and later, when after the death of Eadric of Kent in about 687 this kingdom was ruled by "kings of doubtful title and foreigners",[10] some of those foreigners are shown by charter evidence to have been members of the East Saxon royal house, and, as one of them has his charter confirmed by Ethelred, it seems likely that they established their position in Kent with his help.[11] But his influence in Kent was not unchallenged, for Ceadwalla of Wessex was in a position to grant estates to the Kentish house at Hoo.[12] Ceadwalla was supreme in Surrey in about 686[13] and he conquered Sussex, which he had harried previously when he was a landless atheling in exile, and the Isle of Wight.[14] When he resigned in 688, to go to Rome,[15] he was succeeded by one of the most effective of West Saxon kings, Ine, the author of the first West Saxon code of laws,[16] and soon after, in 690 or 691, the period of uncertain rule in Kent came to an end with the accession of Wihtred. While these two kings reigned south of the Thames, Wihtred till 725, Ine till 726, Mercian overlordship of this area was impossible, especially as Cenred, who succeeded Ethelred of Mercia in 704, had trouble with the Welsh, recorded only in the Life of Guthlac,[17] and as Ceolred, who reigned from 709 to 716, is depicted

---

[1] No. 1, p. 154.   [2] *Life of Wilfrid*, ed. Colgrave, p. 81.
[3] *Aldhelmi Opera*, ed. R. Ehwald (*Mon. Germ. Hist.*, *Auct. Antiq.*, xv), pp. 14f.
[4] No. 151, p. 654.   [5] No. 154, p. 695.   [6] No. 61.
[7] No. 151, p. 662. He also had power in Berkshire and Wiltshire. See F. M. Stenton, *Anglo-Saxon England*, p. 68.
[8] No. 151, pp. 654, 659.   [9] No. 151, p. 653.   [10] No. 151, p. 667.
[11] Birch, No. 42, shows that the Swæfheard whom Bede mentions as ruling in Kent is the son of the East Saxon king Sebbi, and it is confirmed by Ethelred. It is dated 676, but it survives in too late a copy for this to be trusted. Its indiction date would be correct for 691 also, though in that case the signature of Archbishop Theodore would be a later insertion. Birch, No. 89, a composite charter made up from a series of grants by different kings to Hoo, includes among these the East Saxon king Sigehere, who reigned jointly with Sebbi. Birch, No. 35 (which should be dated 690), Nos. 40 and 73, speak of a King Oswine of Kent, otherwise unknown.
[12] Birch, No. 89. See previous note.   [13] No. 58.   [14] No. 151, p. 656.
[15] No. 151, p. 669.   [16] No. 32.   [17] No. 156, p. 711.

as an impious and dissolute king by both Felix and Boniface;[1] he was seen in a vision by a monk of Wenlock suffering for his sins in hell.[2] Ine and he fought at *Wodnesbeorg* in Wiltshire in 715, but the chronicler omits to say who won the battle.[3] Yet, before Bede finished his *Ecclesiastical History* in 731, Æthelbald had re-established Mercian control over all the lands south of the Humber.[4]

It is a matter for deep regret that there is no authority for the great days of Mercia in any way comparable to Bede, nor even a set of annals like that available for eighth-century Northumbria. The Chronicle is a poor record at this time and little interested in Mercia, while no biography exists of Æthelbald or his greater successor Offa. It is only by combining references in a variety of sources that an impression of these kings can be gained. We first meet Æthelbald as a fugitive from Ceolred, in his exile visiting with his faithful followers his kinsman St. Guthlac.[5] The saint's prophecy of a change in his fortunes was fulfilled in 716, when Ceolred, "feasting in splendour amid his companions", died without repentance or confession.[6] Nothing is known of the steps by which Æthelbald won the position Bede accords him in 731. He attacked Wessex in 733 and occupied Somerton,[7] and sometime between 740 and 757 he was in a position to give the Berkshire monastery of Cookham to Christ Church.[8] He took the opportunity of a war between the Picts and Eadberht of Northumbria to raid that kingdom.[9] His charters show him in control of London.[10] It was perhaps as his vassal that Cuthred of Wessex joined with him to fight the Welsh in 743, but later Cuthred "fought stoutly" against him, and defeated him at *Beorhford* in 752.[11] However, the disturbed conditions in Wessex after Cuthred's death must have allowed him to regain control, for Cynewulf of Wessex soon after his accession in 757 witnesses a charter in which Æthelbald makes a grant of land in Wiltshire.[12] In this same year, Æthelbald was murdered by his own followers at night, after a reign of forty-one years.[13] It was a sad end for a man who had been so faithfully followed in his exile, all those years before. As to his character and the nature of his rule, the main source of information is the letter sent in 746 or 747 by Boniface and the bishops of the Anglo-Saxon mission to Germany, which speaks with appreciation of his generosity in alms-giving and his strong maintenance of peace, justice and order in his kingdom, while reprimanding him for his lascivious life and his violation of the privileges of churches.[14] He was perhaps not unmoved by this letter, for in 749 he issued a charter of privileges for the Church.[15] He had not been ungenerous to it earlier, for Felix speaks of his munificence to Crowland, and several charters show him

---

[1] No. 156, p. 712; No. 177, p. 755.   [2] Tangl, No. 10.   [3] No. 1, p. 158.   [4] No. 151, p. 682.
[5] No. 156, pp. 711–713.   [6] No. 177.   [7] No. 1, p. 160.   [8] No. 79.
[9] No. 5 (the Continuation of Bede) dates this 740, the northern additions to the Chronicle (No. 1, p. 160) 737.
[10] No. 66, and references there given.   [11] No. 1, p. 161.   [12] Birch, No. 181.
[13] No. 1, p. 163; No. 3, p. 241.   [14] No. 177. See also Nos. 178, 179.   [15] Birch, No. 178.

making donations to monasteries and churches.[1] However, his reformation was, in the opinion of an anonymous contemporary, inadequate, for he saw him in a vision among the damned in hell.[2] To our scanty sources for knowledge of a king strong enough to hold his throne for forty-one years, one should add the charters that show a striving after a regnal style adequate to the power he possessed,[3] and one that mentions his giving of a large estate to Offa's grandfather,[4] for this suggests that he did not regard with suspicion and hostility all others whose royal descent might give them a claim to rule.

Offa gained the throne by the end of the same year by driving out Æthelbald's immediate successor, Beornred. Narrative sources are singularly poor for his reign. Only Simeon of Durham tells of his conquest of the province of Hastings in 771,[5] and, while the Chronicle records a battle with the people of Kent in 776 at Otford, it does not say who won it. It records the capture of Bensington from Cynewulf of Wessex in 779, the contentious synod when Lichfield was made an archbishopric, the marriage of Offa's daughter to Beorhtric of Wessex in 789, and the bare fact, without any explanation, of the beheading of Ethelbert of East Anglia in 794.[6] Charters allow this scanty record to be expanded. They show no sign that he had influence in Kent before 764, or in the ten years after Otford, which, as Sir Frank Stenton has said, suggests that this was a victory of the men of Kent in revolt.[7] But during the years he was in control, Offa not only confirms the gifts of Kentish kings, but also makes grants without any reference to them,[8] and, as we saw above, revokes a gift made by one of them without his permission.[9] Kent was at this time ruled by a number of kings, sometimes reigning concurrently. The existence of some of them would be unknown except for charters, for the succession of kings of Kent entered in the Chronicle is both inaccurate and incomplete.[10] The most interesting is a King Ealhmund mentioned in a charter of 784,[11] for this is the name of the father of Egbert of Wessex, and thus the remark of the chronicler that the people of Kent had been wrongfully forced away from Egbert's kin[12] receives an explanation.

Offa similarly confirmed South Saxon charters,[13] both before and after his conquest of the *Hæstingas* of East Sussex in 771,[14] and an Osmund who appears as king in 770, is a *dux*, or ealdorman, in 772.[15] Sussex, a small kingdom with much of its territory thickly forested, seems rarely to have been independent.

---

[1] *e.g.* Nos. 64, 66, 67, 79. [2] Tangl, No. 115. [3] See p. 13. [4] No. 78. [5] No. 3, p. 243.
[6] No. 1, pp. 165–167. [7] *Anglo-Saxon England*, p. 206. [8] Birch, Nos. 213 f. [9] See p. 13.
[10] Thus it dates Eadberht's death 748, whereas he appears in two charters of Archbishop Bregowine's time, and hence not before 761 (Birch, Nos. 189 f.). It does not mention Eardwulf, who appears alone or with Ethelbert II (Birch, Nos. 175 f., 199) and who wrote to Lul (Tangl, No. 122); nor Sigered, who appears with Eadberht and with an otherwise unknown Eanmund (Birch, Nos. 193 f.); nor Heahberht and Egbert II, who are subordinate to Offa in 764 and 765 (Birch, Nos. 195 f.), but occur in a text of 766–785 without mention of him (Birch, No. 260), Egbert appearing alone in 778 and 779 (Birch, Nos. 227 f.).
[11] Birch, No. 243. See also No. 1, p. 165.   [12] No. 1, p. 171.
[13] No. 76, and Birch, Nos. 197, 206.   [14] No. 3, p. 243.   [15] Birch, No. 208.

We hear of its kings mainly in charters, though the Chronicle does mention the Nunna who fought along with Ine against the Britons in 710.[1]

But it is on the relations between Offa and Cynewulf of Wessex that charters shed the most interesting light. Soon after Offa's accession, Cynewulf issues a charter with his permission,[2] but his surviving charters between 758 and 778 make no reference to an overlord,[3] though he does appear as witness to a grant of Offa's in 772.[4] Cynewulf must have held part of Berkshire at this time, when he took possession of the monastery of Cookham, but the document that tells us this tells also that he lost it to Offa, presumably after the battle of Bensington in 779.[5] There is a charter of 781 recording a settlement between Offa and the church of Worcester which relates that the church bought from Cynewulf land south of the Avon near Bath to give it to Offa. Offa was presumably wanting a bridge-head across this boundary, but one can hardly believe that Cynewulf was a willing agent in the transaction.[6] Some subservience to Offa is perhaps implied in Cynewulf's presence at Offa's meeting with the legates in 786,[7] when Ælfwold of Northumbria held a meeting of his own with them; but it shows also that Offa could not ignore Cynewulf as he apparently did the kings of other kingdoms, who appear not to have met the legates at all. In fact, it is only from regnal lists, coins, and the reference to the execution of Ethelbert of East Anglia in 794[8] that we are aware that Essex and East Anglia had kings in Offa's reign.

Cynewulf of Wessex was not a negligible person. It was no small feat to retain the West Saxon throne for twenty-nine years against rival claimants, and to hold his own–and, since he held part of Berkshire and some lands in Oxfordshire, perhaps more than hold his own–against Mercia until his defeat at Bensington. Moreover, the Chronicle says he fought with great battles against the Britons, and though no one of these engagements is named or dated, his reference in a charter to war with the men of Cornwall supports the statement.[9] His charters suggest that he was generous to the Church, though he resisted the claims of Canterbury to Cookham;[10] he writes to the missionary Lul in Germany.[11] But what kept his memory alive was the manner of his death: his defence against odds, the refusal of his companions to survive him, the determination of his ealdorman and thegns to avenge him without regard for their kinship with some of the slayers, and the refusal of these kinsmen to accept quarter–these events made up a story of a type dear to the Germanic mind, and made it possible for the chronicler to insert a circumstantial narrative into a barren section of his work.[12] The loyalty of his followers must have seemed all the more impressive in an age which had seen the murders of Æthelbald of

[1] No. 1, p. 158.
[2] Birch, No. 327, assuming that, apart from the date and the boundaries, this is based on a genuine text.
[3] Nos. 55, 70, 71; also Birch, Nos. 185, 224, 225.
[4] Birch, No. 208. This charter survives only in a late cartulary, and has later boundaries added to it.
[5] No. 79.   [6] Birch, No. 241.   [7] No. 191.   [8] No. 1, p. 167.
[9] No. 70.   [10] No. 79.   [11] No. 190.   [12] No. 1, pp. 162 f.

Mercia and Oswulf of Northumbria by their own households. After his death, a king succeeded who married Offa's daughter and no doubt relied on Mercian support against his rival Egbert, who had to live in exile in this reign. This freed Offa from fear of opposition in Wessex.

It is not easy to gain a clear impression of Offa's personality. That he was powerful is certain, and this was recognized abroad also. About 790 Charles the Great negotiated for the marriage of his son Charles with one of Offa's daughters, though this only led to a quarrel, for Offa's request that Charles should let one of his daughters marry his son Ecgferth angered Charles. It is significant that, in his anger, he wished to exclude from his dominions not only Mercians, but Englishmen in general, apparently regarding them all as Offa's subjects; and also that Abbot Gervold of St. Wandrille, who, along with Alcuin, composed the quarrel, is said to have discharged many missions from Charles to Offa.[1] In extant letters, Charles calls Offa "his dearest brother",[2] and treats with him on equal terms on the concerns of their respective nations. He is anxious to explain away any unfriendly act in harbouring exiles from England. Alcuin writes to Offa "you are the glory of Britain", with other terms of high praise,[3] and Cenwulf of Mercia, his successor, refers to him as "king and glory of Britain".[4] It is equally clear that he was ruthless in obtaining what he wished. Alcuin's reference to the blood he shed to secure the succession for his son hints at unrecorded incidents,[5] for the execution of Ethelbert of East Anglia is not alone enough to explain the accusation. Charles envisages the possibility that even at his special request Offa may refuse to allow the return of certain exiles.[6] When Offa wished to obtain papal sanction for the archiepiscopal see of Lichfield, he apparently represented it as the united wish of the English,[7] though he can hardly have been unaware of the opposition which occasioned the 'contentious' synod of 787. He reclaimed Church land when he considered it wrongly alienated from his inheritance.[8] Yet he was no mere tyrant. When he was dead and there was nothing to gain by flattery, Alcuin, in the very letter in which he refers to his bloodshed, speaks with admiration of the excellent 'customs' imposed by Offa "of blessed memory",[9] and King Alfred studied his laws, regrettably lost, before issuing his own code.[10] In one of Alcuin's letters we have mention of some interest in education.[11] He was remembered by several religious houses as a benefactor or founder, and we need not assume that his generosity to St. Peter's at Rome, of which Pope Leo speaks,[12] was an act of policy only; his special devotion to St. Peter there mentioned is borne out by a privilege issued to him by Pope Hadrian, which speaks of his acquiring or founding many monasteries and dedicating them all to St. Peter.[13] His concern for pilgrims emerges in one of Charles's letters to him, which also shows him

---

[1] Nos. 20, 192.   [2] Nos. 196, 197.   [3] No. 195.   [4] No. 80.   [5] No. 202.
[6] No. 196.   [7] No. 205.   [8] No. 77.   [9] No. 202.   [10] No. 33, p. 373.
[11] No. 195.   [12] No. 205.   [13] See Levison, *England and the Continent*, pp. 29 f.

interesting himself in conditions of foreign trade,[1] an interest also indicated by the bringing of the coinage into conformity with that of the Frankish kingdom. And finally, there is the Dyke. This boundary between Wales and England is great in conception, and must have required much driving force and administrative, as well as engineering, skill to bring to completion. It looks as if this massive work were intended to be a memorial—as indeed it has been—to carry down his name to later generations. But in any case, Offa was not soon forgotten; it is obvious that the sword bequeathed some 220 years after his death by the atheling Athelstan carried an enhanced value because it had once been King Offa's.[2]

Mercian power did not crumble on Offa's death. Cenwulf, who succeeded after the few weeks' rule of Offa's son, was still able to protect Brihtric of Wessex, for it was not till the latter's death in 802 that Egbert secured the throne. After a serious Kentish revolt in favour of Eadberht Præn, Cenwulf put his own brother Cuthred on the Kentish throne in 798,[3] and as the archiepiscopal see was now held by Æthelheard, a Mercian placed there by Offa in 792, he brought about the suppression of the unpopular archbishopric of Lichfield.[4] Ecclesiastical synods continued to be held under the presidency of the Mercian king.[5] Moreover, he expanded his territories against the Welsh, and was in Flintshire when he died in 821.[6] This war was continued by his successor Ceolwulf I, but after his deposition in 823 the throne passed to a king not of royal birth, Beornwulf, who lost the battle of *Ellendun* against the rising power of Wessex in 825, and was killed by the East Angles, who had turned to Egbert of Wessex for support, later in the year.[7] We are so utterly devoid of sources for East Anglian history that the name of their king at this date is unknown. Mercian fortunes reached their lowest ebb in 829, when Egbert "conquered the kingdom of the Mercians and everything south of the Humber",[8] a success which caused the chronicler to add his name to the list of Bretwaldas. He received Northumbrian submission on the northern frontier of Mercia. But this proud position was short-lived. Wiglaf re-established Mercian independence in the following year, and was even able to summon bishops from south of the Thames to his councils,[9] though his authority in these regions, now united under Egbert, can never have equalled that of the great Mercian overlords of the eighth century. Mercia remained independent. It was not until after 844 that Berkshire was surrendered to Wessex,[10] and it is as equal monarchs that Burgred of Mercia and Æthelwulf of Wessex combined against the Welsh in

---

[1] No. 196. [2] No. 130.
[3] The main source for Mercian history at this date is the Chronicle, but on Eadberht Præn see also No. 205. [4] See pp. 91 f.
[5] See, for example, Nos. 79, 80, 81, 83. No. 84 is an example of a record of a similar synod held by Beornwulf, and No. 85 shows bishops from Wessex and Sussex witnessing a charter of Wiglaf.
[6] The *Annales Cambriae* are the main source for this Welsh war; but see also No. 1, p. 170, n. 8.
[7] No. 1, p. 171. [8] *ibid.* [9] No. 85. [10] See p. 177, n. 10; p. 480.

853 and arranged a match between their houses.[1] It was the disaster of the Danish invasions, not Egbert's short-lived hegemony, which ended the existence of Mercia as an independent kingdom.

Though the lasting subjugation of Mercia was not among them, the permanent results of Egbert's victories were considerable, namely the acquisition of Cornwall,[2] and of Kent, Surrey, Sussex and Essex.[3] The Chronicle says they had been wrongly taken from his kindred, and we have seen that his father may have ruled for a short time in Kent, that West Saxon kings from time to time were supreme in Surrey, that Ceadwalla conquered Sussex and that Nunna of Sussex was Ine's kinsman. Whether the chronicler's claim was based on these facts or not, the claim to Essex remains obscure. It had kings of its own up to the eve of its submission to Egbert. One called Sigeric had gone to Rome in 798[4] and a *rex* or *subregulus* Sigered witnesses some charters of Cenwulf and Ceolwulf I of Mercia.[5] On Egbert's death, Æthelwulf gave Essex to his son Athelstan,[6] but we never hear of it again until its occupation by the Danes. Egbert's successors ruled all the lands south of the Thames, once his son Æthelwulf had obtained Berkshire. Egbert had also to meet several viking raids, and did so mainly with success, culminating in his victory at Hingston Down.[7] He was undoubtedly an effective ruler, but there is perhaps no king of equal importance of whom we know so little. Genuine charters of his reign are rare, and correspondence non-existent, nor are there any of those chance references that shed a glimmer of light on personality. He must be judged by his achievements alone.

To the warfare occasioned by the attempts of kings to extend their authority and increase their territory at the expense of others must be added much internal strife between rival claimants to a throne. Any man of royal descent might consider that he had a right to rule. Joint rule was not uncommon, especially in Essex, early Wessex and eighth-century Kent, but this practice contained seeds of trouble, and those kingdoms which employed it most take no political lead. Our records show that many kings reigned for only short periods, but even securely established monarchs like Hlothhere of Kent,[8] Ine and Cynewulf of Wessex,[9] and Eadberht Eating of Northumbria[10] had to deal with attempts of rivals to oust them. Young men of royal descent are often met with in exile, as, for example, Sigeberht of East Anglia, fleeing to Gaul to escape Rædwald,[11] Guthlac, who was a scion of the Mercian royal house,[12] Æthelbald of Mercia,[13] Ceadwalla and Egbert of Wessex,[14] in addition to others, like Edwin of Northumbria,[15] the sons of Æthelfrith in Edwin's reign,[16] and Cenwealh of

---

[1] No. 1, p. 174.   [2] See p. 11.   [3] No. 1, p. 171.   [4] Chronicle 'F', No. 1, p. 169.
[5] Birch, Nos. 335, 339f., 373.   [6] No. 1, p. 172.   [7] *ibid.*   [8] No. 151, p. 667.
[9] No. 1, pp. 159, 162.   [10] See p. 16.   [11] No. 151, p. 633.   [12] No. 156, p. 711.   [13] No. 156, pp. 711 f.
[14] No. 151, p. 656; No. 1, p. 172.   [15] No. 151, p. 614; No. 152, p. 689.   [16] No. 151, p. 622.

Wessex when at enmity with Penda,[1] who were driven out by foreign kings. The lot of an exile was not easy, as may be seen from Æthelbald's despair in the Life of Guthlac, and most vividly in the description of the man who "treads the paths of exile" in *The Wanderer*;[2] for it was difficult to find asylum. The harbouring of another king's fugitive was regarded as an unfriendly act and might lead to war; it is the cause of trouble between the East and West Saxons mentioned in Bishop Wealdhere's letter,[3] and it led to war between Wessex and Sussex in 722,[4] and between Northumbria and Mercia in 801.[5] Even Charles the Great found it necessary to explain to Offa his reception of fugitives from England.[6] The reigning families were often connected by marriage alliances, and this lessened the fugitive's chances of a friendly reception at another court.

One can hardly wonder that some bold spirits preferred to collect a force and live by marauding; Ceadwalla was in this position when he killed Æthelwealh of Sussex and temporarily gained his kingdom;[7] Guthlac is another example,[8] and it is at least a possibility that Egbert's father's brief appearance on the Kentish throne in 784[9] may represent a successful attempt of a West Saxon atheling in exile to obtain a footing for himself elsewhere. A potential rival might be rendered harmless if he could be persuaded or forced to enter the Church,[10] and it is possible that the renegade priest Eadberht Præn, whom the men of Kent in revolt against Mercia in 796 set up as their king[11], was an atheling who had been forced unwillingly to take orders. Occasionally, in this prevalence of exile, good could arise out of evil, for the royal youth might find asylum in a place where he could learn things beneficial to his people when he later came to the throne. Sigeberht of East Anglia was converted in Gaul, and wished to imitate the things he approved of there;[12] Oswald was converted in exile at Iona;[13] Aldfrith of Northumbria acquired his interest in scholarship when in exile among the Irish;[14] and it is probable that it was Egbert's three years' stay in the Frankish kingdom that began the intercourse of the West Saxon kings with the Frankish court.[15] It would be a pity to end these remarks on exiles without reference to the poem known as the *Husband's Message*, in which a man of rank who has been driven by hostility from his people joyfully sends for his wife to join him, since he has now overcome his troubles and found wealth and security; it is significant that he has done so "southward across the oceanpath". The Frankish kingdom must at most periods have provided one of the safer refuges for those who had incurred the enmity of an English king.

Assembled together, references to the political history of the Heptarchy convey an impression of continuous warfare and dissension. Yet, when one

---

[1] No. 151, p. 627.   [2] No. 211.   [3] No. 164.   [4] No. 1, p. 159.   [5] No. 3, p. 250.
[6] Nos. 195, 196.   [7] No. 151, p. 656.   [8] No. 156, p. 709.   [9] See p. 22.
[10] Cf. No. 3, pp. 239, 246.   [11] See p. 25.   [12] No. 151, p. 633.   [13] No. 151, p. 624.
[14] *Two Lives of St. Cuthbert*, ed. Colgrave, pp. 104, 236.   [15] No. 1, p. 172; see also Nos. 23, 217 f.

turns to other aspects of the period, it is found to be far from one of unrelieved chaos or stagnation. It would be idle to deny that the various wars disrupted normal life and caused great distress, though the sources rarely go into detail. Bede's account of the burning of villages by Penda[1] would hold good for many places that lay in the line of hostile forces, and the mention of captives in several of our sources reminds us of one possible consequence of defeat. More telling than the individual instances such as that of the Kentish girl whom the abbot of Glastonbury was reluctant to relinquish,[2] or the Northumbrian thegn who narrowly escaped being taken for sale on the Continent,[3] are the regulations in Theodore's penitential concerning remarriage when one partner of the marriage has been led away in captivity,[4] for this shows that such a fate was not uncommon. Nor was Church property always spared by the armies of Christian kings. King Ethelred of Mercia was a founder of churches and himself retired into a monastery, but he profaned churches and monasteries in Kent and despoiled the church of Rochester.[5] Yet many a war mentioned in our records was probably narrowly localized in its effects. In most kingdoms there were long reigns by kings who could maintain peace within their borders. Progress in the arts of government and peace rarely includes datable and spectacular happenings that find their way into chronicles. Much of the period was a time of advance and consolidation in the Church, and it saw great achievements in art, literature and scholarship.

(v) THE VIKING AGE

The first attack fell on the island of Lindisfarne in 793 and is recorded in some detail.[6] Alcuin's letters show the consternation and horror aroused by this event; never before had such terror appeared in Britain, nor had such an inroad been thought possible.[7] Such an attack on this holiest of sanctuaries could surely not occur without a divine warning, and men interpreted in retrospect certain portents seen earlier in the year, flying dragons and bloody rain,[8] as foreshadowing the wrath of God and the imminence of his vengeance. For men of that time believed that no such disaster could befall unless merited by sin, and it is natural enough that Alcuin should recall what Gildas had written on the sins of the Britons and the vengeance God took by sending the English to conquer their land.[9] He was haunted by a fear that history would repeat itself. Were there not sins in plenty to call forth such divine vengeance? And again and again during periods of viking attack writers adopt this attitude: it is shared by Pope John VIII writing to Burgred of Mercia,[10] by Alfred in the

---

[1] No. 151, pp. 631 f.   [2] No. 166.   [3] No. 151, p. 661.
[4] Haddan and Stubbs, III, p. 200.   [5] No. 151, p. 653.
[6] No. 1, p. 167; No. 3, p. 247: *Symeonis Monachi Opera Omnia*, ed. Arnold, I, pp. 50–52.
[7] Nos. 193, 194, 199.   [8] No. 1, p. 167; No. 3, p. 247; No. 193.
[9] Dümmler, Nos. 17, 129.   [10] No. 220.

letter he sent to his bishops along with his translation of the *Pastoral Care*,[1] by the author of the Life of St. Oswald about 1000, when after his account of the battle of Maldon he adds that his countrymen then and now suffer under the same threat as that made to the Jews in Jeremiah, xxv. 8–9 and Ezekiel, vii. 27,[2] and by Archbishop Wulfstan in 1014, when he borrows a passage in one of Alcuin's letters referring to Gildas and the fate of the Britons.[3] The best way to meet the menace is to put one's house in order, by repentance and reform. Writers vary in what they regard as the most serious sins. Alcuin and Wulfstan spread the responsibility widely, the popes are most concerned with breaches of the marriage laws and with cohabitation with nuns, Alfred refers only to neglect of learning, while a ninth-century priest saw a vision threatening destruction by pagans along with other calamities if the observance of Sunday continued to be neglected.[4]

The Lindisfarne raid was followed by an attack on Jarrow in the following year, though it was not made without loss to the raiders.[5] The annals available to Roger of Wendover record raids on Tynemouth and Hartness in 800,[6] and there may have been incidents unrecorded in our scanty records. The only raid on Wessex in this period which our authorities mention, one which took place between 786 and 802, seems to have been a small and isolated incident,[7] whereas we have so little evidence for the other kingdoms that it would be hazardous to assume from the lack of mention of raids that they were immune. At any rate, men were anxious. Alcuin, writing to the clergy and nobles of Kent in 797, bemoans the dissensions between the kings and kingdoms of the English at a time when a great danger is threatening them, since "a pagan people is accustomed to lay waste our shores",[8] and already in 804 Cenwulf of Mercia granted land in Canterbury to the abbess of Lyminge as a place of refuge.[9] At a time prior to the recommencement of attacks which is recorded in the Chronicle, charters are specifying that military service against pagan enemies is to be rendered from estates, and adding the destruction of fortifications to the normal demand for fortress-work.[10] The phrase "as long as the Christian faith may remain in the land", found in an earlier period, must have taken on a more urgent and sinister meaning in view of the viking threat.[11]

After these early raids the next reference to viking attack comes in 835, when they ravaged Sheppey, and from then on the Chronicle gives a reasonably full account in as far as the raids concerned the lands south of the Thames. It is

---

[1] No. 226.   [2] *Historians of the Church of York*, ed. Raine, I, pp. 456 f.   [3] No. 240.
[4] No. 23; cf. No. 214.   [5] No. 3, pp. 247 f.   [6] No. 4.   [7] No. 1, p. 166.
[8] Dümmler. No. 129; Haddan and Stubbs, III, p. 510.   [9] No. 82.
[10] No. 83, and Birch, Nos. 332, 335, which are dated 811.
[11] It occurs in charters of Offa, No. 78 and Birch, No. 236 (from an early eleventh-century cartulary). Also in Birch, No. 396, no later than 832, No. 406, which cannot be dated closer than 833–870, and Birch, No. 407, 833–839. See also Nos. 91, 97, below.

much less detailed about other parts of the country, merely recording in general terms an attack on Lindsey and East Anglia in 841, and on London in 842 and 851, after which the invaders defeated Brihtwulf of Mercia. It records no further incident outside Wessex and Kent until the year of the great invasion, in the autumn of 865, but Roger of Wendover mentions a battle against the pagans at Elvet, in Durham, in 844,[1] while a charter of 855 speaks of them in the Wrekin district.[2] Even as regards Wessex, the Chronicle does not give the whole story, for it omits to mention the raid on Southampton in 842, mentioned by a continental contemporary.[3] We do not know what raids took place in East Anglia or Essex, for these places lie remote from the chronicler's interest and they have left no records of their own.

The invaders were by no means universally successful in their early raids on Wessex. When in 838 they combined with the Britons of Cornwall, Egbert inflicted a great defeat on them at Hingston Down.[4] His son Æthelwulf also had his successes. Thanks to Asser,[5] to Lupus of Ferrières,[6] and to the fuller annals of the Chronicle in this period, more is known of this king than of his predecessors on the West Saxon throne. The emphasis on his piety and his generosity to the Church has sometimes caused his qualities as a ruler to be underestimated.[7] After minor engagements of varying success against the vikings, he certainly won a great victory at *Aclea* in 851, over a force from 350 ships which had had a triumphant career in Kent and Mercia. It was the greatest slaughter of a pagan host that the chronicler had ever heard of,[8] and it is probably the English victory recorded under the year 850 in the *Annals of St. Bertin's*[9] and the success referred to in Lupus's letter to Æthelwulf.[10] After this battle, Æthelwulf was free to turn his attention elsewhere, and to help Burgred of Mercia against the Welsh in 853, though there was a viking raid in Thanet in the same year, and in 854 a Danish force, following a precedent set in the winter of 850–851, remained in the country, this time in Sheppey, over the winter.[11] As nothing is said either of damage wrought by them or of an engagement against them, it is possible that they were bought off. Æthelwulf went to Rome in the following spring, and delayed on his way back to marry the daughter of Charles the Bald.[12] There was an attempt of a faction to replace him by his son during his absence,[13] but we hear of no trouble from vikings in the rest of his reign or in that of his son Æthelbald. In King Ethelbert's reign (860–865) a large force stormed Winchester, but was defeated by the levies of Hampshire and Berkshire,[14] and in 865 the men of Kent tried to buy off an army settled in Thanet.[15] In the autumn of that year, when Ethelbert had been succeeded by Ethelred, there came the

---

[1] No. 4.   [2] No. 90.   [3] No. 22.   [4] No. 1, p. 172.
[5] No. 7, pp. 264 f.   [6] Nos. 217 f.   [7] But see F. M. Stenton, *Anglo-Saxon England*, pp. 242 f.
[8] No. 1, p. 173.   [9] No. 23.   [10] No. 217.   [11] No. 1, p. 174.
[12] No. 1, p. 174; No. 7, p. 265; No. 23.   [13] No. 7, pp. 264 f.
[14] This is probably the raid dated 860 by the *Annals of St. Bertin's* (No. 23).   [15] No. 1, p. 176.

great host which eventually conquered half of England, and led to the settlement of the Danelaw.

The coming of the great army was clearly part of an organized plan of conquest, no mere plundering raid. In later English and Scandinavian traditions (which are not necessarily independent of one another), such an attack was felt to require motivation, and was explained as an act of vengeance for the killing of a ninth-century viking, Ragnar Lothbrok. The murder is located in either Northumbria or East Anglia, and the legends name as leaders certain persons said to be his sons.[1] The names Hubba and Inguar (*i.e.* Ivar) have the support of Abbo, who wrote a Life of St. Edmund as he had heard it told by Dunstan, who had the story from Edmund's sword-bearer,[2] and Ivar is mentioned also by Æthelweard.[3] The King Healfdene mentioned as one of the leaders in the Chronicle is shown to be Ivar's brother by the mention of a brother of theirs killed in Devon in 878.[4] Otherwise there is no early evidence, and the later legends must be used with caution.

The fortunes of this viking host, which first fell on East Anglia in the autumn of 865 and was bought off, up to the defeat by Alfred of the last branch of it to remain in the field, in 878, can be read in the Chronicle,[5] and a few extra particulars can be supplied from elsewhere. It left East Anglia for York in the autumn of 866, and both Simeon of Durham and Roger of Wendover have some details not in the Chronicle, and also tell of the setting up by the Danes of a puppet king, Egbert, in 867.[6] Roger records a rising of the Northumbrians against him in 872, and both he and Simeon mention his death in the next year and the succession of a Northumbrian called Ricsige. These entries explain why the Danish army went to Northumbria in 873, and then retired to Lindsey;[7] this was an unsuccessful attempt to deal with the Northumbrians in revolt. These same northern authorities show that Ricsige managed to hold his position until the appearance of Healfdene with half the great army in 874, when, according to Roger, he died of grief. Simeon says he was succeeded beyond the Tyne by a second Egbert.

After establishing their puppet in York in 867, the army took up winter-quarters in Nottingham, but were content to come to terms when faced with a combination of West Saxon and Mercian forces, and to retire to Northumbria. The Chronicle's entry of the attack on East Anglia and the killing of King Edmund, in 869, is regrettably brief. The early cult of this saint is understandable only on the assumption that something other than his death in battle took place, even though the details of the martyrdom as given in later sources

---

[1] See A. Mawer, "Ragnar Lothbrok and his Sons" (*Saga-Book of the Viking Soc.*, VI, 1908), and A. H. Smith, "The Sons of Ragnar Lothbrok" (*ibid.*, XI, 1936).
[2] *Memorials of St. Edmund's Abbey*, ed. T. Arnold, I, pp. 9f.
[3] No. 1, p. 177, n. 4.   [4] No. 1, p. 180.   [5] No. 1, pp. 176–180.
[6] *Symeonis Monachi Opera Omnia*, ed. Arnold, I, p. 55; No. 3, p. 251; No. 4.   [7] No. 1, p. 178.

cannot be relied on. When the army then turned on Wessex it met stiff resistance, and suffered one severe defeat, which yet seemed to have little result. King Ethelred died in the course of 871, and before it ended his successor Alfred had made peace and the Danes had withdrawn from Wessex to London. While they were there, we are told that the Mercians made peace with them, and from a charter of this year it is clear what sense these words can bear, for in it a bishop of Worcester leases land in order to be able to pay his church's contribution to the tribute to the Danes.[1] Again, the very next year, the Mercians had to 'make peace' again, and in 874 the Danes were able to drive Burgred of Mercia from the kingdom, and set up a nominee of their own. There is no evidence that on this occasion, as in 868, the Mercians received help from the West Saxons. It is interesting to find that the viking invasion had not disrupted communications with the papal see. Only a short extract survives of a letter from Pope John VIII to Burgred, urging him to enforce the Church rules on marriage.[2] One may hope that the rest of the letter included some message of sympathy for a people beset with heathen attack, but the fragment that remains of the same pope's letter to the English archbishops[3] suggests that he had no grasp of the situation in England. If he had, he would hardly have been so eager to enforce correct clerical costume at a time when the question at issue was how long there would be a Church at all in those lands.

The king the Danes set up in Mercia, Ceolwulf II, is called by the West Saxon chronicler "a foolish king's thegn", but charters survive which show him acting, like any other Mercian king, with the support of bishops and ealdormen;[4] and, indeed, it is difficult to see what would have happened in Mercia if no one had been willing to undertake this responsibility, after Burgred had gone to Rome and stayed there. In 877 Ceolwulf's territory was reduced, when the Danes took the north-eastern area for themselves; but he seems to have held the rest until his death. Florence of Worcester seems to imply that he died just before Alfred took London in 886.[5] He was the last king of the Mercians.

Meanwhile, late in 874, the army had divided, and while one part, under Guthrum and two other kings, went to East Anglia, Healfdene went to Northumbria, where Ricsige was reigning.[6] The chronicler's reference to his raids from his headquarters on the Tyne receives support from Irish sources which mention a defeat of the Picts by the 'Black Foreigners' (Danes) at this time;[7] and northern sources record the commencement of the long wanderings of the monks of Lindisfarne with the body of St. Cuthbert and other relics.[8] The following year, however, Healfdene shared out Northumbria to his

---

[1] No. 94.   [2] No. 220.   [3] No. 221.   [4] No. 95, and Birch, No. 541.
[5] See the lists of kings at the end of Florence's work, ed. Thorpe, I, p. 267.
[6] p. 31.   [7] e.g. Annals of Ulster, 874.
[8] No. 3, p. 251; cf. Symeonis Monachi Opera Omnia, ed. Arnold, I, pp. 57, 207.

followers and they began to cultivate their lands. The similar settlement of part of Mercia took place in 877, whereas the force that had gone to East Anglia did not follow this example until after two unsuccessful attempts to conquer Wessex, which are described in the Chronicle, while Asser and Æthelweard supply a little additional information.[1] The second of these attempts came perilously near success, and if, like Burgred, Alfred had "gone to Rome and stayed there", there can be little doubt that all England would have come under Danish rule and the Christian faith no longer have remained in the land. But the king remained to rally the defenders, and his victory at Edington caused Guthrum's army to retire and share out East Anglia, leaving the lands south of the Thames, as well as south-west Mercia, in English hands. The fleet of vikings that arrived in the Thames soon after decided to try its fortunes in the Frankish empire, and though in 885 and again from 892–896 it returned to attack Alfred's kingdom, and Alfred had to meet attacks from Danes settled in Northumbria and East Anglia,[2] there was no repetition of the critical situation of 878. It is no doubt the defence of their lands by Alfred and his son Edward that called forth the praise of Radbod, an early tenth-century biographer of St. Boniface, who says that the English are strong and brave, and that by the aid of the grace of Christ, they defend their lands stoutly, subdue the pirates from the North and drive them from their territories by vigorous fighting.[3]

Much of the material that allows some estimate of Alfred's character to be made is contained in this volume. There is the account of his military achievements in the Chronicle,[4] his laws,[5] his Life by Asser,[6] his will,[7] the letters written in his reign by popes and by Archbishop Fulk of Reims,[8] his own letter circulated with his translation of the *Pastoral Care*,[9] his preface to another work, the *Soliloquies of St. Augustine*, along with some short passages which he added to the works he was translating.[10] Moreover, there are references in later records which show the esteem in which he was held; *e.g.* the concern of the writer of the Fonthill document at the chaos that will result "if one wishes to change every judgment which King Alfred gave";[11] the eagerness of a later Northumbrian writer to claim that a high-reeve of Bamburgh had been a friend of King Alfred;[12] the appeal of later kings to the authority of the 'law-book',[13] by which they mean Alfred's laws with those of Ine attached to them; the actual reissue of some of his statutes in the laws of Cnut;[14] Ælfric's reference to the books which he "wisely translated" and which are still obtainable;[15] and, still more important, the same author's choice of him as one of the three kings signalled out for special mention as victorious by the help of God.[16] Nevertheless,

---

[1] No. 1, pp. 179 f.   [2] No. 1, pp. 181–189.
[3] *Vitae Sancti Bonifatii Archiepiscopi Moguntini*, ed. Levison, p. 66.   [4] No. 1, pp. 177–189.   [5] No. 33.
[6] No. 7.   [7] No. 96.   [8] Nos. 221–225.   [9] No. 226.   [10] No. 237.   [11] No. 102.   [12] No. 6, p. 262.
[13] *e.g.* II Athelstan (No. 35), 5.   [14] II Cnut (No. 50), 57–60.   [15] No. 239(A).   [16] No. 239(I).

not all the material relating to Alfred could be included, and any estimate of him would be incomplete which did not reckon with the bulky volumes of his translations, especially with the *Boethius* and the *Soliloquies*, where he wrestles with theological and philosophical difficulties to bring to his people a knowledge of the eternal truths, in spite of his manifold preoccupations. In view of these works, it cannot be doubted that, though Asser is writing panegyric, his picture of Alfred as a deeply religious man is a true one. In this respect Alfred was a true son of his father. But he is not in the line of kings who relinquished their secular obligations to find salvation in monasteries or at the threshold of the Apostles. He was gifted with unusual ability in government and administration, and brought to large matters and small an experimental type of mind. His invention of a more exact method of recording the passage of time may seem too trivial a matter for the space Asser gives to it, but it is this same practical and inventive ability that led him to reorganize his finances,[1] to arrange for a constant supply of troops,[2] and to plan the defence of the land by boroughs[3] and by larger and better ships.[4] He had to face inertia and opposition to these plans—it may have been in relation to them that he infringed in the pope's opinion the rights of the church of Canterbury[5]—but he had the strength and tenacity to persist, and the full benefit of his measures was reaped in his son's reign. Even leaving aside Asser's discourses on his virtues, there are scattered passages in the sources that seem to bring us near to an attractive personality; he writes with humility and modesty, and there is a poignancy about his hope that others may be able to enjoy at leisure the fruits of their studies as he has not been able to do;[6] he is careful to avoid wounding the self-esteem of his bishops when he sends round his translation of the *Pastoral Care*;[7] he shows his deep sense of the responsibilities of kingship in an addition to *Boethius*.[8] He desired to leave after his life "his memory in good works", and the oral tradition handed down the ages must be reckoned with in any estimate of his character. Whether the story is true or false, the Alfred who patiently suffered the reproaches of a peasant woman whose cakes he had allowed to burn is not at variance with the one in contemporary sources, and such stories grow up about persons who were loved and respected while they lived. He was not the author of the twelfth-century *Proverbs of Alfred*, but it is not without historical interest that this king should have lived so long in the popular mind as the originator of what was regarded as wisdom.

After the death of Ceolwulf II, no English king remained except the West Saxon royal house, but it was not until over half a century after Alfred's death that the last Scandinavian king was expelled. Danish kings ruled in East Anglia

---

[1] No. 7, pp. 274 f.   [2] No. 1, p. 185.   [3] See p. 71.   [4] No. 1, p. 189.
[5] No. 222.   [6] No. 237(A).   [7] No. 226.   [8] No. 237(B).

and southern Northumbria, whereas the districts attached to the Danish
boroughs of Bedford, Huntingdon and Northampton are shown by the
Chronicle to have been in charge of earls,[1] and this was probably true also of
Cambridge, and of the group known as the Five Boroughs, namely Lincoln,
Stamford, Nottingham, Derby and Leicester. Little is discoverable about the
internal history of the Danelaw at this time. A king of East Anglia called
Eohric was killed in 902,[2] and in Northumbria Healfdene was succeeded by
Guthfrith, a Christian, whom later tradition believed to owe his election to
St. Cuthbert's appearance in a vision.[3] He is sometimes identified with a Cnut
who is found on coins, and these afford evidence of a Sigefrith about the same
time. When Æthelwold, the son of Alfred's elder brother King Ethelred, fled
from Wessex after an unsuccessful attempt to get the throne in 899, he was,
according to manuscripts 'B', 'C', and 'D' of the Chronicle, accepted as king
by the Northumbrians, though the West Saxon version, 'A', is at pains to
eradicate any reference to his kingship.[4] When he succeeded in uniting the
East Anglians to his cause in 902, the situation looked threatening; his slaying
at the battle of the Holme, along with another Englishman of royal descent[5]
and with the East Anglian king, must have relieved King Edward of a heavy
anxiety. Our authorities are again at variance as regards the peace he made with
the East Angles and Northumbrians in 906, since the main Chronicle implies
that he dictated terms, whereas 'E' says he made peace "from necessity".[6]
In any case, it was of short duration, and it was not until after the great defeat
of the Northumbrians at Tettenhall in 910, where they lost two kings and many
high officials,[7] that Edward and his sister Æthelflæd, lady of the Mercians, were
able to begin their great concerted action to reconquer the Danelaw.

Their relentless advance, consolidating their gains by the building of
fortresses, can be read in the Chronicle and the Mercian Register.[8] The danger
from viking fleets was not yet at an end; yet the arrival of a large force in
914 did not prevent Edward from building forts at Buckingham and obtaining
the surrender of the Danes of Bedford and Northampton, or Æthelflæd
from building Eddisbury and Warwick; and a great army from East Anglia
failed to obtain their objective in 917 although they enlisted the help of raiding
vikings. Moreover, we can see from the Mercian Register that Æthelflæd was
not free from troubles with the Welsh; nevertheless, by the time of her death in
918, she had taken two of the Five Boroughs, Derby and Leicester, and received
the submission of the men of York. Edward, who had by then won back all
the eastern Danelaw, continued her work by building forts at Nottingham in
918, Thelwall and Manchester in 919, and another at Nottingham in 920, as

[1] No. 1, pp. 195–197. [2] No. 1, p. 191. [3] No. 6. [4] No. 1, p. 190, n. 8; p. 191, n. 8.
[5] Brihtsige, son of Beornoth. These names suggest descent from the Mercian, rather than the West
Saxon royal house.
[6] No. 1, p. 192. [7] No. 1, pp. 192f. [8] No. 1, pp. 192–199.

well as one in the Peak district, at Bakewell. The chronicler may have considered that with the submission he received at the end of 920, of the Scots, the men of York, the northern Northumbrians, and the Strathclyde Welsh, the goal of his work was reached, for he tells us nothing more until he records his death. The Mercian Register shows that Edward was not secure on his northwest frontier, but built *Cledemutha* in 921. He suppressed a revolt at Chester, and he was at Farndon-on-Dee when he died in 924.[1]

The chronicler has done nothing to prepare us for his statement in 920 that Norsemen, as well as Danes and Englishmen, lived in Northumbria, nor does he explain who the Ragnald, first mentioned in this year, is. But from the northern annals used by Simeon and by the northern version of the Chronicle,[2] from the anonymous *History of St. Cuthbert*,[3] from Irish annals, and from place-name evidence, this gap can partially be filled. Place-names reveal a considerable Norse settlement in Lancashire, Westmorland, Cumberland and west and north Yorkshire, and from the other sources we learn of the settlement of the Norse-Irish in Chester and the Wirral in the early tenth century[4] and of the conquest of Northumbria by Ragnald, a Norseman from Dublin, who fought a battle at Corbridge[5] and who captured York, probably in 919. Nothing is known of the Danes of Northumbria between the battle of Tettenhall and their conquest by Ragnald, except that they submitted, apparently willingly, to Æthelflæd in 918. Their readiness is plausibly explained by Dr. Wainwright as rising from their fear of Ragnald.

As long as Æthelflæd lived, Mercia preserved a degree of autonomy, though Edward took the areas attached to London and Oxford under his immediate control on the death in 911 of the ealdorman Ethelred, to whom King Alfred had entrusted the charge of London when he recovered it in 886. Edward clearly had no intention of allowing a new royal line to arise in Mercia from the descendants of Ethelred and Æthelflæd, and therefore removed their daughter into Wessex in the year after her mother's death. The fostering of Athelstan at his aunt's court in Mercia may have been a deliberate move in anticipation of such a situation. For Edward was a man who laid his plans far ahead. This can be seen in two charters of Athelstan's reign,[6] which show that already before 911 Edward was strengthening the English position inside territories then held by the Danes by encouraging English thegns to buy estates from them.

It may be the fault of our rather one-sided sources for his reign that Edward appears merely as an extremely able general, almost completely preoccupied with the reconquest of the Danelaw. There were doubtless other sides to his personality. If, like earlier kings of his line, he maintained intercourse with the

---

[1] No. 1, p. 199; No. 8, p. 279.   [2] No. 1, pp. 199 f.; No. 3, p. 252.
[3] No. 6.   [4] See F. T. Wainwright, *Eng. Hist. Rev.*, LXIII, pp. 145–169.
[5] *Idem, Saga-Book of the Viking Soc.*, XIII, pp. 156–173.   [6] No. 103, and Birch, No. 658.

Scale of Miles

0 10 20   40   60   80   100

3. THE SCANDINAVIAN SETTLEMENTS IN THE EARLY TENTH CENTURY

All boundaries except that contained in the Treaty of Alfred and Guthrum are conjectural only.

lands across the Channel, our sources are too sparse to afford much evidence. Yet one should note that one of the marriage alliances between his daughters and continental princes, that of Eadgifu to Charles the Simple, was made in his lifetime,[1] and that some of his son Athelstan's continental activities also belong to this time. The letter from Radbod of St. Samson's[2] shows that he was generous to at least one continental house, and this is unlikely to have been an isolated instance. It was in his reign that three new sees were created for Wessex, nor was it so blank a period in scholarship as is sometimes supposed.[3] He had himself received an education in letters[4] and in his turn he set store by the education of his son.[5] Nevertheless, the reconquest of the southern Danelaw remains his great achievement, for with half England in Danish control no advance in any other field would have had much chance of permanence. It was left for his son to carry on his work and obtain possession of Northumbria, and thus to become the first king to rule all England.

(vi) THE KINGDOM OF ENGLAND

Athelstan, not long after his accession, when King Sihtric of York, to whom he had given his sister in marriage, died in 927, drove out his brother Guthfrith and his son Olaf, and himself took control of Northumbria.[6] Contemporaries were aware that his position now differed from that of all previous kings; an Old English record of his gifts to Exeter says of him: "Through God's grace, he alone ruled all England, which before him many kings had held between them."[7] Athelstan's charters show that the importance of his position was realized by the king himself.

Much more is known about Athelstan than about his father. Whereas the Chronicle was the main source for the latter's reign, it is a poor record for Athelstan's, though it makes up for its scanty prose entries by preserving the poem on Brunanburh;[8] but in compensation we have the Latin verse panegyric which was available to William of Malmesbury,[9] continental references to his entries into European politics,[10] six law codes,[11] a number of charters,[12] and various minor sources such as lists of relics and notes in manuscripts, which illustrate his generosity to the Church and throw some light on his tastes.

His power was acknowledged by the Celtic princes in Britain. If we may assume that the meeting at Dacre mentioned by William of Malmesbury is the same as that at Eamont in the 'D' version of the Chronicle,[13] Athelstan's

---

[1] See R. L. Poole, "The Alpine Son-in-law of Edward the Elder" (*Eng. Hist. Rev.*, XXVI, 1911).
[2] No. 228.   [3] See p. 96.   [4] No. 7, p. 267.   [5] No. 8, p. 279.
[6] No. 1, p. 200.   [7] Birch, No. 693.   [8] No. 1, pp. 200 f.   [9] No. 8.
[10] Nos. 24–26.   [11] *e.g.* Nos. 35–37.   [12] *e.g.* Nos. 103 f.
[13] Cf. No. 1, p. 200, with No. 8, p. 280. It is possible that the entry in 'D', which was not added until the eleventh century, has confused Owain of Gwent, not mentioned by William, with his namesake of Strathclyde, or the latter may have been omitted by a copyist's error.

suzerainty was acknowledged in 927 by Constantine of the Scots, Owain of Strathclyde, Hywel of Dyfed and Owain of Gwent, as well as by Ealdred, the high-reeve of Bamburgh. Hywel of Dyfed, Idwal of Gwynedd, and Morgan of Morgannwg attended his court on several occasions between 931 and 935,[1] Tewdwr of Brecknock came in 934,[2] and a king called Owain in 931[3] and perhaps in 935.[4] William of Malmesbury takes from the Latin poem an account of a meeting at Hereford at which the Welsh rulers were compelled to promise tribute.[5] There may be some exaggeration of the amount, but the statement that the Wye was fixed as a boundary is accurate. William goes on to relate from the same source how Athelstan strengthened the position of the English in Devon at the expense of his British subjects, expelling these from Exeter.

Athelstan's charters are of great interest in showing that the clerks of his writing office, without doubt at the king's instructions, strive to give expression to their consciousness that this king's position in Britain differed from that of his predecessors. This can be seen in the Amounderness charter,[6] both in the body of the text and in the attestation; another frequently used formula runs: "*basileus* of the English and in like manner ruler of the whole orb of Britain",[7] and the attestation sometimes takes forms such as "king of the whole of Britain".[8] The absurdly inflated and flamboyant language of many of his charters similarly reflects this sense of his great importance. When he died, the *Annals of Ulster* caught the same tone when they referred to him as "the pillar of dignity of the western world".

Athelstan's supremacy did not go unchallenged. Owing to some breach of the peace of 927, he led his army into Scotland in 934. This is one of the few events of his reign recorded in the Chronicle, and a charter shows that one of the occasions when Welsh princes were with him was when he halted at Nottingham on his way to Scotland.[9] Later, in 937, Constantine of the Scots combined with the Norsemen whom Athelstan had ousted from the kingdom of York, now led by Olaf Guthfrith's son, who had succeeded his father in 934,[10] and invaded England with a great force which was defeated at *Brunanburh*. There are several accounts of this battle: the English poem in the Chronicle, the Latin poem quoted by William of Malmesbury, the account in Simeon's *History of the Church of Durham*,[11] also given in briefer form in his *History of the Kings*,[12] that in Florence of Worcester, based on the English poem, but with a few facts from some unknown source,[13] and the entry in the *Annals of Ulster*, which, while it adds little to what is known from other sources, is important in proving that it is not only English writers who regard it as a very great victory

---

[1] No. 104, and Birch, Nos. 675, 677, 702, 703, 716, 718. The two last are doubtful Malmesbury documents, with the incarnation date 937, but the other indications are for 935.
[2] Birch, No. 702.   [3] Birch, No. 675.   [4] Birch, Nos. 716, 718, but see n. 1 above.
[5] No. 8, pp. 280f.   [6] No. 104.   [7] *e.g.* Birch, Nos. 707-709, 714.
[8] *e.g.* Birch, Nos. 682, 694f., 707, 714, 728.   [9] No. 104.   [10] According to Irish annals.
[11] *Symeonis Monachi Opera Omnia*, ed. Arnold, I, p. 76.   [12] No. 3, p. 253.   [13] See p. 200, nn. 3, 5.

for Athelstan.[1] To Ælfric it was the outstanding event of his reign.[2] There are also accounts to which much legendary material has become attached.[3] Simeon says that Owain of Strathclyde was present at the battle, and that the invaders came with 615 ships, and he gives as names for the battlefield *Brunnanwerc* and *Weondun*, Florence adds to what he has learnt from the poem the fact that the invasion was by way of the Humber, the Latin poem shows that the invaders had ravaged far in Athelstan's lands before the armies met, the English poem claims that five kings as well as Constantine's son were slain, and shows that the English force was made up of West Saxons and Mercians. But in spite of all the accounts, the site of the battle cannot be identified.[4] It was certainly not in Wessex, nor in Constantine's territory, and perhaps it was not far from where the invaders had left their ships. Since the site cannot be determined, one cannot decide whether the absence of any mention of Northumbrians implies that they were holding aloof or merely that they could not be mustered in time. Northumbria may be the area meant in the Latin poem when it says: "The natives give way, the whole region yields to the proud."[5]

Athelstan's fame stretched beyond Britain. Very early in his reign he received a continental Latin poem congratulating him on his dealings with Constantine, king of the Scots, and Sihtric, king of York.[6] His sisters were sought in marriage by various continental princes; by the emperor Otto, who presented him with a book of gospels, and perhaps received one from Athelstan as a return gift;[7] by Hugh, duke of the Franks, who sent many relics and valuable gifts;[8] and by Louis of Aquitaine. Another of his sisters was married to a prince by the Alps who was probably Conrad of Burgundy.[9] No fewer than three foreign rulers are known to have been brought up at Athelstan's court, namely his nephew, Louis, nicknamed "From across the Sea", the son of Charles the Simple, whose recall from England is described by Flodoard and Richer;[10] Alan, count of Brittany, his godson, who recovered his land with English help;[11] and Hákon, son of Harold Fairhair of Norway, to whom later Scandinavian tradition gives the nickname "Athelstan's fosterling", claiming that Athelstan supported him with men and ships when he sailed back to Norway to recover his ancestral rights.[12] The accounts in Scandinavian sources have been much embroidered,

---

[1] *Annals of Ulster*, 936 (alias 937).   [2] No. 239(I).
[3] For these, see A. Campbell, *The Battle of Brunanburh*, pp. 147–162.
[4] There have, of course, been various theories, for which see Campbell, *op. cit.*, pp. 57–80.
[5] No. 8, p. 283.
[6] Birch, No. 655. See W. H. Stevenson, "A Latin Poem addressed to King Athelstan" (*Eng. Hist. Rev.*, XXVI, 1911).
[7] Brit. Mus. Cott. Tiber. A. ii, which was given by Athelstan to Christ Church, contains the names of Otto and his mother, while a gospel-book at Gandersheim has the names of Athelstan and his mother Eadgifu. See R. Drögereit, *Niedersächsisches Jahrbuch für Landesgeschichte*, XXI, pp. 46 f.
[8] No. 8, p. 282.
[9] See R. L. Poole, "The Alpine Son-in-law of Edward the Elder" (*Eng. Hist. Rev.*, XXVI).
[10] No. 24.   [11] Nos. 24 f.
[12] See, for example, *Heimskringla*, Saga of Harold Fairhair, chaps. 40 f., Saga of Hákon the Good, chap. 1.

but relations between Athelstan and Harold are supported by William of Malmesbury, who is drawing his information from the Latin poem.[1]

Athelstan's name was well known in continental churches. He helped the exiled canons of St. Samson's at Dol[2] and he made gifts to St. Bertin's at St. Omer;[3] in 929 he sent Cenwold, bishop of Worcester, on a mission with rich gifts to the German churches, and this led to the entry of his name and those of other English persons into the books of confraternity of St. Gall, Reichenau and Pfäfers.[4] One object of this mission may have been the collecting of relics, for a document entered into the Leofric Missal at Exeter says he sent true and wise men overseas to travel as widely as they could to this end.[5] His activities in this direction must have begun before he came to the throne, for he refers to his collection in the manumission performed immediately after his coronation,[6] and his proclivities were well enough known abroad for relics to bulk largely among the gifts brought by the embassy from Hugh, duke of the Franks, no later than 926,[7] while Radbod of St. Samson's accompanied his letter with relics of Breton saints. He acquired books from the Continent also, and gave them to various English churches.[8]

As the first southern king to include Northumbria in his dominions, Athelstan had unprecedented problems of government, but northern sources are too scanty to give a clear idea of how he dealt with them. We have no right to assume that the rule of a West Saxon king was welcome even to the English element of the population, and later events were to show how ready this province was to receive any Scandinavian ruler who might give them a chance to recover independence. During part of his reign Athelstan was in the habit of holding great gatherings attended by both lay and ecclesiastical representatives from the North. The English rulers of the lands north of the Tyne appear at them, and several *duces* with Scandinavian names, whose native title was probably 'earl'. Some of these may, however, belong to East Anglia, so it is impossible to say how many should be located in southern Northumbria. Eight such persons attest in 931,[9] seven in 932 and 934.[10] Three occur in a Malmesbury document which, if it is genuine, probably belongs to 935.[11] After that, none of Athelstan's charters have demonstrably northern signatories, and he may have discontinued the holding of these great assemblies in his last few years. He was himself in Northumbria in 927, and again on his way to and from Scotland in 934,[12] and he was at York in 936 when he received the embassy sent to invite his foster-son Louis back to France.[13] It may have been on one of these occasions that he received at York an embassy from Harold Fairhair of Norway.[14]

[1] No. 8, p. 281.   [2] No. 228.   [3] No. 26.
[4] See J. Armitage Robinson, *The Saxon Bishops of Wells*, pp. 60–62.   [5] Birch, No. 693.
[6] No. 140.   [7] No. 8, p. 282.   [8] See p. 96.   [9] Birch, Nos. 674 f., 677.
[10] No. 104, and Birch, Nos. 689, 692, 701 f.   [11] Birch, No. 716. See p. 39, n. 1.
[12] No. 1, p. 200.   [13] No. 24.   [14] No. 8, p. 281.

While he was in Northumbria, he was generous to the Church to an extent that suggests that he was anxious to strengthen it and win its support. To York, where the archbishop, Wulfstan I, seems to have been his nominee, he gave control of the whole district of Amounderness, bought from the pagans with his own money.[1] To St. Cuthbert's, then at Chester-le-Street, he gave books and a most impressive list of treasures, as well as the royal estate of Wearmouth with its appendant estates.[2] The brothers of this community were still honouring his memory at the end of the eleventh century, when they agreed to celebrate the anniversaries of Malcolm and Margaret of Scotland "as a festival year by year like that of King Athelstan".[3] Ripon and Beverley attributed to him wide-reaching grants of sanctuary. Though no early records survive to prove that these actually dated from his reign, St. Wilfrid's 'mile' at Ripon is mentioned already in surveys entered into the York Gospels in the early eleventh century,[4] while at Beverley there was a similar mile of special sanctuary, according to the evidence of jurors who pronounced on the ancient rights of the church of York in 1106, and the penalties for violating it were increased if the offence were committed on the near side of "Athelstan's cross".[5] This matter should perhaps not be unduly stressed, for Athelstan was a liberal donor to the Church elsewhere, as William of Malmesbury claims[6] and the surviving accounts and lists of his donations prove;[7] Milton Abbas and Muchelney claimed him as their founder.[8] But that he took a special interest in the Church of Northumbria may perhaps be inferred from the appearance in his reign of more suffragans of York than there were in later times, if this indicates an attempt to restore some of the sees destroyed by the Danish invasions.[9]

There was probably also need for reorganization of East Anglia, for between its submission to Edward and his death there were only a few years and those not free from other campaigns; but again, evidence is scanty. By about 932, Athelstan had placed it in the charge of a religiously minded ealdorman, Athelstan Halfking, from an English area, though whether he was of Mercian or West Saxon origin is uncertain. A chance reference in the *Historia Eliensis*[10] speaks of the giving of a monastery at Horningsea to a follower of King Athelstan, and it was in his reign that Theodred was made bishop of London and he may at once have taken charge of part, at least, of the East Anglian diocese, as he certainly did later.[11] But we have no details of either secular or ecclesiastical administration of the areas reconquered from the Danes.

One cannot even know how far the extant laws of this king are meant to apply to the whole kingdom.[12] These laws include many strong and practical

---

[1] No. 104. [2] Birch, No. 685. [3] *Liber Vitae* of Durham, fol. 48v.
[4] See W. H. Stevenson, *Eng. Hist. Rev.*, xxvii, p. 18.
[5] A. F. Leach, *Visitations and Memorials of Southwell Minster* (Camden Soc., 1891), pp. 194f.
[6] No. 8, p. 277. [7] J. Armitage Robinson, *The Times of St. Dunstan*, pp. 51–80.
[8] See p. 97. [9] See p. 95. [10] Ed. D. J. Stewart, p. 146. [11] No. 106. [12] Nos. 35–37.

measures for the suppression of theft, of tyranny by powerful families, and of corruption in administration. They show a desire to encourage trade by ensuring an undebased coinage and by increasing security against fraud. A more personal note comes through in passages which reveal his concern about the too harsh treatment of young offenders.

There are one or two obscure hints that Athelstan's reign was not entirely free from internal troubles. Though one can ignore the embroideries of post-Conquest writers on the statement of the 'E' version of the Chronicle that his brother Edwin was drowned at sea, Folcwin's reference to the same matter certainly suggests that some civil disorder had led to this prince's exile.[1] Again, there may possibly be some grain of truth behind the story William of Malmesbury drew from a spurious document of his house, of an attempt against the king by a certain Alfred.[2]

Finally, in one respect we know more about Athelstan than most Saxon kings: we know something of what he looked like, for William of Malmesbury says he was flaxen-haired, slender and of middle height.[3] The copy of the Lives of St. Cuthbert which he gave to that saint's church contains a picture of him presenting the book to the saint,[4] but it is uncertain how far early representations of this kind are even intended as portraiture.

An Anglo-Saxon poet might well have used the events that immediately followed Athelstan's death late in 939 to illustrate the favourite theme of the transitoriness of earthly success. By the end of 940 a Scandinavian king was again ruling, and not only Northumbria, but Mercia as far as the Watling Street. The relations between the English kings and the North for the next fourteen years can be best seen in the work of Simeon of Durham,[5] for the main Chronicle has, apart from the poem at 942, only a couple of entries, and they would not be intelligible by themselves, while 'E' has only some of the events which Simeon drew from the northern annals, and 'D', which added in the eleventh century matter peculiar to itself, from an unknown source, is unreliable in its dating.[6] The struggle for the possession of Northumbria was a long one. On Athelstan's death his old enemy Olaf, Guthfrith's son, seized Northumbria, made a great raid into Mercia, where at Tamworth, according to the 'D' text of the Chronicle, he took prisoner an important Mercian lady, and was besieged along with Archbishop Wulfstan in Leicester. According to 'D', he and the archbishop escaped by flight, but Simeon only says that peace was made there, the Watling Street to be the boundary between the kingdoms. This was so sudden and great a setback that one cannot wonder that the winning back of the Five

---

[1] No. 26.   [2] No. 8, p. 277.   [3] No. 8, p. 280.
[4] C.C.C.C., MS. 183, reproduced, for example, in D. Talbot Rice, *English Art*, 871–1100, pl. 47.
[5] No. 3, pp. 253 f.   [6] No. 1, p. 202.

Boroughs in 942 was felt to be an occasion worth celebrating in song; the author of the little poem entered in the Chronicle at this point assumes that the Danish population regarded it as a release from captivity. Meanwhile Olaf, Guthfrith's son, had died, and Northumbria was ruled first by Olaf, Sihtric's son, and then by Ragnald, Guthfrith's son, both of whom in turn came to the English court in 943, and Edmund stood sponsor to them. In 944, according to the Chronicle, Edmund drove them both out (Simeon says that the Northumbrians had expelled Olaf the year before) and once again all England is under the West Saxon king. Edmund raided Strathclyde in 945, and the brief entry in the Chronicle can be supplemented with that in Roger of Wendover, telling of help given by a king of Dyfed, of the blinding of the king's sons, and the handing over of the country to Malcolm of Scotland.[1] No further trouble is expressly mentioned in the rest of Edmund's short reign, but the wording of the Chronicle that Eadred 'reduced' Northumbria on his accession in 946 suggests that all was not well. He took oaths from the Scots, and the following year oaths from the Northumbrians at Tanshelf, yet before the end of the year, the Northumbrians had taken as king an exiled king of Norway, Eric Blood-axe. They deserted him on the approach of Eadred's forces in 948, only to receive back Olaf, Sihtric's son, in 949. Three years later he was driven out by Eric, who in his turn was expelled and killed in 954, an incident on which Roger of Wendover supplies some welcome detail.[2] Henceforward the Northumbrians were governed by earls appointed by the kings of England. Scandinavian tradition believed that Eric Blood-axe held his throne by the gift of the English king,[3] but there is no hint of this in English sources, though it is just possible that from 949 to 954 Eadred played off rival claimants against one another.

During this disturbed period, Archbishop Wulfstan of York is suspect of disloyalty to the English king. The case against him is almost entirely in the additions to the 'D' version of the Chronicle, which say he accompanied Olaf on his raid on the Midlands in 940, and was again on the wrong side in 947, when the Northumbrians accepted Eric. It tells of his imprisonment by King Eadred in 952, "because he had often been accused to him", and records his restoration in 954 in words that may mean that he was only allowed to act as bishop in the diocese of Dorchester.[4] Since he attests charters as archbishop of York in 955 and 956, it would at first sight look as if he were fully reinstated, or even as if the whole story in 'D' were untrue, especially when the chronicler Æthelweard attributes to him a share in the driving out of Olaf and Ragnald and appears not to have heard of any alleged Scandinavian sympathies.[5] Yet the accusation cannot be so lightly dismissed, for when manuscript 'B' of the Chronicle records the death of his successor Oscetel in 971,[6] it says that it was

[1] No. 4, p. 257. [2] *ibid.* [3] No. 11.
[4] No. 1, p. 204, n. 5. [5] No. 1, p. 203, n. 1. [6] No. 1, p. 207.

by the will of King Eadred and all his people that Oscetel was made archbishop of York,[1] and, as Eadred died before Wulfstan, this cannot be referring to his succession on the latter's death, unless the name Eadred is an error for Eadwig. It seems possible that he was appointed to look after York during Wulfstan's disgrace, just as in the eleventh century Ælfric of York was given charge of Worcester when Lifing fell into disfavour; and it is conceivable that Eadred was prepared to let Wulfstan retain his metropolitan title, but not to trust him near Yorkshire again. He was buried at Oundle. Whatever is the truth of the matter, one thing is certain: the Anglo-Saxon kings never afterwards appointed a Northumbrian to the see of York.

Of the two English kings who strove to rid Northumbria of Scandinavian kings, one, Edmund, was killed in 946 by a robber, after a reign of less than seven years,[2] in which he had shown good qualities as a ruler. He is mentioned in Ethelred's laws as one of the wise law-givers of the past, and among other things he strove to decrease the prevalence of blood-feuds.[3] Like Athelstan, he concerned himself with continental affairs. There was an embassy from Germany at his court early in his reign,[4] and in 946 he interfered on behalf of his nephew Louis who was being held prisoner by Hugh, duke of the Franks, but his death occurred before Louis's release.[5] As far as we know, his brother and successor Eadred made no entry into continental politics. He was probably too fully occupied with Northumbria. It is worth noting that he had men from this province with him when he visited Abingdon.[6] His will, which shows him anxious to relieve the distress of his subjects in times of calamity, does not include the Northumbrians among his beneficiaries.[7] He was interested in monastic reform, and began the refoundation of Abingdon,[8] and he was a friend of Dunstan.[9]

His will shows that he did not consider the danger from Danish ravages to be over, but they were not renewed in the reigns of his immediate successors. Little is on record for the short reign of Eadwig, who succeeded in 955 as a youth and quarrelled with Dunstan, which gives him a black name in monastic writers. According to the highly coloured story in the oldest Life of Dunstan, he resented the latter's part in forcing him back to his coronation feast from the more congenial society of a lady.[10] The 'D' version of the Chronicle attributes to Archbishop Oda the separation of Eadwig from a lady called Ælfgifu, because they were too closely related.[11] This does not necessarily exclude the possibility of some incident at the coronation, but the account comes from a very biased source. An unusually large number of charters survive from his reign, the most interesting being his grant of Southwell to the church of York;[12] but in

---

[1] 'C' calls the king Edward, and alters the annal in a way that suggests that Oscetel was at first a suffragan bishop of York, before he became archbishop.   [2] No. 1, p. 203.
[3] No. 38.   [4] No. 234, p. 828.   [5] No. 24.   [6] No. 235, p. 834.   [7] No. 107.
[8] No. 235, p. 833.   [9] No. 234, pp. 828 f. [10] No. 234, pp. 829 f. [11] No. 1, p. 205.   [12] No. 108.

957 the Mercians and Northumbrians elected his brother Edgar in his place. The kingdom was therefore divided until Edgar succeeded to the whole on Eadwig's death on 1 October 959.

The absence of warfare during his reign caused Edgar to become known as 'the Peaceable'. His reputation has suffered because some historians, reacting from an earlier unfavourable view of Dunstan, have attributed Edgar's good government to Dunstan, rather than to the king. Whereas Ælfric links together as great and victorious kings Alfred, Athelstan and Edgar,[1] Armitage Robinson writes "Alfred, Athelstan and Dunstan–'these three' were 'mighty men': of all the rest that were before the Norman Conquest it must be written that 'they attained not unto the first three'."[2] Dom Thomas Symons, commenting on the aim of the *Regularis Concordia* to end the vying of monastic houses with one another in elaboration of ritual and devotional practice,[3] accepts without question Robinson's conclusion: "perhaps we may trace the moderating strength of the great archbishop . . . the words of warning are said to have come from the letter of the king; but the king's speech is the speech of his chief minister." But why should they not simply represent the point of view of a sensible layman? And as for Dunstan as the king's 'chief minister', there seems no evidence that he had more political influence than many another archbishop before or later.[4] He was remembered rather for his saintly qualities than his political powers, and one cannot take at their face value all the claims of writers of hagiography regarding the importance and influence of their subject. His biographer 'B', for example, says Eadred trusted him with all the best of his goods,[5] but it is clear from later on in his work, and from Eadred's will,[6] that Dunstan was only one of many whom the king employed in this way; and the same author's claim that Dunstan was chosen bishop in order to give the king the constant benefit of his counsels may well be a similar exaggeration. There is no evidence to show that Dunstan had any special share in the drafting of Edgar's laws, and a set of ecclesiastical regulations which goes under the name of the "Canons of Edgar", once believed to have been issued under Dunstan's influence, has been shown to belong to a later period and to be the work of Archbishop Wulfstan of York.[7] Edgar was on good terms with his archbishop and shared his views on ecclesiastical matters, but it is as well to examine his secular government without a bias in Dunstan's favour.

The documents in this volume include several which in retrospect praise Edgar's reign. The entry, in Archbishop Wulfstan's style, in the 'D' and 'E' versions of the Chronicle,[8] Ælfric's passage in his Life of St. Swithin,[9] and his

[1] No. 239(I).   [2] *The Times of St. Dunstan*, p. 81.
[3] See *Regularis Concordia: The Monastic Agreement*, p. xxv.
[4] R. R. Darlington, *Eng. Hist. Rev.*, LI, p. 387, also doubts Dunstan's political influence.
[5] No. 234, p. 829.   [6] No. 107.   [7] K. Jost, *Anglia*, LVI, pp. 288–301.   [8] No. I, pp. 205 f.   [9] No. 239(G).

addition to *Judges*,[1] the Old English text on the restoration of monasteries,[2] the oldest Life of St. Dunstan,[3] and the anonymous Life of St. Oswald,[4] all speak of the peace and good government in his time. All these writers are, it is true, of the reforming party, and moreover the contrast with what happened later would heighten their appreciation of his reign, but this need not mean that their claims were without foundation. A tradition reached Florence of Worcester that Edgar used to make progresses through his kingdom in order to redress wrongs,[5] and complaints that things have deteriorated since his time are met with.[6] The respect of later generations for his laws is seen in the holding up of him as one of the law-givers whose example should be followed,[7] in their acceptance by the English and Danes in 1018 as the basis of their agreement,[8] and most of all in the great use made of them in the codes of Ethelred and Cnut.[9] While his laws impose penalties of extreme–and, one would think, impracticable–severity for non-payment of Church dues, they otherwise advocate moderation in judgments, lay down excellent principles of just law for rich and poor, and reveal a particular concern with coinage and trade.[10] His concern with the coinage is mentioned also by Roger of Wendover.[11]

Edgar shows a willingness to admit the rights of his Danish subjects to make their own laws;[12] and a desire to gain the goodwill of the Northumbrians may possibly be read into the incident of the ravaging of Thanet, which the northern version of the Chronicle enters without explanation, but which Roger of Wendover explains as a punitory measure after the men of Thanet had ill-treated some York merchants,[13] though such an action could arise simply from a refusal to let lawless acts go unpunished. The one complaint against him, made in the 'D' and 'E' versions of the Chronicle,[14] that he loved foreign customs, introduced heathen manners and attracted foreigners into the country, may have been occasioned by a policy of encouragement of foreign trade and of toleration of Scandinavian customs in the Danelaw.

But it is not so much his laws and administration as his power and his maintenance of peace that impressed the writers mentioned above. Florence of Worcester gives an exaggerated account of his having a fleet of 3,600 ships.[15] Edgar took care to impress his magnificence on his contemporaries by the splendour of his delayed coronation at Bath in 973,[16] and by some sort of spectacular ceremony at Chester later on in the year,[17] at which six kings, or eight according to Ælfric and Florence, came to make submission to him. Ælfric mentions only Cumbrians and Scots, but Florence, who names them, includes two Welsh

---

[1] No. 239(I). [2] No. 238. [3] No. 234, p. 830.
[4] *Historians of the Church of York*, ed. Raine, I, pp. 425 f. [5] Ed. Thorpe, p. 144.
[6] VIII Ethelred (No. 46), 37; No. 240. [7] VIII Ethelred (No. 46), 43.
[8] No. I, p. 228, n. 5; No. 47; No. 48. [9] See p. 333. [10] See Nos. 40 f. [11] No. 4, p. 258.
[12] IV Edgar (No. 41), 2.1, 12. [13] No. I, p. 207; No. 4, p. 257. [14] No. I, p. 206.
[15] Ed. Thorpe, I, p. 144. [16] No. I, pp. 207 f.; *Historians of the Church of York*, ed. Raine, I, pp. 436–438.
[17] No. I, p. 208 and n. I; No. 239(G).

princes as well as two rulers who cannot be identified. Roger of Wendover has preserved an account of the cession of Lothian to Kenneth, king of the Scots, in return for his homage.[1] That he was in communication with the emperor we learn from the Life of St. Oswald, which says he sent gifts to him.[2]

The writers of the monastic reform saw in this attainment of power without warfare a divine reward for his zeal in furthering their cause, and he was certainly wholeheartedly behind the movement.[3] It was not carried out without causing resentment, which flared up immediately after his death. Unfortunately, all our records come from the monastic party, who probably exaggerate the ignorance and viciousness of their opponents, to cover any highhanded action in the course of the reform.

The main evidence for the troubles on Edgar's death is contained in the Chronicle, both in the poem in 'A', 'B' and 'C', and the rhythmical prose in Wulfstan's style in 'D',[4] and in the Life of St. Oswald.[5] Perhaps the failure of Archbishop Oswald to retain the lands recovered for his see by Oscetel should be attributed to the same cause.[6] Edgar left two sons, one a youth, the other a mere child, and there was division among the people as to which should succeed him. The elder, Edward, was elected and crowned before the year ended – Ethelred's charter of about 999, choosing to ignore the contested election, says he was elected unanimously on his father's death by all the leading men[7] – but in the interval there were risings against the monasteries, especially in Mercia. It is not clear how the magnates were divided on the political issue, but Mr. Fisher has recently made a case for associating Ælfhere, whom monastic writers regard as an enemy, with the supporters of Ethelred.[8] Nothing is known of the reason for the exile of Oslac, ealdorman of Northumbria, immediately after Edgar's death.[9]

The politics that underlie the murder of King Edward the Martyr in 978 are as obscure as those behind his accession. Manuscript 'C' of the Chronicle records the mere fact; the passage in 'D' and 'E' was not added until later, when his cult as a saint was established;[10] the most helpful account, that in the Life of St. Oswald, which tells us that he was killed when visiting his brother, is vague – no doubt deliberately vague – in assigning the blame.[11] Post-Conquest writers lay the crime to the charge of Edward's stepmother, Ethelred's mother. Though Ethelred himself was not responsible, being a child at the time, it is probable that the knowledge that his accession was the result of a murder committed on his behalf was responsible for some of the characteristics of his rule.[12] The cult of Edward as a saint was officially encouraged, and in 1008 it was ordained that his feast day was to be celebrated throughout all England.[13]

---

[1] No. 4, p. 258. [2] *Historians of the Church of York*, ed. Raine, I, p. 435. [3] See pp. 97 f.
[4] No. 1, pp. 208 f. [5] No. 236, pp. 839–843. [6] No. 114. [7] No. 123.
[8] *Cambridge Hist. Journ.*, x, pt. III, pp. 254–270. [9] No. 1, p. 209. [10] No. 1, p. 210.
[11] No. 236, pp. 841–843. [12] See F. M. Stenton, *Anglo-Saxon England*, pp. 368 f. [13] V Ethelred (No. 44), 16.

With the reign of Ethelred we again have a full record in the Chronicle, which affords a consecutive narrative of the course of the viking attacks which began in this reign, and ended in the conquest of the country by Cnut. The scaldic poems and the Scandinavian prose narrative based on lost poems add to our knowledge of personalities such as Thorkel the Tall and Earl Eric, and afford evidence of the part played by St. Olaf, on which English sources are silent.[1] The English poem on Maldon,[2] and the account of this battle and of the engagement in Devon given in the Life of St. Oswald,[3] are important as revealing contemporary attitudes to the events, and on one important incident, the martyrdom of St. Ælfheah, there is the account in Thietmar to compare with that in the Chronicle.[4] The same author's account of events around London after Ethelred's death is confused but not without interest, while the survival of the letter from Pope John tells us of unfriendly relations between England and Normandy not recorded in other sources.[5] The other papal letter of this period[6] supports the tirade of Archbishop Wulfstan on the prevalence of disorder and injustice,[7] and there are comments on contemporary affairs in the writings of Abbot Ælfric.[8] The reign is well represented in law-codes,[9] including the full text of a treaty with the Danes and a code concerned with the northern Danelaw, while the charters of this period are unusually informative, indicating not only general disorder and bad government,[10] but also the existence of a plot in Essex to accept Swein as king already in the early years of the viking invasion.[11] They throw valuable light on the character of the king. In short, we are unusually well supplied with material for this unhappy reign.

One could add to this the evidence of the king's nickname, if it were certain that it was given by his contemporaries. It is, however, not recorded before the thirteenth century, and its earliest form is not 'unready', but *unred*. This is a noun, which does not mean 'inaction', but a positive evil, at its best 'folly, foolish counsel' but often 'a treacherous plot', 'an evil deed'. Its application to Ethelred arises from a pun on his name, which means 'noble counsel', and such a pun could have been made by some post-Conquest wit who noticed the discrepancy between his name and his recorded actions. Nevertheless, plenty of these are mentioned in contemporary sources to justify the nickname if it was actually given in his lifetime.

Though there are *unrædas* in plenty in the narrative in the Chronicle, it is the charters that shed the most interesting light on this king. Whereas those of the preceding reigns are usually in a stereotyped form, Ethelred's charters become almost garrulous; sometimes he expatiates on the sins of his youth in terms which one would suppose no clerk would have used without his instructions;[12] or he refers in lachrymose style to the troubles of his reign;[13] often he seems eager

---

[1] Nos. 12–14. [2] No 10. [3] No. 236, p. 843. [4] No. 27. [5] No. 230. [6] No. 231.
[7] No. 240. [8] No. 239. [9] Nos. 42–46. [10] Nos. 117–127. [11] No. 121.
[12] Kemble, Nos. 684, 688, 698, 700. [13] Kemble. No. 706.

to justify his possession of the estates he is granting, by giving detailed accounts of how the lands came into his possession.[1] The most striking example is the narrative of the crimes of Wulfbold,[2] which has proved by the end of its recital that Wulfbold, if really guilty of these things, deservedly lost his land; but it has also revealed something else, the extraordinary feebleness of the government he defied for so long. The charters of Ethelred give away his sense of insecurity and his need for self-justification. The Chronicle gives the impression that he placed in office men he had advanced himself rather than those of old established families, and that his choice was often unfortunate. He was in frequent fear of betrayal, and avenged even suspected betrayal with violence and cruelty, as in the St. Brice's day massacre.[3] Yet the sources do not suggest that he was naturally cruel. He had no hardened conscience and he was deeply concerned for the fate of his soul, being generous to religious establishments and taking the advice of ecclesiastics on the affairs of the Church. But he was not the man to deal with the situation caused by the renewal of viking attack, and nowhere is this more apparent than in his relations with Northumbria.

It is probable that even the strongest and wisest of kings might have found the situation difficult to handle when this heavily Scandinavianized province had a chance of enlisting outside help against southern control; for we do not know how far Edgar's policy of securing its goodwill had been successful, nor what lay behind Ealdorman Oslac's exile in 975. At any rate, the poem on the battle of Maldon suggests that Ethelred's government had thought it desirable to take hostages from Northumbria when the Danish raids began.[4] There is also a possibility that they arranged a diplomatic marriage, for though the evidence that Ethelred's first wife was a daughter of Earl Thored (of Northumbria) is late,[5] such a union would explain why Ethelred's eldest sons had close connexions with the leading men of the northern Danelaw.[6] Wulfric Spott's will[7] shows that men of prominent Mercian family had been penetrating into the area of the Five Boroughs and Yorkshire, and it was one of these, Wulfric's brother Ælfhelm, whom Ethelred chose to succeed Thored as ealdorman about 993. But he was murdered in 1006 and his two sons were blinded, according to Florence of Worcester by the king's orders. The control of southern Northumbria was then given to Uhtred, the ealdorman of northern Northumbria, who is said by later tradition to have been Ethelred's son-in-law, and who had won a victory against the Scots in 1006.[8] The North seems to have yielded easily to Swein in 1013, and even after his death the men of Lindsey were prepared to

---

[1] Nos. 117, 119f., 123.   [2] No. 120.   [3] No. 1, p. 217; No. 127.   [4] No. 10.
[5] Ailred of Rievaulx. See Migne, *Patrologia Latina*, cxcv, col. 741.
[6] No. 1, p. 224; No. 130.   [7] No. 125.
[8] *Annals of Ulster*, 1006. See also *De obsessione Dunelmi, Symeonis Monachi Opera Omnia*, ed. Arnold, I, pp. 215f.

throw in their lot with Cnut and go raiding with him. Ethelred took stern vengeance on them, and in 1015 he again resorted to or at least connived with treacherous murder. For when the thegns of the Seven Boroughs, Sigeferth and Morcar, friends of Ethelred's son Athelstan, were murdered by Eadric Streona, the king took no action to punish the murder, but seized their lands and imprisoned Sigeferth's widow. Up till 1012 he had been loading Morcar with grants of land.[1] Even if he believed these thegns to have been disloyal to him when Swein came, his resort to treacherous murder rather than legal conviction cannot have commended itself to their friends and kin in the North. Ethelred's son, Edmund, in defiance of his father, seized and married Sigeferth's widow, and went north and secured all his estates and those of Morcar, and received the submission of the people. This division between father and son further weakened the English resistance. Cnut received the submission of Northumbria the following year, placing over it his most powerful ally, Earl Eric.

In 1016, once Ethelred was dead, the English put up a good resistance. There are several hints in our sources that the ordinary Englishman could fight for his home when under competent leadership, and the new king, Edmund, whose nickname 'Ironside' is recorded as early as the annal for 1057 in the 'D' manuscript of the Chronicle, supplied it. Even after his defeat at Ashingdon he was formidable enough for Cnut to agree to terms which left the land south of the Thames in Edmund's hands. His death before the end of the year allowed Cnut to obtain the whole kingdom.

For the reigns of Cnut and his sons the Chronicle once again more or less fails us, containing only a few brief entries probably made at a considerably later date. For political events we are helped by Scandinavian poems and traditions,[2] by the material which Florence of Worcester was able to add to the Chronicle he was using,[3] and by an occasional piece of evidence elsewhere. Cnut took steps early in his reign to get rid of possible English rivals, and he placed Northumbria and East Anglia in control of two of his foremost generals, Eric and Thorkel. The former would be not much more than a name to us if it were not for the Scandinavian sources, which show him as Cnut's brother-in-law, earl of Hlathir, who had led the opposition which ended in the overthrow of King Olaf Tryggvason.[4] Thorkel had been the leader of the great Danish host that attacked England in 1009,[5] and entered Ethelred's service with forty-five ships after the martyrdom of Archbishop Ælfheah,[6] which, according to Thietmar, he had tried to prevent.[7] In 1014 he returned to Cnut, with nine ships.[8]

---

[1] There is an unpublished grant to Morcar in 1012 in the William Salt Collection, Stafford.
[2] See Nos. 14–19.   [3] No. 9.   [4] See p. 123.   [5] No. 1, p. 220.   [6] No. 1, p. 222.
[7] No. 27.   [8] *Encomium Emmae Reginae*, ed. Campbell, p. 18; cf. *idem*, pp. 10, 16, 22, 24.

A Scandinavian tradition explained his defection from Ethelred as arising from the slaying of a brother in England.[1] Later sagas make Thorkel one of the leaders of the vikings of Jómsborg, but it is uncertain how much fiction is interwoven into the accounts of this stronghold.[2] He seems to have been left as regent in England in Cnut's absence in 1019–1020,[3] but was exiled in 1021.[4] Two years later he and Cnut were reconciled.[5] Cnut had far more trouble from his own followers than from his English subjects. He married Emma, Ethelred's widow and daughter of Richard of Normandy,[6] and thus ensured that no active support should be given from that quarter to Ethelred's sons, but his own followers Ulf and Eilaf were in arms against him at the Holy River in 1026,[7] and in 1029 he outlawed Earl Hákon, son of Earl Eric.[8] There is little mention of warfare in Britain. The Scots won a victory at Carham-on-Tweed in 1016 or 1018,[9] and Cnut led an expedition to Scotland soon after his return from Rome, receiving the submission of Scottish kings, a fact alluded to in Sighvat's poem as well as in the Chronicle.[10] There may have been intervening incidents unrecorded in our inadequate sources. Some trouble with Wales is implied by entries in the *Annales Cambriae* that "Eilaf laid waste Dyfed" and "Caradauc, son of Rederch, was killed by the English", but Cnut's chief preoccupation was with holding and extending his power in Scandinavia and he drew England into the orbit of northern affairs.

He went to Denmark in 1019, and writes from there of measures to prevent any further threat to England from that quarter.[11] Thietmar[12] and the *Encomium Emmae* show that he had a brother, Harold, unmentioned in English records, and this journey was probably occasioned by his death. After a second journey, from which he returned in 1023,[13] he placed Denmark and one of his sons in Thorkel's charge, though within three years Ulf had replaced Thorkel in Denmark and was regent for Hardacnut.[14] Cnut was threatened by an alliance of Olaf of Norway and Önund of Sweden, with whom his followers Ulf and Eilaf were allied,[15] and received a set-back at the Holy River in 1026.[16] After his return from Rome and his Scottish expedition, he led English forces to Norway and drove out King Olaf;[17] both Florence and the scaldic poems show that he had previously bribed Norwegian chieftains to his side. He set Earl Hákon over Norway,[18] but when Olaf attempted to return and was killed in 1030, an event which the Chronicle records,[19] we learn from Florence and from Scandinavian sources that he placed Ælfgifu of Northampton and his son by her, Swein, over

---

[1] On this story, see A. S. Napier and W. H. Stevenson, *The Crawford Charters*, pp. 140f.
[2] See p. 125.   [3] No. 48.   [4] No. 1, p. 229.   [5] See n. 14, below.
[6] No. 1, p. 228.   [7] No. 1, p. 230.   [8] No. 1, p. 231; No. 9, p. 287.
[9] 1016 according to Simeon's *History of the Church of Durham*, 1018 according to the *History of the Kings*, *Symeonis Monachi Opera Omnia*, ed. Arnold, 1, p. 84, 11, pp. 155f.
[10] No. 1, p. 231; No. 18.   [11] No. 1, p. 228; No. 48.   [12] No. 27.   [13] No. 1, p. 229.
[14] No. 1, p. 229; *Heimskringla*, Saga of St. Olaf, chap. 148.   [15] No. 1, p. 230.   [16] See Nos. 15f.
[17] No. 1, p. 230; No. 9, p. 287; No. 18.   [18] No. 19.   [19] No. 1, p. 231.

Norway, where their rule was extremely unpopular. They lost their kingdom to Magnus, Olaf's son, a little before Cnut's death in 1035.[1]

Something of Cnut's rule in England can be gathered from his laws, his charters, and records of his gifts to the Church. He placed several of his own followers in high places, and Scandinavian names appear among the thegns who witness his charters. He and his earls were guarded by bodies of 'house-carls' which in the early part of his reign would consist of Scandinavians. There survives an interesting list in the Thorney *Liber Vitae*, in which Cnut's earls are followed by thirty-one names of Scandinavian origin without a single English name among them.[2] In eleventh-century records we meet landowners with Scandinavian names outside the Danelaw, such as the Urki who founded the Abbotsbury guild,[3] who presumably owe their land to Cnut's gift. But there was no wide-spread displacement of the English aristocracy, and these same sources depict these Scandinavians behaving in relation to the Church just like English men of rank. Cnut himself acts as a Christian king, as may be seen already in 1018 when he ratifies an agreement with the bishop of Cornwall, using the words "when I succeeded to the kingdom after King Edmund";[4] and his intent to rule as did his predecessors is shown by his choice of Archbishop Wulfstan to draft his laws.[5] Many churches applaud his generosity, and he founded the church at Ashingdon in thanksgiving for his victory, and established Benedictine monks at Holme and Bury St. Edmunds. The author of the *Encomium Emmae* describes at length his humility and religious devotion, which the author himself witnessed at St. Omer,[6] and one of the motives for his Rome pilgrimage was undoubtedly to benefit his soul. But he would not be blind to the political importance of combining it with attendance at the emperor's coronation, and he made good capital out of his contacts with other rulers there.[7] He probably emulated previous English kings in their generosity to continental churches, for it is unlikely that the donation to Chartres mentioned in Fulbert's letter stood alone.[8]

Cnut writes with a touch of naïve pride at the honour he received from pope and emperor. His sons did not maintain his position of dignity, and there is little to admire in the rule of either. The 'E' version of the Chronicle makes it clear that Harold was at first set up as regent, becoming king in 1037 only because of Hardacnut's lingering in Denmark.[9] The statements in the *Encomium Emmae*, that he was chosen king by a few Englishmen and that the archbishop refused to crown him,[10] were written for Emma's benefit and can be discounted. But there are probably some authentic features in the same writer's

---

[1] No. 9, p. 228; *Heimskringla*, Saga of St. Olaf, chaps. 240, 245, 248, 252, Saga of Magnus the Good, chaps. 1–4.

[2] See D. Whitelock, "Scandinavian Personal Names in the *Liber Vitae* of Thorney Abbey" (*Saga-Book of the Viking Soc.*, XII, pp. 127–153).

[3] No. 139.   [4] No. 131.   [5] Nos. 147, 150; see D. Whitelock, *Eng. Hist. Rev.*, LXIII, pp. 433–452.

[6] Ed. Campbell, pp. 36f.   [7] No. 149.   [8] No. 233.   [9] No. 1, p. 232.   [10] Ed. Campbell, pp. 38–41.

version of the murder of the atheling Alfred.[1] This atrocity arose from fear
that the English might readily accept a king of the old royal house. Hardacnut's retention of 60 ships betrays his sense of insecurity. The tax for their
upkeep caused much discontent and at least one unpleasant incident.[2] Other
incidents of this time are a Welsh raid in 1039[3] and an unsuccessful siege of
Durham by the Scots in 1040,[4] but the most interesting feature of these reigns
is that for the first time there emerges the great power wielded by Earl Godwine. In the reluctance of the 'D' version of the Chronicle and of the *Encomium
Emmae* to admit his guilt in the murder of the atheling Alfred which the 'C'
version and Florence lay to his charge, there begins that difference of opinion
on this personage that has continued down to our own time.

When Hardacnut died in 1042, and Edward, son of King Ethelred, succeeded, Denmark passed to Cnut's nephew Swein Estrithson, and the linking
of England with Denmark came to an end. But the incident was not entirely
closed. It left to various Scandinavian kings a belief that they had a right to the
English throne, and this had repercussions later.

(vii) GOVERNMENT AND SOCIETY

The documents in this volume allow us to form some idea of how people
lived and how they were governed, but only if we piece together information
from various sources, for there are no contemporary treatises; and, as in all
other matters, there remain gaps in our knowledge that cannot be filled. The
division of society into three classes, nobles, ordinary freemen and slaves,
seemed to a writer of the later part of our period so ancient, inevitable and in
accordance with the divine scheme that he derives them from the three sons of
Noah.[5] The terminology varies in different localities and at different periods,[6]
as do the rights and obligations of the classes in detail, but the main structure is
constant. The two free classes were distinguished by their wergilds, that is, the
amount to be paid if a member of them were slain; by the value attached to
their oaths; by the size of the compensations to which they were entitled for
injuries, whether bodily injuries or the insult implied by breaches of their
surety or of their rights of protection, or by forcible entry into or fighting
inside their houses; and, on the other hand, by the size of the fines they must
pay if themselves guilty against the law. The details may be seen in the various
law-codes.[7] From these it emerges that in Wessex in the time of Ine and Alfred
there were two classes of noblemen, with wergilds of 1200 and 600 shillings
respectively,[8] but nothing is heard later of the 600 class; moreover, both in Kent

---

[1] No. 28.   [2] No. 1, p. 235; No. 9, p. 291.   [3] No. 1, p. 234; No. 9, p. 290.
[4] *Symeonis Monachi Opera Omnia*, ed. Arnold, 1, pp. 90f.   [5] A. S. Napier, *Anglia*, XI, pp. 2f.
[6] See, for example, p. 334.   [7] Nos. 29-53.   [8] *e.g.* Ine (No. 32), 70; Alfred (No. 33), 26-28.

and early Wessex there were men who possessed wergild and rights, but yet were below the ordinary English freemen, the *ceorl*; in Wessex these are specifically stated to be Welshmen,[1] whereas it is not certain that the Kentish *læt*[2] was a member of a subject British population, though this seems probable. In the absence of laws from the Mercian, East Anglian and Northumbrian kingdoms, it is unknown whether there were Britons above the status of slavery in these areas. Of all the complexus of rights that go to make up a man's status, the wergild was the most important, and the classes sometimes receive their names from it. A puzzling feature emerges that while the Kentish nobleman has a wergild not far different from that of the highest class elsewhere[3] (300 Kentish shillings being equivalent to 6000 pence, while 1200 shillings, the highest wergild outside Kent, equal 4800 pence in early Wessex and in Mercia, 6000 pence in Wessex in later times), the Kentish *ceorl* is reckoned at a third of this,[4] but his West Saxon and Mercian counterpart only at a sixth.[5]

We know most about the upper class, for, with the notable exception of the laws, most of our records are particularly concerned with it. It was considered in late Anglo-Saxon times that men of this class will hold their land as *bookland*,[6] and hence it is mainly they who are mentioned in charters; they were the persons who were in a position to endow religious houses, and who had enough possessions to make it worth while to leave them by written testament and enough resources to procure the writing down of the literature in which they were interested. Much of Old English poetry is aristocratic in its concerns; the tales and poems which entertained the peasants had little chance of being preserved. Thus it happens that any account of the Anglo-Saxon view on life has mainly to be illustrated with examples that relate to the upper orders. Yet one need not assume a difference of attitude in relation to the major obligations of society. Though already in Bede's time noble status could be recognized by distinctions of appearance, speech and bearing,[7] the incident of the avenging of King Sigeberht by his swine-herd,[8] and the speech of the old *ceorl* in *The Battle of Maldon*[9] should prevent our assuming that the exacting obligations of loyalty to a lord were not recognized by the lower as well as the higher orders of society. This code of behaviour is stated fully in this poem, but perhaps equally effective on the subject of loyalty is Aldhelm's letter to Wilfrid's abbots,[10] while many instances of devotion to a lord and sacrifice on his behalf are contained in the documents here given, *e.g.* the faithfulness unto death of the followers of Cynewulf and of his opponent Cyneheard,[11] the exile shared by the followers of Oswald, Æthelbald, and Hringstan,[12] the vengeance taken by Torhtmund for King Ethelred's murder,[13] and the journey of Dunwald to Rome for the good of

---

[1] Ine (No. 32), 23.3, 24.2, 32. [2] Ethelbert (No. 29), 26. [3] Hlothhere (No. 30), 1; Ine (No. 32), 70.
[4] Ethelbert (No. 29), 21. [5] Ine (No. 32), 70; No. 52 (C), 1. [6] Vol. II, p. 813. On *bookland*, see pp. 343 f.
[7] No. 151, p. 660. [8] No. 1, p. 162. [9] No. 10. [10] No. 165. [11] No. 1, pp. 162 f.
[12] No. 151, p. 624; No. 156, p. 711, n. 4; No. 196. [13] No. 3, p. 250; No. 206.

his lord's soul.[1] Acts of treachery such as Hunwold's betrayal of King Oswine,[2] or the murder of Æthelbald of Mercia and Oswulf of Northumbria by their own households,[3] were punishable with death according to the laws.[4] Archbishop Wulfstan speaks with particular horror of treachery,[5] and a writer of about the same period, who claims that a man who observes the due fasts need not fear hell-fire, makes a single exception ,"unless he be a traitor to his lord".[6] The lord on his side defended his man against oppression or accusation.[7] He exacted a payment if his man were killed, in addition to the wergild, which went to the kinsmen. He made him gifts–generosity in a lord is one of the most prized virtues in the poetry–and the heriot mentioned in wills[8] and in Cnut's laws[9] has its origin in the reversion to the lord of gifts of equipment made when the man entered his service. Both *The Wanderer* and a passage in Alfred's translation of the *Soliloquies* illustrate the closeness of the tie between a man and his lord.[10]

Similarly, on upper and lower classes of freemen alike lay the obligations of kinship. Our knowledge of these is incomplete, for the laws rarely deal with family law, and the co-operation of kinsmen in the everyday affairs of life was too much taken for granted for references to be frequent in our sources. We get glimpses of them arranging the terms of marriages[11] and looking after the interests of minors,[12] but the law is interested in them mainly in two capacities: their dealings with an accused or convicted member, and their right to vengeance or wergild. They are to supply food to one of their members in prison,[13] to act as surety in many circumstances,[14] to find a lord for a lordless kinsman,[15] and to pay compensations to save one who has been convicted from the consequences of his crime.[16] They could refuse these offices,[17] and in that case the offender would suffer the death penalty, or go into slavery, or become an outlaw, and the kinsmen would be liable to heavy penalties if they harboured him afterwards.[18] They would also forfeit all right to his wergild. The document on the betrothal of a woman shows how important the protection of kinsmen was felt to be, for it stresses that if she moves into another district her own kinsmen must have the right to protect her and pay if she commits an offence, for a woman did not enter into her husband's kindred when she married.[19] In theory, the king was the protector of foreigners or others without kin in the land,[20] but kinsmen at hand were probably more effective than the officials of a distant authority. Sometimes a kindred might be so powerful locally as to

[1] No. 72.   [2] No. 151, p. 631.   [3] No. 1, p. 163; No. 3, p. 241.
[4] II Athelstan (No. 35), 4.   [5] No. 240, p. 856.   [6] A. S. Napier, *Anglia*, XI, p. 3.
[7] See Ine (No. 32), 50; Alfred (No. 33), 42.5; II Athelstan (No. 35), 3; III Ethelred (No. 43), 4; I Cnut (No. 50), 20.2.
[8] Nos. 106, 121 f., 125 f.   [9] II Cnut (No. 50), 70–71.5, 73.4, 78.   [10] No. 211; No. 237, p. 845.
[11] No. 51; cf. Nos. 128 f.   [12] Hlothhere (No. 30), 6; Ine (No. 32), 38.   [13] Alfred (No. 33), 1.2.
[14] II Athelstan (No. 35), 1.3, 1.4, 6.1; III Athelstan 7.2; VI Athelstan (No. 37), 1.4, 12.2.
[15] II Athelstan (No. 35), 2.   [16] II Athelstan (No. 35), 6.1, 2.   [17] II Edward 6.   [18] II Athelstan (No. 35), 2.2.
[19] No. 51.   [20] Ine (No. 32), 23.1 f., 27; Alfred (No. 33), 1.3, 31; II Cnut (No. 50), 40.

prevent the exercise of justice,[1] and Athelstan takes steps to remove to another district wrongdoers who are being unduly sheltered at home.[2]

But through the laws, as in other sources, we meet kinsmen mainly in connexion with the blood-feud, or with the payment, or receipt, of wergild. Actual vengeance, a theme common in Germanic literature, was a reality in the Anglo-Saxon period, even late on, as is seen very clearly in the regulations of the Cambridge Thegns' Guild.[3] The Mercian captor of the Northumbrian thegn who had fought at the Trent felt he was acting contrary to his duty when he did not kill him, since he had lost kinsmen in the battle,[4] and Bede's admiration for Theodore's settlement between the kings of Mercia and Northumbria after this same battle, without any life being paid for the death of the young prince killed in it, suggests that settlements for persons of exalted station were at that date unusual.[5] The Church was naturally in favour of the prevention of the bloodshed that would result from a lasting vendetta between two kindreds, but there must have been many occasions when the slayer and his kindred were unable to meet the very heavy payments necessary to compound for homicide. Both Alfred and Edmund appear to have made strenuous efforts to limit the effects of the practice. Alfred devotes a long chapter to it, in which he forbids the injured party to take violent action against their adversary without first demanding justice.[6] This law is directed against hasty action against a slayer who is willing to come to terms. The state is willing to assist against the homicide, but time must be given him for settlement to be offered. Originally it was open to the avenging party to refuse to consider settlement. Alfred also forbids vengeance on anyone who has killed a man attacking his lord, or his man, or his kinsman (though not if in so doing he fought against his own lord), or on a man who has found another violating his wife, daughter, sister or mother, and killed him on the spot. Edmund, whose realm included the Danelaw, is distressed at the prevalence of feuds and devotes a whole code to the matter.[7] He extends to a year the thirty days' respite of Alfred's laws; he forbids 'henceforth' vengeance on any except the actual slayer, unless any of the latter's kinsmen, after renouncing him and refusing to pay wergild, give him food and shelter. In this, Edmund may be making new law, and he pronounces a heavy penalty for disobedience. In the Life of Liudger it seems that when a Frisian at York had killed a nobleman's son, it was felt possible that vengeance might be taken on any Frisian whatsoever.[8] The little tract called *Concerning the Mercian Oath*,[9] says that a man of the 1200 wergild is fully avenged on six *ceorls*, in which case five innocent persons would be involved: but at the date of this compilation this may be an antiquarian

---

[1] No. 120 gives a flagrant instance.
[2] III Athelstan, 6; IV Athelstan, 3; VI Athelstan (No. 37), 8.2 f.
[3] No. 136.　　　　　　　　　　　[4] No. 151, p. 661.　　　　　　[5] No. 151, p. 660.
[6] Alfred (No. 33), 42-42.7.　　　[7] No. 38.　　[8] No. 160.　　[9] No. 52(D).

statement.[1] Edmund tried further to discourage the blood-feud by forbidding entrance to his court to a homicide who had not undertaken to do penance and pay wergild. Legislation may have diminished its prevalence, but it did not end the blood-feud. To the end of the Anglo-Saxon period and even beyond, instances of its practice occur.[2] Throughout the period homicide remains primarily the affair of the kindred, and most codes contain clauses relating to it: they never give any comprehensive statement of the rules governing the procedure, but they consider special cases such as slaying of or by ecclesiastics,[3] or persons without kinsmen on one or both sides of the family,[4] or they apportion the responsibility when someone has been killed in a foray,[5] or by a weapon lent for the purpose,[6] or by accident;[7] they make pronouncements on what the kindred must pay if the slayer gets away,[8] and on the time allowed for payment and the priority of the wergild over other compensations incurred by the slaying;[9] and they so often forbid the kindred to avenge a man executed for crime or killed resisting the exercise of law as to suggest that this was a common abuse.[10] The importance of the kindred cannot be doubted.

But there are many signs that in the later part of our period it was not found adequate either to protect the individual from oppression or to produce an accused person to answer a charge. It is the latter aspect that is clearest in the laws, and it leads to the insistence that every man must have a lord who will be responsible for his actions,[11] and eventually to the grouping of men in tithings, the members of which are responsible for one another.[12] Wulfstan complains of the decay of the kindred as a protective force.[13] Already in the early laws one hears of rather mysterious associates who supply the place of the kindred in some circumstances,[14] and in the tenth century there are voluntary guilds, one of whose functions was to afford support and protection similar to that given by the kindred.[15]

The impression of late Anglo-Saxon society given by Domesday Book is that the lesser freemen depended more on the lord to whom they had 'commended' themselves (that is, with whom they had made an agreement to give homage and service in return for protection) than on their kinsmen. Though the *ceorl* had his rights, similar in kind to those of the higher class, but with

· [1] VIII Ethelred (No. 46), 23 contains the words: "kinsmen who must bear the feud with him or pay compensation", which have been taken to contradict Edmund's injunction. But may not those who bear the feud be those who harbour the slayer while refusing to share the wergild?
[2] See D. Whitelock, *The Audience of Beowulf*, pp. 12–17.
[3] Alfred (No. 33), 21; VIII Ethelred (No. 46), 23–26; II Cnut (No. 50), 40f.; *Hadbot* (No. 52(E)).
[4] Ine (No. 32), 23–23.2; Alfred (No. 33), 8.3, 30f.; VIII Ethelred (No. 46), 33f.
[5] Ine (No. 32), 34f.; Alfred (No. 33), 26–28.1.   [6] Alfred (No. 33), 19.
[7] Alfred (No. 33), 36–36.2.   [8] Ethelbert (No. 29), 23; Alfred (No. 33), 30.
[9] Ethelbert (No. 29), 22; Ine (No. 32), 71; II Edmund (No. 38), 7.3. See also p. 336.
[10] Wihtred (No. 31), 25; Ine (No. 32), 21, 28, 35; Alfred (No. 33), 1.5; II Athelstan (No. 35), 6.2f., 20.7; VI Athelstan (No. 37), 1.5; III Edmund, 2; IV Ethelred, 4; V Ethelred (No. 44), 31.1; II Cnut (No. 50), 62.1; *Leges Henrici Primi*, 87.6a.
[11] II Athelstan (No. 35), 2.   [12] II Cnut (No. 50), 20.   [13] No. 240.
[14] Ine (No. 32), 16, 21; Alfred (No. 33), 30f.   [15] Nos. 37, 136–139.

smaller compensations, it may well have been difficult to enforce them against an overbearing thegn, and the backing of some powerful person would seem more valuable than a precarious independence. In the early days the *ceorl* was often on land he owned himself, and might be a person of some substance, though from early times there were others who held their land at a rent from a lord.[1] But in times of disaster, from natural causes or warfare, the *ceorl* stood far less chance of recuperating his losses than did the noble with estates scattered in different areas, and the long ravages of the viking period in particular must have reduced to poverty and dependence many men of the lower orders. Particularly illuminating in this connexion is the statement of Bishop Denewulf on the condition in which his estate at Beddington was left after the ravages of heathen men.[2] The bishop was able to restock it, but what could a *ceorl* have done in such circumstances by his own efforts alone? If he sought assistance from a better-placed person it would be at the cost of independence. Something of the power of a harsh landlord can be seen in the secular parallel drawn in Edgar's fourth code to illustrate the divine wrath to be expected for non-payment of religious dues; if the rent is repeatedly denied, the lord will allow the tenant neither property nor life,[3] that is, will evict him and deprive him of all means of supporting life. The terms on which various classes of tenants hold land on a great estate are set out in the *Rectitudines Singularum Personarum*, included in Volume II of this series:[4] there are *geneatas* who perform mainly riding services, *geburas*, who pay some rent and do various agricultural services, and *cotsetlan* who perform such services for very small holdings. This document belongs to the later part of our period, but already in Alfred's reign the *ceorl* who dwells on rented land is equated for wergild purposes only with a freed-man of the Danes.[5] However, though many once independent peasant families may have found their position deteriorating, there were some in the time of Athelstan strong enough to be a menace in their locality.[6] Moreover, it was possible for a *ceorl* to prosper and to attain the status of a thegn. The necessary qualifications are set out in an eleventh-century compilation,[7] in relation to past practice. Lest this document should be taken to be theorizing merely, one should compare a small treatise on the clergy, which states simply as a fact: "And lo! it often happens that a slave at length earns his freedom from a *ceorl*, and a *ceorl* becomes by the earl's gift entitled to the status of a thegn."[8] Prosperous members of the class may have been able to afford to lease whole estates from others, though in general the holders of *lænland* seem to have been men of the upper class. Alfred gives a pleasant little picture of the man dwelling on this type of land, until such time as his lord lets him have it as bookland, *i.e.* his own possession in perpetuity.[9]

[1] Ine (No. 32), 64–67.   [2] No. 101.   [3] IV Edgar (No. 41), 1.2.
[4] Vol. II, No. 172.   [5] No. 34.   [6] III Athelstan, 6.   [7] No. 52.
[9] M. Ångström, *Studies in Old English Manuscripts* (Uppsala, 1937), p. 125.   [9] No. 237(A).

The slave lies outside all this. He had no wergild, and if he were killed or injured in any way, a price was paid to his master, not a compensation to his kindred. If he himself were guilty of homicide, his master must hand him over to the slain man's lord or kindred, or redeem his life for 60 shillings, the legal price of a slave; if he had free kinsmen, they were not bound to associate themselves with him to pay compensations.[1] For heavy crimes, such as theft, the penalty was usually death,[2] for minor offences the slave was flogged.[3] Running away was punishable by death.[4] A slave was bought and sold as a chattel;[5] a passage which discusses the compensation due to the owner for a stolen slave is similarly worded to one concerning a stolen horse.[6] Most Anglo-Saxons saw nothing wrong in this state of things. The crime of two English priests on the Continent, of whom Bishop Lul complains that one gave men and women in exchange for a horse, while the other sent a man across to England and gave him as a slave to his mother, lay in their appropriation of the property of their churches rather than in their treatment of these individuals.[7] Yet the Church and others worked to improve the lot of slaves, and the laws have some signs of a more humane attitude. There had been a flourishing slave trade with the Continent, as can be seen from Gregory's letter to Candidus,[8] Bede's account of Northumbrian slaves in Rome,[9] and the purchase of a captive by a Frisian merchant in London.[10] The sale of a criminal across the sea is mentioned in Wihtred's law,[11] but Ine's law forbids the sale of Englishmen across the sea.[12] It is forbidden afresh in the laws of Ethelred and Cnut,[13] but was difficult to suppress. Wulfstan complains of the abuse in his sermon,[14] yet later references to its practice occur. Some regulations in the laws, which allow the slave to avoid a flogging by a payment to his master,[15] by implication admit the possibility of the slave having possessions, and certain days were allotted to them to use to their own profit.[16] The *Rectitudines Singularum Personarum* shows that they had acquired certain rights by custom.[17] One of Ethelred's codes includes poor slaves as one of the objects on which tithe should be expended,[18] and the Church encouraged the manumission of slaves for the good of one's soul. It is mentioned already in the laws of Wihtred, where it takes place at the altar,[19] and again and again in other sources. Leofgyth's mother sets free her old nurse who has prophesied the birth of her child.[20] This is a rare glimpse of a household slave and this one at any rate had liberty to advise her mistress and the advice was

---

[1] Ine (No. 32), 74–74.3.   [2] IV Athelstan, 6; III Edmund, 4; I Ethelred, 2.1; II Cnut (No. 50), 32.
[3] Wihtred (No. 31), 10, 13, 15; Ine (No. 32), 3.1, 48; II Athelstan (No. 35), 19; VII Ethelred (No. 45), 3; II Cnut (No. 50), 45.2, 46.2.
[4] Ine (No. 32), 24; VI Athelstan (No. 37), 6.3.   [5] Alfred and Guthrum (No. 34), 4.
[6] VI Athelstan (No. 37), 6.1, 6.3.   [7] Tangl, No. 110.   [8] No. 161.   [9] No. 151, p. 606.
[10] No. 151, p. 661.   [11] Wihtred (No. 31), 26.   [12] Ine (No. 32), 11.
[13] V Ethelred (No. 44), 2; VI Ethelred, 9; II Cnut, 3. Cf. also VII Ethelred (Latin version), 5.
[14] No. 240.   [15] Wihtred (No. 31), 10, 13, 15; Ine (No. 32), 3.1.
[16] Alfred (No. 33), 43; VII Ethelred (No. 45), 5.1, but cf. Latin version 2.3.   [17] Vol. II, p. 815.
[18] VIII Ethelred (No. 46), 6.   [19] Wihtred (No. 31), 8.   [20] No. 159, p. 721.

taken. Lul writes home from Germany asking for two men whom he and his father have freed, if they are willing to join him abroad.[1] Surviving wills often contain a clause about the manumission of some or all of the testator's slaves,[2] and from the tenth and eleventh centuries separate acts of manumission are often entered into the gospels or service books of churches.[3] In the quotation above concerning the *ceorl's* rise in status it says that a slave often gained his freedom. He gained it also, according to a law of Ine, revived by Cnut, if his master forced him to work on a Sunday,[4] and many slaves took the opportunity of escaping from bondage by joining the viking invaders, to judge by Wulfstan's laments[5] and a clause in the treaty of 991.[6]

And who were these people condemned to pass their lives in servitude to others? That some were subject British population is proved by the use of the word for Briton to mean slave. One would expect that the 250 men and women whom Wilfrid found and manumitted on an estate of 87 hides at Selsey were largely of this origin.[7] Later wars added other captives;[8] but the main source of recruitment was from those who lost their freedom as a penalty for crime, or for failure to pay compensations incurred at law. The kindred of such persons lost their right to their wergild if they failed to redeem them within a year.[9] Slavery may be a punishment for theft or for work on Sundays,[10] or for incest.[11] In some contexts it is clear that the criminal remains in slavery only until he is considered to have paid by his labour's the amount of the compensations and fines which would have prevented his enslavement,[12] and this may be meant in places where it is not stated. In Ine's laws, if a man steals with the knowledge of his household, they all go into slavery,[13] and Wulfstan complains of the abuse of law which leads to the enslaving of children in the cradle.[14] Cnut's laws legislate against the practice.[15] Children born of unfree parents are, however, unfree.

There is not a great deal in contemporary records to prove that the Scandinavian settlers in England greatly modified the type of society hitherto described. Themselves a Germanic race, they were similarly divided into the three classes, they recognized the obligations of loyalty to lord and kin, and homicide was the affair of the kindred, to be compounded for or avenged. There were differences in detail in their legal procedure,[16] and in the administrative divisions in areas settled by them. The much greater independence of the Danelaw peasantry in post-Conquest times is legitimately taken to date from

[1] Tangl, No. 49.   [2] Nos. 96, 116, 122, 126, 130.   [3] See pp. 348 f. and Nos. 140–150.
[4] Ine (No. 32), 3; II Cnut (No. 50), 45.3.   [5] No. 240.   [6] II Ethelred (No. 42), 6.2.
[7] No. 151, pp. 655 f.   [8] See p. 28.   [9] Ine (No. 32), 24.1.
[10] e.g. Ine (No. 32), 3.2, 7.1; II Edward, 6; VI Athelstan (No. 37), 12.2.
[11] Edward and Guthrum, 4.   [12] Ine (No. 32), 62; II Edward, 6; VI Athelstan (No. 37), 12.2.
[13] Ine (No. 32), 7.1.   [14] No. 240.   [15] II Cnut (No. 50), 76.2.
[16] The main texts to deal with this part of the country are No. 43, parts of No. 50, and No. 53. The two treaties Nos. 34, 42, and the documents Nos. 104, 108, 114, 125, 136, 150, should be consulted, while Wulfstan's sermon, No. 240, may have the conditions in his northern diocese especially in mind.

the time of the Scandinavian settlements,[1] but the paucity of pre-Conquest records from these areas forbids our illustrating this in this volume, though another peculiarity, the existence of large sokes attached to manors, can be seen already in tenth-century charters such as No. 108. Scandinavian influence is seen on the terminology of some eleventh-century records; thus the word *bonda*, describing a free householder, or replacing *ceorl* in its other sense of 'husband',[2] is found in laws of Ethelred and Cnut drafted by Archbishop Wulfstan of York, who uses in his writings the Scandinavian term 'thrall' instead of the native '*peow*'.[3]

Over a society thus constituted reigned a king. We have already seen the growth in power and splendour first of the Bretwaldas of the Heptarchy, and then of the monarchs of all England. An ecclesiastical consecration seems first to have been used for Offa's son Ecgferth, made king in his father's lifetime. Two coronations are described in some detail in our records, that of Athelstan[4] and the delayed coronation of Edgar.[5] The monarchy was hereditary in the royal family, but there was no fixed rule of succession, which accounts for much of the internal strife in the time of the Heptarchy.[6] Joint rule of two or more members of a family is not met with after this period; indeed, Ælfric evidently regarded the idea with such abhorrence that he could not bring himself to retain in his translations the references to joint rule in the Roman empire.[7] Theoretically, the election lay with the council, but by the late ninth century the succession went normally to the eldest son of the last king, if an adult, otherwise to the next brother. A disagreement among the councillors, as when Edward the Martyr's unpopularity, and perhaps other reasons, led some persons to prefer the younger son, might lead to unrest and strife.[8] The situation in which an assembly of part of the council chose Edmund, and that of another part elected Cnut, was abnormal.[9] The disagreement after the death of Cnut was solved by a compromise.[10]

Behind the laws of Ethelbert of Kent[11] there seems to lie a simple state of things, when much of the business of government could be conducted from the court, and the king visited his subjects in accordance with the ancient right of hospitality. This right is probably the origin of the king's farm,[12] a food-rent due to him from all estates not expressly freed from its payment, and in addition he had many rights such as claiming hospitality for his messengers, huntsmen, fowlers, etc., which were onerous enough for landowners to be willing to pay heavily for immunity from them.[13] In the later part of the eighth century

[1] See Vol. II, p. 74.   [2] VII Ethelred (No. 45), 3; II Cnut (No. 50), 8, 72f., 76.1b
[3] *e.g.* No. 240.   [4] No. 8, p. 279.
[5] No. 1, pp. 207f.; a much fuller account is given in the Life of St. Oswald, *Historians of the Church of York*, I, pp. 436–438.   [6] See pp. 26f.   [7] Preface to *Lives of Saints*.
[8] No. 236, p. 841.   [9] No. 1, p. 226 and n. 2.   [10] No. 1, p. 232.   [11] No. 29.
[12] See Alfred (No. 33), 2; II Cnut (No. 50), 69.1; Nos. 77f.   [13] Nos. 83, 85, 87, 90f., 95.

charters begin to include a clause freeing the land from all royal dues except three, obligations of military service, and of the building and repair of fortifications.[1] The king had the right to tolls and also to inheritance after foreigners and to at least a share in their wergilds, and in those of other kinless folk, if they were slain.[2] He had extensive lands of his own, and another major source of income was the receipt of fines or forfeitures for various offences, which are mentioned continually throughout the laws, while specific instances occur in charters.[3] He had a special wergild,[4] though the amount is known only for Northumbria, where it is fifteen times that of a thegn, and for Mercia, where it is twelve times; in both areas it was divided between the kin and the people.[5] Breach of his protection cost just over four pounds in early Kentish law,[6] five pounds in Wessex in Alfred's time, at which amount it remains later,[7] except that in the Danelaw a very much higher fine, reaching to £48, was attached to the breaking of the king's peace.[8] Lesser offences had lesser fines, 120, 60 and 30 shillings being the commonest sums. But the profits of jurisdiction could be granted by the king to individuals, lay and ecclesiastical; charters often claim this right,[9] and in the Fonthill suit the king's reeve seized Helmstan's property "because he was the king's man"; the implication is that had he been the man of someone else, the forfeiture would not have been to the king.[10] How soon this right to the fines developed into one to hold a private court is controversial, but there is a charter of 816 which implies the existence of a private court,[11] and the wording of injunctions against receiving bribes or giving false judgments in the laws of Athelstan and Edgar does not suggest to me that they were directed against royal officials alone.[12]

The highest official was the ealdorman. He is not mentioned in the Kentish laws, and perhaps so small a kingdom did not require this official in early days. He appears well established in Wessex by the time of Ine, and is probably the person meant when Eddi speaks of *subregulus* and *princeps*.[13] But it is not too easy to equate the terms of Latin sources with Old English, and Brihtfrith, a *princeps* in Eddi, is called *prefectus* by Bede,[14] whose use of *princeps* may be confined to men of royal family. Bede seems to use *dux* as ealdorman as well as in its sense of 'leader', 'general'. *Prefectus* generally renders *gerefa* 'reeve', but the retention of the title high-reeve in the North for the rulers of Bamburgh, one of whom is given the title 'king' in a Celtic source,[15] may suggest that in early times

---

[1] First in No. 74. [2] See p. 56.
[3] *e.g.* Nos. 100, 102, 112, 117, 119, 120, 123. See also No. 238, on the danger that lands leased by monasteries may be wrongly claimed as forfeit for the crimes of the lease-holder.
[4] Alfred (No. 33), 4.1. [5] No. 52. [6] Ethelbert (No. 29), 8.
[7] Alfred (No. 33), 3; VIII Ethelred (No. 46), 5.1; II Cnut (No. 50), 58.
[8] III Ethelred (No. 43), 1–1.2. [9] Nos. 83, 88, 90, 93. [10] No. 102.
[11] Birch, No. 357. See F. M. Stenton, *Anglo-Saxon England*, p. 486.
[12] V Athelstan (No. 36), 1.3f.; III Edgar (No. 40), 3.
[13] No. 154, pp. 693, 696. [14] No. 151, p. 685. [15] *Annals of Ulster*, 912.

gerefa had a wider application and was not used only of officials inferior to the ealdorman. In the attestations to early West Saxon charters, *prefectus* seems to be used of ealdormen.[1] From the second half of the ninth century, ealdorman is also rendered *comes*, but in earlier writers such as Bede this word probably translates *gesith*.[2] Occasionally one gets the term *patricius*, perhaps of an ealdorman of a particularly influential position.[3] In the eleventh century the native word ealdorman was ousted under Scandinavian influence by 'earl'.

The ealdorman was appointed by the king,[4] and in early times in Wessex his sphere of jurisdiction seems to have been the shire. Thus the Chronicle speaks several times of an ealdorman fighting along with the men of a single shire.[5] It is impossible to tell what was the position in the North and Midlands, for reorganization during and after the Danish settlements has concealed what were the earlier administrative areas there. From time to time references occur to the older regions which the shire system superseded, *e.g.* Sonning,[6] *Hemele*,[7] Ismere,[8] the Wrekin-dwellers,[9] Oundle, the *Gyrwe*, the *Feppingas*,[10] the *Wisse* in East Anglia,[11] *Kintis* and *Ahse* in Northumbria.[12] The *Gyrwe* had a *princeps* over them, and Asser mentions a Mercian people called *Gaini* who had an ealdorman,[13] but this is not enough to prove that each region had an ealdorman of its own, though we can see from the attestations to Mercian charters that several ealdormen were in office concurrently in this kingdom. The memory of one ancient region, that of the *Magonsæte* in Herefordshire, who once had a ruling house of their own, survived until quite late,[14] and in the mid eleventh century Ealdorman Hrani took his title from it.[15] From the second half of the tenth century it was common for an ealdorman to have far more than a single shire under him. Athelstan Half-King and his descendants had the whole of East Anglia, Ælfhere was ealdorman of Mercia, all the western shires were under Æthelweard, and Uhtred was in sole charge of Northumbria. Cnut divided the whole of England into four divisions. These arrangements were not stable, and smaller areas were from time to time detached and given a separate ealdorman, but the general tendency in the eleventh century was to leave a vast stretch of country under each earl's control. This was not, however, to repeat the position held by Alfred's son-in-law Ethelred, which was anomalous, for though he retained the title of ealdorman, he and his wife Æthelflæd reigned more as vassal-kings, with ealdormen under them, and presided over meetings of the Mercian council.[16] Asser seems to recognize Ethelred's semi-royal position[17] and Æthelweard actually calls him king.[18]

---

[1] Nos. 69–71. [2] On the *gesith*, see p. 362, n. 3. [3] See p. 244, n. 6.
[4] The passage quoted on p. 59 goes on to say that the thegn becomes an earl by the king's gift, and kings often speak of 'my ealdorman'.
[5] No. 1, pp. 169, 172–175. [6] No. 54. [7] No. 63. [8] No. 67. [9] No. 90.
[10] No. 151, pp. 635, 652, 658, 676. [11] No. 156, p. 713, n. 2.
[12] *Two Lives of St. Cuthbert*, ed. Colgrave, pp. 114, 116. [13] No. 7, p. 267, n. 1.
[14] No. 1, p. 227; No. 109. [15] No. 9, p. 291. [16] See, for example, Birch, No. 574.
[17] No. 7, p. 270. [18] No. 1, p. 186, n. 2.

Like the king, the ealdorman had some rights over lands held by others, which had to be bought out by those who wished for immunity.[1] Also, he had official lands.[2] In the North, his wergild was four times that of a thegn, like a bishop's.[3] For the rest of the country evidence is lacking, but Ealdorman Alfred's will suggests that he had a wergild by reason of his office as well as his ordinary one.[4] The ealdorman received two pounds for breach of his protection, again like the bishop,[5] 60 shillings for breaking into his house.[6] The same amount was due to him for fighting in his house in Ine's laws, but Alfred allows him 100 shillings if fighting occurs or a weapon is drawn in his presence, 120 if this takes place at an assembly.[7] Here we have a reference to his duties in connexion with the administration of justice, and there are many other references to them; he loses his 'shire' if he lets a thief escape;[8] the injured party in a case of homicide can apply to him for assistance;[9] he is to be present at the shire meeting;[10] he is to look out for coiners;[11] he may pronounce the king's peace in the court of the Five Boroughs;[12] he must support the bishops to further the rights of the Church;[13] he has duties with regard to the promulgation of the laws in his district.[14] In return for his services, he received a share of the royal fines. The evidence for his receiving a third is late, but that some share of the fines went to the local officials is shown conclusively by the division of the fine due to the king when anyone in another district takes a man into his service without the cognizance of the ealdorman of the man's earlier district; half is to be paid in the place from which he came, half in the one he has come to.[15] If the whole went to the king, it would be of no consequence where it was paid. The ealdorman appears in his military capacity often enough in the narrative sources, most vividly in the poem on the battle of Maldon,[16] though mention should also be made of Ealdorman Æthelwulf of Berkshire, whom we meet first serving a Mercian king,[17] but who remained in office when this shire passed under West Saxon rule. He led out his forces against the vikings, at first with success, but was killed by them later, and his body was taken back into Mercia to burial.[18] Several ealdormen occur in our sources as benefactors of religious houses, and Æthelweard of the Western Provinces was a patron of letters, as well as the author of a Latin Chronicle.[19] There were, however, some bad appointments to the office, especially in the reign of Ethelred the Unready. The chronicler may be too ready to lay the whole blame for disaster on the ealdormen Ælfric of Hampshire and Eadric of Mercia,[20] but he could not have

---

[1] Nos. 85, 87, 90f.
[2] The evidence for this is mainly from the *Leges Henrici Primi* and Domesday Book, but it is probably implied in I Athelstan, Prologue.
[3] No. 52.
[4] No. 97.
[5] Alfred (No. 33), 3; II Cnut (No. 50), 58.2.
[6] Alfred (No. 33), 40; Ine (No. 32), 45 allows him 80 shillings.
[7] Ine (No. 32), 6.2; Alfred (No. 33), 15, 38.1.
[8] Ine (No. 32), 36.1.
[9] Alfred (No. 33), 42.3.
[10] III Edgar (No. 40), 5.2.
[11] IV Ethelred, 8.
[12] III Ethelred (No. 43), 1.1.
[13] Cnut's Letter (No. 48), 8.
[14] IV Edgar (No. 41), 15, 15.1.
[15] Alfred (No. 33), 37.1.
[16] No. 10; cf. No. 236, p. 843.
[17] No. 87.
[18] No. 1, p. 177 and n. 10.
[19] See pp. 98, 113, 522.
[20] No. 1, pp. 213, 217, 220, 225–227.

done so, so soon after the events, if they had been loyal and competent men; though "the perfidious ealdorman Eadric" became a legend, there was clearly some basis for the way he is depicted.[1] The grounds for the outlawry of the earlier Ælfric, ealdorman of Mercia, are not given,[2] nor is it certain that he should be identified with the one whom Pope John accuses of oppressing Glastonbury;[3] the ealdorman Leofsige who was exiled for killing the king's high-reeve[4] may have had provocation; but certainly all these men compare badly with men like Brihtnoth and Æthelwine, appointed before Ethelred's accession.

It happens that there is no mention of the sheriff in the documents in this volume, though the title is used in Cnut's reign, and a 'shire-man', which represents the same official, occurs in a document of between 964 and 988.[5] Some of the references to the king's reeve may refer to a sheriff, but it is a more general term and includes men in charge of royal estates, whose duties included many concerned with the exercise of justice, as well as the management of the royal estate and the collection of the king's farm. The reeve presides at a popular court[6] (called a hundred court from the mid tenth century, or, in the Danelaw, a wapentake) at which suits are judged and to which traders must bring the men they are taking into the country.[7] By the time of Edward the Elder, this court meets every four weeks.[8] The reeve collects the fines and takes possession of forfeited property; we see one in action in the Fonthill suit.[9] In some circumstances he keeps prisoners at the king's estate.[10] Wilfrid when imprisoned in the royal borough of *Broninis* was in the charge of the reeve Osfrith, and was then moved to that of Tydlin, at Dunbar.[11] The reeve also arranges the execution of a convicted criminal; the kinsmen who have redeemed a thief from death, but cannot prevent him from further stealing, are to return him to the reeve, to be slain.[12] The reeve has also to lead attack against wrong-doers,[13] and to follow the trail of stolen cattle.[14] He is to take an oath or pledge from men in his district that they will obey the king's ordinance,[15] and he is to place suspicious persons under surety.[16] And in addition he is to act as witness at purchases,[17] to help to get the tithe from defaulters,[18] and to assist abbots in their temporal needs.[19] It was a busy life and one full of temptation and opportunities for corruption. The laws mention penalties for reeves who are accessaries to theft,[20] reeves who take bribes,[21] reeves who permit the coining of false money,[22] as well as those who do not carry out the injunctions.[23] Reeves are enjoined to pronounce just judgments,[24] and the judges who so dissatisfied

[1] No. 9, pp. 285 f.   [2] No. 1, p. 212; No. 123.   [3] No. 231.   [4] No. 1, p. 216.
[5] Birch, No. 1097.   [6] Alfred (No. 33), 22, 34; I Edward, Prologue.   [7] Alfred (No. 33), 34.
[8] II Edward, 8.   [9] No. 102.   [10] Alfred (No. 33), 1.3.   [11] *Eddi's Life of Wilfrid*, ed. Colgrave, pp. 72, 76.
[12] VI Athelstan (No. 37), 1.4.   [13] VI Athelstan (No. 37), 8.2 f.   [14] VI Athelstan (No. 37), 8.4 f.
[15] VI Athelstan (No. 37), 10 f.   [16] II Cnut (No. 50), 33.   [17] II Athelstan (No. 35), 10, 12; III Edmund, 5.
[18] II Edgar (No. 40), 3.1.   [19] VIII Ethelred (No. 46), 32.   [20] II Athelstan (No. 35), 3.2.
[21] V Athelstan, 1.3.   [22] II Cnut (No. 50), 8.2.   [23] II Athelstan (No. 35), 25; VI Athelstan (No. 37), 11.
[24] I Edward, Prologue; Cnut's Letter (No. 48), 11.

Alfred, according to Asser, may have been mainly his reeves.[1] It is natural that they were often unpopular. Byrhtferth says in 1011 that "the injustice and robbery and subtleties and wrong judgments and wiles of reeves" will cease at the end of the world,[2] and this and other contemporary complaints are supported by Cnut's injunctions to his reeves who oppress the people.[3]

The king's reeve who could grant the king's peace in the court of the Five Boroughs[4] may have been a sheriff, who was an official in charge of a shire, looking after the king's interests there, and presiding in the absence of the ealdorman over the shire court, which, at least from the time of Edgar, met twice a year.[5] When they controlled large areas the ealdormen must have often been unable to attend all the shire courts in their jurisdiction, but Ealdorman Hrani is present at the shire court of which an interesting account has come down to us.[6] From time to time the sources mention a 'high-reeve'; in Northumbria he has a wergild twice as high as a thegn, and equal to that of a *hold*,[7] which title is of Scandinavian origin, and in Norway it applied to a man who was a noble by birth, not by service with the king. The high-reeves of Bamburgh managed to maintain the independence of northern Northumbria against the Scandinavian kingdom of York, and the title remained hereditary in one family for several generations.[8] But this situation was exceptional. Just what was the position held by a high-reeve in Wessex is obscure; he was a person of enough importance to be mentioned in the Chronicle, and an ealdorman was outlawed for killing a king's high-reeve.[9] Towns also were in charge of reeves, such as those of Oxford and of Buckingham who with more mercy than legality allowed Christian burial to men slain in defence of a thief.[10] Town reeves' duties included much supervision of trade, collecting of tolls and witnessing of purchases, and supervision of the mint in boroughs that were allowed one.[11] They were concerned in the conducting of ordeals, which took place in towns.[12] In seaports, they would need to examine the credentials of incoming ships, and the reeve of Dorchester at the end of the eighth century was killed when making inquiries from Danish ships.[13] The Chronicle occasionally records the death of a town-reeve,[14] and Ceolmund, a London reeve, figures in a mid-ninth-century charter.[15] In later times London and Winchester had more than one reeve at a time. Since the ealdorman complains to the king about the behaviour of the Oxford and Buckingham reeves, it would appear that he had no direct authority over them, but that they were answerable to the king alone.

[1] No. 7, p. 276.   [2] *Byrhtferth's Manual*, ed. S. J. Crawford, p. 242.
[3] Cnut's Letter (No. 49), 12; II Cnut (No. 50), 69.1 f.   [4] III Ethelred (No. 43), 1.1.
[5] III Edgar (No. 40), 5.1.   [6] No. 135.   [7] No. 52.
[8] See references to this family in No. 1, pp. 199 f.; No. 6; No. 105.   [9] No. 1, p. 216.
[10] No. 117.   [11] I Edward, 1; IV Ethelred, 3, 7.3.   [12] III Ethelred (No. 43), 7.
[13] No. 1, p. 166 and n. 6.   [14] No. 1, pp. 188, 192.   [15] No. 92.

When one leaves the royal officials in the shires and towns, and turns to those of the court, who accompanied the king in his perambulations among his residences, the best evidence is afforded by King Eadred's will,[1] with its mention of seneschals, keepers of the wardrobe, butlers, and stewards, these last of a lower order than the preceding. That such offices were held by men of high station is shown by the marriage of King Æthelwulf to his cupbearer's daughter.[2] Eadred refers in general terms to other men of his household, implying that they are of varying degrees of closeness to the royal service, a passage which invites comparison with that of Alfred in his translation of the *Soliloquies* on the differences of position of men in the king's residences.[3] Among the unspecified members of the royal household some were doubtless the king's thegns, men who inherit the position of the king's companions described so vividly in Tacitus and in poetry. Already in Bede it appears that such followers could expect a landed endowment when they reached manhood,[4] and that they were then not always with the king, and Asser tells how Alfred, that great organizer, arranged for a rotation of service.[5] Hence we hear more of the thegns' activities in their own localities than at the king's court. A thief who fled to a thegn (or to an ealdorman or an abbot) had a respite of three days;[6] the thegns are to assist the king in enforcing celibacy on the clergy;[7] the twelve leading thegns form a jury of presentment in the wapentake court, and are to arrest men of ill repute.[8] The king's thegn has a special compensation for breaking into his house,[9] and rights with regard to exculpation.[10] It was thought probable that a thegn would have erected a church on his bookland,[11] and some contexts suggest that some had the right of holding a private court.[12] Cnut's statements concerning heriot show that there were variations in status among the king's thegns,[13] but no one except the king had any right of jurisdiction over them.

Important king's thegns attended the meetings of his council, along with the archbishops, bishops, important abbots, and ealdormen. These councils, which, as far as our evidence goes, were held at irregular intervals, when the king wished to take advice on weighty issues, are well evidenced in our records, for at them charters received their attestations. There are also some interesting examples of them in this volume, such as the deliberation by a Northumbrian council over the acceptance of Christianity,[14] the council on the Nidd over the affairs of Bishop Wilfrid,[15] the assemblies described in the report of the legates in 786,[16] the council summoned by Ethelred to hear what the papal emissary had to say on the hostility with Normandy,[17] and the meeting to establish friendship between Danes and English at Oxford in 1018.[18] One can draw no very hard and

---

[1] No. 107.   [2] No. 7, p. 264.   [3] No. 237.   [4] No. 170, p. 741.   [5] No. 7, pp. 274 f.
[6] IV Athelstan, 6.2.   [7] IV Edgar (No. 41), 1.8.   [8] III Ethelred (No. 43), 3.1.   [9] Ine (No. 32), 45.
[10] Wihtred (No. 31), 20; Alfred and Guthrum (No. 34), 3.   [11] II Edgar (No. 40), 2.
[12] V Athelstan (No. 36), 1.4; III Edgar (No. 40), 3.   [13] II Cnut (No. 50), 71.1–71.5.
[14] No. 151, p. 617.   [15] No. 154, p. 695.   [16] No. 191.   [17] No. 230.   [18] No. 1, p. 228; No. 47.

fast line between meetings of the king's council and ecclesiastical synods. There is no reference to lay members other than the king at the synod of Whitby,[1] nor at the first recorded West Saxon synod, mentioned in the Life of Boniface,[2] but in the days of the Mercian overlords ecclesiastical synods attended by all the bishops south of the Humber were held in the presence of the king and lay councillors of the Mercians.[3] The "great synod" held by Archbishop Æthelgar at London in 989 or 990 was attended by "all the king's councillors", including many from the North who rarely attend councils.[4] The legates in 786 objected to bishops giving judgments at secular councils, but it was not until post-Conquest times that a fixed line was drawn between secular and ecclesiastical causes.

One of the matters on which the king would consult his councillors was the imposing of any abnormal tax. Under ordinary circumstances the expenses of government were met out of the royal income, and the king had the right to call on labour for building or repairing fortresses and bridges, and on military service. Though the duty of serving in the army is often mentioned, and the laws set out the penalties for neglect of it or desertion in a scale graduated according to rank,[5] they do not specify the numbers that could be called out nor the length of service. In the reign of Edward the Confessor, there is evidence that one man went from five hides of land, but the Chronicle shows that in a crisis every able-bodied man might be summoned.[6] Alfred made a reorganization to secure service in rotation, just as he had done with his thegns, so as to be able to have troops in the field as long as required. When great sums were needed to pay tribute to the Danes, or to pay mercenaries, or when it was decided to build a fleet, these expenses could not be met out of the royal income, and the charge was laid on the land, in proportion to its assessment in hides, an assessment probably originally made in connexion with the king's farm. Sometimes it is expressly stated that the decision to pay tribute was made by the king and his councillors, and in 1012 the more important members of the council stayed in London until it was paid.[7]

There must have been a need for a certain amount of routine administration from a central authority, and it could not wait for assemblies of the councillors. Eadred's will shows that there were a number of priests in his service,[8] and some of them would form a sort of secretariat. Athelstan's charters make it clear that some office of this kind was already in existence, and later we hear of documents kept with the king's relics.[9] Eadred leaves a larger legacy to the priests he has put in charge of his relics, and perhaps already these were also in charge of his archives. Moreover, the complicated division of his finances made by Alfred could not have been effected without at least some elementary form of a

[1] No. 151, pp. 640–642; No. 154, pp. 692 f.   [2] No. 158.   [3] e.g. Nos. 77, 79, 81, 84.
[4] No. 120.   [5] Ine (No. 32), 51. Cf. V Ethelred (No. 44), 28 f.   [6] No. 1, p. 225.
[7] No. 1, p. 222.   [8] No. 107.   [9] No. 121.

treasury.[1] But there was as yet no fixed place for it, and Eadred entrusted his belongings to various ecclesiastics.[2]

By far the greatest part of the population was occupied in agricultural pursuits, and, though from this period there are no detailed descriptions of village economy, there is just enough evidence to show that in these days as later the normal practice was the open field system, in which each man held his strips in the common fields, and half or a third of the arable was left fallow each year. Along with a holding in the arable went rights in common meadow and pasture, and in all other amenities of the estate.[3] Ine's laws show men combining to fence common arable or meadow,[4] and Edgar's detailed instructions for the prevention of cattle-stealing are informative about common pasture.[5] There can be no doubt that the arrangement normal in later times, by which the lord's demesne was not a detached block but consisted of strips in the common field, was of great antiquity, and phrases like "every third acre" occur occasionally which suggests this practice.[6] Where estates are favourably placed, we hear of special activities, dairy-farming,[7] horse-breeding,[8] salt-boiling,[9] or fishing.[10] Woodlands are particularly often mentioned. From kings like Alfred,[11] Edmund[12] and Cnut[13] down, the Anglo-Saxons were keen huntsmen, and hunting rights were jealously guarded. But woods were important also as mast pasture, for firewood, and for timber, which was of especial importance in an age when almost all secular building was done in this material; one is grateful for Alfred's brief but vivid little sketch of the selecting and bringing home of timber for various needs.[14]

Not only the slave and the *gebur* "who could not go where he would", but many a freeman of low station, spent his life in his own village and its immediate surroundings, going no farther afield than to the hundred meeting or his lord's court, or perhaps to buy or sell in a nearby town. Most nobles, on the other hand, moved continually; it was customary to move from estate to estate to consume the produce, and many of them held estates scattered over several parts of the country; they attended the shire meeting, and the more important of them went to the royal court; they had the means to journey on pilgrimage to Rome and other distant shrines; they often possessed houses in the towns. From the lord's hall, news of the world outside would percolate to the villagers; those on a royal estate, or that of an important magnate, might have the excitement of a royal visit to their neighbourhood. If the feasts described in our records are characteristic, they would hear accounts of much feasting and drinking.[15]

[1] No. 7, pp. 274 f. [2] No. 107; No. 234, p. 829. [3] For these see, for example, Nos. 56, 58, 83, 85.
[4] Ine (No. 32), 42. [5] IV Edgar (No. 41), 8–11. [6] *e.g.* Kemble, No. 674. [7] No. 93.
[8] Nos. 122, 125. [9] Nos. 64 f., 85, 93, 99. [10] Nos. 115, 125. [11] No. 7, p. 266.
[12] No. 234, p. 828, n. 2. [13] II Cnut (No. 50), 80 f. [14] No. 237.
[15] See, for example, No. 235, p. 834, and *Memorials of St. Dunstan*, ed. Stubbs, p. 18.

But apart from such occasional events, the villagers were not cut off from the world outside. They would learn news from travelling minstrels, men of a lower order than those who performed at Athelstan's coronation,[1] from pedlars, especially those who brought that most essential commodity, salt, over the country, and, if we are to believe various miracle tales, from persons who travelled from shrine to shrine in search of a saint who could cure them. And an unwanted opportunity of travel would come to many a man when the king called out his army.

Town-dwellers were a small minority, even at the end of the period. Our sources are inadequate for tracing the rise of towns or describing the life in them in any detail. In the early period, trade was not of such volume as to bring large concourses of persons together near harbours or where travel routes met, and, though several crafts were carried on, such as those of the goldsmith, the weaponsmith and the blacksmith, the carpenter and the leather-worker, such persons were often in the employ of some lord and did not tend to congregate in towns to any great extent. London, however, was of some significance already in Bede's day;[2] the kings of Kent had a hall in it,[3] and we hear incidentally of a Frisian merchant there.[4] A document of 672–675 calls it "the port where ships come to land",[5] and Æthelbald of Mercia remits toll on ships at London for the benefit of religious houses.[6] In 857 a bishop of Worcester acquires a house and some commercial rights there.[7] York had a community of Frisian merchants in the mid eighth century.[8] Other places for which there is evidence of some degree of urban life in the pre-Viking Age are Canterbury and Rochester;[9] it may merely be the greater number of documents that have survived from Kent that gives the impression that these towns were in advance of those in other parts.

Alfred's plan to protect his kingdom with a ring of fortifications, a plan not completed until his son's reign, was responsible for the rise of some towns, though some of the boroughs of this system were older towns provided with new defences. A document from Edward the Elder's reign gives the names and hidage of these boroughs, as well as the arrangements for manning and repairing them,[10] and there survives a document concerning the similar fortification of Worcester, by Ealdorman Ethelred and his wife, before Alfred's death.[11] It shows that certain dues on loads of salt have 'always' belonged to the king, but allows the bishop half of the fines for offences committed in the market-place or the streets, and some other dues. Outside this area, the bishop's rights are to

[1] No. 8, p. 279.   [2] No. 151, p. 609.   [3] Hlothhere (No. 30), 16 f.   [4] No. 151, p. 661.
[5] No. 54.   [6] No. 66.   [7] No. 92.   [8] No. 160.
[9] Nos. 72, 82, 89. See F. M. Stenton, *Anglo-Saxon England*, pp. 518–520.
[10] The *Burghal Hidage*, best edited by Robertson, *Anglo-Saxon Charters*, Appendix I, No. 1. On Alfred's boroughs see also Asser (No. 7, pp. 272 f.).   [11] No. 99.

remain unchanged. Thus for once we get a little evidence of the rise of the kind of arrangements which are shown by Domesday Book to have been in force in the boroughs. The profits arising from the jurisdiction in a borough by that time are usually divided between the king and the earl, the king taking two-thirds, but there are cases like this one where some church has a share in them. But until one reaches Domesday Book there is little detailed evidence about towns. The borough court met three times a year,[1] and in the area of the Five Boroughs there was a court for the whole five as well as one for each separate borough.[2] Cnut legislates to secure uniformity in legal process in all borough courts.[3] In the early tenth century, both Edward and Athelstan enjoin that all purchases must take place in towns, Athelstan limiting the application of this rule to cases where the goods are worth more than 20 pence.[4] Yet this regulation was dropped later, and replaced with injunctions that purchases must be properly witnessed.[5] Edgar divides boroughs into two classes, large, which must have a body of 36 witnesses, and small, which are to have only twelve, the number required also for the hundred.[6] Only in a town can money be minted, according to a law of Athelstan, which goes on to list the places which are allowed more than one moneyer.[7] This code probably applies only to the south of England, for all the places, except London, are south of the Thames. A code probably belonging to Ethelred's reign allows three moneyers to a principal town, one to others,[8] but coin evidence shows that far more than three moneyers were working simultaneously at some of the largest towns. The laws of the tenth and eleventh centuries have many clauses dealing with debasing of the coinage or coining false money.[9] They are concerned also with the repair of the fortifications,[10] but in general are quite unilluminating on town-life.

We saw above a ninth-century bishop of Worcester acquiring property in London, and later instances of landowners with houses in towns become common. Bishop Theodred bequeathes one in Ipswich, which may be attached to the estate at Waldringfield which he leaves to the same person.[11] For by this time it was becoming a common practice for country estates to have one or more houses in towns attached to them, as one in Hereford is attached to the estate at Staunton granted by Edgar to his thegn Ealhstan.[12] It was at one time thought that these town houses attached to estates were connected with garrison duty in the borough, but it is more likely that they were bought by landowners for convenience or as an investment. Domesday Book shows that some landowners had large holdings in town property. One document of Cnut's

---

[1] III Edgar (No. 40), 5.1.   [2] III Ethelred (No. 43), 1.1.   [3] II Cnut (No. 50), 34.
[4] I Edward, 1; II Athelstan (No. 35), 12, 13.1.
[5] III Edmund, 5; IV Edgar (No. 41), 3.1–7; II Cnut (No. 50), 24.   [6] IV Edgar (No. 41), 4 f.
[7] II Athelstan (No. 35), 14, 14.2.   [8] IV Ethelred, 9.
[9] e.g. III Ethelred, (No. 43), 8, 16; IV Ethelred, 5–9.1.
[10] II Athelstan (No. 35), 13; V Ethelred (No. 44), 26.1; II Cnut (No. 50), 65.   [11] No. 106.   [12] No. 109.

reign shows the reverse process, a citizen of Winchester obtaining a country estate.[1]

Trade was not negligible even in the earliest times. Objects of other than local manufacture are found in heathen burials, some coming, like those placed with Scyld's body in *Beowulf*, "from distant ways". The first extant trade regulation is in the code of Hlothhere and Eadric, and concerns the man of Kent buying in London,[2] and Wihtred's code speaks of the sale of a thief across the sea, thus referring to a slave traffic for which there is other evidence.[3] The same codes as well as that of Ine legislate to meet the problem of offences committed by traders from other lands, as also does Alfred;[4] their protection is guaranteed in English law by the king's right to the wergild of foreigners and to *mund* over them.[5] Already Offa and Charles the Great discuss the position of their nationals trading in the other's country,[6] and this is not the earliest reference to English traders abroad, even apart from the early slave-trade. Saxon merchants were among the traders at the fair of Saint-Denis, near Paris, in the seventh century, and there is an incidental mention of an English merchant settled in Marseilles in the eighth century.[7] By Offa's time English trade across the Channel was considerable enough for Charles to use its suppression as a weapon in a quarrel with Offa,[8] and for the latter to reform the coinage to bring it to a continental standard.[9] Ine's law which states how much of a wergild could be paid in kind suggests that in early days there was a shortage of currency.[10] As trade increased in importance, later kings are much concerned with ensuring a uniform and undebased coinage.[11] They interfere also to standardize weights and measures, and to fix prices,[12] but in our ignorance of the size of a 'wey' of wool, we are no wiser by learning that it must not be sold at more than 120 pence. That by law a sheep was worth fourpence, a pig eightpence or tenpence, a goat twopence, a cow 20 or 24 pence, an ox a mancus (30 pence), a horse 30 shillings, a mare 20 shillings, a slave a pound, is about the full extent of our knowledge of prices.[13] Little though it is, it helps to give some reality to the figures of wergilds, fines and compensations met with so often.

Mention has already been made of foreign merchants in the seventh and eighth centuries in London and York, and by the end of the tenth century the Life of St. Oswald speaks of a great concourse of traders, especially of Danish race, at York,[14] while there survives a text concerning London which refers to traders from Rouen, Flanders, Ponthieu, Normandy, the Isle of France, Huy,

---

[1] No. 132.   [2] Hlothhere (No. 30), 16–16.3.   [3] Wihtred (No. 31), 26; see also p. 60.
[4] Hlothhere (No. 30), 15; Wihtred (No. 31), 28; Ine (No. 32), 20, 25f.; Alfred (No. 33), 34.
[5] See p. 56.   [6] No. 197.   [7] See Levison, *England and the Continent*, p. 7.
[8] No. 20.   [9] See p. 25.   [10] Ine (No. 32), 54.1.
[11] II Athelstan (No. 35), 14f.; III Edgar (No. 40), 8; III Ethelred (No. 43), 8–8.2, 16; IV Ethelred, 5–9.3.
[12] III Edgar (No. 40), 8.1–8.3; V Ethelred (No. 44), 24.
[13] Ine (No. 32), 55; VI Athelstan (No. 37), 6–6.3; *Dunsæte*, 7. The shilling here mentioned is the Mercian shilling of fourpence.
[14] *Historians of the Church of York*, ed. Raine, I, p. 454.

Liège, Nivelles, as well as subjects of the emperor, who were specially privileged.[1] Details are given of the tolls they paid. English traders continued to go abroad; the protection of English ships in foreign harbours is considered in Ethelred's treaty with the vikings,[2] and traders are included among travellers for whom Cnut obtained better terms.[3] International agreement was necessary for trading between the English and Welsh, and the text known as *Dunsæte* regulates traffic on some part of the Welsh border.[4] The eleventh-century statement, that a merchant who has crossed the sea in his own ship three times is entitled to a thegn's rank,[5] hints at a rising mercantile class, of whom one would gladly know more.

(viii) THE CHURCH

The greater part of what we know of the conversion of the English is derived from Bede, and no one can improve on his narrative. Nevertheless, a few additions can be made from other sources. Some of Gregory's letters relating to the mission were unknown to Bede, or at least unused by him,[6] and the anonymous Life of Gregory adds a little to our information.[7] Bede was naturally best informed on the history of the Northumbrian Church, though even here, his account can be supplemented by Saints Lives by others, especially by Eddi's Life of Wilfrid, though this work is too long for inclusion in full in this volume. We have the advantage of knowing what parts of it Bede thought most important and worthy of inclusion in his history,[8] and the selection I have given in this volume shows among other things the value attached to grandeur of architecture and church furnishing by ecclesiastics of Wilfrid's stamp.[9] Bede had received fairly full information about Kent, though he does not mention the foundation of certain early monasteries. The Life of St. Guthlac,[10] who is not mentioned by Bede, shows us that his account of the Church in the Midlands is incomplete, and doubtless more could have been said about East Anglia. One would have liked to know something about the early eighth-century bishop of this province, Cuthwine, a collector of illuminated manuscripts.[11] But it is as regards Wessex that Bede's information was most scanty, and charters, correspondence and Lives of missionary saints tell much that is not in Bede's work. Bede never mentions Boniface.

Nowhere in any of our sources is there given a clear picture of the heathen religion which Christianity replaced. Bede mentions two goddesses by name, Hrethra and Eostre, in his *De Temporum Ratione*, and here and there in the *Ecclesiastical History*, in Eddi and in penitentials one learns a detail or two of heathen practice; place-names survive containing words descriptive of heathen sanctuaries, and in some the names of the gods Woden, Thunor and Tiw are

---

[1] IV Ethelred, 2.5–2.8.   [2] II Ethelred (No. 42), 3.1.   [3] Cnut's Letter (No. 49), 6.
[4] Liebermann, I, pp. 374–379.   [5] No. 52.   [6] See Nos. 161–163.   [7] No. 152.
[8] No. 151, pp. 676–680.   [9] No. 154.   [10] No. 156.   [11] Levison, *op. cit.*, p. 133.

included.[1] But though we know little of the beliefs and the ethical code of the heathen English, it is evident that in some places they were very firmly held. In spite of spectacular initial successes of the missionaries, men were quick to revert to heathenism on the accession of a heathen king or in a time of plague.[2] At the end of the seventh century Wihtred has to legislate against the worship of 'devils', that is, heathen gods,[3] and even later, reformers complain of heathen practices. Thus the synod of *Clofesho* in 747 mentions them specifically among the sins the bishops are to suppress on their visitations,[4] the legates in 786 complain of heathen habits,[5] and Alcuin in 797 advises Archbishop Æthelheard to take action against the wearing of amulets and the holding of assemblies among the hills, for which the churches are being deserted.[6]

It is natural enough that real progress should be slow, for the missionaries were few and the areas served very large. At first there was only one bishop for each kingdom, except that Kent had one at Rochester as well as at Canterbury. The work of evangelization was carried on from the episcopal see. Gregory's instructions show that he meant Augustine and his followers to live a communal, but not monastic life,[7] and the arrangements at Rochester, and at London during the short period of its first conversion, were no doubt similar, as would be those set up by Felix in East Anglia and Birinus in Wessex.[8] Paulinus seems in Northumbria to have worked from various royal estates, and we do not know whether he made permanent arrangement for the serving of the churches he built at York, Lincoln and *Campodunum*.[9] When his mission came to its sudden end, and Oswald reintroduced the faith from Iona, the organization of the Celtic Church was introduced, with its basis the monastery, where bishops might live in subservience to the abbot, though in higher ecclesiastical orders, engaging in long missionary expeditions with no fixed territorial sphere. Aidan therefore made the monastery of Lindisfarne his centre, and when eventually the great diocese of Northumbria was divided, two of its sees, Lindisfarne and Hexham, were established in monasteries. In fact, Bede considered that in 734 so much land was in monastic possession that it would have been difficult to find centres for new sees except in monasteries.[10] Meanwhile, however, the Roman Church had won its victory over the Celtic Church in 663, and most of the sees even in the areas won to the faith by the Celtic Church were not monastic. York was never monastic, but in Bosa's time a communal life was established there.[11] When Archbishop Theodore arrived, the only sees were Canterbury and Rochester in Kent, London in Essex, Dunwich in East Anglia, Winchester in Wessex, Lichfield in Mercia, and York

---

[1] See B. Dickins, *Essays and Studies of the English Association*, XIX, pp. 148–160; F. M. Stenton, *Trans. Royal Hist. Soc.*, 4th Series, XXIII, pp. 1–24. [2] No. 151, pp. 645, 667.
[3] Wihtred (No. 31), 12f [4] Haddan and Stubbs, III, pp. 363f. [5] No. 191.
[6] Dümmler, No. 290. [7] No. 151, p. 600. [8] No. 151, pp. 619f., 627.
[9] No. 151, pp. 618–620. [10] No. 170, p. 740. [11] Alcuin's poem on the saints of York, lines 856–874.

in Northumbria. Before his death he had divided East Anglia between Dunwich and Elmham, the Midlands between Lichfield, Worcester, Hereford, and a see which did not become permanently fixed at Leicester until 737, and, in spite of Wilfrid's opposition, Northumbria between York, Lindisfarne and Hexham. He appointed a separate bishop for Lindsey.[1] Arrangements that proved temporary were the provision of a bishop for the Picts with his see at Abercorn,[2] of a Mercian bishop at Dorchester-on-Thames,[3] and the occasional placing of a bishop at Ripon.[4] In the time of his successor Brihtwold the South Saxons were given a bishop of their own, with his see at Selsey, and Wessex was divided between Winchester and Sherborne.[5] The addition of a see at Whithorn in Galloway in 731[6] provided a third suffragan to York when this was turned into an archiepiscopal see in 735, and the Anglo-Saxon bishops of Mayo also regarded themselves as suffragans of York.[7] There were no further alterations until the Viking Age, except for the temporary raising of Lichfield to an archiepiscopal see.[8]

Bede considered this subdivision inadequate, as far as Northumbria was concerned,[9] and it is obvious that the dioceses were too large to be administered from the sees alone, even when these were held by prelates as conscientious and energetic as Cuthbert was. Some areas were dependent on monastic establishments for their spiritual needs, and from time to time in Bede's writings we hear of noblemen who have founded churches on their estates.[10] But he tells us nothing of how these were served, and the letter to Egbert shows that there was nothing resembling an advanced parochial system in existence. The early history of the parish is wrapped in obscurity. The synod of *Clofesho* in 747 implies that parish priests were not rare,[11] but it is not until the tenth century that we get anything like a clear picture of ecclesiastical organization. Then Edgar's law speaks of old minsters which are entitled to various dues, contrasting them with churches on thegns' estates, which are entitled to part of the thegn's tithe, but only if they have a burial place.[12] These are to be equated with the lesser minsters which Ethelred's laws on sanctuary differentiate not only from chief minsters, *i.e.* cathedral churches, but also from an intermediate rank which must represent the old minsters of Edgar's law. Lowest in Ethelred's scale comes a 'field church', a church without a burial place.[13] Other laws of this reign seem to assume that a village will normally have a church.[14]

One of the earliest measures necessitated by the conversion to Christianity must have been the securing of an income for the newly established Church.

[1] No. 151, pp. 652, 654.   [2] No. 151, p. 666.   [3] No. 151, p. 662.
[4] Eadhæd was translated to it from Lindsey when Ethelred of Mercia recovered that province in 678 (No. 151, p. 654); Wilfrid held this see from 686 to 691. (Eddi's claim that he was restored to York seems false.) See R. L. Poole, "St. Wilfrid and the See of Ripon" (*Eng. Hist. Rev.*, XXXIV, 1919).
[5] No. 151, p. 675.   [6] No. 151, p. 682.   [7] See No. 191.   [8] See pp. 91f.   [9] No. 170.
[10] See p. 669, n. 4.   [11] Haddan and Stubbs, III, p. 365.   [12] II Edgar (No. 40), 1–2.2.
[13] VIII Ethelred (No. 46), 5, 5.1.   [14] VII Ethelred (No. 45), 2.

Only in the very early days could royal munificence, such as that of Ethelbert of Kent,[1] suffice. Conquering kings could be liberal with lands won from enemies, as when Ceadwalla made over to the Church a quarter of the Isle of Wight,[2] an action that may be compared with that of Egbert, who gave a tenth of his conquests in Cornwall to the Church in the early ninth century.[3] One may note also that Wilfrid claimed the possessions of the British Church in areas conquered by Edwin.[4] But in general such methods of endowment were not feasible, and some means had to be sought to make it possible for land to be alienated from the kindred in order to endow a church or a monastery. Though the exact process is obscure, it is likely that bookland owes its creation to this need.[5] It was open for the possessor of land of this type to give it to a monastery or church, or to found a new monastery on it. Anglo-Saxon land-owners tended to regard the house they had founded as a family possession, to be handed down in their kindred. When Benedict Biscop enjoined that no abbot was to be chosen for his foundations by hereditary succession,[6] he was obviously combating a different point of view, and usually all that the Church required was that the abbot or abbess appointed should be suitable. Several instances of hereditary monasteries can be found in these pages, notably that on Spurn Point founded by Wilgils, Willibrord's father, which came to Alcuin by inheritance.[7]

These gifts of land were voluntary; but fairly early we learn of compulsory payments made to the Church. Churchscot is mentioned already in Ine's laws, with very heavy penalties for its non-payment,[8] and Bede's letter to Egbert shows that the bishops in Northumbria were in receipt of compulsory dues by 734.[9] Soulscot, the payment for the sake of the dead person's soul, which came to be regarded as a burial fee to which the Church was entitled, is probably of ancient origin, though first mentioned in Athelstan's laws,[10] where also plough alms first occur. This latter payment, along with churchscot, tithe and Peter's Pence, is enjoined on every Christian man by Edmund's laws,[11] and Edgar prescribes very stringent penalties for non-payment of tithe and hearth-penny (another name for Peter's Pence) while merely referring to the 'law-book' (in this case Ine's law) as regards the penalty for withholding churchscot.[12] The payment of tithe in early days had been a pious Christian duty, mentioned in Theodore's Penitential, which says it should be spent on the poor, on pilgrims, and on churches. The legates in 786 advocate it as a payment all must make,[13] but there is no evidence for its enforcement in England until the tenth century, and Edgar's law reads like new legislation on this matter. Peter's Pence is of obscure origin, but a payment to Rome which may be this due is being made year by year towards the end of Alfred's reign.[14] By the middle of the tenth

[1] No. 151, pp. 598 f., 604. [2] No. 151, p. 656. [3] No. 229. [4] No. 154, p. 693. [5] See pp. 343 f.
[6] No. 155, p. 701. [7] No. 157. [8] Ine (No. 32), 4. [9] No. 170, p. 738. [10] I Athelstan, 4.
[11] I Edmund, 2. [12] II Edgar (No. 40), 1-4. [13] No. 191, p. 771, n. 6. [14] No. 1, pp. 183 f.

century, churchscot and tithe are to be paid to the old parish churches, and care is taken that the founding of new churches shall not unduly rob these of revenue, but the process by which dues had become allotted to the individual churches or minsters and ceased to be administered for the diocese by the bishop is obscure, as, in fact, is the whole history of the rise of the parish church. When later one learns more about it, one finds the priest also in possession of his share in the arable of the community, but no source mentions when and how this arrangement came about.

Another source of revenue came from various fines to which the Church was legally entitled. Even before Christianity became a compulsory religion, it was necessary for the law to take cognizance of the preachers of the new faith, and the earliest written laws begin by protecting the Church and its members from theft.[1] The Church's rights of sanctuary are mentioned already in Ine's laws, and occupy an ever-increasing place in later codes.[2] Members of the clergy had to be fitted into the scale which allowed each man according to his rank a compensation for the breach of his right of protection (mund) or of his surety (borg), and Wihtred allows the Church the same compensation as the king;[3] but by Alfred's time a graduated scale has been fixed, which allows the archbishop three pounds when the king is entitled to five, and places a bishop on a level with the ealdorman, with two pounds, and this scale is still in force in Cnut's time.[4] A similar development is seen in regard to the compensation for breaking into one's premises, for, whereas Ine allows to a bishop the same compensation as to the king, i.e. 120 shillings, provided the offence was committed in his own diocese,[5] Alfred allows only 90 shillings to the archbishop and 60 shillings to a bishop or ealdorman.[6] The compensation is still high, but the Church is no longer put level with the king. Alfred allows a bishop the same compensation as an ealdorman if anyone fights in his presence, and assigns a higher amount to the archbishop, though again leaving him below the king, for such a crime in the king's hall placed the offender's life at the king's mercy.[7]

By the late tenth century, at any rate, a man in priest's orders was entitled to the wergild and other privileges of a thegn.[8] It is uncertain how old this right is, but already the Dialogue of Archbishop Egbert of York (732–766) gives a scale of payments to be made if an ecclesiastic is killed, 800 sicli for a priest, 600 for a deacon, 400 for a monk, and 800 sicli would probably be equivalent to the wergild of a layman of the highest class;[9] but as this text states that this is to be paid to the Church, whereas in later times it is only in the case of a monk that the Church instead of the kindred receives the wergild, this chapter is sometimes

---

[1] No. 29.
[2] Ine (No. 32), 5; Alfred (No. 33), 2, 5, 42.2; IV Athelstan, 6.1, 6.2; II Edmund (No. 38), 2; II Edgar (No. 40), 1, 5.3; VIII Ethelred (No. 46), 1–5.
[3] Wihtred (No. 31), 2.   [4] Alfred (No. 33), 3; II Cnut (No. 50), 58–58.2.   [5] Ine (No. 32), 45.
[6] Alfred (No. 33), 40.   [7] Alfred (No. 33), 7, 15.   [8] e.g. V Ethelred (No. 44), 9.1.
[9] Haddan and Stubbs, III, pp. 408 f. Cf. Chadwick, Studies on Anglo-Saxon Institutions, p. 21.

taken to refer to a payment later called 'altar-compensation'[1] or 'order-compensation' (*Hadbot*)[2] which was due to the Church for offences against the clergy, in addition to the wergild or other compensations due to the kindred. In the diocese of York in the eleventh century,[3] however, 'altar-compensation' was very much lower than the amounts stated in Egbert's *Dialogue*, and than those in the private tract called *Hadbot*, which may represent an ideal rather than an enforced rate of payment.

Another necessity was to decide the value attached to the oath of ecclesiastics. The position in Northumbria is shown in Egbert's *Dialogue*, which in criminal suits allows a priest to swear for 120 hides, a deacon for 60, a monk for 30, and in land disputes equates the oath of a priest with that of two deacons or three monks.[4] Another chapter is concerned with the method of purgation allowed to an accused ecclesiastic. It allows one who has no supporters of his innocence to come forward alone, as long as there are no witnesses of his crime.[5] Wihtred's laws also deal with the case of the accused ecclesiastic, allowing him favourable terms, which place a bishop on a level with the king.[6] Ethelred's laws go into detail on the exculpation of clerics and their injunctions are repeated in Cnut's code.[7] Moreover legislation was necessary for dealing with clerics convicted of crime. For serious crimes the cleric was unfrocked by the bishop and then the secular law took its course; neglect of duty and non-observance of rule was primarily the bishop's concern, but Edgar considered it the function of himself and his thegns to enforce on the clergy obedience to the bishops, and from the middle of the tenth century the State tried to insist on celibacy, Edmund prescribing loss of worldly goods as well as ecclesiastical penalties for non-observance,[8] and Ethelred's laws confining the right to thegnly status to a celibate priest.[9]

Many decisions concerning the status of the clergy would need to be taken in the first period of the conversion. Christianity did not, however, become a compulsory religion in Kent until after 640, when the worship of idols was forbidden and the Lenten fast enforced.[10] In the extant laws, the first statements dealing with the observance of Sunday and of fasts come in the laws of the contemporary kings, Wihtred and Ine, and later codes repeat and add instructions on the observance of fasts and festivals.[11] By Alfred's time, the penalties for crime were increased if any were committed in certain holy seasons.

When a kingdom had accepted Christianity, the clergy became responsible for the conducting of ordeals and the administration of oaths. It is possible that in this they took over functions performed by the priests of the heathen religion.

---

[1] No. 53.   [2] No. 52(E).   [3] No. 53.   [4] Haddan and Stubbs, III, p. 404.
[5] *ibid.*, pp. 404f.   [6] Wihtred (No. 31), 16–19, 21.1–24.
[7] VIII Ethelred (No. 46), 19–24, 27.1; I Cnut, 5–5.4. See also II Cnut (No. 50), 41.1.
[8] I Edmund, 1.   [9] V Ethelred (No. 44), 9.1.   [10] No. 151, p. 628.
[11] Wihtred (No. 31), 9–11, 14f.; Ine (No. 32), 3–3.2; Alfred (No. 33), 40.2; II Edgar (No. 40), 5, 5.1;
V Ethelred (No. 44), 12.3–20; VI Ethelred, 22–25; I Cnut, 14.2–17.3.

As a result, perjury, false witness, and breaking of oaths became regarded as the concern of the Church, which received a share of the fines.[1] It was also entitled to a share in the fines for breaches of the marriage law and for offences against nuns. It was with regard to marriage that the Church came most into conflict with Germanic law, and the battle was a long one; questions on this matter are answered in Gregory's replies to Augustine,[2] and it is one of the subjects dealt with by the synod of Hertford,[3] and in Wihtred's laws,[4] while Bede's account of how Bishop Cedd excommunicated an East Saxon nobleman for his unlawful marriage, but failed to prevent the king from visiting him,[5] is probably typical of the struggle that was going on. Complaints of the prevalence of offences against the marriage law occur in Boniface's and Alcuin's letters,[6] and again in the papal letters that have survived from the ninth century;[7] tenth- and eleventh-century laws refer several times to this topic,[8] and in some memoranda of Archbishop Oswald of York we read of action taken in a flagrant instance.[9] The prevalence of adultery and incest is one of the accusations made by Archbishop Wulfstan in 1014,[10] but later evidence shows that as far as the Scandinavianized North is concerned, prelates preached in vain against divorce and remarriage.[11] Many of the writers who complain of these offences speak also of fornication with consecrated women,[12] a crime of which the atheling Æthelwold was guilty in 900,[13] as also was Earl Swein in the eleventh century. In Alfred's time this offence incurred a fine of 120 shillings, to be shared between the king and the bishop or head of the church;[14] by Cnut's reign, the penalty is increased to loss of all possessions.[15]

There was no separate court in Anglo-Saxon times to deal with ecclesiastical causes, but matters which were the concern of the Church were dealt with in the ordinary courts, and no very clear line was drawn between the responsibilities of the Church and the State. The lay authorities not only assist the Church to obtain her dues and fines from laymen, but are ready to help to secure the clergy's obedience to the bishop's commands;[16] and on the other hand the co-operation of the bishop is expected in matters of no special concern to the Church, such as the insubordination of a reeve, or the discovery of coiners.[17] Purists in the later Anglo-Saxon period express concern at the part played by ecclesiastics in secular judgments.[18]

---

[1] Ine (No. 32), 13; Alfred (No. 33), 1–1.8; II Athelstan (No. 35), 26, 26.1; Cnut's Letter (No. 48), 14; II Cnut (No. 50), 36.   [2] No. 151, p. 600, n. 2.   [3] No. 151, p. 651.   [4] Wihtred (No. 31), 3–6.
[5] No. 151, p. 636.   [6] See Nos. 177, 178, 193, 202.   [7] Nos. 220, 222; cf. No. 223.
[8] V Ethelred (No. 44), 10, 25; VI Ethelred 11–12.1; Edward and Guthrum, 4; I Cnut, 7–7.3; II Cnut (No. 50), 6, 50–55.   [9] No. 114.   [10] No. 240.
[11] This is very clear in a document known as *De Obsessione Dunelmi* (*Symeonis Monachi Opera Omnia*, ed. Arnold, I, pp. 215–220).
[12] *e.g.* Nos. 177, 220, 223. See also Alfred (No. 33), 8; I Edmund, 4; Cnut's Letter (No. 48), 16f.
[13] No. 1, p. 190.   [14] Alfred (No. 33), 8.   [15] Cnut's Letter (No. 48), 16f.
[16] IV Edgar (No. 41), 1.8.   [17] II Athelstan (No. 35), 25.1; IV Ethelred, 8.
[18] See, for example, Ælfric's letter to Archbishop Wulfstan, *Die Hirtenbriefe Ælfrics*, ed. B. Fehr, p. 227; also Ælfric's *Lives of Saints*, ed. Skeat, II, pp. 330f.

The technicalities of the fitting of the new religion into the framework of existing law, and the gradual growth of the parochial system to supply the religious needs of ordinary people, are not the subjects that interested the authors of our early narrative sources. These were monks, and they tell us far more of those men and women whose devotion led them to renounce the world to enter monasteries, or to live as anchorites, often in voluntary exile in foreign lands, in their zeal to inherit an eternal country. The practice of entering foreign monasteries began early. Ceolfrith's brother had gone to Ireland for this purpose about 660,[1] and Bede says that many Northumbrians went there in the time of Finan (651–661) and Colman (661–663);[2] he speaks of English women entering continental houses, especially Brie, Chelles and Andeley, when there were few nunneries in England,[3] and the abbot in Gaul from whom Benedict Biscop got masons for his foundation of Wearmouth has an English name.[4] Benedict himself had intended to spend his life abroad in voluntary exile, but was sent back by Pope Vitalian, since there was work for him at home,[5] and similarly Bishop Aidan prevented Hilda from joining her sister at Chelles, that she might found a nunnery at home.[6] Too much pilgrimage of this kind would leave the Church at home depleted. But even when there were numbers of monastic houses in England, many persons still desired to acquire merit by relinquishing their native land; this attitude helped to fill the monasteries founded by the English missionaries among the German peoples in the eighth century, and an English community continued also at Mayo in Ireland at least until the end of this century, and its members were regarded by Alcuin as 'pilgrims'.

Monasteries began to be established in each English kingdom very soon after the conversion, whether this came from Rome or Iona. Those founded by the Irish Church would follow the pattern of Iona, consisting of separate cells, instead of the communal dormitory and refectory of the continental monasteries, but English sources give few details of life in the early monasteries of the areas won to the faith by the Irish Church. We have fuller information only from the period after the victory of the Roman Church at Whitby, and the foundations of which we know most, the twin monasteries of Wearmouth and Jarrow, were founded by a man of the Roman party. But in any case no very hard and fast line should be drawn at 663; men who sympathized with Rome rather than Iona, men who had studied abroad in areas of Roman observance, were to be found in the lands converted by the Irish Church long before the synod of Whitby, and on the other hand there were Irish elements in kingdoms mainly converted from Rome. Nor did the houses of Irish foundation hastily alter all their earlier practices and conform to the Benedictine rule

---

[1] No. 155, p. 698.   [2] No. 151, p. 644.   [3] No. 151, p. 628.   [4] No. 155, p. 699.
[5] Bede, *Sermo in Natale S. Benedicti Abbatis*, §1.   [6] No. 151, p. 662.

all at once. Owing to Wilfrid's influence, this rule was soon introduced into Northumbria and the Midlands, and naturally the houses established by Augustine and other Roman missionaries would conform to the Benedictine pattern from the first. Moreover, the type of foundation known as a double monastery, that is, a house for nuns with a community of monks alongside, seems to have been introduced from Gaul, but is found all over England, regardless of the source of the conversion.

The first English monastery was that founded at Canterbury by Augustine, dedicated to St. Peter and St. Paul,[1] the first house for women probably Lyminge, since tradition attributed its foundation to Æthelburh, Edwin's widow, after her flight from Northumbria. Lindisfarne was the first northern monastery, being founded by Aidan, and already before his death in 651 Hartlepool had been established as a nunnery.[2] We know most about life in Wearmouth and Jarrow, from the anonymous Life of Ceolfrith[3] as well as from Bede, and some other foundations, e.g. Whitby, Lastingham, Gilling, Melrose, Coldingham, Bardney in Lindsey, Barking in Essex, figure fairly prominently. There are also a number of houses which are referred to only incidentally in accounts of miracles or for some other chance reason. Such, in Bede, are Watton, a nunnery in Yorkshire, Dacre, the unidentified Tunnacæstir and Pægnalæch, an unnamed monastery in Elmet, Partney in Lindsey, Redbridge in Wessex.[4] Other sources show how incomplete even an exhaustive list of monastic houses mentioned in Bede would be. It would be very inadequate for Wessex, excluding places of some importance like Glastonbury,[5] Wimborne,[6] Nursling[7] and Tisbury,[8] as well as smaller places such as Bishop's Waltham,[9] and an unnamed nunnery on the Cherwell.[10] The Kentish houses of Lyminge, two at Minster in Thanet, Minster in Sheppey, Dover, Folkestone and Hoo[11] would all be lacking, as would Farnham,[12] Woking and Bermondsey in Surrey. The evidence for the last two and for Hoo in Kent shows that Medeshamestede (Peterborough) had far greater influence than one would gather from Bede, for these places as well as Breedon-on-the-Hill and probably Brixworth were colonies of this house;[13] and there are other monasteries in Mercian or Hwiccian territory, e.g. Repton,[14] Gloucester[15] and Withington,[16] unmentioned by Bede. From a charter we learn of a nunnery in Sussex.[17] Even Northumbrian houses can be added to those which occur in Bede, who does not mention Cornu Vallis,[18] or the monastery on Spurn Point founded by Willibrord's father,[19] or an unidentified house founded in Osred's

[1] No. 151, p. 604.   [2] No. 151, p. 662.   [3] No. 155.
[4] No. 151, pp. 619, 643, 657, 660.   [5] Nos. 158, 166.   [6] No. 1, p. 159; No. 159.
[7] No. 158.   [8] Nos. 55, 158.   [9] Mentioned in the Vitae Willibaldi et Wynnebaldi, chap. 2.
[10] No. 57.   [11] All these occur in Wihtred's privilege for the churches of Kent, Birch, No. 91.
[12] No. 58.   [13] See F. M. Stenton in Historical Essays in Honour of James Tait, pp. 313–326
[14] No. 156.   [15] Birch, Nos. 60, 535.   [16] Nos. 68, 75.   [17] No. 59.
[18] No. 155, p. 705.   [19] No. 157.

reign, which had a continuous history well on into the ninth century.[1] Many of these places were probably small, but the list is nevertheless an impressive testimony to the zeal for a life of retirement in the early days of Christianity in England, especially since the casual nature of many of the references justifies the belief that many others existed that have no place in our records. Some monasteries reached a great size; the anonymous author of the Life of Ceolfrith, who is not given to wild exaggeration, says that there were more than 600 inmates of Wearmouth and Jarrow by the time Ceolfrith left for Rome.[2] In the later eighth century, after Bede's time, one hears of other monasteries, Muchelney in Wessex,[3] Cookham in Berkshire,[4] Berkeley, Deerhurst and Westbury-on-Trym among the Hwicce,[5] Wenlock in Shropshire,[6] Stonegrave, Coxwold and *Donemutha* in Northumbria,[7] but little is known about these places. And besides the persons who entered religious communities were others who preferred to lead the life of a hermit, such as Cuthbert towards the end of his life[8] and other Lindisfarne saints, Herbert on Derwentwater,[9] Guthlac in Crowland,[10] and later in the eighth century Bealdhere and Etha, whose deaths are entered in the annals used by Simeon.[11]

The appeal of the religious life was felt by peoples of various classes: kings resigned to enter monasteries or go to Rome, and several of the religious leaders belonged to the noble classes. Benedict Biscop had been a thegn of King Oswiu, and Abbot Eastorwine a thegn of King Ecgfrith;[12] Wilfrid started his career in the household of Queen Eanflæd,[13] and Chad's follower Owine had been the chief thegn of Queen Æthelthryth.[14] Ceolfrith had difficulty at Jarrow in inducing monks of noble birth to submit to the discipline of the rule.[15] It was a common practice for queens to take the veil in their widowhood, but some, like Æthelthryt of Ely[16] and Cuthburh of Wimborne,[17] took this step in their husbands' lifetime. Hilda came of a royal family, and her sister, who was married to an East Anglian king, entered a continental nunnery;[18] an abbess mentioned in the Life of St. Guthlac was her granddaughter, being daughter of King Ealdwulf of East Anglia.[19] Sometimes devotion took the form of giving a son or daughter to the Church in infancy, the best known victims of this practice being Bede[20] and Oswiu's daughter Ælfflæd.[21] But monasteries were not filled entirely from the upper levels of society. There were special reasons why the peasant Cædmon should be received into a monastery,[22] but Cuthbert also, who was feeding his master's flocks when he saw a vision of Aidan's soul carried by angels,[23] was presumably of the *ceorl* class, as apparently was Willibrord's father, who founded a monastery on Spurn Point.

[1] On Æthelwulf's poem on this foundation, see p. 570.   [2] No. 155, p. 706.   [3] No. 71.
[4] No. 79. [5] No. 81. [6] See Tangl, No. 10. [7] No. 184. [8] No. 151, pp. 668. [9] No. 151, p. 669, n. 2.
[10] No. 156.   [11] No. 3, p. 241, 243.   [12] Bede, *History of the Abbots*, chaps. I and VIII.
[13] Eddi's *Life of Wilfrid*, ed. Colgrave, p. 6.   [14] No. 151, p. 649, n. 1.   [15] No. 155, p. 699.
[16] No. 151, p. 659.   [17] No. 1, p. 159. [18] No. 151, p. 662. [19] No. 156, p. 711, n. 4. [20] No. 151, p. 686.
[21] No. 151, p. 637.   [22] No. 151, p. 664.   [23] *Two Lives of St. Cuthbert*, ed. Colgrave, pp. 68, 164.

In some of the monasteries scholarship and the arts were soon flourishing. The conversion brought the English into touch with two streams of culture, that from Rome and the Mediterranean, and that from Ireland, where classical and biblical studies had continued to prosper at a time when in most of western Europe they had declined under the stress of barbarian invasions. No fast line should be drawn between the spheres of influence, for one of the most striking features in our records is the amount of intercourse between the ecclesiastics of the different kingdoms of the Heptarchy. This is seen in the range of Aldhelm's correspondence and of Bede's,[1] as well as in many accounts of journeys of prominent persons from one part of England to another, and of friendships such as that between Benedict Biscop and Cenwealh of Wessex,[2] and in little incidental statements, as that Pehthelm, the first bishop of Whithorn, had served under Aldhelm, bishop of Sherborne.[3] Moreover, as was said above, most kingdoms had from the start both Irish and Roman elements in them; nor did the acceptance of Roman usage at the synod of Whitby make any permanent gulf between Northumbria and Ireland. Englishmen continued to go there on voluntary exile, among them the later missionary Willibrord,[4] and the English community in Mayo kept up its connexion with York;[5] it is possible that Alcuin's correspondent Colcu,[6] who had been at York, should be identified with an abbot of this name in charge of the Irish branch of this community, set up by Colman on the island of Inishboffin off the coast of Mayo.[7] From 685 to 704 the Northumbrian throne was occupied by Aldfrith, who had studied among the Irish, and Adamnan, abbot of Iona, made two visits to his court.[8] It illustrates the blending of influences to note that this king was a friend and correspondent of the West Saxon Aldhelm, who had studied under Irish teachers at Malmesbury, but later came under the influence of Archbishop Theodore and Abbot Hadrian at Canterbury. Through Benedict Biscop, their influence reached Wearmouth and Jarrow, where Bede was educated.

Not all those who crossed the sea did so with the intention of not returning; besides the voluntary exiles there were many persons who went on pilgrimages or to study abroad, and returned home laden with books, pictures and other treasures, as well as intangible benefits, the fruits of their experience in foreign lands. The study of Anglo-Saxon art must naturally base itself on surviving objects, metal and ivory work, stone sculpture, and illumination in manuscripts, but the written sources put such works in their context. They show how easy it was for new motifs to be introduced and new standards set by

---

[1] See p. 575.
[2] Bede, *History of the Abbots*, chap. IV.
[3] No. 151, p. 675.
[4] No. 151, pp. 671 f.
[5] No. 3, p. 248; No. 191.
[6] No. 192.
[7] *Annals of Ulster*, 813, refer to a foster son of Colgu, abbot of Inishboffin.
[8] No. 151, p. 674; and cf. p. 690. Adamnan was not the only abbot of Iona to visit Northumbria. He implies (No. 153) that Abbot Seghine had met Oswald after the latter became king of Northumbria. A note in one Nennius manuscript shows that an abbot of Iona visited Ripon in the mid eighth century. See p. 118.

objects brought from abroad by men such as Wilfrid, Benedict Biscop and Acca, and that men eager to see the Church of God beautified with all possible splendour, rich altar-hangings, vessels and adornments of gold and silver, did not solely rely on imported objects. There is no suggestion that the jewellers ordered by Wilfrid to make a magnificent case for the gospels were foreigners,[1] and we learn that Ceolfrith had himself made a cross of gold.[2] Surviving objects prove the skill of the English in metal-work already in heathen times, but for Christian days we have mainly to depend on written evidence, for the objects in precious metals have vanished, as have the elaborate hangings and vestments. It is from accounts given by Eddi,[3] Aldhelm[4] and Bede[5] that some idea can be formed of the richness of church equipment. In architecture also, the finest examples, those at Ripon and Hexham, have not survived, though there is still something to be seen of Benedict Biscop's building, for which he brought masons from Gaul. Fortunately, surviving sculpture and illuminated manuscripts are enough to show the high level of artistic performance attained in the early days of the English Church.

The best productions come from Northumbria, and it is there that the finest scholarship appears; but learning is not confined to this kingdom. The earliest Anglo-Latin writer is the West Saxon Aldhelm, whose work reveals great erudition, and had great influence not only on his contemporaries but on tenth-century writers also. Something of the quality of Northumbrian historical writers can be judged from works included here,[6] three of which, Eddi's Life of Wilfrid, the Life of Gregory and the Life of Ceolfrith, are earlier than Bede. There survives also an anonymous Life of Cuthbert, and Bede used a lost Life of Æthelburh of Barking. Bede wrote other things than history, and his works on chronology and his commentaries on the Bible were influential both at home and on the Continent. No original work has come down to us from Canterbury, though both Bede and Aldhelm speak with great appreciation of the education obtainable there in the time of Theodore and Hadrian, when Greek as well as Latin was studied.[7]

Books were among the imported treasures[8] and some of them survive to this day, including a sixth-century gospel-book from Canterbury, now in Cambridge,[9] a copy of Acts in the Bodleian, generally believed to have been used by Bede,[10] and the sixth-century New Testament, known as the *Codex Fuldensis*, which once belonged to Boniface.[11] The imported books were copied in English scriptoria from an early date. Of particular interest are the description of the ornate gospel ordered by Wilfrid for Ripon,[12] and the account of the

---

[1] No. 154, p. 694. [2] No. 155, p. 704. [3] No. 154. [4] *Aldhelmi Opera*, ed. R. Ehwald, pp. 11–32.
[5] Especially in his *History of the Abbots*, chap. VI. Cf. No. 155, p. 699. [6] Nos. 151, 153–155.
[7] No. 151, pp. 647, 671, 680. [8] See No. 151, p. 680; No. 155, p. 702.
[9] C.C.C.C., MS. 286. [10] Laud, Gr. 35 (Bodl. Cat. No. 1119).
[11] W. M. Lindsay, *Early Irish Minuscule Script*, pp. 4 f. [12] No. 154, p. 694.

copying of the Vulgate at Wearmouth in Ceolfrith's time.[1] The correspondence of the missionaries shows how greatly they relied on the monasteries in the homeland to supply them with books.[2] The assiduity of book-production in English houses in the seventh and eighth centuries is shown most clearly by the numbers of manuscripts or fragments of manuscripts which survive either in English libraries or on the Continent. These manuscripts make clear the extent of Irish influence on early scholarship, for they are normally written in a script which Irish scribes had modified from older continental hands. Another interesting feature of learning and book-production in England at this time is that they were not confined to the male sex. Several nuns correspond in Latin with Boniface and Lul,[3] and there is extant a letter written by Ælfflæd, Hilda's successor at Whitby, to a continental abbess;[4] a fifth-century manuscript of Jerome on *Ecclesiastes* once belonged to an Abbess Cuthswith, probably to be identified with one who received grants of land in Worcestershire about 700,[5] and the account of the learning of Leofgyth given by her biographer shows that the education obtainable in some double monasteries was not different from that in houses for men.[6] Boniface asks an abbess to produce him a manuscript in letters of gold.[7] He clearly did not agree with a gnomic poem that "a woman's place is at her embroidery"; no doubt the author of this would have excluded religious women from its application. In fact, the synod of *Clofesho* in 747 disapproved of elaborate embroidery by nuns.[8]

Already before the death of Bede one meets criticism of the Church. The early simplicity of the Irish missionaries and their lack of organization were not suitable for a fully established Church, but Bede comments more than once with obvious nostalgia on their disregard for worldly goods and their refusal to offer ostentatious hospitality to kings and other men of high station.[9] He may have had in mind entertainments like the three-day feast given by Wilfrid to the king and his great men on the occasion of the dedication of Ripon, which Eddi relates with such pride.[10] Men of Wilfrid's views wished to see a bishop live with dignity, and his own splendour and the size of his retinue aroused the enmity and envy of the queen.[11] A little over a century later we find Alcuin blaming Archbishop Eanbald for travelling with too great a household and overburdening those bound to give him hospitality.[12] Wihtred's laws had to deal with vagrant ecclesiastics,[13] and Bede tells a story of relaxed discipline in the monastery of Coldingham.[14] In his letter to Egbert he says that many so-called monasteries are fraudulent foundations, made to obtain immunity from royal dues, and he advocates their suppression.[15] It would appear from Pope

---

[1] No. 155, p. 702.   [2] Nos. 172, 175f., 179f., 185, 188, 201.   [3] *e.g.* Nos. 168f., 172f.   [4] Tangl, No. 8.
[5] Birch, Nos. 85, 122. See E. A. Lowe, "An Eighth-Century List of Books in a Bodleian MS. from Würzburg", *Speculum*, III, 1928.   [6] No. 159.
[7] No. 172.   [8] Haddan and Stubbs, III, p. 369.   [9] No. 151, pp. 625f., 643.
[10] No. 154, p. 694.   [11] Eddi's *Life of Wilfrid*, ed. Colgrave, p. 48.   [12] No. 208.
[13] Wihtred (No. 31), 7.   [14] No. 151, p. 665, n. 1.   [15] No. 170, pp. 740f.

Paul's letter that his advice was acted on.[1] Bede levels other accusations in 734 against the Church, of failure to supply the religious needs of the people, and of avarice in collecting dues.[2] Throughout the eighth century missionaries abroad write home with criticisms and demands for reform.[3]

In response to letters of admonition from Pope Zacharias, Archbishop Cuthbert called a synod at *Clofesho* in 747, and its injunctions have survived.[4] Several of them merely aim at securing uniformity of observance all over the province, and others are general exhortations on the preserving of Christian unity and the performance of religious duties, but several are specifically directed against contemporary conditions. Bishops are to make annual visitations of their dioceses and among other things suppress heathen customs; they are to hold diocesan synods, and they are to report to a general synod things amiss in their diocese; they are to warn abbots and abbesses to order their communities according to the rule, and are if necessary to visit monasteries in secular control. In ordering bishops, abbots and abbesses to encourage study, the statutes lament that few in these days desire it, and they forbid the presence in monasteries of poets, harpists, musicians and buffoons. They disapprove of layfolk living in monasteries, and they order monks and nuns to wear a proper habit and not indulge in elegant clothing. Bishops are to examine ordinands, and abbots are not to admit persons to the tonsure without due trial of their suitability. Wandering monks and nuns are to return to their monasteries. Priests are to be capable of explaining in the vernacular the Creed and the Lord's Prayer, the Mass and the office of baptism, and of expounding their spiritual significance. They are not to gabble or declaim their services in the manner of secular poets. A special warning is given against drunkenness, which Boniface in one of his letters proclaimed a besetting sin of the English.[5] The laity must not pass the three days before Ascension in games, horse-racing or feasting, instead of in fasting. The synod combats an opinion grown up among the laity that they can expiate their sins by paying money in alms or for the reciting of psalms, without undergoing any personal penance. Alcuin complains later of many of these shortcomings, of show in dress, of immoderation in food and drink,[6] of the practice of fox-hunting and coursing by monks,[7] of their listening to heathen songs,[8] of the decay of learning.[9] He seems afraid that the clergy of York may become guilty of simony at the election of an archbishop.[10]

Nevertheless, as we read our sources we find that there is another side to the picture. Though there was much in eighth-century England to distress idealists, this period cannot be regarded as one of corruption and decadence. It saw a great, though unrecorded, advance in the growth of the parish, it was the

---

[1] No. 184.   [2] No. 170, pp. 738f.   [3] Nos. 177, 179, 193f., 199, 203, 207f.
[4] Haddan and Stubbs, III, pp. 360–376.   [5] Tangl, No. 78, in the version preserved in England.
[6] Nos. 193f., 202f.   [7] Dümmler, No. 19.   [8] Dümmler, No. 124.   [9] See p. 90.   [10] Dümmler, No. 48.

century of the English missions to the Continent, it contains many examples of individual devotion in the founding of monasteries or in pilgrimage to Rome, and it was far from negligible in scholarship and the arts. The beginning of English missionary work abroad by Wilfrid, which is recorded by Eddi and Bede,[1] had only temporary results, and it is to Willibrord, who landed in Friesland in 692 and continued there until his death in 739, that the permanent conversion of the southern part of this area is due. He was a Northumbrian, and thus Bede is well informed on his mission,[2] which is fortunate, for no correspondence from it survives, and the only Life, written by Alcuin,[3] is too late to give much detail. Bede makes no mention of the West Saxon Boniface, though he had finally dedicated himself to mission work as early as 718, and received a papal mandate to preach to the heathen in 719. For three years he helped Willibrord, and then went to preach to the Germans, and was consecrated bishop for them in 722 by Pope Gregory II. After ten years of constant work and considerable success in Hesse and Thuringia, he was granted the *pallium*, but even as archbishop he had no fixed seat until 747, when his see was fixed at Mainz. In the interval he had won converts and founded monasteries, had re-established diocesan organization in Bavaria, and fixed new sees, at Würzburg, Buraburg and Erfurt, for the lands he had won to Christianity, setting Englishmen over two of them. He had brought the rulers of the Franks, Carloman and Pippin, into a new and close relationship with the papacy, and persuaded them to hold synods for the reform of the Frankish Church. After long years of organization, he felt free to head a mission into northern Friesland, which was still heathen, and there, a few months later, he suffered martyrdom on 5 June 754. Boniface's career is known mainly from Lives of him and of some of his helpers,[4] and from the correspondence,[5] which reveals far more than the biographies do the personality of this great man, letting one glimpse the dynamic force of character, the integrity, modesty and absence of self-pity, as well as the gentleness and sympathetic understanding towards his friends. Moreover, one cannot read the sources for his mission without realizing the amount he owed to the support of friends and well-wishers at home, both layfolk and ecclesiastics, and to the numbers of devoted men and women who came to share the hardships of the mission and end their lives on foreign soil. This interest in the conversion of the German peoples did not slacken after Boniface's death. An exchange of letters and gifts continued between Lul, Boniface's successor at Mainz, and many persons, all over England. Further recruits were forthcoming. Northumbria sent Aluberht to Friesland in 767[6] and Willehad about the same time,[7] and there was an Englishman called Leofwine

---

[1] No. 151, p. 678; Eddi's *Life of Wilfrid*, ed. Colgrave, pp. 52 f.   [2] No. 151, pp. 672–674.
[3] See No. 157.   [4] See pp. 569 f.   [5] See pp. 573 f., and Nos. 167–190.
[6] No. 3, p. 243; No. 160.   [7] Anskar, *Vita S. Willehadi*, chap. 1; Haddan and Stubbs, III, p. 433.

working there also.[1] Willehad worked for several years in Friesland, and was sent by Charles the Great to preach to the Old Saxons in 780. After various set-backs, he became bishop of Bremen in 787, and died two years later.

Northumbrian scholarship did not die with Bede. He left at least one scholar at Jarrow who had profited by his teaching, Cuthbert, later abbot of the twin monasteries,[2] who wrote the touching account of his master's last hours; but it was York that now became the centre of Northumbrian scholarship. Alcuin studied there, first under Archbishop Egbert, Bede's pupil and the author of a dialogue on ecclesiastical law, and later under Ethelbert, whom Egbert put in charge of the school. It was Ethelbert who, with Alcuin's help, founded the famous library at York which Alcuin praises in his poem on the saints of York,[3] and speaks of with nostalgia when he had left England for France.[4] Alcuin himself taught in this school when Ethelbert became archbishop in 767, and its fame attracted to it scholars from Friesland, including the Liudger whose Life affords us a glimpse of this period of Alcuin's career.[5] He journeyed more than once to Rome, and it is probable that he made the acquaintance of Charles the Great in 773;[6] in any case he met him in 781, when on his way home from fetching the *pallium* for Archbishop Eanbald,[7] and was then asked by him to take part in his educational reforms. He therefore returned to Charles the following year, though in the report of the legates in 786 we find him in England, accompanying them to Offa's court,[8] and he writes from England from 790 to 793. From then till his death he lived in France. His voluminous correspondence is an important historical source, and his work on the revision of the Bible text and on the liturgy was a permanent contribution to learning; many of his writings were on theological controversy which has lost its interest, and his was not an original mind. Yet he handed on to his continental pupils the traditional English scholarship and paved the way for later writers of the Carolingian renaissance. There were other Englishmen in Charles's kingdom, such as Sigewulf, abbot of Ferrières, Alcuin's pupil at York,[9] Beornred, abbot of Echternach, who became archbishop of Sens,[10] and Fridugis (Frithugils), Alcuin's successor at Tours, who became an important person under Louis the Pious.[11] As in the days of Boniface, England was still sending many of its best men abroad.

Yet the correspondence of Boniface, Lul and Alcuin shows that England itself was not devoid of persons with intellectual interests and attainments, though there are few works that can be dated in this period. There is the Life of St. Guthlac by Felix[12] and some Latin poems on the miracles of St. Ninian.[13]

[1] No. 160   [2] No. 185.   [3] *Historians of the Church of York*, ed. Raine, I, pp. 395 f.
[4] No. 201.   [5] No. 160.   [6] See Levison, *England and the Continent*, p. 154 n.
[7] No. 3, p. 245, and *Vita Alcuini, Mon. Germ. Hist., Scriptores*, XV, pt. I, p. 190.   [8] No. 191.
[9] See pp. 570, 807.   [10] See p. 713.   [11] See Levison, *op. cit.*, pp. 163–166.
[12] No. 156.   [13] *Mon. Germ. Hist., Poetae*, IV, pt. II, pp. 943–962.

Probably we should add the *Liber Monstrorum*.[1] Manuscripts were still being produced in considerable numbers and were in demand abroad. Art was flourishing, and precious gifts were being sent across the Channel in both directions. The rebuilding of the minster at York on a much grander scale was begun by Archbishop Ethelbert, and Alcuin's poem which tells us about it tells also of magnificent altar adornments given by the same prelate.[2] Yet, towards the end of his life, Alcuin was not happy about the state of learning in England: he laments the lack of teachers in Britain, where once they were plentiful;[3] he impresses on Archbishop Æthelheard of Canterbury the importance of renewing the study of the Scriptures,[4] and tells Archbishop Eanbald II of York not to waste the books there,[5] and in another letter he asks: "What use is the abundance of books, if there are none to read and understand them?"[6] It would appear that England had given to the Continent scholars who were needed at home.

Yet it must also be remembered that it is probably in the eighth century that the bulk of extant Old English poetry was composed. This poetry has its roots in the heathen past, but little survives that is not Christian. Bede tells how the inspiration came to Cædmon, a man of the *ceorl* class, to use the native metre for religious themes in the latter part of the seventh century, and how by the time Bede is writing he had been copied by many poets.[7] Bede mentions expressly the didactic intention of Cædmon's work, and though only the hymn quoted in Bede manuscripts can confidently be assigned to this poet, much surviving Old English poetry is clearly intended to teach men the contents of Scripture and the duties of a Christian life. Its value for these purposes was realized by the missionaries to the Old Saxons, for it has long been recognized that the Old Saxon religious poetry, the *Heliand* and the fragmentary *Genesis*, were inspired by English models, and their connexion with Liudger, who had studied under Alcuin at York, is becoming increasingly clear.[8] But there is other religious poetry which is a more spontaneous expression of the poet's own religious emotion, notably the deeply moving poem known as the *Dream of the Rood*, and this personal note is visible in some of the work of a poet called Cynewulf, who lived in the later part of the eighth century or in the early ninth, while the poems called *The Wanderer* and *The Seafarer*, which are included in this volume,[9] express the individual's response to the eternal truths in contrast to the temporal conditions of life. Of even greater interest is the longest poem, *Beowulf*, for though it is not primarily a religious poem, being concerned to tell a story of a hero's fight with monsters against a background of human

---

[1] See K. Sisam, *Studies in the History of Old English Literature*, p. 77.
[2] *Historians of the Church of York*, ed. Raine, I, p. 394.   [3] Dümmler, No. 189.
[4] No. 203.   [5] Dümmler, No. 226.   [6] Dümmler, No. 286.   [7] No. 151, p. 663.
[8] See R. Drögereit, "Werden und die Heliand", *Beiträge zur Geschichte von Stadt und Stift Essen*, LXVI, 1950.   [9] Nos. 211 f.

feud and strife, it hints at a moral dear to the religious poets, the transitoriness of temporal glory, and also it shows how possible it was to reconcile earlier values, the importance of loyalty to kinsmen and lord, even to the avenging of their deaths, the need for liberality to followers, for the keeping of oaths and the fulfilment of boasts, with a Christian view of life. The poem is too long to include here, and though it is valuable in showing the strength with which certain views were held, it is difficult to use as direct historical evidence on points of detail, such as the descriptions of life in the king's hall, as long as there is the present difference of opinion as to how far such things are based on older poetry or drawn from the conditions of the author's time.[1]

The later eighth century saw one attempt to change the organization of the English Church, by creating a third archiepiscopal province. It is a sign of Offa's enormous power that he was able to force through a measure that ran so contrary to the traditions from the time of Gregory's mission. Almost all the documents that have survived relating to the conversion of Lichfield into an archbishopric are contained in this volume.[2] It underlines the paucity of sources for the reign of Offa to note that none of the correspondence relating to its creation has survived, and our knowledge is therefore derived from the documents concerning the abolition of the new province. From these it appears that Offa was led to the course he took by his quarrels with Jænberht, an archbishop of Kentish origin,[3] though he made Pope Hadrian believe that it was the unanimous wish of the English people. His successor Cenwulf began negotiations for the abolition in 797. He was doubtless influenced by its unpopularity, but also by the Mercian sympathies of Archbishop Æthelheard, which made a separate Mercian archbishopric unnecessary. From Alcuin's letter in this year we see that the treatment of Hygeberht, archbishop of Lichfield, was under discussion,[4] and Cenwulf's letter to the pope in 798 shows that he had tried to raise the matter in Rome in 797.[5] This letter hints at the removal of the metropolitan see from Canterbury to London, and it is in this sense that Leo interpreted the request, but he refused to tolerate so great a breach with tradition.[6] Probably Cenwulf did not press the matter, for by the end of 798 Mercian control was re-established in Kent, and Archbishop Æthelheard, whose Mercian sympathies had led to his flight during the Kentish rising, could be reseated in Canterbury. Alcuin had censured Æthelheard for this flight,[7] and written to the clergy and people of Kent exhorting them to recall him, warning them of the risks of internal dissensions in a time of danger from viking attack.[8]

---

[1] On this whole question see D. Whitelock, in *Trans. Royal Hist. Soc.* 4th Series, XXXI, 1949.

[2] Nos. 203–206, 209f.

[3] Three previous archbishops, Tatwine, Nothhelm and Cuthbert, who came from Breedon-on-the-Hill, London and Hereford respectively, were presumably Mercian appointments. The origin of Bregowine, Jænberht's immediate predecessor, is unknown.

[4] No. 203.   [5] No. 204.   [6] No. 205.   [7] No. 203.   [8] Dümmler, No. 129.

Further delay may have been caused by the pope's preoccupation with his own troubles. In 801, Æthelheard went to Rome on this matter, Alcuin writing him a recommendation to Charles the Great,[1] and early in 802 Leo wrote confirming Æthelheard's authority as in former days,[2] sending a letter on the same subject to Cenwulf about the same time.[3] Alcuin's letter of congratulation to Æthelheard is extant.[4] In a synod at *Clofesho* in October, 803, the archbishopric of Lichfield was formally abolished.[5] Hygeberht, the only archbishop of Lichfield, seems to have resigned, since the signature of his successor is followed by that of an Abbot Hygeberht in one of the documents issued at this synod.[6] It is about this time that there begins the enrolment at Canterbury of the series of episcopal professions,[7] one of which, that of Eadwulf of Lindsey, a pupil of Æthelheard, shows by the warmth of its expression of loyalty that feeling ran high among the episcopate regarding the division of the province of Canterbury.[8]

A long drawn-out trouble of this kind cannot have been good for the internal administration of the church of Canterbury, and Alcuin's letter to Æthelheard implies that much could be done to reform it.[9] Æthelheard's successor Wulfred, who succeeded in 805, established at Christ Church a communal way of life on the pattern laid down by Chrodegang of Metz; but it seems probable that he had little opportunity for reforming activities, since he was long occupied in a quarrel with Cenwulf, and was for some years, 817–821, suspended from discharging his functions. The cause of the quarrel is obscure. Alcuin had died in 804, so we have no longer the evidence of his letters, and no papal letters have chanced to survive. Only the Canterbury side is known, from a document of 825,[10] and it says that Cenwulf made charges against the archbishop to the pope. The archbishop had to pay heavily for a reconciliation in 821, the king undertaking to clear him with the pope. How far these dissensions had lowered standards of scholarship at Christ Church can be seen in the bad Latin of this and other documents of the ninth century produced at this house.

The initial viking raids, which began in 793, caused widespread alarm, but did not seriously affect the state of the Church. The letter of Bishop Ecgred of Lindisfarne leaves an impression that the North still had an active and conscientious episcopate, anxious to protect their flock from heresy,[11] and his house was producing its *Liber Vitae* in letters of gold and silver. The library of York was intact, and Lupus of Ferrières asks for a loan from it,[12] and the maintenance of Northumbrian contacts with the Continent is shown also in their art[13] and in the issue by Archbishop Wigmund (837–854) of coins in imitation of those of

[1] No. 206.   [2] No. 209.   [3] Birch, No. 306; Haddan and Stubbs, III, pp. 538 f.
[4] Dümmler, No. 255.   [5] No. 210.   [6] Birch, No. 312.   [7] See p. 578.
[8] Birch, No. 276; Haddan and Stubbs, III, p. 506.   [9] No. 203.   [10] Birch, No. 384.   [11] No. 214.
[12] No. 216.   [13] See T. D. Kendrick, *Anglo-Saxon Art to A.D. 900* (London, 1938), pp. 143–158.

Louis the Pious. Excavation has discovered coins of Wigmund and of King Osbert (849–867) on the site of Whitby Abbey, proving that this was not abandoned before the middle of the century. There are traces of activity in book-production at Lichfield in the early ninth century, including the Book of Cerne; a reasonable standard of scholarship must have been maintained in Mercian houses for Alfred to be able later on to draw from there men adequately educated to help his reforms.

But the great invasion of 865 and the subsequent cession of the north and east of England to Danish rulers had great destructive effect. The two East Anglian sees disappeared, those of Lindsey and Leicester were combined and moved to Dorchester-on-Thames. In Northumbria, the see of Hexham was destroyed and, as far as we know, never revived. The brothers of Lindisfarne wandered for some years with their relics before they settled at Chester-le-Street. Whithorn may have survived rather longer; it was one of the places where the wanderers from Lindisfarne sought an asylum,[1] but its ultimate fate is unknown. Only York seems to have had something like a continuous existence. Most of the monasteries in the areas of Danish settlement were destroyed, and some were never restored, though others were refounded in the tenth century or, in the North, after the Norman Conquest. But a small community at Crayke near York survived at least the first viking settlement, for the monks of Lindisfarne sheltered at it for a time, and since the head of the house, though called by Simeon an abbot, has a woman's name, it was presumably a nunnery or double monastery.[2] There may have been other houses which weathered the storm, but they would be the smaller and poorer places, and they play no recorded part in later developments. West of the Pennines there was still a community at Heversham in the early tenth century, and we hear from the same source of one in Norham in Northumberland,[3] an area which remained under the rule of the English high-reeves of Bamburgh after the Danish settlement of southern Northumbria. There was destruction and demoralization also in the areas which did not become subject to the Danes. Alfred speaks of everything being ravaged and burnt, remembering that before that time he had seen the churches full of treasures and books.[4] We have his evidence for the decline in learning. Asser speaks of the decay of the desire for the monastic life, though he attributes it less to the effect of the viking raids than to the wealth of the English, presumably in comparison with his own barren country.[5] A family who had an estate in Gloucester on condition that it should be held by one of them who was in orders, failed about 900 to find a member willing to take orders.[6] It is to this period that Dunstan is referring

---

[1] See *Symeonis Monachi Opera Omnia*, ed. Arnold, I, p. 67.   [2] *ibid.*, I, pp. 68 f.
[3] No. 6.   [4] No. 226.   [5] No. 7, pp. 273 f.
[6] Birch, No. 582, edited with translation in F. E. Harmer, *Select English Historical Documents of the Ninth and Tenth Centuries*, pp. 25–27, 57–59.

when he speaks of the falling off of teachers.[1] Papal letters complain of offences against the marriage laws,[2] but this complaint is common at all times. What is interesting is that the surviving fragments of correspondence show that contact with Rome was kept up even in the midst of the invasions. In the annals from 887 to 890, when there was little else to record, the chronicler tells us who took to Rome the alms of the king and the West Saxons. The first entry does not read as if this were an innovation.

Alfred's measures to revive monasticism and to raise the standard of learning by inviting scholars from abroad, by insisting that all young men of means should learn to read, and by providing translations from what he considered the most essential Latin works for them to read, are well known from Asser,[3] from Alfred's own works, especially the letter prefaced to the *Pastoral Care*,[4] and from Archbishop Fulk's letter to him.[5] His casual remark that many could read English, taken together with the increasing use of the vernacular in documents from the early ninth century, and with the rapid multiplication of copies of the Chronicle[6] and of the Old English Martyrology,[7] suggests that one reason for the decline of Latin was that it was being superseded for some purposes by English. Vernacular manuscripts of this period had very little chance of survival; subsequent changes in language, spelling and paleography would cause them to be little valued by the generations after the tenth-century revival. The possibility must always be borne in mind that there were more vernacular works from this period than those which have come down, *i.e.* the works by or associated with Alfred, the Chronicle, the Martyrology, and Werferth's translation of Gregory's *Dialogues*.

In Alfred's reign also the conversion of the Danes began, if not as early as Pope Formosus thought it should.[8] The baptism of Guthrum was part of the terms after Edington, and later, in 893, Alfred tried similar means with Hæsten, whose sons were baptized.[9] Guthrum's acceptance of Christianity may have been more than a temporary gesture; at any rate there are signs of a cult of St. Edmund very early in the kingdom Guthrum ruled.[10] We have seen that in the North, the church of York, and a few minor places, survived, and there is no reason to reject the tradition that the Danish king Guthfrith, who became king after Healfdene,[11] and was buried in York Minster when he died,[12] was a Christian. The Danes who settled in the ninth century gradually accepted Christianity, but our records are disappointingly silent on the means by which the conversion was carried out and on the organization of the Church under

---

[1] No. 229. [2] Nos. 220, 222. Cf. No. 223. [3] No. 7, pp. 267–269, 275.
[4] No. 226. [5] No. 225. [6] See pp. 114 f.
[7] See C. Sisam, "An Early Fragment of the Old English *Martyrology*", *Rev. Eng. Stud.*, New Series IV.
[8] No. 227. [9] No. 1, pp. 180, 186.
[10] See D. Whitelock, *Saga-Book of the Viking Soc.*, XII, pp. 159–176. [11] No. 6. [12] See p. 188, n. 7.

Scandinavian rulers in the Danelaw. The complete conversion in Northumbria was retarded by the invasion of Norsemen from Ireland. One of Ragnald's followers swore by Thor and Othin,[1] and as late as 942 the poem on the redemption of the Five Boroughs regards these men as heathen.[2] But it considers the Danes of the relieved boroughs as Christians, though in 926 charters of Athelstan had referred to 'pagans' in Derbyshire as well as in Bedfordshire.[3] However, in the early eleventh century, Archbishop Wulfstan could declare, no doubt in good faith, that elaborate rules on ecclesiastical observances in the Danelaw dated from treaties made in the time of Alfred and his son Edward.[4] Though this cannot have been the case, it shows that the conversion of the Danes was already of remote antiquity in his day; otherwise the claim would have been recognized as false. It is true that he complains of heathen practices,[5] but at least the official adoption of Christianity belonged to times out of mind.

After the reconquest of East Anglia, it seems for a time to have been administered by the bishop of London;[6] it is not until 956 that the series of East Anglian bishops begins again, the see being at Elmham. The dioceses of Leicester and Lindsey were administered from Dorchester after the Danelaw came under English rule, though while the districts of the Five Boroughs were independent these may have been the concern of York. The grant by the English kings of Southwell and Sutton, Nottinghamshire,[7] to the archbishops of York may represent a recognition of an earlier state of things, and the fact that the claim of York to Lindsey in the time of William II had to be bought out shows that it must have had some solid basis.[8] From time to time in the tenth century, there appears a bishop of Lindsey, but the see merges again with Dorchester. When Northumbria is brought back under the English crown, York normally has only one suffragan, the bishop of Chester-le-Street, whose see was later removed to Durham, but during Athelstan's reign the archbishop appears with more suffragans. A charter dated 929 which allows him four is not above suspicion,[9] but an Æscberht, who appears in it alongside Wigred of Chester-le-Street, is a real person enough, attesting many charters, including originals, between 928 and 934,[10] while an Edward who signs in 930 and 931, sometimes along with both of these, may belong to the northern province,[11] as may a Sæxhelm who appears in 934 and 937.[12] They may have been assistant bishops only, but it seems quite possible that an attempt was made to revive more sees in Northumbria at this time, but proved impracticable because of the great impoverishment of the Church in the North. This led to the practice of allowing the archbishop to hold his see in plurality with one in the South. It is not at all clear that Oscetel relinquished Dorchester when he became archbishop of York;

---

[1] No. 6.   [2] No. 1, p. 202.   [3] No. 103.   [4] D. Whitelock, *Eng. Hist. Rev.*, LVI, pp. 1–21.
[5] No. 240.   [6] No. 106.   [7] No. 108; Birch, No. 1044.
[8] *Historians of the Church of York*, ed. Raine, II, pp. 105 f.; III, pp. 21 f.   [9] Birch, No. 665.
[10] Birch, Nos. 663, 674, 675, 677, 689, 702.   [11] Birch, Nos. 669, 674, 677.   [12] Birch, Nos. 702, 716.

it is certain that Oswald, Ealdwulf and Wulfstan held both York and Worcester, an arrangement occasionally revived later. After Athelstan's time, the northern province is usually represented at councils only by its archbishop, though the bishop of Chester-le-Street appears in 949, 955, 958 and 959,[1] and Aldhun, the bishop who moved the see to Durham, witnesses a charter of 1009.[2]

Meanwhile, early in the reign of Edward the Elder, three new sees had been created for Wessex, namely Wells, Ramsbury and Crediton;[3] the latter see sometimes included an assistant bishop for Cornwall, and in 994 this district was made a new bishopric, with its see at St. Germans.[4] There was for a time a separate bishop for Berkshire, but no further permanent additions were made to the number of sees in Anglo-Saxon times.

To the men educated in the reformed monasteries after the mid-tenth-century revival, the first half of the tenth century appeared a time when education and learning was at the lowest possible ebb. Even the scanty sources at our disposal show that this view was exaggerated. It is true that the period produced no great writer, and that the detailed writing of the Chronicle was in abeyance from 924 for some fifty years, but men who hold high office in Athelstan's reign, such as Oda, bishop of Ramsbury and later archbishop of Canterbury, had received no mean education, and manuscripts and fragments of manuscripts of this period survive to prove that religious houses were not completely inactive,[5] but continued to copy the works of Alfred and of the Latin writers of earlier times, while Athelstan's charters betray a revived study of Aldhelm. Several of the books given by Athelstan to religious houses were obtained abroad,[6] but the Life of St. Cuthbert given to Chester-le-Street was English work,[7] and matter was added in England to a continental psalter given to Winchester.[8] The conditions in the churches governed by secular priests must not be judged solely by the statements of their enemies. It is unlikely that intellectual life was completely stagnant in the time of Athelstan, whose court was visited by many embassies and ecclesiastics from the Continent and from Celtic lands. Besides books Athelstan gave treasures, and the list of what he gave to St. Cuthbert's has come down to us, including numbers of vestments

---

[1] Birch, Nos. 883, 911, 1042, 1044, 1052.

[2] An unpublished document in the William Salt collection at Stafford.

[3] See p. 822, and cf. Stubbs, *Registrum Sacrum Anglicanum*, 2nd ed., 1897, pp. 23 f., and R. R. Darlington, *Eng. Hist. Rev.*, LI, pp. 423–426.

[4] See H. P. R. Finberg, *Trans. Royal Hist. Soc.*, 5th Series, III, pp. 115–120.

[5] Among these must be included a fragment of a Latin sermon on Joshua and of a commentary on the 77th Psalm, now at Wrisbergholzen. See R. Drögereit, *Jahrbuch der Gesellschaft für niedersächsische Kirchengeschichte*, LI, pp. 3–15.

[6] *i.e.* the burnt Brit. Mus. Cott. Otho B ix, gospels from France, the Irish gospels of Maelbrighde at Lambeth, Brit. Mus. Cott. Tiber. A ii, probably a gift from the Emperor Otto, another French gospel-book, Brit. Mus. Reg. I. A. xviii, the Acts of the Sixth General Council, Brit. Mus. Cott. Claud. B v. The Gospels at Gandersheim (see p. 40, n. 7) were probably written at Metz. See also J. Armitage Robinson, *The Times of St. Dunstan*, pp. 51–71.

[7] C.C.C.C., MS. 183.

[8] Brit. Mus. Cott. Galba A xviii.

and of vessels, candelabra and other objects of gold and silver.[1] The beautiful stole discovered in St. Cuthbert's coffin belongs to this age. Some light is shed on the practice of the art of embroidery in England by an incident concerning Dunstan, related by his earliest biographer.[2]

The close contacts between England and the Continent made it impossible for Englishmen to be unaware of the monastic reforms that were taking place abroad. Cluny had been founded in 910, and among the houses reformed under its influence was Fleury on the Loire, which was to play a great part in the English reform; while another reform movement, started by Gerard of Brogne, spread through Flanders and affected the abbeys at St. Omer and Ghent. King Edmund had personal reasons for affording asylum to the monks of St. Bertin's at St. Omer who fled from the reform,[3] so his action is not indicative of lack of sympathy with it. We know unfortunately little about the pre-reform houses in England, such as Alfred's foundations at Athelney and Shaftesbury,[4] Athelstan's at Milton Abbas and Muchelney,[5] or the nunneries at Winchester and Wilton mentioned along with Shaftesbury in Eadred's will,[6] while the account of Glastonbury in Dunstan's youth is far from clear.[7] Many former houses had ceased to exist and their lands were in the king's possession. We are not bound to believe the claim of the reforming party that there were no monks except with Dunstan at Glastonbury or Æthelwold at Abingdon,[8] but leading churchmen like Oda of Canterbury and Ælfheah, bishop of Winchester (934–951), were dissatisfied with the position and King Eadred was favourable to reform. When Edgar came to the throne things began to move quickly, and the practices of the reformed houses abroad were followed, for Dunstan had spent his exile at Blandinium in Ghent, Æthelwold had sent a brother of his house to learn the usages of Fleury, and Oswald, the third of the main leaders of the movement, had studied in this house. Monks from both these monasteries came to help to draw up the *Regularis Concordia*, a document which aimed at establishing uniformity of usage for English monasteries. Apart from the annal for 964 in the Chronicle, which describes the expulsion of clerics from the Old and New Minsters in Winchester, from Chertsey and from Milton Abbas, the chief sources for the monastic movement are the Lives of the three main leaders in it.[9] The clearest account is that in the Life of Æthelwold, the restorer of Abingdon and the Fenland monasteries of Ely, Peterborough and Thorney, who replaced the clerics of Winchester by monks. But the biographical writing of this era was greatly inferior to that of the age of Bede, and no very clear picture of the personality of Æthelwold emerges, much of the work consisting of rather dreary miracles. The biographers of Dunstan also concentrate more on his visions and miracles than on other aspects of his

[1] Birch, No. 685.   [2] No. 234, p. 827.   [3] No. 26.   [4] No. 7, pp. 273 f.
[5] William of Malmesbury, *De Gestis Pontificum*, ed. Hamilton, pp. 186, 199.   [6] No. 107.
[7] No. 234, p. 826.   [8] No. 235, p. 835; No. 238.   [9] Nos. 234–236.

character or on details of his administration. The general terms of panegyric tell little of the precise part he took in the reforming of monasteries; they speak of his work at Glastonbury, and there is evidence for his reform of Bath, Malmesbury and perhaps Westminster, but he appears to have made no attempt to place monks at his see at Christ Church, which did not become monastic before the time of Archbishop Sigeric, or perhaps Ælfric.[1] His course of action seems similar to that of Oswald, who only gradually introduced monks into his see at Worcester.[2] He established a small monastery at Westbury-on-Trym,[3] and one at Winchcombe, over which he made Germanus, a fellow pupil from Fleury, abbot, but his most important foundation was Ramsey, at the request of Ealdorman Æthelwine of East Anglia, with whom he formed a life-long friendship. He failed to reintroduce monasticism into his northern diocese when he became archbishop of York, and though his next three successors were Benedictine monks, they were no more able than he had been to found monasteries in the North.

The reformers had the support of King Edgar, and also of many of the leading laymen, especially those in East Anglia, but they were not universally popular, as the reaction on Edgar's death[4] shows. It was temporary, however, and new monasteries continued to be founded in Ethelred's reign. Tavistock was founded by the king's uncle Ordwulf, a supporter of monasteries,[5] and another great family in the south-west, Ælfric's patrons Ealdorman Æthelweard and his son Æthelmær, founded Cerne Abbas and Eynsham.[6] Crowland was founded about this time, and the foundation of Burton-on-Trent in 1004 by the great north-midland thegn Wulfric Spott,[7] with monks brought from Winchester, brought the effects of the revival into an area hitherto lacking such houses. The most important early eleventh-century foundation was Bury St. Edmund's, where Cnut placed Benedictine monks in 1020. It had previously been served by a small community of secular priests. To Ethelred's reign also belongs the introduction of monks into Christ Church, Canterbury, and Sherborne.

During Ethelred's reign efforts were made to impose a communal life on bodies of secular canons. Ethelred's code of 1008 enjoins a common refectory and dormitory wherever the property is adequate for this, and demands celibacy and obedience to rule,[8] and the rule of Chrodogang of Metz was translated into English somewhere about this time. In Cnut's reign Archbishop Ælfric of York began to build communal buildings at Beverley,[9] but the establishment of colleges of secular canons in England belongs mainly to the Confessor's reign.

---

[1] Canterbury tradition attributed the reform to Ælfric (No. 1, p. 214, n. 3), but Florence of Worcester to Sigeric.

[2] In No. 111, which is an early lease by Oswald, there are no monks among the attestations. In Kemble, No. 615, dated 977, there are ten, but this is unique and perhaps suspicious, for other charters of this year and later show only an occasional monk among the signatories. See J. Armitage Robinson, *St. Oswald and the Church of Worcester*, pp. 16-20.

[3] *Historians of the Church of York*, ed. Raine, I, p. 424.   [4] See p. 48.   [5] See No. 123.   [6] See p. 849.

[7] No. 125.   [8] V Ethelred (No. 44), 7.   [9] *Historians of the Church of York*, ed. Raine, II, p. 353.

The reforming prelates of the tenth and eleventh centuries, however, were not interested solely in establishing communities of regular clergy. They concerned themselves also with the instruction of the parish clergy and with the religious and moral condition of the laity. Between 942 and 946 Archbishop Oda issued 'constitutions' dealing with episcopal visitations, the enforcement of a canonical life on the clergy, the observance of the marriage laws by the laity, and the duties of almsgiving, fasting, and payment of tithes.[1] Though the Lives of the reformers give most prominence to their founding of monasteries, they include passages which show that they did not neglect their episcopal duties. Concern with the religion of the nation as a whole is shown in the ecclesiastical laws of successive kings, and in the so-called *Canons of Edgar*;[2] both Bishop Wulfsige of Sherborne and Archbishop Wulfstan of York commissioned the scholar Ælfric to write pastoral letters, which impressed on the clergy the need for celibacy and which give a detailed account of their duties.[3] The homilies of Ælfric were intended to reach the laity through the preaching of the clergy, and many other vernacular homilies of this period have survived. Archbishop Wulfstan preaches directly to the people, while Byrhtferth of Ramsey writes for the instruction of the parish priests. This period also saw great activity in the building of parish churches.[4]

The founding of the reformed monasteries led to a great revival in learning, literature and art. The term 'Winchester School' is often given to its products in sculpture, ivory-carving and manuscript illumination, though this is not meant to imply that they came from there alone. Art historians can study surviving examples of these arts, and written sources, especially lists of donations to churches, tell us about objects in precious metals and gems, and about rich vestments and tapestries. A lot of building went on at this time, but only smaller churches have survived, the great cathedral or monastic churches having been superseded by later buildings.[5] The sources tell us that even the greatest churchmen might practise some craft; Dunstan was skilled in designing and metalwork as well as in music, and even as archbishop spent some of his time in the more laborious task of correcting manuscripts;[6] and Godeman, who produced the famous *Benedictional of St. Æthelwold*, may be identical with the abbot of Thorney of that name. There must have been great activity in the scriptoria to produce even the manuscripts which have survived, both in England and on the Continent, and, naturally, great numbers have been lost.

Only from one of the leaders of the monastic movement have we literary work. There is good evidence for Æthelwold's authorship of the translation of

[1] Wilkins, *Concilia*, I, p. 212.   [2] See p. 46.
[3] Best edited by B. Fehr, *Die Hirtenbriefe Ælfrics*; with English translation by Thorpe, *Ancient Laws and Institutes*, II, pp. 342–393.   [4] On all these matters see R. R. Darlington, *Eng. Hist. Rev.*, LI, pp. 385–422.
[5] See pp. 103 f. for bibliography on these subjects.   [6] No. 234, p. 831.

the Rule of St. Benedict, and I would attribute to him also the Old English account of the establishment of monasteries.[1] Something like a literary renaissance began with the next generation, with the pupils of the first reformers. It is then that the Lives of Æthelwold, Oswald and Dunstan were written[2] – Dunstan's, it is true, by foreigners–while in the vernacular appear the works of the great stylist Ælfric,[3] and of his contemporary Archbishop Wulfstan,[4] the scientific manual of Byrhtferth of Ramsey, the excellent writing of the Chronicle account of Ethelred's reign, and a number of translations or homilies by anonymous writers who in the midst of variety almost all share the characteristic of being able to write good prose. An interest in earlier vernacular poetry is alive in this period, for all the four codices in which the bulk of it has come down were copied not very far from the year 1000.

It is surprising that all this should be taking place during a period of foreign invasion and internal misgovernment. There is no need to doubt the accuracy of the gloomy picture painted by the chronicler and by Archbishop Wulfstan;[5] other records support it.[6] Yet it is not the whole story. In spite of Wulfstan's complaint of disrespect to holy places, there were many pious men among the Anglo-Saxon upper classes, such as Æthelweard, Ordwulf, Wulfric Spott and their families, while the king himself was generous to churches and certainly many excellent appointments to vacant sees and abbacies were made in his time. The Church was not decadent or corrupt, and wretched though the reign of Ethelred the Unready was in many respects, it was a golden age in literature and art.

This should make us chary of using the argument, when trying to establish the date of a work, that political conditions were unfavourable for it. Moreover, it was doubtless the vigour of the Church and the high character of some of the leading ecclesiastics, especially of the two archbishops, that impressed Cnut and caused him to reign as a Christian king and a strong supporter of the Church. And it is to this period that one must assign the missionary work of English ecclesiastics in Scandinavian lands.[7] It is sad that none of the correspondence relating to it has survived, nor any references in English records. Excellent English prose continued to be written throughout the rest of the Anglo-Saxon period and beyond, manuscripts continued to be copied in great numbers, and long after 1066 English styles of illumination remained influential to an extent that is only now being realized. The political troubles of the Confessor's reign did not paralyse the activity in the scriptoria of English churches.

[1] No. 238.   [2] Nos. 234–236.   [3] No. 239.   [4] No. 240.
[5] No. 240.   [6] See, for example, Nos. 27, 120, 121, 127, 231, 236.
[7] On this subject see the works cited on p. 586.

SELECT BIBLIOGRAPHY

of the principal modern works relating to English history between the English Settlement and 1042

(a) BIBLIOGRAPHIES

In addition to the general guides to the literature on this period, *i.e.* C. GROSS, *The Sources and Literature of English History from the earliest times to about 1485* (2nd ed., London, 1915) and T. D. HARDY, *Descriptive Catalogue of Materials relating to the History of Great Britain and Ireland* (vol. I in two parts, R.S., 1862), there is an excellent bibliography in F. M. STENTON, *Anglo-Saxon England* (Oxford, 1943, 2nd ed., 1947). For more recent work, *Writings on British History*, compiled for the Royal Historical Society by A. T. MILNE (London, 1937, *et sqq.*) may be consulted. Bibliographies of the works of some of the foremost scholars are available: of F. M. STENTON in *Sir Christopher Hatton's Book of Seals*, ed. L. C. LOYD and D. M. STENTON (Oxford, 1950); of H. M. CHADWICK in *The Early Cultures of North-West Europe* (H. M. Chadwick Memorial Studies), ed. SIR CYRIL FOX and B. DICKINS (Cambridge, 1950); of W. LEVISON in *Wilhelm Levison, 1876–1947: A Bibliography* (privately printed, O.U.P., 1948).

(b) BOOKS OF REFERENCE

A Handbook of British Chronology, ed. F. M. POWICKE, with the assistance of C. JOHNSON and W. J. HARTE (Royal Hist. Soc., 1939) is specially useful in this period for its lists of English kings, compiled by R. R. Darlington; the list of bishops is taken from W. STUBBS, *Registrum Sacrum Anglicanum* (2nd ed. Oxford, 1897), supplemented by W. G. SEARLE, *Anglo-Saxon Bishops, Kings, and Nobles* (Cambridge, 1899). These lists require revision. The same author's *Onomasticon Anglo-Saxonicum* (Cambridge, 1897), though not exhaustive, is still a most useful work; for Scandinavians in England, one should also consult E. BJÖRKMAN, *Nordische Personennamen in England* (Stud. Eng. Phil., XXXVII, Halle, 1910). H. WANLEY, *Librorum Vett. Septentrionalium, qui in Angliae Bibliothecis extant... Catalogus Historico-Criticus* (vol. II of G. HICKES, *Linguarum Vett. Septentrionalium Thesaurus Grammatico-Criticus et Archaeologicus*, Oxford, 1705), is still an essential guide to vernacular manuscripts. There is no similar catalogue of Latin manuscripts of the period, though E. A. LOWE, *Codices Latini Antiquiores* (Oxford, 1934 *et sqq.*) is supplying the gap for those prior to the ninth century. Much can also be learnt from N. R. KER, *Medieval Libraries of Great Britain* (Royal Hist. Soc., 1941).

(c) GENERAL WORKS

The standard work on this period is F. M. STENTON, *Anglo-Saxon England* (see above). His article "English History: I. The Establishment of English Unity" (*Encycl. Brit.*, 1950) should also be noted. For the period up to the death of Alfred there is also R. H. HODGKIN, *A History of the Anglo-Saxons*, 2 vols. (Oxford, 1933; revised ed. 1952). Of older works, vol. I of SIR JAMES H. RAMSAY, *The Foundations of England* (London, 1898) is useful for its full citations, while F. A. FREEMAN, *History of the Norman Conquest* (5 vols. and index, Oxford, 1867–1879), includes, especially in its appendices, a wealth of detail about eleventh-century personages. For English relations with Scotland the materials edited by A. O. ANDERSON, *Scottish Annals from English Chroniclers A.D. 500 to 1286* (London, 1908) and *Early Sources of Scottish History A.D. 500 to 1286* (vol. I, Edinburgh, 1922) are essential, and for Wales, J. E. LLOYD, *History of Wales from the Earliest Times to the Edwardian Conquest* (2 vols., 3rd ed., London, 1939).

(d) GENERAL WORKS ON PARTICULAR ASPECTS OF THE PERIOD

The most recent comprehensive discussion of the problems of the origin of the English and of the date and course of settlement is that in R. G. COLLINGWOOD and J. N. L. MYRES, *Roman Britain and the English Settlements* (Oxford, 1936). It should be supplemented by J. N. L. MYRES, "The Present State of the Archaeological Evidence of the Anglo-Saxon Conquest" (*History*, N.S., XXI, 1937), and R. DRÖGEREIT, "Ausbreitung der nordwestdeutschen Küstenvölker über See" (*Neues Archiv für Niedersachsen*, XXIII, 1951). Of older works the most important is E. T. LEEDS, *The Archaeology of the Anglo-Saxon Settlements* (Oxford, 1913). Problems relating to individual areas are considered by J. E. A. JOLLIFFE, *Pre-feudal England: the Jutes* (O.U.P., 1933); P. HUNTER BLAIR, "The Origins of Northumbria" (*Arch. Æliana*, 4th Series, XXV, 1947), "The Northumbrians and their Southern Frontier" (*ibid.*, XXVI, 1948), "The Boundary between Bernicia and Deira" (*ibid.*, XXVII, 1949); F. T. WAINWRIGHT, "The Anglian Settlement of Lancashire" (*Trans. Hist. Soc. Lancs. and Cheshire*, XCIII, 1942); W. G. HOSKINS, "Notes on the Anglian and Scandinavian Settlements of Leicestershire" (*Trans. Leics. Arch. Soc.*, XVIII f., 1934–1937); J. N. L. MYRES, "Lincoln in the Fifth century A.D." (*Arch. Journ.*, CIII, 1947). The English penetration of Devon and Cornwall is dealt with by H. P. R. FINBERG in "The Early History of Werrington" (*Eng. Hist. Rev.*, LIX, 1944) and "Sherborne, Glastonbury and the Expansion of Wessex" (*Trans. Royal Hist. Soc.*, 5th Series, III, 1953).

For works on archaeology and place-names relating to these matters, see section (e) below.

The most important articles on the Mercian overlordship are two by F. M. STENTON, "The Supremacy of the Mercian Kings" (*Eng. Hist. Rev.*, XXXIII, 1918) and "Lindsey and its Kings" (*Essays in History presented to R. L. Poole*, 1927), while his "St. Frideswide and her Times" (*Oxoniensia*, I, 1936) and *The Early History of the Abbey of Abingdon* (Reading Studies in Local History, O.U.P., 1913) shed light on the history of the Thames valley during the Heptarchy. The political importance of Offa's Dyke is discussed by SIR CYRIL FOX, "The Boundary Line of Cymru" (*Proc. Brit. Acad.*, XXVI, 1940).

There are two full-length accounts of Alfred; C. PLUMMER, *The Life and Times of Alfred the Great* (Oxford, 1902) and B. A. LEES, *Alfred the Great, the Truth Teller* (New York, 1915). J. ARMITAGE ROBINSON, *The Times of St. Dunstan* (Oxford, 1923) is not confined to ecclesiastical history, though that is its main theme. D. J. V. FISHER, "The Anti-Monastic Reaction in the Reign of Edward the Martyr" (*Camb. Hist. Journ.*, X, Part III, 1952) examines an obscure political situation. For the reign of Cnut, see L. M. LARSON, *Canute the Great* (New York, 1912).

On the general history of the vikings one should consult A. MAWER, *The Vikings* (Cambridge Manuals of Science and Literature, 1913) and T. D. KENDRICK, *A History of the Vikings* (London, 1930), both of which contain select bibliographies of earlier works. On the Danish settlement in England F. M. STENTON, "The Scandinavian Colonies in England and Normandy" (*Trans. Royal Hist. Soc.*, 4th Series, XXVII, 1945) and "The Danes in England" (*Proc. Brit. Acad.*, XIII, 1927) are important. The Norse-Irish invasion is dealt with by F. T. WAINWRIGHT, in "Ingimund's Invasion" (*Eng. Hist. Rev.*, LXIII, 1948), "The Battles at Corbridge" (*Saga-Book of the Viking Soc.*, XIII, Part III, 1949–1950) and "The Submission to Edward the Elder" (*History*, XXXVII, 1952); by A. MAWER, "The Redemption of the Five Boroughs" (*Eng. Hist. Rev.*, XXXVIII, 1923); and by A. CAMPBELL, "Two Notes on the Norse Kingdoms in Northumbria" (*ibid.*, LVII, 1942). The extent of the Norse settlement is discussed by E. EKWALL, "Scandinavians and Celts in the North-West of England" (*Lunds Universitets Årsskrift*, N.F., afd. i, vol. XIV, No. 27, 1918), by F. M. STENTON, "Pre-Conquest Westmorland" (*Royal Comm. Hist. Mon.*, *Westmorland*, 1936), by B. DICKINS in the introduction to *The Place-Names of Cumberland*, Part III (*Eng. Place-Name Soc.*, Cambridge, 1952), and by F. T. WAINWRIGHT, "The Scandinavians in Lancashire" (*Trans. Lancs. and Cheshire Antiq. Soc.*, LVIII, 1945–1946). Other local studies include F. M. STENTON, "York in the Eleventh Century" (*York Minster Historical Tracts*, No. 8, 1927), C. S. TAYLOR, "The Danes in Gloucestershire" (*Trans. Brist. and Glos. Arch. Soc.*, XVII, 1892) and F. T. WAINWRIGHT, "Early Scandinavian Settlement in Derbyshire" (*Derbysh. Arch. and Nat. Hist. Soc. Journ.*, LXVII, 1947). See also introductions to place-name volumes dealing with Danelaw counties. For works dealing with social conditions in the Danelaw, see p. 354.

Though it is primarily concerned with English missions and scholarship, W. LEVISON's *England and the Continent in the Eighth Century* (Oxford, 1946) touches on other contacts with the lands across the Channel, and so does R. DRÖGEREIT, "Sachsen und Angelsachsen" (*Niedersächsisches Jahrbuch für Landesgeschichte*, XXI, 1949) which is especially valuable in assembling evidence for the later Anglo-Saxon periods. Another important work on continental relations is P. GRIERSON, "The Relations between England and Flanders before the Norman Conquest" (*Trans. Royal Hist. Soc.*, 4th Series, XXIII, 1941).

(e) SOURCES OTHER THAN DOCUMENTS
(i) *Archaeology and Art*

The principal general works are G. BALDWIN BROWN, *The Arts in Early England* (6 vols. in 7 parts, London, 1903–1937), *A Guide to the Anglo-Saxon and Foreign Teutonic Antiquities* (British Museum, 1923), E. T. LEEDS, *Early Anglo-Saxon Art and Archaeology* (Oxford, 1936), T. D. KENDRICK, *Anglo-Saxon Art to A.D. 900* (London, 1938), and the same author's *Late Saxon and Viking Art* (London, 1948). A. GOLDSCHMIDT, "English Influence on Medieval Art on the Continent" (*Medieval Studies in memory of A. Kingsley Porter*, ed. W. R. W. KOEHLER, Cambridge, Mass., II, 1939), includes an excellent appreciation of the peculiar qualities of Anglo-Saxon art.

Chapters on the Saxon antiquities of individual counties were contributed by R. A. SMITH to the *Victoria County Histories*; more recent discoveries are often published in the various local antiquarian journals. The *Antiquaries Journal* includes bi-annual surveys of the more important contributions on archaeology and antiquities. There is already a large literature on the subject of Sutton Hoo, the following works being of most general use: *The Sutton Hoo Ship-Burial: A Provisional Guide* (British Museum, 1947); R. L. S. BRUCE MITFORD, "The Sutton Hoo Ship-Burial" (*Proc. Suff. Inst. Arch.*, XXV, 1952), and an appendix contributed by the same author to the new edition of HODGKIN, *A History of the Anglo-Saxons* (see p. 101); for a different point of view, see SUNE LINDQVIST, "Sutton Hoo and *Beowulf*" (*Antiquity*, XXII, 1948). The vexed question of the dating of the coins has been authoritatively discussed by P. GRIERSON, "The Dating of the Sutton Hoo Coins" (*ibid.*, XXVI, 1952).

For viking antiquities in general, use should be made of H. SHETELIG and H. FALK, *Scandinavian Archaeology*, translated by E. V. GORDON (Oxford, 1937), and for those in the British Isles, *Viking Antiquities in Great Britain and Ireland*, ed. H. SHETELIG (5 parts, Oslo, 1940), especially Part IV, "Viking Antiquities in England"; and R. E. M. WHEELER, *London and the Vikings* (London, 1927).

Architecture is excellently dealt with by A. W. CLAPHAM, *English Romanesque Architecture before the Conquest* (Oxford, 1930), a work which takes into account the literary evidence as well as that of the surviving remains. It also discusses the sculpture, on which other outstanding studies are G. BALDWIN BROWN, *op. cit.*, vol. VI, W. G. COLLINGWOOD, *Northumbrian Crosses of the Pre-Norman Age* (London, 1927), J. BRØNSTED, *Early English Ornament* (London and Copenhagen, 1924) and F. SAXL, "The Ruthwell Cross" (in *England and the Mediterranean Tradition*, ed. by the Warburg and Courtauld Institute, O.U.P., 1945).

Among many works dealing with manuscript illumination, the following, in addition to the general works on art, deserve special mention : O. E. SAUNDERS, *English Illumination* (Florence and Paris, vol. I, 1928), O. HOMBURGER, *Die Anfänge der Malschule von Winchester in X. Jahrhundert* (Leipzig, 1912), E. G. MILLAR, *English Illuminated Manuscripts from Xth to XIIIth Century* (Paris and Brussels, 1926), H. WOODRUFF, *The Illustrated Manuscripts of Prudentius* (Cambridge, Mass., 1930), W. OAKESHOTT, *The Sequence of English Medieval Art* (London, 1950), and two works by F. WORMALD, "Decorated Initials in English MSS. from A.D. 900 to 1100" (*Archaeologia*, XCI, 1945) and *English Drawings of the Tenth and Eleventh Centuries* (London, 1952).

Facsimiles of illuminated pages in many MSS. of the period are given in the publications of the Palaeographical Society and of the New Palaeographical Society, and also in J. O. WESTWOOD, *Facsimiles of the Miniatures and Ornaments of Anglo-Saxon and Irish MSS.* (London, 1868), in *Schools of Illuminations : Part I : Hiberno-Saxon and Early English Schools, 700–1100* (British Museum, 1914), in G. F. WARNER, *Illuminated Manuscripts in the British Museum* (British Museum, 1899–1903) and in SIR E. M. THOMPSON, *English Illuminated Manuscripts* (London, 1895). The most important facsimiles of individual illuminated manuscripts are E. G. MILLAR, *The Lindisfarne Gospels* (British Museum, 1923), G. F. WARNER and H. A. WILSON, *The Benedictional of St. Æthelwold, Bishop of Winchester, 963–984*) (The Roxburghe Club, 1910) and SIR I. GOLLANCZ, *The Cædmon Manuscript of Anglo-Saxon Biblical Poetry* (Oxford, 1927).

Other specialist studies are M. H. LONGHURST, *English Ivories* (London, 1926), and R. JESSOP, *Anglo-Saxon Jewellery* (London, 1950).

(ii) *Coins*

The chief catalogue is that of C. F. KEARY, *Catalogue of English Coins in the British Museum : Anglo-Saxon Series* (London, vol. I, 1887, vol. II, 1893), but it must be supplemented by B. E. HILDEBRAND, *Anglosachsiska Mynt i Svenska Kongliga Myntkabinett* (Stockholm, 1881), S. HOLM, *Studier öfver Uppsala Universitets anglosaxiska Myntsamling* (Uppsala, 1917) and B. SCHNITTGER, "Silverskatten från Stora Sojdeby" (*Fornvännen*, X, 1915). JAN PETERSEN lists the English coins found in Norway in Part V, Section IV of *Viking Antiquities in Great Britain and Ireland* (ed. H. SHETELIG, see above), and gives a bibliography.

A general account of the subject is given by G. C. BROOKE, *English Coins from the Seventh Century to the Present Day* (3rd ed., revised by C. A. WHITTON, London, 1950). C. H. V. SUTHERLAND, *Anglo-Saxon Gold Coinage in the light of the Crondall Hoard* (O.U.P., 1948), is of particular value for the early history of Kent and London. Various good monographs, especially on the coins known as *sceattas* and on individual mints, have been appearing in recent years in the *Numismatic Chronicle*, and the *British Numismatic Journal*, which includes also several notes by PHILIP NELSON on unpublished coins. Mention should be made also of P. GRIERSON, "The Gold Solidus of Louis the Pious and its Imitations" (*Jaarboek voor Munt- en Penningkunde*, XXXVIII, 1951), which illustrates the influence of Carolingian coins in England.

(iii) *Place-names*

The principal aids in this study are the publications of the English Place-Name Society and E. EKWALL, *The Concise Oxford Dictionary of English Place-Names* (3rd ed., 1947). For counties not yet surveyed by the Place-Name Society one may use F. M. STENTON, *The Place-Names of Berkshire* (Reading Studies in Local History, 1911), A. MAWER, *The Place-Names of Northumberland and Durham* (Cambridge, 1920), E. EKWALL, *The Place-Names of Lancashire* (Manchester, 1922), J. K. WALLENBERG, *Kentish Place-Names* (Uppsala Univ. Årsskrift, 1931), and *The Place-Names of Kent* (Uppsala, 1934), A. FÄGERSTEN, *The Place-Names of Dorset* (Uppsala Univ. Årsskrift, 1933), H. KÖKERITZ, *The Place-Names of the Isle of Wight* (Nomina Germanica 6, 1940). B. G. CHARLES, *Non-Celtic Place-Names in Wales* (London Med. Stud., Monograph No. I, 1938), deals with names on the Welsh border, and A. MACDONALD, *The Place-Names of West Lothian* (Edinburgh and London, 1941), with an area once part of Northumbria. O. S. ANDERSON, *The English Hundred-Names* (Lund, 1934–1939), provides evidence relating to the origin of the hundred. A series of presidential addresses to the Royal Historical Society by SIR FRANK STENTON (*Trans. Royal Hist. Soc.*, XXI–XXV, 1939–1943) demonstrates how place-name evidence can be used to throw light on historical problems.

(f) PERIODICAL LITERATURE

First in importance is the *English Historical Review*, containing many articles by the foremost scholars in this field of study. The *Transactions of the Royal Historical Society* include several valuable studies relating to this period, as, more occasionally, does *History*, the review of the History Association. *The Saga-Book of the Viking Society* has several articles on the Danes in England as well as on Scandinavian history and culture in general. The principal antiquarian journals which contain articles of interest for this period are *Archaeologia*, the *Antiquaries Journal*, the *Archaeological Journal* and *Antiquity*, but from time to time studies of importance appear in the journals of local societies, and have been referred to in the appropriate place in the bibliographies of this volume. *Speculum* is the American publication to contain most work relating to this period, and *Anglia, Englische Studien*, and *Archiv für das Studium der neueren Sprachen* are the German periodicals which concern themselves most with English affairs. Articles in the *Review of English Studies, Modern Language Review* and *Medium Aevum*, though chiefly concerned with literature, have sometimes a bearing on historical matters also.

NOTE

Except for Nos. 11–19, which are in Old Norse, the original text of all documents printed in this book is, unless otherwise stated, in Latin.

Part I
SECULAR NARRATIVE SOURCES

SECULAR NARRATIVE SOURCES

Introduction

THE first section of this volume contains narrative records which are secular in the sense that they do not set out to tell the life of a saint or the history of a church, but not secular, of course, in the sense of being produced by laymen; for with very few exceptions, such as Æthelweard, Nithard, the scaldic poets, and perhaps the author of the Maldon poem, the writers are ecclesiastics. It is from these sources, with the addition of Bede's *Ecclesiastical History*, that our knowledge of the political history of the Anglo-Saxon period is chiefly obtained, though, as pointed out in the General Introduction, the record has often to be supplemented with incidental references contained in sources not narrative in intent. Nor, on the other hand, is the interest of the texts here given confined to political history; scattered among them are many passages without which any account of the ecclesiastical, social, economic or cultural history of the period would be incomplete.

THE ANGLO-SAXON CHRONICLE

Among the narrative sources of pre-Conquest English history the Anglo-Saxon Chronicle must be given pre-eminence. It is a complicated record, surviving in seven manuscripts (not counting two brief fragments), and for the period covered in this volume it is accurate to describe them as containing versions of the same work, though each has some passages peculiar to it. In the later part of the work, which lies beyond the limit fixed for this volume, the manuscripts differ so greatly that a columnar arrangement of them is essential; but for the portion dealt with in this volume it would entail a tedious amount of repetition if one were to print all the versions in full. The arrangement here adopted is explained in detail in the plan before the translation; it is hoped by the layout chosen to make it possible to distinguish at a glance the common stock of the Chronicle from passages peculiar to individual versions.

The versions of the Chronicle

The extant manuscripts are as follows: Corpus Christi College, Cambridge, MS. 173, often called the Parker manuscript after its donor, cited as 'A'. It is the oldest manuscript, and up to almost the end of 891 it is written in one hand, of the late ninth or very early tenth century. After that, it is kept up in a series of hands, and the eighth scribe, who added annals 925–955, probably not long after the latter year, was certainly writing at Winchester. He enters some events of purely local interest, and for him the word *ceaster* 'the city' means Winchester. It is possible that this manuscript was from the first at the Old Minster, Winchester.[1] This version gives

---

[1] The accession of Frithestan to Winchester in annal 909 is specially marked (see p. 192, n. 4), and his name occurs at the head of the first folio of the *Epistula Sedulii* which is bound up with this manuscript.

a detailed account of events up to 920, and is the only one to give the account of the last campaigns of Edward the Elder. Then it shares in the general decay in historical writing and is the scantiest of our texts, for it uses neither the Mercian Register nor the northern annals. It contains tenth-century poems and royal obits which are in other versions, and some local entries of its own, but it did not receive the excellent record of the reign of Ethelred the Unready found in other versions. Instead, it has an independent entry of some length at 1001, but otherwise only a few scrappy entries after 975. At some time in the eleventh century, it was removed to Christ Church, Canterbury, certainly arriving there by 1075. At Canterbury many interpolations were made, some in the hand of the scribe responsible for version 'F',[1] who also added to the manuscript the Latin *Acts of Lanfranc*. The 'F' scribe had before him when he made interpolations the archetype of the version which we call 'E', and some of his additions into 'A' come from that source. To make room for some of the Canterbury additions, certain erasures were made in 'A', but fortunately, before it was thus tampered with, a copy had been made. This, the burnt manuscript,[2] will be described later. 'A' is the only surviving manuscript early enough for us to be able to distinguish palaeographically the stages of growth, and to separate the original text from the later interpolations. It should warn us to be on our guard when examining versions which survive only in eleventh- or twelfth-century copies, where later alterations are hidden from our sight. 'A' is shown to have remained at Christ Church by the mention of it in later catalogues of the library of that house. In spite of its importance as our oldest manuscript, its value even for the period in which it is a full record must not be overstressed. It is rather carelessly copied, and is at least two removes from the original work. The support of Latin writers who had access to early versions of the Chronicle sometimes proves the superiority of readings in the later manuscripts.

Manuscripts Brit. Mus. Cott. Tiber. A. vi, cited as 'B', and Cott. Tiber. B. i, cited as 'C', are independent copies of a common archetype, which was probably at Abingdon when they were made, for it betrays a connexion with that house in annal 977, and the events of 971 are likely to have been known there. But previous to this annal it shows no special interest in Abingdon; it does not mention the refoundation of that monastery nor the consecration of Æthelwold, the first abbot of the new foundation, as bishop of Winchester in 963. It seems unlikely that Abingdon would have possessed a copy of the Chronicle before that refoundation. Of the two copies, 'B' ends in 977, and a detached leaf,[3] which is commonly believed originally to have been the preface to 'B', breaks off after the mention of Edward the Martyr with the words "and he held", as if the writer could not complete the sentence with the length of the reign. Presumably he was writing before Edward's death in 978. Joscelin calls it "the Saxon History of St. Augustine's, Canterbury", and though there is no evidence before this sixteenth-century statement, it is possible that the monks of Abingdon were content to make a gift of it, seeing that they had another version which they had kept up to date. That other version is represented by 'C', which is an eleventh-century copy, and which breaks off, mutilated, in the middle of the annal for 1066. It has several references to Abingdon affairs, and was doubtless the product of that house.

'B' and 'C' took over the Mercian Register from their archetype, making no attempt to dovetail its annals into those of the Chronicle itself, but inserting it as

---

[1] See p. 112. [2] Brit. Mus. Cott. Otho B. xi. [3] Brit. Mus. Cott. Tiber. A. iii.

a block after a puzzling list of six blank annals that follows on the entry for 915. Both 'B' and 'C' have bungled this list. 'B' has DCCCXVI–DCCCXIX (presumably for DCCCCXVI–DCCCCXIX, to follow its last entry, 915), then DCCC, DCCCI; 'C' starts off with DCCCXCVI and follows on with DCCCXCVII, etc., until it reaches DCCCC; it then has DCCCI (an obvious error for DCCCCI), after which comes the first annal of the Mercian Register, DCCCCII. It looks as if an original list of blank annals beginning 916 has been tampered with in the exemplar to make a better introduction to the Mercian Register, which begins 902. It is not possible to see how far this list of blank annals extended before it was altered. 'B''s version suggests that it went as far as 919, at least. It could have gone as far as 933, for neither 'B' nor 'C' have any entry, apart from the Mercian Register, until 934; in that case all the numbers after 921 (which could be altered to 901) would simply be erased. Hence one cannot tell at what date the Mercian Register was added to the exemplar, except that it was already there when the first copy, 'B', was made.

Besides continuing further, 'C' differs from 'B' in omitting the genealogical preface (if the detached leaf containing this really did once form part of 'B'), which is in 'A' also. Instead, the scribe of the 'C' manuscript seems to have regarded the two texts that precede the Chronicle in his manuscript as forming an introduction to it. They are the *Menologium*, an Old English poem on the Church festivals, and a set of gnomic verses. Did he link them together as a compendium of useful knowledge?

Brit. Mus. Cott. Tiber. B. iv, cited as 'D', and Laud, Misc. 636 in the Bodleian Library, cited as 'E', must also be linked together. Both differ from the versions hitherto discussed in their inclusion in the early part of the Chronicle of much material of northern interest, drawn from Bede and from northern annals which were also accessible to Simeon of Durham. They agree also in having a rhythmical passage in the style of Archbishop Wulfstan at 959; in giving a prose instead of a verse account of Edgar's coronation in 973, and a different poem from that in other manuscripts on his death in 975; in inserting a lengthy passage on the murder of Edward the Martyr; and in innumerable minor matters. Together, they form what is known as the northern recension of the Chronicle, and I have little doubt that the archetype from which they were copied was written at York.[1] But for the later part of the Chronicle the two versions, 'D' and 'E', had a separate history, and each has its individual peculiarities.

'D', which is written in a number of hands, none earlier than the second half of the eleventh century, continues until 1079. It preserves its interest in northern affairs until the end, and is so interested in the career of Archbishop Ealdred of York that it has been suggested that in its later part it originates from a member of his household. In its final portion, it is concerned with Queen Margaret of Scotland and her ancestors, and may, as Sir Frank Stenton suggests, have been intended for the Scottish court. It has also a series of entries relating to the middle of the tenth century which are peculiar to it, and it shares with 'A', 'B' and 'C' the accounts of Alfred's and Edward's wars against the Danes which 'E' omits. It inserts the Mercian Register, but not in a block; it attempts to assign the entries in this to their proper place in the main Chronicle. In the eleventh century, it shows good knowledge of affairs in the Worcester diocese, which has led to its being often described as the 'Worcester Chronicle'. Plummer wished to assign it to Evesham, but Sir Ivor Atkins has shown that the

---

[1] I propose to publish elsewhere the detailed evidence for this view, and to discuss the precise relationship between 'D' and 'E'.

evidence for this is slight. The manuscript was at Worcester in the sixteenth century, but I doubt whether this version left the North before the end of the eleventh century. Archbishops of York were well informed on affairs in the Worcester diocese. Sometimes they held this see in plurality, and they had estates in the area.

'E', on the other hand, ceases to be a northern version about the middle of the eleventh century. There can be no doubt that its archetype reached St. Augustine's, Canterbury, in whose abbots 'E' shows a special interest, beginning in annal 1043.[1] And at Canterbury this version became available to the scribe of 'F', who used it as the basis of the bilingual chronicle he was compiling, and inserted some of its readings into manuscript 'A', as we have already seen. It is uncertain how long this archetype of 'E' remained at St. Augustine's, but eventually it, or a copy of it, was taken to Peterborough. It is very probable that it was taken there some time after the fire at Peterborough in 1116. What is certain is that a copy of it was made there up to 1121, and this copy is our manuscript 'E', which is written in one hand up to this point, and afterwards was kept up at Peterborough until the early days of 1155. The scribe who copied the part up to 1121 betrays his Peterborough preoccupations by inserting into the text he is copying a number of passages about the founding of the abbey and the donations made to it—passages which stand out from the text he is copying by reason of their twelfth-century language. 'E' is thus the version of the Chronicle which continues longest, and it is an independent authority in its later part. For the part with which I am concerned in this volume it is not of first importance, containing little that is not in the other manuscripts, and omitting the sections on the later campaigns of Alfred and the wars of his son Edward. It should, however, be noted that for the additions made to the northern recension of the Chronicle from 286 to the middle of 693 'E' is our sole authority (except in as far as they are in 'F'), for a gathering of manuscript 'D' has been lost at this place.

The version which we have been calling 'F' is Brit. Mus. Cott. Domit. A. viii, a bilingual Latin and English chronicle, produced at Canterbury in the late eleventh or early twelfth century, by a writer who used the archetype of 'E' as his base, but had also before him our 'A'. He occasionally draws on other sources, mainly relating to Canterbury. In its present form this version extends to 1058. It is a greatly abbreviated version, but it has value in sometimes letting us see what was the original reading in the archetype of 'E' in places where the Peterborough scribe of 'E' has altered it.

Reference has been made above to the copy of 'A' which was contained in Brit. Mus. Cott. Otho B. xi, of which only fragments now remain.[2] Before the manuscript was burnt in 1731, it had been published by Whelock in 1644, and a transcript by Nowell has recently been discovered. I propose to refer to this manuscript as 'G'.[3] Its main use is to help to establish the condition of 'A' before the Canterbury additions were made.

Finally, there is the fragment Brit. Mus. Cott. Domit. A. ix, known as 'H'. It deals with the years 1113–1114, and is quite independent of 'E', the only other version to go on so late. It comes from some centre where a more classical Old English could still be written.

---

[1] For 1045.

[2] Brit. Mus. Cott. Otho B. x, fols. 55, 58, 62 and Addit. MS. 34652, fol. 2 probably originally belonged to this manuscript. See N. R. Ker, *Brit. Mus. Quart.*, XIV, 1940.

[3] Plummer calls it 'A', for he uses a special form of 'A' to denote the Parker MS. In this he has not been followed. He objects to 'G' as implying that it was later than 'F'; but after all 'F' is itself earlier than 'E'. Since Otho is the least independent of all the MSS., perhaps the symbol 'G' is not out of place.

In addition to the surviving versions, it is clear that some Latin writers had access to copies of the Chronicle which have not survived. Behind the twelfth-century work known as the *Annals of St. Neots* lies a version free from the chronological error from 756 to 845, which is in all the extant versions and in those used by Latin chroniclers. The West Saxon ealdorman, Æthelweard, a descendant of Alfred's elder brother, who wrote at the end of the tenth century[1] a Latin chronicle for the benefit of his continental kinswoman, Matilda, abbess of Essen, had a version of the Chronicle which, while it had this error in chronology, was in some respects closer to the original than any surviving manuscript. For example, it had not lost by homœoteleuton a whole sentence from annal 885, as all our surviving manuscripts, and the one used by Asser, have done. This implies that Asser, who was writing his *Life of King Alfred* in 893, already had a version at least two removes from the original text. He shows no knowledge of the Chronicle after annal 887, an annal which could not have been composed before 889. The text he used sometimes supports the readings of the other manuscripts against 'A', though there are places where his text, the version used by Æthelweard, and 'A', all agree against the combined evidence of 'B', 'C', 'D', and 'E', to an extent that suggests that all these four manuscripts descend from a common version which contained several new features.

The main version of the Chronicle which Henry of Huntingdon used is very similar to, and may have been our 'E', though the fact that he never uses it after 1121 suggests either that he had a copy of it made before any continuation had been added, or that he had a previous version from which 'E' was copied. He also had access to 'C'. A version like 'E' but lacking some, at least, of its Peterborough entries seems to lie behind the Waverley Annals, while Gaimar in his French verse *History of the English* certainly had a rather better text than 'E' or 'F'. This may be what he calls "the English book of Washingborough", but cannot be the archetype from which 'E' was copied, though it is conceivable that the monks of Peterborough would give away their old version when they had made a new copy for themselves. Gaimar refers also to a copy at Winchester, and I am not convinced that by this he refers merely to the Chronicle in general, as originating from there. There is evidence that in the mid-tenth century there was available at Winchester a version of the Chronicle which was not the Parker manuscript, nor any of our surviving versions, and it may still have been there in Gaimar's time. Its presence may explain why the monks of the Old Minster did not trouble to keep 'A' up to date, and were willing to let it go to Canterbury.[2]

More than one version of the Chronicle underlies the early twelfth-century work known as the *Chronicle of Chronicles* of Florence of Worcester. He had something very like 'A', with the annals about Edward the Elder's campaigns which are peculiar to this version, the Winchester entries in the tenth century and some of its other peculiarities. More often his account has close affinities with 'D', with the northern material, but without showing the same interest in Margaret of Scotland. He may have had a rather older form of the 'D' version than our extant manuscript. Like 'D', he tries to combine the Mercian Register with the main Chronicle, but in a different way; he perhaps had it as a separate document. He also has matter, such as

[1] Only fragments of the burnt manuscript remain. The text as printed by Savile ends at 975, but E. E. Barker has shown (*Bull. Inst. Hist. Research*, XXIV, 46–62) that the chapter-headings in the fragments of Brit. Mus. Otho A. x include the reigns of Edward the Martyr and Ethelred. The work must therefore have been continued later in this version.

[2] D. Whitelock, *Eng. Hist. Rev.*, LVII, pp. 120–122.

annals 979–982, which is in 'C' only. He had sources other than the Chronicle, and for some statements he is the sole authority.

William of Malmesbury several times acknowledges his debt to an English chronicle, or chronicles. He had access to a version very like 'E', which he uses up to about 1120; yet it is unlikely that his text was 'E' itself, for this remained at Peterborough for some time after William was writing. Moreover, he shows no knowledge of the Peterborough additions. Presumably he had a copy of 'E''s archetype, if not the archetype itself. He seems to have had neither 'C' nor 'D', for he remarks that the chronicles are silent about the murder of the atheling Alfred in 1036, which is fully treated in both these versions. One might suspect that when he is nearer to 'D' than to 'E' he is using a form of the latter version in which a closer connexion with 'D' was preserved than in the Peterborough copy, but it is possible that he derives the information he gives from the work of Florence of Worcester. In the early portions of his work William may have used a version of the Chronicle not quite identical with any that survive. But as he also used Æthelweard, genealogies and regnal tables, and makes great efforts to reconcile his various sources, it is difficult to pronounce with certainty on his versions of the Chronicle. His chief addition that may come from a lost version is a reference to a battle fought by Cenwealh against the Britons at *Wirtgernesburg*.[1] He makes no reference to the battle of Bradford-on-Avon fought by this king in 652 (Æthelweard says it was a civil war), which is recorded in 'A', 'B' and 'C' but omitted in 'E';[2] this fact confirms the impression that he was mainly dependent on a Chronicle of the 'E' type.

Simeon of Durham had access to a version of the Chronicle, and among lost manuscripts must be mentioned two entered in an old catalogue of the library of Durham as *cronica duo Anglica*. Moreover it should be noted that one manuscript of Ælfric's Grammar, the Cambridge University Library MS. Hh.1.10, once contained what Archbishop Parker calls in his list of gifts *Hist. Angliae Saxonica*; but the manuscript is now mutilated at the end, and the fate of these annals is unknown.

The composition and circulation of the Chronicle

The fact that Asser, writing in 893, had a manuscript of the Chronicle reaching at least up to 887, which was already two removes from the original text; that the Parker manuscript is copied in one handwriting up to the year 891, and is at a similar remove from the original; that the text used by Æthelweard seems to have lacked the annals from 893 to 915 which record in detail Alfred's last campaigns and those of his son Edward; and that 'E' similarly comes from a version with these annals lacking, all seems to point to a copying and circulation of manuscripts soon after 890. Some of the manuscripts then circulated apparently remained barren, others were continued with later material, in some cases added soon after the events described, in others probably copied in at various later periods by comparison with copies that contained it. For there are various indications that we must reckon with a good deal of collation of different texts and later alteration. The movements of the various versions that have survived have already been discussed.

With even our oldest manuscript in one hand up to 891, it is difficult to ascertain the previous history of the work. Many scholars have taken the elaborate genealogy of King Æthelwulf, entered in 855 after the statement that the king died two years after his return from Rome (*i.e.* 858), to mark the conclusion of an earlier stage of

---

[1] See p. 152, n. 5.   [2] 'D' has lost a gathering at this place.

the compilation. But this is by no means certain. It is likely that a compiler writing in Alfred's reign might think that this was a good place to insert the family tree of the reigning house, for there is reason to believe that this compiler was himself the author of the annals which deal with the latter years of Æthelwulf's reign, annals which have a retrospective tone and which introduce a new method of commencement of the year.[1] It would doubtless have been more logical to put the genealogy at the accession of Egbert, the first king of this dynasty, but it is probable that there was available a set of earlier annals dealing with his reign and the early part of Æthelwulf's. On this view, the compiler put the genealogy at the first suitable place in the part of the record he was himself composing.

The materials the compiler had at his disposal included some epitome of universal history which has not been identified, Bede's *Ecclesiastical History*, the chronological summary at the end being especially useful to him, a few northern annals, some genealogies, lists of regnal years and episcopal lists. He probably also had some sets of earlier West Saxon annals, including one for the first half of the eighth century and another for the reign of Egbert and the early years of his successor. Some of these may have been entered in the margins of Easter tables, *i.e.* the lists drawn up for a series of years to show the date on which Easter would fall, which were then found convenient for the entering of outstanding events, and which sometimes have wide margins left for this purpose. The English missionaries took such tables with annals to the Continent in the eighth century, so we cannot doubt that they were familiar in the homeland also. It cannot be proved that any of these written sources were in the vernacular; certain archaic forms noted by Stevenson are confined to place-names and prove nothing about the original language of the annals.

The events prior to the adoption of Christianity would not be entered on Easter tables; where they are not from Bede, they must go back eventually on oral tradition, perhaps handed down in verse, and the assignment to particular years can have been little more than guesswork. The artificial arrangement of the incidents of the English settlement has often been commented on, and Sir Frank Stenton[2] has shown that one set of incidents has probably been duplicated.

Another type of source seems implied by annal 755, in which the circumstantial account of the feud between Cynewulf and Cyneheard has plainly been added to an annal that once existed without it; its rather archaic prose suggests that it had an earlier written source, though the incident may have been handed down by oral narrative for some time before it was put in writing.

Since Sir Frank Stenton has argued from indications in the surviving text and in Æthelweard that the chronicler was particularly interested in the south-western counties and their nobles, and has postulated some Somerset ealdorman or thegn as patron of the work,[3] the confident attribution of the work to Alfred's instigation cannot be upheld. It is impossible that he should himself have mistaken the ceremony that took place at Rome when he was a child, when he was invested with the insignia of a Roman consul, as a coronation ceremony, as the chronicler does.[4] The rapid dissemination of the work may owe something to his encouragement, but we must not forget that Alfred's own words in the preface to his translation of the *Pastoral Care* imply that there was a reading public for vernacular works. That the Chronicle does not stand entirely apart from the works produced by Alfred, however, is shown by its

[1] See A. J. Thorogood in *Eng. Hist. Rev.*, XLVIII, pp. 353–363.
[2] *Anglo-Saxon England*, pp. 22 f.
[3] *Essays in Medieval History presented to T. F. Tout*, pp. 15–24.
[4] No. 1, p. 174; cf. No. 219.

referring to the Emperor Titus in almost identical words with those used of him in Alfred's translation of Orosius. There are other correspondences between that work and the Chronicle, but unfortunately we have too little early West Saxon prose apart from Alfred's writings to be able to decide whether they are anything more than the natural correspondences in phraseology of contemporary writers on similar themes.

Chronology

The chronology of the Chronicle causes many complications. Mechanical dislocations arise easily out of the habit of numbering a series of years in advance, for it was easy to make an entry against a wrong number, or to take too much space for an entry and fail to adjust the numbers of the subsequent annals; or a copyist might fail to notice a blank annal and so pre-date events for a considerable stretch. Already in pre-Conquest times annal numbers were sometimes altered by a later corrector attempting to get rid of contradictions and inconsistencies. Detailed studies have been made of the alterations to the numbers in 'A'; but 'C' has also been tampered with, while in 'B' the scribe more often than not leaves blanks instead of putting in annal numbers. In all our extant manuscripts there is a dislocation of two, and even three, years from the mid-eighth to the mid-ninth century; in 'C', an entry of seven blank annals, 846–852, where 'A', 'D' and 'E' have only five, throws the chronology out of line, and though a little later the discrepancy was narrowed by the omission of a blank annal, 'C' remains a year in advance until at least 900. And many other instances of dislocation could be given.

Where there is a difference of a single year between the dating of an event in different texts, it is not always possible to decide if one text is in error, or if they are using different styles of beginning the year. The early annals contain no data for deciding this question, but it is clear that annal 794[1] begins at Christmas, as do the additions made into this section of the Chronicle in the northern recension. Christmas seems also the style in 822 and 823,[2] and there is no clear indication of any other usage until 851, which begins in the autumn, presumably on 24 September with the Caesarean Indiction. The change may have begun about 840, when the Alfredian compiler probably began to compose the annals, as we have suggested above. A beginning in the autumn continues at least as far as 889, and is again clear in 900 and 912 'A'.[3] A reversion to Christmas dating for 891–896 has been suggested, though personally I think that the writer of these annals is thinking rather in campaigning years than in calendar years. The Mercian Register begins its year at Christmas, and so undoubtedly does the main Chronicle from 917 'A'.[4] In fact, after this time the only suggestion of a commencement on 24 September comes in the recording of certain obits, where the Chronicle may be using lists drawn up on this system. The clearest instance is the dating of Athelstan's death on 27 October 939 as 940. But in the eleventh century another method competes with Christmas, dating from the Annunciation on 25 March. This is certainly used by 'C' from 1044 to 1053, and again in 1065 and 1066, when 'C' comes to an end. 'D' has it also in these last two years, and, I believe, continued to the end to use this style, which is also visible in 'E' in the first few years after the Conquest. By 1094, however, 'E' has clearly reverted to Christmas dating.[5]

---

[1] For 796.   [2] For 824 and 825.   [3] =913 'C', 'D'.   [4] =915 'C', 'D'.
[5] For a detailed discussion, see Earle and Plummer, *Two of the Saxon Chronicles Parallel*, 2nd edit., 1952, pp. cxxxix–cxlii d.

THE HISTORIA BRITTONUM

Of the Welsh sources for early English history, the *De Excidio Britanniae* of the sixth-century writer Gildas will be considered in Part III of this volume, along with Bede's *Ecclesiastical History*, which incorporated most of the relevant section of it.[1] The *Historia Brittonum*, which goes under the name of Nennius, is a work that has occasioned much controversy, and there is still difference of opinion on many matters regarding its composition, sources and reliability. Its great popularity can be seen by its survival in some thirty-five manuscripts. In several manuscripts the work is anonymous. One group attributes the authorship to Gildas, but two manuscripts of this group[2] have been collated with a lost manuscript which contained the preface of Nennius, and have added other readings, as well as this preface, from this source. The best text of the work is in the Brit. Mus. Harley MS. 3859 (of about 1100), which belongs to a group which contains some genealogies of English kings, with notes of their wars with the Britons.[3] The Durham and Corpus manuscripts contain a note in which the scribe explains that he has omitted these genealogies because his master Beulan considered them useless. They are omitted also in the oldest surviving manuscript, that at Chartres, which omits the preface also, and assigns the work in a rubric to a 'son of Urbgen'. Lot considers that both the antiquity and the importance of this manuscript have been exaggerated. He assigns it to the second half of the tenth century and claims that it consists of excerpts only.

Nennius, or perhaps more correctly Nemnius or Nemnivus (the form in the early eighth-century manuscript Bodley, Auct. F.4.32 which refers to an inventor of an alphabet who must be identical with our author),[4] declares in his preface that he was a disciple of Elvodugus, and in a note in the Durham and Corpus manuscripts he speaks of information given him by this bishop and by Bishop Renchidus. The latter is otherwise unknown, but Elvodugus can be identified with an archbishop who died in 809. The genealogies used in the work go as far as 796. Various attempts have been made to get a more exact date from the various computations contained in his book, but they are contradictory, and are probably to be attributed to various scribes. It is a matter of controversy whether Nennius is the original author of the *Historia Brittonum*, or merely an adaptor of an earlier work. In any case, it is difficult to ascertain how much substratum of fact underlies his romantic stories, such as those about Arthur, or his elaborations on the story of Hengest and Horsa.

But he certainly had access to some English genealogies and regnal lists, which may perhaps be all he means when in his preface he refers to "annals of the Saxons" among his sources. His genealogies are closest to some surviving in the Mercian manuscript Brit. Mus. Cott. Vespas. B. vi, while some of his statements on the length of the reigns of the Northumbriar kings agree with the regnal list in the Moore manuscript of Bede. Nennius has added some notes for which he is the only authority, which have a very different ring from the information in the earlier part of his work. While they are not all trustworthy–for example it can only be a Welsh fiction that a Welsh priest baptized Edwin–some of them may have been derived from early marginal notes or from Welsh poems like the *Gododdin* of Aneirin, which is a lament for a troup of followers sent by the king of the Gododdin (*Votadini*) against the men of Deira and Bernicia from Edinburgh to Catterick, where they met with disaster.[5]

---

[1] No. 151, pp. 590–595. See also p. 588.   [2] Durham, B. II, 35 and C.C.C.C., MS. 139.   [3] See No. 3.
[4] See Thurneysen in *Zeitschr. f. Celt. Phil.*, xx, pp. 97–137; Ifor Williams in *Bull. Board Celt. Stud.*, vii, 4, pp. 380–388.   [5] See p? 131.

I have therefore thought fit to include this section among the materials of English history.

There are also two notes in individual manuscripts of the work that have some interest for English scholars. One is in the Chartres manuscript, and states that Slebhine, abbot of Iona,[1] found the date of the coming of the English at Ripon, thus showing intercourse between Iona and the Northumbrian Church in the mid-eighth century, and the existence at Ripon at that time of some table of computation or some chronicle. The other is in the manuscript now divided between the Vatican and Paris, for this version takes one of its computations as far as the fifth year of King Edmund, *i.e.* 943–944, thus suggesting that it copies a manuscript produced in England in Edmund's reign. We are thus afforded a sign of interest in historical writings, and of activity in manuscript production, in a period generally considered barren of these things.

THE NORTHERN SOURCES

In the above discussion it was necessary from time to time to refer to certain annals written in the north of England. Unfortunately, these have not survived in an original form; this can only be guessed at from passages embodied in the works of later writers, none of whom give a complete set of these annals, the choice of each author being dictated by his individual interests and by the range of other sources available to him. The following works are important in establishing these annals:

(*a*) The Anglo-Saxon Chronicle. The compiler of the main version had access to some northern annals, but either these were very scanty or he made little use of them. At a later date, probably not before the mid-tenth century, the version of the Chronicle which underlies our versions 'D' and 'E' inserted into its text of the main Chronicle a number of annals from a northern source.

(*b*) The *History of the Kings* which goes under the name of Simeon of Durham.[2] This work survives in a single manuscript in which it has been subjected to a revision by a Hexham writer. Some of the latter's insertions can be detected by comparing the chronicle of Roger of Hoveden and the Chronicle of Melrose, both of which used the work before the Hexham additions were made. The *History of the Kings* is a shapeless work that falls into two sections: a part extending to 957, based on material from Bede, from Northumbrian annals for the post-Bede period up to 802, and again from about 900 to 957, with the gap between the sets of annals partly filled up by extensive borrowing from Asser for the years 849–887; and a second section mainly taken from Florence of Worcester, which goes back to 849 and continues to 1129. In the early part of this section, independent additions are rare, but from the later eleventh century they become more common and important. As Florence of Worcester himself drew largely on Asser for the years 849–887, the *History of the Kings* contains two versions of Asser's work. Among the additions made to Florence's work occurs under 1072 an account of the earls of Northumbria from the death of the last king, Eric Blood-axe, to the reign of Henry I.

Roger of Hoveden has been shown by Stubbs to have drawn not directly on the *History of the Kings*, but on a text which survives in manuscript, and is called the *History after Bede*; this attempted to improve on the *History of the Kings*, by getting rid of the repeat of Asser and by using Henry of Huntingdon's chronicle (a work based chiefly on the 'E' version of the Anglo-Saxon Chronicle) from 752 to 860, thus filling in the gap from 802 to 849 in the *History of the Kings*.

[1] 752–767.   [2] See No. 3.

The Chronicle of Melrose has combined still further, and must be used with caution. To the material in the *History of the Kings* it adds matter from Henry of Huntingdon, beginning to use him at 742. Its readings therefore sometimes agree closely with the 'E' manuscript of the Anglo-Saxon Chronicle, but must not be taken to corroborate this, as they are, though indirectly, derived from it. When the Melrose chronicler deals with events recorded both in his northern source and in Henry of Huntingdon, he sometimes has difficulty with discrepancies in their dates. Thus, when he found the death of King Cynewulf of Wessex both in 784 and 786, he solved his problem by dating the king's death 784, and the vengeance which was taken for it on the following day, 786. In his entries for 777 and 778 he has duplicated a single event. He seems to have little of his own to add to material from these two sources. But his relation to Henry of Huntingdon has never, to my knowledge, been fully worked out, and deserves study. It looks as if he had access to a better text than the extant manuscripts; he has the Old English names in a better form.

(c) The *Flowers of History* of Roger of Wendover has made prolific use of the *History of the Kings*. In addition, the author has had access to some annals mainly concerned with York, which seem not to have been used by any other writer. Of particular interest is the one that explains the reason for Edgar's ravaging of Thanet, the bare fact only being entered in the Anglo-Saxon Chronicle ('D', 'E').[1]

(d) The Continuation of Bede. This text is of uncertain date. It seems to draw to some extent on the annals used by the *History of the Kings*, and it also has some matter which is not in that work and which has a genuine ring.

Since the northern version of the Anglo-Saxon Chronicle dovetailed the northern annals somewhat clumsily into its southern text, while the Latin writers all combined them with material from earlier Latin authorities, it is not possible to reconstruct the original condition of the annals; but it seems clear that there was a fairly full set continuing the chronological summary attached by Bede to his *Ecclesiastical History*, and that this extended into the early years of the ninth century. A second set, with its centre of interest at St. Cuthbert's see, then at Chester-le-Street, dealt with events from the end of the ninth century until about 956. I have not attempted to combine into a consecutive series the matter drawn by our various authorities from this source, but I have given the entries as they occur in each of the Latin authorities, for comparison with the text of the Anglo-Saxon Chronicle.

Historical information is contained in another northern source, one of a different kind, the anonymous *History of St. Cuthbert*, a Durham production of about 1050, based mainly on the charters and records of donations to the church of St. Cuthbert, apart from the early portion, which uses Bede. Though it includes some legendary matter, the work supplies some probably authentic information which we should otherwise have missed. It is the earliest source for the account of the election of the Christian Danish King Guthfrith, of interest in spite of its legendary details; it tells something of the survival of monasteries in the tenth-century Danelaw, and of the conquest of Northumbria by Ragnald; and it includes a few welcome references to a part of the country for which information is hard to come by, the land west of the Pennines. The relevant sections are given below.[2] Simeon of Durham used this text when writing his history of the church of Durham.

[1] See No. 1, p. 207; No. 4, p. 257.   [2] No. 6.

ASSER'S "LIFE OF KING ALFRED"

Very little is known of Asser beyond what he tells us in his work. Alfred mentions him among his helpers in the letter he prefixed to his translation of the *Pastoral Care*;[1] William of Malmesbury, who had access to sources lost to us, says that he helped the king with his translation of Boethius; Gerald of Wales refers to him as author of the Life; his death, as bishop of Sherborne, is entered in the Chronicle, 910 (for 909), and in the *Annales Cambriae*, 908. Unfortunately, the only manu- script[2] of his work to survive to modern times was burnt in the fire of 1731. It was seen by Wanley, who dated the oldest hand in it about 1000 or 1001, probably because of its resemblance to a charter of that year. The work had previously been printed by Archbishop Parker in 1574, and later editors based their text on this. Parker had interpolated into Asser's work passages from the *Annals of St. Neots* which he believed to be by Asser, and this caused undeserved suspicions to be cast on the authenticity of the Life. It remained for Stevenson to produce a reliable text, based on the transcripts used by Parker, and on the extracts of the Life incorporated by Florence of Worcester, Simeon of Durham, and the compiler of the *Annals of St. Neots* into their works. Stevenson established the authenticity of the Life both by meeting effectively all the arguments brought against it, and by drawing attention to features that would be inexplicable if the work originated from a later forger. It would be possible to add to these. In recent times a fresh attempt has been made to cast doubt on the genuineness of the work,[3] but only by bringing forward again arguments already disposed of by Stevenson. No one has ever yet produced any convincing motive that might cause anyone to undertake so laborious a task as forging this work.

There is no need to expatiate on the importance of a work written by a man who had lived and worked with King Alfred. The book has its faults: it is written in a verbose and pretentious Latin, which tends to obscure its meaning; it is badly shaped, the material drawn from the author's own experience being combined in a somewhat clumsy manner with a translation into Latin of a version of the Anglo- Saxon Chronicle; there being few models of biographies of laymen at the author's disposal, and many Saints' Lives, it stresses too much, and probably exaggerates, those aspects of the king's character which are more in accord with the latter genre; and it is unfinished. From chapter 91 it may be gathered that the author was writing in 893, and there is no indication of any event that can be dated later. It ends too abruptly for one to believe that it is complete. For all its faults, it tells us much of Anglo-Saxon affairs in the ninth century, and of Alfred in particular, which would otherwise have been unknown, and it lends support to other authorities, the Chronicle, the laws and Alfred's own writings, on many points of interest. Stevenson demonstrated that Asser betrays Frankish influence on his terminology, has used Einhard's *Life of Charles the Great*, and is well informed on affairs in the Frankish empire; but too little is known of Asser's career for us to know the nature of his Frankish contacts.

Mention has been made above of Asser's use of the Anglo-Saxon Chronicle, and where, in the parts he based on this, he has anything of interest to add, this is noted in my notes to that work. Those parts of his work which are drawn from his own knowledge are given below,[4] with the omission only of such wearisome topics as his enlarging on the king's illnesses.

---

[1] No. 226.   [2] Brit. Mus. Cott. Otho A. xii.
[3] J. W. Adamson, *The "Illiterate Anglo-Saxon" and other Essays in Education, Medieval and Modern* (Cambridge, 1946), chapter II.   [4] No. 7.

AUTHENTIC EARLY MATERIAL IN POST-CONQUEST LATIN WRITERS

In as far as they drew on the Anglo-Saxon Chronicle and northern annals, the post-Conquest historians have been mentioned above. It remains to consider the chief instances when they had at their disposal other pre-Conquest material, since lost. William of Malmesbury, who finished his first version of his *De Gestis Regum Anglorum* ("On the Acts of the Kings") about 1125, and issued two revisions after 1135, and whose other main work, *De Gestis Pontificum* ("On the Acts of the Bishops"), seems also to have been completed in 1125, has preserved for us a few important letters, which will be discussed in a later section. He also drew on legends and stories current in his own day, sometimes in a popular verse form, most of which are of little historical value. By far his most important service to Anglo-Saxon history is his paraphrase and partial quotation of a Latin verse panegyric on the reign of Athelstan, an almost contemporary production that adds much to our knowledge of this king's reign, and which is therefore given in full as No. 8.

The *Chronicon ex Chronicis* which goes under the name of Florence of Worcester consists of lengthy additions to a series of annals on world history compiled by Marianus Scotus in the eleventh century and introduced into England by Robert, bishop of Hereford, 1079–1095; these annals have no bearing on English history, and I have omitted them. The additions were made at Worcester, and their attribution to Florence, a monk who died in 1118, depends on a reference to him, in a continuation of this work believed to be by a certain John of Worcester, as the man whose "acute observation and laborious and diligent studies have made this chronicle from chronicles excel all others". Professor Darlington has recently suggested that the whole work up to 1141 is the work of John, whom Ordericus Vitalis saw preparing a Latin chronicle at Worcester, and who might speak thus of an older monk who had given him assistance. For practical convenience, however, I retain the familiar designation, until Professor Darlington gives us in full the result of his research into this work, which badly needs re-editing.

Florence depended for his pre-Conquest history mainly on the Anglo-Saxon Chronicle, Asser, laws and Saints' Lives which still survive. But for the eleventh century he certainly had some sources that have not come down. This is especially true of his account of the reign of Cnut and his sons, and I have therefore given this section of his work in full.[1] This will enable the reader to see how the author combined other material with the Anglo-Saxon Chronicle. The new matter is of unequal value. It would be unwise to accept uncritically the details of the iniquities of the "perfidious ealdorman Eadric", though even here one should note that Eadric plays a very similar rôle in the much earlier work, the *Encomium Emmae* of 1040–1042, which agrees with Florence that the motive for his execution by Cnut was that king's distrust of the men who had been false to their English kings. Much of what Florence has to tell has an authentic ring; some is confirmed by Scandinavian sources,[2] and there are places where one can glimpse Old English expressions behind Florence's Latin. Large portions of this work were incorporated into other Latin histories in the Middle Ages.

The work that goes under the name of Simeon of Durham has been discussed above,[3] as has that of those later writers whose main importance is that they used a lost version of the Anglo-Saxon Chronicle.[4] Apart from this, Henry of Huntingdon knows a lot of legendary matter but little reliable information, while Gaimar, who

[1] No. 9.   [2] Nos. 14–19.   [3] pp. 118 f.   [4] pp. 113 f.

also drew on oral tradition, here and there has preserved a fact of some importance, such as the death-place of King Cenwulf of Mercia,[1] and the dowry, Winchester, Rockingham and Rutland, which he assigns to Emma. Occasionally later monastic chroniclers, such as the writers of the *Historia Eliensis* and the *Historia Ramesiensis*, were able to draw from charters in the archives of their house information that would have been lost otherwise.

THE BATTLE OF MALDON

This famous poem[2] survives only as a fragment, incomplete both at the beginning and end, and it is alone of its kind among surviving Old English records. For, while the tenth-century historical poems included in the Chronicle are celebrating national victories in somewhat general terms, this poem is concerned with the deeds of private individuals, the Ealdorman Brihtnoth and his bodyguard, in a battle which was not a victory, but which the heroism of the defeated turned into a fit subject for song. The death of Brihtnoth at Maldon is mentioned briefly in the Chronicle, 991, and the battle is described more fully in the Life of St. Oswald;[3] but the poem not only adds details of the course of the battle, but dramatically shows us the sentiments of the individual participators, and illustrates how close was the bond that bound a man to his lord even in the troubled days of Ethelred the Unready. It supplies also an important piece of evidence on the relations of the English government with the northern Danelaw; for the presence of a Northumbrian hostage among the followers of an ealdorman of Essex certainly suggests that it had been thought expedient to take hostages from an area of possible pro-Danish sympathies, and to quarter them in loyal households. But the greatest value of the poem is that it warns us that behind the dreary record of incompetence, treachery and defeat in the Chronicle may lie many such incidents, and causes us to attach more weight to occasional statements such as "and they then joined battle stoutly" (999), "there the flower of the East Anglian people was killed" (1004), and to remember that the scaldic poems imply a great English resistance at Ringmere.

It is likely enough that there were once poems of the same type on these or similar incidents. Such poems would have little chance of survival; in fact, they would probably never have been written down. The Maldon fragment is clearly a local poem; it assumes that its hearers are familiar with the persons mentioned and their relationships, using patronymics only to describe men from distant localities–the Mercian Ælfwine, the Northumbrian hostage–or to distinguish persons of the same name. That it should ever have come down to us at all is probably due to Brihtnoth's importance as a benefactor and supporter of monasteries, for the houses with which he was connected would be interested to enter a poem about him in their records. And if it had not caught the attention of Hearne before the manuscript[4] was burnt in 1731, we should have had no evidence that poetry of this kind was composed in Anglo-Saxon times.

SCANDINAVIAN SOURCES

The historical sources of Scandinavia are very bulky, and naturally concern the English historian when they deal with the viking raids and with the persons who play a part in England as well as the Scandinavian North; but they have to be used with great caution, for they were written down at a very late time, and much fabulous matter has become mingled with historical fact.

[1] p. 170, n. 8. [2] No. 10. [3] See No. 236, p. 843. [4] Brit. Mus. Cott. Otho A. xii.

Most important is the scaldic verse, for its very complicated and fixed form resisted change and caused it to be handed on from generation to generation until some of it was written down and has survived to our times. Its preservation is mainly due to its use by the thirteenth-century saga writers who often quote it in their work. This type of verse seems to have been first used a little before the mid-ninth century, and the earliest scalds whose work is preserved belong to the reign of Harold Fairhair of Norway, who had created for himself a united kingdom of Norway before the end of the ninth century, and who had diplomatic dealings with King Athelstan.[1] Fragments of a long poem on him by a scald called Thorbjörn Hornklofi have survived, in which the king's bravery in war, especially at the battle of Hafrsfjörd, is praised in the form of a dialogue between a valkyrie and a raven. This battle, in which Harold utterly defeated the independent chieftains of Norway, is not mentioned at all in English and continental sources, and its importance for English history is only indirect; but several later scaldic poems, or fragments of poems, survive which have a more immediate interest for English historians.

First, there is a group concerned with Eric, Harold Fairhair's son, about whom we should from English sources know nothing beyond his acceptance by the Northumbrians as king, his expulsion and death.[2] There survives in full the poem "Head-Ransom" composed on him by the Icelandic poet Egil Skalla-Grímsson at York to redeem his life when he had come into his power,[3] and also the beginning of a fine poem, Eiríksmál, composed after his death by an unknown poet at his widow's request, which imagines his reception by Othin in Valhalla. The refrain of a dirge on him by his son's scald, Glúm Geirason, "his brand wins Eric gold and land", survives also.

Secondly, the scaldic poetry includes references to the adventures of St. Olaf in England, whereas English sources are silent concerning them. The verses of his scalds Sighvat and Óttar the Black are given below.[4] Both these poets composed also in honour of King Cnut,[5] and there is a poem on the latter's attack on Norway by Thorarin Loftunga,[6] and a fragment of a drápa (a long poem of compliment) by Halvarth Háreksblesi, which speaks of his ruling supreme over England and Denmark, to the betterment of peace there, and of his subjugation of Norway. A poem by Bjarni Gullbráskald, on Kálf Árnason, the leader of the Norwegian forces against St. Olaf, tells of his visit to Cnut, and that before he left, "the lord of London" found land for him. There is also an anonymous poem, or perhaps a collection of separate stanzas, known as Liðsmannaflokkr, "Song of the men of the host", referring to Cnut's attack on England, probably composed in 1016. It concludes: "Since hard battles are ended we can sit in fair London."

Another leader in this invasion would be little more than a name if we had to depend on English records alone, the Earl Eric to whom Cnut gave the earldom of Northumbria. He is Eric of Hlathir, son of Earl Hákon the Bad, and his deeds were celebrated by various scalds. They speak mainly of his career before he came to England, Eyjolf Dadaskald of his campaigns in Gautland, the South Baltic and Russia, Halldór Úkristni and Skúli Thorsteinsson of his prowess in the sea battle against Olaf Tryggvason at Svöld; Thorth Kolbeinsson of his deeds in the battle in which the Jómsviking attack was repelled, as well as at Svöld. He then adds lines of interest for English history.[7]

---

[1] See No. 8, p. 281. [2] No. 1, p. 204; No. 3, p. 253; No. 4, p. 257. [3] No. 11.
[4] Nos. 12, 13, 18. [5] Nos. 15, 16. [6] No. 19. [7] No. 14.

Scalds did not confine their services to Scandinavian kings and chiefs. They some-times took service with English kings, and a poem by Egil, of no great interest, has survived on Athelstan, and the refrain of a poem by Gunnlaug Ormstunga on Ethelred the Unready, which declares that the host fears him as a god, and the race of men does homage to him. A poem on Earl Waltheof of Northumbria, and stanzas dealing with the battles of Fulford and Stamford Bridge, by the scalds of Harold Hardrada and his son Olaf, lie outside the period covered by this volume. One of these scalds composed a poem on Edward the Confessor, but it has not survived.

As to the reliability of scaldic verse as historical evidence, the opinion of Snorri Sturluson is well known. He says: "We find the best evidence in the poems which were offered to the kings themselves or to their sons. . . . It is the way of scalds, of course, to give most praise to him for whom they composed, but no one would dare tell the king himself such deeds of his as all listeners and the king himself knew to be lies and loose talk; that would be mockery, but not praise."[1] This is no doubt sound reasoning; yet it would be possible for a scald to suppress those aspects of a subject that would not be welcome to his hearer, and one cannot regard this type of evidence as free from bias. Harold Hardrada's forces were undoubtedly victorious at Fulford, and no doubt fought well at Stamford Bridge, yet one may wonder whether the epithets "terror of the English", "diminisher of the English", applied by the scalds to Harold's son Olaf, who was allowed after Stamford Bridge to return home to Norway after swearing never to attack England again, would not be misleading to a posterity that had no other sources of information.

The surviving scaldic verse is a mere fraction of what once existed, and much more was available to the twelfth- and thirteenth-century historians than has come down to us. It cannot be doubted that these give a great deal of authentic information from contemporary scaldic verse since lost. Yet it is not easy to assess the value of their information when we cannot compare it with the material on which they based it. For, though the rigid form of the verse minimizes the risk of alteration during transmission, this type of poetry was oblique and obscure in its expression, often lacked precise references, which were unnecessary for a contemporary audience, and gave little help with dating the incidents. It was therefore very liable to misinterpretation. A clear instance of this is given below, where the verses embedded in Snorri's account of St. Olaf's career in England give quite a different picture from that given by Snorri's prose expansion of them.[2] Though it is only fair to assume that in many cases there was handed down with the poems a tradition concerning the occasion on which they were delivered, and fuller information on the events alluded to, from a time when they were still remembered, and hence it is unnecessary to reject all statements not vouched for in surviving poems, the sagas must be used with great caution. They often embody conflicting traditions, their chronology is unreliable, they invent incidents to explain nicknames or create a dramatic situation, and they transfer incidents from one character to another. Yet they are probably trustworthy in their broad outline of Scandinavian history. While this gives them their chief value for the student of English history, it cannot be adequately illustrated in small compass.

The writing of Scandinavian history began in Iceland in the early twelfth century,

[1] *Heimskringla*, Preface, from translation by Erling Monsen, Cambridge, 1932, p. xxxvi.
[2] See pp. 305f.

with the work of two ecclesiastics, Ari Thorgilsson and Sæmund Sigfússon. Ari, who was born about 1067, was the foster-son of Hall who had at one time been a partner of St. Olaf. From him and other aged men Ari could have obtained much reliable information from the early eleventh century, and it is therefore to be regretted that his work on the kings of Norway and Denmark is lost. His surviving work is concerned with Icelandic history, and allows us to form a very high opinion of his historical sense and reliability. The work of his contemporary, Sæmund, a Latin history of the kings of Norway, is lost also, but both it and Ari's work were used by later writers. Towards the end of the twelfth century two Latin histories of the kings of Norway were written in Norway, and about the same period Sven Aageson and Saxo were producing their work on Danish history.[1] Early in the next century a summary (*Ágrip*) of the history of the kings of Norway was written in the vernacular, and it was followed by a much fuller work known as *Fagrskinna*. Meanwhile separate biographies were being produced, including Latin Lives of Olaf Tryggvason by Odd Snorrason and Gunnlaug Leifsson,[2] a vernacular Life of St. Olaf which belongs to about 1160–1180, and survives only in fragments, a short saga about Harold Fairhair and his father, and one on Hákon the Good, and a saga on the earls of Hlathir. There was also a full account of the Life and miracles of St. Olaf by an Icelandic monk Styrmir, lost except in as far as it has been used in later works. It is believed to have included a lost Cnut's saga among its sources. So when Snorri Sturluson came to write his *Heimskringla*, the most important of the histories of the kings of Norway, about 1230, he had the work of several predecessors to draw on, as well as scaldic verse and other oral tradition. Material relating to Danish history was put together in the *Jómsvikingasaga*, mainly about a reputed viking stronghold at *Jómsborg* on the South Baltic coast. Many characters of this saga are certainly historical, including Thorkel the Tall, the leader of the invasion of England in 1009, who appears in English records and in Thietmar,[3] but the existence of the *Jómsborg* settlement has been doubted. No early poem refers to it. This saga was one of the sources of the late-thirteenth-century *Knýtlingasaga*, on the descendants of a legendary Cnut the Foundling, ancestor of Cnut the Great.

The sagas relating the doings of various prominent Icelanders also contain passages of general historical interest. For English history, the most important is Egil's saga, believed to be the work of Snorri Sturluson, earlier than his *Heimskringla*. Egil is there said to have taken service under Athelstan, and to have fought for him at a battle on *Vínheithr* against Olaf 'the Red', which has sometimes been identified with the battle of *Brunanburh*, fought against Olaf Guthfrithsson, which Simeon of Durham says was fought at *Weondun*. If this is the battle meant, the chronology in the saga has become confused, for it places it very early in Athelstan's reign. Mr. Campbell thinks that the saga-writer has muddled this battle with one by the Dvina in Bjarmaland mentioned earlier in the saga.[4] It would therefore be dangerous to use the saga's account as evidence for what took place at *Brunanburh*. But the second place where this saga impinges on English history is of more interest, for, though again the chronology is untrustworthy, the incident of Egil's visit to Eric at York is probably true, supported as it is by two of Egil's poems, and it affords a welcome glimpse into

---

[1] The last event mentioned by Sven is in 1185. Saxo completed his much longer history early in the thirteenth century.
[2] Odd's Life, and part of Gunnlaug's, are known in vernacular translation, the original Latin texts being lost.
[3] No. 1, pp. 220, 223, 227–229; No. 9, pp. 285f.; Nos. 27f.
[4] A. Campbell, *The Battle of Brunanburh*, pp. 68–80.

Northumbria in the days of the Norse rulers at York. I have therefore included this part of the saga, and the poems,[1] to let the reader see scaldic verse in the prose setting supplied by the saga-writer.

CONTINENTAL ANNALS AND CHRONICLES

The writing of annals grew out of the addition of the principal events on to the Easter tables, and as some of these reached the Continent prefixed to Bede's *De temporum ratione*, it need occasion no surprise that continental copies should include some brief references to English affairs, mainly concerned with Northumbria, but some probably originating from Canterbury. But later continental annalists and chroniclers generally deal little with English affairs, as these lay too far outside the orbit of their interests. Here and there, however, there occur references which supplement English records, and I have given the more important of them in the selections which follow.[2] Charles the Great's interference into Northumbrian affairs, the viking raid on Southampton in 842, and Athelstan's excursions into European politics, would all have been unknown to us but for continental sources; while Æthelwulf's marriage into the Frankish royal house for political reasons is much more fully reported there.

I have not included in my selection those continental annals which relate in detail the events of Frankish history entered in brief in the Anglo-Saxon Chronicle between 880 and 891, for their main interest is for Frankish, not English history, though they are useful in helping to determine the true chronology of the Anglo-Saxon Chronicle and also in showing how thin a selection of Frankish events was recorded by the English chronicler. For example, when in 882 the *Annals of St. Vaast* record the burning of Aachen, Trier and Cologne, the English writer is silent. It should also be observed that the continental accounts of the viking activities in the Frankish kingdom increase our confidence in the accuracy of the English chronicler. Thus the latter's statement that the vikings from Fulham went to the land of the Franks, to Ghent, in 880 is confirmed by the *Annals of St. Vaast*, which state that in 879[3] the Northmen across the sea heard of the dissensions within the Frankish empire and came across "with an infinite multitude" and took up winter-quarters in Ghent in November; in 884, the year in which part of the viking force came back to England and part went into the eastern part of the Frankish empire, the same continental authority records a council at Boulogne, after which the vikings divided, part going across the sea, part to Louvain; in 892, the year in which "the great army" came back to England, these annals duly record this crossing, giving the additional information that it was motivated by a famine on the Continent; and finally, in 896, they speak of the Northmen again entering the Seine, in the very year in which, according to the Anglo-Saxon Chronicle, those of the enemy who had no property got themselves ships and went south overseas to the Seine. The continental version supplies the name of the leader, Hundi. Frankish annals of this period show also that the English chronicler Æthelweard had reliable material before him in some places where he has matter not in the extant versions of the Anglo-Saxon Chronicle. His *Escelun* as the name of the Danish camp in the autumn of 881 is the *Haslao*[4] of the *Annals of St. Vaast* at this point; he correctly says that the Danes went to Louvain in 884. It is

[1] No. 11.   [2] Nos. 20–28.
[3] *i.e.* 880 in the Anglo-Saxon Chronicle, which begins its year on 24 September.
[4] *i.e.* Elsloo.

possible that the version of the Anglo-Saxon Chronicle which he used had more detail than any surviving text.

An interest of rather a different kind attaches to the work of the last two continental authors included in this selection, the German chronicler Thietmar of Merseburg and the anonymous St. Omer writer of the *Encomium Emmae*; for though both these writers are very nearly contemporary with the events they relate, their work can be shown to be often wrong.

Thietmar, who was born in 975, became bishop of Merseburg, Saxony, in 1009. His chronicle was perhaps begun in 1012, with additions in the next few years. He died in 1018. Thus his account of events in England in 1012 and 1016 cannot have been written long after they occurred, and he claims an Englishman called Sewold as his authority. Yet it is full of errors. He has confused the martyred archbishop, Ælfheah, with a more widely-known predecessor, Dunstan, who died in 988, and his account of the martyrdom is greatly inferior to that in the Anglo-Saxon Chronicle, having legendary features, though it may be correct in the rôle it allots to Thorkel. In his account of the events of 1016, he says that Edmund (Ironside) was killed in the siege of London, and leaves as leader of the English his brother Athelstan, whom no other source states to have survived his father. Nevertheless, confusion over names does not justify our dismissing out of hand his whole account as worthless. It is likely enough that many rumours were current as to what was happening during the complicated events of 1016, and that many a person left England with only a confused notion of what was going on and who had been killed.

But if we should attribute some of Thietmar's inaccuracies to his writing too near the events, before rumour has been replaced by the truth, we must put him in a different category from the writer of the *Encomium*, whose misstatements are due not only to confusion and error, but also to deliberate misrepresentation. For he is writing with an object, the glorification of Emma, widow of Ethelred and Cnut, during the reign of her son Hardacnut in 1040–1042. He says he is writing at her command; he doubtless hopes for benefits for himself or his community, now that her son is reigning over England and Denmark. What are we to think of the reliability of a writer who can describe Swein Forkbeard, Hardacnut's grandfather, as a generous and religious king, whose end was happy "from both the spiritual and worldly point of view"; who ignores completely Emma's marriage to Ethelred, to whom he refers vaguely as "a certain prince", and thus more than implies in one place that her sons by Ethelred were Cnut's sons? Mr. Campbell, who has produced an excellent edition of the work, believes that he was acting under Emma's instructions in omitting mention of Ethelred; yet his silence could perhaps be adequately explained by the awkwardness of mentioning in a panegyric that this queen had married the enemy of her husband and usurper of her sons' throne. By ignoring Ethelred the author is relieved from the necessity of showing that the reigning king, Hardacnut, had not the best of titles to the throne. It is clear that he is prepared to pervert any evidence for the aggrandisement of Emma and Hardacnut. He is not always well informed, having, for example, a very incomplete account of what happened in 1016; nor very clear-headed, for his attempt to explain that Thorkel was not being treacherous to Cnut in 1014, but was remaining in England by secret arrangement with him, is contradicted by words he puts into Cnut's mouth later on. Yet it may well be that Thorkel's historical defection to the English side was much debated at the time, and that this author has not gone to the trouble of reconciling different theories regarding his motives.

With all its shortcomings, the work cannot be totally disregarded, as Mr. Campbell has shown clearly. The author had seen Cnut, and he gives a picture of his religious fervour not at variance with other evidence. Scandinavian sources support his account of Eric as a great soldier, and his placing him at the siege of London in 1016. His version of the murder of the atheling Alfred, although it may have fictitious additions, supplies a motive for the action taken against him in England, which is lacking from the account in the Anglo-Saxon Chronicle. This section of his work is therefore included in this volume[1] and compared with the accounts of the incident given by the Norman writers, William of Poitiers and William of Jumièges.

[1] No. 28.

SELECT BIBLIOGRAPHY
of Secular Narrative Sources

(a) GENERAL

The bibliographies mentioned in Section A of the General Bibliography, especially HARDY and GROSS, should be consulted, and also, for the general interpretation of these records, the works on Anglo-Saxon history there mentioned, many of which include bibliographies, the best being that in F. M. STENTON, *Anglo-Saxon England*. Reference books mentioned on p. 101 above will be useful for problems of chronology and identification. In addition, recourse should be had to the following works: R. L. POOLE, *Chronicles and Annals* (Oxford, 1926); C. W. JONES, *Saints' Lives and Chronicles in Early England* (Ithaca, New York, 1947).

Collections of chronicle sources by early antiquarian scholars have been largely superseded by works provided with a modern apparatus, though mention should be made of the handsome volume, *Monumenta Historica Britannica*, edited by H. PETRIE (London, 1848), which is still useful for Florence of Worcester and is the most accessible work to include Æthelweard's chronicle. Of works containing selections of narrative sources, the most useful are R. W. CHAMBERS, *England before the Norman Conquest* (London, 1928); M. ASHDOWN, *English and Norse Documents relating to the Reign of Etheired the Unready* (Cambridge, 1930); EDWARD CONYBEARE, *Alfred in the Chroniclers* (London, 1900).

(b) THE ANGLO-SAXON CHRONICLE AND CLOSELY RELATED TEXTS

The sole edition to give the various versions of the Chronicle is *The Anglo-Saxon Chronicle*, ed. by B. THORPE (R. S., London, 1861), vol. I containing the text, vol. II a translation. The edition now most used, *Two of the Saxon Chronicles Parallel*, ed. by C. PLUMMER on the basis of an edition by J. EARLE (Oxford, I, 1892, II, 1899, reprinted 1952, with bibliographical note and note on the commencement of the year by D. Whitelock), is a complete text only of two versions, 'A' and 'E'. Neither of these editions gives the Otho version ('G'), of which the only edition is that of ABRAHAM WHELOCK, in his *Venerabilis Bedae Historia Ecclesiastica* (Cambridge, 1644). Manuscript 'F' is inadequately represented in Thorpe, and has recently been edited by F. P. MAGOUN, Jr., *Annales Domitiani Latini: an Edition* (Mediaeval Studies of the Pontifical Institute of Mediaeval Studies, IX, 1947, pp. 235–295). Separate editions of the other manuscripts are available as follows: a facsimile edition of 'A', *The Parker Chronicle and Laws*, by ROBIN FLOWER and HUGH SMITH (Early Eng. Text Soc., O.U.P., 1941); 'D' in *An Anglo-Saxon Chronicle from British Museum Cotton MS., Tiberius B. iv*, ed. by E. CLASSEN and F. E. HARMER (Manchester, 1926); 'C' in *The C-Text of the Old English Chronicles*, ed. by H. A. ROSITZKE (*Beiträge z. engl. Phil.*, XXXIV, Bochum-Langendreer, 1940). Part of 'A' is edited by A. H. SMITH, *The Parker Chronicle (832–900)* (Methuen's Old English Library, London, 2nd ed. 1939), and the reign of Ethelred from the 'C' text by M. Ashdown, *op. cit.* The best translation is by G. N. GARMONSWAY, *The Anglo-Saxon Chronicle* (Everyman's Library, 1953). The 'E' text is translated by H. A. ROSITZKE, *The Peterborough Chronicle* (New York, 1951).

Æthelweard still awaits a modern editor. As the MS. is lost, the earliest form in which we have this work is the edition by H. SAVILE, in *Rerum Anglicarum Scriptores post Bedam* (London, 1596). It is also in PETRIE, *op. cit.* Asser's *Life of King Alfred* is edited by W. H. STEVENSON (Oxford, 1904). Simeon of Durham's *Historia Regum* should be consulted in *Symeonis Monachi Opera*, ed. T. ARNOLD, II (R. S., London, 1885); the anonymous *Historia de Sancto Cuthberto*, *ibid.*, I, pp. 196–214 (1882): Roger of Wendover's *Flores Historiarum* in the edition by H. O. COXE (London, 1841); the *Continuatio Bedae* in *Venerabilis Baedae Opera Historica*, ed. C. PLUMMER,

1, pp. 361–363 (Oxford, 1896); the *Annals of St. Neots* in STEVENSON's edition of Asser; Florence of Worcester in *Florentii Wigorniensis Monachi Chronicon ex Chronicis*, ed. B. THORPE (London, 1848), and in PETRIE, *op. cit.*; William of Malmesbury's *De Gestis Regum Anglorum* in the edition by W. STUBBS (R. S., London, 1887); Hugo Candidus in *The Chronicle of Hugh Candidus, a Monk of Peterborough*, ed. W. T. MELLOWS (O.U.P., 1949). Gaimar, *Lestorie des Engles*, is edited with translation by SIR THOMAS DUFFUS HARDY and C. TRICE MARTIN (R. S., London, 1888–1889); Henry of Huntingdon's *Historia Anglorum* by T. ARNOLD (R. S., 1879), and the "Waverley Annals", by H. R. LUARD, in *Annales Monastici*, II (R. S., 1865).

Bohn's *Antiquarian Library* (London, 1847–1864) includes translations of the works of Florence of Worcester, Henry of Huntingdon, Roger of Wendover, William of Malmesbury, and, in a volume called *Six Old English Chronicles*, Æthelweard, Asser and Nennius. *The Church Historians of England*, ed. J. STEVENSON (London, 1853–1858), has translations of Florence of Worcester, Asser, Æthelweard, Gaimar, William of Malmesbury and Simeon of Durham. Asser is translated by L. C. JANE (London, 1926) and by CONYBEARE, *op. cit.*

The standard discussion of the origin and transmission of the Anglo-Saxon Chronicle is that by Plummer, as the introduction to vol. II of the above-mentioned *Two of the Saxon Chronicles Parallel*. It should be supplemented by pp. 679–684 of F. M. STENTON, *Anglo-Saxon England*; chapter 2 of H. M. CHADWICK, *The Origin of the English Nation* (Cambridge, 1907, reprinted 1924); pp. 16–24 of J. ARMITAGE ROBINSON, *The Times of St. Dunstan* (Oxford, 1923); F. M. STENTON, "The South-western Element in the Old English Chronicle" (*Essays in Medieval History presented to T. F. Tout*, Manchester, 1925), which is a most important study; SIR IVOR ATKINS, "The Origin of the Later Part of the Saxon Chronicle known as D" (*Eng. Hist. Rev.*, LV, 1940); K. JOST, "Wulfstan und die angelsächsische Chronik" (*Anglia*, XLVII, 1923); N. R. KER, "Some Notes on the Peterborough Chronicle" (*Medium Aevum*, III, 1934); F. P. MAGOUN, Jr., "The Domitian Bilingual of the *Old-English Annals*: The Latin Preface" (*Speculum*, XX, 1945) and "The Domitian Bilingual of the *Old-English Annals*: Notes on the F-text" (*Mod. Lang. Quarterly*, VI, 1945).

Of works dealing with individual parts of the Chronicle the following should be mentioned: on the genealogical tables, A. S. NAPIER, "Two Old English Fragments" (*Mod. Lang. Notes*, XII, pp. 106–114, 1897); B. DICKINS, *The Genealogical Preface to the Anglo-Saxon Chronicle* (Occasional Papers: Number II, printed for the Dept. of Anglo-Saxon, Cambridge, 1952); on annal 755, F. P. MAGOUN, Jr., "Cynewulf, Cyneheard and Osric" (*Anglia*, LVII, 1933), C. L. WRENN. "A Saga of the Anglo-Saxons" (*History*, XXV, 1940–1941); on the poems in the Chronicle, *The Battle of Brunanburh*, ed. by A. CAMPBELL (London, 1938), A. MAWER, "The Redemption of the Five Boroughs" (*Eng. Hist. Rev.*, XXXVIII, 1923), F. HOLTHAUSEN, "Zu dem ae. Gedichte von Aelfreds Tode (1036)" (*Anglia Beiblatt*, L, 1939); on the annals in the mid-tenth century, M. L. R. BEAVEN, "King Edmund I and the Danes of York" (*Eng. Hist. Rev.*, XXXIII, 1918), A. CAMPBELL, "Two Notes on the Norse Kingdoms in Northumbria" (*Eng. Hist. Rev.*, LVII, 1942).

A great number of works deal with the chronology. Besides general works mentioned above,[1] the principal are W. H. STEVENSON, "The Date of King Alfred's Death" (*Eng. Hist. Rev.*, XIII, 1898), R. L. POOLE, "The Beginning of the Year in the Anglo-Saxon Chronicles" (*ibid.*, XVI, 1901), M. L. R. BEAVEN, "The Regnal Dates of Alfred, Edward the Elder, and Athelstan" (*ibid.*, XXXII, 1917) and "The Beginning of the Year in the Alfredian Chronicle", *ibid.*, XXXIII, 1918), R. H. HODGKIN, "The Beginning of the Year in the English Chronicle" (*ibid.*, XXXIX, 1924), A. J. THOROGOOD, "The Anglo-Saxon Chronicle in the Reign of Ecgberht" (*ibid.*, XLVIII, 1933), W. S. ANGUS, "The Chronology of the Reign of Edward the Elder" (*ibid.*, LIII, 1938) and "The Eighth Scribe's Dates in the Parker Manuscript of the Anglo-Saxon Chronicle" (*Medium Aevum*, X, 1941), F. T. WAINWRIGHT, "The Chronology of the 'Mercian Register'" (*Eng. Hist. Rev.*, LX, 1945), D. WHITELOCK, "On the Commencement of the Year in the Saxon Chronicles" (Appendix to Introduction in the reprint of *Two of the Saxon Chronicles Parallel*, 1952). In two articles in *Leeds Studies in English*, VI (1937), "The

[1] p. 101.

day of Byrhtnoth's death and other obits from a twelfth-century Ely kalendar", and "The day of the battle of Æthelingadene", B. DICKINS shows how calendar evidence can supplement the knowledge drawn from chronicles.

The publications of the English Place-Name Society and E. EKWALL's *Oxford Dictionary of English Place-Names*[1] should be used to check identifications of places. Two articles dealing specifically with names in the Chronicle are A. MAWER, "Some Place-Name Identifications in the Anglo-Saxon Chronicles" (*Palaestra*, CXLVII, 1925) and F. P. MAGOUN, Jr., "Territorial, Place- and River-Names in the Old English Chronicle, A-Text" (*Harvard Stud. and Notes in Phil. and Lit.*, XVIII, 1935), D-Text (*ibid.*, XX, 1938).

The importance of Æthelweard is demonstrated by three articles by F. M. STENTON, that on "The South-western Element in the Old English Chronicle", mentioned above, "Æthelwerd's Account of the Last Years of Alfred's Reign" (*Eng. Hist. Rev.*, XXIV, 1909), and "The Danes at Thorney Island in 893" (*ibid.*, XXVII, 1912). E. E. BARKER's "The Cottonian Fragments of Æthelweard's Chronicle" (*Bulletin of the Institute of Historical Research*, XXIV, 1951), not only gives a new reading of the few surviving fragments of this work, but shows that there must once have been a continuation into Ethelred's reign. Little of value has been produced on Asser since Stevenson's edition, but G. H. WHEELER's article "Textual Emendations to Asser's Life of Alfred" (*Eng. Hist. Rev.*, XLVII, 1932) is useful.

On the post-Conquest Latin historians the chapter by W. LEWIS JONES, "Latin Chroniclers from the Eleventh to the Thirteenth Centuries", in vol. I of *The Cambridge History of English Literature* (Cambridge, 1907), may be consulted, and a modern brief study by R. R. DARLINGTON, *Anglo-Norman Historians* (Inaugural Lecture at Birkbeck College, London, 1947). Besides the introductions to the editions cited above, that to W. STUBBS's edition of Roger of Hoveden (R. S., London, 1868) is important for the work attributed to Simeon of Durham, as also is P. HUNTER BLAIR, "Symeon's History of the Kings" (*Archaeologia Aeliana*, 4th series, XVI, 1939); for Roger of Wendover, see C. JENKINS, *The Monastic Chronicler and the Early School of St. Albans* (London, 1922) and V. H. GALBRAITH, *Roger Wendover and Matthew Paris* (David Murray Lecture, Glasgow, 1944). The bearing of evidence from the anonymous *Historia de Sancto Cuthberto* is considered by F. T. WAINWRIGHT, "The Battles at Corbridge" (*Saga-Book of the Viking Soc.*, XIII, pt. III, 1949–1950), whose interpretation differs to some extent from A. CAMPBELL, "The Northumbrian Kingdom of Rægnald" (*Eng. Hist. Rev.*, LVII, 1942).

(c) THE *HISTORIA BRITTONUM*

This text is edited by T. MOMMSEN, in *Mon. Germ. Hist.*, *Auct. Ant.*, XIII, pt. I, 1894; by F. LOT, *Nennius et l'Historia Brittonum* (Bibliothèque de l'école des hautes études, fasc. 263, Paris, 1934); by H. PETRIE, *Monumenta Historica Britannica* (see p. 129). There is an English translation by A. W. WADE-EVANS, *Nennius's "History of the Britons"* together with the "*Story of the Loss of Britain*" (Church Hist. Soc., London, 1938).

In addition to the introductions to the above editions, the following should be consulted: F. LIEBERMANN, "Nennius the Author of the 'Historia Brittonum'" (*Essays in Medieval History presented to T. F. Tout*, Manchester, 1925); R. Thurneysen, "Zu Nennius (Nennius)" (*Zeitschrift für celtische Philologie*, XX, pp. 97–137, 185–191, 1933; p. 374, 1936); IFOR WILLIAMS, "Notes on Nennius" (*Bulletin of the Board of Celtic Studies*, VII, pt. IV, pp. 380–389, University of Wales, Cardiff, 1935), "The Nennian Preface: A Possible Emendation" (*ibid.*, IX, pt. IV, pp. 342–344, 1939), "Mommsen and the Vatican Nennius" (*ibid.*, XI, pt. I, pp. 43–48, 1941). The Arthurian matter is discussed by E. K. CHAMBERS, *Arthur of Britain* (London, 1927).

On the *Gododdin* poem, there is a full study for Welsh readers by IFOR WILLIAMS, *Canu Aneirin* (Cardiff, 1938). In English one may consult the same author's *Lectures on Early Welsh Poetry* (Dublin, 1944); GWYN WILLIAMS, *An Introduction to Welsh Poetry* (London, 1953); K. JACKSON, "The 'Gododdin' of Aneirin" (*Antiquity*, XIII, pp. 25–34, 1939).

[1] See p. 104.

(d) THE POEM ON THE BATTLE OF MALDON

Almost all Anglo-Saxon readers and primers include this poem, but it will be sufficient here to mention the two best editions, that of M. ASHDOWN, *op. cit.*, whose translation I have reprinted, and that of E. V. GORDON, *The Battle of Maldon* (Methuen's Old English Library, London, 1937); both these works include a bibliography. R. W. CHAMBERS prints in his *England before the Norman Conquest* a translation by W. P. KER, whose comments on the poem on pp. 54–57 of his *Epic and Romance* (London, 2nd ed. 1908) should be read. See also E. D. LABORDE, "The Style of the Battle of Maldon" (*Mod. Lang. Rev.*, XIX, 1924) and the same author's important article, "The Site of the Battle of Maldon" (*Eng. Hist. Rev.*, XL, 1925). B. S. PHILLPOTTS, "'The Battle of Maldon': Some Danish Affinities" (*Mod. Lang. Rev.*, XXIV, 1929), sees resemblances to Scandinavian poetry, but her view that the author was familiar with this has won little acceptance. E. V. GORDON, "The Date of Æthelred's Treaty with the Vikings: Olaf Tryggvason and the Battle of Maldon" (*Mod. Lang. Rev.*, XXXII, 1937), argues that the treaty belongs to 994 and cannot be used to support the presence of Olaf at the battle. On Brihtnoth, see D. WHITELOCK, *Anglo-Saxon Wills*,[1] which includes the wills of his father-in-law, sister-in-law, and widow (Nos. II, XIV, XV).

(e) THE SCANDINAVIAN SOURCES

On this subject there is a wealth of literature written in the four Scandinavian languages, both books and articles, and I can only mention a few of the most outstanding of them, and must refer the reader to the following bibliographies: those by HALLDÓR HERMANNSON in *Islandica* (Ithaca, New York), I (1908), *Bibliography of the Icelandic Sagas and Minor Tales* (with supplement, vol. XXIV, 1935), III (1910), *Bibliography of the Sagas of the Kings of Norway and related Sagas and Tales* (with supplement, vol. XXVI, 1937); and the bibliographies given in the periodicals *Acta Philologica Scandinavica* (Copenhagen) and *Arkiv för nordisk Filologi* (Lund). The standard editions of the scaldic poems are FINNUR JÓNSSON, *Den norsk-islandske Skjalde-digtning* (Copenhagen, 1908–1915), of which vols. A, I–II contain the text and variants, vols. B, I–II a normalized text and Danish translation; and a revision of this work by ERNST A. KOCK, under the title *Den norsk-isländska Skaldediktningen*, I (Lund, 1946), which embodies the results of his own *Notationes norroena*, which run through *Lunds Universitetets Årsskrift*, N.F., avd. I, XIX–XXXIV, XXXVII, XXXIX (1923–1943). Translations of the individual stanzas occur in those of the various sagas which quote them. Attention must also be drawn to N. KERSHAW, *Anglo-Saxon and Norse Poems* (Cambridge, 1922), which includes, among other poems, the *Eiríksmál*, and to M. ASHDOWN's work cited above, which has other poems besides those I have borrowed from it. *Corpus Poeticum Boreale*, II: *Court Poetry*, ed. by GUDBRAND VIGFUSSON and F. YORK POWELL (Oxford, 1883), has a spirited translation and gives a good impression of the whole corpus, but its text is out of date.

Egil's saga has been edited several times, best by FINNUR JÓNSSON, in *Altnordische sagabibliothek* (Halle, 2nd ed., 1924) and in *Samfund til Udgivelse af gammel nordisk Literatur* (Copenhagen, 1886–1888) and by S. NORDAL, in *Íslenzk fornrit* (Reykjavík, 1933); it has been translated by W. C. GREEN, *The Story of Egil Skallagrimsson* (London, 1893) and by E. R. EDDISON, *Egil's Saga* (Cambridge, 1930). The *Heimskringla*, the best-known set of sagas on the kings of Norway, is edited by FINNUR JÓNSSON (Copenhagen, 1911) and by BJARNI AÐALBJARNARSON (Reykjavík, 1945), and translated into English by WILLIAM MORRIS and EIRIKR MAGNUSSON (*The Saga Library*, III–VI, London, 1893–1905); by S. LAING in 1844, whose translation of the Olaf sagas was reissued in *Everyman's Library*, 1915, and the remaining sagas in the same series in 1930; and finally by E. MONSEN (Cambridge, 1932). *Ágrip*, a summary of the history of the Norwegian kings, is edited by FINNUR JÓNSSON (*Altnord. Saga-Bibl.*, Halle, 1929); *Fagrskinna*, by the same (Copenhagen, 1902–1903); *Jómsvíkingasaga* by C. AF PETERSENS (Lund, 1879, Copenhagen, 1882), and there is a rendering by G. W. DASENT called *The Vikings of the Baltic Lands* (London, 1875).

[1] See p. 352.

The *Knýtlinga Saga* is in vol. II of *Sögur Danakonunga*, ed. by C. AF PETERSENS and E. OLSON (Copenhagen, 1919–1925), and there is a German translation in *Thule*, XIX (Jena, 1924).

The early Latin histories of Norway, *Historia Norwegiae* and Theodric's *Historia de antiquitate regum Norwagiensium*, are both in G. STORM, *Monumenta Historica Norvegiae* (Christiania, 1880), while the Norse version of ODD SNORRASON's Latin work is in *Saga Óláfs Tryggvasonar*, ed. FINNUR JÓNSSON (Copenhagen, 1932). The best edition of Saxo Grammaticus' *Gesta Danorum* is that of J. OLRIK and H. RAEDER (Copenhagen, 1931). Unfortunately only the first nine books of this work have been translated into English, by O. ELTON (London, 1894), and these deal only with the early, heroic, material. The rather older Danish history, the *Historia Regum Daniae* of Sven Aageson is edited by J. LANGEBEK, *Scriptores Rerum Danicarum Medii Aevi*, I (Copenhagen, 1772).

The sagas edited by GUDBRAND VIGFUSSON and G. W. DASENT, with an English translation, in the Rolls Series (*Icelandic Sagas*, London, 1887–1888) are the *Orkneyinga Saga*, which is of importance for Scottish history rather than for English, and some kings' sagas which lie outside our period. *Gunnlaugssaga Ormstungu*, whose action is partly laid in England, and which is edited by GUÐNI JÓNSSON (Reykjavík, 1934) and by L. M. SMALL (Kendal, 1935), is well known from WILLIAM MORRIS's translation in *Three Northern Love Stories* (London, 1875, 1901).

There are good accounts of historical writing in Scandinavia by G. TURVILLE-PETRE, *The Heroic Age of Scandinavia* (Hutchinson's University Library, London, 1951) and *Origins of Icelandic Literature* (Oxford, 1953); and W. P. KER, "The Early Historians of Norway" (*Saga-Book of the Viking Soc.*, VI, 1910, reprinted in *Collected Essays*, II, 1925). Several books on the sagas are available in English, including W. A. CRAIGIE, *The Icelandic Sagas* (Cambridge Manuals of Science and Literature, 1913), B. S. PHILLPOTTS, *Edda and Saga* (Home University Library, London, 1931), H. KOHT, *The Old Norse Sagas* (New York, 1931). Of more detailed accounts, and studies on the relation between the different texts, the following are important: FINNUR JÓNSSON, *Den islandske litteraturs historie* (Copenhagen, 1907, latest edition, 1920–1924); J. DE VRIES, *Altnordische Literaturgeschichte*, I–II (Berlin and Leipzig, 1941–1942); J. HELGASON, *Norrøn Litteraturhistorie* (Copenhagen, 1934); S. NORDAL, *Om Olaf den Helliges Saga* (Copenhagen, 1914); J. SCHREINER, *Saga og oldfunn: Studier til Norges eldste historie* (Skrifter utgitt av Det Norske Videnskaps-Akademi i Oslo. II, Hist. filol. Klasse, 1927, No. 4); BJARNI AÐALBJARNSSON, *Om de norske kongers sagaer* (ibid., 1936, No. 4); A. CAMPBELL, "Knúts Saga" (*Saga-Book of the Viking Soc.*, XIII, pt. IV, 1950–1951) which summarizes and assesses G. ALBECK's *Knytlinga: Sagaerne om Danmarks Konger* (Copenhagen, 1946). On Saxo, see C. WEIBULL, *Saxo* (Lund, 1915) and E. JØRGENSEN in *Dansk Biografisk Leksikon*, XX (ed. S. DAHL and P. ENGELTOFT, 1941).

There is a good general introduction to scaldic poetry by L. M. HOLLANDER, *The Skalds* (New York, 1945), and the technique is described by M. ASHDOWN, *op. cit.*, pp. 255–272, and by E. V. GORDON, *An Introduction to Old Norse* (Oxford, 1927), pp. xxxix–xliv, 295–297.

Much of the discussion on the reliability of the saga evidence, and on the interpretation of various texts, is in the Scandinavian languages. Thus the work that threw doubt on the existence of a viking community at *Jómsborg* of the type described in the sagas is in Swedish, L. WEIBULL, *Kritiska undersökningar i Nordens historia omkring år 1000* (Lund, 1911), but the question is discussed by S. H. CROSS, "Scandinavian-Polish relations in the late Tenth Century" (*Studies in honor of Hermann Collitz*, Baltimore, 1930). The arguments in S. NORDAL's *Hrafnkatla*, by which he demonstrated the historical inaccuracy and fictitious nature of a saga which had been regarded as based on genuine tradition, are made accessible to English readers by GWYN JONES, "History and Fiction in the Sagas of the Icelanders" (*Saga-Book of the Viking Soc.*, XIII, pt. V, 1952–1953). The dangers of trusting too much to Scandinavian tradition are illustrated by A. CAMPBELL, "Saxo Grammaticus and Scandinavian Historical Tradition" (*Saga-Book of the Viking Soc.*, XIII, pt. I, 1946) and "The Opponents of Haraldr Hárfagri at Hársfjörðr" (ibid., XII, pt. IV, 1942), as well as in the same writer's *Battle of Brunanburh* and *Encomium Emmae Reginae*. Legends[1] that collected round the invasion of 865–878 are conveniently discussed by A. H. SMITH, "The Sons of Ragnar Lothbrok" (*Saga-Book of the Viking Soc.*, XI, pt. II, 1935).

[1] See also J. HELGASON, *op. cit.*, pp. 120–130.

(f) CONTINENTAL SOURCES

As these only occasionally concern English affairs, a lengthy bibliography would be out of place. The following works can be consulted on the various authors: W. WATTENBACH, *Deutschlands Geschichtsquellen im Mittelalter* (6th edit., Berlin, 1893–1894, I, ed. E. Dümmler, Stuttgart and Berlin, 1904), which is being re-edited; the first part by W. LEVISON, *Die Vorzeit von den Anfängen bis zur Herrschaft der Karolinger* (Weimar, 1952), and the second, by H. LÖWE, *Die Karolinger vom Anfang des 8 Jahrhunderts bis zum Tode Karls des Grossen* (Weimar, 1953), have appeared; A. MOLINIER, *Les Sources de l'Histoire de France*, I (Paris, 1901); M. MANITIUS, *Geschichte der lateinischen Literatur des Mittelalters*, I and II (Munich, 1911–1923); M. L. W. LAISTNER, *Thought and Letters in Western Europe A.D. 500 to 900* (London, 1931). For a general account of the period, see J. M. WALLACE-HADRILL, *The Barbarian West, 400–1000* (Hutchinson's University Library, London, 1952); F. LOT, C. PFISTER and F. L. GANSHOF, *Histoire du Moyen Age* (Paris, I, 2nd edit., 1940, II, 1941); and the relevant chapters in the *Cambridge Medieval History*, II (1913), III (1922). There is an important article by P. GRIERSON on "Relations between England and Flanders before the Norman Conquest" (*Trans. Royal Hist. Soc.*, 4th Series, XXIII, 1941). Further bibliographical help is afforded by J. L. A. CALMETTE, *Le Monde Féodal* (New edit., by C. HIGOUNET, Clio 4, Paris, 1951); and L. J. PAETOW, *A Guide to the Study of Medieval History* (Med. Acad. of America, revised edit., New York, 1931).

In addition to the introductions to the various editions cited before the individual texts, the following special studies may be mentioned: F. LOT, *Études critiques sur l'abbaye de Saint-Wandrille* (Bibliothèque de l'école des hautes Études, fasc. 204, 1913); W. LEVISON, "Zu den Gesta abbatum Fontanellensium" (*Revue Bénédictine*, XLVI, 1934) now available in his collected essays, *Aus Rheinischer und Fränkischer Frühzeit* (Düsseldorf, 1948); L. HALPHEN, *Études critiques sur l'histoire de Charlemagne* (Paris, 1921), which discusses the relationships between the annals; O. HOLDER-EGGER, "Zu Folcwin von St. Bertin" (*Neues Archiv*, VI, Hanover, 1881).

I. The Anglo-Saxon Chronicle (60 B.C.–A.D. 1042)

Plan of the present edition

The Anglo-Saxon Chronicle is a complicated record. It is not the aim of this edition to set out in full all the textual variants, for it would be impossible in a translation to make clear the transmission of the text, which can be fully seen only from the Old English texts, and to attempt to do so would only detract from the use of the translation to historians. What is aimed at is an arrangement to make it easier for the reader to distinguish the information common to all or several manuscripts from those additions peculiar to single versions. To have set out in columns (or otherwise) all the manuscripts would not only have entailed a great amount of useless repetition, but, what is more serious, would have obscured from the reader what a lot is common to all or most versions. Where matter is essentially the same in many versions, it is given once only, with significant variations at the foot of the page; but where there are important entries in single versions, use is made of an arrangement in two or more columns. Post-Conquest additions of no importance for pre-Conquest history, such as the Canterbury additions in 'A' and 'F', or the Peterborough additions to 'E', are not included, unless there is reason to believe that they are drawn from pre-Conquest sources and thus have an importance for Anglo-Saxon history.

Unfortunately, the nature of this record varies so greatly in different sections that it is not feasible to adopt precisely the same arrangement throughout. In the sections from 814 to 900, 986 to 1018, the versions are so closely in unison that it is possible to give one only; but from the beginning to 806, the additions made in the tenth century in the northern recension are so important that an arrangement in columns is necessary; again, during most of the tenth century, and from 1019 till the end in 1042, the individual manuscripts have annals of too great importance for them to be relegated to footnotes, and therefore they are set out separately in columns. But even in these periods of greatest divergence, there are passages common to all surviving manuscripts. This common stock can easily be distinguished here from the annals peculiar to single versions, because it reads straight across the page without any distinguishing letter before the date. The basis chosen for this common stock is manuscript 'C', for the earlier manuscripts 'A' and 'B' come to an end too soon; but where these have better readings, this is put in the text, with a footnote to draw attention to it. 'D' is chosen as the better version of the northern recension, though one has to depend on 'E' at the point where a gathering has been lost from 'D'. In the headings, the manuscript which has been taken as the basis is put first; *e.g.* C (A, B) means that the annal is in these three versions, but the translation is based on 'C'.

A further complication is caused by the Mercian Register, a series of consecutive annals from 902 to 924 which 'B' and 'C' insert in a block quite arbitrarily after a set of blank annals perhaps extending to 919, while the compiler of 'D' tries to dovetail them into the main Chronicle. He is not very successful, however, and I have therefore placed each annal beside that of the same year in the main Chronicle. For it seems to me that this is most convenient for the reader wishing to compare these two complementary sources for Edward the Elder's reign.

The date in the left-hand margin is the actual date of the events described,[1] wherever it can be ascertained, so that the reader is relieved of the necessity of correcting chronological dislocations in the manuscripts. Where the date in any manuscript differs from the date in the margin, it is placed in brackets at the beginning of the annal. It may be assumed that a manuscript not mentioned to have a different date has the true one, except in the case of 'B', which usually has no dates at all. My dates for 'C' often differ from those in Thorpe, for I give the original dating, recovered in some places by ultra-violet ray. I give the original, and not the corrected, dates of 'A'.

'G'[2] has mainly been ignored, as being only a late copy of 'A', and similarly I have rarely

[1] Except for the annals taken from an epitome of world history, which are not concerned with English history.   [2] Brit. Mus. Cott. Otho B. xi.

troubled to note the readings and omissions of 'F', for this alone would have required a bulky set of footnotes of no practical value for my purpose – to make accessible the historical information for Anglo-Saxon times contained in the Chronicle. The question what the compiler of 'F' considered important enough to extract has its own interest, but no bearing on this issue. Hence his readings are usually given only when they shed light on the condition of the archetype of 'E'. Minor variations, obvious errors and accidental omissions in texts not used as the base of the translations have frequently been ignored, as too heavy a critical apparatus would defeat the purpose of this volume.

In the footnotes I have referred to passages in Latin writers who had access to copies of the Chronicle now lost. I have sometimes quoted such passages in full. But by the time we reach the reign of Cnut the additional material in Florence of Worcester, whether derived from a lost version of the Chronicle or not, has become too bulky and important to be treated in this way, and is therefore given in full later in the volume, as also are those parts of Simeon of Durham and other writers which depend on northern annals, some of which were accessible to the compiler of the northern recension of the Chronicle. From time to time, it has also been necessary to refer in the footnotes to other sources of information necessary for the elucidation of passages in the Chronicle.

Preface to manuscripts 'A' and (probably) 'B'

[The regnal list and genealogy prefixed to the Chronicle in 'A' exists elsewhere as a separate work. A fragment from the second half of the ninth century (British Museum Additional MS. 23211) is printed by Sweet, *The Oldest English Texts*, p. 179, to which I refer in the following notes as Sw. On the other versions of this text, see Napier in *Mod. Lang. Notes*, XII, pp. 106–114; B. Dickins, *The Genealogical Preface to the Anglo-Saxon Chronicle*.

A single leaf, now folio 178 Brit. Mus. Cott. Tiber. A. iii (called β by Plummer), is generally held to have originally formed the introduction to 'B'. It is printed at pp. 232–233 of Thorpe's edition of the Chronicle. It was presumably written in the reign of Edward the Martyr, for it brings the regnal list up to that point, and does not add the length of his reign. It is not a copy of 'A', for its variant readings are sometimes supported by Sw. The scribe of 'A' seems himself to be responsible for some alterations that bring the information given in the genealogies and list more into line with that in the first paragraph and in the annals themselves. The writer of β seems to have been content to let some of the discrepancies stand.

I give the text of 'A' as far as it goes, calling attention to the variants in Sw. and β; and I then subjoin the continuation to the reign of Edward the Martyr in β.]

In the year when 494[1] years had passed from Christ's birth, Cerdic and his son Cynric landed at *Cerdicesora* with five ships; and Cerdic was the son of Elesa, the son of Esla, the son of Gewis, the son of Wig, the son of Freawine, the son of Frithugar, the son of Brond, the son of Bældæg, the son of Woden.

And six years[2] after they had landed they conquered the kingdom of the West Saxons, and they were the first kings who conquered the land of the West Saxons from the Britons. And he held the kingdom for 16 years, and when he died, his son Cynric succeeded to the kingdom and held it [for 26 years. When he died, his son Ceawlin succeeded and held it][3] for 17[4] years. When he died, Ceol succeeded to the kingdom, and held it for six[5] years. When he died, his brother Ceolwulf succeeded and he reigned 17 years, and their descent goes back to Cerdic. Then Cynegils, the son of Ceolwulf's brother, succeeded to the kingdom and reigned 31[6] years, and he was the first of the kings of the West Saxons to receive baptism. And then Cenwealh succeeded, and held it for 31 years, and Cenwealh was Cynegils's son. And then his

---

[1] The annals date this 495.
[2] Æthelweard's version dated the conquest of Wessex, six years after the landing, 500.
[3] From β, the omission in 'A' being clearly accidental.
[4] All MSS. place his accession in 560 and his expulsion 592.
[5] Five, β.   [6] Twenty, β, but 31 in the text of annal 611, all MSS.

queen Seaxburh held the kingdom for a year after him. Then Æscwine, whose descent goes back to Cerdic, succeeded to the kingdom, and held it for two years. Then Centwine, the son of Cynegils, succeeded to the kingdom of the West Saxons and reigned for seven[1] years. Then Ceadwalla, whose descent goes back to Cerdic, succeeded to the kingdom and held it for three years. Then Ine, whose descent goes back to Cerdic, succeeded to the kingdom of the [West][2] Saxons and held it for 37 years. Then Æthelheard, whose descent goes back to Cerdic, succeeded and held it for 14 years.[3] Then Cuthred, whose descent goes back to Cerdic, succeeded and held it 17 years. Then Sigebriht, whose descent goes back to Cerdic, succeeded and held it one year. Then Cynewulf, whose descent goes back to Cerdic, succeeded to the kingdom and held it 31 years. Then Brihtric, whose descent goes back to Cerdic, succeeded to the kingdom, and held it 16 years. Then Egbert succeeded to the[4] kingdom and held it for 37 years and seven months; and then his son Æthelwulf succeeded and held it for 18 and a half years.

Æthelwulf was the son of Egbert, the son of Ealhmund, the son of Eafa, the son of Eoppa, the son of Ingild, the son of Cenred. And Ine was the son of Cenred, and Cuthburh the daughter of Cenred, and Cwenburh the daughter of Cenred.[5] Cenred was the son of Ceolwold, the son of Cuthwulf, the son of Cuthwine, the son of Ceawlin,[6] the son of Cynric,[7] the son of Cerdic.

And then his son Æthelbald succeeded to the kingdom and held it for five years. Then his brother Ethelbert succeeded and held it for five years. Then their[8] brother Ethelred succeeded to the kingdom and held it for five years.[9] Then their brother Alfred succeeded

A (Sw.)	β
to the kingdom, and then 23 years of his life were passed, and 396 years[10] from when his race first conquered the land of the West Saxons from the Britons.	and held it one and a half years less than thirty. Then Edward, son of Alfred, succeeded, and held it for 24 years. When he died, his son Athelstan succeeded and held it for 14 years, seven weeks and three days. Then his brother Edmund succeeded and held it for six and a half years all but two days. Then his brother Eadred succeeded and held it for nine years and six weeks. Then Eadwig, the son of King Edmund, succeeded and held it for three years and 36 weeks, all but two days. When he died, his brother Edgar succeeded and held it for 16 years, eight weeks and two days. When he died, Edward, Edgar's son, succeeded and held it . . .[11]

[1] Nine, corrected from eight, β.   [2] From β.

[3] Sixteen, β. In the annals 'A' dates his reign 728–741, the other MSS. 726–740.

[4] At this point the fragment Sw. begins.

[5] This whole sentence does not occur in the fragment Sw.

[6] 'A' and β have Celm, a misreading of Celin, an Anglian form of the name Ceawlin. Sw. has Ceaulin.

[7] Both β and Sw. have another link here, adding the name of Crioda (Creoda) as father of Cynric and son of Cerdic. 'A' has brought the genealogy into line with its first paragraph, and with the annals. Similarly 'A' omits Creoda from the genealogy given in annal 855 below.   [8] His, Sw.

[9] β omits this sentence.

[10] This figure must be wrong. Whether we reckon from the conquest of Wessex, i.e. 500, as given above, or from the 'Coming of the English' in 449, we do not arrive at the year of Alfred's accession, 871.

[11] β breaks off here.

Preface to manuscripts D, E *and* F

[It is not possible to know whether the version of the Chronicle which reached the North contained the genealogical preface found in 'A' and originally in 'B'. If it did, the writer who added to the annals a lot of new matter, drawn from Bede and northern annals, preferred to substitute the following preface, which is based on Bede's *Ecclesiastical History*, Book I, chapter 1.]

The island of Britain is 800 miles long and 200 miles broad, and here in the island there are five languages, English, British, Scottish,[1] Pictish and Latin. At first the inhabitants of this island were Britons, who came from Armenia[2] and first occupied southern Britain. Then it happened that the Picts came from the south, from Scythia,[3] with a few warships, and landed first in North Ireland. They asked the Scots to allow them to dwell there, but they would not permit them, for they said that they could not all dwell there together. And then the Scots said: "We can, however, give you advice. We know of another island, east from here, where you can settle if you wish; and if anyone resists you, we will help you to conquer it." The Picts then went away and conquered the north of this land, the Britons, as we have said before, holding the south. The Picts asked for wives from the Scots, [receiving them] on condition that they should always choose their royal line on the female side,[4] and they kept to this for a long time afterwards. Then it happened in the passage of years that a certain portion of the Scots came from Ireland to Britain and conquered a part of the land, and their leader was called Reoda, and from him they are named the people of Dal Riada.[5]

C (B, A)	D (E)
Sixty years before Christ's incarnation, the emperor, Gaius Julius, came to Britain, as the first of the Romans, and defeated the Britons by a battle and overcame them, and nevertheless could not win the kingdom there.	Sixty years before Christ was born, Gaius Julius, emperor of the Romans, came to Britain with 80 ships. There at first he was harassed with cruel fighting and he led to destruction a great part of his army. Then he let his army remain among the Scots and went south to Gaul and collected there 600 ships, with which he returned to Britain. And in the first clash, the emperor's reeve, who was called Labienus, was killed. Then the Britons held the ford of a certain river and staked it all with stout sharp posts below water. That river is called the Thames. When the Romans discovered that, they would not cross the ford. Then the Britons fled to the wild woodlands,[6] and the emperor took very many chief towns, with much fighting, and returned to Gaul.

[1] As in Bede and all texts before the tenth century, the words Scots and Scottish usually refer to the inhabitants of Ireland, though sometimes the Irish colony in the west of Scotland is meant.

[2] This arose from a misreading of Bede's *Armoricano*, *i.e.* Brittany.

[3] Bede does not place Scythia in the south, and in one place seems to use it of Scandinavia.

[4] A legend that has grown up to explain the Pictish matriarchal system of succession.

[5] Approximately equivalent to the modern Argyle.

[6] 'E', "the wood-fastnesses".

C (A, B, D, E)

1 Octavian reigned 66 years and in the 52nd[1] year of his reign Christ was born.

2 The three astrologers came from the East in order to worship Christ, and the children in Bethlehem were slain because of the persecution of Christ by Herod.

3 (4 C; 2 E) In this year Herod died, stabbed by his own hand, and his son Archelaus succeeded to the kingdom.

6 (7 C; 11 E) Five thousand and two hundred years had passed from the beginning of the world to this year.[2]

12 Philip and Herod divided Lycia and Judea into tetrarchies.

16 (15 C) In this year Tiberius succeeded to the throne.

26 (25 C; 27 A[3]) In this year Pilate obtained the rule over the Jews.

30 (29 C) In this year Christ was baptized, and Peter and Andrew converted, and James and John and Philip and the twelve Apostles.

33 In this year Christ was crucified, five thousand two hundred and twenty-six years from the beginning of the world.

34 In this year St. Paul was converted and St. Stephen stoned.

35 In this year the blessed Apostle Peter occupied the see of the city of Antioch.

39 In this year Gaius succeeded to the throne.

44 (45 A, D, E) In this year the blessed Apostle Peter occupied the see of Rome.

45 (46 A, D, E) In this year died Herod, who had killed James one year before his own death.

	C (A, B)	D (E)
47	In this year Claudius came to Britain, the second of the kings of the Romans to do so, and obtained the	In this year Claudius, king of the Romans, went with an army into Britain, and conquered the island and subjected all the Picts and Britons to the power of the Romans. He fought this war in the

[1] Forty-second in 'B', 'D', 'E', corrections in 'A'; 62nd 'G'.
[2] An annal on the accession in 11 of Herod, son of Antipater, was added to 'A' at Canterbury.
[3] This annal in 'A' is a Canterbury addition.

C (A, B)	D (E)
greater part under his control, and likewise subjected the island of Orkney to the rule of the Romans.	fourth year of his reign. And in that year occurred the great famine in Syria, which was foretold in the Acts of the Apostles by the prophet Agabus.[1] Then after Claudius Nero succeeded to the throne, who finally abandoned the island of Britain because of his sloth.

F47 Mark the Evangelist begins to write the gospel in Egypt.
48 In this year was a very severe famine.
49 In this year Nero began to rule.
50 In this year Paul was sent to Rome in chains.

62 In this year James the brother of the Lord suffered martyrdom.

63 In this year Mark the Evangelist died.

69 (68 D) In this year Peter and Paul suffered martyrdom.

70 In this year Vespasian succeeded to the throne.

71 In this year Titus, Vespasian's son, killed 111,000 Jews in Jerusalem.

81 In this year Titus succeeded to the throne–he who said that he lost the day on which he did no good act.[2]

83 (84 D, E) In this year Domitian, Titus's brother, succeeded to the throne.

85 (87 A, D, E; 84 F) In this year John the Evangelist wrote the book of the Apocalypse on the island of Patmos.

100 (99 A[3]) In this year the Apostle Simon was hanged and on that day John the Evangelist went to his rest in Ephesus.

101[3] In this year Pope Clement died.

110 (109 C) In this year Bishop Ignatius suffered martyrdom.

F116 In this year the Emperor Hadrian began to reign.
137 In this year Antoninus began to reign.

D (E)

155   In this year Marcus Antonius and his brother
                         Aurelianus[4] succeeded to the throne.

---

[1] This last sentence was copied into 'A' in a modified form at Canterbury in the eleventh century.
[2] Almost identical words are used of Titus in King Alfred's translation of Orosius (ed. Sweet, p. 264).
[3] In 'A' these annals are Canterbury additions.   [4] Aurelius, 'E'.

C (A, B)   D (E)

167 In this year Eleu-   In this year Eleutherius received the bishopric of Rome
therius received the   and held it with honour for 15 years. To him Lucius,
bishopric of Rome   king of the Britons, sent men and asked for baptism,
and held it gloriously   and he at once sent it to him. And they afterwards
for 15 years. To him   remained in the true faith until Diocletian's reign.[1]
Lucius, king of Bri-
tain, sent letters ask-
ing that he might be
made Christian, and
he carried out what
he asked.

189 In this year Severus   In this year Severus succeeded to the throne and
succeeded to the   journeyed with an army to Britain and conquered a
throne, and he ruled   great part of the island by fighting, and then made a wall
for 17 years. He en-   of turves, with a palisade on top, from sea to sea, as a
closed the land of   protection for the Britons. He ruled 17 years and then
Britain with a dike   died in York. His son Bassianus succeeded to the throne.[2]
from sea to sea.   His other son, who perished, was called Geta.[3]

F200 In this year the Holy Cross was found.

E

286   In this year St. Alban suffered martyrdom.

F343 In this year St. Nicholas died.

C (A, B)   E

379   In this year Gratian succeeded to the throne.

381 In this year the em-   (380) In this year Maximus succeeded to the throne. He
peror Maximus[4] suc-   was born in the land of Britain and he went from there
ceeded to the throne.   into Gaul and there he killed the emperor Gratian and
He was born in the   drove his brother, who was called Valentinian, from his
land of Britain, and   homeland. And Valentinian again collected a force and
he went from there   killed Maximus and succeeded to the throne. In those
into Gaul.[5]   times the heresy of Pelagius arose throughout the world.

410 (409) In this year   (409) In this year Rome was destroyed by the Goths,
the Goths stormed   eleven hundred and ten years after it was built. Then
Rome and the Ro-   after that the kings of the Romans no longer reigned in
mans never after-   Britain. Altogether they had reigned there 470 years
wards reigned in   since Gaius Julius first came to the land.
Britain.[6]

---

[1] The last sentence was added in 'A' at Canterbury.
[2] The last two sentences were added to 'A' in Canterbury.
[3] From this point there is a gap in 'D' until 693.   [4] Maximianus 'A'.
[5] The rest of the annal in 'A' is a Canterbury addition, and is exactly as in 'E'.
[6] A Canterbury addition in 'A' continues the annal as in 'E'.

418 In this year the Romans collected all the treasures which were in Britain, and hid some in the ground, so that no one could find them afterwards, and took some with them into Gaul.

C (A, B)	E
423	In this year Theodosius the younger succeeded to the throne.
430 In this year Bishop Palladius was sent by Pope Celestine to the Scots, that he might strengthen their faith.	In this year Patrick[1] was sent by Pope Celestine to preach baptism to the Scots.
443	In this year the Britons sent across the sea to Rome and begged for help against the Picts, but they got none there, for the Romans were engaged in a campaign against Attila, king of the Huns. And they then sent to the Angles, and made the same request of the chieftains the English.

F444 In this year St. Martin died.

448 In this year John the Baptist revealed his head in the place which once was Herod's dwelling to two monks who had come from the east to pray in Jerusalem.

449 In this year Mauritius[2] and Valentinus succeeded to the throne and ruled for seven years.

C (A, B)	E
In their days Hengest and Horsa, invited by Vortigern, king of the Britons, came to Britain at the place which is called Ebbsfleet, first to the help of the Britons, but afterwards fought against them.[3]	And in their days Vortigern invited the English hither, and they then came in three ships to Britain at the place Ebbsfleet. King Vortigern gave them land in the southeast of this land on condition that they should fight against the Picts. They then fought against the Picts and had the victory wherever they came. They then sent to Angeln, bidding them send more help, and had them informed of the cowardice of the Britons and the excellence of the land. They then immediately sent hither a greater force to the help of the others. Those men came from three tribes of Germany; from the Old Saxons, from the Angles, from the Jutes. From the Jutes came

---

[1] In the absence of 'D', it is unknown how early this change was made. 'F' has Palladius, but may have taken it from 'A', where "or Patricius" is written over Palladius by the Canterbury glossator.

[2] 'A', 'B', 'C' only. 'D', 'E' have correctly Martianus, and this has been added in 'A', above Mauritius, at Canterbury.

[3] There follows a long Canterbury addition in 'A', much as in 'E'.

E

the people of Kent and of the Isle of Wight, namely the
tribe which now inhabits the Isle of Wight and that race
in Wessex which is still called the race of the Jutes. From
the Old Saxons came the East Saxons, the South Saxons
and the West Saxons. From Angeln, which afterwards
remained waste, between the Jutes and the Saxons, came
the East Angles, the Middle Angles, the Mercians and
all the Northumbrians. Their leaders were two brothers,
Hengest and Horsa, who were sons of Wihtgils. Wihtgils was the son of Witta, the son of Wecta, the son of
Woden. From that Woden has descended all our royal
family, and that of the Southumbrians also.[1]

455 In this year Hengest and Horsa fought against King Vortigern at the place which
is called *Ægelesthrep*, and his brother Horsa was killed there; and after that
Hengest and his son Æsc succeeded to the kingdom.

456 (457 A) In this year Hengest and his son Æsc fought against the Britons in the
place which is called *Creacanford*[2] and killed 4,000[3] men; and the Britons then
deserted Kent and fled with great fear to London.

465 (461 B, C; 466 F) In this year Hengest and Æsc fought against the Britons near
Wippedesfleot, and there slew twelve British chiefs, and a thegn[4] of theirs was
slain there whose name was Wipped.

473 In this year Hengest and Æsc fought against the Britons and captured countless
spoils and the Britons fled from the English as from fire.[5]

477 In this year Ælle and his three sons, Cymen, Wlencing and Cissa, came into
Britain with three ships at the place which is called *Cymenesora*,[6] and there they
killed many Britons and drove some into flight into the wood which is called
Andredeslea.[7]

F482 In this year the blessed Abbot Benedict shone with the glory of virtues
for the benefit of this world, as the blessed Gregory relates in the book
of 'Dialogues'.

485 In this year Ælle fought against the Britons near the bank of *Mearcredesburna*.

---

[1] A clear indication that this addition was made in Northumbria.
[2] *Crecganford* 'A', 'E'. Neither form fits the common identification with Crayford.
[3] 'E', 'F': "four troops".
[4] This word supplied from 'A', 'E', 'F'. It is accidentally omitted in 'B', 'C'.
[5] Instead, 'E' has "very grievously".
[6] A place now covered by the sea, south of Selsea Bill.   [7] The Weald.

488 In this year Æsc succeeded to the kingdom and was king of the people of Kent for 24 years.

491 (490 F) In this year Ælle and Cissa besieged *Andredesceaster*,[1] and killed all who were inside, and there was not even a single Briton left alive.

495 In this year two chieftains,[2] Cerdic and his son Cynric, came with five ships to Britain at the place which is called *Cerdicesora*, and they fought against the Britons on the same day.[3]

501 In this year Port and his two sons Bieda and Mægla came to Britain with two ships at the place which is called Portsmouth;[4] and there they killed a [young][5] British man of very high rank.

508 In this year Cerdic and Cynric killed a British king, whose name was Natanleod, and 5,000 men with him. Then the land right up to Charford was called Netley after him.

F508 In this year St. Benedict the abbot, father of all monks, went to heaven.

---

514 In this year the West Saxons came into Britain with three ships at the place which is called *Cerdicesora*; and Stuf and Wihtgar fought against the Britons and put them to flight.

519 In this year Cerdic and Cynric succeeded to the kingdom;[6] and in the same year they fought against the Britons at a place called Charford.[7]

527 In this year Cerdic and Cynric fought against the Britons in the place which is called *Cerdicesleag*.[8]

530 In this year Cerdic and Cynric captured the Isle of Wight and killed a few[9] men in *Wihtgarabyrig*.

[1] The Roman *Anderida*, near Pevensey.
[2] 'Ealdormen', but it is uncertain whether the chronicler is using it in its technical sense.
[3] Æthelweard adds, "and finally were victorious", and then gives an important annal that was probably in his text of the Chronicle: "In the sixth year after their arrival they conquered the western part of Britain which is now called Wessex."
[4] 'E' adds: "and immediately seized the land".
[5] 'B', 'C' omit 'young'.
[6] 'E' and additions to 'A' add: "of the West Saxons".
[7] 'E' and additions to 'A' add: "and princes of the West Saxons ruled from that day onwards".
[8] 'E', erroneously, has Charford.
[9] This was the original reading of 'A', as well as of 'B', 'C' and Æthelweard. 'E' and additions to 'A' wrongly have 'many'.

534 In this year Cerdic died; and his son Cynric ruled for 27[1] years. And they gave the Isle of Wight to their two kinsmen,[2] Stuf and Wihtgar.

538 In this year there was an eclipse of the sun on 16 February from daybreak until nine o'clock in the morning.

540 In this year there was an eclipse of the sun on 20 June, and stars were visible for nearly half an hour after nine o'clock in the morning.

544 In this year Wihtgar died and he was buried in *Wihtgarabyrig*.

547 In this year Ida, from whom the royal family of the Northumbrians took its rise, succeeded to the kingdom.

C (B *and originally* A)

Ida was the son of Eoppa, the son of Esa, the son of Ingui, the son of Angenwit, the son of Aloc, the son of Benoc, the son of Brand, the son of Bældæg, the son of Woden, the son of Freotholaf,[3] the son of Freothowulf, the son of Finn, the son of Godulf, the son of Geat.

E

And he reigned twelve years; and he built Bamburgh, which was first enclosed with a hedge and afterwards with a wall.

552 In this year Cynric fought against the Britons in the place which is called Salisbury,[4] and put the Britons to flight.[5] Cerdic was Cynric's father. Cerdic was the son of Elesa, the son of Esla, the son of Gewis, the son of Wig, the son of Freawine, the son of Freothogar, the son of Brand, the son of Bældæg, the son of Woden.

556 In this year Cynric and Ceawlin fought against the Britons at Barbury.[6]

560 (559 F) In this year Ceawlin succeeded to the kingdom in Wessex and Ælle to the kingdom of the Northumbrians,

C (B, *originally* A)

and held it for 30 years. Ælle was the son of Yffe, the son of Uscfrea, the son of Wilgils, the son of Westerfalca, the son of Sæfugel, the son of Sæbald, the son of Sigegeat, the son of Swefdæg, the son of Sigegar, the son of Wægdæg, the son of Woden.

E

Ida having died; and each of them ruled for 30 years.

---

[1] This is the number in 'B', 'C', 'F' and Æthelweard. 'A' and 'E' have 26.

[2] The word used can mean both 'grandsons' and 'nephews', and would describe the relationship to both Cerdic and Cynric, if, for example, Stuf and Wihtgar were Cerdic's daughter's sons.

[3] 'A', judging by its copy in 'G', omitted this link. The genealogy was erased from 'A' later.

[4] It is believed that references to *Searoburh* apply to Old Sarum, rather than the present Salisbury.

[5] 'E' omits the genealogy. 'F' has the first clause of this annal followed by a mutilated entry of the birth of Ethelbert of Kent.   [6] Barbury Castle, Wilts.

C (B, originally A)

E

565 In this year the priest Columba came from Ireland to Britain, to instruct the Picts, and built a monastery on the island of Iona.

In this year Ethelbert succeeded to the kingdom of the people of Kent[1] and held it for 53 years. In his days Gregory sent us baptism. And the priest Columba came to the Picts and converted them to the faith of Christ. They are the dwellers[2] north of the moors. And their king gave him the island which is called Iona, where, by what men say, there are five hides. There this Columba built a monastery, and he was abbot there 32 years, and died there when he was 77. His heirs still hold that place. The South Picts had been baptized a long time before. Bishop Ninian had preached baptism to them. He was educated in Rome, and his church and monastery is at Whithorn, dedicated in St. Martin's name, and he lies buried there with many holy men. Now in Iona there must always be an abbot, not a bishop, and all the bishops of the Scots must be subject to him, for Columba was an abbot, not a bishop.

C (A, B, E, F)

568 In this year Ceawlin and Cutha[3] fought against Ethelbert, and drove him in flight into Kent, and killed[4] two ealdormen, Oslaf[5] and Cnebba, at *Wibbandun*.

C (A, B, E)

571 In this year Cuthwulf[6] fought against the Britons at *Biedcanford*,[7] and captured four towns, Limbury, Aylesbury, Bensington and Eynsham; and in the same year he died.[8]

577 In this year Cuthwine and Ceawlin fought against the Britons and killed three kings, Conmail, Condidan and Farinmail, at the place which is called Dyrham; and they captured three of their cities, Gloucester, Cirencester and Bath.

E

583

In this year Mauricius[9] succeeded to the rule of the Romans.

584 In this year Ceawlin and Cutha fought against the Britons at the place which is called *Fethanleag*,[10] and Cutha was killed there; and Ceawlin captured many villages and countless spoils,[11] and in anger returned to his own land.

[1] Bede dates his accession 560: 53 is an error for 56. See p. 148, n. 9.

[2] The unusual word, *wærteres*, used here seems to be taken from the place-name which occurs in Simeon of Durham in the form *Wertermorum*. See p. 252.   [3] 'F' adds: "Ceawlin's brother".

[4] This word omitted by 'B' and 'C', supplied from 'A', 'E' and 'F'.   [5] Oslac, 'E' and 'F'.

[6] Cutha, 'E'.   [7] The form of the name is against identification with Bedford.

[8] 'E' adds: "This Cutha was Ceawlin's brother."

[9] 582 is the date usually given for the accession of the eastern emperor, Mauricius Flavius Tiberius.

[10] A place of this name is mentioned in a twelfth-century document relating to Stoke Lyne in north-east Oxfordshire.   [11] 'E' omits the rest of the annal.

588 In this year King Ælle died and Æthelric reigned after him for five years.

591 In this year Ceol[1] reigned for five[2] years.

<table>
<tr><td></td><td>E</td></tr>
</table>

592   In this year Gregory succeeded to the papacy at Rome.[3]
And
In this year there occurred a great slaughter at 'Woden's barrow',[4] and Ceawlin
was driven out.

593 In this year Ceawlin, Cwichelm and Crida perished. And Æthelfrith succeeded
to the kingdom

E

in Northumbria. He was the son of Æthelric, son of Ida.

596[5] In this year Pope Gregory sent Augustine to Britain with a good number of
monks, who preached God's word to the English people.

597 In this year Ceolwulf began to reign in Wessex, and he continually fought and
contended either against the English, or the Britons, or the Picts, or the Scots.[6]
He was the son of Cutha, the son of Cynric, the son of Cerdic, the son of Elesa,
the son of Esla, the son of Gewis, the son of Wig, the son of Freawine, the son
of Freothogar, the son of Brand, the son of Bældæg, the son of Woden.

601 In this year Gregory sent the *pallium* to Britain to Archbishop Augustine, and
many religious teachers to his assistance; and Bishop Paulinus [who][7] converted
Edwin, king of the Northumbrians, to baptism.

C (B, *and originally* A)	E
603 In this year was a battle at *Degsastan*.[8]	In this year Aedan,[9] king of the Scots, fought along with the people of Dal Riada against Æthelfrith,[10] king of the Northumbrians, at *Degsastan*, and almost all his army was slain. There Theodbald, Æthelfrith's brother, was slain with all his troop. No king of the Scots dared afterwards lead an army against this nation. Hering, son of Hussa, led the army thither.[11]

---

[1] 'E' and a late correction in 'A' have Ceolric.   [2] Six, 'E'.
[3] This was added at Canterbury to 'A' at end of annal 592.
[4] Now called Adam's Grave, in Alton Priors, Wilts. 'E' adds "in Britain".
[5] In 'A' this is dated 595 and written in a later hand over an erasure which probably had the same statement dated 596.   [6] 'E' omits the genealogy.
[7] The relative pronoun has probably been omitted by the archetype of all our versions. 'F' supplied "and among them was Paulinus".
[8] Corruptly given as *Egesan stan* in 'B', 'C', and originally in 'A'. The identification with Dawston in Liddesdale, which has been doubted on philological grounds, has recently been defended by Max Förster, *Der Flussname Themse und seine Sippe*, pp. 796–811.
[9] Aedan mac Gabrain, king of the Irish settlement in Argyle from 574 to about 608.
[10] Correcting the manuscript corruption, which reads: "fought against the people of the Dal Riada and Æthelfrith".
[11] This is one of the few places where the northern recension has had access to material not in Bede. Nothing further is known of Hering. On Hussa, see p. 237.

C (B, *and originally* A)   **E**

604 In this year the East Saxons, under King Sæberht[1] and Bishop Mellitus, received the faith and the baptismal bath.

In this year Augustine consecrated two bishops, Mellitus and Justus. He sent Mellitus to preach baptism to the East Saxons, where the king was called Sæberht, the son of Ricule, Ethelbert's sister, and Ethelbert had set him as king there. And Ethelbert gave to Mellitus an episcopal see in London, and he gave to Justus Rochester, which is 24 miles from Canterbury.

604 (606) In this year Gregory died, ten years after he sent us baptism.[2] His father was called Gordianus and his mother Sylvia.

(605) In this year Pope Gregory died; and Æthelfrith led his army to Chester[3] and there killed a countless number of Britons. And thus was fulfilled Augustine's prophecy, by which he said: "If the Britons do not wish to have peace with us, they shall perish at the hands of the Saxons." There also were killed 200 priests who had come there to pray for the army of the Britons. Their leader was called Brocmail,[4] and he escaped with 50 men.[5]

607 In this year Ceolwulf fought against the South Saxons.

611 In this year Cynegils succeeded to the kingdom in Wessex, and held it for 31 years.[6] Cynegils was the son of Ceola, the son of Cutha, the son of Cynric.

614 In this year Cynegils and Cwichelm fought at *Beandun*, and killed 2,045[7] Britons.[8]

616 In this year Ethelbert, king of the people of Kent, died,[9] and his son Eadbald succeeded to the kingdom.

C (B, *and originally* A)   **E**

And that same year 5,800[10] years had passed from the beginning of the world.

He abandoned his baptismal faith and lived by heathen customs, so that he had his father's widow as his wife. Then Laurence, who was then archbishop in Kent, intended to go south across the sea and abandon everything; but the Apostle Peter came to him in the night and scourged him violently, because he wished thus to desert God's flock, and bade him go to the king and preach the true faith to him. He did so, and the king submitted and was baptized. In the days of this king, Laurence, who was archbishop in Kent after Augustine, died, and was buried next to Augustine on 2 February. Then after him Mellitus, who had been bishop of

---

[1] Æthelweard has Sigebyrht.   [2] He died 12 March.
[3] Bede does not date the battle of Chester, but it must have occurred between 613 and 616.
[4] Scromail, 'E'. I have corrected from Bede.
[5] The Old English idiom 'one of fifty', means literally 'with forty-nine'; but from the ninth century it was no longer used precisely, and the chronicler is translating Bede's fifty.
[6] 'E' omits the genealogy.   [7] 2,065 in 'A' and 'E'; 2,040 and more, in Æthelweard.
[8] Instead of this annal, 'F' has a mutilated entry of the accession of Archbishop Laurence.
[9] 'E' adds: "and he had reigned 56 years".   [10] 5616, 'G'.

E

London, succeeded to the archbishopric. Then the
people of London, which had been Mellitus's see,
became heathen. And five years later in Eadbald's
reign, Mellitus departed to Christ. After that Justus
succeeded to the archbishopric, and he consecrated
Romanus for Rochester, where he had been bishop.

617   In this year Æthelfrith, king of the Northumbrians,
was killed by Rædwald, king of the East Angles, and
Edwin, the son of Ælle, succeeded to the kingdom
and conquered all Britain except the people of Kent
alone, and drove out the athelings, Æthelfrith's sons,
namely Eanfrith, Oswald, Oswiu, Oslac, Oswudu,
Oslaf and Offa.

F619 In this year Archbishop Laurence died.

C (A, B)   E

624   In this year Archbishop Mellitus died.

625 In this year Paulinus was   In this year Archbishop Justus consecrated Paulinus
consecrated as bishop   as bishop on 21 July.
for the Northumbrians
by Archbishop Justus.

626 In this year Eanflæd,   In this year Eomer came from Cwichelm, king of the
King Edwin's daughter,   West Saxons, intending to stab to death King Edwin,
was baptized on the   but he stabbed his thegn Lilla and Forthhere, and
holy eve of Pentecost;   wounded the king. And that same night was born
and Penda held his   Edwin's daughter, who was called Eanflæd. Then the
kingdom for 30 years,   king promised Paulinus that he would give his
and he was 50 years old   daughter to God, if he would by his prayers obtain
when he succeeded to   from God that he might destroy his enemy who had
the kingdom.[1] Penda   sent the assassin thither. And he then went into
was the son of Pybba,   Wessex with an army and destroyed there five kings,
the son of Creoda, the   and killed many of that people. And Paulinus bap-
son of Cynewold, the   tized his daughter and twelve[2] people with her at
son of Cnebba, the son   Pentecost. And within a twelvemonth, the king was
of Icel, the son of   baptized at Easter with all his following. Easter was
Eomær, the son of   then on 12 April. This took place at York, where he
Angeltheow, the son   had ordered a church to be built of wood, which was
of Offa, the son of   consecrated in St. Peter's name. The king gave

[1] This would make him eighty when he was killed, but must have arisen from some misunderstanding,
for he left two sons who were minors, nor would he, if so old, have been likely to have a sister young
enough to marry Cenwealh of Wessex who reigned from about 642 to 673. The date 626 for his accession is
also doubtful. Bede implies that he was not king until 632.

[2] Literally 'one of twelve', but see p. 148, n. 5. Some Bede MSS. say eleven, some twelve companions.

C (A, B)	E
Wærmund, the son of Wihtlæg, the son of Woden.[1]	Paulinus an episcopal see there, and afterwards ordered a bigger church to be built there of stone. And in this year Penda succeeded to the kingdom and reigned for 30 years.

627 In this year King Edwin was baptized with his people at Easter.	In this year King Edwin was baptized by Paulinus, and the same Paulinus also preached baptism in Lindsey, where the first to believe was a powerful man named Blæcca, with all his following. And at this time Honorius succeeded to the papacy after Boniface, and sent hither the *pallium* to Paulinus. And Archbishop Justus died on 10 November, and Honorius was consecrated by Paulinus in Lincoln.[2] The pope sent the *pallium* also to this Honorius. And he sent a letter to the Scots, that they should turn to the right Easter.

628 In this year Cynegils and Cwichelm fought against Penda at Cirencester, and afterwards came to terms.

627-8 (632) In this year Eorpwold[3] was baptized.

C (A, B)	E
633 In this year Edwin was slain, and Paulinus returned to Kent and occupied the see of Rochester there.	In this year King Edwin was slain by Cadwallon and Penda at Hatfield[4] on 14 October, and he had reigned for 7[5] years, and his son Osfrith also was slain with him. And then Cadwallon and Penda afterwards advanced and laid waste all the land of the Northumbrians. When Paulinus saw that, he took Æthelburh, Edwin's widow, and went away by ship to Kent, and Eadbald and Honorius received him with great honour and gave him an episcopal see in Rochester, and he stayed there until his death.
634 In this year Bishop Birinus preached baptism to the West Saxons.	In this year Osric, whom Paulinus had baptized, succeeded to the kingdom of the Deirans. He was the son of Ælfric, Edwin's paternal uncle. And Æthelfrith's son Eanfrith succeeded to Bernicia. And also Birinus first preached baptism to the West Saxons under King Cynegils. This Birinus came there by the advice of Pope Honorius, and he was bishop there until the end of his life. And also in this year Oswald succeeded to the kingdom of the Northumbrians, and he reigned for nine years. The ninth year is counted to him because of the heathenism practised by those who reigned the one year between him and Edwin.

---

[1] This genealogy has been erased from 'A'. [2] 'F' adds: "as archbishop of Canterbury".
[3] King of East Anglia. [4] Somewhere in Hatfield Chase. [5] An error for 17.

635 In this year King Cynegils was baptized by Bishop Birinus in Dorchester,[1] and Oswald[2] stood sponsor to him.

636 In this year Cwichelm was baptized in Dorchester, and he died that same year, and Bishop Felix preached the faith of Christ to the East Angles.[3]

639 In this year Birinus baptized King[4] Cuthred in Dorchester, and also received him as his godson.

C (A, B)	E
640 In this year Eadbald, king of the people of Kent, died, and he had reigned 25 years.[5]	(639) In this year Eadbald, king of the people of Kent, who had been king for 24 years, died. Then his son Eorcenberht succeeded to the kingdom, and he demolished all the idols in his kingdom and was the first of the English kings to establish the Easter fast. His daughter was called Eormengota,[6] a holy virgin and a wonderful person, whose mother was Seaxburh,[7] daughter of Anna, king of the East Angles.
641 (642 A[8]) In this year Oswald, king of the Northumbrians, was slain. (643 A) And Cenwealh succeeded to the kingdom of the West Saxons, and held it for 31[9] years.	In this year Oswald, king of the Northumbrians, was slain by Penda, the Southumbrian, at *Maserfeld*[10] on 5 August, and his body was buried at Bardney. His holiness and miracles were afterwards made known in manifold ways throughout this[11] island, and his hands are undecayed in Bamburgh. In this year Cenwealh succeeded to the kingdom of the West Saxons and held it for 21[9] years. The same Cenwealh had the church of Winchester built, and he was the son of Cynegils. And
642 (643 A) The same Cenwealh had the Old[12] Minster built at Winchester.	the same year that Oswald was killed, his brother Oswiu succeeded to the kingdom of the Northumbrians, and he reigned two years less than thirty.
644 (643 B, C) In this year Paulinus, who had been archbishop of York and was afterwards bishop of Rochester, died.	(643) In this year Archbishop Paulinus died in Rochester on 10 October. He had been bishop one year less than twenty, and two months and 21 days. And Oswine, [Edwin's][13] cousin's son, the son of Osric, succeeded to the kingdom of the Deirans, and ruled seven years.

[1] Dorchester-on-Thames, Oxfordshire.   [2] 'E' adds: "king of the Northumbrians".
[3] Felix was preaching there in 630–631.   [4] This title only in 'B', 'C' and 'F'.
[5] The additions to 'A' add: "He had two sons, Eormenræd and Eorcenberht, and Eorcenberht reigned there after his father, and Eormenræd begat two sons who were afterwards murdered by Thunor." This is a reference to a late Canterbury legend.   [6] Abbess of Brie in Gaul.   [7] Abbess of Ely.
[8] From here to 650 'A' is one year in advance of the other versions.
[9] The regnal lists also give 31. His death is entered under 672 below.
[10] Usually identified with Oswestry (Oswald's tree), Shropshire.   [11] The MS. has 'his'.
[12] Only 'B' and 'C' add the word 'old', after the foundation of the New Minster in the early tenth century.   [13] Accepting Earle and Plummer's correction.

645 (644 B, C, E) In this year King Cenwealh was driven out by King Penda.

646 (645 B, C, E) In this year Cenwealh was baptized.

648 (647 B, C) In this year Cenwealh gave to his kinsman Cuthred[1] three thousand hides[2] of land near Ashdown. This Cuthred was the son of Cwichelm, the son of Cynegils.[3]

F648 In this year the minster in Winchester was built, which Cenwealh caused to be made and consecrated in St. Peter's name.

---

650 (649 B, C, E) In this year Agilbert from Gaul received the bishopric in Wessex[4] after the Roman bishop Birinus.

C (A, B)	E
651 In this year King Oswine was slain and Bishop Aidan died.	(650) In this year King Oswiu had King Oswine slain on 20 August, and twelve days later Bishop Aidan died on 31 August.

652 In this year Cenwealh fought at Bradford-on-Avon.[5]

653 (652 E) In this year the Middle Angles, under Ealdorman Peada,[6] received the true faith.

654 (653 E) In this year King Anna was slain, and Botwulf began to build the minster at *Icanho*.[7]

C (A, B)	E
	And in this year Archbishop Honorius died on 30 September.
655 In this year Penda perished and the Mercians became Christians.	(654) In this year Oswiu killed Penda at *Winwædfeld*, and 30 princes with him, and some of them were kings. One of them was Æthelhere, brother of Anna, king of the East Angles.

Then five thousand, eight hundred and fifty[8] years had passed from the beginning of the world. And Peada, the son of Penda, succeeded to the kingdom of the Mercians.[9]

---

[1] Eadred, 'E'.　[2] 'Hides' inserted in 'B', 'C' only.　[3] 'E' omits the genealogy.　[4] "of the Saxons," 'E'.
[5] William of Malmesbury seems to have had access to other matter here, for he makes no mention of Bradford-on-Avon, but speaks of a battle against the Britons at 'Vortigern's *burg*', of which nothing further is known. Æthelweard calls the campaign of 652 'civil war'.　[6] Son of Penda.
[7] This is not, as often suggested, Boston, for the *Life of Ceolfrith* proves that it was in East Anglia. It may have been at Iken, Suffolk. See F. S. Stevenson, *Proc. Suff. Inst. Arch.*, xviii, pp. 29–52.
[8] 5,800, 'E'.　　　[9] Here 'E' has a Peterborough insertion relating to the founding of the abbey.

E

655 In this year Ithamar, bishop of Rochester, consecrated Deusdedit to Canterbury on 26 March.

657 (656 E, F) In this year Peada died,[1] and Wulfhere, son of Penda, succeeded to
the kingdom of the Mercians.[2]

658 In this year Cenwealh fought against the Britons at *Peonnan*,[3] and put them to
flight as far as the Parret. This was fought after he came from East Anglia, and
he had been in exile there for three years. Penda had driven him out and
deprived him of his kingdom because he deserted his sister.

660 In this year Agilbert[4] left Cenwealh, and Wine held the bishopric for three years,
and this Agilbert received the bishopric of the Parisians, by the Seine in Gaul.

661 In this year Cenwealh fought at Easter at *Posentesbyrig*; and Wulfhere, the son
of Penda, harried on[5] Ashdown; and Cuthred, son of Cwichelm, and King
Cenberht died in one and the same year. And Wulfhere, the son of Penda,
harried in the Isle of Wight, and gave the people of the Isle of Wight to
Æthelwold,[6] king of the South Saxons, because Wulfhere had stood sponsor to
him at baptism. And the priest Eoppa was the first man to bring baptism to the
people of the Isle of Wight, by the commands of Wilfrid[7] and King Wulfhere.[8]

C (A, B)

664 In this year there was an eclipse of
the sun, and Eorcenberht, king of
the people of Kent, died. And
Colman went with his companions
to his own land.[9] And the same
year there was a great pestilence.
And Ceadda and Wilfrid were
consecrated.[10] And that same year
Deusdedit died.

E

In this year there was an eclipse of the
sun on 3 May; and in this year a great
pestilence came to the island of Britain,
and in that pestilence Bishop Tuda[11] died,
and was buried at *Wagele*.[12] And Eorcenberht, king of the people of Kent, died,
and his son Egbert succeeded to the kingdom. And Colman went with his companions to his own land. And Ceadda
and Wilfrid were consecrated, and in the
same year Archbishop Deusdedit died.

[1] 'E' says more specifically "was slain".

[2] A long Peterborough insertion about the consecration and endowment of the monastery occurs here
in 'E'.

[3] Usually identified as Penselwood, Somerset. Rositzke suggests Pen Pits, Wiltshire, named from the
same hill (*penn*) from which Penselwood is named.   [4] Bishop of the West Saxons.

[5] So 'B', 'C', 'E'; but 'A' reads "as far as". Ashdown means the line of the Berkshire Downs.

[6] Bede calls him Æthelwealh.   [7] Bishop of Northumbria, in exile.

[8] The three oldest manuscripts ('A', 'B', 'C') have Wulfhere in the nominative instead of the required
genitive case.

[9] This is the only hint the Chronicle gives of the important synod at Whitby held this year. Colman left
after its decisions.

[10] Both to the see of Northumbria, in succession, Ceadda being appointed when Wilfrid delayed abroad.

[11] Of Northumbria.

[12] The *W* is an error for *P*, the letters being similar in Anglo-Saxon script. Bede has *Pægnalaech*. It cannot
be identified.

C (A, B)   E

667   In this year Oswiu and Egbert sent the priest Wigheard to Rome, that he might be consecrated archbishop, but he died immediately he came there.

668 In this year Theodore was consecrated as archbishop.   In this year Pope Vitalian consecrated Theodore as archbishop and sent him to Britain.

669 In this year King Egbert gave Reculver to the priest Bass, to build a minster in it.

670 In this year Oswiu, king of the Northumbrians, died,[1] and Ecgfrith[2] reigned after him; and Leuthere, Bishop Agilbert's nephew, succeeded to the bishopric over the land of the West Saxons, and held it for seven years, and Bishop Theodore consecrated him.[3] Oswiu was the son of Æthelfrith, the son of Æthelric, the son of Ida, the son of Eoppa.

671 In this year there was the great mortality of birds.

672 In this year Cenwealh died, and his queen Seaxburh reigned one year after him.

673 In this year Egbert, king of the people of Kent, died; and in the same year there was a synod[4] at Hertford, and St. Æthelthryth[5] began the monastery at Ely.

674 In this year Æscwine succeeded to the kingdom of Wessex.[6] He was the son of Cenfus, the son of Cenferth, the son of Cuthgils, the son of Ceolwulf, the son of Cynric, the son of Cerdic.

675 In this year Wulfhere, the son of Penda, and Æscwine[7] fought at *Biedanheafde*; and in the same year Wulfhere died[8] and Ethelred succeeded to the kingdom.[9]

676 In this year Æscwine died. And Hædde succeeded to the bishopric,[10] and Centwine succeeded to the kingdom.[11] And Centwine was the son of Cynegils, the son of Ceolwulf. And Ethelred, king of the Mercians, ravaged Kent.

C (A, B)   E

678 In this year the star called 'comet' appeared; and Bishop   In this year the star called 'comet' appeared in August, and shone every morning for three months, like a sunbeam. And Bishop Wilfrid was driven from his bishopric

[1] 'E' adds: "on 15 February".   [2] 'E' adds: "his son".   [3] 'E' omits the genealogy.
[4] "Archbishop Theodore assembled a synod", 'E', 'F'.   [5] "St. Æthelbyrht," 'B', 'C' (wrongly).
[6] 'E' omits the genealogy.   [7] 'E' adds: "son of Cenfus".
[8] Probably in 674, after 23 September, and so recorded in Bede as 675.
[9] 'B' has accidentally omitted this annal. 'E' has a long Peterborough insertion at this point, with Pope Agatho's privilege.
[10] Of Wessex.   [11] 'E' adds: "of the West Saxons" and omits the genealogy.

C (A, B)	E
Wilfrid was driven from his bishopric by King Ecgfrith.	by King Ecgfrith, and two bishops were consecrated in his place, Bosa for Deira and Eata for Bernicia. And Eadhæd was consecrated bishop for the people of Lindsey. He was the first bishop of Lindsey.

679 In this year Ælfwine[1] was slain, and St. Æthelthryth[2] died.

In this year Ælfwine was slain near the Trent, where Ecgfrith and Ethelred were fighting. And St. Æthelthryth died; and Coldingham was burnt by divine fire.

680 In this year Archbishop Theodore presided over a synod in Hatfield, because he wished to correct the faith in Christ; and the same year the Abbess Hilda [of Whitby][3] died.

E

681 In this year Trumberht was consecrated bishop of Hexham and Trumwine for the Picts, because these then were subject to this country.[4]

682 (683 C) In this year Centwine put the Britons to flight as far as the sea.

C (A, B)	E
684	In this year Ecgfrith sent an army into Ireland,[5] and with it Briht his ealdorman, and they miserably injured and burnt God's churches.
685 In this year Ceadwalla began to contend for the kingdom.[6] Ceadwalla was son of Cenberht, the son of Ceadda, the son of Cutha, the son of Ceawlin, the son of Cynric, the son of Cerdic; and Mul, who was afterwards burnt in Kent, was Ceadwalla's brother. And that same year King Ecgfrith was slain.	In this year King Ecgfrith ordered that Cuthbert be consecrated bishop, and Archbishop Theodore consecrated him at York on the first day of Easter[7] as bishop of Hexham,[8] because Trumberht had been deposed from the bishopric. And that same year King Ecgfrith was slain north of the sea[9] on 20 May, and a great army with him. He had been king for 15 years; and his brother Aldfrith succeeded to the kingdom after him. And in this year Ceadwalla began to contend for the kingdom. And that same year Hlothhere, king of the people of Kent, died. And John[10] was consecrated bishop of Hexham, and was there until Wilfrid was restored. Then John succeeded to the bishopric of the city,[11] for Bishop Bosa had died. Then afterwards his priest Wilfrid[12] was consecrated bishop of the city and John went to his monastery in *Derawudu*.[13]

---

[1] Brother of Ecgfrith of Northumbria.   [2] Abbess of Ely.   [3] 'A', 'E', 'F'.
[4] Literally 'hither', *i.e.* Northumbria.   [5] Literally 'among the Scots'.   [6] Of Wessex.
[7] 26 March.   [8] Later he exchanged sees with Eata, bishop of Lindisfarne.   [9] The Firth of Forth.
[10] John of Beverley.   [11] York. This indicates that the writer is a Northumbrian.
[12] Wilfrid II, 718–732.   [13] "The wood of the Deirans." The monastery was at Beverley.

C (A, B)

Ecgfrith was the son of Oswiu, the son of Æthelfrith, the son of Æthelric, the son of Ida, the son of Eoppa. And Hlothhere died that same year.

F685 In this year there occurred in Britain bloody rain, and milk and butter were turned to blood.[1]

---

686 In this year Ceadwalla and Mul[2] ravaged Kent and the Isle of Wight.[3]

687 In this year Mul was burnt in Kent, and twelve other men with him, and that year Ceadwalla again ravaged Kent.

	C (A, B)	**E**
688	In this year Ine succeeded to the kingdom of the West Saxons, and held it for 37 years.[4] And the same year Ceadwalla went to Rome, and received baptism from the pope, and the pope called him Peter. Seven days later he died. Now Ine was the son of Cenred, the son of Ceolwold. Ceolwold was the brother of Cynegils, and they both were the sons of Cuthwine, the son of Ceawlin, the son of Cynric, the son of Cerdic.	In this year King Ccadwalla went to Rome and received baptism from Pope Sergius, and he gave him the name of Peter; and seven days afterwards he died on 20 April, wearing the baptismal robes,[5] and was buried in St. Peter's church. And Ine succeeded to the kingdom of the West Saxons after him. He reigned 27[6] years, and afterwards went to Rome and lived there until the day of his death.
690	In this year Archbishop Theodore died, and Brihtwold succeeded to the bishopric.[7] Hitherto there had been Roman bishops; afterwards they were English.	In this year Archbishop Theodore died. He had been bishop for 22 years, and he was buried in Canterbury.
692		In this year Brihtwold was elected archbishop on 1 July. He had been abbot of Reculver. Hitherto there had been Roman bishops; afterwards they were English. Then there were two kings in Kent, Wihtred[8] and Swæfheard.[9]

[1] This portent is mentioned in *Annales Cambrenses* 689. 'F' continues with a brief reference to Cuthbert's consecration.
[2] 'E' adds: "his brother".
[3] 'E' has a short Peterborough addition, recording an alleged grant to the monastery by Ceadwalla.
[4] An early hand has added in the margin of 'A': "And he built the minster at Glastonbury."
[5] Literally 'Christ's clothes'.   [6] An error for 37.
[7] The other recension is correct in putting his election two years later.
[8] Nihtred, 'E', Wihtred 'F'.   [9] Wæbheard, 'E', Webheard, 'F'.

D (E)

693[1]   In this year Brihtwold was consecrated archbishop by Godwine[2], bishop of the Gauls, on 3 July. Meanwhile Bishop Gefmund[3] had died, and Brihtwold consecrated Tobias in his place. And Dryhthelm[4] was escorted from this life.

694 In this year the people of Kent made terms with Ine, and paid him thirty thousand [pence][5] because they had burnt Mul. And Wihtred succeeded to the kingdom of the people of Kent, and held it for 33 years.[6] Wihtred was the son of Egbert, the son of Eorcenberht, the son of Eadbald, the son of Ethelbert.

D (E)

697   In this year the Southumbrians slew Osthryth, Ethelred's queen and Ecgfrith's sister.

698   (699) In this year the Picts killed Ealdorman Briht [red].[7]

702 (?)   In this year Cenred succeeded to the kingdom of the Southumbrians.[8]

705 (703)[9] In this year Bishop Hædde died, and he had held the bishopric of Winchester for 27 years.

704 In this year Ethelred, son of Penda, king of the Mercians, became a monk. And he had held the kingdom 29 years. Then Cenred succeeded.

	C (A, B)	D (E)

705 In this year died Aldfrith, king of the Northumbrians, and Bishop Seaxwulf.[10]   In this year Aldfrith, king of the Northumbrians, died on 14 December, at Driffield. Then Osred his son succeeded to the kingdom.

[1] Near the beginning of this annal 'D' is resumed.

[2] Archbishop of Lyons. I have corrected to the form of his name in most MSS. of Bede. But the Namur MS. has *Gudune*, which is nearer to the forms here, *Guodune* 'D', *Godune* 'E', 'F'.

[3] Of Rochester.

[4] A man who had a vision of the other world, told by Bede, *Eccles. Hist.*, v, 12. 'E' wrongly calls him Brihthelm.

[5] The text does not name the unit, but pence is certainly meant. 'B' and 'C' replace 'thousands' by 'pounds'.

[6] 'F' has a late Canterbury insertion, on Wihtred's donation to churches at the council of Bapchild. 'E' and 'F' omit the genealogy.

[7] Bede shows that this was his name. The chronicles call him here Berht, which is the same name as that of the leader of Ecgfrith's force to Ireland in 684.

[8] This seems to be recording the same event as 704, from a source two years out, but it is just possible, as Plummer suggests, that Cenred was associated with Ethelred in the kingship two years before the latter's abdication.

[9] An episcopate of 27 years from 676 would bring Hædde's death to 703, but as Bede shows that he was alive in 705, either the date of his accession or the length of his episcopate as given in the Chronicle must be wrong. 'B' and 'C' have 37; the others have 27.   [10] A wrong date: Seaxwulf was dead by 692.

709 (708 C)[1] In this year Aldhelm, who was bishop west of the wood,[2] died. Early in Daniel's time the land of the West Saxons had been divided into two dioceses, whereas it had previously been one. Daniel held the one and Aldhelm the other. Forthhere succeeded Aldhelm. And Ceolred succeeded to the kingdom of the Mercians, and Cenred went to Rome, and Offa[3] with him.

C (B)	D (E)
	And Cenred was there until the end of his life. And that same year Bishop Wilfrid died in Oundle, and his body was taken to Ripon. He was bishop for 45 years, and King Ecgfrith previously drove him to Rome.
710 In this year Ealdorman Brihtferth fought against the Picts.[4] And Ine and Nunna fought against the King Geraint.	In this year Acca, Wilfrid's priest, succeeded to the bishopric which Wilfrid had held. And that year Ealdorman Brihtferth fought against the Picts between the Avon and the Carron. And Ine and his kinsman Nun fought against Geraint, king of the Britons. And that same year Sigbald[5] was killed.

A710 In this year Ealdorman Brihtferth fought against the Picts. And Ine and his kinsman Nun fought against Geraint, king of the Britons.[6]

714 In this year the holy Guthlac died.

715 In this year Ine and Ceolred fought at 'Woden's barrow'.[7]

716 (717[8] (?) C) In this year Osred, king of the Northumbrians, was slain.[9] He held the kingdom for seven[10] years after Aldfrith. Then Cenred succeeded to the kingdom and held it for two years; then Osric, and he held it for eleven years. And in that year Ceolred,[11] king of the Mercians, died, and his body lies in Lichfield, and that of Ethelred, son of Penda, in Bardney. And then Æthelbald succeeded to the kingdom in Mercia, and held it for 41 years. Æthelbald was the son of Alweo, the son of Eawa, the son of Pybba, whose ancestry is given above.[12] And the venerable man Egbert induced the monks on the island of Iona to observe Easter correctly and the ecclesiastical tonsure.[13]

---

[1] 'C' is one year behind here, but from 710 to 715 it was originally in line with the other MSS., though the numbers have since been tampered with. I restore the original dates.
[2] Selwood, which divides East and West Wessex.   [3] King of Essex.
[4] 711, according to Bede's summary.
[5] Hygebald in 'E', but Gaimar supports 'D''s reading. He is unknown.
[6] This annal was originally omitted in 'A', and was copied in at Winchester in the mid-tenth century, from a text like that in 'D' and 'E', only without their additions. Geraint ruled the Cornish Britons.
[7] Now Adam's Grave, in Alton Priors, Wilts.
[8] Though in the printed text 'C' appears to be in line with the other texts, it seems originally to have been a year in advance, and to have been altered by subsequent erasure. The annal numbers assigned by Thorpe to 'B' have no authority.   [9] 'D' and 'E' add: "south of the border".
[10] Eight, 'D'.   [11] 'B' and 'C' have wrongly Ceolwold.   [12] 'D', 'E' omit the genealogy.
[13] "St. Peter's tonsure", 'D', 'E', 'F'. 'F' has only Æthelbald's accession, and the last sentence.

718 In this year Ingild, Ine's brother, died. Their sisters were Cwenburh and
Cuthburh. And Cuthburh founded the monastery at Wimborne. She had
been married to Aldfrith, king of the Northumbrians, and they separated
during their lifetime.

721 In this year Daniel[1] went to Rome; and in the same year Ine slew Cynewulf

D (E)

the atheling. And in this year the holy Bishop John died,
who had been bishop for 33 years, eight months and
13 days; and his body lies in Beverley.

722 In this year Queen Æthelburh demolished Taunton, which Ine had built; and
the exile Ealdberht went away into Surrey and Sussex, and Ine fought against
the South Saxons.[2]

C (A, B)	D (E)
725 In this year, Wihtred, king of the people of Kent, died.[3] [And Ine fought against the South Saxons and there slew Ealdberht].[4]	In this year Wihtred, king of the people of Kent, died on 23 April. He had ruled 34 years. And Ine fought against the South Saxons, and there slew the atheling Ealdberht[5] whom he had banished.[6]

726 (728 A) In this year Ine went to Rome,[7] and Æthelheard[8] succeeded to the
kingdom of the West Saxons, and held it for 14 years.[9] And the same year
Æthelheard and the atheling Oswald fought. Oswald was the son of Æthelbald,
the son of Cynebald, the son of Cuthwine, the son of Ceawlin.

C (A, B)	D (E)
727	In this year Bishop Tobias of Rochester died, and in his place Archbishop Brihtwold consecrated Ealdwulf bishop.
729 In this year the star called 'comet' appeared and St. Egbert[10] died.	In this year two comets appeared; and the same year Osric, who had been king eleven years, died, and the holy Egbert died in Iona. Then Ceolwulf succeeded to the kingdom and held it eight years.

---

[1] Bishop of Winchester.   [2] The last phrase is omitted by 'D', 'E' and 'F'.
[3] 'A' adds: "whose ancestry is given above".
[4] The bracketed portion is not in 'B' or 'C', but as it is in 'A' as well as in 'D' and 'E', it must have
been in the original chronicle.   [5] Eadberht (wrongly), 'D'.
[6] 'F' omits the last sentence. Both it and the Canterbury additions to 'A' add that Wihtred was succeeded
by Eadberht.   [7] Interlined in 'A' is "and there gave up his life". It is also in 'G'.
[8] 'D' and 'E' add "his kinsman".   [9] 'E' and 'F' omit the rest of this annal.
[10] On him, see pp. 671 f., 681, n. 1, 685. His death is entered in Irish annals under 728, but 729 in Bede

730 [In this year atheling Oswald died.][1]

C (A, B)	E (D)[3]
731[2] In this year Osric, king of the Northumbrians, was slain, and Ceolwulf succeeded to the kingdom, and held it for eight years. And Ceolwulf was the son of Cutha, the son of Cuthwine, the son of Leodwold, the son of Ecgwold, the son of Ealdhelm, the son of Ocga, the son of Ida, the son of Eoppa. And Archbishop Brihtwold died, and the same year Tatwine was consecrated as archbishop.	In this year Archbishop Brihtwold died on 13 January. He was bishop 37 years and six months and 14 days.[4] And the same year Tatwine was consecrated as archbishop. He had been priest at Breedon in Mercia.[5] He was consecrated by Daniel, bishop of Winchester, and Ingwold, bishop of London, and Ealdwine, bishop of Lichfield, and Ealdwulf, bishop of Rochester, on 10 June.

733 In this year Æthelbald occupied Somerton,[6] and there was an eclipse of the sun.[7]

D (E)

And Acca was driven from his bishopric.[8]

734 In this year the moon looked as if it were suffused with blood, and Tatwine and Bede died.[9]

D (E)

And Egbert was consecrated bishop.[10]

735   In this year Bishop Egbert received his *pallium* from Rome.

736 In this year Archbishop Nothhelm[11] received the *pallium* from the bishop of the Romans.

737 In this year Bishop Forthhere and Queen Frithogyth[12] went to Rome,

D (E)

and King Ceolwulf received St. Peter's tonsure[13] and gave his kingdom to Eadberht, the son of his paternal uncle, and Eadberht reigned 21 years. And Bishop Æthelwold[14] and Acca[15] died, and Cynewulf was consecrated bishop.[16] And the same year King Æthelbald[17] ravaged Northumbria.

---

[1] Though omitted in 'B' and 'C', this annal, being in 'A', 'D' and 'E', must have been in the original.
[2] 731 is right for Brihtwold's death, but Osric died in 729.
[3] 'E' gives the best text of the northern recension. See n. 4 below.
[4] 'D' inserts at this place almost the whole of the annal as in 'A', 'B' and 'C', including the death of Brihtwold. It thus refers to this twice, and repeats the death of Osric, already given under 729.
[5] Breedon-on-the-Hill, Leics.   [6] In Somerset. Æthelweard calls it a royal vill.
[7] 'F' adds: "and all the circle of the sun became like a black shield".
[8] Hexham. The true date is probably 731.   [9] 735 is probably the true date of Bede's death.
[10] The true date was 732.   [11] Of Canterbury.
[12] Wife of King Æthelheard of Wessex.   [13] *i.e.* took clerical vows.
[14] Of Lindisfarne. Simeon of Durham dates his death and Acca's 740.
[15] Deposed bishop of Hexham.   [16] Of Lindisfarne.   [17] Of Mercia. Æthelwald 'E' (wrongly).

738 In this year Eadberht, son of Eata, son of Leodwold, succeeded to the kingdom of the Northumbrians, and held it for 21 years. And his brother was Archbishop Egbert, son of Eata; and they are both buried in the city of York, in the same chapel.

740 (741 A) In this year King Æthelheard died, and Cuthred[1] succeeded to the kingdom of the West Saxons, and held it 16 years.[2] And he fought stoutly against King Æthelbald.[3] And Cuthbert[4] was consecrated archbishop and Dunn bishop of Rochester.

D (E)

741   In this year York was burnt down.

_____

F742 In this year a great synod was collected at *Clofesho* which was attended by Æthelbald, king of the Mercians, and Archbishop Cuthbert and many other wise men.[5]

_____

743 In this year Æthelbald[3] and Cuthred[6] fought against the Britons.

744 In this year Daniel resigned in Winchester, and Hunfrith succeeded to the bishopric.

D (E)

And shooting stars were frequent. And Wilfrid the younger, who had been bishop of York, died on 29 April. He had been bishop for 30 years.

745 In this year Daniel died. Forty-three[7] years had then passed since he succeeded to the bishopric.

746 In this year King Selred[8] was slain.

748 (747 C) In this year Cynric, an atheling of the West Saxons, was slain, and Eadberht, king of the people of Kent, died.[9]

750 In this year King Cuthred[10] fought against the arrogant ealdorman Æthelhun.

752 In this year, in the twelfth year of his reign, Cuthred[10] fought at *Beorhford* against Æthelbald,

D (E)

king of the Mercians, and put him to flight.

[1] 'D', 'E' add: "his kinsman".   [2] This is the figure in 'A', 'D' and 'E'; 'B' and 'C' have 26, wrongly.
[3] 'D', 'E', add: "king of the Mercians".   [4] Eadberht (wrongly), 'E'.
[5] It is uncertain whether this entry can be relied on. The charter which follows it is dubious.
[6] 'D', 'E', add: "king of the West Saxons".   [7] Forty-six, 'E'. It should be 40.
[8] King of the East Saxons.
[9] A Canterbury addition to 'A' adds that he was succeeded by Ethelbert, King Wihtred's son.
[10] 'D', 'E', add: "king of the West Saxons".

753 In this year Cuthred[1] fought against the Britons.

756 (754)[2] In this year Cuthred[1] died. And Cyneheard succeeded to the bishopric of Winchester after Hunfrith. And Canterbury was burnt down that year. And Sigeberht[3] succeeded to the West Saxon kingdom and held it for one year.

757 (755) In this year Cynewulf[4] and the councillors of the West Saxons deprived Sigeberht[5] of his kingdom because of his unjust acts, except for Hampshire; and he retained that until he killed the ealdorman who stood by him longest; and then Cynewulf drove him into[6] the Weald, and he lived there until a swineherd stabbed him to death by the stream at Privett, and he was avenging Ealdorman Cumbra. And Cynewulf often fought with great battles against the Britons. And when he had held the kingdom 31[7] years, he wished to drive out an atheling who was called Cyneheard, who was brother of the aforesaid Sigeberht. And Cyneheard discovered that the king was at *Meretun* visiting his mistress with a small following, and he overtook him there and surrounded the chamber[8] before the men who were with the king became aware of him.

Then the king perceived this and went to the doorway, and nobly defended himself until he caught sight of the atheling [and thereupon he rushed out against him and wounded him severely].[9] Then they all fought against the king until they had slain him. Then by the woman's outcry, the king's thegns became aware of the disturbance and ran to the spot, each as he got ready [and as quickly as possible].[10] And the atheling made an offer to each of money and life; and not one of them would accept it. But they continued to fight until they all lay dead except for one British hostage, and he was severely wounded.

Then in the morning the king's thegns who had been left behind heard that the king had been slain. Then they rode thither—his ealdorman Osric and his thegn Wigfrith and the men he had left behind him—and discovered the atheling in the stronghold where the king lay slain—and they had locked the gates against them[11]—and they then went thither. And then the atheling offered them money and land on their own terms, if they would allow him the kingdom, and told[12] them that kinsmen of theirs, who would not desert him, were with him. Then they replied that no kinsman was dearer to them than their lord, and they would never serve his slayer; and they offered their kinsmen that they

---

[1] 'D', 'E', add: "king of the West Saxons".

[2] At this point begins the dislocation of chronology mentioned on p. 113 above, by which all extant versions are dated two—or further on even three—years too early up to the annal for 845. The error must therefore have been present in the archetype of all surviving texts, and Æthelweard has it also.

[3] 'D', 'E', add: "his kinsman".

[4] On him, see pp. 23 f.   [5] 'D', 'E', add: "his kinsman".   [6] 'C' has wrongly "from".

[7] Thus MSS. 'A', 'B', 'C', though the length of the reign was 29 years, as given in the *Annals of St. Neots*. 'D' has 21, 'E' 16.

[8] So 'A', 'D' and 'E'. 'B', 'C' have wrongly altered *bur* to *burh*, 'fortress'.

[9] From other MSS.; omitted by 'C'.   [10] Omitted in 'B', 'C'.

[11] Or "on themselves"; but the instances of the idiom are ambiguous. Æthelweard translates *ex adverso*.

[12] 'A' and 'C' have a plural verb here, which would refer to the atheling's party, with an abrupt change of subject. But it is possibly an accidental repetition of the plural ending of the preceding verb, and 'B', 'D' and 'E' may be right to emend to the singular.

might go away unharmed. Their kinsmen said that the same offer had been made to their comrades who had been with the king. Moreover they said that they would pay no regard to it, "any more than did your comrades who were slain along with the king". And they proceeded to fight around the gates until they broke their way in, and killed the atheling and the men who were with him, all except one, who was the ealdorman's godson. And he saved his life, though he was often wounded. And Cynewulf reigned 31 years, and his body is buried at Winchester and the atheling's at Axminster; and their true paternal ancestry goes back to Cerdic.

And in the same year[1] Æthelbald, king of the Mercians, was slain at Secking-ton, and his body is buried at Repton.[2] And Beornred succeeded to the kingdom and held it for but a little space and unhappily. And that same year Offa[3] succeeded to the kingdom and held it for 39 years, and his son Ecgfrith held it for 141 days. Offa was the son of Thingfrith,[4] the son of Eanwulf, the son of Osmod, the son of Eawa, the son of Pybba, the son of Creoda, the son of Cynewold, the son of Cnebba, the son of Icel, the son of Eomær, the son of Angeltheow, the son of Offa, the son of Wærmund, the son of Wihtlæg, the son of Woden.

D (E)

758   (757) In this year Eadberht, king of the Northumbrians, received the tonsure, and his son Oswulf succeeded to the kingdom, and ruled for one year, and the men of his household slew him on 24 July.[5]

760 (758) In this year Archbishop Cuthbert died.[6]

761 (759) In this year Bregowine was consecrated archbishop at Michaelmas.[7]

D (E)

759[8]   And Moll Æthelwold succeeded to the kingdom of the Northumbrians, and reigned six years and then lost it.

762 (760) In this year Ethelbert, king of the people of Kent,[9] died

D (E)

and Ceolwulf died also.[10]

---

[1] 757, the date of the events at the beginning of the annal, not those immediately preceding. The death of Cynewulf has been recorded out of place.

[2] "And he reigned 41 years", 'D', 'E'.   [3] 'D', 'E' add: "put Beornred to flight and".

[4] The rest of the genealogy is omitted in 'D', 'E', 'F'.   [5] So in 'E'; 'D' has "25 July".

[6] 'F' adds: "And he held the bishopric 18 years."   [7] 'F' adds: "and held it for four years".

[8] The parts of these annals peculiar to the northern recension come from a source without the chronological dislocation of the Chronicle, and are therefore usually two years earlier than the events in the parts of the annal common to all versions.

[9] 'F' calls him "son of Wihtred, king of the people of Kent".

[10] He had formerly been king of Northumbria. The exact date of his death is uncertain.

763 (762 C, 761 A, D, E, F) In this year occurred the great winter.

D (E)

761[1]   And Moll, king of the Northumbrians, killed Oswine at 'Edwin's cliff' on 6 August.[2]

765 (763 A, C; 762 D, E, F) In this year Jænberht[3] was consecrated archbishop on the 40th day after Christmas Day.

C (A, B)	D (E)
763[1]	(762) And Frithuwold, bishop of Whithorn, died on 7 May. He had been consecrated in the city[4] on 15 August in the sixth year of Ceolwulf's reign, and was bishop 29 years.[5] Then Pehtwine was consecrated bishop of Whithorn at Elvet on 17 July.[6]

766 (764) In this year Jænberht[7] received the *pallium*.

765[1]   In this year Alhred succeeded to the kingdom of the Northumbrians, and ruled nine years.[8]

D (E)

766   In this year Egbert, archbishop of York, who had been bishop 37[9] years, died on 19 November; and Frithuberht, of Hexham, who had been bishop 34[10] years, died. And Ethelbert was consecrated for York and Alhmund for Hexham.

768   In this year Eadberht, son of Eata, died on 20 August.[11]

774 (772) In this year Bishop Milred[12] died.

D (E)

774   In this year the Northumbrians drove their king Alhred from York at Easter, and took as their lord Ethelred, Moll's son, and he reigned for four years.

---

[1] See p. 163, n. 8.
[2] Cf. Simeon of Durham, p. 242 below, who, in his annal 759, says the battle took place at Eildon.
[3] Eadbriht (wrongly), 'B', 'C'.   [4] York. See p. 155, n. 11.
[5] This would put his accession in 734, and 15 August was a Sunday in that year.
[6] This was a Sunday in 763. Elvet is part of Durham.   [7] Eanbriht, 'B', Eadbriht, 'C', wrongly.
[8] Eight, 'E'.   [9] Thirty-six, 'E'. Both are wrong; it should be 34.   [10] Thirty-three, 'E'.
[11] This statement was added to 'A' at Canterbury. 'E' has 19 August.   [12] Of Worcester.

776 (774 C, D, E, F, G; 773 A) In this year a red cross appeared in the sky after sunset. And that year the Mercians and the people of Kent fought at Otford. And marvellous adders were seen in Sussex.

D (E)

776[1]   In this year Bishop Pehtwine died on 19 September; he had been bishop for 14 years.

779 (777) In this year Cynewulf and Offa fought around[2] Bensington and Offa captured the town.

D (E)

777   And that same year Ethelbert was consecrated bishop of Whithorn at York on 15 June.[3]

778   In this year Æthelbald and Heardberht killed three high-reeves, Eadwulf, son of Bosa, at Coniscliffe, Cynewulf and Ecga at *Helathirnum*, on 22 March. And then Ælfwold succeeded to the kingdom and drove Ethelred from the country;[4] and he reigned for ten years.

782 (780 A, C; 779 D, E) In this year the Old Saxons and the Franks fought.

D (E)

779[5]   And the high-reeves of the Northumbrians burnt Ealdorman Beorn in *Seletun* on 25[6] December. And Archbishop Ethelbert, in whose place Eanbald had previously been consecrated, died in the city;[7] and Bishop Cynewulf[8] of Lindisfarne resigned.

780[9]   In this year Alhmund, bishop of Hexham, died on 7 September, and Tilberht was consecrated in his place on 2 October. And Higbald was consecrated bishop of Lindisfarne at Sockburn; and King Ælfwold sent to Rome for the *pallium* and made Eanbald an archbishop.

782[10]   In this year Werburh, Ceolred's queen, and Cynewulf, bishop of Lindisfarne, died. And there was a synod at *Aclea*.

F (Lat.) 784 At this time King Ealhmund reigned in Kent. (F English) This King Ealhmund was Egbert's father. Egbert was Æthelwulf's father.

---

[1] Simeon, 777.   [2] 'D', 'E', "contested about".
[3] 'E' has a Peterborough addition about donations to Peterborough.   [4] Simeon dates this event 779.
[5] Simeon, 780.   [6] 24, 'E'.   [7] York.   [8] Cynebald (wrongly), 'E'.
[9] Simeon's *History of the Kings*, 781, his *History of the Church of Durham*, 780. 2 October was not a Sunday in either year.
[10] Simeon, *History of the Kings*, 783.

786 (784 A, D, E; 783 C) In this year Cyneheard killed King Cynewulf,[1] and was himself slain and 84 men with him. And then Brihtric succeeded to the kingdom of the West Saxons; and he reigned 16 years, and his body is buried at Wareham; and his true paternal ancestry goes back to Cerdic.

D (E)

786? (785) In this year Abbot Botwine of Ripon died.

787 (785) In this year there was a contentious synod at Chelsea, and Archbishop Jænberht lost a certain part of his province,[2] and Hygeberht was chosen by King Offa. And Ecgfrith was consecrated king.[3]

D (E)

786 (785) And at this time messengers were sent by Pope Hadrian from Rome to England to renew the faith and the friendship which St. Gregory sent us through Bishop Augustine, and they were received with great honour and sent back in peace.[4]

789 (787) In this year King Brihtric married Offa's daughter Eadburh. And in his days there came for the first time three ships of Northmen[5] and then the reeve[6] rode to them and wished to force them to the king's residence, for he did not know what they were; and they slew him. Those were the first ships of Danish men which came to the land of the English.

D (E)

787[7] (788) In this year a synod was assembled in Northumbria at *Pincanheale* on 2 September. And Abbot Ealdberht of Ripon died.[8]

788[9] (789) In this year Ælfwold, king of the Northumbrians, was killed by Sicga on 23 September, and a heavenly light was often seen where he was killed, and he was buried inside the church at Hexham. And a synod was assembled at *Aclea*. And Osred, Alhred's son, who was Ælfwold's nephew, succeeded to the kingdom after him.

---

[1] Cf. annal 757.   [2] *i.e.* Lichfield was made an archbishopric.

[3] Offa's son was consecrated in his father's lifetime. This is the first reference to the 'consecration' of a king in England.

[4] See the report of this legatine mission, No. 191. The last clause of the annal is in 'D' only.

[5] 'A' omits 'of Northmen' but it was in the archetype, for it is also in the *Annals of St. Neots*, which gives the additional information that they landed in Portland. 'D', 'E' and 'F' add: "from Hörthaland" (in Norway).

[6] Æthelweard, whose additions to this annal sound authentic and may be drawn from the early copy of the Chronicle used by him, calls him Beaduheard, and says he was staying in the town of Dorchester. He says that he rode to the harbour with a few men, thinking the strangers to be traders rather than enemies; and that his men were killed with him.

[7] 787. Simeon.   [8] Only 'D' mentions Ripon.   [9] Simeon, *op. cit.*, 788.

792 (790) In this year Archbishop Jænberht[1] died, and Abbot Æthelheard[2] was elected archbishop the same year.

D (E)

790[3] And Osred, king of the Northumbrians, was betrayed and driven from the kingdom, and Ethelred, Æthelwold's son, again succeeded to the kingdom.

791 In this year Badwulf[4] was consecrated bishop of Whithorn by Archbishop Eanbald and by Bishop Ethelbert[5] on 17 July.

794 (792) In this year Offa, king of the Mercians, had Ethelbert[6] beheaded.

D (E)

792[7] And Osred, who had been king of the Northumbrians, was captured after he had returned home from exile, and killed on 14 September, and his body is buried at Tynemouth. And King Ethelred took a new wife, who was called Ælfflæd, on 29 September.

793 In this year dire portents appeared over Northumbria and sorely frightened the people. They consisted of immense whirlwinds[8] and flashes of lightning, and fiery dragons were seen flying in the air. A great famine immediately followed those signs, and a little after that in the same year, on 8 June,[9] the ravages of heathen men miserably destroyed God's church on Lindisfarne, with plunder and slaughter. And Sicga died on 22 February.

796 (794) In this year Pope Hadrian and King Offa died;[10] and Ethelred, king of the Northumbrians, was killed by his own people.[11] And Bishop Ceolwulf[12] and Bishop Eadbald[13] left the country. And Ecgfrith succeeded to the kingdom of the Mercians and died the same year. And Eadberht, whose other name was Præn, succeeded to the kingdom in Kent.

D (E)

794[14] And Ealdorman Æthelheard died on 1 August. And the heathens ravaged in Northumbria, and plundered Ecgfrith's monastery at *Donemuthan*;[15] and one of their

---

[1] Eadbriht (wrongly) 'B', 'C'.   [2] 'F' adds: "of the monastery of Louth".   [3] See p. 163, n. 8.
[4] Or perhaps Baldwulf. The sources vary as to his name.   [5] Of Hexham.
[6] King of East Anglia. He was afterwards regarded as a saint, Hereford Cathedral being one of the places dedicated to him.
[7] See p. 163, n. 8.   [8] Omitted in 'E'.   [9] The MSS. have by mistake January here.
[10] Hadrian died on 25 December 795, Offa on 29 July 796.   [11] 'D', 'E' add: "on 19 April".
[12] Of Lindsey.   [13] Of London.   [14] See p. 165, n. 8.
[15] i.e. 'the mouth of the Don'. Simeon's *History of the Church of Durham* identifies it as Jarrow. It cannot in that case be the *Donemutha* of No. 184. See p. 764, n. 3.

D (E)

leaders was killed there, and also some of their ships were broken to bits by stormy weather, and many of the men were drowned there. Some reached the shore alive and were immediately killed at the mouth of the river.

796   (795) In this year there was an eclipse of the moon between cockcrow and dawn on 28 March, and Eardwulf succeeded to the kingdom of the Northumbrians on 14 May; and he was afterwards consecrated and enthroned on 26 May in York, by Archbishop Eanbald, and Ethelbert, Higbald and Badwulf.[1]

796[2]   In this year Offa, king of the Mercians, died on 29 July.[3] He had reigned 40 years. And Archbishop Eanbald died on 10 August of the same year, and his body is buried in York. And that same year Bishop Ceolwulf[4] died, and Eanbald the second was consecrated in place of the other Eanbald on 14 August.

798   (796) In this year Cenwulf,[5] king of the Mercians, ravaged the people of Kent and of the Marsh,[6] and they seized Præn their king and brought him in fetters into Mercia.

F796   ... and they had his eyes put out and his hands cut off. And Æthelheard, archbishop of Canterbury, arranged a synod, and established and confirmed at the command of Pope Leo all the things relating to God's monasteries which were appointed in the days of King Wihtred and of other kings.[7]

799   (797) In this year the Romans cut out Pope Leo's tongue and put out his eyes and banished him from his see; and then immediately afterwards he could, with God's help, see and speak and was again pope as he had been before.

D (E)

797[8]   And Eanbald received the *pallium* on 8 September, and Bishop Ethelbert[9] died on 16 October, and Heardred was consecrated bishop in his place on 30 October.

[1] Bishops of Hexham, Lindisfarne and Whithorn, respectively.
[2] The northern recension, drawing from a correctly dated source, here duplicates the entries taken from the Chronicle, with its error of two years.
[3] 'E', having 'ides' in mistake for 'kalends', gives the date as 10 August.   [4] Of Lindsey.
[5] So, correctly, 'B' and 'C'. All other MSS. have Ceolwulf.
[6] Romney Marsh. 'A' reads "as far as the Marsh", but all other MSS. and Æthelweard have "the people of the Marsh".
[7] A passage purporting to be the archbishop's speech is then added.
[8] 'F' has this annal, dated 798. His chronology is one year ahead till 802. But note that the 30 October was a Sunday in 798, not 797.   [9] Of Hexham.

D (E)

798   There was a great battle in Northumbria in spring, on
2 April, at Whalley, and Alric, Heardberht's son, was
killed and many others with him.

F798 And Bishop Ælfhun[1] died in Sudbury and was buried in Dunwich, and
Tidfrith was elected to succeed him. And Sigeric, king of the East Saxons,
went to Rome. In the same year the body of Wihtburh was found all
sound and undecayed in Dereham, 55 years after she departed from this
life.

801   (799) In this year Archbishop Æthelheard and Cyneberht, bishop of the West
Saxons, went to Rome.

D (E)

800   In this year there was an eclipse of the moon in the
second hour of the eve of 16 January.

802   (800) In this year King Brihtric and Ealdorman Worr died, and Egbert succeeded
to the kingdom of the West Saxons. And that same day Ealdorman Æthelmund
rode from the province of the Hwiccians across the border at Kempsford. And
Ealdorman Weohstan with the people of Wiltshire met him, and a great battle
took place, and both ealdormen were killed and the people of Wiltshire had
the victory.

D only

804   (801) In this year Beornmod was consecrated bishop of
Rochester.

D (E)

802   In this year there was an eclipse of the moon in the dawn
on 20 May.[2]

804   (802)[3] In this year Beornmod was consecrated bishop of Rochester.

D (E)

803   In this year Higbald, bishop of Lindisfarne, died on
25 May,[4] and Egbert was consecrated in his place on
11 June.

[1] Of Dunwich.
[2] Assuming that the manuscripts, which have the 13th of the kalends of January (20 December) have
written January for June. There was an eclipse on 21 May.
[3] From here to 824, the numbers in 'C' have been tampered with, and are now a year behind the other
MSS., though originally 'C' was in line with the others. I have given the original dating. In the MS. one
minim has been erased where possible, and where numbers end in v or x this has usually been erased, without
anything been added to complete the number. For example, DCCCV now reads DCCC, with a blank; it was
meant to be completed as DCCCIII.
[4] Reading Iunii for Iulii, which would give 24 June.

805 (803) In this year Archbishop Æthelheard died and Wulfred was consecrated archbishop; and Abbot Forthred died.[1]

806 (804) In this year Archbishop Wulfred received the *pallium*.

807 (805) In this year King Cuthred died in Kent, and Abbess Ceolburh[2] and Ealdorman Heahberht.[3]

D (E)

806   In this year there was an eclipse of the moon on 1 September. And Eardwulf, king of the Northumbrians, was driven from his kingdom.[4] And Eanberht, bishop of Hexham, died.

F806   Also in the same year on 31 May the sign of the cross was revealed in the moon, on a Wednesday at dawn. And again in this year on 30 August a wonderful circle was revealed round the sun.

809   There was an eclipse of the sun at the beginning of the fifth hour of the day on 16 July, the second day of the week, the twenty-ninth day of the moon.[5]

814 (812 A, C, D, E; 814 F) In this year King Charles[6] died, and he had reigned 45 years. And both Archbishop Wulfred and Wigberht, bishop of the West Saxons, went to Rome.

815 (813 A, C, D, E; 815 F) In this year Archbishop Wulfred with Pope Leo's blessing returned to his own bishopric. And that year King Egbert ravaged in Cornwall, from east to west.

816 (814 A, C, D, E; 816 F) In this year the noble and holy Pope Leo died, and after him Stephen succeeded to the papacy.

817 (815 E; 816 A, C, D; 817 F) In this year Pope Stephen died, and Paschal was consecrated pope after him; and that same year the English quarter[7] at Rome was burnt down.

821 (819 A, C, D, E; 822 F) In this year Cenwulf, king of the Mercians, died,[8] and Ceolwulf succeeded to the kingdom. And Ealdorman Eadberht died.

---

[1] 'D', 'E', 'F' omit the last clause.   [2] Of Berkeley. See No. 81.   [3] Heardberht in 'D', 'E'.
[4] See Nos. 4, 21. These date this expulsion 808.
[5] 'F''s Latin, "on Sunday, the twelfth day of the moon".   [6] Charles the Great.
[7] Literally 'school', but not in any modern sense of the word. It was first applied to the contingent supplied to the Roman militia by Englishmen in Rome, but by this time had clearly also acquired a local sense. It was on the Vatican Hill and was inhabited by ecclesiastics, pilgrims and others whose business took them to Rome.
[8] Gaimar says he died at Basingwerk, Flintshire. See F. M. Stenton, *Anglo-Saxon England*, p. 228.

823 (821) In this year Ceolwulf was deprived of his kingdom.

824 (822) In this year two ealdormen, Burghelm and Muca, were killed. And there was a synod at *Clofesho.*

825 (823) In this year there was a battle between the Britons and the men of Devon at Galford.[1] And the same year Egbert[2] and Beornwulf, king of the Mercians, fought at Wroughton,[3] and Egbert had the victory and a great slaughter was made there.[4] Then he sent from the army his son Æthelwulf and his bishop Ealhstan[5] and his ealdorman Wulfheard to Kent, with a large force, and they drove King Bealdred north across the Thames; and the people of Kent and of Surrey and the South Saxons and the East Saxons submitted to him because they had been wrongfully forced away from his kinsmen. And the same year the king of the East Angles and the people appealed to King Egbert for peace and protection, because of their fear of the Mercians. And that same year the East Angles killed Beornwulf, king of the Mercians.

827 (825) In this year Ludeca, king of the Mercians, was killed, and his five ealdormen with him; and Wiglaf succeeded to the kingdom.

829 (827) In this year there was an eclipse of the moon on Christmas eve.[6] And that year King Egbert conquered the kingdom of the Mercians, and everything south of the Humber; and he was the eighth king who was 'Bretwalda'.[7] The first who had so great authority was Ælle, king of the South Saxons,[8] the second was Ceawlin, king of the West Saxons, the third was Ethelbert, king of the people of Kent, the fourth was Rædwald, king of the East Angles, the fifth was Edwin, king of the Northumbrians, the sixth was Oswald who reigned after him, the seventh was Oswiu, Oswald's brother, the eighth was Egbert, king of the West Saxons. And Egbert led an army to Dore,[9] against the Northumbrians, and they offered him submission and peace there, and on that they separated.

830 (828) In this year Wiglaf again obtained the kingdom of the Mercians. And Bishop Æthelwold[10] died. And that same year King Egbert led an army among the Welsh, and he reduced them all to humble submission to him.

[1] A Winchester writer who composed or interpolated two charters (Birch, Nos. 389, 390), probably after the Norman Conquest, had some other source of information about this campaign, for he assigns it to its true date and adds matter not in the extant Chronicle. He writes: "The beginning of this document was written in the army when Egbert, king of the *Gewissi* (= West Saxons) advanced against the Britons at the place called *Creodantreow,* in the year of our Lord's incarnation 825, indiction 3, on 19 August. . . . Then the charter of privilege of this estate was written at Southampton on 26 December."
[2] 'D', 'E', add: "king of the West Saxons".   [3] This name has replaced the old *Ellendun.*
[4] Æthelweard's addition is doubtless authentic: "And there was killed Hun, ealdorman of the province of Somerset, and he now rests in the city of Winchester."
[5] Of Sherborne.   [6] It was in the early morning of 25 December.
[7] This is the form that is familiar in history books. It means 'ruler of Britain'. But it is in 'A' (and its copy 'G') only, so that the variant *Brytenwalda* (*Bretenanwealda,* 'C') must go back to the archetype of all the other MSS. and have replaced *Bretwalda* very early. *Brytenwalda* could mean 'mighty ruler'. It is the form used also in some spurious documents. On the powers it implies, see p. 13.
[8] Corrected from 'A', 'D', 'E', "of the West Saxons" 'B', 'C'.
[9] In North Derbyshire, near the Northumbrian boundary.
[10] Of Lichfield. Æthelbald (wrongly) 'D', 'E', 'F'.

832 (829) In this year Archbishop Wulfred died.

F829 And Abbot Feologild was elected after him to the archiepiscopal see on 25 April, and he was consecrated on Sunday, 9 June,[1] and he died on 30 August.

833 (830) In this year Ceolnoth was elected bishop and consecrated, and Abbot Feologild died.

834 (831) In this year Archbishop Ceolnoth received the *pallium*.

835 (832) In this year heathen men ravaged Sheppey.

836 (833) In this year King Egbert fought against the crews of 35 ships[2] at Carhampton, and a great slaughter was made there, and the Danes had possession of the battle-field. And two bishops, Herefrith and Wigthegn,[3] and two ealdormen, Duda and Osmod, died.

838 (835) In this year a great naval force arrived among the West Welsh[4] and the latter combined with them and proceeded to fight against Egbert, king of the West Saxons. When he heard that, he then went thither with his army,[5] and fought against them at Hingston Down, and put both the Welsh and the Danes to flight.

839 (836) In this year King Egbert died. Earlier, before he became king, Offa, king of the Mercians, and Brihtric, king of the West Saxons, had driven him from England to France for three years. Brihtric had helped Offa because he had married his daughter.[6] Egbert reigned 37 years and 7 months, and then Æthelwulf, son of Egbert, succeeded to the kingdom of the West Saxons; and he gave to his son[7] Athelstan the kingdom of the people of Kent and the kingdom of the East Saxons[8] and of the people of Surrey and of the South Saxons.

840 (837) In this year Ealdorman Wulfheard fought at Southampton against the crews of 33[9] ships, and made a great slaughter there and had the victory; and Wulfheard died that year.[10] And the same year Ealdorman Æthelhelm with the people of Dorset fought against the Danish army at Portland, and for a long time he put the enemy to flight;[11] and the Danes had possession of the battle-field and killed the ealdorman.[12]

---

[1] This was a Sunday in 832.   [2] Twenty-five, 'D', 'E', 'F'.
[3] Both occur in the Winchester lists, in succession.   [4] Of Cornwall.
[5] There was probably a minor error in the original here. I use the text of 'B', as doubtless representing best the author's intention. 'A' supplies a redundant "and", 'C' reads "he that" for "then". 'D', 'E', reword the clause.   [6] This explanatory clause is omitted in 'D', 'E', 'F'.
[7] 'D', 'E', 'F', wrongly read "his other son", thus giving rise to the view that Athelstan was Egbert's son, not Æthelwulf's.   [8] "The East Saxons" accidentally omitted in 'D', 'E', 'F'.
[9] Thirty-four, 'C'.   [10] Æthelweard, adds: "in peace".   [11] 'D', 'E', 'F' omit this clause.
[12] 'D', 'E', 'F' omit these last four words; Æthelweard adds: "and his companions with him".

841[1] (838) In this year Ealdorman Hereberht[2] was killed by heathen men and many men with him in the Marsh;[3] and later in the same year [many men][4] in Lindsey, East Anglia and Kent, were killed by the enemy.

842 (839) In this year there was a great slaughter in London and Quentavic[5] and in Rochester.

843? (840 A, D, E, F; 841 C) In this year King Æthelwulf fought against the crews of 35 ships at Carhampton, and the Danes had possession of the battle-field.

845?[6] In this year Ealdorman Eanwulf[7] with the people of Somerset and Bishop Ealhstan and Ealdorman Osric with the people of Dorset fought against the Danish army at the mouth of the Parret, and there made a great slaughter and had the victory.

851 (853 C)[8] In this year Ealdorman Ceorl[9] with the contingent of the men of Devon fought against the heathen army at *Wicganbeorg*,[10] and the English made a great slaughter there and had the victory. And for the first time, heathen men stayed through the winter on Thanet.[11] And the same year 350 ships came into the mouth of the Thames and stormed Canterbury and London[12] and put to flight Brihtwulf, king of the Mercians, with his army, and went south across the Thames into Surrey. And King Æthelwulf and his son Æthelbald fought against them at *Aclea* with the army of the West Saxons, and there inflicted the greatest slaughter [on a heathen army][13] that we have ever heard of until this present day,[14] and had the victory there.

And the same year, King Athelstan and Ealdorman Ealhhere fought in ships[15] and slew a great army at Sandwich in Kent, and captured nine[16] ships and put the others to flight.[17]

---

[1] 'E', 'F' omit this annal.   [2] Ecgbryht, 'D'.

[3] Romney Marsh. 'D' has *Myrc*, 'boundary', in error for *Mersc*, 'marsh'. Hereberht signs Kentish charters.

[4] Supplied from 'A'.   [5] Near Étaples. 'C' alters to Canterbury.

[6] Either here or by the next annal the dating of most MSS. is correct.   [7] Earnulf, 'D', 'E', 'F'.

[8] With two additional blank annals, 'C' gets two years ahead. The lead is reduced to one in 853 by 'C''s omission of a blank annal; but it retains this dating one year in advance of the true date at least for the rest of the century.

[9] Asser adds: "of Devon".

[10] Perhaps, as Magoun suggests, Wigborough, near South Petherton, Somerset; but this is not very near the Devon border, and the name Wicga is so common in Devon names that a 'Wicga's hill' may well once have existed there.

[11] 'A' omits "on Thanet"; Asser has instead "Sheppey". Probably his MS. of the Chronicle agreed with 'A' in omitting the name, and he supplied a different one. Æthelweard has Thanet.

[12] 'D', 'E', 'F' omit the mention of London; so did the MS. of Asser, but accidentally, for its next words are descriptive of London.

[13] These words, being in 'A', 'D', 'E', 'F', must have been in the original version.

[14] 'D', 'E', 'F' omit "until this present day".   [15] 'A' and Asser omit "fought in ships and".

[16] From 'A', 'D', 'E', 'F', Asser and Æthelweard. 'B', 'C' have eight.

[17] This paragraph is in its present place in 'B', 'C', 'D', 'E', 'F' and Asser; 'A' puts it earlier in the annal, after the battle of *Wicganbeorg*, and Æthelweard puts it in his preceding annal, which he dates seven years previously. It looks as if it were a marginal insertion in the original, inserted into the text differently by the various copies. After this annal, 'E' adds a notice of a benefaction to Peterborough.

C (A, B)   D (E)

853 (854 C) In this year Burgred, king of the Mercians, and his council asked King Æthelwulf to help him to bring the Welsh under subjection to him. He then did so, and went with his army across Mercia against the Welsh, and made[1] them all submissive to him. And that same year King Æthelwulf sent his son Alfred to Rome. The lord Leo was then pope in Rome, and he consecrated him king[3] and stood sponsor to him at confirmation.

(852 E) In this year Burgred, king of the Mercians, subjected to himself the Welsh with King Æthelwulf's help.[2]

Then the same year Ealhhere with the people of Kent and Huda with the people of Surrey fought in Thanet[4] against the heathen army, and at first had the victory;[5] and many men on both sides were killed and drowned there, and both the ealdormen killed.[6]

C (A, B)   D (E)

And afterwards, after Easter, King Æthelwulf gave his daughter in marriage to King Burgred,[7] from Wessex to Mercia.

And Burgred, king of the Mercians, married the daughter of Æthelwulf, king of the West Saxons.

855-858[8] (855 A, D, E; 856 C, F) In this year heathen men for the first time stayed in Sheppey over the winter. And the same year King Æthelwulf conveyed by charter the tenth part of his land throughout all his kingdom to the praise of God and his own eternal salvation. And he went to Rome the same year with great state, and remained there a twelvemonth, and then went homewards. And Charles, king of the Franks, gave him his daughter as his queen. And afterwards he came home to his people, and they were glad of it.[9] And two years[10] after he had come from France, he died, and his body is buried in Winchester,[11] and he had reigned 18 years and a half.[12] And Æthelwulf was the son of Egbert,[13] the son of Ealhmund, the son of Eafa, the son of Eoppa, the son of Ingild. Ingild was the brother of Ine, king of the West Saxons, who held the kingdom for 37 years[14] and afterwards went to St. Peter's and ended his life

---

[1] In 'A' the verb is plural, allowing Burgred some share in the campaign.
[2] Note the varying sympathies betrayed by the different emphasis of the two versions.
[3] On this error and its significance for the origin of the Chronicle, see p. 115.
[4] Asser adds that its British name was *Ruim*.   [5] 'D', 'E' omit this clause.
[6] This last clause is omitted by 'A' and Æthelweard.
[7] Asser adds: "in the royal residence which is called Chippenham".
[8] The annal form is temporarily laid aside and the events of three or four years related. For these events, cf. Asser (No. 7, pp. 264 f.) and the *Annals of St. Bertin's* (No. 23).
[9] Instead of this clause, 'D', 'E', 'F' have merely "and came home safe".
[10] Æthelweard says, "one year".
[11] The *Annals of St. Neots* have Steyning, which may come from the copy of the Chronicle they used. If so, Æthelwulf's body was moved to Winchester later.
[12] Nine, 'E', 20, 'F'.
[13] 'E' omits the rest of the genealogy; 'D' similarly reads from the death of Æthelwulf to the notice about his successors at the end of the annal, but then, unlike 'E', 'D' has the genealogy, as in 'A', 'B', 'C'. As it then follows on with the account of the successors, it has this twice, though only its second entry is complete.   [14] The clause giving the length of the reign is not in 'A' or Æthelweard.

there. And they were sons of Cenred. Cenred was the son of Ceolwold, the son of Cutha,[1] the son of Cuthwine, the son of Ceawlin, the son of Cynric, the son of Creoda,[2] the son of Cerdic. Cerdic was the son of Elesa, the son of Esla,[3] the son of Gewis, the son of Wig, the son of Freawine, the son of Freothogar, the son of Brand, the son of Bældæg,[4] the son of Woden, the son of Frealaf,[5] the son of Finn, the son of Godwulf, the son of Geat, the son of Tætwa, the son of Beaw, the son of Sceldwa,[6] the son of Heremod, the son of Itermon, the son of Hathra,[7] the son of Hwala, the son of Bedwig, the son of Sceaf,[8] *i.e.* the son of Noah.[9] He was born in Noah's ark. Lamech, Methuselah, Enoch, Jared, Mahalaleel, Cainan,[10] Enos, Seth, Adam the first man and our father, *i.e.* Christ.[9] [Amen.][11]

And then Æthelwulf's two sons succeeded to the kingdom, Æthelbald to the kingdom of the West Saxons and Ethelbert to the kingdom of the people of Kent [and the kingdom of the East Saxons],[12] and of the people of Surrey, and to the kingdom of the South Saxons, and then Æthelbald reigned five years.[13]

860 (861 C, F) In this year King Æthelbald died, and his body is buried at Sherborne. And then his brother Ethelbert succeeded to the whole kingdom and held it in good harmony [and in great peace].[14] And in his time a great naval force came inland and stormed Winchester; and[15] Ealdorman Osric[16] with the men of Hampshire and Ealdorman Æthelwulf with the men of Berkshire fought against that army, and they put the army to flight and had possession of the battle-field.[17] And Ethelbert reigned five years, and his body is buried in Sherborne.

F860 In this year St. Swithin died.

---

[1] Æthelweard omits Cutha.   [2] 'A' and Æthelweard omit Creoda.   [3] 'D' omits Esla.
[4] Balder in Æthelweard.
[5] 'A' and Æthelweard have two extra names: Frithuwald and Frithuwulf, one before and one after Frealaf.
[6] Æthelweard has Scyld, the form of the name as it occurs in *Beowulf*. He then omits all the names until Sceaf (Scef), again as in *Beowulf*.
[7] Hrawa, 'A', which then omits the next three names, thus making Hrawa born in the ark.
[8] Æthelweard here adds the story of the mysterious arrival of Scef in a ship on the island of Skane as a child, and his acceptance as king—a story which the *Beowulf* poet applied to Scyld. Æthelweard takes the genealogy no farther.   [9] This explanation is in Latin.   [10] Camon in all texts.
[11] This is in 'A' only. Some have seen the end of an older version of the Chronicle here. But see pp. 114 f.
[12] In 'A', 'B', and 'D''s second version; the omission in 'C' is therefore an error. 'E' omits all between "kingdom of the West Saxons" and "and of the people of Surrey", thus omitting all reference to the second son; so does 'D', in its first version, drawn from the same source as 'E', and it also omits "the kingdom of the West Saxons". 'E' omits also "the kingdom of the South Saxons". 'F', however, fills in the lacuna, from 'A'.
[13] The *Annals of St. Neots* add: "Æthelbald his son reigned two and a half years after him, and he previously reigned two and a half years with his father." 'F' adds: "He had sent Alfred his third son to Rome, and when Pope Leo heard that he had died . . . he then consecrated Alfred as king and stood sponsor to him at confirmation, just as his father Æthelwulf asked when he sent him there."
[14] From 'A'. 'D','E', 'F' omit not only this, but "in good harmony" as well. It is freedom from internal dissension that is meant, as we can gather from Asser, but the later versions of the Chronicle may have felt that the remark about peace was contradicted by the next sentence in the annal.
[15] Asser adds: "when they were returning to the ships with immense booty".
[16] So 'A', 'D', 'E', Asser and Æthelweard. 'B' and 'C' unaccountably have "Wulfweard", though this ealdorman died in 840.
[17] This is the engagement mentioned in the *Annals of St. Bertin's*. See No. 23.

865 (866 C) In this year the heathen army encamped on Thanet and made peace with the people of Kent. And the people of Kent promised them money for that peace. And under cover of that peace[1] and promise of money the army stole away inland by night and ravaged all eastern Kent.[2]

866 (867 C) In this year Ethelbert's brother Ethelred succeeded to the kingdom of the West Saxons. And the same year a great heathen army[3] came into England and took up winter quarters in East Anglia; and there they were supplied with horses, and the East Angles made peace with them.

867 (868 C) In this year the army went from East Anglia to Northumbria, across the Humber estuary to the city of York.[4] And there was great civil strife going on in that people,[5] and they had deposed their king Osbert and taken a king with no hereditary right, Ælla. And not until late in the year did they unite sufficiently to proceed to fight the raiding army;[6] and nevertheless they collected a large army and attacked the enemy in York,[7] and broke into the city; and some of them got inside,[8] and an immense slaughter was made of the Northumbrians, some inside and some outside, and both kings were killed, and the survivors made peace with the enemy.[9] And the same year[10] Bishop Ealhstan died, and he had held the bishopric of Sherborne for 50 years, and his body is buried in the cemetery there.[11]

868 (869 C) In this year the same army went into Mercia to Nottingham and took up winter quarters there. And Burgred, king of the Mercians, and his councillors asked Ethelred, king of the West Saxons, and his brother Alfred to help him to fight against the army. They then went with the army of the West Saxons into Mercia to Nottingham, and came upon the enemy in that fortress and besieged them there.[12] There occurred no serious battle there, and the Mercians made peace with the enemy.

869 (870 C) In this year the raiding army returned to the city of York, and stayed there one year.

---

[1] 'D', 'E' omit this phrase.
[2] Asser adds: "for they knew that they would seize more money by secret plunder than by peace".
[3] This is generally known as the 'Great Danish Army', and tradition said it was led by the sons of Ragnar Lothbrok. One of these is mentioned as leader in Æthelweard's version of this annal, namely Igwar (i.e. Ivar).
[4] Simeon, *History of the Church of Durham*, says they took it on 1 November.
[5] Asser adds: "as always happens to a people which has incurred the wrath of God".
[6] The general sense is clear, but the wording ambiguous. A. H. Smith renders: "They resolved upon this, that they would continue fighting."
[7] The anonymous *History of St. Cuthbert* and Roger of Wendover (No. 4) date it Palm Sunday (23 March), Simeon, 21 March.
[8] Asser explains: "For that city had not as yet in those times strong and stout walls."
[9] Simeon says the Northumbrians were led by eight earls as well as the kings.
[10] Æthelweard adds: "Eanwulf, ealdorman of the province of Somerset, died."
[11] Æthelweard adds: "and that of the above-mentioned ealdorman in the monastery which is called Glastonbury".
[12] 'A' omits all reference to this siege. Asser adds: "Since the pagans, defended by the protection of the fortress, refused to give battle, and the Christians could not break the wall, peace was made between the Mercians and the pagans, and the two brothers Ethelred and Alfred returned home with their forces."

870 (871 C) In this year the raiding army rode across Mercia into East Anglia, and took up winter quarters at Thetford. And that winter King[1] Edmund fought against them,[2] and the Danes had the victory, and killed the king[3] and conquered all the land.[4] And the same year Archbishop Ceolnoth died.[5]

871 (872 C) In this year the army came into Wessex to Reading,[6] and three days later two Danish earls rode farther inland.[7] Then Ealdorman Æthelwulf encountered them at Englefield, and fought against them there and had the victory, and one of them, whose name was Sidroc, was killed there.[8] Then four days later King Ethelred and his brother Alfred led a great army to Reading[9] and fought against the army; and a great slaughter was made on both sides and Ealdorman Æthelwulf was killed, and the Danes had possession of the battle-field.[10]

And four days later King Ethelred and his brother Alfred fought against the whole army at Ashdown;[11] and the Danes were in two divisions: in the one were the heathen kings[12] Bagsecg and Healfdene, and in the other were the earls. And then King Ethelred fought against the kings' troop, and King Bagsecg was slain there; and Ethelred's brother Alfred fought against the earls' troop, and there were slain Earl Sidroc the Old,[13] and Earl Sidroc the Younger[14] and Earl Osbearn, Earl Fræna and Earl Harold; and both enemy armies were put to flight and many thousands were killed, and they continued fighting until night.

And a fortnight later King Ethelred and his brother Alfred fought against the army at Basing, and there the Danes had the victory. And two months

[1] "Saint", 'E'.　　　　　　　　　　　　　　　[2] "For a short time", Æthelweard.

[3] Æthelweard adds: "and his body lies buried in the place which is called *Beadoriceswyrth*" (Bury St. Edmunds).

[4] 'F' names the leaders Ingware and Ubba. 'E' has a Peterborough addition, which is not so exclusively local in its interest as most others: "and they destroyed all the monasteries they came to. In this same time they came to *Medeshamstede* (Peterborough), burnt and destroyed it, killed the abbot and the monks and all they found there, and brought it to pass that it became nought that had been very mighty." Æthelweard adds: "and their king Ivar died the same year".

[5] Asser and Æthelweard mention his burial at Canterbury; 'D' in error has "went to Rome" for "died"; a Canterbury addition to 'A' has: "and Ethelred, bishop of Wiltshire, was elected archbishop of Canterbury"; 'F' has a long spurious insertion about the replacement of clerics by monks.

[6] Asser, "a royal residence".

[7] Asser adds: "the remainder making a rampart between the two rivers Thames and Kennet, on the right-hand (*i.e.* southern) side of this same royal residence".

[8] 'A', 'F' and Æthelweard do not mention the death of this earl. Asser does, but he does not name him. It is probable that the name was added in the archetype of the other four MSS. of the Chronicle in error, anticipating the account of the battle of Ashdown.

[9] Asser has details that look like mere embroidery.

[10] Æthelweard has an interesting addition: "Truly the body of the aforesaid ealdorman was stealthily removed and taken into the province of the Mercians to the place which is called *Northworthig*, but Derby in the Danish tongue." Berkshire had been a Mercian area until the reign of King Æthelwulf, and retained its Mercian ealdorman after it came into West Saxon hands.

[11] Asser has a fuller account of this battle than he could have got from the Chronicle. He says that Alfred had to begin the battle alone, since his brother was hearing Mass and refused to leave until it was over; that the Danes had the higher ground, and that the battle raged round a thorn-tree which he had himself seen. Æthelweard, on the other hand, abbreviates the Chronicle account, though when speaking of the Danish losses he adds: "Never before or since has such a destruction been heard of, from the time when the people of the Saxons obtained Britain by war."

[12] Nothing is known of Bagsecg. Healfdene was reputed to be a son of Ragnar Lothbrok.

[13] 'D' accidentally omits the first Sidroc.　　　　[14] So in 'B', 'C'. The rest have "the Young".

later, King Ethelred and his brother Alfred fought against the army at *Meretun*,[1] and they were in two divisions; and they put both to flight and were victorious far on into the day; and there was a great slaughter on both sides; and the Danes had possession of the battle-field. And Bishop Heahmund[2] was killed there and many important men. And after this battle a great summer army came to Reading.[3] And afterwards, after Easter,[4] King Ethelred died, and he had reigned five years, and his body is buried at Wimborne[5] minster.

Then his brother Alfred, the son of Æthelwulf, succeeded to the kingdom of the West Saxons. And a month later King Alfred fought with a small force against the whole army at Wilton[6] and put it to flight far on into the day; and the Danes had possession of the battle-field. And during that year nine[7] general engagements were fought against the Danish army in the kingdom south of the Thames, besides the expeditions which the king's brother Alfred and [single][8] ealdormen and king's thegns often rode on, which were not counted. And that year nine[9] (Danish) earls were killed and one king. And the West Saxons made peace with the enemy that year.

872 (873 C) In this year the army went from Reading to London, and took up winter quarters there; and then the Mercians made peace with the army.

<table>
<tr><td align="center">C (A, B)</td><td align="center">D (E)</td></tr>
</table>

873 (874 C) In this year the army went into Northumbria,[10] and it took up winter quarters at Torksey in Lindsey; and then the Mercians made peace with the army. | In this year the army took up winter quarters at Torksey.

874 (875 C) In this year the army went from Lindsey to Repton and took up winter quarters there, and drove King Burgred across the sea, after he had held the kingdom 22 years. And they conquered all that land. And he went to Rome and settled there; and his body is buried in the church of St. Mary in the English quarter.[11] And the same year they gave the kingdom of the Mercians to be held by Ceolwulf,[12] a foolish king's thegn; and he swore oaths to them and gave hostages, that it should be ready for them on whatever day they wished to have it, and he would be ready, himself and all who would follow him, at the enemy's service.

875 (876 C) In this year the army left Repton: Healfdene went with part of the army into Northumbria and took up winter quarters by the River Tyne. And

---

[1] Asser omits this battle.   [2] Bishop of Sherborne. Æthelweard adds that he was buried at Keynsham.
[3] 'A' and Asser omit this reference to Reading, but it is in 'B', 'C', 'D', 'E' and in Æthelweard.
[4] 15 April.   [5] Sherborne, 'C'.
[6] Æthelweard does not mention this battle by name. He speaks of a battle lost by the smallness of the English force when King Alfred was attending his brother's funeral; but the Chronicle says Alfred was at the battle of Wilton. Asser describes in some detail the flight of the Danes and their turning on their pursuers.
[7] Asser, who omitted *Meretun*, has eight.   [8] In 'A' only.   [9] Æthelweard has eleven.
[10] On the Northumbrian revolt that occasioned this expedition, see No. 4.   [11] See p. 170, n. 7.
[12] 'A' omits the name, but all other MSS., as well as Asser and Æthelweard, have it.

the army conquered the land and often ravaged among the Picts and the Strathclyde Britons; and the three kings, Guthrum, Oscetel and Anwend, went from Repton to Cambridge with a great force, and stayed there a year. And that summer King Alfred went out to sea with a naval force, and fought against the crews of seven ships, and captured one ship and put the rest to flight.

876 (877 C) In this year the enemy army[1] slipped past the army of the West Saxons into Wareham;[2] and then the king made peace with the enemy and they gave him hostages, who were the most important men next to their king in the army,[3] and swore oaths to him on the holy ring[4]–a thing which they would not do before for any nation–that they would speedily leave his kingdom. And then under cover of that, they–the mounted army–stole by night away from the English army to Exeter.

And that year Healfdene shared out the land of the Northumbrians, and they proceeded to plough and to support themselves.

877 (878 C) In this year the enemy army from Wareham came to Exeter; [and the naval force sailed west along the coast][5] and encountered a great storm[6] at sea, and 120 ships were lost at Swanage. And King Alfred rode after the mounted army with the English army as far as Exeter, but could not overtake them [before they were in the fortress where they could not be reached].[7] And they gave him hostages[8] there, as many as he wished to have,[9] and swore great oaths and then kept a firm peace. Then in the harvest season[10] the army went away into Mercia[11] and shared out some of it, and gave some to Ceolwulf.

878 (879 C) In this year in midwinter after twelfth night the enemy army came stealthily to Chippenham,[12] and occupied the land of the West Saxons and settled there, and drove a great part of the people across the sea, and conquered most of the others; and the people submitted to them,[13] except King Alfred.[14] He journeyed in difficulties through the woods and fen-fastnesses with a small force.[15]

[1] Æthelweard adds: "which was in Cambridge".

[2] As usual, Asser describes the location more fully, telling us that it was a nunnery, between the Rivers Frome and Tarrant, with a very secure situation except where, on the west, it joined the mainland.

[3] This passage about hostages is not in 'A', but in all the other MSS. It clearly belongs to the original Chronicle, for both Asser and Æthelweard refer to hostages here.

[4] A sacred ring, normally kept in the inner sanctuary of the heathen temples, and worn by the chief at assemblies, is mentioned in the saga literature of Iceland. According to *Eyrbyggja Saga*, chap. IV, all oaths were sworn on it.

[5] Omitted by 'B', 'C'. [6] From 'A', 'E', 'D'; "mist", 'B', 'C'. [7] Omitted by 'B', 'C'.

[8] 'A', 'D', 'E' read: "preliminary hostages". [9] Æthelweard, "More than were asked for."

[10] Asser says: "in the month of August". Harvest began on 7 August.

[11] Æthelweard supplies the additional information that they built booths in the town of Gloucester.

[12] "A royal residence", Asser. [13] This clause is omitted in 'D', 'E'.

[14] 'A' and 'B': "and conquered and subjected to them most of the others, except King Alfred". 'D' and 'E' simplify by omission of "and subjected to them".

Æthelweard, often well informed on the ealdormen of Somerset, adds: " Also Æthelnoth, ealdorman of the province of Somerset, stayed with a small force in a certain wood."

[15] Asser elaborates this. He places the woods and fens in Somerset, and explains the difficulties: "For he had nothing to live on except what he could seize by frequent raids, either secretly or openly, from the pagans and even from the Christians who had surrendered to the rule of the pagans."

And the same winter the brother of Ivar and Healfdene[1] was in the kingdom of the West Saxons [in Devon],[2] with 23 ships.[3] And he was killed there and 840[4] men of his army with him.[5] And there was captured the banner which they called 'Raven'.[6]

And afterwards at Easter,[7] King Alfred with a small force made a stronghold at Athelney, and he and the section of the people of Somerset which was nearest to it[8] proceeded to fight from that stronghold against the enemy. Then in the seventh week after Easter he rode to 'Egbert's stone'[9] east of Selwood, and there came to meet him all the people of Somerset and of Wiltshire and of that part of Hampshire which was on this side of the sea,[10] and they rejoiced to see him. And then after one night he went from that encampment to Iley,[11] and after another night to Edington, and there fought against the whole army and put it to flight, and pursued it as far as the fortress, and stayed there a fortnight. And then the enemy gave him preliminary hostages and great oaths[12] that they would leave his kingdom, and promised also that their king should receive baptism, and they kept their promise. Three weeks later King Guthrum with 30[13] of the men who were the most important in the army came [to him] at Aller, which is near Athelney, and the king stood sponsor to him at his baptism there; and the unbinding of the chrism[14] took place at Wedmore. And he was twelve days with the king, and he honoured him and his companions greatly with gifts.

879 (880 C) In this year the army went from Chippenham to Cirencester, and stayed there for one year. And the same year a band of vikings assembled[15] and encamped at Fulham by the Thames. And the same year there was an eclipse of the sun for one hour of the day.[16]

[1] Gaimar, a twelfth-century writer, assumes that this brother is Ubba, whom tradition associated with Hingwar (Ivar) in the killing of St. Edmund.   [2] Omitted by 'B', 'C'.
[3] Both Asser and Æthelweard have further information. Asser says he had come from Dyfed (South Wales), where he had spent the winter and massacred many Christians, and gives details of the defence and sortie of the English from a fort he calls *Cynwit* (Countisbury). Æthelweard also refers to the siege of a fort. He names Odda, ealdorman of Devon, as the English leader. Strangely enough, he assigns the victory to the Danes.   [4] 860 in 'B', 'C'.
[5] This is strangely worded in all MSS. as "800 men with him and 40 [60] men of his army". B. Dickins suggests that *here*, 'army', was an error for *hired*, 'retinue', but if so, already the archetype was wrong. M. Hoffmann–Hirtz would read '40 headmen of his army'. Asser has 1200, Æthelweard 800.
[6] The capture of the raven banner is in 'B', 'C', 'D', 'E', but not in 'A', 'F', Asser or Æthelweard. The *Annals of St. Neots* have it also, but it is not certain that they took it from the version of the Chronicle they used, for they add later legendary matter, *e.g.* that the banner was woven by the daughters of Ragnar Lothbrok, and the raven fluttered before victory, drooped before defeat; "and this has often been proved".
[7] 23 March.   [8] Æthelweard says he had no helpers but the members of his household.
[9] This cannot be identified.
[10] Probably this means Hampshire west of Southampton Water, though some scholars follow Asser in interpreting it to mean the men of Hampshire who had not fled abroad. But was it only the people of Hampshire who fled?   [11] Iley Oak (now lost) near Warminster, Wilts.
[12] Asser is fuller: "They sought peace on these terms, that the king should receive from them distinguished hostages, as many as he wished, and should not give one to them. Never before, indeed, had they made peace with anyone on such terms."   [13] Literally 29, but see p. 148, n. 5.
[14] For eight days after baptism, white robes were worn and a white cloth, bound round the head after the anointment with the chrism. The ceremony of its removal is what is meant here. Æthelweard gives Ealdorman Æthelnoth a share in this ceremony.
[15] Asser says that it joined the former army, but nevertheless wintered in Fulham.
[16] Asser adds: "between nones and vespers, but nearer to nones". It is probably the eclipse of 29 October 878.

880 (881 C) In this year the army went from Circencester into East Anglia, and settled there and shared out the land. And the same year the army which had encamped at Fulham went overseas into the Frankish empire to Ghent and stayed there for a year.

881 (882 C) In this year the army went farther inland into the Frankish empire, and the Franks fought against them;[1] and the Danish army provided itself with horses after that battle.

882 (883 C) In this year the army went farther[2] into the Frankish empire along the Meuse,[3] and stayed there a year. And the same year King Alfred went out with ships to sea and fought against four crews of Danish men, and captured two of the ships–and the men were killed[4] who were on them–and two crews surrendered to him. And they had great losses in killed or wounded before they surrendered.

883 (884 C) In this year the army went up the Scheldt to Condé,[5] and stayed there for a year.[6] And Pope Marinus sent some wood of the Cross to King Alfred. And that same year Sigelm and Athelstan took to Rome the alms [which King Alfred had promised thither],[7] and also to India to St. Thomas and St. Bartholomew, when the English were encamped against the enemy army at London; and there, by the grace of God, their prayers were well answered after that promise.

884 (885 C) In this year the army went up the Somme to Amiens, and stayed there a year.

885 (886 C) In this year the aforesaid army divided into two [one part going east],[8] the other part to Rochester, where they besieged the city and made other fortifications round themselves.[9] And nevertheless the English defended the city until King Alfred came up with his army.[10] Then the enemy went to their ships

[1] Probably the Frankish victory of Saucourt, August 881. Æthelweard says that the Franks had the victory, and put the Danes to flight.

[2] 'A' and Asser have "far".   [3] Æthelweard says they camped in *Escelun* (*i.e.* Elsloo).

[4] By a change of the auxiliary verb, 'B', 'C' suggest that the men were killed *after* the capture, whereas in 'A' and Asser it is clear that they were dead before it. 'D', 'E', 'F' go still further and say, "and they slew the men".   [5] Asser adds that there was a nunnery there.

[6] The rest of this annal is not in 'A', Asser or Æthelweard. It has suspicious features. We know of no occasion in or before 883 when the English were encamped against London. Yet as it is in all the MSS. except 'A', it must be an early addition, perhaps misplaced. For what may be meant by India, see Stevenson's edition of Asser, pp. 286–290.

[7] From 'D', 'E'. Something is required to complete the sense in 'B', 'C', but it does not follow that the reading in 'D', 'E' represents the original, rather than an attempt of their common source to make sense of a corrupt passage.

[8] From 'A', 'D', 'E'. Æthelweard says that they went to Louvain.

[9] The last clause is omitted by 'D', 'E'.

[10] Asser's account is fuller and sounds genuine: "And then the pagans left their fortifications and abandoned all the horses which they had brought with them from the Frankish empire, and also left the greater number of their prisoners in the fort, for the king had come there suddenly; and they fled instantly to the ships, and the Saxons at once seized the prisoners and the horses abandoned by the pagans."

and abandoned their fortification, and they were deprived of their horses there, and immediately that same summer they went back across the sea.[1] That same year King Alfred sent a naval force from Kent[2] into East Anglia. Immediately they came into the mouth of the Stour[3] they encountered 16 ships of vikings and fought against them, and seized all the ships and killed the men. When they turned homeward with the booty, they met a large naval force of vikings[4] and fought against them on the same day, and the Danes had the victory.

That same year before Christmas, Charles,[5] king of the Franks, died. He was killed by a boar, and a year previously his brother,[6] who had also held the western kingdom, had died. They were both sons of Louis,[7] who died in the year of the eclipse of the sun.[8] He was the son of that Charles[9] whose daughter Æthelwulf, king of the West Saxons, had married.[10] That same year a large naval force[11] assembled among the Old Saxons and twice in the year there occurred a great battle, and the Saxons had the victory, and with them there were the Frisians.

That same year Charles[12] succeeded to the western kingdom and to all the kingdom on this side of the Mediterranean and beyond this sea,[13] as his great-grandfather[14] had held it, except for Brittany. This Charles was the son of Louis,[15] the brother of the Charles who was the father of Judith whom King Æthelwulf married; and they were sons of Louis.[16] This Louis was the son of the old Charles.[17] This Charles was Pippin's son.

That same year there died the good pope, Marinus,[18] who had freed from taxation the English quarter[19] at the request of Alfred, king [of the West Saxons].[20] And he had sent him great gifts, including part of the Cross on which Christ suffered.

And that same year the Danish army[21] in East Anglia violated their peace with King Alfred.

---

[1] Æthelweard's account of this year is extremely important. See F. M. Stenton, in *Essays presented to T. F. Tout*, pp. 20–21. One can see from it that the original Chronicle must have had two consecutive sentences ending "went across the sea", and all our extant MSS. go back on a text which has accidentally lost the second of them, the scribe having continued after the second, instead of the first occurrence of the words. Unfortunately Æthelweard's Latin is particularly obscure in this annal; yet it is clear that only some of the invaders went back across the sea at this moment. The others came to terms with Alfred, but twice broke them by raiding the country south of the Thames. They received aid from the Danes settled in East Anglia, and they encamped at Benfleet, on the north bank of the Thames estuary. There, however, some sort of quarrel occurred and they went across the sea. This passage, accidentally omitted from the extant versions of the Chronicle, explains Alfred's attack on East Anglia.
[2] 'A' omits "from Kent".
[3] Erroneously written *Stufe* for *Sture* by 'A', 'B', 'C' and Æthelweard. The correct form is in 'D', 'E' and Asser.
[4] Asser adds that it was collected by the pagans inhabiting East Anglia.
[5] Carloman, correctly given by Asser. Also the *Annals of Fulda* call him Charles. He died 12 December 884.
[6] Asser adds his name, Louis. He died 5 August 882.
[7] 'A' adds: "who also had held the western kingdom".
[8] Louis the Stammerer died 10 April 879.   [9] Charles the Bald.
[10] 'E' omits from this point until "Pippin's son".   [11] Asser adds: "from Germany".
[12] The Fat, deposed in 887. Asser calls him "king of the Germans".
[13] Possibly the English Channel. Asser has: "the arm of the sea that lies between the Old Saxons and the Gauls". But it may refer back to the Mediterranean, the lands beyond being in Italy.
[14] Charles the Great.   [15] The German, died 876.   [16] The Pious.   [17] The Great.
[18] He died 15 May 884.   [19] See p. 170, n. 7.   [20] From 'A', 'D' and 'E'.
[21] 'E' has: "went into East Anglia and violated their peace".

886 (887 C) In this year the Danish army which had gone east went west again, and then up the Seine, and made their winter quarters there at the town of Paris.[1]

That same year King Alfred occupied[2] London; and all the English people that were not under subjection to the Danes submitted to him. And he then entrusted the borough to the control of Ealdorman Ethelred.[3]

887 (888 C) In this year the Danish army went up past the bridge at Paris, then up along the Seine to the Marne, and then up the Marne as far as Chézy, and stayed there and in the Yonne area, spending two winters[4] in those two places.

And the same year Charles,[5] king of the Franks, died; and six weeks before he died his brother's son Arnulf had deprived him of the kingdom.[6] The kingdom was then divided into five, and five kings were consecrated to it. It was done, however, with Arnulf's consent and they said that they would hold it under him, for not one of them was born to it in the male line but him alone. Arnulf then lived in the land east of the Rhine, and Rudolf[7] succeeded to the middle kingdom and Odo[8] to the western portion; and Berengar[9] and Guido[10] to Lombardy and the lands on that side of the Alps; and they held it with much discord and fought two general engagements,[11] and ravaged[12] the land again and again, and each repeatedly drove out the other.

And the same year in which the army went up beyond the bridge at Paris, Ealdorman Æthelhelm[13] took to Rome the alms of King Alfred and the West Saxons.[14]

888 (889 C) In this year Ealdorman Beocca took to Rome the alms of the West Saxons and of King Alfred. And Queen Æthelswith, who was King Alfred's sister, died,[15] and her body is buried in Pavia. And the same year Archbishop Ethelred and Ealdorman Æthelwold died in the same month.

889 (890 C) There was no expedition to Rome in this year, but King Alfred sent two couriers with letters.

[1] 'A' and Æthelweard omit the mention of Paris. Asser has it and more detail: "They pitched a camp on both sides of the river near the bridge, to prevent the citizens from crossing the bridge—for that city is situated on a small island in the middle of the river—and besieged the city all that year. But since God compassionately befriended them and the citizens defended themselves manfully, they could not break through the fortifications."

[2] It is clear from Asser's addition, that it was "after the burning of cities and the massacre of people", that Alfred obtained London by warfare, and it is probably implied by Florence of Worcester, using some lost source, when he says: "After his (the last Mercian king, Ceolwulf's) death, Alfred, king of the West Saxons, in order to expel completely the army of the pagan Danes from his kingdom, recovered London with the surrounding areas by his activity, and acquired the part of the kingdom of the Mercians which Ceolwulf had held" (ed. Thorpe, I, p. 267).

[3] The lord of the Mercians, who married Alfred's daughter Æthelflæd. Under their rule, Mercia preserved its autonomy.

[4] The winters of 886–7, 887–8. [5] Charles the Fat, who died in January 888.

[6] On 11 November 887. [7] Count of Upper Burgundy. [8] Count of Paris.

[9] Margrave of Friuli. [10] Duke of Spoleto.

[11] If the battles of Brescia, autumn 888, and Trebbia, spring 889, are meant, this annal cannot have been composed until some way on in the latter year. It does not say they took place in 887.

[12] 'C', "burnt". [13] Asser 'of Wiltshire'. [14] This is the last annal to be used by Asser.

[15] By a minor alteration, 'D', 'E' suggest that she was on her way to Rome, and 'F' says so expressly, but it may be only inference. She was wife of Burgred of Mercia.

890 (891 C) In this year Abbot Beornhelm took to Rome the alms of the West Saxons and of King Alfred. And the northern king, Guthrum, whose baptismal name was Athelstan, died.[1] He was King Alfred's godson, and he lived in East Anglia and was the first[2] to settle that land.

And the same year the Danish army went from the Seine to St. Lô, which lies between Brittany and France; and the Bretons fought against them and had the victory, and drove them into a river and drowned many of them.

F890 In this year Plegmund was elected by God and all the people to the archbishopric of Canterbury.[3]

---

891 (891 A, F; 892 C, D)[4] In this year the Danish army went east, and King Arnulf with the East Franks, the Saxons and Bavarians fought against the mounted force before the ships arrived, and put it to flight.[5]

And three Scots came to King Alfred in a boat without any oars from Ireland, which they had left secretly, because they wished for the love of God to be in foreign lands, they cared not where. The boat in which they travelled was made of two and a half hides, and they took with them enough food for seven days. And after seven days they came to land in Cornwall, and went immediately to King Alfred.[6] Their names were as follows: Dubslane, Machbethu and Maelinmum. And Swifneh, the best scholar among the Scots, died.

(892 A)[7] And the same year after Easter,[8] at the Rogation days[9] or before, there appeared the star which is called in Latin *cometa*. Some men say that it is in English the long-haired star, for there shines a long ray from it, sometimes on one side, sometimes on every side.[10]

892 (892 A, E, F; 893 C, D)[11] In this year the great Danish army, which we have spoken about before, went back from[12] the eastern kingdom westward to Boulogne, and they were provided with ships there, so that they crossed in one journey, horses and all, and then came up into the estuary of the Lympne with 200 [and 50][13] ships. That estuary is in East Kent, at the east end of that great[14]

---

[1] The *Annals of St. Neots* say he was buried at the royal residence at Hadleigh.   [2] *i.e.* of the Danes.

[3] The compiler of 'F' added Plegmund's election into 'A'. It is entered in Latin in 'E'.

[4] 'E' omits this annal. 'C' continues one year ahead. 'D' and 'E' both have a blank annal 891, then 'D' puts this annal under 892 and continues to be in advance of the true date until 914.

[5] This is the great victory on the River Dyle. It used to be held that it occurred in November, in which case the chronicler is no longer beginning his year in September, for November 891 would have been entered under 892. But it is not certain that the battle was so late in the year, one continental opinion putting it in September, or even late August.

[6] Æthelweard says that then they went towards Rome, intending to go to Jerusalem.

[7] The first scribe in the Parker MS. ('A') ends with this annal number. The second scribe, with something to add to the annal, did not delete the number 892, though he begins his next annal 892. This repeat was got rid of later by someone who added one to the original dates of 'A' up to (and including) the blank annal 929. Possibly he compared a text like 'C' that was already one year ahead. As a result of this, 'A', 'C' and 'D' are all, for different reasons, one year in advance. 'E' and 'F' alone are correct for 892, but do not contain the subsequent annals. 'B' has no dates. I give the original dates of 'A', not the corrected ones.

[8] 4 April.   [9] 10–12 May.   [10] 'D' omits the last four words.   [11] On these dates, see n. 4 above.

[12] 'C' writes, "into".   [13] Omitted by 'B', 'C', 'D'. The *Annals of St. Neots* have 350.

[14] So in 'A', 'E', 'F'; "the same wood" 'B', 'C', 'D'.

wood which we call *Andred*.[1] The wood is from east to west 120 miles long, or longer, and 30 miles broad. The river, of which we spoke before, comes out of the Weald. They rowed their ships up the river as far as the Weald, four miles from the mouth of the estuary, and there they stormed a fortress. Inside that fortification[2] there were a few peasants, and it was only half made.

Then immediately afterwards Hæsten[3] came with 80 ships up the Thames estuary and made himself a fortress at Milton,[4] and the other army made one at Appledore.[5]

893[6] (894 C, D) In this year, that was twelve months after the Danes had built the fortress in the eastern kingdom, the Northumbrians and East Angles had given King Alfred oaths, and the East Angles had given six preliminary hostages; and yet, contrary to those pledges, as often as the other Danish armies went out in full force, they went either with them or on their behalf.[7] And then King Alfred collected his army, and advanced to take up a position between the two enemy forces, where he had the nearest convenient site with regard both to the fort in the wood and the fort by the water,[8] so that he could reach either army, if they chose to come into the open country. Then they went afterwards along the Weald in small bands and mounted companies, by whatever side it was then undefended by the English army. And also they were sought by other bands,[9] almost every day, either by day or by night, both from the English army and from the boroughs. The king had divided his army into two, so that always half its men were at home, half on service, apart from the men who guarded the boroughs. The enemy did not all come out of those encampments more than twice: once when they first landed, before the English force was assembled, and once when they wished to leave those encampments.[10] Then they captured much booty, and wished to carry it north across the Thames into Essex, to meet the ships. Then the English army intercepted them and fought against them at Farnham, and put the enemy to flight and recovered the booty. And the Danes fled across the Thames where there was no ford, and up along the Colne on to

---

[1] The Weald. See p. 144, n. 1.

[2] This is the reading of 'B', 'C', 'D'. 'A', 'E', 'F' read: "... stormed a fortress in the fen; inside were a few peasants."

[3] Old Norse Hásteinn (*Hastingus*), a viking leader first heard of c.a the Loire in 866, who afterwards had an active career on the Continent.

[4] Milton Royal, near Sittingbourne, Kent.

[5] After this annal begins the long gap in 'E'. See p. 112. 'E,' 'F' have a Latin entry: "In this year died Wulfhere, archbishop of the Northumbrians."

[6] This annal is not in 'E'. On the dates, see p. 184, n. 4. In this and the next six annals the word *Her* is not used to introduce the annals.

[7] 'C' has, wrongly, "on the other side", but even the correct reading is not free from ambiguity. I take it to mean that they either joined the invading armies or made raids of their own to assist them. But some scholars would render "or on their own behalf".

[8] This is the usual interpretation, but one could render: "where he had the nearest site affording him the protection of wood and water".

[9] From 'A'. 'B', 'C', 'D' have an inferior reading, "peoples".

[10] Here Æthelweard, who has had nothing corresponding to the first part of this annal, supplies some information. He says that after Easter they raided as far as Wessex, and ravaged Hampshire and Berkshire, and that the army which intercepted them at Farnham was led by Alfred's son Edward.

an islet.[1] Then the English forces besieged them there for as long as their provisions lasted; but they had completed their term of service and used up their provisions, and the king was then on the way there with the division which was serving with him. When he was on his way there and the other English army was on its way home, and the Danes were remaining behind there because their king had been wounded in the battle, so that they could not move him,[2] those Danes who lived in Northumbria and East Anglia collected some hundred ships, and went south round the coast [And some 40 ships went north around the coast][3] and besieged a fortress on the north coast of Devon, and those who had gone south besieged Exeter.

When the king heard that, he turned west towards Exeter with the whole army, except for a very inconsiderable portion of the people (who continued) eastwards. They went on until they came to London, and then with the citizens and with the reinforcements which came to them from the west, they went east to Benfleet. Hæsten had then come there with his army which had been at Milton, and the large army which had been at Appledore on the estuary of the Lympne had then also come there. Hæsten had previously built that fortress at Benfleet; and he was then out on a raid, and the large army was at home. Then the English went there and put the enemy to flight, and stormed the fortress and captured all that was within, both goods, and women and also children, and brought all to London; and they either broke up or burnt all the ships, or brought them to London or to Rochester. And Hæsten's wife and two sons were brought to the king; and he gave them back to him, because one of them was his godson, and the other the godson of Ealdorman Ethelred. They had stood sponsor to them before Hæsten came to Benfleet,[4] and he had given the king oaths and hostages, and the king had also made him generous gifts of money, and so he did also when he gave back the boy and the woman. But immediately they came to Benfleet and had made that fortress, Hæsten ravaged his kingdom, that very province which Ethelred, his son's godfather, was in charge of; and again, a second time, he had gone on a raid in that same kingdom when his fortress was stormed.[5]

When the king had turned west with the army towards Exeter, as I have said before, and the Danish army had laid siege to the borough, they went to

[1] Æthelweard calls it Thorney, which has been identified by Sir Frank Stenton as an island near Iver, Bucks.

[2] The chronicler never makes it clear what happened next to these survivors of the great army. We find them a little later with Hæsten at Benfleet. Æthelweard allows us to fill in this gap. He says that Ealdorman Ethelred (whom he wrongly calls king) brought help from London to Edward, who was in charge of the eastward part of the English forces, and that the Danes came to terms, gave hostages and swore to leave Alfred's kingdom; they then joined the ships from the Lympne at Mersea Island.

[3] From 'A'. It is omitted in the other MSS.

[4] Presumably, therefore, Alfred had been in negotiation during the period earlier in the year while he camped between the two armies; but it is just possible that these events took place in 885, where the original Chronicle no doubt had a reference to the sojourn of vikings at Benfleet, though owing to an accidental omission, we have only Æthelweard's garbled version to go by (see p. 182, n. 1). There is, however, no evidence that Hæsten was leading the army in England in that year.

[5] Is it from misunderstanding, or additional information, that the *Annals of St. Neots* have instead of this last sentence: "But when Hæsten came again to Benfleet he repaired there the fortress, which had been destroyed"?

their ships when he arrived there. When he was occupied against the army there in the west, and the (other) two Danish armies were assembled at Shoebury in Essex, and had made a fortress there, they went both together up along the Thames, and a great reinforcement came to them both from the East Angles and the Northumbrians. [They then went up along the Thames until they reached the Severn, then up along the Severn.][1] Then Ealdorman Ethelred and Ealdorman Æthelhelm and Ealdorman Æthelnoth and the king's thegns who then were at home at the fortresses assembled from every borough east of the Parret, and both west and east of Selwood, and also north of the Thames and west of the Severn, and also some portion of the Welsh people. When they were all assembled, they overtook the Danish army at Buttington on the bank of the Severn, and besieged it on every side in a fortress. Then when they had encamped for many weeks on the two sides of the river, and the king was occupied in the west in Devon against the naval force, the besieged were oppressed by famine, and had eaten the greater part of their horses and the rest had died of starvation. They then came out against the men who were encamped on the east side of the river, and fought against them, and the Christians had the victory. And the king's thegn Ordheah and also many other king's thegns were killed, and a very great [slaughter][2] of the Danes was made, and the part that escaped were saved by flight.

When they came to Essex to their fortress and their ships, the survivors collected again before winter a large army from the East Angles and Northumbrians, placed their women and ships and property in safety in East Anglia, and went continuously by day and night till they reached a deserted city in Wirral, which is called Chester. Then the English army could not overtake them before they were inside that fortress. However, they besieged the fortress for some two days, and seized all the cattle that was outside, and killed the men whom they could cut off outside the fortress, and burnt all the corn, or consumed it by means of their horses, in all the surrounding districts. And that was twelve months after they had come hither across the sea.[3]

894 (895 C, D)[4] And then in this year, immediately after that, the Danish army went into Wales from Wirral, because they could not stay there. That was because they were deprived both of the cattle and the corn which had been ravaged. When they turned back from Wales with the booty they had captured there, they went, so that the English army could not reach them, across Northumbria and into East Anglia, until they came into east Essex on to an island called Mersea, which is out in the sea.

And when the Danish army which had besieged Exeter turned homewards, they ravaged up in Sussex near Chichester, and the citizens put them to flight and killed many hundreds of them, and captured some of their ships.

---

[1] Supplied from 'A'. 'D' has the same statement in more concise wording.
[2] Supplied from 'D'. 'A' has omitted the whole clause, but it is necessary for the sense.
[3] Æthelweard makes no reference to the raid on Chester. Instead, after speaking of the capture of Benfleet and the battle of Buttington, he tells us that the pirate Sigeferth came with a fleet from Northumbria and twice ravaged the coast, and then returned home.
[4] On the dating, see p. 184, n. 4. 'E' omits this annal.

Then that same year in early winter[1] the Danes who were encamped on Mersea rowed their ships up the Thames and up the Lea. That was two years after they came hither across the sea.[2]

895 (896 C, D)[3] And in the same year[4] the aforesaid army made a fortress by the Lea, 20 miles above London. Then afterwards in the summer a great part of the citizens and also of other people marched till they arrived at the fortress of the Danes, and there they were put to flight and four king's thegns were slain. Then later, in the autumn, the king encamped in the vicinity of the borough while they were reaping their corn, so that the Danes could not deny them that harvest. Then one day the king rode up along the river, and examined where the river could be obstructed, so that they could not bring the ships out. And then this was carried out: two fortresses were made on the two sides of the river. When they had just begun that work [and had encamped for that purpose],[5] the enemy perceived that they could not bring the ships out. Then they abandoned the ships and went overland till they reached Bridgnorth on the Severn and built that fortress. Then the English army rode after the enemy, and the men from London fetched the ships, and broke up all which they could not bring away, and brought to London those which were serviceable. And the Danes had placed their women in safety in East Anglia before they left that fortress. Then they stayed the winter at Bridgnorth.[6] That was three years after they had come hither across the sea into the estuary of the Lympne.[7]

896 (897 C, D)[8] And afterwards in the summer of this year the Danish army divided, one force going into East Anglia and one into Northumbria; and those that were moneyless got themselves ships and went south across the sea to the Seine.

By the grace of God, the army had not on the whole afflicted the English people very greatly;[9] but they were much more seriously afflicted in those three years by the mortality of cattle and men, and most of all in that many of the best king's thegns who were in the land died in those three years. Of those, one was Swithwulf, bishop of Rochester, and Ceolmund, ealdorman of Kent, and Brihtwulf, ealdorman of Essex [and Wulfred, ealdorman of Hampshire],[10] and Ealhheard, bishop of Dorchester, and Eadwulf, a king's thegn in Sussex, and Beornwulf, the town-reeve of Winchester, and Ecgwulf, the king's marshal, and many besides them, though I have named the most distinguished.

---

[1] So in all MSS. except 'A', which has "before winter".

[2] Æthelweard says that when two years were completed from the arrival at Lympne, Ealdorman Æthelnoth went from Wessex to York against the enemy, who laid waste a large stretch of country in Mercia west of Stamford, between the Welland and the wood called Kesteven. This is probably to be connected with the raids of Sigeferth which he has just mentioned. On the importance of this information, see F. M. Stenton, in *Eng. Hist. Rev.*, XXIV (1909), pp. 79–84.

[3] On the dates, see p. 184, n. 4. 'E' omits this annal.

[4] The first sentence of this annal would have been better placed at the end of the previous one.

[5] 'C' omits this clause.

[6] This is given its full name, *Cwatbrycg*, at this point, only by 'A'. The others call it simply 'Bridge'.

[7] Æthelweard assigns to this year, on St. Bartholomew's day (24 August) the death of Guthfrith, king of the Northumbrians, and says he was buried at York Minster. Cf. pp. 35, 94.

[8] On the dates, see p. 184, n. 4. 'E' omits this annal.

[9] So 'B', 'C', 'D'; "too greatly", 'A'.   [10] From 'A'; omitted by the other MSS.

In the same year the armies in East Anglia and Northumbria greatly harassed Wessex along the south coast with marauding bands, most of all with the warships which they had built many years before. Then King Alfred had 'long ships' built to oppose the Danish warships. They were almost twice as long as the others. Some had 60 oars, some more. They were both swifter and steadier and also higher than the others. They were built neither on the Frisian nor the Danish pattern, but as it seemed to him himself that they could be most useful. Then on a certain occasion of the same year, six ships came to the Isle of Wight and did great harm there, both in Devon and everywhere along the coast. Then the king ordered (a force) to go thither with nine of the new ships, and they blocked the estuary from the seaward end. Then the Danes went out against them with three ships, and three were on dry land farther up the estuary; the men from them had gone up on land. Then the English captured two of those three ships at the entrance to the estuary, and killed the men, and the one ship escaped. On it also the men were killed except five. These got away because the ships of their opponents ran aground. Moreover, they·had run aground very awkwardly: three were aground on that side of the channel on which the Danish ships were aground, and all [the others][1] on the other side, so that none of them could get to the others. But when the water had ebbed many furlongs from the ships, the Danes from the remaining three ships went to the other three which were stranded on their side, and they then fought there. And there were killed the king's reeve Lucuman, Wulfheard the Frisian, Æbba the Frisian, Æthelhere the Frisian, Æthelfrith the king's *geneat*,[2] and in all 62 Frisians and English and 120 of the Danes. Then, however, the tide reached the Danish ships before the Christians could launch theirs, and therefore they rowed away out. They were then so wounded that they could not row past Sussex, but the sea cast two of them on to the land, and the men were brought to Winchester[3] to the king, and he ordered them to be hanged. And the men who were on the one ship reached East Anglia greatly wounded. That same summer no fewer than 20 ships, men and all, perished along the south coast. That same year died Wulfric, the king's marshal, who was [also][4] the Welsh-reeve.[5]

897 (898 C, D)[6] In this year, nine days before midsummer, Æthelhelm, ealdorman of Wiltshire, died; and in this year died Heahstan,[7] who was bishop of London.

	C (A, B)	D (E, F)
900	(901 C)[8] In this year Alfred the son of Æthelwulf died, six days before All Saints' Day. He was king	(901 D, E, F)[8] In this year King Alfred died on 26

---

[1] From 'A'; omitted by the other MSS.   [2] See p. 366, n. 3.   [3] 'D' has wrongly *Wiltunceastre* here.
[4] Supplied from 'A'.   [5] It is very uncertain what this term implies.
[6] On the dates, see p. 184, n. 4. With this annal recommences the beginning of the annals with *Her*. 'E' omits this annal.
[7] From 'A'; all other MSS. make the mistake of calling him Ealhstan.
[8] On the dates, see p. 184, n. 4. Æthelweard records in 899, before Alfred's death, a great discord because of the hosts of the Northumbrians, especially among the places still belonging to the English.

C (A, B)	D (E, F)
over the whole English people except for that part which was under Danish rule, and he had held the kingdom for one and a half years less than thirty; and then his son Edward succeeded to the kingdom.	October; and he had held the kingdom 28 years and half a year; and then his son Edward succeeded to the kingdom.[1]

Then the atheling Æthelwold, his father's brother's son,[2] rode and seized the residence at Wimborne[3] and at *Twinham*,[4] against the will of the king[5] and his councillors. Then the king rode with the army till he encamped at Badbury[6] near Wimborne, and Æthelwold stayed inside the residence with the men who had given allegiance to him; and he had barricaded all the gates against him, and said that he would either live there or die there. Then meanwhile the atheling rode away[7] by night, and went to the Danish army in Northumbria, and they accepted him as king and gave allegiance to him.[8] Then the woman was seized whom he had taken without the king's permission and contrary to the bishops' orders—for she had been consecrated a nun.

And in this same year Ethelred, who was ealdorman of Devon, died four weeks before King Alfred.[9]

901[10] (902 A; 903 B, C, D) In this year Ealdorman Æthelwulf, the brother of Ealhswith, King Edward's mother,[11] died, and Virgilius, an abbot among the Scots, and the priest Grimbald.

902[12] (903 A; 904 B, C, D) In this year Æthelwold[13] came hither across the sea with all the fleet he could procure, and submission was made to him in Essex.[14]

---

[1] 'E' and 'F' end the annal here. 'D' continues with the other events, as in 'A', 'B', 'C'.
[2] He was son of King Ethelred, Alfred's elder brother and predecessor.
[3] This was where his father was buried and probably belonged to his branch of the family.
[4] Now Christchurch, Hampshire.   [5] 'A' reads: "without the king's permission".
[6] Badbury Rings, a prehistoric earthwork.   [7] "He stole away", 'A'.
[8] It is interesting to note that our most West Saxon version, 'A', omits all reference to Æthelwold's acceptance as king. Instead, it says merely: "And the king ordered them to pursue him, and then he could not be overtaken."
[9] Æthelweard, who has no reference to the atheling's rebellion, says that in this year Æthelbald was consecrated archbishop of York, in London.
[10] This annal is not in 'E'. The chronology of this reign is confused. From 901 to 905, 'B', 'C', 'D' and the corrected dates in 'A' are two years ahead, the original dates in 'A' one year. Then 'A' dates 905, 'C' 'D', 906, the peace of Tiddingford, which, judging by Simeon, took place in 906. From then until 912, 'A' is correct, but from 913 to 920 it is three years ahead. 'C', 'D' are one year in advance from 908 to 914, and omit the later annals of Edward's reign. The insertion of the Mercian Register, in a block after a series of blank annals in 'B', 'C' (see pp. 110f.), piecemeal in 'D', causes further complication. I have given its annals under their true years, and I give the original dates of 'A'.
[11] 'A' omits "King Edward's mother"
[12] Probably the autumn of 901. 'E' omits this annal.
[13] *Annals of St. Neots* add: "king of the Danes".
[14] 'A' merely says, "came to Essex with the fleet with which he was"; 'D', "came, with all the fleet which he could procure and which was subject to him, to Essex".

Main Chronicle (A, B, C, D)

903[2] (904 A; 905 B, C, D) In this year Æthelwold induced[3] the army in East Anglia to break the peace so that they harried over all Mercia until they reached Cricklade. And they went then across the Thames, and carried off all that they could seize both in and round about Braydon, and turned then homeward. Then King Edward went after them as soon as he could collect his army, and harried all their land between the Dykes and the Ouse[5], all as far north as the fens. When he wished to go back from there he had it announced over the whole army that they were all to set out together. Then the men of Kent lingered behind there against his command – and he had sent seven messengers to them. Then the Danish army overtook them there, and they fought there. And there were killed Ealdorman Sigewulf and Ealdorman Sigehelm,[6] and the king's thegn Ealdwold, and Abbot Cenwulf, and Sigeberht, Sigewulf's son, and Eadwold, Acca's son, and many besides them, though I have named the most distinguished. And on the Danish side King Eohric[7] was killed, and the atheling Æthelwold, whom they had chosen as their king,[8] and Brihtsige, son of the atheling Beornoth, and Ysopa the *hold*[9] and Oscetel the *hold* and also very many with them, whom we cannot name now. And a great slaughter was made on both sides, but more of the Danes were killed, though they remained in possession of the battle-field. And Ealhswith died in that same year.

Mercian Register[1]

(902) In this year Ealhswith died,[4] and in the same year occurred the battle of the Holme between the people of Kent and the Danes.

F903 In this year Grimbald the priest died, and in the same year the New Minster at Winchester was consecrated, and (there occurred) St. Judoc's arrival.[10]

---

[1] On this document, see pp. 110f.

[2] The events of this annal probably took place at the end of 902, which was reckoned as 903 in a chronicle beginning its year 24 September.

[3] 'A' has "seduced". The *Annals of St. Neots* call Æthelwold "king of the pagans".

[4] 5 December.

[5] The Dykes are the Devil's Dyke and Fleam Dyke. Ekwall thinks the river is the Wissey, but see *The Place-Names of Cambridgeshire*, pp. 12–14.

[6] King Edward's father-in-law.   [7] King of East Anglia.

[8] 'A', which consistently ignores Æthelwold's kingship, has instead of this clause: "who enticed him to that war".

[9] A Scandinavian title, applied to a class of noblemen in the Danelaw, which had a wergild double that of a thegn. See p. 191, n. 9.

[10] *i.e.* of some relics of this seventh-century Breton saint.

Main Chronicle (A, B, C, D)	*Mercian Register*
904	In this year there was an eclipse of the moon.

905	In this year a comet appeared.[1]

906? (905 A; 906 C, D). In this year Alfred, who was reeve at Bath, died. And that same year the peace was established at Tiddingford,[2] just as King Edward decreed, both with the East Angles and the Northumbrians.

E906 In this year King Edward, from necessity, established peace both with the army of the East Angles and the Northumbrians.

Main Chronicle (A, B, C, D)	*Mercian Register*
907	In this year Chester was restored.

908 (909 C, D) In this year Denewulf, who was bishop of Winchester, died.[3]

Main Chronicle (A, B, C, D)	*Mercian Register*
909 (910 C, D) In this year Frithestan[4] succeeded to the bishopric in Winchester, and after that Asser, who was bishop of Sherborne, died. And that same year King Edward sent an army both from the West Saxons and from the Mercians, and it ravaged very severely the territory of the northern army, both men and all kinds of cattle, and they killed many men of those Danes, and were five weeks there.	In this year St. Oswald's body was brought from Bardney into Mercia.[5]
910 (911 C, D) In this year the army in Northumbria broke the peace, and scorned every privilege[6] that King Edward and his councillors offered them, and ravaged over Mercia. And the king had collected about 100 ships, and was then in Kent, and the ships were on their way south-east by sea towards him. Then the Danish army	In this year the English and Danes fought at Tettenhall, and the English were victorious. And that same year Æthelflæd built the borough at *Bremesbyrig*.[7]

[1] 'D' puts this entry at the beginning of the annal it dates 905, adding that it was on 20 October.
[2] Near Leighton Buzzard.
[3] 'F' enters his death 909. Æthelweard records the dedication by Archbishop Plegmund of a 'high tower' in Winchester newly founded in honour of St. Mary, and Plegmund's journey to Rome with the alms of the people and of King Edward.
[4] This name is marked with a small cross in the text of 'A', and there is a red frame round the beginning of the entry, and a large cross in the margin. See p. 109 n.
[5] 'D' places this at the beginning of the annal it dates 906.   [6] 'A', "peace".
[7] 'D' puts this entry at the beginning of the annal it dates 909. It has recorded the battle three times, from the Main Chronicle, from the Mercian Register, and in the annal dated 910 which it shares with 'E'. It adds to the Mercian Register the date, 6 August.

Main Chronicle (A, B, C, D)

thought that the greater part of his forces was
on the ships, and that they could go unopposed
wherever they wished. Then the king learnt that
they had gone on a raid. He then sent his army
both from the West Saxons and Mercians, and
they overtook the Danish army when it was on
its way home and fought against it and put the
army to flight and killed many thousands of its
men.[1] And there were killed King Eowils[2] and
King Healfdene[3] and Earl Ohter and Earl Scurfa,
and Othulf the *hold*,[4] and Benesing the *hold*, and
Anlaf the Black and Thurferth the *hold*, and
Osfrith Hlytta,[5] and Guthfrith the *hold*,[6] and
Agmund the *hold* and Guthfrith.

D, E 910[7] In this year the English army and the Danish army fought at Tettenhall, and Ethelred, lord of the Mercians, died, and King Edward
succeeded to London and Oxford and to all the lands which belonged
to them; and a great naval force came hither from the south from
Brittany, and ravaged greatly by the Severn, but they almost all
perished afterwards.

Main Chronicle (A, B, C, D)	Mercian Register
911 (912 C, D) In this year Ethelred, ealdorman of the Mercians, died,[8] and King Edward succeeded to London and Oxford and to all the lands which belonged to them.	Then the next year Ethelred, lord of the Mercians, died.
912 (913 C, D) In this year about Martinmas, King Edward ordered the northern borough at Hertford to be built, between the Maran, the Beane	In this year Æthelflæd, lady of the Mercians, came on the holy eve of the

[1] Æthelweard has fuller information on this battle, which he seems to date 909. "After one year the
barbarians break their pact with King Edward and with Ethelred, who then ruled the districts of Northumbria and Mercia. The fields of the Mercians are wasted on all sides by the aforesaid disturbance, right up to
the River Avon, where begins the boundary of the West Angles (*i.e.* Saxons) and the Mercians. Thence
they cross over the River Severn into the western districts, and there obtained by plunder no little booty.
But when, exulting in their rich spoils, they withdrew homewards, they crossed a bridge on the eastern side
of the Severn, which is commonly called *Cantbrycg*. A battle-line was formed, and the troops of the Mercians
and the West Saxons suddenly went against them. A battle ensued and the English without delay obtained
the victory at Wednesfield (near Tettenhall), and the army of the Danes was put to flight, overcome by
weapons. These things are said to have been done on the fifth day of the month of August. And it may
rightly be said that in that turmoil or encounter three of their kings fell, namely Healfdene and Eywysl, and
also Ivar lost his sovereignty and hastened to the court of hell, and with them their more distinguished
leaders and nobles."
Both Florence and the *Annals of St. Neots* have the name Wednesfield.
[2] 'A' omits the rest of this annal.   [3] Florence calls them "brothers of King Hinguar" (Ivar).
[4] 'D' omits the rest of the annal except "and Agmund the *hold*". On this title, see p. 191, n. 9.
[5] G. Tengvik, *Old English Bynames*, p. 347, renders this "diviner, soothsayer".
[6] The *Annals of St. Neots* add Eagellus, and omit the second Guthfrith.
[7] This annal, which stands alone in 'E', but in 'D' is added to that from the Main Chronicle which 'D'
dates 910, records the events of several years, 910, 911, 914.
[8] Æthelweard, who dates this 910, adds that he was buried in Gloucester.

Main Chronicle (A, B, C, D)   *Mercian Register*

and the Lea, and then after that in the summer, between Rogation days and midsummer,[2] King Edward went with some of his forces into Essex to Maldon, and camped there while the borough was being made and constructed at Witham,[4] and a good number of the people who had been under the rule of the Danish men submitted to him. And meanwhile some of his forces made the borough at Hertford on the south side of the Lea.[5]

Invention of the Cross[1] to *Scergeat*, and built the borough there, and in the same year that at Bridgnorth.[3]

913 (916 A; 914 C, D) In this year the army from Northampton and Leicester rode out after Easter[6] and broke the peace, and killed many men at Hook Norton and round about there. And then very soon after that, as the one force came home, they met another raiding band[7] which rode out against Luton. And then the people of the district became aware of it and fought against them and reduced them to full flight and rescued all that they had captured and also a great part of their horses and their weapons.

In this year, by the grace of God, Æthelflæd, lady of the Mercians, went with all the Mercians to Tamworth, and built the borough there in the early summer, and afterwards, before Lammas,[8] that at Stafford;[9]

914 (917 A; 915 C, D) In this year a great naval force came over here from the south from Brittany, and two earls, Ohter and Hroald, with them. And they then went west round the coast so that they arrived at the Severn estuary and ravaged in Wales everywhere along the coast where it suited them. And they captured Cyfeiliog, bishop of Archenfield,[11] and took him with them to the ships; and then King Edward ransomed him for 40 pounds. Then after that all the army went inland, still wishing to go on a raid towards Archenfield. Then the men from Hereford and Gloucester and from the nearest boroughs met them and fought against them and put them to flight and killed the earl Hroald and the brother of Ohter, the other earl, and a great part of the

then afterwards in the next year, that at Eddisbury in the early summer, and later in the same year, in the early autumn, that at Warwick;[10]

[1] 2 May.

[2] *i.e.* between 18 May and 24 June. The order of events in this annal, beginning about Martinmas (11 November), suggests that the year is beginning in September.

[3] This annal is not in 'D'.

[4] The *Annals of St. Neots* add: "about the feast of John the Baptist" (presumably the Nativity, 24 June).

[5] Æthelweard has nothing for this year except that he records the death of Eadwulf, who was high-reeve of Bamburgh, in Northumbria.

[6] 28 March.   [7] 'C' has wrongly "band of people".   [8] 1 August.

[9] 'D' enters a brief version of this annal at the beginning of its annal for 913 (real date 912).

[10] 'D' has a brief reference to the building of Warwick at the beginning of its annal 915 (real date 914).

[11] Herefordshire. The name survives as that of a deanery.

Main Chronicle (A, B, C, D)　　　　　　*Mercian Register*

army, and drove them into an enclosure and besieged them there until they gave them hostages, (promising) that they would leave the king's dominion. And the king had arranged that men were stationed against them on the south[1] side of the Severn estuary, from the west, from Cornwall, east as far as Avonmouth, so that they dared not attack the land anywhere on that side. Yet they stole inland by night on two occasions— on the one occasion east of Watchet, on the other occasion at Porlock. Then on both occasions they were attacked, so that few of them got away— only those who could swim out to the ships. And then they remained out on the island of Steepholme[2] until they became very short of food and many men had died of hunger because they could not obtain any food. Then they went from there to Dyfed, and from there to Ireland; and this was in the autumn.[3]

And then after that in the same year, before Martinmas,[4] King Edward went to Buckingham with his army, and stayed there four weeks, and made both the boroughs, on each side of the river, before he went away. And Earl Thurcetel came and accepted him as his lord, and so did all the earls[5] and the principal men who belonged to Bedford, and also many of those who belonged to Northampton.[6]

A *only*[7]

915 (918) In this year King Edward went with his army to Bedford, before Martinmas, and obtained the borough; and almost all the citizens, who dwelt there before, submitted to him. And he stayed there four weeks, and before he went away ordered the borough on the south side of the river to be built.

then afterwards in the next year after Christmas, that at Chirbury and that at *Weardbyrig*; and in the same year before Christmas, that at Runcorn.

916 (919) In this year, before midsummer,[8] King Edward went to Maldon and built and established the borough before he went away. And that same

In this year Abbot Egbert, though innocent, was killed before midsummer

---

[1] 'C' omits "south".　　　　　　　　　　　　　[2] So 'B', 'C', 'D'; 'A' has Flatholme.

[3] Æthelweard refers briefly to these events, which he dates 913. He merely speaks of the arrival of a fleet, of the absence of any heavy engagement, and of its departure for Ireland.

[4] 11 November.　　　　　　　　　　　　　　　[5] So 'B', 'C', 'D'; 'A', *holds*.

[6] Æthelweard has entered the invasion of this year in 913. He then comments on the peacefulness of the winter of 914, when Christmas Day fell on a Sunday.

[7] The account of the latter campaigns of Edward is in 'A' only.　　　　　　[8] 24 June.

A	*Mercian Register*

year Earl Thurcetel went across the sea to France, along with the men who were willing to serve him, with King Edward's peace and support.

on 16 June – that same day was the festival of St. Ciriacus the martyr – with his companions. And three days later Æthelflæd sent an army nto Wales and destroyed *Brecenanmere*,[1] and captured the king's wife and 33[2] other persons.

917 (920) In this year before Easter[3] King Edward ordered the borough at Towcester to be occupied and built; and then after that in the same year at the Rogation days[4] he ordered the borough at *Wigingamere* to be built. That same summer, between Lammas and midsummer,[5] the army from Northampton and Leicester and north of these places broke the peace, and went to Towcester, and fought all day against the borough, intending to take it by storm, but yet the people who were inside defended it until more help came to them, and the enemy then left the borough and went away. And then very quickly after that, they again went out with a marauding band by night, and came upon unprepared men, and captured no small number of men and cattle, between Bernwood Forest and Aylesbury. At the same time the army came from Huntingdon and East Anglia and made the fortress at Tempsford, and took up quarters in it and built it, and abandoned the other fortress at Huntingdon, thinking that from Tempsford they would reach more of the land with strife and hostility. And they went till they reached Bedford; and the men who were inside went out against them, and fought against them and put them to flight, and killed a good part of them. Yet again after that a great army assembled from East Anglia and Mercia, and went to the borough at *Wigingamere* and besieged and attacked it long into the day, and seized the cattle round about; and yet the men who were inside defended the borough. And then the enemy left the borough and went away.

In this year, Æthelflæd, lady of the Mercians, with the help of God, before Lammas obtained the borough which is called Derby, with all that belongs to it; and there also four of her thegns, who were dear to her, were killed within the gates.[6]

---

[1] Langorse Lake, near Brecon. See J. E. Lloyd, *A History of Wales*, 2nd ed., p. 331, n. 41.

[2] The idiom, 'one of thirty-four', may perhaps be meant literally when no round figures are involved. But see p. 148, n. 5.

[3] 13 April.   [4] 19–21 May.   [5] 24 June–1 August.   [6] 'D' has this annal, with the true date.

A

Then after that during the same summer a great host assembled in King Edward's dominions from the nearest boroughs which could manage it[1] and went to Tempsford and besieged the borough and attacked it until they took it by storm; and they killed the king and Earl Toglos and his son Earl Manna, and his brother and all those who were inside and chose to defend themselves; and they captured the others and everything that was inside.

And afterwards, very soon after that, a great (English) host assembled in autumn, both from Kent, from Surrey, from Essex and from the nearest boroughs on all sides; and they went to Colchester and besieged the borough and attacked it until they took it and killed all the people and seized everything that was inside—except the men who fled there over the wall.

Then after that, still in the same autumn, a great army from East Anglia collected, consisting both of the army of the district and of the vikings whom they had enticed to their assistance, and they intended to avenge their injury. And they went to Maldon and besieged the borough and attacked it until more troops came to the help of the citizens from outside; and the army left the borough and went away. Then the men from the borough, and also those who had come to their assistance from outside, went out after them and put the army to flight, and killed many hundreds of them, both of the shipmen and of the others.

Then very soon afterwards in the same autumn King Edward went with the army of the West Saxons to Passenham, and stayed there while the borough of Towcester was provided with a stone wall. And Earl Thurferth and the *holds*[2] submitted to him, and so did all the army which belonged to Northampton, as far north as the Welland, and sought to have him as their lord and protector. And when that division of the English army went home, the other division came on service and captured the borough at Huntingdon, and repaired and restored it by King Edward's command where it had been broken; and all the people of that district who had survived submitted to King Edward and asked for his peace and protection.

Moreover, after that during the same year, before Martinmas, King Edward went with the army of the West Saxons to Colchester, and repaired and restored the borough where it had been broken. And many people who had been under the rule of the Danes[3] both in East Anglia and in Essex submitted to him; and all the army in East Anglia swore agreement with him, that they would (agree to) all that he would, and would keep peace with all with whom the king wished to keep peace, both at

---

[1] Assuming that the singular verb is an error. At this point begin three lines by a very poor scribe. An alternative rendering is: ". . . which could reach it" (Tempsford or the place of assembly?).
[2] See p. 191, n. 9.   [3] Florence adds: "for nearly 30 years".

A   *Mercian Register*

sea and on land. And the army which belonged to Cambridge chose him especially as its lord and protector, and established it with oaths just as he decreed it.

918 (921) In this year, between Rogation days and midsummer,[1] King Edward went with the army to Stamford, and ordered the borough on the south side of the river to be built; and all the people who belonged to the more northern borough submitted to him and sought to have him as their lord. Then during the stay he made there, his sister Æthelflæd died at Tamworth twelve days before midsummer. And then he occupied the borough of Tamworth, and all the nation in the land of the Mercians which had been subject to Æthelflæd submitted to him; and the kings in Wales, Hywel, Clydog and Idwal, and all the race of the Welsh, sought to have him as lord.

Then he went from there to Nottingham, and captured the borough and ordered it to be repaired and manned both with Englishmen and Danes. And all the people who had settled in Mercia, both Danish and English, submitted to him.

In this year, with God's help, she peacefully obtained control of the borough of Leicester, in the early part of the year; and the greater part of the army which belonged to it was subjected. And also the people of York had promised her – and some had given pledges, some had confirmed it with oaths – that they would be under her direction. But very soon after they had agreed to this, she died twelve days before midsummer[2] in Tamworth, in the eighth year in which with lawful authority she was holding dominion over the Mercians. And her body is buried in Gloucester in the east chapel of St. Peter's church.[3]

E918 In this year died Æthelflæd, lady of the Mercians.

A   *Mercian Register*

919 (922 A) In this year after autumn King Edward went with the army to Thelwall and ordered the borough to be built, occupied and manned; and while he stayed there he ordered another army, also from the people of Mercia, to occupy Manchester in Northumbria, and repair and man it. [In this year died Archbishop Plegmund.][6]

In this year[4] also the daughter of Ethelred, lord of the Mercians, was deprived of all authority in Mercia and taken into Wessex, three weeks before Christmas. She was called Ælfwyn.[5]

---

[1] 11 May–24 June.   [2] 'D' adds: "12 June".   [3] This annal is also in 'D', correctly dated.
     [4] It is possible, as Dr. Wainwright, *Eng. Hist. Rev.*, LX, p. 388, suggests, that this is really a continuation of the previous annal.
     [5] This annal is also in 'D', dated 919.   [6] The part in brackets is a late Canterbury addition.

A   *Mercian Register*

920 (923 A) In this year, before midsummer, King Edward went with the army to Nottingham, and ordered to be built the borough on the south side of the river, opposite the other, and the bridge over the Trent between the two boroughs.

Then he went from there into the Peak district to Bakewell, and ordered a borough to be built in the neighbourhood and manned. And then the king of the Scots and all the people of the Scots, and Ragnald, and the sons of Eadwulf and all who live in Northumbria, both English and Danish, Norsemen and others, and also the king of the Strathclyde Welsh and all the Strathclyde Welsh, chose him as father and lord.[1]

921   In this year King Edward built the borough at *Cledemutha*.[2]

E921[3] In this year King Sihtric killed his brother Niall.[4]
D, E923[3] In this year King Ragnald won York.

A (E, F)[5]   *Mercian Register*

924 (925 F) In this year King Edward died[6] and his son Athelstan succeeded to the kingdom.   In this year King Edward died at Farndon in Mercia, and his son Ælfweard died very soon after[7] at Oxford, and their bodies are buried at Winchester. And Athelstan was chosen by the Mercians as king, and consecrated at Kingston,[8] and he gave his sister in marriage[9] [over the sea to the son of the king of the Old Saxons].

E925 In this year Bishop Wulfhelm[10] was consecrated, and in the same year King Edward died.

D

926   (925) In this year King Athelstan and Sihtric, king of the Northumbrians, met together at Tamworth on 30 January and Athelstan gave him his sister in marriage.

[1] Here ends the long entry peculiar to 'A'.
[2] Wainwright, *Eng. Hist. Rev.*, LXV, 203–212, suggests that this is the mouth of the Clwyd. 'D' has this annal.
[3] The true date of both these events is probably 919.
[4] This is an error, for Niall was not related to Sihtric.
[5] This annal could have been added into 'F' and the archetype of 'E' at Canterbury. 'B', 'C', 'D' have only the Mercian Register entry. 'B', 'C' have nothing more until 934.
[6] 17 July.   [7] 'D' adds: "after 16 days".   [8] This did not take place until 4 September 925.
[9] Here the copy used by 'B' and 'C' must have broken off. The conclusion is from 'D', but is probably only a guess. 'D''s reference is to the marriage of Edith to Otto the Great, but the Mercian Register may have gone on to tell of the marriage of another sister to Sihtric.
[10] As archbishop of Canterbury, as in 'F' (and addition to 'A'), which adds that Dunstan was born this year.

D

927

(926) In this year appeared fiery lights in the northern quarter of the sky, and Sihtric died, and King Athelstan succeeded to the kingdom of the Northumbrians; and he brought under his rule all the kings who were in this island: first Hywel, king of the West Welsh, and Constantine, king of the Scots, and Owain, king of the people of Gwent, and Ealdred, son of Eadwulf from Bamburgh. And they established peace with pledge and oaths in the place which is called Eamont, on 12 July, and renounced all idolatry and afterwards departed in peace.[1]

E927 In this year King Athelstan drove out King Guthfrith. And in this year Archbishop Wulfhelm went to Rome.

931[2] In this year Byrnstan was consecrated bishop of Winchester on 29 May, and he held his bishopric two and a half years.

932 In this year Bishop Frithestan died.

E933 In this year the atheling Edwin was drowned at sea.

C (A, B, D, E, F)

934

(933 A) In this year King Athelstan went into Scotland with both a land force and a naval force, and ravaged much of it.[3]

A933 ... and Bishop Byrnstan of Winchester died on All Saints' day.

A934 In this year Ælfheah succeeded to the bishopric.

C (A, B, D)

937[4]

In this year King Athelstan, lord of nobles, dispenser of treasure to men, and his brother also, Edmund atheling, won by the sword's edge undying glory in battle round *Brunanburh*.[5] Edward's sons clove the shield-wall, hewed the linden-wood shields with hammered swords, for it was natural to men of their lineage to defend their land, their treasure and their homes, in frequent battle against every foe. Their enemies perished; the people of the Scots and the pirates fell doomed. The field grew dark (?) with the blood of men, from the time when the sun, that glorious luminary, the bright candle of God, of the Lord Eternal, moved over the earth in the hours of morning, until that noble creation sank at its setting. There lay many a man destroyed by the spears, many a northern warrior shot over his shield; and likewise many a Scot lay weary, sated with battle.

[1] If, as seems probable, the same meeting is meant by William of Malmesbury (No. 8, p. 280), Owain of Strathclyde should be added to those present. See p. 38, n. 13.

[2] Mr. R. Vaughan informs me that this and the three next annals in 'A' were originally dated 932–935.

[3] Florence adds that King Constantine was forced to give his son as a hostage.

[4] The annal is entirely in alliterative verse. Mr. Vaughan says it was originally dated 938 in 'A'.

[5] *Sic* 'A', 'D'; *Brunnanburh*, 'B' and 'C' and a second *n* has been added later in 'A'. Æthelweard calls the place *Brunandun*, Simeon *Wendun*; Florence says Olaf landed in the mouth of the Humber. For William of Malmesbury's account, see No. 8. See also pp. 39f.

C (A, B, D)

The whole day long the West Saxons with mounted companies kept in pursuit of the hostile peoples, grievously they cut down the fugitives from behind with their whetted swords. The Mercians refused not hard conflict to any men who with Olaf had sought this land in the bosom of a ship over the tumult of waters, coming doomed to the fight. Five young kings lay on that field of battle, slain by the swords, and also seven of Olaf's earls, and a countless host of seamen and Scots. There the prince of the Norsemen was put to flight, driven perforce to the prow of his ship with a small company; the vessel pressed on in the water, the king set out over the fallow flood and saved his life.

There also the aged Constantine, the hoary-haired warrior, came north to his own land by flight. He had no cause to exult in that crossing of swords.[1] He was shorn of his kinsmen and deprived of his friends at that meeting-place, bereaved[2] in the battle, and he left his young son on the field of slaughter, brought low by wounds in the battle. The grey-haired warrior, the old and wily one, had no cause to vaunt of that sword-clash; no more had Olaf. They had no need to gloat with the remnants of their armies, that they were superior in warlike deeds on the field of battle, in the clash of standards, the meeting of spears, the encounter of men, and the crossing of weapons, after they had contended on the field of slaughter with the sons of Edward.

Then the Norsemen, the sorry survivors from the spears, put out in their studded ships on to Ding's mere,[3] to make for Dublin across the deep water, back to Ireland humbled at heart. Also the two brothers, king and atheling, returned together to their own country, the land of the West Saxons, exulting in the battle. They left behind them the dusky-coated one, the black raven with its horned beak, to share the corpses, and the dun-coated, white-tailed eagle, the greedy war-hawk, to enjoy the carrion, and that grey beast, the wolf of the forest.

Never yet in this island before this, by what books tell us and our ancient sages, was a greater slaughter of a host made by the edge of the sword, since the Angles and Saxons came hither from the east, invading Britain over the broad seas, and the proud assailants, warriors eager for glory, overcame the Britons and won a country.

E937 In this year King Athelstan led an army to *Brunanburh*.

C (A, B, D)

940[4] (941 A) In this year King Athelstan died[5] on 27 October, 40 years except for one day after King Alfred died; and the atheling Edmund succeeded to the kingdom, and he was then 18 years old. And King Athelstan had reigned for 14 years and 10 weeks.[6]

---

[1] So in 'B', 'C'; 'A' is corrupt; 'D' reads, "meeting of men".
[2] So in all MSS. except 'B', "worsted".   [3] This allusion is quite obscure.
[4] Athelstan died in 939, reckoned 940 by writers who begin the year 24 September. Olaf's election followed soon after, in spite of 'D''s date. According to Mr. Vaughan. 'A''s date was originally 940.
[5] In Gloucester, according to 'D'. Florence says that he was borne to Malmesbury and buried there with great honour.   [6] An addition to 'A' has: "Then Wulfhelm was archbishop in Kent."

D

(941) In this year the Northumbrians were false to their pledges, and chose Olaf from Ireland as their king.

E940 In this year King Athelstan died and his brother Edmund succeeded to the kingdom.

C (A, B, D)

942[1] In this year King Edmund, lord of the English, protector of men,[2] the beloved performer of mighty deeds, overran Mercia, as bounded by Dore, Whitwell gate and the broad stream, the River Humber; and five boroughs, Leicester and Lincoln, Nottingham and likewise Stamford, and also Derby. The Danes were previously subjected by force under the Norsemen, for a long time in bonds of captivity to the heathens, until the defender of warriors, the son of Edward, King Edmund, redeemed them, to his glory.

E942 In this year King Olaf died.[3]

D

940–943[4]

(943) In this year Olaf took Tamworth by storm, and the losses were heavy on both sides, and the Danes were victorious and took away much booty with them. Wulfrun[5] was taken captive in that raid. In this year King Edmund besieged King Olaf and Archbishop Wulfstan in Leicester, and he could have subdued them if they had not escaped by night from the borough. And after that Olaf secured King Edmund's friendship.

C (A, B, D)

943[6] (No date in MSS.) In this year King Edmund stood sponsor to King Olaf at baptism,[7] and the same year, after a fairly big interval, he stood sponsor to King Ragnald at his confirmation.[8]

---

[1] This annal is in alliterative verse. [2] "Kinsmen," 'A'.
[3] Olaf, Guthfrith's son, actually died before the end of 941. He was succeeded by his cousin Olaf, Sihtric's son.
[4] 'D' has placed under 943 events of 940 which precede the recapture of the Five Boroughs which it has already dealt with in the preceding annal. It then tacks on the annal for 943 of the main Chronicle.
[5] See p. 541.
[6] 'A' has run this on to the poem in its previous annal, which ended with "Edmund king", by continuing after the first instead of the second occurrence of these words; 'B' and 'C' appear to start a new annal, but with no number, and 'C' puts a blank annal 943 after this one; 'D' reads straight on from its previous annal, omitting "In this year" and supplying "and".
[7] 'D' adds: "And he bestowed gifts on him royally."
[8] 'F' and an addition to 'A' add: "In this year King Edmund entrusted Glastonbury to St. Dunstan, where he afterwards first became abbot."

C (A, B, D, E, F)

944 In this year King Edmund reduced all Northumbria under his rule, and drove out two kings, Olaf, Sihtric's son, and Ragnald, Guthfrith's son.[1]

945 In this year King Edmund ravaged all Cumberland,[2] and granted it all to Malcolm, king of the Scots, on condition that he should be his ally both on sea and on land.

C (A, B, D)

946 In this year King Edmund died on St. Augustine's day.[3]

D

It was widely known how he ended his life, that Leofa stabbed him at Pucklechurch.[4] And Æthelflæd of Damerham, Ealdorman Ælfgar's daughter, was then his queen.

C (A, B, D)

And he had held the kingdom six years and a half. And then the atheling Eadred, his brother, succeeded to the kingdom and reduced all Northumbria under his rule. And the Scots gave oaths to him that they would agree to all that he wanted.

E948 In this year King Edmund was stabbed to death, and his brother Eadred succeeded to the kingdom, and immediately reduced all Northumbria under his rule; and the Scots swore oaths to him that they would agree to all that he wanted.

D

947 In this year King Eadred came to Tanshelf, and there Archbishop Wulfstan and all the councillors of the Northumbrians pledged themselves to the king, and within a short space they were false to it all, both pledge and oaths as well.

---

[1] 'E', 'F', "two men of royal race, Olaf and Ragnald". Æthelweard seems to be referring to this event under too late a date, when, along with events of 946 (which he dates 948, as he is two years out in this portion of his work) he says: "Bishop Wulfstan and the ealdorman of the Mercians expelled certain deserters', namely Ragnald and Olaf, from the city of York, and brought them into the power of the aforesaid king." He continues: "In the same year died Queen Ælfgifu, King Edmund's wife, and she was afterwards canonized and at her tomb in the nunnery which is commonly called Shaftesbury innumerable miracles have been performed with God's help until the present day."
[2] At this date Cumberland means the kingdom of Strathclyde, not merely the modern county. 'E', 'F' omit the rest of this annal.
[3] 26 May.
[4] Florence is fuller; he says that Edmund was killed when trying to rescue his seneschal from being killed by a base robber, Leofa, and that Pucklechurch was a royal residence; that he reigned five years and seven months, and was buried at Glastonbury by the blessed abbot Dunstan; that Eadred was consecrated on 16 August at Kingston by Oda, archbishop of Canterbury.

D

948   In this year King Eadred ravaged all Northumbria, because they had accepted Eric[1] as their king; and in that ravaging the glorious minster at Ripon, which St. Wilfrid had built, was burnt down. And when the king was on his way home, the army [which] was in York overtook the king's army at Castleford, and they made a great slaughter there. Then the king became so angry that he wished to march back into the land and destroy it utterly. When the councillors of the Northumbrians understood that, they deserted Eric and paid to King Eadred compensation for their act.

E

949   In this year Olaf Cwiran[2] came into Northumbria.

A951 In this year Ælfheah, bishop of Winchester, died on St. Gregory's day.[3]

D   **E**

952   In this year King Eadred ordered Archbishop Wulfstan to be taken into the fortress of *Iudanbyrig*, because accusations had often been made to the king against him. And in this year also the king ordered a great slaughter to be made in the borough of Thetford in vengeance for the abbot Eadhelm, whom they had slain.   In this year the Northumbrians drove out King Olaf, and received Eric, Harold's son.

D (E)

954   In this year the Northumbrians drove out Eric,[4] and Eadred succeeded to the kingdom of the Northumbrians.

D

In this year Archbishop Wulfstan received a bishopric again, in Dorchester. [5]

---

[1] Eric Blood-axe, son of Harold Fairhair of Norway, who came to England as an exile. See No. 11.
[2] *i.e.* Sihtric's son.   [3] 12 March.   [4] See No. 4, p. 257.
[5] This could read: "received back his bishopric (York) at Dorchester".

C (B, E)   **D**

955 (956 B, C) In this year King Eadred died and Eadwig, [Edmund's son],[1] succeeded to the kingdom.

In this year King Eadred died, and he rests in the Old Minster, and Eadwig succeeded to the kingdom of the West Saxons, and his brother Edgar to the kingdom of the Mercians.[2] They were sons of King Edmund and St. Ælfgifu.

A955 In this year King Eadred died on St. Clement's day[3] at Frome and he had ruled nine and a half years; and then Eadwig, the son of King Edmund, succeeded to the kingdom [and exiled St. Dunstan from the land][4].

C (B)   **D (E)**

956

(957D) In this year Archbishop Wulfstan died

D

on 16 December,[5] and he was buried in Oundle. And in the same year Abbot Dunstan was driven across the sea.

957 In this year the atheling Edgar succeeded to the kingdom of the Mercians.[7]

(958)[6] In this year Archbishop Oda separated King Eadwig and Ælfgifu, because they were too closely related.

C (A, B, D, E, F)

959 (958 A, F) In this year King Eadwig died[8] and his brother Edgar succeeded to the kingdom;[9]

C (B)   **D (E, F)[10]**

both in Wessex and in Mercia and in Northumbria, and he was then 16 years old.

in his days things improved greatly, and God granted him that he lived in peace as long as he lived; and, as was necessary for him, he laboured zealously for this; he exalted God's praise far and wide, and loved God's law; and he improved the peace of the people more

---

[1] 'E' only.

[2] This clause is in 'F' also, so it may have been in the archetype of 'E'; but it is wrong, for the division of the kingdom did not take place until 957.   [3] 23 November.

[4] Canterbury addition.   [5] Florence, and York tradition, give 26 December.

[6] If we accept a story in the life of St. Dunstan, this event belongs to 956. In any case 958 is too late.

[7] Florence adds: "and the kingdom of the two kings was divided so that the River Thames should form the boundary between the two kingdoms".

[8] On 1 October, 'A'.   [9] 'A' ends the annal here; 'F' has: "became king over all Britain".

[10] This passage is written in alliterative prose, and is in the style of Archbishop Wulfstan II of York. It is influenced by No. 239 (I).

D (E, F)

than the kings who were before him in the memory of man. And God also supported him so that kings and earls willingly submitted to him and were subjected to whatever he wished. And without battle he brought under his sway all that he wished. He came to be honoured widely throughout the countries, because he zealously honoured God's name, and time and again meditated on God's law, and exalted God's praise far and wide, and continually and frequently directed all his people wisely in matters of Church and State. Yet he did one ill-deed too greatly: he loved evil foreign customs and brought too firmly heathen manners within this land, and attracted hither foreigners and enticed harmful people to this country. But may God grant him that his good deeds may prove greater than his ill-deeds, for the protection of his soul on its everlasting journey.

F (and addition to A) 959 In this year Edgar sent for St. Dunstan, and gave him the bishopric of Worcester, and afterwards the bishopric of London.

F961 In this year the good Archbishop Oda died and Dunstan was elected archbishop.

A[1]

962 In this year Ælfgar, the king's kinsman in Devon, died, and his body rests in Wilton. And King Sigeferth[2] killed himself, and his body is buried at Wimborne. And then during the year there was a very great mortality, and the great and fatal fire occurred in London, and St. Paul's minster was burnt, and was re-built in the same year. And in this same year the priest Æthelmod went to Rome, and died there on 15 August.

E

963 In this year Wulfstan the deacon died on Holy Innocents' day,[3] and after that Gyric the priest died. In that same year Abbot Æthelwold succeeded to the bishopric of Winchester, and he was consecrated on the eve of St. Andrew's day. That day was a Sunday.

In this year St. Æthelwold was chosen for the bishopric of Winchester by King Edgar;[4] and the archbishop of Canterbury, St. Dunstan, consecrated him as bishop on the first Sunday of Advent, which was on 29 November.[5]

---

[1] For the next three years 'A' has fuller and less local annals than in the years preceding.
[2] Nothing is known about him.　　　　　　　　　　　　　　[3] 28 December.
[4] It is remarkable that 'E' and 'F' should be the only MSS. other than the Winchester 'A' to record Æthelwold's accession. 'F' has only a brief entry.
[5] 'E' has a long Peterborough addition, on the refoundation of the abbey.

A

964 In this year King Edgar drove the priests in the city[1] from the Old Minster and from the New Minster; and from Chertsey and from Milton (Abbas); and replaced them with monks. And he appointed Abbot Æthelgar as abbot of the New Minster, and Ordberht for Chertsey, and Cyneweard for Milton.

E

[In this year the canons were expelled from the Old Minster].[2]

D (F)[3]

965 In this year King Edgar took Ælfthryth as his queen. She was the daughter of Ealdorman Ordgar.

D (E, F)

966 In this year Thored, Gunnar's son, ravaged Westmorland, and that same year Oslac succeeded to the aldormanry.

969 In this year King Edgar ordered all Thanet to be ravaged.

C (B)

971 In this year died Archbishop Oscetel, who was first consecrated as a diocesan bishop, of Dorchester, and afterwards consecrated archbishop of York by the consent of King Eadred and of all his councillors;[4] and he was bishop for 22 years, and he died on All Saints' eve, ten days before Martinmas, at Thame. And his kinsman, Abbot Thurcetel, took the bishop's body to Bedford, because he was abbot there at that time.[5]

C (B, D, E, G)

972 (?) (970 D, E; 971 G)[6] In this year the atheling Edmund[7] died.

C (A, B)

973[8] (974 C) In this year Edgar, ruler of the English, with a great company, was consecrated king in the ancient borough, *Acemannesceaster* – the men who dwell in this island also call it by another name, Bath. There great joy had come to all on that blessed day which the children of men call and name the day of Pentecost. There was assembled a crowd of priests, a great throng of

D (E)

(972) In this year the atheling Edgar was consecrated king at Bath on the day of Pentecost, on 11 May, in the thirteenth year after he succeeded to the kingdom, and he was but one year off thirty.

---

[1] Winchester. [2] This annal is in Latin. 'F' has an annal derived from 'A'.
[3] Agreement between 'D' and 'F' implies that the archetype of 'E', used by 'F', had this annal. It must have been omitted when 'E' was copied.
[4] This is the reading in 'B'. 'C' reads: "who was first consecrated as a diocesan bishop for Dorchester, and afterwards for York, by the consent of King Edward [*sic*] and of all his councillors, so that he was consecrated as archbishop." [5] Thurcetel was afterwards abbot of Crowland.
[6] 'A' originally had this annal, and in 'G' (a copy of 'A'), it ends: "and his body is buried at Romsey". It has been erased from 'A'.
[7] Infant son of Edgar and Ælfthryth. [8] The entry in 'A', 'B', 'C' is in alliterative verse.

C (A, B)

learned monks, as I have heard tell. And then had passed from the birth of the glorious King, the Guardian of Light, ten hundred years reckoned in numbers, except that there yet remained, by what documents say, seven and twenty of the number of years, so nearly had passed away a thousand years of the Lord of Victories, when this took place. And Edmund's son, bold in battle, had spent 29 years in the world when this came about, and then in the thirtieth was consecrated king.

975[2] In this year Edgar, king of the English, reached the end of earthly joys, chose for him the other light, beautiful and happy, and left this wretched and fleeting life. The sons of nations, men on the earth, everywhere in this country – those who have been rightly trained in computation – call the month in which the young man Edgar, dispenser of treasure to warriors, departed from life on the eighth day, the month of July. His son then succeeded to the kingdom, a child ungrown, a prince of nobles, whose name was Edward. And ten days before, there departed from Britain a famous man, the bishop, good from his innate virtue, whose name was Cyneweard.[4]

D (E)

And immediately after that the king took his whole naval force to Chester, and six[1] kings came to meet him, and all gave him pledges that they would be his allies on sea and on land.

In this year died Edgar,[3] ruler of the Angles, friend of the West Saxons and protector of the Mercians. It was widely known throughout many nations across the gannet's bath, that kings honoured Edmund's son far and wide, and paid homage to this king as was his due by birth. Nor was there fleet so proud nor host so strong that it got itself prey in England as long as the noble king held the throne.[5]

In this year Edgar's son Edward succeeded to the kingdom. And soon in the same year in harvest time there appeared the star 'comet', and in the next year there came a very great famine and very manifold disturbances throughout England.

---

[1] Florence says: "and his eight sub-kings, namely Kenneth, king of the Scots, Malcolm, king of the Cumbrians, Maccus, king of many islands, and five others, Dufnal (*i.e.* Dunmail), Siferth, Hywel, Jacob (*i.e.* Iago) and Juchil, met him, as he commanded, and swore that they would be faithful to him and be his allies by land and sea. And on a certain day he went on board a boat with them, and, with them at the oars and himself seizing the helm, he steered it skilfully on the course of the River Dee, proceeding from the palace to the monastery of St. John the Baptist, attended by all the crowd of ealdormen and nobles also by boat. And when he had completed his prayers he returned with the same pomp to the palace. As he entered he is reported to have said to his nobles that any of his successors might indeed pride himself in being king of the English, when he might have the glory of such honours, with so many kings subservient to him."
The same incident is referred to by Ælfric. See No. 239 (G).
[2] The entry in 'A', 'B', 'C' is in alliterative metre, of a quality to make one glad that the chroniclers mainly used prose. The passage in 'D' and 'E' is not in this metre, but is strongly rhythmical with some assonance and rhyme.   [3] 'D' adds: "8 July".   [4] Bishop of Wells.   [5] Here the annal reverts to prose.

C (A, B)

Then in Mercia, as I have heard tell, widely, almost everywhere, the praise of the Ruler was cast down to the ground; many of the wise servants of God were dispersed.[2] That was a great cause of mourning for any who bore in his breast and mind an ardent love for the Creator. There the Author of glories, the Ruler of victories, the Governor of the heavens, was too greatly scorned, when his rights were violated. And then also the valiant man Oslac was driven from the country, over the tossing waves, the gannet's bath, the tumult of waters, the homeland of the whale; a grey-haired man, wise and skilled in speech, he was bereft of his lands.

Then was also revealed up in the skies a star in the firmament, which men firm of spirit, wise in mind, skilled in science, wise orators,[3] far and wide call 'comet' by name. The vengeance of the Ruler was manifested widely throughout the people, a famine over the earth, which the Guardian of the heavens, the Prince of the angels, afterwards amended. He gave back bliss to each of the islanders through the fruits of the earth.[4]

D[1]

In his days because of his youth, the adversaries of God, Ealdorman Ælf here and many others, broke God's law and hindered the monastic life,[2] and destroyed monasteries and dispersed the monks and put to flight the servants of God, whom King Edgar had ordered the holy Bishop Æthelwold to institute; and they plundered widows time and again. And many wrongs and evil lawless acts rose up afterwards, and ever after that it grew much worse.

D (E)

And at this time also the famous Earl Oslac was exiled from England.

E (F)

And Ealdorman Ælfhere caused to be destroyed many monastic foundations which King Edgar had ordered the holy Bishop Æthelwold to institute.

---

[1] The passage peculiar to 'D' is in the style of Archbishop Wulfstan.   [2] Cf. No. 236.
[3] 'A' has instead a unique word, literally 'truth-bearers'.
[4] Here ends any agreement between 'A' and the other MSS. Its few later entries are peculiar to it.

C *only*

976 In this year the great famine occurred in England.

C (B)

977 In this year was the great assembly at Kirtlington, after Easter,[1] and Bishop Sideman died there by a sudden death on 30 April. He was bishop of Devonshire, and he had wished his burial to be at Crediton at his episcopal see. Then King Edward and Archbishop Dunstan ordered that he should be conveyed to St. Mary's monastery which is at Abingdon, and this was done, and he is honourably buried at the north side in St. Paul's chapel.[2]

D (E)

(978) In this year all the chief councillors of the English people fell from an upper storey at Calne, except that Archbishop Dunstan alone remained standing upon a beam; and some were very severely injured there, and some did not survive it.

C

978 In this year King Edward was martyred, and his brother Ethelred succeeded to the kingdom and was consecrated king in the same year. In that year Ælfwold, who was bishop of Dorset, died, and his body is buried in the minster at Sherborne.

(979) In this year Ethelred was consecrated king on Sunday, a fortnight after Easter,[4] at Kingston, and at his consecration were two archbishops and ten diocesan bishops. That same year a bloody cloud was often seen in the

D (E)

(979) In this year King Edward was killed at the gap of Corfe[3] on 18 March in the evening, and he was buried at Wareham without any royal honours. And no worse deed than this for the English people was committed since first they came to Britain. Men murdered him, but God honoured him. In life he was an earthly king; he is now after death a heavenly saint. His earthly kinsmen would not avenge him, but his heavenly Father has greatly avenged him. The earthly slayers wished to blot out his memory on earth, but the heavenly Avenger has spread abroad his memory in heaven and in earth. Those who would not bow to his living body, now bend humbly on their knees to his dead bones. Now we can perceive that the wisdom and contrivance of men and their plans are worthless against God's purpose.

In this year Ethelred succeeded to the kingdom, and very quickly after that he was consecrated king at Kingston with much rejoicing by the councillors of the English people.

---

[1] 8 April.   [2] 'B' ends at this point.

[3] The burial at Wareham is in favour of this, the traditional, identification, not of Coryates, which has been suggested. On this murder, see No. 236, pp. 841 f.

[4] *i.e.* 14 April, if 'D' and 'E' are right in placing the coronation soon after the election. If, however, 'C''s date, 979, is correct, the coronation was on 4 May.

C

likeness of fire, and especially it was revealed at midnight, and it was formed in various shafts of light. When day was about to dawn, it disappeared.

A978 In this year King Edward was killed. And in this same year the atheling Ethelred his brother succeeded to the kingdom.

D (E)

979   (980) In this year Ealdorman Ælfhere fetched the holy king's body from Wareham and bore it with great honour to Shaftesbury.

C	D (E)
980 In this year Abbot Æthelgar was consecrated bishop for the see of Selsey on 2 May. And in the same year Southampton was sacked by a naval force, and most of the citizens killed or taken captive; and that same year Thanet was ravaged; and the same year Cheshire was ravaged by a northern naval force.	(981) In this year there first came seven ships and ravaged Southampton.

981 In this year St. Petroc's monastery[1] was sacked, and that same year great damage was done everywhere by the coast both in Devon and also in Cornwall. And in the same year Ælfstan, bishop of Wiltshire, died, and his body is buried in the monastery of Abingdon, and Wulfgar then succeeded to the bishopric. And in the same year Womer, abbot of Ghent, died.

982 In this year three ships of vikings arrived in Dorset and ravaged in Portland. That same year London was burnt down. And in the same year two ealdormen died, Æthelmær of Hampshire and Edwin of Sussex, and Æthelmær's body is buried in the New Minster at Winchester and Edwin's in the monastery of Abingdon. That same year two abbesses in Dorset died, Herelufu of Shaftsbury and Wulfwyn of Wareham. And that same year Odda,[2] emperor of the Romans, went to the land of the Greeks,[3] and he then encountered a great army of the Saracens coming up from the sea, wishing to make

---

[1] Padstow. See W. G. Hoskins and H. P. R. Finberg, *Devonshire Studies* (London, 1952), p. 29, n. 2.
[2] Otto II.
[3] This expression covered all the lands of the eastern emperor, and this expedition was to southern Italy.

C

a raid on the Christian people; and then the emperor fought against them and a great slaughter was made on both sides, and the emperor had control of the field, and yet he was much harassed there before he left. And when he was on his way home, his brother's son died. He was called Odda and was the son of the prince Leodulf, and this Leodulf was the son of the old Odda and of King Edward's daughter.[1]

C (D, E)

983 In this year Ealdorman Ælfhere died,[2] and Ælfric succeeded to the same aldormanry, and Pope Benedict died.[3]

<table>
<tr><td>

A

984 In this year the benevolent Bishop Æthelwold died, and the consecration of the succeeding bishop, Ælfheah, who was called by a second name, Godwine, was on 19 October, and he occupied the bishop's throne in Winchester on the festival of the two apostles, Simon and Jude.[7]

</td><td>

C (D, E)

In this year [the holy][4] Bishop Æthelwold, [father of the monks],[4] died on 1 August,[5] [and in this year Edwin was consecrated as Abbot of Abingdon].[6]

</td></tr>
</table>

C (D, E)

985 In this year Ealdorman Ælfric was driven out of the land. And in the same year Edwin was consecrated abbot of the monastery of Abingdon.[8]

986 In this year the king laid waste the diocese of Rochester. In this year the great murrain first occurred in England.

988 (987 E, F) In this year Watchet was ravaged; (988, all MSS.) and Goda, the Devonshire thegn, was killed,[9] and many fell with him. In this year Archbishop Dunstan died,[10] and Bishop Æthelgar succeeded to the archiepiscopal see, and lived but a short while–one year and three months–after that.

990 (989 E, F) In this year Sigeric was consecrated archbishop,[11] and Abbot Edwin died and Abbot Wulfgar succeeded to the office.[12]

---

[1] Otto the Great married Edith, daughter of Edward the Elder, and they had a son Liodulf.
[2] 'A' has this also, but not the rest of the annal.   [3] 'D', 'E' omit the last clause.
[4] Only in 'D' and 'E'.   [5] The date in 'C' only.   [6] Only in 'E'. Cf. 985, 'C'.
[7] 28 October. 'A' has no further entry until 991; 'F' combines 'A' and 'E' in this annal.
[8] This sentence is only in 'C'. Cf. 984, 'E'.
[9] Florence adds information that may come from the account of this engagement in the *Life of St. Oswald*. See No. 236, p. 843.
[10] "The holy Archbishop Dunstan left this life and attained the heavenly life." 'E'.
[11] 'F' adds: "and afterwards went to Rome for his *pallium*".
[12] 'D' and 'F' omit the reference to the Abingdon abbots. 'E' puts it at the beginning instead of the end of the annal.

A

991[1] In this year Olaf came with 93 ships to Folkestone, and ravaged round about it, and then from there went to Sandwich, and so from there to Ipswich, and overran it all, and so to Maldon. And Ealdorman Brihtnoth came against him there with his army and fought against him; and they killed the ealdorman there and had control of the field.[2] And afterwards peace was made with them and the king stood sponsor to him afterwards at his confirmation.[3]

C (D, E)

In this year Ipswich was ravaged, and very soon afterwards Ealdorman Brihtnoth was killed at Maldon. And in that year it was determined that tribute should first be paid to the Danish men because of the great terror they were causing along the coast. The first payment was 10,000 pounds. Archbishop Sigeric first advised that course.

C (D, E)

992 In this year the holy Archbishop Oswald left this life and attained the heavenly life, and Ealdorman Æthelwine died in the same year. Then the king and all his councillors decreed that all the ships that were any use should be assembled at London. And the king then entrusted the expedition to the leadership of Ealdorman Ælfric and Earl Thored and Bishop Ælfstan[4] and Bishop Æscwig,[5] and they were to try if they could entrap the Danish army anywhere at sea. Then Ealdorman Ælfric[6] sent someone to warn the enemy, and then in the night before the day on which they were to have joined battle, he absconded by night from the army, to his own great disgrace, and then the enemy escaped, except that the crew of one ship was slain. And then the Danish army encountered the ships from East Anglia and from London, and they made a great slaughter there and captured the ship, all armed and equipped, on which the ealdorman was.[7]

And then after Archbishop Oswald's death, Abbot Ealdwulf[8] succeeded to the see of York and to Worcester, and Cenwulf to the abbacy of Peterborough.

993 In this year Bamburgh was sacked and much booty was captured there, and after that the army came to the mouth of the Humber and did great damage there, both in Lindsey and in Northumbria. Then a very large English army was collected, and when they should have joined battle, the leaders, namely Fræna, Godwine and Frythegyst, first started the flight.[9] In this year the king had Ælfgar, son of Ealdorman Ælfric, blinded.

[1] It looks as if 'A' put this at 993, but Mr. Alistair Campbell has called my attention to a caret mark over 991, showing that the scribe, who added it after the numbers from 989 to 992 had been written in a horizontal line, with 993 as the next marginal number, meant the entry to belong to 991.

[2] It looks as if the rest of this annal were added as an afterthought, after the entry for 994 had already been made, for most of it is entered in the margin. It will be noted that the writer does not say that these events took place in 991, but merely *after* an event which did.

[3] A later Canterbury addition here reads: "through the advice of Sigeric, bishop of the people of Kent and of Ælfheah, bishop of Winchester".   [4] Of London or Rochester.

[5] Of Dorchester.   [6] 'F' adds: "one of those in whom the king trusted most".

[7] Florence adds: "and he himself escaped with difficulty by flight".

[8] 'E' adds: "of Peterborough".   [9] Florence: "because they were Danes on the father's side".

A

994 In this year Archbishop Sigeric died, and Ælfric, bishop of Wiltshire, succeeded to the archbishopric.

C (D, E)

In this year Olaf and Swein came to London on the Nativity of St. Mary[1] with 94 ships, and they proceeded to attack the city stoutly and wished also to set it on fire; but there they suffered more harm and injury than they ever thought any citizens would do to them. But the holy Mother of God showed her mercy to the citizens on that day and saved them from their enemies. And these went away from there, and did the greatest damage that ever any army could do, by burning, ravaging and slaying, everywhere along the coast, and in Essex, Kent, Sussex and Hampshire; and finally they seized horses and rode as widely as they wished, and continued to do indescribable damage. Then the king and his councillors determined to send to them and promise them tribute and provisions, on condition that they should cease that harrying. And they then accepted that, and the whole army came then to Southampton and took winter quarters there; and they were provisioned throughout all the West Saxon kingdom, and they were paid 16,000 pounds in money.

Then the king sent Bishop Ælfheah and Ealdorman Æthelweard for King Olaf, and hostages were given to the ships meanwhile. And they then brought Olaf to the king at Andover with much ceremony, and King Ethelred stood sponsor to him at confirmation, and bestowed gifts on him royally. And then Olaf promised – as also he performed – that he would never come back to England in hostility.

C (D, E)

995 In this year the star 'comet' appeared, and Archbishop Sigeric died.[2]

996 In this year Ælfric was consecrated archbishop at Christ Church.[3]

F996 In this year Wulfstan was consecrated bishop of London.

C (D, E)

997 In this year the Danish army went round Devon into the mouth of the Severn and ravaged there, both in Cornwall, in Wales and in Devon. And they landed at Watchet and did much damage there, burning and slaying; and after that they turned back round Land's End to the southern side, and then turned into

---

[1] 8 September.

[2] 28 October 994 is the most probable date. The chronicler may have used an episcopal list which commenced the year on 24 September.

[3] 'F' dates this 995, adding that it was done by King Ethelred and all his councillors on Easter Day at Amesbury. A long spurious passage follows on his replacing canons by monks.

C (D, E)

the mouth of the Tamar, and went inland until they reached Lydford, burning and slaying everything they came across, and burnt down Ordwulf's monastery at Tavistock and took with them to their ships indescribable booty.

F997 In this year Archbishop Ælfric went to Rome for his *pallium*.

C (D, E)

998 In this year the army turned back east into the mouth of the Frome, and there they went inland everywhere into Dorset as widely as they pleased; and the English army was often assembled against them, but as soon as they were to have joined battle, a flight was always instigated by some means, and always the enemy had the victory in the end. And then for another period they stayed in the Isle of Wight, and meanwhile got their food from Hampshire and Sussex.

999 In this year the army came again round into the Thames and turned then up the Medway and to Rochester.[1] And the Kentish levy came against them there, and they then joined battle stoutly; but, alas! they too soon turned and fled [because they had not the support which they should have had],[2] and the Danes had control of the field. And they then seized horses and rode wherever[3] they pleased, and destroyed and ravaged almost all West Kent.[4] Then the king with his councillors determined that they should be opposed by a naval force and also by a land force. But when the ships were ready, one delayed[5] from day to day, and oppressed the wretched people who were on the ships. And ever, as things should have been moving, they were the more delayed from one hour to the next, and ever they let their enemies' force increase, and ever the English retreated inland and the Danes continually followed; and then in the end it effected nothing—the naval expedition or the land expedition—except the oppression of the people and the waste of money and the encouragement of their enemies.

1000 In this year the king went into Cumberland and ravaged very nearly all of it; and his ships went out round Chester and should have come to meet him, but they could not. Then they ravaged the Isle of Man. And the enemy fleet had gone to Richard's kingdom[6] that summer.

A	C (D, E)
1001 In this year there was much fighting in England because of a naval force; and they ravaged and burnt almost everywhere, so that they betook	In this year the army came to the mouth of the Exe and then went inland to

[1] Florence adds: "and surrounded it with a siege for a few days".
[2] In 'E' only.   [3] 'D', 'E', "as widely as".
[4] Literally 'the West Kentings', which implies that it was a separate administrative area.
[5] 'C''s "the judges delayed" is a misreading, as the following singular verb bears out.
[6] Normandy.

A

themselves inland in one journey till they reached Dean;[1] and the people of Hampshire came against them there and fought against them, and there Æthelweard the king's high-reeve was killed, and Leofric of Whitchurch and Leofwine the king's high-reeve, and Wulfhere the bishop's thegn, and Godwine of Worthy, Bishop Ælfsige's son, and 81 men in all; and there were far more of the Danes killed, although they had control of the field. And then they went west from there until they reached Devon; and Pallig came to meet them there with the ships which he could collect, because he had deserted King Ethelred in spite of all the pledges which he had given him. And the king had also made great gifts to him, in estates and gold and silver. And they burnt Teignton and also many other good residences which we cannot name, and afterwards peace was made with them.

Then they went from there to the mouth of the Exe, so that they transported themselves in one journey until they reached Pinhoe; and opposing them there were Kola, the king's high-reeve, and Eadsige, the king's reeve, with what army they could gather, but they were put to flight there, and many were killed, and the Danes had control of the field. And the next morning they burnt the residence at Pinhoe and at Clyst,[4] and also many good residences which we cannot name, and then went back east till they reached the Isle of Wight. And the next morning they burnt the residence at Waltham and many other villages. And soon afterwards terms were made with them and they accepted peace.[5]

C (D, E)

the borough, and proceeded to fight resolutely there, but they were very[2] stoutly resisted. Then they went through the land and did exactly as they were accustomed, slew and burnt. Then an immense army was gathered there of the people of Devon and of Somerset, and they met at Pinhoe; and as soon as they joined battle the people[3] gave way, and the Danes made a great slaughter there, and then overran the land – and ever their next raid was worse than the one before it. And they brought much booty with them to their ships, and turned from there to the Isle of Wight. And there they went about as they pleased, and nothing withstood them, and no naval force on sea, nor land force, dared go against them, no matter how far inland they went. It was in every way grievous, for they never ceased from their evil-doing.

C (D, E)

1002 In this year the king and his councillors determined that tribute should be paid to the fleet and peace made with them on condition that they should cease their evil-doing. Then the king sent Ealdorman Leofsige to the fleet, and he then, by the command of the king and his councillors, arranged a truce with them and that they should receive provisions and tribute. And they then accepted that, and 24,000 pounds were paid to them. Then meanwhile Ealdorman Leofsige killed the king's high-reeve, Æfic, and the king then banished him from the country.

[1] The Æthelinga dene of the text is shown to be in East or West Dean, Sussex, in The Place-Names of Sussex, I, p. xlv; it is near enough to the border of Hampshire to account for the presence of the militia of this shire.   [2] 'E' adds: "resolutely and".   [3] 'D', 'E', "the English army".   [4] Probably Broad Clyst, Devon.
[5] At this point the eleventh-century copy of 'A' (Brit. Mus. Cott. Otho B. xi) came to an end. Subsequent annals in 'A' are Canterbury additions.

C (D, E)

And then in the spring the queen, Richard's daughter,[1] came to this land. And in the same summer Archbishop Ealdwulf died.

And in that year the king ordered to be slain all the Danish men who were in England–this was done[2] on St. Brice's day[3]–because the king had been informed that they would treacherously deprive him, and then all his councillors, of life, and possess this kingdom afterwards.[4]

1003 In this year Exeter was stormed on account of the French *ceorl* Hugh, whom the queen had appointed as her reeve, and the Danish army then destroyed the borough completely and seized much booty there.[5] And in that same year the army went inland into Wiltshire.[6] Then a great English army was gathered from Wiltshire and from Hampshire, and they were going very resolutely towards the enemy. Then Ealdorman Ælfric was to lead the army, but he was up to his old tricks. As soon as they were so close that each army looked on the other, he feigned him sick, and began retching to vomit, and said that he was taken ill, and thus betrayed the people whom he should have led. As the saying goes: "When the leader gives way, the whole army will be much hindered." When Swein saw that they were irresolute, and that they all dispersed, he led his army into Wilton, and they ravaged and burnt the borough, and he betook him then to Salisbury, and from there went back to the sea to where he knew his wave-coursers were.

1004 In this year Swein came with his fleet to Norwich and completely ravaged and burnt the borough. Then Ulfcetel[7] with the councillors in East Anglia determined that it would be better to buy peace from the army before they did too much damage in the country, for they had come unexpectedly and he had not time to collect his army. Then, under cover of the truce which was supposed to be between them, the Danish army stole inland from the ships, and directed their course to Thetford. When Ulfcetel perceived that, he sent orders that the ships were to be hewn to bits, but those whom he intended for this failed him; he then collected his army secretly, as quickly as he could. And the Danish army then came to Thetford within three weeks after their ravaging of Norwich, and remained inside there one night, and ravaged and burnt the borough. Then in the morning, when they wished to go to their ships, Ulfcetel arrived with his troops to offer battle there.[8] And they resolutely joined battle, and many fell slain on both sides. There the flower of the East Anglian people was killed. But if their full strength had been there, the Danes would never have got back to their ships; as they themselves said[9] that they never met worse fighting in England than Ulfcetel dealt to them.

---

[1] 'F', which has part of this annal, adds: "Ymma [Ælfgifu]".   [2] 'D', 'E', omit "this was done".
[3] 13 November. An interesting reference to this massacre is contained in No. 217.
[4] 'F' adds: "without any opposition".
[5] Florence is more explicit, in a passage that seems more than mere surmise from the Chronicle: "Swein, king of the Danes, through the evil counsel, negligence or treachery of the Norman count Hugh, whom Queen Emma had put over Devon, stormed and despoiled the city of Exeter, and destroyed the wall from the east to the west gate."   [6] 'E' omits this sentence.   [7] Florence, "ealdorman of the East Angles".
[8] 'D' and 'E' omit the last phrase.   [9] 'E' ends the annal here.

C (D, E)

1005 In this year occurred the great famine throughout England, such that no man ever remembered one so cruel, and the fleet returned from this country to Denmark this year, and let little time elapse before it came back.

A 1005 In this year Archbishop Ælfric died.

C (D, E)

1006 In this year Archbishop Ælfric died and Bishop Ælfheah succeeded him to the archiepiscopal see [and Bishop Brihtwold succeeded to the bishopric of Wiltshire].[1] In the same year Wulfgeat was deprived of all his property,[2] and Wulfheah and Ufegeat were blinded and Ealdorman Ælfhelm killed.[3] And Bishop Cenwulf[4] died.

Then after midsummer[5] the great fleet[6] came to Sandwich, and did just as they were accustomed, ravaged, burnt and slew as they went.[7] Then the king ordered the whole nation from Wessex and Mercia to be called out, and they were out on military service against the Danish army the whole autumn, yet it availed no whit more than it had often done before; for in spite of it all, the Danish army went about as it pleased, and the English levy caused the people of the country every sort of harm, so that they profited neither from the native army nor the foreign army. When winter approached, the English army went home, and the Danish army then came after Martinmas to its sanctuary, the Isle of Wight, and procured for themselves everywhere whatever they needed; and then towards Christmas they betook themselves to the entertainment waiting them, out through Hampshire into Berkshire to Reading; and always they observed their ancient custom, lighting their beacons as they went. They then turned to Wallingford and burnt it all, and were one night at Cholsey,[8] and then turned along Ashdown to Cuckhamsley Barrow, and waited there for what had been proudly threatened, for it had often been said that if they went to Cuckhamsley,[9] they would never get to the sea. They then went home another way. The English army was then gathered at the Kennet, and they joined battle there, and at once they put that troop to flight, and afterwards carried their booty to the sea. There the people of Winchester could see that army, proud and undaunted, when they went past their gate to the sea, and fetched themselves food and treasures from more than 50 miles from the sea.

Then the king had gone across the Thames, into Shropshire, and received there his food-rents in the Christmas season. Then so great terror of the Danish

[1] In 'E' and 'F' only. 16 November 1005 is probably correct for Ælfric's death.
[2] Florence calls him Leofeca's son, whom Ethelred "had loved almost more than anyone". He attributes the forfeiture to "unjust judgments and arrogant deeds which he had committed".
[3] Florence has details perhaps drawn from a lost saga about Eadric Streona, whom he makes responsible for the crime. He says also that the blinding was at the king's command and took place at Cookham, where he was staying. Ælfhelm was ealdorman of southern Northumbria. Cf. No. 125.
[4] Of Winchester.   [5] Florence: "in the month of July".   [6] "the Danish fleet", 'E'.
[7] Florence adds: "now in Kent, now in Sussex".
[8] 'E' omits this clause.   [9] 'E' omitted this section, from the first Cuckhamsley.

C (D, E)

army arose that no one could think or conceive how to drive them from the country, or to defend this country from them, for they had cruelly left their mark on every shire of Wessex with their burning and their harrying. The king then with his councillors began eagerly to consider what might seem to them all most advisable, that this country could be saved before it was completely destroyed. Then the king and his councillors, for the benefit of the whole nation, determined–hateful though it was to all of them–that tribute must needs be paid to the army. Then the king sent to the army to inform them that he desired that there should be a truce between them, and that tribute should be paid them and provisions given; and then they all accepted that, and they were supplied with food throughout England.

A1006 In this year Ælfheah was consecrated as archbishop.

C (D, E)

1007 In this year the tribute was paid to the army, namely 36,000[1] pounds. In this year also Eadric was appointed ealdorman over the kingdom of the Mercians.[2]

1008 In this year the king ordered that ships should be built unremittingly over all England, namely a warship from 310 hides,[3] and a helmet and corselet from eight hides.

1009 In this year the ships which we mentioned above were ready, and there were more of them than ever before, from what books tell us, had been in England in any king's time; and they were all brought together at Sandwich and were to stay there and protect this country from every invading army. But yet we had not the good fortune or honour that the naval force was of use to this country, any more than it had been on many previous occasions.

Then it happened at this same time, or a little earlier, that Brihtric, Ealdorman Eadric's brother, accused Wulfnoth *Cild* [the South Saxon][4] to the king, and he went away and enticed ships to him until he had 20, and then he ravaged everywhere along the south coast, doing all manner of damage. Then the naval force was informed that they (Wulfnoth's party) could easily be surrounded if people were to set about it. Then the aforesaid Brihtric took with him 80 ships, intending to make a big reputation for himself[5] and to capture Wulfnoth alive or dead. But when they were on their way thither, such a wind blew against them that no man remembered its like, and it beat and dashed to pieces all the ships, and cast them ashore, and at once Wulfnoth came and burnt up the ships.

---

[1] 'E', 'F': "30,000".   [2] 'D' adds: "In this year Bishop Ælfheah went to Rome for the *pallium*."
[3] 'D' has "ships" in error for "hides". 'E' repeats hides after "ten". The order in 'C' "from three hundred hides and from ten" may have puzzled them; 310 is an unusual unit. It is sometimes assumed that something is omitted. Mr. Garmonsway would read: "one large warship from every three hundred hides and a cutter from every ten hides".
[4] From 'D', 'E', 'F'.   [5] 'F' reads: "Then Brihtric wished to earn praise for himself."

C (D, E)

When it became known to the other ships, where the king was, how the others had fared, it was as if everything was in confusion, and the king betook himself home, as did the ealdormen and chief councillors, and deserted the ships thus lightly. And the people who were on the ships took [the ships][1] back to London, and let the toil of all the nation thus lightly come to naught; and no better than this was the victory which all the English people had expected.

When this ship-levy had ended thus, there came at once after Lammas[2] the immense raiding army, which we called Thorkel's army,[3] to Sandwich,[4] and immediately turned their course to Canterbury and would quickly have captured the borough if the citizens had not still more quickly asked them for peace. And all the people of East Kent made peace with that army and gave them 3,000 pounds. And then immediately after that the army turned about till it reached the Isle of Wight, and from there they ravaged and burnt, as is their custom, everywhere in Sussex and Hampshire, and also in Berkshire. Then the king ordered all the nation to be called out,[5] so that the enemy should be resisted on every side; but nevertheless they journeyed just as they pleased.

Then on one occasion the king had intercepted them with all his army, when they wished to go to their ships, and the whole people was ready to attack them,[6] but it was hindered by Ealdorman Eadric, then as it always was. Then after Martinmas[7] they went back again to Kent, and took up winter quarters on the Thames, and lived off Essex and off the shires which were nearest, on both sides of the Thames, and often they attacked the borough of London. But, praise be to God, it still stands untouched, and they always suffered loss there.

Then after Christmas they chose a passage out through the Chilterns, and so to Oxford, and burnt the borough, and made their way then on both sides of the Thames towards their ships. Then they were warned that an army was collected against them at London; they then crossed at Staines. Thus they behaved the whole winter, and during the spring they were in Kent repairing their ships.

1010 In this year the afore-mentioned army came to East Anglia after Easter[8] and landed at Ipswich, and went straightway to where they had heard that Ulfcetel was with his army.[9] That was on Ascension day,[10] and at once the East Angles

---

[1] From 'D', 'E'.   [2] 1 August.
[3] Only 'C' has this clause. The Danish leader Thorkel the Tall is meant.
[4] Florence has an important addition: "The Danish earl Thorkel came with his fleet to England; then, in the month of August, another immense fleet of Danes, which the earls Heming and Eilaf were leading, came to land at the island of Thanet and without delay joined the aforesaid fleet. They then both proceeded to the port of Sandwich."
[5] Florence adds: "and he placed it through the maritime provinces against their attacks".
[6] *Id.:* "prepared to die or to conquer".   [7] 11 November.   [8] 9 April.
[9] Florence says it was at "the place which is called *Ringmere*". Cf. Nos. 12, 13.
[10] 18 May; but Florence puts the battle on 5 May, and this is shown to be correct by the entry of Oswig's death on that date in the Ely calendar discussed by B. Dickins in *Leeds Studies in English*, VI, pp. 14–24.

C (D, E)

fled. The men of Cambridgeshire stood firm against them. The king's son-in-law[1] Athelstan was killed there, and Oswig and his son, and Wulfric, Leofwine's son, and Eadwig, Æfic's brother, and many other good thegns and a countless number of the people. It was Thurcetel Mare's Head who first started that flight. The Danes had control of the field [and there they were provided with horses, and afterwards had control of East Anglia],[2] and ravaged and burnt that country for three months and even went into the wild fens, slaying the men and cattle, and burning throughout the fens; and they burnt down Thetford and Cambridge.

And afterwards they turned back southwards into the Thames valley, and the mounted men rode towards the ships; and quickly afterwards they turned west again into Oxfordshire, and from there into Buckinghamshire, and so along the Ouse until they reached Bedford, and so on as far as Tempsford, and ever they burnt as they went. Then they turned back to the ships with their booty. And when they were journeying[3] to their ships, the English army should have come out again in case they wished to go inland. Then the English army went home. And when they were in the east, the English army was kept in the west, and when they were in the south, our army was in the north. Then all the councillors were summoned to the king, and it was then to be decided how this country should be defended. But even if anything was then decided, it did not last even a month. Finally there was no leader who would collect an army, but each fled as best he could, and in the end no shire would even help the next.

Then before St. Andrew's day[4] the Danish army came to Northampton and at once burnt that town and[5] as much round about it as they pleased, and from there went across the Thames into Wessex, and so towards Cannings marsh,[6] and burnt it all. When they had thus gone as far as they pleased, they came at Christmas to their ships.

1011 In this year the king and his councillors sent to the army and asked for peace, and promised them tribute and provisions on condition that they should cease their ravaging. They had then overrun: (i) East Anglia, (ii) Essex, (iii) Middlesex, (iv) Oxfordshire, (v) Cambridgeshire, (vi) Hertfordshire, (vii) Buckinghamshire, (viii) Bedfordshire, (ix) half Huntingdonshire, (x) much of Northamptonshire;[7] and south of the Thames all Kent, Sussex, Hastings,[8] Surrey, Berkshire, Hampshire and much of Wiltshire. All those disasters befell us through bad policy, in that they were never offered tribute in time nor fought against;[9] but when they had done most to our injury, peace and truce were made with them; and for all this truce and tribute they journeyed none the less in bands everywhere, and harried our wretched people, and plundered and killed them.

[1] Or brother-in-law, *i.e.* brother of Ethelred's first wife. Ethelred's eldest son was called Athelstan, but this was too common a name in the West Saxon house for this fact to be significant in this connexion.
[2] From 'D', 'E'.   [3] 'E', "were dispersing".   [4] 30 November.
[5] 'E' adds: "they seized".   [6] Near All and Bishop's Cannings, Wilts.   [7] Omitted in 'E'.
[8] Not merely the town. Hastings was the name of a district, long regarded as distinct from Sussex.
[9] Only 'C' has these last three words.

C (D, E)

And then in this year, between the Nativity of St. Mary[1] and Michaelmas,[2] they besieged Canterbury,[3] and they got inside by treachery, for Ælfmær,[4] whose life Archbishop Ælfheah had saved, betrayed it. Then they captured there Archbishop Ælfheah, and the king's reeve Ælfweard, and Abbess Leofrun[5] and Bishop Godwine;[6] and they let Abbot Ælfmær[7] escape. And they took captive there all the ecclesiastics, and men and women—it was impossible for any man to tell how much of that people that was[8]—and they stayed afterwards in that borough as long as they pleased. And when they had then ransacked the whole borough, they went to their ships and took the archbishop with them.

He was then a captive who had been head of the English people and of Christendom. There could misery be seen where happiness was often seen before, in that wretched city from which first came [to us][9] Christianity and happiness in divine and secular things. And they kept the archbishop with them till the time when they martyred him.

1012 In this year Ealdorman Eadric and all the chief councillors of England, ecclesiastical and lay, came to London before Easter—Easter Sunday was on 13 April—and they stayed there until the tribute, namely 48,000 pounds,[10] was all paid after Easter. Then on the Saturday the army became greatly incensed against the bishop because he would not promise them any money,[11] but forbade that anything should be paid for him. They were also very drunk, for wine from the south had been brought there. They seized the bishop, and brought him to their assembly on the eve of the Sunday of the octave of Easter, which was 19 April, and shamefully put him to death there:[12] they pelted him with bones and with ox-heads, and one of them[13] struck him on the head with the back[14] of an axe, that he sank down with the blow, and his holy blood fell on the ground, and so he sent his holy soul to God's kingdom. And in the morning his body was carried to London,[15] and the bishops Eadnoth and Ælfhun[16] and the citizens received it with all reverence and buried it in St. Paul's minster. And God now reveals there the powers of the holy martyr.[17]

When that tribute was paid and the oaths of peace were sworn, the Danish army then dispersed as widely as it had been collected. Then 45 ships from that army came over to the king, and they promised him to defend this country, and he was to feed and clothe them.

---

[1] 8 September. [2] 29 September.
[3] Florence adds: "on the twentieth day of the siege part of the city was burnt".
[4] Id. adds: "the archdeacon".   [5] Of St. Mildred's, Thanet. 'E', 'F' have (wrongly) "Leofwine".
[6] Of Rochester.   [7] Of St. Augustine's, Canterbury.
[8] Florence adds: "Then Christ Church was plundered and burnt." He gives an account of further atrocities and of a sickness sent by God on the Danes in vengeance.   [9] From 'D', 'E'.   [10] "8,000": 'E', 'F'.
[11] According to Florence, 3,000 pounds was asked for him.   [12] This last clause is in 'C' only.
[13] Florence adds: "Thrum by name, whom he had confirmed the day before, moved by impious pity."
[14] The interpretation of yr as the blunt end of an axe-head is supported by Leechdoms (ed. Cockayre, III, p. 14), where an yr is used to crush bones.
[15] 'E', by changing the order, makes the bishops bring the body to London.
[16] Of Dorchester and London respectively.
[17] This annal was written before the translation of Ælfheah's body to Canterbury in 1023. Another account of this martyrdom is given by Thietmar. See No. 27.

C (D, E)

1013 In the year after the archbishop was martyred, the king appointed Bishop Lifing to the archbishopric of Canterbury. And in this same year, before the month of August, King Swein came with his fleet to Sandwich, and then went very quickly round East Anglia into the mouth of the Humber, and so up along the Trent until he reached Gainsborough. And then at once Earl Uhtred and all the Northumbrians submitted to him, as did all the people of Lindsey, and then all the people belonging to the district of the Five Boroughs,[1] and quickly afterwards all the Danish settlers[2] north of Watling Street, and hostages were given to him from every shire. When he perceived that all the people had submitted to him, he gave orders that his army should be provisioned and provided with horses, and then he afterwards turned southward[3] with his full forces and left the ships and the hostages in charge of his son Cnut. When he had crossed the Watling Street, they did the greatest damage that any army could do. He then turned to Oxford, and the citizens at once submitted and gave hostages; and from there to Winchester, where they did the same. He then turned eastward to London, and many of his host were drowned in the Thames because they did not trouble to find a bridge. When he came to the borough the citizens would not yield, but resisted with full battle, because King Ethelred was inside and Thorkel with him.

Then King Swein turned from there to Wallingford, and so west across the Thames to Bath, where he stayed with his army. Then Ealdorman Æthelmær[4] came there, and with him the western thegns, and all submitted to Swein, and they gave him hostages. When he had fared thus,[5] he then turned northward to his ships, and all the nation regarded him as full king. And after that the citizens of London submitted and gave hostages, for they were afraid that he would destroy them. Then Swein demanded full payment and provisions for his army that winter, and Thorkel demanded the same for the army which lay at Greenwich, and in spite of it all they ravaged as often as they pleased. Nothing therefore was of benefit to this nation, neither from the south nor from the north.

Then King Ethelred was for a time with the fleet which lay in the Thames, and the queen went across the sea to her brother Richard, and with her Abbot Ælfsige of Peterborough, and the king sent Bishop Ælfhun across the sea with the athelings Edward and Alfred, that he should take care of them. And the king then went from the fleet to the Isle of Wight at Christmas and spent that festival there; and after the festival went across the sea to Richard and was there with him until the happy event of Swein's death.[6]

---

[1] This presumably is the force of 'C''s expression *Fifburhingum*, as opposed to 'D', 'E''s *Fifburgum*, which could mean the boroughs without necessarily including the areas of which they were the centre.
[2] Literally 'the army', used in the sense of the organized inhabitants of an area of Danish settlement in England.
[3] Florence adds: "against the South Mercians".
[4] *Id.* adds: "of Devon".   [5] "When he had won everything thus", 'D', 'E'.
[6] 'E' adds a Peterborough insertion on the collection of relics by Abbot Ælfsige when he was abroad.

C (D, E)

1014 In this year Swein ended his days at Candlemas, on 3 February,[1] and then all the fleet elected Cnut king. Then all the councillors who were in England,[2] ecclesiastical and lay, determined to send for King Ethelred, and they said that no lord was dearer to them than their natural lord, if he would govern them more justly than he did before. Then the king sent his son Edward hither with his messengers, and bade them greet all his people, and said that he would be a gracious lord to them, and reform all the things which they all hated; and all the things that had been said and done against him should be forgiven, on condition that they all unanimously turned to him without treachery. And complete friendship was then established with oath and pledge on both sides, and they pronounced every Danish king an outlaw from England for ever. Then during the spring King Ethelred came home to his own people and he was gladly received by them all.

Then after Swein was dead, Cnut stayed in Gainsborough with his army until Easter,[3] and he and the people in Lindsey came to an agreement that they would provide him with horses and then go out and ravage all together. Then King Ethelred came there to Lindsey with his full force before they were ready, and it was ravaged and burnt, and all the men who could be got at were killed; and Cnut put out to sea with his fleet, and thus the wretched people were betrayed by him. And he then turned south till he reached Sandwich, and he caused to be put ashore the hostages who had been given to his father, and he cut off their hands, ears and noses.[4] And on top of all these evils, the king ordered 21,000 pounds to be paid to the army which lay at Greenwich; and in this year on Michaelmas eve[5] the great tide of the sea flooded widely over this country, coming up higher than it had ever done before, and submerging many villages and a countless number of people.

1015 In this year the great assembly at Oxford took place, and there Ealdorman Eadric betrayed Sigeferth and Morcar,[6] the chief thegns belonging to the Seven Boroughs:[7] he enticed them into his chamber, and they were basely killed inside it. And the king then seized all their property and ordered Sigeferth's widow[8] to be seized and brought to Malmesbury. Then after a short interval, the atheling Edmund went and took the woman against the king's will and married her. Then before the Nativity of St. Mary[9] the atheling went from the west, north to the Five Boroughs, and at once took possession of all Sigeferth's estates and Morcar's, and the people all submitted to him.

---

[1] 'D' adds: "and in the same year Ælfwig was consecrated bishop of London at York, on St. Juliana's day (16 February)". According to Gaimar and Simeon of Durham, Swein was first buried at York. See also No. 27.

[2] This clause is in 'C' only.   [3] 25 April.

[4] Florence adds: "and then he set out for Denmark, to return the next year".   [5] 28 September.

[6] Florence adds: "the sons of Earngrim". On them, see Nos. 125, 130.

[7] The Five Boroughs with the addition of York and probably Torksey.

[8] Florence adds: "Aldgyth".

[9] Id.: "between the Assumption [15 August] and the Nativity [8 September] of St. Mary".

C (D, E)

Then at that same time King Cnut came to Sandwich, and then turned at once round Kent into Wessex, until he reached the mouth of the Frome, and ravaged then in Dorset, in Wiltshire and in Somerset. The king then lay sick at Cosham. Then Ealdorman Eadric collected an army, and so did the atheling Edmund in the North. When they united, the ealdorman wished to betray the atheling, and on that account they separated without fighting, and retreated from their enemies. And then Ealdorman Eadric seduced 40 ships[1] from the king, and then went over to Cnut; and the West Saxons submitted and gave hostages and supplied the Danish army with horses, and it then stayed there until Christmas.

1016 In this year Cnut came with his army,[2] and Ealdorman Eadric with him, across the Thames into Mercia at Cricklade, and they turned then into Warwickshire within the Christmas season, and ravaged and burnt, and killed all they came across. Then the atheling Edmund began to gather the English army. When the army was assembled,[3] nothing would satisfy them except that the king should be there with them and they should have the assistance of the citizens of London. They then desisted from that expedition and each man took himself home. Then after that festival, the army was ordered out again on pain of the full penalty, every man to go forth who was capable of service. And word was sent to the king in London, begging him to come to join the army with the forces which he could muster. When they all came together, it availed nothing, no more than it had often done before. The king was then informed that those who should support him wished to betray him; he then left the army and returned to London.

Then the atheling Edmund rode to Northumbria to Earl Uhtred, and every one thought that they would collect an army against King Cnut. Then they led an army into Staffordshire and into Shropshire and to Chester, and they ravaged on their side[4] and Cnut on his side. He then went out through Buckinghamshire into Bedfordshire, from there to Huntingdonshire, and so into Northamptonshire,[5] along the fen to Stamford, and then into Lincolnshire; then from there to Nottinghamshire and so into Northumbria towards York. When Uhtred learned this, he left his ravaging and hastened northwards, and submitted then out of necessity, and with him all the Northumbrians, and he gave hostages. And nevertheless he was killed by the advice of Ealdorman Eadric,[6] and with him Thurcetel, Nafena's son. And then after that the king[7] appointed Eric for the Northumbrians, as their earl, just as Uhtred had been, and then turned him[8] southward by another route, keeping to the west, and the whole army then reached the ships before Easter.[9] And the atheling Edmund went to

---

[1] Florence adds: "manned by Danish soldiers".
[2] 'E', 'F' add: "of 160 ships". This must be erroneous, for no naval force is in question.
[3] Florence says: "The Mercians would not engage with the West Saxons and Danes."
[4] Florence explains: "because they would not go out to fight the army of the Danes".
[5] This phrase is omitted in 'E'.   [6] Only 'C' connects him with this murder.
[7] Cnut, 'E'.   [8] 'E', "they turned them".   [9] 1 April.

C (D, E)

London to his father. And then after Easter, King Cnut turned with all his ships towards London.

Then it happened that King Ethelred died before the ships arrived. He ended his days on St. George's day,[1] and he had held his kingdom with great toil and difficulties as long as his life lasted.[2] And then after his death, all the councillors who were in London and the citizens chose Edmund as king, and he stoutly defended his kingdom while his life lasted. Then the ships came to Greenwich at the Rogation days,[3] and within a short space of time they turned to London. And the Danes then dug a large ditch on the south side and dragged their ships on to the west side of the bridge, and then afterwards surrounded the borough with a ditch, so that no man could go in or out, and repeatedly attacked the borough, but they withstood them stoutly.[4]

King Edmund had previously gone out and he took possession of Wessex, and all the people submitted to him.[5] And soon after that he fought against the Danish army at Penselwood near Gillingham, and he fought a second battle after midsummer at Sherston;[6] and a great number on both sides fell there, and the armies separated of their own accord. In that battle Ealdorman Eadric and Ælfmær Darling[7] were supporting the Danish army against King Edmund. Then he collected the army for the third time, and went to London, keeping north of the Thames, and so out through *Clayhanger*,[8] and relieved the citizens and sent the enemy in flight to their ships. And then two days after that, the king crossed over at Brentford, and then fought against the army and put it to flight; and a great number of the English people who went ahead of the main force, wishing to get booty, were drowned there through their own carelessness. And the king turned to Wessex after that and collected his army.

Then the Danish army returned at once to London, and besieged the borough, attacking it strongly both by water and by land, but the Almighty God delivered it. The army then turned after that with their ships from London into the Orwell, and went inland there, and went into Mercia, slaying and burning whatever was in their path, as is their custom, and procured provisions for themselves; and they drove both their ships and their herds into the Medway. Then King Edmund collected all his army[9] for the fourth time, and crossed the

---

[1] 23 April.

[2] 'D' and 'E' say only: "on St. George's day, after great toil and difficulties of his life". Florence has important additional information: "His body was buried with great honour in the church of St. Paul the Apostle. And after his death, the bishops, abbots, ealdormen and all the more important men of England assembled together and unanimously elected Cnut as their lord and king; and coming to him at Southampton and repudiating and renouncing in his presence all the race of King Ethelred, they concluded a peace with him, and swore loyalty to him; and he also swore to them that he would be a loyal lord to them, in affairs both of Church and State."   [3] 7-9 May.

[4] Florence: "Therefore, raising the siege for the time, and leaving part of the army to guard the ships, they went away, hastening to Wessex, and gave no time for King Edmund Ironside to raise his army. However, he met them bravely in Dorset with the army which he had been able to collect in so short a time, supported by God's help, and engaging them at a place called Penselwood near Gillingham, he conquered and put them to flight."

[5] *Id.* adds: "with great joy".   [6] *Id.* adds: "In Hwiccia."   [7] *Id.* adds: "and Ælfgar, son of Meaw".

[8] Clayhill Farm in Tottenham, Middlesex. See *The Place-Names of Middlesex*, p. 79. This account of the route taken is only in 'C'.   [9] 'D', 'E', "all the English nation".

C (D, E)

Thames at Brentford, and went into Kent.[1] And the Danish army fled before him with their horses into Sheppey. The king killed as many of them as he could overtake, and Ealdorman Eadric came to meet the king at Aylesford. No greater folly was ever agreed to than that was. The army went again inland into Essex, and proceeded into Mercia and destroyed everything in its path.

When the king learnt that the army had gone inland, for the fifth time he collected all the English nation; and pursued them and overtook them in Essex at the hill which is called Ashingdon, and they stoutly joined battle there.[2] Then Ealdorman Eadric did as he had often done before; he was the first to start the flight with the *Magonsæte*,[3] and thus betrayed his liege lord and all the people of England. There Cnut had the victory and won for himself all the English people. There was Bishop Eadnoth[4] killed, and Abbot Wulfsige,[5] and Ealdorman Ælfric,[6] and Godwine, the ealdorman of Lindsey,[7] and Ulfcetel of East Anglia, and Æthelweard, son of Ealdorman Æthelwine,[8] and all the nobility of England was there destroyed.

Then after this battle King Cnut went inland with his army to Gloucester, where he had learnt that King Edmund was. Then Ealdorman Eadric and the councillors who were there advised that the kings should be reconciled, and they exchanged hostages.[9] And the kings met at Alney[10] and established their friendship there[11] both with pledge and with oath, and fixed the payment for the Danish army. And with this reconciliation they separated, and Edmund succeeded to Wessex and Cnut to Mercia.[12] And the army then went to the ships with the things that they had captured, and the Londoners came to terms with the army and bought peace for themselves; and the army brought their ships into London and took up winter quarters inside.

Then on St. Andrew's day King Edmund died, and his body is buried in Glastonbury along with his grandfather Edgar. And in the same year Wulfgar, abbot of Abingdon, died, and Æthelsige succeeded to the abbacy.[13]

1017   In this year King Cnut succeeded to all the kingdom of England and divided it into four, Wessex for himself, East Anglia for Thorkel, Mercia for Eadric, and Northumbria for Eric. And in this year Ealdorman Eadric was killed,[14] and Northman, son of Ealdorman Leofwine, and Æthelweard, son of Æthelmær the Stout, and Brihtric, son of Ælfheah[15] of Devonshire. And King Cnut exiled

---

[1] Florence adds: "and fought a battle against the Danes by Otford".   [2] 18 October.
[3] The people of Herefordshire; the name survives in Maund Bryan and Rose Maund. See p. 64.
[4] Of Dorchester.   [5] Of Ramsey.   [6] Of Hampshire.   [7] 'D', 'E' omit "of Lindsey".
[8] Ælfwine, 'D', Æthelsige, 'E', 'F'. Æthelwine of East Anglia is meant.
[9] 'D' omits this last clause.   [10] 'D' adds: "by Deerhurst".
[11] 'D' has instead: "and became partners and sworn brothers and established that both with pledge and also with oaths".
[12] Instead of Mercia, 'D' reads: "to the north part". See also No. 9, p. 284.
[13] Only 'C' and 'E' include these Abingdon entries.
   The Chronicle becomes a much scantier record for the reigns of the Danish kings. But we have now come near enough to Florence's lifetime for his account to be a valuable authority, and it is therefore given in full as No. 9.
[14] 'F' says that he was "very rightly" killed, "at London".   [15] Ælfgeat, 'E'.

C (D, E)

the atheling Eadwig[1] and afterwards had him killed. And then before 1 August the king ordered the widow of[2] King Ethelred, Richard's daughter, to be fetched as his wife.[3]

A1017 In this year Cnut was chosen as king.

C (D, E)

1018 In this year the tribute was paid over all England, namely 72,000 pounds in all, apart from what the citizens of London paid, namely ten and a half[4] thousand pounds. Then some of the army went to Denmark, and 40 ships remained with King Cnut, and the Danes and the English reached an agreement at Oxford.[5]

1019 In this year King Cnut returned to Denmark[6] and stayed there all the winter.

D

And in this year[7] died Archbishop Ælfstan, who was called Lifing, and he was a very prudent man, both in matters of Church and State.

C	D	E (F)
1020[8] In this year Archbishop Lifing died, and King Cnut came back to England. And then at Easter[9] there was a great assembly at Cirencester. Then Ealdorman Æthelweard and Eadwig, king of the *ceorls*, were outlawed. And in this year the king went to Ashingdon, and Archbishop	In this year King Cnut came back to England, and then at Easter there was a great assembly at Cirencester. Then Ealdorman Æthelweard was outlawed. And in this year the king and Earl Thorkel went to Ashingdon, and Archbishop Wulfstan and other bishops and also abbots and many monks; and they consecrated the minster at Ashingdon. And the monk Æthelnoth, who was dean at Christ Church, was	In this year King Cnut came to England, and then at Easter there was a great assembly at Cirencester. Then Ealdorman Æthelweard was outlawed. And in this year the king went to Ashingdon,[10] and Archbishop Lifing died. And Æthelnoth, monk and dean of Christ Church, was in that same year consecrated to it as bishop.

[1] Son of King Ethelred. 'D', 'E' add: "and Eadwig, king of the *ceorls*" (see 1020 'C'); they then omit the next clause.
[2] 'D', 'E' add: "the other".   [3] 'F' adds: "namely Ælfgifu in English, Emma in French".
[4] 'E', 'F' have "eleven", misunderstanding the idiom "the eleventh half" = 10½.
[5] 'D' adds: "according to Edgar's law". The preface to what is probably the agreement on this occasion is given as No. 47. 'E' adds: "And in this year Abbot Æthelsige died at Abingdon and Æthelwine succeeded." As later Abingdon sources know only one abbot between Wulfgar and Siward, calling him Æthelwine, Plummer thinks that 'E' has made two abbots out of one called Æthelsige and Æthelwine in different sources.
[6] 'D' adds: "with nine ships".
[7] Only 'D' puts Lifing's death in 1019. He died on 12 June, so the discrepancy cannot be due to a different method of beginning the year.
[8] This annal has the same base in all MSS., but each has its own additions or omissions, which are clearest if the three chief texts are set out in full.   [9] 17 April.
[10] 'F' adds: "and had a minster built there of stone and mortar, for the souls of the men who had been slain there, and gave it to a priest of his who was called Stigand".

C

Wulfstan and Earl Thorkel, and with them many bishops, and they consecrated the minster at Ashingdon.

D

consecrated bishop for Christ Church on 13 November in that same year.

C (D, E)

1021 In this year, at Martinmas,[1] King Cnut outlawed Earl Thorkel.

D

And Ælfgar the charitable bishop[2] died in the early morning of Christmas Day.

C (D, E)

1022 In this year King Cnut went out with his ships to the Isle of Wight, and Archbishop Æthelnoth went to Rome,

D (E, F)

and was received there with much honour by the venerable Pope Benedict, who placed the *pallium* on him with his own hands, and consecrated and blessed him as archbishop with great solemnity on 7 October;[3] and the archbishop immediately on that same day celebrated Mass wearing the *pallium* [as the pope directed him][4] and then afterwards dined in state with the pope himself;

D

and also he himself took the *pallium* from St. Peter's altar. And then he afterwards journeyed happily home to his country.

E (F)

and afterwards returned home with his full blessing. And Abbot Leofwine, who was wrongfully driven from Ely, was his companion, and cleared himself there from everything that had been said against him, as the pope directed him, in the witness of the archbishop and of all the company which was with him.

C

1023 In this year King Cnut came back to England, and Thorkel and he were reconciled, and he entrusted Denmark and his son for Thorkel to maintain and the king took

D

In this year in St. Paul's minster in London, King Cnut gave full permission to Archbishop Æthelnoth and Bishop Brihtwine[5] and to all the servants of God who were with them to take up the archbishop St. Ælfheah from the tomb, and

E (F)

In this year Archbishop Wulfstan died, and Ælfric succeeded. And in the same year Archbishop Æthelnoth moved the relics of St. Ælfheah, the archbishop, from London to Canterbury.[6]

---

[1] 11 November.   [2] Of Elmham.
[3] 'E', 'F', which share some unimportant minor variations from the wording of 'D', do not give this date.   [4] 'E' only.   [5] Of Wells.   [6] 'E' has here a Latin entry relating to Norman history.

C

Thorkel's son with him to England. And afterwards he had St. Ælfheah's relics moved from London to Canterbury.

D

they did so on 8 June. And the illustrious king, and the archbishop and the diocesan bishops, and the earls, and very many ecclesiastics and also lay-folk, conveyed his holy body on a ship across the Thames to Southwark, and there entrusted the holy martyr to the archbishop and his companions. And they then bore him with a distinguished company and happy jubilation to Rochester. Then on the third day Queen Emma came with her royal child Hardacnut, and they then all conveyed the holy archbishop with much glory and joy and songs of praise into Canterbury, and thus brought him with due ceremony into Christ Church on 11 June. Afterwards on the eighth day, on 15 June, Archbishop Æthelnoth and Bishop Ælfsige[1] and Bishop Brihtwine and all who were with them placed St. Ælfheah's holy body on the north side of Christ's altar, to the praise of God and the honour of the holy archbishop, and to the eternal salvation of all those who daily visit his holy body there with devout hearts and with all humility. May Almighty God have mercy on all Christian men, through the holy merits of St. Ælfheah.

1026

D

In this year Bishop Ælfric went to Rome and received the *pallium* from Pope John on 12 November.

E (F)

(1025) In this year King Cnut went with ships to Denmark to the Holme, at the Holy River,[2] and there came against him Ulf and Eilaf and a very great army, both a land force and a naval force, from Sweden. And there very many men on King Cnut's side were destroyed, both Danish and English men, and the Swedes had control of the field.

C (D, E, F)

1028 In this year King Cnut went [from England][3] to Norway with 50 ships,[4]

D (E, F)

and drove King Olaf from the land, and made good his claim to all that land.[5]

---

[1] Of Winchester.   [2] Cf. Nos. 15, 16.   [3] From 'D', 'E', 'F'.
[4] 'F' adds: "of English thegns".   [5] With this annal compare Nos. 18, 19.

C D (E, F)

1029 In this year King Cnut came back home to England.

D (E)

1030 In this year King Olaf was killed in Norway by his own people, and was afterwards holy. And previously in this year the brave Earl Hákon died at sea.

In this year King Olaf came back into Norway and the people gathered against him and fought with him, and he was killed there.

D (E, F)

1027 (1031)[1] In this year King Cnut went to Rome, and as soon as he came home[2] he went to Scotland, and the king of the Scots surrendered to him,

D E (F)

and became his man, but he observed it but little time.

Malcolm, and two other kings, Mælbæth and Iehmarc.[3]

1032 In this year there appeared the wild-fire, such as no man ever remembered before, and also it did damage all over in many places. And in the same year Ælfsige, bishop of Winchester, died, and was succeeded by the king's priest, Ælfwine.

1033 In this year Bishop Leofsige died, and his body is buried in Worcester, and Brihtheah was chosen to his see.

In this year Merehwit, bishop of Somerset,[4] died, and he is buried in Glastonbury.

---

[1] The simplest explanation of this misdating of Cnut's journey by four years is that the chronicler knew that it followed a great battle in Scandinavia, and placed it after Stiklestad, 1030, instead of the Holy River, 1026. Continental evidence fixes the date as 1027. The date of the Scottish expedition is uncertain. With this annal compare Nos. 16, 18.

[2] 'E', 'F' state: "in the same year".

[3] 'E' and 'F' both have a note on Norman history, 'E' in Latin, 'F' in English. Under the date 1031, 'A' mentions Cnut's return, and inserts a spurious charter concerning harbour rights at Sandwich.

[4] The see of Wells is meant.

9

C (D, E)

1034 In this year Bishop Æthelric[1] died,[2] and he is buried in Ramsey.

D

And that same year King Malcolm
of Scotland died.

C (D)

1035 In this year King Cnut died[3] on 12 November at Shaftesbury, and he was brought from there to Winchester and buried there; and Ælfgifu, the queen, then stayed there. And Harold, who said that he was the son of Cnut and the other Ælfgifu[5]– though it was not true–sent there and had all the best treasures taken from her, which she could not keep back,[6] which King Cnut had possessed. Yet she continued to stay there as long as she was allowed.

E (F)

(1036) In this year King Cnut died at Shaftesbury and he is buried in Winchester in the Old Minster; and he was king over all England for very nearly 20 years. And immediately after his death there was an assembly of all the councillors at Oxford. And Earl Leofric and almost all the thegns north of the Thames and the shipmen in London chose Harold to the regency[4] of all England, for himself and for his brother Hardacnut, who was then in Denmark. And Earl Godwine and all the chief men in Wessex opposed it as long as they could, but they could not contrive anything against it. And it was then determined that Ælfgifu, Hardacnut's mother, should stay in Winchester with the housecarls of her son the king, and they should keep all Wessex in his possession; and Earl Godwine was their most loyal man. Some men said about Harold that he was the son of King Cnut and of Ælfgifu, the daughter of Ealdorman Ælfhelm, but it seemed incredible to many men; and yet he was full king over all England.[7]

C (D)

1036 In this year the innocent atheling Alfred, the son of King Ethelred, came into this country, wishing to go to his mother who was in Winchester, but Earl

[1] Of Dorchester.

[2] 'E' ends the annal here.

[3] 'D' inserts here: "and Harold his son succeeded to the kingdom".

[4] The chronicler uses a rather rare word meaning vaguely 'protection', 'support', and avoids any word implying kingly authority. That there was a year of a regency before Harold became king is shown by Hermann's *De miraculis sancti Eadmundi*.

[5] 'D', "and Ælfgifu of Northampton".

[6] This clause is only in 'C'. I am unsure of its implications. Does it mean, "which she was in no position to refuse" or that they took such treasures as she did not manage to secrete?

[7] Cf. Hermann, *De miraculis sancti Eadmundi* (ed. Arnold), pp. 47f.: "England . . . after being bereft of a king for the space of a year, at length received the rule of the two sons of the afore-mentioned king, namely Harold for two and a half years, and after him Hardacnut for three half years" (probably for two and a half, an error due to a misunderstanding of an Old English idiom).

C (D)

Godwine did not allow him, nor did the other men who had great power,[1] because feeling was veering much towards Harold,[2] although this was not right.[3]

But Godwine[4] then stopped him and put him in captivity, and he dispersed his companions and killed some in various ways; some were sold for money, some were cruelly killed, some were put in fetters, some were blinded, some were mutilated,[5] some were scalped.[6] No more horrible deed was done in this land since the Danes came and peace was made here. Now we must trust to the beloved God that they rejoice happily with Christ who were without guilt so miserably slain. The atheling still lived. He was threatened with every evil, until it was decided to take him thus in bonds to Ely. As soon as he arrived, he was blinded on the ship, and thus blind was brought to the monks, and he dwelt there as long as he lived. Then he was buried as well befitted him, very honourably, as he deserved, in the south chapel at the west end, full close to the steeple. His soul is with Christ.[7]

C (D)	**E (F)**

1037 In this year Harold was chosen as king everywhere, and Hardacnut was deserted because he was too long in Denmark; and then his mother, Queen Ælfgifu, was driven out without any mercy to face the raging winter. And she then went across the sea[9] to Bruges, and Earl Baldwin received her well there and maintained her there as long as she had need. And previously in this year, Æfic, the noble dean of Evesham, died.

In this year Ælfgifu, King Cnut's widow, who was King Hardacnut's mother,[8] was driven out. And she then sought Baldwin's protection south of the sea, and he gave her a residence in Bruges and protected and maintained her as long as she was there.

1038 In this year the good Archbishop Æthelnoth died, and Æthelric, bishop of Sussex [who desired of God that he should not let him live

In this year Archbishop Æthelnoth died on 1 November, and a little

---

[1] 'D' has a significant variant; it omits reference to Godwine, reading simply: "but those who had much power in the land did not permit it".

[2] Or perhaps better "the popular cry was greatly in favour of Harold" (Garmonsway).

[3] The rest of this annal is in rhymed verse. In both MSS., but more in 'D', the regularity of the metre is upset here and there.

[4] 'D' again omits to mention Godwine, having 'he' instead, which presumably refers back to Harold.

[5] 'D' omits this clause.　　　　　　　　　　　　　　　　　　　[6] 'D' adds: "shamefully".

[7] Cf. the account of his death in the *Encomium Emmae*, No. 28.

[8] 'F' adds: "and King Edward's".　　　　　　　　　　　　[9] 'D' omits "across the sea".

C (D)

any while after his dear father Æthelnoth, and he also departed within seven days after him],[1] and Ælfric, bishop of East Anglia,[2] and Brihtheah bishop of Worcester, on 20 December.

E (F)

while afterwards Æthelric, bishop of Sussex, and then Brihtheah, bishop of Worcester, before Christmas, and quickly after that Ælfric, bishop of East Anglia. And then Eadsige[3] succeeded to the archbishopric, and Grimcetel to the bishopric of Sussex, and Bishop Lifing to Worcestershire and to Gloucestershire.

C *only*

1039 In this year occurred the great wind, and Brihtmær, bishop of Lichfield, died. And the Welsh killed Edwin, Earl Leofric's brother, and Thurkil and Ælfgeat and very many good men with them. And in this year also Hardacnut came to Bruges, where his mother was.

C (D)

1040 In this year King Harold died. Then they sent to Bruges for Hardacnut, thinking that they were acting wisely, and he then came here with 60 ships, before midsummer, and then imposed a very severe tax, which was endured with difficulty, namely eight marks to the rowlock. And all who had wanted him before were then ill-disposed towards him. And also he did nothing worthy of a king as long as he ruled. He had the dead Harold dug up and thrown into the fen.

E (F)

(1039) In this year King Harold died in Oxford on 17 March, and he was buried at Westminster. And he ruled England four years and sixteen weeks. And in his time 16 ships were paid for at eight marks to each rowlock, just as had been done in King Cnut's time. And in this same year King Hardacnut came to Sandwich seven days before midsummer, and he was immediately received both by the English and the Danes, though his advisers afterwards requited it very sternly, when they decreed that 62 ships should be paid for at eight marks to each rowlock. And in this same year the sester of wheat rose to 55 pence, and even higher.

A1040 In this year Archbishop Eadsige went to Rome, and King Harold died.

---

[1] In 'D' only.   [2] 'D' omits to mention him.   [3] 'F', "the king's priest".

C (D)

1041 In this year Hardacnut had all Worcestershire ravaged for the sake of his two housecarls, who had exacted that severe tax. The people had then killed them within the town in the minster. And soon in that year there came from beyond the sea Edward, his brother on the mother's side, the son of King Ethelred, who had been driven from his country many years before–and yet he was sworn in as king;[1] and he thus stayed at his brother's court as long as he lived. And in this year also Hardacnut betrayed Earl Eadwulf[2] under his safe-conduct and he was then a pledge-breaker. [And in this year Æthelric was consecrated bishop[3] in York on 11 January.][4]

1042 In this year Hardacnut died in this way: he was standing at his drink and he suddenly fell to the ground with fearful convulsions, and those who were near caught him, and he spoke no word afterwards. He died on 8 June. And all the people then received Edward as king,[6] as was his natural right.

E (F)

(1040) In this year the army-tax was paid, namely 21,099 pounds, and later 11,048 pounds were paid for 32 ships. And in this same year Edward, son of King Ethelred, came to this land from France. He was brother of King Hardacnut. They were both sons of Ælfgifu, who was Earl Richard's daughter.

(1041) In this year Hardacnut died at Lambeth on 8 June, and he was king over all England two years all but ten days, and he is buried in the Old Minster with King Cnut his father.[5] And before he was buried, all the people chose Edward as king, in London. May he hold it as long as God will grant him. And all that year was very distressing in many ways. Storms did much damage to the crops; and more cattle were destroyed during this year than anyone remembered before, both through various diseases and through storms. And in this year Ælfsige, abbot of Peterborough, died, and the monk Arnwig was chosen as abbot because he was a very good and very gentle man.[7]

A1042 In this year King Hardacnut died.

[1] These remarks could apply to Ethelred or Edward, but more naturally to the latter. The *Encomium Emmae* says Hardacnut asked Edward to come and hold the kingdom with him.
[2] Of Northumbria.   [3] Of Durham.   [4] In 'D' only.
[5] 'F' adds: "and his mother gave to the New Minster for his soul the head of St. Valentine the martyr".
[6] 'D' reads: "chose Edward and received him as king".
[7] This last sentence, which is not in 'F', is clearly a Peterborough addition.

2. From the *Historia Brittonum*

Since it is very uncertain how much truth lies behind the stories of the English invasion and of Arthur's wars recounted in this work, I have restricted my selection to the section based on the genealogies of the Northumbrian kings, with Nennius's additions, which may probably go back on reliable tradition. They tell us something of the British leaders who resisted Northumbrian expansion, of the nicknames by which the Northumbrian kings were known to their enemies, and of the conquest of Elmet by Edwin.

On the nature of this work, see pp. 117 f., and on editions see bibliography, p. 131. The passages here given are in Mommsen, pp. 202, 204–208, Lot, pp. 197–199, 201–206, and translated by Wade-Evans, pp. 78–83.

. . . Oswiu begat Alhfrith and Ælfwine and Ecgfrith. Ecgfrith is he who made war against his cousin,[1] who was king of the Picts, Brude[2] by name, and he fell there with all the strength of his army; and the Picts with their king were victorious, and the Saxon robbers[3] never continued to demand tribute from the Picts from the time of that battle, which is called "the fight of the pool of *Garan*".[4] Oswiu, however, had two wives, of whom one was called Riemmelth, daughter of Royth, the son of Rum; and the other was called Eanflæd, daughter of Edwin, the son of Ælle. . . .

Osfrith and Eadfrith were two sons of Edwin, and fell with him in the battle of *Meicen*,[5] and the kingdom never returned to his line, because not one of his race escaped from that battle, but all were killed with him by the army of Cadwallon, king of the district of Gwynedd. . . .

Ida, the son of Eoppa, held the districts in the north part of Britain, that is, north of the sea of Humber, and reigned for 12 years, and he joined the fortress, that is *Din Gueirm*, and *Gurd Bernech* [which were two districts, into one district, namely *Deur a Berneich*, in English Deira and Bernicia.].[6]

Then at that time Outigern[7] fought bravely against the race of the English. Then Talhærn Tataguen was renowned in poetry; and Neirin and Taliessin, and Bluchbard and Cian, who is called *Gueinth Guaut*, won fame together at the same time in British poetry.

The great King Mailcun reigned among the Britons, that is in the district of Gwynedd, for his ancestor, namely Cunedag, with his sons who were eight in number, had formerly come from the northern part, that is from the district which is called *Manau Guotodin*,[8] 146 years before Mailcun reigned. And they expelled the Scots[9] from these districts with immense slaughter, and they never returned to inhabit them again.[10]

Adda, the son of Ida, reigned eight years; Æthelric, the son of Adda, reigned four years; Theodric, the son of Ida, reigned seven years; Frithuwald reigned six years.

[1] A. O. Anderson, *Early Sources of Scottish History*, I, p. 193, discusses this relationship, concluding that Brude's maternal grandfather must have been descended from Æthelfrith's son Eanfrith, who married a Pictish princess. [2] Brude mac Bili.

[3] It has been suggested that the word used, *ambronum*, is an error for *Hymbronum*, 'the Humbrians'.

[4] The battle of *Nechtanesmere*, 685, on which see F. T. Wainwright, in *Antiquity*, XXII, pp. 82–97.

[5] The battle of Hatfield, 632.   [6] This is added in the Durham and Corpus MSS.

[7] I. Williams has shown that this is probably the name meant, though the text has Dutigern. See *Bull. Board Celt. Stud.*, VII, pt. I, pp. 387f.

[8] The district at the head of the Firth of Forth.   [9] *i.e.* the Irish settled in North Wales.

[10] On the events in this paragraph, see P. Hunter Blair, *The Origins of Northumbria*, pp. 27–37.

In his time the kingdom of the people of Kent received baptism, sent by Gregory. Hussa reigned seven years. Four kings fought against him,[1] Urbgen, Riderch Hen, Guallauc and Morcant. Theodric fought bravely against that Urbgen with his sons; and in that time sometimes the enemy, sometimes the citizens,[2] were defeated. And he [Urbgen] shut them up for three days and nights in the island of *Metcaud*,[3] and while he was on that expedition he was murdered by Morcant's design out of envy, because in him before all kings there was the greatest courage in carrying on war.

Æthelfrith *Flesaur*[4] reigned 12 years in Bernicia and another 12 in Deira; he reigned 24 between the two kingdoms. And he gave *Dinguoaroy* to his wife who was called Bebbe, and from the name of his wife it took its name, *Bebbanburh* (Bamburgh).

Edwin, the son of Ælle, reigned 17 years, and he occupied Elmet and drove out Ceretic, the king of that district. Eanflæd, his daughter, received baptism on the twelfth day after Pentecost, and all her people, men and women, with her. And at the following Easter, Edwin accepted baptism, and twelve thousand men were baptized with him. If anyone wishes to know who baptized them [thus Bishop Renchidus and Elbobdus, the most holy of bishops, have recounted to me][5] Rum map Urbgen [that is, Paulinus, archbishop of York][5] baptized them, and did not cease for 40 days to baptize the whole race of the robbers [that is, the Old Saxons],[5] and through his preaching many believed in Christ.

Oswald, the son of Æthelfrith, reigned nine years. He is Oswald *Lamnguin*.[6] He killed Cadwallon, king of the district of Gwynedd, in the battle of *Catscaul*,[7] with a great slaughter of his army.

Oswiu, the son of Æthelfrith, reigned 28 years and 6 months. While he reigned, there came a great pestilence upon men, while Catgualart was reigning over the Britons after his father, and he[8] perished in it. And Oswiu killed Penda on the field of *Gai*,[9] and the kings of the Britons were killed who had gone out with Penda on an expedition as far as the city which is called *Iudeu*.[10] [Then Oswiu rendered into Penda's hand all the riches that were with him in the city; and Penda distributed them to the kings of the Britons. That is, the *atbret Iude:i*.][11] And Catgabail, king of the region of Gwynedd, alone escaped with his army, arising by night; on which account he was called Catgabail *Catguommed*.[12]

Ecgfrith, the son of Oswiu, reigned nine years. In his time St. Cuthbert the bishop died in the island of *Metcaud*.[13] Ecgfrith it is who made war against the Picts and fell there.

[1] One MS. (Brit. Mus. Cott. Vespas. D xxi) has 'them' for 'him'.
[2] The Britons, since they had once belonged to the Roman Empire.   [3] Lindisfarne.
[4] From Latin *flexus*, hence 'the Artful'.
[5] These additions are in the Durham and Corpus MSS. The two last are explanatory glosses, and not very happy ones.
[6] Either 'of the fair hand' or 'of the white blade'.
[7] *i.e.* 'enclosure of the young men' and hence a literal translation of *Hagustaldesham* (Hexham). See I. Williams, *Bull. Board Celt. Stud.*, VI, pp. 351–354, and M. Förster, *ibid.*, VII, p. 33.
[8] Catgualart.   [9] This must be another name for the battle of the *Winwæd*, 654.
[10] I. A. Richmond and O. G. S. Crawford, *Archaeologia*, XCIII, 34, suggest that this is to be identified with the *Evidensca* of the Ravenna Cosmography, and is perhaps Inveresk. Older identifications are Inchkeith and Edinburgh.
[11] Literally, 'the restoration of *Iudeu*'. Can it mean 'ransom'? The bracketed portion is from Brit. Mus. Cott. Vespas. D. xxi and Harley 3859.
[12] Wade-Evans translates the name and nickname 'Battle-seizer-battle-shirker'.   [13] Lindisfarne.

Penda, the son of Pybba, reigned for ten years. He first separated the kingdom of the Mercians from the kingdom of the Northerners. And he killed by guile Anna, king of the East Angles, and St. Oswald, king of the Northerners. He fought the battle of *Cocboy*,[1] in which fell his brother Eowa, the son of Pybba, king of the Mercians, and Oswald, king of the Northerners. And he was victorious by diabolical arts. He was not baptized and never believed in God.

---

[1] Bede calls this battle, fought in 641, *Maserfeld*. See No. 151, p. 629.

3. Extracts from *Historia Regum* ("History of the Kings") attributed to Simeon of Durham

This work, on which see p. 118 f. above, is attributed to Simeon in the rubric of the only surviving manuscript, Corpus Christi College, Cambridge, MS. 139, of the late twelfth century. It is a collection of materials rather than a finished work. Simeon is the author of a *History of the Church of Durham* in 1104–1108, but his authorship of the compilation with which we are here concerned has been questioned. I have extracted those sections which seem to be drawn from earlier Northumbrian sources, and have omitted matter taken from Bede, Asser, Florence of Worcester and William of Malmesbury or from late legends. Annals dependent on the Anglo-Saxon Chronicle are included, for they do not come from a surviving version.

The best text is that edited by T. Arnold in the Rolls Series, and there is a translation by J. Stevenson in *Church Historians of England*, III, pt. II. See bibliography, pp. 129–131.

A. Mainly from the first set of northern annals

732[1] Archbishop Brihtwold died. In the same year Tatwine was consecrated the ninth archbishop of the church of Canterbury, in the fifteenth year of the rule of Æthelbald, king of the Mercians. Also in the same year King Ceolwulf was taken captive, tonsured and sent back into his kingdom. . . . Bishop Acca[2] was driven out from his see in the same year, and Cyneberht, bishop of the church of the people of Lindsey, died. In the same year, moreover, Alric and Esc with many others were slain on Thursday, 23 August.

733 Archbishop Tatwine, having received the *pallium* from the apostolic authority, ordained Alwiu[3] and Sigeferth[4] as bishops. There was an eclipse of the sun on 14 August about the third hour of the day, so that almost the whole orb of the sun seemed as if covered with a very black and terrible shield.

734 The moon was suffused with a blood-red colour as it were for a whole hour, about cockcrow on 31 January. Then a blackness followed, and it returned to its own light. In the same year Tatwine, ninth archbishop of the city of Canterbury in Kent, died on 30 July. . . . In the same year Frithuberht was consecrated bishop of the church of Hexham on 8 September.

735 Archbishop Nothhelm was consecrated, and Egbert, bishop of York, received the *pallium* from the apostolic see and was established in the archiepiscopate of the race of the Northumbrians, the first after Paulinus. Bede the teacher died in Jarrow.

736 Nothhelm, having received the *pallium* from the Roman pontiff, consecrated three bishops, namely Cuthbert,[5] Heardwold[6] and Æthelfrith.[7]

[1] This should be 731, as in Bede. 23 August was a Thursday in 731.   [2] Of Hexham.
[3] Aluwioh, of Lindsey.   [4] Or Sicga, of Selsey.   [5] Of Hereford.
[6] Of Dunwich. He is called bishop of the East Angles in the acts of the council of *Clofesho*, 747.
[7] Of Elmham.

737 Bishop Ealdwine, also called Wor,[1] died, and in his place Hwitta[1] and Totta[2] were consecrated bishops for the Mercians and the Middle Angles. In the same year Ceolwulf resigned the kingdom of the Northumbrians, and was made a monk in the island of Lindisfarne, and Eadberht, the son of his father's brother, succeeded in his place.

738 Swæfberht, king of the East Saxons, died.

739 Æthelheard, king of the West Saxons, died, and his brother Cuthred was made king in his place.[3] Also in the same year Archbishop Nothhelm died in peace, four years after receiving the bishopric, and Ealdwulf, bishop of the church of Rochester, ended his days.

740 Æthelwold, bishop of the church of Lindisfarne, departed to the Lord, and Cynewulf replaced him in the bishopric. In the same year Bishop Acca of revered memory was exalted into the land of the living. . . . In the same year Earnwine, son of Eadwulf, was killed on Saturday, 23 December.[4] The history or chronicle of this country[5] says that in the same year Cuthbert, the eleventh archbishop, received the archbishopric of the church of Canterbury; moreover, Dunn accepted the bishopric of the church of Rochester, after Ealdwulf.

741 The minster in the city of York was burnt on Sunday, 23 April.

744 A battle was fought between the Picts and the Britons.

745[6] There were seen in the air fiery flashes such as mortals of that age had never seen before; and they were seen almost the whole night of 1 January. Also in the same year the lord Wilfrid,[7] bishop of the city of York, departed to the Lord on 29 April. . . . In those days also the bishop of the city of London, Ingwold by name, was translated from the Egypt of this world. At the same period, the bishop of the Hwicce died.[8] Also in the same year Abbot Herebald died.

749 Ælfwold, king of the East Angles, died, and Hun, Beonna and Alberht[9] divided the kingdom between them.

---

[1] Of Lichfield.   [2] Or Torhthelm, of Leicester.

[3] The Chronicle (except MS. 'A', which has 741) dates these events 740.

[4] This was not a Saturday in 740, nor in 739 (which would be the year meant by a source beginning the year 24 September). Roger of Hoveden dates the event 24 December, which was a Saturday in 740.

[5] All MSS. of the Chronicle, except 'A', date the events in question 740.

[6] Chronicle 'D', 'E' puts the portents and Wilfrid's death in 744.

[7] He had resigned some years previously.

[8] Wilfrid of Worcester, who died in 743 according to Florence.

[9] The text writes Hunbeanna as one name. The Chronicle of Melrose gives it as Hunbearn. In dividing, I adopt a suggestion of Professor Chadwick. Coins were issued by a King Beonna, who is doubtless the Beorna who follows Ælfwold in the genealogies of Florence.

750 King Eadberht took Bishop Cynewulf as a prisoner to Bamburgh, and had the church of St. Peter in Lindisfarne besieged. Offa, son of Aldfrith, who had been forced to flee to the relics of the holy bishop, Cuthbert, though innocent, was dragged unarmed from the church, almost dead with hunger. In the same year Bishop Alwiu[1] was translated to the contemplation of the other life, and his deacon, Ealdwulf, was consecrated to the bishopric. Also Cuthred, king of the West Saxons, rose against Æthelbald, king of the Mercians.

752 An eclipse of the moon occurred on 31 July. . . .

754 Boniface, archbishop of the Franks, also called Wynfrith, received the crown of martyrdom, together with 53 others.

755[2] Cuthred, king of the West Saxons, died, and Sigeberht received the sceptre of his kingdom.

756 King Eadberht, in the eighteenth year of his reign, and Angus, king of the Picts, led an army against the city of Dunbarton. Hence the Britons accepted terms there, on the first day of the month of August. But on the tenth day of the same month there perished almost the whole army which he led from *Ovania* to Newburgh, that is New City. In the same year the anchorite Bealdhere[3] followed the way of the holy fathers. . . . Moreover the moon fifteen days old, that is the full moon, was on 24 November covered with a blood-red colour; and then the darkness gradually diminished and it returned to its former light. For, most remarkably, a bright star, following and crossing the moon, preceded it when it was illuminated at the same distance as it had followed it before it was obscured.

757 Æthelbald, king of the Mercians, was treacherously killed by his bodyguard, and in the same year the Mercians commenced a civil war among themselves. Beornred being put to flight, King Offa remained victor.

758 Eadberht, king of the Northumbrians,[4] of his own accord gave to his son, Oswulf by name, the kingdom God had conferred on him, and in the course of one year the latter held, lost and forfeited the kingdom; for he was wickedly killed by his household near *Methel Wongtun*[5] on 24 July.

[1] Of Lindsey.
[2] The Chronicle dates this 754, *i.e.* 756, for in this year begins its dislocation of chronology.
[3] Simeon's *History of the Church of Durham* says that he led the life of a hermit at Tyninghame. Alcuin speaks of his visions and miracles in his poem on the saints of York, lines 3118–3186.
[4] The Chronicle of Melrose adds: "having accepted the tonsure for the sake of God, was made a canon at York under Archbishop Egbert".
[5] *Medilwong* occurs in the anonymous Life of St. Cuthbert. It has been suggested that it is one of the Middletons in Ilderton or Middleton in Belford, Northumberland.

759 Æthelwold, who was also called Moll, began to reign on 5 August. At the beginning of his third year, a very severe battle was fought on 6 August at Eildon in which, after three days, Oswine fell, on the Sunday.[1] King Æthelwold, who is called Moll, obtained the victory in the battle. Also in the same year Angus, king of the Picts, died.

762 The aforesaid King Æthelwold married Queen Æthelthryth at Catterick on 1 November.

764[2] An immense snowfall, hardened into ice, unparalleled in all former ages, oppressed the land from the beginning of winter almost until the middle of spring; through its severity the trees and plants for the most part withered, and many marine animals were found dead. Also in the same year Ceolwulf, once king, then servant of our Lord Jesus Christ and a monk, died. . . .[3]

In the same year many towns, monasteries and villages in various districts and kingdoms were suddenly devastated by fire; for instance, the calamity struck *Stretburg*, Winchester, Southampton, the city of London, the city of York, Doncaster and many other places. . . .

In the same year Freohelm, priest and abbot, died; and Totta, bishop of the race of the Mercians,[4] died, and Eadberht was consècrated bishop in his place. Also in these times Frithuwold, bishop of Whithorn, departed from this world, and Pehtwine was appointed bishop in his place.[5]

765 Fiery flashes were seen in the air, such as once appeared during the night of 1 January, as we mentioned above. In the same year Æthelwold lost the kingdom of the Northumbrians on 30 October, at *Pincanheale*.[6] After him Alhred succeeded to the kingdom, sprung, as some say, from the stock of King Ida.

In that year Hemele, bishop of the Mercians, died, in whose stead Cuthred was consecrated bishop of Lichfield. And in the same period Bregowine, archbishop of the city of Kent, was taken from this life, and Jænberht[7] succeeded him in his office. Also Ealdwulf, bishop of Lindsey, in the same year left this life and sought the other. After him Ceolwulf was elected and consecrated.

766 Egbert, archbishop of the city of York, rested in the peace of Christ on 19 November in the thirty-fourth year of his episcopate[8] and Frithuberht, bishop of the church of Hexham, in the same year left this mortal flesh to the eternity of true light on 23 December, in the thirty-second year[9] of his episcopate.

---

[1] This is correct, 9 August being a Sunday in 761. The Chronicle says Oswine was killed at 'Edwin's cliff'.

[2] Most MSS. of the Chronicle put this hard winter in 761, that is 763, allowing for the two-year dislocation.

[3] A passage from Bede's preface addressed to him is quoted.   [4] Of Leicester.

[5] Probably 763, if the Chronicle (762, 'D', 'E') is right in dating his consecration 17 July, for this was a Sunday in 763.

[6] The MS. reads *Winc-*, the letters *w* and *p* being easily confused in Anglo-Saxon script. The old identification with Finchale is not now accepted.

[7] Wrongly called Lamberht here.   [8] This is correct, against the errors of the Chronicle.

[9] Here again, the Chronicle allows too long an episcopate.

767   Ethelbert, bishop of the city of York, and Alhmund, bishop of the church of
      Hexham, were consecrated on 24 April. In the same year Aluberht was consecrated
      bishop for the Old Saxons,[1] and Ceolwulf was consecrated bishop of Lindsey.
      Also in that year, Etha the anchorite[2] died happily in Crayke, a place ten miles
      from the city of York.

768   Eadberht, once king, afterwards cleric, in the tenth year after his resignation of
      his kingdom, in clerk's orders and the service of Almighty God, happily sent
      his soul to heaven at York on 20 August. In the same year Pippin, king of the
      Franks, died. And Hadwine was consecrated bishop of Mayo.[3] And in the same
      period King Alhred married Osgifu.[4]

769   Catterick was burnt by the tyrant Earnred, and by the judgment of God he
      himself perished miserably by fire in the same year.

771   Abbot Sigebald died and the teacher Ecgric departed from the course of this
      transitory life to the fellowship of the elect, where he hears the perpetual song
      of victory. In these days Offa, king of the Mercians, subdued the people of
      Hastings[5] by force of arms. Also in the same year Carloman, the most famous
      king of the Franks, died, cut off by a sudden illness. Moreover, his brother
      Charles, who had previously held half the dominion of his father, hereupon
      obtained the sovereignty of the whole kingdom and the supreme dignity of the
      Frankish peoples with unconquered strength.

772   Ealdorman Pihtel and Abbot Swithwulf died in the Lord. Also, Charles, king
      of the Franks, collected a strong force and assembled the warlike men of his
      dominions, and invaded the Saxon people. Having lost many of his leaders and
      nobles, he retreated to his own land.[6]

773   Hadwine, bishop of the church of Mayo, died, and Leodfrith was chosen bishop
      in his place. In this year also, Wulfhæth, abbot of Beverley, desired to see the day
      of the Lord, which was granted to him, and   [7] succeeded him. In the same
      period, Ethelbert, bishop of the church of York, received the ministry of the
      pallium, sent to him by Pope Hadrian.

774   Ealdorman Eadwulf was taken from the shipwreck of this life; and at the same
      period King Alhred was deprived of the society of the royal household and
      nobles, by the counsel and consent of all his people, and exchanged the majesty

---

[1] *i.e.* as a missionary bishop to convert this continental race. See No. 160.
[2] Mentioned by Alcuin in his poem on the Saints of York, lines 1387–1392.
[3] The see in Northern Ireland founded by the Englishmen who refused to accept the decision of the
Synod of Whitby.
[4] See No. 187. The name is wrongly given by Simeon as Osgearn.
[5] *i.e.* the district of East Sussex. See p. 221, n. 8.
[6] The *Annals of the Frankish Kingdom* do not mention Charles's heavy losses. They speak of his cutting
down the sacred *Irminsul* and returning home with hostages.   [7] There is a gap in the MS.

of empire for exile. He departed with a few companions of his flight, first into Bamburgh, afterwards to the king of the Picts, by name Kenneth. . . .

Also, Ethelred, son of Æthelwold, received the kingdom in his place. Crowned with such great honour, he held it barely five years, as the subsequent account of the writer tells.

At that same period, Charles, the most invincible king of the Franks, who had harassed the most noble city of the Lombards, Pavia, with a long siege, captured it together with King Desiderius himself and the rule of the whole of Italy.

775 The king of the Picts, Kenneth, was snatched from the whirlpool of this polluted life; and Ealdorman Eadwulf, seized guilefully by treachery, was after a short space of time killed, buried and forgotten. Also, Abbot Ebbi paid the debt of nature, departing to go to him who died to grant eternal life.

Lastly, Charles, the most warlike king of the Franks, as we said above, being defended, supported and glorified by all the strength of his army[1] and surrounded by his legions, invaded the people of the Saxons, which region he ravaged with severe battles, great and indescribable, raging with fire and sword, because he was alarmed in mind. And finally he added the two towns of *Syburg*[2] and *Eresburg*[3] and the province of the *Bohweri*,[4] formerly subdued by the Franks, to his supreme empire.

777[5] Pehtwine, bishop of Whithorn, departed this life on 19 September, to the joy of eternal salvation. He had had charge of that church for 14 years. Ethelbert succeeded him.

778 In the fourth year of King Ethelred, namely 778, three ealdormen, namely Ealdwulf, Cynewulf and Ecga, were treacherously killed by the order of that same king by the nobles[6] Æthelbald and Heardberht on 29 September.

779[7] Ethelred was expelled from the royal throne and driven into exile . . . Ælfwold, son of Oswulf, received the kingdom of the Northumbrians when Ethelred had been expelled, and held it ten years. He was indeed a pious and just king, as the following section will show.

---

[1] The text says also that he was *centuriatus*, which must be a corrupt reading.
[2] Hohen-Syburg, at the junction of the Ruhr and Lenne.
[3] A town on the Diemel, remains of which are near the village of Ober-Marsberg.
[4] Presumably the canton called Bucki (*i.e.* round Bückeburg) in the *Annals of the Frankish Kingdom*.
[5] 776 is the date of Pehtwine's death in the Chronicle ('D','E'). His successor's consecration is dated 777.
[6] It is uncertain what contemporary titles Simeon's Latin terms replace. I have translated his *dux* as ealdorman, since this is the normal meaning of the word in Anglo-Latin writers, but in this annal and in 780 the Chronicle ('D', 'E'), I know not on what authority, calls the same individuals 'high-reeves'. It gives no title to the persons called here by Simeon *principes*, sometimes used of ealdormen, sometimes of nobles or magnates in general. Where, in 780, Simeon speaks of a *patricius*, the Chronicle calls him ealdorman; but this word is used elsewhere in a way that suggests that it was confined to very outstanding and powerful men of this office.
[7] The Chronicle ('D', 'E') dates this 778, and in Simeon's *History of the Church of Durham* a date in 780 is said to be in Ælfwold's third year.

780[1] The ealdormen Osbald and Æthelheard, collecting an army, burnt Bearn, a 'patrician'[2] of King Ælfwold in *Seletun* on 24 December. In the same year Archbishop Ethelbert departed from this life to the eternal light, having in his lifetime consecrated Eanbald to the same see. Also in the same year Bishop Cynewulf resigned secular cares and committed the government of his church to Higbald, by the election of the whole community. In the same year also Bishop Eanbald received the *pallium* sent to him from the apostolic see, and, having received it, was solemnly confirmed in his bishopric.[3]

781[4] Higbald was consecrated bishop. Alhmund, bishop of the church of Hexham, a man of outstanding piety and great virtue, after having ruled excellently the aforesaid church for 13 years, ended this life in the reign of the most glorious king of the Northumbrians, Ælfwold, in the third year of his reign, on 7 September, and was made partaker of the eternal bliss on account of his merits. . . . In his place in the bishopric the holy Tilberht was chosen, consecrated and raised to the throne of the episcopal see at the place which is called *Wulfeswelle*, that is, 'well of the wolf'. This was done on 2 October.

783[5] which is the fifth year of King Ælfwold, Werburh, once queen of the Mercians, then an abbess, died, ever, it is right to believe, to remain with Christ. At the same period Bishop Cynewulf, whom we have spoken of before, left the world in the fortieth year of his episcopate, and departed happily to the heavenly country.

786[6] which is the eighth year of King Ælfwold, Botwine, the venerable abbot of the church of Ripon, left the prison of this toilsome life, in the sight of the brethren standing by, receiving the reward of the year of jubilee. And after his death Ealdberht was elected and consecrated abbot in his place. In the same year Ealdwulf was consecrated bishop[7] by Archbishop Eanbald, and by the bishops Tilberht and Higbald, in the monastery called Corbridge, and sent back with honour to his church enriched with treasures and gifts. In these days Ricthryth, formerly queen, then abbess, received the desired reward of the other life, bearing in the holy sight of the Lord oil in her lamp.

At that time,[8] Cynewulf, king of the West Saxons, was killed with a miserable death by a treacherous tyrant Cyneheard, and the cruel slayer was himself killed without pity by Ealdorman Osred[9] in vengeance for his lord, and Brihtric received the kingdom of the West Saxons.

At that time legates[10] were sent to Britain from the apostolic see by Lord Hadrian the pope, among whom the venerable Bishop George held the first

---

[1] 779 in the Chronicle ('D', 'E').   [2] See p. 244, n. 6,
[3] This event is dated 780 in the Chronicle, though rest of the annal is dated 779.
[4] 780, Chronicle ('D', 'E') and *History of the Church of Durham*.   [5] 782, Chronicle ('D', 'E').
[6] 785, Chronicle ('D', 'E').   [7] Of Mayo.
[8] This entry on southern history is taken from a source free from the chronological dislocation of the surviving texts of the Chronicle.
[9] Osric in the Chronicle.   [10] See their report on their mission, No. 191.

place; and they renewed the former friendship with us and the catholic faith which the pope St. Gregory taught us through the blessed Augustine, and were received with honour by kings and by bishops, and by the nobles and magnates of this country, and returned home in peace with great gifts, as was fitting.

787[1] A synod was held at *Pincanheale*[2] on 2 September. At that time Ethelbert, abbot of Ripon, sent his spirit from the fierce storms of this life to the heavenly songs of everlasting bliss. Soon after his death, Sigered was ordained in his place.

788[3] After a conspiracy had been formed by his 'patrician',[4] Sicga by name, King Ælfwold was killed by a miserable death on 23 September at the place called *Scythlescester*[5] near the wall. Then the body of the excellent king was brought to Hexham by a great company of monks and with the chants of the clergy, and was buried with honour in the church of the most holy Apostle Andrew. . . . After the burial of the king, his nephew Osred, the son of King Alhred, reigned in his place for one year. In the place where the just King Ælfwold was slain a light sent from heaven is said to have been seen by many. A church was built there by the faithful of that district, and dedicated in honour of God and St. Cuthbert, the bishop, and St. Oswald, king and martyr.

790 Ethelred was freed from banishment and again enthroned by the grace of Christ on the throne of the kingdom. But King Osred, deceived by the guile of his nobles, taken prisoner and deprived of the kingdom, was tonsured in the city of York, and afterwards, forced by necessity, went into exile.[6] In his second year, Ealdorman Eardwulf was captured and brought to Ripon, and orders were given by the aforesaid king for him to be killed there outside the gate of the monastery. And the brethren carried his body to the church with Gregorian chants, and placed it outside in a tent, and after midnight he was found in the church, alive.

In the same year[7] Badwulf was consecrated bishop of Whithorn at the place which is called *Hearrahalch*, which can be interpreted 'place of lords'. For in the preceding year on the death of the holy Bishop Tilberht, Bishop Ethelbert[8] left his own see and received under his own rule the bishopric of the church of Hexham.

791 The sons of King Ælfwold were taken by force from the city of York, being brought from the principal church by false promises, and were miserably killed by King Ethelred in *Wonwaldremere*; their names were Oelf and Oelfwine. Also in that year[9] Jænberht, archbishop of the church of Canterbury, passed

---

[1] 788, Chronicle ('D', 'E').   [2] See p. 242, n. 6.   [3] 789, Chronicle ('D', 'E').
[4] *Patricius;* see p. 244, n. 6.
[5] Plummer and Mawer both suggest that this is Chesters, a station by the Roman Wall.
[6] Simeon's *History of the Church of Durham* says he fled to the Isle of Man.
[7] The date in the Chronicle ('D', 'E'), 791, is perhaps to be preferred, for 17 July, the day of the consecration, was a Sunday in that year.
[8] Of Whithorn.   [9] 790 (for 792) in the Chronicle. Simeon again calls him Lamberht.

from the darkness of this light to the joy of the true light. Then Æthelheard, abbot of the monastery of Louth, was elected and consecrated bishop for the same see.

792 Charles, king of the Franks, sent to Britain a synodal book, directed to him from Constantinople, in which book—grievous to say—were found many things improper and contrary to the true faith, especially that it had been asserted with the unanimous consent of nearly all the scholars of the East, no fewer—rather more, in fact—than 300 bishops, that images ought to be adored, which the Church of God utterly abhors. Against this Albinus[1] wrote a letter, wonderfully supported by the authority of the Holy Scriptures, and presented it with the same book and in the name of our bishops and nobles to the king of the Franks.

At length in that year Osred came secretly from exile in the Isle of Man, relying on the oaths and good faith of certain nobles; and as his soldiers deserted him, he was captured there by the aforesaid king, namely Ethelred, and killed by his orders at the place which is called *Aynburg* on 14 September. His body was conveyed to Tynemouth and buried in the church of the same noble monastery. In the same year King Ethelred married Queen Ælfflæd, daughter of Offa, king of the Mercians, at Catterick on 29 September.

793 the fourth year of King Ethelred, dreadful prodigies terrified the wretched nation of the English. For horrible lightnings and dragons in the air and fiery flashes were often seen to gleam and fly to and fro; and these signs signified a great famine and the fearful and indescribable slaughter of many men which followed.

In this year also Ealdorman Sicga, who killed King Ælfwold, perished by his own hand, and his body was conveyed to the island of Lindisfarne on 23 April. . . .

In the same year[2] the pagans from the northern regions came with a naval force to Britain like stinging hornets and spread on all sides like fearful wolves, robbed, tore and slaughtered not only beasts of burden, sheep and oxen, but even priests and deacons, and companies of monks and nuns. And they came to the church of Lindisfarne, laid everything waste with grievous plundering, trampled the holy places with polluted steps, dug up the altars and seized all the treasures of the holy church. They killed some of the brothers, took some away with them in fetters, many they drove out, naked and loaded with insults, some they drowned in the sea. . . .

794 The aforesaid pagans, ravaging the harbour of King Ecgfrith, plundered the monastery at the mouth of the River Don.[3] But St. Cuthbert did not allow them to go away unpunished; for their chief was killed by the English with

---

[1] The name by which the scholar Alcuin was often known abroad.

[2] The account of the sack of Lindisfarne is derived from Simeon's *History of the Church of Durham*. This says that it took place on 7 June.

[3] See p. 167, n. 14, p. 764. n. 3. Simeon identifies it with Jarrow in his *History of the Church of Durham*.

a cruel death, and after a short space of time the violence of a storm battered, destroyed and broke to pieces their ships, and the sea overwhelmed many of them. Some were cast on the shore, and soon killed without mercy. And these things befell them rightly, for they had gravely injured those who had not injured them.

At this time Colcu,[1] priest and teacher, passed from this light to the Lord, where he received the glory of happiness in return for his earthly labours. At that time Æthelheard, once ealdorman, but then a cleric, died in the city of York on 1 August.

The venerable Pope Hadrian was in the same year exalted to the sight of God on 26 December, and he had held the see for 26 years, 10 months and 12 days. Also he was buried in the church of St. Peter, Prince of the Apostles, and over his tomb there was fixed to the wall a tablet recording his good deeds in letters of gold and written in verse. King Charles had this marble put there when he was crowned with the royal diadem, for love and memory of the aforesaid father.

795 The same most powerful King Charles with a strong force subdued the people of the Huns, despoiling them by arms, when he had put their king to flight and overcome or destroyed his army. He carried away from there 15 waggons filled with gold and silver and precious robes of silk, each waggon drawn by four oxen. The same king ordered all to be distributed to the churches and the poor on account of the victory granted to him by the Lord Christ, giving thanks to God along with all who fought with him.

796[2] the seventh year of King Ethelred, Alric, once ealdorman, then cleric, died in the city of York. And soon after, that is on 28 March, there was an eclipse of the moon between cockcrow and dawn. In the same year King Ethelred was killed near the Cover on 18 April, in the seventh year of his reign. The 'patrician' Osbald[3] was appointed to the kingdom by some nobles of the nation, and after 27 days was deserted by the whole company of the royal household and the nobles, put to flight and banished from the kingdom, and retired with a few followers to the island of Lindisfarne, and from there he went by ship to the king of the Picts with certain of the brothers. Eardwulf,[4] however, of whom we have spoken before, the son of Eardwulf, was recalled from exile and raised to the crown of the kingdom, and was consecrated on 26 May in York in the church of St. Peter at the altar of the blessed Apostle Paul, where that nation first received the grace of baptism.

And not long after, that is on 26 July, Offa, the most powerful king of the Mercians, died after he had reigned 39 years, and his son Ecgfrith succeeded

[1] Correspondent of Alcuin (No. 192). His death is entered in 796 in the *Annals of the Frankish Kingdom*. See also p. 84.

[2] The eclipse and Eardwulf's accession are put in 795 by 'D', 'E' of the Chronicle. Ethelred's death is entered in the main part of the Chronicle, 794 (for 796). The capture of the Huns' treasure is dated 796 in the *Annals of the Frankish Kingdom*.

[3] See Alcuin's letter to him, No. 200.   [4] See p. 246.

him in the kingdom, and, death befalling him in the same year, unwillingly paid the debt of nature. And Cenwulf, father of St. Cenhelm the martyr, then gloriously received the crown of the kingdom of the Mercians, and held it with unconquered strength by the strong vigour of his government.

Also in the same year Ceolwulf, bishop of Lindsey, despised the times of this life, looking for the consolation of the future world. And a little while after, that is on 10 August, Archbishop Eanbald died in the monastery which is called *Æt Læte*,[1] and his body was conveyed to the city of York, with a large multitude attending it, and honourably buried in the church of the blessed Apostle Peter. And immediately another Eanbald, priest of the same church, was elected to the bishopric, the bishops Ethelbert, Higbald and Badwulf meeting for his consecration at the monastery which is called Sockburn, on Sunday, 15 August.[2]

797 Eanbald the second, having received the *pallium* from the apostolic see, was solemnly confirmed in the archbishopric of the people of the Northumbrians on 8 September, on which day a feast is celebrated, namely the Nativity of St. Mary. . . . In the same year Ethelbert, bishop of Hexham, died on 16 October at the place which is called Barton, and his body was conveyed to Hexham and buried reverently by the brothers of that monastery. In his place Heardred was elected to the bishopric, and after the passage of a few days, namely on 30 October, he was consecrated to the spiritual dignity by Archbishop Eanbald and Bishop Higbald in the place which is called Woodford.

798 A conspiracy having been formed by the murderers of King Ethelred, Ealdorman Wada, in that conspiracy with them, fought a battle against King Eardwulf at the place which is called Billington Moor, near Whalley,[3] and when many had been killed on both sides Ealdorman Wada turned in flight with his men, and King Eardwulf royally won the victory over his enemies.

In the same year London, with a great number of men, was burnt by a sudden fire. In these times Cenwulf, king of the Mercians, invaded the province of the people of Kent with the whole strength of his army, and mightily devastated it with a grievous pillaging almost to its utter destruction. At the same time Eadberht, king of the people of Kent, was captured, and the king of the Mercians ordered his eyes to be torn out and his hands ruthlessly cut off, because of the pride and deceit of those people. Then, having obtained it with the Lord's help, he added the dominion of that kingdom to his own dominions,[4] placing the crown on his head and the sceptre in his hand.

Also in the same year, which was the third year of the aforesaid King Cenwulf, a synod met in the place which is called *Pincanheale*, Archbishop Eanbald presiding. . . .[5]

---

[1] This name seems to mean 'at the crossing'.
[2] A mistake for 14 August, which was a Sunday in 796.
[3] The Chronicle's account of this battle makes no mention of Wada, but has details of its own. See p. 109.
[4] The Chronicle of Melrose adds: "and then Cuthred received it to hold of him".
[5] It passed canons for the Northumbrian Church.

799 Several ships were wrecked by the force of the tempest in the British sea, and shattered or broken to pieces and sunk with a great multitude of men. In the same year Brorda, ealdorman of the Mercians, who was also called Hildigils, died. An abbot called More was killed with a grievous death by his reeve Tilthegn. Also, a little while afterwards, Ealdorman Moll was killed by the urgent order of King Eardwulf. Also at the same period, Osbald, once ealdorman and 'patrician', and for a time king, then indeed abbot, reached his last day, and his body was buried in the church of the city of York. Ealdorman Ealdred, the murderer of King Ethelred, was killed by Ealdorman Torhtmund[1] in vengeance for his lord that same king. . . .

800 Heardred, bishop of the church of Hexham, in the third year of his administration of the bishopric, saw his last day, and in his place Eanberht was elected and consecrated at the place which is called *Cettingaham*. In the same year Alhmund, the son, as some say, of King Alhred, was seized by the guards of King Eardwulf, and by his order was killed along with his fellow fugitives.

Also in the same period, before our Lord's Nativity, on 24 December, an immense wind, arising from the south-west or west, destroyed and threw to the ground by its indescribable force cities, many houses and numerous villages in diverse areas; also countless trees were torn up by the roots and thrown to the earth. In that year an inundation of the sea flowed beyond its bounds. . . . Also a great destruction of cattle occurred in various places. . . .

801 Edwin, who was also called Eda, formerly ealdorman of the Northumbrians, then indeed by the grace of the Saviour of the world an abbot strong in the service of God, ended his last day like a veteran soldier in the sight of the brothers on 15 January; he was also honourably buried in the church of his monastery which is called Gainford.

In these times Eardwulf, king of the Northumbrians, led an army against Cenwulf, king of the Mercians, because of his harbouring of his enemies. And the latter king collected an army and led many forces from other provinces with him. When there had been a long campaign between them, they finally made peace by the advice of the English bishops and nobles on both sides, by the grace of the king of the English.[2] And an agreement of most firm peace was made between them, which both kings confirmed with an oath on the gospel of Christ, calling God as witness and surety that in their lifetime, as long as they should possess this present life and be invested with the insignia of the kingdom, a firm peace and a true friendship should persist between them, unbroken and inviolate. . . .

In the same year Heathuberht, bishop of the city of London, despised the times of this life. And a little later, a great part of that town was burnt by a sudden fire.

[1] See No. 206.
[2] A mysterious reference, probably an error for 'king of the angels'.

802 Brihtric, king of the West Saxons, who had nobly ruled the same race for 17 years, died; and Egbert, from the royal stock of that nation, received and held his dominion and kingdom after him. . . .[1]

B. *Simeon's additions to material drawn from Florence of Worcester relating to the period between the two sets of northern annals*

854 the sixth year after the birth of King Alfred, in the reign of King Osbert over the Northumbrians, Wulfhere received the *pallium* and was confirmed in the archbishopric of York, and Eardwulf received the bishopric of Lindisfarne. . . .[2]

867 . . . When these things[3] had been done, the aforesaid pagans appointed Egbert king under their own domination. Egbert then reigned after this for six years over the Northumbrians beyond the Tyne.

873 Egbert, king of the Northumbrians, dying, had Ricsige as his successor, and he reigned for three years. And Wulfhere was re-instated in his archbishopric.

875 Eardwulf, bishop of Lindisfarne, and Abbot Eadred, carrying the body of St. Cuthbert from the island of Lindisfarne, wandered far and wide for seven years.

876 . . . King Ricsige of the Northumbrians died, and Egbert the second reigned over the Northumbrians beyond the River Tyne.[4]

C. *Material mainly from the second set of northern annals*

892 Wulfhere, bishop of York, died in the thirty-ninth year of his episcopate.[5]

894 . . . In this year King Guthfrith died.

899 King Alfred died when he had reigned 28 years, and his son Edward succeeded him, having been diligently admonished by his father that he should especially honour St. Cuthbert. Also, Bishop Eardwulf died in Chester-le-Street, where he had transferred the body of St. Cuthbert, with which for nine years he had fled before the army of the pagans from place to place in great toil and penury. Cuthbert succeeded him in the bishopric.

900 Æthelbald was consecrated to the bishopric of the church of York.

[1] From this point Simeon appears not to draw on the set of northern annals hitherto available to him, though MSS. 'D' and 'E' of the Chronicle seem to use them until 806. Simeon continues with a story from Asser, then repeats the information about Egbert's accession. He then jumps to 849 and draws on Asser. At the foot of the folio in the manuscript in a different hand are three notices of episcopal successions, with the chronological dislocation of the Chronicle.

[2] A list of the possessions of the see is added and a story about King Ceolwulf as a monk at Lindisfarne.

[3] *i.e.* the Danish invasion of Northumbria and the attack against the Danes at York.

[4] Under the date 883 the story of the election of King Guthfrith is given. See No. 6.

[5] Under 893 and 894 are brief entries taken from a correctly dated copy of the Chronicle.

901 Osbert was expelled from the kingdom.

902 Brihtsige was killed.[1]

906 King Edward, forced by necessity, established a peace with the East Angles and Northumbrians.[2]

910 The English and the Danes fought at Tettenhall. King Edward took London and Oxford and what belonged to it. In that year a large force of pirates attacked with cruel devastation round about the River Severn, but almost the whole of it quickly perished there.

912 King Ragnald and Earl Ottar and Oswulf Crakabain stormed and sacked Dublin.[3]

914 King Niall was killed by his brother Sihtric.[4]

919 King Ragnald[5] took York by storm.[6]

920 King Sihtric destroyed Davonport.

923[7] King Edward died, leaving the rule to his son Athelstan.

925 Bishop Wigred was consecrated to the bishopric of St. Cuthbert.

927 King Athelstan put King Guthfrith to flight from the kingdom of the Britons.

933 King Athelstan ordered his brother Edwin to be drowned at sea.[8]

934 King Athelstan, going towards Scotland with a great army, came to the tomb of St. Cuthbert, commended himself and his expedition to his protection, and conferred on him many and diverse gifts befitting a king, as well as estates, and consigned to the torments of eternal fire anyone who should take any of these from him. He then subdued his enemies, laid waste Scotland as far as Dunnottar and *Wertermorum*[9] with a land force, and ravaged with a naval force as far as Caithness.

---

[1] At the battle of the Holme. See No. 1, p. 191.
[2] A reference to the peace of Tiddingford. See No. 1, p. 192.
[3] A. O. Anderson, *Early Sources of Scottish History*, 1, p. 403, suggests that the occupation of 917 is meant. Oswulf is clearly the same person as Graggabai (Old Norse *Kraka-bein*, 'crow-foot') who, according to the *Annals of Ulster*, was killed along with Ottar by the Tyne in 918.
[4] The *Annals of Ulster* record the death of Niall in 919. He was not Sihtric's brother.
[5] MS. *Inguald* for *Reingwald*.   [6] Wrongly dated 923 in the Chronicle ('D', 'E', 'F').
[7] Should be 924.   [8] Cf. No. 26.
[9] This cannot be identified with certainty. The writer of the northern recension of the Chronicle knew the name and attempted to interpret it. See p. 146, n. 2.

937 King Athelstan fought at *Wendun*[1] and put to flight King Olaf with 615 ships, and also Constantine, king of the Scots, and the king of the Cumbrians with all their host.

939[2] King Athelstan died, and his brother Edmund succeeded him in the kingdom; and in this year King Olaf first came to York, and then, marching south, besieged Northampton. But accomplishing nothing there, he turned his army to Tamworth and ravaged everything round about it. When he reached Leicester on his return, King Edmund met him with an army. There was no severe fighting, for the two archbishops, Oda and Wulfstan, reconciled the kings to one another and put an end to the battle. When peace had thus been made, the Watling Street was the boundary of each kingdom. Edmund held the part to the south, Olaf the kingdom to the north.

941 Olaf, when he had ravaged the church of St. Bealdhere and burnt Tyninghame, soon perished.[3] Therefore the men of York laid waste the island of Lindisfarne and killed many people. Then a son of Sihtric, Olaf by name, ruled over the Northumbrians.

943 The Northumbrians drove out their king, Olaf, from the kingdom.

945[4] King Edmund drove out two kings, and obtained the kingdom of the Northumbrians.

948[5] King Edmund was killed and his brother Eadred received the kingdom, an upholder of justice and virtue. And soon he went about the whole of Northumbria and took possession, but after swearing fealty to him the Northumbrians set up a certain Dane, Eric, as king.

950[6] When King Eadred had ravaged Northumbria and was then returning, the Northumbrians sallied forth and destroyed the rear of his army. The king determined to lead his army back and utterly destroy the province, but the inhabitants cast off the king whom they had appointed, and speedily placated Eadred with gifts.

951[7] Hywel, king of the Britons, died.

---

[1] This alternative name for *Brunanburh* cannot be identified. In the *History of the Church of Durham*, Simeon calls it *Weondun*.

[2] The date is correct for Æthelstan's death, but most events in the annal belong to 940. They are wrongly dated 943 by MS. 'D' of the Chronicle.

[3] His death is recorded under 942 in the Chronicle ('E' and 'F').

[4] This entry is in the common stock of the Chronicle dated 944.

[5] This should be 946. The mistake is also in MSS. 'E' and 'F' of the Chronicle, and was probably in the source common to them and Simeon.

[6] As in the previous annal the date is two years too late.   [7] 950, according to the *Annals of Ulster*.

952[1] Here the kings of the Northumbrians came to an end, and henceforward the province was administered by earls.

953[2] Earl Oswulf received the earldom of the Northumbrians.

955 King Eadred died, and Eadwig, son of the Edmund who had reigned before him, succeeded.

956 The blessed Abbot Dunstan was expelled by Eadwig.

D. *Additions to the material drawn from Florence of Worcester, after the second set of northern annals has come to an end*

968 Bishop Ealdred departed this life at St. Cuthbert's in Chester-le-Street. Ælfsige succeeded him in the bishopric.

995 Bishop Ealdhun translated the body of St. Cuthbert from Chester-le-Street to Durham.

1018 Ealdhun, bishop of Durham, died. A great battle was fought at Carham between the Scots and the English, between the earl of Northumbria, Uhtred, the son of Waltheof, and the king of the Scots, Malcolm, son of Kenneth, with whom in the battle was Owain the Bald, king of the men of Strathclyde.[3]

1020 Edmund received the bishopric of Durham.

1032 Fire raged at many places throughout England, and Ælfsige, bishop of Winchester, died. Ælfwine, the king's priest, succeeded.

1042 Bishop Edmund died, and Eadred succeeded to the bishopric by means of money, and died in the tenth month.

[1] This event seems to be dated two years too early. The Chronicle ('D', 'E') has 954.
[2] Not before Eric was driven out in 954.
[3] Simeon, *History of the Church of Durham*, mentions that it was an overwhelming defeat for the English. If 1018 is correct, Uhtred cannot have been present. See No. 1, p. 225.

4. From Roger of Wendover's *Flores Historiarum* ("Flowers of the Histories")

Roger was a monk of St. Albans writing in the early part of the thirteenth century, and until he comes near to the events of his own time his work is mainly culled from previous writers. But among his sources he clearly had some northern annals, and some of the information he takes from them would otherwise have been lost. His statement about Edgar's coinage is borne out by numismatical evidence, and he must have had an early source also for his account of Kenneth's visit to Edgar, for he could not have given correctly the names of the contemporary bishop and earl who escorted him.

This work is edited by H. O. Coxe (1841) and translated by J. A. Giles in *Bohn's Antiquarian Library* (1892). See bibliography, pp. 129–131.

745 Egbert, archbishop of York, laudably recovered the *pallium*, which had been neglected by eight bishops since the time of Paulinus, the first archbishop of York.

783[1] Ælfwold, king of the Northumbrians, sent to Rome for the *pallium*, and gave it to the archbishop [Eanbald].

800 The most impious army of the pagans cruelly despoiled the churches of Hartness and Tynemouth, and returned with its plunder to the ships.

808[2] Eardwulf, king of the Northumbrians, was put to flight from his kingdom, and Ælfwold succeeded him for two years. The same Ælfwold had put him to flight and occupied his kingdom.

810 Ælfwold, king of the Northumbrians, died, and Eanred reigned in his place for 32 years.

828[3] ... In this year also Egbert, bishop of Lindisfarne, died, and Eardwulf succeeded.

829 When Egbert, king of the West Saxons, had obtained all the southern kingdoms of England, he led a large army into Northumbria, and laid waste that province with a severe pillaging, and made King Eanred pay tribute.

831 ... In the same year, Wulfsige, archbishop of York, paid the debt of nature, and Wigmund succeeded him.

840 Eanred, king of the Northumbrians, died, and his son Ethelred succeeded him, for seven years.

[1] Simeon of Durham dates Eanbald's receiving of the *pallium* 780.
[2] Chronicle ('D', 'E') dates Eardwulf's expulsion 806, but the *Annals of St. Bertin's* have 808.
[3] This entry follows on events dated by the Chronicle 825–828 (really 827–830). Egbert was succeeded by Heathored about 821. Eardwulf did not succeed until 854.

844 In the same year[1] Ethelred, king of the Northumbrians, was expelled from the kingdom, and Rædwulf succeeded to the kingdom; and when, hastily invested with the crown, he fought a battle with the pagans at Elvet,[2] he and Ealdorman Alfred fell with a large part of their subjects, and then Ethelred reigned again.

848 When Ethelred, king of the Northumbrians, had been killed, Osbert succeeded for 18 years. And the same year there was an eclipse of the sun, on 1 October, at the sixth hour of the day.

854 Wigmund, archbishop of York, having died, Wulfhere succeeded. In the same year Eanberht, bishop of Lindisfarne, ended his last day, and Eardwulf succeeded.

867 The abominable army of the Danes moved from East Anglia to the city of York on All Saints' day. At that time also a great discord had arisen among the Northumbrians, and the people, driving out of the kingdom their legitimate king, Osbert, had raised to the crown of the kingdom a certain tyrant, Ælle by name, not born of the royal line. But by the divine counsel, when the Danes came, Osbert and Ælle made peace between them for the common good, and then, uniting copious forces, went to the city of York. On their approach, the pagans straightway took to flight, resolving to defend themselves within the walls of the city; and the Christian kings, pursuing them and making a very fierce attack on the enemy, destroyed the walls of the city. At length, having entered the city, they engaged in a battle against the pagans, very disastrous to themselves; for in that battle there fell the kings Osbert and Ælle, and eight ealdormen with them, with a large multitude of their forces, on Palm Sunday. Then these most abominable victors, the Danes, ravaging the whole province of Northumbia as far as the mouth of the Tyne, brought the country under their rule when they had defeated their enemies. Then, since the kings of the Northumbrians had been killed, a certain Egbert, of English race, acquired the kingdom under the Danish power and ruled it for six years.

872 The people of the Northumbrians drove out from the kingdom their king, Egbert, and Archbishop Wulfhere; and, when expelled, they went to Burgred, king of the Mercians, and were honourably received by him.

873[3] . . . Egbert, king of the Northumbrians, ended his last day, and Ricsige succeeded him in the kingdom for three years. In that same year also, Wulfhere, archbishop of York, was recalled to his see.

876 . . . Healfdene, king of the Danes, occupied Northumbria, and divided it among himself and his thegns, and had it cultivated by his army; then the king of the same province, Ricsige, struck to the very heart with grief, ended his last day, and Egbert succeeded him.

---

[1] *i.e.* as the battle of Carhampton, 843 (?); but though Wendover dates this wrongly, his date for the Northumbrian events may be correct.

[2] Part of the city of Durham.   [3] This annal is also in Simeon's *History of the Kings*.

895[1] . . . Wulfhere, archbishop of York, having died, Æthelbald succeeded.

925 Athelstan, king of the English, joined in matrimony with great ceremony his sister Eadgyth with Sihtric, king of the Northumbrians, sprung from the Danish race; and he gave up the heathen religion for the love of the maiden and received the faith of Christ. But not long afterwards he cast off the blessed maiden and, deserting his Christianity, restored the worship of idols, and after a short while ended his life miserably as an apostate. Accordingly the holy maiden, having preserved her chastity, remained strong in good works to the end of her life, at Polesworth, in fasts and in vigils, in prayers and in zeal for almsgiving. She departed after the passage of a praiseworthy life from this world on 15 July, at this same place, where to this day divine miracles do not cease to be performed.

940[2] Then Olaf[3] married Aldgyth, daughter of Earl Orm, with the support of whose aid and counsel he had obtained the aforesaid victory.[4]

946 . . . King Edmund, relying on the help of Leolin, king of Dyfed, despoiled the whole of Cumbria of all its property, and having deprived the two sons of Dunmail, king of that province, of their sight, he gave the kingdom to Malcolm, king of the Scots, to hold of him, that he might defend the northern parts of England from incursions of enemy raiders by land and sea. . . .

He (King Eadred), as his brother King Edmund had done before, reduced the whole of Northumbria into his power, and received the fealty of the king of the Scots; and moreover he devoutly gave to the metropolitan church of York two large bells. And then, when he had received an oath of fealty from the king of the Cumbrians, and had acquired these regions with security, he hastened south with his troops.

950[5] King Eric was treacherously killed by Earl Maccus[6] in a certain lonely place which is called Stainmore, with his son Haeric and his brother Ragnald, betrayed by Earl Oswulf; and then afterwards King Eadred ruled in these districts.

974[7] . . . About the same time merchants coming from York landed in the isle of Thanet, and were at once taken prisoner by the islanders and robbed of all their goods; whence King Edgar, moved by anger, was so furious with these pillagers that he despoiled all of them of their possessions and even deprived some of life.

---

[1] 892 in Simeon's *History of the Kings*.   [2] This follows on events dated 939 by Simeon.
[3] Guthfrith's son.   [4] His obtaining of all England north of the Watling Street.
[5] This date is too early. It should be 954.
[6] This is probably the name meant by the Macon of the text.
[7] The ravaging of Thanet is dated 969 in the Chronicle ('D', 'E', 'F').

975 . . . Then[1] he ordered a new coinage to be made throughout the whole of England, because the old was so debased by the crime of clippers that a penny hardly weighed a halfpenny on the scales. About the same time, Bishop Ælfsige and Earl Eadwulf conducted Kenneth, king of the Scots, to King Edgar; and when they had brought him to the king, he was given great gifts by the royal munificence; among which the king bestowed on him a hundred ounces of the purest gold, with many adornments of silk and rings with precious stones. He gave besides to the same king all the land which is called Lothian in the native language, on this condition, that every year at the principal festivals, when the king and his successors wore their crowns, they (the kings of the Scots) should come to the court and joyfully celebrate the feast with the rest of the nobles of the kingdom. Moreover, the king gave him many residences on the way, so that he and his successors coming to the festival and returning thence could be lodged there, and these remained in the power of the kings of the Scots until the times of King Henry the Second.[2]

[1] This follows a passage on King Edgar taken from Florence of Worcester.

[2] This should be compared with a passage in *Concerning the First Coming of the Saxons* (*Symeonis Monachii Opera Omnia*, ed. Arnold, II, p. 382): "Then under King Edgar, Oslac was appointed ealdorman over York and the places belonging to it, and Eadwulf, surnamed 'Evil-child', was placed over the Northumbrians from the Tees to *Myreford* (Firth of Forth). These two earls, with Ælfsige, who was bishop at St. Cuthbert's, escorted Kenneth, king of the Scots, to King Edgar. And when he had done him homage, King Edgar gave him Lothian, and sent him back to his own land with much honour."

Wendover has embroidered the account under the influence of later events, but he must have had a source for the kernel of his narrative.

5. From the "Continuation" of Bede

The greater part of the work that goes under this title is not in the early manuscripts of Bede's work which were known to Plummer, and it is not possible to tell from the description in library catalogues of manuscripts not used by Plummer whether in them the *Ecclesiastical History* is followed by the "Continuation". The only manuscripts known to contain this are of twelfth-, fourteenth- and fifteenth-century date, except that the annals for 731–734 occur in some early manuscripts of the *Ecclesiastical History*. The work cannot, therefore, be closely dated, or its relation to the work of Simeon of Durham judged; but it certainly has material not derived from him. This probably comes from eighth-century northern annals. My selection gives all those annals which add to the information we can get from other sources. This text is printed in Plummer's edition of Bede, I, pp. 361–363.

735 . . . Bishop Egbert having received the *pallium*[1] . . . consecrated Frithuberht and Frithuwold bishops.[2] . . .

737 A great drought made the land unfruitful. . . .[3]

740 Cuthbert was consecrated in the place of Nothhelm.[4] Æthelbald, king of the Mercians, through wicked deceit, laid waste the region of the Northumbrians; and their king, Eadberht, was occupied with his army against the Picts. Also Bishop Æthelwold died, and Cynewulf was ordained bishop[5] in his place. Earnwine and Eadberht were killed.

741 A great drought came upon the country. Charles,[6] king of the Franks, died; his sons, Carloman and Pippin, received the kingdom in his stead.[7]

747 The man of God, Herefrith, died.

750 Cuthred, king of the West Saxons, rose against King Æthelbald and Angus.[8] Theudor[9] and Eanred died. Eadberht added the plain of Kyle and other places to his dominions.

754 Boniface, also called Wynfrith, bishop of the Franks, received the crown of martyrdom, with 53 other men; and in his place Redger[10] was consecrated archbishop by Pope Stephen.

757 Æthelbald, king of the Mercians, was wretchedly and treacherously killed at night by his bodyguard; Beornred began to reign. Cynewulf, king of the West

---

[1] Most of this annal is as in Simeon's *History of the Kings*.   [2] Of Hexham and Whithorn respectively.
[3] The rest of this annal, and that for 739, are from Simeon.   [4] Archbishop of Canterbury.
[5] Of Lindisfarne.   [6] Charles Martel.   [7] Annal 745 is from Simeon.
[8] As it is difficult to see any connexion between a king of Wessex and the Pictish king, it is normally assumed that this is corrupt. If not, it may mean that Angus had become an ally of the king of Mercia through fear of a common enemy, Eadberht of Northumbria.
[9] Tewdwr, son of Beli, king of Strathclyde.
[10] Though Boniface was succeeded at Mainz by Lul, it was Chrodogang of Metz who received the archiepiscopal dignity, and the name in the text must be a corruption of Hrothgang, the Old English form of his name. See W. Levison, *Vitae S. Bonifatii Archiepiscopi Moguntini*, p. 60, n. 2.

Saxons, died.[1] In the same year also Offa put Beornred to flight and strove for the kingdom of the Mercians with a bloody sword.

758[2] Oswulf[3] was treacherously killed by his thegns; and in the same year Æthelwold was elected by his people and began to reign. In his second year a great calamity, a pestilence, occurred, which lasted almost two years, diverse grievous sicknesses causing havoc, more especially the disease of dysentery.

761 Angus, king of the Picts, died, who from the beginning of his reign right to the end behaved with bloody crime as a tyrannical slaughterer, and Oswine was killed.[4]

[1] The author has used, and misunderstood, the Anglo-Saxon Chronicle, in which Cynewulf's death in 784 is related in the annal (755) that mentions his accession. He need not, however, have had a correctly dated version, for he may have been able to supply the date 757, instead of 755, from some other source.
[2] Perhaps for 759, since his previous annal is dated 758. It records Eadberht's resignation, as in Simeon.
[3] King of Northumbria.
[4] The text ends by recording Alhred's accession in 765, and the death of Archbishop Egbert and Bishop Frithuberht in 766, as in Simeon.

6. Extracts from the anonymous "History of St. Cuthbert"

The history of the North in the couple of generations following the Danish settlement of 876 is one of the most obscure in our period; hence the implications of some statements in this text (on which see p. 119) assume great significance. The tradition that so soon after the settlement a Christian Danish king should ascend the throne, and owe it to the Church, is itself interesting, but even more so is the survival of a monastery at Heversham on the Kent as late as the early tenth century. Its abbot, however, seems to be securing for himself a safer habitat east of the Pennines, and this chimes in with the information that a secular noble fled from the lands west of the Pennines "from the pirates". Important also is the information on the resistance of Ealdred, the high-reeve of Bamburgh, to Ragnald, leader of the Norse from Ireland. On the chronology and interpretation of this evidence, the article of F. T. Wainwright, *Saga-Book of the Viking Society*, XIII, pp. 156–173 should be consulted.

The text is edited by T. Arnold, *Symeonis Monachii Opera Omnia*, I, pp. 196–214, and paragraph references refer to this edition.

§ 13. At that time[1] St. Cuthbert appeared by night to the holy abbot of Carlisle, whose name was Eadred, firmly enjoining him as follows: "Go", he said, "across the Tyne to the army of the Danes, and say to them that, if they will obey me, they are to point out to you a certain boy, Guthfrith, Hardacnut's son, by name, a purchased slave of a certain widow, and you and the whole army are to give in the early morning the price for him to the widow;[2] and give the aforesaid price at the third hour, and at the sixth hour lead him before the whole multitude, that they may elect him king. And at the ninth hour lead him with the whole army on to the hill which is called 'Oswiu's down', and there place on his right arm a gold armlet, and thus they all may appoint him as king. Also say to him, when he has been made king, that he is to give me the whole territory between the Tyne and the Wear; and whoever shall flee to me, whether on account of homicide, or of any other necessity, is to have sanctuary for 37 days and nights." Resolved as a result of this vision, and strengthened by the reasonable command of the blessed confessor, the holy abbot confidently hastened to the barbarian army; and being honourably received by it, he faithfully carried out in order what had been enjoined on him. For he both found and redeemed the boy, and made him king by the great goodwill of the whole multitude, receiving the land and right of sanctuary. Then Bishop Eardwulf brought to the army and to the hill the body of St. Cuthbert, and over it the king himself and the whole army swore peace and fidelity, for as long as they lived; and they kept this oath well.

§ 21. . . . In the time of the same King Edward (the Elder), Tilred, abbot of Heversham,[3] bought the estate which is called South Eden;[4] half of it he gave to St. Cuthbert, that he might become a brother in his monastery; the other to Norham,[5] that he might be abbot there.

§ 22. In these days[6] Alfred, son of Brihtwulf, fleeing from the pirates, came from beyond the mountains towards the west, and sought the pity of St. Cuthbert and of

---

[1] After the death of Healfdene. Simeon's *History of the Kings* (ed. Arnold, II, p. 114) dates Guthfrith's accession 883.

[2] *Id.* adds that it was at Whittington.   [3] Westmorland.

[4] There is now only one place called Eden, namely Castle Eden, Durham.

[5] Norham-on-Tweed, Northumberland.   [6] *i.e.* when Edward the Elder had come to the throne.

Bishop Cuthheard, that they might grant him some estates. Then Bishop Cuthheard for the love of God and for the sake of St. Cuthbert granted him these estates: Easington, *Seleton*, Thorpe, Horden, (Castle) Eden, the two Shottons, South Eden, Hulam, Hutton, *Twinlingtun*, Billingham with its members, *Scurnfatun*. All these estates, as I have said, the bishop gave to Alfred, that he might be loyal to him himself and the community, and should render full service from them. This also he faithfully did, until King Ragnald came with a great multitude of ships and occupied the land of Ealdred, son of Eadwulf,[1] who was loved by King Edward just as his father Eadwulf had been loved by King Alfred. Therefore Ealdred, being put to flight, went to Scotland, and sought help from King Constantine, and brought him to battle against King Ragnald at Corbridge; in which battle—I know not what sin was the cause—the pagan king was victorious, put Constantine to flight, routed the Scots, and killed Alfred, the faithful subject of St. Cuthbert, and all the English nobility, except Ealdred and his brother Uhtred.

§ 23. When they had been put to flight and the whole land conquered, he divided the estates of St. Cuthbert, and he gave the one part, towards the south, from the estate which is called Eden as far as Billingham, to a certain powerful thegn of his who was called Scula; and the other part, from Eden as far as the River Wear, to one called Olaf Ball. And this son of the devil was hostile in every way he could to God and St. Cuthbert. And thus a certain day, when full of the unclean spirit he entered raging into the church of the holy confessor, he said in the presence of Bishop Cuthheard and the whole community: "What can this dead man Cuthbert do against me, when his threats are daily disregarded? I swear by my mighty gods, Thor and Othin, that from this hour I will be a great enemy to all of you." And when the bishop and the whole congregation knelt before God and St. Cuthbert, and besought them for vengeance for these threats, as it is written: "Vengeance is mine, and I will repay",[2] this son of the devil turned away with great pride and indignation, wishing to depart. But when he had put one foot outside the threshold, he felt as if iron were deeply fixed in the other foot. With this pain piercing his diabolical heart, he fell, and the devil thrust his sinful soul into hell. And St. Cuthbert, as was right, received his land.

§ 24. In the time of the aforementioned King Edward, Wulfheard, son of Hwætred, gave to St. Cuthbert his estate which is called Benwell. At the same time, Eadred, son of Ricsige, rode west beyond the mountains, and killed Ealdorman Eardwulf, and seized his wife in disregard of the peace and the will of the people, and fled to the protection of St. Cuthbert. And there he stayed three years, cultivating in peace the land granted to him by Bishop Cuthheard and the community, from Chester-le-Street as far as the River Derwent, and from there south to the Wear, and from there as far as the road which is called *Deorestrete* to the south-west; and an estate on the Tees which is called Gainford, with whatever belongs to it. This Eadred held this land with loyalty to St. Cuthbert, and rendered his rent faithfully, until the aforesaid King Ragnald, having again collected an army, fought at Corbridge, and killed that same Eadred and a great multitude of the English; and being victorious,

---

[1] High-reeve of Bamburgh.   [2] Romans xii. 19.

he took away from St. Cuthbert all the land which Eadred had held, and gave it to Esbrid, son of Eadred, and his brother Ealdorman Ælstan, who had been stout fighters in this battle. At length this accursed king perished with his sons and his friends, and took with him nothing of what he had stolen from the holy confessor, but only his sins.

7. From Asser's "Life of King Alfred"

For a discussion of this work, see pp. 113, 120. It is a very valuable source for Alfred's reign. It is edited by W. H. Stevenson, Oxford, 1904; and translated by L. C. Jane, *Asser's Life of King Alfred* (Medieval Library), 1926, and by E. Conybeare, *Alfred in the Chroniclers*, London, 1900. Earlier editions do not distinguish between the genuine text and the later interpolations.

To my venerable and most pious lord, ruler of all the Christians of the island of Britain, Alfred, king of the Anglo-Saxons, Asser, lowest of all the servants of God, wishes thousandfold prosperity in both the present and future life, according to his prayers and desires.

Chap. 1. In the year of our Lord's incarnation 849, Alfred, king of the Anglo-Saxons, was born in the royal residence called Wantage, in the shire which is named Berkshire; which shire is thus called from the wood *Berroc*, where box grows very abundantly. . . .[1]

Chap. 2. His mother was called Osburh, a very religious woman, noble in character, noble also by birth; for she was the daughter of Oslac, the renowned cupbearer of King Æthelwulf. This Oslac was by race a Goth, for he was sprung from the Goths and Jutes,[2] namely from the stock of Stuf and Wihtgar, two brothers, and also ealdormen, who received the rule over the Isle of Wight from their uncle King Cerdic and his son Cynric, their cousin.[3] They killed the few British inhabitants of the island whom they could find on it at the place called *Wihtgarabyrig*; for the rest of the inhabitants of the island had either already been killed or had fled as exiles. . . .[4]

Chap. 12. But meanwhile,[5] while King Æthelwulf was lingering beyond the sea for some little time, a certain disgraceful thing, contrary to the practice of all Christians, arose to the west of Selwood.[6] For King Æthelbald, son of King Æthelwulf, and Ealhstan, bishop of the church of Sherborne, and also Eanwulf, ealdorman of Somerset, are said to have plotted that King Æthelwulf should not be received again into the kingship when he returned from Rome. This unhappy business, unheard of in all previous ages, very many persons ascribe to the bishop and the ealdorman alone, by whose counsel it is said this deed was done. But there are also many who impute it solely to the royal pride, because that king was stubborn in this affair and in many other wrong acts, as we have heard from certain men's accounts; and this was proved by the outcome of the affair. For as King Æthelwulf was returning from Rome, his son aforesaid, with all his counsellors, or rather conspirators, tried to commit so great a crime as to keep the king out of his own kingdom; but God did not allow it to happen, neither did the nobles of all the Saxon land consent. For, in order that the irremediable danger to the Saxon land from civil war, with father and

---

[1] Here follows his genealogy, much as in annal 855 of the Chronicle.
[2] As Stevenson suggests, this statement probably arises from a mistaken identification of these peoples.
[3] These remarks are based on annals 530 and 534 of the Chronicle.
[4] Chaps. 3–11 are based on annals 851–855 of the Chronicle.
[5] *i.e.* while Æthelwulf was away on his visit to Rome in 855.
[6] Asser is probably translating the Old English expression, *be westan Selwuda*.

son at war, or rather with the whole people fighting against one or other of them, might not grow more fierce and cruel from day to day, the kingdom previously united was by the indescribable forbearance of the father and the assent of all the nobles divided between father and son; and the eastern districts were assigned to the father, the western, on the other hand, to the son. Thus, where the father ought to have reigned by rights, the wicked and stubborn son reigned; for the western part of the Saxon land has always been more important than the eastern.

Chap. 13. When therefore King Æthelwulf arrived from Rome, all the people, as was fitting, rejoiced so greatly at the coming of their lord, that, if he had allowed it, they wished to deprive his stubborn son Æthelbald, with all his counsellors, of any share in the kingdom. But he, as we have said, exercising great forbearance and prudent counsel, lest danger should befall the kingdom, would not have it done thus. And without any opposition or ill-feeling on his nobles' part, he ordered that Judith, daughter of King Charles, whom he had received from her father, was to sit beside him on the royal throne as long as he lived, contrary to the wrongful custom of that nation. For the people of the West Saxons did not allow the queen to sit next the king, or even to be called queen, but "wife of the king".[1]

Chap. 16. Thus King Æthelwulf lived two years after he came back from Rome. During these years, among many other good endeavours in this present life, meditating on his departure on the way of all flesh, he ordered to be written a testamentary, or rather an advisory, letter, so that his sons should not dispute unduly among themselves after their father's death; in this he took care to command in writing in due form, a division of the kingdom between his sons, that is to say the two eldest, of his own inheritance between his sons and daughter and his relations also, and of the money, which he should leave, between the needs of his soul and his sons and also his nobles. Concerning this prudent policy we have decided to record a few examples out of many, for posterity to imitate, namely such as are understood to belong particularly to the necessities of the soul. It is unnecessary to insert the rest, which belong to human dispensation, in this little book, lest by its length it should arouse disgust in the readers and also in those desiring to hear it. For the benefit of his soul then, which he had been zealous to promote in all things from the first flower of his youth, he enjoined that his successors after him until the Day of Judgment were always to supply with food, drink and clothing, one poor man, whether a native or foreigner, from every ten hides throughout all his hereditary land, provided that that land was occupied by men and herds, and had not become waste land. He gave orders also that a great sum of money was every year to be taken to Rome for his soul, namely 300 mancuses, which were to be divided there thus: 100 mancuses in honour of St. Peter, especially for the purchase of oil to fill all the lamps of that apostolic church on Easter eve and likewise at cockcrow, and 100 mancuses in honour of St. Paul on the same terms, for the purchase of oil for the church of St. Paul the Apostle to fill the lamps on Easter eve and at cockcrow, and 100 mancuses also for the universal apostolic pope.

---

[1] Here follows a story that this custom arose from the evil behaviour of Offa's daughter, Eadburh, wife of Brihtric of Wessex, part of which Asser tells on Alfred's own authority.

Chap. 17. But when King Æthelwulf was dead, his son Æthelbald, contrary to God's prohibition and Christian dignity, and also against the usage of all pagans, ascending the bed of his father, married Judith, daughter of Charles, king of the Franks, earning much infamy from all who heard of it; and ruled the government of the kingdom of the West Saxons for two and a half lawless years after his father's death.[1]

Chap. 21. . . . I think that we should return to what specially incited me to this work; that is to say, that I consider that I should insert briefly in this place the little that has come to my knowledge concerning the character of my revered lord, Alfred, king of the Anglo-Saxons, during his childhood and boyhood.

Chap. 22. Now, he was loved by his father and mother, and indeed by everybody, with a united and immense love, more than all his brothers, and was always brought up in the royal court, and as he passed through his childhood and boyhood he appeared fairer in form than all his brothers, and more pleasing in his looks, his words and his ways. And from his cradle a longing for wisdom before all things and among all the pursuits of this present life, combined with his noble birth, filled the noble temper of his mind; but alas, by the unworthy carelessness of his parents and tutors, he remained ignorant of letters until his twelfth year, or even longer. But he listened attentively to Saxon poems day and night, and hearing them often recited by others committed them to his retentive memory. A keen huntsman, he toiled unceasingly in every branch of hunting, and not in vain; for he was without equal in his skill and good fortune in that art, as also in all other gifts of God, as we have ourselves often seen.

Chap. 23. When, therefore, his mother one day was showing him and his brothers a certain book of Saxon poetry which she held in her hand, she said: "I will give this book to whichever of you can learn it most quickly." And moved by these words, or rather by divine inspiration, and attracted by the beauty of the initial letter of the book, Alfred said in reply to his mother, forestalling his brothers, his elders in years though not in grace: "Will you really give this book to one of us, to the one who can soonest understand and repeat it to you?" And, smiling and rejoicing, she confirmed it, saying: "To him will I give it." Then taking the book from her hand he immediately went to his master, who[2] read it. And when it was read, he went back to his mother and repeated it.

Chap. 24. After this he learnt the daily course, that is, the services of the hours, and then certain psalms and many prayers. He collected these into one book and carried it about with him everywhere in his bosom (as I have myself seen) day and night, for the sake of prayer, through all the changes of this present life, and was never parted from it. But alas, what he principally desired, the liberal arts, he did not obtain according to his wish, because, as he was wont to say, there were at that time no good scholars in all the kingdom of the West Saxons.

Chap. 25. He often affirmed with frequent laments and sighs from the bottom of his heart, that among all his difficulties and hindrances in this present life this was the

---

[1] Chaps. 18–20 and part of 21 are based on the Chronicle.
[2] Accepting Stevenson's suggestion that *et* is an error for a compendium for *qui*.

greatest: that, during the time when he had youth and leisure and aptitude for learning, he had no teachers; but when he was more advanced in years, he did have teachers and writers to some extent, when he was not able to study, because he was harassed, nay, rather disturbed, day and night both with illnesses unknown to all the physicians of this island, and with the cares of the royal office at home and abroad, and also with the invasions of pagans by land and sea. Yet, among all the difficulties of this present life, from infancy unto the present day, he has never abandoned that same insatiable longing, and even now still yearns for it.[1]

Chap. 75. Sons and daughters were born to him by the aforesaid wife,[2] namely Æthelflæd, the first-born, and after her Edward, then Æthelgifu, next Ælfthryth, then Æthelweard, besides those who were snatched away in infancy by an early death. . . . Æthelflæd, when she reached marriageable age, was joined in matrimony to Ethelred,[3] ealdorman of the Mercians. Æthelgifu, devoted to God as a virgin, subjected and consecrated to the rules of the monastic life, entered the service of God. Æthelweard, the youngest, was given over by the divine counsel and the admirable prudence of the king to the pleasures of literary studies, along with almost all the children of noble birth of the whole country, and also many of humble birth, under the diligent care of masters. In that school, books of both languages, Latin, that is, and English, were assiduously read, and they had leisure for writing; so that before they had the strength for manly pursuits, namely hunting and other pursuits which are fitting for noblemen, they were zealous and skilled in the liberal arts. Edward and Ælfthryth were always brought up in the royal court, with great care from their tutors and nurses, and, indeed, with great affection from all; and until this day they continue there, showing humility, affability and gentleness to all, whether their countrymen or foreigners, and great obedience to their father. Nor, indeed, are they allowed to live idly and carelessly without a liberal education among the other occupations of this present life which are fitting for nobles; for they have learnt carefully psalms and Saxon books, and especially Saxon poems, and they frequently make use of books.

Chap. 76. Meanwhile the king, in the midst of wars and frequent hindrances of this present life, and also of the raids of the pagans and his daily infirmities of body, did not cease, single-handed, assiduously and eagerly with all his might, to govern the kingdom, to practise every branch of hunting, to instruct his goldsmiths and all his craftsmen, and his falconers, hawkers and dog-keepers, to erect buildings to his own new design more stately and magnificent than had been the custom of his ancestors, to recite Saxon books, and especially to learn by heart Saxon poems, and command others to do so. He also was in the habit of hearing daily the divine office, the Mass, and certain prayers and psalms, and of observing both the day and the night hours, and of visiting churches at night-time, as we have said, in order to pray without his followers knowing. Moreover, he showed zeal for almsgiving, and

---

[1] Chaps. 26–28, 30–72, are based on the Chronicle, and any important variants and additions have been mentioned in the notes to this work. Chap. 29 mentions Alfred's marriage to the daughter of Ethelred Mucel, ealdorman of the *Gaini*, and his wife Eadburh, a descendant of the Mercian royal line. Chaps. 73 and 74 give a confused account of Alfred's illnesses.

[2] See previous note.

[3] Eadred, erroneously, in the text.

generosity both to his countrymen and to strangers from all nations, and very great and matchless kindness and pleasantness towards all men, and skill in searching into things unknown. And many Franks, Frisians, men of Gaul, pagans, Welsh, Scots and Bretons willingly submitted to his lordship, both noblemen and men of humble rank; and he ruled them all in accordance with his own honourable nature just like his own people, and loved and honoured them, and enriched them with money and rights.[1] Also he was accustomed to listen to the Holy Scripture recited by native clergy, but also, if by chance someone had come from elsewhere, to listen with equal earnestness and attention to prayers along with foreigners. He also loved his bishops and all the ecclesiastical order, his ealdormen and his nobles, his officials and all members of his household, with a wonderful affection. And he himself never ceased among other occupations, day and night, to train their sons, who were being brought up in the royal household, in all good behaviour, and to educate them in letters, loving them no less than his own sons. Yet, as if he had no comfort in all these things and as if he suffered no other disquiet from within or without, he complained in anxious sadness by day and night to God and to all who were bound to him in close affection, and lamented with repeated sighs, that Almighty God had not made him skilled in divine wisdom and the liberal arts; emulating in this the pious and most illustrious and rich Solomon, king of the Hebrews, who, despising all present glory and riches, sought first wisdom from God, and also found both, wisdom and present glory, as it is written: "Seek therefore first the kingdom of God and his justice, and all these things shall be granted unto you."[2] But God, who always sees into the inmost thoughts, and prompts our designs and all good desires, and also most amply ordains that good desires may be obtained, and who never prompts anyone to desire well without also ordaining what each man well and justly desires to have, stirred up the king's mind from within, not without; as it is written: "I will hear what the Lord God will speak in me."[3] Whenever he could, he would acquire assistants in his good design, who could help him to the desired wisdom, that he might obtain what he longed for. Forthwith, like the prudent bee, which arises in the summer-time at dawn from its beloved cells and, directing its course in swift flight through the unknown ways of the air, alights upon many and various blossoms of herbs, plants and fruits, and finds and carries home what pleases it most, he turned afar the gaze of his mind, seeking abroad what he had not at home, that is, in his own kingdom.

    Chap. 77. And then God, suffering no longer his so good and just complaint, sent for the king's goodwill some consolations, certain lights, as it were, namely Wærferth, bishop of the church of Worcester, a man well versed in the divine Scriptures, who at the king's command first translated clearly and beautifully from Latin into the Saxon language the books of the "Dialogues" of Pope Gregory and his disciple Peter, sometimes giving a paraphrase; and then Plegmund, a Mercian by race, archbishop of the church of Canterbury, a venerable man, endowed with wisdom; also Athelstan and Wærwulf, priests and chaplains, learned men, of Mercian race. King Alfred summoned these four to him from Mercia, and advanced them with

---

[1] I suspect that by *potestas*, 'power', here and elsewhere, Asser is meaning rights over land, and not merely an abstract and vague 'authority'.

[2] Matthew vi. 33, from the Old Latin, not the Vulgate, text.   [3] Psalm lxxxiv. 9.

great honours and authority in the kingdom of the West Saxons, in addition to those which Archbishop Plegmund and Bishop Wærferth possessed in Mercia. By the teaching and wisdom of all these men, the king's desire was ceaselessly increased and fulfilled. For by day and night, whenever he had any free time, he ordered books to be read before him by such men, nor indeed did he allow himself to be without one of them. Therefore he obtained a knowledge of almost all books, although he could not as yet by himself understand anything from books, for he had not yet begun to read anything.

Chap. 78. But, since in this matter the royal avarice, praiseworthy as it was, was still unsatisfied, he sent messengers across the sea to Gaul to acquire teachers. From there he summoned Grimbald, priest and monk, a venerable man, an excellent singer, most learned in every way in ecclesiastical studies and the divine Scriptures, and adorned with all good qualities; and also John, likewise a priest and monk, a man of very keen intelligence and most learned in all branches of the art of literature, and skilled in many other arts. By their teaching the king's mind was much enriched, and he endowed and honoured them with great authority.

Chap. 79. At that time I also was summoned by the king, and came to the Saxon land from the western and farthest parts of Wales, and when I had decided to come to him through great tracts of country, I reached the province of the South Saxons,[1] which is called Sussex in the Saxon language, led by guides of that race. There I first saw the king in the royal residence which is called Dean. And when I had been kindly received by him, among other topics of conversation, he asked me pressingly to devote myself to his service and be a member of his court, and to give up for his sake all that I possessed to the north and west of the Severn; and he promised also to give me a greater recompense. And this he did. I replied that I could not make such a promise carelessly and rashly. For it seemed wrong to me to desert for the sake of any worldly honour and power those so holy places in which I had been reared and educated, tonsured, and finally ordained, unless by force and compulsion. To which he said: "If you cannot accede to this, at least grant to me half of your service, so that you may be six months with me and as many in Wales." To which I replied thus: "I cannot promise this easily and rashly without the counsel of my friends." But indeed, since I realized that he desired my services, though I knew not why, I promised that I would return to him six months later, if my life were spared, with such a reply as might be advantageous for me and mine, and acceptable to him. And when this reply seemed good to him, and I had given him a pledge to return at the appointed time, on the fourth day we rode away from him and returned to our own land. But when we had left him, a violent fever laid hold of me in the city of Caerwent and I was grievously afflicted with it day and night for 12 months and a week without any hope of life. And when I did not come to him at the appointed time, as I had promised, he sent letters to me, which urged me to ride to him and inquired the cause of the delay. But as I could not ride to him, I sent another letter to him, which explained to him the reason for my delay and declared that I would perform what I had promised if I could recover from that sickness. Therefore, when

---

[1] Asser uses a Welsh manner of speech, and calls them the "Right-hand Saxons".

the sickness left me, I devoted myself, as I had promised the king, to his service, by the advice and permission of all our people, for the benefit of that holy place[1] and all dwelling in it, on this condition, that I should spend six months of every year with him, either, if I could, six months at a time, or otherwise by turns spend three months in Wales and three in the Saxon land, and that land should be benefited by the teaching of St. David, yet in every case in proportion to our strength.[2] For our brethren hoped that they would suffer fewer tribulations and injuries from King Hyfaidd–who often plundered that monastery and the diocese of St. David's, sometimes by driving out the bishops who were in charge of it, as he at one time among these drove out Archbishop Nobis, my kinsman, and me myself–if I were to come to the notice and friendship of that king by any kind of agreement.

Chap. 80. For at that time, and for a long time before, all the districts of the southern parts of Wales belonged to King Alfred, and still belong to him; for Hyfaidd with all the inhabitants of the region of Dyfed, compelled by the power of the six sons of Rhodri, had submitted to the royal overlordship; also Hywel, son of Rhys, king of Glywyssing, and Brochwel and Ffernfael, the sons of Mewrig, kings of Gwent, compelled by the might and tyranny of Ealdorman Ethelred[3] and the Mercians, of their own accord besought the same king that he would be their lord and protector against their enemies. Also Elise, son of Tewdwr, king of Brecknock, forced by the power of the same sons of Rhodri, of his own accord requested the lordship of the aforesaid king. And Anarawd, son of Rhodri, with his brothers, finally deserted the friendship of the Northumbrians, from which they had had no good, but only injury, and came to the king's presence earnestly beseeching his friendship. And when he had been honourably received by the king, and been accepted by him as his son from the hands of the bishop at confirmation, and been enriched with great gifts, he submitted with all his followers to the king's overlordship, on such terms that he would be obedient to the king in all things, just like Ethelred with the Mercians.

Chap. 81. Nor did they all obtain the king's friendship in vain. For those who desired to increase their earthly power, obtained this; those who desired money, obtained money; those who desired friendship, gained friendship; those who desired both, received both. And all had love and guardianship and protection on every side, in as far as the king with his people could defend himself. When, therefore, I came to him at the royal residence which is called *Leonaford,*[4] I was honourably received by him, and remained with him in his court on that occasion for eight months, during which I read to him whatever books he wished and which we had at hand. For it is his most usual habit either himself to read books aloud or to listen to others who read them, day and night, in the midst of all other occupations of mind and body. And when I had frequently asked his permission to return, and could by no means obtain it, at length when I had made up my mind absolutely to demand his permission, I was summoned to him in the early morning of the eve of our Lord's Nativity, and he

---

[1] St. David's.　　　　　　　　　　[2] See G. H. Wheeler, *Eng. Hist. Rev.,* XLVII, pp. 87f.

[3] As before, the text has in error Eadred.

[4] This place cannot be identified. Stevenson's suggestion of Landford, Wilts., has not been accepted by later place-name scholars. Lenham, Kent, has the same first element.

delivered to me two letters, in which there was a detailed list of all the things belonging to two monasteries, which in Saxon are called Congresbury and Banwell, and on that same day he delivered to me those two monasteries with everything that was in them, and a very costly silk robe, and a strong man's load of incense, adding these words, that he did not give me these small things because he was unwilling to give greater later on. Indeed at a later time he unexpectedly gave me Exeter, with all the diocese belonging to it,[1] in Saxon territory and in Cornwall, besides innumerable daily gifts of all kinds of earthly riches, which it would be tedious to enumerate here, lest it should cause weariness to the readers. But do not let anyone think that I have mentioned such gifts in this place out of any vain glory or in flattery, or for the sake of gaining greater honour; for I call God to witness that I have not done so, but only to make clear to those who do not know, how profuse is his generosity. Then at once he gave me leave to ride to those two monasteries, which were filled with all good things, and thence to return to my own country.[2]

Chap. 87. Also in that same year (887) the oft-mentioned Alfred, king of the Anglo-Saxons, first began by the divine inspiration both to read (Latin) and translate on one and the same day. But, that this may be made clear to those ignorant of it, I will take care to explain the reason for this late start.

Chap. 88. For when we were both sitting one day in the royal chamber talking, as was our wont, on all sorts of subjects, it happened that I read to him a passage from a certain book. And when he had listened to it intently with both his ears, and pondered it carefully in the depths of his mind, he suddenly showed me a little book, which he constantly carried in his bosom, in which were contained the daily course, and certain psalms and prayers which he had read in his youth, and he ordered me to write that passage in the same little book. And I, hearing this and perceiving in part his eagerness of mind and also his devout wish to study the divine wisdom, gave great thanks to Almighty God, although silently, with hands outstretched to heaven, who had planted so great devotion for the study of wisdom in the king's heart. But, when I found no vacant space in that little book, in which I could write the passage –for it was completely filled with various matters– I hesitated for a little while, principally that I might provoke the king's fine understanding to a greater knowledge of the divine testimonies. And when he urged me to write it as quickly as possible, I said to him: "Are you willing that I should write this passage on a separate leaf? For we do not know whether we may not at some time find one or more such passages which may please you; and if this happens unexpectedly, we shall be glad to have kept it apart." And hearing this, he said that it was a good plan. When I heard this, I was glad, and hastened to prepare a quire, at the beginning of which I wrote the passage he had commanded; and on the same day I wrote by his command no fewer than three other passages which pleased him, in the same quire, as I had foretold. And henceforth as we daily talked together, and searching to this end found other

---

[1] Though Exeter did not become a permanent see until 1050, there is no great difficulty in supposing that a smaller diocese was temporarily carved out of the see of Sherborne, later to be merged with it again when Asser became bishop of Sherborne. A parallel case is given by the treatment of Lindsey in the tenth century, when it sometimes is part of the diocese of Dorchester, sometimes a separate see with a bishop of its own. See also H. P. R. Finberg, *Trans. Royal Hist. Soc.*, 5th Series, iii, pp. 115 f.

[2] Chaps. 82–86 are based on the Chronicle, 866–887.

equally pleasing passages, that quire became full; and rightly, as it is written: "The just man builds upon a small foundation and by degrees passes to greater things." Like a most productive bee, travelling far and wide over the marshes in its quest, he eagerly and unceasingly collected many various flowers of Holy Scripture, with which he densely stored the cells of his mind.

Chap. 89. Now, once that passage had been written, he straightway was eager to read and to translate into the Saxon language, and hence to instruct many others. And just as we should learn from that happy thief, who knew the Lord Jesus Christ, his Lord, and indeed the Lord of all, hanging beside him on the venerable gallows of the Holy Cross; for with humble prayers, bending on him his bodily eyes, because he could do nothing else, being all fixed with nails, he called with a lowly voice: "Christ, remember me when thou shalt come into thy kingdom",[1] and on the gallows first began to learn the rudiments of the Christian faith; the king likewise, though in a different way, for he was set in royal power, presumed by the instigation of God to begin his first lessons in holy writings on the festival of St. Martin. And he [began] to learn those flowers, which had been gathered from various masters, and to bring them all into the compass of one book, although in no order, as they came to hand, until it grew almost to the size of a psalter. This book he used to call his 'enchiridion', that is, 'hand-book', because he was most careful to have it at hand by day and night. And he found, as he then said, no little comfort in it. . . .[2]

Chap. 91. The king was pierced by many nails of tribulation, although placed in royal power. For, from his twentieth till his forty-fifth year, in which he now is, he has been constantly afflicted with a most severe attack of an unknown malady, so that he has not a single hour's peace, in which he is not either suffering that infirmity or driven almost to despair by apprehension of it. Moreover he was troubled, and with good reason, by the constant inroads of foreign peoples, which he constantly sustained by land and sea without any peaceful interval. What shall I say of his frequent expeditions and battles against the pagans and the incessant cares of government? What of his daily [solicitude][3] for the nations, which dwell from the Tyrrhenian Sea to the farthest end of Ireland? Indeed, we have even seen and read letters sent to him along with gifts by the patriarch Elias. What of the cities and towns he restored, and the others, which he built where none had been before? Of the buildings made by his instructions with gold and silver, beyond compare? Of the royal halls and chambers constructed admirably in stone and timber at his command? Of the royal residences in stone, moved at the royal command from their ancient sites and beautifully erected in more suitable places? And what[4] of the great trouble and vexation (besides his illness) he had with his own people, who would voluntarily submit to little or no labour for the common needs of the kingdom? Yet, just as a skilful pilot strives to bring his ship, laden with great riches, to the longed-for safe harbour of his native land, though nearly all his sailors are worn out; he, upheld by divine aid, would not allow the helm of the kingdom he had once received to totter or waver, though set alone in the midst of the raging and manifold whirlpools of this present

---

[1] Luke xxiii. 42.   [2] Chap. 90 elaborates the comparison with the thief on the Cross.
[3] Accepting Wheeler's suggestion (*Eng. Hist. Rev.*, XLVII, p. 86) that this is the word omitted in the text here.   [4] Reading *Quid de.*

life. For he most wisely brought over and bound to his own will and to the common
profit of the whole kingdom his bishops and ealdormen and nobles, and the thegns
who were dearest to him, and also his reeves, to whom, after God and the king, the
control of the kingdom seems rightly to belong, by gently instructing, flattering,
urging, commanding them, and, after long patience, by punishing sharply the disobedient, and by showing in every way hatred of vulgar folly and obstinacy. But if,
among these exhortations of the king, his orders were not carried out because of the
slackness of the people, or things begun late in time of need were unfinished and of
no profit to those who undertook them—for I may tell of fortresses ordered by him
and still not begun, or begun too late to be brought to completion—and enemy forces
broke in by land or sea, or, as often happened, on every side, the opponents of the
royal ordinances then were ashamed with a vain repentance when on the brink of
ruin. For by the witness of Scripture I call that repentance vain, by which numberless
men sorrow when afflicted with grievous loss for the many ill-deeds they have
committed. But though—alas, the pity of it—they[1] are sadly afflicted through this, and
moved to tears by the loss of their fathers, wives, children, servants, slaves, handmaids,
their labours and all their goods, what help is hateful repentance, when it cannot
succour their slain kinsmen, nor redeem captives from odious captivity, nor even can
it help them themselves, who have escaped, seeing that they have nought with which
to sustain their own lives? Grievously afflicted, they then repent with too late repentance, and regret that they have carelessly neglected the king's orders, and with one
voice praise the king's wisdom, and promise to fulfil with all their strength what they
have before refused, that is, with regard to the building of fortresses and the other
things for the common profit of the whole kingdom.

    Chap. 92. I do not consider it profitable to pass over in this place his vow and
most well-thought-out scheme, which he was never able to put aside by any means
either in prosperity or adversity. For when in his usual manner he was meditating on
the needs of his soul, among other good acts in which he was actively engaged by
day and night, he ordered the foundation of two monasteries; one for monks in the
place which is called Athelney, which is surrounded on all sides by very great swampy
and impassable marshes, so that no one can approach it by any means except in punts,
or by a bridge which has been made with laborious skill between two fortresses. At
the western end of this bridge a very strong fort has been placed of most beautiful
workmanship by the king's command. In this monastery he collected monks of
various races from every quarter, and set them therein.

    Chap. 93. For at first he had no noble or freeman of his own nation who would
of his own accord enter the monastic life—apart from children, who by reason of
their tender age could not yet choose good or refuse evil—for indeed for many years
past the desire for the monastic life had been utterly lacking in all that people, and
also in many other nations, although there still remain many monasteries founded
in that land, but none properly observing the rule of this way of life, I know not
why; whether on account of the onslaughts of foreigners, who very often invaded
by land or sea, or on account of the nation's too great abundance of riches of every

---

[1] The text, which Stevenson marks as corrupt, has *eulogii* here.

kind, which I am much more inclined to think the reason for that contempt of the monastic life. For this reason he sought to gather together monks of different race in that monastery.

Chap. 94. First, he appointed John, priest and monk, by race an Old Saxon, as abbot, and then some priests and deacons from across the sea. But when he still had not with these the number he wanted, he also procured many of that same Gallic race, some of whom, being children, he ordered to be educated in that same monastery, and to be raised to the monastic order at a later time. In that monastery I also saw one of pagan race, brought up there and wearing the monastic habit, quite a young man, and not the lowest among them.[1]

Chap. 98. The aforesaid king also ordered to be built another monastery by the east gate of Shaftesbury, as a habitation for nuns, over which he appointed as abbess his own daughter, Æthelgifu, a virgin dedicated to God. And along with her dwell many other noble nuns serving God in the monastic life in the same monastery. He richly endowed these two monasteries with estates and wealth of all kinds.

Chap. 99. When all this was thus settled, he meditated according to his usual practice what he could still add that would further his pious intentions. Things wisely begun and profitably conceived were profitably continued. For long ago he had heard that it was written in the law that the Lord had promised to repay his tithe many times over, and had faithfully kept his promise.[2] Inspired by this example and wishing to excel the practice of his predecessors, this pious thinker promised that he would faithfully and devoutly with all his heart give to God a half part of his service, both by day and night, and also the half part of all the riches which reached him every year by moderate and just acquisition; and this resolve he strove to carry out skilfully and wisely in as far as human discernment can observe and keep it. But, as was his habit, in order that he might carefully avoid what we are warned against in another place in Holy Scripture: "If thou offer aright, but dost not divide aright, thou sinnest",[3] he considered how he might rightly divide what he willingly devoted to God, and, as Solomon says: "The heart of the king"—that is his counsel—"is in the hand of the Lord."[4] Taking counsel from on high, he ordered his officers first to divide into two equal parts all his annual revenue.

Chap. 100. When this was done, he adjudged that the first part should be devoted to secular uses, and ordered that this should be further divided into three parts. The first of these shares he bestowed annually on his fighting men, and also on his noble thegns who dwelt by turns in his court, serving him in many offices. Now the royal household was always managed in three relays; for the followers of the aforesaid king were prudently divided into three companies, so that the first company resided one month in the royal court on duty day and night, and when the month was over and another company arrived, the first went home and remained there for two months, each seeing to his own affairs. So also the second company, when its month

---

[1] Chaps. 95–97 describe an attack made on Abbot John by some of his monks, with intent to kill him, but though wounded, he defended himself until help came.

[2] The text continues: "and that he would repay him his tithe many times over", which Stevenson attributes to a scribal blunder in copying both an original and an emended reading.

[3] Genesis iv. 7, in the Old Latin version.　　　　　　　　　　　　　　　　[4] Proverbs xxi. 1.

was over and the third company arrived, returned home and stayed there two months. And also the third, having finished one month of service, went home when the first company arrived, to remain there for two months. And by this arrangement the administration of the royal court is taken in turn at all times of this present life.

Chap. 101. Thus, then, did he grant the first of the three aforesaid shares to such men, to each, however, according to his rank and also to his office; and the second to the craftsmen, whom he had with him in almost countless number, collected and procured from many races, who were men skilled in every kind of earthly craft; and the third share to strangers from every race, who flocked to him from places far and near asking him for money, and even to those who did not ask, to each according to his rank. He gave in a praiseworthy manner with a wonderful liberality, and cheerfully, since it is written: "The Lord loveth a cheerful giver."[1]

Chap. 102. But the second part of all his wealth, which came to him every year from revenue of every kind, and was paid into his treasury, he devoted, as we said a little while back, with all his will, to God, and ordered his officials to divide it most carefully into four equal parts, in such a way, that the first part of this division was to be prudently dispended on the poor of every race who came to him. He used to say in this connexion, that as far as human discretion could ensure it, the saying of the holy Pope Gregory ought to be observed, in which he made a wise observation about the division of alms, saying thus: "Do not give little to whom you should give much, nor much to whom you should give little, nor nothing to whom you should give something, nor anything to whom you should give nothing." And the second part he gave to the two monasteries which he himself had had built, and to those serving God in them, about which we spoke more fully a little way back; and the third to a school which he had collected very zealously from many nobles of his own race and also boys not of noble birth; and the fourth part to the neighbouring monasteries throughout the Saxon kingdom and Mercia. And in some years he also either made gifts, according to his means, to churches in Wales and Cornwall, Gaul, Brittany, Northumbria and sometimes even in Ireland, in turn, and to the servants of God dwelling in them, or else he proposed to give to them later on, provided his life and prosperity continued.[2]

Chap. 105. When these things had been completely set in order, since he desired, as he had vowed to God, to preserve half his service, and to increase it further, in as far as his capacity and his means, and indeed his infirmity, permitted, he showed himself a minute inquirer into the truth of judgments, and this especially because of his care for the poor, on whose behalf he exerted himself wonderfully by day and night in the midst of his other duties in this present life. For except for him alone, the poor had no helpers throughout that kingdom, or indeed very few; since almost all the magnates and nobles of that land had turned their minds more to the things of this world than to the things of God; indeed, in the things of this world each regarded more his own private advantage than the common good.

---

[1] II Corinthians ix. 7.

[2] In chap. 103 Asser repeats his statements about the king's division of his own service, and then, and in the following chapter, describes how the king contrived lanterns to enable him to tell the time, for the purpose of this division.

Chap. 106. Also he gave attention to judgments for the benefit of his nobles and common people, for in the assemblies of the ealdormen and the reeves they disagreed among themselves, so that hardly one of them would allow to be valid whatever had been judged by the ealdormen or reeves. And compelled by this perverse and obstinate dissension, all desired to submit to the king's judgment, and both parties quickly hastened to do so. But yet anyone who knew that on his side some injustice had been committed in that suit, was unwilling to approach the judgment of such a judge of his own accord, but only against his will, though compelled to come by force of law and covenant. For he knew that there he could not quickly conceal any part of his ill-doing, and no wonder, since the king was in truth a most skilled investigator into the exercise of justice, as in all other matters. For he shrewdly looked into almost all the judgments of his whole country which were made in his absence, to see whether they were just or unjust, and if truly he could discover any wrong in those judgments, he would on his own authority mildly inquire of those judges, either in person or by some of his faithful followers, why they had given so wrong a judgment, whether from ignorance or out of any kind of ill-will, that is, for love or fear of one party, or hatred of the other, or even for greed for anyone's money. And then, if those judges admitted that they had given such judgments because they knew no better in those cases, he wisely and moderately reproved their inexperience and folly, saying thus: "I am amazed at your presumption, that you have by God's favour and mine assumed the office and status of wise men, but have neglected the study and practice of wisdom. I command you therefore either to resign on the spot the exercise of the worldly authority you hold, or to apply yourselves much more zealously to the study of wisdom." When they had heard these words, the ealdormen and reeves hastened to turn themselves with all their might to the task of learning justice, for they were terrified and as if they had been severely punished; so that in a marvellous fashion almost all the ealdormen, reeves and thegns, who had been untaught from their childhood, gave themselves to the study of letters, preferring thus toilsomely to pursue this unaccustomed study rather than resign the exercise of their authority. But if anyone were unable to make progress in learning to read, either by reason of his age or the too great slowness of an unpractised mind, he ordered his son, if he had one, or some other kinsman, or even, if he had no one else, his own man, free man or slave, whom he had long before made to learn to read, to read Saxon books to him day and night whenever he had any leisure. And, greatly sighing from the bottom of their hearts that they had not applied themselves to such studies in their youth, they considered the youth of this age happy, who could have the good fortune to be trained in the liberal arts, accounting themselves unhappy indeed, since they had neither learnt in their youth, nor were able to learn in their old age, though they ardently desired it. But we have dwelt on this quickness of old and young to learn to read to add to knowledge of the aforesaid king.

8. Account of the Reign of Athelstan in William of Malmesbury's *De Gestis Regum Anglorum* ("Concerning the Acts of the Kings of the English")

William's account of this king is valuable mainly because of the nearly contemporary poem he came across as he was doing this part of his history, as he tells us himself. One can see from what is here given that, without it, he would have added only legendary matter to our knowledge. On William's work, see pp. 114 and 121. The best and most accessible text is in vol. I of the edition by W. Stubbs (R.S., 1887–1889) to which my paragraph references refer. It has been translated by J. A. Giles, *William of Malmesbury's Chronicle of the Kings of England*, London, 1876.

§ 131. In the year of our Lord's incarnation 924, Athelstan, son of Edward, began to reign, and he held the kingdom for 16 years. His brother Ælfweard, departing this life a few days after his father, had been buried with him at Winchester. Accordingly Athelstan, elected with great unanimity by the nobles in that same place, was crowned at the royal residence which is called Kingston, although a certain Alfred with his seditious supporters—for sedition always finds confederates—tried to oppose it. We shall relate farther on what end he came to in the king's own words.[1] The reason for this opposition was, as they say, because Athelstan was born of a concubine; but, except for this stain, if, indeed, it be true, he had nothing ignoble about him, putting all his predecessors to shade by his piety, and all the glories of their triumphs by the splendour of his own. So much better is it to have that for which you are esteemed from yourself rather than from your ancestors; because the former will be accounted your own, the latter imputed to others. I forbear to write how many and great monasteries he founded. I will not omit to say that there can scarcely have been an old monastery in the whole of England which he did not embellish either with buildings or ornaments or books or estates. Thus he honoured recent foundations avowedly, old ones with tactful kindness as if incidentally. He made a lasting treaty with Sihtric, king of the Northumbrians, giving him one of his sisters in matrimony; and when he died a year later, Athelstan subjected that province to himself, having driven out a certain Ealdwulf who had rebelled.[2] And since a noble spirit, once roused, attempts greater things, he forced Idwal, king of all the Welsh, and Constantine, king of the Scots, to yield their kingdoms. Yet not long afterwards, moved by pity, he restored them to their former position to rule under himself, declaring that it was more glorious to make a king than to be a king. His last contest was with Olaf, son of Sihtric,[3] who crossed his frontiers in the hope of usurping the kingdom, along with the aforesaid Constantine, again in rebellion. And since Athelstan deliberately retired, in order that he might more gloriously defeat the now attacking foe, this most audacious youth,

---

[1] This refers to a spurious charter of this king which William quotes after this extract, in which the king is made to say that Alfred, jealous of his life and happiness, had tried to blind him in Winchester, and was sent for trial to Rome. He was struck down by divine vengeance while swearing a false oath on St. Peter's altar, dying three days later. His lands were confiscated, and the king gave some to Malmesbury.

[2] Probably a member of the ruling house of Bamburgh, though this rebellion is not mentioned elsewhere.

[3] The leader at the battle of *Brunanburh* was Olaf, Guthfrith's son, though Sihtric's son may have been present.

intent on lawless deeds, had proceeded far into England, and was at length opposed at
Brunefeld[1] by the great strategy of the leaders and strong forces of soldiers. When
Olaf perceived such danger to threaten, he cunningly undertook the role of a scout;
laying aside the trappings of kingship and taking in his hands a harp, he reached the
tent of our king, where, singing before the entrance and now and then touching the
resounding strings with a sweet loud sound, he was easily admitted, professing himself
a minstrel who earned his daily livelihood by this art. He captivated the king and the
companions at his board for some time with the musical harmony, while in the midst
of his playing he scrutinized everything with his eyes. When satiety of eating had put
an end to these delights and the nobles' conversation turned again to the stern business
of waging war, he was ordered to depart and received a reward for his song. Disdain-
ing to carry it away, he hid it under him in the ground. This was noticed by a certain
person who had once served under him, and immediately told to Athelstan. When
he blamed the man for not betraying the enemy when he stood before him, he
received this reply: "The same oath which lately, O king, I made to you, I once
gave to Olaf; and if you had seen me violate it against him, you could beware a
similar act against yourself. But condescend to take your servant's advice to move
away your tent; and, if you stay in another place until the rest of your forces arrive,
you will with a moderate delay crush the enemy who is impudently attacking you."
His words were approved and that place was abandoned. Olaf, coming well prepared
by night, killed a certain bishop with all his household, who had reached the army
in the evening and in ignorance of what had occurred had pitched his tent there on
account of the evenness of the green plain. Then proceeding farther, Olaf came upon
the king himself unprepared, for he had given himself up to profound sleep, not
fearing at all that the enemy would dare such an attack. But when, roused from bed
by so great an uproar, he urged his men to battle as much as he could through the
darkness, by chance his sword fell from its scabbard; wherefore, when all things were
full of dread and blind confusion, he invoked God and St. Aldhelm, and replacing
his hand on the scabbard, he found a sword, which today is kept in the kings' treasury
on account of the miracle. It can, as they say, be engraved on one side, but never
inlaid with gold or silver. Relying on this gift from God, and at the same time, because it was now getting light, attacking the Norseman, unwearied he put him to
flight with his army the whole day until evening. There fell Constantine, king of the
Scots,[2] a man of treacherous boldness and vigorous old age, and five other kings and
twelve earls and almost all the host of the barbarians; the few who escaped were
preserved to receive the faith of Christ.

§ 132. Concerning this king, a firm opinion is current among the English, that
no one more just or learned administered the State. A few days ago I discovered that
he was versed in letters, from a certain very old book, in which the author struggled
with the difficulty of his matter, unable to express his meaning as he wished. I would
append here his words for the sake of brevity, if he did not range beyond belief in
praise of the prince, in that kind of expression which Tullius, the king of Roman

---

[1] The same place is meant as the *Brunanburh* of the poem; see No. 1, p. 200.
[2] Older sources show that it was Constantine's son, not himself, who was killed at this battle.

eloquence, in his book on rhetoric calls bombastic. The custom of that time excuses the diction; the affection for Athelstan, who was still alive,[1] lends colour to the excess of praise. I shall add, therefore, in a familiar style a few matters which may seem to augment the record of his greatness.

§ 133. King Edward, after many noble achievements both in war and in peace, a few days before his death repressed the contumacy of the city of Chester, which was in revolt in alliance with the Britons; and having placed there a garrison of soldiers, he was seized by sickness, and ended the present life at the residence of Farndon, and, as I have said above, was buried at Winchester. Then, by his father's command and testament, Athelstan was acclaimed king, recommended by his age, of thirty years, and the maturity of his wisdom. For also his grandfather Alfred had formerly prayed for a prosperous reign for him, seeing and affectionately embracing him when he was a boy of handsome appearance and graceful manners; and he had him made a knight at a very early age, giving him a scarlet cloak, a jewelled belt, and a Saxon sword with a gold scabbard. Afterwards he had arranged that he should be brought up in the court of his daughter Æthelflæd and his son-in-law Ethelred; and there, reared by the great care of his aunt and that most famous ealdorman, in expectation of a kingdom, he trampled down and destroyed envy by the glory of his virtues, and after the death of his father and the decease of his brother he was crowned king at Kingston. Hence, at the glory of such happy events and the joy of that day, the poet exclaims, not without cause:

"A royal son prolonged a noble line, when a splendid gem illumined our darkness, the great Athelstan, glory of the country, way of rectitude, noble integrity, unable to be turned from the truth. Given at his father's command to the learning of the schools, he feared stern masters with their clattering rod, and, avidly drinking the honey of learning, he passed not childishly the years of childhood. Soon, clad in the flower of young manhood, he practised the pursuit of arms at his father's orders. Nor in this did the duties of war prove him remiss, as later his care of the state showed also. His father, famed to every age, fulfilled his destiny, to conquer all ages with eternal fame; then the young man's name was acclaimed in omen of the kingdom, that he might hold auspiciously the hereditary reins. The nobles assemble and place the crown, pontiffs pronounce a curse on faithless men; fire glows among the people with more than wonted festivity, and by various signs they disclose their deepest feelings. Each burns to show his affection to the king; one fears, one hopes, high hope dispels fear; the palace seeths and overflows with royal splendour. Wine foams everywhere, the great hall resounds with tumult, pages scurry to and fro, servers speed on their tasks; stomachs are filled with delicacies, minds with song. One makes the harp resound, another contends with praises; there sounds in unison: 'To thee the praise, to thee the glory, O Christ.' The king drinks in this honour with eager gaze, graciously bestowing due courtesy on all."

[1] The last line of the poem as given by William shows that Athelstan was dead when it was composed.

§ 134. When the ceremony of consecration had been performed, lest he should belie the hope of the citizens and fall short of their opinion, Athelstan entirely subjugated all England by the terror of his name alone, except only the Northumbrians. For a certain Sihtric ruled over them, a barbarian by race and disposition, a kinsman of that Gurmund[1] of whom we read in the history of King Alfred, and though he had scoffed at the power of preceding kings, he voluntarily sought affinity with Athelstan with humble messengers; and himself hastily followed and confirmed the words of the envoys. Therefore he was honoured both by union with his sister and by manifold gifts, and laid the basis of a perpetual treaty. But, as I recall what was said above, being cut off from life a year later, he gave Athelstan the opportunity of joining Northumbria, which belonged to him both by ancient right and recent marriage alliance, to his own part. Then Olaf, son of Sihtric, fled to Ireland, and his brother Guthfrith to Scotland; the king's men followed at once, being sent to Constantine, king of the Scots, and Owain, king of the Cumbrians, to demand the fugitive under threat of war. The barbarians had no intention of refusing, but on the contrary, coming without delay to a place which is called Dacre, they surrendered themselves and their kingdoms to the king of the English. By virtue of this treaty, the king himself stood sponsor to the son of Constantine whom he had ordered to be baptized. Yet Guthfrith escaped, slipping away by flight in the midst of the preparations for the journey, with a certain Thurferth, earl of various regions, and soon he besieged York and urged the townsfolk to rebellion, now with entreaties and now with threats; and, succeeding with neither, he went away. And not long afterwards both were shut up in a certain fortress, but eluded the vigilance of the guards in flight. Of these two, Thurferth soon died, shipwrecked on the shore, left as a prey to fishes; Guthfrith, driven about with many hardships by land and sea, finally came to court a suppliant. He was there peacefully received by the king and sumptuously feasted with him for four days, and then, an inveterate pirate, accustomed to live in water like a fish, he went back to his ships. Meanwhile Athelstan razed to the ground the fortress which the Danes had formerly fortified in York, that there might be nowhere for perfidy to shelter; the booty which had been found in the fortress, and which was indeed most plentiful, was generously divided, to each man his share. For this man had laid this charge on himself, to rake no wealth into his own money-bags, but liberally to expend all his acquisitions either on monasteries or on his loyal followers. By this, throughout his life, he emptied his paternal treasury, by this, the lawful gains of his own victories. He was affable and kind to the servants of God, pleasant and courteous to the laymen, serious, out of regard for his majesty, to the magnates, kind and moderate to the lesser folk, out of condescension for their poverty, putting aside the pride of kingship. He was, as we have learnt, not beyond what is becoming in stature, and slender in body; his hair, as we have ourselves seen from his relics, flaxen, beautifully mingled with gold threads. He was much beloved by his subjects out of admiration of his courage and humility, but like a thunderbolt to rebels by his invincible steadfastness. He forced the rulers of the North Welsh (*i.e.* the Northern Britons)[2]

---

[1] William has previously explained that his countrymen (the Normans) call Guthrum by this name.
[2] The people of Wales, as opposed to the West Welsh, the people of Cornwall.

to meet him at the city of Hereford and to submit after they had resisted for
some time; thus he carried into effect what no king before him had even dared to
think of, that they were to pay to him annually in the name of tribute 20 pounds of
gold, 300 of silver, to add 25,000 oxen, besides as many dogs as he chose, which
could discover with their keen scent the dens and lurking-places of wild beasts, and
birds which were trained to make a prey of other birds in the air. When he had
departed from there, he turned himself to the West Britons, who are called Corn-
Welsh; who, being situated in the west of Britain, look across at Cornouaille.[1]
Attacking them also with vigour, he compelled them to leave Exeter, which they
had up to that time inhabited with equal rights with the English; fixing the boundary
of their province beyond the River Tamar, just as he had established the River Wye
as the frontier for the North Britons. Accordingly, when he had cleansed that city
by purging it of that vile people, he fortified it with towers and surrounded it with
a wall of squared stone. And although that barren and unfruitful soil can scarcely
produce poor oats, and frequently the empty husk without the grain, yet because of
the magnificence of the city and the wealth of the inhabitants, and also of the great
concourse of strangers, there so abounds there every kind of merchandise that you
may desire nothing in vain which you think conducible to human profit. Many noble
traces of him are to be seen both in the city and in the neighbouring district, which
are better described by the tongue of the natives than by my pen.

§ 135. On this account all Europe proclaimed his praises, extolled his excellence
to the skies; foreign kings rightly considered themselves fortunate if they could buy
his friendship either by marriage alliance or gifts. A certain Harold, king of the
Norwegians, sent him a ship which had a gold beak and purple sail, surrounded
inside with a dense rank of gilded shields. The names of his envoys were Helgrim
and Osfrid; who, being royally entertained in the city of York, were compensated
for the labours of their journey with fitting gifts. Henry the First, son of Conrad
(for there were many of this name), king of the Germans and emperor of the Romans,
demanded Athelstan's sister for his son Otho, passing over so many neighbouring
kings, since from a distance he perceived in Athelstan nobility of lineage and greatness
of mind; for these two qualities had so taken up a united abode in him that there
could be no one either more illustrious or noble of race or more courageous or
powerful of disposition. Wherefore, when he had considered carefully that he had
four sisters, in whom, except for difference in age, there was no disparity of beauty,
he sent two to the emperor at his suit; it has already been related how he disposed of
them in marriage.[2] The third was chosen in wedlock by Louis, prince of Aquitaine,
a descendant of Charles the Great. The fourth, in whom was united by nature the
whole essence of beauty which the others had in part, Hugh, king of the Franks,[3]
sought for from her brother by messengers. The leader of this embassy was Adelolf,
son of Baldwin, count of Flanders, by Æthelswith, daughter of King Edward.[4]

[1] In Brittany.
[2] In §§ 112 and 126, we are told that one was married to Otto, the other to a 'duke' near the Alps. R. L.
Poole (Eng. Hist. Rev., XXVI, pp. 313–317) suggests that he was Conrad of Burgundy.
[3] Hugh was duke, not king, of the Franks.
[4] This is an error. Her name was Ælfthryth and she was daughter of King Alfred, and sister, not daughter,
of Edward.

When he had set forth the wooer's requests in an assembly of nobles at Abingdon, he offered indeed most ample gifts, which might instantly satisfy the cupidity of the most avaricious: perfumes such as never before had been seen in England; jewellery, especially of emeralds, in whose greenness the reflected sun lit up the eyes of the bystanders with a pleasing light; many fleet horses, with trappings, "champing", as Maro says, "on bits of ruddy gold";[1] a vase of onyx, carved with such subtle engravers' art that the cornfields seemed really to wave, the vines really to bud, the forms of the men really to move, and so clear and polished that it reflected like a mirror the faces of the onlookers; the sword of Constantine the Great, on which could be read the name of the ancient owner in letters of gold; on the pommel also above thick plates of gold you could see an iron nail fixed, one of the four which the Jewish faction prepared for the crucifixion of our Lord's body; the spear of Charles the Great, which, whenever that most invincible emperor, leading an army against the Saracens, hurled it against the enemy, never let him depart without the victory; it was said to be the same which, driven by the hand of the centurion into our Lord's side, opened by the gash of that precious wound Paradise for wretched mortals; the standard of Maurice, the most blessed martyr and prince of the Theban legion, by which the same king was wont in the Spanish war to break asunder the battalions of the enemies, however fierce and dense, and to force them to flight;[2] a diadem, precious certainly for its quantity of gold, but more for its gems, whose splendour so threw flashes of light on the onlookers that the more anyone strove to fix his gaze on it, the more was he driven back and forced to give in; a piece of the holy and adorable Cross enclosed in crystal, where the eye, penetrating the substance of the stone, could discern what was the colour of the wood and what the quantity; a portion also of the crown of thorns, similarly enclosed, which the madness of the soldiers placed on Christ's sacred head in mockery of his kingship.

The most august king, delighted with such great and exquisite gifts, responded with hardly inferior presents, and moreover gladdened the heart of the eager suitor by union with his sister. And, indeed, he enriched succeeding kings with these gifts, but on Malmesbury he bestowed part of the Cross and the crown, by the support of which, I believe, the place still flourishes, though it has suffered so many shipwrecks of its liberty, so many injuries from claimants. For he also ordered to be honourably buried in this place the sons of his uncle Æthelweard, Ælfwine and Æthelwine, whom he had lost in the battle against Olaf, declaring also that the repose of his own body was to be there. Concerning this battle, it is time that we should give the account of that poet from whom we have excerpted all these particulars.

"He had passed five and three and four years ruling his subjects by law, subduing tyrants by force, when there returned that plague and hateful ruin of Europe. Now the fierce savagery of the North couches on our land, now the pirate Olaf, deserting the sea, camps in the field, breathing forbidden and savage threats. At the will of the king of the Scots, the northern land lends a quiet assent

---

[1] *Aeneid*, VII, 279.
[2] See L. H. Loomis, "The Holy Relics of Charlemagne and King Athelstan: the Lances of Longinus and St. Mauricius", *Speculum*, XXV, 1950.

to the raving fury; and now they swell with pride, now frighten the air with words. The natives give way, the whole region yields to the proud. For since our king, confident and eager in youth, deeming his service done, had long spent slow leisure hours, they despoiled everything with continuous ravages, driving out the people, setting fire to the fields. The green crops withered in the fields, the blighted cornfield mocked at the husbandman's prayers. So great was the force of foot-troops, so fierce that of horsemen, a host of countless coursers. At length the complaining rumour roused the king, not to let himself thus be branded that his arms gave way before the barbarian axe. There is no delay; he fiercely unfolds in the wind standards, leading victorious cohorts, a hundred banners. A vigorous force of men, a hundred thousand strong, follow their standards to the scene of battle. The mighty report of their approach terrified the raiders, the din so shook the legions of the plunderers, that, dropping their spoils, they sought their own lands. But the multitude left behind, destroyed with a pitiable slaughter, polluted the thirsty air with foul stench. Olaf fled, one of so many thousands, a hostage of death, fortune's noble pledge, to hold power when Athelstan was dead."[1]

---

[1] Olaf occupied York before the end of the year in which Athelstan died, and by a treaty in 940 he became for a short time ruler of all England north and east of Watling Street.

9. The reigns of the Danish kings of England, from Florence of Worcester

In view of the scantiness of the entries in the Anglo-Saxon Chronicle for this period, this is an important authority, and its statements should be compared with those in the material from Scandinavian sources given on pp. 309–312. On the work from which this section is taken, see pp. 113 f., 121. This part is edited by B. Thorpe, *Florentii Wigorniensis Monachi Chronicon ex Chronicis*, 1848, I, pp. 178–197; H. Petrie, *Monumenta Historica Britannica*, 1848, pp. 592–600. It is translated by J. Stevenson in *Church Historians of England*, II, pt. I, 1853, and by T. Forester in *Bohn's Antiquarian Library*, 1854.

When a few days had passed after these events,[1] and King Edmund Ironside still wished to contend with Cnut, the perfidious ealdorman Eadric and certain others would on no account suffer this to be done, but counselled him to make peace with Cnut and divide the kingdom. And when at last he consented, though unwillingly, to their suggestions, messengers passed between them and hostages were exchanged, and both kings met together at the place which is called Deerhurst; Edmund encamped with his party on the west bank of the Severn, and Cnut with his on the east bank. Then the two kings were carried by boats on to an island called Alney–and it is situated in the middle of that same river; and there, when peace, friendship and fraternity had been confirmed both with pledge and oaths, the kingdom was divided. [Edmund obtained] Wessex, East Anglia, Essex with London [and all the land on the southern bank of the River Thames], Cnut [obtaining the northern parts of England]; the crown of the kingdom, however, remained with Edmund.[2] Then, having exchanged arms and clothing, and decided the tribute which was to be paid to the naval force, they separated. But the Danes returned to the ships with the booty which they had seized, and the citizens of London made peace with them, giving a sum of money, and allowed them to stay the winter with them.

After these events, King Edmund Ironside died about the feast of the Apostle St. Andrew,[3] the fifteenth indiction,[4] at London, but was buried at Glastonbury with his grandfather, Edgar the Peaceable. And after his death, King Cnut gave orders that all the bishops and ealdormen and leading men, and all the nobles of the English people, were to be assembled at London. When they had come before him, he, as if in ignorance, questioned shrewdly those who had been witnesses between him and Edmund when they had made the pact of friendship and the division of the kingdom between them, how he and Edmund had spoken together concerning the latter's brothers and sons; whether his brothers and sons should be allowed to reign after their father in the kingdom of the West Saxons, if Edmund were to die in Cnut's lifetime. And they said that they knew beyond doubt that King Edmund had entrusted no portion of his kingdom to his brothers, either in his life or at his death;

[1] *i.e.* the battle of Ashingdon, 1016.
[2] The MSS. of Florence are corrupt at this point, and so, presumably, was the version used by Simeon of Durham, for he omits the details of the division entirely. The portions within brackets are supplied from Roger of Wendover, but I doubt whether his version represents the original text of Florence. It is at variance with the Chronicle, which allows only Wessex to Edmund. The name Cnut is not in the Lambeth and Dublin MSS. of Florence, and is a later addition in the Corpus MS. This omits also the words *corona tamen.*   [3] 30 November.   [4] The fifteenth indiction began on 24 September 1016.

and they said that they knew that Edmund wished Cnut to be the supporter and protector of his sons, until they were old enough to reign. In truth, God is to witness, they gave false testimony, and lied deceitfully, imagining both that he would be more gracious to them because of their lying, and that they would receive a big reward from him. Some of these false witnesses were put to death not long afterwards by that same king. Then after the above-mentioned inquiry, King Cnut tried to obtain from the aforesaid nobles oaths of fealty. And they swore to him that they would elect him as their king and humbly obey him, and make a payment to his army; and, accepting a pledge from his bare hand, along with oaths from the leading men of the Danes, they utterly renounced the brothers and sons of Edmund, and repudiated them as kings.

Now one of the aforesaid athelings was Eadwig, the illustrious and much honoured brother of King Edmund, and by most evil counsel they there resolved that he should be exiled. And when King Cnut had heard the servile flattery of the above-mentioned persons, and the contempt which they expressed for Eadwig, he entered his chamber rejoicing, and, calling to him the perfidious ealdorman Eadric, he inquired of him how he might entrap Eadwig, to endanger his life. And he said in reply that he knew another man, Æthelweard by name, who would be able to betray him to death more easily than he; he could have a talk with him and promise him a great reward. When he learnt the man's name, the king called him to him, saying craftily: "Thus and thus has Ealdorman Eadric spoken to me, saying that you can lay a trap for the atheling Eadwig in order to kill him. Agree now to our counsels, and you shall possess all the honours and dignities of your ancestors; and get me his head, and you will be dearer to me than my own brother." He indeed said that he would seek him out and kill him, if he could by any means. Nevertheless, he did not intend to kill him, but promised this by way of pretence; for he was sprung from a most noble English family.[1]

1017 In this year King Cnut received the dominion of the whole of England, and divided it into four parts: Wessex for himself, East Anglia for Earl Thorkel, Mercia for Ealdorman Eadric, Northumbria for Earl Eric. Also he made a treaty with the leading men and all the people, and they with him, and they established a firm friendship between them with oaths, and laid aside and put an end to all ancient enmities.[2] Then, by the counsel of the perfidious ealdorman Eadric, King Cnut outlawed the atheling Eadwig, brother of King Edmund, and Eadwig who was called "king of the *ceorls*". Yet in the course of time Eadwig was reconciled with the king, but Eadwig the atheling, deceived by the treachery of those whom he had considered hitherto his closest friends, was killed, though guiltless, in the same year by the command and request of King Cnut. Eadric advised him to kill also the young athelings, Edward and

---

[1] If, as seems probable, the person concerned is the Æthelweard whose death is mentioned in 1017, this last remark is true, for he was of royal race, a descendant of Alfred's elder brother, Ethelred.

A marginal entry in one MS. adds here: "The reverend man Leofsige, abbot of Thorney, received the bishopric of the church of Worcester."

[2] With this wording compare the proem to Cnut's laws, No. 47.

Edmund, the sons of King Edmund; but because it would be a great disgrace to him for them to perish in England, he sent them after a short passage of time to the king of the Swedes to be killed.[1] He would by no means acquiesce in his requests, although there was a treaty between them, but sent them to the king of the Hungarians, Solomon by name, to be preserved and brought up there. One of them, namely Edmund, ended his life there in the course of time; but Edward received in matrimony Agatha, daughter of the brother of the Emperor Henry, by whom he had Margaret, queen of the Scots, and the consecrated virgin Christina, and the atheling Edgar.

In the month of July, King Cnut married the widow of King Ethelred, Queen Ælfgifu. And at the Lord's Nativity, when he was in London, he gave orders for the perfidious ealdorman Eadric to be killed in the palace, because he feared to be at some time deceived by his treachery, as his former lords Ethelred and Edmund had frequently been deceived; and he ordered his body to be thrown over the wall of the city and left unburied. Along with him were killed, though guiltless, Ealdorman Northman, son of Ealdorman Leofwine and thus brother to Earl Leofric, Æthelweard, son of Ealdorman Æthelmær, and Brihtric, son of the Devonshire magnate Ælfheah. The king appointed Leofric ealdorman in the place of his brother Northman, and afterwards held him in great esteem.

1018   In this year 72,000 pounds were paid to the Danish army from the whole of England and 10,500 from London; and 40 ships remained with King Cnut, but the rest returned to Denmark. The English and the Danes came to an agreement at Oxford concerning the observance of King Edgar's law.[2]

1019   In this year Cnut, king of the English and the Danes, went to Denmark, and stayed there through the whole winter.[3]

1020   King Cnut returned to England and held a great council at Easter at Cirencester, and outlawed Ealdorman Æthelweard. Lifing, archbishop of Canterbury, departed this life, and Æthelnoth, who was called 'the Good', the son of the noble man Æthelmær, succeeded him. In the same year the church which King Cnut and Earl Thorkel had erected on the hill which is called Ashingdon was dedicated with great ceremony and glory in their presence by Wulfstan, archbishop of York, and many other bishops.[4]

1021   Cnut, king of the English and Danes, before the feast of St. Martin,[5] expelled from England Thorkel, the oft-mentioned earl, with his wife Edith. Ælfgar, bishop of the East Angles, died, and Ælfwine succeeded him.

---

[1] All accounts of the flight of the athelings have legendary features, and the name and nationality of their protectors vary considerably. All that is certain is that they did find a refuge in Hungary, and that Edward married Agatho, a kinswoman of the Emperor.   [2] See No. 1, p. 228; No. 47.
[3] One MS. adds: "Ælfmær, bishop of Selsey, having died, Æthelric succeeded."
[4] I omit a passage on the election of a bishop of Durham, summarized from the account given in Simeon's *History of the Church of Durham*. It is only in the margin of the main MS.   [5] 11 November.

1022   Æthelnoth, archbishop of Canterbury, went to Rome, and Pope Benedict received him with great honour, and gave him the *pallium*.

1023   The body of St. Ælfheah, the martyr, was translated from London to Canterbury. Wulfstan, archbishop of York, died at York on Tuesday, 28 May, but his body was removed to Ely and buried there. Ælfric Puttuc, prior of Winchester, succeeded him.

1025   Edmund, a most religious man, received the bishopric of Lindisfarne.[1]

1026   Ælfric, archbishop of York, went to Rome and received the *pallium* from Pope John. Richard II, duke of the Normans, died, and Richard III succeeded him and died in the same year. His brother Robert succeeded him.

1027   Since it was intimated to Cnut, king of the English and Danes, that the Norwegians greatly despised their king, Olaf, for his simplicity and gentleness, his justice and piety, he sent a large sum of gold and silver to certain of them, requesting them with many entreaties to reject and desert Olaf, and submit to him and let him reign over them. And when they had accepted with great avidity the things which he had sent, they sent a message back to him that they would be ready to receive him whenever he pleased to come.

1028   Cnut, king of the English and the Danes, sailed to Norway with 50 great ships, and drove out King Olaf and subjected it to himself.

1029   Cnut, king of the English and Danes and Norwegians, returned to England, and after the feast of St. Martin he sent into exile, under pretence of an embassy, the Danish earl, Hákon, who had married the noble lady, Gunnild, daughter of Cnut's sister and Wyrtgeorn,[2] king of the Wends; for he was afraid he might be either deprived of life or expelled from the kingdom by him.

1030   The aforesaid Earl Hákon perished at sea; but some say that he was killed in Orkney.[3] St. Olaf, king and martyr, son of Harold, king of the Norwegians, was unjustly killed in Norway by the Norwegians.

1031   Cnut, king of the English, Danes and Norwegians, went in great state from Denmark to Rome, and offered to St. Peter, Prince of the Apostles, immense gifts in gold and silver and other precious things, and procured from Pope John that the English quarter[4] should be freed from all taxation and toll; and on his

---

[1] This repeats, under a wrong date, what was said above *s.a.* 1020 (see p. 286, n. 4). The retention of the old name for the see, by this time at Durham, is noteworthy.

[2] The form of the name seems influenced by that of the fifth-century British king, which occurs in the Chronicle Florence had before him. It has been suggested that the Wrytsleof who witnesses a charter of Cnut's in 1026 is the same individual.

[3] Theodric, the Norwegian author of a late twelfth-century history of the kings of Norway, says that he perished in the Pentland Firth when returning from fetching his bride from England.

[4] See p. 170, n. 7.

way there and back he disbursed liberal alms to the poor, and by paying an enormous price he did away with many barriers on the way, where toll was exacted from pilgrims. Also he vowed to God before the tomb of the Apostles to emend his life and conduct; and he sent from there to England a memorable letter by a most prudent man, Lifing, who was at that time abbot of the church of Tavistock, but soon afterwards in the same year the successor of Eadnoth in the see of the church of Crediton, and who was his companion on the journey, and by his other messengers; while himself he returned from Rome by the way he had come, visiting Denmark before England.[1]

1032 The church of St. Edmund, king and martyr, was dedicated in this year.

1033 A man of great piety and modesty, Leofsige, bishop of the Hwicce, died in the episcopal residence of Kempsey on Tuesday,[2] 19 August, and, as it is right to believe, migrated to the heavenly kingdom; and his body was buried with honour in the church of St. Mary of Worcester. The abbot of Pershore, Brihtheah, the son of a sister of Wulfstan, archbishop of York, was elevated to his see.

1034 Æthelric, bishop of Lincoln,[3] died, and was buried in the monastery of Ramsey; and Eadnoth succeeded him. Malcolm, king of the Scots, died.

1035 Cnut, king of the English, before his death, appointed as king over the Norwegians Swein, who was said to be his son by Ælfgifu of Northampton, daughter of Ealdorman Ælfhelm and the noble lady Wulfrun; but some asserted that he was not the son of the king and this Ælfgifu, but that this same Ælfgifu wished to have a son by the king, but could not, and therefore ordered to be brought to her the newly born infant of a certain priest, and made the king fully believe that she had just borne him a son. He also appointed Hardacnut, his son by Queen Ælfgifu, as king over the Danes. And afterwards in this year, on Wednesday, 12 November, he ended his life at Shaftesbury, but was buried with very great ceremony in the Old Minster at Winchester. Queen Ælfgifu resided there after he had been buried.

Harold, indeed, said that he was the son of King Cnut and Ælfgifu of Northampton, although it was not true;[4] for some say that he was the son of a certain shoemaker, but that Ælfgifu had behaved in the same way with regard to him as she is said to have done in the case of Swein. For our part, since the matter is in doubt, we cannot settle what is certain about the birth of either. Harold, however, when he had seized the royal authority, sent his guards in haste to Winchester, and tyrannically deprived Queen Ælfgifu of the greater

---

[1] The letter is then given in full. We have placed it with Cnut's other enactments, as No. 49.
[2] 19 August was a Sunday, not a Tuesday, in 1033.
[3] i.e. of Dorchester. The see was not moved to Lincoln until after the Norman Conquest.
[4] The *History of the Kings* of Simeon of Durham not only omits the stories of the birth of Swein and Harold, but asserts that Cnut before he died appointed Harold as king of the English.

and better part of the treasures and riches which King Cnut had left to her, and allowed her, thus despoiled, to reside there as she had begun. And with the consent of very many of the nobility of England, he began to reign as if the legitimate heir; not, however, as powerfully as Cnut, because the more rightful heir, Hardacnut, was expected. Hence, after a short time, the kingdom of England was divided by lot, and the north part fell to Harold, the south to Hardacnut. Robert, duke of the Normans, died, and his son, William the Bastard, then a minor, succeeded him.

1036 The innocent athelings Alfred and Edward, sons of Ethelred, formerly king of the English, joining to them many Norman soldiers and crossing with a few ships from Normandy, where they had dwelt with their uncle Richard for a long time, to England, came in order to confer with their mother, who was living in Winchester. This some men in power bore with indignation and concern, because, though it was not right, they were much more devoted to Harold than to them; and especially, it is said, Earl Godwine. He, indeed, detained Alfred as he was hastening towards London to a parley with King Harold, as he had commanded, and placed him in close confinement; and of his companions some he dispersed, some he put in fetters and afterwards blinded, some he tortured by scalping and punished by cutting off their hands and feet; many also he ordered to be sold, and he killed by various and miserable deaths 600 men at Guildford. But we believe that their souls now rejoice in Paradise with the saints, whose bodies were so cruelly slain on earth, though they were free from guilt. When Queen Ælfgifu heard this, she sent her son Edward, who remained with her, back to Normandy with great haste. Then, by the orders of Godwine and certain others, the atheling Alfred was taken tightly bound to the island of Ely; but as the ship touched land, immediately, on board ship, his eyes were very cruelly torn out; and he was led thus to the monastery and given to the custody of the monks. There a short time afterwards he departed from this world, and his body was buried with fitting ceremony in the south chapel, in the western part of the church; his soul truly enjoys the bliss of Paradise.

1037 Harold, king of the Mercians and Northumbrians, was elected king by the leading men and all the people, to rule all England. Hardacnut indeed was entirely rejected, because he lingered in Denmark, and put off coming to England as he was asked; and his mother, Ælfgifu, formerly queen of the English, was expelled from England without pity at the beginning of winter. A vessel was soon prepared, and she crossed to Flanders and was received with honour by the noble Count Baldwin. As became such a man, he took care freely to supply her needs for as long as necessity demanded. In the same year, a little earlier, Æfic, the dean of Evesham, a man of great piety, died.

1038 Æthelnoth, archbishop of Canterbury, departed this life on 29 October; the seventh day after his death Æthelric, bishop of the South Saxons, died; for he had besought God that he should not live long in this world after the death of his most beloved father, Æthelnoth. He was succeeded in his bishopric by Grimcetel, and Æthelnoth in his archbishopric by the king's chaplain Eadsige. In the same year also Ælfric, bishop of the East Angles, died, and Brihtheah, bishop of the Hwicce, ended his life on Wednesday, 20 December. King Harold gave his bishopric to Lifing, bishop of Crediton; and in Ælfric's place Stigand, the king's chaplain, was appointed, but he was afterwards ejected, and Grimcetel was elected for gold,[1] and held then two dioceses, of the South Saxons and the East Angles. But Stigand was again restored and Grimcetel ejected. [And Stigand indeed held the bishopric of the South Saxons, and acquired the bishopric of the East Angles for his brother Æthelmær. And accounting this little for his ambition, Stigand ascended the thrones of Winchester and Canterbury, and was hardly and with difficulty prevailed on to let a bishop of their own be ordained for the South Saxons. After Æthelmær, Arfast was bishop of Elmham, and, lest he should appear to have done nothing—since the Normans are most eager for future fame—he transferred the see of Elmham to Thetford.][2]

1039 In this year there was a very severe winter. Brihtmær, bishop of Lichfield, died, and Wulfsige succeeded him. The Welsh killed Edwin, brother of Earl Leofric, and the noble king's thegns Thurkil and Ælfgeat, son of Eadsige, and many men with them. Hardacnut, king of the Danes, sailed to Flanders and came to his mother, Ælfgifu.

1040 Harold, king of the English, died at London, and was buried in Westminster. After his burial, the nobles of almost the whole of England sent envoys to Hardacnut at Bruges, where he was staying with his mother, and, thinking that they were acting advisably, asked him to come to England and take the sceptre of the kingdom. He prepared 60 ships, and manned them with Danish troops, sailed over to England before midsummer, and was received with rejoicing by all, and was soon raised to the throne of the kingdom; but during the time of his rule he did nothing worthy of royal power. For, as soon as he began to reign, being not unmindful of the injuries which his predecessor King Harold, who was reputed his brother, had done either against him or against his mother, he sent to London Ælfric, archbishop of York, Earl Godwine, Stir, the master of his household, Eadric his steward, Thrond his executioner, and other men of high position, and ordered the body of this Harold to be dug up and thrown into a marsh; and when it had been thrown there, he gave orders for it to be pulled out and thrown into the River Thames. But a short

---

[1] *pro auro* is the reading of one MS. The others have instead *pro eo*, 'in his place'. William of Malmesbury has *pro auro*.

[2] The passage in brackets is only in the margin of the main MS. Simeon of Durham omits all that relates to the East Anglian see. Florence has taken his information from William of Malmesbury (*De Gestis Pontificum*, ed. Hamilton, p. 150), and it is full of errors, on which see R. R. Darlington, *Eng. Hist Rev.*, LI, p. 400 n. Stigand was not bishop of Selsey and did not become bishop of Elmham until 1043. He was deposed but soon afterwards restored, and was succeeded by Æthelmær in 1047. Grimcetel was bishop of Selsey until his death in 1047.

time afterwards it was picked up by a certain fisherman and borne in haste to the Danes, and buried by them with honour in the cemetery which they had in London.

When this was done, he enjoined that eight marks were to be paid to each oarsman of his fleet, and twelve to each steersman, from the whole of England, a tribute so heavy, indeed, that hardly anyone could pay it; on which account he became extremely hateful to all who had before greatly desired his coming.

Besides these things, he burned with great anger against Earl Godwine and Lifing, bishop of Worcester, because of the killing of his brother Alfred, of which Ælfric, archbishop of York, and some others accused them. For that reason he deprived Lifing of the bishopric of Worcester and gave it to Ælfric; but the next year he took it from Ælfric and graciously gave it back to Lifing, who had made his peace with him. But Godwine gave to the king for his friendship a skilfully made galley, having a gilded prow, and furnished with the best tackle, handsomely equipped with suitable weapons and 80 picked soldiers, each of whom had on his arms two gold armlets, weighing 16 ounces, wore a triple mail-shirt, a partly gilded helmet on his head, and had a sword with a gilded hilt fastened round his loins, and a Danish battle-axe rimmed with gold and silver hanging from his left shoulder, and in his left hand a shield, whose boss and studs were gilded, in his right hand a spear which in the English language is called *ætgar*.[1] Moreover, he swore to the king, with the ealdormen and the more important thegns of almost the whole of England, that it was not by his counsel nor his will that his brother was blinded, but that his lord King Harold had ordered him to do what he did.

1041 In this year Hardacnut, king of the English, sent his housecarls through all the provinces of his kingdom to collect the tax which he had imposed. Two of them, namely Feader and Thurstan, were killed on Monday, 4 May, by the people of Worcestershire and the citizens, in an upper room of a tower of the monastery of Worcester, to which they had fled to hide themselves when a riot had broken out. Hence the king, moved to anger, sent there to avenge their slaying Thuri of the Midlanders,[2] Leofric of the Mercians, Godwine of the West Saxons, Siward of the Northumbrians, Hrani of the *Magonsæte*,[3] and the other earls of the whole of England, and almost all his housecarls, with a great army, while Ælfric was still holding the bishopric of Worcester; ordering them to kill, if they could, all the men, to plunder and burn the city and to lay waste the whole province. When the 12 November arrived, they began to lay waste both the city and the province, and did not cease to do so for four days; but they captured or killed few either of the citizens or of the men of the province, because, having notice of their coming, the people of the province had fled in

---

[1] Apparently a sort of javelin.
[2] It is uncertain just what this earldom comprised. It seems to have included Huntingdonshire; the name may be from its position between East Anglia and Mercia, or it may be a reminiscence of the old Middle Anglia.
[3] The inhabitants of an area roughly approximating to modern Herefordshire. See p. 64.

all directions; a great number of the citizens, however, took refuge in a certain small island which is called Bevere, situated in the middle of the Severn, and having made a fortification, defended themselves manfully against their enemies until peace was restored and they were allowed to return home freely. Accordingly, on the fifth day, when the city had been burnt, everyone went off to his own parts with much booty, and the king's wrath was at once appeased. Not long afterwards, Edward, the son of Ethelred, formerly king of the English, came from Normandy, where he had lived in exile for many years, to England, and being honourably received by his brother, King Hardacnut, remained in his court.

1042 At a feast at the place called Lambeth, at which Osgod Clapa, a man of great power, was giving his daughter Gytha in marriage to Tofi, surnamed the Proud, a Dane and an influential man, with much rejoicing, Hardacnut, king of the English, while he stood cheerful, in health and high spirits, drinking with the aforesaid bride and certain men, fell suddenly to the ground by a sad fall in the midst of his drinking, and remaining thus speechless, expired on Tuesday, 8 June, and was borne to Winchester and buried next his father, King Cnut. And his brother Edward was raised to the throne in London, chiefly by the exertions of Earl Godwine and Lifing, bishop of Worcester. His father was Ethelred, whose father was Edgar, whose father was Edmund, whose father was Edward the Elder, whose father was Alfred.

10. The poem on the battle of Maldon

That the 325 lines which survive deal with the engagement at Maldon mentioned in 991 in the Chronicle is proved by their mention of Brihtnoth's death. Mr. Laborde has localized the fight more closely from the indications in the poem, placing it some distance east of the town. He thinks that the Danes were at the beginning on the island of Northey in the estuary of the Blackwater (*Pante*), and were allowed by Brihtnoth to cross to the mainland by a causeway (called both 'bridge' and 'ford') which was passable at low tide. The beginning of the poem is lost, and we do not know how long it originally was. There are some passages in the poem to suggest that before deciding on battle Brihtnoth had held a meeting earlier in the day, and it may have been at that that Eadric and Offa had made the vows mentioned in the poem. Probably the poem is incomplete at the end also, and this fact weakens the argument that it could not have been composed by anyone present at the battle, since no one would wish to advertise his own survival, 'lordless'. Some of the loyal thegns may have recovered from wounds, or have remained fighting until the Danes withdrew, at nightfall or before. Whoever the poet was, the information in the latter part of the poem can only come from one who did not share in the general flight, unless, of course, it is fictitious. Possibly the poem was commissioned by Brihtnoth's widow, whom we know to have given to Ely a tapestry depicting the deeds of her husband. See also p. 121.

The Danish leaders are said by Florence and writers dependent on him to be Justin and Guthmund, Steita's son, whereas MS. 'A' of the Chronicle mentions Olaf (*i.e.* Tryggvason) as leader. Florence may have taken his information from the treaty (see No. 42) which mentions all three. He may have omitted Olaf as the other versions of the Chronicle do not mention him until 994. The absence of Olaf's name from the poem is no argument against his presence; the poem is a fragment, and in any case Olaf's importance would not be realized in 991.

Calendar evidence shows that the battle was fought on 10 or 11 August.

Almost all Anglo-Saxon Readers include this poem. There is also a convenient edition by E. V. Gordon, in Methuen's Old English Library, 1937, and it is very well edited with translation by M. Ashdown, *English and Norse Documents*, pp. 3–37, 72–90. By her kind permission I reproduce here her translation.

Then he bade each warrior leave his horse, drive it afar and go forth on foot, and trust to his hands and to his good intent.

Then Offa's kinsman first perceived that the earl would suffer no faintness of heart; he let his loved hawk fly from his hand to the wood and advanced to the fight. By this it might be seen that the lad would not waver in the strife now that he had taken up his arms.

With him Eadric would help his lord, his chief in the fray. He advanced to war with spear in hand; as long as he might grasp his shield and broad sword, he kept his purpose firm. He made good his vow, now that the time had come for him to fight before his lord.

Then Brihtnoth began to array his men; he rode and gave counsel and taught his warriors how they should stand and keep their ground, bade them hold their shields aright, firm with their hands and fear not at all. When he had meetly arrayed his host, he alighted among the people where it pleased him best, where he knew his body-guard to be most loyal.

Then the messenger of the vikings stood on the bank, he called sternly, uttered words, boastfully speaking the seafarers' message to the earl, as he stood on the shore. "Bold seamen have sent me to you, and bade me say, that it is for you to send treasure quickly in return for peace, and it will be better for you all that you buy off an attack with tribute, rather than that men so fierce as we should give you battle. There is no need that we destroy each other, if you are rich enough for this. In return for the gold we are ready to make a truce with you. If you who are richest determine to redeem your people, and to give to the seamen on their own terms wealth to win their friendship and make peace with us, we will betake us to our ships with the treasure, put to sea and keep faith with you."

Brihtnoth lifted up his voice, grasped his shield and shook his supple spear, gave forth words, angry and resolute, and made him answer: "Hear you, searover, what this folk says? For tribute they will give you spears, poisoned point and ancient sword, such war gear[1] as will profit you little in the battle. Messenger of the seamen, take back a message, say to your people a far less pleasing tale, how that there stands here with his troop an earl of unstained renown, who is ready to guard this realm, the home of Ethelred my lord, people and land; it is the heathen that shall fall in the battle. It seems to me too poor a thing that you should go with our treasure unfought to your ships, now that you have made your way thus far into our land. Not so easily shall you win tribute; peace must be made with point and edge, with grim battle-play, before we give tribute."

Then he bade the warriors advance, bearing their shields, until they all stood on the river bank. Because of the water neither host might come to the other. There came the tide, flowing in after the ebb; the currents met and joined. All too long it seemed before they might clash their spears together. Thus in noble array they stood about Pante's stream, the flower of the East Saxons and the shipmen's host. None of them might harm another, unless a man should meet his death through a javelin's flight.

The tide went out, the seamen stood ready, many a viking eager for war. Then the bulwark of heroes appointed a warrior, hardy in war, to hold the bridge, Wulfstan was his name, accounted valiant among his kin.[2] It was he, Ceola's son, who with his javelin shot down the first man that was so hardy as to set foot upon the bridge. There with Wulfstan stood warriors unafraid, Ælfhere and Maccus, a dauntless pair; they had no thought of flight at the ford, but warded themselves stoutly against the foe, as long as they might wield their weapons. When the vikings knew and saw full well that they had to deal with grim defenders of the bridge, the hateful strangers betook themselves to guile, craved leave to land, to pass over the ford and lead their men across. Then the earl, in his pride, began to give ground all too much to the hateful folk; Brihthelm's son called over the cold water (the warriors gave ear): "Now is the way open before you; come quickly, men, to meet us in battle. God alone knows to whom it shall fall to hold the field."

The wolves of slaughter pressed forward, they recked not for the water, that viking host; west over Pante, over the gleaming water they came with their bucklers, the seamen came to land with their linden shields.

There, ready to meet the foe, stood Brihtnoth and his men. He bade them form the war-hedge with their shields, and hold their ranks stoutly against the foe. The battle was now at hand, and the glory that comes in strife. Now was the time when those who were doomed should fall. Clamour arose; ravens went circling, the eagle greedy for carrion. There was a cry upon earth.

[1] Perhaps ironically, Brihtnoth uses a term that describes the payment to a lord on his thegn's death, the 'heriot', originally, and usually, paid in weapons and horses.
[2] Or, "a bold man of a bold kin".

They let the spears, hard as files, fly from their hands, well-ground javelins. Bows were busy, point pierced shield; fierce was the rush of battle, warriors fell on either hand, men lay dead. Wulfmær was wounded, he took his place among the slain; Brihtnoth's kinsman, his sister's son, was cruelly cut down with swords. Then was payment given to the vikings; I heard that Edward smote one fiercely with his blade, and spared not his stroke, so that the doomed warrior fell at his feet. For this his lord gave his chamberlain thanks when time allowed.

Thus the stout-hearted warriors held their ground in the fray. Eagerly they strove, those men at arms, who might be the first to take with his spear the life of some doomed man. The slain fell to the earth.

The men stood firm; Brihtnoth exhorted them, bade each warrior, who would win glory in fight against the Danes, to give his mind to war.

Then came one, strong in battle; he raised his weapon, his shield to defend him, and bore down upon the man; the earl, no less resolute, advanced against the 'churl'. Each had an evil intent toward the other. Then the pirate sent a southern spear, so that the lord of warriors was stricken. He pushed with his shield so that the shaft was splintered, and shivered the spear so that it sprang back again. The warrior was enraged; he pierced with his lance the proud viking who had given him the wound. The warrior was deft; he drove his spear through the young man's neck; his hand guided it so that it took the life of his deadly foe. Quickly he shot down another, so that his corselet burst asunder; he was wounded through his mail in the breast, a poisoned point pierced his heart. The earl was the more content; then the proud man laughed, and gave thanks to his Creator for the day's work that the Lord had granted him.

Then one of the warriors let a dart fly from his hand, so that it pierced all too deeply Ethelred's noble thegn. By his side stood a warrior not yet full grown, a boy in war. Right boldly he drew from the warrior the bloody spear, Wulfstan's son, Wulfmær the young, and let the weapon, wondrous strong, speed back again; the point drove in so that he who had so cruelly pierced his lord lay dead on the ground. Then a man, all armed, approached the earl, with intent to bear off the warrior's treasure, his raiment and his rings and his well-decked sword. Then Brihtnoth drew his blade, broad and of burnished edge, and smote upon his mail. All too quickly one of the seamen checked his hand, crippling the arm of the earl. Then his golden-hilted sword fell to the earth; he could not use his hard blade nor wield a weapon. Yet still the white-haired warrior spoke as before, emboldened his men and bade the heroes press on. He could no longer now stand firm on his feet. The earl looked up to heaven and cried aloud: "I thank thee, Ruler of Nations, for all the joys that I have met with in this world. Now I have most need, gracious Creator, that thou grant my spirit grace, that my soul may fare to thee, into thy keeping, Lord of Angels, and pass in peace. It is my prayer to thee that fiends of hell may not entreat it shamefully."

Then the heathen wretches cut him down, and both the warriors who stood near by, Ælfnoth and Wulfmær, lay overthrown; they yielded their lives at their lord's side.

11

Then those who had no wish to be there turned from the battle. Odda's sons were first in the flight; Godric for one turned his back on war, forsook the hero who had given him many a steed. He leapt upon the horse that had been his lord's, on the trappings to which he had no right. With him his brothers both galloped away, Godwine and Godwig, they had no taste for war, but turned from the battle and made for the wood, fled to the fastness and saved their lives, and more men than was fitting at all, if they had but remembered all the favours that he had done them for their good. It was as Offa had told them[1] on the field when he held a council, that many were speaking proudly there, who later would not stand firm in time of need.

Now was fallen the people's chief, Ethelred's earl. All the retainers saw how their lord lay dead. Then the proud thegns pressed on, hastened eagerly, those undaunted men. All desired one of two things, to lose their lives or to avenge the one they loved.

With these words Ælfric's son urged them to go forth, a warrior young in years, he lifted up his voice and spoke with courage. Ælfwine said: "Remember the words that we uttered many a time over the mead, when on the bench, heroes in hall, we made our boast about hard strife. Now it may be proved which of us is bold! I will make known my lineage to all, how I was born in Mercia of a great race. Ealhhelm was my grandfather called, a wise ealdorman, happy in this world's goods. Thegns shall have no cause to reproach me among my people that I was ready to forsake this action, and seek my home, now that my lord lies low, cut down in battle. This is no common grief to me, he was both my kinsman and my lord."

Then he advanced (his mind was set on revenge), till he pierced with his lance a seaman from among the host, so that the man lay on the earth, borne down with his weapon.

Then Offa began to exhort his comrades, his friends and companions, that they should press on. He lifted up his voice and shook his ash-wood spear: "Lo! Ælfwine, you have exhorted all us thegns in time of need. Now that our lord lies low, the earl on the ground, it is needful for us all that each warrior embolden the other to war, as long as he can keep and hold his weapon, hard blade, spear and trusty sword. Godric, Odda's cowardly son, has betrayed us all. Too many a man, when he rode on that horse, on that proud steed, deemed that it was our lord. So was our host divided on the field, the shield-wall broken. A curse upon his deed, in that he has put so many a man to flight!"

Leofsunu lifted up his voice and raised his shield, his buckler to defend him, and gave him answer: "This I avow, that I will not flee a foot-space hence, but will press on and avenge my liege-lord in the fight. About Sturmer the steadfast heroes will have no need to reproach me now that my lord has fallen, that I made my way home, and turned from the battle, a lordless man. Rather. shall weapon, spear-point and iron blade, be my end." He pressed on wrathful and fought sternly, despising flight.

Dunhere spoke and shook his lance; a simple churl, he cried above them all, and bade each warrior avenge Brihtnoth: "He that thinks to avenge his lord, his chief in the press, may not waver nor reck for his life." Then they went forth, and took no

---

[1] I take the words *on dæg*, omitted in this translation, not as a tag but as significant. This expression normally means 'on that day' and may here imply a meeting and discussion before the battle, probably described in the lost beginning of the poem.

thought for life; the retainers began to fight hardily, those fierce warriors. They prayed God that they might take vengeance for their lord, and work slaughter among their foes.

The hostage began to help them eagerly; he came of a stout Northumbrian kin, Æscferth was his name, Ecglaf's son. He did not flinch in the war-play, but urged forth the dart unceasingly. Now he shot upon a shield, now he hit his man; ever he dealt out wounds, as long as he could wield his weapons.

Still in the van stood Edward the Long, bold and eager; he spoke vaunting words, how that he would not flee a foot-space or turn back, now that his lord lay dead. He broke the shield-wall and fought against the warriors, until he had taken due vengeance upon the seamen for his lord. Then he himself lay among the slain.

So too did Æthelric, Sigebriht's brother, a noble companion, eager and impetuous, he fought right fiercely, and many another. They clove the hollow shield and defended themselves boldly. The buckler's edge burst and the corselet sang a fearful song.

Then Offa smote a seaman in the fight, so that he fell to the earth. Gadd's kinsman too was brought to the ground, Offa himself was quickly cut to pieces in the fray. Yet he had compassed what he had promised his chief, as he bandied vows with his generous lord in days gone by,[1] that they should both ride home to the town unhurt or fall among the host, perish of wounds on the field. He lay, as befits a thegn, at his lord's side.

Then came a crashing of shields; seamen pressed on, enraged by war; the spear oft pierced the life-house of the doomed. Wigstan went forth, Thurstan's son, and fought against the men. Wighelm's child was the death of three in the press, before he himself lay among the slain.

That was a fierce encounter; warriors stood firm in the strife. Men were falling, worn out with their wounds; the slain fell to the earth.

Oswold and Eadwold all the while, that pair of brothers, urged on the men; prayed their dear kinsmen to stand firm in the hour of need, and use their weapons in no weak fashion.

Brihtwold spoke and grasped his shield (he was an old companion[2]); he shook his ash-wood spear and exhorted the men right boldly: "Thoughts must be the braver, heart more valiant, courage the greater as our strength grows less. Here lies our lord, all cut down, the hero in the dust. Long may he mourn who thinks now to turn from the battle-play. I am old in years; I will not leave the field, but think to lie by my lord's side, by the man I held so dear."

So too Godric, Æthelgar's son, emboldened them all to battle. Often he launched his javelin, his deadly spear, upon the vikings; thus he advanced in the forefront of the host; he hewed and laid low, until he too fell in the strife. It was not the same Godric that fled from the battle.

---

[1] Or perhaps only earlier on in the day.   [2] geneat. See p. 366, n. 3.

II. From the Saga of Egil Skalla-Grímsson

The following extract is included as giving a glimpse of Northumbria in the days of the Scandinavian kings, a period for which English sources are scanty. Though the saga belongs to the early thirteenth century (most scholars think it a work of Snorri Sturluson), there can be no doubt that Egil was a historical person of the tenth century, and that the poem "Head-Ransom" is genuine. The saga's account of the occasion of its composition is based on some stanzas from another poem, which I have given after the saga for comparison. It shows that the incident can be accepted as true in outline, and it is open for the reader to form his own opinion as to whether the rest is solely the expansion and invention of the saga writer, or based on lost sources or oral tradition. The poems give no help with the precise dating, and hence the incorrect chronology is understandable. English sources know of Eric at York in Eadred's reign, not Athelstan's. Eric's rule in York is vouched for by a Celtic source, the Latin "Life of St. Catroe", according to which the saint came from the land of the Cumbrians to the city of Leeds, which it calls the boundary between the Northmen and the Cumbrians, and was from there led by a certain Gunderic to King Eric in the town of York. This is placed in Edmund's reign, but the chronology of the Life is unreliable, as also is the statement that Eric's wife was related to St. Catroe. (See A. O. Anderson, *Early Sources of Scottish History*, I, pp. 441 f.).

It is not possible to show in translation that Egil's "Head-Ransom" is a metrical *tour de force*. It obeys the strict rules of stress and alliteration, but it is unusual in its consistent employment of rhyme, every four consecutive half-lines rhyming. It has been suggested that Egil was influenced in this practice by Latin hymns heard in England. In content, on the other hand, it consists entirely of generalities, with no special details of Eric's career, perhaps because Egil was an unwilling panegyrist of this king.

On editions and translations of this saga, see bibliography (p. 132). Most of the portion given here is in E. V. Gordon's *Introduction to Old Norse* (Oxford, 1927). The poems are edited separately in the collections of scaldic verse (see p. 132), F. Jónsson, I A, pp. 35–39, 43 f., I B, pp. 30–33, 38 f.; Kock, I, 19–21, 24–26; Vigfusson and Powell, I, 266–275.

Chap. 59. . . . They (Eric Blood-axe and his followers) first went west over the sea to the Orkneys. There he gave his daughter Ragnild in marriage to Earl Arnfinn. Then he went south by Scotland with his troop and harried there. Then he went south to England and harried there. And when King Athelstan learnt that, he gathered an army and went against Eric. And when they met, terms were arranged between them, and it was settled that King Athelstan appointed Eric in charge of Northumbria, and he was to be protector of the land for King Athelstan against the Scots and the Irish. King Athelstan had made Scotland tributary to him after the fall of King Olaf,[1] but yet that race was always disloyal to him. King Eric always had a royal residence in York. . . .[2]

And when they[3] met men to talk to, they learnt tidings which seemed perilous to Egil, that King Eric Blood-axe was near there, and Gunnhild, and they had the kingdom in their charge, and he was not far away in the borough of York. He learnt also that the *hersir* Arinbjörn[4] was there with the king and in great good favour with the king. And when Egil was sure of this news, he made a plan. It seemed to him very unlikely that he would get away, even though he should try to conceal himself and go in disguise as long a journey as it would be before he came out of Eric's kingdom. He was easily recognizable to any who might see him. It seemed base to him to be taken in flight. He then summoned up his courage and straightway in the night when

---

[1] The saga teller makes the mistake of thinking that Olaf, who allied himself with Constantine, king of Scotland, and was defeated at *Brunanburh*, was king of Scotland.

[2] Egil, drawn from Iceland by the spells of Gunnhild, Eric's wife, was wrecked in the Humber when on his way to King Athelstan. No lives were lost.   [3] Egil and his men.

[4] A *hersir* was a member of the old, independent nobility. Arinbjörn was a life-long friend of Egil.

they had come there he reached a decision; then he got him a horse and rode at once to the borough.

He came there in the evening and rode at once into the borough. He had a hood hanging down over his helmet and was fully armed. Egil asked where the house was which belonged to Arinbjörn. This was told him. He rode there into the court. But when he came to the hall, he got off his horse and found a man to talk to. He was then told that Arinbjörn was sitting at a meal. Egil said: "I should like you, my good fellow, to go into the hall and ask Arinbjörn whether he would rather talk indoors or out with Egil Skalla-Grímsson."

The man said: "It is not much trouble for me to perform that errand."

He went into the hall and spoke quite loudly: "A man has come outside the door here", he said, "as big as a troll, and he told me to go in and ask whether you would rather talk indoors or out with Egil Skalla-Grímsson."

Arinbjörn said: "Go and ask him to wait outside, and he will not have to wait long." He did as Arinbjörn said, went out and repeated the message.

Arinbjörn ordered the tables to be removed. Then he went out and all his house-carls with him. And when Arinbjörn met Egil, he greeted him and asked why he had come there. Egil told him very clearly in a few words about his journey; "but now you must consider what course I am to take, if you are willing to give me help".

"Have you met any men in the borough", said Arinbjörn, "who will have recognized you before you came into the court here?"

"None", said Egil.

"Then let men take their weapons", said Arinbjörn.

They did so, and when they and all Arinbjörn's housecarls were armed, he went into the king's house. When they came to the hall, Arinbjörn knocked on the doors and ordered them to be opened, saying who was there. The door-keepers immediately opened the door. The king sat at table. Arinbjörn then ordered 12 men to go in, naming for this purpose Egil and ten other men.

"Now you, Egil, must give yourself up to King Eric and take hold of his foot, and I will plead your suit."

Then they went in. Arinbjörn went before the king and greeted him. The king welcomed him and asked what he wanted.

Arinbjörn said: "I come here with a man who has come a long way to visit you at home and be reconciled with you. It is a great honour to you, sire, when your enemies come of their own free will from other lands and seem unable to bear your anger, even when you are nowhere near. Behave now in princely fashion towards this man; let him have good terms from you, since he has made your honour as great as can now be seen, has crossed many seas and difficult ways from his home. No necessity compelled him to this journey, only goodwill towards you."

Then the king looked round and saw where Egil towered above the heads of men, and he glared at him and said: "Why are you so bold, Egil, as to dare to come to meet me? You departed from me last time in such a way that you had no hope of life from me."

Then Egil went to the table and took hold of the king's foot.[1] . . . King Eric said:

---

[1] Egil speaks an impromptu stanza here, saying that he has crossed the sea to visit him.

"I need not count up the charges against you, but yet they are so many and serious that each can well be sufficient cause that you never leave here alive. You have nothing to hope for except to die here. You might have known before that you would get no terms from me."

Gunnhild spoke: "Why should Egil not be killed at once? Or have you forgotten, king, what Egil has done—killed your friends and kinsmen, and in addition your son, and insulted you yourself? And where have men ever heard of such things committed against a man of royal rank?"

Arinbjörn said: "If Egil has spoken ill of the king, he can make amends for it in words of praise that will last for all time."

Gunnhild spoke: "We will not listen to his praise. Have Egil led out and killed, king. I do not wish to hear his words or to see him."

Then said Arinbjörn: "The king will not let himself be egged on to all your villainy. He will not have Egil killed at night, for night-slayings are murders."

The king said: "It shall be as you ask, Arinbjörn; Egil shall live tonight. Take him home with you and bring him to me in the morning."

Arinbjörn thanked the king for his words. "We hope, sire, that from this Egil's case may take a turn for the better. But though Egil has done you great injuries, take into account that he has lost a lot through your kinsmen. King Harold, your father, took the life of a famous man, Thorolf, his father's brother, at the slander of wicked men, not for any good reason; and you, king, broke the law as regards Egil for the sake of Berg-Önund. And moreover you tried to take Egil's life, and slew men of his, and deprived him of all his possessions, and in addition made him an outlaw and drove him from the land. And Egil is not a man to put up with insult. And in every case which is to be judged, the provocation must be taken into consideration. I will now", said Arinbjörn, "have Egil home with me tonight in my house."

And so it was; and when they reached the house, the two of them went into a little upper room and discussed the situation. Arinbjörn said thus: "The king was very angry now, but it rather seemed to me that his mood softened somewhat before the end, and luck must now decide what happens. I know that Gunnhild will put her whole heart into wrecking your suit. Now I will give you advice, to stay awake tonight and compose a panegyric on King Eric; it would seem to me a good idea if it were to be a *drápa*[1] of twenty stanzas, and if you could recite it in the morning when we come before the king. Thus did Bragi, my kinsman, when he was exposed to the wrath of Björn, king of the Swedes; he made a *drápa* of twenty stanzas about him in one night, and received for it his head. Now it may happen that we have good luck with the king, so that it may bring about your reconciliation with the king."

Egil said: "I shall try to follow this advice, if you wish, but I have never prepared myself to compose praise on King Eric."

Arinbjörn told him to try. Then he went away to his men. They sat over their drink until midnight. Then Arinbjörn and his company went to the sleeping-quarters, and before he undressed he went up to the upper room to Egil and inquired how the

---

[1] A long poem, with at least one refrain. Such poems were usual in praise of kings and other great persons.

poem was getting on. Egil said that nothing was composed – "a swallow has perched here by the window and twittered all the night, so that I have had no peace because of it".

Then Arinbjörn went away and out by the doors where one could get up on to the building, and he set himself by that window of the upper room where the bird had perched. He saw that some shape-changer[1] left the building by another way. Arinbjörn sat all night there by the window, until it grew light. And after Arinbjörn had come there, Egil composed the whole *drápa*, and had it by heart so that he could recite it in the morning when he met Arinbjörn. They kept watch for when it should be time to go to the king.

King Eric went to table according to his habit, and there was a great crowd with him. And when Arinbjörn was aware of this, he went with all his company fully armed into the king's house, when the king was sitting at table. Arinbjörn asked for admittance into the hall and leave was given him. He and Egil went in with half the company; the other half stood outside the doors. Arinbjörn greeted the king and the king received him well. Arinbjörn said: "Egil has now come here; he has not tried to escape in the night. Now we wish to know, sire, what shall be his lot. I expect well of you. I have so behaved, as was fitting, that I have spared nothing in deed or word, to make your honour greater than before. Also I have left all my possessions and the kinsmen and friends I had in Norway, and followed you, when all your nobles deserted you; and that is only right, for you have done many things exceeding well for me."

Then said Gunnhild: "Stop, Arinbjörn, and do not talk so long about that. You have done much for King Eric, and he has fully rewarded it. You are under a much greater obligation to King Eric than to Egil. It is not for you to ask that Egil should go away unpunished from his meeting with King Eric, considering the things he has been guilty of."

Then said Arinbjörn: "If you, king, and Gunnhild and you together, have determined that Egil shall get no terms here, it is a noble thing to give him leave to go, and a respite of a week, to save himself, seeing that he has journeyed here to meet you of his own free will, and expected peace on that account. Then your dealings can still be as they may, henceforward."

Gunnhild spoke: "I can see in this, Arinbjörn, that you are more loyal to Egil than to King Eric. If Egil is to ride away from here for a week in peace, he will in this time reach King Athelstan. And King Eric has no need to hide from himself that all kings are now men of greater power than he; but a little while ago it would not have been likely that King Eric would lack the will and energy to avenge his wrongs on every man such as Egil is."

Arinbjörn said: "No one will call Eric a greater man even if he kill a foreign yeoman's son, who has walked into his power. But if he wishes to grow famous by this, I must help him to make these tidings seem the more worth telling, for Egil and I shall now back one another, so that we must both be dealt with at the same time.

---

[1] It was believed that certain persons had the power to change themselves into animals or birds, and Gunnhild herself was reputed to have learnt sorcery.

You will then buy Egil's life dearly, king, when we are all laid on the field, I and my followers. I would have expected other treatment from you, than that you would rather fell me to the ground than let me receive the life of one man when I ask it."

Then the king said: "You put very much zeal, Arinbjörn, into helping Egil. I shall be very reluctant to do you injury, if it comes to this, that you will rather give up your life than see him killed. Yet there are sufficient charges against Egil, whatever I choose to have done with him."

And when the king had spoken thus, Egil went before him and began the poem, and recited it loudly and got a hearing.

"I came west over the sea and I bring the sea of the Storm-ruler's breast.[1] Thus has it gone with me; I launched my oaken ship at the time of the ice-breaking; I loaded with a share of poetry the stern-cabin of my soul's ship.[2]

"I offered myself to the king as guest.[3] It is my duty to sing his praise. I bore Othin's mead to the land of the English. I have composed a poem about the king, truly I praise him. I ask him for a hearing, since I have composed a poem of praise.

"Pay heed, king–it becomes you well–how I utter my song, if I get a hearing. Most men have heard what battles the king fought, but the Storm-ruler saw where lay the slain.

"There arose the crash of swords against the shield's rim; battle grew fierce round the king; the prince pressed on. Then could be heard there the fateful song of the storm of battle; the stream of swords roared as it flowed on mightily.

"The weaving of spears did not miss its mark before the king's gay shield-ranks; the seals' plain[4] roared in fury under the banners, where it wallowed in blood.

"Men sank to the ground through the clash of javelins. From that Eric won renown.

"I will tell further, if men are silent. I have heard more of their deeds of prowess. Wounds grew frequent in the prince's battle, swords splintered against the dark shield-rims.

"Sword clashed against sword, the wound-engraver bit–that was the point of the sword. I learnt that there fell the oaks of Othin[5] before the flashing sword[6] in the play of iron.

"There was thrusting of points and gnashing of edges. From that Eric won renown.

---

[1] *i.e.* poetic art, poetry being the mead stolen by Othin from the dwarfs. The Storm-ruler is Othin.
[2] His breast.
[3] Thus E. V. Gordon; Finnur Jónsson and S. Nordal, accepting a slightly different reading, interpret "the prince offered me hospitality". This hardly fits the incident as given in the prose.
[4] The sea.   [5] Warriors.
[6] Thus E. V. Gordon, literally, 'the ice of the sword-girdle'.

"The prince reddened the sword; there was food for ravens; the javelin took life, blood-stained spears flew. The destroyer of the Scots fed the giantess's steeds,[1] Nari's sister[2] trod on the eagle's evening meal.[3]

"The battle-cranes flew over the rows of the slain; the beaks of the birds of prey[4] were not free from blood; the wolf tore wounds, and the sword-wave[5] surged against the raven's beak.

"There came for Gjálp's steed[6] the destroyer of hunger. Eric offered corpses to the wolves from his fight at sea.

"The swordsman[7] wakens the maid of battle, and shatters the hedge of the ski of the sea-king's domaine.[8] Darts splintered and points bit; bow-strings sped arrows from the bow.

"The flying javelin bit, peace was broken; the elm-bow was spanned, the wolf rejoiced at it. The leaders of the host defied death. The yew-bow twanged when swords were drawn.

"The prince bent the yew, arrows[9] flew. Eric offered corpses to the wolves from his fight at sea.

"Still do I wish to declare before men the disposition of the generous ruler. I shall hasten with my praise. He scatters the fire of the river[10] and the prince holds lands in his grip.[11] He is most deserving of praise.

"The giver of gold armlets deals out gold;[12] the distributor of rings will not endure niggardliness. Freely is spent by him the gravel of the hawk's land;[13] he gladdens many seamen with Frothi's meal.[14]

"The inciter of sword-play throws the shield[15] with his arm.[16] He is a generous giver of rings. Both here and everywhere Eric's deeds grow greater, I speak advisedly, it is known east across the sea.

"Pay heed, prince, how I have succeeded in my poem. I am glad that I received a hearing. With my mouth I have drawn Othin's sea from the bottom of my heart concerning this maker of battle.

"I have brought the prince's praise to the end of the poem.[17] I know the true measure in the company of men. I have brought praise of the king from the abode of laughter.[18] It has come about that all have heard it."

---

[1] Wolves.   [2] Hel.   [3] The slain.   [4] Literally, 'wound-mews'.   [5] Blood.
[6] The wolf, Gjálp being a giantess's name.
[7] Literally, 'sword-Freyr'. The name of any god is used to mean 'chief, man'.
[8] i.e. shields, which used to be hung round ships. 'Ski of the sea' is a common kenning for ship.
[9] Literally, 'wound-bees'.   [10] Gold.
[11] Out of this passage, by reading Joforlandi, instead of jöfurr löndum, Vigfusson and Powell, op. cit., I, p. 270, get "holds the land of York", and they take the subject to be horn-klofi and to mean a raven-banner.
[12] Literally, 'arm-stone', the metal worn on the arm.
[13] Gold, since the land, or dwelling-place of the hawk, is a man's wrist.
[14] Gold, because Frothi ordered gold to be ground out for him from a magic quern.
[15] Literally, 'field of points'.   [16] Literally, 'seat of rings'.
[17] E. V. Gordon's rendering of "to the breaking of silence".   [18] His breast.

King Eric sat upright while Egil recited the poem, and glared at him. And when the poem was ended, the king said: "The poem is excellently recited. And now I have decided, Arinbjörn, what shall happen in the matter between Egil and me. You have pleaded Egil's case with great eagerness, when you threaten to raise trouble against me. Now shall be done for your sake what you have asked, that Egil shall leave my presence whole and unhurt. But you, Egil, so arrange your journeyings in future, when you go from my presence out of this hall, that you never come into my sight or my sons', and never be before me or my people; but for this time I give you your head. Because you walked into my power, I will not commit a villain's deed against you, but you must know as a truth that this is no reconciliation with me or with my sons or with any kinsmen of ours, who wish to take due vengeance."

From Egil's Arinbjarnarkviða

3. I had once drawn on me the wrath of the son of the Ynglings,[1] the mighty king; I pulled the hat of boldness over my dark head, and went to seek the nobleman (Arinbjörn),

4. where the king, the protector of the people, sat and ruled under the helmet of terror;[2] the king ruled with unyielding heart in York over a wet land [?].[3]

5. To look on the gleam that came from the stars of Eric's brows was not safe or without terror, when the serpent-glistening moon of the king's forehead shone with fearful rays.

6. Yet I dared to bring forward my poem[4] before the prince of the salmon's land,[5] so that Othin's foaming cup[6] reached the mouth of every man's hearing.

7. My reward for the poem in the prince's house did not seem to men handsome, when I received from the king my wolf-grey head for Othin's mead.

8. I received it, and with the gift [?] there followed the dark pits of my broad brows and the mouth which delivered my Head-Ransom before the king's knees.

9. I received besides the tongue and a crowd of teeth and the ears, endowed with hearing; and the gift of the song-praised king was called better than gold.

10. At my side there stood my loyal friend, better than many generous men, on whom I could rely in every plan, a man rich in honour;

11. Arinbjörn, the best of men, who alone delivered me from the king's hatred, the prince's friend who never lied in the court of the warlike king.

---

[1] The dynastic name of the royal house of Norway.   [2] *i.e.* held people in awe.
[3] The last word is uncertain.
[4] "Pillow-mate-ransom", *i.e.* "Head-Ransom", according to Vigfusson and Powell. Finnur Jónsson considers the passage obscure.
[5] Vigfusson and Powell render this "the Humbers-march".   [6] Poetry.

12-13. Poems about St. Olaf in England

The poems of Sighvat and Ottar are most fully preserved in Snorri's *Heimskringla*, but neither Snorri nor the sources he used have interpreted them correctly. From Ottar's reference to the help given by Olaf to Ethelred, it was assumed that all the battles in England were fought on Ethelred's behalf, and therefore are to be dated after his return. But it is clear enough from the poems themselves that Olaf was fighting against the English at Ringmere and at Canterbury, and it is safe to assume that the battle against Ulfcetel in 1010 and the capture of Canterbury in 1011 are the occasions referred to. In that case the incident of London Bridge, which Sighvat puts before Ringmere, most probably belongs to the unsuccessful attack on London in 1009. Neither poem says that London surrendered on this occasion, though the prose context, which has taken the stanza to refer to an incident of Ethelred's return, says the citizens surrendered to Ethelred as a result. That Olaf actually took part in Thorkel's invasion of 1009 is supported by the statement in the "Legendary Saga of St. Olaf", probably drawing on the older (mainly lost) saga of this king, that Olaf joined Thorkel, as well as by a tradition in many continental authorities that Olaf helped Swein and Cnut to win England, though they date his participation too late, in the campaigns of 1013 or even 1016. There is, however, no reason to doubt the accuracy of Ottar's verses on help afforded to Ethelred in 1014, on his return from Normandy. Like Thorkel, Olaf can have changed sides. The reluctance of the saga-writers to believe that he fought against the English may be due to a sense that it was unfitting for a sainted king to have made viking raids against the people from whom tradition said he brought missionaries to his people. For a detailed discussion of the whole matter, see A. Campbell, *Encomium Emmae Reginae*, pp. 76-82.

These verses can conveniently be seen in their prose context in the *Heimskringla* (Saga of St. Olaf, chaps. 13-15, 27-29) in Miss Ashdown's *English and Norse Documents*, pp. 154-173. An elaborate account is there given of the destruction of London Bridge, according to which Olaf fastened his ships to its supports, which broke when the ships were rowed away.

Two further battles are mentioned in the prose, based on lost stanzas of Sighvat. We are told that Olaf met Ethelred's sons in Normandy and agreed to help them to win back England in return for a promise of Northumbria. He sent his foster-father Rani to win men by money and offers of friendship. Next spring Olaf and Ethelred's sons landed at *Jungafurtha* and captured the town, but when Cnut appeared with a superior force Ethelred's sons fled to Normandy. Olaf sailed to Northumbria and won a battle at *Furuvald* and much treasure. He then left his warships and sailed to Norway in two merchant ships. Though this information may be from lost stanzas, it is wrongly placed in the *Heimskringla*, after Ethelred's death in 1016, by which time Olaf was back in Norway.

For editions of the *Heimskringla*, see bibliography, p. 132. The text of the poems is in F. Jónsson, I A, pp. 224-225, 291-294, I B, pp. 214f., 269-271; Kock, I, pp. 112, 138f. Vigfusson and Powell, II, pp. 125f., 153f. My translation is that of M. Ashdown, *English and Norse Documents*, pp. 159-167.

12. *From* Ólafsdrápa, *by Sighvat the scald*

6. It is true that the sixth attack[1] was where Olaf attacked London's bridge. The valiant prince offered Ygg's[2] strife to the English. Foreign swords pierced, but there the vikings guarded the dike. A part of the host had their booths in level Southwark.

7. Moreover once more Olaf brought about the meeting of swords a seventh time in Ulfcetel's land, as I relate. All the race of Ella[3] stood arrayed at Ringmere Heath. Men fell in battle, when Harold's heir stirred up strife.

8. I know that the warrior, a terror to men,[4] fought at the stronghold his eighth battle. The protector of the retinue advanced in his might. The governors could not defend their town of Canterbury from the noble Olaf. Much woe befell the *Portar*.[5]

---

[1] The previous battles did not concern England.   [2] A name for Othin, meaning 'the terrible'.
[3] The English, regarded as the descendants of the king of Northumbria whom legend said to have killed Ragnar Lothbrok.
[4] A variant reading gives "to the Wends".   [5] Citizens?

9. The young king undaunted gave the English bloody pates. At *Newmouth* swords were reddened once more with blood. Now have I, O stirrer up of conflicts, reckoned nine battles. There fell the Danish host from the East, in the place where spears were wielded most fiercely against Olaf.

13. *From the 'Head-Ransom' of Ottar the Black*

7. And further, O prover of the serpent of Ygg's storms,[1] valiant in war, you broke down London's bridge. It was granted to you to win lands. Iron ring-swords, swung fiercely in the war-meeting, had their course, while old shields sprang asunder. Battle waxed fierce at that.

8. You came to the land, guardian of the realm, and, mighty in your strength, assured his realm to Ethelred. The true friend of warriors was thus your debtor. Hard was the meeting, by which you brought the kinsman of Edmund back to the protection of his country. The support of his race had ruled that land before.[2]

9. I learn that your host, Prince, far from the ships, piled up a heavy heap of slain. Ringmere Heath was reddened with blood. The people of the land, ere all was done, fell to the earth before you in the din of swords, and many a band of English fled terrified away.

10. Prince, you made a great onslaught on the children of kings. Gracious lord, you took wide Canterbury in the morning. Fire and smoke played fiercely upon the dwellings. I learn that you destroyed the lives of men. You had the upper hand, Prince's offspring.

11. Lord wide-renowned, the people of English race might not stand against you, undaunted one, when you took tribute. Not seldom did man pay gold to the gracious prince. I learn that great treasures went ever and again down to the shore.[3]

13. Companion of Princes, bold in the storm of the corpse-fire, you launched two ships from the west. Often have you put yourself in danger. The fierce flow of the waters would surely have harmed those merchant ships as they crossed the waves, if a crew less doughty had been on board.

14. You did not fear the ocean. You crossed a heavy sea. No ruler of men will ever find better followers. A voyage had to be made before you reached mid-Norway, offspring of Harold, but the ship flung back, again and again, the high waves from its sides.

---

[1] Ygg's storms are battle; the serpent of battle is the sword.
[2] If the view expressed above is correct, this stanza is misplaced, for it relates to a later time than the following stanzas.
[3] The twelfth stanza speaks of a battle in Poitou.

14. The "Eiríksdrápa" of Thord Kolbeinsson

The previous portion of this poem deals with Eric's prowess in the battle against the Jómsvikings and in that at Svöld, and of the division of Norway after Olaf Tryggvason's death, when Eric was given one half and his brother Swein the other. Eric held it under King Swein of Denmark, whose daughter he had married. Of the stanzas here given, 8 and 11 are preserved in *Heimskringla*, Saga of St. Olaf, chaps. 24 and 25, stanzas 9–13 in *Knýtlingasaga*, chaps. 8, 13 and 15; stanza 14 in Snorri's *Edda*. For the text, see F. Jónsson, 1 A, pp. 215 f., 1 B, pp. 205 f.; Kock, 1, pp. 107 f., Vigfusson and Powell, 11, pp. 104 f.

The presence of Eric at the siege of London in 1016 is vouched for by the *Encomium Emmae*.

8. Next I begin my praise, how, as I have heard, famous men sent to the helm-adorned chieftain, Earl Eric, a liege lord's summons that he should dutifully come to a friendly meeting with them. I understood what the king intended.[1]

9. The glorious marriage alliance between the princes proved its worth in men's battles, as I have learnt. Many ships of various sizes steered up the estuary. The wielder of the sword, of high lineage, sailed with his dark beasts so near the land that the English plains could be seen.

10. Moreover Cnut, the Scylding, who furrowed the keel-track, let his warships sail out to the shallows of the shore. The meeting of the helmeted earl and the prince came about easily on the day when both men wished to come over the sea.[2]

11. The tester of gold joined battle west of London; the steerer of the sea-horse fought for the land. Ulfcetel, brave in the rain of battle, got ugly blows, where the dark swords shook above the Danish soldiers.[3]

12. The brave warrior, who frequently gave swollen flesh to the raven, marked men with the print of the sword's edge. The bold Eric often diminished the host of the English and brought about their death. The army reddened Ringmere Heath.

13. The givers of plenty to the raven, who long were hateful to the English, went up into the land from the ships. But the natives, who meant to defend their homesteads, made an expedition against them. The king's following repaid them with sword-play.

14. Gjálp's stud-horses[4] waded in blood, and the wolf-pack got plenty of wolves' fodder.[5] The wolves enjoyed the grey beasts' ale.[6]

---

[1] On this stanza, see Kock, *Notationes Norroena*, § 2922.
[2] See *ibid.*, § 584.
[3] Or, "The brave in the rain of battle got ugly blows from the Danish soldiers, where Ulfcetel's dark swords shook." See Kock, *op. cit.*, § 285, where variant manuscript readings are preferred.
[4] Gjálp was the name of a giantess, and her horses are wolves.
[5] Literally, 'wheat'.   [6] *i.e.* blood.

15. The "Knútsdrápa", a poem in praise of King Cnut, by Ottar the Black

Ottar was one of St. Olaf's scalds, who later seems to have entered Cnut's service. This poem is chiefly concerned with Cnut's conquest of England, though it mentions the battle of the Holy River in its final stanza. All except this last stanza is preserved in chaps. 8, 10 and 12 f. of the *Knýtlingasaga*, while the last stanza is in chap. 150 of St. Olaf's saga in the *Heimskringla*. On editions of these works, see pp. 132 f. The poem is edited by F. Jónsson, 1 A, pp. 296–298, 1 B, pp. 272–275; by Kock, 1, pp. 140 f.; by Vigfusson and Powell, 11, pp. 155 f.; and by M. Ashdown, pp. 136–139, whose translation I print here.

1. Destroyer of the chariot of the sea, you were of no great age when you pushed off your ships. Never, younger than you, did prince set out to take his part in war. Chief, you made ready your armoured ships, and were daring beyond measure. In your rage, Cnut, you mustered the red shields at sea.

2. The Jutes followed you out, they who were loath to flee. You arrayed the host of the men of Skane, free-handed adorner of Van's reindeer of the sail.[1] The wind filled the canvas, Prince, above your head. You turned all your prows westward out to sea. Where you went, you made your name renowned.

3. You carried the shield of war, and so dealt mightily, chief. I do not think, O Prince, that you cared much to sit at ease. Lord of the Jutes, you smote the race of Edgar in that raid. King's son, you dealt them a cruel blow. You are given the name of stubborn.

4. Dwellings and houses of men burned, Prince, as you advanced, young though you were. Many a time you caused the people to give warning of deadly attack.

5. You made war in green Lindsey, Prince. The vikings wrought there what violence they would. In your rage, withstander of the Swedes, you brought sorrow upon the English, in *Helmingborg* to the west of the Ouse.

6. Young leader, you made the English fall close by the Tees. The deep dyke flowed over the bodies of Northumbrians. You broke the raven's sleep, waker of battle. Bold son of Swein, you led an attack at Sherstone, farther to the south.

7. There, I know, you took the Frisians' lives, breaker of the peace of shields. You shattered Brentford with its habitations. Edmund's noble offspring met with deadly wounds. The Danish force shot down the men with spears, but you pursued the flying host.

8. Mighty Scylding,[2] you fought a battle beneath the shield at *Assatun*.[3] The blood-crane got morsels brown (with blood). Prince, you won renown enough with your great sword, north of *Danaskogar*, but to your men it seemed a slaughter indeed.

9. Gracious giver of mighty gifts, you made corslets red in Norwich. You will lose your life before your courage fails.

[1] A sailing ship. Van is Njörthr, a sea-god.　　　[2] An ancient Danish dynastic name.
[3] Ashingdon, Essex.

10. Still you pressed on, blunting swords upon weapons; they could not defend their strongholds when you attacked. The bow screamed loud. You won no less renown, driver of the leaping steed of the roller, on Thames's bank. The wolf's jaw knew this well.

11. King bold in attack, you smote the Swedes in the place called Holy River, and there the she-wolf got much wolf's food. Terrible staff of battle, you held the land against two princes,[1] and the raven did not go hungry there. You are swift to deal with the race of men.

16–19. Poems on Cnut's dealings in Norway

The poems in this section mainly illustrate the strife between Cnut and St. Olaf, which is only briefly alluded to in the Anglo-Saxon Chronicle; but attention should be drawn also to the reference in one of Sighvat's poems to Cnut's pilgrimage to Rome and to a stanza in another which supports the entry in the Anglo-Saxon Chronicle on the submission of Scottish kings to him.

Sighvat's *Tøgdrápa* deals with the campaign in which occurred the battle of the Holy River, which is mentioned by name in the last stanza of Ottar's *Knútsdrápa* (No. 15), as well as in the Anglo-Saxon Chronicle, *sub anno* 1025 'E'. According to the prose context in the *Heimskringla*,[2] Olaf harried Zealand and Önund of Sweden harried Skane, Cnut came with Earl Hákon from the west, and found that Earl Ulf had treacherously been trying to replace him by his son Hardacnut on the throne of Denmark. He sailed to where Olaf and Önund were assembled in the Holy River, in Skáne, and there many of his ships were destroyed when his enemies burst a dam they had constructed. At this point arrived Earl Ulf, to Cnut's assistance according to his own claim later on. The battle seems to have been indecisive, and both sides withdrew. Later Cnut had Ulf murdered in Denmark. Saxo has a rather different account; he too speaks of treachery on Ulf's part, though differently motivated, but he makes Ulf flee to Sweden and himself engineer the alliance against Cnut. At the battle the Danes meet with disaster by trying to cross a bridge in too great numbers, so that it collapsed and many were drowned. Ulf fled, and was later executed by Cnut's orders.[3]

Sighvat's "Western Travel Verses" include a description of a visit to Cnut's court, and of his reception by Olaf when he returned. The first four stanzas are preserved in chap. 146 of St. Olaf's saga in the *Heimskringla*, which dates the occasion in the summer before the battle of the Holy River; stanza 5, however, is in chap. 131, and assigned to an earlier visit to Cnut, and stanzas 6 and 7 are in chap. 160, but referred to the same journey as stanzas 1–4. Vigfusson and Powell include as part of this poem the stanzas I have called 'occasional verses', which Finnur Jónsson prints as stanzas 15–20 of Sighvat's "Loose Verses" (*Skjaldedigtning*, I A, pp. 269–271, I B, pp. 249–250). Stanza 15 should be compared with Anglo-Saxon Chronicle, 1031; the others with Florence's account of the bribing of the Norwegian chieftains by Cnut (see No. 9, p. 287). All are preserved in the *Heimskringla*, Saga of St. Olaf; stanza 15 in chap. 131, as a verse uttered by Sighvat to Cnut's messengers who had come to Olaf at Tunsberg to demand that he should become Cnut's man; stanzas 16–18 in chap. 161, assigned to the period after the battle of the Holy River; stanza 19 in chap. 168, which describes the period just prior to Cnut's expedition to Norway of 1028.

It is this expedition, with its successful issue and the granting of Norway to Earl Hákon, that is celebrated in Thorarin's poem, stanzas 2–7 of which are in chap. 172 of the Saga of St. Olaf in the *Heimskringla*.[4] There we learn that Thorarin had angered Cnut by composing merely a *flokk* (a short poem) on him, and therefore composed a long poem to recover his favour, which was called "Head-Ransom"; only the refrain of this survives: "Cnut guards his land as the Shepherd of Greece (Christ) does the heavenly kingdom." But a second long poem survives by being quoted in this chapter, taking its name (*Tøgdrápa*) from the metre. There is extant also a stanza by Halvarthr Hareksblesi which celebrates Cnut's success without adding anything to our knowledge, and

---

[1] St. Olaf and King Önund of Sweden.

[2] Saga of St. Olaf, chaps. 145–153; stanzas 3 and 4 are in chap. 145, stanzas 7 and 8 in chap. 147, stanzas 6 and 9 in chap. 149. Stanza 2 is in chap. 26, stanza 1 in *Hauksbok*. Stanzas 3–11 are also in the *Fagrskinna*, Saga of St. Olaf, chap. 27, and stanzas 2 and 11 also in *Knýtlingasaga*, chap. 16 f.

[3] Saxo, Book X, chap. XVI, ed. J. Olrik and H. Ræder, pp. 288–293.

[4] Stanza 1 is in *Knýtlingasaga*, chap. 19, stanza 8 in Snorri's *Edda*.

several poems deal with Olaf's return and his death at Stiklastadir, but they are not closely enough connected with English history to warrant their inclusion here. Thorarin also addressed a poem to Cnut's son Swein, whom Cnut set over Norway after Olaf's death, but it is mainly concerned with Olaf's miracles, advising Swein to pray to him. The *Heimskringla* has much to say about the unpopularity of this son of Cnut, about whom we learn little from English sources, and of his mother, Ælfgifu; it records his death in the same year as his father, after he had lost Norway to Magnus the Good.

For texts and translations, see editions of *Heimskringla*, etc., and collections of verse, in bibliography, pp. 132f.; Sighvat's poems are in F. Jónsson, 1 A, pp. 241–243, 248–251, 269–271, 1 B, pp. 226–228, 232–234, 249–250; Kock, 1, pp. 117f., 120f., 129; Vigfusson and Powell, 11, pp. 133–136; Thorarin's poem in F. Jónsson, 1 A, pp. 322–324, 1 B, pp. 298f.; Kock, 1, pp. 151f.; Vigfusson and Powell, 11, pp. 159f.

16. *From the* Tøgdrápa[1] *on King Cnut, by Sighvat the Scald*

1.[2] And Ivar, who dwelt at York, carved the eagle on Ella's back.

2. And thereupon Cnut killed or drove away all Ethelred's sons, every one.

3. I know from what I have heard that courage was not lacking in Harold's son in the army; Olaf, the prince blessed with fair seasons, let his force traverse the ocean south from the Nid.

4. The cold keels sped with the king from the north to flat Zealand. This has been learnt. And Önund came with another, a Swedish army at the oars, against the Danes.[3]

6. The gallant kings could not entice Denmark to them by warfare. Then the vanquisher of the Danes ravaged Skane severely.

Cnut is the foremost sovereign under heaven.[4]

7. The fair, keen-eyed son of the Danish king learnt of an army from the east. The shining sea-timber sailed from the west, bearing thence the enemy of Ethelred.[5]

8. And the king's dragons carried blue sails on their sailyards in a fair wind. Splendid was the king's voyage, and the sails that came from the west sped over the sea-path to Limfjord.

9. The ruler of Jutland let nothing be taken for him when he had come to his land. Men were pleased at that. The buckler of the Danes would have no plundering of the land.

Cnut is the foremost sovereign under heaven.

10. To the king who had been intent on war came a longing for travel, bearing a [pilgrim's] staff. The lord, dear to the emperor, friend of Peter, reaped a portion of Rome's glory.[6]

[1] This word applies to a poem in a special metre.
[2] This stanza and the next are detached scraps, quoted by themselves.
[3] Stanza 5 is obscure and indefinite.
[4] This refrain is split into two parts, the first half coming before stanzas 3 and 7, the completion at the end of stanzas 6 and 9. The second half comes again at the end of stanza 11, but the stanza with the first half has in this instance been lost.   [5] Cnut.
[6] Accepting Kock's suggestion that *vegr* in this stanza is 'glory, honour', not 'way'. Otherwise one must render 'traversed quickly some of the way to Rome'. See *Notationes Norroena*, §652.

11. Few generous princes will thus have measured the southward path with their feet.

Cnut is the foremost sovereign under heaven.

17. *From the* Vestrfarar Visor (*'Western Travel Verses'*) *of Sighvat the Scald*

1. Berg, many a morning have we called to mind how I moored my ship's prow at the western end of Rouen on a journey.

2. I had to inquire outside the door of the hall before I could get speech with the lord of the Jutes [Cnut]; I saw the hall barred before me. But, once within the hall, the descendant of Gorm graciously discharged my suit. Often I bear iron armour on my arms.

3. The generous Cnut, who uses all his power, and Hákon prepare to threaten Olaf's life. I may fear the king's death. The protector [Olaf] may yet live, though Cnut and the earls wish otherwise. It were better . . . if he himself escape.[1]

5. O bear-cub,[2] the noble Cnut, who is greatly famed for his achievements, has splendidly decked the arms of both of us, when we visited the king. To you he, the very wise man, gave a mark of gold or more, and a keen sword, and to me half a mark. God himself rules all things.

6.[3] I, thy Staller,[4] am come home hither. Give heed, prince of warriors. Men mark my words as I utter them. Say, king of the people, where you have intended a seat for me among your men. Anywhere inside your hall is agreeable to me.

7. Cnut, liberal with jewels, asked me if I would serve him as well as Olaf, the generous with rings. I said it became me to have but one lord at a time, and I meant my answer truthfully. Enough examples are given to every man.

18. *Occasional verses by Sighvat the Scald*

15. The most famous princes in the North from the midst of Fife have brought their heads to Cnut; that was to buy peace. Olaf the Stout never thus yielded his head to anyone in this world. He often fought till victory.

16. The king's enemies are walking about with open purses; men offer the heavy metal for the priceless head of the king. Everyone knows that he who takes gold for the head of his good lord has his place in the midst of black hell. He deserves such punishment.

17. It was a sad bargain in heaven, when they who betrayed their lord went to the deep-lying world of flaming fire.[5]

---

[1] Following in the main Finnur Jónsson, who considers some words unintelligible. There follows an obscure stanza, which I omit, which seems to refer to some attempt of Hákon to mediate between the Norwegian freeholders and King Olaf.   [2] Bersi (Skáldtorfússon), another scald.
[3] According to the chapter in the *Heimskringla* which has preserved this stanza and the next, Sighvat was coldly received when he returned to Olaf, and said stanza 6. When Olaf asked him if he had become Cnut's man, he replied with stanza 7.   [4] A man with a place at court.
[5] Kock would interpret this last clause as "when those who practised treachery against the home in heaven went hence to the deep power of the high flame".

18. The housecarls of the Harda-king [Olaf] would be too accommodating to the earl [Hákon] if they took money for Olaf's life. It does not honour his household to be talked of thus. Better is it with us if we are all clear of treason.

19. The king of England calls out a levy, but we have got a little army and smaller ships; [yet] I do not see our king afraid. It will be an ugly business if the men of the land let the king be short of men. Money makes men break their faith.

19. The Tøgdrápa on King Cnut, by Thorarin Loftunga

1. I have certainly borne off a reward of 50 marks in the presence of the warlike chief,[1] which the warrior, well practised in battle, gave me for the poem, when I met the prince.

Cnut is under the sun's *seat the best of kings.*[2]

2. My courteous patron came hither with a very great host. The brisk prince led out of Limfjord no small ocean-fleet.

3. The people of Agder, though stern in battle, were filled with dread of the journey of this fierce craver of carnage.[3] The prince's ship was all decked with gold; the sight of it was to me grander than any report.

4. And the coal-black vessels of the roaring sea[4] sped fast over the ocean past Lister. All Egersund was thronged within, in the south, with ships, with skis of the sea.

5. And the sworn housecarls sailed quickly past Tjörnaglen's ancient howe, where the wave-coursers drove past Stad. The leader's journey was not cheerless.

6. Strong against the storm,[5] the slender sea-beasts bore their long sides past Stim; the steeds of the cold sea so journeyed from the south that the valiant urger of the host came north to Nid.

7. Then the brisk ruler of the noble Jutes gave to his nephew the whole of Norway; and to his son—I say it—he gave Denmark, the dark dwellings in the swan's dale[6] (the sea).

8. I have got a generous prince; a *tøgdrápa* is composed on the sword-bearing warrior.[7]

---

[1] This poet uses elaborate kennings that cannot be translated without sounding ridiculous. His phrase here is "the maple-tree (*i.e.* man, chief) of the din of swords (battle)".

[2] As in Sighvat's poem in this metre, the two halves of the refrain were separated, and as it happens no stanza with the second half has survived, and so its content can only be guessed.

[3] Literally, "of rows of the battle-swan (bird of prey)", *i.e.* 'ranks of slain men'.

[4] A variant reading is taken by B. Aðalbjarnarson as "over the sea of Hadyr (a mountain south of Egersund)".

[5] Kock, *op. cit.*, §2016, has a variant reading, *byrrauhn*, "the wind's steeds".

[6] This is Kock's interpretation (*op. cit.*, §1792), as a phrase descriptive of woody islands. Vigfusson and Powell, "the dale of the dark halls of the swan (Sealand)". F. Jónsson, by emendation, "waster of the sun of the swan's dale", the sun of the sea being gold. The whole would mean 'dispenser of gold', and apply to Cnut.

[7] Another very elaborate kenning: "the tree of the flame of the storm of the paths of battle-beacons". Battle-beacons are swords, their paths shields, the storm of shields is battle, the flame of battle is the sword, the tree of the sword is its bearer.

20. From the "Acts of the Abbots of Fontenelle" (St. Wandrille)

This work, which was composed between 833 and 845, contains one passage of interest for English history, illustrating the relations between Charles the Great and Offa. It gives the cause of the quarrel between these kings mentioned in Alcuin's correspondence. (See No. 192.) The best edition is that of F. Lohier and J. Laporte, *Gesta sanctorum patrum Fontanellensis* (Soc. de l'hist. de Normandie), Rouen and Paris, 1936.

XII, 2. This Gervold[1] was appointed an administrator of the affairs of the kingdom for many years, exacting the imposts and taxes at various ports and cities, especially in Quentavic.[2] Hence he is known to have been closely connected in friendship to Offa, the most mighty king of the English or Mercians. There are still extant letters sent from the latter to him, Gervold, in which he declares that he will be his friend and dearest intimate. For he many times discharged diplomatic missions to the aforesaid King Offa by order of the most invincible King Charles; finally one on account of the daughter of the same king, who was sought in marriage by the younger Charles;[3] but as Offa would not agree to this unless Berta, daughter of Charles the Great, should be given in marriage to his son, the most mighty king being somewhat enraged gave orders that no one from the island of Britain and the English race was to land on the sea-coast of Gaul for the sake of commerce. But he was restrained from doing this by the advice and supplication of the aforesaid Father Gervold.

21. From the "Annals of the Frankish Kingdom"

These annals are sometimes called the *Royal Annals*, or *Annales Laurissenses maiores* (the greater annals of Lorsch), or the *Annals of Einhard*. They deal with events from 741; in one manuscript they stop at 788, in another at 813, while others contain a working over of them and a continuation up to 829. It is generally held that they were compiled at court. I quote the one passage of importance for English history, concerning Charles the Great's support of Eardwulf of Northumbria. The annals are edited by F. Kurze in *Script. rer. Germ. in usum scholarum*, 1895.

808 Meanwhile the king of the Northumbrians from the island of Britain, Eardwulf by name, being expelled from his kingdom and native land, came to the emperor while he was still at Nijmegen, and after he had made known the reason for his coming, he set out for Rome; and on his return from Rome he was escorted by envoys of the Roman pontiff and of the lord emperor back into his kingdom. At that time Leo III ruled over the Roman Church, and his messenger, the deacon Ealdwulf from that same Britain, a Saxon by race, was sent to Britain, and with him two abbots, Hruotfrid the notary[4] and Nantharius of St. Omer, sent by the emperor.

809 . . . After King Eardwulf of the Northumbrians had been conducted back into his kingdom and the envoys of the emperor and the pope had returned, one of them, the deacon Ealdwulf, was captured by pirates, while the others crossed the sea without danger, and being taken by them into Britain he was redeemed by a certain man of King Cenwulf, and he returned to Rome.

[1] Abbot of St. Wandrille.   [2] Near Étaples.   [3] Charles the Great's son.   [4] Abbot of St. Amand.

22. From Nithard's "History of the Sons of Louis the Pious"

Nithard was a layman, the son of Bertha, daughter of Charles the Great, and of Angilbert. Charles the Bald asked him in 841 to write this history, which extends until 843. Nithard was killed in 844. His work contains this contemporary reference to a viking raid on Southampton which is not mentioned in English sources. The best edition is that of Ph. Lauer, *Nithard (Les classiques de l'histoire de France au moyen âge)*, Paris, 1926.

BOOK IV, 3. About the same time (842) the Northmen ravaged *Quentavic*,[1] and then crossed the sea and likewise plundered *Hamwig* (Southampton) and *Nordhunnwig* (Northam).[2]

23. From the "Annals of St. Bertin's"

These annals received their usual title from the fact that an early manuscript came from this house. For the latter part of the period they cover, they occupy much the same position as the *Annals of the Frankish Kingdom* for the preceding period. They can be divided into three sections; from 741 to 835 they are the work of an author devoted to Louis the Pious, writing on the left side of the Rhine, before 840; from 835 to 861, they are by Prudentius of Troyes, who was chaplain to the Empress Judith from 830 to 831, became bishop of Troyes in 843, and died in 861; the last section, 862–882, is by Hincmar, who was archbishop of Reims from 845 to 882. I have selected only the references to the English, which deal with the relations between Æthelwulf and Charles the Bald, and with the viking raids. This text is edited by G. Waitz, in *Script. rer. Germ. in usum scholarum*, 1883.

839   After the holy Easter, the king of the English sent messengers to the emperor as he returned to the Frankish kingdom, asking that a passage through the Frankish kingdom on the way to Rome for the sake of prayer might be granted him by the emperor; and also warning him that careful attention should be given to the safety of the souls of those subject to him, since a vision revealed to a certain person among them had struck no little terror in their hearts. He took care to send to the emperor an account of this vision.[3]

844   ... The Northmen attacked with war the island of Britain, especially in the part which is inhabited by the Anglo-Saxons, and fighting for three days were victorious, committed plunder, rapine and slaughter everywhere, and possessed the land at their pleasure.

850   [*Lothaire had made peace with the Danes under Rorich, giving them Duurstede.*] Part of the others ravaged the *Menapii*,[4] the *Tarvisii*[5] and other maritime peoples,

---

[1] Near Étaples.

[2] I owe to Sir Frank Stenton this identification. Northam is near Southampton. Presumably the form in the text is corrupted from *Nordhamwic*.

[3] The vision is then described: a religious priest was visited in his sleep by a man who led him into an unknown country where there were wonderful buildings, including a church in which were many boys reading books written in black and blood-red letters in alternate lines. He was told that the blood-red lines represented the sins of Christian men, who would not obey the precepts of holy writ; the readers were the souls of the saints, whose incessant intercession retards the final punishment. He is reminded of the failure of crops, and told that unless Christians quickly repent of their sins and observe the Lord's day better, a great and terrible danger will befall them: there will be dense darkness for three days, and an immense heathen fleet will ravage with fire and sword most of the Christian peoples and lands.

[4] The inhabitants of the district of *Mempiscus*, east of Thérouanne.   [5] The inhabitants of Thérouanne.

while part, attacking the island of Britain and the English, were defeated by them with the help of our Lord Jesus Christ.

855 . . . Charles also received with honour Æthelwulf, king of the English, as he was hastening to Rome, and presented him with everything belonging to royal estate, and had him escorted to the frontiers of his kingdom with the attendance fitting for a king . . .

856 . . . Æthelwulf, king of the West Saxons, on his way back from Rome, was married on 1 October in the palace of Verberie to Judith, daughter of King Charles, to whom he had been betrothed in the month of July; and, when the diadem had been placed on her head, Ingmar, bishop of Reims, giving the blessing, he honoured her with the name of queen, which hitherto had not been customary with him and his people; and when the marriage had been solemnized with royal magnificence on both sides and with gifts, he returned by ship with her to Britain, to the control of his kingdom.

858 . . . Æthelwulf, king of the West Saxons, died. His son Æthelbald married his widow, Queen Judith.

860 . . . The Danes stationed on the Somme, since the aforesaid tribute was not paid to them, took hostages and sailed to the Anglo-Saxons. Overthrown and driven back by them, they sought other parts.

Part III (by Hincmar)

861 The Danes who had formerly burnt the city of Thérouanne, returning from the English under the leadership of Weland with 200 ships and more, went up the Seine and besieged the fort constructed by the Northmen on the island which is called *Oscellus*, and those Northmen.

24. From Flodoard's Annals

A few references to English affairs occur in the annals of Flodoard, who lived from 893 to 966 and was a canon of Reims, and who, besides this work, wrote a history of the church of Reims, extending to 948. His work was used by Richer, another monk of Reims, who came there after 966 and was still alive in 998. I have referred in footnotes to additions made by him where they seem likely to be based on authentic information. The main interest of these authors for us is their information about King Athelstan's continental relations. Flodoard's annals are best edited by Ph. Lauer, *Les Annales de Flodoard*, Paris, 1905; Richer's history is edited by G. Waitz, in *Script. rer. Germ. in usum scholarum*, 1877, and by R. Latouche, in *Les classiques de l'histoire de France au moyen âge* (Paris, 1930), with French translation.

921 . . . Many English on the way to Rome were struck down with stones by the Saracens in the passes of the Alps . . .

923 . . . A multitude of the English travelling to the thresholds of St. Peter for the sake of prayer were killed by the Saracens in the Alps . . .

926 ... Hugh, son of Robert,[1] married the daughter of Edward, king of the English, Charles's[2] wife's sister.

936 ... The Bretons, returning from the lands across the sea with the support of King Athelstan, came back to their country.[3] Duke Hugh sent across the sea to summon Louis, son of Charles, to be received as king; and King Athelstan, his uncle,[4] first taking oaths from the legates of the Franks, sent him to the Frankish kingdom with some of his bishops and other followers. Hugh and the other nobles of the Franks went to meet him and committed themselves to him immediately he disembarked on the sands of Boulogne, as had been agreed by both sides. From there he was conducted by them to Laon, and, endowed with the royal benediction, he was anointed and crowned by the lord Archbishop Artold, in the presence of the chief men of the kingdom, with 20 bishops and more ...[5]

939 ... An English fleet, sent by King Athelstan, their king, in aid of King Louis, crossed the sea and ravaged certain places near the coast of Thérouanne. They went back across the sea and returned home without having carried out any of the business for which they came.[6]

946 ... Edmund, king of the English, sent messengers to Duke Hugh about the restoration of King Louis,[7] and the duke accordingly made a public agreement with his nephews and other leading men of his kingdom. ... Hugh, duke of the Franks, allying himself with Hugh the Black, son of Richard, and the other leading men of the kingdom, restored to the kingdom King Louis. ... Edmund, king across the sea, died, and the wife of King Otto, sister of the same Edmund, died also.

[1] Hugh, duke of the Franks, was the son of Robert, count of Paris, who was made king in 922 and died in 923. Cf. No. 8, p. 280.

[2] Charles the Simple, king of the West Franks.

[3] This refers to Athelstan's support of another fosterling, Alan of Brittany. See p. 40, and No. 25.

[4] Louis, who was surnamed "from across the sea", was the son of Athelstan's sister Eadgifu and Charles the Simple.

[5] Richer, though he uses Flodoard, has a fuller account. Some of his additions are rhetorical flourishes, but he has some extra facts, and, as his father was in Louis's service, they are probably reliable. Thus he knows that Athelstan received the Frankish embassy at York, and gave them gifts, and that the arrival of the parties on the respective sides of the Channel was made known to each other by beacons, and that Bishop Oda (afterwards archbishop of Canterbury) was sent over to negotiate and to secure full safeguards before Athelstan would let Louis cross.

[6] Louis was in difficulties in this year when Otto, king of the Germans, invaded Lotharingia. Richer says that the fleet was sent because it was thought that the people had risen against Louis.

[7] According to Richer, Louis's mother had written of her son's plight both to Edmund and Otto, and Edmund sent fierce threats against Hugh which were treated with contempt. Hugh was keeping Louis in custody, after having redeemed him from the Northmen of Rouen who had captured him in the previous summer.

25. From the Chronicle of Nantes

This extract tells us about Athelstan's connexions with the Continent about which English sources are silent. His support of the Breton exiles is referred to by Flodoard under the year 936 (see above, No. 24). The Latin work known as the Chronicle of Nantes has not survived, except in a late fifteenth-century French translation of the greater part of it by a certain Pierre le Baud, and for some passages inserted into other works. For the part with which we are concerned there is extant not only the French translation, but also some Latin excerpts in the early fifteenth-century "Chronicle of St. Brieuc". Merlet has brought forward good reasons for assigning the composition of the Chronicle of Nantes to the years 1050-1059, and has shown that the author had annals and narratives before him for the early part of his work. The work is edited by R. Merlet, *La Chronique de Nantes*, Paris, 1896.

Chap. 27. . . . Among the nobles who fled for fear of the Danes,[1] Mathuedoi, the count of Pohel, put to sea with a great multitude of Bretons, and went to Athelstan, king of the English, taking with him his son, called Alan, who was afterwards surnamed 'Crooked Beard'. He had had this Alan by the daughter of Alan the Great, duke of the Bretons, and the same Athelstan, king of England, had lifted him from the holy font. This king had great trust in him because of this friendship and the alliance of this baptism.

Chap. 29. . . . The city of Nantes remained for many years[2] deserted, devastated and overgrown with briars and thorns, until Alan Crooked Beard, grandson of Alan the Great, arose and cast out those Normans from the whole region of Brittany and from the River Loire, which was a great support for them. This Alan was brought up from infancy with Athelstan, king of the English, and was strong in body and very courageous, and did not care to kill wild boars and bears in the forest with an iron weapon, but with a wooden staff. He collected a few ships and came by the king's permission with those Bretons who were still living there, to revisit Brittany.[3]

26. From the "Acts of the Abbots of St. Bertin's" by Folcwin the deacon

The author of this work was brought up at St. Bertin's, and finished this history in 962. Later, in 965, he became abbot of Laubach. He wrote also a life of his uncle and namesake Folcwin of Thérouanne and then the *Lives of the Abbots of Laubach*. He died in 990. The passage here given should be read in connexion with the reference in the 'E' version of the Anglo-Saxon Chronicle, 933, to the drowning of the Atheling Edwin at sea, an event to which much later legendary matter was attracted. This work is edited by O. Holder-Egger, *Folcwini diaconi gesta abbatum S. Bertini Sithensium*, in Mon. Germ. Hist., Scriptores, XIII (1881), pp. 600-635.

Chap. 107. Arnulf, the aforesaid abbot and count, grieving that the religious life of the monastery, which had flourished there in former times, as founded by the blessed Bertin, was at that time decayed, began to consider how he might set up the former religion and make the place famous for its ancient holiness. On this account, therefore,

---

[1] In the early part of the tenth century, after Brittany had been devastated by the Northmen.
[2] After it has been sacked by the Northmen.
[3] His reconquest of his dukedom and subsequent career are outside the subject of this book.

he called to him a certain Abbot Gerhard, and began to treat with the monks themselves, to see if perchance he could incline their hearts to consent to good counsel. But since they remained obdurate and were moved neither by threats nor blandishments, he ordered them to leave the monastery in the year of the holy Nativity of Jesus Christ our Lord 944, on 15 April; and he gave the monastery to the same Abbot Gerhard, who almost alone and first in the western districts in recent times observed the pattern of regular life, for him to govern it according to the rule, with monks collected from diverse places. And people in no small number were assembled for this spectacle, and there was to be seen very great and universal grief at the monks' departure, and tears in the eyes of many, and confusion among the servants of the monastery along with the rest of the crowd of people, who wished to rise against the regular monks and against the count himself. But the count sent after them, and asked them to return, promising that he would give them all things needful, if only they would return to their own place and promise to observe the monastic order. But persevering in their opinion, they went out with a great multitude of people following, and stayed some little time at a village called Longuenesse belonging to the same monastery. But after a short time, the greater part of them took ship on the ocean and were borne to the land across the sea. King Athelstan[1] received them kindly, and at once gave them the monastery which is called Bath, mainly because King Edwin, the brother of this same famous king, had been buried in the monastery of St. Bertin. For in the year of the Incarnate Word 933, when the same King Edwin, driven by some disturbance in his kingdom, embarked on a ship, wishing to cross to this side of the sea, a storm arose and the ship was wrecked and he was overwhelmed in the midst of the waves. And when his body was washed ashore, Count Adelolf, since he was his kinsman,[2] received it with honour and bore it to the monastery of St. Bertin for burial. After his death his brother King Athelstan sent several gifts to this place as alms for him, and on this account he received graciously the monks of the same monastery when they came to him.

27. From the Chronicle of Thietmar of Merseburg

In spite of all his errors (on which see the discussion of this work on p. 127), Thietmar is an almost contemporary writer on the events of 1012–1016, and his account is included for comparison with that in the Anglo-Saxon Chronicle. It may well be reliable in its account of Thórkel's attitude to the murder of Archbishop Ælfheah, and if we accept less readily his statements on Emma's behaviour at the siege of London, they nevertheless have historical value in showing that contemporaries believed her capable of handing over her stepsons to obtain terms for herself.

The chronicle is edited by F. Kurze, in *Script. rer. Germ. in usum scholarum*, 1889; and by R. Holtzmann, in *Script. rer. Germ.*, New Series, IX, Berlin, 1935. I have followed the latter's numbering of the chapters.

BOOK VII, 36. I have heard that the English, so called from their angelic, *i.e.* beautiful, appearance, or else because they are situated on an angle of this earth, have very often suffered indescribable misery from Swein, the son of Harold, the fierce king of the

---

[1] The writer does not know that Athelstan had been succeeded by his brother Edmund in 939.
[2] He was son of King Alfred's daughter Ælfthryth and Baldwin II, count of Flanders.

Danes, and have been driven to such a pass that they, who were formerly payers of tribute to Peter, Prince of the Apostles, and spiritual sons of their holy father, Gregory, have paid to unclean dogs the tribute yearly imposed on them, and have unwillingly relinquished the greater part of their kingdom, after the inhabitants had been captured or killed, for it then to be boldly inhabited by the enemy. Since the Lord consented to this to punish the sins of some who were unfaithful to him, and instigated the aforesaid enemies, the persecutor, who had never even learnt to spare his own, raged thus greatly. For this above-mentioned man, not a ruler, I say, but a destroyer, when after the death of his father he had been captured by revolting Northmen[1] and redeemed at an immense price by his subjects, and found that on this account he was called a slave in the secret whisperings of the worst sort of men, determined unrestrainedly to avenge to the common injury—and, if he had been willing to realize it, to his own damage—what he could profitably have avenged on a few. For, leaving his power to foreign enemies, he exchanged security for wandering, peace for war, a kingdom for exile, God of heaven and earth for the devil; and, laying waste all habitations, he boasted frequently that he was no hired and beneficent lord, but of his own will an enemy of his own people, ruling, alas, far and wide.

37. But after he had been preserved for a long time with great labour to himself and his contemporaries, an infidel among the faithful, he, the death of many, was by the divine will overcome by a tardy death, and, since his companions at once fled, buried there.[2] When Ethelred, king of the English, who had been a fugitive from there for a long time, discovered this for certain, he joyfully, giving thanks to God, came back to his country, and, assembling all his soldiers, he attempted to destroy the body of his enemy. But to prevent this, a certain woman who had been previously warned by her followers, though she was a native of the country, took up from the ground Swein's remains, and sent them by ship to their native *arctos*,[3] *i.e.* to the northern region.[4]

39. The sons of Swein . . . were born to him by the daughter of Earl Miseco,[5] the sister of Bolizlav, Miseco's son and successor. She was long divorced from her husband,[6] and with others endured no little trouble. Her offspring, who in all things took much after their father, received with mourning the body of their father when it was brought, and buried it; and preparing ships, were eager to avenge whatever insult against their father the English had intended to commit. Passing over the many crimes which are ascribed to them, because they are unknown to me, I will briefly disclose with my pen what a certain person told me as known by him to be true.

40. Ethelred, king of the English, died in the year of our Lord 1016; and in the month of July the aforesaid brothers Harold and Cnut, with their general, Thurgut,[7]

[1] Adam of Bremen (ed. B. Schmeidler, p. 91) says Swein was taken prisoner twice, but by the Slavs.
[2] In England.   [3] The Great and Little Bear.
[4] Simeon of Durham and Gaimar say he was buried at York, and Gaimar adds that ten years or more later his bones were taken to Norway and buried at St. Olaf's.   [5] Of Poland.
[6] Scholars differ as to whether this means Swein, or a previous husband. Scandinavian sources, who call Swein's wife Sigrid, say that she was first married to Eric the Victorious of Sweden. The author of the *Encomium Emmae* agrees with Thietmar in bringing Cnut's mother from *Slavia*.
[7] No leader of this name is known, and hence this is often taken to refer to Thorkel; but the latter is correctly named later on, and was not killed in 1016.

and with 340 ships, set out and besieged a certain city, London by name, where the queen, grieving for the death of her husband and defender, was staying with a garrison, along with her sons, Athelstan and Edmund,[1] and with two bishops and the other leading men; and, bringing their ships, each holding 80 men, up the river which is called the Thames, they attacked it for six months. But then the queen was worn out by constant war, and sent messengers to ask for peace and to inquire diligently what they required of her. They at once received the reply from the insatiable enemies, that if the queen would give up her sons to death and redeem herself with fifteen thousand pounds of silver, and the bishops with twelve thousand, and with all the coats-of-mail, of which there was the incredible number of twenty-four thousand, and would give 300 picked hostages as security for these things, she could gain for herself and her companions peace with life; if not, all cried out three times that they should perish by the sword. The venerable queen with her followers was extremely agitated at this message, and after long deliberation in a vacillating mind replied that she would do thus, and confirmed it with the soldiers mentioned above.

41. Meanwhile, the two brothers escaped in the silence of the night from the threatened peril in a little boat, and gathered together whomsoever they could to the defence of their country and the rescue of their mother, while the enemy was still unaware. But when Thurgut, the leader of the pirates, went out one day to harry the neighbouring districts with a host, he unexpectedly came across the enemy and attacked them; catching sight of them from a distance, he approached them, exhorting his comrades boldly. And of the two parties there fell Edmund and Thurgut[2] with a great number of their companions. And neither to them nor to the others was there any hope of the victory they desired, but they separated of their own accord, wounded, and only lamenting that things had chanced to fall out thus. But the Scriptures forbid us to believe that anything occurs by fate or chance. The Danes, then, though weakened, came to their confederates' ships, and when they understood that relief was being brought to the city by the survivor, Athelstan, and the approaching Britons, they mutilated their hostages and fled. And may God the protector of those who trust in him, destroy and scatter them, that they may not continue to harm these or other faithful people. Let us rejoice in the relief of the city, but lament over the rest.

42. I have learnt also from the account of the aforesaid man Sewald of a miserable and memorable deed; that the perfidious force of the Northmen, led by Thorkel, took captive the noble prelate of the city of Canterbury, called Dunstan,[3] along with others, and ill-treated them with chains and hunger and indescribable torments after their abominable custom. Moved by human weakness, he promised them money and fixed a term for the obtaining of it, so that if he could not escape death by an acceptable ransom, he might meanwhile cleanse himself with frequent groans as a living sacrifice to be offered up to the Lord. Then, when all the appointed period was ended, the voracious Charybdis of thieving magpies summoned the servant of God, and

[1] Not her sons, but her stepsons. No other source says Athelstan survived his father.
[2] Edmund was not killed in battle, and if Thurgut is an error for Thorkel, the statement that he was killed is erroneous also.
[3] An error for Ælfheah.

quickly demanded of him with threats the payment of the promised tribute. And gentle as a lamb, he said: "I am ready at once for anything you now dare to do to me; but, by the love of Christ, that I may deserve to become an example to his servants, I am untroubled today. It is not my wish, but dire poverty, that makes me seem a liar to you. This my body, which in this exile I have loved immoderately, I offer to you, guilty as it is, and I know that it is in your power to do what you wish with it; but as a suppliant I commit my sinful soul to the Creator of all, for it does not concern you."

43. The troop of wicked men surrounded him as he spoke these words, and collected various weapons to kill him. When their leader, Thorkel, saw this from a distance, he ran quickly, and said: "Do not, I beg you, do this. I will give to all of you with a willing heart gold and silver and all that I have here or can get by any means, except only my ship, on condition that you do not sin against the Lord's anointed." The unbridled anger of his comrades, harder than iron or stone, was not softened by such gentle words, but it was appeased only by the shedding of innocent blood, which together they forthwith shed by the heads of oxen and showers of stones and a constant stream of blocks of wood. Among so many attacks of the raging folk, he received the heavenly joy, as the working of the following sign at once proved. For one of the leaders became crippled in his limbs, and realized that he had sinned against Christ's elect, as it is written: "'Vengeance is mine,' saith the Lord, 'and I will repay.'"[1] In this triumph of the martyr of Christ his wretched persecutors were vanquished, and they have lost God and also the money offered them by the leader, and finally, unless they repent and make amends, their souls; whilst he, with a stole made white hitherto by innocence of mind and body, and then dyed with red blood, has appeased the divine sight. Let us sinners acquire this intercessor by constant prayers, and believe that he has much power with the divine majesty.

BOOK VIII, 7. In England the crews of 30 pirate ships were slain,[2] thanks be to God, by their king, the son of King Swein; and he, who formerly with his father was an invader and assiduous destroyer of the province, now remained its sole defender, as in the desolate Lybian desert [reigns] the basilisk.[3]

28. From the "Encomium Emmae Reginae"

This tendentious work, which is discussed on pp. 127f. above, was written at St. Omer between 1040 and 1042, and thus is at most only half a dozen years after the event described in this section. I include it for comparison with the Anglo-Saxon Chronicle, 1036. By making Alfred's visit one of political intention, it supplies a motive for his molestation in England, which is lacking from the account in the Chronicle, where his sole purpose is to visit his mother. It is possible that the English writer considered it impolitic to state in the reign of the Confessor that his brother's murderers had any sort of provocation. Norman traditions, best represented by William of Poitiers and William of Jumièges, are in agreement with the *Encomium* on this matter, though differing in detail. They describe an earlier attempt by Edward to recover his throne, in which he came with 40 ships to Southampton, was met by an English force, and, though victorious, retired to Normandy with his booty, because of the superiority of the forces opposed to him. Harold's cruel treatment of Alfred,

---

[1] Romans xii. 19.   [2] In 1018.   [3] Lucan ix. 726.

who is said to have made better preparations for attack, and, sailing from the port of *Icius* (Wissant ?), to have come to Canterbury, is explained as an attempt to frighten Edward from making any further effort. Like the 'D' version of the Anglo-Saxon Chronicle, the author of the *Encomium* seems anxious to avoid laying the crime on Earl Godwine. He may have been unwilling to make an enemy of a man who was in power at the time of his writing, whereas Harold was dead and could safely be vilified. The Norman versions lay great stress on the deliberate treachery of Godwine, who pretended to receive Alfred as a friend, in order to hand him over to his enemies. They are, however, obviously actuated by a wish to justify William the Conqueror's attack on England by all possible means, and seize this opportunity of making it an act of vengeance for the murder of Alfred by the machinations of Godwine, King Harold II's father.

A. Campbell, *Encomium Emmae Reginae* (Royal Hist. Soc., 1949), has superseded all earlier editions. The best edition of William of Poitiers is that by R. Foreville, *Guillaume de Poitiers* (*Les classiques de l'histoire de France au moyen âge*, Paris, 1952). William of Jumièges is edited by J. Marx, *Gesta Normanorum Ducum* (Société de l'histoire de Normandie, Rouen and Paris, 1914). Both works were composed some thirty-five years after Alfred's murder. With Mr. Campbell's permission I reprint his translation.

BOOK III, § 2. But Emma, the queen of the kingdom, silently awaited the end of the matter,[1] and for some little time was in her anxiety daily gaining God's help by prayer. But the usurper[2] was secretly laying traps for the queen, since as yet he dared not act openly, but was allowed to hurt her by nobody. Accordingly, he devised an unrighteous scheme with his companions, and proposed to kill the children of his lady, that henceforth he might be able to reign in security and live in his sins. He would, however, have effected nothing whatever in this matter if, helped by the deceit of fraudulent men, he had not devised what we are about to narrate. For having hit upon a trick, he had a letter composed as if from the queen to her sons, who were resident in Normandy, and of this I do not hesitate to subjoin a copy:

§ 3. "Emma, queen in name only, imparts motherly salutation to her sons, Edward and Alfred. Since we severally lament the death of our lord, the king, most dear sons, and since daily you are deprived more and more of the kingdom, your inheritance, I wonder what plan you are adopting, since you are aware that the delay arising from your procrastination is becoming from day to day a support to the usurper of your rule. For he goes round hamlets and cities ceaselessly, and makes the chief men his friends by gifts, threats and prayers. But they would prefer that one of you should rule over them, than that they should be held in the power of him who now commands them. I entreat, therefore, that one of you come to me speedily and privately, to receive from me wholesome counsel, and to know in what manner this matter, which I desire, must be brought to pass. Send back word what you are going to do about these matters by the present messenger, whoever he may be. Farewell, beloved ones of my heart."

§ 4. This forgery, when it had been composed at the command of Harold the tyrant, was sent to the royal youths by means of deceitful couriers, presented to them as being from their unwitting mother, and received by them with honour, as a gift from their parent. They read its wiles in their innocence, and alas too trustful of the fabrication, they unwisely replied to their parent that one of them would come to her, and determined upon day and time and place for her. The messengers, accordingly, returned and told the foes of God what answer had been made to them by the most noble youths. And so they awaited the prince's arrival, and schemed what they

[1] The election of Harold to succeed Cnut.   [2] Harold.

should do to him to injure him. Now on the fixed day, Alfred, the younger prince, selected companions with his brother's approval, and beginning his journey came into the country of Flanders. There he lingered a little with Marquis Baldwin, and when asked by him to lead some part of his forces with him as a precaution against the snares of the enemy, was unwilling to do so, but taking only a few men of Boulogne, boarded ship and crossed the sea. But when he came near to the shore, he was soon recognized by the enemy, who came and intended to attack him, but he recognized them and ordered the ships to be pushed off from that shore. He landed, however, at another port, and attempted to go to his mother, deeming that he had entirely evaded the bane of the ambush. But when he was already near his goal, Earl Godwine met him and took him under his protection, and forthwith became his soldier by averment under oath. Diverting him from London, he led him into the town called Guildford, and lodged his soldiers there in separate billets by twenties, twelves and tens, leaving a few with the young man, whose duty was to be in attendance upon him. And he gave them food and drink in plenty, and withdrew personally to his own lodging, until he should return in the morning to wait upon his lord with due honour.

§ 5. But after they had eaten and drunk, and being weary, had gladly ascended their couches, behold, men leagued with the most abominable tyrant Harold appeared, entered the various billets, secretly removed the arms of the innocent men, confined them with iron manacles and fetters, and kept them till the morrow to be tortured. But when it was morning, the innocent men were led out, and were iniquitously condemned without a hearing. For they were all disarmed and delivered with their hands bound behind their backs to most vicious executioners, who were ordered, furthermore, to spare no man unless the tenth lot should reprieve him. Then the torturers made the bound men sit in a row, and reviling them beyond measure, followed the example of that murderer of the Theban Legion, who first decimated guiltless men, though more mercifully than they did. For that utterly pagan ruler spared nine of the Christians and killed the tenth, but these most profane and false Christians killed nine of the good Christians and let the tenth go. That pagan, though he massacred Christians, nevertheless ordered that they should be beheaded on an open plain unfettered by bonds, like glorious soldiers. But these, though they were in name Christians, were nevertheless in their actions totally pagan, and butchered the innocent heroes with blows from their spears bound as they were, like swine. Hence all ages will justly call such torturers worse than dogs, since they brought to condemnation the worthy persons of so many soldiers not by soldierly force but by their treacherous snares. Some, as has been said, they slew, some they placed in slavery to themselves; others they sold, for they were in the grip of blind greed, but they kept a few loaded with bonds to be subjected to greater mockery. But the divine pity did not fail the innocent men who stood in such peril, for I myself have seen many whom it snatched from that derision, acting from heaven without the help of man, so that the impediments of manacles and fetters were shattered.

§ 6. Therefore, since I am dealing briefly with the sufferings of the soldiers, it remains that I should curtail the course of my narrative in telling of the martyrdom of their prince, that is to say the glorious Alfred, lest perchance if I should choose to go over all that was done to him in detail, I should multiply the grief of many people and particularly of you, Lady Queen. In this matter I beg you, lady, not to ask more than this, which I, sparing your feelings, will briefly tell. For many things could be told if I were not sparing your sorrow. Indeed there is no greater sorrow for a mother than to see or hear of the death of a most dear son. The royal youth, then, was captured secretly in his lodging, and having been taken to the island called Ely, was first of all mocked by the most wicked soldiery. Then still more contemptible persons were selected, that the lamented youth might be condemned by them in their madness. When these men had been set up as judges, they decreed that first of all both his eyes should be put out as a sign of contempt. After they prepared to carry this out, two men were placed on his arms to hold them meanwhile, one on his breast, and one on his legs, in order that the punishment might be more easily inflicted on him. Why do I linger over this sorrow? As I write my pen trembles, and I am horror-stricken at what the most blessed youth suffered. Therefore I will the sooner turn away from the misery of so great a disaster, and touch upon the conclusion of this martyrdom as far as its consummation. For he was held fast, and after his eyes had been put out, was most wickedly slain. When this murder had been performed, they left his lifeless body, which the servants of Christ, the monks, I mean, of the same Isle of Ely, took up and honourably interred. However, many miracles occur where his tomb is, as people report who even declare most repeatedly that they have seen them. And it is justly so: for he was martyred in his innocence, and therefore it is fitting that the might of the innocent should be exercised through him. So let Queen Emma rejoice in so great an intercessor, since him, whom she formerly had as a son on earth, she now has as a patron in the heavens.

Part II
CHARTERS AND LAWS

CHARTERS AND LAWS

Introduction

THE documents considered in this section constitute the main source for our knowledge of Anglo-Saxon administration, social and economic history, though this must be supplemented by reference to some statements in narrative sources, and in literature, correspondence and other records in Part III. Moreover, the political historian cannot afford to ignore the evidence of charters, which may supply references to events on which narrative sources are silent. Useful as these records are, it must never be forgotten that they are utilitarian documents, and the historical evidence they afford is only incidental, and not part of their purpose; or that we have only a fraction of what once existed, a fact which makes it dangerous to argue from silence. The relation of surviving records of this kind to what once existed is therefore considered at some length in the following pages.

THE ANGLO-SAXON LAWS

The preservation of the laws

Already at the time of the English settlement of Britain the invaders had a developed legal system, agreeing in its main principles with that of other Germanic peoples, but it was not until after the adoption of Christianity that any of this mass of legal custom was written down. Then, as Bede tells us, King Ethelbert of Kent "among the other benefits which in his care for his people he conferred on them, also established for them with the advice of his councillors judicial decrees after the example of the Romans, which, written in the English language, are preserved to this day and observed by them; in which he first laid down how he who should steal any of the property of the Church, of the bishop, or of other orders, ought to make amends for it, desiring to give protection to those whom, along with their teaching, he had received".[1] These laws are extant, though only in a twelfth-century manuscript, and a number of later codes, issued by various kings, and some treatises of private origin, have also come down to us. We may first consider what relation surviving legal records have to what once existed.

It is not the official law-books, if such there were, kept by the kings at some headquarters, that have come down to us. It is to the activity of ecclesiastical scribes that we owe our extant laws. When a code was promulgated, many copies must have been circulated, in order that the decisions should become known to all whose concern they were. One of Edgar's codes[2] gives instructions about the circulation of copies "in all directions" by the ealdormen in their individual provinces, while among the legal texts that survive from an earlier reign, that of Athelstan, one is a reply from the bishops and other councillors of Kent accepting and putting into force the measures enacted by the king and his councillors,[3] and another shows how the Londoners

[1] See No. 151, p. 160.   [2] See No. 41.   [3] III Athelstan.

proposed to apply in detail to the area of their own jurisdiction the general injunctions they had received on the maintenance of the peace.[1] In both these cases ecclesiastical authorities unite with laymen in these measures, and it is only the copies kept by religious institutions that had any chance of survival to our times. Thus, for example, the Kentish laws, which survive only in the *Textus Roffensis*, compiled at Rochester, probably at the instigation of Bishop Ernulf (1115–1124), are doubtless derived from a copy kept at Canterbury, where Ernulf had previously been prior. Another important manuscript of laws[2] once belonged to St. Paul's.

But it should be noted that we do not owe all our extant codes simply to a tendency to preserve and re-copy, out of respect for the past, sets of laws that were no longer in force; some codes have come down to us in compilations made for a practical use. The clergy were not only the preservers and transcribers of the laws; they were also often the drafters of it, and therefore required copies of earlier statutes for their guidance. This is particularly clear in the early eleventh century, when the actual form taken by several of Ethelred's codes and by those of Cnut is due to Wulfstan, archbishop of York and bishop of Worcester, and it is therefore of interest to find in several manuscripts, which on other grounds we can connect with him, collections of earlier statutes, some of which he has used for his own compilations. It is easy to conceive that when a text is being copied, not out of antiquarian interest, but with the intention of incorporating it in new legislation, absolute fidelity to the ancient wording is not felt necessary, and, in fact, if one compares different versions of codes which survive more than once in the Wulfstan manuscripts, or in some other source besides these, one occasionally finds that Wulfstan's own terminology has been substituted for that of the original text. This makes one doubt whether one always has the unchanged version in codes, such as IV Edgar, which are preserved only in the Worcester manuscripts.

Ine's code constitutes a more important instance of the survival of an early code because it was used as a basis for later legislation; it survives because it was copied as a sort of appendix to Alfred's laws, of which it was one of the main sources, as the king tells us himself. We are left in uncertainty whether, as there copied, it represents Ine's code exactly and completely, or whether it has already been partially edited for the king's immediate purpose. He tells us that he rejected many of the observances of his forefathers which he did not like,[3] and for all we know some of these may have been omitted from the copy of Ine's code appended to his own. But, though one must always bear in mind this possibility of modification in the course of transmission of texts which survive only in versions of much later date, it must not be assumed that there was a widespread practice of modernization, for the presence of much archaic diction and syntax proves that in general the text was rendered much as it stood.

The laws of Alfred and Ine survive in a manuscript of the early tenth century[4] and a fragment of Ine's laws in another pre-Conquest manuscript;[5] fragments remain of the early eleventh-century Brit. Mus. Cott. Otho B. xi, which once contained Alfred and Ine,[6] but was almost entirely destroyed in the fire of 1731, only part of the list of rubrics and Alfred 40–42.7, Ine 66–76.2, having escaped. Several codes have come down in pre-Conquest form in the Wulfstan manuscripts mentioned above, of which Brit. Mus. Cott. Nero A. i, in its oldest part, has I Athelstan, a fragment of I Edmund,

---

[1] No. 37.   [2] C.C.C.C., MS. 383.   [3] See p. 373.
[4] C.C.C.C., MS. 173.   [5] Brit. Mus. Burney MS. 277.
   [6] This MS. contained also II Athelstan, and chaps. 7–25 survive, but according to Liebermann they are in a later hand than the Alfred and Ine fragments, and belong to the end of the eleventh century.

most of III Edgar, V Ethelred (twice), the beginning of VIII Ethelred, and the private treatises known as *Griō* and *Norōhymbra cyricgriō*; Brit. Mus. Harley MS. 55 in its pre-Conquest portion has II and III Edgar; C.C.C.C., MS. 190, has three short texts, *Be Mircna lage*, *Aō*, *Hadbot*; C.C.C.C., MS. 201, about the time of the Conquest, has I Athelstan, I Edmund, II and III Edgar, V, VII and VIII Ethelred, an early draft of Cnut's laws, the "Law of the Northumbrian Priests", and the small texts *Be Geōyncuōm, Norōleoda laga, Be Mircna lage, Aō*, and *Hadbot*. IV Edgar survives only in two pre-Conquest manuscripts, both from Worcester, Brit. Mus. Cott. Nero E. i and C.C.C.C., MS. 265, neither of which contains any other legal texts. Then there is a fragment, X Ethelred, on a detached leaf of unknown provenance in a Vatican manuscript; while Cnut's letter of 1020 was inserted at the end of the York gospels along with some of Wulfstan's homilies, perhaps already while Wulfstan was holding the see. Pre-Conquest are also the Latin and Old English versions of VI Ethelred, in Brit. Mus. Cott. Claud. A. iii; *Romscot* and *Judex*, if the part of Nero A. i in which they occur is just before, rather than after, the Norman Conquest, in which case another version of II and III Edgar, and of the rubrics and beginning of Alfred, must be added to texts in manuscripts of Anglo-Saxon date; and finally there is *Episcopus* from a Worcester manuscript, Junius 121, about 1065.[1]

Although this may seem a long list, it should be noted how little of it would be left if we were to remove all those items which owe their survival to the interest taken in the law at Worcester and the fortunate preservation of the manuscripts of this see. And we should note also that several codes are not included at all, but have come down in post-Conquest manuscripts only; namely all the laws of the Kentish kings, the treaty between Alfred and Guthrum, both the codes of Edward the Elder, most of II Athelstan, V and VI Athelstan, II Edmund, the Hundred Ordinance, I, II, III Ethelred, and the so-called Laws of Edward and Guthrum, which belong to this reign, Cnut's 1027 letter, and a number of anonymous pieces, including such important documents as *Rectitudines* and *Gerefa*, the agreement with the *Dunsæte*, and many smaller texts and formulae. We owe all of these, as well as the later versions of texts which do survive in pre-Conquest manuscripts, to the interest taken in Anglo-Saxon law in Norman times, especially in the reign of Henry I, which saw the compilation of the two great codices, the *Textus Roffensis* and the St. Paul's manuscript of about 1125–1130, now C.C.C.C., MS. 383. A certain amount of agreement in arrangement between these two codices, shared also with the Latin *Quadripartitus*, indicates that they were not compiled from separate codes, but that there were already available earlier compilations of sets of codes. About the same time as these two codices were compiled, the laws of Cnut, in Brit. Mus. Harley MS. 55, were copied; another version, Brit. Mus. Nero A. i, is dated by Liebermann about 1070.

The interest in Anglo-Saxon law at this period found further expression. A collection was made and translated into Latin in an ambitious work of about 1114, called by its author *Quadripartitus*, though the last two books, if ever written, have not survived. Only the first book of his work was concerned with Anglo-Saxon law, and for it he managed to assemble the greater number of those texts known to us, and a few that have not survived. His Latin versions are all that we have to represent the following:[2] Athelstan's Ordinance on Almsgiving, III Athelstan, except for a

[1] Rituals for use at ordeals or excommunications are excluded from this discussion.

[2] I accept throughout Dr. Sisam's view that Lambard had not access to a lost vernacular MS. of laws, and that when he has Old English versions not otherwise extant they are his own translations from the Latin of *Quadripartitus*.

fragment preserved in Old English in the *Textus Roffensis*, IV Athelstan, III Edmund, IV Ethelred, a version of VII Ethelred which differs considerably from the only Old English text, and a short document mainly on the suppression of theft, which goes under the name of Appendix to Alfred and Guthrum, since it follows this treaty, but which Liebermann would assign to the mid-tenth century. The author of *Quadripartitus* included all the laws in either the *Textus Roffensis* or the St. Paul's manuscript, except the Kentish laws and the anonymous texts *Becwæð* and *Gerefa*; in addition, he had access to some codes not in these manuscripts, but which survive only in the Worcester manuscripts, *e.g.* I Athelstan, II and III Edgar, VII Ethelred, and *Episcopus*, but he has not used, and perhaps did not know, IV Edgar, V, VI, VIII–X Ethelred, Cnut's letters, the "Law of the Northumbrian Priests", *Grið* and *Norðhymbra Cyricgrið*. The author was probably not an Englishman, and did not always understand his originals; this makes it difficult to accept without reservation his authority in those codes where the English version has not survived. He may himself have been the author of the so-called "Laws of Henry I", which makes extensive use of *Quadripartitus*. It takes its name from its beginning with the coronation charter of Henry, but it is actually an attempt to state the law of England, using the older laws, but taking passages also from foreign sources such as the *Lex Salica*, the *Lex Ribuaria* and Frankish capitularies. It has probably preserved some genuine fragments of English legal practice, which would otherwise not have reached us, but in view of the multiplicity of its sources it has to be used with caution.

The author of *Quadripartitus* set the laws of Cnut first, and the respect paid to this king's legislation is shown also by two Latin translations of his laws produced in this period, the *Consiliatio Cnuti*, about 1110–1130, which also used VIII Ethelred, and to which the small texts "Incendiaries", "(Legal) Seizure" (*Forfang*) and the Hundred Ordinance are appended; and, probably rather earlier, about 1103–1120, the "Institutes of Cnut and other Kings of the English", which inserts amongst Cnut's laws passages from Ine, Alfred, II Edgar, and some of the anonymous texts, including *Grið* which *Quadripartitus* did not use. Both writers include a little material of unknown provenance. A very different type of document is the so-called "Laws of Edward the Confessor", probably written towards the end of Henry I's reign, by a writer ready to romance in favour of ecclesiastical interests, who pretends that he is giving the laws of Edward the Confessor as stated by juries to William I. In striking contrast to the honour in which the other Norman writers had held Cnut's laws, we are here told that law had slumbered between the reigns of Edgar and Edward the Confessor. Finally, there is a document in Old French and Latin, which, though called "the Laws of William", is a private document, of which the first part consists of apparently reliable statements on English law. Liebermann considers this text to be no later than 1135, and perhaps as early as 1090. All these works, along with the compilation of the two codices of Old English laws mentioned above, show how great an interest was taken in ascertaining Anglo-Saxon law at this date, and but for it our knowledge of Anglo-Saxon law would have been much poorer.

Even so, several codes have been lost. One certain and very regrettable loss is that of the laws of Offa of Mercia. Alfred claims to have used them when drawing up his own code, and it is possible that Alcuin is referring to them in a letter written just after Offa's death.[1] One of Edward the Elder's codes refers to treaties with the Danish

---

[1] No. 202.

parts of England, which are not among our surviving records. It is highly probable that Eorcenberht's injunctions in 640 regarding the destruction of idols and the keeping of Lent were issued in written form, but, if so, they have perished. Athelstan's second code (chap. 11) refers to some previous enactment that does not survive; and references in both I and III Ethelred to an assembly at *Bromdun* are easier to understand if measures against theft were promulgated at it, though they have not come down to us. We should not have known of the way code followed on code in Ethelred's reign if most of them had not been drawn up by a literary man who inserted them in manuscripts containing his other writings, and who happened to be connected with a church whose manuscripts had a fair chance of survival. It would not be safe therefore to see in the number of codes of this reign a sign of Ethelred's ineffectual government, though this may have something to do with it; other kings may have issued more codes than we know.

Yet, even if we were fortunate enough to possess all the Anglo-Saxon laws that were put into writing, it is probable that we should be a long way from a complete statement on the subject. The written laws are generally enactments, when it was necessary to re-state rules that were being disregarded, to clarify matters on which there could be uncertainty, or to modify existing rules. A great amount of customary law, such, for example, as that relating to inheritance and other family matters, was probably never put into writing at all, being too well known and too fixed to require written statement. It is here that the charters may sometimes be helpful, letting one get a glimpse of certain aspects of the law in its working, and similarly the written laws can sometimes be reinforced by evidence from Domesday Book, and occasionally from odd references in literary sources. But when all has been put together, there remain many topics on which one would welcome further evidence.

The extant laws

In the following selection of laws, those of early date may seem to have too great a preponderance; but, if one omits the tedious tariffs on compensation for injuries—as I have done—they have a more varied interest than the later codes which frequently repeat what has been said before. The laws of Kent show us the attempt to fit the obligations of the new religion into the framework of a Germanic legal system, and they give us information about a people and a period for which other evidence is none too plentiful. It is remarkable to find in the latest of these Kentish codes that active heathenism had still to be reckoned with as late as the end of the seventh century in the kingdom which was the first to be converted. It may have been Wihtred's example that fired his contemporary, King Ine of Wessex, to issue written laws; there was certainly some connexion between the two kings, for both insert an almost identical chapter. Ine's laws throw such light on late seventh-century Wessex that I have included them in full; they do not, like Wihtred's, mention penalties for worship of 'devils', but before we assume from this that Christianity had more readily been received in Wessex, we must remember that we possess Ine's laws only in Alfred's edition of them. They do, however, reveal an attempt to encourage men to become full members of the Church by allowing greater weight to the oath of a communicant.

Offa's laws being lost, we next come to Alfred, whose great interest in the administration of justice is vouched for by Asser. It is characteristic of that king that before he issued his law-book he should have examined the law-giving in the bible in an attempt to get at some general principles. His introduction begins with the decalogue and continues with many statements of Hebrew law from Exodus xx–xxiii, then, after referring to Christ's words "Think not that I am come to destroy the law, &c." and the letter of the Apostles to Antioch, Syria and Cilicia,[1] it briefly sketches what it supposes to be the history and activity of synods in England, and thus comes to the king's own intentions. Of this introduction I have selected a few passages where the additions and changes show that the king was seriously considering the law of Exodus with a view to its applicability to the conditions of his own time, and I have added to these extracts his account of synods and of his own investigations. I have given all his code except for some sections on detailed compensations. His treaty with Guthrum is also included.

The two extant codes of Alfred's son and successor are short and of no great interest. Their content is repeated in Athelstan's laws, and so I have been content to refer to them in the notes to Athelstan. The so-called treaty of Edward and Guthrum is not included; for it is actually a text of a century later. Six codes and a short ordinance on almsgiving survive from Athelstan's reign, though two are only in Latin versions. I have chosen the second, 'at Grateley' and the fifth, 'at Exeter', since between them they include most of the new matter in his legislation, and also the sixth, which is of particular interest in showing how the general instructions given by the king were put into practice in one district by detailed arrangements. As this district is that dependent on the city of London, it throws a little light on the organiza- tion of this city, and it introduces us to one of those artificial organizations for the maintenance of order and for mutual assistance which we meet again in the later guild-statutes.[2] Of the codes omitted, I Athelstan is concerned entirely with the payment of tithe, and the content of III and IV is almost entirely covered in the codes selected. Moreover, they survive (except for a fragment of IV) only in the Latin of *Quadripartitus*, and its author has not fully understood them.

Edward the Elder was legislating for the English part of England only, for he mentions that an offence which is to be paid for "according to the law-book" if it occur "herein", is to be paid for according to "the treaties" if committed in the north and east. Athelstan's laws do not state how far the area extends for which they are intended. But by the middle of the century it seems likely that the kings of England must have had to give thought to the advisability of attempting some measure of uniformity over the whole country now under their control. The most interesting of Edmund's codes is directed at controlling the vendetta, and is definitely stated to apply "throughout all my dominion", and it is at least a probability that it was the prevalence of blood-feuds in the areas of Scandinavian settlement that brought home to him the need for this action. It is noteworthy that some Scandinavian loan- words, *e.g. griŏ, sehtan* and *hamsocn*, first appear in this code. His other two codes are of less interest; I Edmund mainly stresses the need to pay dues to the Church, but it has two statements of wider interest. Its insistence on clerical celibacy reminds us that we are at the period when monastic revival was in the air, and its refusal to allow a homicide in the king's neighbourhood marks a movement to emphasize the sanctity of kingship, discernible in other texts in this century. It is one of the ironies of history that this very king should have met his death going to the help of his seneschal who was trying to prevent the entry of a criminal into the king's presence. In this reign or just after it, comes the Hundred Ordinance, and in either case II Edmund

---

[1] Acts xv. 23 ff.   [2] See Nos. 136–139.

shows that the hundred was a recognized institution in his time. It may be part of an attempt to secure greater uniformity over the various parts of the kingdom, and be not unconnected with the division of the midlands into shires during this century.

By the time one reaches Edgar, the legal autonomy of the Danish districts has been accepted, at least in principle. I include the code, IV Edgar, which states this, partly on this account but also for its interest in affording a glimpse of how laws were circulated, and, again, because it is the first instance of the enjoining of religious observances to stave off national calamity. It is not without interest that the code should have been preserved for us in manuscripts accessible to Archbishop Wulfstan, who is loud in advocating similar measures during the Danish invasions. Throughout his writings, Wulfstan is full of praise of Edgar's legislation, and it was no doubt at his instigation that it was made the basis of the agreement between the English and Danes after Cnut's conquest. But Wulfstan did more than praise: he imitated, and the laws of Edgar that he so frequently used are II and III Edgar. It seems only right, therefore, to print such influential laws here.

Of the ten codes, or fragments of codes, of Ethelred's reign—and as one should add the so-called "Laws of Edward and Guthrum" there are really eleven—the first four have no sign of Wulfstan's influence. Ethelred's laws at Woodstock (I Ethelred), issued for an English area, are unremarkable, but a code of somewhere about the same time (III Ethelred) issued at Wantage to apply to a Danish area, is of great interest, and is printed here, as is also the treaty made with Olaf Tryggvason and other viking leaders (II Ethelred). There is also a set of trade regulations for London, known as IV Ethelred, though it contains no king's name. Of the codes drawn up by Wulfstan, namely V–X and the "Laws of Edward and Guthrum", I have included V, VII and part of VIII, which between them contain almost all that is of interest.

I have recently suggested that Wulfstan continued to draft laws after Ethelred's death.[1] I have given here the preface of what I confidently believe to be the first draft of Cnut's laws, got ready in haste for the meeting between Danes and English in 1018. I have included also his two interesting and important letters from abroad, and since his main code was the last issued in pre-Conquest England, and was held in great honour in Norman times, it seems right that it should be well represented, though with omission of those sections where it is merely repeating laws already included in this selection, and also of some of the homiletic matter.

The choice among the anonymous pieces was more difficult, for most would have qualified for admission on grounds of interest. The five pieces on ranks have the additional interest of being very probably a collection by Wulfstan himself. The "Law of the Northumbrian Priests" is a fortunate survival from an area with few documents, and the text on the betrothal of a woman belongs to a branch of law of which we should be glad to know more. It is useful for comparison with surviving marriage agreements.[2]

The translation

The translation of the Anglo-Saxon laws has its special difficulties. They are frequently, especially in the earlier times, very briefly and even cryptically expressed, being composed for persons familiar with the general circumstances and thus requiring guidance on a particular issue only. They may therefore merely state what is to be

---

[1] See *Eng. Hist. Rev.*, LXIII, pp. 433–452.   [2] See Nos. 128, 129.

paid on a certain occasion without saying by whom or to whom, and it is not in all cases possible to expand their laconic statements without committing oneself to an interpretation which was not necessarily the author's meaning. There are many places also where there can be doubt as to what antecedent a pronoun refers. But the greatest difficulty of all is in the interpretation of some of the terminology. The laws are spread over a period of four centuries; the meanings of words can change over so long a stretch of time. Even in contemporary documents, or, in fact, in the same code, a term may be used in its general, wider sense, as well as in a technical sense, and it is not always clear how one should take it in a given instance. For example, the word *gesith* originally means simply a companion, and Liebermann would thus interpret it in Ine 23.1, whereas it came to be applied particularly to members of the king's retinue, and so to members of an upper class, who themselves had men under them. This, its usual sense in the laws, may well be its meaning in Ine 23.1. One may compare the position with the word *gegilda*: by the late tenth century it certainly means a member of a guild, but by etymology it should mean simply "a person who pays along with someone". When we read in Ine 16 that the *gegildan* of a slain thief have no right to an oath to clear the thief, are we to take it, with Liebermann, that this could refer to a guild such as those evidenced later, and thus assume the existence of such associations in the late seventh century? Or, since in Ine 21, 21.1, it seems to be interchangeable with 'kinsmen', should we, with Attenborough, take it in its original sense, to mean those persons who by reason of kinship or any other cause were united with the thief for purposes of payment, and so were entitled to receive compensation for him if any were due? These would in normal cases be the kinsmen, but in the absence of these, there were *gegildan* who were not kinsmen, as we can see from Alfred 30.1.

Another difficulty is to know whether, when two different words are used, they are variant methods of referring to the same thing, or whether a distinction is being made. The breach of one's *borg* or 'security' was probably only one of many acts which could be regarded as violation of *mund* or '(power of) protection', but the terms seem used without distinction. In many contexts, *gesith* and *gesith-born* man could be interchanged, but the former would probably not be used of a member of a *gesith-born* family not yet in possession of a household of his own.[1] The same conceptions may be described by different words at different periods, but it would be unwise to state dogmatically that nothing has altered but the name. The term for noble birth in the earliest Kentish laws, *eorl-cund*, is replaced in the latest Kentish code by *gesith-cund*, the term current in contemporary Wessex, to judge by Ine's laws. The change may be more than a matter of terminology, and express a recognition that noble rank is now mainly gained through personal service to the king. King Alfred seems to have preferred to speak of the nobility in terms of their wergilds, though he does use *gesith-cund*, and the term is used with reference to rank in non-legal writings of his time. After his reign, it appears to have been superseded by the term 'thegn'. But throughout this time, the original name for a noble, *eorl*, was kept alive by the rhyme formula *eorl and ceorl*, and was used in poetry. The interest taken, whether for practical or antiquarian reasons, in previous laws by later writers, may sometimes preserve a term in an older sense at a later date. In the following translations the more serious cases of obscurity or ambiguity are discussed in the footnotes, in which, as well as in many of the renderings in the text itself, I am frequently

[1] See p. 362, n. 2.

indebted to the work of previous editors, especially Liebermann, Attenborough and Miss Robertson.

The working of the legal system

A few general explanations on the working of the Anglo-Saxon legal system are desirable as an introduction to the laws themselves. Lawsuits were brought before the public assemblies, before something which is simply denoted by 'folk-moot' in the earlier laws, but before the assembly of the hundred, borough or shire at any rate from the mid-tenth century onwards, except when the right to hold a court had been granted to some private magnate, lay or ecclesiastical. Even when a thief had been caught in the act and killed, it was necessary for the slayer to declare with a public oath that he had slain him as a thief. In all other suits, the plaintiff summoned the defendant to answer to a charge, and failure to appear after due summons meant outlawry. In the majority of cases, the defendant in criminal suits, the possessor of the disputed property in civil cases, was allowed to produce an oath with the help of compurgators, who were willing to swear with him to his innocence in a criminal charge, or to his rightful ownership in a civil suit. There was little attempt to investigate the facts and weigh the evidence, as in modern suits, but there were, however, certain circumstances which would rob the defendant of his right to come to the oath and allow this to the plaintiff instead. If the man accused had been found in possession of stolen goods, or in other suspicious circumstances, or if he were a notorious bad character; or if the claimant of land had the title-deeds in his possession; in cases such as these the plaintiff with his oath-helpers was allowed to produce his oath, and if he did so successfully, all that was left for the defendant was to pay the penalties or to go to the ordeal. The same alternative was open for the defendant who, having the right to produce an oath, proved unable to get the full number of oath-helpers. The number of these required, no matter which party had the right to bring the oath, varied with the charge; it is fixed by the laws, usually in relation to the amount of the penalty attached to the particular crime, as, for example, when we are told in Ine 30 that the accused is to clear himself by his wergild, and if he cannot, to pay his wergild. The size of the oath is often expressed in hides in Ine's law, and once in Alfred's, and it is clear that when it is, the number of hides in the oath is the same as the number of shillings in the fine for the offence in question; but what is not clear is the precise meaning of an oath expressed in hides, or, rather, what it was that entitled a man to swear for a certain number of hides. It was certainly not simply the possession of land of that amount. The value of a man's oath was graded on the same ratio as his wergild; thus we are told that in Mercian law, the oath of a man with a twelve hundred wergild is worth that of six *ceorls*, and there are signs that the *ceorl* was entitled to swear for five hides,[1] though it could only have been a rare occurrence that a man of this class would possess so much land as this, an amount which was believed in some quarters to entitle a man to some of the privileges of a thegn.[2] Early Northumbrian law probably expressed oaths in terms of hides, like that of Wessex, to judge by the *Dialogue* of Egbert, Archbishop of York (732–766), which declares the values of the oaths of the clergy as 120 *tributarii* for a priest, 60 *manentes* for a deacon, 30 *tributarii* for a monk,[3] thus using the same Latin terms for hide as do Latin charters. The

---

[1] See H. M. Chadwick, *Studies on Anglo-Saxon Institutions*, pp. 143–153.
[2] See No. 52. Liebermann (*Glossar*, s.v. *Eideshufen*) suggests that the *ceorl* swore for five hides because he was regarded as representing a community of this size, just as in later times, at any rate, one man represented five hides for the performance of military service.   [3] Haddan and Stubbs, III, p. 404.

Kentish laws, on the other hand, state the actual number of helpers required, and so do the later laws from the "Treaty of Alfred and Guthrum" on, except for a reference to an oath of a pound in I Ethelred 1.3, a mode of reckoning which occurs also in charters. If, as seems likely. the correspondence of one shilling to one hide seen in the laws of Ine still holds, and the amount became traditional at the time when fourpence was calculated to the shilling in Wessex as well as Mercia,[1] the oath of one pound would be the same thing as an oath of 60 hides, probably equivalent to an oath sworn by twelve *ceorls*.

If the accused went to the ordeal, it was left for the accuser to decide whether this was to be the ordeal of water or of iron. In the former case, the cold water ordeal might be chosen, in which the accused was thrown, fastened on a rope, into some convenient tank, pond or river, after this had been adjured in God's name to accept the innocent and cast out the guilty. If he floated, his guilt was considered established. In the hot water ordeal, the accused had to seize a stone from the bottom of a cauldron of water, in the ordeal of iron, he had to carry a heated weight of iron a certain distance; in either case he was considered cleared if after three days his hand had healed without festering. Both these forms of ordeal took place within a church, and elaborate rituals for their performance are preserved in various ritual books. Just as the size of oath required for compurgation increased in proportion to the seriousness of the charge, so also the ordeal could be simple or threefold; in the latter case, the hand must be plunged into the cauldron up to the elbow, instead of the wrist, in the ordeal of hot water, while the weight of iron was three pounds instead of one in the ordeal of iron. Another form of ordeal, the swallowing of a consecrated morsel, after it had been adjured to choke the guilty, was used when the accused was a cleric. In all cases, if the accused were convicted at the ordeal, he must then pay the penalty laid down by the law for the offence in question, but one should note that this was sometimes lighter than that imposed for the same act if the criminal had been caught red-handed.

Occasional mention is made of a 'fore-oath'. This was produced by the plaintiff to prove that he had a bona fide case sufficient to force the defendant to come to answer to the charge, and that he was not merely trumping one up out of envy or malice.

After a conviction, the majority of offences could be compounded for, if the accused – or his kinsmen or his lord, if they were willing to assist him – could discharge all the claims, namely the fine to the king (or to the holder of the profits of jurisdiction if these had been granted into private hands), and the compensation to the injured parties, which in many cases included not only those who had been injured or robbed, but also persons whose surety or rights of protection had been violated by the action. In a case of homicide, the wergild had to be paid to the kindred, and it took precedence over the other claims, *e.g.* that of the lord to compensation for his man, that of the State to the fine for fighting, that of the owner of the house if the killing had taken place in one.[2] If the accused could not satisfy all claims, he went into penal slavery, to work for those whose claims he could not satisfy. If the crime were one which incurred the death penalty, the criminal's goods were forfeit, but the widow retained her third of them if she were innocent of complicity. The few great crimes for which the penalty was death, with no option of redemption, were sometimes called *botleas*

---

[1] The West Saxon shilling was later calculated as equivalent to fivepence, while that of Mercia remained at fourpence.

[2] At least, this seems implied by Ine 71, but in a later tract, called *Wergild*, it is only the *healsfang* which must be paid before the compensation to the lord and the fine for fighting.

crimes, *i.e.* crimes beyond compensation. Naturally nothing more could be paid than life and all possessions, but all other offences could be aggravated by involving breach of sanctuary, breach of the special Church festivals, or breach of the king's peace.

If, after these few paragraphs of explanation, one reads the extracts here chosen, it is obvious that the main difficulties with which the legislators were concerned were twofold: to bring to justice men of small competence who had little to lose by flight, and to make difficult the disposal of stolen property, especially cattle. The first difficulty led to various statutes making other persons, kinsmen, lord, and, later, members of artificial associations, responsible with their possessions for the production of an offender, and also to regulations which would make an employer think twice before he took an unknown man into his service, and thus would make it difficult for the fugitive from justice to get a living anywhere. The second consideration produced masses of regulations about the need for witnesses at purchases, and the procedure of vouching the vendor to warranty when goods in one's possession were attached. With these preliminary explanations, it is best to let the laws speak for themselves.

CHARTERS

The number and authenticity of extant charters

The two great collections of Anglo-Saxon documents, Kemble's *Codex Diplomaticus* and Birch's *Cartularium Saxonicum*, contain between them some 1,500 different charters, in addition to manumissions, papal and other letters, detached boundaries, dedications to books, and a few other texts that are not charters. There are also in print in scattered places over a hundred charters not in these works and some still lurk in unprinted sources. Charters form a most valuable source of Anglo-Saxon history, affording information of most varied kinds; but before this information can be used with safety, it is necessary to assure oneself of the genuineness of the document containing it, and it is therefore desirable to preface the selection here given with a few general remarks on the question of authenticity, especially since Kemble's opinions on individual documents, expressed by attaching an asterisk to those he considered spurious, are frequently out of agreement with modern views.

Some 200 charters survive in contemporary, or nearly contemporary, form, mainly on separate parchments, but sometimes on fly-leaves or blank spaces of gospels or other religious books. Another 40 or so are copies on separate parchments made in later, but still pre-Conquest, times; and Mr. N. R. Ker has recently suggested that the first part of the Worcester cartulary which is known as Hemming's cartulary is a pre-Conquest compilation.[1] Some originals have been lost since they were first printed. Wanley in 1705 notes that 92 documents (86 of pre-Conquest date) were listed by Dugdale as being at Worcester in 1643.[2] Seventeen Worcester charters, all, except one, of pre-Conquest date, had been printed by Hickes before their disappearance. There is only one contemporary charter of this date at Worcester now; but fortunately Smith printed in an appendix to his edition of Bede,[3] in 1722, 24 Worcester charters which in Wanley's day were in the possession of Lord Somers, but which were destroyed in a fire at Lincoln's Inn in 1752. Similarly, a set of 12 Abingdon documents, no longer extant, had been transcribed by Talbot, and his transcripts are

---

[1] See *Studies in Medieval History presented to F. M. Powicke*, pp. 49–75.
[2] *Thesaurus*, II, 299 f.   [3] *Baedae Historia Ecclesiastica Latine et Saxonice*, pp. 764–782.

now bound up with Corpus Christi College, Cambridge, MS. 111.[1] Most of the Rochester charters printed by J. Thorpe in his *Registrum Roffense* in 1769 from the archives of that church have found their way to the British Museum, but Birch found no version of his Nos. 439 and 460, dated 842 and 850 respectively, and had to print from Thorpe. No. 460, however, is shown by its spelling to have been a post-Conquest text, and it is of doubtful authenticity. Somner, the Kentish antiquary, appears now to be the oldest authority for Birch, No. 342, and Kemble, Nos. 732 and 745, while it is possible that he had older versions of Birch, Nos. 317 and 344, and of Kemble, No. 782, than the texts in the Canterbury cartularies which survive.[2]

Thus, though the great majority of charters have come down to us only in post-Conquest cartularies, or in the Charter, Patent and Confirmation Rolls of later kings, there exists a reasonable amount of contemporary material by which the authenticity of late versions can be tested. That these can be accurate copies may be shown by a comparison of originals with late versions when both happen to survive. Exact copies are to be found not only in cartularies of good repute like the *Textus Roffensis* or Hemming's cartulary, but even in less reliable sources; *e.g.* the *Codex Wintoniensis* has exact versions of some original charters,[3] and a number of texts that survive either in contemporary form or in Talbot's copies were closely rendered in an Abingdon cartulary. Sometimes, however, the copy shortens the original, by omission of words or even of whole clauses, especially of the attestations of witnesses. The Chichester register in its version[4] of an original of 780[5] omits the names of ten signatories of the grant and three of the confirmation, and also abbreviates the anathema; otherwise it gives an accurate text. The Worcester cartulary, Brit. Mus. Cott. Nero E. i, gives shortened versions, while the Burton-on-Trent cartulary[6] usually omits all but the first few attestations. Such curtailment should not throw doubt on the authenticity of a text, but may make it more difficult to establish this with certainty when no full version has survived.

Some later versions can be shown to have been guilty of interpolation. It was the practice of some cartularies to add the incarnation date to early charters dated only by the indiction, and there are also instances of the interpolation of clauses which claim the possession of privileges or immunities which, at the date of the charter, were either not known, or else taken for granted without specific mention. Thus the clause of immunity from all royal dues except the three regular exceptions of military service, bridge and fortress making, is added to the cartulary versions of several Canterbury charters whose originals survive without any clause of this nature. Hence it is clear that the presence of a later feature of this kind need not impugn the genuineness of a text as a whole. Detailed boundaries in the vernacular first occur in a possible text in 814;[7] they become normal in the tenth century; but they are frequently added in cartularies to charters too early for this feature.

The number of texts to be entirely rejected as spurious is probably not so great as is sometimes supposed. Many texts that survive only in a later source are couched in the formulae used by extant contemporary documents of about the same time, and have a list of witnesses consistent with their date. No forger could produce such a text unless he had an original of this date before him; he might conceivably copy

---

[1] See Wanley, *op. cit.*, p. 150.

[2] Madox, *Formulare Anglicanum*, 1702, has preserved the Westminster charter, Birch No. 1309. Birch, Nos. 882, 1145 and 1336 are printed from seventeenth-century paper copies of lost documents.

[3] Brit. Mus. Harley Charters 43 C2 and C11.   [4] Birch, No. 237.

[5] No. 76, Birch, No. 1334.   [6] National Library of Wales, Peniarth MS. 390.   [7] Birch, No. 346.

such an original, substituting the name of a different estate or a different donee from those in his exemplar; if he did, his text would in all other respects represent a genuine text, and even the substituted matter need not necessarily be untrue. Most religious houses kept lists of their benefactors, and therefore the claim that a certain grant was made by a particular person may be correct even when the charter making the grant is not free from suspicion. It is improbable, however, that forgers were often careful enough to search for an original of the required date; their work was not to be subjected to the searching scrutiny of modern methods of detection. No one possessed our modern apparatus for ascertaining whether the formulae were permissible or the witnesses alive at the alleged date. There would be little incentive to go to tremendous trouble to produce a flawless text, and there can be little doubt that the great majority of unexceptionable cartulary versions are copies of genuine originals which have not been preserved. Even texts to which exception can be taken because of the presence of suspicious clauses may nevertheless have a genuine base, although with some later additions. Such interpolations, and in fact forgeries in general, were by no means always in support of false claims; often they were to meet a demand in later days for written evidence of rights of various kinds which were lawfully held, though such written evidence had either disappeared or never existed. Yet a too remote antiquity may often be claimed for various rights, and evidence may be fabricated to support freedom from royal or episcopal control.

Many of the charters in cartularies may be accepted as genuine even without the support of similar phraseology in contemporary documents. When the cartularies of different religious houses agree in their phrasing in texts of about the same date, we must assume either that they have contemporary texts before them, or that there has been collu̇sion between different houses to produce forged documents. Such collusion did on occasion take place: Dr. Levison has recently traced in detail the career of a twelfth-century forger called Guerno, who fabricated documents for religious houses in Soissons and Rouen, for St. Augustine's at Canterbury and probably for Peterborough,[1] and the Westminster school of forgers was influential outside its own house. St. Paul's and Chertsey must have combined to produce spurious documents,[2] and there is a connexion between the Bath and Malmesbury forgeries,[3] while a Worcester document dated 972[4] is copied from a Pershore text,[5] and so on. But such documents are generally elaborate affairs that make wider claims than genuine texts and frequently give themselves away by the use of expressions–sometimes of Frankish origin–quite alien to those in pre-Conquest texts. It is very unlikely that there ever existed a class of more subtle forgers, capable of producing texts with many of the normal features of an Anglo-Saxon charter, who worked for various houses and were careful to vary their phraseology on a consistent scheme according to the alleged date of the charter they were fabricating. It is much easier to believe that in general, agreement between texts of the same period preserved in different sources arises from independent reproduction of genuine texts, even when, by accident, no surviving contemporary version contains the phrases in question. We are especially dependent on such criteria for testing authenticity in periods for which contemporary evidence is scanty. A couple of examples will illustrate this.

There is a dearth of contemporary charters of the reigns of Alfred and his son,

---

[1] *England and the Continent in the Eighth Century*, pp. 210–220.
[2] Birch, Nos. 737, 1195; Kemble, No. 812.   [3] Birch, Nos. 670, 671.
[4] Birch, No. 1284.   [5] Birch, No. 1282.

Edward the Elder. In the twelfth-century Winchester cartulary, however, there is a charter of the latter king, dated 901,[1] which includes details that would be pointless in a later fabrication and which has before its dating clause and attestations a vernacular addition. I suspect it of being a reference to a marriage settlement, but the wording is too ambiguous for certainty, and the point of this addition would be clear only to persons who knew the relationship of the people mentioned in it. If the charter were the invention of a later age we should surely have been given more explicit information. This charter is unusual in that its list of witnesses, although a long one, contains no ecclesiastics. A forger would have been unlikely to omit so regular a feature as episcopal signatures, and it is to be noted that there are other texts purporting to come from this period in which the ecclesiastical element in the attestations is very slight, while it is absent altogether from an original of Ethelbert of Wessex of 858[2] and from a charter of Alfred preserved in the Abingdon cartulary,[3] which is a grant to one of the persons concerned in the charter of Edward's under consideration and is somewhat similar in type, having, like it, a vernacular addition before the attestations. On general grounds, therefore, Edward's charter may be adjudged genuine. Its authenticity is further supported by the occurrence of some of its formulae in a text of the very same year preserved in the Wilton cartulary,[4] especially since both charters use a derivative of a Greek word not employed, as far as our evidence goes, elsewhere. This agreement suggests that the Wilton charter is at least based on a genuine text of this date, though its proem has agreements with rather later charters, e.g. with a Winchester original of 948,[5] and still more with a Muchelney original of 995.[6] It would surely be an odd coincidence if a forger accidentally used this rare word when concocting a text which he dates the very year of the only other occurrence of it.

My second illustration comes from a group of tenth-century documents which differ considerably in their phraseology from the bulk of the charters of this period, being drawn up in rhythmical Latin and containing a number of formulae peculiar to them. Eight of them occur in the Burton-on-Trent cartulary,[7] and as they differ so signally from any documents that have been preserved in contemporary form, one might have regarded them as Burton forgeries, if odd specimens of this type did not crop up in the records of other religious houses; three are from Worcester,[8] two from Thorney, whereas Glastonbury, Winchester, Peterborough and Ely are represented by one each. They are mainly concerned with lands and donors in the midlands, and it seems probable that they are authentic, odd though their phrasing may be.

A great deal of detailed study is still necessary before any pronouncement can be made as to the number of spurious texts purporting to come from the Anglo-Saxon period. Glaring forgeries of the type mentioned above cause little trouble. These tend to attribute grants to kings such as Ine or Ethelwulf of Wessex, Offa of Mercia, Athelstan and others known to be generous to religious houses, but they are expressed in terminology very alien to the authentic texts issued by these kings. They sometimes try to add verisimilitude by introducing events of whose existence they have learnt from Bede, the Anglo-Saxon Chronicle, Asser or William of Malmesbury, not realizing how rare such references are in genuine texts of most periods. An authentic charter of Athelstan issued at Nottingham in 934 makes no mention at all of the

---

[1] No. 100.   [2] Birch, No. 496.   [3] Birch, No. 581.   [4] Birch, No. 588.   [5] Birch, No. 862.
[6] E. H. Bates, *Two Cartularies of the Benedictine Abbeys of Muchelney and Athelney*, pp. 43–45.
[7] Peniarth MS. 390.   [8] One is No. 105 below, and is one of the Somers charters printed in Smith.

expedition to Scotland on which the king is actually engaged, but two charters that are obviously spurious on other counts contain quite gratuitous reference to the battle of *Brunanburh*. Kemble declared "as the truth always feels itself to be strong, but a lie always feels itself to be weak, the great pains taken to make us believe something, lead us naturally to suspect a consciousness that that something was in reality not worthy of belief".[1]

But between blameless texts on the one hand and obvious fabrications on the other, there lies a large group where decision is not so easy. Suspicion may be roused by a discrepancy between the various methods of dating, or between the date and the witnesses, or between either of these and the name of the king supposed to have issued the charter; or the formulae, though genuine in themselves, may seem too early or too late for the supposed date. Some such documents may represent the work of later fabricators who had inadequate material before them or who did not trouble to take as the basis of their work an original of the proper period, and thus, for example, copied the forms normal in Athelstan's charters in texts issued in Edgar's name. Yet all such texts should not be hastily dismissed; it is easy to misread or miscopy Roman numerals, and some discrepancies are of this origin; when a charter is contradicted by chronicle evidence with regard to the accession to office of a witness, or his death, one must not assume without investigation that it is necessarily the charter which is wrong; some kings' names, moreover, were easily confused by later copyists, and a 'spurious' charter of Cenwulf of Mercia may prove to be an authentic text of Cynewulf of Wessex,[2] while the peculiarities of Birch, No. 873, are explained when we realize that the Abingdon scribe confused Ethelred (Æðered) I of Wessex with Eadred, so that the date belongs to the latter, though the forms and witnesses are of Ethelred's reign. Even the test of anachronistic use of formulae must not be applied too rigidly; there is no abrupt change in style from reign to reign; modifications creep in gradually, and from time to time formulae are revived after apparently being discontinued for a long period, so that one may meet an undoubtedly authentic charter couched in conservative terms. We need to know more than we yet do about the conditions in which Anglo-Saxon charters were drawn up before we can pronounce with confidence on the authenticity of a cartulary text in all cases.

It is a suspicious feature when an Anglo-Saxon charter mentions the name of the person who drew it up. Such statements are not normal in the pre-Conquest period, and they occur mainly in those forgeries mentioned above which are influenced by Frankish diplomatic practice. The forger's motive is obvious when a document claims the sanctity of having been drawn up by St. Dunstan himself. Yet it is as well to be careful even in applying this test. Four cartulary texts purporting to come from the late seventh or very early eighth century, one from Shaftesbury,[3] one from Abingdon[4] and two from Malmesbury,[5] claim to have been written by Wynberht, later abbot of Nursling. The Malmesbury texts are highly suspicious, and as they occur in William of Malmesbury's *De Gestis Pontificum* may have influenced the compilers of the other two cartularies; but, as W. H. Stevenson has pointed out, this unusual feature may well be geniune at a date when the West Saxon see was held by a Frankish bishop, who is likely to have introduced a practice of his own country. It is also worth noting that there is a charter of 1008 in the cartulary of the monastery of Abingdon,[6] which states "*Ego Wulfgar abbas hanc kartulam gaudenti corde composui*", and another

---

[1] *Codex Diplomaticus*, I, pp. lxxxixf.   [2] Birch, No. 327.   [3] No. 55, Birch, No. 107.
[4] Birch, No. 100.   [5] Birch, Nos. 37, 103.   [6] Kemble, No. 1305.

Abingdon charter,[1] dated 993, has "*Ego Uulfgar abbas abbandunens coenobii hoc sintagma triumphans dictaui*". It is possible that such phrases are later expansions, owing to a misunderstanding of the use in Ethelred's charters of the verbs *composui, dictavi*, and others like them simply to give variety to the attestation clauses of the witnesses; in a lost Abingdon charter copied by Talbot,[2] Wulfgar witnesses "*gaudens dictavi*" when all the other abbots add their names alone, and this may have given rise to a belief that he himself drew up the documents. Yet there would not be anything incredible in the performance of this task by so important a dignitary; there is unimpeachable evidence that even an archbishop could be asked by the king to draw up a charter,[3] and a writ of Edward the Confessor stating that he has granted Taynton, Oxfordshire, to St. Denis in Paris concludes "and it is my will that the bishop[4] compose a 'book' to it, with my full permission".[5] This 'book' is extant. It is therefore possible that the Abingdon charters are correct in their claim to Wulfgar's authorship. These charters should be compared with Kemble, No. 736, a contemporary charter of Cnut, from Evesham, in which, while all the other bishops attest with a simple formula, such as 'have acquiesced', 'have subscribed', or the like, Bishop Æthelric of Dorchester is made to say: *in nomine saluatoris iubente rege sub testimonio optimatum hanc scedulam dictitando perscribere iussi*.

Finally, before pronouncing any document to be an out and out forgery, it is always as well to consider whether there was any possible motive for its fabrication. As Sir Frank Stenton remarks: "Even an Anglo-Norman monk did not engage wantonly in the fabrication of documents useless to his house."[6] Documents which show a community alienating the lands of their house are unlikely to have been invented, and one should hesitate to pronounce a document a forgery if it merely describes temporary arrangements that have long come to an end at the date of the alleged fabrication.

For the purposes of this volume I have mainly avoided texts that present difficulties of this kind, using, except where otherwise stated, those that I consider beyond doubt, but I have not, other things being equal, shown a strong preference for a contemporary text above one extant in a later form, for in some cases the evidence of these cartulary texts has been too little used.

It remains to be noted, however, that even a proved forgery need not be without interest. It may tell us something about the period in which it was fabricated, or it may use sources of information that have not come down to us. For example, whoever fabricated or interpolated two Winchester charters[7] had access to some material about Egbert's campaign in Devon which is not in the Anglo-Saxon Chronicle and which avoids the incorrect date of that record.[8]

When drawing conclusions from the extant charters, it must always be borne in mind that only those that found their way into ecclesiastical archives had any chance of survival. The comparative rarity of grants to laymen is probably to be explained simply by this fact; it would be unsafe to assume that such grants were rare.

The origin and development of the Anglo-Saxon charter

The use of writing to record the transfer of land and the gift of privileges was due to the influence of the Church, and men of later times assumed that the practice began

---

[1] Brit. Mus. Cott. Aug. ii 38 = Kemble, No. 684.
[2] Kemble, No. 703.   [3] Kemble, No. 898.   [4] *i.e.* Wulfwig of Dorchester.
[5] The latest discussion on this question is contained in F. E. Harmer, *Anglo-Saxon Writs*, pp. 38–41.
[6] *The Early History of the Abbey of Abingdon*, p. 13.   [7] Birch, Nos. 389, 390.   [8] See p. 171, n. 1.

immediately after the conversion and that the first Christian king, Ethelbert of Kent, issued donation charters to Canterbury and Rochester. But the charters said to be issued in his name are obvious forgeries and no charter survives in a contemporary form before one of Hlothhere of Kent of 679.[1] Cartulary versions couched in early formulae do not begin more than a few years before this date, the earliest being Birch, No. 28, dated the fourteenth year of Wulfhere of Mercia, i.e. 670–671 (its witnesses seem to have been copied from No. 57 and to belong to 681). From the last quarter of the seventh century, authentic charters are extant from Surrey, Mercia, Sussex, Essex, the kingdom of the Hwicce, and especially from Kent, while there are a few texts relating to Wessex[2] which employ some early formulae and may have a genuine base. Written grants were known in Northumbria from about the same period, as we know from Eddi, who tells how Wilfrid read out on the day of the dedication of Ripon (671–678) "a list of the lands which the kings, for the good of their souls, had previously, and on that very day as well, presented to him, with the agreement and over the signatures of the bishops and all the chief men",[3] and Bede, writing in 734, refers to the deeds procured by false monasteries in confirmation of their possessions, authenticated by the signature of bishops, abbots and secular authorities.[4] It has been suggested that grants were made by charter from the earliest days of the English Church, but that the early ones were written on papyrus and thus perished easily; but there is no evidence that papyrus was ever used in this country, and it would be odd if churchmen of subsequent generations did not copy out of piety the papyrus charters of their earliest benefactors on to more permanent material. Hence the alternative opinion is more probable, that the use of the written record was an introduction of Archbishop Theodore of Tarsus, who organized the English Church so thoroughly during his episcopate of 668–690. Donations to churches were certainly made before his time; the innovation lay in the drawing up of a document to record the act. This view is easier to accept since the opinion has been discarded in late years that the Anglo-Saxon formal charter was 'dispositive', i.e. that its delivery to the donee constituted the act of donation. It is now generally held that it was merely 'evidentiary', a precautionary record of an act performed before witnesses, an act valid and complete whether a charter was made or not. The earliest grants were probably made by some sort of symbolic act of transfer, such as the placing of a sod on the altar, which is occasionally mentioned in early charters.

Charters can be conveniently divided into two classes, royal and private, and the first of these groups subdivided into the 'diploma' and the 'writ'. The diploma is a solemn document, almost always in Latin. In fact, there is only one reliable example of a document of this kind being issued in the vernacular, namely a grant by Brihtwulf of Mercia to his thegn Forthred in 845;[5] a handful of other vernacular diplomas exist, but arouse a suspicion of being later translation from Latin originals by their stilted English, their retention of Latin tags, or the late form of their language. The diploma is issued by the king, often with the expressed consent of his council, and it records the creation or transfer of 'bookland'—a term whose interpretation has occasioned controversy, but which probably describes land which was freed from payment of the king's farm and certain other royal dues, originally with the intention that it should be devoted to religious purposes, and which was held with the power to

[1] No. 56.   [2] e.g. Birch, Nos. 65, 71, 74, 100.   [3] See No. 154.
[4] See No. 170, p. 741.   [5] Birch, No. 452.

alienate it freely.[1] The 'book', or title-deed, usually states that the donee may leave the land to whom he chooses, and in the literary usage of the tenth century, at any rate, the term bookland is employed to denote land owned freely at one's own disposal. We know little about the holding of land in pre-Christian England, but it can hardly be doubted that there, as in other Germanic lands, there might be difficulties in the way of alienating it from the kindred, and that new arrangements might have to be made after the conversion to Christianity before landowners could make permanent endowments to religious bodies. It is not surprising that the agreement of the councillors should often be obtained for an act which diminished the royal revenue, and which probably ran counter to traditional rules of inheritance; nor that, before very long, ecclesiastics, being accustomed to the use of writing, should introduce the written record as a better security against the claims of the donor's descendants or of later kings; nor, finally, that the instrument they introduced should have a much more pronounced ecclesiastical flavour than the late Roman private deeds which served as their models. The diploma begins with an invocation, usually followed by a religious proem; in the body of the grant itself the donor often mentions that he is acting for the good of his soul, or that the gift is made for the foundation or augmentation of a monastery; a sanction follows, consigning to the torments of hell anyone who dares to infringe the donation, and sometimes calling down the blessing of God on all who support it; the witnesses attest it with the sign of the Cross. Disputes concerning 'bookland' are often dealt with at Church synods in the eighth and ninth centuries. As time goes on, the religious element in the diploma becomes more elaborate–by the reign of Ethelred (978–1016) the proem has sometimes swollen into a homily of considerable length–even though it had become common to make grants of bookland to laymen without any intention of its being devoted to religious uses. Sometimes we are frankly told that a price has been paid for the grant, and this may have happened in cases where it is not mentioned. It is possible that the granting of bookland afforded a means by which the kings could raise ready money, at the cost of loss of future income from their farm.

As has been said above, the earliest charters were based on the late Roman private deed. They are comparatively short and simple; if boundaries are given, they are brief and in Latin; no attempt is made to vary the formulae by which the witnesses attest. In the eighth century, Kentish charters remain conservatively faithful to the early formulae, but in Mercia, especially under Offa, various new features are found, which henceforward become a permanent part of the normal Anglo-Saxon diploma. For example, we have in a Mercian text of 770[2] the first authentic instance of a clause which later is almost invariably present, which excepts the three public charges of military service, bridge and fortress work from the general exemption from royal dues. Boundaries begin to be given more fully in the eighth century, and a West Saxon charter of 778[3] has them in considerable detail, but still in Latin; it is not until the next century that we get genuine instances of boundaries set out in detail in the vernacular. There are signs also of a striving after a more inflated style, as in a charter of Offa of 779,[4] and this tendency steadily increases until one reaches the absurdly elaborate and florid style of Athelstan's charters, which, with their rare words,

---

[1] See F. M. Stenton, *Anglo-Saxon England*, pp. 302–308, and for earlier views, F. W. Maitland, *Domesday Book and Beyond*, pp. 270 ff., P. Vinogradoff, "Folkland" (*Eng. Hist. Rev.*, VIII, 1893), Liebermann, II, *Glossar*, s.v. *Bocland*, G. J. Turner, "Bookland and Folkland" (*Historical Essays in honour of James Tait*, Manchester, 1933), J. E. A. Jolliffe, "English Bookright" (*Eng. Hist. Rev.*, L, 1935).

[2] No. 74.   [3] Birch, No. 225.   [4] Birch, No. 230.

bombastic expressions, and references to classical mythology, are under the influence of Aldhelm. Athelstan's charters use certain proems again and again, and he also has certain established variants for the other parts of his charters. Texts have come down to us from various archives that have identical passages of considerable length, and it can be regarded as established that by his time at least there was some sort of royal chancery or secretariat that produced these documents, though it is not until Ethelred's reign that we get an express reference to a king's writer.[1] About the same period, a donation charter of a lady called Wulfrun to Wolverhampton is stated to have been *Scriptum per calamum et atramentum et manum notarii et scriniarii Ethelredi regis Anglorum.*[2] Athelstan's most florid types soon went out of favour, but some of his others continued in frequent use, and his successors followed the practice of using stereotyped forms–so much so, in fact, that most of their texts are of little interest, being in something very like common form. They do introduce several new proems, however, of which the most interesting are some which speak of the end of the world as imminent, quoting texts such as "nation shall rise against nation". This type begins in Edgar's reign and is much used.

The position changes soon after the accession of Ethelred; a cult of originality seems to have set in and ready-made proems are avoided–even if on occasion an appearance of novelty is obtained by the simple process of substituting a synonym for many of the words of an existing proem. Some of the new proems reach enormous length. In the rest of the document, while the format varies little, the wording of the clauses tends to differ from one charter to another, as if repetition were being avoided. Many of Ethelred's charters show another change: they are extremely communicative.

They discourse on contemporary events, or give long accounts of how the estates in question came into the king's possession, often by forfeiture, and occasionally they go into the vernacular for this purpose; some speak in detail of his repentance for usurpation of Church lands in his youth and blame the influence of bad advisers. This type seems to begin with the Tavistock foundation charter of 981, and becomes fairly common later. If only an isolated document of this type had survived, its authenticity would have been suspect; but they are preserved by various religious houses–Tavistock, Rochester, Abingdon, Canterbury, Shaftesbury, the Old and New Minsters at Winchester, St. Frideswides at Oxford, and St. Albans. The charter from this last house (Crawford Charter XI) is a contemporary document, but even without this evidence that this kind of charter is genuine, we could never have supposed that all these foundations could have conspired to fabricate such charters and assign them to this one king. It is simplest to assume that they emanate from the royal clerks, and that these were acting under the king's instructions; for it is hard to conceive of any individual on his own responsibility using the phrases about former sins which Ethelred is made to employ of himself in some of them. There is a rather similar charter of Cnut very early in his reign,[3] but most charters after Ethelred's reign revert to the more stereotyped forms which have much less interest for the historian.

In the reign of Ethelred we get the first genuine example of the second kind of royal charter, the writ.[4] This is a much simpler type of document, a letter,

[1] F. M. Stenton (*Anglo-Saxon England*, p. 349), refers to an unpublished grant in Peniarth MS. 390 by Ethelred II to Ælfwine, his 'writer'.   [2] Dugdale, *Monasticon*, VI, pp. 1443f.   [3] No. 132.
[4] All extant pre-Conquest writs have recently been excellently edited with a translation and commentary by F. E. Harmer, *Anglo-Saxon Writs*, and the introduction is not only a full treatment of these documents but a mine of information on Anglo-Saxon diplomatic as a whole.

authenticated by a seal, from the king to the local authorities of the area in which he has made a grant of land or privilege to a certain donee, informing them that he has done so. Some such announcement, though not necessarily in writing, must have been an essential accompaniment to any grant, and a chance reference in King Alfred's translation of the *Soliloquies of St. Augustine* reveals that the king's writ and seal was a familiar thing well over a century before our earliest surviving example.[1] It is reasonable to assume that the writ was from the beginning written in English, and in the simple epistolary style of our extant examples. It was destined eventually to supersede the formal diploma, though the latter continued to be sometimes issued even after the Norman Conquest. The Lincolnshire section of Domesday Book contains the following statement which is interesting in this connexion: "this land was delivered to Bishop Odo by charter [*per cartam*]; but they (the men of the Riding) have not seen the king's writ [*breuem regis*] for it".[2]

The earliest private deed with any claim to authenticity is in 670–676,[3] but as it is probable that the donor in this case was King Ine's father, and so of royal blood, and as I am not certain that the donor of a charter of 681[4] was not a sub-king of the Hwicce, it is perhaps safest to begin our list with a lease issued by a bishop of Worcester between 718 and 743,[5] which is the first of a large series of leases by ecclesiastical communities to laymen for a term of lives, usually three. The greater number of extant leases of this kind have been preserved in the archives of the church of Worcester, but there are some from other churches, and transactions of this kind are sometimes referred to in Domesday Book. A grant of land by a layman not of royal rank in 762[6] is probably genuine, although it survives only in a late authority. A grant by an abbot between 757 and 775 to the church of Worcester[7] shows the influence of royal charters, having a proem and anathema like these, and the king's name at the head of the attestations; later examples occur of private deeds drawn up on the lines of royal charters, such as Birch, Nos. 490, 515, 519, 539, all of the second half of the ninth century, or an original deed of 995[8] which is issued in a bishop's name, although the king in his attestation states that he has conceded the donation at the desire of Bishop Æscwig. Practice was not uniform when private persons made grants of land that required the king's permission; a Winchester transaction of 961[9] is drawn up exactly like a royal charter with the king as the donor, though it is stated that he is acting with the permission of Bishop Brihthelm and the community of the church; whereas the English lease referring to the same transaction says it was done by the bishop and all the community of Winchester, with King Edgar's consent. Sometimes, however, the donations of private individuals are made by means of simple endorsements on existing royal charters, as when Ealdorman Oswulf and his wife added a grant to Lyminge on a Kentish original of 798.[10]

. This is in Latin, but in the first half of the ninth century it became common to make such additions on Kentish charters in English, one of the earliest being the will of the reeve Æthelnoth and his wife, of 805 or soon afterwards.[11] In 822 or 823 an English document was endorsed on a Worcester lease of 803,[12] and in 825 English is used for the first time to record the settlement of a dispute before a synod.[13] English

---

[1] No. 237 (A).
[2] C. W. Foster and T. Longley, *The Lincolnshire Domesday and the Lindsey Survey*, p. 209.
[3] No. 55. [4] No. 57. [5] Birch, No. 166. [6] No. 72.
[7] Birch, No. 220. [8] Kemble, No. 691. [9] No. 110. [10] Birch, No. 289.
[11] Birch, No. 318. [12] Birch, No. 308. [13] Birch, No. 386.

documents that claim an earlier date than these seem to be either later translations of Latin documents or spurious. Before long English superseded Latin for recording lawsuits about land, for wills, records of sales, exchanges and private agreements; many documents of these kinds that have come down to us in Latin are post-Conquest translations from the vernacular; the monasteries of St. Albans, Ramsey and Ely, for example, made Latin translations or abstracts of their vernacular deeds. Leases of ecclesiastical lands are drawn up in either language, or even in a combination of both. Only in the formal diploma did Latin—except for the boundaries—remain unchallenged. English documents of the later Saxon period are fairly numerous, and are often of greater and more varied interest than the formal Latin diplomas of the period.

The historical interest of the charters

The documents that follow have been chosen for the information they afford the historian in various fields. They tell us of the relations between the kingdoms of the Heptarchy, and show that a Bretwalda was an overlord in more than his title; they afford incidental information on the effects of the viking invasions and shed occasional light on the policy of English kings towards the Danish settlers; they are indispensable for the study of ecclesiastical history, not only enabling us to supplement the history of the episcopal sees and the great abbeys, but informing us of the existence of otherwise unknown communities; they supplement the laws and let us see them in action, both the criminal laws and those relating to the holding of land; much of what we know of the king's rights comes from them; the economic historian cannot dispense with their evidence on agrarian arrangements, or on the salt and lead industries, or with their occasional references to trade and town life; something can be learnt from them as regards the standards of material culture, and some of them bring us into close touch with men and women of the time. In this volume the outstanding interest of each text is indicated before it, but other things will emerge if the selection is read as a whole. It will, however, only be by accident if the selection should occasionally happen to perform one important service rendered by charters, namely the checking of the dates given by other sources, for in general one requires for this the whole body of the evidence, to be able to compare the signatures of different charters.

Guild regulations

In the tenth century we begin to get evidence that men were entering into voluntary, artificial associations for mutual protection and benefits of various kinds, temporal and spiritual. The earliest extant regulations are those of the London 'peace-guild', a text often known as Athelstan's sixth code,[1] but which is not a royal code but mainly a record of the arrangements made by this guild for carrying out the royal decrees to suppress cattle-lifting. But though this subject looms largest, the document concerns itself also with the administration of the common finances of the guild and the arrangements for a monthly feast, with the contributions to be made by each member to help one of their number who has suffered misfortune, with their joint responsibility to support a member concerned in a feud, and finally with the obligations of each individual with regard to the soul of a deceased member. This text, with its pre-occupation with the laws against theft, is preserved in a manuscript of laws; all the other sets of regulations concentrate much more on the religious

[1] No. 37.

duties. Some are entered in gospels; one from Ely contains the Cambridge thegns' regulations,[1] and other guild-regulations survive in gospels from Exeter and from Bedwyn,[2] both from the end of the tenth century, while the records of later, apparently small and purely religious associations at Woodbury and ten other places in the diocese of Exeter were added at the end of the eleventh century or in the early twelfth to another Exeter gospel-book, along with a number of manumissions.[3] One set of statutes from the first half of the eleventh century survives on a contemporary parchment.[4] It is for the guild founded by a thegn of Cnut called Urki, at Abbotsbury, Dorset.

There are references to guilds in other sources. A writ of Edward the Confessor[5] speaks of an "English knights' guild" in London as existing in the reign of Edgar, and the Winton Domesday speaks of a hall in Winchester where "the knights drank their guild", with reference to the reign of Edward the Confessor.[6] The existence of a similar guild at Canterbury already in the ninth century is shown by a charter.[7] Domesday Book mentions a guildhall at Dover. But no statutes survive for any of these, nor is it certain what was the meaning of 'knight' in this connexion, whether an armed retainer of a lord, or a young man of noble family.[8]

Manumissions

The redemption of captives and freeing of slaves was one of the Christian acts of mercy, and many Anglo-Saxon wills contain instructions about the freeing of some of the testator's slaves. A written record of the act of manumission was not essential to its validity, but many persons took the precaution of having their act recorded in the gospels or some other church book of a neighbouring church, to make it more difficult for anyone afterwards to deprive the manumitted slave of his freedom and the manumittor of the eternal reward he hoped to receive. In some cases the act itself took place before the altar; but sometimes it had been performed elsewhere, at crossroads or at some public assembly. Most surviving manumissions are too late for inclusion in this volume. The earliest extent manumission is the one performed by King Athelstan immediately after he was crowned king, in 925,[9] which is preserved in a gospel-book from St. Augustine's. From Exeter several manumissions survive, two from the tenth century in Brit. Mus. Cott. Tiber. B. v, a leaf which once formed part of a gospel,[10] several from the eleventh century, in the Leofric Missal,[11] and another set, from the first half of the twelfth century, on some pages now bound up with the Exeter Book,[12] but which originally belonged to the gospel-book now Cambridge University Library, MS. Ii, 2.11, which contains one manumission.[13] From Bodmin also there is a large set, entered in the gospels, Brit. Mus. Addit. MS. 9381, dating, apart from one or two late additions, from the reign of Edmund

---

[1] No. 136.   [2] Nos. 137, 138.
[3] See *The Exeter Book of Old English Poetry*, ed. R. W. Chambers, M. Förster and R. Flower, fol. 7a–b; Thorpe, *Diplomatarium*, pp. 608–610.
[4] No. 139.   [5] Harmer, *op. cit.*, No. 51.
[6] See *Vict. County Hist. Hants*, I, 532.   [7] Birch, No. 515.
[8] On this matter see C. Gross, *The Gild Merchant* (Oxford, 1890), I, pp. 174–191, J. Tait, *The Medieval English Borough*, pp. 119–123, F. M. Stenton, *Norman London*, pp. 13f., and *Anglo-Saxon England*, pp. 519f., F. E. Harmer, *Anglo-Saxon Writs*, pp. 231–235.
[9] No. 140.   [10] No. 149, and Kemble, No. 1353.
[11] Birch, Nos. 1245–1253, Thorpe. *Diplomatarium*, pp. 638–640.
[12] Fol. 4a–6b; Thorpe, *op. cit.*, pp. 631–638.
[13] Thorpe, *op. cit.*, p. 622. See also F. Rose-Troup, "Exeter Manumissions and Quittances of the Eleventh and Twelfth Centuries", *Trans. Devon. Assoc.*, LXIX (1937).

(939–946) to the early eleventh century.[1] Then there are some in the gospels which once belonged to Great Bedwyn, now Berne Stadtbibliothek, MS. 671, probably of the first half of the eleventh century,[2] and another set of eleventh-century entries originally belonged to gospels from Bath, now C.C.C.C., MS. 140, fol. 1 and MS. 111, fol. 3 v.[3] The North is represented only by some manumissions from Durham, one in the *Liber Vitae*,[4] and three in the burnt manuscript, Otho B. ix, a gospel-book given by Athelstan to St. Cuthbert's, into which four eleventh-century manumissions were added. Three of them have survived in transcripts made by Richard James, and have been published by H. H. E. Craster in *Arch. Aeliana*, 4th Series, I, pp. 190–191. The only manumission to come down to us from a source other than a gospel or ritual book is one of 1058–1075 in the *Textus Roffensis*.[5]

[1] Nos. 141–148. The Bodmin manumissions have been frequently edited. See Kemble, No. 981, Whitley Stokes, in *Revue celtique*, I (1872), Haddan and Stubbs, I, pp. 676–683, Earle, pp. 271–274, M. Förster, in *A Grammatical Miscellany offered to Otto Jespersen*, pp. 77–99, Thorpe, *op. cit.*, pp. 623–631.

[2] First edited by H. Meritt, *Journ. Eng. Germ. Phil.*, XXXIII (1934), then by M. Förster, *Der Flussname Themse und seine Sippe*, pp. 794 f. See also H. C. Brentnall, "Bedwyn in the Tenth Century", *Wilts. Arch. and Nat. Hist. Mag.*, LII (1948).

[3] Kemble, Nos. 933–937, Thorpe, *op. cit.*, pp. 640–644.

[4] No. 150.   [5] Kemble, No. 975; Thorpe, *op. cit.*, p. 644.

SELECT BIBLIOGRAPHY
of Laws and Charters and Modern Works relating to
Administration, Social and Economic History

(a) THE LAWS

The great edition of F. LIEBERMANN, *Die Gesetze der Angelsachsen* (Halle, 1903–1916: vol. I, Texts; vol. II, pt. I, Glossary, pt. II, Commentary; vol. III, Introduction and Notes) has superseded earlier editions, but as it is an expensive and not easily accessible book, references have also been given to B. THORPE, *Ancient Laws and Institutes of England* (London, 1840: vol. I, Secular Laws; vol. II, Ecclesiastical Laws) which supplies a modern English translation, though in some respects out of date. More up-to-date translations and useful commentaries accompany the texts of the royal codes in *The Laws of the Earliest English Kings*, ed. F. L. ATTENBOROUGH (Cambridge, 1922) and *The Laws of the Kings of England from Edmund to Henry I*, ed. A. J. ROBERTSON (Cambridge, 1925), but for the private codes one must still go to Thorpe for an English translation, while for several ecclesiastical codes he remains the only printed source. The chief developments since Liebermann's edition are K. Sisam's demonstration that Lambard had no lost manuscript for his versions of Athelstan's "Ordinance on Charities" and first code, a fact which casts doubt on the existence of such a manuscript (*Mod. Lang. Rev.*, XVIII (1923), pp. 100–104; XX (1925), pp. 253–269; conveniently re-issued in *Studies in the History of Old English Literature* (Oxford, 1953), pp. 232–258) and the re-dating of certain codes by D. WHITELOCK, "Wulfstan and the so-called Laws of Edward and Guthrum", *Eng. Hist. Rev.*, LVI (1941), pp. 1–21; "Wulfstan and the Laws of Cnut", *ibid.*, LXIII (1948), pp. 433–452. The objections raised against the views in the latter article by K. JOST, *Wulfstanstudien* (Berne, 1950), pp. 94–103, will be answered in a forthcoming article in *Eng. Hist. Rev.*

(b) THE CHARTERS
(i) *Editions*

There are two main collections of charters, J. M. KEMBLE, *Codex Diplomaticus Aevi Saxonici* (6 vols., London, 1839–1848) and W. DE G. BIRCH, *Cartularium Saxonicum* (3 vols. and index, London, 1885–1893), which adds many documents to those in Kemble, but deals only with the period up to 975. B. THORPE, *Diplomatarium Anglicum Ævi Saxonicum* (London, 1865), includes translations of the Old English documents contained in it, and is still useful for its collection of guild-statutes, but has in the main been superseded by later editions of the small amount of material it adds to Kemble. J. EARLE, *A Hand-book to the Land-Charters and other Saxonic Documents* (Oxford, 1888), similarly has little not also in Kemble and Birch, and nothing not available elsewhere; but nevertheless reference has been made to these two works since they may be accessible to persons who have no easy access to the big collections. Several of the charters of the earlier period are included in vol. III of *Councils and Ecclesiastical Documents*, ed. A. W. HADDAN and W. STUBBS (Oxford, 1871); and many of those relating to monastic houses are in the *Monasticon Anglicanum*, compiled by William Dugdale and others in the seventeenth century and re-issued in the nineteenth (6 vols. in 8, London, 1817–1830, reprinted 1846). A handful of charters in this work were missed by Kemble, the most important being a charter of Edgar to Wilton (II, p. 323) and Wulfrun's charter to Wolverhampton (VI, p. 1443). There are two collections of facsimiles: *Facsimiles of Ancient Charters in the British Museum*, ed. E. A. BOND (4 parts, London, 1873–1878), and Ordnance Survey, *Facsimiles of Anglo-Saxon*

Manuscripts, ed. W. B. SANDERS (3 parts, Southampton, 1878–1884). The former includes eleven charters not in Kemble and Birch, of which all but three are in Earle, while the latter has thirteen not in any work previously mentioned. There are some separate facsimiles of other documents: a lease for three lives by Bishop Cuthwulf of Hereford (Birch, No. 429) by C. S. GREAVES and J. LEE-WARNER in *Arch. Journ.*, xxx (1873); W. DE G. BIRCH, *The Anglo-Saxon Charter of Oslac* (London, 1892); the Thorndon Hall charter of Edgar, in *Trans. Devon. Assoc.*, LXI (1929); a late *inspeximus* of a charter of the Confessor, *ibid.*, LXXI (1939); Exeter manumissions in *ibid.*, LXIX (1937), and in *The Exeter Book of Old English Poetry* (published for the Dean and Chapter of Exeter Cathedral, 1933); a manumission from Durham, in the facsimile of the *Liber Vitae* of Durham (Surtees Soc., CXXXVI, 1923); a Muchelney charter of Ethelred II, frontispiece to *Two Cartularies of the Benedictine Abbeys of Muchelney and Athelney* (see below); *The Sunbury Charter*, ed. W. H. TAPP (printed by Thomasons Ltd., the Cedar Press, Hounslow); a Kentish vernacular charter (Kemble, No. 1315) in *Arch. Cantiana*, I (1858), p. 63; Wihtred's charter of 699, recently given to the Kent County Council, in an article by Gordon Ward in *ibid.*, LX (1948).

There are modern editions of the vernacular documents, provided with translation and commentary, as follows: F. E. HARMER, *Select English Historical Documents of the Ninth and Tenth Centuries* (Cambridge, 1914); D. WHITELOCK, *Anglo-Saxon Wills* (Cambridge, 1930); A. J. ROBERTSON, *Anglo-Saxon Charters* (Cambridge, 1939); F. E. HARMER, *Anglo-Saxon Writs* (Manchester, 1952). The last two include some material not previously printed.

Documents not in the above works are to be found in the following: *The Crawford Collection of Early Charters and Documents*, ed. A. S. NAPIER and W. H. STEVENSON (Oxford, 1895), which is a model of what an edition of charters should be; *Liber Monasterii de Hyda*, ed. E. EDWARDS (Rolls Series, London, 1866); *Two Cartularies of the Benedictine Abbeys of Muchelney and Athelney*, ed. E. H. BATES (Somerset Rec. Soc., London, 1899); J. B. DAVIDSON, "On some Anglo-Saxon Charters at Exeter", *Journ. Brit. Arch. Assoc.*, XXXIX (1883); M. FÖRSTER, *Der Flussname Themse und seine Sippe* (Munich, 1941), pp. 767–795; M. GIBBS, *Early Charters of the Cathedral Church of St. Paul, London* (Royal Hist. Soc., London, 1939), pp. 1–8. There are also a few scattered documents that the collections have missed, such as two of Ethelred II in S. SHAW, *The History and Antiquities of Staffordshire* (London, 1798–1801), I, pp. 19, 28; Cnut's charter to Fécamp, ed. C. H. HASKINS in *Eng. Hist. Rev.*, XXXIII (1918), pp. 342–344; the grant of Taynton to St. Denis by Edward the Confessor, ed. M. BOUQUET, *Recueil des historiens des Gaules et de la France*, XI (Paris, 1769), pp. 655; and Ethelred II's grant to *deowiesstow* (probably Dewstow, Monmouth) recovered by N. R. KER (*Studies in Medieval History presented to F. M. Powicke*, p. 73).

Some of the cartularies which contain Anglo-Saxon documents have been published. In addition to the Hyde Abbey and Muchelney and Athelney cartularies mentioned above, the following should be noted: *Chronicon Monasterii de Abingdon*, ed. J. STEVENSON (Rolls Series, London, 1858); *Two Chartularies of the Priory of St. Peter at Bath*, ed. W. HUNT (Somerset Rec. Soc., 1893); *The Great Chartulary of Glastonbury*, ed. A. WATKIN (Somerset Rec. Soc., 1947–1952); *The Cartulary of the Monastery of St. Frideswide at Oxford*, ed. S. R. WIGRAM (2 vols., Oxford Hist. Soc., 1895–1896); *Textus Roffensis*, ed. T. HEARNE (Oxford, 1720); *Registrum Wiltunense, Saxonicum et Latinum, A.D. 893–1045*, ed. R. C. HOARE (London, 1827); *Hemingi Chartularium ecclesiae Wigorniensis*, ed. T. HEARNE (2 vols., Oxford, 1723).

(ii) *Topographical and Local Studies*

It is obvious that persons familiar with the localities concerned have much to add to the study of the charters, and attention must first be called to the excellent little monograph by H. P. R. FINBERG, "The Early Charters of Devon and Cornwall" (*Occasional Papers*, No. 2, Dept. of English Local History, University College of Leicester, 1953), which lists with accurate identification the charters from this area and works out fully the boundaries of two of the most important. Other collections of charters by localities are: W. H. STEVENSON and W. H. DUIGNAN, "Anglo-Saxon Charters relating to Shropshire" (*Trans. Shropsh. Arch. and Nat. Hist. Soc.*, 4th Series, I, 1911), and C. G. O. BRIDGEMAN, "Staffordshire Pre-Conquest Charters" (*Will.*

Salt Arch. Soc., 1916), both of which, however, give translations only; both text and translation are given by E. E. BARKER, "Sussex Anglo-Saxon Charters" (*Sussex Arch. Collections*, LXXXVI–LXXXVIII, 1947–1949), text only by W. FARRER, *Early Yorkshire Charters*, I (Edinburgh, 1914). Dr. G. B. GRUNDY confines himself to studying the boundaries, dealing with Wiltshire in *Arch. Journ.*, LXXVI–LXXVII (1919–1920), with Hampshire in *ibid.*, LXXVIII–LXXXV (1921–1928), Berkshire in *Berks., Bucks., and Oxon. Arch. Soc. Journ.*, XXVII–XXXII (1922–1928), Somerset in *Proc. Somerset Arch. and Nat. Hist. Soc.*, LXXIII–LXXX (1927–1934), Oxford in *Saxon Oxfordshire* (Oxfordshire Rec. Soc., XV, 1933), Dorset in *Proc. Dorset Nat. Hist. and Arch. Soc.*, LV–LVII (1933–1935), Gloucestershire in *Saxon Charters and Field-names of Gloucester*, published by the Brist. and Glos. Arch. Soc., 1935–1936, Worcestershire in *Trans. Birm. Arch. Soc.*, LII–LIII (reprinted separately, Oxford, 1931). Large-scale studies of this kind, from maps, have not the value of detailed perambulations on the spot, such as lie behind Mr. Finberg's work. Reference must also be made to several important contributions to the study of Kentish charters by GORDON WARD, in *Arch. Cantiana*, XLI–LX (1929–1949); to F. ROSE-TROUP's articles on Devon charters in *Trans. Devon. Assoc.*, LXI–LXXIV (1929–1942), especially "The New Edgar Charter and the South Hams", LXI; to the work of the Rev. C. S. TAYLOR in *Trans. Brist. and Glos. Arch. Soc.*, especially "Berkeley Minster", XIX (1894–1895), "Bath, Mercian and West Saxon" and "The Pre-Domesday Hide of Gloucester", XVIII (1893–1894); to F. G. GURNEY's "Yttingaford and the Tenth-Century Bounds of Chalgrave and Linslade", in *Trans. Beds. Hist. Rec. Soc.*, V (1920), which contains also an article by G. H. FOWLER on "Some Saxon Charters".

(iii) *The Criticism and Study of Charters*

While there are various manuals for the study of charters in general, notably H. BRESSLAU, *Handbuch der Urkundenlehre für Deutschland und Italien* (2nd ed., Berlin and Leipzig, 1915–1931) and A. GIRY, *Manuel de Diplomatique* (Paris, 1894), the criticism of Anglo-Saxon documents is very scattered. W. H. STEVENSON's pronouncements are to be found throughout his notes to the *Crawford Charters* and his edition of Asser, and in his following important articles: "An Old-English Charter of William the Conqueror in favour of St. Martin's-le-Grand, London, A.D. 1068" (*Eng. Hist. Rev.*, XI, 1896); "Yorkshire Surveys and other Eleventh-Century Documents in the York Gospels" (*ibid.*, XXVII, 1912); "Trinoda Necessitas" (*ibid.*, XXIX, 1914). Stevenson tended to be over-suspicious, and it was left to Sir Frank Stenton to establish the genuineness of several documents; for his work on charters, see especially *The Early History of the Abbey of Abingdon* (Reading Studies in Local History, O.U.P., 1913); "The Supremacy of the Mercian Kings" (*Eng. Hist. Rev.*, XXXIII, 1918); "Medeshamstede and its Colonies" (*Historical Essays in honour of James Tait*, Manchester, 1933); "St. Frideswide and her Times" (*Oxoniensia*, I, 1936). W. LEVISON, *England and the Continent in the Eighth Century* (Oxford, 1946), Appendices I and IV, is important for the origin as well as the criticism of Anglo-Saxon charters, and there is an excellent account of their origin and employment supplied by H. D. HAZELTINE as a preface to WHITELOCK, *Anglo-Saxon Wills*. V. H. GALBRAITH, *Studies in the Public Records* (London, 1948), may also be consulted, and F. E. HARMER, *Anglo-Saxon Writs*, which includes a most important introduction dealing with tests of authenticity as well as with many general matters of the history of diplomatic. Other important articles are R. DRÖGEREIT, "Gab es eine angelsächsische Königskanzlei?" (*Archiv für Urkundenforschung*, XIII, pp. 335–436, Leipzig, 1935), and the same author's "Kaiseridee und Kaisertitel bei den Angelsachsen" (*Zeitsch. der Savigny-Stiftung für Rechtsgeschichte*, LXIX, pp. 24–73, Weimar, 1952); M. TREITER, "Die Urkundendatierungen in angelsächsischer Zeit nebst Überblick über die Datierung in der anglo-normannischen Periode" (*Archiv für Urkundenforschung*, VII, 1921); H. P. R. FINBERG, "The House of Ordgar and the Foundation of Tavistock Abbey" (*Eng. Hist. Rev.*, LVIII, 1943), which establishes the authenticity of the foundation charter of this house; N. R. KER, "Hemming's Cartulary" (*Studies in Medieval History presented to F. M. Powicke*, Oxford, 1948); C. E. WRIGHT, "Sir Edward Dering: a seventeeth-century antiquary and his 'Saxon' charters" (*The Early Cultures of North-West Europe*, H. M. Chadwick Memorial Studies, Cambridge, 1950); A. CAMPBELL, "An Old English Will" (*Journ. Eng. Germ. Phil.*, XXXVII, 1938).

(c) MODERN WORKS

For the aspects of Anglo-Saxon history specially considered in this section reference should be made to F. M. STENTON, *Anglo-Saxon England* (see p. 101). The following works should also be noted.

There is an excellent sketch of Anglo-Saxon law in chap. 2 of vol. I of *The History of English Law* by F. POLLOCK and F. W. MAITLAND (2nd ed., Cambridge, 1923), which should be supplemented by W. S. HOLDSWORTH, *A History of English Law* (vol. I, 6th ed., 1938, vol. II, 3rd ed., 1923, London), and T. F. T. PLUCKNETT, *A Concise History of the Common Law* (4th ed., London, 1948). A detailed study of the various legal institutions is contained in H. M. CHADWICK, *Studies on Anglo-Saxon Institutions* (Cambridge, 1905); and there is a wealth of detailed knowledge in the second volume of Liebermann's great work, though the method of its distribution among the various headings of his commentary makes it a laborious task to ascertain in full his views on a particular topic. Various topics concerning the king's peace and private jurisdiction have been reopened by J. GOEBEL, Jr., *Felony and Misdemeanour* (New York, 1937), though his view that a grant of jurisdiction did not carry with it the right to hold a court in Saxon times has not won general acceptance. See reviews by T. F. T. PLUCKNETT, *Law Quart. Rev.*, LIV (1938), pp. 295–298, and H. M. CAM, *Amer. Hist. Rev.*, XLIII (1938), pp. 583–587, and also N. D. HURNARD, "The Anglo-Norman Franchises" (*Eng. Hist. Rev.*, LXIV, 1949).

For a general survey of Anglo-Saxon society, see D. WHITELOCK, *The Beginnings of English Society* (vol. II of *The Pelican History of England*, Harmondsworth, 1952) and chapters by W. J. CORBETT in *Camb. Med. Hist.*, III (1922). A picture of society in the migration period is given in H. M. CHADWICK, *The Heroic Age* (Cambridge, 1912), while the same author's *Studies on Anglo-Saxon Institutions* deals with the social classes in England and with several questions relating to administration. The commentary in vol. II of Liebermann's edition of the laws is a mine of information on this as on other topics. Among studies of separate institutions may be mentioned F. LIEBERMANN, *The National Assembly in the Anglo-Saxon Period* (Halle, 1913), L. M. LARSON, *The King's Household in England before the Norman Conquest* (Madison, 1904), W. A. MORRIS, "The Office of Sheriff in the Anglo-Saxon Period" (*Eng. Hist. Rev.*, XXXI, 1916), and *The Medieval English Sheriff to 1300* (Manchester, 1927), H. M. CAM, "Manerium cum Hundredo: The Hundred and the Hundredal Manor" (*Eng. Hist. Rev.*, XLVII, 1932).

Social and agrarian history cannot be separated in this period. F. W. MAITLAND, *Domesday Book and Beyond* (Cambridge, 1897), remains a very stimulating book, though some of his suggestions have not proved tenable. P. VINOGRADOFF, *Villeinage in England* (Oxford, 1892), includes a summary of older views on English society, as well as first laying down the lines that most later scholars have followed. The relevant chapters in vol. I of the *Cambridge Economic History* (Cambridge, 1941) make it easier to relate English to continental conditions, and the importance of geographical factors is brought out in *An Historical Geography of England before A.D. 1800*, ed. by H. C. DARBY (Cambridge, 1936). Among studies of individual areas J. E. A. JOLLIFFE, *Pre-Feudal England: The Jutes* (Oxford, 1933), is important, and the same author's article, "Northumbrian Institutions" (*Eng. Hist. Rev.*, XLI, 1926); H. P. R. FINBERG, *Tavistock Abbey: a Study in the Social and Economic History of Devon* (Cambridge, 1951), throws light on the special features of this part of the country.

The introductory chapters to the Domesday survey of individual counties, contained in the Victoria County Histories, are often of value for the late Saxon period. On conditions in the Danelaw there are several valuable studies by F. M. STENTON, including *Types of Manorial Structure in the Northern Danelaw* (Oxford Studies in Social and Legal History, II, 1910), "The Free Peasantry of the Northern Danelaw" (*Bulletin de la Société royale des Lettres de Lund*, 1925–1926), "The Danes in England" (*Proc. Brit. Acad.*, XIII, 1927), and the introduction to *The Lincolnshire Domesday and the Lindsey Survey*, ed. C. W. FOSTER and T. LONGLEY (Lincoln Rec. Soc., 1924); while any study of East Anglia in pre-Conquest times must work back from D. C. DOUGLAS, *The Social Structure of Medieval East Anglia* (Oxford, 1927), and make use also of H. C. DARBY, *The Medieval Fenland* (Cambridge, 1940).

The working of the open-field system of agriculture is seen clearest in C. S. and C. S. ORWIN, *The Open Fields* (Oxford, 1938), and various systems used in England are discussed in H. L. GRAY, *English Field-Systems* (Cambridge, Mass., 1915).

On towns, the standard work is J. TAIT, *The Medieval English Borough* (Manchester, 1936), which has re-established the early beginning of urban life, against the views of C. STEPHENSON, *Borough and Town* (Cambridge, Mass., 1933), who would attribute it mainly to post-Conquest conditions.

A. THE LAWS

29. From the laws of Ethelbert, king of Kent (602–603?)

This code is mentioned in Bede's *Ecclesiastical History* (see No. 151, p. 610), and can be dated between the adoption of Christianity in 597 and the king's death in 616. Liebermann suggests 602–603 as a likely date. Like all the Kentish laws, it is found only in the *Textus Roffensis*. I have omitted the section dealing with compensations for injuries. The text is in Liebermann, I, pp. 3–8; Attenborough, pp. 4–17; Thorpe, I, pp. 2–25. The two last contain an English translation.

These are the decrees which King Ethelbert established in Augustine's day.

1. The property of God and the Church [is to be paid for] with a twelve-fold compensation; a bishop's property with an eleven-fold compensation; a priest's property with a nine-fold compensation; a deacon's property with a six-fold compensation; a cleric's property with a three-fold compensation; the peace of the Church with a two-fold compensation; the peace of a meeting with a two-fold compensation.

2. If the king calls his people to him, and anyone does them injury there, [he is to pay] a two-fold compensation and 50 shillings to the king.

3. If the king is drinking at a man's home, and anyone commits any evil deed there, he is to pay two-fold compensation.

4. If a freeman steal from the king, he is to repay nine-fold.

5. If anyone kills a man in the king's estate, he is to pay 50 shillings compensation.

6. If anyone kills a freeman, [he is to pay] 50 shillings to the king as 'lord-ring'.[1]

7. If [anyone] kills the king's own smith[2] or his messenger,[3] he is to pay the ordinary wergild.[4]

8. The [breach of the] king's protection,[5] 50 shillings.

9. If a freeman steals from a freeman, he is to pay three-fold, and the king is to have the fine or[6] all the goods.

10. If anyone lies with a maiden belonging to the king, he is to pay 50 shillings compensation.

11. If it is a grinding slave, he is to pay 25 shillings compensation; [if a slave of] the third [class], 12 shillings.

12. The king's *fedesl*[7] is to be paid for with 20 shillings.

[1] Presumably what is called elsewhere a *manbot*. The term used here is obviously ancient, belonging to a time when payments were more often in rings than in currency. Several of the words in this code are either unique, or used otherwise only in poetry, which was conservative in its vocabulary.

[2] Literally, 'service-smith'.

[3] The word *ladrinc* 'leading-man, escort' is unique, and its meaning therefore uncertain; one is tempted to compare the official called in *Beowulf ar* 'herald, messenger', who escorts strangers into the king's presence, but he is clearly of noble rank, whereas the point of the present law seems to be to give an ordinary man's wergild to persons who—but for their service to the king—would not be entitled to so much; presumably, therefore, they are not freemen.

[4] The term used, *leodgyld*, differs from that used for wergild elsewhere.

[5] Offences against anyone or any place under the king's protection, but also including various acts showing lack of respect. Other persons than the king had their *mund(byrd)* ('right of giving') protection'.

[6] As Liebermann suggests, the *and* in the text is probably used with an alternative sense. The king has all the goods if these are not enough to cover the fine.

[7] Liebermann interprets this as 'Kostgänger', *i.e.* 'boarder', and this derives support from 25, where a *ceorl* receives compensation if his 'loaf-eater' is slain. *Fedesl* occurs elsewhere only in the sense 'a fatted animal'.

13. If anyone kills a man in a nobleman's estate, he is to pay 12 shillings compensation.

14. If anyone lies with a nobleman's serving-woman,[1] he is to pay 20 shillings compensation.

15. The [breach of a] ceorl's[2] protection: six shillings.

16. If anyone lie with a ceorl's serving-woman, he is to pay six shillings compensation; [if] with a slave-woman of the second [class], 50 sceattas;[3] [if with one of] the third [class], 30 sceattas.

17. If a man is the first to force his way into a man's homestead, he is to pay six shillings compensation; he who enters next, three shillings; afterwards each [is to pay] a shilling.

18. If anyone provides a man with weapons, when a quarrel has arisen, and [yet] no injury results, he is to pay six shillings compensation.

19. If highway-robbery is committed, he[4] is to pay six shillings compensation.

20. If, however, a man is killed, he[4] is to pay 20 shillings compensation.

21. If anyone kills a man, he is to pay as an ordinary wergild 100 shillings.

22. If anyone kills a man, he is to pay 20 shillings at the open grave, and within 40 days the whole wergild.

23. If the slayer departs from the land, his kinsmen are to pay half the wergild.

24. If anyone binds a free man, he is to pay 20 shillings compensation.

25. If anyone kills a ceorl's dependant,[5] he is to pay six shillings compensation.

26. If [anyone] kills a læt,[6] he is to pay for one of the highest class 80 shillings; if he kills one of the second class, he is to pay 60 shillings; if one of the third class, he is to pay 40 shillings.

27. If a freeman breaks an enclosure,[7] he is to pay six shillings compensation.

28. If anyone seizes property inside, the man[8] is to pay three-fold compensation.

29. If a freeman enters the enclosure,[9] he is to pay four shillings compensation.

30. If anyone kill a man, he is to pay with his own money and unblemished goods, whatever their kind.

31. If a freeman lies with the wife of a freeman, he is to atone with his wergild,[10] and to obtain another wife with his own money, and bring her to the other's home.

32. If anyone thrusts through a true hamscyld,[11] he is to pay for it with its value.

---

[1] Literally, 'a female cup-bearer'.

[2] Though Modern English 'churl' is the direct descendant of this word, the sense has changed so much that to use it would be misleading. Its normal Old English meaning is a peasant proprietor.

[3] A sceat was a coin later replaced by the penny. A Kentish shilling was made up of twenty of them.

[4] The man who provided the weapon.

[5] Thus Attenborough translates hlafæta 'loaf-eater'.

[6] Only in Kent is there reference to classes of men lower than the ceorl, but above the slave. Liebermann translates 'half-free'. A læt may be a manumitted slave, or perhaps a member of a subject (pre-English) population.

[7] Or perhaps already eodor means a homestead, as probably in Alfred 40.

[8] The one who broke the enclosure?

[9] The difference from the offence in 27 presumably lies in the unauthorized entry not being accompanied by breaking of the fence. But cf. chap. 17.

[10] Grammatically, it is possible that her wergild is meant.

[11] This is obscure. Attenborough suggests tentatively, "damages the enclosure of a dwelling". See also Liebermann, Archiv für das Studium der neueren Sprachen, cxv, pp. 389–391.

33. If hair-pulling occur, 50 *sceattas* [are to be paid] as compensation.[1]

73. If a freewoman, with long hair,[2] commits any misconduct, she is to pay 30 shillings compensation.

74. The compensation for [injury to] a maiden is to be as for a freeman.

75. [Breach of] guardianship over a noble-born widow of the highest class is to be compensated for with 50 shillings;

75.1. that over one of the second class, with 20 shillings; over one of the third class, with 12 shillings; over one of the fourth, with six shillings.

76. If a man takes a widow who does not belong to him, the [penalty for breach of the] guardianship is to be doubled.

77. If anyone buys a maiden, she is to be bought with a [bride] payment, if there is no fraud.

77.1. If, however, there is any fraud, she is to be taken back home, and he is to be given back his money.

78. If she bears a living child, she is to have half the goods, if the husband dies first.

79. If she wishes to go away with the children, she is to have half the goods.

80. If the husband wishes to keep [the children], [she is to have the same share] as a child.

81. If she does not bear a child, [her] paternal kinsmen are to have [her] goods and the 'morning-gift'.[3]

82. If anyone carries off a maiden by force, [he is to pay] to the owner 50 shillings, and afterwards buy from the owner his consent [to the marriage].

83. If she is betrothed to another man at a [bride] price, he[4] is to pay 20 shillings compensation.

84. If a return[5] [of the woman] takes place, [he is to pay] 35 shillings and 15 shillings to the king.

85. If anyone lies with the woman of a servant[6] while her husband is alive, he is to pay a two-fold compensation.

86. If one servant kills another without cause, he is to pay the full value.

87. If a servant's eye or foot is destroyed, the full value is to be paid for him.

88. If anyone binds a man's servant, he is to pay six shillings compensation.

89. Highway robbery of [or by?] a slave is to be three shillings.

90. If a slave steals, he is to pay two-fold compensation.

---

[1] The next 39 chapters deal with the compensations for wounds and injuries of all conceivable kinds.
[2] This is generally taken to be a distinguishing feature of a free, as opposed to a bond, woman.
[3] The gift made by the husband to the bride the morning after the consummation of the marriage.
[4] The man who ran off with her.
[5] Liebermann considers the possibility that this word means that the woman came to meet him willingly. It glosses *obviatio* in the Durham Ritual. But, as he says, it is difficult to see why a fine should be paid to the king only if the woman is a willing victim.
[6] *esne*, a word of vague meaning, in legal use normally denotes an unfree labourer, and sometimes seems interchangeable with *peow* 'slave', though Alfred 43 seems to distinguish the two, placing them, however, on a level with regard to holidays. Outside the laws the meaning 'slave' can be found: Bede's *servus* is translated *esne*, and elsewhere the word *esnecund* glosses *condictiorius*; but it also means 'young man' or simply 'man', especially when qualified by some complimentary adjective, such as 'bold' or 'learned'.

30. The laws of Hlothhere and Eadric, kings of Kent (673–685?)

This code must be dated between 673 and 685, if it was issued jointly by the two kings mentioned in it, for Hlothhere came to the throne in the summer of 673 and was killed by the South Saxons, who were brought against him by his nephew, Eadric, in February 685. It is nowhere stated that Eadric ever reigned jointly with his uncle, but such combined rule is not uncommon at this period. However, it is possible that Eadric re-issued a code of his predecessor during his own short reign of a year and a half. Of particular interest in this code is its concern with Kentish men trading in London, and its reference to possession by the king of a hall in that East Saxon city. The code survives in the *Textus Roffensis*. It is edited by Liebermann, I, pp. 9–11; and, with English translation, by Attenborough, pp. 18–23, and Thorpe, I, pp. 26–35.

These are the decrees which Hlothhere and Eadric, kings of the people of Kent, established.

PROLOGUE. Hlothhere and Eadric, kings of the people of Kent, added to the law which their forefathers had made these decrees which are stated hereafter.

1. If a man's servant[1] kills a man of noble birth, who has a wergild of 300 shillings, the owner is to give up the slayer and pay in addition the value of three men.

2. If the slayer escapes, he is to add the value of a fourth man, and is to clear himself with good oath-helpers, that he could not capture the slayer.

3. If a man's servant[1] kills a freeman, who has a wergild of 100 shillings, the owner is to give up the slayer, and the value of another man in addition.

4. If the slayer escapes, he is to be paid for with the value of two men, and [the owner] is to clear himself with good oath-helpers, that he could not capture the slayer.

5. If a freeman steals a man, if the latter comes back as informer, he is to accuse him to his face; he is to clear himself, if he can; each man [so charged] is to have a number of free oath-helpers, and one with him in the oath from the village to which he belongs;[2] if he cannot do that, he is to pay as he can afford.[3]

6. If a husband dies leaving wife and child, it is right that the child should accompany the mother, and he is to be given one of his paternal kinsmen as a willing protector, to look after his property until he is ten years old.

7. If anyone steals the property of another man, and the owner afterwards attaches it, he [the accused] is to vouch to warranty at the king's hall, if he can, and produce him who sold it to him; if he cannot do that, he is to relinquish it, and the owner to succeed to it.

8. If a man brings a charge against another, and he meets the man at an assembly or a meeting, the man is always to give surety to the other, and to do him such right as the judges of the people of Kent shall prescribe for them.

9. If he then refuses him surety, he is to pay 12 shillings to the king, and the suit is to remain as open as it was before.

10. If a man charges another, after he has given him surety,[4] then three days later

---

[1] *esne.* See note on p. 359.

[2] This is a difficult clause. With Attenborough I take *æghwilc man* 'each man', since it is nominative, to be the subject, in spite of its late place in the sentence. Liebermann refers it to all the oath-helpers, making it requisite that all should come from his own village, and thinks that the accused is to have a number of these present, but swear with only one of them.

[3] The MS. *gono hage* is normally amended to *genoh age* to give this sense. The copyist may have been influenced by the verb *onhagian* which can mean 'to afford'. Presumably if he had not enough he would suffer other penalties. This law is altogether rather vague, leaving the number of oath-helpers unspecified also.

[4] The MS. has 'and' which the editors delete.

they are to seek for themselves an arbitrator, unless a later term be preferable to him who brings forward the charge. After the suit has been settled, the man is to do right to the other within seven days; he is to satisfy him with money or with oath, whichever he prefers. If then he will not do that, he shall then pay 100 shillings, without an oath,[1] one day after the arbitration is over.

11. If anyone in another's house calls a man a perjurer, or shamefully accosts him with insulting words, he is to pay a shilling to him who owns the house, and six shillings to him to whom he spoke that word, and to pay 12 shillings to the king.

12. If anyone removes a cup from another where men are drinking, without provocation, he shall according to ancient law pay a shilling to him who owns the house, and six shillings to him whose cup was removed, and 12 shillings to the king.

13. If anyone draws a weapon where men are drinking, and yet no injury is done there, [he is to pay] a shilling to him who owns the house and 12 shillings to the king.

14. If the house is stained by bloodshed, he is to pay to the man[2] [the price for breach of] his protection, and 50 shillings to the king.

15. If anyone harbours a stranger, a trader or any other man who has come across the frontier, for three nights in his own home, and then supplies him with his food, and he then does any injury to any man, the man[3] is to bring the other to justice or to discharge the obligations for him.

16. If a man of Kent buys property in London, he is to have then two or three honest *ceorls*, or the king's town-reeve, as witness.

16.1. If then it is attached in the possession of the man in Kent, he is to vouch to warranty the man who sold it to him, at the king's hall in that town, if he knows him and can produce him at that vouching to warranty.

16.2. If he cannot do that, he is then to declare at the altar with one of his witnesses or with the king's town-reeve, that he bought that property openly by a public transaction[4] in the town, and he is then to be given back his price.

16.3. If, then, he cannot declare that with proper exculpation, he is to relinquish it, and the owner is to succeed to it.

31. The laws of Wihtred, king of Kent (695)

Wihtred reckoned his reign from some date in 690–691 (July 694 is in his fourth year). His code was issued on the sixth day of *Rugern* (probably 'rye-harvest') in the fifth year of his reign, and in the ninth indiction, which begins on 1 September 695 if the Greek indiction is meant. This seems to point to 6 September, for a date in the autumn, after 24 September (the commencement of the Caesarean indiction), would be too late to be in *Rugern*, and a date in the 'rye-harvest' of 696 would not be in Wihtred's fifth year. Wihtred died on 23 April 725, after a reign of thirty-four and a half years. It is interesting to note that in the early years of his reign he had still to regard the practice of heathenism as a menace. The last clause of his code occurs also in the laws of his contemporary Ine, and so we must assume some measure of collaboration between the two rulers. The code has come down to us only in the *Textus Roffensis*, but it was used by the compiler of Cnut's laws, who repeats the statute concerning foreigners who do not conform to the marriage laws of the Church; presumably the presence in the England of Cnut's time of heathen Danes has created afresh the situation with which Wihtred had to deal. The text is edited by Liebermann, I, pp. 12–14; and with English translation by Attenborough, pp. 24–31, Thorpe, I, pp. 36–43.

---

[1] *i.e.* he has lost his right to bring an oath. [2] The owner of the house.
[3] The host. [4] Or "with goods known to be his" (Attenborough).

These are the decrees of Wihtred, king of the people of Kent.

PROLOGUE. When the most gracious king of the people of Kent, Wihtred, was reigning, in the fifth year of his reign, the ninth indiction, on the sixth day of *Rugern*,[1] in the place which is called *Berghamstyde*,[2] there was collected a deliberative assembly of leading men. Brihtwold, archbishop of Britain, was there, and the above-named king; also the bishop of Rochester, who was called Gefmund, was present; and every order of the Church of that nation spoke in unanimity with the loyal people. There, with the consent of all, the leading men devised these decrees and added them to the lawful usages of the people of Kent, as it says and declares hereafter.

1. The Church [is to be] free from taxation.

1.1. And the king is to be prayed for, and they are to honour him of their own free-will without compulsion.

2. The [breach of] the Church's protection is to be 50 shillings like the king's.

3. Men living in illicit cohabitation are to turn to a right life with repentance of sins, or to be excluded from the fellowship of the Church.

4. Foreigners, if they will not regularize their marriages, are to depart from the land with their goods and their sins.

4.1. Our own men, in this people, are to forfeit the fellowship of the Church, without confiscating their goods.

5. If after this meeting, any *gesith-born*[3] man chooses to enter into an illicit union in spite of the command of the king and the bishop and the decree of the books,[4] he is to pay to his lord 100 shillings according to ancient law.

5.1. If it is a *ceorl*, he is to pay 50 shillings; and both of them are to abandon the union, with repentance.

6. If a priest permits an illicit union, or neglects the baptism of a sick person, or is so drunk that he cannot [perform it], he is to abstain from his ministration until the bishop's sentence.

7. If a tonsured man, who is under no [ecclesiastical] authority[5] seeks hospitality, he is to be given it once; and it is not to happen that he is harboured longer, unless he has permission.

8. If anyone gives his man freedom at the altar, he is to have the rights of a freeman of that people;[6] his manumittor is to have his inheritance and his wergild and

---

[1] Probably September. The word means 'rye-harvest'.

[2] Birch, No. 88, dated 696, is also issued at this place. Bearsted, near Maidstone, may be meant, for its early forms show that it is derived from the same name, whereas Barham, Kent, which has been suggested, is an earlier *Bioraham*.

[3] This is the only occurrence in Kentish law of a term common in the West Saxon code of Ine, contemporary with Wihtred. It seems to refer to the same class which the earlier Kentish laws called *eorlcund*. The word *gesith* means 'companion' and is applied in poetry and elsewhere to the members of a king's *comitatus*. But it is clear from the term *gesith-cund* 'born a *gesith*' that it has come to denote a member of a class, and from Ine's laws we find this had a wergild of either twelve or six hundred shillings. After the time of Alfred the six-hundred wergild disappears, and men of the twelve-hundred wergild are called thegns, and not *gesiths*. A man of *gesith* rank was usually in charge of a household of his own, and it is in his capacity of lord of other men that he appears in Ine 23.1 and 50.   [4] Books of ecclesiastical canons.

[5] Like clauses 4–6 of the canons of Hertford of 672, this law is directed against clergy who wander from diocese to diocese. It is probably not meant to apply only to monks outside their cloister.

[6] Literally, 'to be folk-free'.

protection over his household, even if he live beyond the boundary, wherever he wishes.

9. If a servant,[1] against his lord's command, do servile work between sunset on Saturday evening and sunset on Sunday evening, he is to pay 80 *sceattas*[2] to his lord.

10. If a servant rides on his own business on that day, he is to pay six [shillings] to his lord, or be flogged.

11. If, however, a freeman [works] in the forbidden time, he is to be liable to his *healsfang*;[3] and the man who discovers it is to have half the fine and half the [profit from the] work.

12. If a husband sacrifice to devils without his wife's knowledge, he is to be liable to pay all his goods and[4] *healsfang*; if they both sacrifice to devils, they are to be liable to pay *healsfang* and[4] all their goods.

13. If a slave sacrifices to devils, he is to pay six shillings compensation or be flogged.

14. If anyone gives meat to his household in time of fasting, he is to redeem both freeman and slave with *healsfang*.

15. If a slave eat it of his own accord [he is to pay] six shillings or be flogged.

16. The word of the bishop and the king without an oath is to be incontrovertible.

17. The head of a monastery is to clear himself with a priest's exculpation.

18. A priest is to purge himself with his own asseveration in his holy vestments before the altar, saying thus: "I speak the truth in Christ, I do not lie."[5] Similarly a deacon is to purge himself.

19. A cleric is to purge himself with three of the same order, and he alone is to have his hand on the altar; the others are to stand by and discharge the oath.

20. A stranger is to purge himself with his own oath on the altar; similarly a king's thegn;

21. a *ceorl* with three of the same class on the altar; and the oath of all these is to be incontrovertible.

21.1. Then the Church's right of exculpation is as follows:

22. If anyone accuses a bishop's servant[6] or a king's, he is to clear himself by the hand of the reeve: the reeve is either to clear him or deliver him to be flogged.

23. If anyone accuses an unfree servant of a community in their midst, his lord is to clear him with his oath alone, if he is a communicant; if he is not a communicant he is to have in the oath another good oath-helper, or pay for him or deliver him to be flogged.

24. If the servant of a layman accuses the servant of an ecclesiastic or the servant of an ecclesiastic accuses the servant of a layman, his lord is to clear him with his oath alone.

25. If anyone kill a man who is in the act of thieving, he is to lie without wergild.

---

[1] *esne*, here and in chap. 10. See p. 359, n. 6.

[2] Accepting Attenborough's emendation from 'shillings'. Liebermann, however, emends 'lord' into the nominative, and therefore alters in the first line to 'by his lord's command'.

[3] A proportion of the wergild which went to the nearest relatives of the slain man. When the wergild was 1200 shillings it was 120 shillings, and it may be that this ratio applies to other wergilds.

[4] 'And' is probably for 'or'.   [5] This formula is in Latin.

[6] Here and in the following chapters, the word translated 'servant' is *esne*. See p. 359, n. 6.

26. If anyone captures a freeman with the stolen goods on him, the king is to choose one of three things; he is either to be killed or sold across the sea or redeemed with his wergild.

26.1. He who discovers and captures him, is to have the right to half of [the payment for] him; if he is killed, 70 shillings is to be paid to them.[1]

27. If a slave steals and is redeemed, [this is to be at] 70 shillings, whichever the king wishes.[2] If he is killed, half is to be paid for him to the possessor.[3]

28.[4] If a man from a distance or a foreigner goes off the track, and he neither shouts nor blows a horn, he is to be assumed to be a thief, to be either killed or redeemed.

32. The laws of Ine (688–694)

We owe the survival of the laws of the West Saxon king, Ine, who reigned from 688 to 726, solely to their being added as a supplement to the laws of Alfred, who expressly mentions his use of them. They belong to the episcopate of Eorcenwold of London. They are of particular interest, as being the earliest we possess, apart from those of the Kentish kings. It is not, however, safe to assume that we have them complete, for King Alfred may have had copied only such as were useful for his purpose, and have ignored any which time had made a dead letter. Ine's laws survive in the same manuscripts as those of Alfred (see pp. 328 f). In view of their especial interest, I have given them in full. The text is edited by Liebermann, I, pp. 88–123; and with English translation by Attenborough, pp. 36–61, Thorpe, I, pp. 102–151.

PROLOGUE. I, Ine, by the grace of God, king of the West Saxons, with the advice and with the instruction of my father Cenred, and my bishop Hædde, and my bishop Eorcenwold, along with all my ealdormen and the chief councillors of my people, and also a great assembly of the servants of God, have been inquiring about the salvation of our souls and about the security of our kingdom, that true law and true statutes might be established and strengthened throughout our people, so that none of the ealdormen or of our subjects might afterwards pervert these our decrees.

1. First we enjoin that the servants of God rightly observe their proper rule.

1.1. After that, we enjoin that the law and decrees of all the people are to be observed thus:

2. A child is to be baptized within 30 days; if it is not, 30 shillings compensation is to be paid.

2.1. If it then die without being baptized, he is to compensate for it with all that he possesses.

3. If a slave works on Sunday at his master's command, he is to be free, and the master is to pay 30 shillings as a fine.

3.1. If, however, the slave works without his knowledge, he is to be flogged.[5]

3.2. If then a freeman works on that day without his lord's command, he is to forfeit his freedom.[6]

---

[1] His capturers, who would otherwise lose by the king's choice of the death-penalty. But if *heom* is a mistake for the singular, *him*, it could mean 'for him' and the situation envisaged might be if the capturer took the law into his own hands, killed the thief, and thus robbed the king of his choice. He would have to compensate for it.

[2] This law is awkwardly expressed if the alternative is the death-penalty. But some alternative price of redemption may perhaps have been accidentally omitted.

[3] Presumably the man who captured him.   [4] Almost identical with Ine 20.

[5] C.C.C.C., MS. 383, adds: "or (pay) the 'hide-price'", *i.e.* the sum to save him from being flogged.

[6] *Ibid.* adds: "or 60 shillings, and a priest is doubly liable".

4. Church-scot is to be given by Martinmas; if anyone does not discharge it, he is to be liable to 60 shillings and to render the church-scot twelve-fold.

5. If anyone is liable to the death penalty and he reaches a church, he is to retain his life and to compensate as the law directs him.

5.1. If anyone is liable to be flogged, and reaches a church, the flogging is to be remitted.

6. If anyone fights in the king's house, he is to forfeit all his possessions, and it is to be at the king's judgment whether he is to keep his life or not.

6.1. If anyone fights in a minster, he is to pay 120 shillings compensation.

6.2. If anyone fights in the house of an ealdorman or other important councillor, he is to pay 60 shillings compensation and is to give another 60 shillings as a fine.

6.3. If then he fights in the house of a rent-payer[1] or a gebur,[2] he is to pay 120 shillings as a fine and six shillings to the gebur.

6.4. And even if the fighting is in the midst of the open country, 120 shillings is to be given as a fine.

6.5. If, however, they quarrel at their drinking, and one of them bears it with patience, the other is to pay 30 shillings as a fine.

7. If anyone steals without his wife and his children knowing, he is to pay 60 shillings as a fine.

7.1. If, however, he steals with the knowledge of all his household, they are all to go into slavery.

7.2. A ten-year-old boy can be [considered] privy to a theft.

8. If anyone asks for justice in the presence of any official[3] or other judge, and can not obtain it, and [the accused] will not give him a pledge, he [the accused] is to pay 30 shillings compensation, and within seven days make him entitled to justice.

9. If anyone has recourse to distraint[4] before he asks for justice for himself, he is to give back what he seized and pay as much again and pay 30 shillings compensation.

10. If anyone within the boundaries of our kingdom commit robbery and rapine, he is to give back the plunder and give 60 shillings as a fine.

11. If anyone sells his own countryman, bond or free, even if he is guilty, across the sea, he is to pay for him with his [own] wergild.[5]

12. If a thief is caught [in the act], he is to die the death, or his life is to be redeemed by his wergild.

---

[1] The term used is gafolgelda. On its meaning, see next note.

[2] The gebur is called by Sir Frank Stenton "a free, but economically dependent peasant". He received his land and stock from a lord and rendered agricultural services and other dues. If Ine's law were meant to cover all classes of free peasant in this chapter, gafolgelda would have to be applied to the peasant who farmed land of his own; but, though Alfred 39 speaks simply of ceorl in this connexion, it is not safe to assume that this was Ine's meaning. Alfred need not merely be repeating Ine's ruling, but may be improving on it. Ine's list here of compensations for fighting in houses is surely not meant to be exhaustive; the gesith-cund classes are omitted, so it would not be odd if the peasant farming his own land received no mention. The law is probably confined to cases about which there could be uncertainty, or where it was desired to make an alteration. If we assume this, we may take the gafolgelda to be, as the word suggests, one who holds land from a lord at a rent; and both he and the gebur can be included in the phrase in Alfred's treaty with Guthrum, "the ceorl who occupies gafolland" (see p. 381).

[3] scirman.

[4] The word wracu frequently means 'vengeance', but from what follows, it is clear that it is here used in a narrower meaning, of illegal distraint.

[5] C.C.C.C., MS. 383, adds: "and atone for it deeply with God".

13. If anyone in the bishop's presence bears false witness and breaks his pledge, he is to pay 120 shillings compensation.

13.1. We call up to seven men 'thieves'; from seven to thirty-five a 'band'; above that it is an 'army'.

14. He who is accused of [complicity with] a band [of marauders] is to clear himself by [an oath of] 120 hides, or compensate correspondingly.[1]

15. He who is accused of [taking part in] the raid of any army is to redeem himself with his wergild or clear himself by [an oath of the amount of] his wergild.

15.1. With communicants, the oath shall be [only] half as much.

15.2. A thief, when he is in the king's bonds, has then no right to purge himself.

16. He who slays a thief may declare with an oath that he slew him as a guilty man, by no means the associates.[2]

17. He who finds stolen and hidden meat, may, if he dares, declare with an oath that he owns it; he who traces it has the reward due to an informer.

18. If a ceorl is often accused, and if at the last he is taken [in the act], his hand or foot is to be struck off.

19. A king's geneat,[3] if his wergild is 1200 shillings, may, if he is a communicant, swear for 60 hides.

20.[4] If a man from a distance or a foreigner goes through the wood off the track, and does not shout nor blow a horn, he is to be assumed to be a thief, to be either killed or redeemed.

21. If anyone then asks for the wergild of the slain man, [the slayer] may declare that he slew him as a thief; by no means the associates or the lord of the slain man.[5]

21.1. If he [the slayer], however, conceals the deed and it is revealed long after, he opens the way to the oath for the dead man, so that his kinsmen may prove him guiltless.

22. If your geneat[6] steals and escapes from you, if you have a surety, demand the compensation from him; if he has no surety, pay you the compensation, and he is not to be any nearer a settlement on that account.

23. If a foreigner is slain, the king has two-thirds of the wergild, his son or kinsmen the third part.

23.1. If, however, he is without kinsmen, half [goes to] the king, half to the gesith.[7]

---

[1] When an oath is expressed in hides, their number often corresponds to the number of shillings in the fine, so a fine of 120 shillings is meant.

[2] This obscure statement probably means that the thief's associates have no right to swear to his innocence. These associates (gegildan) have been variously interpreted. Liebermann thinks that already we have a guild like that in VI Athelstan (see No. 37); he notes that in Ine 21, 21.1, the term seems to interchange with 'kinsmen', but suggests that the latter word is being used widely. But it may be gegildan which is vague, denoting "those associated with him in payment" (Attenborough), primarily his kinsmen. See p. 334.

[3] This word denotes originally 'a member of a household' and may in these early laws be being used quite generally. By the eleventh century it is used of men who hold land from a lord and pay rent and certain honourable services (especially riding duties), and who seem to correspond to a class called 'radcnihts' in Domesday Book. In its technical sense a geneat differs from a gesith in not normally being of the noble class. On gesith, see p. 362, n. 3.

[4] Almost identical with Wihtred 28.

[5] i.e. they are not to have a prior right to produce an oath.   [6] See n. 4 above.

[7] Liebermann takes gesith here in the general sense of 'companion', comparing the gegildan of Alfred 31, but it is more probable that Attenborough is right in taking it as 'the man under whose protection he has been', which makes better sense of the next clause. On gesith, see also p. 362, n. 3.

23.2. If, however, it is an abbot or an abbess,[1] they are to share in the same way with the king.

23.3. A Welsh rent-payer[2] [has a wergild of] 120 shillings, his son, 100; a slave [is to be paid for with] 60, some with 50; a Welshman's hide with 12 [shillings].[3]

24. If a penally enslaved Englishman runs away, he is to be hanged and nothing paid to his master.

24.1. If anyone kills him, nothing is to be paid to his kinsmen if they have not redeemed him within twelve months.

24.2. A Welshman, if he has five hides, is a man of a six-hundred wergild.

25. If a trader buys among the people in the countryside,[4] he is to do it before witnesses.

25.1. If stolen property in a trader's possession is attached, and he has not bought it before good witnesses, he is to declare by [an oath of the amount of] the fine, that he was neither accessory nor confederate to the theft; otherwise he is to pay 36 shillings as a fine.

26. For the maintenance of a foundling six shillings is to be paid[5] for the first year, 12 for the second, 30 for the third, and afterwards according to its appearance.

27. Whoever begets an illegitimate child and does not acknowledge it, has no right to the wergild at its death, but its lord and the king [have it].

28. He who captures a thief has a right to 10 shillings, and the king to the thief; and the kinsmen are to swear to him oaths that they will wage no feud.

28.1. If he, however, runs away and gets out of sight, then he [who captured him] is liable to the fine.

28.2. If he wishes to deny it, he is to do so by [an oath corresponding to] the property and the fine.

29. If anyone lends a sword to another's servant,[6] and he runs away, he is to pay for him a third; if he gives him a spear, half; if he lends him a horse, he is to pay his full value.

30. If a *ceorl* is accused of harbouring fugitives, he is to exculpate himself by [an oath of the amount of] his own wergild; if he cannot, he is to pay for [harbouring] him his own wergild; and the man of *gesith* rank similarly by his wergild.[7]

31. If one buys a wife, and the marriage does not take place, the money is to be paid back, and as much again, and the surety is to receive compensation, as much as the breach of his surety[8] costs.

32. If a Welshman has a hide of land, his wergild is 120 shillings; if, however, he has a half hide, 80 shillings; if he has none, 60 shillings.

---

[1] i.e. who has previously protected the foreigner.
[2] Apparently the highest class of Welsh peasant. See p. 365, n. 1.
[3] i.e. a Welshman must pay this sum to save himself from a flogging.
[4] Outside the ports or towns. With the use of the word *up* in this sense should be compared the adjective *uplendisc* 'rural, rustic'.
[5] Probably by the king's representative, for it was the king who would be entitled to the wergild of a person of unknown kin.
[6] *esne*, usually an unfree servant. See p. 359, n. 6.
[7] i.e. if he is accused of this crime he swears or pays according to his wergild. On *gesith*, see p. 359, n. 2.
[8] *borgbryce*; this term is often used to cover the same complex of rights as *mundbryce*. On *mund*, see p. 334.

33. The king's Welsh horseman,[1] who can carry his messages, his wergild is 200 shillings.

34. Whoever was present on the expedition made for the purpose of killing a man,[2] is to clear himself of the killing and pay compensation for the expedition according to the wergild of the slain man.

34.1. If his wergild is 200 shillings, he is to pay 50 shillings compensation; and one is to proceed with the same proportion in the case of the nobler born.

35. He who slays a thief may declare with an oath that he slew him fleeing as a thief, and the kinsmen of the dead man are to swear to him an oath not to carry on a feud. If, however, he conceals it and it is revealed later, he is then to pay for him.

35.1. If one vouches to warranty for property a man who had previously denied it on oath, and wishes to deny it again, he is to deny it with an oath equivalent to the fine and to the value of the property; if he will not deny it on oath, he is to pay double compensation for the false oath.

36. He who captures a thief, or is given a captured thief, and he then lets him get away, or conceals the theft, is to pay for that thief with his[3] wergild.

36.1. If he is an ealdorman, he is to lose his office, unless the king wishes to pardon him.

37. The *ceorl*, who has often been accused of theft, and then at last is proved guilty at the ordeal or else in obvious guilt, is to have hand or foot struck off.

38. If a husband[4] and wife have a child together, and the husband dies, the mother is to have her child and rear it; she is to be given six shillings for its maintenance, a cow in summer, an ox in winter; the kinsmen are to take charge of the paternal home,[5] until the child is grown up.

39. If anyone goes away from his lord without permission, or steals into another 'shire',[6] and is discovered there, he is to return to where he was before and pay 60 shillings to his lord.

40. A *ceorl*'s homestead must be fenced winter and summer. If it is not fenced, and his neighbour's cattle get in through his own gap, he has no right to anything from that cattle; he is to drive it out and suffer the damage.

41. Anyone can deny bail[7] by oath if he knows that he is doing right.

42. If *ceorls* have a common meadow or other land divided in shares to fence, and some have fenced their portion and some have not, and [if cattle] eat up their common crops or grass, those who are responsible for the gap are to go and pay to the others, who have fenced their part, compensation for the damage that has been

---

[1] *horswealh*. The word *wealh* is ambiguous in Old English, meaning either a 'Welshman' or a 'slave'. From the context, I assume the former meaning here, the king's service raising the status of the Welshman so that he is entitled to the wergild of an English freeman. By itself, the law could mean that an unfree horse-servant in the king's service was to be paid for as a freeman, which would then remind us of Ethelbert 7.
[2] I take the subjunctive mood after 'that' to suggest purpose rather than result.   [3] *i.e.* the thief's?
[4] Or *ceorl* may be being used in its usual sense of the ordinary freeman. The amounts paid are low enough to suggest that it is this class that the law has in mind, but it may not intend to exclude the nobility in the first part of the regulation.
[5] *frumstol*, literally 'first seat', therefore 'principal (or 'original') residence'.
[6] In the early laws it is uncertain whether 'shire' already bears its later definite meaning, or is used more generally of 'jurisdiction', or 'district under one's jurisdiction'.   [7] Or perhaps 'a debt'.

done there. They are to demand with regard to¹ those cattle such reparation as is proper.

42.1. If, however, it is any of the cattle which breaks the hedges and enters anywhere, and he who owns it would not or could not control it, he who finds it on his arable is to seize it and kill it; and the owner is to take its hide and flesh and suffer the loss of the rest.

43. If anyone burns down a tree in the wood, and it is disclosed who did it, he is to pay full fine; he is to pay 60 shillings, for fire is a thief.

43.1. If anyone fells in the wood quite a number of trees, and it afterwards becomes known, he is to pay for three trees at 30 shillings each; he need not pay for more of them however many they were, for the axe is an informer, not a thief.

44. If, however, anyone cuts down a tree under which 30 swine could stand, and it becomes known, he is to pay 60 shillings.

44.1. The blanket paid as rent from each household² shall be worth sixpence.

45. Forcible entry into the residence of the king or the bishop, within his own diocese, one shall compensate with 120 shillings; [into that] of an ealdorman, with 80 shillings; [into that] of a king's thegn, with 60 shillings; [into that] of a *gesith-born* man who owns land, with 35 shillings; and deny it correspondingly.

46. When anyone accuses a man that he stole cattle or received stolen cattle, he must deny the theft by [an oath of] 60 hides, if he is entitled to give an oath.³

46.1. If, however, the accusation is produced by an Englishman, it is to be denied with an oath of double this size; if it then is a Welshman's accusation, the oath is no greater on that account.

46.2. Every man may deny by oath harbouring [of stolen goods?] and homicide, if he can and dare.

47. If anyone attaches stolen cattle, [the accused] may not vouch a slave to warranty.

48. If any man is a newly enslaved penal slave, and he is accused of having stolen before he was enslaved, the accuser then has the right to give him one flogging; he can compel him to the flogging by [an oath of the amount of the stolen] goods.

49. If anyone finds swine on his mast-pasture without his permission he is to take then a pledge worth six shillings.

49.1. If, however, they were not there more often than once, the owner is to pay a shilling, and declare that they have not been there more often, by [an oath of] the value of the swine.

49.2. If they were there twice, he is to pay two shillings.

49.3. If one takes pannage in pigs, [one is to take] the third with the bacon three fingers thick, the fourth with it two fingers thick, the fifth with it a thumb thick.

50. If a *gesith-born* man intercedes with the king or the king's ealdorman or with

¹ Or 'from'. The sentence can be variously interpreted, to mean either that those whose property has been injured are to assess their damages as is proper, or that those who neglected the fence may have some claim against the owner of the damaging cattle.
² Or perhaps *hiwisc* means here, as sometimes elsewhere, a hide of land. I am uncertain whether the meaning is that a 'blanket' was paid from each household with at least one hide of land, or else one had to be rendered for every hide.
³ *i.e.* if he has not forfeited his right to swear an oath by previous conviction for crime, especially perjury.

his lord for members of his household, slaves or freemen, he, the *gesith*,[1] has no right to any fines, because he would not previously at home restrain them from wrong-doing.

51. If a *gesith-born* man, who owns land, neglects military service, he is to give 120 shillings and to forfeit his land; one who owns no land, 60 shillings, a *ceorl* 30 shillings, as fine for [neglect of] military service.

52. He who is accused of secret compacts, is to clear himself of [complicity] in the compacts with [an oath of] 120 hides, or pay 120 shillings.

53. If anyone attaches a stolen slave in the possession of another, and the person is dead who sold him to the man in whose possession he was attached, he is to vouch the grave of the dead man to warranty for the slave, as for other property, whatever it may be, and declare in that oath of [the amount of] 60 hides that the dead man sold him to him. Then with that oath he has done away with the fine; he is to give the slave back to the owner.

53.1. If, however, he knows who has the dead man's inheritance, he is then to vouch the inheritance to warranty, and ask the person that has the inheritance to make that purchase[2] incontestable, or to declare that the dead man never owned that property.

54. He who is accused of homicide, and wishes to deny the slaying with an oath –then there shall be in the hundred [hides][3] a man entitled to swear a king's oath at 30 hides, both in the case of a *gesith-born* man or a *ceorl*,[4] whichever it be.

54.1. And if wergild is paid, then he may give in each of the hundreds [of the wergild] a slave, and a coat-of-mail and a sword, if he need.

54.2. A penally enslaved Welshman shall be compelled to [suffer] a flogging as a slave by [an oath of] 12 hides, an Englishman by [an oath of] 34 hides.[5]

55. A ewe with her lamb is worth a shilling until 12[6] days after Easter.

56. If anyone buys any cattle and he then finds any unsoundness in it within 30 days, he is to hand it back to the seller, or [the latter] is to swear that he knew of no fraud when he sold it to him.

57. If a husband steals any cattle and brings it into his house, and it is seized therein, he is guilty for his part, but without his wife, for she must obey her lord; if she dare declare with an oath that she did not taste of the stolen meat, she is to receive her third portion.[7]

58. The horn of an ox is valued at tenpence.

59. The horn of a cow [is valued at] twopence; the tail of an ox is valued at a shilling; that of a cow at fivepence; the eye of an ox is valued at fivepence, that of a cow at a shilling.

---

[1] See p. 362, n. 3. This passage seems to imply that a *gesith* may have a lord other than the king. The lord envisaged in this passage may be someone to whom the king has granted rights of jurisdiction.

[2] *ćeap* will refer either to the transaction of purchasing, or to the thing purchased. Attenborough translates here "[his title to] the chattel".

[3] *e.g.* if an oath, expressed in hides, was to be given in a suit where the fine involved was a freeman's wergild of 200 shillings, there would have to be two men entitled to swear for 30 hides; if the highest wergild were involved, of 1200 shillings, there would have to be twelve of them.

[4] Does this refer to the slayer, or the slain man?

[5] The original reading may have been 24, double the oath for a Welshman.

[6] Fourteen in the later MSS.　　　　[7] *i.e.* if his possessions are forfeit, a third is retained by her.

59.1. As barley-rent, six weys must always be given for each labourer.

60. The *ceorl* who has hired another's yoke [of oxen], if he has enough to pay for it entirely in fodder–let one see that he pays in full; if he has not, he is to pay half in fodder, half in other goods.

61. Church-scot is to be paid from the haulm[1] and the hearth where one resides at midwinter.[2]

62. When a charge is brought against a man, and he is driven to the ordeal, and he himself possesses nothing to give, in order to avoid the ordeal; and another man comes forward and gives his goods instead, on what terms he can obtain, on condition that he becomes subject to him until he can restore his property to him; and then he is again a second time accused and driven to the ordeal; if he who before gave goods on his behalf will not support him further, and he [the accuser] takes him, he [the creditor] is to lose his goods, which before he paid on his behalf.

63. If a *gesith-born* man moves elsewhere, he may then have with him his reeve and his smith and his children's nurse.

64. He who has 20 hides must show 12 hides of sown land when he wishes to leave.

65. He who has 10 hides, must show six hides of sown land.

66. He who has three hides is to show one and a half.

67. If anyone covenants for a yardland or more at a fixed rent, and ploughs it, if the lord wishes to increase for him the [rent of the] land by demanding service as well as rent, he need not accept it, if he does not give him a dwelling; and he is to forfeit the crops.[3]

68. If a *gesith-born* man is evicted, he is to be evicted from the dwelling, but certainly not from the cultivated land.

69. A sheep must go with its fleece until midsummer, or else the fleece is to be paid for at twopence.

70. For a man of a two-hundred wergild there is to be paid a compensation to the lord of 30 shillings; for a man of a six-hundred wergild, 80 shillings; for a man of a twelve-hundred wergild, 120 shillings.

70.1. As a food-rent from 10 hides: 10 vats of honey, 300 loaves, 12 'ambers' of Welsh ale, 30 of clear ale, 2 full-grown cows, or 10 wethers, 10 geese, 20 hens, 10 cheeses, an 'amber' full of butter, 5 salmon, 20 pounds[4] of fodder and 100 eels.

71. If anyone is accused on a charge involving payment of wergild, and he then admits it before the oath, and has previously denied it, one is to wait for the fine until the wergild has been paid.

72. If a thief who would be liable to pay his wergild[5] is captured, and he escapes

---

[1] The phrase *healme and heorðe* is an alliterative formula to refer to the whole homestead, its dwelling-place and its cultivated land. The *healm* 'stubble' refers to the fields from which the harvest was garnered.

[2] This term usually means Christmas, but as church-scot was due at Martinmas (11 November), it probably has a wider meaning here.

[3] I assume that the situation considered is when the original agreement has expired, and the lord will not renew it on the old terms.

[4] Liebermann translates 'Wispel', a German measure of about 24 bushels.

[5] Literally, 'a wergild-thief'. Liebermann takes it to mean any criminal who would have to pay his wergild to redeem himself.

on the same day from the men who have caught him, yet he is recaptured the same night, one has no right to more than full fine from them.[1]

73. If, however, the theft is now a night old, those who caught him are to pay compensation for their fault[2] as they may compound with the king and with his reeve.

74. If a Welsh slave kills an Englishman, then he who owns him shall surrender him to the lord and kinsmen [of the slain man], or pay 60 shillings for his life.

74.1. If, however, he will not pay the price for him, the master must then set him free; his kinsmen are then to pay the wergild if he has a free kindred; if he has not, the avengers are to deal with him.

74.2. The freeman need not pay money for his kinsman[3] along with a slave, unless he wishes to redeem him from a vendetta; nor the slave along with the freeman.

75. If anyone attaches stolen property, and the person with whom it is attached vouches another man to warranty, if that man will not admit it and says he never sold it to him, but sold him something else, then he who is vouching that person to warranty may declare that he sold him nothing other than that same thing.

76. If anyone kills the godson or godfather of another, the compensation for the [spiritual] relationship is to be the same as that to the lord; the compensation is to increase in proportion to the wergild, the same as the compensation for his man does which has to be paid to the lord.

76.1. If, however, it is the king's godson, his wergild is to be paid to the king the same as to the kindred.

76.2. If, however, he was resisting him who slew him, then the compensation to the godfather is remitted, in the same way as the fine to the lord is.

76.3. If it is a spiritual son at confirmation, the compensation is to be half as much.

33. The laws of Alfred (871–899)

On Alfred as a law-giver, see p. 331 above. His laws survive in full in two manuscripts, the early tenth-century C.C.C.C., MS. 173, and the twelfth-century *Textus Roffensis*. The twelfth-century C.C.C.C., MS. 383 has lost the introduction and the beginning of the laws themselves, while only fragments are now left of what were doubtless complete versions in the early eleventh-century British Museum manuscripts, Cott. Otho B. xi and Cott. Nero A. i; there was probably once a version also in the pre-Conquest British Museum manuscript Burney 277, for, though only a fragment of the laws of Ine now survives, it is likely that this code was preceded by Alfred's, as in all other manuscripts which contain it. The code probably belongs to the middle of the reign. Alfred's laws were used by later Saxon codes, and were translated into Latin in *Quadripartitus*. I have given only a small selection from the introduction, but a full version of the laws themselves, except for some details on the tariffs for injuries. The text is edited by Liebermann, I, pp. 15–89; with English translation by Attenborough, pp. 62–93, Thorpe, I, pp. 44–101. Attenborough omits Alfred's introduction.

Int. 28.[4] If anyone entrust property to his friend, if he steal it himself, let him repay two-fold. If he knows not who stole it, let him clear himself, that he committed

---

[1] Those who let him escape. 'Full fine' is 120 shillings. Since *þeah* could mean 'even if' instead of 'yet', and *him* could be 'him' as well as 'them', this passage could read: "even if he is recaptured the same night, one has no right to more than full fine from him", *i.e.* the thief can no longer be regarded as one caught in the act, and is liable only to the fine of 120 shillings. But the first interpretation fits better with the following clause.   [2] In letting him escape.

[3] *mid þam þeowan mæg gieldan.* Liebermann suggests that *mæg* here means 'payment for kindred' (cf. *wer* for *wergild*), or that we have a compound verb *mæg gieldan*. But possibly *mæg* is an error for the dative *mæge*, when we could read: "a freeman need not pay along with a servile kinsman".

[4] Cf. Exodus xxii. 7, 8, 10, 11.

no fraud there. If it then were livestock, and he says that an army took it, or that it killed itself, and he has witness, he need not pay for it. If then he have no witness, and he [the owner] will not believe him, let him bring an oath.

Int. 30.[1] The women who are in the habit of receiving wizards and sorcerers and magicians, thou shalt not suffer to live.

Int. 40.[2] Do not thou heed the word of the false man, to obey therefore, nor consent to his judgments, nor say any witness after him.

Int. 41. Do not thou turn thyself to the folly and unjust will of the people in their speech and clamour, against thy right [judgment], and do not yield for them to the teaching of the most foolish.

Int. 43.[3] Judge thou very fairly. Do not judge one judgment for the rich and another for the poor; nor one for the one more dear and another for the one more hateful.

Int. 49.6. A man can think on this one sentence alone, that he judges each one rightly; he has need of no other law-books. Let him bethink him that he judge to no man what he would not that he judged to him, if he were giving the judgment on him.

Int. 49.7. After it came about that many peoples had received the faith of Christ, many synods were assembled throughout all the earth, and likewise throughout England, after they had received the faith of Christ, of holy bishops and also of other distinguished wise men; they then established, for that mercy which Christ taught, that secular lords might with their permission receive without sin compensation in money for almost every misdeed at the first offence, which compensation they then fixed; only for treachery to a lord they dared not declare any mercy, because Almighty God adjudged none for those who scorned him, nor did Christ, the Son of God, adjudge any for him who gave him over to death; and he charged [everyone] to love his lord as himself.

Int. 49.8. They then in many synods fixed the compensations for many human misdeeds, and they wrote them in many synod-books, here one law, there another.

Int. 49.9. Then I, King Alfred, collected these together and ordered to be written many of them which our forefathers observed, those which I liked; and many of those which I did not like, I rejected with the advice of my councillors, and ordered them to be differently observed. For I dared not presume to set in writing at all many of my own, because it was unknown to me what would please those who should come after us. But those which I found anywhere, which seemed to me most just, either of the time of my kinsman, King Ine, or of Offa, king of the Mercians, or of Ethelbert, who first among the English received baptism, I collected herein, and omitted the others.

Int. 49.10. Then I, Alfred, king of the West Saxons, showed these to all my councillors, and they then said that they were all pleased to observe them.

1. First we direct, what is most necessary, that each man keep carefully his oath and pledge.

---

[1] From Exodus xxii. 18, but only wizards are mentioned there.
[2] This and the next clause are from Exodus xxiii. 1, 2.   [3] Elaborated from Exodus xxiii. 3.

1.1. If anyone is wrongfully compelled to either of these, promising treachery to his lord or any illegal aid, then it is better to leave it unfulfilled than to perform it.

1.2. [If, however, he pledges what it is right for him to perform,]¹ and leaves it unfulfilled, let him with humility give his weapons and his possessions into his friends' keeping and be 40 days in prison at a king's estate, endure there what penance the bishop prescribes for him, and his kinsmen are to feed him if he has no food himself.

1.3. If he has no kinsmen and has not the necessary food, the king's reeve is to feed him.

1.4. If he has to be forced thither, and will not go otherwise, and he is bound, he is to forfeit his weapons and his possessions.

1.5. If he is killed, he is to lie unpaid for.

1.6. If he escapes before the end of the period, and he is caught, he is to be 40 days in prison, as he should have been before.

1.7. If he gets clear, he is to be outlawed, and to be excommunicated from all the churches of Christ.

1.8. If, however, there is secular surety for him, he is to pay for the breach of surety as the law directs him, and for the breach of pledge as his confessor prescribes for him.

2. If anyone for any guilt flees to any one of the monastic houses to which the king's food-rent belongs,² or some other privileged community which is worthy of this honour, he is to have a respite of three days to protect himself, unless he wishes to be reconciled.

2.1. If during that respite he is molested with slaying or binding or wounding, each of those [who did it] is to make amends according to the legal custom, both with wergild and with fine, and to pay to the community 120 shillings as compensation for the breach of sanctuary, and is to have forfeited his own [claim against the culprit].

3. If anyone violates the king's surety, he is to pay compensation for the charge as the law directs him, and for the breach of the surety with five pounds of pure pennies. The breach of the archbishop's surety or of his protection is to be compensated with three pounds; the breach of the surety or protection of another bishop or an ealdorman is to be compensated with two pounds.

4. If anyone plots against the king's life, directly or by harbouring his exiles or his men,³ he is liable to forfeit his life and all that he owns.

4.1. If he wishes to clear himself, he is to do it by [an oath equivalent to] the king's wergild.

4.2. Thus also we determine concerning all ranks, both *ceorl* and noble:⁴ he who plots against his lord's life is to be liable to forfeit his life and all that he owns, or to clear himself by his lord's wergild.

5. Also we determine this sanctuary for every church which a bishop has consecrated: if a man exposed to a vendetta reaches it running or riding, no one is to drag

---

¹ Supplied from *Textus Roffensis* to fill a lacuna in the oldest MS.

² Asser mentions that the king gave part of his income to monasteries.

³ Liebermann takes this to mean the men of any one of the exiles, but the natural antecedent is the king, as Attenborough takes it. Presumably disloyal men are meant.

⁴ An old rhyming formula, *ge ceorle ge eorle*, is used, in which *eorl* retains its otherwise obsolete sense of nobleman.

him out for seven days, if he can live in spite of hunger, unless he himself fights [his way] out.[1] If then anyone does so, he is liable to [pay for breach of] the king's protection and of the church's sanctuary–more, if he seizes more from there.

5.1. If the community have more need of their church, he is to be kept in another building, and it is to have no more doors than the church.

5.2. The head of that church is to take care that no one gives him food during that period.

5.3. If he himself will hand out his weapons to his foes, they are to keep him for 30 days, and send notice about him to his kinsmen.

5.4. Further sanctuary of the church: if any man has recourse to the church on account of any crime which has not been discovered, and there confesses himself in God's name, it is to be half remitted.

5.5. Whoever steals on Sunday or at Christmas or Easter or on the Holy Thursday in Rogation days; each of those we wish to be compensated doubly, as in the Lenten fast.

6. If anyone steals anything in church, he is to pay the simple compensation and the fine normally belonging to that simple compensation, and the hand with which he did it is to be struck off.

6.1. And if he wishes to redeem the hand, and that is allowed to him, he is to pay in proportion to his wergild.

7. If anyone fights or draws his weapon in the king's hall, and he is captured, it is to be at the king's judgment, whether he will grant him death or life.

7.1. If he escapes, and is afterwards captured, he shall always pay for himself with his wergild, and compensate for the crime, with wergild as with fine, according to what he has done.

8. If anyone brings a nun out of a nunnery without the permission of the king or the bishop, he is to pay 120 shillings, half to the king and half to the bishop and the lord of the church which had the nun.

8.1. If she outlives him who brought her out, she is to have nothing of his inheritance.

8.2. If she bears a child, it is not to have any of the inheritance, any more than the mother.

8.3. If her child is killed, the share of the maternal kindred is to be paid to the king; the paternal kindred are to be given their share.

9. If a woman with child is slain when she is bearing the child, the woman is to be paid for with full payment, and the child at half payment according to the wergild of the father's kin.

9.1. The fine is always to be 60 shillings until the simple compensation rises to 30 shillings; when the simple compensation has risen to that, the fine is afterwards to be 120 shillings.

9.2. Formerly, [the fine] for the stealer of gold, the stealer of stud-horses, the stealer of bees, and many fines, were greater than others; now all are alike, except for the stealer of a man: 120 shillings.

---

[1] According to Liebermann, commits himself a breach of sanctuary by fighting in the doorway to defend himself.

10. If anyone lies with the wife of a man of a twelve-hundred wergild, he is to pay to the husband 120 shillings; to a man of a six-hundred wergild 100 shillings is to be paid; to a man of the *ceorl* classs 40 shillings is to be paid.[1]

12. If a man burns or fells the wood of another, without permission, he is to pay for each large tree with five shillings, and afterwards for each, no matter how many there are, with fivepence; and 30 shillings as a fine.

13. If at a common task a man unintentionally kills another [by letting a tree fall on him] the tree is to be given to the kinsmen, and they are to have it from that estate within 30 days, or else he who owns the wood is to have the right to it.

14. If anyone is born dumb, or deaf, so that he cannot deny sins or confess them, the father is to pay compensation for his misdeeds.

15. If anyone fights or draws a weapon in the presence of the archbishop, he is to pay 150 shillings compensation; if this happens in the presence of another bishop or an ealdorman, he is to pay 100 shillings compensation.

16. If anyone steals a cow or a brood-mare and drives off a foal or a calf, he is to pay a shilling compensation [for the latter], and for the mothers according to their value.

17. If anyone entrusts to another one of his helpless dependants, and he dies[2] during that time of fostering, he who reared him is to clear himself of guilt, if anyone accuses him of any.

18. If anyone in lewd fashion seizes a nun either by her clothes or her breast without her leave, the compensation is to be double that we have established for a lay person.

18.1. If a betrothed maiden commits fornication, if she is of *ceorl* birth, 60 shillings compensation is to be paid to the surety; and it is to be paid in livestock, cattle[3] [only], and one is not to include in it any slave.

18.2. If she is a woman of a six-hundred wergild, 100 shillings are to be given to the surety.

18.3. If she is a woman of a twelve-hundred wergild, 120 shillings are to be paid to the surety.

19. If anyone lends his weapon to another that he may kill a man with it, they may, if they wish, join to pay the wergild.

19.1. If they do not join, he who lent the weapon is to pay a third part of the wergild and a third part of the fine.

19.2. If he wishes to clear himself, that in making the loan he was aware of no evil intent, he may do so.

19.3. If a sword-polisher receives another man's weapon to polish it, or a smith a man's tool, they both are to give it back unstained,[4] just as either of them had

[1] Chap. 11 is concerned with compensations for assaults of various kinds and in various circumstances against women.

[2] So Liebermann, but the dictionaries and Attenborough take the expression *hine forferie*, which seems unique, to mean 'cause or allow to die', and the subject would then be the guardian.

[3] *feogodum*. Liebermann suggests that this was originally only a gloss to *cwicæhtum* 'livestock', or, alternatively, that it is an antithesis to this and means 'valuables (other than livestock)' with a preceding 'and' omitted.

[4] Without it having been used to commit a crime.

received it; unless either of them had stipulated that he need not be liable to compensation for it.

20. If anyone entrusts property to another man's monk, without the permission of the monk's lord, and it is lost to him, he who owned it before is to bear its loss.

21. If a priest slays another man, he is to be handed over, and all of the [minster] property which he bought for himself,[1] and the bishop is to unfrock him, when he is to be delivered up out of the minster, unless his lord is willing to settle the wergild on his behalf.

22. If anyone brings up a charge in a public meeting before the king's reeve, and afterwards wishes to withdraw it, he is to make the accusation against a more likely person, if he can; if he cannot, he is to forfeit his compensation.[2]

23. If a dog rends or bites a man to death, [the owner] is to pay six shillings at the first offence; if he gives it food, he is to pay on a second occasion 12 shillings, on a third 30 shillings.

23.1. If in any of these misdeeds the dog is destroyed,[3] nevertheless this compensation is still to be paid.

23.2. If the dog commits more offences, and the owner retains it, he is to pay compensation for such wounds as the dog inflicts, according to the full wergild.

24. If a neat wounds a man, [the owner] is to hand over the neat, or to make terms.

25. If anyone rapes a *ceorl*'s slave-woman, he is to pay five shillings compensation to the *ceorl*, and 60 shillings fine.

25.1. If a slave rape a slave-woman, he is to pay by suffering castration.

26 (29).[4] If anyone with a band of men kills an innocent man of a two-hundred wergild, he who admits the slaying is to pay the wergild and the fine, and each man who was in that expedition is to pay 30 shillings as compensation for being in that band.

27 (30). If it is a man of a six-hundred wergild, each man [is to pay] 60 shillings as compensation for being in that band, and the slayer the wergild and full fine.

28 (31). If he is a man of a twelve-hundred wergild, each of them [is to pay] 120 shillings, and the slayer the wergild and the fine.

28.1 (31.1). If a band of men does this and afterwards wishes to deny it[5] on oath, they are all to be accused; and then they are all collectively to pay the wergild, and all one fine, as is accordant to the wergild.

29 (26). If anyone rapes a girl not of age, that is to be the same compensation as for an adult.

30 (27). If a man without paternal kinsmen fights and kills a man, and if then he

---

[1] Or "and everything with which he bought for himself a living" (or a place in a monastery). Thus Liebermann interprets it. In either case, the intention is to give the man his property for him to use it towards paying the wergild. Liebermann compares the *Dialogue of Egbert*, chap. 14, which, in treating of this very situation, says that the man cast out is to have any things he offered to the church "that he may have something to redeem him with". Later MSS. have 'brought' for 'bought'.

[2] The *Textus Roffensis* adds: "and he [the reeve] is to succeed to the fine".

[3] Perhaps merely 'escapes'.

[4] The figures in brackets are those retained by Liebermann from earlier editors who rearranged the MS. order. Attenborough numbers straight on.

[5] *i.e.* each wishes to deny being the actual slayer.

has maternal kinsmen, those are to pay a third share of the wergild, [and the associates[1] a third; for the third part][2] he is to flee.[3]

30.1 (27.1). If he has no maternal kinsmen, the associates are to pay half, and for half he is to flee.

31 (28). If anyone kills a man so placed, if he has no kinsmen, he is to pay half to the king, half to the associates.

32. If anyone is guilty of public slander, and it is proved against him, it is to be compensated for with no lighter penalty than the cutting off of his tongue, with the proviso that it be redeemed at no cheaper rate than it is valued in proportion to the wergild.

33. If anyone charges another about a pledge sworn by God, and wishes to accuse him that he did not carry out any [promise] of those which he gave him, he [the plaintiff] is to pronounce the preliminary oath in four churches, and the other, if he wishes to clear himself, is to do it in twelve churches.

34. Moreover, it is prescribed for traders: they are to bring before the king's reeve in a public meeting the men whom they take up into the country with them, and it is to be established how many of them there are to be; and they are to take with them men whom they can afterwards bring to justice at a public meeting; and whenever it may be necessary for them to have more men out with them on their journey, it is always to be announced, as often as it is necessary for them, to the king's reeve in the witness of the meeting.

35. If anyone binds an innocent *ceorl*, he is to pay him six shillings compensation.

35.1. If anyone scourges him, he is to pay him 20 shillings compensation.

35.2. If he places him in the stocks,[4] he is to pay him 30 shillings compensation.

35.3. If in insult he disfigures him by cutting his hair, he is to pay him 10 shillings compensation.

35.4. If, without binding him, he cuts his hair like a priest's, he is to pay him 30 shillings compensation.

35.5. If he cuts off his beard, he is to pay him 20 shillings compensation.

35.6. If he binds him and then cuts his hair like a priest's, he is to pay him 60 shillings compensation.

36. Moreover, it is established: if anyone has a spear over his shoulder, and a man is transfixed on it, the wergild is to be paid without the fine.

36.1. If he is transfixed before his eyes, he is to pay the wergild; if anyone accuses him of intention in this act, he is to clear himself in proportion to the fine, and by that [oath] do away with the fine,

36.2. if the point is higher[5] than the butt end of the shaft. If they are both level, the point and the butt end, that is to be [considered] without risk.

37. If anyone from one district[6] wishes to seek a lord in another district, he is to do so with the witness of the ealdorman, in whose shire he previously served.

---

[1] On the *gegildan*, see p. 366, n. 2. Here, at any rate, persons who are not kinsmen are meant.

[2] From the *Textus Roffensis*, since it has been omitted in the oldest MS.

[3] This shows that the payment of their proper share frees the kinsmen from the dangers of a vendetta, even if the whole wergild is not paid. The slayer himself remains exposed if his own third is unpaid.

[4] *hengen*; perhaps it should be rendered 'prison'.

[5] C.C.C.C., MS. 383, and the Latin translation known as *Quadripartitus* add here: "three fingers".

[6] *boldgetale*, literally 'a number of houses'. Bishop Wærferth uses it several times to translate *provincia*.

37.1. If he do it without his witness, he who accepts him as his man is to pay 120 shillings compensation; he is, however, to divide it, half to the king in the shire in which the man served previously, half in that into which he has come.

37.2. If he has committed any wrong where he was before, he who now receives him as his man is to pay compensation for it, and 120 shillings to the king as fine.

38. If anyone fights in a meeting in the presence of the king's ealdorman, he is to pay wergild and fine, as it is fitting, and before that, 120 shillings to the ealdorman as a fine.

38.1. If he disturbs a public meeting by drawing a weapon, [he is to pay] 120 shillings to the ealdorman as a fine.

38.2. If any of this takes place before the deputy of the king's ealdorman, or before the king's priest, [there shall be] a fine of 30 shillings.

39. If anyone fights in the house of a *ceorl*, he is to pay six shillings compensation to the *ceorl*.

39.1. If he draws a weapon and does not fight, it is to be half as much.

39.2. If either of these things happens to a man of a six-hundred wergild, it is to amount to three-fold the compensation to a *ceorl*; [if] to a man of a twelve-hundred wergild, to double that of the man of the six-hundred wergild.

40. Forcible entry into the king's residence shall be 120 shillings; into the archbishop's, 90 shillings; another bishop's or an ealdorman's, 60 shillings; that of a man of a twelve-hundred wergild, 30 shillings; of a man of a six-hundred wergild, 15 shillings; forcible entry into a *ceorl*'s enclosure, five shillings.

40.1. If any of this happens when the army has been called out, or in the Lenten fast, the compensations are to be doubled.

40.2. If anyone openly neglects the rules of the Church in Lent without permission, he is to pay 120 shillings compensation.

41. The man who holds bookland, which his kinsmen left to him – then we establish that he may not alienate it from his kindred if there is a document or witness [to show] that he was prohibited from doing so by those men who acquired it in the beginning and by those who gave it to him; and that is then to be declared[1] in the witness of the king and of the bishop, in the presence of his kinsmen.

42. Moreover we command: that the man who knows his opponent[2] to be dwelling at home is not to fight before he asks justice for himself.

42.1. If he has sufficient power to surround his opponent and besiege him there in his house, he is to keep him seven days inside and not fight against him, if he will remain inside; and then after seven days, if he will surrender and give up his weapons, he is to keep him unharmed for 30 days, and send notice about him to his kinsmen and his friends.

42.2. If, however, he reaches a church, it is then to be [dealt with] according to the privilege of the church, as we have said above.

42.3. If he [the attacker] has not sufficient power to besiege him in his house, he

---

[1] By whoever is contesting the alienation of the land.
[2] A man against whom he has a legitimate blood-feud.

is to ride to the ealdorman and ask him for support; if he will not give him support, he is to ride to the king, before having recourse to fighting.

42.4. Likewise, if a man run across his opponent, and did not previously know him to be at home, if he will give up his weapons, he is to be kept for 30 days and his friends informed; if he will not give up his weapons, then he may fight against him. If he is willing to surrender, and to give up his weapons, and after that anyone fights against him, he [who does] is to pay wergild or compensation for wounds according to what he has done, and a fine, and is to have forfeited [the right to avenge] his kinsman.[1]

42.5. Moreover we declare that a man may fight on behalf of his lord, if the lord is being attacked, without incurring a vendetta. Similarly the lord may fight on behalf of his man.

42.6. In the same way, a man may fight on behalf of his born kinsman, if he is being wrongfully attacked, except against his lord; that we do not allow.

42.7. And a man may fight without incurring a vendetta if he finds another man with his wedded wife, within closed doors or under the same blanket, or with his legitimate daughter or his legitimate sister, or with his mother who was given as a lawful wife to his father.

43. These days are to be given to all free men, but not to slaves or unfree labourers:[2] 12 days at Christmas, and the day on which Christ overcame the devil,[3] and the anniversary of St. Gregory,[4] and seven days at Easter and seven days after, and one day at the feast of St. Peter and St. Paul,[5] and in harvest-time the whole week before the feast of St. Mary,[6] and one day at the feast of All Saints.[7] And the four Wednesdays in the four Ember weeks are to be given to all slaves, to sell to whomsoever they choose anything of what anyone has given them in God's name, or which they can earn in any of their leisure moments.[8]

34. The treaty between Alfred and Guthrum (886–890)

This extremely interesting document, which, since London is left on the English side of the boundary, was probably drawn up after Alfred obtained London in 886, survives in two versions, both in C.C.C.C., MS. 383. I give here the longer of the two versions, which also occurs in the Latin of *Quadripartitus*. The code is certainly no later than 890, for in this year Guthrum died. The text is edited by Liebermann, I, pp. 126–129; and with English translation by Attenborough, pp. 98–101, Thorpe, I, pp. 152–157.

PROLOGUE. This is the peace which King Alfred and King Guthrum and the councillors of all the English race and all the people which is in East Anglia have all agreed on and confirmed with oaths, for themselves and for their subjects, both for the living and those yet unborn, who care to have God's grace or ours.

1. First concerning our boundaries: up[9] the Thames, and then up the Lea, and along the Lea to its source, then in a straight line to Bedford, then up the Ouse to the Watling Street.

---

[1] Accepting Liebermann's interpretation of this passage.   [2] *esnewyrhtan.* See p. 359, n. 6.
[3] 15 February.   [4] 12 March.   [5] 29 June.
[6] 15 August (the Assumption) or 8 September (the Nativity).   [7] 1 November.
[8] The rest of the code merely consists of a tariff of the compensations to be paid for wounds of various kinds and for other injuries.   [9] For *up on* meaning 'up' cf. the Chronicle 895.

2. This is next, if a man is slain, all of us[1] estimate Englishman and Dane at the same amount, at eight half-marks[2] of refined gold, except the *ceorl* who occupies rented land,[3] and their [the Danes'] freedmen; these also are estimated at the same amount, both at 200 shillings.

3. And if anyone accuses a king's thegn of manslaughter, if he dares to clear himself by oath, he is to do it with 12 king's thegns; if anyone accuses a man who is less powerful then a king's thegn, he is to clear himself with 12 of his equals and with one king's thegn—and so in every suit which involves more than four mancuses—and if he dare not [clear himself], he is to pay three-fold compensation, according as it is valued.

4. And that each man is to know his warrantor at [the purchase of] men or horses or oxen.

5. And we all agreed on the day when the oaths were sworn, that no slaves nor freemen might go without permission into the army of the Danes, any more than any of theirs to us. But if it happens that from necessity any one of them wishes to have traffic with us, or we with them, for cattle or goods, it is to be permitted on condition that hostages shall be given as a pledge of peace and as evidence so that one may know no fraud is intended.[4]

35. King Athelstan's laws issued at Grately, Hampshire (II Athelstan, 924–939)

This is a comprehensive code, covering many of the main problems faced by English kings in their attempt to preserve good order, and reference is made back to it in other legislation of this reign. The exact date of the code cannot be ascertained. It has been preserved for us in the *Textus Roffensis* and the C.C.C.C., MS. 383, and fragments of it survive in the remains of Brit. Mus. Cott. Otho B. xi. These are written in a later hand than that which wrote the laws of Alfred and Ine in this manuscript, and probably should be dated late eleventh century. A Latin version is in *Quadripartitus*.
    The text is edited by Liebermann, I, pp. 150–167; and with English translation by Attenborough, pp. 126–143, Thorpe, I, pp. 194–215.

ATHELSTAN'S ORDINANCE[5]

Concerning thieves. First, that no thief is to be spared who is caught with the stolen goods, [if he is] over twelve years and [if the value of the goods is] over eightpence.

1.1. And if anyone does spare one, he is to pay for the thief with his wergild—and the thief is to be no nearer a settlement on that account—or to clear himself by an oath of that amount.

[1] Liebermann, however, takes 'all' as adverbial, *i.e.* 'precisely we estimate'.
[2] A mark was a Scandinavian weight, by the end of the next century, and perhaps already, about 3440–3520 grains. The amount here stated may represent a recognized Scandinavian wergild, but, if the ratio of gold to silver was approximately 10 : 1 at this time, it would not be very far from the wergild of the highest English class. See Chadwick, *Studies on Anglo-Saxon Institutions*, pp. 50 f.
[3] It is perhaps best to interpret this, as does Sir Frank Stenton (*Anglo-Saxon England*, pp. 258 f.), as meaning all of the *ceorl* class who do not farm land of their own. Those of this class who do are then classed with Englishmen of noble rank as level with all free classes of Danes. One should perhaps compare the treaty with the Danes in Ethelred's reign (see p. 402), where similarly Danish and English free men are set level and paid for at the highest wergild (£25 = 1200 West Saxon shillings). It would not be in itself inconceivable that the Danes might insist, in the land they had conquered, on lowering all English *ceorlas* to the level of their own half-free class, but if that were what was meant here, the relative clause would seem redundant.
[4] Literally, "that one has a clean back".
[5] This heading is in the *Textus Roffensis* only. C.C.C.C., MS. 383, has "Concerning Thieves".

1.2. If, however, he [the thief] wishes to defend himself or to escape, he is not to be spared [whether younger or older than twelve].[1]

1.3. If a thief is put into prison, he is to be in prison 40 days, and he may then be redeemed with 120 shillings; and the kindred are to stand surety for him that he will desist for ever.

1.4. And if he steals after that, they are to pay for him with his wergild, or to bring him back there.

1.5. And if anyone defends him, he is to pay for him with his wergild, whether to the king or to him to whom it rightly belongs; and everyone of those who supported him is to pay 120 shillings to the king as a fine.

2. Concerning lordless men[2]. And we pronounced about those lordless men, from whom no justice can be obtained, that one should order their kindred to fetch back[3] such a person to justice and to find him a lord in public meeting.

2.1. And if they then will not, or cannot, produce him on that appointed day, he is then to be a fugitive afterwards, and he who encounters him is to strike him down as a thief.

2.2. And he who harbours him after that, is to pay for him with his wergild or to clear himself by an oath of that amount.

3. Concerning the refusal of justice.[4] The lord who refuses justice and upholds his guilty man, so that the king is appealed to, is to repay the value of the goods and 120 shillings to the king; and he who appeals to the king before he demands justice as often as he ought, is to pay the same fine as the other would have done, if he had refused him justice.

3.1. And the lord who is an accessory to a theft by his slave, and it becomes known about him, is to forfeit the slave and be liable to his wergild on the first occasion; if he does it more often, he is to be liable to pay all that he owns.

3.2. And likewise any of the king's treasurers or of our reeves, who has been an accessory of thieves who have committed theft, is to be liable to the same.

4. Concerning treachery to a lord. And we have pronounced concerning treachery to a lord, that he [who is accused] is to forfeit his life if he cannot deny it or is afterwards convicted at the three-fold ordeal.

5. And we have pronounced concerning breaking into a church; if he [who is accused] be convicted at the three-fold ordeal, he is to pay according to what the law-book[5] says.

6. Concerning witchcraft. And we have pronounced concerning witchcrafts and

---

[1] The last six words are not in the *Textus Roffensis*, but can be put together from the C.C.C.C., MS. 383, and the *Quadripartitus*. Without some such qualification, the whole clause seems a meaningless repetition of 1, for a thief is not to be spared whether he flee or not.

[2] From C.C.C.C., MS. 383.

[3] *gehamettan* is assumed from this context and from its etymology to mean 'to domicile', but one should compare the O.E. version of the *Capitula of Theodulf* (ed. A. S. Napier, 1916, pp. 115 f.), where the words *omnes debitores uestros repetitis* (Douai version: "you exact of all your debtors") of Isaiah lviii. 3, are rendered *ealle eowre gyltendras ge hametaδ*. A rendering 'bring back', or 'bring home' would suit very well the only other recorded instance, *i.e.* Birch, No. 599; *he moste þa inberδan menn hamettan to Eblesburnan*, "he might bring home to Ebblesbourne the persons born on the estate".

[4] From *Textus Roffensis*.

[5] By this is probably meant the laws of Alfred, with those of Ine as an appendix. The reference in this chapter is to Alfred 6.

sorceries and secret attempts on life,[1] that, if anyone is killed by such, and he [who practised them] cannot deny it, he is to forfeit his life.

6.1. If, however, he wish to deny it, and is convicted at the three-fold ordeal, he is to be 120 days in prison; and his kinsmen are afterwards to take him out and to pay 120 shillings to the king, and to pay the wergild to the kinsmen [of the dead person], and to stand surety for him that he will desist from such for ever.

6.2. Concerning incendiaries.[2] Incendiaries and those who avenge a thief are to be subject to the same penalty.

6.3. And he who wishes to avenge a thief, and yet does not wound anyone, is to pay 120 shillings to the king for the assault.

7. And we have pronounced concerning the simple ordeal, with regard to those men who have often been accused, and were convicted, and know no one to stand surety for them; they are to be brought to prison, and they are to be released as it is said here above.

8. Concerning landless men. And we have pronounced, that if any landless man took service in another shire, and afterwards returns to his kinsmen, he [any kinsman] is to harbour him [only] on condition that he brings him to justice if he commits any offence there, or he is to pay the compensation on his behalf.

9. Concerning the attaching of livestock. He who attaches livestock is to have nominated for him five men among his neighbours, and from those five get one who will swear with him that he is attaching it according to the common law. And he who wishes to maintain his right to it, is to have 10 men nominated for him, and to get two of them and to give the oath that it was born in his possession, without the oath of the whole number. And this selected oath is to be valid [in cases where] over 20 pence [is involved].

10. Concerning exchange. And no one is to exchange any livestock without the witness of the reeve or the priest or the lord of the estate or the treasurer or other trustworthy man. If anyone does so, he is to pay 30 shillings as a fine, and the lord of the estate is to succeed to the exchanged property.

10.1. Concerning false witness. If it is then discovered that any of them gave false witness, his witness is never again to be valid; and also he is to pay 30 shillings as a fine.

11. Concerning him who should demand payment for a slain man. We have pronounced that he who should demand payment for a slain thief, is to come forward with three others,[3] two from the paternal kindred and one from the maternal, and they are to give the oath that they knew of no theft committed by their kinsman, for which guilt he deserved to lose his life; and they[4] are afterwards to go with twelve others and prove him liable[5] as it was ordained before. And if the kinsmen of the dead

---

[1] Literally, 'murders'. Open killing was not reckoned as murder in Anglo-Saxon law.
[2] From *Textus Roffensis*.
[3] The phrases, literally 'one of three', 'one of twelve', probably mean 'with three (twelve) others' in this law. See p. 148, n. 5.
[4] Liebermann takes this to refer to the party which has slain the man. See next note.
[5] *gescyldigan* is a rare verb, and Liebermann takes it to mean that the slain man's guilt was to be proved. But I do not think we should exclude the possibility that it means 'liable to be paid for', and that the oath supported by three kinsmen is a preliminary oath, after which a day is appointed for a larger oath to be brought to establish his innocence, and therefore his right to have a wergild paid for him.

man will not come thither on the appointed day, each who brought forward the suit is to pay 120 shillings.

12. [That one is not to buy outside a town.]¹ And we have pronounced that no goods over 20 pence are to be bought outside a town, but they are to be bought there in the witness of the town-reeve or of another trustworthy man, or, again, in the witness of the reeves in a public meeting.

13. And we pronounce that every borough is to be repaired by a fortnight after Rogation days.

13.1. Secondly, that all buying is to be within a town.²

14. Concerning moneyers. Thirdly, that there is to be one coinage over all the king's dominion, and no one is to mint money except in a town.

14.1. And if a moneyer is convicted, the hand with which he committed the crime is to be struck off, and put up on the mint. And if, however, there is an accusation, and he wishes to clear himself, he is then to go to [the ordeal of] hot iron, and redeem the hand with which he is accused of having committed the crime; and if he is convicted at the ordeal, the same is to be done as it said here above.

14.2. In Canterbury [there are to be] seven moneyers; four of the king, two of the bishop, one of the abbot; in Rochester three, two of the king, one of the bishop; in London eight; in Winchester six; in Lewes two; in Hastings one; another at Chichester; at Southampton two; at Wareham two; [at Dorchester one];³ at Exeter two; at Shaftesbury two; otherwise in the other boroughs one.

15. Fourthly: that no shieldmaker is to put any sheepskin on a shield, and if he does so, he is to pay 30 shillings.

16. Fifthly: that every man is to have two mounted men for every plough.⁴

17. Sixthly: if anyone accepts a bribe from a thief and ruins the rights of another, he is to be liable to pay his wergild.

18. Seventhly: that no one is to sell a horse across the sea, unless he wishes to give it.

19. And we have pronounced with regard to a slave, that, if he is convicted at the ordeal, the price of the goods is to be paid, and he is to be flogged three times or the price is to be paid a second time. And the fine is to be at a half-rate where slaves are concerned.

20. If anyone fails to attend a meeting three times, he is to pay the fine for disobedience to the king; and the meeting is to be announced seven days before it is to take place.

20.1. If, however, he will not do justice nor pay the fine for disobedience, the leading men are to ride thither, all who belong to the borough, and take all that he owns and put him under surety.

20.2. If, however, anyone will not ride with his fellows, he is to pay the fine for disobedience to the king.

¹ From *Quadripartitus*. This chapter repeats a regulation of Edward the Elder (I Edward I).
² This repetition, and the new numbering of the clauses, suggests that a separate set of statutes is here being incorporated. It may end with 18; it is mainly concerned with trading regulations.
³ This is from *Quadripartitus*.
⁴ If this refers to military service, the demand is much heavier than in later times, when one man from every five hides is a not uncommon rate.

20.3. And it is to be announced in the meeting that everyone is to be at peace with everything with which the king will be at peace, and to refrain from theft on pain of losing his life and all that he owns.

20.4. And he who will not cease for these penalties–the leading men are to ride thither, all who belong to the borough, and take all that he owns. The king is to succeed to half, to half the men who are on that expedition. And they are to put him under surety.

20.5. If he knows no one to stand surety for him, they are to take him prisoner.

20.6. If he will not permit it, he is to be killed, unless he escapes.

20.7. If anyone wishes to avenge him or carry on a feud against any of them, he is to be at emnity with the king and all the king's friends.

20.8. If he escapes, and anyone harbours him, he is to be liable to pay his wergild, unless he dares to clear himself by the [amount of the] fugitive's wergild, that he did not know that he was a fugitive.

21. If anyone compounds for the ordeal, he is to compound what he can for the price of the goods, and not for the fine, unless he to whom it belongs will concede it.

22. And no one is to receive the man of another man, without the permission of him whom he served before.

22.1. If anyone does so, he is to give back the man and pay the fine for dis-obedience to the king.

22.2. And no one is to dismiss his man who has been accused, before he has rendered justice.

23. If anyone pledges [to undergo] the ordeal, he is then to come three days before to the priest whose duty it is to consecrate it, and live off bread and water and salt and vegetables until he shall go to it, and be present at Mass on each of those three days, and make his offering and go to communion on the day on which he shall go to the ordeal, and swear then the oath that he is guiltless of that charge according to the common law, before he goes to the ordeal.

23.1. And if it is [the ordeal of] water, he is to sink one and a half ells on the rope; if it is the ordeal of iron, it is to be three days before the hand is unbound.

23.2. And each man is to obtain [the right to pursue] his charge by a preliminary oath, as we have said before; and each of those of both parties who is present is to be fasting, according to the command of God and of the archbishop; and there are not to be on either side more men than twelve. If the accused man then is one of a larger company than twelve,[1] the ordeal is then invalidated, unless they will leave him.

24. And he who buys livestock with a witness, and has to vouch to warranty afterwards – then he from whom he bought it is to take it back, whether he be slave or free, whichever he is.

24.1. And there is to be no trading on Sundays; if then anyone does it, he is to forfeit the goods and pay 30 shillings fine.

25. If any of my reeves will not carry out this [ordinance] and is less zealous about

---

[1] From the ambiguity of the expression *twelfa sum* (see p. 148, n. 5), it is uncertain whether this figure is inclusive of the defendant or not.

it than we have pronounced, he is then to pay the fine for disobedience to me, and I shall find another who will.

25.1. And the bishop in whose diocese it lies is to exact the fine for disobedience from the reeve.

25.2. He who deviates from this ordinance is to pay on the first occasion five pounds, on the second occasion his wergild, on the third occasion he is to forfeit all that he owns and the friendship of us all.

26. And he who swears a false oath, and it becomes known against him, is never afterwards to be entitled to an oath, nor is he to be buried in a consecrated cemetery when he dies, unless he has the witness of the bishop in whose diocese he is that he has done penance for it as his confessor has prescribed for him.

26.1. And his confessor is to inform the bishop within 30 days whether he was willing to submit to that penance. If he does not do so, he is to pay in accordance with what the bishop will allow him.

[All this was established at the great assembly at Grately, at which Archbishop Wulfhelm was present and all the nobles and councillors whom King Athelstan could gather together.][1]

36. King Athelstan's laws issued at Exeter (V Athelstan)

This little code illustrates both the need of strong measures to prevent defiance of the law and corruption among judges, and the readiness of a king like Athelstan to take them. It survives in the *Textus Roffensis* and in Latin in *Quadripartitus*. The text is edited by Liebermann, I, pp. 166–169; and with English translation by Attenborough, pp. 152–155, Thorpe, I, pp. 220–225.

PROLOGUE. I, King Athelstan, make known that I have learnt that our peace is worse kept than I should like and than it was pronounced at Grately; and my councillors say that I have borne it too long.

Prol. 1. Now I have concluded, along with the councillors who have been with me at Christmas at Exeter, that all [the disturbers of the peace] are to be ready, themselves, their wives and their cattle and all things, to go whither I wish – unless they are willing to desist after this – on condition that they never come back into their native district.

Prol. 2. And if they are ever met with in the district, that they are to be liable [to the same penalty] as he who is caught with stolen goods.

Prol. 3. And he who harbours them, or any of their men, or sends anyone to them, is to forfeit his life and all that he owns. That is then because the oaths and the pledges and the sureties which were given there are all disregarded and broken, and we know no other things to trust to, except it be this.

1. And he who receives the man of another man, whom he dismisses for his wrong-doing, and cannot clear[2] him from [the charge of] evil-doing, is

---

[1] This is from the Latin of *Quadripartitus*, which probably got the information from the lost prologue to this code. Athelstan's other legislation refers several times to the laws promulgated at Grately. Lambard's 'Old English' version of this passage is probably an Elizabethan translation from the Latin.

[2] On the authority of the alleged lost manuscript known to Lambard, *getruwian* is sometimes emended to *steoran* and the clause translated: 'to restrain him from evil doing'; but Lambard was probably only translating the *castigare* of *Quadripartitus*, and it is not certain that the author of this understood the passage. It makes good sense as it stands: if the new lord can prove that the man was innocent of the charge on which he was dismissed, he is not liable to penalty for engaging him.

to pay for him to the man whom he followed before, and give 120 shillings to the king.

1.1. If the lord, however, wishes wrongfully to ruin the man, he is then to justify himself, if he can, in a public meeting; and if he is innocent, he is to seek such lord as he will in the witness of that meeting, because I grant that each of those who are innocent may serve such lord as he wishes.

1.2. And such reeve as neglects this and will not be zealous about it is to pay to the king the fine for disobedience to him, if he is truly accused of it.

1.3. And such reeve as accepts a bribe, and through that ruins the rights of another, is to pay the fine for disobedience to the king and bear also the degradation, as we have pronounced.[1]

1.4. And if it is a thegn who does it, it is to be the same.

1.5. And in the district of every reeve as many men are to be nominated as are known to be trustworthy, that they may be witnesses in every suit; and the oaths of them,[2] the trustworthy men, are to be in proportion to the value of the property [in dispute], without selection.

2. And he who tracks cattle into the land of another—he who owns the land is to follow the trail out [of his land], if he can; if he cannot, the trail is to serve instead of the preliminary oath, if he [the loser] accuses anyone on that estate.

3. And every Friday at every minster all the servants of God are to sing 50 psalms for the king and for all who desire what he desires, and for the others, as they may deserve.

37. The ordinance of the bishops and reeves of the London district (VI Athelstan)

The importance of this text for studying the history of London can hardly be overstressed. It clearly does not concern only the city itself, but a wider area attached to it; otherwise one would not have more than one bishop implicated. Some lands outside the diocese of London, probably in Surrey and Kent, must be included. Reference is made to a 'peace-guild', which has police duties for the common security of the district, various arrangements about mutual help among its members, and a somewhat elaborate organization, which includes a common purse. The ordinance seems to be a combination of a set of rules for the running of this guild and an undertaking to observe the king's enactments, with some arrangements as to the putting of them into force. The code is preserved in the *Textus Roffensis*, with the Latin rubric *Iudicia ciuitatis Londoniae*, and there is a Latin text in *Quadripartitus*. The code is edited by Liebermann, I, pp. 173–183; and with English translation by Attenborough, pp. 156–169, Thorpe, I, pp. 228–243.

PROLOGUE. This is the ordinance which the bishops and the reeves who belong to London have agreed to and confirmed with pledges in our peace-guild, both nobles and *ceorls*,[3] in addition to the statutes which were established at Grately and at Exeter and at Thunderfield.[4]

1.1. First, namely: that no thief [who steals] over 12 pence and [who is] over 12 years old is to be spared, whom according to the common law we have discovered to be guilty and to be unable to deny it; we are to kill him and take all that he owns,

---

[1] Loss of office is probably meant, as in II Athelstan 25.

[2] *i.e.* the number requisite in a particular suit.

[3] A rhyming formula: *ge eorlisce ge ceorlisce.* See p. 374, n. 4.

[4] Probably Thunderfield, Surrey, which has the proper early form in King Alfred's will and in Birch, No. 820. An O.E. fragment of laws issued there exists, and a longer Latin text. This code is cited as IV Athelstan.

and first we are to take the value of the [stolen] property from his possessions, and what is left is to be divided into three, one part for the wife, if she is innocent and was not privy to the crime, and the remainder [is to be divided] into two; the king is to succeed to half, the fellowship to half. If it is bookland or bishops' land, then the lord of the estate has a right to that half part in common with the fellowship. . . .[1]

2. Secondly: we pronounced that each of us was to contribute four pence for our common necessities within twelve months, and we were to compensate for the property that should be taken after we had contributed that money; and we were to have all the searching[2] for ourselves in common. And each man was to pay his shilling who had property that was worth 30 pence, except for a poor widow, who had no one working[3] for her and no land.

3. Thirdly: that we always are to reckon 10 men together—and the senior is to have charge of the nine in all those dues which we have all agreed on—and afterwards a hundred of them together, and one hundred-man, who is to admonish those 10 men to the common benefit of us all; and those 11 are to have control of the money of the hundred, and to note what they pay out, when one has to pay, and what on the other hand they receive, if money comes to us from our common suit; and they are to see to it also that each due is forthcoming which we have all agreed to for the benefit of us all, on penalty of 30 pence or one ox, so that all may be performed which we have agreed in our ordinances and which is set out in the terms of our constitution.[4]

4. Fourthly: that each man of those that heard the summons was to be helpful to the rest both in following the trail and in riding with them, as long as the trail could be seen; and after the trail had been lost, a man was to be procured [from two tithings][5] where the population was large, from one tithing where it was more sparse—unless more are required—to ride or go on foot whither there is then greatest need, and they have all agreed.

5. Fifthly: that no search is to be abandoned either north of the boundary or south of it, until every man who has a horse has ridden out once; and he who has no horse is to work for the lord who rides or goes on foot instead of him, until he comes home, unless justice can be obtained earlier.

6.1. Sixthly: concerning our compensation, a horse [is to be paid for] with half a pound, if it is worth so much, and if it is inferior it is to be paid for according to its value, judging by its appearance, and to the value the owner sets on it,[6] unless he has witness that it was as good as he says; and he[7] is to have the additional payment that we obtain there.

6.2. And an ox [is to be paid for] at a mancus; and a cow at 20 [pence]; and a pig at 10 [pence]; and a sheep at a shilling.

[1] Chaps. 1.2–1.5 merely repeat with some amplification rules concerning theft from the other codes. I have therefore omitted them.
[2] The quests after stolen cattle, but here more particularly the profits arising from them or from any litigation about stolen goods.
[3] The precise meaning of *forwyrhta* in this context is doubtful. It usually means 'advocate', 'agent'.
[4] Attenborough's rendering.   [5] Supplied from *Quadripartitus*.
[6] Liebermann explains this as the value he swears to by oath, in contrast to his mere statement if he has witnesses.
[7] *Quadripartitus*, "we are to have".

6.3. And concerning our slaves, we pronounced to those who owned slaves that, if anyone were to steal a slave, half a pound was to be paid for him; if, however, we obtained compensation, he [the owner] was to be paid above that according to his value, judging by his appearance; and we were to have for ourselves the surplus of what we obtained there. If, however, he ran away, he was to be taken and stoned as it was formerly agreed; and each man who possessed a man was to contribute a penny or a halfpenny, according to the number of people in the association, so that the full sum should be reached. If, however, he should get away, he was to be paid for according to his value, judging by his appearance, and we were all to search for him. If we then should come across him, the same was to be done to him as was done to an unfree[1] thief, or he is to be hanged.

6.4. And the price [paid in compensation] for goods worth over 30 pence is always to mount as far as half a pound,[2] after we search for it, further, if we obtain compensation at the full value; and the search is to go on, as was agreed before, although it [the sum involved] is less.

7. Seventhly: we pronounced that, no matter who did the deeds which avenged the injury of us all, we were all in one friendship and in one emnity, whichever should result; and he who was before others in killing a thief, should be the better off by 12 pence from the money of us all for the deed and for the enterprise. And he who owned the cattle for which we pay compensation is not to give up the search, and the claim that goes with it, until we obtain payment, on pain of [the fine for] disobedience to us; and we then should also recompense him for his trouble from our common property, according to what the proceedings had cost, lest the claim should be neglected.

8.1. Eighthly: that we, the hundred-men and those who have charge of the tithing, shall always assemble once a month, if we can and have leisure, whether at the time of the filling of the butts or else when it suits us, and take note how our agreement is being observed; and then 12[3] men shall dine together and shall supply themselves as they think fitting, and distribute all the leavings for God's sake.

8.2. And if it then happens that any kindred is so strong and so large, within the district or outside it, whether men of a twelve-hundred wergild or of a two-hundred, that they refuse us our rights and stand up for a thief, we are to ride thither with all our men with the reeve in whose district it is.

8.3. And also we are to send in both directions to the reeves and request help from them of as many men as may seem to us suitable in so great a suit, so that the guilty men may stand in greater awe on account of our association; and we are all to ride thither and avenge our injury and kill the thief and those who fight with him and support him, unless they will desert him.

8.4. And if one follows a trail from one shire into another, the men who are nearest are to take up and follow the trail, until it is announced to the reeve; he then is to take it up with [the men of] his district, and follow the trail out of his shire, if he can; if, however, he cannot, he is to pay the price of the cattle, and the two reeves'

---

[1] *Wylisc* is ambiguous, meaning 'Welsh, foreign, servile'; but the distinction here is between the treatment of a slave and that of a freeman, when convicted of theft.

[2] Liebermann (III, p. 120) interprets differently.   [3] One would have expected eleven.

districts[1] are to have the full suit in common, no matter where it is, whether north of the boundary or south; so that even from one shire to another each reeve is to help the next for the sake of the peace of us all, on pain of the [fine for] disobedience to the king.

8.5. And also everyone is to help the others, as it is agreed and confirmed with pledges; and such man as neglects it beyond the boundary is to be liable to pay 30 pence or one ox, if he disregards any of that which stands in our document and which we have confirmed with our pledges.

8.6. And we pronounced also with regard to each man who has given his pledge in our guild, that if death befalls him, each guild-brother is to give a loaf with its accompaniment[2] for his soul, and to sing or cause to be sung 50 psalms within 30 days.

8.7. And we charge all subject to us that each man is to note when he has his cattle and when he has not, with his neighbours' witness, and if he cannot find it, to point out the trail to us within three days; for we believe that many heedless men do not care how their cattle wander, out of over-confidence in the peace.

8.8. Again, we charge that, if he wishes to ask for the value of the cattle, he is to inform his neighbours within three days; and nevertheless the search is to go on, as it was stated before; for we will not pay for stray cattle, unless it is stolen; many men bring forward impudent claims. If he cannot point out the trail, he is to declare on oath with his three neighbours that it has been stolen within three days, and to ask afterwards for its value.

8.9. And let it not be uttered in vain or passed over in silence, if our lord or any of our reeves can suggest to us any addition to our peace-guild; [rather] let us accept it joyfully, as becomes us all and is necessary for us. Then we trust in God and our royal lord, that, if we carry it all out thus, the condition of all the nation will be better as regards theft than it was before. If, however, we become negligent about this peace and this pledge which we have given and which the king has laid on us, we can expect or know well that these thieves will prevail still more than they have previously done. But let us keep our pledge and the peace, as it may please our lord; there is great need for us to carry out what he wishes, and if he commands and directs us further, we are humbly ready to obey.

9. Ninthly: we have pronounced concerning those thieves that we cannot hastily[3] prove guilty; if such a one is afterwards proved guilty and liable, the lord or the kinsmen are to redeem him on the same terms as one redeems those men who are convicted at the ordeal.

10. Tenthly: all the councillors all together gave their pledge to the archbishop at Thunderfield, when Ælfheah Stybb and Brihtnoth, Odda's son, came to that assembly at the king's command, that every reeve should receive the pledge in his own shire, that they would all maintain that peace as King Athelstan and his councillors had enacted it, first at Grately and again at Exeter, and afterwards at Faversham, and a fourth time at Thunderfield in the presence of the archbishop and all the bishops and his councillors, whom the king himself nominated, who were present; that the

---

[1] i.e. where the owner lives, and where the trail has ended.
[2] i.e. meat, or cheese, or beans, or whatever one eats with bread according to the season.
[3] i.e. on the spot.

decrees which were established in this assembly should be observed, except those which had been repealed: namely Sunday marketing, and that one might with full and true witness buy outside a town.

11. Eleventhly: Athelstan commands his bishops and his ealdormen and all his reeves over all my dominion, that you observe the peace just as I and my councillors have enacted it. If any of you neglects and will not obey me, and will not take the pledge from those subject to him, and if he consents to secret compacts, and will not so concern himself with keeping order as I have commanded and as it stands in our writings, then is the reeve to be without his office and without my friendship, and to pay me 120 shillings, and half that each of my thegns [is to pay] who owns land and will not so maintain order as I have commanded.

12.1. Twelfthly: the king has now again spoken to his councillors at Whittlebury, and has sent word to the archbishop by Bishop Theodred that it seemed too cruel to him that a man should be killed so young, or for so small an offence, as he had learnt was being done everywhere. He said then, that it seemed to him and to those with whom he had discussed it, that no man younger than fifteen should be killed unless he tried to defend himself or fled, and would not surrender; in that case he was to be struck down, whether for a greater or smaller offence, whichever it then might be. But if he would surrender, he was to be put in prison, as it was agreed at Grately, and was to be redeemed on the same conditions.

12.2. Or, if he is not put in prison, none being available, they are to stand surety for him at the amount of his full wergild, that he evermore will cease from all wrong-doing. If the kindred will not redeem him nor stand surety for him, he is then to swear as the bishop directs him that he is willing to cease from all wrong-doing, and he is to be in servitude for the amount of his wergild. If he then steals after that, he is to be killed or hanged, as an older man would have been.

12.3. And the king said also, that no one was to be killed for a [theft of] property worth less than 12 pence, unless he tried to flee or defend himself; in that case one was not to hesitate, although the amount involved were less. If we maintain it thus, then I trust to God that our peace will be better than it was before.

38. Edmund's code concerning the blood-feud (II Edmund, 939–946)

This important document, which shows how widely current was the practice of private vengeance in the mid-tenth century, survives in the early twelfth-century manuscripts, C.C.C.C., MS. 383, and the *Textus Roffensis*, and in the Latin of *Quadripartitus*. It is edited by Liebermann, I, pp. 186–191; and with English translation by Robertson, pp. 8–11, Thorpe, I, pp. 246–251.

PROLOGUE. King Edmund informs all people, both high and low, who are in his dominion, that I have been inquiring with the advice of my councillors, both ecclesiastical and lay, first of all how I could most advance Christianity.

Prol. 1. First, then, it seemed to us all most necessary that we should keep most firmly our peace and concord among ourselves throughout my dominion.

Prol. 2. The illegal and manifold conflicts which take place among us distress me and all of us greatly. We decreed then:

1. If henceforth anyone slay a man, he is himself to bear the feud, unless he can

with the aid of his friends within twelve months pay compensation at the full wergild, whatever class he [the man slain] may belong to.

1.1. If, however, the kindred abandons him, and is not willing to pay compensation for him, it is then my will that all that kindred is to be exempt from the feud, except the actual slayer, if they give him neither food nor protection afterwards.

1.2. If, however, any one of his kinsmen harbours him afterwards, he is to be liable to forfeit all that he owns to the king, and to bear the feud as regards the kindred [of the man slain], because they previously abandoned him.

1.3. If, however, anyone of the other kindred takes vengeance on any man other than the actual slayer, he is to incur the hostility of the king and all his friends, and to forfeit all that he owns.

2. If anyone flees to a church or my residence, and he is attacked or molested there, those who do it are to be liable to the same penalty as is stated above.

3. And I do not wish that any fine for fighting or compensation to a lord for his man shall be remitted.

4. Further, I make it known that I will allow no resort to my court before he [the slayer] has undergone ecclesiastical penance and paid compensation to the kindred, [or][1] undertaken to pay it, and submitted to every legal obligation, as the bishop, in whose diocese it is, instructs him.

5. Further, I thank God and all of you who have well supported me, for the immunity from thefts which we now have; I now trust to you, that you will support this measure so much the better as the need is greater for all of us that it shall be observed.

6. Further, we have declared concerning *mundbryce*[2] and *hamsocn*,[3] that anyone who commits it after this is to forfeit all that he owns, and it is to be for the king to decide whether he may preserve his life.

7. Leading men[4] must settle feuds: First, according to the common law the slayer must give a pledge to his advocate, and the advocate to the kinsmen, that the slayer is willing to pay compensation to the kindred.

7.1. Then afterwards it is fitting that a pledge be given to the slayer's advocate, that the slayer may approach under safe-conduct and himself pledge to pay the wergild.

7.2. When he has pledged this, he is to find surety for the wergild.

7.3. When that has been done, the king's *mund*[5] is to be established; 21 days from that day *healsfang*[6] is to be paid;[7] 21 days from then the compensation to the lord for his man; 21 days from then the first instalment of the wergild.

---

[1] Following the interpretation of a rather corrupt passage, given by Liebermann, III, p. 127.

[2] This term means the violation of anyone's right of protection over others, but here it is clearly the king's right which is meant. This is the first occurrence of the term in the laws.

[3] Literally, 'attack on a homestead'. It includes forcible entry, and injury of persons inside a house. The term is a Scandinavian loan-word and this is its earliest occurrence.

[4] *witan* 'wise men' seems here to be used more widely than its usual meaning of 'councillors'.

[5] 'Protection.' This clause means that any act of violence after that will be regarded as a breach of the king's special protection.

[6] A part of the wergild which went to the nearest kin. See p. 363, n. 3.

[7] It is possible that the clause "twenty-one days from then the fine for fighting" has been omitted at this point. It occurs in a document of very similar content to much of this code usually cited as *Wergild*. Nevertheless, it remains a possibility that an intentional alteration is being made by one of these texts.

39. The Hundred Ordinance (939–about 961)

The only manuscript to preserve this code in Old English is C.C.C.C., MS. 383, where it is entered on p. 2, following two short texts, *Blaseras* 'Incendiaries' and *Forfang* '(Legal) Seizure'; the code survives also in two Latin versions, the *Quadripartitus* and the appendix to the *Consiliatio Cnuti*, and in both of these it follows on these same two texts. All versions must therefore come from a collection in which these three were already assembled. The last two chapters of the code, which obviously have no connexion with it, are probably added to it by the same compiler from some separate sources, although they have no new rubrics.

This code is sometimes cited as I Edgar, but it is not certain that it was issued by him. Personally, I do not find even the argument showing it to be at any rate later than the reign of Edmund to be fully convincing. It rests almost entirely on the assumed implications of one clause: chap. 2 declares that when a thief has been pursued and taken, he is to be given his deserts "as it was Edmund's decree previously". It is assumed that this implies that the present ordinance is being promulgated after Edmund's death; and, taken like this, it involves the further conclusion that the ordinance cannot be establishing the hundred as a new thing, for another of Edmund's codes (III Edmund 2) refers to the hundred as an organized body. Even so, the ordinance cannot definitely be assigned to Edgar, for the intervening kings Eadred and Eadwig might have issued it. After Edmund, Edgar is certainly the most likely king, since no reference is ever made to his two immediate predecessors as law-givers, not even by Edgar himself, who does refer to his father's legislation; yet this argument establishes merely a probability, not a certainty.

It is, perhaps, the most natural interpretation of the crucial clause to take it as a reference to a previous king, and it would be strengthened if one could be sure that the absence of a king's name at the beginning of the ordinance is a mere accident of transmission; for, if the code had gone out in Edmund's name, one would have expected him to refer to himself in the first person in this clause. This is, however, not quite conclusive, for another code (III Edmund), of which only a Latin text has survived, begins in the third person, but changes to first person singular in chap. 3, and to first person plural in chap. 4 and for the rest of the code, and, in fact, similar inconsistency is not uncommon. If, however, this ordinance was not originally drawn up in a king's name, it would be natural that the reigning king should be referred to by name. In that case all that the clause in question need mean is that Edmund had made a decree on the penalty for theft at some date before this ordinance. This decree has been lost, for there is no precise reference to the treatment of a thief in the extant laws of Edmund. Liebermann suggests that the Hundred Ordinance used III Edmund, *i.e.* the code which refers to the hundred as an established body; but, though there certainly seems a connexion between III Edmund 3 and chap. 6 of the ordinance, the borrowing could be the other way round, or both codes may have drawn from a common original.

I do not think, therefore, that we can absolutely exclude the possibility that the ordinance did in fact precede any of the references to the hundred elsewhere, though, since the clause referring to Edmund will certainly bear the interpretation usually put upon it, it cannot be proved that it did.

There were certainly courts which met every four weeks before the time of this ordinance, and the places at which the hundreds held their meetings often have names which prove them to have been meeting-places from very early times. There is evidence from early times, too, of the assessment of the country in round figures of a hundred or multiples of a hundred hides, but no early evidence for administrative areas called hundreds or assessed at a hundred hides. While several of the midland counties are made up of hundreds which have this assessment, there is no such neat correspondence in the southern districts. It seems probable, therefore, that the institution of hundreds in the Midlands either was on a different principle from that current in the South, or took place at a much later date, when any original correspondence between the name and the assessment had in the South been obliterated by later developments. It seems simplest to regard this ordinance as part of a movement to secure some uniformity of administrative arrangements when, after the re-conquest of the Danelaw, the kings of Wessex were ruling all England. It might then be part of the same reorganization of the Midlands that produced the modern shires. The name 'hundred' for the smallest juridical area may have been an innovation of this reorganization, applied for the sake of uniformity to divisions serving the same purpose in the South, even though these did not receive the same artificial assessment. This smallest juridical area seems originally to have been administered from a royal estate.[1]

The code is edited by Liebermann, I, pp. 192–195; and with English translation by Robertson, pp. 16–19, Thorpe, I, pp. 258–261.

This is the ordinance on how the hundred shall be held.

1. First, that they are to assemble every four weeks and each man is to do justice to another.

[1] On the relation between the hundreds and the royal manors, see H. M. Cam, *Eng. Hist. Rev.*, XLVII, pp. 353–376.

2.[1] If the need is urgent, one is to inform the man in charge of the hundred, and he then the men over the tithings; and all are to go forth, where God may guide them, that they may reach [the thief]. Justice is to be done on the thief as Edmund decreed previously.

2.1. And the value of the stolen property is to be given to him who owns the cattle, and the rest is to be divided into two, half for the hundred and half for the lord–except the men; and the lord is to succeed to the men.

3. And the man who neglects this and opposes the decision of the hundred–and afterwards that charge is proved against him–is to pay 30 pence to the hundred, and on a second occasion 60 pence, half to the hundred, half to the lord.

3.1. If he does it a third time, he is to pay half a pound; at the fourth time he is to forfeit all that he owns and be an outlaw, unless the king allows him [to remain in] the land.

4. And we decreed concerning strange cattle, that no one was to keep any, unless he have the witness of the man in charge of the hundred or of the man over the tithing; and he [the witness] is to be very trustworthy.

4.1. And unless he has one of them, he is not to be allowed to vouch to warranty.

5. Further, we decreed, if one hundred follows up a trail into another hundred, that is to be made known to the man in charge of that hundred, and he is then to go with them.

5.1. If he neglects it, he is to pay 30 shillings to the king.

6. If anyone evades the law and flees, he who supported him in that injury[2] is to pay the simple compensation.[3]

6.1. And if he is accused of abetting his escape, he is to clear himself according as it is established in the district.

7. In the hundred, as in any other court, it is our will that in every suit the common law be enjoined, and a day appointed when it shall be carried out.

7.1. And he who fails to appear on the appointed day–unless it is through his lord's summons–is to pay 30 shillings compensation, and on a fixed day perform what he should have done before.

8.[4] A cow's bell, a dog's collar [?], a blast-horn; each of these three is worth a shilling, and each is reckoned an informer.

9. The iron which belongs to the three-fold ordeal is to weigh three pounds.

40. King Edgar's code at Andover (?) (II and III Edgar, 959–963)

What is usually cited as II and III Edgar seems to have formed a single act of legislation, the first part being concerned with ecclesiastical affairs, the second with secular matters. It survives in full in Old English in three manuscripts, Brit. Mus. Harley, MS. 55, C.C.C.C., MS. 201, and Brit. Mus. Cott. Nero A. i, and there is a fourth version of most of the secular part in another part of Nero A. i,

---

[1] A rubric is added in the margin: "That men go without delay in pursuit of thieves" (accepting Miss Robertson's reading).

[2] This is an ambiguous passage: *se ðe hine to ðam hearme geheold.* Thorpe translates: "who held him to answer for the offence". If this means the person whose business it was to see that he came to answer the charge, it does not differ in essence from Liebermann, who compares III Edmund 3, a chapter dealing with the lord's responsibility for the deeds of men in his service. This code is only in Latin, in *Quadripartitus*, but the phrase *qui aliquem manutenebit et firmabit ad dampnum faciendum* may be translating something very like our text. The meaning seems to be "he who by maintaining him made it possible for him to commit that injury".   [3] *i.e.* the value of the stolen goods.

[4] This and the following chapter obviously have no connexion with the rest of the ordinance, and are presumably detached statements which the scribe wrongly joined on to this code.

which may once have contained at this place a complete text of the whole, for the preceding folios have been lost. This part of Nero A. i, as well as the Harley and Corpus manuscripts, has connexions with Worcester, and thus it is mainly to this place that we owe the preservation of this legislation. The absence of Edgar's codes from the great post-Conquest compilations from Rochester and St. Paul's may perhaps be ascribed to the incorporation of the greater part of them in the laws of later kings. Both II and III Edgar are contained in the Latin work, *Quadripartitus*. The code seems to have been used by IV Edgar (No. 41), and, if so, must be earlier than 963, the latest date for the latter code. The place of promulgation was Andover, if we can assume that IV Edgar 1.4 is referring to II and III Edgar.

The text is edited by Liebermann, I, pp. 194–201 (II Edgar), pp. 200–207 (III Edgar); and with English translation by Robertson, pp. 20–23 (II Edgar), pp. 24–29 (III Edgar), Thorpe, I, pp. 262–265 (II Edgar), pp. 266–271 (III Edgar).

A. *Ecclesiastical*

PROLOGUE. This is the ordinance which King Edgar determined with the advice of his councillors, for the praise of God and for his own royal dignity and for the benefit of all his people.

1. First, namely, that God's churches are to be entitled to their rights.

1.1. And all payment of tithe is to be made to the old minster,[1] to which the parish belongs, and it is to be rendered both from the thegn's demesne land and from the land of his tenants[2] according as it is brought under the plough.

2. If, however, there is any thegn who has on his bookland a church with which there is a graveyard, he is to pay the third part of his own tithes into his church.

2.1. If anyone has a church with which there is no graveyard, he is then to pay to his priest from the [remaining] nine parts[3] what he chooses.

2.2. And all church-scot[4] is to go to the old minster, from every free hearth.

[2.3. And plough-alms are to be rendered when it is 15 days after Easter.][5]

3. And the tithe of all young stock is to be rendered by Pentecost, and of all the fruits of the earth by the Equinox, and all church-scot is to be rendered by Martinmas, under pain of the full fine, which the law-book[6] prescribes.

3.1. And if then anyone will not render the tithes, as we have decreed, the king's reeve is to go there, and the bishop's reeve and the priest of the minster, and they are to seize without his consent the tenth part for the minster to which it belongs, and to assign to him the next tenth; and the [remaining] eight parts are to be divided into two, and the lord of the estate is to succeed to half and the bishop to half, whether he [the defaulter] be a king's man or a thegn's.

4. And every hearth-penny[7] is to be paid by St. Peter's day.[8]

4.1. And he who has not rendered it at that appointed day is to take it to Rome, and 30 pence in addition, and to bring back a document showing that he has handed

---

[1] The Harley and Corpus texts use the plural here, without altering the sense, for the Nero text is thinking of each case individually. 'Minster' is used to describe the old parish churches, often served by a small community of priests, to distinguish them from the later churches built within their parishes.

[2] *geneatland*.   [3] The Nero text has "from the ninth part".

[4] This due is first mentioned in Ine's laws, with heavy penalties for refusing it. It was paid by free men in proportion to their holding, and was commonly paid in grain.

[5] This chapter is missing from the Nero text and from *Quadripartitus*, so that it occurs only in those manuscripts connected with Archbishop Wulfstan. I suspect it of being an insertion made when he worked over Edgar's laws for his own drafts. A similar injunction occurs in several of the codes he compiled, closest in VIII Ethelred 12.

[6] The reference is probably to Ine 4. By 'law-book' the laws of Alfred with Ine's laws following them are usually meant.

[7] A penny paid from every house, by this time identical with Peter's pence.   [8] 1 August.

over that amount there. And when he then comes home, he is to pay 120 shillings to the king.

4.2. And if again he will not pay it, he is again to take it to Rome, with another such compensation; and when he comes home, he is to pay 200 shillings to the king.

4.3. On the third occasion, if he still will not do it, he is to forfeit all that he owns.

5. And every Sunday shall be observed as a festival from Saturday noon until dawn on Monday, under pain of the fine which the law-book prescribes;[1] and every other festival as it is enjoined.

5.1. And every ordained fast is to be observed with all diligence [and the fast every Friday, unless it is a festival.].[2]

[5.2. And payment for the soul is to be paid for every Christian man to the minster to which it belongs.

5.3. And every right of sanctuary is to be maintained as it best has been.]

B. *Secular*

1. This now is the secular ordinance which I wish to be observed.

1.1. Namely, then, that it is my will that every man, whether poor or rich, is to be entitled to the benefit of the common law, and just judgments are to be judged for him.

1.2. And there is to be such remission in the compensation as is justifiable before God and supportable in the State.

2. And no one is to apply to the king in any suit, unless he may not be entitled to right or cannot obtain justice at home.

2.1. If that law is too severe, he is then to apply to the king for alleviation.

2.2. In crimes that admit of compensation, no one is to forfeit more than his wergild.

3. And the judge who pronounces a wrong judgment on another is to pay to the king 120 shillings as compensation, unless he dare declare on oath that he knew not how to do it more justly—and he is always to forfeit his thegnly status,[3] unless he may redeem it from the king, according as he will allow him. And the bishop of the diocese is to exact the compensation on the king's behalf.

4. And he who wishes to accuse another falsely, so that he suffer loss either of property or of life,[4] if the other can then prove what one would charge him with to

---

[1] Ine 3 is probably what is meant.

[2] This, and the next two clauses, are not in the Nero text nor in *Quadripartitus*, and may represent additions under Archbishop Wulfstan's influence. See p. 395, n. 5. The word used here for right of sanctuary occurs elsewhere in the laws only in the codes issued under his influence. The addition to chap. 5.1 appears in I Cnut 16a, and with slight variation in V Ethelred 17 (= VI Ethelred 24); 5.2 is mainly in V Ethelred 12.1 (= VI Ethelred 21 = I Cnut 13.1); these are all codes in Wulfstan's style.

[3] Literally, 'his thegnship'. This word normally means 'the rank and privileges of a thegn'. I take it that a more general term than *folgað* 'office' was chosen in order to make the clause apply to holders of private jurisdictions and not to appointed officials alone.

[4] This is the reading of the complete version in the Nero text; one of the Worcester versions glosses *feore* 'life' as *vel freme*, while the two other Worcester texts read *freme* instead of *feore*. *Fremu* means 'benefit', though the post-Conquest interpretation 'reputation' may be possible. The laws of Cnut using this passage support *freme*, but as I believe them to have been drawn up by Wulfstan, it is natural that they should have the Worcester reading. It should be noted that in one MS. group of Wulfstan's "Sermon to the English" the phrase occurs: *ge æt freme ge æt fostre ge æt feo ge æt feore*. *Quadripartitus* reads "life or *commodo*" which seems to translate *freme* rather than *feo* 'property', and so agrees with none of the Old English texts; but for this occurrence, I should be inclined to dismiss *freme* as a Worcester alteration.

be false, he [the accuser] is to forfeit his tongue, unless he redeem himself with his wergild.

5. And the hundred court is to be attended as it was previously established.

5.1. And the borough court is to be held thrice a year and the shire court twice.

5.2. And the bishop of the diocese and the ealdorman are to be present, and there to expound both the ecclesiastical and the secular law.

6. And each man is to provide himself with a surety, and the surety is to produce and hold him to every legal duty.

6.1. And if anyone then commits a crime and escapes, the surety is to incur what he [the criminal] would have incurred.

6.2. And if it is theft,[1] and if he can lay hold of him within twelve months, he is to surrender him to justice and to be given back what he previously paid.

7. And he who is frequently accused and is unworthy of the people's trust, and who fails to attend these meetings[2] – then men are to be chosen from the meeting to ride to him; and he may still provide a surety, if he can.

7.1. If, however, he cannot, one is to secure him however one can, alive or dead, and seize all that he owns, and pay to the accuser simple compensation for his goods, and the lord of the estate is[3] to succeed to half, and the hundred to half.

7.2. If either kinsman or stranger refuses to go on that ride, he is to pay 120 shillings to the king.

7.3. And no matter what refuge the proved thief, or the man who is discovered in treason against his lord, may reach, they are never to save their lives.[4]

8. And one coinage is to be current throughout all the king's dominion, and no man is to refuse it;

8.1. and the system of measurement, as is observed in Winchester.[5]

8.2. And a wey of wool is to be sold at half a pound,[6] and no one is to sell it more dearly.[7]

[8.3. And if anyone sells it cheaper, whether openly or secretly, both he who sells and he who buys are to pay 60 shillings to the king.][8]

41. Edgar's code issued at "Wihtbordesstan" (IV Edgar, 962–963)

This extremely interesting code, which throws light both on how the statutes were circulated and on Edgar's relations with the Danelaw, survives in Old English only in two manuscripts from Worcester, namely Brit. Mus. Cott. Nero E. i and C.C.C.C., MS. 265, which contains much source material used by Archbishop Wulfstan. This manuscript also has a Latin version. The code seems to have been unknown to the compiler of *Quadripartitus*.

It is an interesting code also from a stylistic point of view, for it departs considerably from the

---

[1] The three Worcester texts read "a thief" instead of 'theft'.

[2] The Worcester MSS. add: "three times"; and this is also in Cnut's laws which use this chapter. It is missing from *Quadripartitus*, and is probably a Worcester addition.

[3] The Worcester versions, and Cnut's laws, add here the favourite Wulfstan word *elles* 'otherwise'.

[4] One Worcester MS. (C.C.C.C., 201) adds: "unless the king allows them to preserve their life".

[5] This clause is much extended in the Worcester MSS., whereas *Quadripartitus* supports the text as above. The extended text runs: "And one standard of measurement and one standard of weight is to be current, as is observed in London and in Winchester."   [6] The 120 pence of the Worcester MSS. is the same thing.

[7] Liebermann takes this to be an error for *undeoror* 'more cheaply', the reading of the Worcester MSS.; but it is supported by *Quadripartitus*, and may represent the original text. By the time the alterations were made in the Worcester MSS., the position may have changed.

[8] This chapter is lacking from the Nero main text, and from *Quadripartitus*. It is therefore in the Worcester texts only, and may be a later addition.

succinct, often obscure, style of earlier legal documents, and gives us an example of a homiletic style
before the period of the great homilists Ælfric and Wulfstan. It is a rather individualistic style, and it
is very tempting to associate it with one of the great churchmen who surrounded King Edgar.
Though the code applies expressly to the whole kingdom, it refers in one place to 'the archbishop'
in the singular; this must refer to the archbishop of Canterbury, at that date Dunstan, and as in
a later reign we find an archbishop himself drafting the laws, it is not impossible that here we have
Dunstan's work.

 The plague which occasioned the issue of these injunctions is presumably that entered in the
Anglo-Saxon Chronicle under 962'A', and a date soon after this is consonant with what we know of
the personages mentioned towards the end of the code, where arrangements are made for its
circulation in Northumbria, Mercia and East Anglia. Presumably a separate version would be
circulated throughout Wessex and Kent.

 The code is edited by Liebermann, I, pp. 206–215; and with English translation by Robertson,
pp. 28–39, Thorpe, I, pp. 270–279.

PROLOGUE. ✠ Here it is made known in this document how King Edgar inquired
what could be a remedy in the sudden pestilence which greatly oppressed and reduced
his people far and wide throughout his dominion.

1. First, namely, that it seemed to him and his councillors that a calamity of this
kind was merited by sins and by contempt of God's commands, and especially by the
withholding of the tribute which Christian men ought to render to God in their tithes.

1a. He has pondered and considered the ways of God by comparison with
worldly usage:

1.1. If any tenant[1] disregards the rent to his lord, and does not pay it to him at the
appointed day, it is to be expected, if the lord is merciful, that he may forgive the
neglect and take his rent without exacting a penalty.

1.2. If, however, he frequently through his bailiffs demands his rent, and the
other then proves obstinate and intends to withhold it with defiance, it is to be expected
that the lord's anger will so increase that he may grant him neither possessions nor life.

1.3. It is to be expected that our Lord will act in like manner on account of the
audacity with which the laymen have resisted the frequent admonitions which our
teachers have given about our Lord's tribute, namely our tithes and church-scot.

1.4. Therefore I and the archbishop command that you do not anger God, nor
merit either sudden death in this present life or indeed the future death in everlasting
hell by any withholding of God's dues; but both poor man and rich, who has any
produce, is to render his tithes to God with all gladness and with all willingness, as the
ordinance directs which my councillors decreed at Andover, and have now again
confirmed with pledging at *Wihtbordesstan*.

1.5. Moreover, I command my reeves, on pain of losing my friendship and all that
they own, that they punish each of those who does not perform this and who wishes
to break the pledge of my councillors by any remissness, just as the aforesaid ordinance
directs them; and there is to be no remission of that punishment.

1.5a. If he is so contemptible, that he either curtails God's [dues] to the perdition
of his soul, or with reluctance at heart attends to them less diligently than to what he
accounts his own; then[2] much more his own is what endures for him for ever into
eternity if he would pay it with willingness and full gladness.

1.6. Further, it is my will that these dues of God shall be alike everywhere in my
dominion.

---

[1] *geneatmann.*
[2] Miss Robertson supplies "he ought to realise that", to make the sequence of thought clearer.

1.7. And those servants of God who receive the dues which we pay to God, are to live a pure life, that through that purity they may intercede for us to God.

1.8. And I and my thegns shall compel our priests to that[1] which the pastors of our souls direct us, namely our bishops whom we should never disobey in any of the things which they prescribe for us for God's sake, that through that obedience by which we obey them for God's sake, we may merit the eternal life to which they draw us by teaching and by example of good works.

2. ✠ It is my will that secular rights be in force in every province, as good as they can best be devised, to the satisfaction of God, and for my full royal dignity and for the benefit and security of poor and rich;

2a. and that I have in every borough and in every shire the rights belonging to my royal dignity, as my father had; and my thegns are to have their dignity in my time as they had in my father's.

2.1. And it is my will that secular rights be in force among the Danes according to as good laws as they can best decide on.

2.1a. Among the English, however, that is to be in force which I and my councillors have added to the decrees of my ancestors, for the benefit of all the nation.

2.2. Nevertheless, this measure is to be common to all the nation, whether Englishmen, Danes or Britons, in every province of my dominion, to the end that poor man and rich may possess what they rightly acquire, and a thief may not know where to dispose of stolen goods, although he steal anything, and against their will they be so guarded against, that few of them shall escape.

3. Namely, then, it is my will that every man is to be under surety both within the boroughs and outside the boroughs.

3.1. And witness is to be appointed for each borough and for each hundred.

4. Thirty-six are to be chosen as witness for each borough;

5. twelve for small boroughs and for each hundred, unless you wish for more.

6. And every man is with their witness to buy and sell all goods that he buys and sells, in either a borough or a wapentake.[2]

6.1. And each of them, when he is first chosen as a witness, is to take an oath that never, for money or love or fear, will he deny any of the things for which he was a witness, and will never declare anything in his testimony but that alone which he saw and heard.

6.2. And two or three of the men thus sworn in are to be witness at every transaction.

7. And he who rides out to make any purchase is to inform his neighbours what he is going for; and when he comes home he is also to announce in whose witness he bought the goods.

8. If, however, when out on any journey, he unexpectedly makes a purchase, without having announced it when he set out, he is to announce it when he comes home; and if it is livestock, he is to bring it on to the common pasture with the witness of his village.

---

[1] The enforcement of clerical celibacy is probably meant here.
[2] The Latin version reads: *in civitate, rure aut hundrede.*

8.1. If he does not do so within five days, the villagers are to inform the man in charge of the hundred, and both themselves and their herdsmen are to be immune from penalty; and he who brought it there is to forfeit the cattle, because he would not announce it to his neighbours; and the lord of the estate is to succeed to half, and the hundred to half.

9. If, however, it remains on the common pasture more than five days unannounced, he is to forfeit the cattle, as we have said above, and each of the herdsmen is to be flogged; and there is to be no remission of that, no matter what refuge they reach; and he is nevertheless to declare in whose witness he bought that cattle.

10. If then he declares that he bought it with the witness of the men who are nominated as witnesses, either in a borough or in a hundred, and the man in charge of the hundred discovers that it is true, he is nevertheless to forfeit the cattle, because he would not announce it to his neighbours nor to the man in charge of his hundred; and he is to suffer no more loss in this matter.

11. If, however, he declares that he bought it with witness, and that is false, he is to be regarded as a thief and to lose his head and all that he owns. And the lord of the estate is to keep the stolen cattle or the value of the stolen cattle, until the owner discovers it and proves his right to the cattle with witness.

12. Further, it is my will that there should be in force among the Danes such good laws as they best decide on, and I have ever allowed them this and will allow it as long as my life lasts, because of your loyalty, which you have always shown me.

12.1. And I desire that this one decree concerning such an investigation shall be common to us all, for the protection and security of all the nation.

13. And it is my will that villagers and their herdsmen may hold the same investigation among my livestock and among that of my thegns, as they hold among their own.

13.1. If then my reeve or any other man, in high or low position, refuses it, and offers indignity either to the villagers or their herdsmen, the Danes are to decide by law what punishment they wish to apply in that matter.

14. Among the English, I and my councillors have decided what the punishment shall be, if any man offers resistance or goes to the length of slaying any one of those who are concerned in this investigation and who inform about concealed cattle, or any of those who give true witness and by their truthfulness save the innocent and lawfully bring destruction upon the guilty.

14.1. It is, then, my will that what you have decided on for the improvement of public order, with great wisdom and in a way very pleasing to me, shall ever be observed among you.

14.2. And this addition is to be common to all of us who inhabit these islands.

15. Now Earl Oslac[1] and all the host[2] who dwell in his aldormanry are to give their support that this may be enforced, for the praise of God and the benefit of the souls of all of us and the security of all people.

15.1. And many documents are to be written concerning this, and sent both to

[1] Of Northumbria.

[2] The word *here*, originally meaning a raiding army, came to be used of the inhabitants of the Danish settlements, without any military significance.

Ealdorman Ælfhere[1] and Ealdorman Æthelwine,[2] and they are to send them in all directions, that this measure may be known to both the poor and the rich.

16. I will be a very gracious lord to you as long as my life lasts, and I am very well pleased with you all, because you are so zealous about the maintenance of the peace.

42. King Ethelred's treaty with the viking army (II Ethelred, 991)

It is interesting to compare this treaty with Alfred's treaty with Guthrum (No. 34). Some of the problems faced by the kings are identical, but it is noteworthy how this later treaty is concerned with the safety of English ships in foreign ports, which indicates the expansion of English trade between these two reigns. This peace was probably made after the events described in the Chronicle, 991; this could be stated with certainty if it could be established beyond doubt that Archbishop Sigeric died in 994, and not 995, as stated in some inferior sources; for if the earlier date is accepted, he died before the conclusion of the viking invasion of 994 and could not have negotiated its treaty. See pp. 214, n. 2, 252f. The treaty is known only from the post-Conquest manuscript, C.C.C.C., MS. 383, and, in Latin, from *Quadripartitus*. The rubrics, being in Lambard only, have no manuscript authority. It is edited by Liebermann, I, pp. 220–225; and with English translation by Robertson, pp. 56–61, Thorpe, I, pp. 284–289.

PROLOGUE. These are the peace terms and conditions which King Ethelred and all his councillors have made with the army with which were Olaf and Jostein and Guthmund, Steita's son.

1. Firstly, that a general[3] peace be established between King Ethelred with all his people and all the army to which the king gave the tribute, according to the terms which Archbishop Sigeric,[4] Ealdorman Æthelweard[5] and Ealdorman Ælfric[6] made, when they obtained permission from the king to purchase peace for the areas which they had rule over, under the king.

1.1. And that, if any fleet harry in England, we are to have the help of them all; and we must supply them with food as long as they are with us.

1.2. And any region which gives asylum to any of those who are harrying England is to be treated as an enemy by us and the whole army.

2. And every trading ship which enters an estuary is to have peace, even if it belongs to a region outside this truce, provided it is not driven ashore.[7]

2.1. And even if it is driven ashore, and takes refuge in any borough included in the truce, and the men escape into the borough, the men and what they bring with them are to have peace.

3. And each of the men to whom the truce applies is to have peace both on land and on water, both within the estuary and outside.

3.1. If a subject of King Ethelred to whom this truce applies comes into a district where it does not apply, and the army comes there, his ship and all his goods are to enjoy peace.

3.2. If he has drawn his ship ashore or built a shed or pitched a tent, he and all his goods are to enjoy peace there.

[1] Of Mercia.   [2] Of East Anglia.

[3] Literally, 'world-peace', a unique compound. 'World' as a first element has various meanings: it may mean secular, or it may be little more than an intensitive, referring to size, and here contrasting this truce with those of limited application to single districts. So Miss Robertson.

[4] Of Canterbury.   [5] Of the Western Provinces.   [6] Of Hampshire.

[7] Wrecks were considered the property of the king or of privileged landowners, on whose land they were wrecked.

3.3. If he brings his goods into a house among the goods of men outside the truce, he is to forfeit his goods, but himself to have peace and his life, if he announces himself.

3.4. If the man to whom the truce applies flees or fights, and will not announce himself, he is to lie uncompensated for, if he is killed.

4. If a man is robbed of his goods, and he knows by which ship, the steersman is to give back the goods, or to go with four others, being himself the fifth, and deny [the charge, swearing] that he took it lawfully, as it was agreed upon above.

5. If an Englishman slays a Dane, a freeman a freeman, he is to pay for him with 25 pounds, or the actual slayer is to be surrendered; and the Dane is to do the same for an Englishman, if he slays one.

5.1. If an Englishman slays a Danish slave, he is to pay for him with one pound, and the Dane the same for an English slave, if he slays one.

5.2. If eight men are slain, then it is a breach of the truce, within a borough or outside. For less then eight men the full wergild is to be paid as compensation.

6. If the breach of the truce is committed within a borough, the citizens are to go themselves and take the slayers, alive or dead—[or] their nearest kinsmen[1]—head for head. If they will not, the ealdorman is to go there; if he will not, the king is to go; if he will not, that aldormanry is to be excluded from the truce.

6.1. Concerning all the slaughter and all the harrying and all the injuries which were committed before the truce was established, all of them are to be dismissed, and no one is to avenge it or ask for compensation.

6.2. And neither they nor we are to receive the other party's slave, or thief, or person concerned in a feud.

7. And if anyone charges a man of our country that he stole cattle or slew a man, and the charge is brought by one viking[2] and one man of this country, he is then to be entitled to no denial.[3]

7.1. And if their men slay eight of us, they are then to be outlawed both by them and by us, and are to be entitled to no compensation.

7.2. Twenty-two thousand pounds in gold and silver were paid from England to the army for this truce.[4]

43. King Ethelred's code issued at Wantage (III Ethelred, 978–1008)

This code is mainly concerned with an area of the Danelaw and gives important information on its organization. It is probable that it was issued about the same time as a code issued at Woodstock (I Ethelred), which is expressly said to be "according to the law of the English". The date of both codes is uncertain; they are almost certainly before Ethelred's flight in 1013, and the absence of any trace of the influence of Wulfstan, archbishop of York, suggests that they were earlier than 1008, from which time he drafted several codes. There was an assembly at Wantage in 997 (Kemble,

---

[1] In agreement with earlier editors, I differ from Liebermann and Robertson here, who take 'their nearest kinsmen' in apposition to 'citizens' and as referring to the kinsmen of the slain men. I take it that a situation is envisaged in which fewer slayers can be seized than the number of dead men. Though Edmund's law forbade vengeance except on the actual doer of the deed, this arrangement may well be a sop to the Danes, to prevent a fresh outbreak of hostilities. The chapter seems to concern itself only with the position when the English are the slayers.

[2] Literally, 'ship-man', the word for ship being an Old Norse one.

[3] This means that he would have to go to the ordeal to clear himself.

[4] The chapters that follow immediately have no original connexion with this truce, being concerned with details of procedure when vouching to warranty.

No. 698), but it naturally does not follow that this was the only time the witan were assembled at this royal residence.

This code survives in Old English only in the *Textus Roffensis*, and in Latin in *Quadripartitus*. It is edited by Liebermann, I, pp. 228–233; and with English translation by Robertson, pp. 64–71, Thorpe, I, pp. 292–299.

PROLOGUE. These are the laws which King Ethelred and his councillors have decreed at Wantage, for the improvement of public security.

1. Namely, in order that his peace may remain as firm as it best was in the days of his ancestors, [breach of] that peace which he gives with his own hand[1] is not to be atoned for by compensation.

1.1. And the peace which the ealdorman and the king's reeve give in the meeting of the Five Boroughs,[2] that is to be atoned for with twelve hundred.[3]

1.2. And the peace which is given in the meeting of one borough is to be atoned for with six hundreds; and that which is given in a wapentake, is to be atoned for with a hundred, if it is broken;[4] and that which is given in an alehouse, is to be atoned for, if a man is killed, with six half marks, and if no one is killed, with twelve ores.[5]

2. And no man is to pervert what is declared with witness, no more when the persons[6] are still alive than when they are dead.

2.1. And each man is to come forward as witness [only] of what he dares to swear to on the relics which are placed in his hand.

3. And the purchase of land,[7] and the lord's gift which he has the right to give, and the purchase of legal rights,[8] and agreements[9] and witness, are to be valid, so that no one may pervert them.

3.1. And that a meeting is to be held in each wapentake, and the twelve leading thegns,[10] and with them the reeve, are to come forward and swear on the relics which are put into their hands that they will accuse no innocent man nor conceal any guilty one.

3.2. And they are then to seize the men who have frequently been accused, against whom the reeve is taking proceedings,[11] and each of them is to pay six half marks as pledge, half to the lord of the estate and half to the wapentake.

3.3. And each of them shall buy for himself [the benefit of the] law with twelve ores, half to the lord of the estate, half to the wapentake.

---

[1] *i.e.* declared by him in person. Hence the expression "the king's hand-peace".

[2] Lincoln, Stamford, Nottingham, Derby and Leicester.

[3] The reckoning is in long hundreds (120) of silver ores. By the time of Domesday Book, and perhaps already, 16 pence were reckoned to the ore, so that a hundred of silver is equivalent to £8, a very high figure when the purchasing power of money is remembered. The highest fine in English England was £5.

[4] *i.e.* whether anyone is killed or not.   [5] A mark consists of eight ores.

[6] The Old English phrase is obscure: "with regard to the living no more than to the dead". Liebermann at first took it to apply to the witnesses, later to the parties.

[7] The term used is Scandinavian. I take the meaning to be that sale with the proper legal formalities is not to be revoked later, by the kindred. In Scandinavian laws there is usually a clause allowing kinsmen a right of pre-emption.

[8] The sum paid by an outlaw to obtain readmission to legal status. The term used is Scandinavian in origin.

[9] It is uncertain whether one should take this Scandinavian word, *witword*, as 'agreement, contract', as in Middle English, or as 'demonstrable title to possession', as in later Scandinavian law.

[10] This institution is generally considered to be one of the origins of the jury system.

[11] The Old English text is corrupt here; this rendering (which is Miss Robertson's) is based on *Quadripartitus*

3.4. And each man frequently accused is to go to the three-fold ordeal, or to pay four-fold.

4. If, however, the lord is willing to clear him, along with two good thegns, that he never paid compensation for theft since the assembly was held at *Bromdun*,[1] nor was accused, he is to go to the simple ordeal or to pay three-fold.

4.1. If then he is convicted, he is to be struck so that his neck is broken; and if he fails to appear at the ordeal, he is to pay the simple value of the stolen goods to the owner and 20 ores to the lord of the estate, and go to the ordeal afterwards.

4.2. And if the owner will not attend the ordeal, he is to pay 20 ores, and his suit shall be lost; and yet he [the accused] is to go to the ordeal for the lord of the estate, or to pay two-fold.

5. And if anyone has cattle without surety, and the lords of the estate attach it, he is to give up the cattle and pay 20 ores.

6. And every accuser is to have the choice whether he wishes the ordeal to be of water or of iron.

6.1. And every vouching to warranty and every ordeal is to take place in a royal borough.

6.2. And if he flees from the ordeal, the surety is to pay for him with his wergild.

7. And if anyone wishes to clear a thief, he is to lay down a hundred [of silver] as a pledge, half for the lord of the estate and half for the king's reeve in the town, and to go to the three-fold ordeal.

7.1. And if he is proved right[2] at the ordeal, he is to take up his kinsman [from unconsecrated ground]; if he, however, is proved wrong, [the slain thief] is to lie where he lay before, and he himself is to pay a hundred [of silver].

8. And every moneyer who is accused of coining false money, since it was forbidden, is to go to the three-fold ordeal; if he is proved guilty, he is to be slain.

8.1. And no one except the king is to have a moneyer.

8.2. And every moneyer who is accused is to buy for himself [the benefit of] law with 12 ores.

9. And no one is to slaughter an ox, unless he has the witness of two trusty men; and he is to keep the hide and the head for three days, and those of a sheep likewise.

9.1. And if he gives away the hide before that, he is to pay 20 ores.

10. And every fugitive, who is a fugitive in one district, is to be so in every district.

11. And no one is to have any jurisdiction over a king's thegn except the king himself.

12. And in a king's suit one is to put down six half-marks as a pledge, in an earl's and bishop's 12 ores as a pledge, and at any thegn's six ores as a pledge.

13. And if anyone is charged with feeding a man who has broken our lord's

---

[1] Too common a name for identification. Brandon in Norfolk, Suffolk, Warwickshire, Durham, all go back on this form, as also does Brendon, Devon, Bromden, Shropshire, Brundon, Suffolk.

[2] Literally, "if he be clean". Liebermann seems to take the pronoun to refer to the thief, but the text 'Ordeal' uses the term 'clean' to describe that condition of the hand three days after the ordeal which ensured victory for the man who had undergone it.

peace, he is to clear himself with three twelves; and the reeve is to nominate the compurgators.

13.1. And if he is discovered with him, they are both liable to the same penalty.

13.2. And a sentence where the thegns are unanimous is to be valid; if they disagree, what eight of them say is to be valid; and those who are outvoted there, are each to pay six half-marks.

13.3. And where a thegn has a choice of two things, amicable settlement or legal process,[1] and he then chooses settlement, that is to be as binding as a legal sentence.

13.4. And he who in spite of it admits exculpation, or he who offers it, is to pay six half-marks.

14. And if anyone dwells undisturbed by charges and claims on his estates during his lifetime, no one is to bring an action against his heirs after his death.

15. And he who robs a man in daylight, and the latter announces it in three villages, is to be entitled to no asylum.

16. And those moneyers who work in the wood or elsewhere are to forfeit their lives, unless the king wishes to spare them.

44. King Ethelred's code of 1008 (V Ethelred)

This is the first datable code written in the highly individual style of Archbishop Wulfstan. It survives in C.C.C.C., MS. 201, which contains many of his works, and twice in another manuscript with Worcester connexions, Brit. Mus. Cott. Nero A. i. It does not occur in the work of any of the post-Conquest compilers or translators.

The date is given by the rubric of one version. Because a code known as VI Ethelred is very similar, and has a Latin paraphrase which says it was promulgated at Enham, it is usually assumed that V Ethelred is a slightly different version of statutes issued at Enham in 1008. Yet the differences between V and VI Ethelred are considerable, and relate to matters of fact, not merely of expression. I consider that the best solution of this problem is that given by Dr. Sisam,[2] who suggests that after the Council of Enham had decided on the statutes to be issued, it was left to Archbishop Wulfstan to produce a version for the northern part of the country with some modifications, and that VI Ethelred represents this modified version. Dr. Sisam would see in the Latin paraphrase the document Wulfstan drew up for circulation among the higher ecclesiastics. This version expressly states Wulfstan's part in the drafting of it, but his style is obvious in the vernacular versions also.

I have taken as the basis of my text the first of the two versions in Nero A. i. This has the Latin rubric: "In the name of the Lord, in the year of our Lord's incarnation 1008." The second version in this manuscript has merely, in Old English: "Concerning the ordinance of the English councillors." The Corpus manuscript has the Latin invocation, but no reference to the date.

The code is edited by Liebermann, I, pp. 236–247; and with English translation by Robertson, pp. 78–91, Thorpe, I, pp. 304–313.

PROLOGUE. This is the ordinance which the king of the English and both ecclesiastical and lay councillors have approved and decreed.

1. First, namely, that we all shall love and honour one God and zealously hold one Christian faith and entirely cast off every heathen practice;[3] and we all have confirmed both with word and with pledge that we will hold one Christian faith under the rule of one king.

1.1. And it is the decree of our lord and his councillors that just practices be

---

[1] Literally, 'love or law'.

[2] *Studies in the History of Old English Literature* (Oxford, 1953), pp. 278–287.

[3] VI Ethelred, after speaking of heathenism, has the following chapter (7): "And if wizards or sorcerers, magicians or whores, murderers or perjurers are caught anywhere in the land, they are to be zealously driven out of this country, and this nation is to be purified, or they are to be completely destroyed in this country, unless they desist and atone very deeply."

established and all illegal practices abolished, and that every man is to be permitted the benefit of law;

1.2. and that peace and friendship are to be rightly maintained in both religious and secular concerns within this country.

2. And it is the decree of our lord and his councillors that no Christian and uncondemned[1] men are to be sold out of the country, and especially not among the heathen people, but care is earnestly to be taken that those souls be not destroyed which God bought with his own life.

3. And it is the decree of our lord and his councillors that Christian men are not to be condemned to death for all too small offences.

3.1. But otherwise life-sparing[2] punishments are to be devised for the benefit of the people, and God's handiwork and his own purchase which he paid for so dearly is not to be destroyed for small offences.

4. And it is the decree of our lord and his councillors that men of every order are each to submit willingly to that duty which befits them both in religious and secular concerns.

4.1. And especially God's servants–bishops and abbots, monks and nuns, priests and women devoted to God–are to submit to their duty and to live according to their rule and to intercede zealously for all Christian people.

5. And it is the decree of our lord and his councillors that every monk who is out of his monastery and not heeding his rule, is to do what behoves him: return readily into the monastery with all humility, and cease from evil-doing and atone very zealously for what he has done amiss; let him consider the word and pledge which he gave to God.

6. And that monk who has no monastery is to come to the bishop of the diocese, and pledge himself to God and man that from that time on he will at least observe three things, namely his chastity, and monastic garb, and the service of his Lord, as well as ever he can.

6.1. And if he keeps that, he is then entitled to the greater respect, no matter where he dwell.

7. And canons, where there is property such that they can have a refectory and dormitory, are to hold their minster with right observance and with chastity, as their rule directs; otherwise it is right that he who will not do that shall forfeit the property.

8. And we pray and instruct all priests to protect themselves from God's anger.

9. They know full well that they may not rightly have sexual intercourse with a woman.

9.1. And whoever will abstain from this and preserve chastity, may he have God's mercy and in addition as a secular dignity, that he shall be entitled to a thegn's wergild and a thegn's rights, in life as well as in the grave.

---

[1] *unforworhte*, taken by Liebermann as meaning "not having incurred the death-penalty", by Miss Robertson as "innocent of crime".

[2] The word *friðlic* seems unique in Old English, though *friðligr*, 'peaceable', occurs in Old Norse. I imagine the meaning here refers to any penalties which do not put the offender outside the *frið*, *i.e.* do not cause him to be executed, or, if he escapes, make him an outlaw, to be killed with impunity.

9.2. And he who will not do what belongs to his order, may his dignity be diminished both in religious and secular concerns.

10. And also every Christian man is zealously to avoid illegal intercourse, and duly keep the laws of the Church.

10.1. And every church is to be under the protection of God and of the king and of all Christian people.

10.2. And no man henceforth is to bring a church under subjection, nor illegally to traffic with a church,[1] nor to expel a minister of the church without the bishop's consent.

11. And God's dues are to be readily paid every year.

11.1. Namely, plough-alms 15 days after Easter, and the tithe of young animals by Pentecost, and of the fruits of the earth by All Saints' day, and 'Rome-money'[2] by St. Peter's day and light-dues three times a year.

12. And it is best that payment for the soul be always paid at the open grave.

12.1. And if any body is buried elsewhere, outside the proper parish, the payment for the soul is nevertheless to be paid to the minster to which it belongs.

12.2. And all God's dues are to be furthered zealously, as is needful.

12.3. And festivals and fasts are to be properly observed.

13. The Sunday festival is to be diligently observed, as befits it.

13.1. And one is readily to abstain from markets and public meetings on the holy day.

14. And all the festivals of St. Mary are to be diligently observed, first with a fast and afterwards with a festival.

14.1. And at the festival of every Apostle there is to be fasting and festivity, except that we enjoin no fast for the festival of St. Philip and St. James, because of the Easter festival.[3]

15. Otherwise other festivals and fasts are to be kept diligently just as those kept them who kept them best.

16. And the councillors have decreed that St. Edward's[4] festival is to be celebrated over all England on 18 March.

17. And there is to be a fast every Friday, except when it is a feast-day.

18. And ordeals and oaths are forbidden on feast-days and the legal Ember days, and from the Advent of the Lord until the octave of Epiphany, and from Septuagesima until 15 days after Easter.

19. And at these holy seasons, as it is right, there is to be peace and unity among all Christian men, and every suit is to be laid aside.

20. And if anyone owes another a debt or compensation concerning secular matters, he is to pay it readily before or after [these seasons].

---

[1] Not necessarily simony, but the bartering of churches among laymen such as that Ælfric complains of. See *Lives of Saints*, I, p. 430, where he says that men deal with churches as with mills.

[2] *i.e.* Peter's Pence.

[3] It is only rarely that the feast of St. Philip and St. James (1 May) falls in the octave of Easter. It did not in 1008, when Easter was 28 March, nor in 1009, when it was 17 April. But in this latter year it came within the fifteen days after Easter mentioned in chap. 18 below. It seems to me likely, therefore, that this code was issued when Easter 1008 was already over, with an eye to conditions the following Easter.

[4] King Ethelred's brother, murdered in 978. See No. 1, p. 210; No. 236, pp. 841 f.

21. And every widow who conducts herself rightly is to be under the protection of God and the king.

21.1. And each [widow] is to remain unmarried for twelve months; she is then to choose what she herself will.

22. And every Christian man is to do what is needful for him; heed zealously his Christian duties, and form the habit of frequent confession, and freely confess his sins and willingly atone for them as he is directed.

22.1. And everyone is to prepare himself often and frequently for going to communion;

22.2. and to order words and deeds rightly, and keep carefully oath and pledge.

23. And every injustice is to be zealously cast out from this country, as far as it can be done.

24. And deceitful deeds and hateful abuses are to be strictly shunned, namely, false weights and wrong measures and lying witnesses and shameful frauds,

25. and horrible perjuries and devilish deeds of murder and manslaughter, of stealing and spoliation, of avarice and greed, of over-eating and over-drinking, of deceits and various breaches of law, of injuries to the clergy and of breaches of the marriage law, and of evil deeds of many kinds.

26. But God's law henceforth is to be eagerly loved by word and deed; then God will at once become gracious to this nation.

26.1. And people are to be zealous about the improvement of the peace, and about the improvement of the coinage everywhere in the country, and about the repair of boroughs[1] in every province and also about military service, according to what is decreed, whenever it is necessary,

27. and about the supplying of ships, as zealously as possible, so that each may be equipped immediately after Easter every year.[2]

28. And if anyone deserts from an army which the king himself is with, it is to be at the peril of his life and all his property.[3]

28.1. And he who otherwise deserts from the army is to forfeit 120 shillings.

29. And if any excommunicated man—unless it be a suppliant for protection—remain anywhere in the king's neighbourhood before he has submitted readily to ecclesiastical penance, it is to be at the peril of his life and all his possessions.

30. And if anyone plots against the king's life, he is to forfeit his life; and if he wishes to clear himself, he is to do it by [an oath of the value of] the king's wergild or by the three-fold ordeal in [the area under] English law.[4]

31. And if anyone commit ambush[5] or open resistance anywhere against the law

---

[1] The other two versions, as well as VI Ethelred, add: "and about the repair of bridges".

[2] VI Ethelred 34 adds: "And if anyone damages a warship of the people, he is diligently to make reparation and pay the king for (breach of his) protection; and if one damages it so that it becomes useless, he is to pay its full value and the (fine for) breach of his protection to the king."

[3] The other MSS. have 'wergild' instead of 'all his property'.

[4] VI Ethelred 37 adds to a very similar statute: "and in the law of the Danes by what their law is". The Corpus MS. of the present code replaces the explicit statements with the general instruction: "unless he clear himself by the heaviest (oath) which the councillors decree".

[5] *forsteal*, originally meaning 'obstruction', became specialized in meaning to 'lying in wait'.

of Christ or the king, he is to pay either wergild or fine or *lahslit*,[1] ever in proportion to the deed.

31.1. And if he illegally offers resistance with assault, and so brings it about that he is killed, no wergild is to be paid to any of his friends.

32. And ever henceforth the abuses are to cease which hitherto have been too common far and wide.[2]

33. And every abuse is to be zealously suppressed.

33.1. For [only] as a result of suppressing wrong and loving righteousness will there be improvement at all in the country in religious and secular concerns.

34. We must all love and honour one God and entirely cast out every heathen practice.

35. And let us loyally support one royal lord, and all together defend our lives and our land, as well as ever we can, and pray Almighty God from our inmost heart for his help.[3]

45. The edict when the 'Great Army' came to England (VII Ethelred, probably 1009)

The Old English version is preserved only in the C.C.C.C., MS. 201. The Latin version in *Quadripartitus* has considerable differences in arrangement and wording, but was clearly issued on the same occasion and has almost the same content, except that it ends with some general prohibitions against the selling of men abroad and theft, similar to some in previous codes. The discrepancies between the versions are capable of more than one explanation: the Old English may represent Wulfstan's first draft, kept at Worcester, or it may be a version modified by him later, with an eye to using it again; or possibly the edict went out in varying forms, taking into consideration the circumstances of those to whom it was addressed. The Latin version is more specific on the duties of ecclesiastics. I translate the Old English version, but refer to the significant variations of the Latin text in the footnotes. Two Wulfstan homilies (Napier, Nos. xxxv and xxxvi) use this code.

In the year in which it was issued, Michaelmas (29 September) fell between Thursday and Sunday. Liebermann points out that this was so in 992–995, 998–1000, 1004–1006, 1009–1011 and 1015. It seems most likely that the edict refers to the army that came in August 1009. (See Anglo-Saxon Chronicle.) The text is edited by Liebermann, I, pp. 260–262; with English translation by Robertson, pp. 108–117. Thorpe, I, pp. 336–339, has the Latin version only.

This was decreed when the great army came to the country.[4]

PROLOGUE. All of us have need eagerly to labour that we may obtain God's mercy and his compassion and that we may through his help withstand our enemies.

---

[1] *lahslit* 'breach of the law' is the term given in the Danelaw to a fine varying with the rank of the offender, 10 half-marks for the king's thegn, 6 half-marks for other landowners, 12 ores for the *ceorl*.

[2] The Corpus MS. words this clause differently, and adds some instances of the abuses in question. It runs:

32. And ever henceforth are the abuses to cease which our lord himself has again and again ordered to be suppressed.

32.1. First, namely, concerning the attaching of property, which deceiving rogues have readily practised in the West, who have harassed and wrongfully afflicted many a man.

32.2. And the second is, that witnesses were not allowed to be valid, although they were fully reliable and declared [only] what they were willing to swear to.

32.3. The third concerns silence, that a man would remain silent, and afterwards claim from a successor what had never been claimed from his predecessor.

32.4. And in the North the abuse was current, that homicide might be laid to the charge of a guiltless person, and that should be held valid if it were announced thus at once on the same day.

32.5. But our lord has suppressed that abuse. May he do more.

VI Ethelred omits this whole chapter, having instead (39): "And if anyone defiles a nun or ravishes a widow, he is to atone for it deeply both to the Church and the State."

[3] The other two MSS. end with a Latin benediction: "The Lord's name be blessed."

[4] This rubric is only in the Old English version; the Latin says instead that this was decreed by King Ethelred and his councillors at Bath.

1. Now it is our will that all the nation [shall fast] as a general penance for three days on bread and herbs and water, namely on the Monday, Tuesday and Wednesday before Michaelmas.

2. And every man is to come barefoot to church, without gold and ornaments, and to go to confession.

2.1. And all are to go out with the relics[1] and to call on Christ eagerly from their inmost hearts.

2.2. And one penny or the value of one penny is to be paid from each hide.

2.3. And it is to be brought to church and then divided into three with the witness of the confessor and the reeve of the village.[2]

3. And if anyone does not perform this, then he is to compensate for it as it is legally ordained: the freeman[3] with 30 pence, the slave with a flogging, the thegn with 30 shillings.[4]

4. And wherever this money has to be paid, every penny is to be distributed for God's sake.

4.1. And the food also, which each would have consumed if the fast had not been ordained, is all to be willingly distributed for God's sake after the fast to needy men and bedridden persons and men so afflicted that they are unable to fast thus.

5. And each member of a household is to pay a penny as alms, or his lord is to pay it for him, if he has not got it himself; and men of rank[5] shall pay a tithe.

5.1. And slaves during those three days are to be freed from work, in order to go to church, and in order that they may the more willingly observe the fast.[6]

6. And in every minster all the community are to sing their psalter together during those three days.

6.1. And every priest is to say Mass for our lord and for all his people.

6.2. And in addition one Mass is to be said every day in each minster with special reference to the need which is now urgent for us,[7] until things become better.

6.3. And at each service the whole community, prostrate before God's altar, is to sing the psalm: "Why, O Lord, are they multiplied"[8] and the prayers and collects.[9]

7. And all in common, ecclesiastics and laymen, are to turn eagerly to God and to deserve his mercy.

8. And every year henceforth God's dues are to be paid at any rate correctly, to

---

[1] Presumably what is meant by the Latin (2.2), which says that priest and people are to go barefoot in procession each of the three days. It then adds: "And in addition every priest is to sing 30 masses and every deacon and cleric 30 psalms."

[2] This clause is not in the Latin version, but is replaced with a more general injunction: "And every priest and reeve of a village and the men of the tithing are to be witnesses that this almsgiving and fasting is carried out, as they would be able to swear to it on the relics" (2.5).

[3] The term used is *bunda*, a Scandinavian term commonly used of the peasant proprietor. The Latin version has 'poor freeman' (2.4). As it is clear from the context, it is meant to include all freemen below the rank of thegn.   [4] The Latin version has 120 shillings, to be paid by a king's thegn.

[5] *heafodmen*. The Latin version (1.3) understands it to mean thegns. It means men who maintain households of followers.

[6] The Latin version allows the three days for a different motive: "that they may work for themselves what they wish" (2.3).

[7] The Latin version is specific: the Mass is entitled "Against the heathen" (3).   [8] Psalm iii.

[9] The Latin version says "the collect against the heathen", and then adds a clause missing in the Old English: "And in every foundation and convent of monks every priest severally is to celebrate 30 Masses for the king and all the people, and every monk 30 psalters" (3.1).

the end that Almighty God may have mercy on us and grant that we may overcome our enemies.

God help us. Amen.[1]

46. Extracts from King Ethelred's 1014 code (VIII Ethelred)

One of the chief features of interest of this code is that it shows how far the Christian conception of kingship had developed. It also shows the respect paid to certain former kings as legislators. It is another of the codes in Archbishop Wulfstan's style, and, like the previous code, it survives in full only in the C.C.C.C., MS. 201, connected with him. The first five chapters survive in another Wulfstan manuscript, Brit. Mus. Cott. Nero A. i.

The date is given by the Latin rubric in the Corpus MS. As the code begins "this is one of the ordinances", and as it is entirely concerned with Church matters, it seems probable that it was once accompanied by a companion ordinance on secular concerns, now lost.

The code is edited by Liebermann, I, pp. 263–268; and with English translation by Robertson, pp. 116–129, Thorpe, I, pp. 343–351.

In the year 1014 from the incarnation of our Lord Jesus Christ.

PROLOGUE. This is one of the ordinances which the king of the English composed with the advice of his councillors.

1. First, namely, that it is his will that all God's churches are to be entitled to full right of sanctuary.

1.1. And if ever henceforth any man so violates the sanctuary of God's Church that he commits homicide within the church walls, that then is beyond compensation, and each of those who are friends of God are to be at enmity with him, unless it happen that he escapes from there and reaches so important a sanctuary that the king grants him his life on that account, in return for full compensation both to God and to men.

2. And namely, first that he is to give his own wergild to Christ and the king, and with it buy for himself the right to make compensation.

2.1. For a Christian king is Christ's deputy in a Christian people, and he must avenge very zealously offences against Christ.

3. And if then it comes to compensation, and the king allows it, the violation of sanctuary is to be compensated for to the church at the amount of the full [fine for] breach of the king's protection, and the purification of the church is to be secured as befits it,[2] and he is indeed to supplicate earnestly to God.

4. And if the sanctuary is violated without anyone being slain, compensation is eagerly to be paid in proportion to the deed, whether it arises from fighting, or from robbery, or from unlawful sexual intercourse, or whatever it arises from.

4.1. And always first the church is to be compensated for the violation of sanctuary, in proportion to the deed and in proportion to the status of that church.

5. All churches are not entitled to the same status in a temporal sense, although they have the same consecration in regard to religion.

[1] Besides the differences already mentioned, the Latin text is supplied with a general introduction, that men shall love God and obey the king as their ancestors did, and defend with him the kingdom; with some details on church dues, mainly from II Edgar 2.2; with a prohibition against selling men out of the country, with an anathema on those who do; with some clauses on theft, including one that is new (6.3): "And if any reeve has done it, he is to pay double the compensation prescribed for another."

[2] Probably the words of the Nero text have been accidentally omitted: "and he is to pay compensation to the kindred in full and the price for his man (to the lord)".

5.1. Violation of the sanctuary of a chief minster, in case of a crime that admits of compensation, is to be atoned for at the rate of the [breach of the] king's protection, namely with five pounds in English law; and that of a rather smaller minster with 120 shillings, that is, at the rate of the king's fine; and that of one still smaller,[1] with 60 shillings; and that of a field-church with 30 shillings.

5.2. Ever by rights must judgment accord with the deed, and the amount of the fine with the status [of the church].[2]

18.[3] And the status of the ministers of the altar is to be respected for fear of God.

19. And if a priest, who lives according to a rule, is charged with a simple accusation, he is to say Mass, if he dares, and alone clear himself on the host itself;

19.1. and at a three-fold accusation, he is to clear himself, if he dares, also on the host with two supporters in the same orders.

20. And if a deacon, who lives according to a rule, is charged with a simple accusation, he is to take two supporters in the same orders, and clear himself with them.

20.1. And if he is charged with a three-fold accusation, he is to take six supporters in the same orders and clear himself with them, and he himself is to be the seventh.

21. And if a secular priest who does not live by a rule is accused, he is to clear himself like a deacon who lives according to a rule.

22. And if a minister of the altar who is without friends and who has no oath-helpers is accused, he is to go to the ordeal of the consecrated bread, and then experience there what God wishes, unless he is allowed to clear himself on the host.

23. And if a man in orders is charged with a blood-feud and accused of being either the actual slayer or the instigator, he is to clear himself with his kinsmen who must bear the feud with him or pay compensation for it.

24. And if he is without kinsmen, he is to clear himself with his associates, or fast before the ordeal of the consecrated bread, and experience at it what God decrees.

25. And no cloistered monk anywhere may lawfully demand compensation in a feud nor pay compensation in a feud; he leaves the obligations of kinship when he submits to the monastic rule.

26. If a priest becomes a homicide or otherwise commits too grave a crime, he is then to forfeit both his ecclesiastical orders and his country, and to go on pilgrinage as far as the pope may prescribe for him, and zealously to make atonement.

27. If anywhere a priest takes part in false witness or perjury, or is the accessory and accomplice of thieves, he is then to be cast out from the fellowship of those in orders, and to forfeit both the society and friendship and every dignity, unless he atone for it deeply towards God and towards men, in full as the bishop instructs him, and find for himself a surety that he will from that time forth cease from such things.

27.1. And if he wishes to clear himself, he is to clear himself in proportion to the deed, whether with a three-fold [or with a simple] process of exculpation, in proportion to the deed.

---

[1] The Nero text adds, perhaps correctly, from Edgar's law: "where nevertheless there is a burial-place".

[2] Agreeing with Liebermann that in this context *mæþ* has the same sense as in the previous clauses, the status of the church, and is not in its vaguer sense of 'moderation, due measure'. But cf. *Hadbot* (No. 52 E), 10.

[3] The intervening chapters have been occupied by injunctions on the payment of tithe and other dues to the Church, taken with little modification from earlier legislation.

28. If a minister of the altar order his own life rightly according to the instruction of the books [of canon law], he is then to be entitled to the full wergild and dignity of a thegn, both in life and in the grave.

29. And if he orders his life amiss, his dignity is to diminish in proportion to the deed.

30. Let him know, if he will, that he has no concern with a wife or with worldly warfare, if he wishes rightly to obey God and keep God's laws, as it becomes his orders by rights.

31. But we eagerly direct and lovingly pray that men in every order will lead the life which belongs to them.

31.1. And henceforth we desire that abbots and monks live more in accordance with the rule than they have been in the habit of doing up till now.

32. And the king commands all his reeves in every place, that you protect the abbots in all worldly needs as you best can, and, as you wish to have God's friendship and mine, assist their stewards everywhere to obtain their rights, so that they themselves may the more often remain secure in their monasteries and live according to the rule.

33. And if a man in holy orders or a foreigner is for any reason defrauded of property or of life, or is bound or beaten or insulted in any way, the king shall then be for him in the place of a kinsman and protector, unless he has another.

34. And compensation is to be paid both to him and to the king, as is fitting, in proportion to the deed, or he is to avenge the deed very severely.

35. It belongs very rightly to Christian men to avenge very zealously offences against God.

36. And wise were the secular councillors who appointed secular laws to uphold religious rights, for the control of the people, and assigned the compensations to Christ and the king, whereby many should thus be forced by necessity to do right.

37. But in the assemblies, although they took place designedly in famous places, since the days of Edgar, Christ's laws have waned and the king's laws dwindled.

38. And then was separated what had been common to Christ and the king in secular penalties, and ever things grew the worse in Church and State; may they now improve, if it is God's will.

39. And yet improvement can still come, if one will begin it zealously and in earnest.

40. And if one wishes rightly to cleanse the country, one must inquire and eagerly investigate, where the criminals have their dwelling, who will not cease or make amends to God; but wherever they are found, they are to be brought to justice, willingly or unwillingly, or be utterly expelled from the land, unless they submit and turn to right-living.

41. And if a monk or a priest becomes altogether an apostate, he is ever to be excommunicated, unless he more sensibly return to his duty.

42. And he who keeps under his protection God's outlaw[1] beyond the term which the king has set, risks forfeiting himself and all his property to the deputies of Christ,

---

[1] An excommunicated person. But cf. p. 428, n. 1.

who maintain and control the Christian faith and the kingdom as long as God grants.

43. But let us do as is necessary for us; let us take as our example what former rulers wisely decreed, Athelstan and Edmund, and Edgar who came last—how they honoured God and kept God's law and paid God's tribute, as long as they lived.

43.1. And let us love God with our inmost heart and heed God's laws as well as ever we can.

44. And let us zealously honour the true Christian religion and utterly despise all heathen practices.

44.1. And let us loyally support one royal lord, and let each of our friends love the next with true fidelity and support him rightly.

47. Preface to the version of Cnut's laws contained in the Corpus Christi College, Cambridge, MS. 201 (1018)

For reasons which I have stated in full in *Eng. Hist. Rev.*, LXIII, pp. 433–444, I believe this version of Cnut's laws to be the one brought before the assembly of English and Danes at Oxford in 1018. The statutes which follow the preamble are drawn mainly from VI Ethelred, though Edgar's laws are used also. The contents of this version with some rearrangement and much additional material were later promulgated as Cnut's full code. This preface is edited by Liebermann, I, p. 278, Robertson, p. 154, footnote. It is translated in my above-mentioned article, and I repeat this translation here. The whole code can only be read by reassembling it from scattered places in Liebermann's edition of the laws, *i.e.* I, pp. 278, 280, 308–312, 288–291, 252–258.

This is the ordinance which the councillors determined and devised according to many good precedents; and that took place as soon as King Cnut with the advice of his councillors completely established peace and friendship between the Danes and the English and put an end to all their former strife. In the first place, the councillors determined that above all things they would ever honour one God and steadfastly hold one Christian faith, and would love King Cnut with due loyalty and zealously observe Edgar's laws. And they agreed that they would, with God's help, investigate further at leisure what was necessary for the nation, as best they could. Now we wish to make clear what can benefit us in religious and secular concerns, let him pay heed who will. Let us very resolutely turn from sins and eagerly atone for our misdeeds and duly love and honour one God and steadfastly hold one Christian faith and diligently avoid every heathen practice.

48. Cnut's Letter to the people of England (1019–1020)

From the Anglo-Saxon Chronicle it appears that Cnut went to Denmark in 1019 and returned in the following year. Florence of Worcester says that he held a council at Cirencester at Easter (17 April) 1020. Since only Earl Thorkel is instructed to deal with those who defy the laws, it seems probable that the letter was sent to him while he was acting as regent in Cnut's absence; otherwise surely all the earls would have received this injunction. I do not understand why Liebermann assumes that the letter must have been written after Cnut's return to England. It is more probable that he wrote it from Denmark at the end of 1019 or the very beginning of 1020. In any case, it cannot have been written between Archbishop Lifing's death on 12 June 1020 and the consecration of his successor on 13 November, for it speaks of archbishops, in the plural. Earl Thorkel was banished in 1021.

The letter, which employs some of Wulfstan's phraseology and makes use of the laws drafted by that prelate, is preserved solely in a copy entered at the end of the York Gospels, along with some Wulfstan texts, in a hand which could be as early as Wulfstan's lifetime. It is edited by Liebermann, I, pp. 273–275, Earle, *A Hand-book to the Land-Charters*, pp. 229–232; and with English translation by Robertson, pp. 140–145.

1. King Cnut greets in friendship his archbishops[1] and his diocesan bishops, and Earl Thorkel and all his earls, and all his people, whether men of a twelve hundred wergild or a two hundred, ecclesiastic and lay, in England.

2. And I inform you that I will be a gracious lord and a faithful observer of God's rights and just secular law.

3. I have borne in mind the letters and messages which Archbishop Lifing brought me from Rome from the pope, that I should everywhere exalt God's praise and suppress wrong and establish full security, by that power which it has pleased God to give me.

4. Since I did not spare my money as long as hostility was threatening you, I have now with God's help put an end to it with my money.

5. Then I was informed that greater danger was approaching us than we liked at all; and then I went myself with the men who accompanied me to Denmark, from where the greatest injury had come to you, and with God's help I have taken measures so that never henceforth shall hostility reach you from there as long as you support me rightly and my life lasts.

6. Now I thank Almighty God for his help and his mercy, that I have so settled the great dangers which were approaching us that we need fear no danger to us from there; but [we may reckon] on full help and deliverance, if we need it.

7. Now it is my will, that we all thank Almighty God humbly for the mercy which he has shown for our help.

8. Now I pray my archbishops and all my diocesan bishops, that they all may be zealous about God's dues, each in the district which is entrusted to him; and also I charge all my ealdormen that they help the bishops in furthering God's rights and my royal dignity and the benefit of all the people.

9. If anyone, ecclesiastic or laymen, Dane or Englishman, is so presumptuous as to defy God's law and my royal authority or the secular law, and he will not make amends and desist according to the direction of my bishops, I then pray, and also command, Earl Thorkel, if he can, to cause the evil-doer to do right.

10. And if he cannot, then it is my will that with the power of us both he shall destroy him in the land or drive him out of the land, whether he be of high or low rank.

11. And also I charge all my reeves, on pain of losing my friendship and all that they possess and their own lives, that everywhere they maintain my people justly, and give just judgments with the witness of the bishops of the dioceses, and practise such mercy therein as seems just to the bishop of the diocese and can be supported.[2]

12. And if anyone gives asylum to a thief or interferes on his behalf, he is to be liable to the same penalty to me as the thief, unless he can clear himself of liability to me with the full process of exculpation.

[1] The MS. uses an abbreviation that is usually singular; but in chap. 8 the same abbreviation is used when the accompanying possessive shows that the plural 'archbishops' is intended, and doubtless this is meant here also.

[2] *i.e.* by the State. I accept Liebermann's emendation of *se* to *þe*, on the assumption that the same thing is meant as in III Edgar 1.2. (See p. 396, above.) If the text is kept unchanged the last clause must be rendered "and the man himself can bear"; but in that case *mildheortnesse* cannot bear its normal meaning of 'mercy'. Miss Robertson renders it 'mitigated penalties'.

13. And it is my will that all the nation, ecclesiastical and lay, shall steadfastly observe Edgar's laws, which all men have chosen and sworn to at Oxford.

14. For all the bishops say that the breaking of oaths and pledge is to be very deeply atoned for with God.

15. And also they teach us further that we must with all our strength and all our might earnestly seek, love and honour the eternal merciful God, and shun all evil-doing, namely [the deeds of] homicides and murderers, and perjurers and wizards and sorceresses, and adulterers, and incestuous deeds.

16. And also we command in the name of God Almighty and of all his saints, that no man is to be so presumptuous as to take to wife a woman consecrated to a life of chastity or a nun.

17. And if anyone has done so, he is to be an outlaw before God and excommunicated from all Christendom, and to forfeit to the king all that he owns, unless he desists quickly and atones very deeply to God.

18. And moreover we admonish that the Sunday festival is to be observed and honoured with all one's might from Saturday noon until dawn on Monday, and that no one is to be so presumptuous as either to practise any trade or to attend any meeting on that holy day.

19. And all men, poor and rich, are to go to their church and make supplication for their sins, and to observe zealously every appointed fast, and honour readily those saints whose feasts the priests shall enjoin on us,

20. so that all together through the mercy of the eternal God and the intercession of his saints we can and may come to the bliss of the heavenly kingdom and dwell with him who liveth and reigneth ever without end. Amen.

49. Cnut's letter of 1027

It is this letter, preserved only in Latin translation in the chronicles of Florence of Worcester and William of Malmesbury, that allows us to date Cnut's journey to Rome, for the coronation of the Emperor Conrad by Pope John XIX on Easter Day (26 March), 1027, is certainly the assembly referred to in paragraph 5 of the letter. The Anglo-Saxon Chronicle dates Cnut's journey to Rome 1031, and this has led Mr. A. Campbell (*Encomium Emmae Reginae*, pp. lxiif.) to argue that Cnut made two journeys to Rome. But see p. 231, n. 1.

The letter is of outstanding importance for our knowledge of Cnut's reign, of his international dealings, his troubles in Scandinavia, and his concern from abroad for the governance of England, and it also shows that foreign trade was considerable enough for the king to interest himself in the matter.

It is to be regretted that the Old English version has not survived. We do not know where Florence and William got their information that the bearer of the letter was Lifing, then abbot of Tavistock (see No. 9, p. 288), but there may have been a rubric to the text of the letter. If, however, we accept the statement that Lifing was not yet a bishop, we must reject the date of a charter in the *Codex Wintoniensis* (Kemble, No. 743) in which he appears as bishop already in 1026.

The letter is edited by Liebermann, I, pp. 276–277, and with English translation by Robertson, pp. 146–153. It is given in Thorpe's edition of Florence, I, pp. 185–189, and in Stubbs's edition of William of Malmesbury, I, pp. 221–224. For translations of these works, see pp. 277, 284.

Cnut, king of all England, and of Denmark, and of the Norwegians, and of part of the Swedes, sends greeting to Æthelnoth the metropolitan, and to Ælfric, archbishop of York, and to all the bishops and leading men, and to the whole race of the English, whether nobles or *ceorls*.

1. I make known to you that I have recently been to Rome, to pray for the

remission of my sins and for the safety of the kingdoms and of the peoples which are subjected to my rule.

2. I had long ago vowed this journey to God, but I was not able to perform it until now because of the affairs of the kingdom and other causes of hindrance.

3. But now I give most humble thanks to my Almighty God, who has granted me in my lifetime to visit his holy Apostles, Peter and Paul, and every sacred place which I could learn of within the city of Rome and outside it, and in person to worship and adore there according to my desire.

4. Especially have I accomplished this because I learned from wise men that the holy Apostle Peter had received from the Lord great power to bind and to loose, and was the keeper of the keys of the kingdom of heaven, and I considered it very profitable diligently to seek his special favour before God.

5. Be it known to you, that there was there a great assembly of nobles at the celebration of Easter, with the lord Pope John and the Emperor Conrad, namely all the princes of the nations from Mount Garganus[1] to the sea nearest [to us] ;[2] and they all both received me with honour and honoured me with precious gifts; and especially was I honoured by the emperor with various gifts and costly presents, with vessels of gold and silver and silk robes and very costly garments.

6. I therefore spoke with the emperor and the lord pope and the princes who were present, concerning the needs of all the peoples of my whole kingdom, whether English or Danes, that they might be granted more equitable law and greater security on their way to Rome, and that they should not be hindered by so many barriers on the way and so oppressed by unjust tolls; and the emperor and King Ródulf,[3] who chiefly had dominion over those barriers, consented to my demands; and all the princes confirmed by edicts that my men, whether merchants or others travelling for the sake of prayer, should go to and return from Rome in safety with firm peace and just law, free from hindrances by barriers and tolls.

7. Again, I complained before the lord pope and said that it displeased me greatly that my archbishops were so much oppressed by the immensity of the sums of money which were exacted from them when according to custom they came to the apostolic see to receive the *pallium*. It was decided that this should not be done in future.

8. Indeed, all the things which I demanded for the benefit of my people from the lord pope and from the emperor and from King Rodulf and the other princes through whose lands our way to Rome lies, they most willingly granted, and also confirmed what they had conceded with an oath, with the witness of four archbishops and twenty bishops and an innumerable multitude of dukes and nobles who were present.

9. Therefore I give most hearty thanks to Almighty God, that I have successfully accomplished all that I had desired, just as I had designed, and have carried out my vows to my satisfaction.

10. Now, therefore, be it known to you all, that I have humbly vowed to Almighty

---

[1] Monte Gargano, in the province of Foggia.

[2] Cnut composed this letter on his homeward journey to Denmark, perhaps, as Liebermann suggests, in Flanders or Hamburg. The nearest sea would therefore be the North Sea.

[3] Of Burgundy.

God to amend my life from now on in all things, and to rule justly and faithfully the kingdoms and peoples subject to me and to maintain equal justice in all things; and if hitherto anything contrary to what is right has been done through the intemperance of my youth or through negligence, I intend to repair it all henceforth with the help of God.

11. For this reason I implore and command my councillors, to whom I have entrusted the councils of the kingdom, that from now on they shall not in any way, either for fear of me or for the favour of any powerful person, consent to any injustice, or suffer it to flourish in any part of my kingdom.

12. I command also all the sheriffs and reeves over my whole kingdom, as they wish to retain my friendship and their own safety, that they employ no unjust force against any man, neither rich nor poor, but that all men, of noble or humble birth, rich or poor, shall have the right to enjoy just law; from which there is to be no deviation in any way, neither on account of the royal favour nor out of respect for any powerful man, nor in order to amass money for me; for I have no need that money should be amassed for me by unjust exaction.

13. And therefore I wish to make known to you, that, returning by the same way that I went, I am going to Denmark, to conclude with the counsel of all the Danes peace and a firm treaty with those nations and peoples who wished, if it had been possible for them, to deprive us both of kingdom and of life, but could not, since God indeed destroyed their strength. May he in his loving-kindness preserve us in sovereignty and honour, and scatter and bring to nought the power and strength of all our enemies from henceforth.

14. Then, when peace has been concluded with the nations which are round about us, and all our kingdom here in the east has been set in order and pacified, so that we need fear no war or enmity from anyone from any quarter, I intend to come to England as early in the summer as I can get a fleet equipped.

15. But I send ahead this letter, in order that all the people of my kingdom may be gladdened at my success, because, as you yourselves know, I have never spared—nor will I spare in the future—to devote myself and my toil for the need and benefit of all my people.

16. Now, therefore, I command and implore all my bishops and reeves of the kingdom, by the faith which you owe to God and to me, that you bring it about before I come to England that all the dues, which according to ancient law we owe to God, shall be paid in full, namely plough-alms and tithe of livestock born that same year, and the pence which we owe to St. Peter at Rome, whether from the towns or the villages, and in the middle of August tithe of the fruits of the earth, and at the feast of St. Martin the first-fruits of the grain[1] (which are called 'church-scot' in English) to the church of the parish where each man resides.

·17. If these dues, and others like them, are not paid in full when I come, the royal collectors are to obtain them according to the laws, sternly and without remission, from him who is in fault.

---

[1] Liebermann considers this is merely a misunderstanding of the Old English word *cyricsceat*, with confusion of *sceat* with *sæd* 'seed'. It should, however, be noted that church-scot was often paid in grain.

50. Extracts from the laws of Cnut (1020–1023)

This code, which falls into two parts, an ecclesiastical and a secular (cited respectively as I and II Cnut), is much the longest of Old English law codes. It is, however, largely made up of extracts from previous kings' legislation plus homiletic matter. I have therefore confined my selection to such parts as are original, or at least from no known source, except when it is necessary to retain a statute borrowed from elsewhere in order to preserve the sequence of thought. The footnotes explain how the gaps are filled in.

The code is undated, and I have set out at length elsewhere[1] my reasons for believing that it at any rate reached its general shape, and was perhaps promulgated, before Wulfstan's death in 1023. His style is clearly distinguishable, and his own works figure prominently among its sources. In Old English it survives in three manuscripts, two of which, the Brit. Mus. MSS., Harley 55 and Cott. Nero A. i, have it bound up with matter which certainly came from Worcester. The third manuscript is C.C.C.C., MS. 383, and its version is incomplete at the beginning.

The great respect paid to Cnut's laws in post-Conquest times has been mentioned above. Moreover in 1065 when Earl Harold was sent to conciliate the northern rebels at Northampton, the 'D' manuscript of the Anglo-Saxon Chronicle tells us that "he renewed there Cnut's law".

The code is edited by Liebermann, I, pp. 278–371; and with English translation by Robertson, pp. 154–219, Thorpe, I, pp. 358–425.

I Cnut: Ecclesiastical

This is the ordinance which King Cnut, king of all England and king of the Danes and king of the Norwegians,[2] and his councillors decreed, for the praise of God and for his own royal dignity and benefit; let one resolve whichever [course] one will.[3]

PROLOGUE. This is the ordinance which King Cnut[4] determined with the advice of his councillors, for the praise of God and for his own royal dignity and benefit; and it took place at the holy Christmas season at Winchester.

1. First, namely, that above all other things they would ever love and honour one God and steadfastly hold one Christian faith, and love King Cnut with due loyalty.[5]

20. Let us also perform zealously what we wish to enjoin further: let us ever be loyal and true to our lord and ever with all our might exalt his dignity and do his will.

20.1. For all that ever we do out of just loyalty to our lord, we do it all to our own great benefit, for assuredly God will be gracious to him who is duly loyal to his lord.

20.2. And also every lord has very great benefit from treating his men justly.[6]

II Cnut: Secular

PROLOGUE. This is now the secular ordinance which I, with the advice of my councillors, wish to be observed over all England. . . .[7]

---

[1] *Eng. Hist. Rev.*, LXIII, pp. 433–452.

[2] If this were original, it would make the code later than Cnut's victory over the Norwegians in 1030, or at least than his claims on Norway in 1027. But it is confined to the Harley MS. and is usually regarded as a later addition.   [3] Only the Harley MS. has this superscription. The last clause is rather cryptic.

[4] The Nero text adds here: "king of all England and king of the Danes"; but as without this the prologue is exactly in the form of that of II Edgar, I suspect this of being an accretion.

[5] I omit most of I Cnut. It contains VIII Ethelred 1.1–5.1, on sanctuary, and 19–27.1, on accusations against men in orders; clauses from V and VI Ethelred on the behaviour of ecclesiastics follow, and then a number of injunctions on payment of church dues, partly from II Edgar and partly from VIII Ethelred. The section on observance of festivals from VI Ethelred has the addition that St. Dunstan's day is to be kept on 19 May. The rest is homiletic, and I give only its first and most interesting part.

[6] I omit the rest of this code.

[7] I have omitted clauses drawn mainly from VI Ethelred, 8.1–9, since they differ little from V Ethelred 1.1–1.2, though the source of this, III Edgar, has been used also. These general principles are then followed by prohibitions of too ready application of the death-penalty, and of the sale of men abroad. See V Ethelred 2, 3. Then VI Ethelred 7 (see p. 405, n. 3) is repeated.

5. And we earnestly forbid every heathen practice.

5.1. It is heathen practice if one worships idols, namely if one worships heathen gods and the sun or the moon, fire or flood, wells or stones or any kind of forest trees, or if one practises witchcraft or encompasses death by any means, either by sacrifice[1] or divination, or takes any part in such delusions.

6. Homicides and perjurers, injurers of the clergy and adulterers, are to submit and make amends or to depart from their native land with their sins.

7. Hypocrites and liars, robbers and plunderers, shall incur God's anger, unless they desist and atone very deeply.

7.1. And he who wishes to purify the country rightly and to put down wrong-doing and to love righteousness, must diligently correct and shun such things.

8.[2] And also let us all take thought very earnestly about the improvement of the peace and the improvement of the coinage; about the improvement of the peace in such a way as may be best for the householder[3] and most grievous for the thief; and about the improvement of the coinage in such a way that one coinage is to be current throughout all this nation without any debasement, and no man is to refuse it.

8.1.[4] And he who after this coins false money is to forfeit the hand with which he coined the false money, and he is not to redeem it at any price, neither with gold nor with silver.

8.2. And if the reeve is accused, that it was with his permission that he coined the false money, he is to clear himself with the three-fold process of exculpation; and if this exculpation fails, he is to incur the same sentence as he who coined the false money.[5]

12. These are the rights which the king possesses over all men in Wessex, namely *mundbryce*[6] and *hamsocn*,[7] *forstal*[8] and [the fine for] the harbouring of fugitives[9] and the fine for neglecting military service, unless he wishes to honour anyone further.[10]

13. And if anyone commits a deed punishable by outlawry, the king [alone] is to have power to grant him peace.

13.1. And if he has bookland, it is to be forfeited into the king's possession, no matter whose man he be.

13.2. And whoever feeds or harbours the fugitive is to pay five pounds to the king, unless he clear himself, that he did not know him to be a fugitive.

14. And in Mercia he possesses just what is written here above, over all men.

15. And in the Danelaw he possesses the fine for fighting and that for neglecting

---

[1] *blote* is the reading supported by the Law of the Northumbrian Priests (No. 53). The Harley text has *hlote* 'lot-casting'.

[2] This section is taken from VI Ethelred 32, 32.1 (cf. V.26.1), the latter clause being itself from III Edgar 8.

[3] *bonda*. See p. 410, n. 3. In this context the word refers to any law-abiding member of society. As in the laws of the Scandinavians, the free peasant proprietor is taken as the normal person to benefit from the law.

[4] This is based on II Athelstan 14.1.

[5] Here follow VI Ethelred 32.2 (=III Edgar 8.1), 32.3 (=V Ethelred 26.1), concerned with weights and measures and the duties of the repair of boroughs and bridges, and military service. Then come the last two clauses of VI Ethelred (40, 40.1) the second of which =V Ethelred 33.1. The Nero and Corpus versions of Cnut's laws retain the 'Amen' which was in place at the end of VI Ethelred.

[6] Breach of the king's protection.　　　　　　　　[7] See p. 392, n. 3.

[8] See p. 408, n. 5.　　　　　　　　　　　　[9] This is mentioned only in the Nero version.

[10] *i.e.* further than by giving the usual grant of private jurisdiction, which did not include these special royal pleas. The Nero version adds here: "and he grants him this privilege".

military service, *griðbryce* (breach of the peace) and *hamsocn* unless he wishes to honour anyone further.

15*a*. And if then anyone maintains or harbours an outlawed man,[1] he is to pay compensation for it as the law was before.

15.1.[2] And he who promotes an abuse or gives a wrong judgment henceforth, owing to hatred or bribery, is then to forfeit 120 shillings to the king in the area under English law, unless he dare declare on oath that he knew not how to do it more justly; and he is always to forfeit his thegnly status,[3] unless he may redeem it from the king, according as he will allow him.

15.1*a*. And in the Danelaw he is to forfeit *lahslit*,[4] unless he clear himself–that he knew no better.

15.2. And he who refuses to follow just law and just judgment, is to be liable to pay [a fine] in the area under English law to him who has a right to it, either to the king 120 shillings, or to the earl 60 shillings, or to the hundred 30 shillings, or to each of them, if it so happens.

15.3. And he who violates just law in the Danelaw is to pay *lahslit*. . . .[5]

19. And no one is to distrain on property either within the shire or outside it until he has demanded his rights three times in the hundred.

19.1. If on the third occasion he cannot obtain right, he is then the fourth time to go to the shire-meeting, and the shire is to appoint for him the fourth term [for settlement].

19.2. And if this then fails, he is to get permission either from this court or that,[6] that he may seize his own.

20. And it is our will that every free man who wishes to be entitled to right of exculpation and to a wergild if anyone slays him,[7] be brought, if he is over twelve years old, into a hundred or tithing; otherwise he is not to be entitled to any rights of free men.

20*a*. Whether he has a home of his own, or is in the following of another, each is to be brought in a hundred and under surety, and the surety is to hold him and bring him to every legal duty.

20.1. Many an overbearing man will, if he can and may, defend his man whichever way it seems to him that he can defend him more easily, whether as a free man or a slave; but we will not allow that abuse.

21. And it is our will that every man over twelve years of age is to give an oath that he will not be a thief or accessory to a theft.

22. And every trustworthy man, who has not been frequently accused, and has failed neither at oath nor at ordeal, is to be entitled to the simple process of exculpation within his hundred.

---

[1] The Nero version inserts "or a fugitive".

[2] This is largely based on III Edgar 3. The Harley MS. has the significant difference that the penalty has arisen from 120 shillings to the delinquent's wergild. [3] *þegnscipe*. See p. 396, n. 3.

[4] See p. 408, n. 6. The *lahslit* for a king's thegn was 10 half-marks, rather higher than 120 West Saxon shillings. [5] Here the code inserts III Edgar 2, 4, 5–5.2, with unimportant variations.

[6] Literally, "hence or thence" which, judging by the order, seems to go with the permission (*sic* Miss Robertson), though *Quadripartitus* and Liebermann take it in the next clause, where it would mean that the distraint might be made anywhere on the defaulter's property.

[7] The Nero MS. and *Quadripartitus* have instead: "if anyone accuses him".

22.1. And for an untrustworthy man one is to select a simple oath within three hundreds, and a three-fold oath from the area which belongs to the borough;[1] or he is to go to the ordeal.

22.1a. And a simple process of exculpation is to be set on foot by a simple preliminary oath, and a three-fold process of exculpation by a three-fold preliminary oath.

22.2. And if a thegn has a trustworthy man to give the preliminary oath in his stead, that may be so done; if he has not, he is himself to set on foot his suit.

22.3. And no preliminary oath is ever to be remitted.

23. And no man is to be entitled to vouch to warranty unless he has trustworthy witness as to where he obtained what is being attached.

23.1. And that witness is to declare, by God's favour and the lord's, that they stand with him in true testimony, as they saw with their eyes and heard with their ears, that he obtained it rightly.

24. And no one is to buy anything worth more than fourpence, neither livestock nor other goods, unless he has the trustworthy witness of four men, whether it is in the borough or in the country.

24.1. And if it is then attached, and he has not such witness, there is to be no vouching to warranty, but the owner is to be given back his own and the additional payment,[2] and he who has the right to it is to be given the fine.

24.2. And if he has witness, as we have said above, one may vouch to warranty three times; on the fourth occasion he is either to make good his claim to it or give it back to the owner.

24.3. And it does not seem right to us that any man should make good his claim where there is witness[3] and it can be shown that there has been fraud; so that no one ought to make good his claim until at least six months after it was stolen. . . .[4]

27. And he who defends himself or his man in court by a counter-charge shall have spoken this all in vain, and is to answer the other as seems right to the hundred.

28.[5] And no one is to entertain any man for more than three days, unless he whom he previously served commits him to him.

28.1. And no one is to dismiss his man, before he is cleared of every charge with which he had been accused.

29. And if anyone comes across a thief and willingly lets him escape without raising hue and cry, he is to pay compensation at the rate of the thief's wergild, or clear himself with a full oath that he did not know him guilty of crime.

29.1. And if anyone hears the hue and cry and ignores it, he is to pay [the fine for] disobedience to the king or to clear himself fully.

30. And if any man is so regarded with suspicion by the hundred and so frequently

---

[1] This means that he is not allowed to choose his own compurgators, but the court appoints them, according to whether the case demands a simple or three-fold oath.

[2] The word *æftergyld* is unique. The Latin translators understood it to mean 'as much again'.

[3] For the man who claims that it is stolen property.

[4] Here Cnut's laws insert III Edgar 7–7.3, on the treatment of men of bad reputation. A clause is added which repeats in other words the statement in the previous clause that no refuge is to save the life of a manifest thief.

[5] This and the following clause are like II Athelstan 22, 22.2, in content, but not in wording.

accused, and three men together then accuse him, there is then to be nothing for it but that he is to go to the three-fold ordeal.

30.1. If the lord then says that he has failed neither at oath nor at ordeal since the assembly was held at Winchester, the lord is to take with him two trustworthy men from within the hundred and swear that he failed neither at oath nor at ordeal, nor did he pay any compensation for theft, unless the lord have a reeve who is entitled to do this on his behalf.[1]

30.2. And if the oath is then forthcoming, the man who is there accused is to choose which he will have, whether simple ordeal or an oath worth a pound within the three hundreds, in a case of [stolen goods of] over 30 pence.

30.3. And if, however, they dare not give that oath, he is to go to the three-fold ordeal.

30.3a. And the three-fold ordeal is to be set on foot thus: he[2] is to take five men and be himself the sixth.

30.3b. And if he is then convicted, on the first occasion he is to pay two-fold compensation to the accuser and his wergild to the lord who is entitled to his fine, and to appoint trustworthy sureties that he will afterwards cease from all evil-doing.

30.4. And on the second occasion there is to be no other compensation, if he is convicted, but that his hands, or feet, or both, in proportion to the deed, are to be cut off.

30.5. And if, however, he has committed still further crimes, his eyes are to be put out and his nose and ears and upper lip cut off, or his scalp removed, whichever of these is then decreed by those with whom the decision rests; thus one can punish and at the same time preserve the soul.

30.6. If, however, he runs away and avoids the ordeal, the surety is to pay to the accuser the value of his property, and his wergild to the king or to the man who is entitled to his fine.

30.7. And if the lord is then accused that it was by his advice that he ran away, having previously committed a crime, he is to take with him five trustworthy men[3] and be himself the sixth, and clear himself of it.

30.8. And if the exculpation succeeds, he is to be entitled to the wergild.

30.9. And if it does not succeed, the king is to succeed to the wergild, and the thief is to be an outlaw as regards the whole people.

31.[4] And each lord is to have the men of his household under his own surety.

31a. And if he[5] is accused of anything, he is to answer within the hundred, where he is charged, as the true law is.

31.1. And if he is accused and he escapes, the lord is to pay the man's wergild to the king.

31.1a. And if the lord is then accused, that it was by his advice that he ran away, he is to clear himself with five thegns, and be himself the sixth.

---

[1] This chapter repeats I Ethelred 1.2 (cf. also III Ethelred 4), except that Winchester is substituted for *Bromdun*, and that Ethelred required the oath-helpers to be thegns.
  The following chapters also are mainly from I Ethelred, but paragraphs 30.3a and 5 are new, and 4 substitutes mutilation for the death-penalty.   [2] *i.e.* the accuser.
[3] 'Men' added only in the Corpus MS. Probably the original had 'thegns', as in Ethelred's law.
[4] The following section is from I Ethelred also (1.10–1.13), except that 31a is new.
[5] Any man of the household.

31.2. And if the exculpation fails, he is to pay his [own] wergild to the king and the man is to be an outlaw.

32.[1] And if a slave[2] is convicted by the ordeal, on the first occasion he is to be branded.

32.1. And on the second occasion, there is to be no compensation except his head.

33. And if there is any man regarded with suspicion by all the people, the king's reeve is to go thither and put him under surety, that he may be brought to do justice to those who bring charges against him.

33.1. If, however, he has no surety, he is to be slain and to lie in unconsecrated ground.

33.1a. And if anyone offers resistance on his account, they are both to share the same penalty.

33.2. And he who neglects this and will not carry it out as it is decreed by us all, is to pay to the king 120 shillings.

34. And one and the same law is to be valid in boroughs as regards exculpation.

35. And if a friendless man, or a stranger from a distance, becomes so afflicted by his friendless state that he has no surety, he is then, at a first charge, to go to prison and stay there until he goes to God's ordeal, and experience there what he may.

35.1. Assuredly, he who pronounces a worse judgment on a friendless man or a stranger from a distance than on his own fellows, injures himself.

36. And if anyone swears a false oath on the relics, and is confuted, he is to forfeit his hands or half his wergild; and it is to be divided by the lord and the bishop.

36.1. And from thenceforth he is not to be entitled to an oath, unless he atones for it very deeply with God, and finds surety for himself that he will desist from such ever afterwards.

37. And if anyone notoriously takes part in false witness, and he is confuted, his testimony is afterwards to be worthless, but he is to compensate the king or the lord of the estate[3] with his *healsfang*.[4]

38.[5] Wrong-doing is not permitted at any time; and yet it should be especially guarded against at festival seasons[6] and in sacred places.

38.1. And ever as a man is mightier or of higher rank, he must atone the deeper for wrong-doing both to God and to men.

38.2. And ecclesiastical amends are always to be diligently demanded according to the instruction in books [of penance] and secular amends according to the secular law.

39. If anyone slays a minister of the altar, he is to be an outlaw before God and men, unless he atone for it very deeply, by exile and also towards the kindred, or clear himself by an oath equal to the wergild.

---

[1] For this chapter and the next, as far as 33.2, the source is still I Ethelred (2, 2.1, 4–4.3). I Ethelred 3, which deals with security and witness at sales, is omitted, presumably because it breaks the sequence of ideas. With 4.3 I Ethelred comes to an end.

[2] The Harley and Corpus texts have wrongly "a thief".

[3] The Nero text adds: "who owns jurisdiction over him".   [4] See p. 363, n. 3.

[5] This and the next clause are drawn from an ecclesiastical tract known as "Concerning Confession".

[6] The Nero text adds: "and fasting seasons", which is also in the source.

39.1. And he is to begin to make amends both to God and to men within 30 days, on pain of losing all that he owns.

40.[1] If a man in holy orders or a foreigner is for any reason defrauded of property or of life, the king shall then be for him in the place of a kinsman and protector, unless he has another.

40.1. And compensation is to be paid to the king, as is fitting, or he is to avenge the deed very severely.

40.2. It belongs very rightly to a Christian king[2] to avenge very zealously offences against God, in proportion to the deed.

41.[3] If a minister of the altar becomes a homicide or otherwise commits too grave a crime, he is then to forfeit both his ecclesiastical orders and his native land, and to go on a pilgrimage as far as the pope may prescribe for him, and zealously to make atonement.

41.1.[4] And if he wishes to clear himself, he is to clear himself with three-fold process of exculpation.

41.2. And unless he begins to make amends to God and to men within 30 days, he is to be an outlaw.

42.[5] And if anyone binds or beats or greatly insults a man in holy orders, he is to pay compensation to him as is right, and to the bishop the fine for sacrilege in proportion to his status, and to the lord or the king the full [fine for] breach of his protection; or he is to clear himself by full process of exculpation.

43.[6] If a man in holy orders commits a capital crime, he is to be seized and kept for the bishop's judgment, according to the nature of the deed.

44.[7] And if a condemned man desire confession, it is never to be refused him.

44.1. And if anyone does refuse it to him, he is to pay 120 shillings compensation to the king; or, to clear himself, he is to take five men and be himself the sixth.

45.[8] And if it can be arranged, no condemned man should ever be put to death during the Sunday festival, unless he flees or resists; but he is to be seized and kept until the feast-day is over.

45.1.[9] If a freeman work on a feast-day, he is to pay his *healsfang*[10] in compensation and indeed to atone for it deeply to God, as he is directed.

45.2.[11] A slave, if he work, is to suffer a flogging or redeem himself from one, in proportion to the deed.

45.3.[12] If a master compels his slave to work on a feast-day, he is to forfeit the slave,

---

[1] From here to 48.3, the code draws mainly on VIII Ethelred and a related code of Wulfstan's composition called erroneously "The treaty of Edward and Guthrum"; but it sometimes curtails, and sometimes expands from other sources, so I consider it best to give it in full; 40, 40.1, 40.2, are from VIII Ethelred 33, 34, 35, with omissions.

[2] Ethelred's code said "Christian men".   [3] Almost exactly as in VIII Ethelred 26.

[4] VIII Ethelred 27.1 (27 is not used by Cnut's law). But Ethelred allowed either simple or triple oath according to the crime involved.   [5] Expanded from VIII Ethelred 33.

[6] From "Edward and Guthrum", 4.2.   [7] Ibid., 5.   [8] Ibid., 9.1.

[9] Though this and the following clauses are based on "Edward and Guthrum", other legal texts have been used. In this chapter the penalty of *healsfang* comes from Wihtred 11, where Ine 3.2 and "Edward and Guthrum" 7.1 prescribe loss of freedom, to be redeemed, according to the latter code, by payment of *lahslit* or fine, and according to some MSS. of Ine, by payment of 60 shillings.   [10] See p. 363, n. 3.

[11] From "Edward and Guthrum" 7.1, in agreement with Ine 3.1.

[12] From *ibid.*, 7.2, but with the addition of the clause about the freeing of the slave from Ine 3.

who is afterwards to be a free man; and the master is to pay *lahslit* among the Danes, a fine among the English, in proportion to the deed; or to clear himself.

46.[1] If a free man break a legally ordained fast, he is to pay *lahslit* among the Danes, a fine among the English, in proportion to the deed.

46.1. It is wrong that one should eat during a time of fast before the mealtime, and still worse, that one should defile oneself with fleshmeat.

46.2.[2] If a slave do it, he is to suffer a flogging or redeem himself from one, in proportion to the deed.

47.[3] If anyone openly commits a breach of the Lenten fast by fighting or intercourse with women or by robbery[4] or by any other grave crime, double compensations are to be paid, as in a high festival, in proportion to the deed.

47.1. And if anyone denies it, he is to clear himself with the three-fold process of exculpation.

48.[5] And if anyone refuses with force to pay church dues, he is to pay *lahslit* among the Danes, full fine among the English; or, to clear himself, he is to take eleven [men] and be himself the twelfth.[6]

48.1. And if he wounds a man, he is to pay compensation for it and pay full fine to the lord, and redeem his hand from the bishop or forfeit it

48.2. If he slays a man, he is to be an outlaw, and each of those who wish to uphold the law are to pursue him with hostility.

48.3. If he so acts that he is slain because he offered resistance against the law, and that is proved true, no wergild is to be paid for him.

49. If anyone commits an offence against a man in holy orders, he is to pay compensation for it in proportion to the latter's status, whether by wergild or by fine or by *lahslit* or by all his possessions.

50. If anyone commits adultery, he is to pay compensation for it in proportion to the deed.

50.1. It is wicked adultery that a married man should commit fornication with a single woman, and much worse if with another's wife or with a woman consecrated [to God].

51. If anyone commits incest, he is to pay compensation according to the degree of the relationship, whether by wergild or by fine or by all his possessions.

51.1. It is by no means on a level whether a man has intercourse with his sister, or with a more distant relation.

52. If anyone ravishes a widow, he is to compensate for it with the wergild.

52.1. If anyone ravishes a maiden, he is to compensate for it with the wergild.

53. If a woman during her husband's lifetime commits adultery with another man, and it becomes known, let her afterwards become herself a public disgrace and her lawful husband is to have all that she owns, and she is to lose her nose and ears.

---

[1] From "Edward and Guthrum", 8.   [2] From *ibid.*   [3] Cf. Alfred 5.5, 40.1.
[4] Robbery is omitted in the Nero version and originally in *Quadripartitus.*
[5] From here to 48.3 is taken from "Edward and Guthrum" 6.4–6.7, but with a significant alteration in 48.1, for the source prescribed the payment of wergild for this offence.
[6] The source said nothing about the method of exculpation.

53.1. And if an accusation is brought, and the exculpation fails, the bishop is then to take control and to judge sternly.

54. If a married man commits fornication with his own slave-woman, he is to forfeit her and make amends for himself with God and with men.

54.1. And if anyone has a lawful wife and also a concubine, no priest is to do for him any of the offices which must be done for a Christian man, until he desists and atones for it as deeply as the bishop directs him, and desists from such for ever.

55.[1] Foreigners, if they will not regularize their marriages, are to depart from the land with their goods and their sins.

56. If manifest murder occur,[2] so that a man is murdered, the murderer is to be given up to the kinsmen.

56.1. And if an accusation is brought, and the accused fails at the exculpation, the bishop is to give judgment.

57.[3] And if anyone plots against the king or his lord, he is to forfeit his life and all that he owns, unless he goes to the three-fold ordeal.

58.[4] If anyone violates the king's surety, he is to compensate for it with five pounds.

58.1.[5] If anyone violates the archbishop's or the atheling's surety, he is to compensate for it with three pounds.

58.2.[6] If anyone violates a diocesan bishop's or an ealdorman's surety, he is to compensate for it with two pounds.

59.[7] If anyone fight in the king's court, he is to forfeit his life, unless the king wishes to spare him.

60. If anyone illegally disarms a man, he is to compensate him with *healsfang* ;[8] and if he binds him, he is to compensate with half the wergild.[9]

61. If anyone commits a full breach of the peace in the army, he is to forfeit his life or his wergild.

61.1. If he commits a partial breach,[10] he is to compensate in proportion to the deed.

62. If anyone commits *hamsocn*,[11] he is to compensate for it with five pounds to the king in the area under English law,[12] and in the Danelaw as it stood before.

62.1. And if he is slain there, no wergild is to be paid for him.

63. If anyone commits robbery, he is to restore and pay as much again, and forfeit his wergild to the king.[13]

64. House-breaking[14] and arson and obvious theft and manifest murder and betrayal of a lord are beyond compensation according to the secular law.

---

[1] This clause is taken unchanged from the laws of the Kentish king, Wihtred (4). It is probably the influx of Scandinavians in the reign of Cnut that caused the revival of this ancient statute.

[2] Murder to the Anglo-Saxons meant killing by secret means.

[3] While this clause is based on VI Ethelred 37 (= V Ethelred 30), it omits some of the phrases, and it uses also Alfred 4.2, taking from there the inclusion of plotting against a lord who is not the king. Alfred's code is used for the next chapters (up to 60), so this agreement is not likely to be accidental.

[4] From Alfred 3.　　[5] Cf. Alfred 3, where, however, the atheling is not mentioned.　　[6] From Alfred 3.

[7] Cf. Alfred 7.　　[8] See p. 363, n. 3.　　[9] Cf. Alfred 35, but here binding cost only ten shillings.

[10] *i.e.* by a minor offence.　　　　[11] See p. 392, n. 3.

[12] The Nero version adds here: "and in Kent in a case of *hamsocn*, five pounds to the king and three to the archbishop".　　　　　　　　　　[13] *Ibid.* "or to him who owns the jurisdiction".

[14] It is clear from the penalty that this is a different and a graver offence than *hamsocn*, presumably including the destruction of buildings.

65. If anyone neglects the repair of fortresses or bridges, or military service, he is to pay 120 shillings compensation to the king in the area under English law, and in the Danelaw as it stood before; or to clear himself; fourteen men are to be nominated to him, and he is to get [the support of] eleven.

65.1. All people should by rights help to repair the church.

66. If anyone wrongfully maintains a fugitive from an ecclesiastical process,[1] he is to surrender him to the law and pay compensation to whom it belongs; and he is to pay to the king the amount of the wergild.

66.1.[2] And if anyone maintains and keeps an excommunicated person or an outlaw, it is to be at the peril of his life and all his property.

67. If anyone eagerly wishes to turn from wrong-doing back to right behaviour, one is to be merciful to him very readily, as best one can, for the fear of God.

68. And let us do, as is profitable for us, always help quickest those who need it most; then shall we receive our reward for it where it will be most pleasing to us.

68.1.[3] For the weak man must always be judged and prescribed for more leniently than the strong, for the love of God;

68.1a. for we know full well that the feeble cannot bear a burden like the strong, nor the sick man like the sound.

68.1b. And therefore we must moderate and distinguish reasonably between age and youth, wealth and poverty, freedom and slavery, health and sickness.

68.1c. And these things are to be distinguished both in religious penances and in secular judgments.

68.2. Also in many a deed, when a man acts under compulsion, he is then the more entitled to clemency in that he did what he did out of necessity.

68.3. And if anyone acts unintentionally, he is not entirely like one who does it intentionally.

69. Now this is the mitigation by which I wish to protect all the people from what they were hitherto oppressed with all too greatly.

69.1. First, namely, that I charge all my reeves, that they lawfully provide for me from my own property, and support me from it, and that no one need give anything to them to my provisioning unless he himself wishes.

69.2. And if anyone after this demands a fine, he is to forfeit his wergild to the king.

70. And if anyone departs from this life intestate, be it through his heedlessness, or through sudden death, the lord is then not to take more from his possessions than his legal heriot.

70.1. But by his direction, the property is to be very justly divided among the wife, the children and the close kinsmen, each in the proportion which belongs to him.

---

[1] The actual words are "God's fugitive". Miss Robertson translates 'an excommunicated person', but some distinction seems to be drawn between him and the excommunicated person of the next chapter. What is meant is probably anyone who flees rather than appear to answer a charge in which the rights of the Church are involved. [2] Cf. VIII Ethelred 42.

[3] This and the following clauses (up to 68.3) make use of a tract added at the end of VI Ethelred, which also survives in some MSS. as a separate work, and which deals with legal principles; and also of a treatise "Concerning Confession" (Thorpe, II, pp. 260–265).

71. And heriots are to be so determined as befits the rank:

71a. an earl's as belongs thereto, namely eight horses, four saddled and four unsaddled, and four helmets and four coats of mail and eight spears and as many shields and four swords and 200 mancuses of gold;

71.1. and next, the king's thegns, who are closest to him: four horses, two saddled and two unsaddled, and two swords and four spears and as many shields, and a helmet and coat of mail and 50 mancuses of gold;

71.2. and of the lesser thegns: a horse and its trappings, and his weapons or his *healsfang* in Wessex; and two pounds in Mercia and two pounds in East Anglia.

71.3. And the heriot of the king's thegn among the Danes, who has right of jurisdiction; four pounds.

71.4. And if he has a more intimate relation with the king: two horses, one saddled and one unsaddled, and a sword and two spears and two shields and 50 mancuses of gold.

71.5. And he who is of lower position: two pounds.

72.[1] And where the householder dwelt undisturbed by charges and claims, the wife and children are to dwell on the same [property] unmolested by litigation.

72.1. And if the householder was cited before he died, then the heirs are to answer as he would have had to, if he were alive.

73.[2] And each widow is to remain unmarried for 12 months; she is afterwards to choose what she herself will.

73a. And if she chooses a husband within the year's space, she is then to forfeit the morning-gift and all the possessions which she had through her former husband; and the nearest kinsmen are to succeed to the lands and to the possessions which she had before.

73.1. And he[3] is to be liable to pay his wergild to the king or to him to whom he has granted the jurisdiction.

73.2. And even if she was married by force, she is to forfeit those possessions, unless she wishes to leave the man and return home and never afterwards become his.

73.3. A widow is never to be consecrated [as a nun] too hastily.

73.4. And each widow is to pay the heriot within 12 months, without fine, unless it is convenient to her to do so sooner.

74. And neither a widow nor a maiden is ever to be forced to marry a man whom she herself dislikes, nor to be given for money, unless he chooses to give anything of his own freewill.

75. And I consider it right, if anyone sets his spear at the door of another man's house, and himself has an errand inside, or if other weapons are laid in orderly fashion where they could remain quietly, if they were allowed, and any man then takes that weapon and does some injury with it; it is then right, that he who did the injury shall also compensate for the injury.

75.1. And he who owns the weapon is to clear himself, if he dare, that it was never either his wish or his intention or his advice or his cognisance; then it is the law of God that he should be clear.

---

[1] Cf. III Ethelred 14.   [2] From VI Ethelred 26.1 (= V Ethelred 21.1).   [3] The second husband.

75.2. And the other, who did the deed, is to understand that he is to pay compensation for it as the laws direct.

76.[1] And if any man brings home stolen property to his cottage, and he is found out, it is right that he [the owner] should have what he has tracked.

76.1. And unless it has been brought under the wife's lock and key, she is to be clear.

76.1a. But she must look after the keys of the following: namely her store-room, her chest and her coffer; if it is brought inside any of these, she is then guilty.

76.1b. And no wife can forbid her husband to place inside his cottage what he pleases.

76.2. Up till now it happened that the child which lay in the cradle, although it had never tasted food, was reckoned by avaricious folk as being as guilty as though it had discretion.

76.3. But I earnestly forbid this henceforth, and likewise many things which are very hateful to God.

77. And the man, who in his cowardice deserts his lord or his comrades, whether it is on an expedition by sea or on one on land, is to forfeit all that he owns and his own life; and the lord is to succeed to the possessions and to the land which he previously gave him.

77.1. And if he has bookland, that is to pass into the king's possession.

78. And the heriot is to be remitted for the man who falls before his lord in a campaign, whether it is within the land or outside the land; and the heirs are to succeed to the land and to the possessions and divide it very justly.

79. And he who has performed the obligations on an estate with the witness of the shire[2] is to have it uncontested for his lifetime and to give it to whom he pleases after his lifetime.

80. And it is my will that every man is to be entitled to his hunting in wood and field on his own land.

80.1. And everyone is to avoid trespassing on my hunting, wherever I wish to have it preserved, on pain of full fine.

81. And *drincelean*[3] and the lord's legal gift[4] are to remain ever unperverted.

82. And it is my will that every man is to be entitled to peace, going to a meeting and from a meeting, unless he is a manifest thief.

83. And he who violates these laws which the king has now given to all men, whether he be Danish or English, is to forfeit his wergild to the king.

83.1. And if he violates it again, he is to pay his wergild twice.

83.2. And if he then is so presumptuous that he violates it a third time, he is to forfeit all that he owns.[5]

---

[1] With this and the next clauses, cf. Ine 57.

[2] The Nero text adds: "and he who owned it before would not or could not".

[3] This is a word of uncertain meaning. It may be 'granting of drink' and refer to the custom of drinking to mark the conclusion of a compact, or it may, like its Old Norse equivalent, *drekkulaun*, refer to a gift (in Scandinavia, of land from the king) made in return for hospitality, thus meaning 'reward for drink'.

[4] Cf. III Ethelred 3.

[5] Some concluding chapters follow, taken from a little treatise "Concerning the priesthood" contained in C.C.C.C., MS. 201. They are merely homiletic.

51. Concerning the betrothal of a woman

As family law and inheritance are subjects on which we are particularly badly informed, this short text, which survives in the *Textus Roffensis* and the C.C.C.C., MS. 383, and in Latin in *Quadripartitus*, is particularly welcome. The text bears no clear indication of date. Liebermann would place it 975–1030, with a preference for the latter part of this period. The stressing of the need that the woman herself is to accept the suitor suggests that it is not early. It is edited by Liebermann, I, pp. 442–444, and with English translation by Thorpe, I, pp. 254–257.

How a man shall betroth a maiden, and what agreement there ought to be.[1]

1. If a man wishes to betroth a maiden or a widow, and it so pleases her and her kinsmen, then it is right that the bridegroom first according to God's laws and proper secular custom should promise and pledge to those who are her advocates, that he desires her in such a way that he will maintain her according to God's law as a man should maintain his wife; and his friends are to stand surety for it.

2. Next, it must be known to whom belongs the remuneration for rearing her. The bridegroom is then to pledge this, and his friends are to stand surety for it.

3. Then afterwards the bridegroom is to announce what he grants her in return for her acceptance of his suit, and what he grants her if she should live longer than he.

4. If it is thus contracted, then it is right that she should be entitled to half the goods–and to all, if they have a child together–unless she marries again.

5. He is to strengthen what he promises with a pledge, and his friends are to stand surety for it.

6. If they then reach agreement about everything, then the kinsmen are to set about betrothing their kinswoman as wife and in lawful matrimony to him who has asked for her, and he who is leader of the betrothal is to receive the security.

7. If, however, one wishes to take her away from that district into that of another thegn, then it is to her interest that her friends have the assurance that no wrong will be done to her, and that if she commits an offence, they may be allowed to stand next in paying compensation, if she has not possessions with which she can pay.

8. At the marriage there should by rights be a priest, who shall unite them together with God's blessing in all prosperity.

9. It is also well to take care that one knows that they are not too closely related, lest one afterwards put asunder what was previously wrongly joined together.

52. A compilation on status (probably 1002–1023)

The texts I include under this heading are those called by Liebermann *Geþyncðo, Norðleoda laga, Mircna laga, Að* and *Hadbot*, and printed by him, I, pp. 456–469. Thorpe has the three first, in a different order, I, pp. 186–193.

The five texts occur in C.C.C.C., MS. 201, a manuscript with connexions with Archbishop Wulfstan of York (1002–1023), and Miss D. Bethurum has produced good reasons for assigning the collection to this prelate, who was deeply interested in this matter.[2] The last three are also in C.C.C.C., MS. 190, another manuscript to contain texts connected with Wulfstan. All five, but not as a group or in order, are in the *Textus Roffensis*, and the authors of both *Quadripartitus* and the *Instituta Cnuti* use them. Much of what is known of status in Anglo-Saxon times comes from these texts, which should not be regarded as official enactments but as a private compilation.

---

[1] This heading is only in C.C.C.C., MS. 383.

[2] "Six Anonymous Old English Codes", *Journ. Eng. and Germ. Phil.*, XLIX, pp. 449–463.

(A) CONCERNING WERGILDS AND DIGNITIES (Geþyncðo)

1. Once it used to be that people and rights[1] went by dignities, and councillors of the people were then entitled to honour, each according to his rank, whether noble or *ceorl*, retainer or lord.[2]

2. And if a *ceorl* prospered, that he possessed fully five hides of land of his own,[3] a bell and a castle-gate, a seat and special office in the king's hall, then was he henceforth entitled to the rights of a thegn.

3. And the thegn who prospered, that he served the king and rode in his household band[4] on his missions,[5] if he himself had a thegn who served him, possessing five hides on which he discharged the king's dues,[6] and who attended his lord in the king's hall, and had thrice gone on his errand to the king – then he[7] was afterwards allowed to represent his lord with his preliminary oath,[8] and legally obtain his [right to pursue a] charge, wherever he needed.

4. And he who had no such distinguished representative, swore in person to obtain his rights, or lost his case.

5.[9] And if a thegn prospered, that he became an earl, then was he afterwards entitled to an earl's rights.

6.[9] And if a trader prospered, that he crossed thrice the open sea at his own expense, he was then afterwards entitled to the rights of a thegn.

7. And if there were a scholar who prospered with his learning so that he took orders and served Christ, he should afterwards be entitled to so much more honour and protection as belonged by rights to that order, if he kept himself [chaste] as he should.[10]

8. And if anyone, anywhere, injured an ecclesiastic or a stranger by word or deed, then it was the concern of the bishop and the king, that they should atone for it as quickly as they could.

(B) THE LAW OF THE NORTH PEOPLE (Norðleoda laga)[11]

1. The payment for a king of the North people[12] is 30,000 *thrymsas*;[13] 15,000 *thrymsas* belong to the wergild, 15,000 to the kingship; the wergild belongs to the kinsmen and the royal-compensation to the people.

2. The wergild of the archbishop and the atheling is 15,000 *thrymsas*.

3. That of a bishop and an ealdorman 8,000 *thrymsas*.

---

[1] This code uses many alliterative and rhymed formulas, in which words may be used vaguely, or sometimes with an older sense than they have in separate use. The word used here is simply 'law'. It is used to cover all the complex of rights and obligations which varied according to the rank of the person concerned.

[2] In this pair of formulas, *ge eorl ge ceorl*, *ge þegen ge þeoden*, *eorl* retains its archaic meaning of 'noble', not its current sense of *ealdorman*, and 'thegn' retains the element of service rather than of high rank.

[3] The version in the *Textus Roffensis* adds here: "church and kitchen".   [4] The king's bodyguard.

[5] The word *radstefn* is unique. It probably refers to important errands undertaken by a mounted messenger.

[6] The Corpus MS. accidentally omits *utware*. This word means not merely military service, but all public charges.   [7] The intermediate thegn.

[8] The *Textus Roffensis* adds: "at various necessities". Cf. II Cnut 22.2.

[9] These chapters are only in the *Textus Roffensis*.

[10] The *Textus Roffensis* reads instead of this last part: "unless he should commit an offence, so that he could not practise that priestly office". But the original meant to allow full rights only to the celibate clergy.

[11] *Textus Roffensis* has instead: "Concerning Wergild."

[12] *Textus Roffensis* replaces the reference to the North with "by folk-law among the English".

[13] One *thryms* is equal to three pennies.

4. That of a *hold*[1] and a king's high-reeve 4,000 *thrymsas*.

5. That of a mass-thegn[2] and a secular thegn 2,000 *thrymsas*.

6. A *ceorl*'s wergild is 266 *thrymsas*, which is 200 shillings according to the law of the Mercians.

7. And if a Welshman prospers, that he has a hide of land and may produce the king's tribute, then his wergild is 120 shillings.[3]

7.1. And if he does not prosper beyond half a hide, then his wergild is to be 80 shillings.

8. And if he has no land and nevertheless is free, one is to pay for him with 70 shillings.

9. And if a *ceorl* prospers, that he has five hides of land on which he discharges the king's dues, and anyone kills him, he is to be paid for with 2,000 *thrymsas*.

10. And even if he prospers so that he possesses a helmet and a coat of mail and a gold-plated sword, if he has not the land, he is a *ceorl* all the same.

11. And if his son and his son's son prosper, so that they have so much land, then the offspring is of *gesith-born* class, at 2,000 [*thrymsas*].

12. And if they have it not, and cannot prosper sufficiently, one is to pay at the *ceorl*'s rate.

(c) CONCERNING THE LAW OF THE MERCIANS (*Mircna laga*)

1. In the law of the Mercians a *ceorl*'s wergild is 200 shillings.

1.1. A thegn's wergild is six times as much, namely 1200 shillings.

2. Then a king's simple wergild is the wergild of six thegns by the law of the Mercians, namely 30,000 *sceattas*,[4] which is 120 pounds in all.

3. So great is [the size of] the wergild in the common law according to the law of the Mercians;

3.1. and on account of the kingship there belongs a second equal sum as compensation in payment for a king.

4. The wergild belongs to the kinsmen and the royal-compensation to the people.

(D) CONCERNING THE MERCIAN OATH (*Að*)[5]

The oath of a man of a 1200 wergild is equivalent to the oath of six *ceorls*; for, if a man of a 1200 wergild is to be avenged, he is fully avenged on six *ceorls*, and his wergild is the wergild of six *ceorls*.

(E) CONCERNING THE OATH OF ECCLESIASTICS AND CONCERNING THE COMPENSATION FOR OFFENCES AGAINST [THOSE IN] HOLY ORDERS (*Að and Hadbot*)[6]

The oath of a mass-priest and a secular thegn is in the law of the English reckoned equally valuable, because of the seven orders of the Church which the priest, prospering through the grace of God, has obtained.[7]

---

[1] See p. 191, n. 1.   [2] i.e. a priest.   [3] *Textus Roffensis* '220'.   [4] To be precise, it should be 28,800.
[5] 'Law', not oath, in C.C.C.C., MS. 190; no rubric in *Textus Roffensis*.
[6] Liebermann takes the first chapter of this along with what precedes (D) and calls the two together 'Oath'. But the best manuscripts have here this new rubric, and go straight on to what Liebermann calls *Hadbot*; it is clear that they regarded this first chapter as connected with what follows and not with what preceded. I keep the MS. division. The *Textus Roffensis* puts this first paragraph before the text I have numbered D.   [7] The *Textus Roffensis* adds: "so that he may become worthy of a thegn's rights".

1. Seven-fold are the gifts of the Holy Spirit; and there are seven steps of the ecclesiastical degrees and holy orders, and seven times a day should the servants of God praise God in church and intercede zealously for all Christian people.

1.1. And to all friends of God it belongs very rightly that they love and honour God's church and protect and defend God's servants.

1.2. And he who injures them by word or deed is to atone for it eagerly with seven-fold compensation, in proportion to the deed,[1] if he wishes to deserve God's mercy.

1.3. For relics and holy orders and the consecrated houses of God must always be zealously honoured for the fear of God.

2. And in compensation for [an offence against a man in] orders, if loss of life occur, one must pay for the first degree with a pound, in addition to the legal wergild, and intercede zealously with ecclesiastical penance. . . .[2]

9. And in compensation for [an offence against a man in] orders, if there occur [only] a half breach,[3] one is to compensate eagerly in proportion to the deed.

9.1. And compensation for [offences against those in] orders [belongs] by rights a third to the bishop, the second part to the altar, the third to the community.

10. There must always by rights be sentence according to the deed and apportioning [of the penalty][4] according to the degree, in ecclesiastical and secular concerns.

11. And the secular councillors were wise who added to the ecclesiastical right laws these laws for the control of the people, and honoured relics and holy orders for the love of God, and greatly privileged God's houses and God's servants.

53. The law of the Northumbrian priests (probably 1020–1023)

I include this text because evidence relating to the north of England in the later Saxon period is scanty. It shows us that heathen practices had still to be reckoned with, and it reveals a three-fold division of society for certain purposes, giving us a unique term to describe the lowest free class, for it seems to talk indescriminately of a *ceorl*, a *tunesmann* 'villager', and a mysterious *færbena*. (See note on p. 437, below.) It reveals also the organization of the priests of York into a community with common obligations and a common chest, the existence of the office of archdeacon in the northern province, and the toleration of the marriage of the clergy in this area.

As Liebermann points out, the text falls into two parts which were probably originally distinct. Only chaps. 1–45 constitute a priests' law proper, and it may be that chaps. 19–24, which do not, like the others, begin "If a priest . . .", are a later accretion. The second part of the text, chaps. 46 to the end, concerns itself with the behaviour of the laity in religious concerns, not with that of priests. Liebermann dates this second portion between 1028 and about 1060 (the date of the manuscript, C.C.C.C., MS. 201), but his earlier limit depends on his dating of the laws of Cnut, which this portion seems to use. This prevents him from assigning the document as a whole to the period when it was most likely to have come into being, the episcopate of Archbishop Wulfstan of York. As I have stated above (p. 419), I believe that Cnut's laws had come into being much earlier than 1028, during Wulfstan's lifetime, and there is to my thinking nothing to prevent our assigning this code to his episcopate.

The reasons for so doing are as follows: the text survives only in a manuscript which contains many of his writings and some of his sources, and which, on that account, is commonly assigned to Worcester, though the claims of York should also be considered. After Wulfstan's time, the connexion between the two sees was broken, except for the years 1040–1041, when Bishop Lifing of Worcester had incurred the royal disfavour and his see was given to Archbishop Ælfric of York

---

[1] C.C.C.C., MS. 190, and the *Textus Roffensis* add: "and in proportion to the orders".
[2] Six very similar chapters follow in which the compensation is increased by a pound for each of the higher grades in turn.
[3] *i.e.* if no fatal injury is inflicted.   [4] C.C.C.C., MS. 190, has instead 'mercy'.

for a year, and again in 1060–1062, when Ealdred tried to retain the see of Worcester after his election to York, but was forced by the pope to relinquish it. Secondly, all the known sources used in either part of the work are those written by Wulfstan, except for III Ethelred, a code for part of the Danelaw with which any archbishop of York would have to be familiar. It is also worth noting that a special point is made that a priest must not celebrate Mass without wine. Now this is not specifically signalled out in the so-called *Canons of Edgar* which have been used for this section, nor in the original text of Ælfric's first pastoral letter for Wulfstan; but in the revision of this text in Wulfstan's style, almost certainly by him himself, a clause is added: "And one is never to celebrate Mass without wine." As this version of the letter occurs in the same manuscript as the Priests' Law, the clause in the latter could have been inserted by a later compiler; but surely it is more probable that it was a familiar abuse in this northern diocese in Wulfstan's time, and hence its addition to the letter, and its specific mention in the statutes drawn up for observance in his diocese. The connexion with the so-called *Canons of Edgar*, which Jost has shown to be a work of Wulfstan's, proves that the text is not earlier than his episcopate, and I see no necessity to put it later.

The code is edited by Liebermann, I, pp. 380–385; and with English translation by Thorpe, II, pp. 290–303.

1. If anyone offer wrong to any priest, all his colleagues are to be zealous about obtaining the compensation with the help of the bishop, and in every matter of law they are to be, just as it is written, "as if one heart and one soul".[1]

2. And by virtue of God's prohibition we forbid that any priest shall either buy or receive another's[2] church, unless anyone becomes guilty of a capital crime so that he is henceforth unworthy to minister at the altar.

2.1. And if any priest does so in any other circumstance, he is to forfeit his dignity and the friendship of his colleagues, and he is not to celebrate Mass anywhere until he who rightly owns the church is in possession of it.

2.2. And he who did that wrong is to pay 20 ores to the bishop, 12 ores to the priest whom he ousted from his church, 12 ores to all the colleagues, and he is also to forfeit the money if he gave any wrongly for the church of another priest.

2.3. And each priest is to provide himself with 12 sureties,[3] that he will rightly observe the priests' law.

3. And if any priest commits an offence, and he celebrates Mass in spite of the bishop's prohibition, he is to pay 20 ores for disregard of the prohibition, and in addition make amends for the offence which he previously committed.

4. If a priest neglects the bishop's own summons, he is to pay 20 ores.

5. If a priest refers a case to a layman which he ought to refer to an ecclesiastic, he is to pay 20 ores.

6. If a priest neglects the archdeacon's summons, he is to pay 12 ores.

7. If a priest commits an offence and he celebrates Mass in spite of the archdeacon's prohibition, he is to pay 12 ores.

8. If a priest refuses anyone baptism or confession, he is to pay 12 ores compensation for it, and above all to make zealous supplication to God.

9. If a priest does not fetch the chrism at the proper time, he is to pay 12 ores.

10. We instruct that every child is to be baptized within nine days, under penalty of 6 ores.

---

[1] Acts iv. 32. It is quoted in Latin. Wulfstan quotes this text in his *Polity* (Thorpe, II, p. 316).

[2] Emending to *oðres*.

[3] *festermen*. A list of 72 *festermen* for a certain Ælfric is entered on an end-leaf of the York Gospels. They are printed by Jón Stefansson in *Saga-Book of the Viking Club*, IV, pp. 296–310, by W. H. Stevenson in *Eng. Hist. Rev.*, XXVII, pp. 11–13, and by W. Farrer in *Yorkshire Charters*, I, No. 9.

10.1. And if a child dies heathen within nine days, through carelessness, amends are to be made to God, without a secular fine; and if it occur after nine days, amends are to be made to God, and 12 ores to be paid for the [lack of] care, that it remained heathen so long.

11. If a priest misdirect the people regarding a festival or a fast, he is to make amends to God and pay 12 ores.

12. If a priest wrongly obtain ordination outside the diocese, he is to pay 12 ores, and a deacon 6 ores; and each is to lose his orders unless the bishop of the diocese acknowledges the ordination.

13. If a priest celebrates Mass in an unconsecrated building, he is to pay 12 ores.

14. If a priest celebrates Mass without a consecrated altar, he is to pay 12 ores.

15. If a priest consecrates the host in a wooden chalice, 12 ores.

16. If a priest celebrates Mass without wine, he is to pay 12 ores.

17. If a priest neglects the host, he is to pay 12 ores.

18. If a priest celebrates Mass more often than three times in one day, he is to pay 12 ores.

19. If anyone violates sanctuary, he is to pay compensation in proportion to the status of the church and according to what its right of protection is.

20. If anyone traffics with a church, he is to pay compensation with *lahslit*.[1]

21. If anyone brings a church under subjection, he is to pay compensation with *lahslit*.

22. If anyone wrongfully drives a priest from his church, he is to pay compensation with *lahslit*.

23. If anyone wounds a priest, he is to pay compensation for the wounds and to pay 12 ores to the bishop[2] as compensation for [insult to] the altar on account of his orders; and for a deacon six ores as compensation for [insult to] the altar.

24. If anyone slays a priest, he is to pay compensation for him with the full wergild, and 24 ores to the bishop as compensation for [insult to] the altar; for a deacon 12 ores as compensation for [insult to] the altar.

25. If a priest treats disrespectfully the church from which all his dignity must spring, he is to compensate for it.

26. If a priest puts unsuitable things in the church, he is to compensate for it.

27. If a priest removes church-goods, he is to compensate for it.

28. If a priest of his own free will deserts the church to which he was ordained, he is to compensate for it.

29. If a priest scorns or insults another by word or deed, he is to compensate for it.

30. If a priest fights another, he is to pay compensation to him and to the bishop.

31. If a priest gives assistance to another in wrong-doing, he is to compensate for it.

32. If a priest refuses lawful help to another, he is to compensate for it.

---

[1] See p. 408, n. 6.

[2] Accepting Liebermann's emendation. The scribe has written the abbreviation for 'that' instead of the very similar one for 'bishop'.

33. If a priest leaves another unwarned of what he knows will harm him, he is to compensate for it.

34. If a priest neglects the shaving of beard or hair, he is to compensate for it.

35. If a priest leaves a woman[1] and takes another, let him be anathema![2]

36. If a priest does not ring the hours or sing the hours at the appointed time, he is to compensate for it.

37. If a priest comes with weapons into the church, he is to compensate for it.

38. If a priest performs in a wrong order the annual services of the church, by day or night, he is to compensate for it.

39. If a priest conducts the ordeal wrongly, he is to compensate for it.

40. If a priest covers up fraud,[3] he is to compensate for it.

41. If a priest practises drunkenness or becomes a gleeman or a tavern-minstrel,[4] he is to compensate for it.

42. If a priest conceals what wrong is rife among men in his parish, he is to compensate for it.

43. If a priest leaves the yearly dues undemanded, he is to compensate for it.

44. If a priest stays away from a synod, he is to compensate for it.

45. If a priest will not submit to what is right, but resists the bishop's ordinance, he is to compensate for it or to be cut off from the community of those in holy orders, and to forfeit both fellowship and every privilege, unless he submits and atones for it deeply.

46. If anyone violates God's law or the secular law, he is to compensate for it eagerly.

47.[5] We must all love and honour one God and zealously hold one Christian faith and entirely cast out every heathen practice.

48.[6] If, then, any man is discovered who henceforth carries on any heathen practice, either by sacrifice or divination, or practises witchcraft by any means, or worship of idols, he is to pay, if he is a king's thegn, 10 half-marks, half to Christ, half to the king.

49. If it is otherwise a landowner, he is to pay six half-marks, half to Christ and half to the lord of the estate.

50. If it is a *færbena*,[7] he is to pay 12 ores.

51. If a king's thegn denies it, then 12 [thegns] are to be nominated for him, and

---

[1] Though marriage of the clergy had to be tolerated, the author cannot bring himself to use a word meaning legal wife.   [2] *Anathema sit!*

[3] I do not, with Liebermann, consider the reading *searwaδ bewinde* corrupt, but take *searwaδ* as an abstract noun. Bosworth-Toller reads *searwaδ be winde*, taking *searwaδ* as a verb, rendering "uses deceit in respect to the wrapping up of the hand". But there is no other case of *wind* in this sense.

[4] Literally, 'an ale-minstrel', one who performs where men are drinking.

[5] Cf. the prologue to the earliest version of Cnut's laws (No. 47).   [6] Cf. II Cnut 5.1.

[7] From the context, it is clear that this word denotes a freeman who is not a landowner; etymologically it means a 'journey-petitioner', presumably as in Bosworth-Toller, "one that has to ask leave to go from his lord", or, in the terminology of Domesday Book, one who "could not recede". The distinction is then being drawn between men with land at their own disposal and those who are merely tenants on the land of another. But Liebermann, III, p. 224, seems to take it in the opposite sense, "one who claims the right to go", in which case the highest type of *ceorl* is meant. This seems to me a forcing of the sense of *bena*, 'a suppliant'. This word is confined to this code, except for a single occurrence in the Erfurt Glossary, where it is used in a different sense, as a 'passenger', 'one that requests a passage'.

he is to take 12 of his kinsmen and 12 compurgators selected for him [?];[1] and if his [oath] fails, he is then to pay *lahslit*: 10 half-marks.

52. If a landowner denies it, then as many selected compurgators, his equals, are to be nominated for him as for a king's thegn; if that fails, he is to pay *lahslit*: 6 half-marks.

53. If a man of the *ceorl* class denies it, then as many selected compurgators of his equals are to be nominated for him as for the others; if that fails, he is then to pay *lahslit*: 12 ores.

54. If there is on anyone's land a sanctuary round a stone or a tree or a well or any such nonsense, he who made it is then to pay *lahslit*, half to Christ and half to the lord of the estate.

54.1. And if the lord of the estate will not help in the punishment, then Christ and the king are to have the compensation.

55. Sunday market we forbid everywhere, and every public assembly and all work and all carrying [of goods], whether by wagon or by horse or on one's back.

56. He who does any of these things is to pay the penalty: a freeman 12 ores, a slave with a flogging; except for travellers, who are permitted to carry sustenance for their needs; and in case of hostility one may travel because of necessity between York and a distance of six miles on the eve of festivals.

57. He who violates a festival or a legal fast is to pay 12 ores fine.

57.1. And it is our will that every Rome-penny is to be paid to the bishop's see by St. Peter's day.

57.2. And it is our will that two trusty thegns and one priest be nominated in each wapentake, to collect it and hand it over, as they dare to swear to it.

58. If a king's thegn or any lord of an estate withholds it, he is to pay 10 half-marks, half to Christ and half to the king.

59. If any villager conceals or withholds any penny, the lord of the estate is to pay the penny and take an ox from the man; and if the lord of the estate neglects this, then Christ and the king are to succeed to the full compensation: 12 ores.

60. If anyone withholds tithes and he is a king's thegn, he is to pay 10 half-marks; a landowner [is to pay] six half-marks, a *ceorl* 12 ores.

61. And by virtue of God's prohibition we forbid that any man should have more wives than one; and she is to be legally betrothed and wedded;

61.1. and that any man should marry a nearly related person, [any nearer] than outside the fourth degree. And no man is to marry anyone spiritually related to him.[2]

61.2. And if anyone does so, may he not have God's mercy, unless he desists and atones as the bishop directs.

62. If, however, he dies in that sin, he is to forfeit Christian burial and God's mercy.

63. If anyone lies with a nun, both are to be liable to pay their wergild, both he and she.

---

[1] The meaning of the term *wallerwente* (simply *wente* in later chapters) is reasonably clear, though its form has not been fully explained. Liebermann suggests that it is a corruption of Old Norse *valinvitni* 'chosen (unrelated) witness'.

[2] *e.g.* a co-sponsor, a god-daughter, or a godmother of his child.

63.1. And if they die in that [sin] without desisting from it, they are to forfeit Christian burial and God's mercy.

64. If anyone abandons a living legal wife, and wrongly takes to wife another woman, may he not have God's mercy, unless he atones for it.

65. But each is to keep rightly his legal wife as long as she lives; unless it comes about that they both choose to separate with the bishop's advice and wish thenceforth to preserve chastity.

66. If anyone henceforth violates just laws, he is to compensate for it eagerly.

67. We must all love and honour one God and zealously hold one Christian faith and entirely cast out every heathen practice.

67.1.[1] And it is our will, that the purchase of land and the purchase of legal rights and agreements and trustworthy witness, and just judgment and final settlement[2] and first statement of a case [?][3] are to remain valid, and *drincelean*[4] and the lord's legal gift, and above all ever one Christianity and one royal authority in the nation.

Epilogue. Blessed be the name of the Lord from now and into eternity.[5]

---

[1] This is a combination of III Ethelred 3 and II Cnut 81.   [2] This term, *fulloc*, occurs here only.
[3] Another unique word, *frumtalu*. It may mean that the accuser is not allowed to change his charge later.
[4] On this, see p. 430, n. 3.   [5] This is in Latin.

B. THE CHARTERS

54. Grant by Frithuwold, sub-king of Surrey, to Chertsey (672–674)

This is one of the earliest of authentic charters. Though it is preserved only in a late Chertsey cartulary (Brit. Mus. Cott. Vitell. A. xiii), its formulae agree with those of early documents, and there seems no reason to reject it. In the cartulary it is followed by lengthy boundaries in the vernacular, certainly of much later date, which I have not included. It is of historical interest in showing the relationship of Surrey to Mercia in early times. It is No. 987 in Kemble, No. 34 in Birch.

✠ In the name of the Lord Saviour Jesus Christ.

I, Frithuwold, concede this donation of my right for the liberty of every single thing.

How often so ever we devote any thing to the members of Christ as an act of piety, we trust to benefit our soul, because we render to him his own property, and do not bestow ours.

Wherefore I, Frithuwold, of the province of the men of Surrey, sub-king of Wulfhere, king of the Mercians, of my own free will, being in sound mind and perfect understanding, from this present day grant, concede, transfer and assign from my rightful possession into yours, land for increasing the monastery which was first constructed under King Egbert, 200 hides[1] for strengthening the same monastery, which is called Chertsey, and five hides in the place which is called Thorpe. I not only give the land, but confirm and deliver myself and my only son in obedience to Abbot Eorcenwold. And the land is, taken together, 300 hides, and moreover by the river which is called the Thames, the whole along the bank of the river as far as the boundary which is called the ancient ditch, that is *Fullingadic*; again, in another part of the bank of the same river as far as the boundary of the next province, which is called Sonning.[2] Of the same land, however, a separate part, of 10 hides, is by the port of London, where ships come to land, on the same river on the southern side by the public way. There are, however, diverse names for the above-mentioned land, namely Chertsey, Thorpe, Egham, Chobham, *Getinges*,[3] Molesey, Woodham and *Hunewaldesham*,[4] as far as the above-mentioned boundary. I grant it to you, Eorcenwold, and confirm it for the foundation of a monastery, that both you and your successors may be bound to intercede for the relief of my soul–along with fields, woods, meadows, pastures, and rivers and all other things duly belonging to the monastery of St. Peter, Prince of the Apostles, at Chertsey. Therefore all things round about, belonging to the aforesaid monastery, just as they have been granted, conceded and confirmed by me, you are to hold and possess, and both you and your successors are to have free license to do whatever you wish with the same lands. Never, at any time, shall this charter of my donation be contravened by me or my heir. If anyone shall try to contravene this my donation and confirmation, may he be cut off from all Christian society and deprived of participation in the celestial kingdom; and in order that this

---

[1] The terms which I have translated hide in this charter are *manens* and *mansa*.
[2] On the old province of Sonning, see F. M. Stenton, *Anglo-Saxon England*, pp. 291, 298.
[3] The name survives in Eaton Farm, Cobham. See *Place-Names of Surrey*, p. 88.
[4] This name survived, as Hundulsam, into the sixteenth century. It was in Weybridge. See *ibid.*, p. 98.

charter of my donation and confirmation may be firm, stable and unshaken, I have asked witnesses to subscribe whose names are added below.

> And I, Frithuwold, who am the donor, together with Abbot Eorcenwold, have formed the sign of the Holy Cross ✠ on account of my ignorance of letters.
> Sign of the hand of Frithuric, witness. ✠
> Sign of the hand of Ebbe, witness. ✠
> Sign of the hand of Ecgwold, witness ✠
> Sign of the hand of Baduwold, witness. ✠
> Sign of the hand of Ceadda, witness. ✠
> Likewise Bishop Hunfrith,[1] asked by Abbot Eorcenwold, has subscribed with his own hand. ✠
> And these are the sub-kings who all have subscribed under their sign.
> Sign of the hand of Frithuwold, witness. ✠
> Sign of the hand of Osric, witness. ✠
> Sign of the hand of Wigheard, witness. ✠
> Sign of the hand of Æthelwold, witness. ✠
>
> And in order that this donation may be secure and the confirmation stable, this charter is confirmed by Wulfhere, king of the Mercians, for he both placed his hand on the altar in the residence which is called Thame and subscribed with the sign of the Holy Cross with his own hand. ✠

55. Grant by Cenred to Abbot Bectun of land on the River Fontmell, Dorset (670–676), with confirmation by Cyneheard, bishop of Winchester, and Cynewulf, king of Wessex (759)

An early West Saxon charter, with a later confirmation which illustrates the difficulty that arose when several estates had been granted by one donation charter and only one was to be alienated. In this instance, the original grant seems to have been copied at the time of the later transaction, with the name of a single estate where originally there had been more. This would explain the unexpected plural "the above-mentioned lands". At the time of this copying, it would be easy for the words "of blessed memory" to be added after Leuthere's name. Their presence need not be accounted a suspicious feature, therefore. The grant ends, before its signatories, with a Frankish formula, and it copies Frankish practice in naming the scribe; but as Leuthere was a Frank, these characteristics do not invalidate the charter. It has correspondences with early authentic texts, and motive for forgery seems lacking.

The charter and its confirmation survive only in the fourteenth-century cartulary of Shaftesbury Abbey (Brit. Mus. Harley MS. 61), into whose possession the land must have come.

The donor is very probably King Ine's father, whom he associates with him in the prologue to his legislation. The cartulary, late though it is, has preserved an early spelling of his name, as Coinred. Nothing is known about the donee, Abbot Bectun, nor am I sure what seventh-century name this represents. Of the signatories, Leuthere was bishop of Wessex from 670 to 676, Cyneberht is probably the abbot of Redbridge, Hants, mentioned by Bede in connexion with the conquest of the Isle of Wight by Ceadwalla in 686 (see No. 151, p. 657). Abbot Hædde may be Leuthere's successor in the see of Winchester, and Wynberht was afterwards abbot of Nursling (see No. 158). He is named as the scribe of other charters, Birch, No. 100, from Abingdon, and Nos. 37, 103 from Malmesbury. All are suspicious documents, and as two are in William of Malmesbury's *De Gestis Pontificium* they may have been known to the Abingdon writer. Yet the fabricators may well have had before them genuine material when they allow Wynberht to be named as scribe in charters drawn up in Leuthere's episcopate.

On Wintra, abbot of Tisbury, Hants, see No. 158.

---

[1] Probably an error for Wynfrith of Lichfield.

Nothing is known of Bectun's successor Catwali, whose name suggests British origin, nor of the latter's successor Tidbald, nor of the Ecgwold who was abbot of Tisbury at the date of the confirmation, unless he should be the Abbot Ecga who witnesses a charter of Æthelbald of Mercia along with other West Saxon signatories in 757 (Birch, No. 181).

The proem of the original grant is found elsewhere, e.g. in a St. Paul's charter of 706–709, and in a Westminster charter about Battersea (dated 693), spurious as it stands, but with early Barking material behind it. It continued to be used at a later date, e.g. in Brit. Mus. Stowe Charter XIII, a charter of Archbishop Wulfred of 824 (Birch, No. 381).

This document is No. 104 in Kemble, and is divided as Nos. 107 and 186 in Birch.

In the name of our Lord Jesus Christ the Saviour. Those things which are profitably defined according to ecclesiastical teaching and synodal decrees, although the word alone suffices, ought yet to be committed to most trustworthy writings and documents, to avoid uncertainty in future time.

Wherefore I, Cenred, for the relief of my soul and the remission of my sins, have decided to grant a certain small portion of land to the venerable man, Abbot Bectun, i.e. 30 hides[1] north of the stream Fontmell by name; it has on the south the land of Bishop Leuthere of blessed memory. Now I have placed for more complete security sods of the above-mentioned lands on the gospels, so that from this day he may have in all things free and secure power of holding, having, possessing.

If, indeed, any one of the bishops or kings shall try to contravene this defining charter by his own temerity, or rather by sacrilegious fury, may he especially incur the wrath of God, and be cut off from the thresholds of Holy Church, and not be able to make good his claim to this which he demands.

> I, Cenred, who have signed this charter of my donation in all things in my own hand, and have given it to trustworthy witnesses for corroboration. ✠
>
> I, Leuthere, bishop,[2] although unworthy, have subscribed this charter of donation. ✠
>
> I, Cyneberht, abbot, have subscribed. ✠
>
> I, Hædde, abbot, have subscribed. ✠
>
> I, Wynberht, priest, who at the request of the above-mentioned abbot, have written and subscribed this charter. ✠ etc.

✠ I, Cyneheard, an unworthy bishop, have impressed this sign for the confirming and strengthening of this charter which I declare to have been drawn up in this way: the successor of the afore-named Abbot Bectun, Catwali by name, gave the above-designated land of 30 hides to Abbot Wintra for his money, and wrote another deed of this donation and the above-written possession. He withheld, however, both the charter of the original donation and the subscriptions of kings, bishops, abbots and leading men, because, since this portion of land had been enrolled among the other testimonies of their lands, it could not easily be detached, nor can it yet. And therefore, after the original witnesses were dead, a long strife arose between the communities of the two monasteries and lasts until now. For, from the time when it was given to Wintra by the aforesaid abbot, his successors held this land, and the successors of the other community had the original deed which is strengthened by the hands of the aforesaid witnesses.

---

[1] manentes.   [2] Of Winchester.

Therefore I now, and our king, and the rest whose witness and subscription is noted below, have made a peaceful reconciliation between them, partly through the giving of money, partly through the performance of an oath, to the extent that hereafter the successors of Abbot Wintra, *i.e.* Ecgwold and his community which is in the monastery which is called Tisbury, are to have and possess for ever, with the permission of the other community over which Abbot Tidbald presides, the land about which there long was a dispute; and I have transcribed the present deed and made excerpts from that originally given to Abbot Bectun, with the consent namely of Abbot Tidbald and his community; and I have given this writing to Abbot Ecgwold, with the witnesses named below consenting and confirming it, but rejecting other writings which have been drawn up about this land.

And these things were done 759 years from the incarnation of our Lord, the twelfth indiction.

✠ of Cynewulf, the king.
✠ of Herewold the bishop.[1]
✠ of Scilling the priest.[2]
✠ of Cerdic the priest,[2] etc.

56. Grant by Hlothhere, king of Kent, to Abbot Brihtwold, of land in Thanet (679)

This is the earliest charter of which the original (Brit. Mus. Cott. Augustus, II. 2) is preserved. It is written in uncials. There is a facsimile in *Brit. Mus. Facs.*, I, plate I. It is No. 16 in Kemble, No. 45 in Birch, and in Earle, p. 8.

✠ In the name of our Lord and Saviour Jesus Christ. I, Hlothhere, king of the people of Kent, grant for the relief of my soul land in Thanet which is called *Westan ae*[3] to you, Brihtwold[4] and to your monastery, with everything belonging to it, fields, pastures, marshes, small woods, fens, fisheries, with everything, as has been said, belonging to that same land. As it has been owned hitherto, by the well-known boundaries indicated by me and my reeves, we confer it in the same way to you and your monastery. May you hold and possess it, and your successors maintain it for ever. May it not be contradicted by anyone. With the consent of Archbishop Theodore and Eadric, my brother's son, and also of all the leading men, as it has been granted to you, hold it thus, you and your successors. May whoever attempts to contravene this donation be cut off from all Christendom, and debarred from the body and blood of our Lord Jesus Christ, this charter of donation remaining nevertheless in its firmness. And I have both formed the sign of the Cross for its confirmation with my own hand and asked witnesses to subscribe.

Done in the city of Reculver, in the month of May, the seventh indiction.

On the same afore-mentioned day I added another estate in Sturry, by well-known boundaries indicated by me and my reeves, with fields and woods and meadows. Just as we stated before about the above-mentioned land, so this is to be granted by me

---

[1] Of Sherborne.
[2] This is an error. These men were lay members of the king's household, and it is probable that the compiler of the cartulary has wrongly expanded to *presbiter* an abbreviation which meant *prefectus*.
[3] This name, which means 'west of the river', cannot be identified.
[4] Abbot of Reculver, who became archbishop of Canterbury in 692.

in the same way, with everything belonging to it. May it be in the power of the abbot for ever; granted by me, may it be contradicted—which God forbid—by no one, neither by me nor by my kindred nor by others. If anyone does otherwise, let him know that he is condemned by God, and shall render account to God in his soul on the Day of Judgment.

✠ Sign of the hand of King Hlothhere, the donor.
✠ Sign of the hand of Gumberht.
✠ Sign of the hand of Gefred.
✠ Sign of the hand of Osfrith.
✠ Sign of the hand of Irmenred.
✠ Sign of the hand of Æthelmær.
✠ Sign of the hand of Hagan.
✠ Sign of the hand of Ealdred.
✠ Sign of the hand of Ealdhod.
✠ Sign of the hand of Guthheard.
✠ Sign of the hand of Beornheard.
✠ Sign of the hand of Welhisc.

57. Grant by Æthelmod to Abbess Beorngyth of land by the River Cherwell (681)

This charter survives only in a cartulary of the abbey of Bath (C.C.C.C., MS. 111), but its authenticity is indicated by its sharing formulae of early Kentish originals; nor does there seem any motive for its fabrication. It is one of the very earliest charters referring to Mercia. The same abbess is the recipient of a grant of land at *Slæpi* (possibly Islip) by Wulfhere, king of the Mercians, in the fourteenth year of his reign, *i.e.* 670–671 (Birch, No. 28), which is preserved in the same manuscript, and which has a list of witnesses presumably added from this later charter, for they fit 681 but not 670–671. Both charters are important, for information about this part of the country in early days is very scanty. This document is No. 21 in Kemble, No. 57 in Birch.

In the name of the Lord God our Saviour Jesus Christ.

I, Æthelmod, with the consent of King Ethelred, grant for the relief of my soul to you, Beorngyth, venerable abbess, and to Folcburh, and through you to your monastery, 20 hides[1] by the river which is called Cherwell, that you may hold it by right and your authority, as much as you may claim for your monastery. If indeed anyone shall try to contravene this charter of my donation, let him know that he shall render account on the Day of Judgment. And in order that this my donation may continue in its firmness, I have made below with my own hand the sign of the Holy Cross, and I have asked the most holy Archbishop Theodore to subscribe, and King Ethelred to subscribe as well.

Done in the month of October, the ninth indiction.

Sign of the Holy Cross of Æthelmod. ✠
Ethelred, king by the grace of God, have subscribed.[2] ✠
Theodore, by the grace of God archbishop, have subscribed. ✠
Putta, by the grace of God bishop,[3] have subscribed. ✠
Bosel, by the grace of God bishop,[4] have subscribed. ✠

[1] *manentes.*
[2] Taking *ascriptio* as error for *ascripsi* or *subscripsi.*
[3] Of Hereford.
[4] Of Worcester.

58. Grant by Ceadwalla, king of Wessex, of land at Farnham, Surrey, for a monastery (685–687)

A charter of particular interest in showing a West Saxon king with authority in Surrey, whereas No. 54 above showed that this area was earlier under Mercian control, and earlier still, Kentish. We see also that part of the land which he gives for religious purposes had been a heathen sanctuary. The date 688 cannot be right, for Wilfrid had left for the North by 687, at latest.

The charter is preserved only in the twelfth-century cartulary of Winchester Cathedral (Brit. Mus. Addit., MS. 15350), into whose possession the estate of Farnham later came; but it contains the formulae of early charters, sharing, among other things, the same proem.as the Surrey charter from the Chertsey cartulary (No. 54). The scribe, who misreads a minuscule open *a* as *u*, must have had an eighth- or early ninth-century exemplar before him. The incarnation date was probably a later addition. The charter is No. 994 in Kemble, No. 72 in Birch.

✠ In the name of our Lord Jesus Christ the Saviour.

How often so ever we devote anything to the members of Christ as an act of piety, we trust to benefit our soul, because we render to him his own property, and do not bestow ours.

Wherefore I, Ceadwalla, by the dispensation of the Lord, king of the Saxons, for the relief of my soul, confer on you, *i.e.* Cedde, Cisi and Criswa, into your possession for the construction of a monastery the land whose name is Farnham, of 60 hides,[1] of which 10 are in Binton, 2 in Churt, and the rest are assigned to their own places and names, that is *Cusanweoh*;[2] with everything belonging to them, fields, woods, meadows, pastures, fisheries, rivers, springs. You are to have from me free permission to give and exchange and it is to be placed under your authority. Never, at any time, shall I and my heirs try to contravene this charter of donation.

And if anyone shall presume with proud incursion to infringe or diminish through tyranny this donation which I have made, may he be cut off from all Christian society; [this donation] remaining nevertheless in its firmness.

Done in the place whose name is *Besingahearh*, in the year of our Lord Jesus Christ's incarnation 688, first indiction.

Sign of the hand of Ceadwalla king and donor.

I, Wilfrid, bishop,[3] have subscribed this donation.
I, Eorcenwold, bishop,[4] have subscribed this same donation.
I, Hædde, bishop,[5] have subscribed the donation made by the king.
I, Aldhelm, unworthy abbot,[6] have subscribed this cyrograph.

I, Hagona, abbot.	Sign of the hand of Headda.
I, Eadberht, abbot.	Sign of the hand of Eadberht.
I, Wadda, priest.	Sign of the hand of Coen.
I, Guda, priest.	Sign of the hand of Rewe [?].
I, Bada, priest.	Sign of the hand of Theoda.
I, Bicca, priest.	Sign of the hand of Oswine.
I, Welisc, priest.	Sign of the hand of Snocca.
Sign of the hand of Wadda.	Sign of the hand of Mocca.

[1] *cassati.*
[2] Neither this name, nor *Besingahearh* below, can be identified. Both are of heathen origin, meaning 'the sanctuary of Cusa' and 'the sanctuary of the Besings' respectively.
[3] St. Wilfrid, while in exile from Northumbria. See p. 679, n. 4.
[4] Of London.   [5] Of Winchester.   [6] Of Malmesbury.

59. Grant by Nothhelm, king of the South Saxons, to his sister Nothgyth, of land at Lidsey and other places to found a monastery (688–705, perhaps 692)

We should know little of the kings of Sussex but for charter evidence. This early charter is preserved only in the fourteenth-century Register B. xviii of the Dean and Chapter of Chichester. The date, 692, is probably a later addition. So also may be the title of bishop given to Eadberht, for according to Bede the see of Sussex was not created until after Aldhelm, who here signs as abbot, became bishop of Sherborne in 705. Moreover, Cenred, father of King Ine of Wessex, is not given the title of king anywhere else. But even if the list of witnesses has to this extent been altered, there is no good reason to reject the document as a whole. It is No. 995 in Kemble, and No. 78 in Birch.

✠ In the name of our Lord Jesus Christ the Saviour.

I, Nothhelm, king of the South Saxons, for the relief of my soul, knowing that whatever I devote from my own possessions to the members of Christ will benefit me in the future, will gladly give to you, my sister Nothgyth, some portion of land for the founding of a monastery on it and the building of a church which may be devoted to the divine praises and honouring of the saints; namely 38 hides[1] in the places which are named: in Lidsey and Aldingbourne 12, in *Genstedesgate*[2] 10, in Mundham 11, on the east bank 2, on the west 3; that you may hold and possess it, with all things belonging to it, fields, woods, meadows, pastures.

If anyone dare to diminish this donation assigned to you, in anything great or small, let him know that he will incur the penalty of his presumption in the stern judgment of Almighty God.

This charter was written in the year of Christ's incarnation, 692.

✠   I, Nunna, king of the South Saxons, have consented and subscribed.
✠   I, Watt, king, have consented and subscribed.
✠   I, Cenred, king of the West Saxons, have consented and subscribed.
✠   I, Ine, have consented and subscribed with my own hand.
✠   I, Eadberht, bishop,[3] have consented and subscribed.
✠   I, Aldhelm, abbot, have subscribed.
✠   I, Hagona, abbot, have subscribed.

60. Grant by Œthelræd to the Abbess Æthelburh, of land at "Ricingaham", etc. (685–694, probably 690–693)

This is the earliest extant East Saxon charter (Brit. Mus. Cott. Augustus, II. 29), and is probably for Barking Abbey, though this is not mentioned by name in the text. A later, but still pre-Conquest endorsement, calls it "the title-deed for Barking", and Æthelburh, abbess of *Beddanham*, can hardly be other than the saint of that name, sister of Eorcenwold, abbot of Chertsey and bishop of London. This Æthelburh was the foundress of Barking Abbey at about this time, and the only identifiable estate mentioned in this charter is Dagenham, the next parish to Barking, on the east. The name Barking is one of those plural names in *ing* which often designate a region, rather than a single settlement, and it seems to me likely that it was this very substantial grant that may have caused the abbey of *Beddanham* henceforth to be known as Barking, and have brought about the subsequent loss of the name *Beddanham*.[4] It is unfortunate that the only one of the boundaries of the present grant which can certainly be identified is the Thames; for, though *The Place-Names of Essex* identifies the *Writolaburna* with the Wid, this is surely too far away to the north, to form the

---

[1] *cassati.*

[2] *The Place-Names of Sussex*, I, p. 64, suggests that this place is now represented by Westergate, in Aldingbourne.   [3] Of Selsey.

[4] Bede, it is true, says that Eorcenwold founded Barking for his sister before he became bishop in 675, but it does not follow that it bore this name from the first.

eastern boundary of an estate whose southern boundary is the Thames. One would have expected it to be about where the Bean is, and it is noteworthy that the old name of this river was *Mar-* or *Marke-dic, i.e.* 'boundary ditch'. [1]

That the Æthelburh concerned is St. Æthelburh is further supported by the interesting fact that the charter has close resemblances in its phraseology to the charter granted to Chertsey in the time of her brother, Eorcenwold (No. 54).

The charter used to be considered an original, but is now generally believed to be about a hundred years later. It is in formal, rather stiff uncials, and the production of a copy of this kind at a later date is easier to understand if, as I suspect, it represents the first substantial grant to the house, which turned it from an obscure community to the important abbey it became.

Florence of Worcester says that St. Æthelburh died on 11 October 664, but, as Plummer observes, there is no certainty about the year, which is based on the insecure assumption that she died in the plague of 664. Her successor, Hildelith, to whom Aldhelm dedicated his *De Virginitate*, was alive in 709. If the present charter is, as I believe, issued to St. Æthelburh, Florence's date is a long way out, for Eorcenwold, who witnesses as bishop, did not become one until 675, while Hædde became bishop of Winchester in 676. If Wilfrid's signature belongs to the time when he was administering the see of Leicester, the charter cannot be before 691, and a late date in Sebbi's reign is suggested by his witnessing along with his two sons; he first appears as joint king with an older kinsman, in 664, and reigned 30 years, so that 694 is the latest date for his death. Bishop Eorcenwold predeceased him. An Abbot Hagona witnesses in 686–687 and 692, but it is not certain that he is the priest named in this document.

I am not certain that this evidence allows as precise a dating of this charter as is commonly given, 692–693. Wilfrid was in the south of England in earlier periods of his stormy career, and, as the West Saxon bishop of Winchester witnesses the deed, there is nothing to prevent our assuming that Wilfrid could have done so in 685–687, when staying under the protection of King Ceadwalla of Wessex. A date 690–692 would explain the absence of any archiepiscopal signature, for Theodore died in 690, and there was a gap before Brihtwold succeeded, but then other early documents survive without the archbishop's signature which were certainly not issued *sede vacante.* The outside limits, therefore, are 685–694, probably towards the end of that period.

There survives also a charter (Birch, No. 87), dated 695,[2] of doubtful authenticity, which purports to be from Eorcenwold to Barking. The fabricator clearly had access to early material, including the present deed, though he strangely says that Œthelræd's grant was of 75 hides at the places named, and turns the grant of 40 hides into a donation by King *Swidfrid* of land called Barking and Beddanham. He attributes another donation to Œthelræd, of 10 hides at *Celta,* and speaks of donations at other places by the kings Wulfhere and Ethelred of Mercia, and Ceadwalla of Wessex. From the latter king, this charter says, the house obtained Battersea, and that it did receive this estate about this time is suggested by the fact that the spurious eleventh-century Westminster charter claiming that this was granted to them in 693 is witnessed by several of the signatories of Œthelræd's grant to Æthelburh.

There is a facsimile of Œthelræd's grant in *Brit. Mus. Facs.,* I, pl. 2. It is No. 35 in Kemble, No. 81 in Birch, and is in Earle, p. 13.

✠ In the name of our Lord Jesus Christ the Saviour.

As often as we seem to offer anything to your holy and venerable places, we render to you your own, not bestow ours. Wherefore I, Œthelræd, kinsman of Sebbi of the province of the East Saxons, with his consent, of my own free will, being in sound mind and perfect understanding, deliver to you, Abbess Æthelburh, for ever and transfer from my rightful possession into yours for increasing your monastery which is called *Beddanham,* the land which is called *Ricingaham, Budinham,* Dagenham, *Angenlabeshaam,* and the field in the wood which is called Widmund's field; which are, taken together, 40 hides[3] as far as the boundaries which belong thereto; with everything belonging to it, with fields and woods, meadows and marsh; that both you and your successors may hold and possess and have free power to do whatever you wish with that same land.

---

[1] Since this book went to press a detailed study has appeared of this and other charters, by C. Hart, *The Early Charters of Barking Abbey* (Colchester, 1953). Mr. Hart and I have independently reached similar conclusions.

[2] Mr. Hart has shown that this date results from a misreading and should be corrected to 687.

[3] *manentes.*

Done in the month of March, and I have asked witnesses in suitable number to subscribe.

If anyone attempts to contravene or mar this charter of donation, let him know that he is condemned before the Almighty God and his son Jesus Christ and the Holy Spirit, that is the Indivisible Trinity, and cut off from all Christian society; this charter of donation remaining nevertheless in its firmness. And that the gift may be firm and unshaken, the boundaries of this land with which it is surrounded are these: on the east *Writolaburna*,[1] on the north Centing's tree and *Hanchemstede*, on the south the River Thames.

If, however, anyone shall wish to increase this donation, may God increase his benefits in the land of the living with his saints without end. Amen.

✠ I, Sebbi, king of the East Saxons, have subscribed in confirmation.

I, Œthelræd, the donor, have subscribed.

✠ I, Eorcenwold, bishop,[2] have consented and subscribed.

I, Wilfrid, bishop, have consented and subscribed.

✠ I, Hædde, bishop,[3] have consented and subscribed.

I, Guda, priest and abbot,[4] consenting, have subscribed.

✠ I, Ecgbald, priest and abbot, have consented and subscribed.

✠ I, Hagona, priest and abbot, consenting, have subscribed.

✠ I, Hoc, priest and abbot, consenting, have subscribed.

Sign ✠ of the hand of King Sebbi.

Sign ✠ of the hand of King Sigeheard.

Sign ✠ of the hand of King Swæfred.

Endorsed in a later hand: This is the deed for Barking.

61. Grant of Ethelred, king of Mercia, of land at Ealing to Wealdhere, bishop of London (693–704)

This is only a quotation from a charter which has been lost, but as it reveals a Mercian king dealing with land in Middlesex at least as early as 704, and also throws light on the early constitution of St. Paul's, I adjudged it worthy of inclusion. It, and Nos. 62 and 63, are all taken from a series of extracts from St. Paul's documents made by Richard James before 1638 and preserved in the Bodley MS., James 23. They were first noted by Miss Gibbs, and, as the originals have disappeared and they contain important information, the discovery is of great interest. Many of the documents that were transcribed into the St. Paul's registers and have survived are of doubtful authenticity, but most of these extracts from a lost charter roll seem genuine, their phrasing being supported by that in documents of the same date issued for and preserved by other religious houses. See *Early Charters of the Cathedral Church of St. Paul, London,* ed. M. Gibbs, p. 4.

In the name of the supreme God.

I, Ethelred, king of the Mercians, with the consent and permission of my councillors, give to you, Bishop Wealdhere, a portion of land in the place which is called Ealing, that is, 10 hides[5] for the increase of the monastery[6] in the city of London.

---

[1] The old name of the River Wid (see *Place-Names of Essex*, p. 278), but this seems too far away.
[2] Of London.   [3] Of Winchester.   [4] Of Hoo, Kent.   [5] *manentes.*
[6] Literally, 'monastic life'. The vernacular *munuclif* 'monk-life' also was used as a synonym for 'monastery'.

62. Grant by Tyrhtil, bishop of Hereford, of land at Fulham to Wealdhere, bishop of London (704–709)

On the provenance of this extract, see introduction to No. 61. Tyrhtil, bishop of Hereford, held the see from 688, and Florence of Worcester says he died in 710. The date of the death of Wealdhere is uncertain, the first reliable charter to be signed by his successor Ingwold being Birch, No. 91, in 716. Cenred of Mercia reigned only from 704 to 709. One wonders why a bishop of Hereford should have had property so far away as Fulham, but he may, of course, have been a man of Middlesex in origin. See M. Gibbs, *op. cit.,* p. 3.

In the name of our Lord Jesus Christ.

I, Bishop Tyrhtil, have resolved to offer and bestow a small portion of land on Wealdhere, bishop of London, in return for his acceptable money, with the consent and permission of Sigeheard, king of the East Saxons, and of Cenred, king of the Mercians, that by these benefits willingly conferred on the church I may be able to purge the guilt of my sins and obtain the remedy conferred by the divine goodness. The possessions of this land are 50 hides[1] in the place which is called Fulham, etc.

63. Grant by Offa, king of the East Saxons, to Wealdhere, bishop of London, of land at Hemel Hempstead, Hertfordshire (about 704–709)

On the provenance of this extract, see introduction to No. 61. The interest of this brief extract lies in its reference to one of those ancient regions which were superseded by later administrative arrangements. Offa is the king who gave up his throne to retire to Rome in 709. The date of his accession is uncertain; Swæfred and Sigeheard are alive in 704, but Essex was so often under kings ruling jointly that it is unsafe to assume that Offa's reign can only begin after that time. Wealdhere became bishop between 691 and 694, and he was still alive in 705. The first reliable signature of his successor is in 716. See M. Gibbs, *op. cit.,* p. 5.

In the name of our Lord Jesus Christ the Saviour.

Although the word of priests and the decrees of royal ordinances remain in unshaken stability for ever, yet, because commonly the storms and whirlwinds of secular concerns beat also at the gates of the Church. . . .[2]

I, Offa, king of the East Saxons, [give] a portion of land in the region which is called Hæmele[3] to you Wealdhere, bishop of London, etc.

64. Exchange by Æthelbald, king of Mercia, of some salt-works with the Church of Worcester (716–717)

This is a very early reference to the salt industry, which was of very great importance for Worcestershire. This must have been one of Æthelbald's earliest charters, for Ecgwine, bishop of Worcester, who witnesses it, died in 717, and Æthelbald came to the throne in the previous year after long exile, in which one of his followers was the Ofa who witnesses this charter as *minister* 'king's thegn', and who was later made an ealdorman. See also p. 711, n. 4.

The manuscript (Brit. Mus. Cott. Tiber. A. xiii) in which this text survives is generally known as 'Hemming's cartulary', and, though not every text in it is above reproach, it has preserved a great number of undoubtedly authentic records which would otherwise have been lost. On this cartulary, see N. R. Ker, 'Hemming's Cartulary', in *Studies in Medieval History presented to F. M. Powicke,* where it is claimed that only fols. 119–200 are the compilation of Hemming, who was a monk of Worcester in the time of Bishop Wulfstan II (1062–1095), whereas the preceding folios constitute an earlier manuscript, and date from the early eleventh century. This charter is on fol. 195b. It is No. 67 in Kemble, No. 137 in Birch, and on p. 15 of Thorpe's *Diplomatarium.*

---

[1] *manentes.*

[2] The proem no doubt went on to stress the importance of written evidence. A rather similar proem occurs in Birch, No. 1121.   [3] The name survives in Hemel Hempstead.

In the name of the Lord Jesus.

I, Æthelbald, by divine dispensation king of the Mercians, having been asked by the holy community of Christ dwelling in the place whose name is Worcester, will concede and grant into their free liberty of possession for the redemption of my soul a certain portion of ground on which salt is wont to be made, at the south side of the river which is called Salwarp, in the place which is called *Lootwic* and *Coolbeorg*,[1] for the construction of three salthouses and six furnaces; receiving in exchange from the afore-mentioned community of Christ six other furnaces in two salthouses in which likewise salt is made, namely on the north side of the said river whose name is Salwarp. And we agreed to make this mutual exchange because it seemed more convenient to us both.

And this liberty I, Æthelbald, king of the Mercians, will confirm with the sign of the Holy Cross.

I, Ecgwine, bishop.[2]   I, Sigeberht, king's thegn.
I, Wilfrid, ealdorman.   I, Eadberht, king's thegn.
I, Æthelweard, ealdorman.   I, Ofa, king's thegn.
I, Stronglic, ealdorman.[3]   I, Eadwulf, king's thegn.

65. Grant by Ethelbert II, king of Kent, to Dunn, priest and abbot, of land by the River Lympne, Kent (20 Feb. 732)

This is the first charter of undoubted authenticity to contain a clause of immunity. Like No. 64, it concerns the production of salt, this time from salt-pans in coastal areas. Dunn became bishop of Rochester in 740 or 741.

The charter is Brit. Mus. Cott., Augustus, II. 91, and there is a facsimile in *Brit. Mus. Facs.*, I, pl. 6. It is No. 77 in Kemble, No. 148 in Birch, and on p. 20 in Thorpe's *Diplomatarium*.

✠ In the name of our Lord God and Saviour Jesus Christ.

There is a small piece of land, *i.e.* a quarter of one ploughland by the River Lympne, suitable for the boiling of salt, which I, Ethelbert, king of the people of Kent, formerly presented to your predecessor, Hymbra;[4] and you, O Dunn, abbot and priest, have used the same gift now for a long time with my assent. I now bestow and grant that same small piece of land of my rightful ownership to you and to the church of the Blessed Mary[5] over which you preside with your care, not in exchange for any worldly money but solely for the relief of my soul; in such a way that from the present day and season, it is to be in your power ever to have and possess it, just as you please. And next, no royal right is to be obtained in it at all, except only such as is general in all the ecclesiastical lands which are known to be here in Kent. And that this same donation of mine may constantly keep its firmness, I have formed below it the sign of the Holy Cross, and I ask witnesses of it to subscribe.

This was done on the twentieth day of the month of February, in the seventh year of our reign, the fifteenth indiction, at Canterbury.

---

[1] These places cannot now be identified. There is a place called Lutwyche, but it is in Shropshire, not by the Salwarp in Worcestershire.   [2] Of Worcester.

[3] Stronglic witnesses Birch, No. 157, another of Æthelbald's charters, and also a spurious Abingdon charter purporting to come from Ine of Wessex (Birch, No. 101), where the forger has added several names drawn from a Mercian charter of Æthelbald.

[4] This name is almost illegible. The *Brit. Mus. Facs.* read *Hymora*, but the ultra-violet ray shows the fourth letter to be *b*.   [5] At Lyminge.

And in addition, I, King Ethelbert, have added to this donation, which I have made for the relief of my soul, every year 120 loaded wagons of wood for boiling the salt; also, I have given to it 100 acres of the same estate, in the place which is called Sampton.[1] And the boundaries of that land are these: in the east the king's land, in the south the river which is called Lympne, in the west and in the north *Hudanfleot*.

✠ The sign of the Holy Cross, which Ethelbert, king and donor, has written.
✠ I, Tatwine, bishop,[2] have subscribed at the request of King Ethelbert.
✠ I, Albinus, abbot,[3] have subscribed at the order of the most faithful King Ethelbert.
✠ Sign of the hand of Bealdheard.
✠ Sign of the hand of Bynna.
✠ Sign of the hand of Eanberht.
✠ Sign of the hand of Æthelgeard.

66. Grant by Æthelbald, king of Mercia, of remission of toll on one ship at London for the Church of Rochester (734). With confirmation by Brihtwulf, king of Mercia (about 844–845)

This is a good example of a type of grant not uncommon about this time, which is of interest for the history of English trade. This king made a similar grant about 732–733 to the abbess of Minster, Thanet, in a charter (Birch, No. 149) whose proem is identical with that of the present document, and it was confirmed to the abbess by Offa early in his reign (Birch, No. 188). Æthelbald similarly remitted in 748 half the dues on one ship for the abbey of Minster (Birch, No. 177), and a year or two earlier he had freed from toll two ships at London for the benefit of Worcester, in a charter which survives only in an Old English translation (Birch, No. 171). An extract from a similar document granted to St. Paul's has come down to us in one of James's transcripts (see p. 448, above, and M. Gibbs, *op. cit.*, p. 6f.), and its genuineness is supported by its close agreement with a charter by which King Eadberht of Kent freed a ship at Fordwich for the benefit of the abbey of Reculver (Birch, No. 173) and with another issued by the same king for Minster, freeing a ship at Sarre (Birch, No. 189). These last three documents, and also that of Æthelbald to Minster in 748, differ from the present document in including a clause that allows the same privilege to a new ship if the original one is shipwrecked or worn out.

The indictional date of this charter is 734. This can be the seventeenth year of Æthelbald's reign only if his accession in 716 took place after 23 September. The confirmation of this charter is later than Tatnoth's accession to the see of Rochester. His predecessor was still signing in 842, and he himself is called 'elect' in 844. Though the witnesses do not let a precise date be given, the list as a whole is in close agreement with lists of 844–845.

One surviving version of this charter (Brit. Mus. Cott. Charter XVII.1) is in a ninth-century hand, perhaps a copy made at the time of its confirmation. There is also a version in the *Textus Roffensis*. It is of interest to note that the second half of its proem occurs in a charter of King Egbert of Kent granted to Rochester in 766–785 (Birch, No. 260). There is a facsimile of the Cotton Charter in *Brit. Mus. Facs.*, II, pl. 1. This document is No. 78 in Kemble, No. 152 in Birch.

✠ In the name of our Lord and Saviour Jesus Christ.

If those things which each bestows and grants to men by his word, in order to receive a reward from God, could remain constantly stable, it would seem unnecessary that they should be recounted and strengthened in writing; but since in truth nothing would seem stronger to prove donations and to refute the man wishing to infringe donations than [charters] of donation strengthened by the hands of donors and witnesses, many, not without cause, seek to have the things which are known to

[1] A lost place in West Hythe.   [2] Archbishop of Canterbury.
[3] Of St. Peter and St. Paul (later St. Augustine's), Canterbury.

have been conferred on them confirmed in a document; and consent ought to be granted to their demands all the more willingly and the more quickly, in that a more useful thing is conferred now in the visible world to those who are suppliants, and also a richer harvest will be given afterwards in the invisible world to those who are grantors, in return for the conferred gift of piety.

For this reason, I, Æthelbald, king of the Mercians, announce by these present letters that I have given for my soul to Ealdwulf, bishop of the church of the blessed Apostle Andrew, which he governs, the entrance, *i.e.* the toll, of one ship, whether one of his own or of any other man, hitherto belonging to me or my predecessors by royal right in the port of London, just as he has asked our clemency; and in order that this donation may be firm and stable for ever, so that nobody, kings or nobles or tax-gatherers or also any of their deputies whatsoever, may presume or be able to invalidate it in part or wholly, I will make with my own hand the sign of the Holy Cross below on this page and will ask witnesses to subscribe. Whoever, therefore, shall permit what I have granted or has been granted for my soul to remain un-impaired, may he have the blessed communion with the present and future Church of Christ; but if anyone will not permit it, may he be cut off from the society not only of holy men but also of the angels, this our donation remaining nevertheless in its firmness.

Done in the month of September, on the day of the second indiction,[1] in the seventeenth year of our reign.

✠   I, Æthelbald, king, have subscribed.
✠   I, Daniel, bishop,[2] have written.
✠   Sign of the hand of Ofa.
✠   Sign of the hand of Sigebed.

✠   This also was again confirmed by Brihtwulf, king of the Mercians, in the royal residence *Werburgewic*.[3]

✠   I, Brihtwulf, king of the Mercians, have confirmed this donation of me and my predecessor King Æthelbald with the sign of the Holy Cross of Christ, these witnesses consenting whose names are contained here, for the pardon of my offences and those of my predecessor King Æthelbald. If, indeed, any of my successors, kings or nobles or tax-gatherers, should wish to infringe or diminish this our donation, let him know that he will be cut off from the congregation of all saints on the dreadful Day of Judgment, unless he has previously made suitable amends.

✠ I, Brihtwulf, king of the Mercians.	✠ I, Tatnoth, bishop.[5]
✠ I, Ceolnoth, archbishop.	✠ I, Hunberht, ealdorman.
✠ I, Sæthryth, queen.	✠ I, Mucel, ealdorman.
✠ I, Ceolred, bishop.[4]	✠ I, Hunstan, ealdorman.

[1] I take this to mean on 24 September, the first day of the second indiction.

[2] Of Winchester. It is surprising to find a West Saxon bishop as the sole episcopal signatory, but I suspect that the copyist has greatly curtailed this list of signatures.

[3] Gordon Ward, *Arch. Cantiana*, XLVII, pp. 117–125, suggests that this refers to Hoo, Kent, which was dedicated to St. Werburh.   [4] Of Leicester.   [5] Of Rochester.

Tenth-century endorsement (partly in Old English, partly in Latin)

The entry of one ship into London, Æthelbald, king of the Mercians . . . of St. Andrew the Apostle at Rochester, and Beorn . . . bishop, in inheritance.

67. Grant by Æthelbald, king of Mercia, to Ealdorman Cyneberht, of land at Stour in Ismere, Worcestershire (736)

This charter (Brit. Mus. Cott. Augustus, II. 3) was at one time bound up with the Vespasian Psalter, and was taken out of it by the orders of Sir Robert Cotton; but it was undoubtedly originally a separate document. It bears the marks of folding, and has a tenth-century archive mark on that section of the reverse side whose discoloration shows that it was the part exposed when the charter was folded.

It is the earliest Worcestershire document to survive in a contemporary form. It has the added interest that, if it is compared with a later charter (Birch, No. 220), an interesting example is obtained of a privately owned monastery. In the present document, Cyneberht is given land to found a monastery. In the later charter we find his son, Abbot Ceolfrith, granting the inheritance of his father in these places (Hanbury and Stour, in the province of the people of Ismere) to Worcester, with some fear that his kindred may intervene, which causes him expressly to mention in his anathema 'anyone . . . of my *parentela*'. This charter belongs to 757–775, and Cyneberht was still alive in 757, if he is the abbot of this name who witnesses a charter of King Æthelbald of that year (Birch, No. 181).

Abbot Ceolfrith's fears that his gift might be interfered with seem to have been justified: Stour in Ismere was one of the places which King Offa claimed from the bishop of Worcester, as having been wrongly alienated from the inheritance of King Æthelbald (No. 77, below). The monks of Worcester came to terms with him in 781, relinquishing to him the abbey of Bath to settle this and other claims.

Once again, we get in a charter a glimpse of one of those ancient districts which were superseded by later administrative arrangements. It now survives only in the name of Ismere House, between Kidderminster and Wolverley.

The charter is important also for its regnal styles, as pointed out by Sir Frank Stenton in "The Supremacy of the Mercian Kings" (*Eng. Hist. Rev.*, XXXIII, pp. 433–452). Æthelbald attests as *rex Britanniæ* 'king of Britain', which probably corresponds to the Old English term *Bretwalda* of the Chronicle, whereas in the text he shows what is covered by this term by calling himself "king not only of the Mercians but also of all provinces which are called by the general name 'South English'". The kings to whom the Chronicle allots the title *Bretwalda* are those who Bede said had empire over all the territories south of the Humber.

There is a facsimile of this charter in *Brit. Mus. Facs.*, I, pl. 7. It is No. 80 in Kemble, No. 154 in Birch.

✠ I, Æthelbald, by the gift of God king not only of the Mercians but also of all provinces which are called by the general name 'South English', for the relief of my soul and the remission of my sins, make over, liberally granting into ecclesiastical possession, to my venerable companion Cyneberht for the construction of a monastery a small piece of land, namely 10 hides,[1] in the province to which was applied by the men of old the name Ismere, by the river called Stour, with all necessities belonging to it, with fields and woods, with fisheries and meadows. Thus that, as long as he shall live, he is to have the power of holding and possessing it, and, whether during his lifetime or indeed after his death, of leaving it to whom he shall wish. And the aforesaid estate is bounded on two sides by the above-named river, and has on its northern side the wood which they call Kinver, but on the west another of which the name is Morfe, the greater part of which woods belongs to the aforesaid estate.

If anyone, however, tries to violate this donation, let him know that he will make to God a reckoning in fearful fashion for his act of tyranny and his presumption at the terrible Judgment.

[1] *cassati.*

And this charter was written in the year of the incarnation of our Lord Jesus Christ 736, the fourth indiction.

✠ I, Æthelbald, king of Britain, confirming my own donation, have subscribed.

✠ I, Wor, bishop,[1] have consented and subscribed.

✠ I, Wilfrid, bishop,[2] have subscribed at King Æthelbald's order.

✠ I, Æthelric, sub-king[3] and companion of the most glorious prince Æthelbald, have consented to this donation and subscribed.

✠ I, Ife, abbot, though unworthy, have consented and subscribed.

✠ I, Heardberht, brother and ealdorman of the aforesaid king, have consented and subscribed.

✠ I, Ebbella, giving my consent, have subscribed.

✠ I, Onoc, companion, have subscribed.

✠ I, Ofa, have consented and subscribed.

✠ I, Sigebed, have consented and subscribed.

✠ I, Bercol, have consented and subscribed.

✠ I, Ealdwulf,[4] have consented and subscribed.

✠ I, Cusa, have consented and subscribed.

✠ I, Pede, have consented and subscribed.

The charter continues overleaf

There is, moreover, an estate in the above-mentioned wood Morfe which is called *Brochyl*.[5] This I, Æthelbald, king of the South English, have granted, conferring it on my faithful ealdorman and companion Cyneberht with the above-mentioned estate into ecclesiastical right.

Tenth-century endorsement: North Stour.

68. Archbishop Nothhelm in a synod decides the succession to a family monastery in Gloucestershire (736–737)

This charter affords another instance of a privately owned monastery, and shows how disputes concerning church lands were brought before an ecclesiastical synod. If this text is compared with No. 75, we find that the monastery was called Withington. Bishop Mildred of Worcester gave it in 774 to Abbess Æthelburh, daughter of Alfred, it having been granted to him by Abbess Hrothwaru. An Abbess Æthelburh occurs elsewhere, but it is difficult to keep apart Alfred's daughter from the abbess of the same name who was daughter of King Offa. Birch, No. 238, records the grant of Fladbury to Abbess Æthelburh, and Levison assumes this to be Offa's daughter. This may be so, but an Alfred had been concerned with previous arrangements about this estate. The present charter survives in Brit. Mus. Cott. Tiber A. xiii, fol. 25 (on this MS., see p. 449). It is No. 82 in Kemble, No. 156 in Birch, and edited by Earle, p. 31, Thorpe, *Diplomatarium*, p. 23, Haddan and Stubbs, III, 337.

WITHINGTON[6]

✠ Ethelred, the most glorious king of the Mercians, with his companion, Oshere, sub-king of the Hwicce, having been asked by him, conferred into ecclesiastical right with free possession land of 20 hides[7] by the river whose name is *Tillath*[8] to two nuns

---

[1] Of Lichfield.　　　　　[2] Of Worcester.　　　　　[3] Son of King Oshere of the Hwicce.
[4] This is probably the name meant by the scribal blunder Ealduuft. Aldwulf signs Birch, No. 157.
[5] Brockhill occurs three times in Worcestershire place-names, but not in the required area.
[6] The heading was added by the compiler of the cartulary.
[7] *cassati*.　　　　　　　　　　　　　　　　　　　　　[8] Now the Upper Coln, Glos.

namely Dunne and her daughter Bucge, for the construction of a monastery on it, for the forgiveness of his sins, and strengthened this their donation with the subscription of his own hand. But the aforesaid handmaid of God, Dunne, granted indisputably the monastery which had been built on the aforesaid estate, with its lands and also the charter descriptive of the land, over which she at that time alone presided, into the possession of her daughter's daughter, when herself on the point of death. But because this grand-daughter was still young in age, she entrusted the keeping of the charter of the enrolled land, and also all the charge of the monastery until she should reach a riper age, to the girl's mother, a married woman. When the grand-daughter asked that the charter should be given back, her mother, not wishing to give it back, replied that it had been stolen. When at length the whole business was brought to the holy synod of the sacerdotal council, the whole venerable council decreed, along with the most reverend Archbishop Nothhelm, that the charter of donation, either of the kings or of the above-mentioned handmaid of God, Dunne, was to be most clearly written out[1] and given to the aforesaid abbess, Hrothwaru, and that her possession of the monastery was to be most secure; the person who presumed to withdraw that original charter of the assignment of the land, either by theft or by fraudulently removing it by any means whatever, having been undoubtedly condemned and accursed by the decree of the most holy synod. And the holy synod decrees this, that after her death, this deed with the land is to be given back to the episcopal see of the city of Worcester, as it was settled before by her ancestors.

✠ I, Nothhelm, archbishop by the grace of God, have subscribed canonically.
✠ I, Daniel, bishop,[2] have subscribed.
✠ I, Wor, bishop,[3] have subscribed.
✠ I, Ingwold, bishop,[4] have subscribed.
✠ I, Wilfrid, bishop,[5] have subscribed.[6]
[✠ I, Ealdwulf, bishop,[7] have subscribed.
✠ I, Ælfwig, bishop,[8] have subscribed.
✠ I, Forthhere, bishop,[9] have subscribed.]
✠ I, Cuthbert, bishop,[10] have subscribed.
[✠ I, Herewold, bishop, have subscribed.[11]]

69. Grant by Æthelheard, king of Wessex, to Forthhere, bishop of Sherborne, of land at Crediton (10 April 739)

This charter (Bodleian Library, Crawford Charter I) is in a hand of the mid-eleventh century, and it has some suspicious features. It has lengthy boundaries in Old English, such as never occur in an original of this date. They may, however, have been added to a genuine early text, and the immunity clause, of a type unusual so early, may also be interpolated. The list of witnesses could hardly be

---

[1] *describi*.   [2] Of Winchester.   [3] Of Lichfield.   [4] Of London.   [5] Of Worcester.
[6] Birch omits the next three signatures from his text, quoting them from earlier editors, in his footnotes. There survives no earlier source than Dugdale.
[7] Of Rochester   [8] Of Lindsey.   [9] Of Sherborne.   [10] Of Hereford.
[11] This last witness also is relegated by Birch to his footnotes. His signature causes some difficulty, for he was successor at Sherborne of Forthhere, who signs the same document. But the Chronicle records that the latter went to Rome in 737, and it is possible that arrangements were made about a successor before his departure; or Herewold may have held part of the diocese.

fabricated, nor would a late forger have spelt the king's name with *i* instead of *e* (*Athil-*). The proem occurs in a charter of about 693 (Birch, No. 85) as well as in two rather dubious texts dated 682 and 688 (Birch, Nos. 62, 70); its second part occurs in undoubtedly authentic eighth-century charters. I include this document because of its importance for the history of the West Saxon conquest of Devon. This has recently been demonstrated afresh by H. P. R. Finberg, *The Early Charters of Devon and Cornwall* (1953), pp. 20–31. A detailed study of the boundaries, on the spot, has enabled him to sketch them on the map and show how they avoid an area of land, Treable in Cheriton Bishop, which is dealt with in a charter of Edward the Martyr, under the name *Hyples eald land* (*Journ. Brit. Arch. Assoc.*, XXXIX, p. 280). He suggests that this territory was avoided in the early grant because it was still in Cornu-British hands.

Æthelheard's charter is No. 1 in *The Crawford Collection of Early Charters and Documents*, edited by A. S. Napier and W. H. Stevenson; it is No. 1331 in Birch.

✠ In the name of the Lord God Jesus Christ the Saviour.

All things which are seen are, according to the Apostle, temporal, and those which are not seen are eternal.[1] Therefore with earthly and transitory things ought to be bought perpetual and lasting things, God granting his support. For which reason I, King Æthelheard, have taken care to bestow for ever on our Bishop Forthhere some land for the construction of a monastery, *i.e.* 20 hides[2] in the place which is called Creedy,[3] with all the advantages existing in it; and I have corroborated this donation in the presence of suitable witnesses, that no one may without danger to his soul be able to infringe what has been performed in the presence of such distinguished counsellors.

And these are the boundaries:[4] First from Creedy Bridge on to the highway, along the highway to *Sulhford* to the Exe, then along the Exe until *Focgan* eyots,[5] from *Focgan* eyots along the boundary ridge, from the boundary ridge to Luha's tree, from Luha's tree to the enclosure gate, from the enclosure gate to Dodda's ridge, from Dodda's ridge to Grendel's pit, from Grendel's pit to the ivy-grove, from the ivy-grove to *Hrucgancumb's* ford, from *Hrucgancumb's* ford to *Fearnburg*, from *Fearnburg* to *Earneshrycg*, from *Earneshrycg* to *Wealdancumb's* ford, from *Wealdancumb* to *Tettenburn*,[6] from *Tettenburn* upstream to the Lilly Brook, from the Lilly Brook to the middle ridge, from the middle ridge to the ford on the highway,[7] from the ford on the highway to *Cyrtlan* gate, from *Cyrtlan* gate to the crab-apple tree, from the crab-apple tree to the green way, from the green way to the wolf-pit, from the wolf-pit upstream to where the brooks meet, then up to the middle of the ridge, along the ridge to the path, from the path straight as a shaft to the alder, southward over to the precipice, from the precipice to the head of *Byrccumb*, from the head of *Byrccumb* to Hana's ford, thence to the broad ash, from the broad ash to the head of *Foxcumb*, thence to the stone ford on the Yeo, from the stone ford to the alder-thicket, from the alder-thicket to the landslip, thence to the green down, from the green down to the highway[8] to Putta's post, thence to Beornwynn's tree, from Beornwynn's tree to the stone ford on the Yeo, thence to Bucga's ford, from Bucga's ford to Brunwold's tree, thence to *Æsccumb*, from *Æsccumb* to *Wonbroc*, along the stream to

---

[1] II Corinthians iv. 18.   [2] *cassati*.   [3] Crediton means the town on the Creedy.

[4] The boundaries, which are in English, have been translated from Crawford Charter II, as this represents a tenth-century copy. I have made extensive use of the notes in Stevenson and in Finberg, *op. cit.*

[5] The name survives in Foghays near Exwick Barton.

[6] Stevenson suggests that this is an old name of the Kelland Brook.

[7] Literally, 'army-path' (*herepæð*). The name may survive in Lower and Higher Harford, hamlets near by.   [8] According to Stevenson this is the Exeter-Okehampton road.

the Teign, upstream on the Teign to *Path-ford*,[1] thence to Franca's combe, from Franca's combe to the head of Drascombe, thence to *Deormere*, from *Deormere* to the long stone, thence to the head of Hurra's combe, from the head of Hurra's combe to *Riscford* on the *Nymet*, thence to Hillerton, from Hillerton to Wærna's fortress, thence to *Ciddanford* to Cæfca's grove, thence to Cain's acre, from Cain's acre to the head of *Wylfcumb*, thence to the stone hill, from the stone hill to the cress well, from the cress well to *Dythford*, thence to the gate of the dyke, from the gate of the dyke to Unna's hill, thence to *Swincumb*, from *Swincumb* to Egesa's tree, thence on *Riscbroc* downstream until *Scipbroc*, on *Scipbroc* downstream until *Nymed*, on *Nymed* downstream to the Dalch, from the Dalch upstream until the willow slade, from the willow slade to eight oaks, thence to *Hafoccumb*, from *Hafoccumb* to the enclosure gate, thence out on the precipice, thence to Binneford on the Creedy, thence on the stream until *Hafoccumb*, thence to the enclosure gate, thence to the old highway until the east Creedy, thence along the stream to Creedy Bridge.

And to this land I will add this liberty and I firmly ordain that it is to be immune and eternally secure from all fiscal causes and royal concerns and secular works, except only matters pertaining to military service.

Whoever increases it, may his benefits be increased, and whoever diminishes or alters it, may his joy be turned into sorrow, and may he suffer for ever the infernal torments.

This donation was done in the year of the incarnation of our Lord Jesus Christ 739, the seventh indiction, on 10 April:

✠ Sign of the hand of Æthelheard, king.
✠ Sign of the hand of Cuthred.[2]
✠ Sign of the hand of Frithogyth.[3]
✠ I, Daniel, bishop,[4] have subscribed canonically.
✠ I, Forthhere, bishop,[5] have consented and subscribed.
✠ Sign of the hand of Herefrith, 'prefect'.[6]
✠ Sign of the hand of Dudd, abbot.
✠ Sign of the hand of Ecgfrith, 'prefect'.
✠ Sign of the hand of Puttoc, 'prefect'.

70. Grant by Cynewulf, king of Wessex, of land on the River Wellow to the Church of Wells (757–778, perhaps 766)

The king who issued this charter is the hero of annal 755 in the Anglo-Saxon Chronicle (No. 1, pp. 162 f.), and the statement made there that he fought against the Britons receives confirmation from this charter. Cynewulf (on whom see also Nos. 55, 71, 79, 190, and 191) seems to have been

---

[1] Finberg says the name survives in Parford and Great Pafford.
[2] This must be Æthelheard's successor, who succeeded him about 740.
[3] Æthelheard's wife. The Chronicle records that she and Bishop Forthhere went to Rome in 737. If this charter is genuine, it shows that a pilgrimage, and not a retirement from the world, is meant. On this and the difficulty that arises from Forthhere's signing charters contemporaneously with his successor Herewold, see Napier and Stevenson, pp. 40 f., and R. R. Darlington, *Eng. Hist. Rev.*, LI, p. 425.
[4] Of Winchester.
[5] Of Sherborne.
[6] Early West Saxon charters seem to use this term for ealdorman.

a generous donor to religious houses. Besides this and the following grant, he makes donations to Bath, Malmesbury and Sherborne, and we know of three grants to laymen of lands which eventually came into monastic hands, and may have been given for that end. One would like to identify Wigfrith, who witnesses here as 'prefect' with the man of this name who helped to avenge Cynewulf's slaying in 786, but the Chronicle calls him 'thegn' only, whereas 'prefect' in early West Saxon charters seems to mean ealdorman.

The indications of date in this charter are inconsistent, for the twelfth indiction would in Cynewulf's reign give either 759 or 774, not 766, which is the fourth indiction. It is possible that III has been miscopied XII. A date fairly early in the reign is suggested by the appearance of the same seven 'prefects' in 757 and 762. The boundaries of the charter, which survives only in the register of the Dean and Chapter of Wells, could be a later addition, but it is in their favour that they are in Latin; the only charter of this king to survive in a contemporary form (Birch, No. 225), which is unfortunately too mutilated for reproduction, has long Latin boundaries. Lengthy boundaries seem, as far as our evidence goes, to have begun with this king.

The evidence of charters permits us to supplement the scanty account of the Chronicle on the relations between this king and Offa of Mercia (see p. 23). Here, as in No. 71, he acts without reference to Offa. This charter is No. 115 in Kemble, No. 200 in Birch.

✠ In the name of our Lord Jesus Christ.

Since it is agreed by all catholics and true believers in the Lord that the times of this temporal life far and wide throughout the globe daily pass away by uncertain and divers causes, and also men, overcome by sudden sickness, immediately give up and end their lives and lose at the same time all transitory things; for that reason we here expend and bestow the Lord's benefits to the poor without any delay, in order that there we may receive the harvest of reward in the eternal country with the Lord happily without end;

Therefore I, Cynewulf, king of the West Saxons, will grant and humbly make over to the Apostle and servant of God, St. Andrew, with the consent of my bishops and magnates, for the love of God and for the expiation of my sins, and also, what is sad to relate, because of some harassing from our enemies, the race of the Cornish men, some portion of land, that is 11 hides[1] near the river which is called Wellow, for the increasing of the monastery which is situated by the great spring which they call Wells, in order that they may the more diligently serve God in the church of St. Andrew the Apostle; it is surrounded by these boundaries:

On the south from the valley which is called *Asancumb*, on the west side to a spring which is named *Diornanwiel*, then to the hill which the natives call Thornhill, then to the waste land to Picela's thorn; and then beyond the River Wellow to the spring *Holanwielle*, and thence to the waste land to a ditch which is by the source of a stream which the natives call *Saltbroc*, and then on the same stream as far as the River Wellow, then on the bank of the river as far as the ford of the Wellow, and then on the public way as far as the elder which they call 'Elder-tree', and thence along the muddy torrent to the east ford, thence back through the plain between two rocky ways to the above-named valley, *Asancumb*.

✠ If anyone should dare to infringe or diminish this, let him know that he must render account in the presence of Christ and his holy angels in the Last Judgment.

✠ This document was written in the year of our Lord's incarnation 766, the twelfth indiction.

[1] *manentes.*

✠ I, Cynewulf, king of the Gewisi,[1] have strengthened this my donation with the sign of the Holy Cross.

✠ I, Herewold, bishop,[2] have signed this charter of munificence with my own hand.

✠ I, Cyneheard, bishop,[3] have consented to this liberality and subscribed.

✠ Sign of the hand of Scilling, 'prefect'.

✠ Sign of the hand of Heahfrith, 'prefect'.

✠ Sign of the hand of Eoppa, 'prefect'.

✠ Sign of the hand of Æthelric, 'prefect'.

✠ Sign of the hand of Hemele, 'prefect'.

✠ Sign of the hand of Wigfrith, 'prefect'.

✠ Sign of the hand of Cerdic, 'prefect'.

71. Grant by Cynewulf, king of Wessex, to Muchelney Abbey (762)

I include this charter because, taken together with No. 70, it throws light ón West Saxon rule in Somerset, and because it is very little known, since it is in none of the collections of Anglo-Saxon charters. Both in it and No. 70 the actual grant is couched in very general terms, which suggests that the county was not thickly populated and that precise boundaries were unnecessary. With these charters of Cynewulf should also be compared Birch, No. 327, which has been wrongly taken for a charter of Cenwulf of Mercia and dated 808. It is in favour of Bath, and belongs to 757–758. In it, and in Birch, No. 181, a charter of 757, Mercian kings appear as Cynewulf's over-lords, whereas here, in 762, and in No. 70, which cannot be precisely dated, Cynewulf acts without reference to an overlord (see p. 23). This charter survives, probably in an abbreviated form, in the Muchelney cartulary, and is edited by the Rev. E. H. Bates, *Two Cartularies of the Benedictine Abbeys of Muchelney and Athelney*, p. 47.

In the name of our Lord Jesus Christ.

I, Cynewulf, king of the West Saxons, have granted willingly for the remedy of my sins and in the presence of my counsellors whose names are contained below, to the monastery which is called Muchelney, to Abbot Eadwold, some portion of land, *i.e.* eight hides[4] between the two rivers *Earn*[5] and Isle, and it has on the west the hill which is called *Dun Meten*.

And this document of privilege was written in the year of our Lord's incarnation 762, the fifteenth indiction, in the place which is called *Pentric*.[6]

✠ Sign of the hand of Cynewulf the king.

✠ Sign of the hand of Herewold, bishop.[7]

✠ Sign of the hand of Cyneheard, bishop.[8]

✠ Sign of the hand of Scilling, 'prefect'.

✠ Sign of the hand of Hemele, 'prefect'.

✠ Sign of the hand of Cerdic, 'prefect'.

✠ Sign of the hand of Heahfrith, 'prefect'.

✠ Sign of the hand of Æthelric, 'prefect'.

✠ Sign of the hand of Eoppa, 'prefect'.

✠ Sign of the hand of Wigfrith, 'prefect'.

[1] According to Bede, this was an old name of the West Saxons. It was sometimes revived in antiquarian mood in later times.
[2] Of Sherborne.   [3] Of Winchester.   [4] *cassati*.
[5] Ekwall says this is the old name of the stream which joins the Isle north-east of Isle Abbots.
[6] Perhaps Pentridge, Dorset.   [7] Of Sherborne.   [8] Of Winchester.

72. Grant by Dunwald of land in Canterbury to the monastery of St. Peter and St. Paul, Canterbury (762)

This is a very early instance of a grant by a private person. It survives in a late cartulary (Trinity Hall MS., Cambridge), but one which contains a number of genuine early documents; nothing in its wording gives grounds for suspicion, nor is there any obvious motive for the invention of circumstantial detail such as it contains. The original may well have been added to Ethelbert's charter to Dunwald (which has not survived), in the same way as many private grants are added to royal charters surviving from the Christ Church archives. The charter affords an interesting example of the personal devotion of a thegn to his king. The date seems correct. Jænberht, abbot of St. Peter and St. Paul (later St. Augustine's), Canterbury, succeeded Bregowine as archbishop of Canterbury in 765. King Ethelbert II died in 762. Bealdheard is a name that occurs in Ethelbert's charters.

Dunwald does not occur under this name elsewhere, but it is tempting to regard this form as the late scribe's error either for Dunwalh, since King Ethelbert had a cup-bearer of that name, who attests a contemporary charter (Birch, No. 160) or for Dunwalla, another witness of the same charter.

This charter is No. 109 in Kemble, No. 192 in Birch, and on p. 36 of Thorpe's *Diplomatarium*.

✠ In the name of our Lord Jesus Christ.

I, Dunwald, the thegn of King Ethelbert of glorious memory, while he lived, now indeed desiring to convey his money for the safety of his soul to the threshold of the Apostles at Rome, along with others, assign after my death, unless perchance it should please me to carry it out in my lifetime, a residence which is situated in the market-place at the Queen's gate of the city of Canterbury, and which Hringwine now holds – the same which the aforesaid king granted with other small lands in his own right for me to possess with his tribute, and to give to whomsoever I should wish – to the church of the blessed Peter and Paul, situated near by, where the body of the same King Ethelbert, my lord, rests, for his soul and for my salvation, by an eternal donation, to be possessed with his tribute. And in order that there should be no contention about this in the future, I have set out this same transaction on the deed of the original donation to me. And, therefore, with the consent of our venerable Archbishop Bregowine, I have now caused to be set out this deed of this my donation and have strengthened it with my own hand, and I invite him and other religious witnesses to do the same.

Done in the year of Christ's incarnation 762.

✠   I, Bregowine, by the grace of God archbishop, have subscribed the sign of the Holy Cross.

✠   I, Dunwald, have strengthened my aforesaid donation with the sign of the Holy Cross.

✠   I, Bealdheard, ealdorman, have subscribed.

✠   I, Cyneheard, priest, have consented and subscribed.

✠   I, Jænberht, abbot, have subscribed as a witness.

This land is surrounded by these boundaries: from Queen's gate in the south, having three perches in extent, and thence west a most straight line divides the land of the king and this, for 23 perches as far as the walled enclosure[1] which adjoins the city wall on the north side, having 33 rods.

[1] *maceria.*

73. Exchange of lands in Middlesex between Offa, king of Mercia, and Abbot Stithberht (767); with endorsement of Pilheard, 'comes' of Cenwulf, king of Mercia (801)

This charter, Brit. Mus. Cott. Augustus II. 26, 27, survives in a contemporary form. The first part has an interesting reference to 'the sanctuary of the Gumenings' (Harrow), descriptive of a tribal temple in heathen days. The endorsement has an early mention of the three public dues, and a reference to popular assemblies. The incarnation date is given as 764, but the indiction is for 767. As Jænberht's accession to Canterbury and Cuthfrith's to Lichfield belong to 765, the indiction date is to be preferred. There is a facsimile in Brit. Mus. Facs., I, pl. 9. The charter is No. 116 in Kemble, No. 201 in Birch.

In the name of the Triune Deity.

Our Lord reigning for ever. I, Offa, by the divine controlling grace king of the Mercians, will concede and grant most willingly, to Stithberht, a venerable man possessed of an abbot's charge, land of 30 hides[1] in Middlesex, between the sanctuary of the Gumenings (Harrow-on-the-Hill) and the Lidding;[2] and six hides and a dwelling are east of the River Lidding. And the aforesaid Stithberht has made over to me in exchange land of the same number of hides, i.e. 30, in the Chilterns [?][3] in a place which is called Wycombe [?].

If anyone, however – which God forbid – tries to infringe this our exchange, let him know that he must render account in the presence of Christ and his angels.

And in the year of our Lord's incarnation 767,[4] the fifth indiction, this giving of a donation and exchange of a gift was accomplished, these witnesses consenting and subscribing whose names are inscribed below.

✠ I, Offa, king of the Mercians, subscribe.
✠ I, Jænberht, by the grace of God archbishop.
✠ I, Eadberht, bishop.[5]
✠ I, Cuthfrith, bishop.[6]

Endorsement

When, therefore, these charters of donations or exchanges of the afore-mentioned kings, namely Æthelbald and Offa, came down to me, I, Pilheard, unworthy companion of Cenwulf, king of the Mercians, received them, obtaining them most justly, and brought them forward in the synodal assembly near the place which is called Chelsea, in the presence of the already mentioned king of the Mercians and the bishops of the churches of God, and also of the ealdormen or leading men, and acquired the privilege of these lands from the most pious king of the Mercians, now my lord, for money, i.e. with 200 shillings, and afterwards 30 every year in my days and those of my successors; and that they were to be free for ever from the rendering of all fiscal dues, works and burdens and also of popular assemblies, except only 'price for price'.[7] Yet the due amount of the three public causes is to be paid, that is,

---

[1] The word used for 'hides' is *manentes*.   [2] The old name of Wealdstone Brook.

[3] If this is what is meant, the form, *Ciltinne*, is perhaps a scribal error, for the normal form is *Ciltern*. It is clear that a district, not a village is meant. Ekwall, who suggests one of the Wycombes for *Wicham*, nevertheless does not include *Ciltinne* in his forms of Chiltern.

[4] Corrected from 764 of the text.   [5] Of Leicester.   [6] Of Lichfield.

[7] i.e. the simple value of any stolen property is to be paid to the owner, but nothing in addition, and no fines. These remain with the holder of the immunity.

the construction of bridges and forts, and also, in the necessity of military service, only five men[1] are to be sent. These were present as trustworthy witnesses of this transaction whom this charter includes.

And now I, Cenwulf, by the dispensation of God, king of the Mercians, subscribe the privilege of my own donation most willingly with the sign of the Holy Cross. ✠

✠ I, Æthelheard, by the gift of God archbishop, have imprinted the venerable sign of the Cross.

✠ I, Unwona, bishop,[2] have consented.

✠ I, Wigberht, bishop,[9] have consented.

✠ I, Ealdwulf, bishop,[3] have consented.

✠ I, Ealhheard, bishop,[10] have consented.

✠ I, Utol, bishop,[4] have consented.

✠ I, Tidfrith, bishop,[11] have consented.

✠ I, Eadwulf, bishop,[5] have consented.

✠ I, Wihthun, abbot.

✠ I, Deneberht, bishop,[6] have consented.

✠ I, Beonna, abbot.

✠ I, Hathoberht, bishop,[7] have consented.

✠ I, Foldred, abbot.

✠ I, Cyneberht, bishop,[8] have consented.

✠ I, Cenwulf, by the gift of God, king of the Mercians, consent and subscribe.[12]

✠ I, Hathoberht.

✠ I, Cuthred.[13]

✠ I, Æthelmund.

✠ I, Oswulf.

✠ I, Esne.

✠ I, Beornnoth.

✠ I, Heardberht.

✠ I, Cynehelm.

✠ I, Ceolmund.

✠ I, Wigga.   ✠ I, Cydda.

74. Grant by Uhtred, sub-king of the Hwicce, to Æthelmund, son of Ingild, of land at Aston Fields in Stoke Prior, Worcestershire (770)

This charter, which is in the possession of the Dean and Chapter of Worcester, is the earliest undoubtedly genuine document to mention the three public dues, the so-called *Trinodo* (or *Trimodo*) *necessitas*. It also illustrates the relations of Offa with the ruling house of the Hwicce. On Æthelmund, see No. 81.

The charter is damaged, but most of the blanks can be filled from Hickes' version (*Thesaurus*, I, p. 170) of a lost charter granting Aston to the same donee, in 767, which, except that it is briefer, is couched in identical terms (Birch, No. 202). Among the blanks in the present charter is the name of the estate, and the endorsement reads "To Aston, *i.e.* Stoke." There are facsimiles of this charter in *Ord. Surv. Facs.*, II, Worcester Charter; *Trans. Royal Soc. Lit.*, New Series, XI (1878), p. 338; C. H. Turner, *Early Worcester Manuscripts*, pl. 31. It is No. 203 in Birch.

✠ In the name of our Lord Jesus Christ.

It is most certainly evident and thus free from doubt that all things which are seen are temporal, and the things which are not seen are eternal.

---

[1] Assuming that *vires* is in error for *viri*.   [2] Of Leicester.   [3] Of Lichfield.
[4] Of Hereford.   [5] Of Lindsey.   [6] Of Worcester.   [7] Of London.
[8] Of Winchester.   [9] Of Sherborne.   [10] Of Elmham.   [11] Of Dunwich.
[12] Cenwulf's second attestation heads the lay signatories, which begin in the third column.
[13] This last column, of four names, is placed in the bottom margin.

Therefore I, Uhtred, by the gift of God sub-king[1] of the Hwicce, have meditated that, out of the portion of the earthly kingdom which I have received from the Giver of all good things, I should expend something, however unworthy, for the profit of ecclesiastical liberty, for the relief of my soul. Hence [I will grant] most willingly for the sake of the Lord Almighty to my faithful thegn, namely Æthelmund, son of Ingild, who was ealdorman and 'prefect' of Æthelbald, king of the Mercians, with the advice and permission of Offa, king of the Mercians, and also of his bishops and leading men, land of five hides,[2] i.e. the village which is called [Aston], by the river which is called Salwarp, on its eastern side, to possess by ecclesiastical right; that as long as he lives he may possess it, and leave it to two heirs after him, whomsoever he shall wish. And when these have departed from the world, the land with the deeds is to be given back to the church of Worcester, for their table, without any contradiction, as alms for me and for us all, [for the love of the celestial] country and for their intercession to the living and true God. Moreover, as a fitting price has been received from the aforesaid Æthelmund, [let everyone know] that this land is free from every tribute, small or great, of public matters, and from all services whether of king or ealdorman, except the building of bridges or the necessary defences of fortresses against enemies. Also in every way [we forbid] in the name of God Almighty, [that, if] anyone in this aforenamed land steals anything outside it, anything [be paid] to anyone except specifically 'price for price'[3] [as a settlement, nothing outside as a fine].

May the Almighty God not cease to increase the benefits in eternity of him who increases this my injunction; may he who diminishes it—which [we hope no one will—let him know that he] must render account [before] the judgment-seat of Christ, unless he has previously made sufficient amends to God and men.

[This donation] was drawn up [in the year] of the incarnation of our Lord Jesus Christ 770, the ninth indiction,[4] the eleventh decenoval, the eighth of the lunar cycle.

[✠ I, Offa, by the gift of God king] of the Mercians, have consented to this, my sub-king's, donation and have placed on it the sign of the Holy Cross.

[✠ I, Mildred, the grace of Christ] conceding, humble bishop of the Hwicce, have consented and subscribed.

[✠ I, Uhtred], by the grant of the dispensation of [the merciful God], sub-king of my own people, corroborating this my donation of privilege conceded for the sake of the Lord, have written the sign of salvation.

[✠ I, Ealdred, sub-king[5]] of the Hwicce, subscribe consenting to this donation conceded by my brother.

[✠ I, Eata, have consented and] subscribed.

[✠ I, Brorda have con]sented and subscribed.

✠ I, Eadbald, have consented and subscribed.

---

[1] regulus.   [2] tributaria.
[3] i.e. simple compensation, by repaying the amount stolen. See p. 461, n. 7.
[4] This is miscalculated; 770 was the eighth indiction.   [5] subregulus

These are the boundaries of this donation: Salwarp, *Cymedes halh*, 'White stone', 'Red pool'.

Continued overleaf

✠ I, Cynethryth, queen of the Mercians, have consented and subscribed.

✠ I, Ecgfrith, son of them both, have consented and subscribed.

✠ I, Ælfflæd, daughter of them both, have consented and subscribed.

Endorsed: To Aston, *i.e.* Stoke.

Of King Offa.

75. Grant by Mildred, bishop of Worcester, to Abbess Æthelburh, of land at Withington, Gloucestershire (774)

This charter should be compared with No. 68 above. It gives the later history of the family monastery which was the subject of dispute. It follows it in the same manuscript, Brit. Mus. Cott. Tiber. A. xiii, on which see p. 449. It is No. 124 in Kemble, No. 217 in Birch, and is in Earle, p. 52.

WITHINGTON

✠ Our Lord and Saviour reigning for ever.

I, Mildred, by the gift of the grace of God humble bishop of the Hwicce, [grant] the land of the monastery which is called Withington, which is situated on the west side of the river which is called *Tillnoth*,[1] 21 hides[2] – which land, to wit, Oshere, sub-king of the Hwicce bestowed on Dunne, the handmaid of God, that it might be in legal possession of the Church, with the consent of Ethelred, king of the Mercians; she, however, bequeathed the aforesaid land to her daughter's daughter to possess after her, namely Abbess Hrothwaru, with the knowledge and permission of the most reverend Bishop Ecgwine, and the aforesaid Abbess Hrothwaru has granted it to me by right of my own privilege and possession. Now, therefore, with the permission of the servants of God who by the providence of God are under my governance, I willingly deliver it to the honourable Abbess Æthelburh, daughter of Alfred, in such a way, however, that while she lives she is to have and possess it, and after her death return it again for the eternal redemption of my soul to the church of the blessed Peter, Prince of the Apostles, which is situated in Worcester, where also is the pontifical see of the Hwicce.

This charter was written in the year of Christ's incarnation 774, the twelfth indiction, these witnesses confirming it.

✠ I, Mildred, bishop, will confirm this my donation with the sign of the Cross, on condition that Æthelburh shall also return the monastery at Withington[3] with all the goods that are there, after her day to the church of Worcester, as was the injunction of her father, Alfred.

76. Grant by Oslac, ealdorman of the South Saxons, of land at Earnley, Sussex (780). With confirmation by Offa, king of Mercia (786-796)

This is the earliest South Saxon charter to survive in contemporary form. It belongs to Chichester Cathedral. It helps to illustrate Offa's dealings with Sussex. Oslac issues the charter in his own name at Selsey, but it needs confirmation by Offa, as overlord, and this confirmation takes place in

---

[1] Now the Upper Coln.   [2] *manentes.*   [3] The scribe wrote 'Worcester' by mistake.

Mercian territory, at Irthlingborough, Northants. Sir Frank Stenton has drawn attention to the contrast between the provincial script of the text and the practised hand of the endorsement. Between 759 and 770 Offa had confirmed South Saxon grants made by men who called themselves kings, Ealdwulf (Birch, No. 197) and Osmund (*ibid.*, No. 206), but who appear later attesting charters with the title of *dux* 'ealdorman' only. Oslac may have been a member of the same family. The confirmation is some years later than the grant; Gislhere, who signs in 781, has been replaced as bishop of Selsey by Wihthun, whose first signature is in 789, and who was not the immediate successor, since a certain Tota attests in 786.

It is not known where in the diocese of Selsey the church of St. Paul was situated. The monastery of Selsey itself was dedicated to St. Peter.

There is a facsimile of the charter by Birch, *The Anglo-Saxon Charter of Oslac*, 1892. This version is No. 1334 in Birch. An inferior version, from a register of Chichester Cathedral, is No. 1012 in Kemble, No. 237 in Birch.

✠ Our Lord Jesus Christ reigning and governing for ever.

I, Oslac, ealdorman of the South Saxons, willingly grant for the relief of my soul to the venerable church of St. Paul the Apostle a certain portion, *i.e.* with two names, Earnley and *Tielæsora*, with all things belonging to it, fields, woods.

In the year of the incarnation of the Lord 780, it was done in the place which is called Selsey. ✠

✠ I, Oslac, have subscribed this donation with my own hand.
✠ I, Gislhere, bishop,[1] have consented and subscribed.
✠ I, Ealdwulf, have consented and subscribed.
✠ I, Ælfwold, have consented and subscribed.
✠ I, Wærmund, have consented and subscribed.
✠ I, Beornmod, have consented and subscribed.
✠ I, Wærfrith, have consented and subscribed.
✠ I, Wiohstan, have consented and subscribed.
✠ I, Beffa, have consented and subscribed.
✠ I, Bealdheard, have consented and subscribed.
✠ I, Æthelmund, have consented and subscribed.
✠ I, Beornheard, have consented and subscribed.
✠ I, Brihtnoth, have consented and subscribed.

✠ Thus also all royal dignity says: if anyone indeed shall try, relying on tyrannical power, violently to make void this decree, he is to know that he must render account in the presence of Christ at the terrible Judgment of all men, and have his part with Judas the betrayer of our Lord in lower hell. . . . ✠

Endorsed
✠ I, Offa, by the gift of God king of the Mercians, ✠ corroborating the aforesaid land at the petition of Wihthun, bishop of the South Saxons, subscribe and will confirm with the impression of the dominical Cross.
✠ I, Cynethryth, queen, have consented and subscribed.
✠ I, Brorda, 'prefect', have consented and subscribed.
✠ I, Unwona, bishop,[2] have consented and subscribed.

This was duly performed in the place which is called Irthlingborough.

[1] Of Selsey.   [2] Of Leicester.

77. The settlement at the synod of Brentford of a claim made by Offa, king of Mercia, against the Church of Worcester (781)

This document, which is preserved in Brit. Mus. Cott. Tiber. A. xiii, fol. 106, suggests that some land could not permanently be alienated from the kindred, but it would have been interesting to know on what grounds Offa chose to regard as invalid the acts of his predecessor in alienating lands. The estate of 14 hides at Stour in Ismere is presumably the one of this size granted to Worcester by Abbot Ceolfrith (see p. 453 above), and this probably included the 10 hides which Ceolfrith's father, Cyneberht, had been given by King Æthelbald with the right to bequeath to whom he wished (see No. 67). Probably the church of Worcester did not think it politic to cling to their rights and resist the king's claim as they might have done that of a less formidable adversary. Hampton is probably Hampton Lucy, Warwickshire, which in December 780 Worcester leased to King Offa's kinswoman, Eanburh (Birch, No. 239). The large estate at Stour was by the river of that name in east Worcestershire and Warwickshire which flows into the Avon, whereas Stour in Ismere is the river that joins the Severn at Stourport. The other estates are Bredon, Worcestershire, and Stratford-on-Avon, Warwickshire.

The purchase by the church from Cynewulf of Wessex on Offa's account of a stretch of land on the West Saxon side of the Avon is of great interest. It suggests that Offa is strengthening the southern boundary of his kingdom, and one wonders whether Cynewulf, who at times admitted Offa's overlordship, was an entirely willing party to the transaction. See p. 23.

The charter is No. 143 in Kemble, No. 241 in Birch, and is also in Haddan and Stubbs, III, p. 438.

✠ In the name of the supreme God.

Seasons follow seasons, and it happens in periods of change that things said in former times may be made void unless we confirm them with writings.

For which reason I, Hathored, by the dispensation of God humble bishop of the Hwicce, with at the same time the consent and advice of all my community which is settled in the city of Worcester, have, investigating most diligently, considered and pondered about the peace and condition of the Church. Verily, we have had a dispute with Offa, king of the Mercians, our most beloved lord, about certain estates. For he said that we were wrongly holding in our power without hereditary right the inheritance of his kinsman, to wit King Æthelbald, i.e. 90 hides[1] in the place which is called Bath, and in many other places, namely 30 hides[2] at Stratford, 38 at Stour, also 14 hides[1] at a place of like name, Stour in Ismere, 12 at Bredon, 17 hides[2] at Hampton. But the aforesaid cause of dissension being settled in the synodal council at the place which is called Brentford, we restored also to the already mentioned King Offa that most famous monastery at Bath, without any hindrance or objection, for him to possess or even to deliver to whom he should consider fit, and we conceded it most willingly to his lawful heirs to enjoy for ever; and we added 30 hides near by on the south side of the river which is called Avon, which land we bought at a proper price from Cynewulf, king of the West Saxons. On that account, the aforesaid King Offa, as a payment of compensation, and for the concord of a very firm peace, willingly conceded the aforesaid places at Stratford, Stour, Bredon, Hampton, Stour in Ismere, without any cause of controversy or exaction, to our aforesaid church, that is, in Worcester, with this liberty that these lands were to be subjected to no greater payment of any kind than the afore-mentioned episcopal see. Also he willingly conceded and bestowed the food-rents[3] for three years belonging to him, that is, six 'entertainments'.[4]

Now, therefore, I, Offa, by the grace of God king, and also all bishops, abbots and

---

[1] *manentes.*   [2] *cassati.*   [3] *pastiones.* I presume this refers to the king's farm.
[4] Probably this refers to the assessment of the king's farm in units of 'the farm of one night', *i.e.* the amount considered adequate to maintain the king and his household for a day.

leading men, have consented to and subscribed the afore-written privilege of the lands, which was conceded for the relief of my soul in the synod at Brentford, Archbishop Jænberht presiding along with me. I have written with my own hand the sign of the most sacred Cross of Christ for establishing the security.

This charter was drawn up at Brentford, in the year of the incarnation of Christ 781, the fourth indiction.

✠ Offa, king of the Mercians.

✠ Brorda, ealdorman.

✠ Brihtwold, ealdorman.

✠ Eadbald, ealdorman.

✠ Esne, ealdorman.

✠ Eadbald, ealdorman.

✠ Eadberht, ealdorman.

✠ Diera, bishop.[1]

✠ Æthelwulf, bishop.[2]

✠ Heardred, bishop.[3]

✠ Jænberht, archbishop.

✠ Eadberht, bishop.[4]

✠ Hygeberht, bishop.[5]

✠ Æthelmod, bishop.[6]

✠ Ecgbald, bishop.[7]

✠ Ceolwulf, bishop.[8]

✠ Hathored, bishop.[9]

✠ Gislhere, bishop.[10]

✠ Eadberht, bishop.[11]

✠ Ealdberht, bishop.[12]

78. Grant by Offa, King of Mercia, to the Church of Worcester of land at Westbury and Henbury, Gloucestershire (793–796)

This charter is the only surviving statement of the amount the king could draw from an estate as his farm. It survives both in Brit. Mus. Cott. Tiber. A. xiii, fol. 48 (on this manuscript, see p. 449), and Brit. Mus. Cott. Nero E. i, a Worcester cartulary perhaps later than part of 'Hemming's cartulary', and one which gives abbreviated versions only. The Tiberius version is No. 166 in Kemble, No. 273 in Birch, and in Thorpe's *Diplomatarium*, p. 39. The Nero version is No. 272 in Birch. My text is translated from the Tiberius version.

✠ In the name of our Lord Jesus Christ.

I, Offa, bestow the land at Westbury, with everything duly belonging to it, *i.e.* 60 hides,[13] and 20 hides in another place, Henbury, on Worcester for the relief of my soul and the souls of my parents, after my death and that of my son Ecgfrith, and it is rightly to remain in all things with the same power and freedom with which King Æthelbald granted it by charter to my grandfather, Eanwulf; *i.e.* that it is to be so free in the donation of lands and is to remain unshaken in all causes, small or great, for ever, as long as the Christian faith remains among the English in Britain. We enjoin in the name of the supreme God that it is to be released from all compulsion of kings and ealdormen and their subordinates except these taxes; that is,[14] of the tribute at Westbury, two tuns full of pure ale and a coomb[15] full of mild ale and a coomb full of Welsh ale, and seven oxen and six wethers and 40 cheeses and six long *þeru*[16] and 30 'ambers'[17] of unground corn and four 'ambers' of meal, to the royal estate. This, accordingly, with the consent and advice of my bishops and councillors, they decided by a firm agreement, that no authority of king or ealdorman or of any

[1] Of Rochester. [2] Of Elmham. [3] Of Dunwich. [4] Of Leicester. [5] Of Lichfield.
[6] Of Sherborne. [7] Of Winchester. [8] Of Lindsey. [9] Of Worcester. [10] Of Selsey.
[11] Of Hereford. [12] Of London. [13] *manentes.*
[14] The amount of this food-rent is given in English. [15] A measure of uncertain size.
[16] The neuter plural of a word of unknown meaning. [17] Another measure of uncertain size.

secular kind should demand or strive to get by force or petition from our inheritance anything more than these things, in much or in little, except this only which this present charter contains.

✠ I, Offa, by the grace of God king, confirm with the mark of my own hand this fixed yearly rent to the king.

✠ I, Ecgfrith, son of the same king, have consented and subscribed.

✠ I, Æthelheard, archbishop, have consented and subscribed.

✠ I, Hathored, bishop,[1] have consented and subscribed.

✠ I, Unwona, bishop,[2] have consented and subscribed.

✠ The sign of Brorda, 'patrician'.

✠ The sign of Beonna, abbot.

✠ The sign of Alhmund, abbot.

✠ The sign of Wigmund, abbot.

✠ The sign of Forthred, abbot.

✠ The sign of Bynna, ealdorman.

✠ The sign of Esne, ealdorman.

✠ The sign of Æthelmund, ealdorman.

✠ The sign of Alhmund, ealdorman.

✠ The sign of Wigberht, ealdorman.

✠ The sign of Wicga, ealdorman.

✠ The sign of Edgar, ealdorman.

✠ The sign of Alhmund, ealdorman.

79. Agreement between Archbishop Æthelheard and Abbess Cynethryth at a synod of "Clofesho", ending a long dispute over the monastery of Cookham, Berkshire (798)

Among other things, this document gives information about the possession of the debatable lands on the middle Thames in the eighth century. Cookham, in Berkshire, is controlled by a Mercian king, Æthelbald, who reigned from 716 to 757; but Cynewulf of Wessex had control of this region at some time in his reign (757–786), until it was wrested from him by Offa, perhaps as a result of the battle of Bensington in 779. Soon after his accession, Cynewulf issued charters which are witnessed by the Mercian king, and in 772 he is present at Offa's court (Birch, No. 208), but his acknowledgment of Mercian supremacy seems to have been intermittent. See p. 23.

The Abbess Cynethryth may be Offa's widow (see Levison, *England and the Continent in the Eighth Century*, pp. 251 ff.). If so, she was mother of the King Ecgfrith who had given *Pectanege* monastery to the archbishop. Neither *Bedeford* nor *Pectanege* can be identified with certainty.

This agreement survives only in later cartularies, Lambeth MS. 1212 and Brit. Mus. Cott. Claud. D. ii. It is No. 1019 in Kemble, No. 291 in Birch, and is in Thorpe, *Diplomatarium*, p. 40, Haddan and Stubbs, III, p. 512, Earle, p. 65.

✠ Our God and Lord Jesus Christ reigning for ever.

I, Æthelheard, by the grant of the abundant grace of Almighty God metropolitan of the church of Canterbury, with our most excellent King Cenwulf, summoning together all our provincial bishops, ealdormen and abbots and men of whatever high rank, to a synodal council in the place which is called *Clofesho*, there asked of them by careful inquiry how the catholic faith was held among them, and how the

---

[1] Of Worcester. [2] Of Leicester.

Christian religion was practised. To these inquiries it was unanimously replied thus: "Be it known to thy Paternity that exactly as it was set down in the beginning by the holy Roman and apostolic see, by the direction of the most blessed Pope Gregory, thus we believe, and we endeavour as much as we can to practise what we believe without equivocation." But after these things had been dealt with more fully, I began thus: "It is necessary, dearest brothers, to make restitution to the churches of God and the venerable men who for a long time now have been miserably afflicted by the loss of lands and the removal of title-deeds."[1]

After these words, the documents of the monastery which is called Cookham, and of the lands adjacent to it, were produced in the midst. This monastery, namely with all the lands belonging to it, Æthelbald, the famous king of the Mercians, gave to the church of the Saviour which is situated in Canterbury, and in order that his donation might be the more enduring, he sent a sod from the same land and all the deeds of the afore-mentioned monastery by the venerable man Archbishop Cuthbert, and ordered them to be laid upon the altar of the Saviour for his everlasting salvation. But after the death of the aforesaid pontiff, Dægheah and Osbert, whom the same pontiff had brought up as pupils, impelled by the evil spirit, stole these same documents, and delivered them to Cynewulf, king of the West Saxons. And he, receiving immediately the evidence of documents, took over for his own uses the aforesaid monastery with all things duly belonging to it, disregarding the words and actions of the aforenamed Archbishop Cuthbert. Again, archbishops Bregowine and Jænberht complained through their various synods concerning the injury sustained by the church of the Saviour, both to Cynewulf, king of the West Saxons, and to Offa, king of the Mercians, who seized from King Cynewulf the oft-mentioned monastery, Cookham, and many other towns, and brought them under Mercian rule.

At length, King Cynewulf, led by a tardy penitence, sent back to the church of Christ in Canterbury the charters, that is to say, the deeds which he had wrongfully received from the above-mentioned men Dægheah and Osbert, with a great sum of money, humbly asking that he might not be imperilled under an anathema of so great authority. Truly, King Offa as long as he lived retained the afore-mentioned monastery, Cookham, without documents, just as he had received it, and left it to his heirs after him without the evidence of documents.

But in the second year of King Cenwulf, a synod was held at *Clofesho*, as has been indicated above. And I, Æthelheard, by the grace of God archbishop of Canterbury, and Cufa my dean with me, and many other seniors of that church of Christ, brought the deeds of the aforesaid monastery of Cookham into the council; and when they had been read through in the presence of the synod, it was decided by the voice of all that it was right that the metropolitan church should receive the oft-mentioned monastery, Cookham, whose title-deeds it had in its possession; because it had been so wrongly despoiled for such a long time.

Then, however, it pleased me, Æthelheard, by the grace of God archbishop, and Abbess Cynethryth, who at the time was in charge of the oft-mentioned monastery, and the elders assembled for this purpose from both sides, Kent, namely and *Bedeford*,

---

[1] 'Chirographs.'

that the same Cynethryth should give to me in exchange for the oft-mentioned monastery land of 110 hides[1] in the region of Kent: 60 hides,[2] namely in the place which is called Fleet, and 30 in the place which is called Tenham, and 20 in a third place which is called the source of the Cray. These lands, truly, King Offa formerly caused to be assigned to himself while he was alive and to his heirs after him, and after the course of their life, he ordered them to be consigned to the church which is situated at *Bedeford*. This also we decided in the presence of the whole synod that the abbess should receive from me the oft-mentioned monastery with its documents, and I should receive from her the lands and the deeds of the lands which she gave to me in Kent, to the end that no controversy may arise in the future between us and our heirs and those of King Offa, but that what was confirmed between us with the testimony of so noble a synod may be kept for ever by an unbroken covenant. I, Archbishop Æthelhëard, also concede to the possession of Abbess Cynethryth the monastery which is situated in the place which is called *Pectanege*, which the good King Ecgfrith gave and granted by charter for me to possess with hereditary right.

80. Restoration by Cenwulf, king of Mercia, to Christ Church, Canterbury, of lands in Kent granted by Egbert, king of Kent, and revoked by Offa, king of Mercia (799)

This document (Brit. Mus. Stowe Charter VII) is of singular interest in showing what was Offa's conception of his rights as overlord. The reason for his objection to the grant is expressed less ambiguously in Birch, No. 332: "and King Egbert had given the land to Ealdhun by charter, but after him, King Offa took away the aforesaid land from our community, as if, in fact, Egbert were not allowed to bestow by charter lands by hereditary right". This shows that it is a subject king, Egbert, to whom Offa refers as his *minister* 'thegn' in the present text. From Birch, No. 319, we learn that Ealdhun had been reeve in the royal vill in the city (Canterbury), and from Birch, No. 332, that he was a kinsman of Archbishop Jænberht.

There is a facsimile of this charter in *Ord. Surv. Facs.*, III, pl. 7. It is No. 293 in Birch, while No. 1020 in Kemble is from inferior versions preserved in the late Canterbury registers, Lambeth MS. 1212 and Register A of Christ Church, Canterbury.

In the name of the Redeemer of the world.

I, Cenwulf, by the grace of God king of the Mercians, at the request of Æthelhëard our archbishop, restore to the metropolitan church of the Saviour in the hope of future recompense, land of 44 ploughlands, at a place named thus: at Charing, 30 ploughlands, at *Seleberhtes cert*,[3] or *Bryninglond*, 10; which lands, in fact, King Egbert formerly bestowed on the afore-named church for a recompense of great riches; also four ploughlands at a place called *Humbinglond* in Barham, which land also the aforesaid Egbert made over to his thegn, Ealdhun by name, and he when setting out across the sea gave his estate aforesaid to the community which dwelt at the church of the Saviour, for him and them into their own right and control to have and enjoy happily in the Lord for their common necessities. But afterwards Offa, king and glory of Britain, transferred the possession of these lands, and distributed them to his thegns, saying that it was wrong that his thegn should have presumed to give land allotted to him by his lord into the power of another without his witness. But now, however, I, King Cenwulf, at the request of the aforesaid pontiff, with the

---

[1] *manenses.*   [2] *cassati.*   [3] Now simply Chart.

consent of all our bishops and leading men, for my everlasting salvation and the peace and victory of the most loyal race of the Mercians, and also because of the payment of money, whose estimation amounts to 100 mancuses, will grant in the same way and on the same terms the possession of those lands, both the church of Christ and also the four ploughlands at [Bishops]bourne, to the congregation and community of the church of Canterbury to be held in their own right for ever, just as it was ordained and granted before under King Egbert; and I confirm this my donation, under the testimony of illustrious living men, with the sign of the Holy Cross, that they may remain thus.

This donation of both was made in the year of our Lord's incarnation 799, which is the third year of our rule and the seventh indiction, in the royal town at Tamworth.

✠   I, Cenwulf, king, will grant and subscribe as witness.
✠   I, Hygeberht, archbishop,[1] have consented and subscribed.
✠   I, Æthelheard, archbishop,[2] have subscribed as witness.
✠   I, Unwona, bishop,[3] have subscribed.
✠   I, Cyneberht, bishop,[4] have subscribed.
✠   I, Ealhheard, bishop,[5] have subscribed.
✠   I, Hathored, bishop,[6] have subscribed.
✠   I, Utol, bishop,[7] have subscribed.
✠   I, Tidfrith, bishop,[8] have subscribed.
✠   I, Eadwulf, bishop,[9] have subscribed.
✠   I, Wihthun, bishop,[10] have subscribed.
✠   I, Hathoberht, bishop,[11] have subscribed.

✠   I, Ealhmund, abbot.   ✠   I, Forthred, abbot.
✠   I, Beonna, abbot.   ✠   I, Wigmund, abbot.

These venerable witnesses have consented and subscribed. Turn the leaf and you see the names of the ealdormen who consenting to this placed the sign of their hands.

✠   Brorda, ealdorman.[12]   ✠   Edgar, ealdorman.
✠   Esne, ealdorman.[12]   ✠   Wicga, ealdorman.
✠   Æthelmund, ealdorman.   ✠   Beornmod, ealdorman.
✠   Wigberht, ealdorman.   ✠   Hygeberht, ealdorman.
✠   Heardberht, ealdorman.   ✠   Cuthred, ealdorman.
✠   Ceolmund, ealdorman.   ✠   Lulling, ealdorman.

81. Æthelric, son of Æthelmund, declares before the synod of "Aclea" how he bequeathes his inheritance, confirmed to him by a previous synod (804)

This document is important among other things in containing a nuncupative will. Æthelric is perhaps the son of the donee of No. 74, who received five hides at Aston, or Stoke, from Uhtred, sub-king of the Hwicce, in 770. He is certainly son of the thegn Æthelmund to whom Offa gave 55 hides at Westbury by the Avon between 793 and 796, in perpetual liberty (Birch, No. 274). This grant is difficult to reconcile with No. 78 above, in which Offa gives 60 hides at Westbury and 20 at

---

[1] Of Lichfield.   [2] Of Canterbury.   [3] Of Leicester.   [4] Of Winchester.   [5] Of Elmham.
[6] Of Worcester.   [7] Of Hereford.   [8] Of Dunwich.   [9] Of Lindsey.   [10] Of Selsey.
[11] Of London.   [12] In these two signatures, the title used is *princeps*, in all the others *dux*.

Henbury to Worcester after the death of himself and his son. The Rev. C. S. Taylor, in an article on Berkeley Minster in *Trans. Brist. and Glos. Arch. Soc.*, XIX (1894–1895), pp. 70–84, assumes that Offa granted to Æthelmund his own life interest only, but there is no hint of this in the document, and Æthelmund's son is in possession of the estate. It is possible that Æthelmund is the ealdorman killed at Kempsford in 802 (see No. 1, p. 169). Æthelric's mother, Ceolburh, is presumably the abbess whose death is recorded in the Chronicle, 805 (for 807), and who is said by Florence of Worcester to have been abbess of Berkeley. Her son's suggestion that she may need protection from "the Berkeley people" may indicate a fear that the community will try to possess themselves of her inherited land. Berkeley did give trouble, and No. 84 records the settlement at *Clofesho* in 824 of their dispute with the church of Worcester concerning this monastery of Westbury. Berkeley was still in possession of an estate at a place called Stoke in 883, when they relinquished it to Ealdorman Ethelred in return for privileges, and he made arrangements for it eventually to go to Worcester (Birch, No. 551); but it does not follow that this is the same Stoke as that mentioned in the present document. The Stoke held by Berkeley is generally identified with Stoke Bishop, Gloucestershire; the one given to Æthelmund by Uhtred is undoubtedly Stoke Prior, Worcestershire.

    This document survives in the two Brit. Mus. Cott. MSS., Tiber. A. xiii and Nero E. i (on which see pp. 449, 467). It is No. 186 in Kemble, No. 313 in Birch, in Thorpe, *Diplomatarium*, p. 54, Haddan and Stubbs, III, p. 548.

WESTBURY AND STOKE[1]

✠ In the name of the supreme Lord God, who—King of Kings—dwells in the heights and looks over all things, celestial and terrestrial.

In the year of the incarnation of Christ 804, the twelfth indiction.

I, Æthelric, son of Æthelmund, having with the knowledge of the synod been summoned to the synod and to appear for judgment in the place which is called *Clofesho* with the deeds of the estate, *i.e.* 'Westminster',[2] which previously my kinsmen delivered and granted to me, Archbishop Æthelheard directed me and gave judgment there with the witness of King Cenwulf and his chief men in front of the whole synod when they perused my documents, that I was free to give my land and title-deeds wherever I wished.

Afterwards I entrusted them for my friends to keep when for the relief of my soul I sought St. Peter and St. Paul. And when I came back to my country, I received back my land and repaid the price as we previously agreed, that we might be mutually at peace. But a few years later another synod was held, at *Aclea*. Then in that synod in the presence of the bishops, the king and his leading men, I recalled my former privilege, which was adjudged to me before, and with their permission I testified with the present witness how I wished to give my inheritance. And I spoke thus:

"These are the names of those lands which I will give to the place which is called Deerhurst, for me and for Æthelmund my father, if it befall me that my body shall be buried there: Todenham, and Stour, Shrawley and *Cohhanleah*; on condition that that community carries out their vows as they have promised me. Again, I will give to Wærferth 11 hides[3] at Bromsgrove and Feckenham, so that he may have them for his life and afterwards give them to Worcester. Also, indeed, I give to Gloucester 30 hides under Over. And when the end of my life befalls me, I will give to my mother, Ceolburh, if she live longer than I, the land at 'Westminster' and at Stoke, that she may have it for her life and afterwards give it to the church of Worcester; that on this account she may while she lives have there protection and defence against the claims of the Berkeley people. And if any man in any dispute decrees from her an oath against the Berkeley people, she will be most free to give it with the true

---

[1] A marginal addition in the cartulary.   [2] This monastery was at Westbury-on-Trym.   [3] *manentes.*

counsel of my kinsfolk, who granted me the inheritance, and with mine, with which I will give it to her. And if she does not get protection in the city of Worcester, she is afterwards first to seek it from the archbishop in Kent, and if she does not get it there, she is to be free with her deeds and estates to choose protection where it shall please her. If it shall happen otherwise–as I hope it will not–that any man contends dishonourably against my title-deeds and inheritance, then Bishop Ealdwulf has in Lichfield the duplicate of this charter, and my close and most faithful friends have others, namely Eadberht, son of Edgar, and Æthelheah, son of Esne, in confirmation of this matter.

Also I, Æthelric, ask, for the love of Almighty God, and enjoin and beseech by all the powers of heaven, that no man dare to diminish this placing of the Cross of Christ, which is confirmed by the testimony of such great men. If anyone dares to infringe this confirmation, may he be effaced from the praise of God, if he has not made amends.

✠ I, Cenwulf, king of the Mercians, have subscribed this munificence with the sign of the Holy Cross.

✠ I, Æthelheard, archbishop of the city of Canterbury, have subscribed the sign of the Holy Cross.

✠ I, Ealdwulf, bishop of Lichfield, have consented.

✠ I, Wearnberht, bishop,[1] have consented.

✠ I, Deneberht, bishop,[2] have consented.

✠ I, Wulfheard, bishop,[3] have consented.

✠ I, Eadwulf, bishop,[4] have consented.

✠ I, Heahberht, ealdorman, have subscribed.

✠ I, Beornnoth, ealdorman, have subscribed.

✠ I, Ceolweard, ealdorman, have subscribed.

✠ I, Cynehelm, ealdorman, have subscribed.

✠ I, Wicga, ealdorman, have subscribed.

✠ I, Wigheard, ealdorman, have subscribed.

✠ I, Byrnwold, ealdorman, have subscribed.

✠ I, Ealdred, ealdorman, have consented and subscribed.

82. Grant by Cenwulf, king of Mercia, and Cuthred, king of Kent, to the abbess of Lyminge, of land in Canterbury as a refuge (804)

The chief interest of this charter is its evidence of uneasiness about the monasteries exposed to raiding on the coast. The vikings had sacked Lindisfarne in 793, Jarrow in the next year, and raided the coast of Dorset between 787 and 802, and there may have been unrecorded raids.

The charter is No. 188 in Kemble, No. 317 in Birch. These editors print from W. Somner, *Antiquities of Canterbury*, ed. Battely (1703), App. No. LXIV, p. 68, evidently unable to find any manuscript source.

✠ The Lord God Almighty directing and governing.

I, Cenwulf, king of the Mercians, and Cuthred, my brother, king of the people of Kent, in the year of our Lord's incarnation 804, have conceded to the venerable

[1] Of Leicester.   [2] Of Worcester.   [3] Of Hereford.   [4] Of Lindsey.

Abbess Selethryth and her community at the church of St. Mary, ever Virgin, which is situated in the place which is called Lyminge, where rests the body of the blessed Eadburh, a small piece of land in the city of Canterbury as a refuge in necessity; this is, six acres belonging to the church which is situated in honour of the blessed Mary[1] in the western part of the city, and whose boundaries are seen to encompass it thus: in the east, the River Stour, in the west and south, the wall of the city; from the site of the church it extends to the north with a projection, it is said, of about fifteen rods.

If, however, anyone shall try to infringe or diminish this our donation, let him know that he must render account on the Day of Judgment, unless he wish to make amends before to God and men with worthy compensation. And these are the names of the witnesses which are written below.

✠   I, Cenwulf, king of the Mercians, confirm this my donation with the sign of Christ's Cross.

✠   I, Cuthred, king of the people of Kent, confirm with the sign of the Cross.

✠   I, Æthelheard, by the grace of God archbishop, have consented and subscribed.

✠   I, Eadwulf, bishop,[2] have consented and subscribed.

✠   I, Deneberht, bishop,[3] have consented and subscribed.

83. Grant by Ceolwulf I, king of Mercia, to Archbishop Wulfred, of land at "Mylentun", near Kemsing, Kent (17 September 822)

This charter, Brit. Mus. Cott. Augustus, II. 93, gives the exact date of Ceolwulf's coronation, and suggests that a gift to the consecrator may have been normal on such an occasion. It gives a very comprehensive list both of the appurtenances of an estate and of the charges with which land can be burdened. There is a facsimile in Brit. Mus. Facs., II, pl. 15. The charter is No. 216 in Kemble, No. 370 in Birch, and also in Earle, p. 100.

✠ In the name of Jesus Christ the Saviour of the World, who is and who was and who will be, through whom kings rule and divide the kingdoms of the world.

Just as the Governor of the whole world has made distribution according to the measure of his own will, so, the grace of the same God permitting, I, Ceolwulf, king of the Mercians and also of the people of Kent, will give and concede to Wulfred, the venerable archbishop, some portion of land of my rightful possession, i.e. five plough-lands in the province of Kent at a place called *Mylentun*, into his own power, to have, possess and exchange, or also leave after his death to whomsoever of those dear to him he shall please, with all the advantages duly belonging to it, with fields, woods, meadows, pastures, waters, mills, fisheries, fowling-grounds, hunting-grounds, and whatever is contained in it. Moreover I will free the aforesaid land from all servitude in secular affairs, from entertainment of king, bishop, ealdormen, or of reeves, tax-gatherers, keepers of dogs, or horses, or hawks; from the feeding or support of all those who are called *fæstingmen*;[4] from all labours, services, charges or burdens,

---

[1] Gordon Ward, in *Arch. Cantiana*, LIV, pp. 62–68, identifies this with the church of St. Mildred, but R. V. Potts, in *ibid.*, LVI, pp. 19 f., disputes this, contending that St. Mary's has disappeared, probably being destroyed by the Danes.   [2] Of Lindsey.   [3] Of Worcester.

[4] This term occurs only in charters, and seems to refer to those who had the right to claim lodging as they went about the king's business.

whatever, more or less, I will enumerate or say. It is to remain freed everywhere for ever from all burdens, greater or smaller, specified or unspecified, except from these four causes which I will now name: military service against pagan enemies, and the construction of bridges and the fortification or destruction of fortresses among the same people, and it is to render single payment outside,[1] according to the custom of that people, and yet pay no fine to anyone outside, but it is ever to remain free and secure in its integrity, without any violence for any reason, for Wulfred the archbishop and his heirs in the future, with its most certain boundaries:[2] in the east, Kemsing, in the south, the spring in the hollow, and in the west the Darent, in the north, Shoreham; likewise the wood which is called Chart at the west and at the north, Greatness, at the east, the 'Chart' of Kemsing, and in the south, Andred.[3] Again, in Andred, food and pasture for swine and cattle or goats in its places Ewehurst [?], *Sciofingden* and *Snadhyrst*.

And if anyone should desire to know why I have given and freed this gift so devoutly, let him know that it is recited to him chiefly for the love of Almighty God, and for the venerable degree of the aforesaid pontiff, and also of my consecration which, through the grace of God, I have received from him the same day, and also for his acceptable money, *i.e.* a gold ring containing 75 mancuses, as I received it from him.

It is done in the year of our Lord's incarnation 822, the fifteenth indiction, on 17 September, in the royal place which is called *Bydictun*, these witnesses consenting and writing whose names are contained below.

✠   I, Ceolwulf, king of the Mercians, subscribe this my donation with my own hand.

✠   I, Wulfred, archbishop, consenting, subscribe.

✠   I, Œthelwold, bishop,[4] have consented and subscribed.

✠   I, Hrethhun, bishop,[5] have consented and subscribed.

✠   I, Wulfheard, bishop,[6] have consented and subscribed.

✠   I, Heahberht, bishop,[7] have consented and subscribed.

✠   I, Sigered, ealdorman, have consented and subscribed.

✠   I, Eadberht, ealdorman, have consented and subscribed.

✠   I, Wulfred, ealdorman, have consented and subscribed.

✠   I, Muca, ealdorman, have consented and subscribed.

✠   I, Eadfrith, ealdorman, have consented and subscribed.

✠   I, Bofa, ealdorman, have consented and subscribed.

✠   I, Piot, 'prefect', have consented and subscribed.

✠   I, Eadbald.

✠   I, Cyneberht.   ✠   I, Baduheard.

✠   I, Wighelm.   ✠   I, Tunred.

[1] *i.e.* the simple value of stolen goods.
[2] On these, see E. G. Box, in *Arch. Cantiana*, XLIII, pp. 120–122.
[3] The Weald.   [4] Of Lichfield.   [5] Of Leicester.
[6] Of Hereford.   [7] Of Worcester.

84. Settlement at the synod of "Clofesho" of the dispute over Westbury between Worcester and Berkeley Abbey (824)

I have included this document partly in order that it may be compared with No. 81 above, with which it is connected, but partly also for its illustration of the workings of the law. It applies the principle that, in land-litigation, the possessor has the right to come to the oath. As in some other documents, a respite of 30 days is given during which the compurgators can be collected.

The witnesses include a brother of King Beornwulf, who also witnesses a contemporary charter of 825 (Birch, No. 384), and a papal *praeco* Nothhelm, otherwise unknown.

The charter is preserved in the Brit. Mus. MSS. Cott. Tiber. A. xiii, fol. 47, and Cott. Nero E. i, fol. 387. On these manuscripts, see pp. 449, 467. It is No. 218 in Kemble, No. 379 in Birch. There is a translation of part of it in *Select Essays in Anglo-Saxon Law*, p. 323.

✠ Our Lord Jesus Christ reigning for ever, who governs the monarchy of the world by his strength ever into eternity.

In the year of the incarnation of our Lord Jesus Christ 824, the second indiction, in the reign of Beornwulf, king of the Mercians, a pontifical and synodal council was held in the place which is called *Clofesho*, the aforesaid king presiding there, and the venerable man, Archbishop Wulfred, directing and guiding that meeting. There, having been assembled, were present all our bishops and abbots and all the ealdormen of the Mercians and many of the wisest men. There among many other discussions, a certain dispute was brought forward between Bishop Heahberht and the community of Berkeley, concerning the inheritance of Æthelric, son of Æthelmund, *i.e.* the monastery which is called Westbury. Now the afore-named bishop had the land with the title-deeds, just as Æthelric had ordered that it was to revert to the church of Worcester. That agreement, however, was settled and decreed by the archbishop and by all the holy synod, that the bishop, who had the monastery and territory with the deeds, was to swear the land into his own possession with an oath of the servants of God, priests, deacons and many monks. And when the dispute had been thus concluded and written down in the presence of the bishop, that oath was given 30 days later at 'Westminster'.[1] Wherefore if anyone attempts to remove this estate from that church in the city,[2] let him know that he is acting against the decrees of the holy canons, because the holy canons decree that whatever a holy universal synod with its catholic archbishop has adjudged ought not to be made null or void in any way. And these things were done on 30 October; these are the witnesses and confirmers of this transaction, whose names are noted here below:

✠ I, Beornwulf, king of the Mercians, have confirmed this charter of the synodal decree with the sign of the Holy Cross of Christ.

✠ I, Wulfred, archbishop, have corroborated this synodal judgment with the sign of the glorious Cross.

✠ I, Œthelwold, bishop,[3] have consented.   ✠ At the oath at 'West-
✠ I, Hrethhun, bishop,[4] have consented.   minster' there were as many
✠ I, Eadwulf, bishop,[5] have consented.   as 50 priests and 10 deacons
✠ I, Heahberht, bishop,[6] have consented.   and 160 other priests.[8]
✠ I, Beonna, bishop,[7] have consented.

[1] *i.e.* Westbury.   [2] The Old English word, *ceaster* 'Chester', is used.   [3] Of Lichfield.
[4] Of Leicester.   [5] Of Lindsey.   [6] Of Worcester.   [7] Of Hereford.   [8] This note is in Old English.

✠   I, Wigthegn, bishop,[1] have consented.

✠   I, Ceolberht, bishop,[2] have consented.

✠   I, Wærmund, bishop,[3] have consented.

✠   I, Cynred, bishop,[4] have consented.

✠   I, Hunberht, bishop,[5] have consented.

✠   I, Eanmund, abbot, have consented.

✠   I, Cuthwulf, abbot, have consented.

✠   I, Wihtred, abbot, have consented.

✠   I, Wilfrid, abbot, have consented.

✠   I, Beornnoth, ealdorman.   ✠   I, Eadberht, ealdorman.

✠   I, Sigered, ealdorman.   ✠   I, Egbert, ealdorman.

✠   I, Eadwulf, ealdorman.   ✠   I, Ealhheard, ealdorman.

✠   I, Mucel, ealdorman.   ✠   I, Uhtred, ealdorman.

✠   I, Ludeca, ealdorman.

✠   Bynna, the king's brother.

✠   Piot, priest.

✠   Cyneberht.

✠   Nothhelm, messenger[6] from the lord Pope Eugenius.

✠   Bola.   ✠   Aldred the toll-collector have

✠   Wighelm   consented.

✠   Eadbald have consented.   ✠   Baduheard.

✠   Here are the names of the priests who stood and were concerned in the
     oath.[7]

85. Grant by Wiglaf, king of Mercia, of a privilege for the lands of the monastery of Hanbury, Worcestershire (836)

This charter, Brit. Mus. Cott. Augustus, ɪɪ. 9, is interesting in the full list it gives of the privileges of an estate, but its chief value lies in its indication that the ealdormen of the districts concerned required to be compensated when a comprehensive privilege of this kind was granted.

Mucel Esne's son is probably son of Ealdorman Esne who attests from 779 to about 810. King Alfred's father-in-law was called Mucel, ealdorman of the Gaini, but as two ealdormen of this name were in office concurrently, one cannot be sure that he was Esne's son.

The charter is also in Brit. Mus. Cott. Tiber. A. xiii, fol. 21, on which manuscript see p. 449. There is a facsimile of the original charter in *Brit. Mus. Facs.*, ɪɪ, pl. 24. The charter is No. 237 in Kemble, No. 416 in Birch, and in Earle, p. 111.

✠ The kingdom of God ought to be sought above the entire riches of the world, the Apostle testifying: "For the things which are seen are temporal; but the things which are not seen are eternal."[8] "What doth it profit a man, if he gain the whole world and suffer the loss of his own soul?"[9]

Wherefore I, Wiglaf, king of the Mercians, with my bishops and ealdormen and magistrates, liberally free to the celestial height for the whole race of the Mercians in

---

[1] Of Winchester.   [2] Of London.   [3] Of Dunwich.
[4] Of Selsey.   [5] Of Elmham.   [6] *praeco*, literally, 'herald'.
[7] This sentence is in Old English. It is followed by a list of 56 names, which it seemed pointless to print here. Three are abbots (Freomund, Eadberht, Egbert), 47 are priests, 6 are deacons.
[8] II Corinthians iv. 18.   [9] Matthew xvi. 26.

common and for the absolution of our sins, the monastery at Hanbury, complete with the wood belonging to it and with fields and meadows, and with all appurtenancies, and with salt-pits and lead-furnaces, and villages and all things belonging thereto, from small and from great causes, specified and unspecified, except the construction of ramparts and bridges.

This donation was made at Croft,[1] in the year of our Lord's incarnation 836, the fourteenth indiction, and in the seventh year of our reign granted by God. For the redemption of my soul, with a willing and agreeable mind, I will free the aforesaid places, with all the villages[2] which are subject to all those places, in this way for ever; I will free them from entertainment of king and ealdormen, and from all building of the royal residence, and from that burden which we call in Saxon *fæstingmen*.[3] All these things I concede with a willing mind. Know, therefore, you who may obtain this fleeting kingdom after me, why I have written and ordered to be written this gift and this privilege; because I desire of my God and trust in his ineffable mercy that our Lord Jesus Christ may cause to be deleted my sins which I committed through ignorance. I believe that he may deign to cleanse me from all, through this good deed, because it is written: "Amend sin where it was committed." Now I humbly beseech my successors by the glorious and wonderful name of our Lord Jesus Christ, that you will graciously allow the charitable gift to stand which I have given into the height of the summit of the heavens into the hand of the Lord for myself and for the whole race of the Mercians in common, and condescend to add to it.

✠　I, Wiglaf, king of the Mercians.

✠　Cynethryth, queen.

✠　Ceolnoth, archbishop.

✠　Cynefrith, bishop.[4]

✠　Hrethhun, bishop.[5]

✠　Eadwulf, bishop.[6]

✠　Heahberht, bishop.[7]

✠　Eadwulf, bishop.[8]

✠　Ealhstan, bishop.[9]

✠　Beornmod, bishop.[10]

✠　Husa, bishop.[11]

✠　Cunda, bishop.[11]

✠　Ceolberht, bishop.[12]

✠　Cynered, bishop.[13]

✠　Eanmund, abbot.

✠　Wihtred, abbot.

✠　Beornhelm, abbot.

✠　I, Sigered, ealdorman, have confirmed this donation with the sign of Christ's Cross.

✠　Mucel, ealdorman.

✠　Tidwulf, ealdorman.

✠　Æthelheard, ealdorman.

✠　Cyneberht, ealdorman.

✠　Æthelwulf, ealdorman.

✠　Ealhhelm, ealdorman.

✠　Hunberht, ealdorman.

✠　Ælfstan, ealdorman.

✠　Mucel, ealdorman.

✠　Wicga.

---

[1] Leics.　　　　[2] *casallis*. Is this translating Old English *cotlif* 'cottage, hamlet, village'?
[3] See p. 474, n. 4.　　[4] Of Lichfield.　　[5] Of Leicester.　　[6] Of Lindsey.
[7] Of Worcester.　　[8] Of Hereford.　　[9] Of Sherborne.　　[10] Of Rochester.
[11] Neither of these names occur elsewhere. Stubbs suggested that they represent bishops of the two East Anglian sees of Elmham and Dunwich, but R. R. Darlington, *Eng. Hist. Rev.*, LI, p. 425, has shown that this is improbable.
[12] Of London.　　[13] Of Selsey.

☩ Ealdred.   ☩ Wiglaf.
☩ Ealdberht.   ☩ Eanwulf.
☩ Alfred.   ☩ Ealhmund.
☩ Hwithyse.   ☩ Brihtwulf.
☩ Wearnberht.   ☩ Ecgheard.
☩ Wulfred.

☩ This privilege was obtained from King Wiglaf with the 20 hides at Idsall[1] and the privilege of the land at *Haeccaham* with the estate of 10 hides at 'Field' by the *Weoduma*, and to Mucel, son of Esne, the estate of 10 hides at Crowle.[2] They are to have them for their lifetime, and after their lifetime the land is to be given back into the holy foundation at Worcester.[3]

Contemporary endorsements[4]

This is the privilege of Hanbury which was obtained with the land at Idsall and 10 hides of the land at Hanbury, and 10 hides in the beanfields at 'Field'.

And the bishop gave to Ealdorman Sigered 600 shillings in gold.

And to Ealdorman Mucel 10 hides of land at Crowle.

86. Restoration by Brihtwulf, king of Mercia, of various estates to the Church of Worcester (28 March 840)

This is probably another instance of a clash between family and ecclesiastical claims on land. King Offa had given in 780 to the monastery of Bredon in Worcestershire, which had been founded by his grandfather, Eanwulf, and which became the possession of the church of Worcester, land in four places, including the Washbourne and Cutsdean mentioned in the present document. Offa states that the monastery is to remain in his kindred (Birch, No. 236). Brihtwulf's reasons for taking back this property may have been like those of Offa in similar circumstances (see No. 77 above.)

The charter is in the Brit. Mus. MSS., Cott. Tiber. A. xiii, fol. 12, and Cott. Nero E. i, fol. 183. On these manuscripts, see pp. 449, 467. It is No. 245 in Kemble, No. 430 in Birch, and in Thorpe's *Diplomatarium*, p. 90. It is translated by C. G. O. Bridgeman in *Will. Salt. Arch. Soc.*, 1916, pp. 72f.

WASHBOURNE

☩ To our high and holy and most omnipotent God and the holy and glorious Trinity be strength, honour and power for ever. Amen.

In the year of the incarnation of the same God, our Lord Jesus Christ, 840, the third indiction.

It happened indeed that Brihtwulf, king of the Mercians, took from us and gave away our land which had been given and conceded and confirmed rightly and legally to the episcopal see, *i.e.* to the church of Worcester, into its own power and free possession by a firm donation. The aforesaid king granted it to his own men just as hostile men instructed him, that is Stoulton, Washbourne, Kemerton, Taddington, Cutsdean.

Then the Bishop Heahberht proceeded with his seniors with him to Tamworth at Easter, having with them their privileges and charters of the lands before

---

[1] Now Shifnal, Shropshire.   [2] Worcs.
[3] This paragraph is in Old English. The last sentence seems in a later hand.
[4] The endorsements are in Old English, and in contemporary hands.

mentioned, and they were read out there before the king and his nobles, and there the leading men of the Mercians gave judgment for him that they had been wrongly and illegally despoiled of their own.

Then their land was returned to them in peace, and at the same time also the bishop made a gift to this granting king in return in Wellesbourne:[1] *i.e.* four very choice horses and a ring of 30 mancuses and a skilfully wrought dish of three pounds, and two silver horns of four pounds; and he gave to the queen two good horses and two goblets of two pounds and one gilded cup of two pounds.

And then the king before witnesses firmly freed these lands for ever, in the presence of his magnates, from every compulsion and charge of maintenance, and strengthening it also with the sign of the Holy Cross of Christ with his own hand, he wrote and confirmed it.

If, truly, anyone, king or ealdorman or man of any rank, be deceived by diabolical avarice that he shall try to violate or diminish this our alms and privilege, let him know that he will be cut off from the company of all the saints of God on the day of the great Judgment before the judgment-seat of Christ, unless he has here made amends to God and men with full compensation.

And these witnesses were present and consented and subscribed to this whose names shine[2] on the other side of the charter.

✠ I, Brihtwulf, king of the Mercians, fortify this my privilege and donation with the standard of the Holy Cross, that it may remain fixed for ever.
✠ I, Sæthryth, queen, have consented.
✠ I, Cynefrith, bishop,[3] have consented.
✠ I, Heahberht, bishop,[4] have consented.
✠ I, Brihtred, bishop,[5] have consented.
✠ I, Cuthwulf, bishop,[6] have consented.
✠ I, Eanmund, abbot.
✠ I, Hunberht, ealdorman.
✠ I, Mucel, ealdorman.
✠ I, Cyneberht, ealdorman.
✠ I, Æthelwulf, ealdorman.
✠ I, Eadwulf.
✠ I, Wicga.
✠ I, Eadwulf.

✠ I, Æthelheard, ealdorman.
✠ I, Dudda, ealdorman.
✠ I, Sigered, ealdorman.
✠ I, Mucel, ealdorman.
✠ I, Alfred.
✠ Hwithyse.
✠ I, Ealdberht.

87. Grant by Ceolred, bishop of Leicester, of land at Pangbourne, Berkshire, to Brihtwulf, king of Mercia, who then grants it to Ealdorman Æthelwulf (843 or 844)

The historical importance of this charter was pointed out by F. M. Stenton, *The Early History of Abingdon*, pp. 25–27. It shows that Berkshire was under Mercian control at this time. The ealdorman concerned retained his position when Berkshire a little later passed into West Saxon hands. He was killed fighting the Danes in 871. See No. 1, p. 177, and n. 10.

The incarnation date does not agree with the indiction, which gives 843. The charter is preserved in the Abingdon cartulary, Brit. Mus. Cott. Claud. B. vi, fol. 11. It is No. 257 in Kemble, No. 443 in Birch, and in Thorpe's *Diplomatarium*, p. 93.

---

[1] Warw. [2] Literally, 'are yellow'. [3] Of Lichfield. [4] Of Worcester. [5] Of Lindsey. [6] Of Hereford.

✠ Our Lord Jesus Christ reigning for ever.

I, Bishop Ceolred, with the knowledge and permission of my venerable communities, will give to Brihtwulf, king of the Mercians, the territory of 14 hides[1] at Pangbourne by the river which is called Thames, in return for the liberty of these monasteries, that he may have, enjoy and possess that same land for his life and leave it to whomsoever he shall wish after him in perpetual inheritance.

I, Brihtwulf, king of the Mercians, will grant to Ealdorman Æthelwulf the liberty and territory of Pangbourne in perpetual inheritance. That is, for instance, that they are to be freed from the entertainment of ealdormen and from that burden which we call in Saxon *fæstingmen*;[2] neither are to be sent there men who bear hawks or falcons, or lead dogs or horses, but they are to be freed perpetually for ever.

If, however, anyone shall observe this or wish to increase it, may he receive blessing from the Lord God of heaven here and in the future; if, however, anyone – which we hope will not happen – shall wish to violate or diminish it in any part, let him know that he will render account before the judgment-seat of our Judge, unless he has previously made amends to God and men.

This was done in the year of our Lord's incarnation 844, and the sixth indiction, and in the fourth year of the reign of King Brihtwulf. These witnesses attesting and writing have corroborated with the sign of the Holy Cross, whose names are noted below:

✠ I, Brihtwulf, king, have conceded and subscribed.

✠ I, Sæthryth, queen, have consented and subscribed.

✠ I, Ceolred, bishop,[3] have consented and subscribed.

✠ I, Hunberht, bishop,[4] have consented and subscribed.

✠ I, Heahberht, bishop,[5] have consented and subscribed.

✠ I, Eanmund, abbot, have consented and subscribed.

✠ I, Mucel, ealdorman, have consented and subscribed.

✠ I, Hunberht, ealdorman, have consented and subscribed.

✠ I, Ælfstan, ealdorman, have consented and subscribed.

✠ I, Cyneberht, ealdorman, have consented and subscribed.

✠ I, Æthel[wulf?], ealdorman, have consented and subscribed.

✠ I, Beornnoth, have subscribed.

✠ I, Alfred, have subscribed.

✠ I, Wulfred, have subscribed.

88. Grant of land at the South Hams, Devon, by Æthelwulf, king of Wessex, to himself (26 December 846)

This charter, Brit. Mus. Cott. Charter VIII. 36, is a most important document for understanding the meaning of 'bookland', for it implies that until the king had an estate of his own formally 'booked' to him, he could not leave or give it to whom he pleased, nor free it from tribute and services for the sake of his beneficiary. King Edgar similarly grants an estate to himself in 963 (Birch, No. 1118).

---

[1] *manentes*.   [2] See p. 474, n. 4.   [3] Of Leicester.
[4] Of Elmham, unless it is an error for Tunberht, bishop of Lichfield.   [5] Of Worcester.

The land concerned in the present charter is a great stretch of country in South Devon (see *Place-Names of Devon*, pp. 264f.). The boundaries have been examined by Mrs. Rose-Troup in *Transactions of the Devonshire Association*, LXI, pp. 266–276. She concludes that they surrounded an estate along the coast from the Dart to the Plym, and that it included Plympton, which was in the possession of the church of Sherborne by 904 (Birch, No. 610). 26 December 846 would be dated 847 since the year probably began at Christmas.

There is a facsimile in *Brit. Mus. Facs.*, II, pl. 30. The charter is No. 260 in Kemble, No. 451 in Birch, and is in Earle, p. 119.

Ｐ Our Lord Jesus Christ reigning for ever.

Since inserted in sacred volumes[1] ... by whose excellent and very salutary oracle, we are daily instructed that this alone survives man "of all his labour which he taketh under the sun"[2] and of all things which he possesses in the days of his vanity, if he should bestow anything in generosity of alms-giving, intent on pious works, and by sharing the needs of his neighbours to the full extent of his powers "make for himself", according to the Saviour's precept, "friends of the mammon of iniquity, who may receive him into everlasting dwellings";[3] therefore I, Æthelwulf, by the help of God, king of the West Saxons, with the consent and permission of my bishops and chief men, have ordered some portion of land, of 20 hides,[4] to be ascribed to myself into my own inheritance; *i.e.* for me to have and enjoy with meadows and pastures, with fields and woods, with waters, running and stagnant, and again, for me to leave eternally to anyone whatever as it may be pleasing to me. And the aforesaid land is to remain free and secure from all things, *i.e.* from tribute of king and ealdorman, and from services exacted by force and from penal causes, and from the capturing of a thief and from every secular burden, except military service and the building of bridges.

The deed of this donation was written in the year of our Lord's incarnation 847, the tenth indiction.

These indeed are the boundaries of these 20 hides[5] in Ham[6] which his councillors conceded to King Æthelwulf, in the place which is called Dorchester, on the second day of Christmas, in the presence of suitable witnesses whose names inscribed below are made clear to the eyes of beholders:[7] First into *Mercecumb*, then into the green pit, then on to the tor at *Mercecumbes* spring, then to Denewald's[8] stone, then to the ditch where Esne dug across the road, thence down to the source of the spring, then down from there by the brook, as far as *Tiddesford*, then up the brook as far as Heott's ditch to the stream, from the stream down where the vixen's[9] ditch meets the brook, and then down the brook to the sea. Then from Thurlestone[10] up the brook as far as *Mollycombe*, from the head of *Mollycombe* to the grey stone, then up above the source of the spring into *Odencolc*, thence on the old way towards the white stone,[11] thence to the hill[12] which is called 'at the holly', thence to the hoary stone, thence to the

[1] Some sixteen letters are illegible here.   [2] Ecclesiastes i. 3.   [3] Luke xvi. 9.
[4] *manentes.*   [5] *cassati.*   [6] Part of the territory now known as the South Hams.
[7] The boundaries are then given in English.
[8] This man's name may survive in Dendles Wood, in the parish of Cornwood.
[9] Mrs. Rose-Troup points out that a place called Wixenford is somewhere near where one would expect this boundary mark. No early forms of this name are known.
[10] Mrs. Rose-Troup considers that the boundaries begin again here on Dartmoor, in which case the pierced stone is not the surviving Thurlestone. But see *Place-Names of Devon*, p. 264.
[11] Not 'with the white stones', as Mrs. Rose-Troup interprets it.
[12] Or 'barrow'.

source of *Secgwell*, thence eastward into the fort,[1] thence westward to the little fort, thence to the paved road,[2] thence below the wood straight out to the reed pool, then up the Avon until the old swine-enclosure runs out to the Avon, then by that enclosure on to a hill,[3] then on to Sorley, thence to the source of 'Wolf-well', thence along the 'wall-way' to the stone at the stream, from the stone on along the high-way to the ditch, thence down to *Wealdenesford*, thence on to the hollow way, thence down the brook to *Hunburgefleot*, and there to the sea.

If anyone, however, at any time or for any reason, and of whatever dignity, profession or order, shall with sacrilegious presumption attempt to pervert or to make invalid the conferment of this munificence, may he be separated from the community of the Church of Christ and from the fellowship of the saints here and in the future, and may his part be set with misers and robbers and may he be associated with Judas Iscariot who betrayed the Lord; if anyone, however, possessed rather with pious intent, shall be anxious to strengthen and defend these things here, may God increase his portion in the inheritance of the righteous, and may he rejoice with all [the blessed][4] without end.

✠   I, King Æthelwulf, for the confirmation of this donation have reverently written down the sign of victory of the Holy Cross.

✠   Sign of the hand of Æthelbald, the king's son.

✠   Sign of the hand of Osric, ealdorman.

✠   Sign of the hand of Osmund, king's thegn.

✠   Sign of the hand of Ecgheard, king's thegn.

✠   Sign of the hand of Lulling, abbot.

✠   Of Wulflaf, abbot.

✠   Sign of the hand of Ecgwulf, king's thegn.

✠   Sign of the hand of Lulluc, king's thegn.

✠   I, Ealhstan, bishop,[5] have consented and subscribed.

✠   Sign of the hand of Ceorl, ealdorman.[6]

✠   Sign of the hand . . .

✠   Sign of the hand of Wulfred, king's thegn.

     Sign of the hand of Ealhstan, king's thegn.

✠   Sign of the hand of Mildred, king's thegn.

Endorsed: To Ham.

89. Grant by Æthelwulf, king of Wessex in connexion with the tithing of his land, of land near Rochester to his thegn Dunn (855), with the addition of an Old English grant of the land by the latter to his wife

King Æthelwulf's 'booking' of the tenth part of his land 'to the praise of God and his own eternal salvation' is mentioned in the Anglo-Saxon Chronicle (No. 1, p. 174), and there survive many charters which purport to be grants by this king to various religious houses in fulfilment of this

---

[1] Mrs. Rose-Troup suggests Ugborough, but older forms of this name show that it was not a *burg* 'fort', but a *beorg* 'hill, barrow'.

[2] Literally 'street'.   [3] Or 'barrow'?   [4] A word is illegible here.   [5] Of Sherborne.   [6] *princeps*.

decision. But, with this one exception, they are of doubtful authenticity. It would appear from this charter that what the king did was to grant land to his thegns so that they could leave it freely to religious houses. On this whole question, see W. H. Stevenson's edition of *Asser*, pp. 186–191.

The charter is preserved in the *Textus Roffensis*. It is No. 276 in Kemble, No. 486 in Birch. The Old English portion is No. 9 in Robertson, *Anglo-Saxon Charters*, with translation.

✠ In the name of the Triune Deity.

I, Æthelwulf, king of the West Saxons and also of the people of Kent, on account of the tithing of lands which, by the gift of God, I have decided to do for some of my thegns, will give to you, Dunn, my thegn, one dwelling which we call in Saxon a *haga*,[1] to the south of Rochester, and 10 acres adjacent on the south side of that dwelling, and also 2 acres of meadow and 10 wagons loaded with wood on the king's hill, and the rights of common in the marsh which rightly belonged to that dwelling of old. And we concede and grant this for you to have and possess, and you are to have the power to leave it with full liberty after your days to whatever heir you please.

I, Æthelwulf, king by the gift of God, have completed this aforesaid donation and privilege in the year of our Lord's incarnation 855, the third indiction, *i.e.* when by the grant of divine grace I proceeded across the sea to Rome; in the presence of these witnesses who have consented and subscribed with me to this:

✠ I, King Æthelwulf, have strengthened and subscribed this my donation and privilege with the sign of the Holy Cross of Christ.

✠ I, Ceolnoth, archbishop, have consented and subscribed.

✠ I, Ethelbert, king, have consented and subscribed.

✠ I, Lullede, ealdorman, have consented and subscribed.

✠ I, Æthelmod, ealdorman, have consented and subscribed.

✠ I, Alfred, the king's son, have consented and subscribed.

✠ I, Eadred, ealdorman, have consented and subscribed.

✠ I, Æthelric, ealdorman, have consented and subscribed.

✠ I, Cyneheah, king's thegn,[2] have consented and subscribed.

✠ I, Mildred, king's thegn, have consented and subscribed.

✠ I, Ceolmund, king's thegn, have consented and subscribed.

✠ I, Lulla, king's thegn, have consented and subscribed.

✠ I, Ethelred, king's thegn, have consented and subscribed.

✠ I, Wulflaf, king's thegn, have consented and subscribed.

✠ I, Ethelred, king's thegn, have consented and subscribed.

✠ I, Wihtgar, king's thegn, have consented and subscribed.

✠ I, Duduc, king's thegn, have consented and subscribed.

✠ I, Osbert, king's thegn, have consented and subscribed.

✠ I, Sigenoth, king's thegn, have consented and subscribed.

In the name of the Lord.[3] Dunn has given this deed and the land which is written thereon to his wife, in God's favour, that she may have it and enjoy it for her day, and give it after her day in the name of the holy Apostle St. Andrew to the community

[1] A fenced plot, usually a town-property.
[2] Throughout this list the term used is *miles* instead of the more common *minister*.
[3] The rest of this document is in English.

with the consent of God and of all his saints, for us both and for all our ancestors;[1] unless they may hold it with the consent of the community at a fair rent as they can agree on, without any deceit or fraud. And they, the community, shall deserve it with their divine services over the year, and the deed is always to remain with the bequest in the community's possession.

90. **Grant by Burgred, king of Mercia, to Ealhhun, bishop of Worcester, of a privilege for lands in Gloucestershire (855)**

This charter has great historical importance because of its reference to the pagans in the Wrekin district in 855, for we should otherwise not have suspected that the viking raids affected West Mercia at this period. It serves as a salutary reminder that the Anglo-Saxon Chronicle does not give a complete account of the Danish raids.

Of the estates mentioned, the six hides at Barnsley can be shown to have belonged to Worcester about 802 (Birch, No. 304).

The charter is entered twice, on fol. 39 and 194b, in Brit. Mus. Cott. Tiber. A. xiii, on which see p. 449. It is No. 277 in Kemble, No. 487 in Birch. It is translated by W. H. Stevenson and W. H. Duignan, *Trans. Shropsh. Arch. and Nat. Hist. Soc.*, 4th Series, i, pp. 3 f.

ABLINGTON, POULTON, BARNSLEY, EISEY

✠ In the name of Almighty God and our Lord Jesus Christ, who lives for ever. Amen.

I, Burgred, by the help of God and the concession of the Ruler of all realms, king of the Mercians, in bestowing in perpetual alms for myself the agreement and privilege of this liberty on my eminent pontiff and faithful friend Ealhhun and his community at Worcester, with the advice and license of all my chief men, will securely grant and write this liberty for them, in these territories and places, *i.e.*: 10 hides[2] at Ablington by the Coln, and nine hides[2] at Poulton, and likewise six hides[3] at Barnsley and five hides[2] at Eisey. Thus these lands are to be freed from all services and fiscal dues, great and small, of king or ealdorman or their deputies for ever in every matter except only four causes, bridges and fortresses and military service against enemies, and simple compensation is to be paid to another, and nothing outside in fines. And I will also free the land of three hides[2] in Bentley, on the west side of the Severn, from the pasturing of the king's swine, which is called 'fern-pasture'. The afore-named bishop has granted to me on account of the delivery of this privilege two gold armlets of skilled workmanship, which weigh 45 mancuses.

If anyone, indeed, with a benevolent mind, shall wish to increase or support or preserve the donation of this privilege and the grant of our alms, may he be placed, crowned, and blessed with the righteous here in the present and in the future. And he who shall try with any fraud or deception to violate or diminish this privilege through diabolical greed, let him know that he is united with robbers and sinners and damned without any honour in eternal damnation with the devil and his companions, unless he shall make amends here with compensation to God and men.

And the donation of this privilege was done in the year of our Lord's incarnation

---

[1] Miss Robertson suggests that *eldran* 'ancestors' is an error for *cildran* 'children', or that words such as 'and children' have been omitted by the copyist.   [2] *manentes*.   [3] *cassati*.

855, the third indiction, in the place which is called *Oswaldesdun*, when the pagans were in the province of the Wrekin-dwellers.

✠ I, Burgred, king of the Mercians, have consented to and subscribed with my hand this above-written privilege.

✠ I, Æthelswith, queen, have consented to this privilege.

✠ I, Ceolred, bishop,[1] have consented and subscribed.

✠ I, Ealhhun, bishop,[2] have consented and subscribed.

✠ I, Brihtred, bishop,[3] have consented and subscribed.

✠ I, Cuthwulf, bishop,[4] have consented and subscribed.

✠ I, Hunberht, ealdorman.	✠ I, Mucel, ealdorman.
✠ I, Æthelheard, ealdorman.	✠ I, Æthelwulf, ealdorman.
✠ I, Beornnoth, ealdorman.	✠ I, O[s]mund, ealdorman.
✠ I, Beornnoth, ealdorman.	✠ I, Beornheard, ealdorman.
✠ I, Ealdberht, ealdorman.	✠ I, Ceolmund.
✠ I, Wærberht, ealdorman.	✠ I, Bealdred.
✠ I, Edgar.	✠ I, Mucel.
✠ I, Eadwulf.	✠ I, Æthelwulf.
✠ I, Wærberht.	✠ I, Bealdred.
✠ I, Ealdberht.	✠ I, Æthelheard.

91. Grant of a privilege by Burgred, king of Mercia, to Ealhhun, bishop of Worcester, concerning the monastery at Blockley (855)

This is a charter illustrating the royal rights, and it shows also that a distinction between Mercian and Hwiccian territory was kept up after the latter ceased to have rulers of its own. It survives in the Brit. Mus. MSS. Cott. Tiber. A. xiii, fol. 14b, Cott. Nero E. i, fol. 183. On these manuscripts, see pp. 449, 467. The Tiberius version is No. 278 in Kemble, No. 489 in Birch; the Nero version, No. 488 in Birch.

✠ Our holy and high progenitor, the Creator of the universe, reigning for ever and ever. Amen.

I, indeed, Burgred, by the grant of the most omnipotent Lord, king of the Mercians, will grant and deliver for the redemption of my soul and for the absolution of my sins and for the hope of heavenly remuneration, to my faithful and very dear bishop and friend Ealhhun, the gift and donation of this privilege, *i.e.* the monastery which is called Blockley. I will free it from the feeding and maintenance of all hawks and falcons in the land of the Mercians, and of all huntsmen of the king or ealdorman except only those who are in the province of the Hwicce; likewise even from the feeding and maintenance of those men whom we call in Saxon 'Walhfæreld[5] and from lodging them and from lodging all mounted men of the English race and foreigners, whether of noble or humble birth. They are to be freed from all these afore-mentioned things for ever, as long as the Christian faith may last among the English in the island of Britain. Bishop Ealhhun bestowed on me on account of the donation of this

---

[1] Of Leicester.   [2] Of Worcester.   [3] Of Lindsey .   [4] Of Hereford.
[5] The significance of this term, which means literally 'Welsh expedition', is uncertain. It could mean the messengers who passed between England and Wales, or possibly an English patrol of the borders.

aforesaid privilege an acceptable sum of money, namely 300 shillings in silver, in order that they may the more freely enjoy this my alms for ever.

If anyone, however, shall attempt with goodwill to increase or preserve or protect in all things this my donation or privilege, let him know that he will have fellowship in heaven with the righteous, and his rest in eternity with God and his angels; and if there be anyone–as indeed we hope there is not–who shall wish to change this and prefer to alter it to evil servitude or constraint, let him know that he will be separated and excommunicated from the fellowship of all the saints of God in heaven, and damned in eternity without end with the devil and his angels, unless previously he shall make amends here with compensation to God and men.

The charter of this privilege was made in the year of our Lord's incarnation 855, the third indiction, in the famous town which is called by many Tamworth, and these witnesses were present whose names are noted here below.

✠ I, Burgred, king of the Mercians, fortify this my donation and alms with the sign of the Cross of Christ.

✠ I, Æthelswith, queen, have consented.

✠ I, Tunberht, bishop,[1] have consented.

✠ I, Ceolred, bishop,[2] have consented.

✠ I, Ealhhun, bishop,[3] have consented.

✠ I, Brihtred, bishop,[4] have consented.

✠ I, Cuthwulf, bishop,[5] have consented.

✠ I, Hunberht, ealdorman.   ✠ I, Ealdberht, ealdorman.

✠ I, Æthelheard, ealdorman.   ✠ I, Wearnberht, ealdorman.

✠ I, Beornnoth, ealdorman.   ✠ I, Mucel, ealdorman.

92. Grant by Burgred, king of Mercia, to Ealhhun, bishop of Worcester, of a house and commercial rights in London (18 April 857)

It is extremely interesting to find as distant a landowner as the church of Worcester eager to secure property in London at so early a date. One should compare Birch, No. 561, by which a later bishop of Worcester, Wærferth, acquired in 889 a 'court' at 'Hwætmund's stone' in London with various privileges.

It is possible that the 'prefect' Ceolmund from whom Bishop Ealhhun had bought this property is the 'prefect' of this name to whom Æthelwulf of Wessex granted land near Rochester in 842 (Birch, No. 439).

This charter is preserved in Brit. Mus. Tiber. A. xiii, fol. 19, on which see p. 449. It is No. 280 in Kemble, No. 492 in Birch.

✠ In the name of the Lord God Most High, who is the hope of all the ends of the earth and in the sea afar off.[6]

I, indeed, Burgred, by the concession of the most omnipotent God, king of the Mercians, will grant and deliver to Ealhhun my bishop for the relief of my soul with the consent of my counsellors a certain small portion of a liberty, of a profitable little estate in the town of London, i.e. at a place called *Ceolmundinghaga*,[7] which is situated not far from the west gate; for the bishop to have in his own liberty, or

---

[1] Of Lichfield. [2] Of Leicester. [3] Of Worcester. [4] Of Lindsey. [5] Of Hereford. [6] Psalm lxiv. 6.

[7] This seems to be a clear instance of the use of the ending *-ing* with merely genitival force, for the *haga* presumably takes its name from the Ceolmund mentioned in the charter.

17

belonging to the city of Worcester, with all the things which rightly belong to it, great and small; *i.e.* that he is to have therein to use freely the scale and weights and measures as is customary in the port. The liberty of this estate was bought from the king with 60 shillings of silver, and had been purchased before with the same amount of money–one pound–from Ceolmund the 'prefect'.[1] Peace and security be to all observing this privilege, and may the vengeance of the eternal King fall on those opposing or denying it, if they have not made worthy amends to God and men.

These things were done in the year of our Lord's incarnation 857, and the fifth indiction, in the famous place called Tamworth, on the holy Easter of the Lord. And 12 pence a year is to be paid to the king as rent from that little estate. These were witnesses whose names are here.

✠　I, Burgred, king of the Mercians, fortify and confirm this privilege which I have given to the bishop, with the sign of the Cross of Christ.

✠　I, Æthelswith, queen, have consented and subscribed this donation of the king.

✠　I, Tunberht, bishop.[2]　　　　　✠　I, Beornnoth, ealdorman.

✠　I, Ceolred, bishop.[3]　　　　　　　I, Ealdberht, ealdorman.

　　I, Ealhhun, bishop.[4]　　　　　　　I, Mucel, ealdorman.

✠　I, Brihtred, bishop.[5]　　　　　✠　I, Æthelwulf, ealdorman.

　　I, Cuthwulf, bishop.[6]　　　　　　　I, Beornheard, ealdorman.

　　I, Hunberht, ealdorman.　　　　　　I, Eadred, ealdorman.

93. Exchange between Ethelbert, king of Kent, and his thegn Wulflaf of land at "Wassingwell" and Mersham, and conversion of the latter into folkland (858)

This document, Brit. Mus. Cott. Augustus II. 66, is important because of its use of the rare term folkland. The estate of *Wassingwell* must hitherto have been folkland, yielding full royal dues and services. When therefore the king grants it by charter to Wulflaf, and thus turns it into bookland –*i.e.* land held by title-deed–he reconverts to folkland the estate at Mersham which he obtains in exchange.

There is a facsimile in *Brit. Mus. Facs.*, II, pl. 33. The charter is No. 281 in Kemble, No. 496 in Birch, and is in Thorpe, *Diplomatarium*, p. 119, Earle, p. 125.

✠ Our Lord Almighty God of Hosts reigning for ever.

I, King Ethelbert, with the consent and permission of my secular nobles and religious dignitaries, with willing heart will give and concede to my faithful thegn Wulflaf some portion of land of my rightful possession, namely five ploughlands in the place which is called *Wassingwell*,[7] in exchange for other land, namely at Mersham. I, Ethelbert, will free eternally this above-mentioned land at *Wassingwell* from all liability to royal service just as the afore-mentioned land at Mersham was before. These indeed are the marshes which duly and rightly belong to that same land, which marshes Hega had before: *i.e.* one dairy-farm of the people of Wye, which before

---

[1] In this context 'prefect' may mean 'reeve'.　　　　[2] Of Lichfield.　　　　[3] Of Leicester.
[4] Of Worcester.　　　　[5] Of Lindsey.　　　　[6] Of Hereford.
[7] Westwell, according to J. K. Wallenberg, *Kentish Place-Names*, pp. 197ff.; but Gordon Ward, in *Arch. Cantiana*, LIII, pp. 24–28, considers that it means the whole manor of *Wella*, later divided into Eastwell and Westwell.

was subject[1] to Wye and to Lenham, and one salthouse at Faversham, and the right for two wagons to go with the king's wagons to Blean wood, and pasture for four oxen with the king's oxen; in the dairy-farm of the people of Wye 30 weys of cheese, and also 10 weys in the other dairy-farm of the people of Wye, and 20 lambs and 20 fleeces. And the above-written land at *Wassingwell* [has] from of old these well-known boundaries lying round it: in the west, the king's folkland,[2] which Wighelm and Wulflaf hold; in the north, 'Cuthric's down', *Heregetheland*;[3] in the east, Wighelm's land;[4] in the south, the bishop's land at Chart; and two mills belonging to the same land, one in *Wassingwell*, the other in *Hwitecelde*. These are the swine-pastures which we call in our language *denbera*, namely *Lamburnan-den*, *Orricesden*, Tilden, *Stanehtan-den*, and the wood called *Sandhurst* which belongs to *Wassingwell*. And I have willingly granted this privilege to this same piece of land at *Wassingwell* and likewise to the said Wulflaf, with the consent and permission of my chief men, that it may remain free and immune from all royal tribute, and services exacted by force and penal matters, from the domination of the ealdorman and the capturing of a thief and every secular burden, except military service only, and the building of bridges and fortification of fortresses.

If, however, anyone–which God forbid–deceived by diabolical fraud and allured by worldly cupidity, shall attempt to infringe this or make it invalid, let him know that he is separated from the community of catholics and that on the day of the great Judgment when heaven and earth are moved he will render account in the presence of Christ and the celestial host unless he has previously made amends.

This was done in the year of our Lord's incarnation 858, the sixth indiction, these witnesses consenting and subscribing whose names are inscribed below.

These are the meadows[5] belonging to *Wassingwell*: half *Stocmead*, north of *Hegford*, by Stour mead, as belong thereto.

✠ I, King Ethelbert, will strengthen and do subscribe this my donation with the sign of the Holy Cross of Christ.

✠ I, Æthelmod, ealdorman, have consented and subscribed.

✠ I, Eastmund, *pedesecus*,[6] have consented and subscribed.

✠ I, Wulflaf, have consented and subscribed.

✠ I, Ethelred, have consented and subscribed.

✠ I, Sigenoth, have consented and subscribed.

✠ I, Beagmund, have consented and subscribed.

✠ I, Ese, have consented and subscribed.

✠ I, Dunn, have consented and subscribed.

✠ I, Oslac, have consented and subscribed.

✠ I, Dudda, have consented and subscribed.

✠ I, Mucel, have consented and subscribed.

---

[1] From here to '20 fleeces' below, the text is mainly in English.   [2] Probably Kingsland.
[3] Wallenberg suggests that this is Challock, for Heregyth was the name of a previous holder of land there, and it is in the required place.   [4] Wallenberg suggests Wilmington.
[5] The rest of this somewhat unintelligible remark is in Old English.
[6] This word occurs from time to time in charters. Its precise significance is uncertain, but it presumably refers to some specially close attendant on the king.

✠ I, Burgnoth, have consented.
✠ I, Æthelwold, have consented.
✠ I, Eadwold, have consented.
✠ I, Lulla, have consented.
✠ I, Acca, have consented.
✠ I, Cynelaf, have consented.

✠ I, Æthelhere, have consented.
✠ I, Wighelm, have consented.
✠ I, Nothmund, have consented.
✠ I, Sigemund, have consented.
✠ Hunfrith, have consented.

Endorsed

These are the deeds of the land at *Wassingwell* which King Ethelbert gave to his thegn Wulflaf in exchange for other land of the same size at Mersham. The king gave and granted by charter to Wulflaf five ploughlands of land at *Wassingwell* in exchange for the five ploughlands at Mersham, and the king made the land at Mersham into folkland for himself when they had exchanged the lands, except for the marshes and except for the salthouse at Faversham and except for the wood which belongs to the salthouse.[1]

94. Lease by Wærferth, bishop of Worcester, of Nuthurst, Warwickshire, in order to obtain money to pay the tribute to the Danes (872)

This charter should be compared with the annal for 872 in the Anglo-Saxon Chronicle. It shows the far-reaching effects of taxation to buy off the Danes. It is preserved in Brit. Mus. Cott. Tiber. A. xiii, fol. 108, and Brit. Mus. Cott. Nero E. i, fol. 184. On these manuscripts, see pp. 449, 467. The Tiberius text is No. 303 in Kemble, No. 534 in Birch; the Nero text is No. 533 in Birch.

✠ Our Lord Jesus Christ reigning for ever, and by his rule[2] governing all things not only celestial but also terrestrial by the laws of equity.

In the year of whose human incarnation 872, the fifth indiction, I, Wærferth, by the abundant grace of God and the gratuitous gift of him who thunders and rules, bishop of the Hwicce, and with the unanimous permission of his community in Worcester, give and deliver to Eanwulf, a king's thegn, for his friendship and acceptable money—20 mancuses of tested gold—a certain estate of our rightful ownership, *i.e.* two hides[3] in Nuthurst, for him to possess happily for his life and to leave to three heirs after him such as he shall choose; on condition, however, that when the lives of the above-mentioned heirs are ended, the aforesaid land is to be given back to the monastery which is called Stratford without contradiction of anyone whatever. This, however, the above-mentioned bishop agreed to chiefly because of the very pressing affliction and immense tribute of the barbarians, in that same year when the pagans stayed in London. And now, therefore, we ask and entreat men of whatever status that this our agreement may continue unviolated and stable in the future. May divine blessing be increased to those who add to and preserve this gift; may diabolical vengeance be laid on those who diminish and despoil it, unless—as we hope—he shall make amends with fitting compensation before God and men.

These witnesses consenting whose names are inscribed below with the sign of the gracious Cross.

---

[1] All this paragraph is in Old English.   [2] Emending *imperium* to *imperio*.   [3] *mansiones*.

✠ I, Werferth, by the grant of the mellifluous gift of Almighty God, bishop, confirm this donation with the sign of the Holy Cross.

✠ I, Æthelheard, prior, have consented.

✠ I, Beornferth, priest, have consented.

✠ I, Eadferth, priest, have consented.

✠ I, Wulfhere, priest, have consented.

✠ I, Ealhhere, priest, have consented.

✠ I, Eadwold.

✠ I, Brihthelm.

✠ I, Burgheard.

✠ I, Wigheard.

✠ I, Beornferth.

✠ I, Heahred.

✠ I, Eared.

✠ I, Wigberht.

✠ I, Ethelred.

✠ I, Wynhelm.

95. Privilege of Ceolwulf II of Mercia, freeing the diocese of Worcester from the charge of feeding the king's horses, in return for spiritual benefits and the lease for four lives of land at Daylesford, Worcestershire (875)

The main interest of this charter is that it shows that Ceolwulf II, though the Anglo-Saxon Chronicle, 874, may call him "a foolish king's thegn", and regard him as a puppet king, was accepted as true king of Mercia by his subjects; otherwise one would not get the signatures of bishops and ealdormen to his charter. It survives in Brit. Mus. Cott. Tiber..A. xiii, fol. 27, on which see p. 449. It is No. 306 in Kemble, No. 540 in Birch.

DAYLESFORD

✠ In the name of the holy and indivisible Trinity.

In the year of the human incarnation of the same, 875, the seventh[1] indiction, I, Ceolwulf, by the grant of the gratuitous grace of God, king of the Mercians, have premeditated giving something in alms for myself that I may receive a share of the eternal reward. Therefore, having been asked by Wærferth, bishop of the Hwicce, and the community in Worcester, I have granted in perpetuity this privilege with the unanimous consent of all my bishops and ealdormen and also of all the chief men of our race, that the whole diocese of the Hwicce is to remain absolved and secure from feeding the king's horses and those who lead them. And the bishop has given to King Ceolwulf six hides[2] at the place which is called Daylesford; and they determined this divine service for the expiation of the sins of King Ceolwulf, that in those monasteries in which the afore-mentioned charge should have been rendered, commemoration and the Lord's Prayer were daily to be raised to heaven as long as the Christian faith should be observed in this race. Then also the above-mentioned king gave to the afore-named bishop 60 mancuses of gold on condition that he himself should hold this land and leave it after him to three heirs whom he should choose, and after the lifetime of these heirs the aforesaid land was to return to Worcester for the soul of King Ceolwulf and his successors, and nevertheless the above-mentioned privilege was to remain in perpetuity. May the Almighty God defend those who deign to defend this gift, and let those who try to violate it know that they shall render account on the day of the dreadful Judgment.

[1] 875 is the eighth indiction.   [2] *manentes*.

These are witnesses and confirmers of this donation whose names are noted below, by the sign of the Holy Cross.

✠ I, Ceolwulf, king of the Mercians, confirm this agreement with my own hand.

✠ I, Eadberht, bishop,[1] have consented.

✠ I, Wærferth, bishop,[2] have consented.

✠ I, Deorlaf, bishop. [3]

✠ I, Brihtnoth, ealdorman.

✠ I, Æthelhun, ealdorman.

96. The will of King Alfred (873–888)

This will, which is in Old English, is the earliest surviving will of an English king, though we know something of the contents of King Æthelwulf's will from Asser's account of it (see No. 7, p. 265). Any remains of so great a king as Alfred are important, and this document will be found to have many features of interest. The date lies between the succession of Bishop Wærferth and the death of Archbishop Ethelred.

The oldest version of the will is Brit. Mus. Stowe MS. 944, fol. 29b–33, edited by Birch, *Liber Vitae of New Minster and Hyde Abbey* (Hants Rec. Soc., 1892), pp. 74–80. This is in an early eleventh-century hand; there is a later and inferior version, with a Middle English and a Latin translation, in the *Liber Monasterii de Hyda*, a late fourteenth- or early fifteenth-century manuscript, edited by E. Edwards (Rolls Series, 1866). There is a facsimile of the Stowe text in *Ord. Surv. Facs.*, III, pl. 22. The best edition of the will is that by F. E. Harmer, *Select English Historical Documents of the Ninth and Tenth Centuries*, pp. 15–19, with translation, pp. 49–53. It is No. 314 in Kemble, Nos. 553–555 in Birch, and is in Thorpe, *Diplomatarium*, p. 484, Earle, p. 144.

I, King Alfred, by the grace of God and on consultation with Archbishop Ethelred and with the witness of all the councillors of the West Saxons, have been inquiring about the needs of my soul and about my inheritance which God and my ancestors gave to me, and about the inheritance which my father, King Æthelwulf, bequeathed to us three brothers, Æthelbald, Ethelred and myself; that whichever of us should live longest was to succeed to the whole. But it happened that Æthelbald died; and Ethelred and I, with the witness of all the councillors of the West Saxons, entrusted our share to our kinsman King Ethelbert, on condition that he should return it to us as fully at our disposal as it was when we entrusted it to him; and he then did so, both that inheritance, and what he had obtained from the use of the property we two held jointly, and what he had himself acquired.

Then it so happened that Ethelred succeeded, and I asked him in the presence of all the councillors that we might divide that inheritance and he should give me my share. He then told me that he could not divide it easily, for he had very often before attempted it; and he said that he would leave after his death to no person sooner than to me whatever he held of our joint property and whatever he acquired. And I gave a ready assent to that. But it happened that we were all harassed by the heathen army; then we spoke about our children, that they would require some property, whatever might happen to the two of us in those troubles. Then we were at an assembly at

---

[1] The lists of the Mercian sees of Lichfield, Leicester and Lindsey are incomplete at this date, but as the two latter were in territory already in Danish hands, the present witness is almost certainly bishop of Lichfield. No bishop of this see is known for certain between Tunberht (last in 857) and Ælfwine (first in 926).

[2] Of Worcester.

[3] Of Hereford.

Swinbeorg[1] and we then agreed in the witness of the councillors of the West Saxons that whichever of us should live longer should grant to the other's children the lands which we had ourselves obtained and the lands which King Æthelwulf gave to us in Æthelbald's lifetime, except those which he bequeathed to us three brothers. And each of us gave to the other his pledge, that whichever of us lived longer should succeed both to lands and treasures and to all the other's possessions except the part which each of us had bequeathed to his children.

But it happened that King Ethelred died. Then no one made known to me any will or any testimony that the position was any other than as we had both agreed with witness. When we now heard many disputes about the inheritance, I brought King Æthelwulf's will to our assembly at *Langanden*[2] and it was read before all the councillors of the West Saxons. When it had been read, I begged them all for love of me–and offered them my pledge that I would never bear any of them a grudge because they declared what was right–that none of them would hesitate either for love or fear of me to pronounce the common law, lest any man should say that I wronged my young kinsfolk, the older or the younger. And then they all rightly pronounced and declared that they could not conceive any juster title nor hear of one in the will. "Now that everything in it has come into your possession, bequeath it and give it into the hand of kinsman or stranger, whichever you prefer." And they all gave me their pledge and signature[3] that as long as they lived no man should ever change it in any way other than as I myself bequeath it at my last day.

I, Alfred, king of the West Saxons, by the grace of God and with this witness, declare how I wish to dispose of my inheritance after my death. First, I grant to Edward my elder son the land at Stratton in Trigg[4] and Hartland[5] and all the booklands which Leofheah holds, and the land at Carhampton and at Kilton and at Burnham and at Wedmore–and I beseech the community at Cheddar to choose him on the terms which we have already agreed on–along with the land at Chewton and what belongs to it. And I grant him the land at Cannington[6] and at Bedwyn[7] and at Pewsey[7] and at Hurstbourne[8] and at Sutton and at Leatherhead[9] and at Alton.[10]

And all the booklands which I have in Kent and at the lower Hurstbourne and at Chiseldon[11] are to be given to Winchester on the terms on which my father bequeathed it, and my private property which I entrusted to Ecgwulf at the lower Hurstbourne.

And to my younger son the land at Arreton[12] and that at Dean[13] and that at Meon[14] and at Amesbury[15] and at Dean[16] and at Sturminster[17] and at Yeovil[18] and at Crewkerne[18] and at Whitchurch[19] and at Axmouth[19] and at Branscombe[19] and

---

[1] The identification of this place by H. G. Tomkins in *Academy*, 24 May 1884, p. 368, as Swanborough Tump, Wilts., is not borne out by the *Place-Names of Wiltshire*, p. 320, for the early form of this name is recorded as *Swanabeorh*.   [2] Unidentified.
[3] The names of the witnesses were written by the scribe, but the individual witnesses probably touched the cross by the signature in token of his attestation.   [4] A district in Cornwall.
[5] Devon.   [6] The last seven places are in Somerset.   [7] Wilts.
[8] Hurstbourne Tarrant, Hants, the lower Hurstbourne mentioned below being Hurstbourne Priors.
[9] Surrey.   [10] Either the Hants or Wilts. place of this name.   [11] Wilts.   [12] Isle of Wight.
[13] Probably the place where Asser first met Alfred, in Sussex (see No. 7, p. 269).   [14] Hants.
[15] Wilts.   [16] Perhaps West Dean, Wilts.   [17] Dorset.   [18] Somerset.   [19] Devon.

at Cullompton[1] and at Tiverton[1] and at Milborne[2] and at Exminster[1] and at Suðeswyrðe[3] and at Lifton,[1] and the lands which belong to it, namely all that I have in Cornwall[4] except Trigg.

And to my eldest daughter the residence at Wellow;[5] and to my middle daughter that at Kingsclere[6] and at Candover;[6] and to the youngest the estate at Wellow[7] and at Ashton[8] and at Chippanham.[8] And to my brother's son Æthelhelm the estate at Aldingbourne[9] and at Compton[10] and at Crondall[6] and at Beeding[9] and at Beddingham[9] and at Burnham[10] and at Thunderfield[11] and at Eashing.[11] And to my brother's son Æthelwold[12] the residence at Godalming[11] and at Guildford[11] and at Steyning.[13] And to my kinsman Osferth the residence at Beckley and at Rotherfield and at Ditchling and at Sutton and at Lyminster and at Angmering and at Felpham,[14] and the lands which belong thereto. And to Ealhswith[15] the estate at Lambourn[16] and at Wantage[16] and at Edington.[17]

And to my two sons 1,000 pounds, 500 pounds to each; and to my eldest daughter and my middle daughter and the youngest and to Ealhswith, 400 pounds to the four of them, 100 pounds to each. And to each of my ealdormen 100 mancuses, and likewise to Æthelhelm and Æthelwold and Osferth; and to Ealdorman Ethelred a sword worth 100 mancuses. And the men who serve me, to whom I have now given money at Eastertide, are to be given 200 pounds, and it is to be divided among them, to each as much as will fall to him according to the manner in which I have just now made my distribution. And to the archbishop 100 mancuses and to Bishop Esne and to Bishop Wærferth and to the bishop of Sherborne.[18] And there is to be distributed for me and for my father and for the friends for whom he used to intercede and I intercede, 200 pounds, 50 to priests throughout my kingdom, 50 to poor servants of God, 50 to poor men in need, 50 to the church in which I shall be buried. I know not for certain whether there is so much money, nor do I know if there is more, but I think so. If there is more, it is to be shared among all to whom I have bequeathed money; and it is my will that my ealdormen and my officials shall all be included and shall distribute it thus.

Now I had previously written differently about my inheritance when I had more property and more kinsmen, and I had entrusted the documents to many men, and in these same men's witness they were written. Therefore, I have now burnt all the old ones which I could discover. If any one of them shall be found, it has no validity, for it is my will that now it shall be as here stated, with God's help.

And it is my will that the men who hold those lands shall observe the directions

---

[1] Devon.
[2] Mr. Finberg has suggested to me that this is not the Somerset Milborne, but the Domesday Borna, Silverton, Devon.
[3] J. J. Alexander, *Trans. Devon Assoc.*, LXIII, 349–358, suggests that this is Lustleigh.
[4] Literally, 'among the Welsh'.   [5] Either in Hants, Wilts., or Somerset.   [6] Hants.
[7] Perhaps in the Isle of Wight.   [8] Wilts.   [9] Sussex.
[10] Too common a name for certain identification.   [11] Surrey.   [12] On him, see No. 1, pp. 190f.
[13] Sussex. King Æthelwulf was first buried at this place (see p. 171, n. 11).
[14] All the lands given to Osferth lie in Sussex.   [15] Alfred's wife.
[16] Berks. Alfred was born at Wantage.   [17] Wilts. The scene of Alfred's victory over Guthrum.
[18] The absence of the bishop's name suggests that the see was vacant when the will was made, or that its holder seemed unlikely to outlive the king.

which stand in my father's will to the best of their power. And if I have any unpaid debt to any one, I desire that my kinsmen certainly pay it. And it is my will that the men to whom I have bequeathed my booklands shall not give it away from my kindred after their death, but I wish that after their death it shall pass to my nearest of kin unless any of them have children; in that case I prefer that it should pass to the child born on the male side as long as any is worthy of it. My grandfather had bequeathed his land in the male line and not in the female line.[1] If then I have given to anyone on the female side what he acquired, my kinsmen are to buy it back, if they wish to have it during their[2] lifetime. If not, let it go after their death as we have already stated. For this reason I say that they are to pay for it, that they succeed to my lands, which I may give on the female as well as the male side, whichever I choose.

And I pray in the name of God and of his saints that none of my kinsmen or heirs oppress any of the dependants[3] whom I have supported. And the councillors of the West Saxons pronounced it right for me to leave them free or servile, whichever I choose; but I desire for the love of God and the good of my soul that they shall be entitled to their freedom and free choice. And I command in the name of the living God that no one is to harass them either by demands of money or by any thing, so that they may not choose such lord as they wish. And I desire that the community at Damarham[4] be given their title-deeds and freedom to choose whatever lord they prefer, both for my sake and for Ælfflæd and for the friends for whom she used to intercede and I intercede. And from my livestock let such payment be made for the good of my soul as is possible and is also fitting and as you wish to give on my behalf.

97. The will of Ealdorman Alfred (871–888)

Besides its interest as an early example of an ealdorman's will, this Old English document, Stowe Charter xx, has claims on our attention because it contains one of the three passages concerned with folkland. Unfortunately its interpretation is not certain. The king's consent seems necessary before Alfred's son may hold it, but the way in which Alfred refers to this son, giving him a very secondary place to his daughter, the child of his wife Wærburh, together with his hope of begetting a male heir closer to him, can only mean that the son in question was illegitimate, and it may be this which prevents Alfred from leaving him folkland without a special permission from the king. The ealdorman's reference to his two wergilds is important also, for it suggests that an ealdorman may have had a wergild by nature of his office, as well as his ordinary one. Alfred was probably ealdorman of Surrey. His will is drawn up after King Alfred's accession in 871 and before the death of Archbishop Ethelred in 888.

There is a facsimile in *Ord. Surv. Facs.*, iii, pl. 20. The best edition is in Harmer, *op. cit.*, pp. 13–15, with translation, pp. 47–49. It is No. 317 in Kemble, No. 558 in Birch, and is in Thorpe, *Diplomatarium*, p. 480, Earle, p. 149.

✠ *Christus.* I, Ealdorman[5] Alfred command to be written and made known in this document to King Alfred and all his councillors and advisors, and likewise to my kinsmen and friends, the names of the persons to whom I most readily grant my

---

[1] The Old English is picturesque: "on the spear side and not on the spindle side".

[2] *i.e.* of the present owners, on the female side.

[3] The only other recorded instance of the term here used, *cyrelif*, refers to a body of canons dependent on a bishop for their support. (See Old English version of the *Rule of Chrodegang*, ed. A. S. Napier, pp. 76f., where *þe on cyrelife sittað* translates *qui victu et vestitu potiantur*.) Etymologically, the word seems to imply voluntary subjection to a lord, and Alfred may be referring to the various types of person described in Asser as entering his service (see No. 7, p. 275), laymen as well as ecclesiastics.

[4] Hants.   [5] *dux.*

inheritance and my bookland, namely my wife Wærburh and the child of us both. That is, then, first 32 hides in Sanderstead[1] and Selsdon,[1] and 20 hides in Westerham[2] and 30 hides in Clapham[1] and 6 hides in Lingfield[1] and 10 hides in Horsley[1] and 6 hides in Nettlestead.[2] I, Ealdorman Alfred give to Wærburh and to Ealhthryth, the child of us both, these lands after my death with livestock and with crops and with everything which belongs to those lands–and I give them 2,000 swine along with the lands–if Wærburh remains unmarried as we verbally agreed. And she is to take to St. Peter's my two wergilds, if it be God's will that she may perform that journey. And after Wærburh's death the land at Sanderstead and Selsdon and at Lingfield is to pass uncontested to Ealhthryth. And if she has a child, that child is to succeed to the land after her; if she has no child, the nearest of kin descended from her direct paternal ancestry is to succeed to the land and to the stock. And any one of my paternal kinsmen who may have the means and the desire to obtain the other lands is then to buy the lands from her at half price. And whatever man it may be who shall have the use of the land at Clapham after my death, let him pay 200 pence every year to Chertsey as a help to their provisions for the sake of Alfred's soul.

And I give to my son Æthelwold three hides of bookland: two hides at Waddon,[1] one hide at Gatton;[1] and I give to him with them 100 swine. And if the king is willing to grant him the folkland along with the bookland, let him have it and use it; if that may not be, then she is to give to him whichever she prefers, either the land at Horsley or that at Lingfield. And I give to my kinsman Brihtsige a hide of bookland at Lingfield, and 100 swine with it. And she is to give 100 swine to Christ Church for me and for my soul, and 100 to Chertsey; and the surplus is to be divided among the monasteries of God's churches in Surrey and in Kent, as long as they choose to remain monasteries[3] [?]. And I give to my kinsman Sigewulf the land at Nettlestead after Wærburh's death; and Sigewulf is to pay from the land 100 pence to Christ Church; and each of the heirs who succeed to the land after him is to render the same alms to Christ Church for Alfred's soul, as long as the Christian faith lasts and the money can be raised from that land. And I give to my kinsman Eadred the land at Farley[4] after Ethelred's death, if he will hold it under him; and he is to pay from that land 30 ambers of corn to Rochester every year. And after Eadred's death this land is to be assigned in writing and without dispute to Alfred's direct maternal kindred, as long as the Christian faith remains on the English island.

This provision and these statements which are written here above–I, Alfred, desire and wish that they be henceforward truly confirmed for me and my heirs. If then Almighty God has ordained and shall grant me as a gift that a nearer male heir shall be born to me, I grant to him all my inheritance after my death to enjoy as he pleases. And whatsoever man will rightly observe and perform these benefactions and gifts and these written and verbal statements, may the King of Heaven preserve him in this present life and also in the life to come; and whatsoever man may lessen or

---

[1] Surrey.   [2] Kent.

[3] This seems to be the most likely meaning for the ambiguous þa hwile þe hio lestan willen "as long as they will last". For 'will' is unusual as a simple future at this date, as it would be if one rendered "as far as they (the swine) will go round".

[4] Probably in Surrey.

infringe them, may God Almighty lessen his worldly possessions and also the glory of his soul for ever and ever.

✠ Here[1] are written the names of the men who are witnesses of these provisions:

✠   I, Ethelred, archbishop, confirm and inscribe these statements and provisions with the sign of the Holy Cross of Christ.

✠   Alfred, ealdorman.[2]

✠ Brihtwulf, ealdorman.	✠ Eardwulf, priest.
✠ Beornhelm, abbot.	✠ Beornoth, deacon.
✠ Eardwulf, abbot.	✠ Wealdhelm, deacon.
✠ Wærburh.	✠ Wine, sub-deacon.
✠ Sigefrith, priest.	✠ Sæfrith.
✠ Beonheah, priest.	✠ Ceolmund, king's thegn.
✠ Beagstan, priest.	✠ Edmund, king's thegn.
✠ Wulfheah.	✠ Eadwold, king's thegn.
✠ Æthelwulf, priest.	✠ Sigewulf, king's thegn.

Endorsement in a contemporary hand: This is Alfred's will.

98. The presentation of the 'Golden Gospels' to Christ Church

This Old English text is entered on fol. 10a of an illuminated manuscript now in the Royal Library at Stockholm, usually known as the Golden Gospels of Stockholm. It is unknown how this manuscript got there. It is English work of the eighth century, and until recently was assigned to Canterbury; but Kuhn has made a plea for Lichfield as the place of origin (*Speculum*, XXIII, pp. 591–629).

The ealdorman in question is the one whose will has come down to us (see No. 97). There is no closer indication of the date of this entry. The Danes could have obtained this loot in any of their raids, for we need not assume that the book remained at its place of origin.

There is a facsimile in J. O. Westwood, *Facsimiles of the Miniatures and Ornaments of Anglo-Saxon Manuscripts* (1868), pl. II. It is edited by Harmer, *op. cit.*, pp. 12f., with translation, pp. 46f., and is No. 634 in Birch.

✠ In the name of our Lord Jesus Christ.[3] I, Ealdorman Alfred and Wærburh my wife obtained these books from the heathen army with our pure money, that was with pure gold, and this we did for the love of God and for the benefit of our souls and because we did not wish these holy books to remain longer in heathen possession. And now they wish to give them to Christ Church to the praise and glory and honour of God, and in gratitude for his Passion, and for the use of the religious community which daily raises praise to God in Christ Church; on condition that they shall be read every month for the sake of Alfred and Wærburh and Ealhthryth, for the eternal remedy of their souls, as long as God has foreseen that the Christian faith shall continue at that place. Moreover I, Ealdorman[4] Alfred and Wærburh beg and implore in the name of Almighty God and of all his saints, that no man be so presumptuous as to give away or remove these holy books from Christ Church, as long as the Christian faith may endure.

Alfred.   Wærburh.   Ealhthryth their [daughter].

---

[1] This list is on the back of the document.   [2] This and all the following titles are in Latin.
[3] This invocation is in Latin.   [4] In this place he uses the Latin title, *dux*.

99. Arrangements about the building of fortifications at Worcester (about 889–899)

This is an Old English document of great importance in relation to Alfred's 'burghal system', and to the organization of a town. It survives in Brit. Mus. Cott. Tiber. A. xiii, fol. 1b, on which see p. 449. A paper manuscript of the sixteenth century, Brit. Mus. Cott. Vespas. A. v, is useful for filling the lacunae where the Tiberius text is now illegible. The best edition is by Harmer, *op. cit.*, pp. 22 f., with translation, pp. 54 f. It is No. 1075 in Kemble, No. 579 in Birch, and is edited with translation in Thorpe, *Diplomatarium*, pp. 136–139.

To Almighty God, the True Unity and the Holy Trinity in heaven, be praise and honour and thanksgiving for all the benefits which he has granted us. For whose love in the first place, and for that of St. Peter and of the church at Worcester, and also at the request of Bishop Wærferth their friend, Ealdorman Ethelred and Æthelflæd ordered the borough at Worcester to be built for the protection of all the people, and also to exalt the praise of God therein. And they now make known, with the witness of God, in this charter, that they will grant to God and St. Peter and to the lord of that church half of all the rights which belong to their lordship, whether in the market or in the street, both within the fortification and outside; that things may be more honourably maintained in that foundation and also that they may more easily help the community to some extent; and that their memory may be the more firmly observed in that place for ever, as long as obedience to God shall continue in that minster.

And Bishop Wærferth and the community have appointed these divine offices before that which is done daily, both during their life and after their death; *i.e.* at every matins and at every vespers and at every tierce, the psalm *De profundis* as long as they live, and after their death *Laudate Dominum*; and every Saturday in St. Peter's church thirty psalms and a Mass for them, both for them living and also departed.

And moreover Ethelred and Æthelflæd make known that they will grant this to God and St. Peter with willing heart in the witness of King Alfred and of all the councillors who are in the land of the Mercians; except that the wagon-shilling and the load-penny[1] at Droitwich go to the king as they have always done. But otherwise, land-rent, the fine for fighting, or theft, or dishonest trading, and contribution to the borough-wall, and all the [fines for] offences which admit of compensation, are to belong half to the lord of the church, for the sake of God and St. Peter, exactly as it has been laid down as regards the market-place and the streets. And outside the market-place, the bishop is to be entitled to his land and all his rights, just as our predecessors established and privileged it.

And Ethelred and Æthelflæd did this in the witness of King Alfred and of all the councillors of the Mercians whose names are written hereafter.[2] And they implore all their successors in the name of Almighty God that no one may diminish this charitable gift which they have given to that church for the love of God and St. Peter.

[1] The payments on a cart-load or pack-load of salt.
[2] These were omitted in the cartulary.

100. Grant by King Edward the Elder of land in Wylye to Æthelwulf, with a vernacular agreement made by the latter (901)

I have given my reasons on p. 340 for believing this to have a genuine base, although it survives only in the Winchester cartulary, Brit. Mus. Addit. MS., 15350; and, if it is genuine, it is important, because texts of this king are so rare. It has an interesting notice of the forfeiture of land for desertion, and one would imagine that it was during the Danish invasion that the crime was committed. The man concerned, Ealdorman Wulfhere, may be the one who witnesses charters from 854 to 871, and who received Buttermere, Wiltshire, in 863.

I suspect the vernacular agreement between Deormod and Æthelwulf to be a marriage agreement, for Deormod gets nothing for himself, but only for a woman, whose name, Deorswith, suggests that she is either his daughter or his sister; moreover, the agreement seems one-sided, if not a marriage agreement, for we are not told that Æthelwulf received anything in return. Deormod is probably King Alfred's 'faithful man' to whom he gave Appleford, Berkshire, in exchange for *Harandum* (Birch, No. 581). He occurs in the Fonthill charter (No. 102), and witnesses many charters of doubtful authenticity, usually as thegn, twice, in doubtful Winchester texts, as ealdorman, once in a spurious Wilton text as cellarer (Birch, No. 567). Æthelwulf is too common a name for certain identification. He is wrongly called bishop in the rubric in the cartulary.

This charter is No. 1078 in Kemble, No. 595 in Birch.

✠ In the name of the High Thunderer, Creator of the world.

Truly the foreseeing and powerful arrangement of the Churches long ago resolved, and decreed with most careful definition to be observed by those succeeding, that the gifts of most pious kings should be delivered with the records of charters on account of the changeable vicissitudes of the times, and concluded with the testimony of a title-deed, lest the source of truth should be brought to nought by the assault of misty oblivion.

On that account it is declared to all present, absent, and those who come after, by the contents of this document, that [I], Edward, by the gift of God's grace king of the Anglo-Saxons, give and concede to Æthelwulf a certain portion of land of my own rightful ownership into his perpetual possession by hereditary right; and on account of his pleasing obedience I confirm to him the more securely the extent of the aforesaid estate, *i.e.* 10 hides[1] in the place which is called 'by the Wylye',[2] with all things duly belonging to it, *i.e.* meadows, pastures, woods, waters and water-courses; that he may have and possess and happily present it to whomsoever he shall choose, in all things with free-will. We write the aforesaid land to him, indeed, free in all things, except the fortification of fortresses and the construction of bridges and military service.

Truly this afore-named estate was originally forfeited[3] by a certain ealdorman, Wulfhere by name, and his wife, when he deserted without permission both his lord King Alfred and his country in spite of the oath which he had sworn to the king and all his leading men. Then also by the judgment of all the councillors of the Gewisse[4] and of the Mercians he lost the control and inheritance of his lands. And now it is made clear at the foot of this document to all who read and hear it, that all those ancient deeds—if anyone has any—are to be proscribed and to be of no further avail, whether in great or in small affairs.

This aforesaid land, indeed, is seen to be surrounded by these boundaries:[5] first to Codford, then down along the Wylye to *Hyssapol*, then on the bend, then east of

---

[1] *cassati.*   [2] Wilts. There is now a village as well as a river Wylye.
[3] The Old English verb *forwyrcan* has two meanings, 'obstruct' and 'forfeit'. The composer of this charter has used the Latin *praepeditus* 'obstructed' when what he means is 'forfeited'.
[4] An old name of the West Saxons.   [5] The boundaries are in Old English.

Cynelmingham over the meadow to *Hafocwyll*, then along the boundary furrow to the great thorn, then along the way to the boundary linch, then along the boundary linch to *Aldercombe*, then over the neck of 'Roe-down' over Roakham[1] to *Trindlea*, then so to Wiglaf's tree, then over the heathland to the dyke gate [or gap], then west along the dyke to the well-way, then along the well-way to the wide valley, then along the way back to *Odenford*, from *Odenford* to Codford.

If anyone, however, shall wish to increase or amplify the charter of this our donation, may God increase his benefits in the land of the living; if, however, it shall happen—as we hope it will not—that anyone of any status whatever shall appear who shall wish to infringe or change this, let him know that he is cut off[2] from the fellowship of God and his saints, unless he have first made emends with sufficient compensation to God and all.

This writing[3] makes known the agreement between Deormod and Æthelwulf about the land at Wylye, namely that Æthelwulf gave it to Deorswith into her own possession to deal with as was most pleasing to her both in her life and after her life, and gave her the title-deeds on the same day on which they were given to him,[4] in the witness of these men.

This charter was written in the year of our Lord's incarnation 901, the fourth indiction, these witnesses consenting and attaching the standard of the Holy Cross, whose names are seen to be inscribed below.

✠ I, Edward, the king.
✠ I, Æthelweard, ætheling.
✠ I, Ordgar, ealdorman.   ✠ I, Buga, king's thegn.
✠ I, Ordlaf, ealdorman.   ✠ I, Cufa, king's thegn.
✠ I, Sigewulf, ealdorman.   ✠ I, Athelstan, king's thegn.
✠ I, Heahferth, ealdorman.   ✠ I, Wulfhun, king's thegn.
✠ I, Ordgar, ealdorman.   ✠ I, Witwulf, king's thegn.
✠ I, Deormod, ealdorman.   ✠ I, Ælfheah, king's thegn.
✠ I, Ælfstan, ealdorman.   ✠ I, Uffa, king's thegn.
✠ I, Beornstan, ealdorman.   ✠ I, Wulfhere, king's thegn.
✠ I, Æthelferth, ealdorman.   ✠ I, Brihtric, king's thegn.
✠ I, Ælfheah, ealdorman.   ✠ I, Dudig, king's thegn.
✠ I, Alfred, ealdorman.   ✠ I, Brihtsige, king's thegn.
✠ I, Brihtsige, king's thegn.   ✠ I, Wulfsige, king's thegn.
✠ I, Occa, king's thegn.   ✠ I, Wihtbord, king's thegn.
✠ I, Wulfhere, king's thegn.   ✠ I, Odda, king's thegn.
✠ I, Ælfhere, king's thegn.   ✠ I, Eardwulf, king's thegn.
✠ I, Alfred, king's thegn.   ✠ I, Ælfstan, king's thegn.
✠ I, Alfred, king's thegn.

[1] This is suggested in *The Place-Names of Wiltshire* (Eng. Pl.-N. Soc.), p. 230, assuming that the *nacum* of the text is an error for *racumbe*, i.e. roe-valley.
[2] *epicarmai*, for Greek ἐπίκερμα. An attempt at the same form is made in Birch, No. 588, a suspicious Wilton charter of Edward, dated 901.   [3] This paragraph is in Old English.
[4] The Old English is ambiguous here. It could mean "on which she was given to him", but since the witnesses referred to are presumably those of the charter, I consider the first interpretation more likely.

101. Old English lease of Beddington, Surrey, by Denewulf, bishop of Winchester, to King Edward the Elder (899–908)

The twelfth-century scribe of this Old English text, with its interesting reference to the havoc of the Danish invasions, had difficulty in reading his exemplar, mistaking the open *a* for a *u*. The man who translates it into Latin misunderstands it in places, and uses post-Conquest phrases. The lease shows the dilemma of ecclesiastical landowners when kings wish to obtain estates whose alienation has been forbidden under pain of anathema. It is preserved in the Winchester cartulary, Brit. Mus. Addit. MS. 15350. It is No. 1089 in Kemble, No. 619 in Birch (Latin version No. 618), and in Thorpe, *Diplomatarium*, pp. 161–163, with translation.

I, Bishop Denewulf, inform my lord King Edward about the land at Beddington which you were desirous I should lease to you. I have then, my dear lord, now procured from the community in Winchester, both young and old, that they grant it to me with all goodwill, to give it by charter for your lifetime, whether to use yourself or to let on lease to whomsoever you please.

Then there is 70 hides of that land, and it is now completely stocked, and when my lord first let it to me it was quite without stock, and stripped bare by heathen men. And I myself then acquired the stock for it which was afterwards available there. And now we very humbly grant it to you. Moreover, my dear lord, the community are now desirous that it be given back to the foundation after your death. Now, of the cattle which has survived this severe winter there are 9 full-grown oxen and 114 full-grown pigs and 50 wethers, besides the sheep and the pigs which the herdsmen have a right to have, 20 of which are full grown; and there are 110 full-grown sheep, and 7 bondsmen, and 20 flitches; and there was no more corn there than was prepared for the bishop's farm, and there [are] 90 sown acres.

Then the bishop and the community at Winchester beg that in charity for the love of God and for the holy church you desire no more land of that foundation, for it seems to them an unwelcome [?][1] demand; so that God need blame neither you nor us for the diminishing in our days; for there was a very great injunction of God about that when men gave those lands to the foundation.

102. Old English letter to King Edward the Elder explaining the history of an estate at Fonthill, Wiltshire (899–924, probably early in the reign)

This account of the career of the thief Helmstan is full of human interest as well as of information on the working of Anglo-Saxon law. It can be left to speak for itself; yet it may be pointed out how well it supports Asser's statements about the interest taken by Alfred in the administration of justice, and about the readiness of litigants to appeal to him. The writer is probably the Ordlaf who is mentioned as succeeding to the forfeited estate because it had been held on lease from him. It is not unparalleled for a drafter of a document to vary between the first and the third person. Though Birch, No. 590, which records an exchange between Ealdorman Ordlaf and Bishop Denewulf of Fonthill for Lyddiard in 900, may have suspicious features (see Stevenson, *Eng. Hist. Rev.*, XIII, p. 73, n.), it suggests at least that the community at Winchester had some reason for connecting Ordlaf with Fonthill.

The original letter is at Canterbury, Chart. Antiq. Cantuar. C. 1282. There is a facsimile in *Ord. Surv. Facs.*, I, pl. 13. It is edited with translation by Harmer, *op. cit.*, pp. 30–32, translation, pp. 60–63, Thorpe, *Diplomatarium*, pp. 169–174, *Select Essays in Anglo-Saxon Law*, pp. 338–342. It is No. 328 in Kemble, No. 591 in Birch, and in Earle, pp. 162–165.

---

[1] Taking *ynbædune* as *unbeden* perhaps meaning 'unrequested'; Kemble and Thorpe take it as *ymbe dine*, interpreting "it seems to them concerning thy demand", but this does not fit well with what follows.

✠ Sire, I will inform you what happened about the land at Fonthill, the five hides which Æthelhelm Higa is claiming. When Helmstan committed the crime of stealing Ethelred's belt, Higa at once began to bring a charge against him, along with other claimants, and wished to win the land from him by litigation. Then he came to me and begged me to intercede for him, because I had stood sponsor to him at his confirmation before he committed that crime. Then I spoke on his behalf and interceded for him with King Alfred. Then–may God repay his soul–he allowed him to be entitled to prove his right against Æthelhelm as regards the land, because of my advocacy and true account. Then he ordered that they should be brought to agreement, and I was one of the men appointed to do it, and Wihtbord and Ælfric, who was then keeper of the wardrobe, and Brihthelm and Wulfhun the Black of Somerton, and Strica and Ubba and more men than I can now name. Then each of them gave his account, and it then seemed to us all that Helmstan should be allowed to come forward with the title-deeds and prove his right to the land, that he had it as Æthelthryth had sold it into Oswulf's possession at a suitable price; and she had told Oswulf that she was entitled to sell it to him because it was her 'morning-gift' when she married Æthelwulf. And Helmstan included all this in the oath. And King Alfred had given his signature to Oswulf, when he bought the land from Æthelthryth, that it might thus remain valid, and Edward gave his and Æthelnoth his and Deormod his, and so did each of the men whom one then wished to have. And when we were reconciling them at Wardour, the deed was produced and read, and the signatures were all written on it. Then it seemed to all of us who were at that arbitration that Helmstan was the nearer to the oath on that account.

Then Æthelhelm would not fully assent until we went in to the king and told exactly how we had decided it and why we had decided it; and Æthelhelm stood himself in there with us. And the king stood in the chamber at Wardour–he was washing his hands. When he had finished, he asked Æthelhelm why what we had decided for him did not seem just to him; he said that he could think of nothing more just then than that Helmstan should be allowed to give the oath if he could. I then said that he wished to attempt it, and asked the king to appoint a day for it, and he then did so. And on that appointed day he performed the oath fully. He asked me to help him, and said that he would rather give [the land to me]¹ than that the oath should fail or it ever . . .² Then I said that I would help him to obtain justice, but never to any wrong, on condition that he granted it to me; and he gave me a pledge to that.

And then we rode on that appointed day, I–and Wihtbord rode with me, and Brihthelm rode there with Æthelhelm; and we all heard that he gave the oath in full. Then we all said that it was a closed suit when the sentence had been fulfilled. And, Sire, when will any suit be ended if one can end it neither with money nor with an oath? And if one wishes to change every judgment which King Alfred gave, when shall we have finished disputing? And he then gave me the title-deed just as he had pledged to do, as soon as the oath was given; and I promised him that he might use the land as long as he lived, if he would keep himself out of disgrace.

---

¹ There is a hole in the MS. at this point, but the sense can be supplied with reasonable certainty.
² There is a hole, with space for some twelve letters, at this point.

Then on top of that–I do not know whether it was a year and a half or two years later–he stole the untended oxen at Fonthill, by which he was completely ruined, and drove them to Chicklade, and there he was discovered, and the man who tracked him rescued the traced cattle [?]. Then he fled, and a bramble scratched him in the face; and when he wished to deny it, that was brought as evidence against him. Then Eanwulf Peneard's son, who was the reeve, intervened, and took from him all the property that he owned at Tisbury. I then asked him why he did so, and he said that he was a thief, and the property was adjudged to the king, because he was the king's man. And Ordlaf succeeded to his land; because what he was occupying was held on lease from him, he could not forfeit it. And you then pronounced him an outlaw.

Then he sought your father's body, and brought a seal[1] to me, and I was with you at Chippenham. Then I gave the seal to you, and you removed his outlawry and gave him the estate to which he still has withdrawn [?]. And I succeeded to my land, and then in your witness and that of your councillors I gave it to the bishop, five hides in exchange for the land of five hides at Lyddiard. And the bishop and all the community granted me the four hides, and the fifth was land subject to tithe. Now, Sire, it is very necessary for me that it may remain as it now is arranged and was before. If it shall be otherwise, then I must and will be satisfied with what seems right to you as a charitable gift.

Endorsement

✠ And Æthelhelm Higa retired from the dispute when the king was at Warminster, in the witness of Ordlaf and Osferth and Odda and Wihtbord and Ælfstan the Bald and Æthelnoth.

103. **Grant by King Athelstan to his thegn Ealdred of land at Chalgrave and Tebworth, Bedfordshire, which the latter had bought from the 'pagans' at King Edward's orders (926)**

The importance of this document and of Birch, No. 658, a charter of the same date and identical phrasing granting lands in Derbyshire to Uhtred, has been demonstrated by Sir Frank Stenton (*Types of Manorial Structure in the Northern Danelaw*, pp. 74f.). They make it clear that some time before 911, before he began his re-conquest of the Danelaw, Edward was encouraging his thegns to buy estates in Danish territory. Chalgrove was given to Abingdon by a woman called Ælfgifu in 972–992, which explains the presence of this charter in the cartulary of that house, Brit. Mus. Cott. Claud. B. vi. It is No. 1099 in Kemble, No. 659 in Birch.

✠ In the name of our Lord Jesus Christ. All undertakings of transitory affairs, which are clearly seen by human eyes, decay; those truly which are hidden and invisible remain for ever by the government of the eternal Judge. It is not to be doubted but that the divine teachings of the Scriptures promise to those deserving it that they can acquire and buy these things by the gift of the abundant grace of God.

Therefore I, Athelstan, king of the Anglo-Saxons, adorned and elevated with no small dignity, prompted by desire from on high, will grant to my faithful thegn Ealdred the land of five hides[2] which is called Chalgrave and Tebworth, which he

---

[1] Probably a document authenticated by a seal, to show that he had taken an oath at the king's tomb.
[2] *manentes.*

bought with sufficient money of his own, namely ten pounds of gold and silver, from the pagans by the order of King Edward and also of Ealdorman Ethelred along with the other ealdormen and thegns; conceding with it the freedom of hereditary right, to have and possess as long as he lives, and to give after his death to whatever heirs, acceptable to himself, he shall wish.

These are the boundaries of the aforesaid land:[1] Where the dyke runs into Watling Street, along Watling Street to the ford, then along the brook to the other ford, then from that ford up to the spring, and thence into the valley, thence from the valley to the dyke, from the dyke to the second dyke, then from that dyke to the brook, then from the brook to Kimberwell, then along the dyke to *Eastcote*, then thence to the old brook, up from the old brook parallel with the little stream, then straight up to the highway, along the highway to the dyke, along the dyke to Watling Street.

And the donation of the aforesaid land is to be free from every secular burden except military service and the construction of bridges and fortresses, in return for an adequate sum of money which I have received from him, *i.e.* 150 mancuses of pure gold.

If anyone, indeed, incited by impudence, shall try to infringe or change or diminish this generous munificence, let him know that, on the day of the great Judgment, when the hinges of the pole and the foundations of the earth as well as the deepest dens of hell shall quake and tremble, on which each shall reveal his work and conscience, what he did, good or ill . . .[2] if he have not previously made emends with compensation.

In the year of the incarnation of our Lord Jesus Christ 926, the fourteen indiction.

These are the estates which King Athelstan granted by charter to Ealdred in return for his pure money, in the witness which is herein.[3]

✠ I, King Athelstan, have inscribed below with the sign of the Holy Cross.
✠ I, Wulfhelm, archbishop, have subscribed.
✠ I, Wynsige, bishop,[4] have consented and subscribed.
✠ I, Theodred, bishop,[5] have consented and subscribed.
✠ I, Beornheah, bishop,[6] have consented and subscribed.
✠ I, Sigehelm, bishop,[7] have consented and subscribed.
✠ I, Eadwulf, bishop,[8] have consented and subscribed.
✠ I, Edgar, bishop,[9] have consented and subscribed.
✠ I, Ælla, bishop,[10] have consented and subscribed.
✠ I, Cyneferth, bishop,[11] have consented and subscribed.
✠ I, Ordgar, ealdorman, have consented and subscribed.
✠ I, Ælfwold, ealdorman, have consented and subscribed.
✠ I, Osferth, ealdorman, have consented and subscribed.
✠ I, Wulfgar, ealdorman, have consented and subscribed.
✠ I, Wulfhelm, the king's seneschal.

[1] On these, see F. G. Gurney, *Publ. Beds. Hist. Rec. Soc.*, v, 163–170. They are in Old English.
[2] Some clause seems to be omitted here, such as 'he will perish with Judas', or 'in the flames of Hell'.
[3] This clause, which is in English, reads like an endorsement. There is nothing corresponding to it in the companion charter, Birch, No. 659.

[4] Of Dorchester.	[5] Of London.	[6] Of Selsey.	[7] Of Sherborne.
[8] Of Crediton.	[9] Of Hereford.	[10] Of Lichfield.	[11] Of Rochester.

✠ I, Alfred, king's thegn, have consented and subscribed.

✠ I, Ceolstan, king's thegn, have consented and subscribed.

✠ I, Ælfric, king's thegn, have consented and subscribed.

✠ I, Ælfric, king's thegn, have consented and subscribed.

✠ I, Eadwulf, king's thegn, have consented and subscribed.

✠ I, Helmstan, king's thegn, have consented.

✠ I, Alfred, king's thegn, have consented and subscribed.

✠ I, Æthelhelm, king's thegn, have consented and subscribed.

104. Grant by King Athelstan, of Amounderness to the Church of York (7 June 934)

The genuineness of this charter was doubted by W. H. Stevenson, because of the error of its dating and some unusual features in its clauses; but the discrepancy in the various parts of the date may be due to later tampering, and the fact that precisely the same discrepancy occurs in a suspicious Worcester charter (Birch, No. 701) need not be significant in this connexion, for the Worcester text survives only in an eleventh-century cartulary possibly drawn up when the dioceses of York and Worcester were held in plurality, and it could easily have been based on this very document. It seems to me likely that the discrepancy arose from an attempt to make the original date, 934, agree with the statement that the grant was made when Wulfstan was appointed archbishop. That 934 is correct is shown by the issue of a charter with an almost identical set of witnesses at Winchester on 28 May 934, and it is doubtless the expedition to Scotland recorded in this year which has brought the company to Nottingham ten days later. As for the unusual features, it must be remembered that the conditions were unusual also. Athelstan, the first West Saxon king to rule in Northumbria, was faced with an unprecedented situation, and it seems to me quite likely that he should have tried to strengthen the English hold on the North, and the Christian Church there, by purchasing a large area in the north of Lancashire, recently settled by Norsemen, and handing it over to the authority from whom he might reasonably expect loyal support, the metropolitan see of the North. The grant may have been made at Wulfstan's accession, although the document was not drawn up till the king's journey north in 934; or the clause about Wulfstan's accession could be a later insertion. The document is phrased in the formulae of Athelstan's charters, and as Farrer has pointed out, the church of York neither possessed, nor made any recorded claim on this estate in later times. There is no known motive for forgery, and it would be an odd story to invent.

If it is genuine, as I believe, it is a very important document for the history of the dealings of the English kings with the northern Danelaw, and for the relations between the kings and that intriguing but mysterious personality, Wulfstan I of York. In any case, it undoubtedly has a genuine list of witnesses, and so allows us to form some idea of the company the king had with him when on his way to Scotland, and the presence on such an occasion of the Welsh sub-kings and so many ealdormen with Scandinavian names is interesting.

Moreover, the charter is a good specimen of the strange, flamboyant and inflated style favoured by Athelstan's writing-office. The florid style, partly derived from the writings of Aldhelm, reaches its height in this reign, which in itself is a fact of historical interest. The proem is identical with that of Birch, No. 702, a contemporary parchment.

The charter survives only in a late form, in Reg. Mag. Alb. of the Dean and Chapter of York, where it has been entered twice, in part I, fol. 59, and part II, fol. 78b. It is No. 352 in Kemble, Nos. 703, 1344 in Birch, No. 1 in W. Farrer, *Early Yorkshire Charters*, where W. H. Stevenson's comments are added.

The wanton fortune of this deceiving world, not lovely with the milk-white radiance of unfading lilies, but odious with the gall-steeped bitterness of lamentable corruption, raging with venomous wide-stretched jaws, bitingly rends the sons of stinking flesh in this vale of tears; and although by its smiles it may be able to draw unfortunates to the bottom of Acherontic Cocytus, unless the Creator of the roaring deep lend his aid, it is shamelessly fickle; and therefore, because this ruinous fortune falls and mortally decays, one should chiefly hasten to the pleasant fields of indescribable

joy, where are the angelic instruments of hymn-singing jubilation and the mellifluous scents of blooming roses are perceived with inconceivable sweetness by
the nostrils of the good and blessed and harmonies are heard by their ears for ever.[1]
Allured by love of that felicity–when now depths disgust, heights grow sweet–and
in order to perceive and enjoy them always in unfailing beauty, I, Athelstan, king of
the English, elevated by the right hand of the Almighty, which is Christ, to the throne
of the whole kingdom of Britain, assign willingly in fear of God to Almighty God
and the blessed Apostle Peter, at his church in the city of York, at the time when
I constituted Wulfstan its archbishop, a certain portion of land of no small size, in the
place which the inhabitants call Amounderness; that the bishop may [hold] it without
the yoke of hateful servitude, with meadows, pastures, woods, streams, and all conve-
niences duly belonging to it, for as long as he may use the breatheable air with his
nostrils and the visible world with the glance of his eyes, and may leave it to sacred[2]
heirs after him, ever to his church in eternal inheritance. This aforesaid donation
I have bought with no little money of my own; I have granted in perpetuity not
only it, but rather all the estates of that afore-named church, namely of St. Peter,
Prince of the Apostles, bought with refined gold.

If, however–which God forbid–anyone puffed up with the pride of arrogance
shall try to destroy or infringe this little document of my agreement[3] and confirmation, let him know that on the last and fearful day of assembly, when the trumpet of
the archangel is clanging the call and bodies are leaving the foul graveyards, he will
burn with Judas the committor of impious treachery and also with the miserable Jews,
blaspheming with sacrilegious mouth Christ on the altar of the Cross, in eternal
confusion in the devouring flames of blazing torments in punishment without end.

Truly the record of this our intention, by the inspiration, favour and help of our
God and Lord Jesus Christ, was written in the year of our Lord's incarnation 930,[4]
and in the sixth year of the reign committed to me, the seventh indiction, the third
epact, the second concurrent, 7 June, the twenty-first day of the moon, in the city
well known to all which is called Nottingham, all the body of chief men rejoicing,
under the wings of royal generosity. The authority also of its unshaken firmness was
strengthened by these witnesses, whose names are entered below depicted with letters.

But first the boundaries are traversed, and when these have been traversed the
promises of the confirmers are set forth. First from the sea up along the Cocker to
the source of that river, from that source straight to another spring which is called
in Saxon Dunshop, thus down the riverlet to the Hodder, in the same direction to
the Ribble and thus along that river through the middle of the channel back to the sea.

Now, as I said before, the agreements of nobles, lest they should be given to
oblivion, seem fit to be inserted with letters used in charters.

✠   I, Athelstan, king, endowed with the rule of special privilege, have
        corroborated and subscribed the head of this list with the sign of the
        holy and ever to be adored Cross.

[1] This clause includes a genitive plural *clivipparum* of a word of unknown meaning.
[2] Birch, No. 1344, has *sacius*, for *sacris*?   [3] [*sic*] Birch, No. 1344; 703 reads 'purchase'.
[4] The other indications are for 934.

✠ I, Wulfhelm, archbishop of the church of Canterbury, have consented and
      subscribed.
✠ I, Wulfstan, archbishop of the church of York.
✠ I, Hywel, sub-king, have consented and subscribed.
✠ I, Morgan, sub-king, have consented and subscribed.
✠ I, Idwal, sub-king, have consented.
✠ I, Ælfwine, bishop,[1] have consented.
✠ I, Theodred, bishop,[2] have consented.
✠ I, Wulfwig, bishop,[3] have consented.
✠ I, Ælfheah, bishop,[4] have consented.
✠ I, Oda, bishop,[5] have consented.
✠ I, Alfred, bishop,[6] have consented.
✠ I, Tidhelm, bishop,[7] have consented.
✠ I, Burgric, bishop,[8] have consented.
✠ I, Alfred, bishop,[9] have consented.
✠ I, Conan, bishop,[10] have consented.
✠ I, Cynesige, bishop,[11] have consented.
✠ I, Wulfhelm, bishop,[12] have consented.
✠ I, Wigred, bishop,[13] have consented.
✠ I, Eadwulf, bishop,[14] have consented.
✠ I, Cenwold, bishop,[15] have consented.
✠ I, Beornstan, bishop,[16] have consented.
✠ I, Ælfwold, ealdorman, have consented.
✠ I, Osferth, ealdorman, have consented.
✠ I, Athelstan, ealdorman, have consented.
✠ I, Oswulf, ealdorman, have consented.
✠ I, Uhtred, ealdorman, have consented.
✠ I, Ælfstan, ealdorman, have consented.
✠ I, Uhtred, ealdorman, have consented.
✠ I, Ragnald, earl,[17] have consented.
✠ I, Ivar, earl, have consented.
✠ I, Hadder, earl, have consented.
✠ I, Scule, earl, have consented.
✠ I, Thurferth, earl, have consented.
✠ I, Halfden, earl, have consented.
✠ I, Odda, king's thegn, have consented.
✠ I, Wulfgar, king's thegn, have consented.
✠ I, Ælfheah, king's thegn, have consented.
✠ I, Athelstan, king's thegn, have consented.

---

[1] Of Lichfield.   [2] Of London.   [3] Of Selsey.   [4] Of Wells.   [5] Of Ramsbury.
[6] Of Sherborne.   [7] Of Hereford.   [8] Of Rochester.   [9] See unknown.   [10] Of Cornwall.
[11] Birch, No. 687, speaks of Bishop Cynesige of Berkshire.
[12] If he is the bishop of Hereford of this name, it is odd that he should sign along with his predecessor
Tidhelm.   [13] Of Chester-le-Street.   [14] Of Crediton.   [15] Of Worcester.   [16] Of Winchester.
[17] I have translated *dux* as earl where Scandinavian persons are concerned, for this, not ealdorman, was
doubtless the title by which they were known.

✠ I, Æthelmund, king's thegn, have consented.

✠ I, Æthelnoth, king's thegn, have consented.

✠ I, Ælfsige, king's thegn, have consented.

✠ I, Wulfmær, king's thegn, have consented.

✠ I, Helmstan, king's thegn, have consented.

✠ I, Wulflaf, king's thegn, have consented.

✠ I, Wulfhelm, king's thegn, have consented.

✠ I, Wulfnoth, have consented.

✠ I, Wulfbold, have consented.

✠ I, Ælfhere, have consented.

✠ I, Æthelwold, have consented.

✠ I, Eadric, have consented.

✠ I, Wynsige, have consented.

✠ I, Sigered, have consented.

✠ I, Æthelweard, have consented.

✠ I, Ælfhere, have consented.

✠ I, Eadric, have consented.

✠ I, Æthelsige, have consented.

✠ I, Ælfric, have consented.

✠ I, Æthelferth, have consented.

105. Grant by King Eadred to Wulfric, of land in Warkton, Northamptonshire (946).

This is one of the Worcester charters that belonged to Lord Somers in Wanley's time, and have since been lost (see p. 337). It belongs to a small group which share marked differences from the usual tenth-century texts, being couched in a strongly rhythmical, alliterative Latin (see p. 340). They mainly belong to the Midlands. Birch, and after him Ekwall, in the *Dict. Eng. Place-Names*, wrongly assigns this to Workington, Cumberland.

This charter supports No. 83 above in suggesting that kings made grants on the day of their coronation, or soon after. It should also be noted that it calls the Scandinavians 'pagans', presumably with reference to the Norsemen from Dublin, as in the poem in the Anglo-Saxon Chronicle, 942.

Since the manuscript has been lost, the oldest text is given by Wanley, in Hickes, *Thesaurus*, II, p. 302, but most of the signatures are omitted. The complete text was edited by J. Smith, in the appendix to his edition of Bede (1722), p. 772. It is No. 815 in Birch.

✠ The grace of God conceding, in the year of our Lord's incarnation 946, after the death of King Edmund who royally guided the government of kingdoms, of the Anglo-Saxons and Northumbrians, of the pagans and the Britons, for a space of seven years, it happened that Eadred, his uterine brother, chosen in his stead by the election of the nobles, was in the same year by the pontifical authority orthodoxly consecrated king and ruler to the sovereignty of the quadripartite rule. And then he, the king, constantly presented many gifts to many, in the king's residence which is called Kingston, where also the consecration was performed. This Wulfric the *pedisequus*[1] can for certain readily extol, whom the same king honourably gladdens with abundant generosity, conceding to him land of seven hides[2] at Warkton to enjoy with perpetual right, limited by known bounds as is said below, acquired with great things and small, apart from bridge and fortress and service in battle.

[1] See p. 489, n. 6. [2] *manentes.*

✠ Moreover this grant in the year of our Lord's incarnation 946, and the first period in the temporal cycle in which he guided the government of the diadems of the Anglo-Saxons with the Northumbrians, and of the pagans with the Britons, was performed in this way, with these witnesses writing with `im whose names follow below:

✠   King Eadred, with the archbishops and the other prelates, granted this land with the triumphal sign of victory.

✠ Oda, archbishop.	✠ Morgan.
✠ Wulfstan, archbishop.	Cadmo.[11]
✠ Theodred, bishop.[1]	✠ Æthelmund, ealdorman.
✠ Ælfheah, bishop.[2]	✠ Ealhhelm, ealdorman.
✠ Wulfgar, bishop.[3]	✠ Athelstan, ealdorman.
✠ Cenwold, bishop.[4]	✠ Eadric, ealdorman.[12]
✠ Ælfric, bishop.[5]	✠ Oswulf, high-reeve.
✠ Wulfhelm, bishop.[6]	✠ Orm, and Morcar, earl.
✠ Wulfsige, pontiff.[7]	✠ Grim and Coll, earl.
✠ Alfred, pontiff.[8]	✠ Eadred, abbot.
✠ Æthelgar, pontiff.[9]	✠ Wigstan, abbot.
✠ Æthelwold, pontiff.[10]	✠ Dunstan, abbot.
✠ Hywel, sub-king.	✠ Uhtred.

May those who increase the royal benefaction receive an increase of the blessed reward of the Eternal King. Amen.

106. Old English will of Theodred, bishop of London (942–951)

A little light is thrown by this document on a very obscure subject, the ecclesiastical organization of the Danelaw soon after its re-conquest by the English crown. The pre-Viking Age sees had been destroyed, and we learn here that a bishop of London was also in charge of a see with its centre at Hoxne, Suffolk. Theodred was probably a man from this area, for all the estates which he leaves to his kindred belong to it. He left a good reputation, being surnamed 'the Good', and we find him concerned in Athelstan's legislation which mitigated the severity of the laws against young thieves (see No. 37). The reference to his see in Suffolk explains why in Abbo's "Life of St. Edmund" it should be he who passes judgment on men caught attempting to rob St. Edmund's church. The will also shows the existence of minsters, or collegiate churches, at Hoxne and Mendham, and also suggests that there was a considerable German element in the clergy at St. Paul's, for Gosebriht, Gundwine, and possibly Odgar, are German names. It is also interesting that the only religious house outside his own dioceses which Theodred mentions is the recently reformed Glastonbury, and that the bishop should have been in Pavia, presumably on his way to or from Rome.

The will survives in a fourteenth-century cartulary of Bury St. Edmunds, Camb. Univ. Lib. MS. Ff., 2, 33. It is No. 957 in Kemble, No. 1008 in Birch, and is edited with translation in Thorpe, *Diplomatarium*, p. 512, and as No. 1 in Whitelock, from which the present translation is taken.

---

[1] Of London.   [2] Of Winchester.   [3] Of Lichfield.
[4] Of Worcester.   [5] Of Hereford.   [6] Of Wells.
[7] Of Sherborne.   [8] Of Selsey.   [9] Of Crediton.
[10] His see is unknown. There is room for him at Dorchester or Rochester.
[11] This is probably a miscopying of Caducan; i.e. Cadwgan, brother of Hywel and Morgan, the two previous signatories. They were sons of Owain, king of Gwent, mentioned in the Anglo-Saxon Chronicle, 926 (see No. 1, p. 200). See Lloyd, *History of Wales*, 1, p. 338 and note.
[12] In his search for variety the writer has used four words for ealdorman, *dux, ealdorman, comes, princeps*.

In the name of our Lord Jesus Christ.[1]
    I, Theodred, bishop of the people of London, wish to announce my will concerning my property, what I have acquired and may yet acquire, by the grace of God and his saints, for my soul and for that of my lord under whom I acquired it and for my ancestors' souls, and for the souls of all the men for whom I intercede, and from whom I have received alms, and for whom it is fitting that I should pray.

First, he grants his lord his heriot, namely 200 mancuses[2] of red gold, and two silver cups and four horses, the best that I have, and two swords, the best that I have, and four shields and four spears; and the estate which I have at Duxford,[3] and the estate which I have at Illington,[4] and the estate which I have at Arrington.[3] And I grant to Eadgifu 50 mancuses[2] of red gold.

And to St. Paul's church I grant the two best chasubles that I have, with all the things which belong to them, together with a chalice and one cup. And my best Mass-book, and the best relics that I have, [are to go] to St. Paul's church. And I grant to St. Paul's church the estate at St. Osyth,[5] as an estate to provide sustenance for the community, with all that is on it, except the men who are there; they are all to be freed for my soul's sake. And I grant the estate at Southery,[4] with all the fishing which belongs to it, to the community at St. Paul's church, and the men are to be freed for the bishop's soul. And Bishop Theodred grants the estate at Tillingham[5] to St. Paul's church to be the property of the community, and the men are to be freed for my soul. And I grant the estate at Dunmow[5] after my death to St. Paul's church for the community.

And I grant the estate at Mendham[6] to my sister's son Osgod after my death, except that I desire that the minster and a hide of land at Mendham [shall belong?] to the church. And I grant the estate at Shotford[6] and Mettingham[6] to God's community at Mendham church. And I grant to Osgod the estates at Syleham,[6] and at Instead,[6] and at Chickering[6] and at Ashfield,[6] and at *Wortinham*, and all the small estates which are attached to these.

And I grant the estates at Horham[6] and at Athelington[6] to God's community at St. Ethelbert's church at Hoxne. And I grant the estate at Lothingland[6] to Offa, my sister's son and his brother, and half the men are to be freed there, and also at Mendham, for the bishop's soul. And I grant to my kinsman Osgod, Eadwulf's son, the estates at Barton, and at Rougham, and at Pakenham.[7]

And I grant the estates at Nowton and at Horningsheath and at Ickworth and at Whepstead to St. Edmund's church, as the property of God's community, for Bishop Theodred's soul. And I grant to Osgod my sister's son, the estate at Waldringfield and my house[8] in Ipswich, which I bought. And I grant to Wulfstan the estate at Wortham just as it stands.

And I grant to every bishop's see five pounds to be distributed for my soul. And I grant to the archbishop five mancuses[2] of gold. And I grant that ten pounds be distributed for my soul at my episcopal demesne, in London and outside London.

---

[1] The invocation is in Latin.   [2] The text has marks in error for mancuses.
[3] Cambs.   [4] Norfolk.   [5] Essex.   [6] Suffolk.
[7] All these places and those in the next paragraph are in Suffolk.
[8] OE. *haga* 'haw', 'town-house', 'close'.

And I grant that ten pounds be distributed for my soul at my episcopal demesne at Hoxne. And it is my will that the stock which is at Hoxne, which I have acquired there, be taken and divided into two parts, half for the minster, and [half] to be distributed for my soul. And as much as I found on that estate is to be left on it, but all the men are to be freed for my soul. And it is my wish that at London there be left as much as I found on the estate, and that what I have added to it be taken and divided into two, half for the minster and half for my soul, and all the men are to be freed. And the same is to be done at Wimbledon[1] and at Sheen.[1] And at Fulham[2] everything is to be left as it now stands, unless one wishes to free any of my men. And at Dengie[3] let there be left as much as I found on the estate and let the rest be divided into two, half for the minster and half for my soul.

And I grant to Glastonbury five pounds for my soul. And I grant to Theodred my white chasuble which I bought in Pavia, and all that belongs to it, and a chalice for festivals and the Mass-book which Gosebriht bequeathed to me. And I grant to Odgar the yellow chasuble which I bought in Pavia, and what belongs to it. And I grant to Gundwine the other yellow chasuble which is unornamented, and what belongs to it. And I have bequeathed to Aki[4] the red chasuble and all that belongs to it. And whosoever detracts from my testament, may God deprive him of the kingdom of heaven, unless he make amends for it before his death.

107. Old English will of King Eadred (951–955)

This will affords information about the constitution of the king's household, and shows that the possibility of viking raids was in men's thoughts even in the middle of the tenth century. It is of interest to compare this will with the account in the "Life of St. Dunstan" of how this king, near death, sent the various persons to whom he had entrusted his treasure to fetch it so that he could distribute it, but died before Dunstan, at any rate, returned with that part entrusted to him (see No. 234, p. 829).

The will survives in the *Liber Monasterii de Hyda*, and is on pp. 153–161 of Edward's edition. The best edition is in Harmer, pp. 34f., with translation, pp. 64f. It is No. 912 in Birch.

In the name of the Lord.[5] This is King Eadred's will; first, namely, that he grants to the place where he wishes his body to rest two gold crosses and two gold-hilted swords, and 400 pounds. Then he grants to the Old Minster at Winchester three estates, namely Downton, Damarham and Calne.[6] Then he grants to the New Minster three estates, namely Wherwell, Andover and Kingsclere;[7] and to the Nuns' Minster Shalbourne[6] and Thatcham[8] and Bradford.[6] Then he grants to the Nuns' Minster at Winchester[9] 30 pounds, and 30 to Wilton, and 30 to Shaftesbury.

Then he grants for the redemption of his soul and the benefit of his people 1600 pounds, to the end that they may redeem themselves from famine and from a heathen army if they need. The archbishop at Christ Church is to receive 400 pounds for the relief of the people of Kent and Surrey and Sussex and Berkshire;

[1] Surrey.   [2] Middlesex.   [3] Essex.
[4] The reading of the text, *spracacke*, is corrupt; I hazard a guess that the original read *spræc Ake*. Aki, an Old Norse loan, occurs commonly in Danish England, including the eastern counties.
[5] The invocation is in Latin.   [6] Wilts.   [7] Hants.
[8] Accepting Miss Harmer's emendation of *þæt ham* to *þæcham*. It is in Berks.
[9] Like the Parker text of the Chronicle, 964, he refers to this place merely as 'Chester'.

and if anything happen to the bishop, the money is to remain in the minster, by the witness of the councillors who are in the shire. And Ælfsige, bishop at the see of Winchester, is to receive 400 pounds, 200 for Hampshire, 100 for Wiltshire, and the other for Dorset; and if anything happen to him, let it remain, as it says above, in the witness of the councillors who are in the shire. And Abbot Dunstan is to receive 200 pounds, and to keep it at Glastonbury for the people of Somerset and Devon; and if anything happen to him, let it be as it is said here above. And Bishop Ælfsige is to receive the 200 pounds which is left over, and keep it at the see of Winchester, for whichever shire may need it. And Bishop Oscetel is to receive 400 pounds, and keep it at the see of Dorchester, for the Mercians, as it is said here above. And Bishop Wulfhelm has that 400 pounds.[1] And 2000 mancuses of gold are to be taken and minted into mancuses;[2] and the archbishop is to receive one part, the second Bishop Ælfsige, the third Bishop Oscetel, and they are to distribute them throughout the bishoprics, for the sake of God and the redemption of my soul.

Then I grant to my mother the land at Amesbury[3] and Wantage[4] and Basing,[5] and all the booklands which I have in Sussex and Surrey and Kent, and all those which she held before. And I grant to the archbishop 200 mancuses of gold, reckoning the hundred at a hundred and twenty; and to each of my diocesan bishops 120 mancuses of gold; and to each of my ealdormen 120 mancuses of gold; and to each appointed seneschal and each appointed keeper of the wardrobe, and each appointed butler, 80 mancuses of gold. And to each of my chaplains whom I have put in charge of my relics 50 mancuses of gold and five pounds in pence; and to each of the other priests five pounds. And to every appointed steward 30 mancuses of gold, and to every man in priest's orders who has been employed [?][6] since I came to the throne, and each of those who are in my household, in whatever office he is employed, unless he be little connected with the royal dwellings [?].[7]

Then it is my wish that from each of these estates twelve almsmen shall be chosen, and if anything happen to any one of them, another is to be put in his place. And this is to continue as long as Christianity shall last, for the praise of God and the redemption of my soul. And if anyone will not do this, the land is then to go to the place where my body shall rest.

108. Grant by King Eadwig, of Southwell to Oscetel, Archbishop of York (956)

On this estate the archbishops of York founded the great minster of Southwell. It is uncertain how the religious needs of the people of Nottinghamshire had been supplied during the time of the independent Danelaw, and it may be that in granting to York this great estate, and following it with a grant of Sutton a couple of years later, the English kings were only strengthening a position

---

[1] Wulfhelm was bishop of Wells. From the "Life of St. Dunstan" it is clear that Eadred had placed his treasures in the charge of various persons.

[2] A mancus was normally a weight, but was also applied to a gold coin. Very few of these survive, and it is possible that they were minted in large numbers only for a ceremonial purpose, as here.

[3] Wilts.   [4] Berks.   [5] Hants.

[6] If *gepeodad* is for *gepeoded*, it presumably means 'associated, attached (to the court)'.

[7] *he sy lit inbynde to þam cynestolum*. This is perhaps corrupt; no word *inbynde* is known. *Cynestol* usually means a throne, but it can hardly mean this here where it is plural. Does the king mean that he does not include persons employed on royal estates whose business hardly brings them into contact with the king?

of authority in the county which was already held by the northern primate. However this may be, the county henceforward forms part of the archbishop's diocese. The indiction date, 956, should be preferred to the incarnation date, for in 958 Eadwig was no longer king of this part of England, which had chosen his brother Edgar instead.

The document throws some light on the tenurial arrangements of the northern Danelaw. Already the central estate has many places attached to it with sake and soke, an arrangement very prominent in Domesday Book. See F. M. Stenton, *Types of Manorial Structure in the Northern Danelaw,* especially pp. 78–81.

The charter is preserved in the Reg. Mag. Alb. of the Dean and Chapter of York. It is No. 472 in Kemble, Nos. 1029, 1348 in Birch, No. 2 in W. Farrer, *Early Yorkshire Charters.*

✠ Our Lórd Jesus Christ reigning for ever; things visible and invisible, temporal and eternal, are to be distinguished by him.

And therefore I, Eadwig, king of the English, for the love of our Lord Jesus Christ concede to my beloved bishop, Oscetel, in inheritance, part of my land at a place called Southwell, 20 hides[1] with pastures, meadows, woods and all things, great or small, duly belonging to it. He is to possess it profitably for as long as he lives and after his death to leave it to whomever he sees fit, whether to persons known or unknown. This aforesaid donation of the king is to be [free] from every worldly hindrance apart from these three: preparing of bridges, and the construction of fortresses, and military service.

If indeed anyone of the catholic or orthodox shall wish to increase this donation of the king, may God increase for him his temporal goods; if truly [anyone shall wish] to diminish or violate it, let him know that he will be plunged into lower hell with the apostates, unless he shall make amends before his death in this mortal life for what he did wickedly.

The aforesaid donation was made in the year of our Lord's incarnation 958,[2] the fourteenth indiction.

The land is seen to be surrounded with these boundaries:[3] . . . These are the villages which belong to Southwell with sake and with soke:[4] Farnsfield, Kirtlington, Normanton, Upton, Morton, Fiskerton, Gibsmere, Bleasby, Goverton, Halloughton, Halam. In Farnsfield two manslots of land belong to Southwell; in Halam every sixth acre and three manslots; in Normanton every third acre; in Fiskerton the two parts and four manslots of all the land.

✠   I, King Eadwig, with the consent of my bishops and advisors have expressed with the holy sign.

✠   I, Oda, archbishop, have confirmed.

✠   I, Edgar, the king's brother, have subscribed.

✠   I, Oscetel, archbishop, have corroborated.

Ælfsige, bishop.[5]	Wulfsige, bishop.[9]
Daniel, bishop.[6]	Æthelwulf, bishop.[10]
Brihthelm, bishop.[7]	Eadmund, ealdorman.
Ælfwold, bishop.[8]	Athelstan, ealdorman.

---

[1] *mansae.*   [2] Error for 956, which is the year of the indiction.

[3] Boundaries are given for Southwell, Normanton, Upton and Fiskerton. They are given in a slightly better form in Birch, No. 1348, but as they are debased, and of no special interest, I have omitted them. They have been translated by Stevenson in Farrer's edition.   [4] Rights of private jurisdiction.

[5] Of Winchester.   [6] Of Cornwall.   [7] Of London.

[8] Of Crediton.   [9] Of Sherborne.   [10] Of Elmham.

Gunner, earl.[1]	Ælfsige, king's thegn.
Æthelsige, ealdorman.	Eadric, king's thegn.
Æthelmund, ealdorman.	Eadwold, king's thegn.
Orm, earl.	Ælfwold, king's thegn.
Ælfhere, ealdorman.	Ælfsige, king's thegn.
Æthelwold, ealdorman.	Oswulf, king's thegn.
Leot, earl.	Osweard, king's thegn.
Uhtred, ealdorman.	Ælfwine, king's thegn.
Alfred, ealdorman.	Oswig, king's thegn.
Ælfheah, king's thegn.	Wulfric, king's thegn.
Wulfric, king's thegn.	Byrnric, king's thegn.
Ælfsige, king's thegn.	Æthelsige, king's thegn.
Ælfric, king's thegn.	

109. Grant by King Edgar to his thegn Ealhstan, of land at Staunton, Herefordshire, and a house in Hereford (958)

This charter has several points of interest. It shows an ancient regional name still in use in the West Midlands, instead of the shire name, which suggests that the organization into shires was not yet complete; it illustrates the granting of a town-house in the nearest country town, along with an estate; it shows also Edgar's regnal style when he was king only of part of England; it suggests that Oscetel had not yet become archbishop of York, for if he had, he would surely have headed the episcopal signatures. Bishop Wulfric is probably bishop of Hereford, for though this name does not appear in the list of this see, there has doubtless been an omission between Ælfric, who last appears in 951, and Æthelwulf, who first signs about 972, earlier signatures with this name belonging to the bishop of Elmham. Bishop Wulfric signs from 961 to 970, and is probably the recipient of *Stanton* (likely to be in the West Midlands, since the deed was preserved at Burton Abbey) in 968 (Birch, No. 1211).

This is a contemporary charter belonging to the Dean and Chapter of Wells. There is a facsimile in *Ord. Surv. Facs.*, II. It is No. 1040 in Birch.

✠ The Almighty Father, occupying the heavenly citadel, observing the declining and fleeting frailty of the human race, sent to us his only-begotten Son, through whom he ordered the ages with ineffable redemption, for the deletion of our sins. For the will of the same gracious Creator resolved, and his mercy conceded, that anyone could buy with the lowest things the highest, with the terrestrial things the celestial, [and] with the things that perish, acquire those which will last for ever.

Therefore I, Edgar, by the favour of the divine grace obtaining the monarchy of the whole kingdom of the Mercians, bestow and willingly concede to my faithful thegn Ealhstan for his acceptable money, namely 40 mancuses of refined gold, a certain estate in the province of the *Magonsæte*,[2] *i.e.* six hides in the place which is called by the inhabitants of the place Staunton, that he may have it and always possess it eternally, with all benefits duly belonging to that land, and that he may have the power to do with it whatever he shall wish to do.

And this land is surrounded by these boundaries: First from the mill ford along the Arrow, then to *Washford*; from *Washford* along the Arrow round the top of *Holneig*; from the top of *Holneig*[3] to the top of the oak edge, then along the top of

---

[1] See p. 507, n. 17.　　　　　　　　　　　　　　[2] Part of Herefordshire. See p. 64.
[3] From here to '*snaed* way' has been added later.

the oak edge, then to the front of the *snaed* way, from the *snaed* way round *Hanley* to *aecna*-bridge, up along the brook, then to the dyke,[1] along the dyke to *Tanesbæc*, from *Tanesbæc* along the boundary-fence, then to the boundary of the community of *Lene*,[2] along the boundary of the community of *Lene*, then to Æthelwold's hedge, from Æthelwold's hedge to *Heanoldan*, from *Heanoldan* to the boundary thorn, from the boundary thorn along the fence to the swing-gate, from the swing-gate along the paved road to the dyke-gate, from the dyke-gate to the third gate, then along the paved road back to *Milford*.

And King Edgar grants by charter to his thegn Ealhstan a house in Hereford, in eternal inheritance for ever.[3]

Also this land is to be free from all tribute, great and small, and from royal service, except the construction of bridges, the building of fortresses and military expedition. If, however, anyone shall wish to break or diminish this my gift and concession, may the Almighty God lessen his days in this world, and may he incur in the future world the wrath of God, unless he have previously made good amends with compensation.

And this my donation was made in the year of our Lord's incarnation 958, in the first indiction, the second year of my reign.

✠ These witnesses were present and consented and subscribed and strengthened this with the triumphal standard of the Holy Cross.[4]

✠   I, Edgar, king of the Mercians and Northumbrians and Britons, have consented and ordered this to be written and have strengthened it with the standard of the Holy Cross.

✠   I, Cynesige, bishop,[5] have consented and subscribed.

✠   I, Oscetel, bishop,[6] have consented and subscribed.

✠   I, Dunstan, bishop,[7] have consented and subscribed.

✠   I, Wulfric, bishop,[8] have consented and subscribed.

✠   I, Æthelwulf, bishop,[9] have consented and subscribed.

✠   I, Leofwine, bishop,[10] have consented and subscribed.

✠   I, Ælfhere, ealdorman, have consented and subscribed.

✠   I, Athelstan, ealdorman, have consented and subscribed.

✠   I, Æthelmund, ealdorman, have consented and subscribed.

✠   I, Uhtred, ealdorman, have consented and subscribed.

✠   I, Æthelwold, ealdorman, have consented and subscribed.

✠   I, Brihtnoth, have consented and subscribed.

✠   I, Ælfwine, king's thegn, have consented and subscribed.

✠   I, Wulfhelm, king's thegn, have consented and subscribed.

✠   I, Æthelsige, king's thegn, have consented and subscribed.

---

[1] Is this the Rowe Ditch?

[2] This is the name of an old district on the Arrow and Lugg, which survives in the names Eardisland, Kingsland, Lyonshall, Monkland and Leominster.

[3] The boundaries and this statement are in English.

[4] The list (after the king) is arranged in four columns of six names of each rank.

[5] Of Lichfield.   [6] Of Dorchester.   [7] Of Worcester.

[8] Of Hereford.   [9] Of Elmham.   [10] Of Lindsey (?).

✠ I, Wærstan, king's thegn, have consented and subscribed.

✠ I, Wulfgar, king's thegn, have consented and subscribed.

✠ I, Wulfstan, king's thegn, have consented and subscribed.

110. **Lease by King Edgar with the permission of the bishop and community of Winchester of land at Kilmeston, Hampshire, to Æthelwulf, with the addition of an Old English lease of the same estate by the bishop and community (961)**

The main interest of this document is that it shows that what at first sight looks like a royal grant is in fact merely a royal permission to a religious house to lease their own property. Also, it is perhaps the last time we find the 'priests' of Winchester acting as a body. In 964 they were driven out and replaced by monks.

The text is preserved in the Winchester cartulary, Brit. Mus. Addit. MS. 15350. It is No. 1231 in Kemble, Nos. 1077, 1078 in Birch. Robertson, *Anglo-Saxon Charters*, No. 33, gives the Old English part only, with translation.

Our Lord Jesus Christ reigning for ever. Now, therefore, while there is a time of grace, let us hasten with all efforts to avoid the snare of death, and, while we possess a carnal patrimony, let spiritual trade be practised, in order that we may deserve to obtain among the angelic choirs the joys that will last for ever.

Therefore I, Edgar, king, governor and ruler of the whole of Britain, have given to a certain faithful thegn of mine, whom some call by the well-known name of Æthelwulf, 10 hides[1] in the place to which the inhabitants of that region assigned of old the name of Kilmeston, with the permission of Bishop Brihthelm and the community of the church, on condition that he renders the dues of the church, *i.e.* one church-scot, and five shingles and one plank[2] every year; so that he may have and possess it as long as he lives, and may leave it to two heirs after him, and after the lives of the three of them, he shall leave it to the church of St. Peter, by which it was conceded before.

And the aforesaid land is to be free from every worldly hindrance, with all things duly belonging to it, fields, pastures, meadows, woods; except public work, military service and the building of bridges and fortresses.

If, however, any depraved person shall try by false machinations to overthrow our grant by any document, may he be himself delivered in fiery bonds into the abyss of Chaos, and his memory hidden with the mist of death, unless with assiduous prayers he shall previously deserve to obtain here the wished-for pardon.[3] The aforesaid estate is surrounded by these boundaries:

These are the boundaries to Kilmeston: first from the white stream near Millbarrow, thence north to *Yferlea* by Brihtwold's boundary to *Brochanger*, to *Terhealcan* through *Hormeswood* out to three acres, on past the wood to *Æpshanger* to the linch, and so by the dyke over the brook north of *Eallanford* to the post, thence east to the boundary linch, and so east by the bishop's boundary below *Cadanhanger* to Wulfferth's homestead, thence to *Thornhurst*, down by *Thryfesdene*, by Brihtswith's boundary up

---

[1] *mansae.*
[2] These terms are expressed in English.
[3] From this point to the dating clause English is used. As none of these names except Millbarrow can be identified for certain, little definite has come from Dr. Grundy's examination of these boundaries in *Arch. J.*, LXXXIII, pp. 160ff.

to Sigeberht's footpath, thence west by it, over the highway[1] to the white dyke, west along the dyke back to the white stream.

And eight acres of meadow under *Wanexan dun*, which belong to Kilmeston, and the house in the town within the south wall [?] which belongs to the estate.

. This is the boundary of the wood south of Millbarrow: first from the ash-stump at *Hunlafinghamm*, south along the boundary to *Lammære*, to the swing-gate, then west by the bishop's boundary to *Higleag*, thence north along the highway by Brihtwold's boundary, out into the open country, past the *wyrttruma* back to the ash-stump.

This charter was written in the year of our Lord's incarnation 961, the fourth indiction.

> I, Edgar, king of the English, have conceded the aforesaid donation.
> I, Dunstan, archbishop of the church of Canterbury, have confirmed the donation of the same king with the sign of the Holy Cross.
> I, Brihthelm, bishop of the church of Winchester, have imprinted the triumphal victory-sign of the Holy Cross.
> I, Oswulf, bishop,[2] have signed.
> I, Oswald, bishop,[3] have consented.
> I, Æthelwulf, bishop,[4] have subscribed.
> I, Ælfwold, bishop,[5] have concluded.
> I, Æthelwold, abbot.[6]

I, Ælfhere, ealdorman.	I, Oswulf, king's thegn.
I, Ælfheah, ealdorman.	I, Æthelweard, king's thegn.
I, Athelstan, ealdorman.	I, Æthelwine, king's thegn.
I, Æthelwold, ealdorman.	I, Æthelsige, king's thegn.
I, Brihtnoth, ealdorman.	I, Wulfstan, king's thegn.
I, Ælfgar, king's thegn.	I, Alfred, king's thegn.
I, Brihtferth, king's thegn.	I, Eanwulf, king's thegn.
I, Ælfwine, king's thegn.	I, Ordgar, king's thegn.
I, Ælfsige, king's thegn.	I, Witsige, king's thegn.
I, Osweard, king's thegn.	I, Ælfwig, king's thegn.

Old English addition[7]

Bishop Brihthelm and all the community in the Old Minster at Winchester let the land at Kilmeston to Æthelwulf with the consent of King Edgar and the witness of all the councillors whose names stand here above, and also of both the communities, whether priests or nuns, here in the town, free from every service except the ecclesiastical service which the charter includes, and the secular service which all the people must ever perform, for the lives of two men after him. Then I beseech in the name of God and of St. Peter and of all his saints that no man be so presumptuous as to keep it longer from the church. If, then, anyone do so, that he be cut off from God and from all his elect, unless he fittingly make amends before his death.

[1] Literally, 'army-path'.   [2] Of Ramsbury.   [3] Of Worcester.
[4] Of Elmham.   [5] Of Crediton.   [6] Of Abingdon.
[7] This would probably be on the same original parchment as the Latin charter.

111. Lease in Latin and Old English by Oswald, bishop of Worcester, of land in Cotheridge, Worcestershire (963)

Oswald issued a great number of leases and many of them have been preserved, some in original form, more in the cartulary drawn up at Worcester in the eleventh century, Brit. Mus. Cott. Tiber. A. xiii, where this text survives. Some are in Latin, some in Old English, some, like this one, in a combination of the two languages. This one is early in the series, and the clergy of Worcester, who witness it, have not yet begun to include the monks whom Oswald gradually introduced into their midst. It is noteworthy how few of them are in the higher priest's orders. Church-scot in the diocese of Worcester at the time of Domesday Book was one load of grain from every hide.

This is No. 508 in Kemble, No. 1106 in Birch, No. 35 in Robertson, *Anglo-Saxon Charters*, where there is a translation.

✠ I, Oswald, having been ordained bishop by the chrism of Christ, in the year of our Lord's incarnation 963, with the consent of Edgar, king of the English, and of Ælfhere, ealdorman of the Mercians, and also of the community of the church of Worcester, have granted in eternal inheritance a certain portion of land, namely one hide in the place which is called by the inhabitants by the well-known name of Cotheridge, to a certain thegn of mine by name Ælfric; and after the end of his life he is to leave it unburdened to two heirs only, and when they are dead it is to be restored to the church of God in Worcester.[1]

On condition that each year he plough two acres of that land and sow therein his church-scot, and afterwards reap and garner it. And I grant him each year twelve loads of wood in my woodland without payment.

These are the boundaries to Cotheridge: First up the Teme and due north along the bishop's boundary to the Atchen way; from the Atchen way to Cotheridge stream, and along the stream to *Bridgeburnan* ford, thence along the paved road until it comes below Oba's tree, thence due south along the hedgerow to the *Rixuc*,[2] along the *Rixuc* to *Hihtesgehaeg*, thence due south to the paved road, and then along the paved road to Bransford, up along the Teme, then back to the bishop's boundary.

This charter was written with these witnesses consenting whose names are noted below:

✠ I, Wulfric, priest.
✠ I, Ælfric, priest.
✠ I, Edgar, deacon.
✠ I, Alfred, cleric.
✠ I, Wulfhun, cleric.
✠ I, Cynesige, cleric.
✠ I, Cynestan, cleric.
✠ I, Cynethegn, cleric.

✠ I, Wynstan, cleric.
✠ I, Edwin, cleric.
✠ I, Brihtstan, cleric.
✠ I, Wulfgar, cleric.
✠ I, Athelstan, sacrist.
✠ I, Æthelwold, cleric.
✠ I, Wulfheah, cleric.

I, Ælfric, make known to my dear lord that I grant to my son Æthelsige the land which I acquired of you, after my death to have for his lifetime and after his death to give to whom may be most pleasing to him, and that is to be in the male line.[3]

---

[1] The next two paragraphs are in Old English.
[2] A stream name probably surviving in the name Rushwick.
[3] This paragraph is in Old English.

112. Old English deed of exchange in which Æthelwold, bishop of Winchester, obtained an estate forfeited by a woman for practising witchcraft (963–975)

The main feature of this little record is the manner in which one of the estates the bishop obtained had come into the king's possession. On the penalty for witchcraft, see pp. 382, 405 n. 6. It survives in a twelfth-century Peterborough cartulary, Soc. Ant. Lond. MS. 60. It is best edited, with translation, by Robertson, *Anglo-Saxon Charters*, No. 37. It is No. 591 in Kemble, No. 1131 in Birch, and, with translation, in Thorpe, *Diplomatarium*, p. 229.

Here it is made known in this document that Bishop Æthelwold and Wulfstan Uccea exchanged lands in the witness of King Edgar and his councillors. The bishop gave Wulfstan the land at Washington[1] and Wulfstan gave to him the land at Yaxley[2] and at Ailsworth.[3] Then the bishop gave the land at Yaxley to Thorney and that at Ailsworth to Peterborough. And a widow and her son had previously forfeited the land at Ailsworth because they drove iron [?] pins[4] into Wulfstan's father, Ælfsige. And it was detected and the murderous instrument dragged from her chamber; and the woman was seized, and drowned at London Bridge, and her son escaped and became an outlaw. And the land came into the king's possession, and the king gave it to Ælfsige, and his son Wulfstan gave it to Bishop Æthelwold, as it says here above.

113. Grant by King Edgar of land at Kineton, Warwickshire, to his thegn Ælfwold (969)

This is one of the lost Worcester originals (see p. 337). Its main historic interest comes in the boundaries, for these show that even as late as this, the original distinction between the Mercians proper and the Hwicce was still felt; for the boundary of the Mercians mentioned is not that of the great kingdom ruled by the kings of Mercia from the eighth century, but the line of demarcation separating the original Mercians from the settlers in the Severn valley. The administrative reorganization which created the counties of the Midlands ignored this division, but it still separates the dioceses.

The charter has a diplomatic interest also, for there survives an original charter (Birch, No. 1229) issued to the same grantee in the same year, which is couched in identical terms and has exactly the same witnesses in the same order, except that it omits Ealdorman Æthelwine. The estate concerned is Apsley, Bedfordshire, and the two charters must have been issued on the same occasion.

This charter was printed by J. Smith in the appendix to his edition of Bede (1722), p. 774, before the original was burnt. It is No. 548 in Kemble, No. 1234 in Birch.

✠ In the name of our Lord Jesus Christ. Truly every generous donation of kings ought to be strengthened by the testimony of letters, lest the line of posterity falls, in ignorance, into paltry niggardliness. For this reason, I, Edgar, by the pleasure of the divine grace, king and chief ruler of all Albion, bestow a certain portion of land, namely 10 hides[5] at the place which is commonly called Kineton, on my faithful thegn who is called by the knowledgeable people of this island by the well-known name of Ælfwold, as an eternal inheritance, that he himself, while his life lasts, may have it to his satisfaction with all advantages, namely meadows, pastures, woods; and

---

[1] Sussex.   [2] Hunts.   [3] Northants.

[4] That the offence meant is that of sticking pins into a wax image of a person in the belief that this will cause injury is shown by reference to this sin in penitential literature. For example, in a tract known as *Modus Imponendi Poenitentiam*, in a context dealing with witchcraft and magic arts, occurs the phrase "if anyone drive pins into a man".

[5] *cassati*.

after the conclusion of his life leave it unburdened to whatsoever heirs he shall wish. Also the aforesaid estate is to be free from every yoke of earthly service except three, namely fixed military service and the restoration of bridges and fortresses.

If anyone, therefore, shall wish to transfer this our donation into anything other than we have decreed, may he, cut off from the fellowship of the Holy Church of God, be punished perpetually by the eternal flames of the doleful abyss together with Judas the betrayer of Christ and his associates, if he has not made amends with fitting compensation for what he committed against our decree.

This aforesaid estate is encompassed by these bounds on all sides:[1] these are the boundaries to Kineton: from Wellesbourne[2] to the gully, from the gully to the ditch, from the ditch on the boundary to the paved road,[3] from the paved road to the *morth-hlaw*,[4] from the *morth-hlaw* to the foul pit, from the foul pit to the springs, from the springs to the boundary of the Mercians,[5] from the boundary of the Mercians to *Succan-pit*, from *Succan-pit* to *Grundlinga-brook*, along the stream, from that stream to *Fidestan*, from that stone to *Hragra-thorn*, from *Hragra-thorn* back to Wellesbourne.

In the year of the incarnation of our Lord Jesus Christ 969, the charter of this donation was written, these witnesses consenting whose names are inscribed below.

✠   I, Edgar, king of the English, with the consent of my advisors, have strengthened it with the sign of the Holy Cross.

✠   I, Dunstan, archbishop of the church of Canterbury, have consented[6] and subscribed.

✠   I, Oscetel, archbishop, have speedily consented.

✠   I, Ælfstan, bishop,[7] have joined in signing.

✠   I, Æthelwold, bishop,[8] have consented.

✠   I, Oswulf, bishop,[9] have confirmed.

✠   I, Wynsige, bishop,[10] have consolidated.

✠   I, Oswald, bishop,[11] have strengthened.

✠   I, Wulfric, bishop,[12] have consented.

✠ I, Æscwig, abbot.	✠ I, Ordgar, ealdorman.
✠ I, Osgar, abbot.	✠ I, Athelstan, ealdorman.
✠ I, Ælfstan, abbot.	✠ I, Æthelwine, ealdorman.
✠ I, Æthelgar, abbot.	✠ I, Brihtnoth, ealdorman.
✠ I, Ælfric, abbot.	✠ I, Brihtferth, king's thegn.
✠ I, Cyneweard, abbot.	✠ I, Ælfwine, king's thegn.
✠ I, Ælfhere, ealdorman.	✠ I, Wulfstan, king's thegn.
✠ I, Ælfheah, ealdorman.	✠ I, Æthelweard, king's thegn.

---

[1] The boundaries that follow are in Old English.
[2] The stream is now Dene Brook, but the name survives as that of two villages.
[3] The Warwick–Banbury road.   [4] This should mean 'murder barrow, or hill'.
[5] See *The Place-Names of Warwickshire* (Eng. Pl.-N. Soc.), p. 272, where it is pointed out that this name survives in the field-name Martimow in Radway. The boundary between the dioceses of Worcester and Coventry (earlier Lichfield) still separates Radway and Kineton.
[6] Both in this text and Birch, No. 1229, the word used is *possedi*, 'have possessed', which must be corrupt. The version of Birch, No. 1229, in Brit. Mus. Cott. Vitell. C. ix, fol. 126b, has *consensi* 'I have consented'.
[7] Of London.   [8] Of Winchester.   [9] Of Ramsbury.
[10] Of Lichfield.   [11] Of Worcester.   [12] Of Hereford.

✠ I, Eanwulf, king's thegn.   ✠ I, Ælfweard, king's thegn.
✠ I, Oswulf, king's thegn.   ✠ I, Æthelmund, king's thegn.
✠ I, Wulfstan, king's thegn.   ✠ I, Osweard, king's thegn.
✠ I, Leofwine, king's thegn.   ✠ I, Leofwine, king's thegn.

114. Archbishop Oswald's Old English memoranda on the estates of the see of York (972–992)

Because of the destruction of so much of the York material just after the Norman Conquest, it is rare to get a document that throws light on conditions in this province. This record may help to correct any impression one might receive that those archbishops of York who held the see in plurality with that of Worcester were uninterested in the affairs of their northern diocese. It has another feature of interest, for certain interlineations have been made in a hand that occurs in many manuscripts connected with Archbishop Wulfstan, the homilist, and may well be his own, as Mr. N. R. Ker has suggested (*Studies in Medieval History presented to F. M. Powicke*, pp. 70f.). The manuscript, Brit. Mus. Harley MS. 55, is probably from Worcester, and this portion belongs to the early eleventh century. The document is edited with translation, Robertson, *Anglo-Saxon Charters*, No. 54. It is Nos. 1278, 1279 in Birch.

Archbishop Oswald composed this declaration and had it written.

These are the villages which have been taken from Otley: the first is Addingham, the second Ilkley, the third Menston, the fourth half of Burley, the fifth Guiseley, the sixth Chevin, the seventh Middleton, the eighth half of Denton, the ninth Timble, the tenth Lindley, the eleventh Stainburn, the twelfth Beckwith, the thirteenth half of *Byllinctun*.[1]

These villages have been taken from Ripon: the first is Hewick, the second Hewick,[2] the third *Ansætleh*,[3] the fourth one hide at Stainley, the fifth Helperby, the sixth at Myton. Two hides from Poppleton.

This has been taken from Sherburn: half of *Ceoredesholm* and half of Cawood – and *Gisferþesdæll* has always belonged to Sherburn – and half the soke[4] which belongs to Sherburn.

These are the lands which Archbishop Oscetel obtained in Northumbria with his money and which were given to him in compensation for illegal marriage: one is Appleton, which he bought for 24 pounds from Deorwulf. He bought Everingham for 44 pounds from Osulf's father, when he was at the point of death,[5] and he bought the estate at Newbold for 120 mancuses of red gold from King Edgar; and Helperby was given to him in compensation for illicit cohabitation – there were two brothers who had one wife – and to Helperby belong two parts of Myton and the soke of Wide Open and Tholthorpe and Youlton and Thorpe. And he bought Skidby for 20 pounds, and three hides at Bracken he bought from King Edgar, and he granted it to him by charter for St. John's.[6] *I, Archbishop Oswald, declare that*[7] all these lands which *the* Archbishop Oscetel obtained in Northumbria – and my lord granted

---

[1] Bilton near Harrogate?
[2] Copt and Bridge Hewick.   [3] This lost name means 'hermit's lea'.
[4] Though originally this meant jurisdiction, it came to be used of the territory over which one had jurisdiction.
[5] Accepting Miss Robertson's interpretation of *fæge* 'doomed' in this context.
[6] Beverley.
[7] The italicized parts are not part of what was first written, but added by the hand mentioned above.

them to me *for St. Peter's* when he was at Nottingham – [and] these other lands which are entered here besides, I had them all until [Ethelred ?][1] ascended. Then St. Peter was afterwards robbed [of them]. May God avenge it as he will.

115. Grant by King Edward the Martyr to Ealdorman Æthelweard of lands in Cornwall (977)

This charter is included partly because there are very few texts from this short reign, partly for its interest in showing a king granting a large holding in Cornwall to a person of considerable importance, Ealdorman Æthelweard, who wrote the Latin chronicle referred to frequently above (see p. 65). He was the representative of an older branch of the royal family than the reigning house, and the patron of the homilist Ælfric. One should note that on this coastal estate, maritime guard has taken the place of bridgework in the dues reserved from the general immunity. The boundaries are in English, as is usual, but many of the names are in Cornish. For their interpretation, I am indebted to Davidson, *op. cit.*, and M. Förster, *Der Flussname Themse und seine Sippe.*

This text, which belongs to the Dean and Chapter of Exeter, is a copy made on the back of a charter of 1059 by which Edward the Confessor grants these same lands to Bishop Ealdred of Cornwall (Earle, pp. 300–302), without referring, however, to the maritime guard. There is a facsimile in *Ord. Surv. Facs.*, II, Exeter Charters, No. 14 (d). It is edited by J. B. Davidson, *Journ. Brit. Arch. Assoc.*, XXXIX, pp. 282–285, Earle, pp. 295–297.

✠ Our Lord Jesus Christ reigning for ever. It is known by firm reason to almost all who pursue the study of wisdom, that, as the dangers of the present existence are threatening and the cares of evanescent things unexpectedly increasing, human knowledge of mortal affairs, vanishing like dew, fades away, and is at length given to oblivion, unless it is noted down before by some secure means, because the things which are seen here are not eternal but temporal, as the Apostle, inspired with speech of the Thunderer, says.[2] Now, like a shadow, the corporeal things quickly flee; but the eternal glory stands more certain than all that is visible.

On this account, I, Edward, by the gift of the grace of God, king of the English and of the other nations on every side, with the counsel and consent of my bishops and chief men, willingly concede to my faithful ealdorman Æthelweard by name certain portions of land situated in diverse places, namely Treraboe,[3] Trevallock, Grugith[4] and *Trethewey*;[5] in perpetual inheritance with all things duly belonging to them, fields, woods, meadows and fisheries, free from all royal dues except military service and the fortification of fortresses and maritime guard; and after he goes the way of all flesh, he is to leave at will the aforesaid land to whoever he shall wish.

And this donation was done in the year 977 from the incarnation of our Lord, the fifth indiction, 6[6] concurrents, 28 epacts, in the seventeenth[7] year of the cycle of nineteen years, in the second year of my reign; these witnesses consenting whose names are seen to be inscribed below.

[1] The text is illegible here. The paper MS., Harley 6841, reads *oþ þerað in com.* My suggested rendering requires *oþ æperæd in com.* Unfortunately it seems certain that there is ð, not *d*, before *in*, but as this text writes *hyrðe* for *hyrde*, this is not an insuperable obstacle. [2] Cf. II Corinthians iv. 18.
[3] A farm in the parish of St. Keverne, according to Davidson. Trevallock is half a mile west of St. Keverne.
[4] This is Davidson's identification of *Trefgrued*, called *Crucwæð* in the boundaries. All three places are in St. Keverne.
[5] In St. Martin-in-Meneage. This identification is by J. E. Gover. [6] This should be seven.
[7] This should only be 'ninth'. The error may be miscopying or miscalculation.

This is the boundary to Treraboe: First at *Pollicerr*, then by the dyke along the way, then from the way, then on the little dyke on the east side of the way to *Pollhæscen*, down by the brook to the fort of the Durra, then along the brook to *Carn-Nithbran* to *Deumæncoruan*, thence along the way to *Cruc-Drænoc*, thence to *Carrecwynn* and from there back to *Pollicerr*.

This is the boundary to Trevallock: First to the dyke, then from the dyke down to the brook, from the brook to *Crouswrach*, along the way on to the dyke, thence to *Mayn-biw*[1] to *Cruc-mur*, thence to *Carn-wlicet*, along that to the brook, thence along the stream until *Tuow-water*, back by the dyke.

This is the boundary to Grugith: first at *Nant-Buorthtel*;[2] along the stream to *Lenbrunn*,[3] thence to *Cestelmerit*,[3] thence west to *Wucou*, down west along the dyke as far as the brook, thence to *Fonton-Morgeonec*, thence down to the brook where it started.

This is the boundary to Trethewey: first at *Penhal-Meilar*,[4] south to the way, thence to the ford, straight to *Erliwet*, thence forth along the stream to *Lyncenin*, thence up to *Penhal-Meilar*.

✠ I, Edward, king of the English [confirm] this gift with the triumphal sign of the Holy Cross.

✠ I, Dunstan, archbishop, have confirmed.

✠ I, Æthelwold, bishop,[5] testify.

I, Ælfstan, bishop,[6] have assented.

I, Wulfsige, bishop,[7] have agreed and subscribed.

✠ I, Ælfhere, ealdorman.[8]

I, Æthelwine, ealdorman.

I, Brihtnoth, ealdorman.

I, Leofwine, ealdorman.

I, Ælfweard, king's thegn, testify.

I, Ælfsige, king's thegn, testify.

I, Leofwine, king's thegn, testify.

I, Brihtmær, king's thegn, testify.

I, Ælfgar, king's thegn, testify.

Whoever, therefore, shall eagerly desire to preserve, nay rather to increase, this our gift, may his life be prolonged and may he deserve to go after his death happily to the kingdom of the heavens. But if, which God forbid, anyone forgetting God and himself shall try to alter it, may he be anathema, and may he not live out half his days,[9] and may he by no means see the glory of God with the choirs of angels in the land of the living.

---

[1] 'Stone of life', according to Förster, *op. cit.*, p. 29.   [2] 'Valley of the good [?] fold', *op. cit., loc. cit.*
[3] These two boundary marks occur also in a charter of 967 in the bounds of *Lesneage* in St. Keverne, in the forms *leinbroinn* and *cestell merit* respectively. The Durra is also mentioned in these bounds.
[4] 'Head of the moor of the Meilar', Förster, *op. cit., loc. cit.*   [5] Of Winchester.
[6] London, Rochester and Ramsbury all had bishops of this name at this date.   [7] Of Sherborne.
[8] One signature is illegible here.   [9] Cf. Psalm liv. 24.

116. Old English will of Wulfwaru (984–1016)

I include this document as a specimen of a woman's will to illustrate the type of evidence for social conditions that can be gathered from the will of a woman of no historic importance. Nothing is known of Wulfwaru or her family elsewhere. All her identifiable estates are in Somerset. The will is preserved in a Bath cartulary, C.C.C.C., MS. III. It is No. 694 in Kemble, and, with translation, in Thorpe's *Diplomatarium*, p. 528, and Whitelock, No. 21, from which the present translation is taken.

I, Wulfwaru, pray my dear lord King Ethelred, of his charity, that I may be entitled to make my will. I make known to you, Sire, here in this document, what I grant to St. Peter's monastery at Bath for my poor soul and for the souls of my ancestors from whom my property and my possessions came to me; namely then, that I grant to that holy place there an armlet which consists of 60 mancuses of gold, and a bowl of two and a half pounds, and two gold crucifixes, and a set of Mass-vestments with everything that belongs to it, and the best dorsal that I have, and a set of bed-clothing with tapestry and curtain and with everything that belongs to it. And I grant to the Abbot Ælfhere the estate at Freshford with the produce and the men and all the profit which is obtained there.

And I grant to my elder son Wulfmær the estate at Claverton, with produce and with men and with all profits; and the estate at Compton with produce and men and all profits; and I grant him half the estate at Butcombe with produce and men and all profits, and half of it I grant to my younger daughter Ælfwaru, with produce and men and all profits. And they are to share the principal residence between them as evenly as they can, so that each of them shall have a just portion of it.

And to my younger son Ælfwine I grant the estate at Leigh, with produce and men and all profits; and the estate at Holton, with produce and men and all profits; and the estate at *Hocgestun*,[1] with produce and men and all profits; and 30 mancuses of gold.

And I grant to my elder daughter, Gode, the estate at Winford, with produce and men and all profits; and two cups of four pounds; and a band of 30 mancuses of gold and two brooches and a woman's attire complete. And to my younger daughter, Ælfwaru, I grant all the women's clothing which is left.

And to my son Wulfmær and my second son Ælfwine and my daughter Ælfwaru –to each of the three of them–I grant two cups of good value. And I grant to my son Wulfmær a hall-tapestry and a set of bed-clothes. To Ælfwine my second son I grant a tapestry for a hall and tapestry for a chamber, together with a table-cover and with all the clothes which go with it.

And I grant to my four retainers[2] Ælfmær, Ælfweard, Wulfric and Wulfstan, a band of 20 mancuses of gold. And I grant to all my household women, in common, a good chest well decorated.

And I desire that those who succeed to my property provide 20 freedmen, 10 in the east and 10 in the west; and all together furnish a food-rent for Bath every year for ever, as good as ever they can afford, at such season as it seems to all of them that

---

[1] This is the same name as Hoggeston, Bucks., but if this place is meant, Wulfwaru possessed one isolated estate far from her other lands.

[2] The term used, *cniht*, meant a mounted retainer at this time. See F. M. Stenton, *The First Century of English Feudalism*, pp. 133 f.

they can accomplish it best and most fittingly. Whichever of them shall discharge
this, may he have God's favour and mine; and whichever of them will not discharge
it, may he have to account for it with the Most High, who is the true God, who
created and made all creatures.

117. Grant by King Ethelred to his thegn Æthelwig, of land at Ardley, Oxford-shire, forfeited by certain brothers for fighting in defence of a thief (992–995)

Like several of Ethelred's charters, this text, which is preserved in the Abingdon cartulary, Brit.
Mus. Cott. Claud. B. vi, sheds light on the workings of Anglo-Saxon law, showing among other
things that the right of Christian burial was forfeited by anyone killed resisting the law, and that an
ealdorman could not himself deal with a breach of law by the king's reeve, but only appeal to
the king.

If one could accept the incarnation date, 995, this text would show that Archbishop Sigeric was
alive in 995; but, as the evidence for his death in 994 is considerable,[1] one cannot rely on the
accuracy of this date in a late copy, particularly as it is not supported by the indiction date, which
has either been miscopied or miscalculated. The fourteenth indiction gives either 986 or 1001,
both of which are impossible for the list of witnesses. This belongs to 992–995, or, if one could be
certain that Sigeric died in 994, 992–994.

The charter is No. 1289 in Kemble, and is in Thorpe, *Diplomatarium*, pp. 290ff.

✠ Whatever is transacted by men of this world to endure for ever ought to be
fortified securely with ranks of letters, because the frail memory of men in dying
forgets what the writing of letters preserves and retains.

Hence I, Ethelred, by the grace of God, king of the English, wish it to be known
to all my faithful subjects, that I deliver in hereditary right to a certain of my thegns,
Æthelwig by name, five hides in the residence which is called by those who know,
Ardley, that he may possess them while his life lasts, and after his last day has closed
his eyes, may leave them to whichever friend he shall wish in perpetual possession.
And the present donation is to be absolved from every servile yoke, except, however,
three things, namely national military service, the construction of fortresses, the
restoration of bridges. I will make clear in a brief account how, indeed, the present
estate came into my possession.

There were three brothers sharing a certain establishment, one of whose men, by
name Leofric, stole a bridle at the instigation of the devil; and when it was discovered
in his bosom, those who had lost the bridle, and the three brothers, the masters of the
aforesaid thief, rose up hurriedly and made war on one another. Two of the brothers,
namely Ælfnoth and Ælfric, were killed in the fight, and the third, Æthelwine,
barely escaped along with the aforesaid robber, entering the church of St. Helen.[2]
But when the people around heard of these things, Æthelwig, my reeve in Buckingham, and Wynsige, the reeve in Oxford, gave the aforesaid brothers Christian burial.
Therefore Ealdorman Leofsige, having got word of this, came to my presence
accusing the aforesaid reeves, as the slain brothers had been illegally given Christian
burial. I, however, not wishing to sadden Æthelwig, because he was dear and precious
to me, at the same time both allowed those who had been buried to repose with

[1] On this question, see K. Sisam, *Rev. Eng. Stud.*, VII, pp. 15f., re-issued in *Studies in the History of Old
English Literature*, pp. 157f.
[2] At Abingdon.

the Christians, and also conceded to him the afore-mentioned land in perpetual inheritance.

If, truly, anyone, swollen with the lust of cupidity, shall attempt to destroy this my charter of donation, let him be anathema, maran-atha[1] – *i.e.* alienation from the fellowship of Christians – unless he comes to his senses and, repenting, does penance for what he tried to do fraudulently. This, however, I strongly enjoin, that no document of other title-deeds may seem to be superior to our charter, but such is to lie hidden for ever and be destroyed.

These are the boundaries of the five hides at Ardley :[2] first from the great dyke,[3] then to Æthelwold's lea to the boundary, from the boundary thus along the valley to *Sexig-broc*,[4] from *Sexig-broc* to *Uffewell* brook, from the brook to the green dyke, from the dyke south of the earthwork until Cwichhelm's barrow,[5] from the barrow then to the town-highway, from the town-highway towards Little *Cyltun*[6] for the breadth of an acre, then on the green way which leads to Heyford, along the green way opposite Cynewynn's well, from the well to the great dyke, along the dyke to the Bune,[7] along the Bune to the old ford, from the ford into Ardley, from the lea back to the great dyke.

This document was written in the year from the incarnation of the Lord 995, the fourteenth indiction, these witnesses consenting whose names are inscribed below.

✠ I, Ethelred, king, *basileus*[8] of the English, holding the summit of the whole kingdom, freely concede, or bestow and consent, or cheerfully confirm, the privilege of this gift.

✠ I, Sigeric.[9]

✠ I, Ælfstan, bishop of the church of London, have corroborated.

✠ I, Ælfheah, bishop of the church of Winchester, have confirmed.

✠ I, Æscwig, bishop of the church of Dorchester, have pronounced.

✠ I, Ælfric, bishop of the church of Wilton, have strengthened.

✠ I, Ealdwulf, bishop of the church of Worcester, have assented.

✠ I, Osberht, bishop of the church of the South [Saxons], have completed.

✠ I, Ælfheah, bishop of the church of Lichfield, have joyfully consented.

✠ I, Æthelwulf, bishop of the church of Hereford, have supported.

✠ I, Ælfwold, bishop of the church of Crediton, have upheld.

✠ I, Wulfsige, bishop of the church of Sherborne, have granted, glad at the request.

[1] I Corinthians xvi. 22.

[2] The boundary paragraph is in Old English. I am indebted to Mrs. M. J. Gelling for some of the identifications.

[3] Ash Bank, Wattle Bank or Aves Ditch. See *The Place-Names of Oxfordshire* (Eng. P.-N. Soc.), p. 5.

[4] The parish of Bucknell contains a lost name, *Saxinton*, with which this stream-name should probably be connected.

[5] This is the same name as that of Cuckamsley, Berks., the *Cwicelmeshlæwe* of the Anglo-Saxon Chronicle, *s.a.* 1006.

[6] This name should be connected with *Chilgrove*, the old name of Ballard's Copse in Ardley.

[7] An older name for the Claydon Brook.

[8] This Greek title was sometimes used in the regnal styles of the tenth century.

[9] Archbishop of Canterbury; the copyist either omitted his attestation formula inadvertently or could not read it.

✠ I, Æthelweard, ealdorman, joyfully fortify or affirm, and stand present as a witness.

✠ I, Ælfric, ealdorman, imprint the sign of the Cross, or uphold.

✠ I, Ælfhelm, ealdorman.	✠ I, Ælfsige, king's thegn.
✠ I, Leofwine, ealdorman.	✠ I, Ordwulf, king's thegn.
✠ I, Leofsige, ealdorman.	✠ I, Leofric, king's thegn.
✠ I, Ælfweard, abbot.	✠ I, Wulfheah, king's thegn.
✠ I, Ælfsige, abbot.	✠ I, Wulfric, king's thegn.
✠ I, Brihtnoth, abbot.	✠ I, Wulfgeat, king's thegn.
✠ I, Brihthelm, abbot.	✠ I, Æthelnoth, king's thegn.
✠ I, Leofric, abbot.	✠ I, Æthelric, king's thegn.
✠ I, Ælfhere, abbot.	✠ I, Æthelsige, king's thegn.
✠ I, Cenwulf, abbot.	✠ I, Æthelmær, king's thegn.
✠ I, Ælfric, abbot.	✠ I, Ceolmund, king's thegn.
✠ I, Ælfhun, abbot.	✠ I, Wihtsige, king's thegn.
✠ I, Germanus, abbot.	✠ I, Æthelwig, king's thegn.

118. Ratification by King Ethelred for Æscwig, bishop of Dorchester, of an estate at Risborough, Buckinghamshire, granted to him by Archbishop Sigeric in exchange for money to buy off the Danes (994 or 995)

This charter, which is preserved in Register B of Christ Church, Canterbury, illustrates the seriousness of the Danish menace, and gives details not in the chroniclers. The occasion on which the archbishop had to buy immunity for the metropolitan church of the kingdom must have been the raid of 994, when Kent was one of the counties ravaged (see No. 1, p. 214). Later, Æscwig returned Risborough to Christ Church (Kemble, No. 690).

The witnesses and attestation clauses are almost identical with those of Kemble, No. 691, a contemporary document by which Bishop Æscwig grants Cuxham, Oxfordshire, to his man. This should not cast suspicion on the present document, for Æscwig's charter is not likely to have been available for the monks of Canterbury to imitate, nor would they have forged a charter alienating an estate; and if it were forged in favour of Dorchester, it could hardly have found its way into a Christ Church register. The agreement points rather to the two documents having been drawn up on the same occasion. Both texts give the date as 995, and this raises again the question of the date of Sigeric's death (see p. 526). Yet the indiction date of this present document is correct for 994, while Kemble, No. 691, gives no indiction. The present charter is No. 689 in Kemble.

✠ In the name of the Holy Saviour, who justly governs all things, created by him out of nothing, and mightily brings them together to the sway of his power by the strength of his rule, lest, reduced to nothing, they perish, and worthily preserves them. Since, indeed, we know that it has often and repeatedly been recounted by wise men that all perishable things are seen to hasten to their ruinous fall, it seems that each of the faithful ought especially to endeavour constantly to practise good deeds in the present life, as is possible, so that he may rejoice in the future reward of recompense.

For which reason, I, Ethelred, ruler of the English and governor of the other adjoining nations round about, concede most willingly to a certain bishop of mine, very faithful to me, with the familiar name of Æscwig, to the control of his possession a certain portion of land, namely 30 hides[1] in the place which is called by the inhabitants

---

[1] *mansiunculae.*

by the name of Risborough;[1] but also we are anxious to intimate to all faithful people whatsoever, as we deem it necessary, by what course the aforesaid estate was granted into the possession of the afore-mentioned bishop. For when the pagan race, raging with its slaughters, was devastating Kent, and raving in hostility was destroying it, they threatened that they would come to the church of the Holy Saviour, which is situated in the city of Canterbury, and raze it to the ground with their fires, unless the money which had been promised to them by Archbishop Sigeric was given to them in full. Hence the archbishop, perturbed by many anxieties, since he had not so much as a single penny, took counsel, and, sending to the aforesaid prelate, Æscwig, that is, both asked him urgently with many prayers to give him for the earnestness of his love the money which was lacking, and beseeched him with much prayer not to refuse to accept the aforesaid estate into the control of his possession in exchange for this. Hence the aforesaid prelate, deeply moved by such distress, gave his consent, obtaining the money, namely 90 pounds of refined silver and 200 mancuses of the purest gold, and sending it to the archbishop by the same messengers by whom the message was brought. When he had received it, the archbishop called to him the enemy and paid in full what he had previously, though under compulsion, promised; and he gave the title-deed of the aforesaid estate to Bishop Æscwig, in my presence and in the witness of my chief men, granting it with a most willing mind, that he was to have it and possess it as long as he remained in this world, and to grant it to what heir he pleased after him. The aforesaid estate is to be free from every worldly hindrance, with all things which are known to belong to it, both in great things as in small, in fields, pastures, meadows, woods, except these three, namely military service, the building of bridges and fortresses. And the aforesaid estate is surrounded by such boundaries as are contained in the original title-deed, written in Saxon letters and the Saxon language, etc.

May those attempting to change, diminish, or violate this privilege of our generous grant truly have their portion with those to whom it is said: "Depart from me, ye workers of iniquity, into the flame-vomiting fire, where there shall be weeping of the eyes and gnashing of the teeth";[2] unless he previously make amends before his departure from bodily life diligently and canonically with fitting penance and legal compensation.

The present charter was drawn up in the year of the incarnation of our Lord 995, the seventh indiction, these witnesses consenting whose names are seen written below:

✠ I, Ethelred, king of the English, guiding the government of the whole
 sovereignty, have willingly granted the donation of this privilege.

✠ I, Sigeric, archbishop of the church of Canterbury, have corroborated it
 with the sign of the Holy Cross.

✠ I, Ælfheah, bishop of the church of Winchester, have confirmed.

✠ I, Ælfstan, bishop of the church of London, have strengthened.

✠ I, Æscwig, bishop of the church of Dorchester, have approved.

✠ I, Ælfstan, bishop of the church of Rochester, have joined in signing.

---

[1] Monks Risborough, Bucks. Cf. No. 126.   [2] Cf. Luke xiii. 27f.

✠ I, Ordberht, bishop of the church of Selsey, have impressed [my mark].

✠ I, Sigegar, bishop of the church of Wells, have assented.

✠ I, Ælfric, bishop of the church of Wilton, have concurred.

✠ I, Æthelweard, ealdorman. ✠ I, Ordwulf, king's thegn.

✠ I, Ælfric, ealdorman. ✠ I, Wulfgeat, king's thegn.[1]

✠ I, Leofsige, ealdorman. ✠ I, Wulfheah, king's thegn.[1]

✠ I, Leofwine, ealdorman. ✠ I, Ælfsige, king's thegn.

✠ I, Ælfsige, abbot. ✠ I, Fræna, king's thegn.

✠ I, Leofric, abbot. ✠ I, Wulfric, king's thegn.

✠ I, Brihtnoth, abbot.

✠ I, Æthelmær, king's thegn.

119. Grant by King Ethelred to Wulfric, Wulfrun's son, of land in Dumbleton, Gloucestershire, forfeited by Æthelsige for theft (995)

The grantee of this charter is the Wulfric Spott whose will is given as No. 125. It is from this charter that 'we learn of his ancestry. Besides showing the working of the law, the text shows also in its Old English portion that a more complicated transaction can lie behind a Latin charter than would appear from the Latin text.

Wulfric left Dumbleton to Archbishop Ælfric, "along with the other", by which probably is meant 24 hides at Dumbleton which Ethelred granted to the archbishop in 1002 (Kemble, No. 1295; see also No. 126). This land also had fallen to the king by forfeiture, this time by a woman for fornication. The archbishop left Dumbleton to Abingdon.

The original charter has been lost, but Talbot's transcript is in C.C.C.C., MS. 111, p. 175. It belonged to Abingdon, and was copied into the cartulary of that house, Brit. Mus. Cott. Claud. B. vi. There exists also a twelfth-century transcript, Brit. Mus. Cott. Augustus, ii. 48. The charter is No. 692 in Kemble.

✠ The Disposer of heaven and earth and Vanquisher of hell reigning from age to age. The condition of the tottering universe declines on every side and is shaken with severe whirlwinds, but by the help of the divine omnipotence it is nevertheless strengthened with the support of great men, lest it should seem improvidently to be ruined by feeble vacillation; while it is regulated by the authority of such great primates as long as the strength of the Christian name prevails and the rights of kingdoms are governed by provident dispensation; whence those whom the fortune of this age sports with by its feeble motion, ought especially to be vigilant to acquire those joys which are not for one year but for ever, that by the distribution of temporal treasures they may deserve to gain the support of the eternal bounty.

On this account, I, Ethelred, emperor by the providence of God of all Albion, concede as a perpetual inheritance to a certain thegn most dear to me, on whom nobility of kindred conferred the name of Wulfric, on account of the most faithful obedience with which he has courteously served me, a certain parcel of land, namely two and a half hides[2] in the place which the inhabitants call Dumbleton; in order that he may enjoy it well and possess it in prosperity, as long as he is seen to pass through the habitation of this life with vital spirit and rotary course; and after his departure from this fleeting life, that he may leave it to whatever successor he shall please. The

---

[1] These two names are garbled in the text in the register as Wolfryð and Wolfeby respectively. The contemporary list of Kemble, No. 690, shows what should have been written.

[2] *mansae.*

aforesaid estate, which is situated on public land, is moreover to be free from every worldly obstacle, along with all things which are known to belong to that place, both in great things as in small, in fields, pastures, meadows, woods, except these three, military service, construction of bridges and fortresses.

For those, indeed, diminishing or violating this my donation – which, I desire, may be far from the minds of the faithful – may their portion be with those against whom it was said: "Depart from me, you cursed, into everlasting fire which was prepared for Satan and his satellites";[1] unless previously they obtain pardon by making amends with fitting penance to God and with legal compensation.

For, what the memory of man lets slip, the circumscription in letters preserves; hence it ought to be made known to readers that this aforesaid estate came into the control of my possession through a crime of unspeakable presumption of a certain man, to whom his parents gave the name of Æthelsige, although he disgraced the name[2] by a base and shameful act; in that he did not shrink from audaciously committing theft; and, as I have said above, it was conferred by me on the honourable thegn. We have approved that the account of his crime should be noted here with a report in English:

Thus was the land at Dumbleton forfeited which Æthelsige forfeited into King Ethelred's possession: it was because he stole the swine of Æthelwine, the son of Ealdorman Æthelmær; then his men rode thither and brought out the bacon from Æthelsige's house, and he escaped to the wood. And he was then outlawed and his land and his goods were assigned to King Ethelred. Then he granted the land in perpetual inheritance to his man Hawas; and Wulfric, son of Wulfrun, afterwards obtained it from him by exchange with what was more convenient to him, with the king's permission and the witness of his councillors.

This aforesaid donation was made in the year of the incarnation of our Lord 995, the eighth indiction, and in the seventeenth year of the aforesaid king this charter was written, those consenting who are noted below.

✠ I, Ethelred, king of the English, have conceded unchangeably and strengthened the aforesaid donation with the sign of the Holy Cross.

✠ I, Ælfric, by the grace of God, archbishop elect of the church of Canterbury, have established the king's donation with the marvel of the Cross.

✠ I, Ealdwulf, archbishop elect of the church of York, have corroborated the king's donation with the blessed impression of the Holy Cross.

✠ I, Ælfstan, bishop of the church of London, have made the sign.

✠ I, Ælfheah, bishop of the church of Winchester, have marked the sign.

✠ I, Æscwig, bishop of the church of Dorchester, have put my mark.

✠ I, Æthelwulf, bishop of the church of Hereford, have set my mark.

✠ I, Wulfsige, bishop of the church of Sherborne, have concluded.

✠ I, Æthelweard, ealdorman.　　✠ I, Leofsige, ealdorman.

✠ I, Ælfric, ealdorman.　　✠ I, Leofwine, ealdorman.

✠ I, Ælfhelm, ealdorman.　　✠ I, Ælfweard, abbot.

---

[1] Matthew xxv. 41.　　　　[2] The name means 'noble victory'.

✠ I, Ælfsige, abbot.
✠ I, Leofric, abbot.
✠ I, Brihthelm, abbot.
✠ I, Wulfgar, abbot.
✠ I, Æthelmær, king's thegn.
✠ I, Ordwulf, king's thegn.
✠ I, Ælfsige, king's thegn.
✠ I, Brihtwold, king's thegn.
✠ I, Wulfheah, king's thegn.

✠ I, Wulfric, king's thegn.
✠ I, Wulfgeat, king's thegn.
✠ I, Leofric, king's thegn.
✠ I, Æthelnoth, king's thegn.
✠ I, Æthelric, king's thegn.
✠ I, Leofric, king's thegn.
✠ I, Æthelweard, king's thegn.
✠ I, Wulfmær, king's thegn.
✠ I, Fræna, king's thegn.

120. Grant by King Ethelred to his mother, of Brabourne and other estates in Kent which had been forfeited by a certain Wulfbald for many crimes (996)

The major interest of this document is the picture it gives of the weakness of Ethelred's régime, but it is also important in its recording a great synod at London, which was attended by many magnates from the North who do not usually witness charters. The boundaries show the attaching of town houses to country estates. It is of interest, too, to find that Ælfthryth had possessed Cholsey, for this was one of the estates that had been held by Æthelflæd, widow of King Edmund, and it seems possible that it was one of the estates which tended to be assigned to the support of the queen.

The charter is wrongly dated 993; the regnal year, the indiction and the list of witnesses, all fit 996, which is the first possible date for Wulfstan to sign as bishop of London. The great assembly mentioned must have been held in 989 or 990.

It is not easy to see how this document came to be in the New Minster cartulary, *Liber Monasterii de Hyda*, for there is no record of their holding any of these lands. The queen may have entrusted her deeds to the care of this house. The whole charter is in E. Edwards, *Liber Monasterii de Hyda* (Rolls Series), pp. 242–253. The Old English account of Wulfbald is No. 63 in Robertson, *Anglo-Saxon Charters*, with translation.

In the name of our God and Lord Jesus Christ, in the year of our Lord's incarnation 993,[1] the ninth indiction, I, Ethelred, king of the English and governor of the whole orbit of Britain, with the divine approval pre-ordained by the grace of the same our God and Lord, as king for the peoples and tribes, in the eighteenth year of my rule, have conceded by a grant to my venerable mother, Ælfthryth by name, certain pieces of land in different places, namely seven ploughlands, [three and a half][2] in the place which is called Brabourne, and three and a half in the same place which is called Evegate; moreover two also in the field of the citizens, and three in addition in the place which the inhabitants are accustomed to call Nackington; and also three at Chalk[3] and one at *Wirigenn*;[4] on condition that she is to have and possess these aforesaid lands as long as she may retain the vital spirit unextinguished in the mortal flesh; and then, indeed, she is to leave it to what heir she pleases in succession to her, just as we have indicated above, in eternal inheritance. May therefore this our gift remain immovable, and pleasant with eternal liberty, with all things which are known to belong to that place, both in specified as in unspecified causes, in small things and in great, in fields, pastures, woods, water-courses, except these three things, military

---

[1] Probably 996, with misreading of *ui* as *iii*, an easy and common error.
[2] The boundaries show that this figure has been omitted.
[3] The strange form in the text, *Cealconæt*, arises from taking the *æt* (for Latin *et* 'and') as part of the name. The place is probably Chalk, which was assessed at just three ploughlands in Domesday Book.
[4] J. K. Wallenberg (*Kentish Place-Names*, pp. 336–351) suggests that this is an error for Perry. This was assessed at one ploughland in Domesday Book.

service and the building of bridges and fortresses. And we enjoin this command in the name of the Father and the Son and the Holy Spirit, that no man, puffed up with pride or by any spiteful instigation, shall come up and endeavour to evade this afore-said liberty by the annoyance of any sort of burden, and refuse to consent to the afore-written decrees; let him know that he is alienated from the fellowship of the Holy Church of God by the authority of the blessed Apostle Peter and all his associates, unless he make amends here with fitting penance, before his death, for what he has done with spiteful machination against our decree; because it is said by the psalmist: "Touch ye not my anointed",[1] etc.

Truly, these aforesaid lands a certain man, by name Wulfbald, is known to have held, and they were awarded to the control of my right by the most just judgment of all my chief men, on account of the guilt of his crime, as is found written in what follows in an account in English. And I concede to her these territories in exchange for the land which she previously gave to me, *i.e.* Cholsey, requiting a gift with a gift, desiring to obtain the divine promise: "Give, and it shall be given to you."[2]

These are the crimes which Wulfbald committed against his lord: first, when his father was dead, he went to his stepmother's land, and seized there everything that he found, inside and outside, great and small. Then the king sent to him and ordered him to pay back the plundered goods; then he ignored that, and his wergild was assigned to the king. Then the king sent immediately to him and made the same demand; then he ignored that, and then a second time his wergild was assigned to the king. On top of that, he rode and seized the land of his kinsman, Brihtmær of Bourne.[3] Then the king sent to him and ordered him to vacate that land; then he ignored that, and his wergild was assigned to the king a third time. And the king sent to him yet again, and ordered him off; then he ignored that, and his wergild was assigned to the king a fourth time. Then took place the great assembly at London; Ealdorman Æthelwine was there and all the king's councillors. Then all the councillors who were there, both ecclesiastical and lay, assigned to the king all Wulfbald's property, and also placed him at the king's mercy, whether to live or to die. And he retained all this, uncompensated for, until he died. Afterwards, when he was dead, on top of all this, his widow went, with her child, and killed the king's thegn Eadmær, the son of Wulfbald's father's brother, and fifteen of his companions, on the land at Bourne[4] which Wulfbald had held by robbery despite the king. And when Arch-bishop Æthelgar held the great synod at London, he and all his property were assigned to the king.

These are the men who were present at that award: Archbishop Æthelgar, and Archbishop Oswald, and Ælfstan, bishop of London, and Bishop Sigeric,[5] and Ælfstan, bishop of Rochester, and Bishop Ordberht,[6] and Bishop Ælfheah,[7] [and Bishop Æthelsige,[8] and Ælfwold, bishop of Devonshire, and Bishop Ealdred,[9] and

---

[1] Psalm civ. 15.   [2] Luke vi. 38. The rest, up to the signatures, is in English.
[3] Possibly Brabourne, since the holder of this estate in Domesday Book is called Godric of Bourne, and an alternative name for his holding in Brabourne is 'Godric's Bourne'.
[4] Brabourne.   [5] Of Ramsbury.   [6] Of Selsey.
[7] Of Lichfield.   [8] Of Sherborne.   [9] Of Cornwall.

Bishop Sigegar,[1] and Bishop Æscwig,[2] and Bishop Theodred,[3] and Bishop Ælfheah],[4] and Bishop Æthelwulf,[5] and Ealdorman Æthelwine, and Ealdorman Brihtnoth, and Ealdorman Æthelweard, and Ealdorman Ælfric, Earl Thored, and Abbot Eadwulf, and Abbot Brihtnoth, and Abbot Germanus, and Abbot Wulfsige, [and Abbot Leofric, and Abbot Sigeweard], and Leofric, abbot of Muchelney, and Leofric, abbot of Exeter, and Abbot Ælfhun, and Ælfhelm, and Wulfheah, and Wulfric, Wulfrun's son, and Stir, Ulf's son, and Nafena and Northman his brother, and Leofwine, Leoftæte's son, and Leofsige of Mordon, and Bondi, and Ælfhelm Polga, and Æthelwold, and Leofric, and Sigeweard of Kent, and Leofsunu, and Æthelwold the Stout, and Ælfgar, the man of Honiton, and Wulfgeat,[6] and Æthelmær, and Æthelric, and Æthelnoth, Wigstan's son,[7] and Leofwine, Æthelwulf's son, and Sigeberht, and Leofstan of Sussex.

These are the boundaries of the three and a half ploughlands belonging to Brabourne itself: namely first from *Hreodburne* to the hollow way, from the hollow way up across the down to the common at *Cuwara* wood, from *Cuwara* wood to the king's lower copse, from the king's lower copse to Bodsham, to the bishop's boundary, from the bishop's boundary to *Hægmere*, from *Hægmere* south to *Stoccesgata*, from *Stoccesgata* to Viking's field, from Viking's field to *Colheapytt*, from *Colheapytt* to the east corner of *Clænandun*, from the east corner of *Clænandun* to the boundary of *Sibbanburne*, from the boundary of *Sibbanburne* to the boundary of *Ulhæma*[8]—and 25 acres east of *Ubanham* belongs to Brabourne—from the boundary of *Ulhæma* west to 'Deep-gate', west by *Haran-strod* to the ford, from the ford to Bockham, to the mill, from the mill to *Sandhurst*, from *Sandhurst* to the king's oak-wood,[9] from the oak-wood to *Gysinghyrne*, from *Gysinghyrne* east to the ford, from the ford, over the common to *Thornacre*, from *Thornacre* to *Hreodburne* back where it started. And there are mills within these boundaries. And this is the meadow belonging to Brabourne which lies outside the boundaries: there are five acres at *Syathford*, and one acre at *Wifelesbeorg*, and two at Ouseley, and two at Bronesford, and two at *Milancamp*, and one mill was bought from Hastingleigh for Brabourne; and three houses in Lympne, three in Canterbury; and [there are] six swine-pastures in the Weald which belong to Brabourne: one is *Crudenhole*; the second Hemsted; the third *Beginge* [Baynden?]; the fourth *Hereburne*; the fifth *Strætden*; the sixth Biddenden.

These are the boundaries of the three and a half ploughlands at Evegate, of the *geneatland*:[10] first, to the north of Bircholt, to *Eastinge*, to the plank-bridge, to the mill, from the mill between *Heortesstede* and *Stanstede*, to *Wminungabire*,[11] north to the Stour, to the bridge; thence west to the Stour as far as Leofstan's meadow, from

---

[1] Of Wells.   [2] Of Dorchester.   [3] Of Elmham.
[4] Of Winchester. The names in brackets are from the Middle English version of the text, since, as Miss Robertson points out, the scribe omitted them when copying the Old English.
[5] Of Hereford.   [6] From the Middle English version, instead of Wulfgar.
[7] Ethelred's envoy to Richard of Normandy. See No. 230.
[8] This seems to mean the boundary of the people of *Ulaham*, an unidentified place mentioned in other charters. See Gordon Ward, *Arch. Cantiana*, XLVII, pp. 149 f.   [9] Now Nackholt.
[10] Land let to *geneatas*, a class of land-holders who rendered riding-services and other services of a somewhat aristocratic kind, but not agricultural labour.
[11] This is obviously corrupt. Wallenberg suggests connecting it with Gibbins Brook (earlier *æt Gimmincge*).

the meadow to *Scobbing*, from *Scobbing* to 'Noithwood'; from 'Northwood' to *Weliscing*, from *Weliscing* back to 'Northwood'.

These are the boundaries of the two ploughlands at the field of the citizens: first, to *Rammeshirst*, from *Rammeshirst* to *Wirestede*,[1] from *Wirestede* to *Lurdingadene*, from *Lurdingadene* to *Ealdrigseath*, from *Ealdrigseath* to Akhurst, from Akhurst to *Ælfrucg*, from *Ælfrucg* to *Peallestede*, from *Peallestede* to 'Southland', back to *Rammeshirst*; and one swine-pasture which is called *Bingdene*.

These are the boundaries to the three ploughlands at Nackington: first, to Leofsige's boundary, from Leofsige's boundary to the emperor's [?] paved road, along the paved road to the cross, from the cross on along the emperor's paved road to the hill at *Hlothgewirpe*, from *Hlothgewirpe* to Wulfric's mill at his borough-gate,[2] from the mill, along Wulfric's paved road, out to *Sethehlinc*, from *Sethehlinc* out to Hardres, from Hardres to South Nackington, to Siweard's boundary, back again to the boundary of Leofsige the Black. This is the house that belongs to Nackington; [that] which Leofstan built within the queen's gate.[3] This is the swine-pasture belonging to Nackington: *Wigreding* acres; and at *Wirege* [Perry?] there is one ploughland which Wulfstan of Saltwood has.

✠ I, Ethelred, king of the whole of Britain, have confirmed the aforesaid donation with the sign of the Holy Cross.

✠ I, Ælfric, archbishop of the church of Canterbury, have joined in signing.

✠ I, Ealdwulf, archbishop of the church of York, have corroborated.

✠ I, Ælfheah, bishop of the church of Winchester, have consented.

✠ I, Wulfstan, bishop of the church of London, have impressed [my mark].

✠ I, Æscwig, bishop,[4] have joined in signing.

✠ I, Ælfheah, bishop,[5] have consented.

✠ I, Æthelwulf, bishop,[6] have joined in writing.

✠ I, Ordberht, bishop,[7] have joined in signing.

✠ I, Ælfwold, bishop,[8] have consented.

✠ I, Ælfweard, abbot.	✠ I, Leofwine, ealdorman.
✠ I, Wulfsige, abbot.	✠ I, Brihtwold, king's thegn.
✠ I, Wulfgar, abbot.	✠ I, Wulfheah, king's thegn.
✠ I, Leofric, abbot.	✠ I, Wulfric, king's thegn.
✠ I, Brihthelm, abbot.	✠ I, Wulfgeat, king's thegn.
✠ I, Ælfhere, abbot.	✠ I, Æthelmær, king's thegn.
✠ I, Brihtnoth, [abbot].	✠ I, Ordwulf, king's thegn.
✠ I, Germanus, abbot.	✠ I, Æthelric, king's thegn.
✠ I, Ælfwold, abbot.	✠ I, Æthelnoth, king's thegn.
✠ I, Æthelweard, ealdorman.	✠ I, Æthelwine, king's thegn.
✠ I, Ælfric, ealdorman.	✠ I, Æthelweard, king's thegn.
✠ I, Ælfhelm, ealdorman.	✠ I, Fræna, king's thegn.
✠ I, Leofsige, ealdorman.	✠ I, Leofric, king's thegn.

[1] Wallenberg suggests that *W* is the common error for *P*, and that the place is Pested.
[2] This survives as Burgate. By 'borough' a fortified house is meant.
[3] On this, see G. M. Livett, "Queningate and the Walls of Durovernum", *Arch. Cantiana*, XLV, pp. 92–115.
[4] Of Dorchester.   [5] Of Lichfield.   [6] Of Hereford.   [7] Of Selsey.   [8] Of Crediton.

121. Old English charter of King Ethelred confirming the will of Æthelric of Bocking (995–999)

But for this document we should never have known just how serious was the menace during the later Scandinavian invasions from internal unrest and pro-Danish sympathies. Essex had been one of the parts of the Danelaw first to be recovered from the Danes, and yet there is this reference to a conspiracy to receive Swein Forkbeard, as an acknowledged fact, the point at issue not being whether there was such a conspiracy, but whether Æthelric had a share in it. The statement also raises the question of the date of Swein's first arrival. The Chronicle first mentions him by name in 994, but Æthelric, who lived for many years after this suspicion of conspiracy, was dead by 999, at the latest. It seems possible that Swein was already leading the Danes in the attack on Essex of 991. Æthelric's will is extant (Whitelock, No. 16 (1); Kemble, No. 699; Thorpe, p. 516; Earle, p. 215)́, but it is of no great interest. He leaves everything to his wife, Leofwynn, for her lifetime, with reversions to Christ Church, St. Paul's, St. Edmund's, and St. Gregory's at Sudbury. If a man of this religious bent really wished to accept Danish rule, it affords some measure of the disgust with Ethelred's rule even early in his reign; but one wonders why the king apparently took no action in Æthelric's life, reviving the 'terrible accusation' when he could no longer deny it. The incident makes one wonder whether others among the many persons in this reign who lost their estates by forfeiture had fair trial. One would like to identify Æthelric with the man of this name, Sigebriht's brother, who fought at Maldon (which lies close to his estates) in 991 (see No. 10), but this cannot be done with certainty.

This document is also of importance in containing the first datable reference to the keeping of documents with the king's relics. It survives as a contemporary parchment, the Red Book of Canterbury, No. 18, with halves of the word 'cyrograph' at the top and bottom, thus supporting the statement that there were three copies. There is a facsimile in *Ord. Surv. Facs.*, I, pl. 17. It is No. 704 in Kemble, and in Earle, pp. 216f. It is edited with translation in Thorpe, *Diplomatarium*, p. 539, *Select Essays in Anglo-Saxon Law*, pp. 362f., Whitelock, No. 16 (2), from which the present translation is taken.

It is shown here in this document how King Ethelred granted that the will of Æthelric of Bocking should stand.

It was many years before Æthelric died that the king was told that he was concerned in the treacherous plan that Swein should be received in Essex when first he came there with a fleet; and the king before many witnesses informed Archbishop Sigeric of it, who was then his advocate for the sake of the estate at Bocking which he had bequeathed to Christ Church. Then, both during his life and afterwards, he was neither cleared of this charge, nor was the crime atoned for, until his widow brought his heriot to the king at Cookham, where he had gathered his council from far and wide. Then the king wished to bring up the charge before all his council, and said that Ealdorman Leofsige and many others were cognisant of the charge. Then the widow begged Archbishop Ælfric, who was her advocate, and Æthelmær, that they would beseech the king that she might give her marriage-gift to Christ Church, for the sake of the king and all his people, to the end that the king would give up the terrible accusation, and Æthelric's will might stand; *i.e.* as it says above, the estate at Bocking to Christ Church, and his other landed property to other holy places as his will specifies. Then may God repay the king! He consented to this for the sake of Christ and of St. Mary and of St. Dunstan and of all the saints who rest at Christ Church, the terms being that she should carry out this and his will should remain valid.

This declaration was straightway written and read before the king and the council. These are the names of the men who witnessed this:

Archbishop Ælfric, and Ælfheah, bishop of Winchester, and Wulfsige, bishop of Dorset, and Godwine, bishop of Rochester, and Ealdorman Leofsige, and Ealdorman

Leofwine, and Abbot Ælfsige, and Abbot Wulfgar, and Abbot Brihthelm, and Abbot Ælfwold and Æthelmær and Ordwulf and Wulfgeat and Fræna and Wulfric, Wulfrun's son; and all the thegns who were gathered there from far and wide, both West Saxons and Mercians, Danes and English.

There are three of these documents: one is at Christ Church, the second at the king's sanctuary; the widow has the third.

122. Old English will of Bishop Ælfwold of Crediton (997–1012)

This will is included for its varied interest. The bishop bequeathes a ship, armour, horses, vestments, tapestries, etc., and books, and it is particularly interesting that two of these go to a layman. This layman, mentioned immediately after the king, and before the atheling, must be a person of great importance, and we can hardly be wrong in identifying him with Ordwulf (son of Ordgar, who had been ealdorman of Devon), the founder of Tavistock, and uncle to King Ethelred. He signs from 975 to 1005. This is one of the Crawford Charters in the Bodleian Library, and is No. 10 in Napier and Stevenson, *The Crawford Charters*, with translation on p. 126.

This is Bishop Ælfwold's will: that is that he grants the land at Sandford to the minster in Crediton as payment for his soul, with produce and men just as it stands except for the penally enslaved men; and he grants one hide of it to Godric, and a plough-team of oxen. And he grants to his lord four horses, two saddled and two unsaddled, and four shields and four spears and two helmets and two coats of mail, and 50 mancuses of gold which Ælfnoth of Woodleigh owes him, and a sixty-four-oared ship; it is all ready except for the rowlocks. He would like to prepare it fully in a style fit for his lord if God would allow him. And to Ordwulf two books, Hrabanus and the Martyrology; and to the atheling 40 mancuses of gold and the wild horses on the land at Ashburton, and two tents; and to Ælfwold the monk 20 mancuses of gold and a horse and a tent; and to Brihtmær the priest 20 mancuses of gold and a horse; and to his three kinsmen, Eadwold, Æthelnoth and Grimcetel, to each of them 20 mancuses of gold and to each of them a horse; and to his kinsman Wulfgar two tapestries and two seat-coverings and three coats of mail; and to his brother-in-law Godric two coats of mail; and to Edwin the priest five mancuses of gold and his cope; and to Leofsige the priest the man whom he relinquished to him before, called Wunstan; and to Cenwold a helmet and coat of mail; and to Boia a horse; and to Mælpatrik five mancuses of gold; and to Leofwine Polga five mancuses of gold; and to Ælfgar the scribe a pound of pennies, [which] he[1] lent to Tun and his brothers and sisters. They are to pay him. And to his sister Eadgifu a *strichrægel*[2] and a dorsal and a seat-covering; and to Ælfflæd the *offestre*[3] five mancuses of pennies; and to Spila three mancuses of gold and 60 pennies; and to Leofwine Polga and Mælpatrik and Brihtsige, to each of the three of them a horse; and to each man of his household his mount which he had lent him; and to all his household retainers five pounds to divide, to each according to his degree.

And to Crediton three service-books, a missal, a benedictional and an epistle-book,

---

[1] *i.e.* the bishop.

[2] A unique word, for which the dictionaries' suggestion 'a cloth for rubbing' seems most unlikely: such would hardly be a valuable article, and one would rather expect the *stric* to be something which the *hrægel* will cover. It may be noted, however, that O.N. *strik* means a kind of cloth.

[3] Another unique word, denoting a female worker of some kind.

and a set of Mass-vestments. And on each episcopal estate freedom to every man who was a penal slave or whom he bought with his money. And to Wilton a chalice and a paten of 120 mancuses of gold all but three mancuses. And to his chamberlains his bed-clothes.

And to witness of this are: Wulfgar, Ælfgar's son, and Godric of Crediton, and Edwin the priest, and Ælfwold the monk, and Brihtmær the priest.

123. Grant by King Ethelred of lands at Farnborough, Berkshire, Wormleighton, Warwickshire, South Cerney, Gloucestershire, and Perry, to Abingdon, to make up for the withdrawal from them of lands at Hurstbourne, Hampshire, Bedwyn and Burbage, Wiltshire (990–1006, perhaps 999)

The information given by this charter, which survives in Brit. Mus. Cott. Claud. B. vi, C. xi, that estates were earmarked for the support of the athelings (lit., 'royal sons') is interesting, and there is no reason to doubt its accuracy. Hurstbourne and Bedwyn are both entered as royal lands in Domesday, and the main estate at Burbage is probably included in the Domesday account of Bedwyn. This last place had belonged to Cynewulf of Wessex, and it was left by King Alfred to his son and successor, as also was Hurstbourne. According to Birch, No. 1080, Hurstbourne included 13 houses in Winchester, and 25 burghers are entered in the Domesday account of Bedwyn, so I have assumed that the unique expression of the present text, *in praediorum municipiis*, refers to town-properties.

The text as recorded in the Abingdon cartularies has no list of witnesses; but its last paragraph suggests that the king issued on the same occasion separate charters for each of the estates he is giving to Abingdon, and, if so, we should perhaps be justified in dating this charter 999, the year in which Kemble, No. 703, a grant of South Cerney to Abingdon, was issued. Neither this place nor Wormleighton were held by Abingdon in 1066, but the abbey had 10 hides in Farnborough.

The Abingdon cartulary also includes charters purporting to be grants by King Edgar of the estates which were afterwards withdrawn (Birch, Nos. 1213, 1067, 1080). They have been regarded with some suspicion, and Birch, No. 1213 in particular is more elaborate than Edgar's charters which survive in contemporary form. Its anathema agrees with that of Ethelred's charter to Abingdon; yet it should be noted that the same form appears in texts attributed to Edgar which were preserved at Pershore and Winchester, and there seems a possibility that more elaborate charters than those 'in common form' were sometimes drawn up for important houses. The alternative would be to consider these Abingdon texts of Edgar as forgeries based on Ethelred's charters, but in that case the Abingdon affair becomes complicated, for we should be assuming that the abbey forged three texts to prove their right to estates they no longer possessed. If it did so in order to get some compensation out of Ethelred, it was surely too soon after the supposed grants for the fraud to have gone undetected; and at a later date would the monks have forged documents to show their former right to lands which they no longer claimed?

The present charter, though unique in some ways, has in my opinion the authentic ring of Ethelred's phraseology, and I do not find it difficult to believe that Edgar, in his very great zeal for the endowment of monasteries, may have overstepped the limits of what was legally permissible; the taking back of the estates would no doubt be part of the reaction on his death recorded in many of our sources.

The forfeiture of Ælfric's lands is mentioned also in Kemble, No. 703, and his outlawry is recorded in the Anglo-Saxon Chronicle, 985. It is of interest that one of the forfeited estates, Wormleighton, had been granted to his predecessor, Ealdorman Ælfhere, in 956 (Birch, No. 946), for this lends support to the statement of Florence of Worcester that Ealdorman Ælfric was Ælfhere's son; but as nothing is known of the widow Eadflæd from whom Ælfric is said to have seized this and other lands, this cannot be established with certainty. Neither is anything known of Æthelweard, Ceolflæd's son, who bought back Ethelred's friendship with the gift of an estate at Perry (perhaps Water- or Wood-Perry, Oxfordshire), after some unspecified crime committed by him and his brother.

This charter is No. 1312 in Kemble.

✠ Our Lord Jesus Christ reigning for ever, and guiding the kingdoms of all ages with the empire of his great government.

I, Ethelred, by his saving grace king of the English, in the midst of the various vicissitudes of this fleeting age, called to mind how in the time of my boyhood an act was done on my behalf, when my father, King Edgar, going the way of the whole universe, departed to the Lord old and full of days; namely that all the leading men of both orders unanimously chose my brother Edward to guide the government of the kingdom, and gave over to me for my use the lands belonging to kings' sons. Some of which lands, in truth, my father, while he reigned, had granted for the redemption of his soul to the omnipotent Christ and his Mother St. Mary, to the monastery which is called Abingdon: *i.e.* Bedwyn, with all things belonging to it, Hurstbourne, with all its appurtenancies, Burbage and all renders belonging to it. These lands were at once withdrawn by force, by the decree and order of all the leading men, from the aforesaid holy monastery, and, by the order of these same, placed under my power. Whether they did this thing justly or unjustly, they themselves may know. Then, when my brother left this miserable world and received the reward of everlasting life predestined to him by God, I, by Christ's consent, received the control both of the royal lands and at the same time those belonging to kings' sons.

Now, however, because it seems to me very grievous to incur and bear the curse of my father, by retaining this offering which he made to God for the redemption of his soul, and because the grace of God has deigned to bring me to an age of understanding, and has granted me through the decrees of my leading men an abundant and copious share of lands, I therefore determine both to honour the aforesaid holy monastery with a suitable gift out of my own inheritance, and to enrich it with an opportune bestowal of possessions; first for the love of Almighty God and of his blessed Mother, that she may deign to be a faithful intercessor for me to our Lord God; then for the love of my father's soul and for the eternal redemption of my own soul, and also for the sake of my children, who intend to take to themselves and subject to their own control the same aforesaid lands. Truly, the names of the lands which I concede with willing mind to the aforesaid monastery are these: one, namely, is at Farnborough, a second at Wormleighton, the third at Cerney.

These portions of land Ælfric, surnamed 'Child', forcibly withdrew from a certain widow called Eadflæd, but later, when in his office of ealdorman he was convicted of crime against me and against all my people, these portions which I have mentioned and also all the landed possessions which he owned, were assigned to my control, when all my leading men assembled together to a synodal council at Cirencester, and expelled the same Ælfric, guilty of high treason, as a fugitive from this country; and all with unanimous consent decreed that I ought by right to possess all things possessed by him. Then with merciful kindness I allowed the aforesaid widow to possess her inheritance, for the love of my leading men who were her advocates to me, and she finally in her last words when dying left back to me the possession of the same lands, with kind and willing heart, as a perpetual inheritance.

And the estate at Perry,[1] which also I concede to that aforesaid monastery, is well known to be one of the lands which Æthelweard, Ceolflæd's son, gave for me

---

[1] Perhaps Wood- or Water-Perry, Oxon.

to possess eternally, to obtain my friendship. It is well known to all people far and wide how he and his brother committed a crime against me, and how both incurred my hostility which their crimes demanded.

This deed of the aforesaid lands was made at the admonition of my uncle Ordwulf and of Æthelmær, closely tied to me by kinship, and of my beloved thegn Wulfgeat, and also of my abbot, Wulfgar, friendly to me with complete devotion, who reminded me with frequent suggestion, along with the persuasion of the other loyal men, that I should take care to renew and increase in some part the inheritance of God Almighty; which also I have done for the love of Christ, who raised me to my kingdom, and of those who exhort me with friendly assiduity for my necessary and eternal safety; and because of the humble and friendly obedience which the aforesaid abbot is wont loyally and joyfully to show me.

Also, I make known before all this favour from my goodwill, that I grant that the lands of the same possessions, in every province to which they belong, with all things appertinent to them, whether in the town-properties[1] of the estates, or in tribute, or in toll, or in whatever service it is customary to exact in diverse ways on each estate, are to be free with full liberty from every yoke of earthly servitude, exactly as my father granted that the portion of the above-mentioned lands was to be free from all servitude of worldly things, except three, namely fixed military service, the restoration of bridges and fortresses.

This I enjoin also with the authority of the Holy Trinity and the Indivisable Unity and of the Blessed Mary, Ever-Virgin, that no man shall presume to change this donation for any reason, or to bring forward a title-deed or the writing of a chirograph against the document of my donation; but all those old deeds, since the above-mentioned crime necessitates it, are to be reckoned invalid for ever after, and, reduced to nothing and exposed to the contempt of all, are to be trampled under foot; and the decrees of this privilege are to be strengthened with firm and unshaken solidity.

If anyone, indeed, by the instigation of the devil, shall presume to violate these decisions, corroborated by the divine authority as well as by mine, whether it be my son, or ealdorman, or bishop, or thegn, or of whatever dignity he be, may Almighty God and his holy Mother and Ever-Virgin Mary, and all the holy strength of the heavenly hosts praising the divine majesty with unceasing voice, despise him in this life, and destroy him, despised, in the future world without end, unless he shall make amends with fitting compensation before his death for what he offended against God and St. Mary. Amen.

The deed of this privilege is to be kept continuously in the aforesaid monastery, that this liberty may be apart from the title-deeds for all the possessions of the aforesaid lands, which I have granted with kind and willing heart to the same monastery to the Almighty God and his holy Mother Mary, and being granted, have committed with eternal stability.

---

[1] *municipiis.*

124. Grant by King Ethelred of a small property in and outside Canterbury to his man Ethelred (1002)

This is a little known charter, Stowe Charter xxxv, which tells something about Canterbury at this time. Though dated 1003, the other indications of date are for 1002, and as there is evidence else-where that Wulfstan, who signs here as bishop of London, became archbishop of York in 1002, it is preferable to accept the earlier date, although this is a contemporary text. It is not included in any of the collections of charters, but there is a facsimile in *Ord. Surv. Facs.*, III, pl. 36.

P Since, indeed, every momentary pleasure of mortals must end with the grief of lamentable bitterness, and, drooping like the flower of the field, withers away, the invisible and eternally enduring joys of heaven are to be bought with the visible and transitory delights of favouring fortune. Therefore I, Ethelred, chief ruler and *basileus* of the race of the English, make over to a certain faithful man of mine, by name Ethelred, for his days and his wife's, a certain portion of my small estate, *i.e.* 15 rods in length and 8 in breadth within the precincts of the city of Canterbury, six acres for ploughing outside the wall, on account of his humble service and his sufficient payment, namely seven pounds; a condition of this kind having been inserted that after their day it is to be restored to the holy church of Christ in perpetual right for the relief of my soul.

And the land is surrounded by these boundaries:[1] first on the east side is the king's land, and on the south side the borough-street, and on the west side the land of the community of Christ Church, and on the north side the cemetery. Now this is the boundary of the two acres: on the east side lies the land of the community of Christ Church, and on the south side that of the abbot of Appledore,[2] and on the west side the land of the townsmen, and on the north side king's street. Now, again, this is the boundary of the other two acres: on the east side lies Athelstan's land, and on the south side king's street, and on the west side and the north side the land of the community of St. Augustine's. Now this is the boundary of one acre: on the east side lies Athelstan's land, and on the south side and the west side, king's street, and on the north side that of the community of St. Augustine's. Now this is the boundary of the sixth acre: on the east side lies king's street, and on the south side the cattle-market, and on the west side and the north side, Athelstan's land.

If, however—which we do not wish—anyone puffed up with the pride of arrogance shall try to annul this my charter of donation, let him know that he must render account to the Lord on the Day of Judgment, unless he has previously made amends with fitting compensation. It is written in the year 1003,[3] the fifteenth indiction, the fourth epact; dated 11 July, the 27th day of the moon. It was written in the city of Canterbury which is the metropolis of the people of Kent.

✠ I, Ethelred, king of the English, have strengthened and subscribed this my donation with the standard of the Holy Cross of Christ.

✠ I, Ælfric, archbishop of the church of Canterbury, have confirmed this donation of King Ethelred with a willing mind.

[1] The boundaries are in English.
[2] Birch, No. 1212, dated 968, refers to a community at Appledore.
[3] The indiction and the epact are for 1002, and in that year 11 July was the 27th day of the moon.

✠ I, Ælfheah, bishop of Winchester, have strengthened.

✠ I, Wulfstan, bishop of London, have acquiesced.

✠ I, Godwine, bishop of Rochester, have impressed [my mark].

✠ I, Ordberht, bishop of [Selsey],[1] have consented.

✠ I, Æthelric, bishop of Sherborne, have put my mark.

✠ I, Ælfwold, bishop of Crediton, have concluded.

✠ I, Wulfric, abbot.	✠ I, Wulfgeat, king's thegn.
✠ I, Ælfweard, abbot.	✠ I, Leofwine, king's thegn.
✠ I, Ælfsige, abbot.	✠ I, Æthelric, king's thegn.
✠ I, Wulfgar, abbot.	✠ I, Lifing, king's thegn.
✠ I, Leofric, abbot.	✠ I, Leofstan, king's thegn.
✠ I, Wigheard, abbot.	✠ I, Sigeweard, king's thegn.
✠ I, Ælfric, ealdorman.	✠ I, Wulfstan, king's thegn.
✠ I, Leofwine, ealdorman.	✠ I, Sigered, king's thegn.
✠ I, Ælfhelm, ealdorman.	✠ I, Wulfstan.
✠ I, Æthelmær, king's thegn.	✠ I, Wærhelm.
✠ I, Ordwulf, king's thegn.	✠ I Guthwold.[2]
✠ I, Wulfric, king's thegn.	

Endorsed in English: This is the deed of the *haga*.[3]

125. Old English will of Wulfric Spott, the founder of the abbey of Burton-on-Trent (1002–1004)

This will is of considerable historical interest. It throws light on a part of the country for which information is scanty, and it records the foundation of the one important Benedictine house in the North-West Midlands. The testator is sprung from a great Mercian house. His mother, Wulfrun, was of sufficient importance for her capture by the Danes to be recorded in the Chronicle (No. 1, p. 202), and his brother is that Ælfhelm, ealdorman of southern Northumbria, who was murdered in 1006 (see No. 1, p. 218); Ælfhelm's sons Wulfheah and Ufegeat are also mentioned in the will. This will lets us see the extent and range of influence of a prominent thegn; while the bulk of his lands lie in Staffordshire and Derbyshire, he has estates also in Shropshire, Leicestershire, Nottinghamshire, Warwickshire, Gloucestershire, Lincolnshire and South Yorkshire, and he refers in general terms to lands in South Lancashire and Cheshire. It is interesting to find a Mercian thegn with so strong a stake in the northern Danelaw, and his grant of an estate along with all the *socn* (jurisdiction) belonging to it suggests that in this part of England the arrangement was already in force by which a manor had an area of 'sokeland' attached to it, as so commonly in the Domesday account of these areas. The Morcar who appears so prominently in this will is very probably the thegn 'of the Seven Boroughs' who was murdered in 1015 (see No. 1, p. 224).

The parchment containing this will belongs to the Marquis of Anglesey.[4] There is a facsimile in *Ord. Surv. Facs.*, III, last plate. It has often been edited, *e.g.* by Kemble, No. 1298, Earle, pp. 218 ff.; and with translation by Thorpe, *Diplomatarium*, pp. 543 ff., Bridgeman in *Hist. Collections for Staffs.* (Will, Salt Arch. Soc., 1916), pp. 1 ff., Whitelock, No. 17, from which the present translation is taken.

I n the name of the Lord.[5]
     Wulfric here declares his will to his dear lord and to all his friends. First I grant to my lord 200 mancuses of gold, and two silver-hilted swords and four horses, two

[1] A space is left blank for the name of his see.

[2] These last three signatures are in the last column, and there is no room for any title to be given them.

[3] Town-property, a house and surrounding area.

[4] It is now Anglesey Document I in the Public Library, Burton-on-Trent.

[5] The invocation is in Latin.

saddled and two unsaddled, and the weapons which are due with them. And I grant to every bishop five mancuses of gold and to each of the two archbishops ten mancuses of gold. And I grant to every monastic order one pound, and to every abbot and every abbess five mancuses of gold. And I grant to Archbishop Ælfric the land at Dumbleton[1] along with the other, for my soul, in the hope that he may be a better friend and supporter of the monastery which I have founded.

And I grant to Ælfhelm and Wulfheah the lands between the Ribble and the Mersey, and in Wirral, that they may share them between them as evenly as they can—unless either of them wishes to have his own—on condition that when it is the shad season, each of them shall pay 3,000 shad to the monastery at Burton. And I grant to Ælfhelm Rolleston[2] and Harlaston.[2] And I grant to Wulfheah the estates at Barlaston[2] and Marchington.[2] And I grant to Ælfhelm the estate at Conisbrough,[3] on condition that he arrange that the monks shall have each year a third of the fish, and he two thirds. And I grant Wulfheah the estate at Alvaston,[4] and I grant Ufegeat the estate at Norton in the hope that he may be a better friend and supporter of the monastery.

And I grant to my poor daughter the estate at Elford[2] and that at Oakley,[5] with all that now belongs there, as long as her life lasts, and after her death, the land is to go to the monastery at Burton. And she shall not possess it on such terms that she can forfeit it for any reason, but she is to have the use of it as long as she can deserve[6] it, and afterwards it is to go to the monastery at Burton because it was my godfather's gift. And I desire that Ælfhelm may be protector of her and of the land. And the land at Tamworth is not to be subject to any service nor to any man born, but she is to have the lordship.

And I grant to my retainer Wulfgar the estate at Balterley[2] just as his father acquired it for him. And I bequeath to Morcar the estates at *Walesho*,[7] *Theogendethorp*, Whitwell, Clowne, Barlborough, Duckmanton, Mosborough, Eckington, Beighton,[8] Doncaster and *Morlington*. And to his wife I grant Austrey,[9] just as it now stands with the produce and the men. And I grant to my kinsman Ælfhelm the estate at Palterton,[10] and that which Scegth bequeathed to me. And I grant to Æthelric the estate at Wibtoft[9] and that at Tong,[11] for his day, and after his day it is to go to Burton for my soul and for my mother's and for his.

And these are the estates which I grant to Burton: first Burton on which the monastery stands, and Stretton[2] and Bromley[2] and *Bedinton*[12] and Gailey[2] and Whiston[2] and Longford[13] and Stirchley[13] and Newton by the *wic*,[14] and *Wædedun*; and the little estate which I have in the other Newton; and Winshill[2] and Sutton[10] and Ticknall,[10] and Shangton,[15] and Wigston,[15] and Hales[16] and Romsley,[13] and Shipley[13] and Sutton ;[13]

---

[1] See Nos. 119, 126. [2] Staffs. [3] Yorks. [4] Or else Elveston, Derbys.
[5] Survives as a farm near Elford.
[6] Or perhaps "perform the services due from it". [7] Perhaps Walsall, Staffs., or Wales, Yorks.
[8] These seven estates are in Derbys. [9] Warws. [10] Derbys.
[11] Tonge, Leics., or Tong, Shropshire.
[12] A lost name; the place is probably Pillaton, Staffs. [13] Salop.
[14] Probably Newton near Middlewich, Cheshire. The salt-towns were often referred to simply as *wic*; but this word may mean only 'dairy-farm' in some contexts.
[15] Leics. [16] Perhaps Halesowen, Worcs.

and Acton[1] for two lives as the terms state; and Darlaston[2] and what belongs to it, namely Rudyard[2] and my little estate in Cotwalton;[2] and Leigh[2] with all that belongs to it; Okeover[2] with what belongs to it, Ilam,[2] and Caldon[2] and Castern;[2] and the heriot-land at Sutton,[3] and Morley[3] and Breadsall,[3] and Morton[3] and all the jurisdiction which belongs to it, and the land included in it at Pilsley,[3] and Ogston[3] and Wingfield[3] and *Snodeswic* along with Morton; and the estate at Tathwell;[4] and the estate at Appelby[5] which I bought with my money, and that at Weston[6] and Burton;[6] and the hide at Sharnford[5] along with Wigston; and Harbury[7] and Aldsworth[8] and Alvington[9] and Eccleshall[10] and *Waddune*[11] and one hide at Sheen.[2]

And I grant to the community at Tamworth the estate at Longdon[2] just as they have let it to me, and they are to have half the usufruct, and the monks of Burton half, both of the produce and the men and the stock, and of all things

And the bishop is to take possession of his estate at Bupton,[3] and the monks at Burton are to take what is on the land, both produce and men, and all things; and the land at the mire [is to go] to the bishop.

And I desire that the king be lord of the monastery which I built and of the estates which I bequeathed to it to the glory of God and the honour of my lord and for my soul; and that Archbishop Ælfric and my brother Ælfhelm be protectors and friends and advocates of that foundation against any man born, not as their own possession, but [as belonging] to St. Benedict's order.

And I grant to my god-daughter, [the daughter] of Morcar and Ealdgyth, the estate at Stretton[3] and the brooch [?] which was her grandmother's. And to the monastery at Burton 100 wild horses, and 16 tame geldings, and besides this all that I possess in livestock and other goods except those which I have bequeathed.

And whoever perverts this, may God Almighty remove him from all God's joy and from the communion of all Christians, unless it be my royal lord alone, and I believe him to be so good and so gracious that he will not himself do it, nor permit any other man to do so.

Farewell in Christ.[12] Amen.

Endorsed[13]

This is the charter of freedom to the monastery at Burton which King Ethelred freed eternally, to the glory of God and the honour of all his saints, just as Wulfric re-established it for his own sake and for the souls of his ancestors, and filled it with monks in order that men of that order under their abbot might ever serve God in that place, according to St. Benedict's teaching. Thus be it.[12]

126. Old English will of Ælfric, archbishop of Canterbury (1002–1005)

The cost of opposing Danish invasions hangs heavily over this document, which is preserved in the Abingdon cartularies, the Brit. Mus. MSS. Claud. B. vi and C. ix. The gift of ships to two counties is obviously to help them to meet their obligations to a ship-levy (cf. No. 1, p. 219), and the debts which the counties of Kent, Surrey and Middlesex had contracted were doubtless for a similar

---

[1] Salop.   [2] Staffs.   [3] Derbys.   [4] Lincs.
[5] Leics.   [6] Probably Warws.   [7] Warws.   [8] Glos., or else Awsworth, Notts.
[9] Glos.   [10] Staffs., or Exhall, Warws., or Eccleshall Yorks.   [11] Perhaps Whaddon, Glos.
[12] In Latin.   [13] This refers to the foundation charter which precedes the will on the parchment.

purpose, or to pay tribute to the Danes. According to St. Albans records, *Eadulfingtun* had been leased to the abbey by the king in exchange for 100 pounds with which to buy off the Danes. This will lends point, therefore, to the action of Ælfric's successor, the Bishop Ælfheah of this will, in refusing in 1012 to let a ransom be paid for him by an already overburdened people (see No. 1, p. 222).

Ælfric was successively a monk at Abingdon, abbot of St. Albans, bishop of Ramsbury and archbishop of Canterbury, and his will reveals his interest in all these places. His executors are his brother Leofric, abbot of St. Albans after him, and Wulfstan, the homilist, archbishop of York and bishop of Worcester (see No. 240).

The will is No. 716 in Kemble, and is edited with translation in Thorpe, *Diplomatarium*, pp. 549 f., and in Whitelock, No. 18, from which the present translation is taken.

Here it is made known how Archbishop Ælfric drew up his will. First, as his burial fee,[1] he bequeathed to Christ Church the estates at Westwell[2] and Bourne,[2] and Risborough.[3] And he bequeathed to his lord his best ship and the sailing tackle with it, and 60 helmets and 60 coats of mail. And if it were his lord's will, he wished that he would confirm to St. Albans the estate at Kingsbury,[4] and himself retake possession of *Eadulfington* in return.

And he bequeathed to Abingdon the estate at Dumbleton,[5] and three hides of it to Ælfnoth for his life, which afterwards [are to belong] to Abingdon with the rest. And he bequeathed him ten oxen and two men, and they are to be subject to the lordship to which the land belongs. And he bequeathed the estate which he bought at Wallingford[6] to Ceolweard, and after his death to Cholsey.

And he bequeathed to St. Albans the estate at Tew,[7] and the terms were to remain unchanged between the abbot and Ceolric which had been agreed upon with the archbishop; namely that Ceolric was to hold the portion of the estate which he has for his life, and also that portion which the archbishop let to him in return for his money; that was seven and a half hides for five pounds and 50 mancuses of gold; and after his day all of it together is to go to St. Albans. And their terms were that Osney[7] also should go to that monastery after Ceolric's day. And he bequeathed to St. Albans the estate in London which he bought with his money, and all his books he also bequeathed there, and his tent.

And he arranged that what money there was should be taken and first every debt paid, and afterwards what was due was to be provided for his heriot. And he granted a ship to the people of Kent and another to Wiltshire. And as regards other things besides these, if there should be any, he bade that Bishop Wulfstan and Abbot Leofric should act as seemed best to them. And the estates in the west, at Fiddington[8] and Newton,[8] he bequeathed to his sisters and their children. And the land of Ælfheah, Esne's son, is always to remain in his family.

And he bequeathed to Archbishop Wulfstan a pectoral cross, and a ring and a psalter; and to Bishop Ælfheah a crucifix. And in accordance with God's will he forgave the people of Kent the debt which they owed him, and the people of Middlesex and Surrey the money which he paid on their behalf. And it is his will that after his day every penally enslaved man who was condemned in his time be set free.

If anyone change this, may he have it to account for with God. Amen.

---

[1] Literally, 'soul-payment'.   [2] Kent.   [3] Monks Risborough, Bucks. Cf. No. 118.
[4] Middlesex.   [5] See Nos. 119, 125.   [6] Berks.   [7] Oxon.   [8] Glos.

127. Renewal by King Ethelred for the monastery of St. Frideswide, Oxford, of a privilege for their lands at Winchendon, Buckinghamshire, and White-hill, Cowley, and Cutslow, Oxfordshire, after their church and deeds had been burnt down during the massacre of the Danes (7 December 1004)

The authenticity of this extremely important document has been demonstrated by F. M. Stenton, "St. Frideswide and her Times", *Oxoniensia*, I (1936), pp. 105f. It contains the one reference, outside chronicles, to the massacre of the Danes, presumably referring to St. Brice's day, 1002 (see No. 1, p. 217). The boundaries need not necessarily be of the same date as the Latin text, but nevertheless behind their form in the charter roll lies an exemplar in good West Saxon. This remark does not, however, apply to the last paragraph of the vernacular portion, which clearly has a different textual history. It must have been copied from a version in Middle English, with greatly decayed inflectional endings, and *u* for Old English *y*. I suspect it of being a spurious addition, to support the canons' rights to tithes, chapels, etc., not mentioned in their original privilege. In 1122 the (spurious?) foundation charter of Henry I includes a reference to the chapels of Headington, Marston, Elsfield and Binsey.

Some of the boundaries in this document are considered by G. B. Grundy in *Saxon Oxfordshire* (Oxford Rec. Soc., xv, pp. 15ff.).

The fourteenth-century charter roll, Rot. Cart. 6, E. ii, which is used by S. R. Wigram for his text of this document in *The Cartulary of the Monastery of St. Frideswide at Oxford* (Oxford Hist. Soc., 1895), I, pp. 2–9, contains a better version than the abbey cartularies, which were used by Kemble, No. 709.

In the year of the incarnation of our Lord 1004, the second indiction, in the 25th year of my reign, by the ordering of God's providence, I, Ethelred, governing the monarchy of all Albion, have made secure with the liberty of a privilege by the royal authority a certain monastery situated in the town which is called Oxford, where the body of the blessed Frideswide rests, for the love of the all-accomplishing God; and I have restored the territories which belong to that monastery of Christ with the renewal of a new title-deed; and I will relate in a few words to all who look upon this document for what reason it was done. For it is fully agreed that to all dwelling in this country it will be well known that, since a decree was sent out by me with the counsel of my leading men and magnates, to the effect that all the Danes who had sprung up in this island, sprouting like cockle amongst the wheat, were to be destroyed by a most just extermination, and this decree was to be put into effect even as far as death, those Danes who dwelt in the afore-mentioned town, striving to escape death, entered this sanctuary of Christ, having broken by force the doors and bolts, and resolved to make a refuge and defence for themselves therein against the people of the town and the suburbs; but when all the people in pursuit strove, forced by necessity, to drive them out, and could not, they set fire to the planks and burnt, as it seems, this church with its ornaments and its books. Afterwards, with God's aid, it was renewed by me and my subjects, and, as I have said above, strengthened in Christ's name with the honour of a fresh privilege, along with the territories belonging to it, and endowed with every liberty, regarding royal exactions as well as ecclesiastical dues.

If, however, by chance it shall happen at any time – which God forbid – that anyone, ensnared by the slothfulness of an insane mind, defrauds the gift of this our donation, by [the devil's] efforts, may he receive the eternal anathema of death from the Holy Church of God, unless before his end he brings so false a claim to a desirable compensation.

The estates of the aforesaid monastery are known to be surrounded by these boundaries. These are the boundaries of the ten hides at Winchendon :[1] first from Æscwulf's well to the borough ditch, from the ditch to the hundred tree, from the tree to the two moors, from the moors to the headland, from the headland to *Tenwell* streamlet, from the streamlet to Bica's brook,[2] from the brook to the Thame, along the Thame to *Ebbeslade*, from the slade to *Merwell*, from *Merwell* to the rough hill,[3] from the hill to the dirty pit, from the pit to the rushbrook, from the brook to Wott's brook,[4] from Wott's brook back to Æscwulf's well.

These are the boundaries to the three hides at Whitehill: namely from the old *Hensingeslade*[5] over the cliff to the stony way, from the way, to the long barrow,[6] from the barrow to the Port Way, from the highway to the River Cherwell, and so along the river, till one comes back to *Hensingeslade*.

These are the boundaries of the three hides at Cowley: from the Cherwell bridge along the river to the little stream, by *Hacelingescroft*, straight along east until one reaches the upper furlong, which runs up northwards to the head of the wheat furlong; from the head to the little stream eastward to the boundary hedge, from the hedge to the brook, from the brook to the acres,[7] from the acres to Hockmere, from that boundary[8] to Iffley, from Iffley to the brook, from the brook back to the Cherwell.

These are the boundaries of the three hides at Cutslow: first from the Port Way to *Trille-well*,[9] from the well to the small stream, from the small stream to the bishop's boundary, from the boundary to *Wifeleslac*[10] to the slade, from the slade to *Wifeleshill*, from the hill to *Hyne*.

This privilege was composed at Headington, where I granted to my own monastery at Oxford, in which St. Frideswide rests, all the liberty that any free monastery has most freely, with sake and soke, toll and team, infangen-thef,[11] on highway and on stream, and my tithes from Headington and from all the lands which belong to it, in wood and field and in all the things and rights which belong to a free monastery, in chapels and in [dues from] the living and the dead,[12] and in all things.[13]

This document was written by the order of the aforesaid king in the royal residence which is called Headington, on the day of the octave of the blessed Apostle Andrew, these nobles consenting who are seen noted below:

> I, Ethelred, king of the English, have granted this privilege for Christ's name with perpetual liberty to the aforesaid [monastery].

[1] The boundaries are given in English.
[2] Beachendon Farm, near Winchendon, preserves the same personal name.
[3] Or perhaps mound. The same name survives as Rowley (Hundred), but this is too far away to be the place meant here.   [4] The same personal name occurs in the neighbouring Waddesdon.
[5] The same first element occurs in Hensington, Oxon., close by. Ekwall suggests that it may be a wood or stream name from *hens* 'hens'.   [6] Or perhaps 'hill'.
[7] This is assuming that the MS. *den* is a corruption of the definite article; but as acres are not distinguishable as boundary marks, it may be that a name 'Den-acre' is intended.
[8] Assuming that the second element in *Hoccemære* is *mære* 'boundary' rather than *mere* 'lake'. Grundy notes a Hockmere Farm and cottages due south of Cowley village, near the parish boundary.
[9] *The Place-Names of Oxfordshire*, p. 11, records a Trill Mill Stream, south of Oxford.
[10] The same name occurs in Great Wilsey, a field-name in Marston. See *id.*, p. 181.
[11] This formula, which is common in eleventh-century charters and writs, means rights of private jurisdiction, the receiving of tolls and the profits arising from the process of vouching to warranty when an object was claimed to be stolen property, and the right to execute summary justice on a thief caught on one's own land.   [12] *i.e.* all church dues including burial-fees.
[13] On the question of the authenticity of this last paragraph, see p. 545.

I, Ælfric, archbishop of the church of Canterbury, have corroborated it under pain of anathema.

I, Wulfstan, archbishop of the city of York, have confirmed.

I, Ælfgifu, consecrated to the royal couch, have promoted this donation.

I, Athelstan, first-born of the king's sons, with my brothers, was present as a favourable witness.

I, Ælfheah, bishop of Winchester, have joined in signing.

I, Ælfstan,[1] bishop of the church of Wells, have strengthened.

I, Ælfhun, bishop of the church of London, have consecrated.

I, Godwine, bishop of the church of Lichfield, have fortified.

I, Ordberht, bishop of the South Saxons, have concluded.

I, Æthelric, bishop of the church of Sherbourne, have consented.

I, Ælfwold, bishop of the church of Crediton, have invigorated.

I, Ælfric, ealdorman.	I, Goda, king's thegn.
I, Leofwine, ealdorman.	I, Æthelweard, king's thegn.
I, Wulfgar, abbot.	I, Ethelwine, king's thegn.
I, Ælfsige, abbot.	I, Æthelric, king's thegn.
I, Cenwulf, abbot.	I, Ælfgar, king's thegn.
I, Ælfsige, abbot.	I, Leofwine, king's thegn.
I, Æthelmær, king's thegn.	I, Godwine, king's thegn.
I, Ordwulf, king's thegn.	I, Leofwine, king's thegn.
I, Æthelmær, king's thegn.	I, Ordmær, king's thegn.

128. Old English marriage agreement between Wulfric and Archbishop Wulfstan's sister (1014–1016)

This and the following document are included for comparison with the treatise "Concerning the betrothal of a woman" (see No. 51). The estates concerned are in Worcestershire.

This is one of the Worcester charters printed in the Appendix to Smith's *Bede* before they were destroyed; it is on p. 778 of that work, and it had previously been printed in Hickes, *Dissertatio Epistolaris*, p. 76, and by Wanley, *Thesaurus*, II, pp. 302f. It is Kemble, No. 738; Thorpe, *Diplomatarium*, p. 320; Robertson, *Anglo-Saxon Charters*, No. 76. There are translations in Thorpe and Robertson.

✠ Here in this document it is made known about the terms which Wulfric and the archbishop[2] made when he obtained the archbishop's sister as his wife, namely that he promised her the land at Orleton and Ribbesford for her lifetime, and he promised her the land at Knightwick, that he would obtain it for her from the community of Winchcombe for three men's lives; and he gave her the land at Alton to give and to grant to whomsoever she pleased during her lifetime or after her death; and he promised her 50 mancuses of gold and 30 men and 30 horses.

Now these were witnesses that these terms were thus made: Archbishop Wulfstan and Ealdorman Leofwine and Bishop Athelstan[3] and Abbot Ælfweard[4] and Brihtheah the monk,[5] and many good men besides them, both ecclesiastics and laymen.

[1] He usually signs by his other name of Lifing.
[2] Wulfstan was archbishop of York and bishop of Worcester. [3] Of Hereford.
[4] Of Evesham. [5] Wulfstan's sister's son, later abbot of Pershore, and then bishop of Worcester.

Now there are two copies of these terms. One is with the archbishop in Worcester, and the other with Bishop Athelstan in Hereford.

129. An Old English marriage agreement from Kent (1016–1020)

This document, which should be compared with No. 128, was printed by Somner, *A Treatise of Gavelkind*, p. 196, from a Canterbury cyrograph which seems since to have been lost. It is No. 732 in Kemble, and in Earle, p. 228; with translation, Thorpe, *Diplomatarium*, p. 312, Robertson, *Anglo-Saxon Charters*, No. 77.

Here in this document is made known the agreement which Godwine made with Brihtric when he wooed his daughter; first, namely, that he gave her a pound's weight of gold in return for her acceptance of his suit, and he granted her the land at Street with everything that belongs to it, and 150 acres at Burmarsh and in addition 30 oxen, and 20 cows, and 10 horses and 10 slaves.

This was agreed at Kingston in King Cnut's presence in the witness of Archbishop Lifing and of the community of Christ Church, and of Abbot Ælfmær and the community of St. Augustine's, and of Æthelwine the sheriff, and Sigered the Old, and Godwine, Wulfheah's son, and Ælfsige Child, and Eadmær of Burham, and Godwine, Wulfstan's son, and Karl the king's retainer.

And when the maiden was fetched from Brightling,[1] there acted as surety for all this Ælfgar, Sigered's son, and Frerth, the priest of Folkestone, and Leofwine the priest of Dover, and Wulfsige the priest, and Eadred, Eadhelm's son, and Leofwine, Wærhelm's son, and Cenwold Rust, and Leofwine, son of Godwine of Horton, and Leofwine the Red, and Godwine, Eadgifu's son, and Leofsunu his brother; and whichever of them shall live the longer is to succeed to all the possessions both in land which I have given them and in all things. Every trustworthy man in Kent and Sussex, thegn or *ceorl*, is aware of these terms.

And there are three of these documents; one is at Christ Church, the second at St. Augustine's, the third Brihtric has himself.

130. Old English will of the Atheling Athelstan, eldest son of King Ethelred (1015)

This prince predeceased his father. His will lets us glimpse the separate household of an adult member of the royal family. One should note how widely scattered are his estates. He mentions in his will many persons of importance: Godwine, Wulfnoth's son, might be the later earl; the testator's brother Edmund is, of course, the later king, and Eadwig is the unfortunate prince murdered by Cnut's orders. But perhaps most interesting is the connexion of the atheling with several magnates of the northern Danelaw, Morcar and Sigeferth (see No. 1, annal 1015, and cf. No. 125), and Thurbrand, who engineered the murder of Earl Uhtred in 1016 (see No. 1, p. 225).[2] Athelstan's brother Edmund had close connexions with these parts also (see No. 1, p. 224). The testator took great interest in his weapons, but the precise meaning of some of the terms in which he describes them cannot be recovered. Of especial interest is the sword handed down for over 200 years from King Offa. It is tempting to equate it with the Avar sword sent to Offa by Charles the Great (see No. 197).

The will survives in two early eleventh-century versions, Brit. Mus. Stowe Charter xxxvii,

---

[1] Sussex.
[2] For Thurbrand, see *Symeonis Monachi Opera Omnia*, ed. Arnold, I, p. 218, II, pp. 197, 383.

which has the top halves of the word 'cyrograph' at the foot, and Christ Church, Canterbury, MS. AA. H. 68. It was also entered twice into the Winchester cartulary, Brit. Mus. Addit. MS. 15350. There is a facsimile of the Stowe charter in *Ord. Surv. Facs.*, III, pl. 38, and of the Christ Church charter in *ibid.*, I, pl. 18. It is No. 722 in Kemble, and in Earle, pp. 224f.; with translation in Thorpe, *Diplomatarium*, p. 557, Whitelock, No. 20, from which the present translation is taken.

✠ In the name of Almighty God. I, Athelstan the atheling, declare in this document how I have granted my estates and my possessions, to the glory of God and for the redemption of my soul and of my father's, King Ethelred's, from whom I acquired the property.

First, I grant that every penally enslaved man whom I acquired in the course of jurisdiction be freed. And to Christ and St. Peter, at the place where I shall be buried, I grant along with my body the estate at Adderbury[1] which I bought from my father for 200 mancuses of gold, by weight, and for five pounds of silver. And the estate at Marlow[2] which I bought from my father for 250 mancuses of gold, by weight; and the estate at Morden[3] which my father let to me, I grant to that foundation for the souls of us both—and I beseech him, that for God's sake and for St. Mary's and for St. Peter's, my bequest may stand—and the sword with the silver hilt which Wulfric made, and the gold belt and the armlet which Wulfric made, and the drinking-horn which I have bought from the community at the Old Minster.

And I desire that the money which Æthelwold's widow ought to pay me, which I have contributed towards her income, *i.e.* twelve pounds by tale, be taken and entrusted to Bishop Ælfsige at the Old Minster for my soul. And I grant to Christ Church in Canterbury the estate at Hollingbourne[4] and what belongs to it, except the one ploughland which I have given to Sigeferth; and the estate at *Garwaldingtun*.[5] And I grant the estate at Rotherfield[6] to the Nunnery, for St. Mary's sake, and a silver bowl[7] of five pounds; and to the New Minster a silver cauldron, of five pounds, in the name of the Holy Trinity, to whom the foundation is dedicated. And I give to the Holy Cross and St. Edward at Shaftesbury the six pounds about which I have given directions to my brother Edmund.

And to my father, King Ethelred, I grant the estate at Chalton[8] except the eight hides which I have granted to my retainer Ælfmær; and the estate at Norton; and the estate at Mollington;[1] and the silver-hilted sword which belonged to Ulfketel; and the coat of mail which Morcar has; and the horse which Thurbrand gave to me; and the white horse which Leofwine gave to me.

And to my brother Edmund I grant the sword which belonged to King Offa; and the sword with the 'pitted' hilt; and a blade and a silver-coated trumpet; and the estates which I obtained in East Anglia; and the estate in the Peak valley [?].[9] And I wish that each year there shall be paid one day's food-rent from this property to the community at Ely on the festival of St. Æthelthryth; and that 100 pence shall be given to that monastery, and 100 poor people fed there on that day; and may this charitable bequest be for ever performed yearly, whoever shall hold the estates, as long as

---

[1] Oxon.   [2] Bucks.   [3] Cambs.   [4] Kent.
[5] Perhaps Garrington, Kent; see Wallenberg, *Place-Names of Kent*, pp. 314f.   [6] Oxon, or Sussex.
[7] Probably not *mæl* 'cross', as I translated in 1930, but the rare word *mæle*, which from its use in glosses appears to mean 'bowl, dish'; see Swaen, in *Neophilologicus*, XXVIII, pp. 42–49.
[8] Hants.   [9] Derbys.

Christianity shall last. And if they who have the estates will not discharge these charities, the property shall go to St. Æthelthryth's.

And I grant to my brother Eadwig a silver-hilted sword. And I grant to Bishop Ælfsige a gold crucifix which Eadric, Wynflæd's son, has, and a black stallion. And I grant to Ælfmær the estate at Hambleton[1] which he had before: and I beseech my father, for God Almighty's sake and for mine, that he will permit this grant which I have made to him. And I grant to Godwine, Wulfnoth's son, the estate at Compton[2] which his father possessed. And I grant to my foster-mother, Ælfswith, because of her great deserts, the estate at Weston,[2] which I bought from my father for 250 mancuses of gold, by weight. And to my chaplain Ælfwine I grant the estate at Harleston[2] and the inlaid sword which belonged to Withar, and my horse with the harness. And I grant to my seneschal Ælfmær the eight hides at Catherington,[1] and a pied stallion and my round shield, and the notched [?] sword. And to Sigeferth I grant the estate at Hockliffe,[3] and a sword and a horse and my curved [?] shield. And I grant to Æthelweard the Stammerer and Lifing the estate at Tewin.[4] And I grant to Leofstan, the brother of Leofwine Cwatt, the landed property which I have taken from his brother. And to Leofmær of Bygrave[4] I grant the estate which I have taken from him. And I grant to Godwine the Driveller the three hides at Lurgershall.[5] And I grant to Eadric, the son of Wynflæd, the sword on which the hand is marked. And I grant to my retainer Æthelwine the sword which he has given to me. And I grant to Ælfnoth my sword-polisher the notched [?] inlaid sword, and to my staghuntsman the stud which is on Coldridge.[6] And let Ælfric of Barton and Godwine the Driveller be paid from my money as much as my brother Edmund knows that I ought rightly to pay them.

Now I thank my father in all humility, in the name of Almighty God, for the answer which he sent me on the Friday after the feast of Midsummer by Ælfgar, Æffa's son; which, as he told me in my father's words, was that I might, by God's leave and his, grant my estates and my possessions as seemed to me most advisable in fulfilment of my duties to God and men. And my brother Edmund and Bishop Ælfsige[7] and Abbot Brihtmær and Ælfmær, Ælfric's son, are witnesses of this answer.

Now I pray all the councillors, both ecclesiastical and lay, who may hear my will read, that they will help to secure that my will may stand, as my father's permission is stated in my will.

I now declare that all those things which I have granted to God, to God's Church and God's servants, are done for the soul of my dear father, King Ethelred, and for mine, and for the soul of Ælfthryth, my grandmother, who brought me up, and for the souls of all those who shall give me their help with these benefactions. And may he who by any means perverts this will, have to account with Almighty God, and with St. Peter, and with all those who praise God's name.

---

[1] Hants.   [2] Too common a name for certain identification.   [3] Beds.   [4] Herts.

[5] Sir Allen Mawer, in *Studia Neophilologica*, XIV, pp. 93 f., has shown that Lurgershall, Wilts., is a more likely identification of this name than Lurgershall, Bucks., Ludgarshall, Glos., or Lurgashall, Sussex. See next note.

[6] On the borders of Lurgershall, Wilts., an identification made by Sir Allen Mawer.

[7] Of Winchester.

131. Grant by King Cnut of lands at Landrake and Tinnel, Cornwall, to Burhwold, bishop of Cornwall, with an Old English addition showing that this was a ratification of arrangements made by his predecessor King Edmund Ironside (1018)

This is an early charter of Cnut, belonging to the Dean and Chapter of Exeter, and it illustrates the readiness of this king to rule like his Saxon predecessors, and to be generous to the Church. It shows also that Edmund, even in his short and troubled reign, had time to carry out this transaction, and that Burhwold, whose first datable signature occurs in 1018, was already bishop of Cornwall in 1016. There is a facsimile in *Ord. Surv. Facs.*, II, Exeter Charters, No. 9. The only edition otherwise to give the boundaries and Old English addition is that of J. B. Davidson, *Journ. Brit. Arch. Assoc.*, XXXIX, 285–289. Kemble, No. 728, and Haddan and Stubbs, I, pp. 686–688, give the Latin part only.

✠ In the name of the Holy Trinity. Since the course of the world, as we discern daily, tends to its end with various and uncertain hazards, it is necessary for each mortal so to pass through this fleeting life that he may at some time possess the perpetual life, aided by the favour of God, and, as long as he breathes the breath of this life, bring within the safe bounds of writing all things which are established by just consideration; lest perchance they fall into oblivion for those succeeding, and thus the dispositions of the elders be despised by their juniors. On this account, I, Cnut, enthroned king of the English, grant to a certain most faithful bishop of mine who is called by the well-known name of Burhwold, in right of eternal inheritance a certain portion of land, namely four hides divided among two places, at a place called by the inhabitants Landrake, and the other the estate of Tinnel; that he may have it as long as the vital spirit sustains the fragile body in this wretched life, and after his death he is to commit the land at Landrake to St. German in perpetual liberty for his soul and the king's; and the bishop is to do with Tinnel what shall seem to him fitting. And this gift is to remain, just as I have already said, exempt from every secular service, with all things duly belonging to it, fields, woods, pastures, meadows; except only military service, if necessity compels, and the capture of thieves; and he is to possess the liberty, as is indicated above.

As for those, truly, who diminish or violate this my donation—which I wish may be far from the minds of the faithful—may their part be with those against whom it was said: "Depart from me, you cursed, into everlasting fire, etc.",[1] unless they previously make compensation here before their death.

The aforesaid land is surrounded on all sides with these boundaries:[2] first on *Poldrisoc*, up along the rivulet to 'Horsewell', thence to the pierced stone, thence to Ælmarch's spring, on the rivulet to the Tiddy, up along the Tiddy to the little rivulet, then west to *Cructerlan*, then west to the rivulet, down the rivulet as far as *Botfuysc*, then north to the barrow, straight on to the forked stump, then east on to the rim of the ridge to the head of the moor, to the brook, to the Tiddy, up along the Tiddy to *Difrod*,[3] then up the rivulet to the ford, then east to the head of the moor, down the brook to *Bryhter*, up along the brook to the highway, then due north to the little ford, then up to the head of the valley, then north along the way as far as the slade, then east to the valley, on the rivulet as far as the junction of the streams, up along

---

[1] Matthew xxv. 41.   [2] The boundaries are in English.   [3] Probably a corruption of Tidiford.

the brook to the head of the valley, then to the highway, then north along the way till level with the little fort, then due east to the spring, down the brook to the Lynher, down the stream to *Poldrysoc.*

These are the boundaries of the hide at Tinnel: First from *Carrecron* along the rivulet west to the source of the spring, thence west to the way, then north along the way to the stump, then west to the spring, down the rivulet to the creek, up to the king's mill, up the brook to *Nantnewiou*, then due south to 'Behrat's spring', on the rivulet to the junction of the streams, then up the brook to the plank bridge, north along the way to the dyke, then west on the rim to the spring, on the rivulet to the junction of the streams, then west along the old boundary, then north to the rivulet, then east along the slade to the brook, then east to the way, along the stream[1] to the spring, down the brook as far as the Tamar, down to *Carrecron.*

Here it is made known in this document[2] how King Edmund asked Bishop Burhwold for the land at Throwleigh.[3] When the king received it from him, he gave him the four hides at Landrake and the one hide at Tinnel in return for Throwleigh, and when I, King Cnut, succeeded to the kingdom after King Edmund, the bishop told me how they had exchanged lands, as it says here above. Then I, King Cnut, informed Bishop Burhwold that I granted the same lands just as King Edmund had granted them to him, ever uncontested for his lifetime, and after his lifetime the estate of Landrake is to go to St. German's minster for the support of the community for as long as Christendom shall last; and the bishop shall do with the land at Tinnel as God may direct him. And I grant that the lands are to be free from every service which is ever rendered from land, for the praise of God and St. German, except only military service and prayers for my soul.

The document of this gift was written in the year 1018 of the incarnation of our Lord, these witnesses consenting whose names are seen to be inscribed below:

✠ I, Cnut, monarch of the whole of Britain, have strengthened the gift of my liberality with the miraculous sign of the Holy Cross.

✠ I, Lifing, bishop of the church of Canterbury, have consented and subscribed.

✠ I, Wulfstan, archbishop of the church of York, have subscribed with the sign of the Holy Cross.

✠ I, Ælfgifu, queen, most humbly have assisted.

✠ I, Ælfsige, bishop,[4] have not opposed.

✠ I, Brihtwold, bishop,[5] have acquiesced.

✠ I, Æthelwine, bishop,[6] have confirmed.

✠ I, Brihtwine, bishop,[7] have counselled.

✠ I, Eadnoth, bishop,[8] have strengthened.

✠ I, Burhwold, bishop,[9] have concluded.

✠ Thorkell, earl.   ✠ Eilaf, earl.

✠ Eric, earl.

[1] Taking *hric* as error for *ric.*   [2] This document is in Old English.   [3] Devon.
[4] Of Winchester.   [5] Of Ramsbury.   [6] Of Wells.
[7] Of Sherborne.   [8] Of Crediton.   [9] Of Cornwall.

✠ Ranig, ealdorman.[1]
✠ Æthelweard, ealdorman.
✠ Godwine, ealdorman.
✠ Brihtwig, abbot.
✠ Æthelsige, abbot.
✠ Brihtmær, abbot.
✠ Ælfsige, abbot.
✠ Ælfhere, abbot.

✠ Æthelwold, abbot.
✠ Thored, king's thegn.
✠ Aslac, king's thegn.
✠ Tofi, king's thegn.
✠ Ælfgar, king's thegn.
✠ Odda, king's thegn.
✠ Ælfgar, king's thegn.[2]

Contemporary Old English endorsement

This is the title-deed of the lands at Landrake and Tinnel, of the four hides which King Cnut granted by charter to Bishop Burhwold in eternal inheritance.

132. Restoration by King Cnut to New Minster, Winchester, of land at Drayton, Hampshire, which he had wrongfully granted to a citizen of Winchester (1019)

Most of the Latin charters of Cnut which have come down to us present no features of especial interest, but this one shows him carrying on the tradition of Ethelred in recounting the previous history of the property concerned, illustrates his anxiety to do justly by the Church, and introduces us to an inhabitant of Winchester eager to secure landed property in the country. The place meant is shown by the boundaries to be near Whitchurch, and the name seems to be preserved in Drayton Lodge, south of Middleton, near Longparish. The charter belongs to Winchester College, and there is a facsimile in *Ord. Surv. Facs.*, II, Winchester College Charters, No. 4. It is printed in E. Edwards, *Liber Monasterii de Hyda*, Appendix C, pp. 324–326.

Christ Jesus our Saviour, true and highest God, three in Unity, one in Trinity, born by an incomprehensible birth of one substance with his co-eternal Father – who, most beautiful of things, bearing with profound mind the beautiful empyrean before the material formation of heaven, earth and ocean, brought forth by the power of a mere word alone the shining hierarchy of the angels, and the bright clear vessels of the sun, the moon and the fiery stars, and the various decoration and adornment of the four quarters of the universe, and the inconceivable abundance of fish in Neptune's tempestuous element – reigning continually and triumphing and perpetually guiding all things: I, Cnut, ruler and *basileus* of the noble and fair race of the English, have ordered this parchment to be inscribed by the furrowing reed with the forms of letters, on behalf of the minster which is called 'New', situated in the famous and populous city of Winchester, in which the wonderful bodies of the illustrious confessors Judoc and Grimbald to this day are efficacious in miracles; for an estate containing in it the extent of five hides,[3] which the tongue of the natives is accustomed to call Drayton, that this land may be applied for the benefit of the monks dwelling in the aforesaid minster, just as it was a long time before. This land, indeed, a certain inhabitant of the aforesaid city, young, daring and inconstant, acquired for himself

---

[1] This is just about the time when the native term ealdorman was giving place to the title earl, so that the translation of the Latin *dux* presents difficulty. The first three names with this title are those of Scandinavians, always called earl in vernacular texts, whereas the native term was still sometimes used of English officials.

[2] The last 24 names are arranged in four columns, with six representatives of each rank.

[3] *cassati.*

from me with cunning and lying, saying that the land was mine and that I could easily give it to him, which also I did. But when I realized the truth, I caused the inheritance of God rather to be restored to worthy heirs, and ordered this to be manifested for testimony and confirmation in the present charter. And since we have discovered that there are in the possession of the afore-mentioned youth letters contrary to this privilege, and acquired by fraudulent investigation, we both condemn those under pain of anathema, and hold as worthless any other such if there are any anywhere; and we endow only this writing with perpetual liberty and confirm it.

Moreover, we desire that Christ will grant blessing and mercy to those consenting to this privilege; and we wish that the everlasting pains of hell will threaten those opposing it, unless they the more quickly come to their senses from the wickedness of their malice and from injustice.

The sides, truly, of the aforesaid estate thus extend their limits for the country-men:[1] first from the *Humera* east by the boundary of the men of Middleton[2] to Tidbury,[3] from Tidbury to Micheldever,[4] and so along Micheldever to Leofwine's boundary, from Leofwine's boundary to the heathen barrow; and from the heathen barrow back into Drayton.

For indeed the authorative page of this title-deed was drawn up in the year of our Lord's incarnation 1019, the first week of Easter, in the presence of the king, for the confirmation and testimony of illustrious great men, whose names follow:

✠ I, Cnut, king of the English, have granted and strengthened this gift with a willing mind.

✠ I, Lifing, archbishop of the church of Canterbury, have confirmed the stability of the testimony.

✠ I, Wulfstan, archbishop of York, have consented.

✠ I, Ælfgifu, consort of the same king, have assisted.

✠ I, Ælfsige, bishop,[5] have placed [my mark].

✠ I, Brihtwold, bishop,[6] have made it secure.

✠ I, Ælfmær, bishop,[7] have put my mark.

✠ I, Eadnoth, bishop,[8] have impressed [my mark].

✠ I, Godwine, bishop,[9] have acquiesced.

✠ I, Thorkel, earl	✠ I, Brihtwig, abbot.
✠ I, Eric, earl.	✠ I, Brihtmær, abbot.
✠ I, Godwine, ealdorman.	✠ I, Ælfhere, abbot.
✠ I, Eilaf, earl.	✠ I, Brihtwold, abbot.
✠ I, Leofwine, ealdorman.	✠ I, Sihtric, king's thegn.
✠ I, Regnold, earl.[10]	✠ I, Hakon, king's thegn.
✠ I, Æthelsige, abbot.	✠ I, Halden, king's thegn.

---

[1] The boundaries are in English.
[2] Quite near to Drayton Lodge is a Middelton, and I assume that this is meant by *Middelhæma* 'the Middle-dwellers'.   [3] Tidbury Ring, south of Whitechurch, according to Ekwall.
[4] This place-name originally described a river; it survives only as a village name
[5] Of Winchester.   [6] Of Ramsbury.   [7] Of Selsey.   [8] Of Crediton.
[9] Of Rochester.   [10] This earl does not appear elsewhere.

✠ I, Thored, king's thegn.   ✠ I, Æthelweard, king's thegn.
✠ I, Atsere, king's thegn.   ✠ I, Sigered, king's thegn.
✠ I, Ælfgar, king's thegn.   ✠ I, Oslac, king's thegn.
✠ I, Thurkil, king's thegn.   ✠ I, Leofwine, king's thegn.
✠ I, Brihtric, king's thegn.

Glory and riches and happiness and blessing in the tabernacles of the righteous be granted to all promoting this privilege.

133. Old English letter of Wulfstan, archbishop of York, informing King Cnut and Queen Ælfgifu that he has consecrated Æthelnoth archbishop of Canterbury (1020)

This and the following document show part of the correspondence that went on about the appointment of an archbishop. Letters in the vernacular from private individuals rarely survive, and this has the additional interest of coming from a man important in the sphere of literature as well as of public affairs. The original document has not come down, but an early copy was made in a Christ Church book, the MacDurnan Gospels (now at Lambeth Palace), fol. 69b. The best edition, with translation, is that of F. E. Harmer, *Anglo-Saxon Writs*, No. 27. It is No. 1314 in Kemble, Earle, p. 232, Thorpe, *Diplomatarium*, p. 313.

✠ Archbishop Wulfstan greets humbly King Cnut his lord and the Lady Ælfgifu. And I inform you both, beloved, that we have acted concerning Bishop Æthelnoth according as notice came from you: that we have now consecrated him. Now I pray for the love of God and for all God's saints that you may show that respect to God and to the holy order that he may be entitled to all those things which the others before him were, Dunstan who was good, and many another; that this man also may be entitled to rights and dignities. That will be profitable for you both in religious concerns and also becoming in secular concerns.

134. Old English writ of King Cnut to ensure Archbishop Æthelnoth of the temporalities of his see (1020)

This is the earliest writ to survive in contemporary, or nearly contemporary, form. It should be compared with No. 133. Like this, it is entered in the MacDurnan Gospels, on fol. 114b. There is a facsimile in J. O. Westwood, *Palaeographia Sacra Pictoria*, pl. 14. It is best edited, with translation, by F. E. Harmer, *Anglo-Saxon Writs*, No. 28. It is in Earle, pp. 233 f.

✠ King Cnut greets in friendship all my bishops and my earls and my reeves in every shire in which Archbishop Æthelnoth and the community at Christ Church hold land. And I inform you that I have granted him that he is to be entitled to his sake and soke, and [fines for] breach of the peace, *hamsocn*,[1] *forsteal*,[2] to [the right to do justice on] the thief caught on his land, and to [the fine for] harbouring of fugitives; over his own men within borough and outside, and over Christ Church, and over as many thegns as I have relinquished to him. And I do not wish any man to withdraw anything there except him and his officials; for I have granted these rights to Christ for the eternal redemption of my soul, and I will not permit that any man ever violate this on pain of forfeiting my friendship.

[1] See p. 392, n. 2.   [2] See p. 408, n. 5.

135. Old English record of a family lawsuit in Herefordshire (1016–1035)

This is one of the most vivid of the accounts of lawsuits that have come down to us. It illustrates the procedure at a shire meeting and it shows how freely a woman could dispose of land in Anglo-Saxon times. It affords an example of a will declared orally before witnesses, who then announced it at the meeting. The writing of it in the gospels at Hereford, where it still remains, was only an additional precaution. Both Thurkil the White and his wife Leofflæd are mentioned in Domesday Book, Thurkil as the pre-Conquest holder of Wellington, one of the estates here mentioned. Dr. O. von Feilitzen has shown in *Mod. Lang. Notes*, LXII (1947), pp. 155–165, that the name of the father of the unsuccessful claimant, Enneawn, hitherto taken as corrupt and altered to the feminine name Eanwene, is actually the Welsh masculine name Enniaun.

Part of this document is facsimiled in *New Palaeographical Society*, part X, pl. 234. It is No. 755 in Kemble, and is edited with translation in Thorpe, *Diplomatarium*, p. 336, *Select Essays in Anglo-Saxon Law*, pp. 365–367, and Robertson, *Anglo-Saxon Charters*, No. 78.

Here in this document it is declared that a shire meeting met at *Ægelnothesstan* in King Cnut's time. There were present Bishop Athelstan and Ealdorman Ranig, and Edwin the ealdorman's [son] and Leofwine, Wulfsige's son, and Thurkil the White; and Tofi the Proud came there on the king's business. And there was Bryning the sheriff, and Æthelgeard of Frome, and Leofwine of Frome, and Godric of Stoke, and all the thegns of Herefordshire. Then there came journeying to that meeting Edwin, Enniaun's son, and brought a charge against his own mother for a piece of land, namely Wellington and Cradley. Then the bishop asked who was to represent his mother. Then Thurkil the White replied and said that it was for him to do so, if he knew the case. When he did not know the case, three thegns, namely Leofwine of Frome, and Æthelsige the Red, and Wynsige the shipman, were appointed by that meeting to go to where she was. And when they came to her, they asked her what was her case concerning the land which her son was claiming. Then she said that she had no land which belonged to him at all, and she became extremely angry with her son, and called to her her kinswoman, Leofflæd, the wife of Thurkil the White, and spoke thus to her in front of them: "Here sits my kinswoman Leofflæd, to whom I grant after my death my land and my gold, and my clothing and my raiment, and everything that I possess." And she then said to the thegns: "Act like thegns, and announce well my message to the meeting before all the good men, and inform them to whom I have granted my land and all my possessions, and to my own son never a thing; and ask them to be witness of this." And they did so; they rode to the meeting and announced to all the good men what she had charged them with. Then Thurkil the White stood up in that meeting, and asked all the thegns to give to his wife clear from the claim the lands which her kinswoman had granted her, and they did so. And Thurkil rode then with the permission and witness of all the people to St. Ethelbert's minster,[1] and had it entered in a gospel-book.

[1] Hereford Cathedral.

C. GUILD REGULATIONS

136. The Thegns' Guild in Cambridge

In many ways this is the most interesting set of guild regulations, especially in its evidence for the survival of the blood-feud at so late a date. Its interpretation is not free from problems. It is unfortunate that the author should have used an ambiguous expression, *wylisc*, to describe the man for whom a wergild less than that of a *ceorl* is to be paid. According to the laws of Ine there were classes of Welshmen with wergilds from 120 to 60 shillings; but that was two centuries earlier and in Wessex. It would be very interesting if we could use our present document to prove that even in the east of England at this late date there existed a class of Welshmen with lower wergilds than Englishmen of the same rank; but such an assumption is not justified. The same term is used in Old English of a foreigner and of a man of servile status. All our author may have in mind is the price to be paid to the owner if one kills a slave, normally 60 shillings. But even if he really meant a Welshman, it must be noted that the members of this guild are clearly men of substance, likely to hold estates in various parts of the country, and to travel to attend the king's council and on other business. We cannot assume that the feuds which they carry on are always in the Cambridge district.

These regulations are entered on a detached leaf of a gospel-book, which probably once belonged to the abbey of Ely. It is now Brit. Mus. Cott. Tiber. B. v, fol. 74. A grant by a certain Ælfhelm to his goldsmith (Kemble, No. 1352, Robertson, No. 71) between 970 and 999, was already written on this leaf before the regulations were added. They were first edited by Hickes, *Dissertatio Epistolaris*, pp. 20f., and this is the only source for the words at the end, for the leaf has since crumbled. They are edited with translation by Thorpe, *Diplomatarium*, pp. 610–613.

Here in this writing is the declaration of the enactment which this fellowship has determined in the thegns' guild in Cambridge. Firstly, that each was to give to the others an oath of true loyalty, in regard to religious and secular affairs, on the relics; and all the fellowship was ever to aid him who had most right. If any guild-brother die, all the guildship is to bring him to where he desired, and he who does not come for that purpose is to pay a sester of honey; and the guildship is to supply half the provisions for the funeral feast in honour of the deceased; and each is to contribute twopence for the almsgiving, and from it the fitting amount is to be brought to St. Æthelthryth's.[1] And if then any guild-brother have need of his fellows' help and it is made known to the reeve of the nearest guild-brother—unless the guild-brother himself be at hand—and the reeve neglects it, he is to pay one pound. If the lord neglects it, he is to pay one pound, unless he is engaged on the necessary business of his lord, or is on a bed of sickness. And if anyone kill a guild-brother, nothing other than eight pounds[2] is to be accepted as compensation. If the slayer scorn to pay the compensation, all the guildship is to avenge the guild-brother and all bear the feud. If then one avenges him, all are to bear the feud alike. And if any guild-brother slays a man and does it as an avenger by necessity and to remedy the insult to him, and the slain man's wergild is 1200 [shillings], each guild-brother is to supply half a mark to his aid; if the slain man is a *ceorl*, two ores; if he is servile [or Welsh?], one ore. If, however, the guild-brother kill anyone foolishly and wantonly, he is himself to be responsible for what he has done. And if a guild-brother slay a guild-brother through his own folly, he is himself to be responsible towards the kindred for the offence he

[1] At Ely.

[2] This figure represents a long hundred (120) ores, reckoned at 16 pence to the ore, and is a fine found elsewhere in the Danelaw. See p. 403, n. 3.

has committed, and to buy back his membership of the guild with eight pounds, or he is to forfeit for ever fellowship and friendship. And if a guild-brother eats or drinks with the man who slew his guild-brother–unless it be in the presence of the king, or the bishop of the diocese, or the ealdorman–he is to pay one pound, unless he can deny with two of his bench-fellows that he knew him. If any guild-brother insult another, he is to pay a sester of honey,[1] unless he can clear himself with two of his bench-fellows. If a retainer draws a weapon, the lord is to pay one pound, and the lord is to get from him what he can, and all the guildship is to assist him to recover his money. And if a retainer wound another, the lord is to avenge it, and all the guildship together; that–no matter what advocacy he seek–he shall not keep his life. And if a retainer sits within the *stig*[2] he is to pay a sester of honey. And if anyone have a *fotsetla*,[3] he is to do the same. And if any guild-brother dies outside the district, or is taken ill, his guild-brothers are to fetch him and bring him, dead or alive, to where he wishes, on pain of the same fine which has been stated in the event of his dying at home and a guild-brother failing to attend the body. And the guild-brother who does not attend his morning conference[4] is to pay his sester of honey.

137. The Exeter Guild Statutes

Perhaps the most interesting of these regulations is that relating to pilgrimage to Rome. The statutes survive in Brit. Mus. Cott. Tiber. B. v, fol. 75, a leaf of a gospel-book from Exeter. They are in Thorpe, *Diplomatarium*, pp. 613 f.

This association is assembled at Exeter for the love of God and for our souls' need, having regard both to the prosperity of our life and also to the days thereafter which we wish to be allotted to us at God's Judgment. We have then agreed that our meeting shall take place three times in twelve months, once at Michaelmas,[5] the second time at the feast of St. Mary after Christmas,[6] the third time on the feast of All Saints after Easter.[7] And each guild-brother is to have two sesters of malt and each retainer one, and a *sceat* of honey. And the priest is always to sing two Masses at each meeting, one for the living friends, the other for the departed; and each brother of ordinary rank[8] two psalters of psalms, the one for the living friends, the other for the departed. And after a death, each man [is to pay for] six Masses or six psalters of psalms; and at a pilgrimage south,[9] each man [is to contribute] fivepence; and at the burning of a house, each man a penny. And if any man fails to observe the appointed day, [he is to pay] on the first occasion three Masses, on the second occasion

---

[1] This clause is repeated in error in the MS.

[2] This word is of uncertain meaning in this context; it may refer to some railed-off dais. In other contexts it has its modern meaning 'sty', but as the first element of 'steward' it probably has some connotation as here.

[3] This word occurs here only. It may mean a personal attendant, for -*setla* means 'one who sits', or 'dwells', as in *ansetla* 'a dweller alone', 'hermit', or *cotsetla* 'a cottager'. In poetry certain types of attendant, a spokesman or a minstrel, are described as sitting at the feet of their lord.

[4] This is from Hickes, for the MS. has crumbled away at the foot.

[5] 29 September.   [6] The Purification, 2 February.

[7] It is obvious that this cannot mean the usual All Saints' day, 1 November. It may mean 13 May, the Feast of All Martyrs, established to celebrate the dedication of the Pantheon to St. Mary and all Christian Martyrs, though this is normally entered in calendars as "dedication of the basilica of St. Mary".

[8] Does this mean laymen, or clerics below priests' orders?   [9] To Rome.

five, on the third occasion no man is to clear himself unless it be for sickness or his lord's needs. And if any man neglects the appointed day for his contribution, he is to pay double. And if any man of this fellowship insult another, he is to pay 30 pence in compensation. Then we pray for the love of God that every man observe this assembly rightly, as we have rightly ordered it. May God help us thereto.

138. The Bedwyn Guild Statutes

This was first published by H. Meritt in *Journ. Eng. Germ. Phil.*, XXXIII, pp. 343-351, from MS. 671 in the Stadtbibliothek, Berne, and then by M. Förster, *Der Flussname Themse und seine Sippe*, pp. 791 f. My translation is from Förster's text.
On the history of the estate at Bedwyn, see No. 123.

The enactment of this guildship is as follows: if death befalls any one of them, each is to obtain five Masses or five psalters for the soul; and on the thirtieth day, pair by pair, five loaves and a pennyworth of something to eat with it, such as he can get. And at their meeting, pair by pair, they shall contribute a penny for their soul. And at the burning of a house, pair by pair, [they shall contribute] a load of building-material[1] or twopence. And at the Rogation days two members of the guild are to contribute to the priest a young sheep or twopence. And if anyone charge his guild-brother with lying or cheat him on his guild-bench, he is to make compensation with five ambers of ale and with three . . .[2]

139. The Abbotsbury Guild Statutes

The founder of this guild appears in eleventh-century records as Orcy, Orecy, Urki, Urk and Ork, probably representing a Scandinavian *Urkir*.[3] He received a grant of Portisham, the next village to Abbotsbury, from Cnut in 1024 (Kemble, No. 741) and one of Abbott's Wootton from Edward the Confessor in 1044 (Kemble, No. 772). In a writ between 1053 and 1058 (Kemble, No. 871; Harmer, No. 1), King Edward directs that his 'housekarl' Urk is to have full strand rights along the extent of his lands – rights that the abbey of Abbotsbury, which succeeded to them, were jealously guarding in 1268. A fragment remains (*Ord. Surv. Facs.*, II, Earl of Ilchester, No. 5) of a grant by his wife, Tole (who gave her name to Tolpuddle), to Abbotsbury, and it cannot be later than 1045. Between 1058 and 1066, King Edward issued a writ (Kemble, No. 841; Harmer, *Anglo-Saxon Writs*, No. 2) in which he speaks of Tole as the widow of his man Urk and gives her permission to bequeath her land and goods to St. Peter at Abbotsbury according to the agreement made by her and her husband that it should go there after their two lives. Urki does not sign after 1043. Domesday Book shows Abbotsbury in possession of Portisham and Abbott's Wootton, known to have been his, and also of Tolpuddle.
We cannot be certain of the precise date at which the guild was founded. If it was at the very end of Urki's life, it is just beyond the date limit of this volume. But it may well have been some years earlier, and it seems desirable to include it for comparison with the other sets of statutes. The statutes survive on a parchment belonging to the Earl of Ilchester, of which there is a facsimile in *Ord. Surv. Facs.*, II, Earl of Ilchester's charters, No. 4. They are No. 942 in Kemble, and are edited with translation by Thorpe, pp. 605-608.

Here it is made known in this document that Urki has given the guildhall and the site at Abbotsbury to the praise of God and St. Peter and for the guildship to own in his lifetime and after it, in lasting memory of himself and of his wife. Whoever

---

[1] A rather later hand has added "and work it".   [2] The text breaks off here.
[3] See E. Björkman, *Nordische Personennamen in England*, p. 171. For the forms without a final vowel, see O. von Feilitzen, *The Pre-Conquest Personal Names of Domesday Book*, pp. 71 f. To the examples there given can be added *Scul*, for *Skúli*, in the Thorney *Liber Vitae*.

wishes to pervert this, may he have to account with God at the great Judgment. Then these are the terms which Urki and the guild-brothers at Abbotsbury have agreed on for the praise of God and the honour of St. Peter and the need of their souls. Firstly, three days before St. Peter's Mass,[1] from each guild-brother one penny or one pennyworth of wax, whichever there is the greater need of, to the minster; and on the eve of the feast from every two guild-brothers one broad loaf, of good quality and well supplied with something to eat with it, for our common alms-giving; and five weeks before St. Peter's Mass each guild-brother is to contribute a guild-sester full of pure wheat and it is to be paid within two days on pain of paying the entrance fee, namely three sesters of wheat. And the wood is to be paid within three days after the corn-contribution, from each true guild-brother a burden of wood, and two from the man who is not a full member, or a guild-sester of corn is to be paid. And he who undertakes a brewing and does not do it satisfactorily is to be liable to his entrance fee, and there is to be no remission.[2] And the guild-brother who insults another deliberately inside the guild is to make amends to the whole fellowship with his entrance fee, and afterwards to the man whom he insulted, just as he can arrange it. And if he will not submit to compensation, he is to forfeit the fellowship and every other guild-privilege. And he who brings in more men than he ought without the permission of the steward and of the purveyors is to pay his entrance fee. And if death befall any of our fellowship, each guild-brother is to contribute a penny at the body for the soul, or to pay as much as three guild-brothers. And if any one of us becomes ill within 60 miles, we are then to find 15 men to fetch him – 30 if he be dead – and these are to bring him to the place which he desired in his life; and if he dies in the neighbourhood, the steward is to be informed to what place the body ought to be taken, and the steward is then to inform the guild-brothers, as many as he can possibly ride to or send to, that they are to come there and worthily attend the body and bring it to the minster, and pray earnestly for the soul. That will be rightly called a guildship which we observe thus, and it well befits it, both in spiritual and temporal concerns; for we do not know which of us will first depart. Then we believe, by God's help, that the terms pronounced above will benefit us all, if we observe it rightly. Let us pray God Almighty eagerly from our inmost heart, that he have mercy on us, and also his holy Apostle St. Peter, that he intercede for us and clear our way to the eternal rest, because we have assembled this guild for his sake. He has the dominion in heaven, that he may admit into heaven whom he will and exclude whom he will not, just as Christ himself said to him in his gospel: "Peter, I will give to thee the keys of the kingdom of heaven, and whatsoever thou shalt bind on earth, it shall be bound in heaven, and whatsoever thou shalt loose on earth, it shall be loosed in heaven."[3] Let us have trust and hope in him that may ever watch over us here in the world and after death help our souls. May he bring us to eternal rest. Amen.

---

[1] 1 August.   [2] Literally, 'gift', perhaps 'favouritism'.   [3] Matthew xvi. 19.

D. MANUMISSIONS

140. Old English manumission by King Athelstan (925)

This is the earliest Anglo-Saxon manumission on record, in Brit. Mus. Royal MS. I. B. vii. J. Armitage Robinson suggested that the St. Augustine's gospel-book in which it is entered was the one on which Athelstan took his coronation oath. It is No. 639 in Birch, and, with translation, in Thorpe, *Diplomatarium*, p. 622.

King Athelstan freed Eadhelm immediately after he first became king. Ælfheah the priest and the community, Ælfric the reeve, Wulfnoth the White, Eanstan the prior, and Byrnstan the priest were witness of this. He who averts this–may he have the disfavour of God and of all the relics which I, by God's mercy, have obtained in England. And I grant the children the same that I grant the father.

141-148. Manumissions in a gospel-book from Bodmin

The following eight manumissions are selected from a large number in Brit. Mus. Addit. MS. 9381, fol. 1–7, 133b, 141. As one would expect, many of the names are Celtic. The manumissions are sometimes in Latin, sometimes in English. They are edited by Kemble, No. 981, Haddan and Stubbs, 1, pp. 676–683, Thorpe, *Diplomatarium*, pp. 623–631, Earle, pp. 271–274, M. Förster, in *A Grammatical Miscellany offered to Otto Jespersen*, pp. 77–99.

141. Manumissions by King Edmund (939-946)

These are the names of the women, Medhuil, Adlgun, whom King Edmund freed on the altar of St. Petroc in the presence of these witnesses: Cangueden the deacon, Ryt the cleric, Anaoc, Tithert.

These are the names of the men whom King Edmund freed for his soul on the altar of St. Petroc–Tancwoystel, Wenerieth–before these witnesses: Wulfsige the priest, Adoyre, Milian the cleric.

And on the same day he delivered this woman, Arganteilin, with the same witnesses.

142. Old English manumission for King Eadred

This cannot be before Eadred's accession in 946. He died in 955, and Bishop Æthelgar of Crediton in 953, but it is not clear whether the manumission was performed in their lifetime or for their souls.

Wuennmon and her offspring, Moruiw, her sister, and her offspring, and Wurgustel and his offspring, were freed here in the village for King Eadred and for Bishop Æthelgar in the witness of the community which is here in the village.

143. Old English manumission for King Eadwig

Eadwig reigned from 955 to 959, but the manumission may have been done for his soul after his death.

Marh freed Lethelt and all her offspring for King Eadwig on his own relics; and he had her brought hither to the minster and freed here on Petroc's relics in the community's witness.

144. Establishment of free status (959–967)

This is not a manumission, but a record of a defence of status.

These are the names of the sons – Wurcon, Aethan, Iudnerth, Wurfothu, Guruaret –whose sons and grandsons and all their posterity defended themselves by oath with the permission of King Edgar, since their fathers were said by the accusation of evil men to have been the king's serfs; with Bishop Comoer witness, Ælfsige the ealdorman witness, Dofagan witness, Marh witness, Ælfnoth witness, Brihtsige the priest witness, Matiuth the priest witness, Abel the priest witness.

145. Manumission by Bishop Wulfsige for King Edgar

This is one of several manumissions which Bishop Wulfsige of Cornwall performs for King Edgar. If we could be sure that this was done for his soul after his death, we could date between 975 and 989, the date when Wulfsige's successor first signs. Wulfsige signs between 963 and 981. Two witnesses are shared with No. 146.

Bishop Wulfsige freed Iudprost with his sons for the soul of King Edgar and for his own soul before these witnesses: Brihtsige the priest, Electus the priest, Abel the priest, Morhatho the deacon, Canretheo the deacon, Riol the deacon.

146. Manumission by the priests of St. Petroc for King Edgar

Judging by the witnesses, this is approximately contemporary with No. 145.

These are the names of the men—Sulleisoc, Ourduythal—whom the clerics of St. Petroc's freed for the soul of King Edgar on the altar of St. Petroc on the festival of St. Michael, before these witnesses: Brihtsige the priest, Osian the priest, Austius the lector, Riol the deacon.

147. Old English record of establishment of free status

Palaeographical evidence suggests that this is from the second half of the tenth century. Like No. 144, it is not a manumission but a record of a settlement concerning a man's freedom. It should be noted that the legal price of a slave was a pound, the equivalent of eight oxen.

Here it is made known in this book that Ælfric, Ælfwine's son, wished to subject Putrael to him as a slave. Then Putrael came to Boia and begged for his intercession with his brother Ælfric. Then Boia settled the suit with Ælfric, namely that Putrael gave to Ælfric eight oxen at the church door at Bodmin, and gave 60 pence to Boia for his advocacy, and made himself and his offspring for ever free and secure from contention from that day as regards Ælfric and Boia and all Ælfwine's children and their offspring in this witness: Isaac the priest and Wunning the priest and Sæwulf the priest and Godric the deacon and Cufure the prior and Wincuf and Wulfweard and Gestin the bishop's steward and Artaca and Kinilm and Godric Map and Wulfgar and more good men.

148. *Manumission of a woman by Æthelflæd, wife of Earldorman Æthelweard*

Burhwold cannot have become bishop before 1002, in which year his predecessor's signature occurs. He was bishop by 1016. Ealdorman Æthelweard may be the one who signs in 1018 and was exiled in 1020, but we do not know the date of the death of an earlier ealdorman of the name, the chronicler, and ealdorman of the western provinces. His signatures cease in 998, but he could have taken part in local activities such as this one for some years after he ceased to be active at court.

This is the name of the woman, Ælfgyth, whom Æthelflæd freed for her soul and for the soul of her lord, Ealdorman Æthelweard, on the bell of St. Petroc in the residence which is called Liskeard, in the presence of these witnesses looking on: Athelstan the priest, Wine the priest, Dunstan the priest, Goda the thegn, Ælfweard Scirlocc, Æthelwine Muf, Ealdred his brother, Eadsige the writer. And these are the witnesses from the clerics of St. Petroc's: Prudens the priest, Boia the deacon, Wulfsige the deacon, Brihtsige the cleric, in order that freedom . . . And afterwards Ealdorman Æthelweard came to the minster of St. Petroc and freed her for his soul on the altar of St. Petroc in the presence of these witnesses looking on: Bishop Burhwold, Abbot Germanus, Tittherd the priest, Wulfsige the deacon, Wurgent, son of Samuel, Ylcaerthon the reeve, Tethion the 'consul' . . . the son of Mor. And he affirmed that whosoever shall observe this liberty shall be blessed, and whosoever shall infringe it shall be cursed by the Lord God of heaven and by his angels. Amen.

149. Old English manumission by King Eadwig at Exeter (956–959)

This entry is on a leaf which once formed part of a gospel-book at Exeter, and is now fol. 75 of Brit. Mus. Cott. Tiber. B. v. It was written after the guild-statutes, No. 137, were already there. Daniel was bishop of Cornwall, and Ealdorman Æthelwold succeeded his father, Athelstan Half-King, to East Anglia, about 956. This text is in Thorpe, *Diplomatarium*, p. 623, and with facsimile, *Trans. Devon. Assoc.*, LXIII, p. 184.

King Eadwig ordered Ælfnoth the sacrist to free Abunet at Exeter, free and with the right to depart, in the witness of Ealdorman Æthelwold and Bishop Daniel and Brihtric the prior and Wulfric the sacrist. And King Eadwig ordered Brihtric to put it here in Christ's book.

150. An Old English manumission from Durham, freeing those who had sold themselves for food

This is an entry into the Durham *Liber Vitae*, Brit. Mus. Cott. Domit. A. vii, that is the book containing lists of benefactors to the church of St. Cuthbert. The main part of the volume was an elaborate production in letters of silver and gold of the ninth century, but other lists were added until the twelfth century. The manumission occurs on fol. 43 and is in a hand of the late tenth century. It looks to me as if its beginning had been erased to make way for a list of names added later, and as if what is usually taken to be the name of the woman manumittor is really only the last name of a much later list.

This little text sheds a grim light on conditions in time of famine and upheaval. There is a facsimile in the *Surtees Society*, CXXXVI (1923). It is No. 925 in Kemble, in Earle, p. 275, and, with translation, in Thorpe, *Diplomatarium*, p. 621, and edited by H. H. E. Craster, in *Arch. Acliana*, 4th series, I, p. 189.

[Geatfleda] has given freedom for the love of God and for the need of her soul: namely Ecceard the smith and Ælfstan and his wife and all their offspring, born and unborn, and Arcil and Cole and Ecgferth [and] Ealdhun's daughter, and all those people whose heads she took for their food[1] in the evil days. Whosoever perverts this and robs her soul of this, may God Almighty rob him of this life and of the heavenly kingdom, and may he be accursed dead and alive ever into eternity. And also she has freed the men whom she begged from Cwaespatric, namely Ælfwold and Colbrand and Ælfsige and his son Gamal, Ethelred Tredewude and his stepson Uhtred, Aculf and Thurkil and Ælfsige. Whoever deprives them of this, may God Almighty and St. Cuthbert be angry with them.

[1] *i.e.* whom she accepted as slaves to save them from starvation.

Part III
ECCLESIASTICAL SOURCES

ECCLESIASTICAL SOURCES

Introduction

BECAUSE of the conditions of survival of Anglo-Saxon records, it is natural
that those dealing specifically with religion and the affairs of the Church should
far outdo all other kinds, and this greatly increases the difficulty of giving a
selection which will be representative of the various types of document and at the
same time include not only those of prime importance for ecclesiastical history but
those whose incidental information is necessary for the understanding of political and
social history. The following selection has been made for these diverse ends, but to
keep this volume within reasonable compass it has been necessary to exclude many
documents that might well have qualified for inclusion. Certain types of record,
however, are unsuitable in a work of this kind, because of their length and the nature
of their contents: penitentials, pastoral letters, rules of monastic observances, various
liturgical documents, are usually concerned with points of detail of little interest to
the general reader. Though such documents are often of value to the Church historian
who studies their interrelationships and the provenance of their injunctions, they
cannot be printed in selection.

The material relating to the pre-Viking Age Church is greater both in bulk and
interest than that available for later periods. The end of the Alcuin correspondence
seems a natural line of division, for, though the first raids had begun a few years
earlier, they seemed isolated incidents and had not yet seriously dislocated ecclesiastical
organization. From then on, until we come to the biographies of the saints of the
tenth-century reformation, there remain only scattered and sometimes fragmentary
materials.

BEDE'S "ECCLESIASTICAL HISTORY OF THE ENGLISH NATION"

The commencement of this section of the volume with large selections from
Bede's great work requires no defence. It is the primary authority for early Church
history, and though it is at the same time the major source for our knowledge of
political history up to 731, the placing of it here, rather than in Part I, may serve as
a useful reminder that Bede was not writing a political history and that it is therefore
unsafe to assume from his silences his ignorance of certain events that have no bearing
on ecclesiastical affairs. In fact, we learn from him of certain major political happenings
only incidentally: he tells us of the battle of Chester merely to show the fulfilment of
Augustine's prophecy; of the war between the East Saxons and West Saxons, in
which Sæberht's sons were killed, to illustrate their punishment for disobeying
Bishop Mellitus; of Edwin's war with the West Saxons because of this king's vow
to accept Christianity if victorious; of Oswald's rule in Lindsey to explain the
Bardney monks' reluctance to receive his body; of Penda's siege of Bamburgh as
the occasion of a miracle of Aidan's; of the ravaging of Kent by Ethelred of Mercia
because it brought to an end Putta's episcopate at Rochester; of the battle of the

Trent because the peace after it was engineered by Archbishop Theodore. This will show how dangerous it is to use the argument *e silentio* when dealing with this text.

To bring the work into the compass of the present volume I have omitted visions, most of the lengthy section on Augustine's questions and Gregory's replies, some papal letters, some passages from secondary authorities, much of the detail on the Easter controversy, miracles which tell little or nothing of contemporary life or events, and a few minor matters. The nature of the omissions is made clear in footnotes, for even when the material may seem of slight interest to us, it nevertheless forms part of what, after Bede's day, educated Englishmen knew of the previous history of their land. It may be of interest to compare my selection with that made by the Alfredian translator. He passed over papal letters, most of the matter relating to the Easter controversy, including the account of the synod of Whitby, chapters dealing with the Celtic churches, and the account of the holy places which Bede took from Adamnan. He retained all the miracles, and the full text of Augustine's questions with Gregory's replies.

SAINTS' LIVES

Saints' Lives can be divided for the purpose of historical studies into several categories. First in importance naturally come the Lives of persons who played a great part in the history of their time, especially when such Lives were written by authors who had first-hand knowledge of the saint in question, or at least derived their information direct from his disciples and contemporaries. Contemporary or nearly contemporary Lives of men or women of less historical importance may still shed valuable light on the history of their day. In general, the value to a historian of the Life of a saint diminishes as the gap between the time he lived and the time of writing increases, but each must be weighed on its own merits, with a consideration of the sources, written or oral, at the author's disposal, as well as of his competence. At the lowest end of the scale come those Lives in which the author, with little or no knowledge of the saint, merely gives a generalized account of his or her virtues, often borrowed from other Saints' Lives, or repeats apocryphal legends concerning them, or even gives play to his own invention, in answer to a demand for precise information not contained in the material at his disposal. Some such Lives are completely valueless, and have been ignored in the following survey; but there are others which make up for ignorance of the Life of the saint by including accounts of miracles which contain interesting detail on social conditions of the writer's own time. To give one example out of many: Ælfric's homily on St. Swithin is of no use at all for the history of the ninth century, when Swithin lived, but is a valuable source for the later tenth century when the cult of this saint had become important. Before we pass on to review briefly the more important Saints' Lives referring to pre-Conquest times, it is as well to remember that the authors were not writing history, but for the edification of their readers, so that even the best contemporary Lives may omit much that we would have liked to know, concentrating on the qualities that emphasize the sanctity of the saint and spur men to emulation, rather than on his actions in the world of temporal affairs.

Saints' Lives are one of the earliest forms of Anglo-Saxon literature. They begin before Bede, with the anonymous Life of Gregory by a monk of Whitby,[1] the anonymous Lives of Cuthbert[2] and of Ceolfrith,[3] and Eddi's Life of Wilfrid,[4] all of

---

[1] No. 152.   [2] Ed. B. Colgrave, *Two Lives of Saint Cuthbert*.   [3] No. 155.   [4] No. 154.

which were known to Bede. He used also a Life of St. Æthelburh of Barking which has not survived; the writing of Saints' Lives, therefore, was not confined to Northumbria. Bede himself has left us the Life of St. Cuthbert both in verse and in prose, and a *History of the Abbots of Monkwearmouth and Jarrow*, in addition to the many accounts of saints given in his *Ecclesiastical History*. These works belong to that class of Life produced by the generation which has known the saint, and they are more like historical biography, more concerned with the actual life of the saint, than is often the case. The miraculous element is not allowed to swamp the narrative–from Bede's *History of the Abbots* it is entirely absent–and thus they form an important source for early English history.

The Life of another contemporary of Bede, Guthlac, the hermit of Crowland, who died in 714, was written from information derived from men who had known him, by Felix, in the middle of the eighth century.[1] It affords a considerable amount of information about the early Mercian kingdom, a subject on which material is scanty.

Then there is a whole crop of Lives of the Anglo-Saxon missionary saints. All are written on the Continent, and to my knowledge no English manuscript of any of them has survived. The earliest Life of St. Boniface was written at Mainz by a man called Willibald, from information obtained from Lul, Boniface's successor, and others who had known him.[2] Though Boniface was worthy of a better biographer, this work does give the facts of his career, and is the main authority for the circumstances of his martyrdom. Moreover, its earlier portion tells something of early Christian Wessex. The early tenth-century Life by Radbod adds a detail to the account of the martyrdom which sounds authentic, of his raising a volume of the gospels in defence against the blow that killed him. It contains also an interesting little passage expressing admiration for the recent defence by the English of their land against viking invasion.[3] The later Lives of Boniface improve on Willibald only in as far as they draw on the letters.[4]

There are, however, three other Lives in which something can be learnt of Boniface's personality. Two are Lives of continental pupils of his: the Life of Gregory of Utrecht, written by his pupil Liudger, and the Life of Sturmi, first abbot of Fulda, by his pupil Egil. Both not only tell of Boniface's activities, but give some idea of the impression he made on those he worked with. And something of his character can also be gathered from the Life of Leoba by Rudolf of Fulda.[5] Leofgyth (Leoba), Boniface's chief woman helper, was an Englishwoman, and Rudolf's Life of her includes a picture of life in the double monastery of Wimborne. Rudolf did not write until 836, but he obtained his knowledge from persons who remembered Leofgyth. The Life of the other great missionary, Willibrord, was unfortunately not written until the time of Alcuin, whose Life of this saint is of the type which gives more prominence to the sanctity of the saint's character than to the events of his life.[6] Even so, the account of Willibrord's parentage affords a welcome glimpse into conditions in Northumbria, and there is also described Willibrord's attempt to convert the Danes and his adventure at the heathen sanctuary on Heligoland.

Far more interesting are the Lives of two other English missionaries, the brothers Willibald and Wynnebald, members of Boniface's mission. They were written, mainly from Willibald's own recital, by an English nun of Heidenheim, Hygeburh by name. In spite of her inadequate control of the Latin language, she manages to

[1] No. 156. [2] No. 158. [3] See p. 33. [4] See p. 573 f. [5] No. 159. [6] No. 157.

convey a wealth of information, which is especially interesting when it deals with Willibald's travels in the Levant, but which also covers conditions in the Anglo-Saxon homeland in the early part of her work. The Lives that deal with other Anglo-Saxon missionary saints are much later works, and only occasionally have details of value for our purpose. We learn of an Anglo-Saxon hermit called Sola, in Willibald's diocese, from a mid-tenth-century Life written at Elwangen; and of Leofwine, who came to Gregory of Utrecht and worked among the heathen at Deventer. The Life of him, written in the mid-ninth century, perhaps at Werden contains a vivid sketch of his attendance at a heathen assembly at Marklo. There is little of interest in Lupus of Ferrière's Life of St. Wigberht, the Anglo-Saxon abbot of Fritzlar, written some ninety years after his death, in the ninth-century Life of St. Burghard, bishop of Würzburg, in the late ninth-century Life of St. Wealdburh, the sister of Willibald and Wynnebald, or in the eleventh-century Life of Lul, by Lambert of Hersfeld. The Life of St. Berhtwine, the founder of Malonne, begins with the saint in England, where, it says, he was educated at *Otbellum* and became a bishop; but the statements in this ninth-century Life are too legendary for any reliance to be placed on them.[1]

Reliable information on English affairs is, however, to be found in the Life of Liudger,[2] the author of the Life of Gregory of Utrecht, and himself a missionary bishop to the Old Saxons. He was a Frisian, sent by Gregory to study under Alcuin at York, and his Life, which was written by Altfrid before 849, contains evidence of a Frisian trading community at that city in the middle of the eighth century. It was Liudger who finally destroyed the sanctuary of the god Forseti on Heligoland which Willibrord had desecrated. Another missionary to the Old Saxons was a Northumbrian called Willehad, whose Life by Anskar tells of his appointment to this mission by a Northumbrian synod under King Alhred of Northumbria. And, finally, there is a Life of Alcuin, written at Ferrières between 821 and 829, which derives its information from Alcuin's friend and countryman Sigewulf, and which has a little to tell us about the school of York. It adds to our list of Englishmen who travelled on the Continent the name of the priest Autbert (*i.e.* Eadberht), who took his nephew Sigewulf abroad to study the Roman practice and to learn chanting at Metz.[1]

Meanwhile, in the English homeland, the writing of biography seems to have been in abeyance. No early Lives of Bede or Aldhelm have survived. The Life of their contemporary, Ecgwine, bishop of Worcester and reputed founder of Evesham, is also late and valueless except in as far as the author had an occasional document, such as a copy of Boniface's letter to Æthelbald of Mercia, at his disposal. No Life of St. Swithin, the chief ninth-century saint, seems to have been written while the facts of his life were remembered. Ælfric obviously could discover nothing about him, even at Winchester. The earliest Life of Grimbald, King Alfred's helper, was not written before the second half of the tenth century, and has little definite information beyond what could be learnt from Asser and from Fulk's letter to Alfred. The gap between the early period of biographical writing and that of the late tenth century is, however, bridged a little by two long poems: that by Alcuin on the Saints of York, and that by a certain Æthelwulf, who wrote in the early ninth century a poem on the abbots of his monastery, at some unidentified place in Northumbria.[1]

It is not until after the monastic revival that once again we get almost contemporary accounts. The two earliest Lives of Dunstan, one by an anonymous author whose name began with a B,[3] the other by Adelard, give too much miracle and too

---

[1] For editions of these works see p. 582.   [2] No. 160.   [3] No. 234.

little history. It is difficult to obtain from them any clear impression of Dunstan's character, but B does give from time to time some important information on events in the mid-tenth century. The Life of Æthelwold of Winchester, by his pupil, Ælfric,[1] is by comparison a sober work which gives a sound account of the monastic revival, especially when it is supplemented by the picture of the church of Winchester in the middle of the tenth century given in the same author's homily on Swithin. It has recently been plausibly argued that another Life of Æthelwold, which Armitage Robinson believed to be a post-Conquest fabrication, is, in fact, that ascribed by William of Malmesbury to Wulfstan, precentor of Winchester, and hence a work written in the lifetime of men who had known the saint.[2] In that case, the material peculiar to it is worthy of respect. Perhaps the most interesting of the Saints' Lives of the monastic revival is that of Oswald, archbishop of York, part of which, at least, was written at Ramsey between 995 and 1005.[3] Though a shapeless work, it gives details on obscure matters of contemporary politics.

As examples of this type of source, two Lives have been given in full, the anonymous Life of Ceolfrith and Ælfric's Life of Æthelwold, to represent the early and late periods of hagiographical writing respectively. Passages of outstanding interest for English history have been selected from the others.

LETTERS

Correspondence is often a source of the utmost importance. More than any other type of material it may shed light on personality. Often it will give a contemporary opinion on events when other authorities give the mere facts. For some events it is our sole source of information, and often its references are the more valuable in being made incidentally by correspondents whose main concern is with other matters and who thus have no motive for misrepresentation. But there is no type of document that has slighter chances of survival, and what has come down can only be a minute proportion of what once existed. The great mass of letters must have seemed both to sender and recipient of ephemeral interest, and a motive for preserving them, so obvious in the case of charters, was lacking. Private letters between laymen had practically no chance of survival; it must not be too readily assumed that such were rare. But even where ecclesiastics are concerned, it is a fortunate chance when letters have survived the many forces of destruction between the time of writing and the present day. Apart from one or two lucky survivals of the original, such as Bishop Wealdhere's letter[4] and that to Edward the Elder on the Fonthill dispute,[5] which is something of a legal record, letters have come down in copies made for various reasons. They may have been embedded in historical works, such as the writings of Bede, Eddi and William of Malmesbury. A register or drafts of outgoing correspondence may have been kept by the sender, as in the case of papal correspondence. Sometimes the recipient made a collection of letters received, as Boniface appears to have done with the letters he received from the papal see. But only rarely have such collections reached us, even in part; they were subjected to various vicissitudes in later times. Papal registers, for example, are known to have existed as early as the mid-fourth century, but none remain in the papal archives from earlier than the pontificate of Innocent III (1198–1216); for the various misfortunes of the papal see, combined with the moving of the archives to new repositories, and the Lateran fire

[1] No. 235. [2] See pp. 831 f. [3] No. 236. [4] No. 164. [5] No. 102.

of 1307, have caused the destruction of records, and thus we owe to copies those registers and fragments of registers which are available. We read of researches into the papal archives on behalf of Bede[1] and Boniface,[2] and of the presence of fourteen papyrus rolls of the register of Gregory the Great in the Lateran in the time of Hadrian I (772-795), who fortunately had them, or a selection from them, copied into two volumes. It is believed that this work is now represented by a collection of 686 letters, surviving in several manuscripts. Two smaller collections of Gregory's letters, with respectively 200 and 54 letters, survive, and appear to have been known to Alcuin. Even so, these manuscripts do not contain all this pope's letters. For English readers the most interesting of Gregory's letters are those on the English mission,[3] some of which, but not all, are given by Bede, who also has two of his letters not in the extant collections.

Excerpts from the registers of Popes Leo IV (847-855), John VIII (872-882) and Stephan V (885-891)[4] were made by a compiler interested in their canonical importance, and his collection survives in a twelfth-century manuscript (Brit. Mus. Addit. MS. 8873), and is known as the British collection. It has fragments of Leo's letters to Æthelwulf,[5] and to Brihtwulf of Mercia and Archbishop Ceolnoth,[6] and of John VIII's letter to Burgred of Mercia.[7] Another collection of canons, that of Cardinal Deusdedit, has preserved part of that pope's letter to the two archbishops.[8] The excerpts from this pope's register come from the first years of his pontificate; for the later years the register survives in a manuscript from Monte Cassino, and contains the letter to Archbishop Ethelred.[9] Since this part was not available to the compiler of the British collection, it would appear as if the original rolls were not returned to the papal repository after copying. By the fortunate inadvertence of the scribe of the papal formula-book, the *Liber Diurnus*, the name of Cynethryth, Offa's queen, was left standing in a privilege confirming to some person and his wife and offspring certain monasteries which he had consecrated in the name of St. Peter. We can tell therefore that the formula is based on a lost privilege of Pope Hadrian to King Offa.[10]

Other papal letters concerned with English affairs we owe to preservation by the recipient. A collection of the letters sent by popes from Gregory III to Hadrian I to the Frankish rulers from Charles Martell to Charles the Great, made at the latter's orders in 791 for fear that, being on papyrus, they should perish, and known as the *Codex Carolinus*, includes a letter in which Hadrian says that he now knows to be false a rumour that Offa was scheming to depose him.[11] In the Wolfenbüttel manuscript of this collection, letters from Leo III (795-816) have been added, among them two referring to Charles's interference in the affairs of Northumbria.[12] But there is no similar collection of papal correspondence with English kings, and the few others that are extant, those between Leo III and Cenwulf of Mercia,[13] and that of John XV to Ethelred the Unready,[14] have survived because they were available to the compilers of the eleventh-century manuscripts Brit. Mus. Cott. Vespas, A. xiv and Tiber. A. xv, or else to William of Malmesbury.

[1] No. 151, p. 589.   [2] No. 179.   [3] *e.g.* Nos. 161-163.
[4] As well as some others whose pontificates lie outside the limits of this volume. See P. Ewald, *Neues Archiv,* v, pp. 277-414, 505-596.
[5] No. 219.   [6] See p. 810.   [7] No. 220.   [8] No. 221.   [9] No. 222.
[10] Levison, *England and the Continent,* pp. 29f.   [11] Haddan and Stubbs, III, pp. 440-443.
[12] *ibid.,* III, pp. 562-566. Cf. also Nos. 4, 21.
[13] Nos. 204, 205 and Haddan and Stubbs, III, pp. 538f. There are also parts of privileges issued by this pope and Paschal I for Cenwulf's monasteries, preserved in Brit. Mus. Cott. Tiber. E. iv.   [14] No. 230.

Papal letters to persons not kings, apart from those in the correspondence of Boniface, are not numerous. Some are included in one or both of the eleventh-century manuscripts just mentioned, which are to some extent based on a common source. Though consisting mainly of Alcuin's letters, they have some others. In the Tiberius manuscript there is a letter of Sergius I to Abbot Ceolfrith of Jarrow about 701, asking for a monk of his house to be sent to Rome,[1] and both manuscripts have the interesting letter of Paul I to Eadberht of Northumbria and Archbishop Egbert.[2] The Tiberius manuscript has preserved also the letter of a Pope John to an Ealdorman Ælfric.[3] Other papal letters are to be found in the cartularies or other books of religious houses, though not all are genuine. There can be no doubt of the genuineness of a letter of Constantine I (708–715) to Hædde, abbot of Bermondsey and Woking, entered in the twelfth-century cartulary of Peterborough, the mother-house of these foundations.[4] A letter of Agatho was available at St. Augustine's;[5] a letter of Sergius I to Aldhelm with privileges for Malmesbury at least has many correct formulae;[6] Glastonbury had in William of Malmsbury's time an Old English translation of a letter from Leo III, which William renders into Latin;[7] Canterbury has kept for us Formosus's letter to the English bishops,[8] though in a form that has been tampered with; a letter of John XII to Dunstan survives both in a genuine form in the Sherborne Pontifical and with a spurious insertion in a Canterbury manuscript.[9] In these two cases there can be no doubt that the text has been altered, but one must guard against a too ready assumption that any strong expressions in favour of a particular house are suspect; one could easily have suspected the monks of Canterbury of having tampered with John VIII's letter to Archbishop Ethelred,[10] if the circumstances of its preservation did not make such tampering completely impossible. For the tenth century there is a great paucity of papal letters. It would be difficult to decide whether it is entirely an accident that so few survive, or whether the popes of that period, busily engaged in holding their position against rival claimants, were in less frequent intercourse with England. Just before the Saxon period closes, outside the limits of this volume, papal letters become less rare. Leo IX writes about the removal of the see of Crediton to Exeter, Victor II issues a privilege for Chertsey, Nicholas II writes to Giso of Wells, to Wulfwig of Dorchester, and to Archbishop Ealdred of York, and there is a fragment of a letter of Alexander II to Abbot Ordric of Abingdon.

The collection of Boniface's correspondence with the popes, mentioned above, has come down to us along with other letters written to, or by, him or other members of his mission. We owe the preservation of this invaluable source for eighth-century history almost entirely to activities at Mainz in the time of his pupil and successor, Lul. It was there that the 'minor' collection, of the papal letters, was combined with the 'major' collection, of other correspondence. There too was written the manuscript now at Munich, once at Fulda, with 82 letters of these two collections, and the Karlsruhe manuscript also from Fulda, with 91; while the third important

---

[1] In later versions of this letter, in the twelfth-century MSS. of the *Liber Pontificalis*, Harley MS. 633 and Camb. Univ. Lib., Kk. iv, 6, and in William of Malmesbury, the name Bede has been inserted as that of the monk asked for. The oldest version of this letter is in Haddan and Stubbs, III, pp. 248–250, and is No. 104 in Birch.

[2] No. 184.   [3] No. 231.   [4] See F. M. Stenton, *Historical Essays in Honour of James Tait*, pp. 319–322.

[5] See Levison, *England and the Continent*, p. 189.

[6] Birch, No. 105, only in William of Malmesbury, but there was an Old English translation in Brit. Mus. Cott. Otho C. i, a copy of West Saxon Gospels, probably from Malmesbury. This is Birch, No. 106.

[7] See Levison, *op. cit.*, p. 251. It is Birch, No. 284, and confirms the monastery of Glastonbury to Cynehelm.   [8] No. 227.   [9] See Levison, *op. cit.*, p. 201 n.   [10] No. 222.

manuscript, at Vienna, which omits the 'minor' collection, but has a fuller 'major' collection, with more letters connected with Lul, is believed to have used the drafts and originals in the Mainz archives.[1] But for Lul's loyalty to his master's memory, all that we should have known of this whole correspondence would have been the exhortation to Æthelbald of Mercia,[2] from William of Malmesbury and the author of the Life of St. Egwine, and the letter to Archbishop Cuthbert[3] informing him of the decisions taken at a Frankish synod. This was known to Archbishop Wulfstan and to William of Malmesbury, and moreover it was copied into Brit. Mus. Cott. Otho A. i, along with the decisions of the council of *Clofesho* perhaps based on it, and printed by Spelman before the manuscript was burnt in the Cottonian fire. A letter of Boniface describing a vision related to him was also remembered in England, for it was translated into English.[4] But we should have known nothing of his more intimate correspondence, and none of Lul's. Moreover, Tangl has noted ninety references to letters which do not survive.

Similarly, continental manuscripts are our chief authorities for the only other bulky correspondence of the period, that of Alcuin, who was a most prolific letter-writer, to kings and members of royal families, archbishops, bishops, abbots, abbesses, religious communities, priests, lesser clergy, noblemen, in England and the Frankish kingdom, in Italy, Spain and Ireland. Dümmler's edition contains 311 letters, to which two more can be added,[5] and 85 of them are concerned with English affairs. The chief manuscripts come from continental houses governed by his friends and pupils, such as Corbie, where Adelhard was abbot, Salzburg, the see of his friend Arno, etc. But it was not only out of piety to his memory that his letters were copied, for in some manuscripts they are preserved as examples of style, with the names replaced by an abbreviation for *ille*. This motive for preserving letters is not uncommon, and accounts for the survival of some letters of no great contemporary significance. Some other manuscripts select those of Alcuin's letters directed against heresy or dealing with astronomical questions. Several of Alcuin's letters occur in pre-Conquest English manuscripts also; in the eleventh-century compilations Cott. Vespas. A. xiv and Tiber. A. xv, mentioned above, and in a Lambeth manuscript.[6] The Vespasian manuscript is connected with Archbishop Wulfstan, and two manuscripts at Corpus Christi College, Cambridge (190 and 265), both with material collected by or for him, contain some of Alcuin's letters that had a particular interest for this prelate, who makes use of Alcuin's writings in his own work. Though many of Alcuin's letters concerned with England have survived in continental manuscripts alone, it should be noted that the report of the legates of 786, of which no English manuscript is known, was used by Wulfstan. It seems likely, therefore, that more Alcuin material was available in England than our extant manuscripts would suggest. The cathedral of York, where one would expect most interest to be taken in this scholar, was burnt down by the Normans, and many of its treasures, books and documents destroyed.

---

[1] Altogether, there are close on 150 letters of this correspondence.   [2] No. 177.   [3] Tangl, No. 78.

[4] See K. Sisam, "An Old English Translation of a Letter from Wynfrith to Eadburga (A.D. 716–17) in Cotton MS. Otho C. i", *Mod. Lang. Rev.*, XVIII (1923), reprinted in *Studies in the History of Old English Literature*, 1953.

[5] One to Offa (see Levison, *England and the Continent*, pp. 245 f.) and one to Beatus of Liébana (*ibid.*, pp. 314–323).

[6] Lambeth MS. 218, part 3. Dümmler dates it eleventh century, but M. R. James, *A Descriptive Catalogue of the Manuscripts in the Library of Lambeth Palace*, Part III, pp. 350 f., says it is in a ninth-century hand of a Northumbrian type. But it is not, as one would have hoped, a collection made in England; it consists almost entirely of letters to Charles the Great, and 18 of its 21 letters are in the same order as in a MS. from Troyes, and must come from a common source.

We owe both these bulky sets of letters to fortunate circumstances. The fact that they stand alone must not be taken as a sign that most Anglo-Saxon ecclesiastics wrote few letters. One has only to read the preface to Bede's *Ecclesiastical History* to realize that a considerable interchange of letters must have taken place in collecting material for that work; and of all the letters relating to it we have only a single letter, to Albinus, abbot of the monastery of St. Peter and St. Paul, Canterbury, which accompanied a copy of the *Ecclesiastical History*–and even this letter is now known from a printed source alone, for the manuscript of St. Vincent's in Metz, from which Mabillon printed it in his *Vetera Analecta*, cannot now be found.[1] The letters which Bede mentions in his list of works, which are really treatises, and his long letter to Archbishop Egbert on problems of Church government,[2] are extant, but of his casual correspondence nothing survives. The letter of his pupil Cuthbert, describing his last moments, has come down in several English and continental manuscripts.

We are rather better off with regard to his older contemporary, Aldhelm. This is partly because William of Malmesbury found some letters surviving, and included eight, whole or in part, in his works. Only one of these is known from another source. Five Aldhelm letters, only one of which occurs elsewhere, are in the Vienna manuscript of the Boniface correspondence along with poems to or by Aldhelm; it seems likely that they may have been sent to Lul in response to his request to his former master, Dealwine, for some of Aldhelm's works;[3] and, if so, it may be that two Sherborne letters in the same manuscript, that of Archbishop Brihtwold to Bishop Forthhere,[4] and a letter from Bishop Daniel to Forthhere, recommending the Deacon Merwealh,[5] reached Lul at the same time. Only one of Aldhelm's letters, that to a certain Heahfrith, congratulating him on his return from Ireland, and speaking with appreciation of the school of Canterbury, comes down in several manuscripts, those containing his prose treatise on *Virginity*. But even the few and often fragmentary remains of Aldhelm's correspondence are enough to indicate the wide range of his epistolary activity; besides Heahfrith, he writes to Geraint, king of the Cornish Britons, Hadrian, abbot of St. Peter and St. Paul, Canterbury, the abbots of Wilfrid's monasteries,[6] a bishop of Wessex (Leuthere?), an Abbess Sigegyth, a scholar Wihtfrith, a certain Æthelwold, who writes Latin poems, an unknown Scot, and Cellan, abbot of Pèronne. A long letter to Aldfrith of Northumbria, whom he calls Acircius, is actually a treatise on metre. One cannot doubt that much of his correspondence has been lost. William of Malmesbury had access to letters of Bishop Hædde of Winchester (676–705), as well as to letters of Aldhelm to him,[7] but he does not quote them and none have survived.

Eddi has preserved a letter from Archbishop Theodore to King Ethelred of Mercia in 686 or 687,[8] on Wilfrid's behalf. Theodore's reorganization and administration of the English Church must have entailed numbers of letters, but this is the sole survivor. It is greatly to be regretted that no other letters are available to show the personality of this remarkable man, and a similar great loss is that of all the correspondence relating to Willibrord's mission to the Frisians—whether because it was never collected, or because the collection was destroyed later, we cannot know. And how much we may be the poorer by the disappearance of the letters which passed between

---

[1] In a Hague MS. the letter of Cuthbert reporting Bede's death is preceded by the last few lines of a letter from some unknown person to Albinus, who has been variously identified with this abbot (Brotanek, *Anglia*, LXIV, pp. 161 f.) or with Alcuin (N. R. Ker, *Med. Aev.*, VIII, p. 40).

[2] No. 170. [3] No. 176. [4] No. 166. [5] Tangl, No. 39.

[6] No. 165. [7] *De Gestis Pontificum*, ed. Hamilton, p. 159. [8] Ed. Colgrave, p. 89.

the archbishops of Canterbury and their suffragans in the normal course of affairs is brought home to us by the very great interest of a unique survival, the letter of Wealdhere of London.[1] Another chance survival is a letter among the correspondence of Boniface and Lul which was written by Ælfflæd, abbess of Whitby, to a continental abbess called Adola, recommending a nun travelling to Rome.[2] A letter from the anchorite Alchfrid, the author of certain prayers in the Book of Cerne, to Higbald, priest and *lector* of a Northumbrian monastery in the second half of the eighth century, survives in Cott. Vespas. A. xiv as the sole example of correspondence between the less important Northumbrian churchmen.[3]

Yet, in spite of such great gaps, the period from the time of Aldhelm to the death of Alcuin is well represented in comparison with the rest of the Anglo-Saxon period. From this there are only a few scattered letters, no major collection having survived. There are the papal letters already mentioned; the four letters of Lupus of Ferrières dealing with English affairs,[4] extant in a single manuscript; and one letter[5] and two abstracts of letters[6] from Fulk, archbishop of Reims, in Alfred's reign. Of all these, only Fulk's complete letter comes to us from an English source.[7] Cott. Tiber. A. xv supplies us with the letter of Egred, bishop of Lindisfarne, on Pehtred's heresy,[8] some lines of verse addressed to Wulfhelm, archbishop of Canterbury (926–942), and a few letters from the Continent to Dunstan or King Edgar in the period of the monastic revival, namely from Count Arnulf of Flanders, the abbey of St. Ouen at Rouen, that of St. Geneviève in Paris, Wido, abbot of Blandinium, and various unnamed persons; it has also letters from Falrad, abbot of St. Vedast at Arras, Odbert, abbot of St. Bertin's at St. Omer, and a person designated by the letter B, to Dunstan's successor, Archbishop Æthelgar, and one from the same Odbert to Archbishop Sigeric, who receives one from Abbot Ælfweard of Glastonbury also. The manuscript contains in addition a couple of anonymous letters, and one to the brothers of the Old Minster, Winchester, from Landferth, the author of the Latin *Miracles of St. Swithin*; this letter is also in Cott. Vespas. A. xiv, as are the letters to Æthelgar, and those of Wido and Odbert. This manuscript is the sole source of a letter from an unnamed writer to Wulfstan, while he was still only bishop of London,[9] and it includes also the letter sent by the bishops of England to the pope, in protest against the demands in connexion with the bestowal of the *pallium*, which Levison has shown to date from about 1000, and which may, as Miss Bethurum has suggested, have been drafted by Archbishop Wulfstan.[10] A manuscript now at Boulogne contains an answer by Abbot Ælfric to a lost letter from this archbishop which had asked queries on some matters of ecclesiastical observance,[11] and various Wulfstan manuscripts contain a set of penitential letters, from or to Wulfstan, or to Ælfric, archbishop of Canterbury, which were probably collected as formulae for copying.[12] Two other letters of this type are in the Sherborne Pontifical,[13] along with a letter from an unnamed archbishop to Wulfsige,[14] bishop of Sherborne. A letter from Wulfric, abbot of St. Augustine's, to Abbo of Fleury, asking him to versify B's Life of St. Dunstan, is preserved in a St. Gall manuscript of the Life in question.[15]

[1] No. 164.   [2] Tangl., No. 8.   [3] Ed. by Levison, *England and the Continent*, pp. 297–302.
[4] Nos. 215–218.   [5] No. 225.   [6] Nos. 223, 224.   [7] A tenth-century evangeliary.
[8] No. 214.   [9] All these are edited by Stubbs, *Memorials of St. Dunstan*, pp. 354–405.
[10] Haddan and Stubbs, III, pp. 559–561; Levison, *op. cit.*, pp. 241–248; D. Bethurum, in *Philologica: the Malone Anniversary Studies*, pp. 97–104.
[11] B. Fehr, *Die Hirtenbriefe Ælfrics*, pp. 222–227.   [12] M. Bateson, *Eng. Hist. Rev.*, x, pp. 727–730.
[13] Paris MS. Lat. 943. Stubbs, *op. cit.*, pp. 408f., prints as one letter.
[14] Stubbs, *op. cit.*, pp. 406–408.   [15] *ibid.*, p. 409.

Most of these tenth- and eleventh-century letters are inferior in historical interest to many from the earlier period. Perhaps the most interesting survival is one which William of Malmesbury found at Milton Abbas.[1] It is from Radbod, prior of St. Samson's at Dol, Brittany, to King Athelstan, sending him relics and reminding him that his father, Edward the Elder, had entered into confraternity with their house. It thus affords evidence of continental connexions during a period when information is hard to come by. Mention should be made in this connexion of a set of verses in praise of Athelstan, sent from abroad, which are preserved in Brit. Mus. Cott. Nero A. ii.[2] It is, in fact, mainly as proof of continued intercourse between the English and continental churches that the correspondence of the later period interests us. Several letters show that foreign houses looked hopefully to English kings for financial support. The single letter to Cnut, surviving among the correspondence of Fulbert of Chartres,[3] thanks him for a donation.

The survival of these letters seems to have been a matter of chance, and there is no evidence of any systematic enrolment of incoming or outgoing correspondence by the great figures of the monastic revival, a circumstance all the more to be regretted in that their biographers are far from giving a full and clear picture of them. And among these sparse remains, not a single fragment has come down relating to the reconversion of the lands settled by the Scandinavians in the Viking Age, nor to the missions carried on by the English in the Scandinavian countries. One must suppose that both of these activities would occasion a considerable interchange of letters, but conditions cannot have been favourable for their survival.

All the letters hitherto discussed have been in Latin. Surviving letters in the vernacular are very rare. Apart from prefaces to literary works couched in epistolary form, from pastoral letters of bishops to their clergy, from official writs by which the king communicated his will to various officials and assemblies, and a few legal records which are in the form of a letter,[4] there are very few to be considered, namely Dunstan's letter to King Ethelred about the see of St. Germans,[5] a letter entered into a gospel-book from Bedwyn, written by Bishop Æthelric of Sherborne to Æthelmær, almost certainly the ealdorman of that name, about some encroachment on the rights of his see,[6] Archbishop Wulfstan's letter to inform Cnut and Emma that he has consecrated Æthelnoth archbishop,[7] and the fragment to 'Brother Edward'.[8] But it would be wrong to assume that letters in the vernacular were rare in the later part of our period. Among the Latin letters not one is from an English ecclesiastic to a layman, all being either addressed to clerics or written from the Continent. It seems justifiable to assume from the surviving material that English ecclesiastics, when writing to laymen, from the tenth century at any rate, normally wrote in English,[9] and to attribute the rarity of extant vernacular letters to the smallness of the chances of survival of letters to laymen. It cannot have been unusual for kings to correspond with individual laymen, for Ælfric in one of his homilies says casually: "If the king

---

[1] No. 228.
[2] Birch, No. 655, with the MS. wrongly cited as Nero A. xi. See W. H. Stevenson, *Eng. Hist. Rev.*, XXVI, pp. 482–487. Stevenson dates the hand not much later than the middle of the tenth century, and refers to a late twelfth-century version in a Durham MS.
[3] No. 233. [4] Especially the record of litigation addressed to Edward (No. 102).
[5] No. 229. [6] See M. Förster, *Der Flussname Themse und seine Sippe*, pp. 781–783.
[7] No. 133. [8] No. 232.
[9] The question whether the letter about St. Germans is or is not a genuine letter of Dunstan does not affect this matter, for a forger would not have written it in English if it were abnormal for an archbishop to communicate with the king in English.

sends his writ to any of his thegns", as if this were a very ordinary occurrence; but not a single writ to an individual thegn is extant. With letters, as with charters, it must be borne in mind that we are unlikely to have anything remaining unless some religious house has had an interest in its preservation. This is true even of the State correspondence of kings with one another. Nothing has come down from royal archives, and we should not know of the letters of Charles the Great to Offa if they had not been entered into collections of Alcuin's letters; he probably was responsible for their drafting.[1] Simeon of Durham knew that Pippin had sent letters to Eadberht of Northumbria,[2] and the author of the *Acts of the Abbots of Fontenelle*[3] had seen letters from Offa to Abbot Gervold, who had more than once been employed by Charles as a diplomatic envoy, but not one of these survives. These were not likely to have been isolated exchanges.

A few words should be said about another type of letter, the professions of faith made by bishops on their appointment to their sees. These survive for the province of Canterbury in two manuscripts, the early twelfth-century Brit. Mus. Cott. Cleo. E. i, and a later Canterbury register. The earliest extant examples are from the end of the eighth century, and it was doubtless Offa's attempt to make Lichfield an archbishopric that brought home to the archbishops of Canterbury the desirability of preserving these professions. During the first two thirds of the ninth century they are common, but after 870 the only one known to me from pre-Conquest times is that of a bishop of Elmham in the mid-tenth century. It looks as if the enrolment was discontinued during the disorganization caused by Danish raids. After the Conquest they were used to support the Canterbury claim against York. In fact, in the earliest of them, Eadwulf of Lindsey, who speaks in very strong terms of his attachment to Canterbury, is called bishop of York by the copyist.[4] There may have been genuine confusion with Archbishop Ealdwulf of York (995–1002), but it would certainly strengthen the Canterbury claim to have a bishop of York professing obedience. The archbishop of York also received professions from his suffragans; Archbishop Cynesige received them from two bishops whom he consecrated to Glasgow, if we may believe the statement of the twelfth-century *Chronicle of the Archbishops of York*, but these professions perished along with the ornaments, books, privileges and other charters of the church when it was burnt by the Normans.[5] The professions which survive are not without value to the historian. They sometimes help to establish the succession of bishops in the various sees, and they allow some judgment to be formed of the standard of Latin composition. But they are not of sufficient interest individually to be worth including in this volume.

Small though the number of extant letters may be in proportion to what once existed, it is large enough for a selection to present difficulty. I have aimed at variety, and at giving not only documents which add to our knowledge of major ecclesiastical concerns or political events, but also some that shed light on humbler aspects of daily life. And with regard to the Boniface correspondence, I have tried to include enough to give some idea of the personality of this great man. It is for this reason that I have

---

[1] It is for this reason that I have preferred to leave the letter of Charles to Offa (No. 197) among Alcuin's letters, though strictly speaking it is not an ecclesiastical record, rather than to put it in a category by itself.

[2] *Symeonis Monachi Opera Omnia*, ed. T. Arnold, I, p. 48.   [3] No. 20.

[4] Birch, No. 276; Haddan and Stubbs, III, p. 506.

[5] J. Raine, *Historians of the Church of York*, II, pp. 343 f.

included one or two of his letters that have no direct bearing on English affairs. If the preponderance of eighth-century letters seems excessive, it must be remembered that they are more interesting in themselves and that we are badly off for other sources for this period.

VERNACULAR LITERATURE

Though this survives in bulk, not much of it is of direct importance to the historian. Most of it can come under the heading of ecclesiastical documents in that, whether written by clerics or laymen, it is intended for religious instruction and edification. Of the verse literature, I have chosen two poems which, while revealing the attitude to the Christian faith, also shed light on social life, and I have added one example of the verse catalogues in which men examine the allotment of divine benefits to men in this temporal world, and in so doing afford an occasional welcome glimpse into contemporary society. One of the difficulties of dealing with Old English poetry is that it can rarely be dated with any precision, but most would agree that these three poems are pre-Viking Age.

Prose literature, on the other hand, survives only from Alfred's time and later. The bulk of it consists of sermons or translations of Latin authors. I have confined my selection to Alfred's original prefaces and his additions to his sources, to similar original passages by Ælfric which have a historic interest, and to Wulfstan's famous sermon of exhortation to his countrymen in the time of the Danish invasion.

SELECT BIBLIOGRAPHY

of Ecclesiastical Records and Modern Works relating to the History of the Church and of Scholarship

I. ORIGINAL SOURCES AND MODERN WORKS DEALING SPECIFICALLY WITH THEM

(a) COLLECTIONS

For the period up to 870, there is a large and representative selection in vol. III of HADDAN and STUBBS, *Councils and Ecclesiastical Documents* (see p. 351), but for the later period the only work of this kind is D. WILKINS, *Concilia Magnae Britanniae et Hiberniae*, vol. 1 (London, 1737), in many respects out of date. Many Saints' Lives and collections of correspondence are edited in the *Monumenta Germaniae Historica*, ed. G. H. PERTZ and others, which, beginning in 1826, is still continuing: the Saints' Lives in the series *Scriptores* and *Scriptores rerum Merovingicarum*, and correspondence in *Epistolae* and *Epistolae Selectae*. Materials relating to individual religious houses are collected in DUGDALE's *Monasticon* (see p. 351). Many ecclesiastical canons and penitential writings are collected in vol. II of B. THORPE, *Ancient Laws and Institutes of England* (London, 1840), and the law-codes of the English kings (on which see p. 351) include much matter relating to the Church. Documents relating to the Gregorian mission are given with translation in A. J. MASON, *The Mission of St. Augustine to England according to the Original Documents* (Cambridge, 1897); and R. W. CHAMBERS, *England before the Norman Conquest* (London, 1928), includes several passages translated from ecclesiastical records.

(b) BEDE

The standard edition of the *Historia Ecclesiastica*, the *Historia Abbatum* and the letter to Egbert is that of C. PLUMMER, *Venerabilis Baedae Opera Historica* (Oxford, 1896), with full and excellent commentary. On translations of these works, see pp. 588, 697, 735.

The prose *Life of St. Cuthbert* has been edited, along with the anonymous life of this saint, by B. COLGRAVE, *Two Lives of St. Cuthbert* (Cambridge, 1940), with translation and commentary; Bede's verse Life is edited by W. JAAGER, *Bedas metrische Vita sancti Cuthberti* (Leipzig, 1935), and the works on chronology by C. W. JONES, *Bedae Opera de Temporibus* (Med. Acad. Amer. XLI, Cambridge, Mass., 1943). Except for M. L. W. LAISTNER, *Bedae venerabilis Expositio Actuum Apostolorum et Retractatio* (Med. Acad. Amer. XXXV, 1939), the other writings of Bede have to be consulted in old editions, *Venerabilis Bedae Opera*, ed. J. A. GILES (12 vols., London, 1843–1844) or *Patrologia Latina*, ed. J. MIGNE, vols. XC–XCV (1850–1862). See also W. LEVISON, "Modern Editions of Bede" (*Durham Univ. Journ.*, XXXVII, 1945).

The following are the more important of the numerous works on Bede and his writings: *Bede: his Life, Times, and Writings*, ed. A. HAMILTON THOMPSON (Oxford, 1935); R. W. CHAMBERS, "Bede" (*Proc. Brit. Acad.*, XXII, 1936); "Bede of Jarrow", in E. S. DUCKETT, *Anglo-Saxon Saints and Scholars* (New York, 1947). Specialist studies include M. L. W. LAISTNER and H. H. KING, *A Hand List of Bede Manuscripts* (Ithaca, N.Y., 1943); P. F. JONES, *A Concordance to the Historia Ecclesiastica of Bede* (Med. Acad. Amer., II, 1929).

Of the works embodied by Bede in his *Historia Ecclesiastica* the *De Excidio Britanniae* of Gildas is edited by T. MOMMSEN (*Mon. Germ. Hist., Auct. Ant.*, XIII, pt. I, 1894), also by PETRIE in *Monumenta Historica Britannica* (see p. 129), pp. 1–46, and, with translation, by HUGH WILLIAMS in *Cymmrodorion Record Series*, No. 3 (London, 1899). There are translations by J. A. GILES, *Six Old English Chroniclers* (Bohn's Antiquarian Library, 1891) and by A. W. WADE-EVANS, *Nennius's "History of the Britons" together with "The Story of the Loss of Britain"*

(Church Hist. Soc., London, 1938). On its historical value, see F. Lot, "De la valeur du *De Excidio*", in *Medieval Studies in memory of Gertrude Schoepperle* (Paris, N.Y., 1927); G. H. Wheeler, "Gildas de Excidio Britanniae, Chapter 26" (*Eng. Hist. Rev.*, XLI, 1926); and C. E. Stevens, "Gildas Sapiens" (*ibid.*, LVI, 1941). The best edition of Constantius's *Life of St. Germanus of Auxerre* is that of W. Levison, in *Mon. Germ. Hist.*, *Script. rer. Merov.*, VII, pt. I, 1919.

(c) SAINTS' LIVES (APART FROM THOSE BY BEDE)

On Adamnan's *Life of St. Columba*, see p. 690; on the *Life of St. Gregory* by a monk of Whitby, see p. 687; on the anonymous *Life of Ceolfrid*, see p. 697; on the *Life of St. Wilfrid* by Eddius Stephanus, see p. 692; and on Felix's *Life of St. Guthlac*, see p. 709. The anonymous *Life of St. Cuthbert* is edited by B. Colgrave, *op. cit.*

Of the Lives of the Anglo-Saxon missionaries and their pupils the following are most important for English history: *Vitae Sancti Bonifatii archiepiscopi Moguntini*, ed. W. Levison (*Script. rer. Germ. in usum scholarum*, 1905), the oldest of which (Willibald's) is translated by G. W. Robinson, *The Life of St. Boniface by Willibald* (Cambridge, Mass., 1916); *Vitae Willibaldi et Wynnebaldi* by Hugeburc (Hygeburh), ed. O. Holder-Egger (*Mon. Germ. Hist.*, Scriptores, XV, pt. I, 1887); *Vita Leobae* by Rudolf (see p. 719); Alcuin's *Vita Willibrordi* (see p. 713); *Vita Liudgeri* by Altfrid (see p. 724); *Vita Willehadi* by Anskar, ed. G. H. Pertz (*Mon. Germ. Hist.*, Scriptores, II, 1829); *Vita Alcuini*, ed. by W. Arndt (*ibid.*, XV, pt. I, 1887); *Vita Lebuini antiqua*, ed. by A. Hofmeister (*ibid.*, XXX, pt. II, 1934); *Vitae Burchardi episcopi Wirziurgensis*, ed. O. Holder-Egger (*ibid.*, XV, pt. I, 1887).

Important for the light they throw on Boniface are the *Vita Gregorii abbatis Traiectensis* by Liudger, ed. O. Holder-Egger (*ibid.*, XV, pt. I, 1887), and the *Vita Sturmi abbatis Fuldensis* by Eigil, ed. G. H. Pertz (*ibid.*, II, 1829). The *Vita Bertuini* is edited by W. Levison (*ibid.*, Scriptores rer. Merov.*, VII, pt. I, 1919).

Alcuin's poem *De Pontificibus et Sanctis Ecclesiae Eboracensis* is edited by E. Dümmler (*Mon. Germ. Hist.*, *Poetae latini aevi Carolini*, I, 1881) and by J. Raine, *Historians of the Church of York* (R.S., I, 1879); Æthelwulf's poem on the abbots of his monastery is in *Symeonis Monachi Opera Omnia*, ed. T. Arnold, I, pp. 265-294.

On the saints of the tenth-century monastic revival, the Lives of St. Dunstan are collected in W. Stubbs, *Memorials of St. Dunstan*, R.S., 1874. The earliest of them, by B (see No. 234), is discussed by D. Pontifex, "The First Life of St. Dunstan" (*Downside Review*, LI, 1933). On the *Life of St. Æthelwold* by Ælfric and that by Wulfstan the Precentor, see pp. 831f. On the anonymous *Vita Oswaldi Archiepiscopi Eboracensis*, see p. 839. Some tenth-century Lives of much earlier saints add little to our knowledge of the saints concerned, but illustrate contemporary life; these include the *Life of St. Swithin* in Ælfric's *Lives of Saints* (see p. 849) and the metrical account of this saint's life and miracles by Wulfstan the Precentor, ed. A. Campbell, along with the mid-tenth-century verse *Life of Wilfrid* by Frithegod in *Thesaurus Mundi* (Zürich, 1950).

Finally, there is valuable material in the *De Gestis Pontificum Anglorum* of William of Malmesbury (ed. N. E. S. A. Hamilton, R.S., 1870).

(d) LETTERS

P. Jaffé, *Regesta Pontificum Romanorum ad annum* 1198 (2nd ed. revised by W. Wattenbach and others, Leipzig, 1881-1888) is a catalogue of papal letters. The Register of Gregory the Great is edited by P. Ewald and L. M. Hartmann (*Mon. Germ. Hist.*, Epistolae, I-II, 1887-1889), and discussed by E. Posner, "Das Register Gregors I" (*Neues Archiv*, XLIII, 1921). The *Codex Carolinus* is edited by P. Jaffé in *Bibliotheca rerum Germanicarum*, IV (Berlin, 1867), and by W. Gundlach in *Mon. Germ. Hist.*, *Epist. Karol. Aevi*, I (1892). On the letters in the 'British Collection' of canons, see P. Ewald, "Die Papstbriefe der Brittischer Sammlung" (*Neues Archiv*, V, 1880, pp. 277-414, 505-596). Those of Leo IV are edited by A. de Hirsch-Gereuth in *Mon. Germ. Hist.*, *Epist. Karol. Aevi*, III (1898), and all the letters of John VIII are edited by

E. CASPAR in *ibid.*, *Epist. Karol. Aevi*, V (1928). On the register of this pope, see E. CASPAR, "Studien zum Register Johanns VIII" (*Neues Archiv*, XXXVI, 1911) and H. STEINACKER, "Das Register Papst Johanns VIII: Ein Beitrag zum Problem des älteren päpstlichen Registerwesens" (*Mitteil. d. österreich. Instituts f. Geschichtsforschung*, LII, 1938). On papal letters in general, see R. L. POOLE, *Lectures on the History of the Papal Chancery* (Cambridge, 1915).

The letters of Aldhelm are best edited by R. EHWALD in *Mon. Germ. Hist., Auct. Ant.*, XV (1919), pp. 475–503, and those of Boniface and Lul by M. TANGL in *Mon. Germ. Hist., Epistolae Selectae*, I, 1916. Most of this correspondence has been translated by E. EMERTON, *The Letters of Saint Boniface* (Columbia University Records of Civilization, XXXI, 1940), and many of those of chief interest for English historians by E. KYLIE, *The English Correspondence of Saint Boniface* (London, 1911). I have not seen G. W. ROBINSON, "Letters of Saint Boniface to the Popes and Others" (*Papers of the Amer. Soc. of Church History*, 2nd Series, VII, 1923). H. HAHN, *Bonifaz und Lul; ihre angelsächsischen Korrespondenten* (Leipzig, 1883) is an important study, and TANGL has made some additions to his edition in his "Studien zur Neuausgabe der Bonifatius-Briefe" (*Neues Archiv*, XL, 1915–1916, XLI, 1917–1919). See also W. LEVISON, *England and the Continent*, pp. 280–290. The Alcuin correspondence is best edited by E. DÜMMLER in *Mon. Germ. Hist., Epist. Karol. Aevi*, II, 1895); two letters that have since come to light can be read in LEVISON, *op. cit.*, pp. 245 f., 314–323. On the letters of Lupus of Ferrières, see p. 807; on Fulk's letters, see pp. 813 f. Most of the letters of the tenth and eleventh centuries are collected in STUBBS, *Memorials of St. Dunstan*, pp. 354–412.

(e) LITERARY SOURCES

For editions of Old English texts not mentioned in this volume, one should consult *The Cambridge Bibliography of English Literature*, ed. F. W. BATESON (Cambridge, 1940), the bibliographies in G. K. ANDERSON, *The Literature of the Anglo-Saxons* (Princeton University Press, 1949), and *The Year's Work in English Studies*, edited for the English Association (Oxford, 1921 et sqq.).

Poetic texts can be read in translation in the following works: A. S. COOK and C. B. TINKER, *Select Translations from Old English Poetry* (Boston, 1902); N. KERSHAW, *Anglo-Saxon and Norse Poems* (Cambridge, 1922); B. DICKINS, *Runic and Heroic Poems* (Cambridge, 1915); R. K. GORDON, *Anglo-Saxon Poetry* (Everyman's Library, 1926); *The Exeter Book* (Early Eng. Text. Soc., pt. I, ed. I. Gollancz, 1895, pt. II, ed. W. S. MACKIE, 1934); and in several works of C. W. KENNEDY, *The Poems of Cynewulf* (London, 1910), *The Cædmon Poems* (London, 1916), *Old English Elegies* (Princeton, 1936), *Early English Christian Poetry* (London, 1952). *Beowulf* is translated into modern prose by J. R. CLARK HALL, revised by C. L. WRENN (London, 1940). There are numerous verse translations.

The historical value of the verse literature is discussed by D. WHITELOCK, "Anglo-Saxon Poetry and the Historian" (*Trans. Royal Hist. Soc.*, 4th Series, XXXI, 1949). Among modern works on these poems should be noted C. W. KENNEDY, *The Earliest English Poetry* (O.U.P., 1943); W. W. LAWRENCE, *Beowulf and Epic Tradition* (Cambridge, Mass., 1928); R. W. CHAMBERS, *Beowulf: An Introduction* (2nd ed., Cambridge, 1932); A. BONJOUR, *The Digressions in Beowulf* (Medium Aevum Monographs, V, Oxford, 1950); D. WHITELOCK, *The Audience of Beowulf* (Oxford, 1951); K. SISAM, several studies collected in his *Studies in the History of Old English Literature* (Oxford, 1953), especially "Cynewulf and his Poetry".

Alfred's works can be read in translation in the books mentioned on pp. 818, 844, where reference is made also to some articles and monographs on them. To these may be added F. KLAEBER, "Zu König Ælfreds Vorrede zu seiner Übersetzung der Cura Pastoralis" (*Anglia*, XLVII, 1923); S. POTTER, "The Old English 'Pastoral Care'" (*Trans. Phil. Soc.*, 1947); P. F. VAN DRAAT, "The Authorship of the Old English Bede" (*Anglia*, XXXIX, 1915); S. POTTER, "King Alfred's Last Preface" (*Philologus*, XCVII, 1949); K. MALONE, "King Alfred's North: A Study in Mediaeval Geography" (*Speculum*, V, 1930), and "On King Alfred's Geographical Treatise" (*ibid.*, VIII, 1933); R. EKBLOM, "Alfred the Great as Geographer" (in *A Philological Miscellany presented to Eilert Ekwall*, Uppsala, 1942=*Studia Neophilologica*, XIV); J. I'A BROMWICH, "Who was the translator of the prose portion of the Paris Psalter?" (in *The Early Cultures of North-West Europe*, H. M. Chadwick Memorial Studies, Cambridge, 1950). For WÆRFERTH's translation of the *Dialogues of Gregory the Great*, see H. Hecht ("Bibliothek der angelsächsischen Prosa, V, 1900–1907). For the Old English version of Bede's *Ecclesiastical History*, see p. 588.

Of the works of the tenth-century reformers, the *Regularis Concordia* has recently been well edited by T. Symons (Nelson's Medieval Classics, London, 1953), with translation and intro-duction. Æthelwold's translation of the *Benedictine Rule* is edited by A. SCHRÖER (Bibliothek der angelsächsischen Prosa, II, Kassel, 1885). Old English translations of continental rules are edited by A. S. NAPIER, *The Enlarged Rule of Chrodegang, the Capitula of Theodulf, and the Epitome of Benedict of Aniane* (Early Eng. Text Soc., 1916). See also M. BATESON, "Rules for Monks and Secular Canons after the Revival under King Edgar" (*Eng. Hist. Rev.*, IX, 1894). Old English translations of continental penitentials are edited by J. RAITH, *Die altenglische Version des Halitgar'schen Bussbuches* (Bibliothek der angelsächsischen Prosa, XIII, 1933), and R. SPINDLER, *Das altenglische Bussbuch* (Leipzig, 1934).

For editions and translations of Ælfric's *Catholic Homilies, Lives of Saints, Heptateuch*, etc., see p. 849. His *Colloquy*, with its Old English gloss, is edited by G. N. GARMONSWAY (Methuen's Old English Library, 1939), and translated by A. S. COOK and C. B. TINKER, *Select Translations from Old English Prose* (Boston, 1908), by S. H. GEM, *An Anglo-Saxon Abbot* (Edinburgh, 1912), and by A. R. BENHAM, *English Literature from Widsith to the Death of Chaucer* (New Haven, 1916). ÆLFRIC's *Grammar* is edited by J. ZUPITZA (Berlin, 1880), his *Pastoral Letters* by B. FEHR, *Die Hirtenbriefe Ælfrics* (Bibliothek der angelsächsischen Prosa, IX, 1914), his *De Temporibus Anni* by H. HENEL (Early Eng. Text Soc., 1942), several minor works by B. ASSMANN, *Angelsächsische Homilien und Heiligenleben* (Bibliothek der angelsächsischen Prosa, III, 1889) and by R. BROTANEK, *Texte und Untersuchungen zur altenglischen Literatur und Kirchengeschichte* (Halle, 1913), his Old English version of Alcuin's *Interrogationes Sigewulfi in Genesin* by G. E. MacLEAN (*Anglia*, VI, 1883, VII, 1884), his version of the *Hexameron* by S. J. CRAWFORD (Bibliothek der angelsächsischen Prosa, X, 1921), his version of "Job" by B. ASSMANN in *Anglia*, IX, 1886. Most of what is of general interest in E. DIETRICH's great study, "Abt Aelfrik" (*Zeitsch. f. hist. Theol.*, XXV, 1855, XXIV, 1856), is reproduced in C. L. WHITE, *Ælfric: A New Study of his Life and Writings* (Yale Stud. in English, 1898), whereas the most recent general work, M.-M. DUBOIS, *Ælfric, Sermonnaire, Docteur et Grammairien* (Paris, 1943), makes a number of statements it would be very difficult to substantiate. The most important recent work on this author is that of K. SISAM, "MSS. Bodley 340 and 342: ÆLFRIC's *Catholic Homilies*" (*Rev. Eng. Stud.*, VII–IX, 1931–1933, now available in his *Studies in the History of Old English Literature*). The main works on his sources are M. FÖRSTER, *Über die Quellen von Ælfrics exegetischen Homiliae Catholicae* (Berlin, 1892, and *Anglia*, XVI, 1894), J. H. OTT, *Ueber die Quellen der Heiligenleben in Ælfrics Lives of Saints* (Halle, 1892) and GRANT LOOMIS, "Further Sources of Ælfric's Lives of the Saints" (*Harvard Stud. and Notes in Phil. and Lit.*, XIII, 1931).

The homilies of the other great writer of this period, Wulfstan, are published along with many falsely ascribed to him by A. [S.] NAPIER, *Wulfstan: Sammlung der ihm zugeschriebenen Homilien* (Berlin, 1883). For the other works of Wulfstan, and studies on him, see p. 854 and bibliographies in the works there cited.

The other principal literary sources of the tenth and eleventh centuries are as follows: *The Blickling Homilies*, edited with translation by R. MORRIS (Early Eng. Text Soc., 1880); the Vercelli Homilies, ed. M. FÖRSTER, "Der Vercelli-Codex CXVII" (*Stud. z. engl. Phil.*, L, 1913), and *Die Vercelli-Homilien* (Bibliothek der angelsächsischen Prosa, XII, 1932); Byrhtferth's *Manual*, edited with translation by S. J. CRAWFORD (Early Eng. Text Soc., 1929). On this author, who has been suggested as the author of the anonymous *Life of Oswald*, see p. 839, and also G. F. FORSEY, "Byrhtferth's *Preface*" (*Speculum*, III, 1928). A little text of some interest for Church history, on the resting-places of the English saints, is edited by F. LIEBERMANN, *Die Heiligen Englands* (Hanover, 1889) and is also in W. DE G. BIRCH, *Liber Vitae . . . of New Minster and Hyde Abbey* (Hants Rec. Soc., 1892, pp. 83–94). There survives also an Old English *Martyrology* edited by G. HERZFELD (Early Eng. Text Soc., 1900).

II. MODERN WORKS ON THE ANGLO-SAXON CHURCH AND ANGLO-SAXON LEARNING

(a) GENERAL WORKS AND BOOKS OF REFERENCE

In addition to works cited p. 101 above, the following books of reference may be mentioned: *A Dictionary of Christian Biography*, ed. W. SMITH and H. WACE (London, 1877–1878, abridged in one volume by H. WACE and W. C. PIERCY, London, 1911); *A Dictionary of Christian Antiquities*, ed. W. SMITH and S. CHEETHAM (London, 1876–1880), in as far as it has not been superseded by the *Dictionnaire d'Archéologie Chrétienne et de Liturgie*, ed. F. CABROL and H. LECLERCQ (14 vols., Paris, 1907 et sqq.).

F. M. STENTON, *Anglo-Saxon England*, deals fully with the ecclesiastical history as well as other subjects. For Church history alone there is W. HUNT, in vol. 1 of the *History of the English Church* (ed. W. R. W. STEPHENS and W. HUNT, London, 1907), and a useful account of the English Church in relation to the Church as a whole is given in M. DEANESLY, *A History of the Medieval Church, 590–1500* (London, 6th ed., 1950).

(b) WORKS ON SPECIAL PERIODS AND TOPICS

The most important work on the Celtic Church is J. F. KENNEY, *Sources for the Early History of Ireland, Vol. I: Ecclesiastical* (Columbia, 1929); see also L. GOUGAUD, *Christianity in Celtic Lands* (London, 1932), and J. A. DUKE, *The Columban Church* (Oxford, 1932). There is a detailed account of the Celtic form of monasticism in J. RYAN, *Irish Monasticism: Origins and Early Development* (London, etc., 1931).

Important studies on the early Church in England are contained in *Bede: his Life, Times and Writings*, ed. A. HAMILTON THOMPSON (Oxford, 1935), in E. S. DUCKETT, *Anglo-Saxon Saints and Scholars* (New York, 1947), which deals with Aldhelm, Wilfrid, Bede and Boniface, and in R. L. POOLE, *Studies in Chronology and History* (ed. A. L. POOLE, Oxford, 1934). M. BATESON's valuable monograph, "Origin and Early History of Double Monasteries" (*Trans. Royal Hist. Soc.*, N.S., XIII, 1899), should be supplemented by S. HILPISCH, "Die Doppelklöster" (*Beitr. z. Gesch. des alten Mönchtums u. des Benediktinerordens*, XV, Münster, 1928). D. J. V. FISHER, "The Church in England between the Death of Bede and the Danish Invasions" (*Trans. Royal Hist. Soc.*, 5th Series, II, 1952), covers a rather obscure period. On the missionaries to the Continent, S. J. CRAWFORD's excellent survey, *Anglo-Saxon Influence on Western Christendom 600–800* (O.U.P., 1933), was followed by the detailed work of W. LEVISON, *England and the Continent in the Eighth Century* (Oxford, 1946). Among books and articles on special topics or individual missionaries the following are noteworthy: W. LEVISON, "St. Willibrord and his place in History"(*Durham Univ. Journ.*, XXXII, 1940, reprinted along with other Willibrord studies in his collected papers, *Aus rheinischer und fränkischer Frühzeit*, Düsseldorf, 1948); T. SCHIEFFER *Angelsachsen und Franken* (Akad. d. Wissenschaften u. d. Literatur in Mainz: Abhandlungen der Geistes- u. Sozialwissenschaftlichen Klasse, No. 20, 1950), which consists of two studies on Boniface and Lul; R. DRÖGEREIT, "Werden und der Heliand" (*Beitr. z. Gesch. von Stadt u. Stift Essen*, LXVI, 1950), which demonstrates the extent of the Anglo-Saxon influence exercised through Liudger; J. JUNG-DIEFENBACH, "Die Friesenbekehrung bis zum Martertode des hl. Bonifatius" (*Missionswissenschaftliche Studien*, ed. J. SCHMIDLIN, N.R. I, 1931). A comprehensive and up-to-date study of Alcuin is now available in E. S. DUCKETT's *Alcuin, Friend of Charlemagne* (New York, 1951), where a full bibliography may be found.

Light has been thrown on the Church in Alfred's time by P. GRIERSON, "Grimbald of St. Bertin's" (*Eng. Hist. Rev.*, LV, 1940), and on the recovery from the Danish invasions by D. WHITELOCK, "The Conversion of the Eastern Danelaw" (*Saga-Book of the Viking Society*, XII, pt. III, 1941). For the tenth-century Church there is the excellent work of J. ARMITAGE ROBINSON, *The Times of St. Dunstan* (Oxford, 1923), and a very thorough study of the monastic revival and its results in M. D. KNOWLES, *The Monastic Order in England* (Cambridge, 2nd ed. 1949). See also T. SYMONS, "The English Monastic Reform of the Tenth Century" (*Downside*

Rev., LX, 1942). The reaction on the death of Edgar has been ably discussed by D. J. V. FISHER, "The Anti-Monastic Reaction in the Reign of Edward the Martyr" (*Cambridge Hist. Journ.*, X, pt. III, 1952), while the belief in a degenerate English Church in the eleventh century has been dispelled by R. R. DARLINGTON, "Ecclesiastical Reform in the Late Old English Period" (*Eng. Hist. Rev.*, LI, 1936), and P. G. CARAMAN, "The Character of the late Saxon Clergy" (*Downside Rev.*, LXIII, 1945). H. BOEHMER's article, "Das Eigenkirchentum in England" (*Festgabe für Felix Liebermann*, Halle, 1921), discusses private ownership of churches throughout the period.

English missions to Scandinavia and their effects are dealt with in K. MAURER, *Die Bekehrung des norwegischen Stammes zum Christenthume* (Munich, 1855); A. TARANGER, *Den Angelsaksiske Kirkes Indflydelse paa den Norske* (Christiania, 1890); E. JØRGENSEN, *Fremmed Indflydelse under den Danske Kirkes tidligste Udvikling* (Copenhagen, 1908); K. GJERSET, *History of the Norwegian People* (New York, 1927); C. J. A. OPPERMANN, *The English Missionaries in Sweden and Finland* (Church Hist. Soc., London, 1937).

Mention should also be made of A. M. RYAN's *Map of Old English Monasteries and Related Ecclesiastical Foundations, A.D. 400–1066* (Cornell Studies in English, XXVIII, 1939).

(c) WORKS DEALING WITH INDIVIDUAL CHURCHES AND MONASTERIES

Material relating to the general history of various establishments is included in the works listed on pp. 351 f. above. The following monographs are important: M. DEANESLY, "The Familia at Christchurch, Canterbury" (*Essays in Medieval History presented to T. F. Tout*, 1925) and "The Archdeacons of Canterbury under Archbishop Ceolnoth" (*Eng. Hist. Rev.*, XLII, 1927); M. D. KNOWLES, "The Early Community at Christ Church, Canterbury" (*Journ. Theol. Stud.*, XXXIX, 1938); R. A. L. SMITH, "The Early Community of St. Andrew at Rochester, 604 – c. 1080" (*Eng. Hist. Rev.*, LX, 1945); J. ARMITAGE ROBINSON, *The Saxon Bishops of Wells* (Brit. Acad. Supplementary Papers, No. 4, 1918), *St. Oswald and the Church of Worcester* (ibid., No. 5, 1919), *Somerset Historical Essays* (Oxford, 1921), which deals with Glastonbury; F. M. STENTON, *The Early History of the Abbey of Abingdon* (Reading Studies in Local History, O.U.P., 1913); SIR IVOR ATKINS, "The Church of Worcester from the Eighth to the Twelfth Century" (*Antiq. Journ.*, XVII, 1937); H. P. R. FINBERG, "The House of Ordgar and the Foundation of Tavistock Abbey" (*Eng. Hist. Rev.*, LVIII, 1943) and "Sherborne, Glastonbury, and the Expansion of Wessex" (*Trans. Royal Hist. Soc.*, 5th Series, III, 1953).

(d) LITERATURE AND LEARNING

The following histories of literature will be found useful: vol. I of the *Cambridge History of English Literature* (Cambridge, 1907); K. MALONE in Book I of *A Literary History of England*, ed. A. C. BAUGH (New York, 1948); P. G. THOMAS, *English Literature before Chaucer* (London, 1924); W. L. RENWICK and H. ORTON, *The Beginnings of English Literature to Skelton 1509* (London, 1939). For Anglo-Latin culture, M. L. W. LAISTNER, *Thought and Letters in Western Europe* (London, 1931) and J. D. A. OGILVY, *Books known to Anglo-Latin Writers from Aldhelm to Alcuin* (Cambridge, Mass., 1936), should be used. On individual authors, see works mentioned above, pp. 583 f. There is an important article by P. F. JONES on the earliest period, "The Gregorian Mission and English Education" (*Speculum*, III, 1928). D. WHITELOCK, *The Audience of Beowulf* (see p. 583), attempts to assess the culture of the later eighth century. For the later Old English period one may consult R. GRAHAM, "The Intellectual Influence of English Monasticism between the Tenth and the Twelfth Centuries" (*Trans. Royal Hist. Soc.*, N.S., XVII, 1903), and M. D. KNOWLES, "The Cultural Influence of English Medieval Monasticism" (*Cambridge Hist. Journ.*, VII, pt. III, 1943). The high quality of English culture is well demonstrated by R. W. CHAMBERS in *On the Continuity of English Prose from Alfred to More and his School* (in Harpsfield's *Life of More*, ed. E. V. HITCHCOCK, Early Eng. Text Soc., 1932, and printed separately, Oxford, 1933) and by F. E. HARMER, "The Intellectual Background" in her *Anglo-Saxon Writs* (Manchester, 1952).

A. THE PRE-VIKING AGE CHURCH

(a) BEDE'S "ECCLESIASTICAL HISTORY OF THE ENGLISH NATION"

151. From Bede's "Ecclesiastical History of the English Nation"

On the nature of this work, whose importance cannot be exaggerated, see pp. 567f. It should be added that Bede's works carried the fame of Anglo-Saxon learning to continental lands, and through the ages down to our own time (see Nos. 179f., 185, 188, 216). This can be seen by the multiplication of manuscripts, down to the era of print, the first printed edition of the *Ecclesiastical History* appearing in Strasburg in 1475. On the manuscripts, see M. L. W. Laistner and H. H. King, *A Handlist of the Bede Manuscripts* (Cornell University Press, 1943), which lists many manuscripts unknown to Plummer, including, for the *Ecclesiastical History*, the Leningrad MS. (on which see the facsimile edition by O. Arngart, *The Leningrad Bede*, Copenhagen, 1952), which is only a few years later than the Moore MS. at Cambridge, and an eighth-century manuscript from Fulda, now at Kassel (see *Zentralblatt für Bibliothekswesen*, Beiheft, LXIV, p. 184, and W. M. Lindsay, *Nota Latinae*, p. 452). The bearing of these early manuscripts on the problem of the transmission of the text has not yet been worked out. Plummer, basing his views mainly on the four early manuscripts known to him, the Moore MS. of 737 (M), the eighth-century Namur MS. (N), Brit. Mus. Cott. Tiber. A. xiv (B) and Cott. Tiber. C. ii (C), both of the eighth century, was able to distinguish two main types or recensions, the second of which, represented by MS. C, omits Book IV, chap. 14, embodies in the chronological summary the entries for 733 and 734 which in the M group of manuscripts occur after the close of the whole work, omits from Bede's bibliography of his works the excerpts from Jerome on the Prophets, and has minor differences in text and arrangement. Plummer suggests that there was a still earlier recension from which chap. 32 of Book IV was absent. It should be noted that the preface states that already a version had been sent to King Ceolwulf for his judgment, and it is probable that Bede himself made some revision after 731; for, though he says he finished the work in this year, all extant manuscripts include what is probably a reference to the battle of Tours, which took place in 732.

The *Ecclesiastical History* was one of Bede's latest works. He seems to have begun his literary career about 700, or a few years earlier, with text-books, and his *De Temporibus* of 703 included his short chronicle (*Chronica minora*), which represents his first excursus into historical writing. Between that date and the issue of the *Ecclesiastical History* he had written many commentaries on the books of the Bible, Saints' Lives, including both prose and verse Lives of St. Cuthbert, and his history of the abbots of his own monastery, scientific works and his long chronicle (*Chronica maiora*). It was therefore as an experienced writer that he undertook the present work. He had spent his life from childhood in the monastery, so his own part in affairs had been slight; but little of what went on in Northumbria would fail to reach the ears of the inmates of this important house, and Bede has given us his own account in his preface of his efforts to obtain information of the previous history of the other English kingdoms. And in other parts of his work he often tells us of the source of his information: some has reached him directly from Wilfrid and from Acca; his teacher Trumberht was a disciple of Chad; his fellow-priest Eadgils had lived in Coldingham before its destruction; he had talked with a priest who was with Jaruman when he won back the East Saxons to the faith, and so on.

He had written sources also. He made use of his own previous writings about St. Cuthbert and the abbots of his own monastery, and his work based on Adamnan's book on the Holy Places; of Eddi's Life of Wilfrid, a Life of Fursa and a lost Life of Æthelburh of Barking and a *Passio* of St. Alban. He had papal letters and records of synods. For his description of Britain and its history in Roman times he used various classical authors, such as Pliny, Eutropius, Orosius, Prosper and Marcellinus Comes, and he draws on Constantius's Life of Germanus for the period after the departure of the Romans. But his biggest debt is to the *Liber Querulus de Excidio Britanniae*, written by the British author Gildas near the middle of the sixth century. This is not a history, but a denunciation of the sins of his countrymen, and it gives few names or dates; but in the course of it a general account of the English conquest is given, which, coming from a writer born some fifty years after its commencement, is our chief source for this obscure period. From it Bede selected almost everything relating to this theme, compressing it to some extent, and adding to it the names of Vortigern, Hengest and Horsa, which probably reached him from traditional sources.

Bede was the first writer to use for historical purposes the dating by the incarnation, and owing to Anglo-Saxon influence this spread on the Continent and eventually became general. As with the Anglo-Saxon Chronicle, there is some uncertainty about the date of the commencement of the year. The opinion of R. L. Poole (*J. Theol. Stud.*, xx, 1918, reprinted in his *Studies in Chronology and History*, 1934), that Bede commenced the year on 24 September, still seems to me to present fewest difficulties, though it has been attacked by W. Levison, *England and the Continent in the Eighth Century*, pp. 265–279, and C. W. Jones, *Saints' Lives and Chronicles in Early England*.

The standard edition is by C. Plummer, *Venerabilis Baedae Opera Historica*, Oxford, 1896. The Old English version, of Alfred's time, is edited by T. Miller for the Early Eng. Text Soc., 1890–1898, and by J. Schipper, *König Alfreds Übersetzung von Bedas Kirchengeschichte* (Bibliothek der angelsächsischen Prosa, 1897). Among modern English translations may be noted: Thomas Stapleton, *The History of the Church of Englande* (Antwerp, 1565, St. Omer, 1622); J. A. Giles in Bohn's *Antiquarian Library*, 1840 (on which my translation is partly based); L. C. Jane, in *The Temple Classics* (1903), *Everyman's Library* (1910); A. M. Sellar, a revision of Giles (revised edition, London, 1912).

Bede's Preface

To the most glorious King Ceolwulf, Bede, servant of Christ and priest.

I formerly, at your request, most readily sent to you the *Ecclesiastical History of the English Nation*, which I had recently produced, for you to read and examine; and I now send it again to be transcribed and more fully considered at your leisure. And I esteem greatly the sincerity and zeal, with which you not only diligently give ear to the words of the Holy Scripture, but also industriously endeavour to become acquainted with the actions and sayings of former men of renown, especially of our own nation. For if history relates good things of good men, the attentive hearer is incited to imitate what is good; or if it recounts evil things of wicked persons, nevertheless the devout and godly hearer or reader, shunning that which is hurtful and wrongful, is the more earnestly kindled to perform those things which he knows to be good and worthy of God. You also, most carefully observing this, are desirous that the said history should be made more fully familiar to yourself and to those over whom the Divine Authority has set you to rule, from your regard to the general welfare.

But to remove all occasion for doubting the things I have written, both from yourself and from other hearers or readers of this history, I will state briefly from what authorities I chiefly learnt them.

My principal authority and helper in this work was the most reverend Abbot Albinus, a man most learned in all things; who, having been educated in the church of the people of Kent by those venerable and learned men, Archbishop Theodore of blessed memory, and Abbot Hadrian, diligently investigated either from written records or the traditions of the elders all the things that were done in that same province of the people of Kent, or also in the regions adjacent to it, by the disciples of the blessed Gregory; and who sent to me by the pious priest of the church of London, Nothhelm,[1] those of them which seemed worth recording, either in writing, or by word of mouth of the same Nothhelm. Nothhelm afterwards went to Rome, and with the permission of the Pope Gregory who is now set over that Church[2] searched into the archives of the holy Roman Church, and found there some letters of the blessed Pope Gregory and of other pontiffs. And, returning home, he brought them to me by the advice of the aforesaid most reverend Father Albinus, to be inserted in my history. Thus, from the beginning of this volume to the time when the English nation received the faith of Christ, we have learnt what we have discovered mainly from the writings of former men, collected from various quarters; but from then until the present time, what was transacted in the church of the people of Kent by the disciples of the blessed Pope Gregory or their successors, and under what kings the same happened, has been conveyed to us by Nothhelm through the zeal of the aforesaid Abbot Albinus. They also partly informed me by what bishops and under what kings the provinces of the East and West Saxons, as also of the East Angles and the Northumbrians, received the grace of the gospel. In short, I was chiefly encouraged to undertake this work by the exhortations of the same Albinus. In like manner, Daniel, the most reverend bishop of the West Saxons, who is still living, communicated to me in writing some things relating to the ecclesiastical history of that province, and also that of the South Saxons adjoining it, as also of the Isle of Wight. But how, by the ministry of the pious priests of Christ, Cedd and Chad, the province of the Mercians was brought to the faith of Christ, which it knew not before, and how the province of the East Saxons recovered the faith they had rejected, and how those fathers lived and died, we diligently learnt from the brethren of the monastery which was built by them and is called Lastingham. Moreover, what things concerning the Church occurred in the province of the East Angles, we discovered partly from the writings and tradition of those before us, partly from the account of the most reverend Abbot Esi. What was done towards promoting the faith, and what was the episcopal succession, in the province of Lindsey, we learnt either from the letters of the most reverend Bishop Cyneberht, or by word of mouth from other persons of good credit. As for what was done in the Church through the various regions in the province of the Northumbrians, from the time when they received the faith of Christ until the present, I learnt it not from any one authority, but by the faithful testimony of innumerable witnesses, who might know or remember the same; besides what I had of my own knowledge. Among these it is to be observed that I in part took what I have written concerning our most holy father and bishop, Cuthbert, either in this volume, or in the little book of his acts, from what I formerly found written about him by the brethren of the church of Lindisfarne, accepting without reserve the account which I read; but in part I took care wisely

---

[1] See No. 171.   [2] Gregory II, 715 to 11 February 731.

to add such things as I could myself find out by the most reliable testimony of trust-worthy men. And I humbly entreat the reader, if in these things that I have written he find anything not delivered according to the truth, he will not impute this to me, who, as the true rule of history requires, have laboured sincerely to commit to writing such things as I could gather from common report, for the instruction of posterity.

Moreover, I humbly beseech all to whom this same history of our nation shall chance to come, readers or hearers, that they will remember to offer frequent inter-cessions to the heavenly mercy for my infirmities of mind and body; and that each in their own provinces may repay me with this reward, that I, who have endeavoured diligently to record what concerning the several provinces or places of importance I believed to be worthy of note and pleasing to the inhabitants, may receive among them all the benefit of their pious intercession.

BOOK I

CHAPTER XI.[1] . . . Rome was stormed by the Goths in the year from its foundation, 1164, and from that time the Romans ceased to rule in Britain, almost 470 years after Gaius Julius Caesar came to the same island. They lived within the rampart, which, as we have mentioned, Severus made across the island, on the south side of it, as the cities, lighthouses,[2] bridges and paved roads made there testify until this day; yet they had a right of dominion over the farther parts of Britain, as also over those islands which are beyond Britain.

CHAPTER XII.[3] *The Britons, being ravaged by the Scots and Picts, sought help from the Romans, who, coming a second time, built a wall across the island; but when this was imme-diately broken through by the aforesaid enemies, they were reduced to greater distress than before.*

From that time Britain, in the part held by the Britons, being robbed of all armed soldiers, of all military stores, and of all the ardour of vigorous youth, which had been led away by the rashness of the tyrants[4] and never again returned home, was wholly exposed to rapine, as being totally ignorant of the practice of war. Whereupon suddenly it was aghast and groaned for many years from two very savage nations across the sea, the Scots from the north-west, the Picts from the north. We call these nations 'across the sea', not on account of their being settled outside Britain, but because they were remote from that part of it which was possessed by the Britons; two inlets of the sea lying between them, of which one from the eastern sea, the other from the western, run far and with broad extent into the lands of Britain, although they do not reach so far as to touch one another.[5] The eastern has in the midst of it

---

[1] Up to this point Bede has drawn on classical sources, but this is a passage of his own added to a chapter taken from Orosius.

[2] Plummer suggests that watch-towers may be meant.   [3] Here Bede uses Gildas. See p. 588.

[4] The various Roman governors of Britain who had crossed to Gaul to try to make themselves emperor. Gildas, who has the singular, meant Maximus.

[5] This attempt to explain *transmarinas* is Bede's addition to his source.

the city of *Giudi*;[1] the western has on it, that is, on its right bank, the city of *Alcluith*,[2] which in their language signifies the rock of the Clyde, for it is close by the river of that name.

Owing to their persecution by these nations, the Britons sent messengers to Rome with letters, beseeching their help with tearful prayers, and promising perpetual submission, provided that the threatening enemy should be kept off. An armed legion was immediately sent to them, which, when it arrived in the island and engaged the enemy, slew a great multitude of them, and drove the rest out of the territories of their allies; and, having meanwhile delivered them from that most cruel oppression, they advised them to build a wall across the island between the two seas, which might be a defence for them in keeping off the enemy; and thus they returned home with great triumph. The islanders, raising the wall which they had been told to build, not of stone, since they had no workman capable of such a work, but of turves, made it of no use. However, they made it for many miles between the two bays, or inlets of the sea, of which we have spoken; so that, where the protection of the water was lacking, they might defend their frontiers from the enemies' invasion with the help of the rampart. Clear traces of the work erected there, that is of a very broad and high rampart, can be seen at this day. It begins at about two miles' distance from the monastery of Abercorn, on the west at a place which is called *Peanfahel* in the speech of the Picts, but *Penneltun* in the language of the English; and running westwards, it ends near the city of *Alcluith* [Dunbarton].

But the former enemies, when they perceived that the Roman soldiers were gone, immediately came by sea, broke through the boundaries and destroyed everything, and trampled and overran all before them, as if mowing down ripe corn. Therefore messengers were again sent to Rome, imploring aid with lamenting voice, lest their wretched country should be utterly extirpated, and the name of a Roman province, which had so long been renowned among them, should become utterly contemptible, overthrown by the wickedness of foreign races. A legion was sent again, which arrived unexpectedly in autumn, made great slaughter of the enemy, and drove all those who could escape in flight across the sea; whereas they were wont before to carry off yearly booty across the sea without opposition.

Then the Romans declared to the Britons that they could not in the future undertake such troublesome expeditions for their protection; they advised them rather to arm and exert themselves to contend against the enemies, who would not prove stronger than they unless they themselves became effeminate from idleness. Moreover, since they thought that it might be some advantage to the allies whom they were forced to abandon, they constructed strongly in stone a wall from sea to sea, in a straight line between the towns which had been built there for fear of the enemy, where also Severus had once built a rampart. This wall, famous and visible even yet, they constructed at public and private expense, the Britons also lending their assistance. It is eight feet broad and twelve high, in a straight line from east to west, as is visible to onlookers until today. This being quickly finished, they gave good advice to the

---

[1] It is uncertain what place is meant. It is generally identified with Nennius's *Iudeu*. See p. 237.
[2] Dunbarton, on the Clyde.

dispirited people, and supplied patterns for manufacturing arms. Besides, they erected towers at intervals along the sea-coast towards the south, where their ships lay, to keep a look-out to sea, because there also an invasion of the barbarians was feared, and they took leave of their allies as men never to return.

As they were returning to their own land, the Scots and Picts, aware of their refusal to return, speedily came back themselves, and having grown more confident than ever, seized from the natives all the northern and farthest part of the island as far as the wall. A timorous guard was placed against their attacks on the top of the fortification, where it languished day and night, dazed and with a quaking heart. On the other side, the barbed weapons of the enemies were not idle; the cowardly defenders, dragged miserably from the wall, were dashed to the ground. What more need be told? Forsaking their cities and wall, they took to flight and were dispersed. The enemy pursued, and there swiftly followed a slaughter more cruel than all before; for as lambs are torn by wild beasts, the wretched citizens[1] were torn in pieces by the enemies. Hence, expelled from their dwellings and holdings, they saved themselves from the pressing danger of starvation by robbing and plundering one another, adding their domestic broils to the calamities without, till the whole country was left destitute of food, except what relief could be procured by hunting.

CHAPTER XIII. *In the reign of Theodosius the Younger, in whose time Palladius was sent to the Scots who believed in Christ, the Britons begging assistance from Aetius the consul did not obtain it.*

In the year of our Lord's incarnation 423, Theodosius the younger, receiving the rule after Honorius, the 45th from Augustus, held it 26 years. In the eighth year of his reign, Palladius was sent by Celestinus, the pontiff of the Roman Church, to the Scots who believed in Christ, as their first bishop.[2] And in the 23rd year of his reign, Aetius, a man of renown, who was also a patrician, discharged his third consulship along with Symmachus. To him the wretched remnants of the Britons sent a letter, whose beginning is this: "To Aetius, thrice consul, the groans of the Britons"; and in the course of the letter they thus unfolded their calamities: "The barbarians drive us to the sea, the sea drives us back to the barbarians; between them spring two sorts of death: we are either slaughtered or drowned." Yet, though they did all this, they could not get any assistance from him,[3] seeing that he was engaged at that time in most serious wars with Blædla and Attila, kings of the Huns; and although the year before this Blædla had been murdered by the treachery of his brother Attila, yet Attila himself remained so intolerable an enemy to the republic, that he ravaged almost all Europe, attacking and laying waste cities and fortresses. At the same time a famine befell Constantinople, and was quickly followed by a pestilence; moreover, several of the walls of that city, with 57 towers, fell to the ground.[4] Also many cities had fallen into ruin, and famine and the pestilential stench of the air destroyed many thousands of men and cattle.

[1] Bede keeps Gildas's term, which means subjects of the Roman Empire and is opposed to barbarians.
[2] This statement is taken from Prosper of Aquitaine. What follows is from Gildas.
[3] The rest of the chapter is based on Marcellinus Comes.
[4] Plummer notes that there was an earthquake in 447.

CHAPTER XIV.[1] *The Britons, compelled by the great famine, drove the barbarians from their territories; soon after there ensued, along with plenty of corn, loose-living, pestilence, and the downfall of the nation.*

In the meantime, the aforesaid famine distressed the Britons more and more, leaving to posterity a lasting memory of its evil effects, and forced many of them to submit to the raiding plunderers; not so some others, however, but rather, putting their trust in divine help, when human help failed, they continually waged war from the very mountains, caves and woods; and then for the first time began to inflict heavy losses on their enemies, who had plundered the land for many years. Thereupon the impudent Irish marauders returned home, to come again before long; the Picts then, for the first time, and afterwards, remained in the farthest part of the island, but did not cease to plunder and harass the people of the Britons from there from time to time.

When, however, the ravages of the enemy were abating, the island began to abound with such plenty of grain as no previous age remembered; with this plenty, loose-living increased, and was immediately attended with a plague of all sorts of crimes; in particular, cruelty, hatred of truth, and love of falsehood; to such an extent that if any one of them seemed to be milder than the rest and in some measure more inclined to truth, the hatred and weapons of all were regardlessly hurled against him as if he were the subvertor of Britain. Nor were the laity alone guilty of these things, but even our Lord's own flock, and its pastors, casting off the light yoke of Christ and giving themselves over to drunkenness, animosity, quarrelsomeness, strife, envy and other such sins. In the meantime, a grievous plague suddenly fell upon the corrupt men, which in a short time destroyed such a multitude of them, that indeed the living did not suffice to bury the dead; yet, those that survived could not be recalled from the death of the soul, which they had incurred by their sins, either by the death of their friends, or by fear of death. Whereupon, not long after, a more severe vengeance for their dire wickedness fell upon the sinful nation. For they held a council, as to what was to be done, and where help was to be sought to prevent or repel the cruel and frequent incursions of the northern nations; and they all agreed along with their King Vortigern to call over to their aid from regions across the sea the race of the Saxons; which, as the event showed more clearly, was brought about by the Lord's will, that evil might befall the wicked.

CHAPTER XV.[2] *The race of the Angles, being invited to Britain, at first drove away the enemy; but not long afterwards, joining in league with them, turned their weapons upon their allies.*

In the year of our Lord's incarnation 449, Marcian came to the throne along with Valentinian, the 46th from Augustus, and held it for seven years. Then the nation of the Angles, or Saxons, being invited by the aforesaid king, arrived in Britain with three warships, and received by the order of the same king a place of settlement in the eastern part of the island, as if they were to fight on behalf of the country, but

---

[1] This chapter is entirely taken from Gildas.

[2] Much of this chapter is Bede's own, though he takes from Gildas the tradition of three ships, the location of the settlement in the east, and the outline of his account of the revolt.

really intending to conquer it. Accordingly they engaged with the enemy, who had come from the north to give battle, and the Saxons had the victory. When this was announced in their homeland, as well as the fertility of the island and the cowardice of the Britons, a more considerable fleet was quickly sent over, bringing a stronger force of armed men, which, added to the band sent before, made up an invincible army. The newcomers received by the gift of the Britons a place to inhabit among them, on condition that they should wage war against their adversaries for the peace and security of the country, and the Britons were to give them the pay due to soldiers.

They came from three very powerful nations of the Germans, namely the Saxons, the Angles and the Jutes. From the stock of the Jutes are the people of Kent and the people of Wight, that is, the race which holds the Isle of Wight, and that which in the province of the West Saxons is to this day called the nation of the Jutes, situated opposite that same Isle of Wight. From the Saxons, that is, from the region which now is called that of the Old Saxons, came the East Saxons, the South Saxons, the West Saxons. Further, from the Angles, that is, from the country which is called *Angulus*,[1] and which from that time until today is said to have remained deserted between the provinces of the Jutes and the Saxons, are sprung the East Angles, the Middle Angles, the Mercians, the whole race of the Northumbrians, that is, of those peoples who dwell north of the River Humber, and the other peoples of the Angles. Their first leaders are said to have been two brothers, Hengest and Horsa, of whom Horsa was afterwards killed by the Britons in battle, and has still in the eastern parts of Kent a monument inscribed with his name. They were the sons of Wihtgils, the son of Witta, the son of Wecta, the son of Woden, from whose stock the royal race of many provinces trace their descent.

In a short time, as bands of the aforesaid nations eagerly flocked into the island, the people of the newcomers began to increase so much that they became a source of terror to the very natives who had invited them. Then suddenly they entered into a league with the Picts, whom by this time they had driven away by warfare, and began to turn their weapons against their allies. And first they forced them to supply them with a greater quantity of provisions, and, seeking an occasion for a quarrel, they protested that unless supplies of food were given them more plentifully, they would break the treaty and devastate all the island. Nor were they backward in putting their threats into execution. Indeed, to speak briefly, the fire kindled by the hands of the pagans wreaked God's just vengeance for the crimes of the people; not unlike that which, being once lighted by the Chaldeans, consumed the walls, and even all the buildings, of Jerusalem. For here also, by the act of the pitiless victor, or rather by the disposition of the just Judge, it laid waste all the neighbouring cities and fields, continued its burning course from the eastern to the western sea, without any opposition, and covered almost the whole surface of the doomed island. Public as well as private buildings were overturned; everywhere the priests were cut down before the altars; without any respect for rank, prelates were destroyed with the people, with fire and sword; nor was there any to bury those who had been thus cruelly slaughtered. And thus some of the miserable survivors, being captured in the mountains, were

---

[1] Angeln in Schleswig.

butchered in heaps; others, spent with hunger, came forth and submitted to the enemy, to undergo perpetual servitude for the sake of obtaining food, if they were not killed on the spot; some, with sorrowing hearts, sought regions across the sea; others, remaining in their own country, led a miserable life with fearful and anxious hearts among the mountains, woods and steep rocks.

CHAPTER XVI.[1] *The Britons obtained their first victory over the people of the Angles under the leadership of Ambrosius, a Roman.*

When the hostile army had destroyed and dispersed the natives of the island and returned home,[2] the Britons began by degrees to take heart and gather strength, sallying out of the lurking-places where they had concealed themselves, and unanimously imploring divine assistance, that they might not everywhere be utterly exterminated. They had at that time for their leader Ambrosius Aurelianus, a worthy man, who alone of the Roman nation had chanced to survive the aforesaid storm, in which his parents, who had borne the royal name and badge, had perished. Under this leader the Britons revived, and offering battle to the victors, themselves gained the victory by the favour of God. And from that time, sometimes the citizens, sometimes the enemy, prevailed, until the year of the siege of *Mons Badonicus,*[3] when they made no small slaughter of those enemies, about 44 years after their arrival in Britain.[4]

CHAPTER XXII.[5] *The Britons, being at peace for a time from foreign wars, wasted themselves in civil wars, and gave themselves up to greater crimes.*

Meanwhile, in Britain, there was some respite from foreign, but not from civil wars. The ruins of cities, destroyed by the enemy and abandoned, still remained. The citizens who had escaped the enemy fought against each other. However, the kings, priests, private persons and nobles, still remembering the late calamity and slaughter, observed their own station. But as these died and a generation succeeded which was ignorant of that time, and acquainted only with the present peaceful state of things, all the bonds of truth and justice were so shattered and overturned, that, not to speak of traces, not even a memory of them was to be found, except in very few people.[6] Among other unutterable deeds of crime, which their own historian Gildas relates in mournful words, they also added this, that they never undertook the preaching of the

---

[1] This chapter is from Gildas.   [2] *i.e.* to their own settlement.
[3] In spite of many suggestions, this place cannot be identified. As for the date of the battle, Bede's evidence would imply about 493, but the passage in Gildas is obscure and this may merely be Bede's interpretation of it. Gildas says he was born in the year of the battle, but opinions differ whether he means to go on to say that this battle was 44 years and one month before the time of writing, or after some previous event, as Bede takes it. The *Annales Cambriae* date it 516, but we do not know on what evidence.
[4] Chapters XVII–XXI are almost entirely drawn from Constantius's Life of St. Germanus of Auxerre, and relate how this saint and St. Lupus of Troyes came a few years before this to repel the Pelagian heresy. The main interest of these chapters for English history is their bearing on the chronology of the English invasions (see p. 7). Chapter XX speaks of divine help brought by these bishops in a battle of the Britons with the Picts and Saxons, and if this is more than a pious legend, and is correctly assigned to Germanus's first visit, it shows the Saxons and Picts combined already about 428. Chapter XXI relates a later visit of Germanus to Britain when the heresy had sprung up again.
[5] Bede now returns to the account in Gildas.
[6] The rest of the chapter is Bede's own, as are the chapters that follow.

word of the faith to the race of the Saxons or Angles who inhabited Britain with them. But nevertheless the goodness of God did not desert his people, whom he foreknew,[1] but on the contrary he sent much worthier heralds of the truth to the aforesaid nation, to bring it to the faith.

CHAPTER XXIII. *The holy Pope Gregory, sending Augustine with his monks to preach to the nation of the English, also comforted them with a letter of exhortation, not to cease from their labours.*

In the year of our Lord's incarnation 582, Mauricius, the 54th from Augustus, ascended the throne and held it 21 years. In the tenth year of his reign, Gregory, a man pre-eminent in learning and action, was promoted to the pontificate of the Roman and apostolic see, and ruled it for 13 years, 6 months and 10 days. He, moved by divine inspiration, in the fourteenth year of this same emperor, and about 150 years from the coming of the English into Britain, sent the servant of God, Augustine, and several other God-fearing monks with him, to preach the word of God to the nation of the English. When in obedience to the pontifical commands they had undertaken the said work and had already travelled a little of the way, they were struck with a cowardly fear, and considered returning home, rather than proceeding to a barbarous, fierce, and unbelieving nation, whose very language they did not know; and by common consent they decided this to be the safer course. At once they sent back home Augustine, whom Gregory had appointed to be consecrated their bishop, if they should be received by the English, that he might by humble prayers obtain of the blessed Gregory that they should not be obliged to undertake so dangerous, so toilsome, and so uncertain a journey. Gregory sent to them a letter of exhortation, persuading them to proceed in the work of preaching the word, putting their trust in the divine help. This letter was in the following form:

"Gregory, servant of the servants of God, to the servants of the Lord.

"Forasmuch as it had been better not to begin good works, than to think of desisting from these which have been begun, it behoves you, my beloved sons, to fulfil with the greatest zeal the good work, which, by the help of the Lord, you have begun. Let not, therefore, the toil of the journey, nor the tongues of evil-speaking men, deter you; but with all earnestness, with all fervour, perform what, by God's direction, you have begun; knowing that great labour is followed by the greater glory of an eternal reward. When Augustine, your superior, returns, whom also we constitute your abbot, obey him humbly in all things; knowing that whatsoever you shall do by his direction will in every respect be profitable to your souls. The Almighty God protect you with his grace, and grant that I may see the fruits of your labour in the eternal country; to the end that, though I cannot labour with you, I may yet partake in the joy of the reward, because indeed I am willing to labour. God keep you safe, my most beloved sons.

"Given the 23 July, in the 14th year of the reign of our most religious lord, Mauricius Tiberius Augustus, the 13th year after the consulship of the same our lord, the 14th indiction."[2]

[1] Romans xi. 2.   [2] Some MSS., including the Moore MS., have 13th indiction.

CHAPTER XXIV. *He sent a letter to the bishop of Arles about their entertainment.*

The same venerable pope then sent a letter also to Etherius, archbishop of Arles,[1] that he might receive Augustine kindly on his journey to Britain; this is the text of it:

"To his most reverend and holy brother and fellow-bishop Etherius, Gregory, the servant of the servants of God.

"Although religious men stand in need of no recommendation with priests who have the charity which is pleasing to God, yet, because a fit occasion for writing has occurred, we thought good to send to you, our brother, our letter, advising you that by the help of God we have directed thither for the good of souls the bearer of these presents, Augustine, the servant of God, of whose zeal we are assured, with other servants of God; whom it is necessary that your Holiness hasten to assist with priestly zeal, and afford him your comfort. And, that you may be the more ready in your assistance, we have also enjoined him to inform you minutely of the occasion of his coming; knowing that when you are acquainted with it, you will for God's sake dispose yourself with complete devotion for his solace, as the matter requires. We recommend also to your charity in all things the priest Candidus, our common son, whom we have transferred to the government of a small patrimony of our church. God keep you safe, most reverend brother.

"Given the 23 July, the 14th year of the reign of our most religious lord, Mauricius Tiberius Augustus, the 13th year after the consulship of the same our lord, the 14th indiction."

CHAPTER XXV. *Augustine, coming into Britain, first preached in the island of Thanet to the king of the people of Kent; and thus, having received permission from him, entered Kent to preach there.*

Thus strengthened by the encouragement of the blessed Father Gregory, Augustine, with the servants of Christ who were with him, returned to the work of preaching the word, and reached Britain. At that time Ethelbert was king in Kent, with very great power, for he had extended the frontiers of his empire as far as the boundary of the great River Humber, by which the southern and northern peoples of the Angles are divided. There is at the eastern side of Kent a large island, Thanet; it is in size, according to the English custom of reckoning, of 600 hides,[2] and is separated from the mainland by the River Wantsum, which is about three furlongs[3] broad, and is fordable in only two places; for both ends of it run into the sea. The servant of the Lord, Augustine, and his companions, nearly 40 men, it is said, landed on this island. They had taken interpreters of the Frankish nation, by the orders of the blessed Pope Gregory; and sending to Ethelbert, Augustine announced that he had come from Rome, and had brought the best of messages, which promised without a doubt

---

[1] Bede is in error here, for Etherius was bishop of Lyons, while the archbishop of Arles was called Vergilius.

[2] Literally 'families'. The word 'hide' is from a root meaning family, and it denotes the amount of land considered adequate for a household.

[3] A Roman *stadium* was a little shorter than an English furlong, but if Bede had an English term in mind it would doubtless be this.

to those who obeyed it eternal joy in heaven and a kingdom that would last without end with the living and true God. When the king heard this, he ordered them to stay in that island where they had landed, and necessaries to be supplied to them, until he saw what to do with them. For report of the Christian religion had already reached him, seeing that he had a Christian wife of the royal family of the Franks, Berhta by name, whom he had received from her parents on condition that she should be allowed to preserve inviolate the rites of her faith and religion, with the bishop, Liudhard by name, whom they gave her to help her in her faith.

Accordingly, some days after, the king came to the island, and sitting in the open, ordered Augustine and his companions to come to a conference with him there. For he had taken care that they should not come to him in any house, yielding to an ancient superstition, for fear that, on their entry, if they practised any magical art, they might get the better of him and deceive him. But they came endowed with divine, not demoniacal power, bearing a silver cross as a standard and the image of our Lord and Saviour painted on a panel, and, chanting litanies, they entreated the Lord for their own eternal salvation, and for that of those for whom and to whom they had come. And when at the king's orders they sat and preached the word of life to him and to all his followers who were present, he replied, saying: "Fair, indeed, are the words and promises which you bring; but because they are new and uncertain, I cannot give assent to them and abandon those which I along with all the nation of the English have followed for so long a time. But because you have come from far hither as strangers, and, as I conceive, have desired to impart to us also those things which you yourselves believe to be true and best, we do not wish to harm you; rather, we will receive you with friendly entertainment, and supply you with things necessary for your sustenance; nor do we forbid you to gain to your religious faith all whom you can by your preaching." Accordingly he gave them an abode in the city of Canterbury, which was the metropolis of his whole realm, and, as he had promised, besides seeing to their temporal sustenance, he did not withhold permission for them to preach. It is said that as they approached the city, after their manner, with the Holy Cross and the image of the great King, our Lord Jesus Christ, they were singing in unison this litany: "We beseech ye, O Lord, in all thy mercy, that thy wrath and thy indignation may be turned away from this city, and from thy holy house, because we have sinned. Alleluia."[1]

CHAPTER XXVI. *Augustine in Kent followed both the doctrine and the way of life of the primitive Church, and received an episcopal see in the king's city.*

And when they had entered the lodging given to them, they began to imitate the apostolic life of the primitive Church; that is, by serving God with continual prayers, vigils and fastings, preaching the word of life to whom they could, despising all things of this world as not their concern, receiving from those whom they taught only the things necessary for their sustenance; themselves living in all things according to what they taught, and ever ready to suffer any adversity, or even to die for the truth which they preached. In short, several believed and were baptized, admiring the

[1] This antiphon, belonging to the Rogation Days, is based on Daniel ix. 16.

simplicity of their innocent way of life, and the sweetness of their heavenly doctrine. There was near to that city, on the east, a church built of old in honour of St. Martin, while yet the Romans inhabited Britain, in which the queen, who, as we have said, was a Christian, was wont to pray. In this they also first began to meet, to chant psalms, to pray, to celebrate Mass, to preach and to baptize; until, after the king had been converted to the faith, they received a wider permission to preach everywhere, and to build or restore churches.

And when he, among the rest, was attracted by the pure life of the holy men, and by their pleasant promises, the truth of which they had confirmed also by the mani-festation of many miracles, and, believing, was baptized, greater numbers began daily to flock to hear the word, and abandoning the practices of heathenism, to join them-selves by faith to the unity of the Holy Church of Christ. It is said that the king, while he rejoiced greatly in their faith and conversion, would compel no one to Christianity; only he showed more affection to the believers, as fellow-citizens with him of the kingdom of heaven. For he had learnt from those who taught and led him to salvation, that the service of Christ should be voluntary, and not by compulsion. Nor was it long before he granted to his teachers a place for their see, suitable to their degree, in his capital of Canterbury, along with possessions of various kinds that were necessary for them.

CHAPTER XXVII. *Augustine, having been made bishop, informed Pope Gregory of what had taken place in Britain, and sought and received replies to his urgent questions.*

Meanwhile the man of the Lord, Augustine, went to Arles, and according to the orders that they had received from the holy Father Gregory was consecrated arch-bishop of the nation of the English by Etherius,[1] archbishop of that city; and on his return to Britain he sent at once to Rome the priest Laurence and the monk Peter, to report to the blessed Pope Gregory that the nation of the English had received the faith of Christ, and that he had been made bishop; at the same time beseeching his solution of those questions which seemed urgent. He soon received fitting answers to his inquiry; which we have also thought fit to insert in this our history:[2]

I. The first question of the blessed Augustine, bishop of the church of Canter-bury: Concerning bishops, how are they to live with their clergy? and concerning the things which are brought to the altar by the offerings of the faithful, into how many parts are they to be divided? and how is the bishop to act in church?

Gregory, pope of the city of Rome, replies: . . . all emoluments which accrue, ought to be divided into four portions; one, namely, for the bishop and his household, for hospitality and entertainment, the second for the clergy, the third for the poor, the fourth for the repair of churches. But because you, brother, brought up under monastic rules, ought not to live apart from your clerics in the Church of the English, which has lately been by the will of God brought to the faith, you ought to establish that way of life which our forefathers did in the begin-ning of the early Church, among whom no single one of them said that aught of

---

[1] Bede repeats here the error he made in chapter XXIV; the name should be Vergilius.

[2] Augustine's questions and Gregory's responses occupy many pages, and are often concerned with details of practice no longer of great interest. I give only a small selection of parts of wider interest.

the things which they possessed was his own, but all things were common unto them. . . .[1]

II. Augustine's question: Since the faith is one, are there diverse customs in the churches, and one custom of Masses held in the holy Roman Church, and another in that of Gaul?

Pope Gregory replies: You know, brother, the custom of the Roman Church, in which you remember that you were reared. But it pleases me, if you have found anything whether in the Roman, or in the Gallican, or in any other Church, which may be more acceptable to Almighty God, that you make careful choice, and impart by special institution in the Church of the English, which is still new in the faith, what you have been able to collect from many Churches. For things are not to be loved for the sake of places, but places for the sake of good things. . . .

III. Augustine's question: I beseech you, what punishment should be inflicted if anyone steals anything from the Church?

Gregory replies: You can judge, brother, from the standing of the thief, how he ought to be corrected. For there are some, who, though they have substance, commit theft; and there are others who transgress in this point through want; whence it is necessary that some be corrected with fines, some with stripes, some more severely, and others more mildly. And when it is done with rather more severity, it is to arise from charity, and not from passion; because this is done for him who is corrected, that he may not be delivered to the flames of hell. . . . You may add also how they ought to restore those things which they have stolen from the Church. But God forbid that the Church should receive more than it has lost of earthly goods, and seek gain out of such vanities. . . .[2]

CHAPTER XXIX. *Pope Gregory sent to Augustine the* pallium *and a letter and several ministers of the word.*

Moreover, the same Pope Gregory, because Bishop Augustine had told him that his harvest indeed was great, but the labourers few,[3] sent to him with the aforesaid messengers several fellow-workers and ministers of the word; first and foremost among whom were Mellitus, Justus, Paulinus and Rufinianus; and by them all things in general which were necessary for the worship and service of the Church, namely sacred vessels, and coverings for the altar, also ornaments for the churches, vestments for the bishops and clerics, likewise relics of the holy apostles and martyrs, besides many books. He also sent a letter, in which he informed him that he had sent the *pallium* to him, and at the same time he directed how he should constitute bishops in Britain. This is the text of the letter:

"To the most reverend and holy brother Augustine, his fellow-bishop, Gregory, servant of the servants of God.

[1] Acts iv. 32.

[2] This is in striking contrast to the Laws of Ethelbert (see No. 29), and one wonders whether Augustine's question was connected with the drawing up of those laws. Anglo-Saxon law shows no attempt to follow Gregory's injunction to consider motive. This was too advanced a conception for early law. Following questions deal with problems of marriage with relations, the number of bishops necessary at the consecration of a bishop, Augustine's relations with the bishops of Gaul and Britain, the latter being placed under Augustine's authority, and other matters. Chapter XXVIII consists of Gregory's letter asking Vergilius of Arles to support Augustine.   [3] Matthew ix. 37; Luke x. 2.

"Though it is certain that the indescribable rewards of the eternal kingdom are reserved for those who labour for Almighty God, yet is it necessary for us to bestow on them the benefit of honours, that they may by this recompense be enabled to toil harder in devotion to their spiritual work. And because the new Church of the English has been brought to the grace of the Almighty God, by the gift of the same Lord and your labour, we grant you the use of the *pallium* in that Church, only for the celebration of the solemnities of the Mass; so that you may ordain in different places twelve bishops, who are to be subject to your authority, in order that the bishop of the city of London[1] shall in the future always be consecrated by his own synod, and receive the *pallium* of this honour from this holy and apostolic see, which, by the will of God, I serve. We desire you to send to the city of York a bishop whom you shall think fit to ordain; yet so, that if that city with the neighbouring places should receive the word of God, he also is to ordain twelve bishops, and to enjoy the metropolitan dignity; because we design, if we live, to bestow the *pallium* on him also by the favour of the Lord; but yet we wish him to be subject to your direction, brother. But after your death he is so to preside over the bishops whom he shall have ordained as to be in no way subject to the jurisdiction of the bishop of London. But in the future there is to be this division of honour between the bishops of the cities of London and York, that he is to take precedence who has first been ordained; but they are to arrange harmoniously by common counsel and agreed action whatever is to be done in zeal for Christ; let them decide rightly and then carry out their decision without dissension.

"But you, brother, by the will of our Lord and God Jesus Christ, are to have authority not only over those bishops whom you shall ordain, and those who shall be ordained by the bishop of York, but also over all the bishops of Britain; to the end that from the words and life of your Holiness they may learn a pattern of right belief and good living, and, performing their office with faith and morality, they may, when it shall please God, attain to the heavenly kingdom. God keep you safe, most reverend brother.

"Given 22 June in the 19th year of the reign of our most religious lord, Mauricius Tiberius Augustus, the 18th year after the consulship of this same lord, the fourth indiction."

CHAPTER XXX. *A copy of the letter which Pope Gregory sent to Abbot Mellitus, then going to Britain.*

When the aforesaid messengers had set out, the blessed Father Gregory sent after them a letter worthy to be recorded, in which he plainly shows how carefully he watched over the salvation of our nation, writing thus:

"To his most beloved son Abbot Mellitus, Gregory, servant of the servants of God.

"We have been very anxious since the departure of our people that are with you, because we have heard nothing of the success of your journey. When,

[1] Gregory was expecting Augustine to make London his see.

therefore, Almighty God has led you to the most reverend man, our brother Bishop Augustine, tell him what I have decided after long deliberation concerning the affair of the English: namely that the temples of the idols in that nation ought not to be destroyed; but let the idols, which are in them, be destroyed; let water be blessed and sprinkled in the said temples, altars erected and relics placed there. For, if those temples are well built, it is needful that they should be converted from the worship of devils to the service of the true God; that the nation, seeing that their temples are not destroyed, may remove error from their hearts, and, knowing and adoring the true God, may the more familiarly resort to the places to which they have been accustomed. And because they are accustomed to slaughter many oxen in sacrifice to devils, some solemnity ought to be given to them in exchange for this also; as that, on the day of dedication, or the nativities of the holy martyrs, whose relics are deposited there, they should make themselves booths of boughs round those churches which have been converted from temples, and celebrate the solemnity with religious feasting; and no longer sacrifice animals to the devil, but kill cattle for their food and to the praise of God, and give thanks to the Giver of all for their sustenance; that, while some outward rejoicings are preserved for them, they may be able the more easily to consent to the inward joys. For there is no doubt that it is impossible to cut off everything at once from their obdurate hearts, for he who strives to ascend to the highest place, rises by degrees or steps, not by leaps. Thus the Lord indeed made himself known to the people of Israel in Egypt, but yet he retained for them in his own worship the use of sacrifices, which they were wont to offer to the devil, charging them to offer animals in sacrifice to him, to the end that with changed hearts they might lay aside one part of the sacrifice, whilst they retained another; and although the animals were the same as they had been accustomed to offer, yet, when they sacrificed them to God and not to idols, they would no longer be the same sacrifices. Therefore it behoves you, beloved, to say this to the aforesaid brother, that he, placed there at present, may consider how he ought to order all these things. God keep you safe, most loved son.

    "Given 17 June. . . ."[1]

CHAPTER XXXI. *Pope Gregory exhorted Augustine by a letter not to glory in his miracles.*

    At that time he also sent to Augustine a letter about the miracles which he had heard had been wrought by him, in which he exhorts him in these words not to incur the danger of elation in their great number:[2]

    "I know, dearest brother, that Almighty God reveals great miracles through you, beloved, to the nation whom he has been pleased to choose; wherefore you must rejoice in that same heavenly gift with fear, and fear with rejoicing. You may rejoice that the souls of the English are drawn by outer miracles to inward grace; but yet fear, lest amidst the signs which are wrought, the weak mind may be

[1] The rest of the date is exactly the same as that of the previous letter, but 17 June must be wrong, for it makes this letter earlier than that of chapter XXIX. Plummer shows that the true date is 18 July.
[2] For the full text of this letter, see Hadden and Stubbs, III, pp. 14-17. In the parts omitted by Bede, Gregory warns Augustine further with biblical examples.

puffed up in its own presumption, and, as it is externally raised to honour, may fall inwardly through vain-glory. For we ought to remember that when the disciples returned with joy from preaching, and said to their heavenly master: 'Lord, the devils also are subject to us in thy name',[1] they immediately heard: 'Rejoice not in this, but rejoice in this, that your names are written in heaven.'[2] For they who rejoiced in the miracles had set their minds on private and temporal joy, but they are recalled from the private to the general, from the temporal to the eternal joy, when it is said to them: 'Rejoice in this, that your names are written in heaven.' For not all the elect work miracles, but nevertheless the names of all of them are preserved written in heaven. For the disciples of truth should take no joy except in the good which they have in common with all, and in which there is no end to their gladness.

"And thus it remains, dearest brother, that amidst the things which by the operation of God you do outwardly, you always carefully judge yourself within, and carefully understand both what you are yourself, and how great grace there is towards that nation, for whose conversion you have received even the gift of working miracles. And if you remember any time when you have offended against our Creator either by word or by deed, you are always to call this to mind, that the memory of your guilt may crush the rising vain-glory in your heart. And whatever gifts of working miracles you shall receive, or have received, you are to reckon them not granted to you, but to those for whose salvation they are conferred on you."

CHAPTER XXXII. *Pope Gregory sent a letter and gifts to King Ethelbert.*

The same blessed Pope Gregory also sent at the same time a letter to King Ethelbert, together with several gifts of various kinds, being desirous also to glorify the king with temporal honours when he rejoiced that he had attained to the knowledge of the heavenly glory through his own labour and zeal. This is a copy of the aforesaid epistle:

"To the most glorious lord and his most excellent son Ethelbert, king of the English, Bishop Gregory.

"For this reason does Almighty God advance good men to the government of nations, that he may impart by means of them the gifts of his mercy to all over whom they are placed. We know this to have taken place in the nation of the English over whom your glory has been raised, in order that through the blessings granted to you, heavenly benefits may also be conferred on the nation subject to you. And therefore, illustrious son, guard with careful heart that grace which you have received from heaven, hasten to spread the Christian faith among the peoples subject to you, increase your righteous zeal for their conversion, suppress the worship of idols, cast down the buildings of the temples, build up the morals of your subjects by great purity of life, exhorting, terrifying, persuading, correcting, and setting an example of good works; that you may find a rewarder in heaven in him whose name and knowledge you will have spread on

---

[1] Luke x. 17.   [2] Luke x. 20.

earth. For he, whose honour you seek and maintain among the nations, will also render the fame of your glory more glorious even to posterity. . . .[1]

"Besides, we would have your Highness know, that, as we find in Holy Scripture from the words of the Almighty Lord, the end of the present world, is already at hand, and the kingdom of the saints is about to come, which will never end. But as the end of the world draws near, many things threaten us which have not been before; namely changes in the air, and terrors from the sky, and tempests against the order of the seasons, wars, famines, pestilences, earthquakes in divers places; which, however, will not all come in our days, but will all follow after our days. If, therefore, you perceive any of these to happen in your land, by no means let your mind be perturbed, for these signs of the end of the world are sent before, for this reason, that we should take heed to our souls, on the watch for the hour of death, and may be found prepared with good actions for the coming of the Judge. . . .

"Given the 22 June. . . ."[2]

CHAPTER XXXIII. *Augustine repaired the church of our Saviour, and built the monastery of the blessed Peter the Apostle; and concerning Peter, its first abbot.*

When, as we have said, Augustine had received an episcopal see in the royal city, he restored in it with the king's support a church which he had learnt had been built there of old by the work of the Roman believers, and consecrated it in the name of the holy Saviour our Lord and God Jesus Christ, and established there a residence for himself and all his successors. And he also built a monastery not far from that city, to the east, in which at his instigation Ethelbert built from the foundation the church of the blessed Apostles Peter and Paul, and enriched it with divers gifts; in which the bodies of Augustine himself and of all the bishops of Canterbury, and likewise of the kings of Kent, might be buried. But Augustine himself did not consecrate that church, but his successor Laurence.

The first abbot of that monastery was the priest Peter, who, being sent on a mission to Gaul, was drowned in the bay of the sea called Ambleteuse, and was committed to a mean tomb by the inhabitants of that place. But, in order that the Almighty God might show of what merit he was, a heavenly light appeared all night over his tomb, until the neighbours, who saw it, perceiving that he had been a holy man who had been buried there, and inquiring whence and who he was, removed the body and placed it in the church in the city of Boulogne with honour fitting such a man.

CHAPTER XXXIV. *Æthelfrith, king of the Northumbrians, vanquished the nations of the Scots in war and drove them from the territories of the English.*

At this time the very valiant King Æthelfrith, most eager for glory,[3] ruled over the kingdom of the Northumbrians, and more than all the chieftains of the English

---

[1] A comparison with the Emperor Constantine follows, and exhortations to spread the faith and to obey Augustine.

[2] The rest of the date as for the letter in chapter XXIX.

[3] This sounds like a translation of the Old English term of praise, *domgeornost*.

ravaged the nation of the Britons; so that he might be compared to Saul, once king of the Israelites, save only in this, that he was ignorant of the divine religion. For none of the leaders,[1] none of the kings, caused more of their lands either to pay tribute to the race of the English, or be settled by them, after they had exterminated or subdued the inhabitants. To him might justly be applied what the patriarch said when blessing his son in the person of Saul: "Benjamin a ravenous wolf, in the morning shall eat the prey, and in the evening shall divide the spoil."[2]

Hence Aedan, king of the Scots who dwell in Britain, alarmed by his success, came against him with an immense and strong army; but was defeated and fled with a few men; for almost all his army was cut down in that most famous place which is called *Degsastan*, that is, Degsa's stone.[3] Theobald, Æthelfrith's brother, perished also in that battle with all the army which he was leading. Æthelfrith brought this war to an end in the year of our Lord's incarnation 603, and in the 11th year of his reign, which lasted 24 years; moreover in the first year of Phocas, who then ruled the Roman empire. And from that time none of the kings of the Scots dared come into Britain to make war against the English even to this day.

BOOK II

CHAPTER I. *Of the death of the blessed Pope Gregory.*

At this time, that is, in the year of our Lord's incarnation 605, the blessed Pope Gregory, after he had ruled most gloriously the see of the Roman and Apostolic Church for 13 years, 6 months and 10 days, died, and was translated to an eternal see in the heavenly kingdom. It is fitting for us to discourse more at large concerning him in our *Ecclesiastical History*, seeing that by his zeal he converted our nation, that is, the nation of the English, from the power of Satan to the faith of Christ; and we can rightly, and should, call him our apostle. For as soon as he first ruled the pontificate of the whole world, and was placed over the Churches long since converted to the true faith, he made our nation, till then given up to idols, the Church of Christ, so that we may be permitted to apply to him the Apostle's words, that, if unto others he be not an apostle, yet to us he is, for we are the seal of his apostleship in the Lord. . . .[4]

To his works of piety and righteousness belongs also this, that he snatched our nation, through the preachers whom he sent hither, from the teeth of the ancient enemy and made it partaker of eternal freedom. And rejoicing in its faith and salvation, and commending it with worthy praise, he says himself in his exposition on the blessed Job: "Behold, the tongue of Britain, which only knew how to grind out barbarous sounds, has long since begun to resound the Hebrew Alleluia in the praise of God. Behold, the once swelling ocean now serves prostrate at the feet of the saints,

---

[1] Literally 'tribunes'. The O.E. version translates 'ealdormen'.
[2] Genesis xlix. 27.   [3] See p. 147, n. 8.
[4] Cf. I Corinthians ix. 2. Bede here proceeds to tell the life of Gregory, which I omit until, in the last paragraphs of it, he deals with the English mission. This should be compared with No. 152.

and its barbarous motions, which earthly princes could not subdue with the sword,
are now through the fear of God bound by the mouths of priests with words alone;
and the heathen who had no fear of troops of fighting men, now as a believer stands
in awe of the tongues of the humble. For since he has perceived the heavenly words,
and miracles also have been revealed, the strength of the divine knowledge is poured
into him, and he is held in check by the terror of that divinity, that he fears to do
evil, and longs with all his desires to come to the eternal grace." With these words
the blessed Gregory shows this also, that St. Augustine and his companions brought
the nation of the English to the acknowledgment of the truth, not alone by the
preaching of words, but also by the showing of celestial signs. . . .

Nor ought we to pass by in silence a story which has reached us from the tradition
of our ancestors concerning the blessed Gregory;[1] which tells why he was prompted
to such great care for the salvation of our nation. They say that one day, when
merchants had recently arrived, and many things for sale were collected in the market-
place, and many people had assembled to buy them, Gregory came himself with the
rest, and saw among other wares some boys put up for sale, white of body, pleasing
in countenance, and also with very beautiful hair. When he saw them, he inquired,
they say, from what region or country they had been brought. And he was told that
they were from the island of Britain, whose inhabitants were of such appearance.
Again, he asked whether the islanders were Christians, or still bound in pagan errors.
He was told that they were pagans. And, drawing a deep sigh from the depths of his
heart, he said: "Alas, the pity, that the author of darkness should possess men of such
bright countenances, and that so graceful an outward form should contain a mind
destitute of internal grace." Accordingly, he inquired again, what was the name of
that nation. He was answered that they were called Angles. And he said: "Good, for
they have angelic faces, and such are meet to be co-heirs with the angels in heaven.
What is the name of the province, from which they have been brought?" He was
answered that the people of that province were called the *Deire*. "Good", he said,
"Deire; snatched from wrath,[2] and called to the mercy of Christ. How is the king
of that province named?" He was told that he was called Ælle. And, playing on the
name, he said: "Alleluia, the praise of God the Creator ought to be sung in those
parts."

And he went to the bishop of the Roman and apostolic see, for he had not yet
been made bishop himself, and asked him to send some ministers of the word to the
nation of the English in Britain, by whom they might be converted to Christ; saying
he was himself ready to accomplish the work with the Lord's help, if it pleased the
apostolic pope that this should be done. While he could not carry this out, because,
though the pope was willing to grant him what he asked, the citizens of Rome could
not permit him to depart so far from the city, he accomplished the long desired work
as soon as he held the office of the pontificate; sending other preachers, indeed, but
helping their preaching to bear fruit by his exhortations and prayers. These things we
have thought fit to insert into our *Ecclesiastical History* according to the story which
we have received from the ancients.

---

[1] Cf. No. 152.   [2] *i.e. de ira*, punning on the name.

CHAPTER II. *Augustine admonished the bishops of the Britons on behalf of catholic peace, having also wrought a miracle in their presence; and what vengeance came upon them when they spurned him.*

Meanwhile Augustine, with the help of King Ethelbert, summoned to a conference with him the bishops and teachers of the nearest province of the Britons, at the place which to this day is called Augustine's oak in the language of the English, on the borders of the Hwicce and the West Saxons; and began to persuade them with brotherly admonition that, preserving catholic unity with him, they should under-take for the Lord's sake the common labour of preaching the gospel to the heathens. For they did not keep Easter Sunday at the proper time, but from the 14th to the 20th of the moon, which computation goes by a cycle of 84 years. Moreover, they did many other things contrary to the unity of the Church. When, after a long discussion, they would not comply with the prayers or exhortations or rebukes of Augustine and his companions, but preferred their traditions to all the Churches which throughout the world agree in Christ, the holy Father Augustine put an end to this troublesome and long contention, saying: "Let us beseech God, 'who makes men of one manner to dwell in the house'[1] of his Father, that he will deign to signify to us by heavenly signs which tradition is to be followed, and by what ways we are to hasten to enter his kingdom. Let some sick man be brought, and let us believe that the faith and practice of him through whose prayers he shall be healed are acceptable to God and ought to be followed by all." When the adversaries agreed to this, though unwillingly, a man of English race, who had lost the sight of his eyes, was brought. And when he was presented to the bishops of the Britons, and found no benefit nor cure from their ministry, at length Augustine, compelled by strict necessity, bowed his knees to the Father of our Lord Jesus Christ,[2] imploring that he would restore his lost sight to the blind man, and by the bodily enlightenment of one man would kindle the grace of spiritual light in the hearts of many of the faithful. Immediately the blind man received sight, and Augustine was hailed by all as the true herald of the highest light. The Britons then admitted that they perceived that it was the true way of righteousness which Augustine preached; but said they could not renounce their ancient customs without the consent and permission of their people. They therefore asked that a synod might be held a second time which more might attend.

When this was arranged, there came, it is said, seven bishops of the Britons and many very learned men, especially from their most celebrated monastery, which is called in the language of the English, the fort of Bangor,[3] over which Abbot Dinoot is said to have presided at that time. They that were to go to the aforesaid council came first to a certain holy and discreet man, who led the life of an anchorite among them, to consult with him whether they ought to desert their own traditions at the preaching of Augustine. He replied: "If he is a man of God, follow him." They said: "And how can we prove that?" And he said: "The Lord says: 'Take my yoke upon you and learn of me, because I am meek and humble of heart.'[4] If therefore that Augustine is meek and humble of heart, it is to be believed that he himself bears Christ's yoke, and offers it for you to bear; but if he is stern and proud, it is evident

---

[1] Psalm lxvii. 7.   [2] Ephesians iii. 14.   [3] Bangor-is-coed, Flintshire.   [4] Matthew xi. 29.

that he is not of God, nor are we to regard his words." They said again: "And how shall we tell even this?" "Contrive", he said, "that he may first arrive with his company at the place of the synod, and if on your approach he rises to meet you, hear him submissively, knowing that he is a servant of Christ; but if he despises you, and will not rise up in your presence, when you are more in number, let him also be despised by you."

They did as he said. And it happened that as they came, Augustine was sitting on a chair. Seeing this, they immediately became angry, and charging him with pride, they laboured to contradict everything he said. But he said to them: "You act in many things contrary indeed to our custom, nay, rather to that of the universal Church; but yet, if you will comply with me in these three things, to celebrate Easter at the proper time, to complete the ministry of baptism, by which we are re-born to God, according to the custom of the holy Roman and Apostolic Church, and to preach together with us the word of God to the nation of the English, we will calmly endure all the other things which you do, although contrary to our practices." But they replied that they would do none of those things, and would not have him for their archbishop, saying among themselves: "If he would not rise for us now, how much more will he despise us as of no account, if we begin to be in subjection to him?"

The man of the Lord, Augustine, is said to have foretold with threats that, if they would not have peace with their brethren, they would have war from their enemies; and, if they would not preach the way of life to the nation of the English, they would undergo the vengeance of death at their hands. This came about by the dispensation of the divine judgment, in every point just as he had foretold.

For afterwards, that most powerful king of the English of whom we have spoken, Æthelfrith, collected a mighty army and made a very great slaughter of that heretical nation at the city of the legions, which is called by the nation of the English *Legacaestir*,[1] but by the Britons more correctly *Carlegion*. And when he was about to give battle, and he saw their priests, who were come together to offer up their prayers to God for the soldiers who fought in the battle, standing apart in a safer place, he inquired who they were, and to what end they had gathered there. Most of them were of the monastery of Bangor, in which, it is said, there was so great a number of monks, that, though the monastery was divided into seven parts with superiors set over each, none of those parts had fewer than 300 men, who all lived from the labour of their hands. Many of these, having observed a fast of three days, assembled with others at the aforesaid battle to pray, and they had a defender, Brocmail by name, who was to protect them from the barbarians' swords whilst they were intent on prayer. When King Æthelfrith understood the reason of their coming, he said: "If then they cry to their God against us, in truth, though they do not bear arms, they fight against us, seeing that they assail us with curses." And so he commanded them to be attacked first, and then destroyed the rest of the impious army, not without much loss to his own army. They say that about 1,200 of those who came to pray were destroyed in that fight, and that only 50 escaped by flight. Brocmail turned his back with his men at the first approach of the enemy, and left those whom he ought to have defended,

[1] Chester.

unarmed and exposed to the attacking swords. And thus was fulfilled the prediction of the holy Bishop Augustine, although he himself had a long time before been taken up into the heavenly kingdom, that the heretics should feel the vengeance of temporal death also, because they had spurned the offer of eternal salvation.

CHAPTER III. *Augustine made Mellitus and Justus bishops; and concerning his death.*

In the year of our Lord's incarnation 604, Augustine, archbishop of Britain ordained two bishops, namely Mellitus and Justus; Mellitus to preach to the province of the East Saxons, who are divided from Kent by the River Thames and border on the eastern sea, and whose metropolis is the city of London, situated on the bank of the aforesaid river, and a mart of many nations coming to it by land and sea. In that nation at that time Sæberht, nephew to Ethelbert by his sister Ricule, reigned, although subject to the same Ethelbert, who, as has been said above, was supreme over all the races of the English as far as the River Humber. But when this province also received the word of truth by the preaching of Mellitus, King Ethelbert built in the city of London the church of St. Paul the Apostle, in which place both Mellitus and his successors were to have their episcopal see. But Justus Augustine ordained bishop in Kent itself, in the city of *Dorubrevis*, which the nation of the English call Rochester,[1] after a former chief of it, who was named Hrof. It is almost 24 miles west of the city of Canterbury, and in it King Ethelbert built a church of the blessed Apostle Andrew, and he also offered many gifts to the bishops of both these churches, as well as of Canterbury, adding lands and possessions for the use of those who were with the bishops.

But the beloved of God, our father Augustine, died, and his body was laid outside, close to the church of the blessed Apostles Peter and Paul, which we mentioned above, because it was not yet finished or dedicated. But as soon as it was dedicated, the body was brought in, and fittingly buried in its northern chapel;[2] in which were buried also the bodies of all following archbishops except two only, namely Theodore and Brihtwold, whose bodies were placed in the church itself, because the aforesaid chapel could not hold any more. Almost in the middle of it, it has an altar dedicated in honour of the blessed Pope Gregory, on which every Saturday their memorial Masses are solemnly celebrated by a priest of that place. Inscribed upon the tomb of Augustine is this epitaph: "Here rests the Lord Augustine, the first archbishop of Canterbury, who, being formerly sent hither by the blessed Gregory, bishop of the city of Rome, and supported by God with the working of miracles, brought King Ethelbert and his nation from the worship of idols to the faith of Christ, and having fulfilled in peace the days of his office, died on 26 May, in the reign of the same king."[3]

[1] *Hrofæscæster.*
[2] *Porticus.* The plan of this Canterbury church, which has been uncovered by excavation, shows that it had *porticus* both on the north and south sides. Other early Saxon churches also had one or more *porticus*, i.e. small chambers attached to the church, usually entered only by a narrow door. They were commonly used as burial chapels.
[3] Chapter IV tells how Laurence succeeded Augustine as archbishop, and sent letters on the observance of Easter to the Britons and to the Scots; and how Mellitus attended a synod in Rome and brought back its decrees to the English churches.

CHAPTER V. *After the death of the kings Ethelbert and Sæberht, their successors restored idolatry, on which account Mellitus and Justus left Britain.*

In the year of our Lord's incarnation 616, which is the 21st year after Augustine with his companions was sent to preach to the nation of the English, Ethelbert, king of the people of Kent, after his temporal kingdom which he had held most gloriously for 56 years, entered into the eternal joys of the heavenly kingdom. He was indeed the third of the kings in the nation of the English to hold dominion over all their southern provinces, which are divided from the northern by the River Humber and the boundaries adjoining it; but the first of them all to ascend to the heavenly kingdom. For the first who had sovereignty[1] of this kind was Ælle, king of the South Saxons; the second Caelin, king of the West Saxons, who in their language is called Ceawlin; the third, as we have said, Ethelbert, king of the people of Kent; the fourth, Rædwald, king of the East Angles, who, even while Ethelbert was alive, had been obtaining the leadership for his own race; the fifth, Edwin, king of the nation of the Northumbrians, that is, of that nation which dwells on the north side of the River Humber, ruled with greater power over all the peoples who inhabit Britain, the English and Britons as well, except only the people of Kent, and he also reduced under English rule the Mevanian islands[2] of the Britons, which lie between Ireland and Britain; the sixth, Oswald, also a most Christian king of the Northumbrians, held a kingdom with these same bounds; the seventh, his brother Oswiu, governing for some time a kingdom of almost the same limits, also subdued for the most part and made tributary the nations of the Picts and Scots, who hold the northern parts of Britain. But of this hereafter.[3]

King Ethelbert died on 24 February, 21 years after receiving the faith, and was buried in the chapel of St. Martin within the church of the blessed Apostles Peter and Paul, where also Queen Berhta lies buried. Among the other benefits which in his care for his people he conferred on them, he also established for them with the advice of his councillors judicial decrees after the example of the Romans, which, written in the English language, are preserved to this day and observed by them;[4] in which he first laid down how he who should steal any of the property of the Church, of the bishop, or of other orders, ought to make amends for it, desiring to give protection to those whom, along with their teaching, he had received.

This Ethelbert was the son of Eormenric, whose father was Octa, whose father was Oeric, surnamed Oisc,[5] after whom the kings of the people of Kent are wont to be called Oiscings; whose father was Hengest, who, invited by Vortigern, was the first to enter Britain with his son Oisc, as we have related above.

But after the death of Ethelbert, when his son Eadbald had received the government of the kingdom, this proved very harmful to the still tender growth of the Church there. For he not only refused to accept the faith of Christ, but also was defiled with fornication of such a kind as, the Apostle testifies,[6] was unheard of even among the Gentiles, that one should have his father's wife. By both these crimes he gave occasion for those to return to their former vomit who, under the rule of his

---

[1] *imperium.*   [2] Man and Anglesey.   [3] pp. 626, 638.   [4] No. 29.
[5] The Æsc of the Anglo-Saxon Chronicle, No. 1, p. 143.   [6] I Corinthians v. 1.

father, had accepted the laws of faith and chastity either for favour or fear of the king. Nor were the scourges of the heavenly severity lacking to punish and correct the unbelieving king; for he was seized by frequent attacks of madness, and possessed by an unclean spirit.

The storm of this disturbance was increased by the death of Sæberht, king of the East Saxons, who, when he sought the everlasting kingdom, left as heirs to a temporal kingdom his three sons, who had remained heathen. They began immediately to practise openly the idolatry which during his lifetime they seemed to have left off a little, and freely to give permission to their subjects to worship idols. And when they saw the bishop, in celebrating the solemnities of the Mass in the church, give the Eucharist to the people, they said, as it is commonly reported, puffed up with ignorant folly: "Why do you not give us also that white bread which you used to give to our father, Saba"—for thus they used to call him—"and still continue to give to the people in church?" To whom he replied: "If you will be washed in that font of salvation in which your father was washed, you can also be partakers of the holy bread of which he partook; but if you despise the laver of life, by no means can you receive the bread of life." And they said: "We will not enter that font, because we know that we have no need of it, but yet we will be fed with that bread." And when they had been earnestly and often admonished by him, that it could on no account be, that anyone should share in the sacred oblation without the sacred purification, they finally were moved to anger and said: "If you will not comply with us in so light a matter, as we request, you shall not stay any longer in our province." And they expelled him, and ordered him to leave their kingdom with his followers.

Being expelled from there, he went to Kent, to confer with Laurence and Justus, his fellow-bishops, what should be done in that case. And they decided by common consent that it was better for them all to return to their own land and serve God there with a free mind, than to remain to no purpose among barbarians revolted from the faith. And thus Mellitus and Justus departed first and withdrew into the regions of Gaul, intending to await the issue of events there. But the kings who had driven away from them the herald of the truth did not follow the worship of devils for very long with impunity. For they went out to battle against the nation of the Gewisse[1] and all fell together, along with their army. Yet, the people whom they had turned to wickedness, although the authors of it had perished, could not be corrected and recalled to the simplicity of the faith and charity, that is in Christ.[2]

CHAPTER VI. *Laurence, being reproved by the Apostle Peter, converted King Eadbald to Christ, and he immediately recalled Mellitus and Justus to their preaching.*

But when Laurence[3] was about to follow Mellitus and Justus and to leave Britain, he ordered a bed to be prepared for him for that night in the church of the blessed Apostles Peter and Paul, of which we have already often spoken. And when, after pouring out many prayers and tears to the Lord for the state of the Church, he laid himself to rest on it and fell asleep, the most blessed Prince of the Apostles appeared to him and, scourging him severely in the dead of night, inquired of him with apostolic

---

[1] An old name for the West Saxons.   [2] II Corinthians xi. 3.   [3] Augustine's successor as archbishop.

sternness why he was abandoning the flock which he had committed to him, or to what shepherd he was leaving the sheep of Christ in the midst of the wolves, when he himself was fleeing. "Have you", he said, "forgotten my example, who for the sake of the little ones of Christ, whom he had committed to me in token of his love, endured at the hands of infidels and enemies of Christ, bonds, stripes, imprisonment, afflictions, and finally death itself, even the death of the cross, to be crowned with Christ?" Roused by the stripes and also the exhortations of the blessed Peter, Laurence, the servant of Christ, went immediately in the morning to the king, and drawing back his garment showed with what stripes he had been torn. The king was greatly astonished, and asked who had dared to inflict such stripes upon so great a man; and when he heard that for the sake of his salvation the bishop had suffered such torments and blows from the Apostle of Christ, he was greatly afraid; and cursing all the idolatrous worship, and renouncing his unlawful marriage, he accepted the faith of Christ, and, being baptized, took care to promote and favour the interests of the Church in all matters as much as he could.

He sent also to Gaul, and recalled Mellitus and Justus, and bade them return freely to govern their churches; and they came back a year after they had gone away. Justus returned to the city of Rochester, where he had presided before; but the Londoners would not receive Bishop Mellitus, choosing rather to serve idolatrous high priests. For Eadbald had not the same kingly power as his father had had, that he could restore the bishop to his church with the pagans refusing and opposing it. However, he and his nation, after his conversion to the Lord, were zealous to obey the divine precepts. Lastly, he built the church of the holy Mother of God in the monastery of the most blessed Prince of the Apostles, which was consecrated by Archbishop Mellitus.[1]

CHAPTER IX. *Concerning the reign of King Edwin, and how Paulinus, coming to preach the gospel to him, first initiated his daughter with others in the sacraments of the Christian faith.*

At that time the race of the Northumbrians also, that is, the nation of the English which dwells on the north side of the River Humber, with their king, Edwin, received the word of the faith by the preaching of Paulinus, whom we mentioned above.[2] This king, as a presage of his acceptance of the faith and of the heavenly kingdom, received increased power of earthly dominion; so that he reduced under his control—what none of the English had done before him—all the territories of Britain, where there were provinces either of the English or the Britons. What is more, he subjugated to the rule of the English the Mevanian islands, as has been said above; the first of these, which is to the south, is both larger in extent and more fruitful in the yield and richness of its crops, and measures 960 hides according to the English computation; the second contains 300 and more.

The occasion of this nation's receiving the faith was that the aforesaid king was allied to the kings of the people of Kent, having taken to wife Æthelburh, who was

[1] Chapters VII and VIII record the accession of Mellitus (619), his miraculous quenching of a fire in Canterbury, his death in 624 and Justus's succession, and give the text of the letter from Pope Boniface to the latter, with the *pallium*, in which the pope mentions letters received from King Eadbald.
[2] p. 600.

otherwise called Tate, the daughter of King Ethelbert. When first he sent suitors to ask for this alliance from her brother, Eadbald, who was then ruling the kingdom of the people of Kent, he received the reply that it was not lawful for a Christian maiden to be given in marriage to a pagan, lest the faith and sacraments of the heavenly King should be profaned by union with a king who was entirely ignorant of the worship of the true God. When the messengers brought back these words to Edwin, he promised that he would do nothing in any way to oppose the Christian faith which the maiden practised; but that he would allow her to preserve the faith and practices of her religion according to Christian custom, with all who came with her, men or women, priests or thegns. Nor did he refuse to submit to that same religion himself, if when examined by his councillors it should be found to be more holy and more worthy of God.

And thus the maiden was promised, and sent to Edwin, and in accordance with what had been agreed, Paulinus, a man beloved of God, was ordained bishop to accompany her, and to confirm her and her companions both with daily exhortation and celebration of the heavenly sacraments, lest they should be corrupted by the society of the pagans.

Paulinus was consecrated bishop by Archbishop Justus on 21 July, in the year of our Lord's incarnation 625, and thus came with the said maiden to King Edwin as if an attendant at their union in the flesh; but rather with his whole mind he was intent on calling the nation to which he was going to the knowledge of the truth and, according to the words of the Apostle, presenting it as a chaste virgin to the one true husband, Christ.[1] And when he had come to that province, he laboured much, both to retain those who had come with him, by the help of the Lord, lest they should fall from the faith, and, if by chance he could, to convert some of the pagans to the grace of the faith by his preaching. But, as the Apostle says, although he laboured a long time in preaching the word: "The god of this world hath blinded the minds of unbelievers, that the light of the gospel of the glory of Christ should not shine unto them."[2]

The next year there came into the province a certain assassin, Eomer by name, sent by the king of the West Saxons called Cwichelm, hoping to deprive King Edwin of his kingdom and his life. He had a two-edged dagger, poisoned, so that if the wound made by the blade were not sufficient to kill the king, it would be helped by the deadliness of the poison. He came to the king on the first day of Easter, near the River Derwent, where there was a royal residence, and entered as if bearing a message from his lord; and while he was artfully delivering his pretended embassy, he started up suddenly, and, unsheathing his dagger under his mantle, made an attack on the king. And when Lilla, a most devoted king's thegn, saw this, not having a shield at hand with which to defend the king from death, he at once interposed his own body to receive the striker's blow. But the enemy thrust with such force that he also wounded the king through the body of the slain thegn. And when he was immediately attacked with swords on all sides, he also killed with his abominable dagger in that tumult another of the thegns, whose name was Forthhere.

[1] II Corinthians xi. 2.   [2] II Corinthians iv. 4.

On that same holy night of Easter, the queen had given birth to the king's daughter, whose name was Eanflæd. And when the king in the presence of Bishop Paulinus gave thanks to his gods for the birth of his daughter, the bishop, on the other hand, began to give thanks to the Lord Christ, and to assure the king that he by his prayers had obtained from him that the queen should bring forth the child in safety and without much pain. The king was delighted with his words, and promised that he would renounce idols and serve Christ if he granted him life and victory when fighting against that king by whom the murderer who had wounded him had been sent; and as a pledge for the fulfilment of his promise, he delivered up that same daughter to Bishop Paulinus to be dedicated to Christ. She was baptized on the holy day of Pentecost, first of the nation of the Northumbrians, with eleven others[1] from her household.

At that time, when the king had been healed from the wound inflicted some time before, he collected an army and marched against the nation of the West Saxons, and joining battle, either killed or forced to surrender those whom he had learnt to have plotted his death. And thus returning a victor to his own land, he would not immediately and unadvisedly receive the sacraments of the Christian faith, although from the time when he had promised that he would serve Christ he no longer served idols. But first he took heed both to learn more diligently at leisure the doctrine of the faith from that venerable man Paulinus, and to discuss with those whom he knew to be the wisest of his leading men what they thought ought to be done in this matter. And since he was himself a man of great natural shrewdness, he often sat long alone, silent indeed, but communing with himself in the depths of his heart what he ought to do, and which religion ought to be followed.[2]

CHAPTER XII. *Edwin was persuaded to believe by a vision once shown to him as an exile.*[3]

. . . Also a heavenly vision, which the divine goodness had been pleased once to reveal to him when an exile with Rædwald, king of the Angles, helped his mind not a little to grasp and understand the counsel of the doctrine of salvation. For when Paulinus saw that it was with difficulty that the haughtiness of the king's mind could be inclined to the humility of the way of salvation, and to the reception of the mystery of the life-giving Cross, he employed for the salvation of him and at the same time of the people over whom he was set, both words of exhortation among men and words of supplication to the divine goodness; at length, it seems probable, he learnt in the spirit what was the nature of a prophecy formerly revealed from heaven to the king. Nor did he lose any time, but immediately admonished the king to carry out his vow, which, when he received the oracle, he had promised to perform if he were delivered from his trouble at that time and advanced to the throne.

The prophecy was as follows: When he was being persecuted by Æthelfrith, who

---

[1] Some manuscripts have twelve. Possibly the tradition used the ambiguous expression *twelfa sum*, on which see p. 148, n. 5.

[2] Chapters x and xi are entirely taken up with letters of Pope Boniface to King Edwin and Queen Æthelburh, of general exhortation.

[3] Cf. No. 152.

reigned before him, he wandered for a space of many years through many places and kingdoms in hiding as an exile, and at length came to Rædwald, beseeching him to save his life by protecting him from the snares of so great an enemy; and he received him willingly and promised to do what he asked. But after Æthelfrith learnt that he had appeared in that province and was living in the king's following with his companions, he sent messengers to offer Rædwald a great sum of money to slay him; but with no effect. He sent a second and a third time, offering more plentiful gifts of money, and threatening war on him if he refused. And Rædwald, whether weakened by the threats or corrupted by the gifts, complied with his requests and promised either to kill Edwin himself or to hand him over to the envoys. When a certain very loyal friend discovered this, he went to the chamber where he was going to bed, for it was the first hour of the night, and calling him out, told him what the king had promised to do with him, adding: "If, therefore, you are willing, I will this very hour lead you out of this province and bring you into a place where neither Rædwald nor Æthelfrith will ever be able to find you." He replied: "I thank you indeed for your goodwill; but yet I cannot do what you suggest, and be the first to make void the agreement I entered into with so great a king, when he has done me no harm, nor as yet shown me any hostility. But, on the contrary, if I am to die, let him, rather than some baser person, deliver me to death. For whither may I now flee, when for the course of so many years and seasons I have been a wanderer through all the provinces of Britain to escape the snares of enemies?" When his friend had gone, Edwin remained alone outside, and sitting with a heavy heart before the palace, he began to be overwhelmed by vacillating thoughts, not knowing what to do or which way to turn.

And when, for a long time in silent anguish of mind, he "was consumed with a hidden fire",[1] he suddenly saw in the silence of the dead of night a man of unknown face and habit approaching him; and when he saw him, thus unknown and unexpected, he was not a little afraid. But the man approaching greeted him and asked why at that hour, when others were at rest and fast asleep, he alone should sit there watchful and sad on a stone. He, in his turn, asked what concern it was of his whether he spent the night indoors or out. The stranger said in reply: "Do not think that I am ignorant of the cause of your grief and sleeplessness and sitting alone outside; for I know most surely who you are and why you grieve and what evils you fear will fall upon you shortly. But tell me, what reward would you give to the man, if such there were, who should deliver you from these troubles and persuade Rædwald not to do you any harm himself nor deliver you to perish at your enemies' hands?" And when he replied that he would give everything he could in reward for such a service, the stranger added: "What if he promised also that you should in truth destroy your enemies and become king, so that you should surpass in power not only all your ancestors, but all who were kings before you in the nation of the English?" And Edwin, encouraged by his questioning, did not hesitate to promise that he would make a recompense worthy of the favours to him who should grant him such great benefits. Then the other spoke a third time: "But if", he said, "he who foretells

---

[1] Virgil, *Aeneid* iv. 2.

truly that so many and great gifts are to befall you, could also give you better and more useful counsel for your life and safety than any of your ancestors or kinsmen ever heard of, do you consent to obey him and receive his salutary advice?" Edwin did not hesitate to promise at once that he would follow in all things the teaching of him who should bring him out from so many and great calamities and advance him to the throne. And when he had received this reply, the man who was speaking with him suddenly placed his right hand on his head, saying: "When this sign shall be given you, remember this time and our talk, and do not delay to carry out what you now promise." And when he had said this, he is said to have suddenly vanished, that the king might understand that it was not a man who had appeared to him, but a spirit.

And whilst the royal youth still sat there alone, glad, indeed, at the consolation offered him, but very anxious, and carefully pondering who he who had said these things to him might be, and where he had come from, his aforesaid friend came to him, and greeting him with a joyful face said: "Rise and go inside, and calmly and relieved of your fears set your body and mind at rest, for the king has had a change of heart, and designs to do you no harm, but rather to keep his plighted faith; for when he showed the queen in secret his plan of which I told you before, she dissuaded him from his purpose, reminding him that it was on no account fitting for so great a king to sell for gold his best friend placed in distress, and thus to lose for money his honour, which was more precious than all treasures." In short, the king did as has been said; not only did he refuse to give up the exile to the enemy messengers, but he also helped him to gain his kingdom. For, as soon as the messengers returned home, he collected a mighty army to war against Æthelfrith, and when the latter met him with a very inferior force, for Rædwald had not given him time to summon and assemble his whole army, he killed him in the territories of the Mercian people on the east bank of the river which is called Idle. In this fight there was killed also a son of Rædwald, Regenhere by name. And thus, in accordance with the prophecy which he had received, Edwin not only escaped the snares of the king, his enemy, but also succeeded to the glory of the kingdom after he was killed.

When therefore Paulinus was preaching the word of God and the king delayed his acceptance, and for some time, as we have said, was wont to sit alone at fitting hours and investigate carefully what he ought to do and what religion ought to be followed, the man of God came to him one day, and laid his right hand on his head and asked whether he recognized that sign. And when, trembling, the king would have fallen at his feet, Paulinus raised him up, addressing him in a voice he seemed to recognize, and said: "Behold, you have escaped by the gift of God from the hands of the enemies whom you feared; behold, by his bounty, you have obtained the kingdom which you desired. Take heed not to delay to do the third thing, which you promised, by receiving the faith and observing the precepts of him, who, besides delivering you from temporal adversity, has raised you to the dignity of a temporal kingdom; and if henceforth you are willing to obey his will, which he signifies to you through me, he will also deliver you from the perpetual torments of the wicked, and make you to be partaker with him in the eternal kingdom of heaven."

CHAPTER XIII. *How the same king held a council with his chief men about the reception of the faith of Christ; and how his high priest profaned his own altars.*

When the king had heard these words, he replied that he was both willing and bound to receive the faith which he taught. Still, he said that he would confer about it with his loyal chief men and counsellors, so that if they also were of his opinion they might all be consecrated to Christ together in the font of life. And with Paulinus's assent, he did as he had said. For, holding a council with his wise men, he asked of each in turn what he thought of this doctrine, previously unknown, and of this new worship of God, which was preached.

The chief of his priests, Coifi, at once replied to him: "See, king, what manner of thing this is which is now preached to us; for I most surely admit to you, what I have learnt beyond a doubt, that the religion which we have held up till now has no power at all and no use. For none of your followers has applied himself to the worship of our gods more zealously than I; and nevertheless there are many who receive from you more ample gifts and greater honours than I, and prosper more in all things which they plan to do or get. But if the gods were of any avail, they would rather help me, who have been careful to serve them more devotedly. It remains, therefore, that if on examination you find these new things, which are now preached to us, better and more efficacious, we should hasten to receive them without any delay."

Another of the king's chief men, assenting to his persuasive and prudent words, immediately added: "Thus, O king, the present life of men on earth, in comparison with that time which is unknown to us, appears to me to be as if, when you are sitting at supper with your ealdormen and thegns in the winter-time, and a fire is lighted in the midst and the hall warmed, but everywhere outside the storms of wintry rain and snow are raging, a sparrow should come and fly rapidly through the hall, coming in at one door, and immediately out at the other. Whilst it is inside, it is not touched by the storm of winter, but yet, that tiny space of calm gone in a moment, from winter at once returning to winter, it is lost to your sight. Thus this life of men appears for a little while; but of what is to follow, or of what went before, we are entirely ignorant. Hence, if this new teaching brings greater certainty, it seems fit to be followed." The rest of the nobles and king's counsellors, by divine inspiration, spoke to the same effect.

But Coifi added that he would like more attentively to hear Paulinus speak about the God whom he preached. And when by the king's orders he did so, Coifi, having heard his words, called out: "I long since perceived that what we worshipped was naught; for the more zealously I sought for truth in that worship, the less I found. But now I confess openly that there shines in this preaching that truth which can confer on us the gifts of life, health and everlasting happiness. Therefore I suggest, O king, that we quickly condemn and deliver to the flames the temples and altars which we have consecrated without reaping any profit." To cut a long story short, the king gave open consent for Paulinus to preach the gospel, and, renouncing idolatry, acknowledged that he received the faith of Christ. And when he inquired of the aforesaid high priest of their rites, who should first profane the altars and temples of the idols, with the precincts which surrounded them, he answered: "I will; for who may now more fittingly destroy the things which I worshipped through folly, as an example to all others through the wisdom truly granted to me by God?" And immediately, abjuring vain superstitious folly, he asked the king to give him weapons and a stallion on which to mount and ride to destroy the idols. For the high priest had not been allowed either to carry weapons or to ride on anything but a mare. Accordingly he bound on his sword and took a spear in his hand, and mounting the king's stallion he proceeded to the idols. When the multitude saw this, they thought he had gone mad. And as soon as he drew near to the temple, he did not hesitate to profane it, throwing into it the spear which he held; and rejoicing greatly in the knowledge of the worship of the true God, he ordered his fellows to destroy and set fire to the temple with all its precincts. The former place of the idols is still shown, not far from York, to the east, beyond the River Derwent, and it is today called Goodmanham, where the high priest himself, at the inspiration of the true God, defiled and destroyed those altars which he himself had consecrated.[1]

CHAPTER XIV. *The same Edwin became Christian with all his nation; and where Paulinus baptized.*

So King Edwin with all the nobility of his nation and many of the people received the faith and the laver of holy regeneration in the eleventh year of his reign, which was the year of our Lord's incarnation 627, and about 180 years from the coming of the English into Britain. He was baptized at York on the holy day of Easter, 12 April, in the church of the Apostle Peter which he himself had hastily built there in wood, while he was a catechumen receiving instruction for his baptism. In that city also he gave an episcopal see to his teacher and bishop, Paulinus. But as soon as he was baptized, he was eager by Paulinus's direction to construct in that place a larger and more majestic church of stone, in the middle of which might be enclosed the oratory which he had made before. When the foundations had been laid around the former oratory, he began to build the church foursquare. But before the walls reached their full height the king himself was wickedly killed, and left the work to be completed by his successor, Oswald. However, for six years on end from that time, that is, until the end of the reign of the king, Paulinus by his consent and favour preached the word of God in that province; and as many as were fore-ordained to eternal life believed and were baptized, among whom were the sons of King Edwin, Osfrith and Eadfrith, who had both been born to him in his exile by Cwenburh, daughter of Ceorl, king of the Mercians.

Afterwards his other children, born of Queen Æthelburh, were baptized, Æthelhun and a daughter Æthelthryth, and a second son Uscfrea, of whom the first two were seized from this life while still in the white baptismal robes, and buried in the church of York. Yffi, son of Osfrith, was also baptized, besides not a few other noble and royal persons. It is said that the fervour of the faith of the people of the Northumbrians and their desire for the laver of salvation were so great that on one occasion Paulinus, coming with the king and queen to the royal residence which is called Yeavering,

[1] Virgil, *Aeneid* ii. 502.

spent 36 days with them there fully occupied in catechizing and baptizing; during which days he did nothing else from early morning till evening but instruct the people, who flocked to him from all villages and places, in Christ's saving word, and wash them after instruction with the laver of remission in the River Glen, which was near by. This residence was deserted in the time of later kings, and another was made instead of it in the place which is called *Maelmin*.[1]

These things happened in the province of the Bernicians; but in the province of the Deirans also, where he was often wont to stay with the king, he baptized in the River Swale, which flows by the village of Catterick. For oratories or baptisteries could not yet be built in the early infancy of the Church there. However, in *Campodunum*,[2] where also there was then a royal residence, he built a church, which afterwards, with the whole of the place, was burnt by the pagans who killed King Edwin; in its place later kings made for themselves a residence in the region which is called Leeds. But the altar, since it was of stone, escaped the fire, and it is still kept in the monastery of the most reverend abbot and priest, Thrythwulf, which is in the forest of Elmet.

CHAPTER XV. *The province of the East Angles received the faith of Christ.*

King Edwin had so great devotion to the true worship that he also persuaded the king of the East Angles, Eorpwold, son of Rædwald, to abandon the idolatrous superstitions and receive, along with his province, the faith and sacraments of Christ. And indeed, his father, Rædwald, had long before been admitted in Kent to the sacraments of the Christian faith, but in vain; for on his return home he was seduced by his wife and certain perverse teachers, and being turned from the sincerity of his faith, his later state was worse than the former; so that after the manner of the ancient Samaritans, he seemed to serve both Christ and the gods which he had served before; and in the same temple he had both an altar for the Christian sacrifice and a small altar[3] for offering victims to devils. Ealdwulf, king of that same province, who lived in our time, testifies that that temple lasted until his time, and that he saw it in his boyhood.

The aforesaid King Rædwald was noble by birth, although ignoble in his actions; he was the son of Tytil, whose father was Wuffa, after whom the kings of the East Angles are called Wuffings.

But Eorpwold was killed not long after he had received the faith, by a heathen called Ricberht; and for three years from then the province was given over to error, until the brother of Eorpwold, Sigeberht, succeeded to the kingdom, a man most Christian in all ways and most learned, who during his brother's lifetime, when an exile in Gaul, had been initiated into the sacraments of the faith, and was eager to make all his province partake of them as soon as he began to reign. His exertions were splendidly promoted by Bishop Felix, who, when he had come from the districts of the Burgundians, where he had been reared and ordained, to Archbishop

---

[1] Unidentified.

[2] The Roman station of *Cambodunum*, which is now believed to have been near Dewsbury. See *Archaeologia*, XCIII, p. 43.

[3] The diminutive, may, however, be contemptuous rather than an indication of size.

Honorius, and had told him his desire, was sent by him to preach the word of life to the aforesaid nation of the Angles. Nor were his wishes in vain; for the pious husbandman of the spiritual field found there a large harvest of believers. Indeed, according to the inner meaning of his name he freed all that province from long iniquity and unhappiness and brought it to the faith and works of righteousness and the gifts of perpetual happiness, and received an episcopal see in the city of Dunwich; and after he had presided over that province with pontifical authority for seventeen years, he ended his life in peace there.

CHAPTER XVI. *How Paulinus preached in the province of Lindsey, and of the nature of Edwin's rule.*

Paulinus preached the word also in the province of Lindsey, which is the first on the south bank of the River Humber, reaching as far as the sea; and he first converted to the Lord the reeve[1] of the city of Lincoln, whose name was Blæcca, with his household. He likewise built in that city a church of splendid workmanship in stone. Though its roof has fallen either through long neglect or the hands of enemies, its walls may be seen standing yet, and every year some miracles of healing are wrought in that place, for the benefit of those who seek them with faith. In that church, after Justus had departed to Christ, Paulinus consecrated Honorius bishop in his stead, as we shall later relate in its place.

Regarding the faith in this province, a most trustworthy man, priest and abbot of the monastery of Partney, by name Deda, has told me that an old man informed him that he was baptized by Bishop Paulinus at midday, in the presence of King Edwin, along with a great crowd of people, in the River Trent by the city which is called in the English language *Tiowulfingacæstir*.[2] The old man was also wont to describe the person of the same Paulinus, that he was a man tall of stature, a little stooping, with black hair and a thin face, a hooked and thin nose, his aspect both venerable and awe-inspiring. He had also with him in his ministry James the deacon, a truly zealous man and renowned in Christ and in the Church, who survived to our days.

It is said that there was such great peace at that time in Britain, wherever the dominion of King Edwin extended, that, as it is proverbially said until today, if a woman with her new-born babe chose to wander throughout the island from sea to sea, she could without molestation. That king took such care for the good of his people, that in many places where he saw clear springs near the highways, he caused stakes to be fixed, with copper cups hanging on them, for the refreshment of travellers; and no one dared touch them except for their proper use because of their great fear of him, nor wished to, because of their affection. Truly he kept such great state in his kingdom, that not only were his banners borne before him in war, but even in time of peace his standard-bearer always went before him as he rode between his cities, his residences and provinces with his thegns. Also, when he walked anywhere along the

---

[1] *praefectus.*
[2] Identified with Littleborough, Notts., the only place on the Trent below Newark with a Roman settlement large enough to be called a 'city'.

streets, that sort of banner which the Romans call 'tufa'[1] and the English 'thuuf' was usually borne before him.[2]

CHAPTER XX. *When Edwin had been killed, Paulinus, returning to Kent, received the bishopric of the church of Rochester.*

But when Edwin had ruled most gloriously over the nation of the English and of the Britons as well for seventeen years, for six of which, as we have said, he also was a soldier for the kingdom of Christ, Cadwallon,[3] king of the Britons, rebelled against him, supported by Penda, a very vigorous man of the royal stock of the Mercians, who from that date ruled over the kingdom of that nation for twenty-two years with varying fortune; and when an important battle was fought on the plain which is called Hatfield,[4] Edwin was killed on 12 October, in the year of our Lord's incarnation 633,[5] when he was 48 years old, and his whole army was either killed or dispersed. In the same battle one of his sons, Osfrith, a warlike youth, was killed before him, another, Eadfrith, forced by necessity, went over to King Penda, and was afterwards killed by him in Oswald's reign, contrary to the faith of his oath.

At this time a great slaughter was made in the Church and nation of the Northumbrians, especially because one of the leaders, by whom it was made, was a pagan, and the other a barbarian more cruel than a pagan. For Penda, with all the nation of the Mercians, was devoted to idols, and a stranger to the name of Christ; but Cadwallon, although he had the name and profession of a Christian, was yet so barbarous in mind and behaviour that he spared neither women nor innocent children, but with bestial cruelty gave all over to death by torture, and overran in his fury all their provinces for a long time, intending to exterminate the whole race of the English from the territories of Britain. Nor did he pay any respect to the Christian religion which had sprung up among them. Indeed it is the custom of the Britons to this day to hold of no account the faith and religion of the English, and to have no intercourse with them any more than with pagans. King Edwin's head was brought to York and afterwards placed in the church of the blessed Apostle Peter, which he himself had begun, but which his successor Oswald finished, as we said above.[6] It was laid in the chapel of the holy Pope Gregory, from whose disciples he had received the word of life.

The affairs of the Northumbrians being thus thrown into confusion at this moment of disaster, when there seemed no safety anywhere except in flight, Paulinus took with

---

[1] On this word see M. Deanesly in *Eng. Hist. Rev.*, LVIII. pp. 136–142. She shows that Bede took it from Vegetius's *Epitome de re militari*, where it is probably an early scribal error, and no doubt associated it with the Old English word meaning 'tuft' merely because of its similarity in form.

[2] Chap. XVII contains the letter written by Pope Honorius to King Edwin, congratulating him on his conversion; he sends the *pallium* both to Paulinus and the newly consecrated archbishop of Canterbury, so that on the death of either, the survivor may consecrate a successor without the long and dangerous journey to Rome. Chap. XVIII mentions again the death of Justus and the consecration of his successor Honorius by Paulinus, and then gives Pope Honorius's letter to Archbishop Honorius of Canterbury, repeating the arrangement about the consecration of archbishops. It is dated 11 June 634. It was apparently not yet known at Rome that Edwin had been killed on 12 October 632 (if Bede begins his year on 24 September), and Paulinus had fled to Kent. Chap. XIX gives extracts from letters of Popes Honorius and John to the Scots on the Easter question, along with warning against the Pelagian heresy.

[3] King of Gwynedd.   [4] Some place in Hatfield Chase.

[5] 632 in our reckoning, if Bede is beginning his year in September.   [6] p. 618.

him Queen Æthelburh, whom he had originally brought there, and returned to Kent by ship, and was received with great honour by Archbishop Honorius and King Eadbald. He came there conducted by Bass, a very brave thegn of King Edwin, having with him Edwin's daughter Eanflæd and his son Uscfrea, and also Yffi, the son of the king's son Osfrith; these boys the mother afterwards, in fear of the kings Eadbald and Oswald, sent to Gaul, to be brought up by King Dagobert, who was her friend; and there they both died in infancy, and were buried in the church with the honour due to royal children and to innocents of Christ. Paulinus also brought away with him many precious vessels of King Edwin's, including a great gold cross and a chalice of gold, consecrated for the service at the altar, which are still kept and shown in the church of Kent.

At this time the church of Rochester had no pastor, for Romanus, its bishop, being sent by Archbishop Justus as an envoy to Pope Honorius, was drowned in the Italian sea; thus the aforesaid Paulinus received his charge at the invitation of the prelate Honorius and King Eadbald, and held it until he in his time ascended to the heavenly kingdom with the fruit of his glorious labours. Dying in that church, he left there the *pallium* which he had received from the Roman pope.

But he left in his church at York James the deacon, truly a holy man and one fully versed in the rites of the Church; who, continuing in that church for a long time after, rescued much prey from the ancient enemy by teaching and baptizing. The village where he mainly used to dwell, near Catterick, is named after him to this day. And since he was very highly skilled in singing in church, when peace was restored in the province, and the number of the faithful increased, he began also to teach to many the ecclesiastical singing according to the manner of the Romans and the men of Kent. And, old and full of days, as the Scriptures say, he went the way of his fathers.

BOOK III

CHAPTER I. *The next successors of King Edwin betrayed both the faith of their nation and the kingdom, but the most Christian king, Oswald, restored both.*

When Edwin had been killed in battle, he was succeeded in the kingdom of the Deirans, to which province his family belonged, and where he had first begun to reign, by the son of his uncle Ælfric, Osric by name, who had been admitted to the sacraments of the faith through the preaching of Paulinus. But the kingdom of the Bernicians—for the nation of the Northumbrians was of old divided into these two provinces—passed to Eanfrith, the son of Æthelfrith, who derived his origin and right to reign from that province. For all the time that Edwin reigned, the sons of the aforesaid Æthelfrith, who had reigned before him, lived in exile with a large band of young nobles among the Scots or the Picts, and there were instructed according to the doctrine of the Scots and renewed with the grace of baptism. And as they were allowed to return to their country when the king their enemy was dead, the aforesaid Eanfrith, the eldest of them, received the kingdom of the Bernicians. Both these kings, when they received the dignity of an earthly kingdom, renounced and betrayed the sacraments of the heavenly kingdom, into which they had been initiated, and again delivered themselves up to defilement and damnation through their former idolatrous abominations.

Not long after, Cadwallon, king of the Britons, killed them both, with impious hand, but righteous vengeance. And first, in the next summer, when Osric was rashly besieging him in the municipal town,[1] he suddenly sallied out with all his troops and destroyed him, taken by surprise, with all his army. Then, when for a whole year he had possessed the provinces of the Northumbrians, not like a victorious king, but despoiling them as a raging tyrant, and harrying them with fearful slaughter, he at length condemned Eanfrith, who unadvisedly came to him with twelve of his chosen thegns to sue for peace, to a like fate. To this day, that year is looked upon as unhappy and hateful to all good men, as well on account of the apostasy of the kings of the English who had cast off the sacraments of the faith, as of the outrageous tyranny of the British king. Hence it has been agreed by all who reckon the dates of kings, to abolish the memory of those faithless monarchs and assign that year to the reign of the succeeding king, namely Oswald, a man loved of God; who, after the slaying of his brother Eanfrith, advanced with an army, small, but strengthened·with the faith of Christ; and the impious leader of the Britons with those immense forces, which he boasted nothing could resist, was killed in the place which is called in the language of the English, *Denisesburna*,[2] that is, the brook of Denis.

CHAPTER II. *Among other innumerable miracles of healing by the wood of the cross which that king erected when about to fight against the barbarians, a certain man was cured of a broken arm.*

The place is still pointed out to this day, and held in great veneration, where Oswald raised the sign of the Holy Cross when about to engage in this battle, and prayed to God on his knees, that he should succour with heavenly help his worshippers in such sore need. Then, it is said, when the cross had been made in haste and the hole dug in which it was to be put, the king himself, burning with faith, laid hold of it and placed it in the ditch, and held it upright with both hands until the earth was heaped up by the soldiers and it was made fast. When this was done, uplifting his voice he proclaimed to the whole army: "Let us all kneel, and together beseech the almighty, living and true God to defend us in his mercy from the proud and savage enemy; for he knows that we have undertaken a just war for the safety of our nation." All did as he had ordered, and thus, advancing on the enemy as dawn was breaking, they obtained the victory as their faith deserved.[3] In the place where he prayed innumerable miraculous cures are known to have been revealed, as a sign and memorial of the king's faith. For even until today many are wont to cut off shavings of the wood of that sacred cross, which they put in water, and give it for sick men or cattle to drink, or sprinkle them with it, and they are at once restored to health.

That place is called in the English language 'Heavenfield', which can be rendered *caelestis campus* in Latin, which name it obviously received of old as a presage of future events, denoting, surely, that the heavenly trophy was to be erected there, a heavenly

---

[1] York.   [2] Now called Rowley Water, Northumberland.
[3] Cf. the account of this battle in No. 153.

victory begun, and heavenly miracles performed until today. The place is near the wall in the north by which the Romans once shut off the whole of Britain from sea to sea to prevent the attacks of the barbarians, as we have said above. And the brothers of the church of Hexham, which is not far away, have now for a long time made it their custom to come every year on the day before that on which King Oswald was afterwards slain, and keep vigils in that place for the salvation of his soul, and, having sung many psalms of praise, to offer for him the next morning the sacrifice of the holy oblation. And as that good custom has spread, they have lately by building a church there made the place more sacred and more honoured by all men; and this with good reason, for we have ascertained that no symbol of the Christian faith, no church, no altar was erected in the whole nation of the Bernicians before the new leader of the army, prompted by the devotion of his faith, set up this standard of the Holy Cross when about to give battle to that most savage enemy. . . .[1]

CHAPTER III. *The same king asked for a bishop from the people of the Scots and received Aidan, and gave to him an episcopal see on the island of Lindisfarne.*

Accordingly the same Oswald, as soon as he received the kingdom, desired that all the nation which he began to rule should be imbued with the grace of the Christian faith, of which he had already had very great proof in defeating the barbarians, and sent to the chief men of the Scots, among whom he had himself in exile received the sacrament of baptism with those of his thegns who were with him, asking them to send him a bishop, that the nation of the English whom he was ruling might by his teaching and ministry both learn the gifts and receive the sacraments of the faith of the Lord. Nor were they slow in granting what he asked; for he received Bishop Aidan, a man of the greatest gentleness, godliness and moderation, and possessing the zeal of God, although not entirely according to knowledge. For he was accustomed to observe the day of the Lord's Easter according to the manner of his nation, as we have frequently mentioned, from the 14th to the 20th of the moon. Indeed at that time the northern province of the Scots and all the nation of the Picts still celebrated the Lord's Easter after that manner, thinking that in this observance they were following the writings of the holy and praiseworthy Father Anatolius. Whether this is true, every skilled person may easily discover. But the Scots who dwelt in the southern parts of Ireland had long before learnt to observe Easter by the canonical rite, by the admonition of the bishop of the apostolic see.

On the arrival of the bishop, the king gave him a place for an episcopal see on the island of Lindisfarne, where he himself desired. This place, as the tide ebbs and flows, is twice a day enclosed by the waves of the sea like an island, and twice becomes connected with the land when the shore is left dry. And humbly and willingly paying heed to his admonitions in all matters, the king industriously applied himself to building and extending the Church of Christ in his kingdom. It was a beautiful sight to see the king acting there as interpreter of the heavenly word to his ealdormen and thegns when the bishop was preaching the gospel, since the bishop did not know the English language thoroughly; for the king had fully learnt the language of the Scots during

[1] Here follows the account of the healing of a monk of Hexham who broke his arm by falling on the ice.

his long exile. From that time there came many every day from the region of the Scots to Britain, and preached the word of the faith with great devotion to those provinces of the English over which Oswald reigned, and those of them who had received priests' orders ministered the grace of baptism to believers. Churches were built in various places; the people joyfully flocked to hear the word; possessions and estates were given by the gift of the king for the founding of monasteries; English children, as well as older people, were instructed by Scottish masters in study and the observance of monastic discipline.

For those who came to preach were mainly monks. Bishop Aidan himself was a monk, having been sent out from the island which is called Iona, whose monastery was for a long time the chief of almost all monasteries of the northern Scots and of all the Picts, and had the direction of their people. That island indeed belongs to Britain, being separated from it by a small arm of the sea, but the monastery had long before been bestowed on the monks of the Scots by the gift of the Picts who inhabit those parts of Britain, because they received the faith of Christ from their preaching.[1]

CHAPTER v. *Of the life of Bishop Aidan.*

From this island, from the community of these monks, Aidan was sent to instruct the province of the English in Christ, having received bishop's orders. At that time the abbot and priest Seghine was over that monastery. Among other lessons on how to live, Aidan left to the clerics a most salutary example of abstinence and continence; and it specially commended his teaching to all, that he taught nothing that he did not practise with his followers. For he cared neither to seek anything of this world nor to love it. Everything which was given to him by kings or rich men of the world, he took pleasure in bestowing at once on any poor men whom he met. He used to travel both through town and country on foot, not on horseback, unless perhaps compelled by great necessity; to the end that wherever he saw anyone, rich or poor, as he went, he might instantly turn aside to them and either invite them, if they were unbelievers, to receive the mystery of the faith, or, if they were believers, strengthen them in that faith, and incite them to almsgiving and the performance of good works by his words and actions.

His manner of life was so different from the slothfulness of our times that all those who bore him company, whether clerics or laymen, had to study, that is, to be engaged in either reading the Scriptures or learning psalms. This was the daily employment of himself and all who were with him, wherever they went. And if by chance it happened, which however happened rarely, that he was summoned to the king's table, he went with one cleric or two; and, when he had eaten a little, he hastened to leave, either to read with his followers, or to pray. Influenced by his

---

[1] Chap. IV describes the mission of Columba to the northern Picts and of Ninian to the southern Picts, which resulted in the building of a church dedicated to St. Martin, where Ninian was buried. In Bede's time it belonged to the Bernicians and was called 'At the White House' (Whithorn), from the church being built in stone. Particulars are added on the constitution of Iona, and on the winning over of the monastery to the catholic Easter by the Englishman Egbert in 715. In his chronological summary Bede assigns this to 716.

example, all religious men and women at that time adopted the custom of prolonging their fast on Wednesdays and Fridays throughout the year until the ninth hour, except for the relaxation in the fifty days after Easter. He never out of respect or fear kept silent about the rich, if any of them sinned; but he corrected them with harsh reproof. He never used to give any money to powerful men of the world, but only food, if he was entertaining them, but rather expended for the use of the poor the gifts of money which were bestowed on him by the wealthy, as we have said, or employed them in ransoming those who had been wrongfully sold. Moreover, he afterwards made many of those whom he had ransomed into his disciples, and, teaching and instructing them, advanced them to priests' orders. . . .[1]

CHAPTER VI. *Of the religion and wonderful goodness of King Oswald.*

King Oswald, being instructed, with the nation of the English which he governed, by the teaching of this bishop, not only learned to hope for heavenly realms unknown to his fathers, but obtained earthly realms greater than those of any of his ancestors, from the one God, who made heaven and earth. In short, he received under his dominion all the nations and provinces of Britain, which are divided among four languages, that is, the Britons, the Picts, the Scots and the English.

When raised to that height of power, nevertheless, wonderful to relate, he was always humble, kind and generous to poor men and strangers. It is said, in fact, that on one occasion, when he was sitting at dinner with the aforesaid bishop on the holy Easter Day, and there was placed on the table before him a silver dish filled with royal delicacies, and they were already about to put forth their hands to bless the bread, there entered suddenly his thegn to whom was committed the charge of receiving the poor, and he informed the king that a great multitude of poor people, come from all quarters, was sitting in the streets begging some alms of the king. He at once ordered that the food placed in front of him should be carried to the poor, and also that the dish should be broken up and divided in portions among them. At which sight the bishop who sat by him, delighted at such an act of piety, seized his right hand and said: "May this hand never decay." And it happened according to his prayer. For when he had been killed in battle, and his hands and arms were cut off from his body, it happens that they remain incorrupt until this day; and they are kept enclosed in a silver coffer in the church of St. Peter in the king's town which is called after a certain former queen, Bebbe by name,[2] and they are venerated with due honour by all.

By this king's labours the provinces of the Deirans and the Bernicians, which till then had been at variance, were reconciled and bound together as if they were one people. For he was the nephew of King Edwin, by his sister Acha, and it was fitting that so great a predecessor should have in his own family such an heir to his religion and his kingdom.

---

[1] The chapter concludes with a story that Aidan had been preceded by a priest of harsher character, who had no success, but returned to Iona reporting that the English were intractable and barbaric. Aidan, who suggested that milder and more patient methods should have been used, was then sent himself.
[2] *i.e.* Bamburgh.

CHAPTER VII. *The province of the West Saxons received the word of God at the preaching of Birinus; and concerning his successors Agilbert and Leuthere.*

At that time the people of the West Saxons, who were of old called the Gewisse, accepted the faith of Christ in the reign of Cynegils, at the preaching of Bishop Birinus, who had come to Britain by the advice of Pope Honorius, having promised in his presence that he would sow the seed of the holy faith in the remotest inland regions of the English, where no teacher had preceded him. Hence at the bidding of the same pontiff he was consecrated to the degree of bishop by Asterius, bishop of Genoa. But on arriving in Britain and first coming to the nation of the Gewisse, where he found all to be confirmed pagans, he thought it more useful to preach the word there, rather than to go farther looking for people to whom he should preach.

And thus as he preached the gospel in the aforesaid province, when the king himself had been instructed and was being baptized at the font with his people, it happened that at that time the most holy and victorious king of the Northumbrians, Oswald, was present, and received him as he came forth from baptism, and, by a most seemly alliance pleasing to God, first received as his son dedicated to God by this second birth, the man whose daughter he was about to receive in marriage. The two kings gave to the bishop the city which is called Dorchester,[1] to make therein his episcopal see; and there, after building and dedicating churches, and calling many people to the Lord by his pious labours, he departed to the Lord, and was buried in that same city; but many years later, by the agency of Bishop Hædde, he was translated from there to Winchester, and laid in the church of the blessed Apostles Peter and Paul.

When the king died, his son Cenwealh succeeded him in the kingdom, but refused to accept the faith and sacraments of the heavenly kingdom, and not long after lost also the dominion over an earthly kingdom. For he put away the sister of Penda, king of the Mercians, whom he had married, and took another wife; and thus, attacked in war and deprived of his kingdom by him, he withdrew to the king of the East Angles, whose name was Anna. He lived there three years in exile, and learned and received the true faith. For the king with whom he dwelt in exile was himself a good man, and happy in a good and holy offspring, as we shall show later on.[2]

But when Cenwealh was restored to his kingdom, there came from Ireland into that province a certain bishop, Agilbert by name, a Gaul by race indeed, but one who had then lived no short time in Ireland for the sake of studying the Scriptures; and he attached himself to the king of his own accord, taking up the ministry of preaching. The king, observing his learning and industry, asked him to accept the episcopal see there and to remain as the bishop of his people; and he assented to his requests and for many years he presided over that nation as their bishop. At length the king, who only knew the language of the Saxons, grew weary of his outlandish speech, and secretly brought into the province another bishop speaking his own language, Wine by name, who also had been ordained in Gaul; and dividing the province into two dioceses, he gave to him an episcopal see in the city of *Wenta*, which is called

---

[1] Dorchester-on-Thames.   [2] pp. 628f., 658f.

Winchester by the nation of the Saxons. Hence Agilbert was seriously offended, because the king had done this without consulting him, and went back to Gaul, and received the bishopric of the city of Paris, and died there an old man and full of days. When not many years had passed after his departure from Britain, Wine was expelled from his bishopric by the same king, and took refuge with the king of the Mercians called Wulfhere, and bought from him the see of the city of London for money, and remained its bishop until the end of his life. And thus the province of the West Saxons was without a bishop for no short time.

During that time also the aforesaid king of that nation, since he was very often afflicted by his enemies with most serious losses in his kingdom, at last bethought himself that his unbelief had formerly expelled him from his kingdom, and his acknowledgment of the faith of Christ had recalled him to his kingdom; and he understood that then also the province deprived of a bishop was rightly likewise deprived of divine support. He therefore sent messengers to Agilbert in Gaul, beseeching him with humble apologies to return to the bishopric of his nation. But he excused himself, and affirmed that he could not come, because he was bound to the bishopric of his own city and diocese; yet, lest he should give no sort of help to so earnest an appeal, he sent to him instead of himself a priest Leuthere, his nephew, who, if he wished, might be ordained his bishop, saying that he judged him worthy of a bishopric. When he had been honourably received by the king and the people, they asked Theodore, then archbishop of the church of Canterbury, to consecrate him as their bishop, and he was consecrated in that same city and for many years sedulously governed alone the bishopric of the Gewisse by synodal authority.

CHAPTER VIII. *Eorcenberht, king of Kent, ordered the idols to be destroyed; and concerning his daughter Eorcengota and his kinswoman Æthelburh, virgins dedicated to God.*

In the year of the incarnation of our Lord 640, when Eadbald, king of the people of Kent, departed from this life, he left the government of the kingdom to his son Eorcenberht; and he, receiving it, held it most nobly for twenty-four years and some months. He was the first of the kings of the English to order by his supreme authority that the idols over his whole kingdom were to be abandoned and destroyed, and that the fast of forty days was to be observed. And so that it could not lightly be neglected by anyone, he appointed proper and adequate penalties for the offenders. His daughter Eorcengota, a fit offspring of such a parent, was a virgin of great virtues, serving God in the monastery which had been founded in the country of the Franks by the most noble abbess named Fara, in a place which is called Brie.[1] For at that time, when few monasteries had been founded in the country of the English, many persons were accustomed to go from Britain to the monasteries of the Franks or Gauls for the sake of the monastic life; and they also sent their daughters to be instructed there, and united to the Heavenly Bridegroom; especially to the monasteries in Brie, and in Chelles, and in Andeley. Among these was Sæthryth, daughter of the wife of Anna, king of the East Angles, whom we have mentioned above, and Æthelburh, the same king's own daughter; both of whom, although they were foreigners, were appointed

[1] Faremoûtier-en-Brie.

abbesses of the monastery of Brie on account of their virtues. Seaxburh, that king's elder daughter, wife of Eorcenberht, king of the people of Kent, had a daughter Eorcengota. . . .[1]

CHAPTER IX. *In the place where King Oswald was killed, frequent miracles of healing were performed; first, a certain traveller's horse was cured, and then a paralysed girl.*

Oswald, the most Christian king of the Northumbrians, reigned for nine years, including also that year which the brutal cruelty of the king of the Britons, and the insane apostasy of the kings of the English, had made detestable. For, as we have said above,[2] it was decided by the unanimous consent of all that the names and memory of the apostates ought to be completely erased from the list of the Christian kings, and no date ascribed to their reign. At the end of those years a great battle was fought, and Oswald was killed by that same pagan nation and pagan king of the Mercians, by whom also his predecessor Edwin had been slain, at the place which is called in the English language 'Maserfield',[3] in the 38th year of his age, on the fifth day of the month of August. . . .[4]

CHAPTER XI. *There stood a heavenly light the whole night above his relics, and those possessed by devils were cured by them.*

Among the rest, I think we ought not to pass over in silence the power and heavenly miracles shown when his bones were discovered and translated to the church in which they are now kept. This was done by the zeal of Osthryth, queen of the Mercians, who was the daughter of his brother, that is, Oswiu, who held the throne after him, as we shall tell later on.

There is a noble monastery in the province of Lindsey, Bardney by name, which that queen and her husband Ethelred loved greatly, venerated and enriched, and in this she desired to lay the revered bones of her uncle. When the wagon, in which these bones were brought, arrived towards evening at the aforesaid monastery, the men who were in the monastery would not willingly admit them; for, although they knew him to be a holy man, yet they retained their ancient hatred for him when he was dead, because he was a native of another province and had obtained dominion over them. Hence it happened that the relics brought there remained outside for that night, with only a large tent spread over the wagon in which they lay. But the manifestation of a heavenly miracle revealed with what reverence they ought to be received by all the faithful. For all that night a column of light stretched from the wagon up to the sky, and was visible in nearly all places in the province of Lindsey. Whereupon, in the morning, the brothers of the monastery who had refused it the day before, began themselves eagerly to beg that the holy relics, so beloved of God, should be deposited among them. Accordingly, the bones were washed and placed in a shrine which they had prepared for them, and set with due honour in the church;

---

[1] The rest of the chapter speaks of her sanctity, and of that of her aunt Æthelburh.

[2] p. 623.

[3] This seems to have been identified with Oswestry 'Oswald's tree', Shropshire, already in the twelfth century, and this derives support from Welsh poems that retain some memory of fighting in this area. If the identification is correct, Oswald was the invader. Bede's account is non-committal on this point.

[4] The rest of the chapter deals with miracles worked by this king after his death, as does chap. x.

and that there might be a perpetual memorial of the royal character of this holy man, they placed over his tomb a banner made of gold and purple. . . .[1]

CHAPTER XII. *A little boy was cured of a fever at his tomb.*[2]

. . . It is not to be wondered at that the prayers of that king, who is now reigning with the Lord, should be very efficacious with him, since, while yet governing a temporal kingdom, he was more wont to labour and pray for the eternal kingdom. In fact, they say that he often continued standing in prayer from the time of matins till it was day; and that by reason of his constant habit of praying or giving thanks to the Lord, he used always, wherever he sat, to hold his hands on his knees with upturned palms.

It is also commonly said and has become proverbial that he even ended his life in prayer. For when he was surrounded with weapons and enemies, and saw that he must immediately perish, he prayed for the souls of his army. Hence people say in a proverb: "'God have mercy of their souls', said Oswald, as he fell to the ground."

His bones were translated and placed in the monastery, as we have said; but the king who killed him ordered his head, hands and arms to be cut off, and set upon stakes. But one year later, Oswiu, the successor to his kingdom, came with an army and took them away, and buried the head in the cemetery of the church of Lindisfarne, and the hands and arms in his royal city.[3]

CHAPTER XIV. *On the death of Paulinus, Ithamar received the bishopric of Rochester in his place; and of the wonderful humility of King Oswine, who was killed by King Oswiu by a cruel death.*

When King Oswald had been translated to the heavenly realms, his brother Oswiu, a young man of about thirty, received the throne of his earthly kingdom in his place, and held it with much trouble for twenty-eight years, being attacked by the pagan nation of the Mercians, which had killed his brother, and also by his own son Alhfrith, as well as by his nephew, Œthelwald, the son, that is, of his brother who had reigned before him.

In his second year, that is, in the year of the incarnation of our Lord 644, the most reverend father, Paulinus, formerly bishop of York, but then of the city of Rochester, went to the Lord on 10 October, having held the bishopric 19 years, 2 months and 21 days; and was buried in the sacristy of the blessed Apostle Andrew, which King Ethelbert had built from the foundation in the same city of Rochester. In his place Archbishop Honorius ordained Ithamar, sprung, indeed, from the Kentish nation, but the equal of his predecessors in his way of life and his learning.

During the first years of his reign Oswiu had a partner in the royal dignity, Oswine by name, of the stock of King Edwin, being a son of that Osric, of whom we spoke before, a man of outstanding godliness and devotion, who governed the

---

[1] The rest of the chapter relates a miracle told to this queen by Abbess Æthelhild, still living in Bede's day, sister of Bishop Æthelwine of Lindsey and of Abbot Ealdwine of Partney. She had herself seen the miraculous light.

[2] The account of this miracle precedes the general explanation which I have included here.

[3] Bamburgh. The following chapter, omitted here, recounts a miracle performed in Ireland by a relic of his, told on the authority of Acca, who had heard it from the missionary Willibrord.

province of the Deirans for seven years with great prosperity in all things, himself much loved of all. But Oswiu, who ruled the other, northern, part of the nation across the Humber, that is, the province of the Bernicians, could not keep peace with him; but on the contrary, as the causes of dissension increased, he killed him by a most wretched death. For when they had raised armies against one another, and Oswine saw that he could not contend against one who had greater forces, he thought it better at that time to lay aside any intention of fighting, and reserve himself for better times. Accordingly he dismissed the army which he had assembled, and ordered all the men to go home from the place which is called *Wilfaresdun*, that is, 'the hill of Wilfare', and is almost ten miles distant from the village of Catterick, to the north-west. And himself, with only one very faithful thegn, Tondhere by name, turned aside to hide himself in the house of the *gesith* Hunwold, whom also he thought to be most loyal to him. But alas! it was far otherwise; for he was betrayed by that same *gesith*, and Oswiu slew him and his aforesaid thegn by means of his reeve Ethelwine by a death to be detested by all. This happened on 20 August, in the ninth year of his reign, in the place which is called Gilling, where afterwards, in atonement for this crime, a monastery was constructed,[1] in which prayers were to be daily offered up to the Lord for the redemption of the souls of both kings, both of him who had been slain and of him who had ordered the slaying. . . .[2]

CHAPTER XVI. *Aidan, by his prayers, kept off from the royal town the fire kindled by the enemy.*

Another notable miracle of the same father is told by many who were in a position to know. For during his episcopate, the hostile army of the Mercians, led by Penda, cruelly ravaged the country of the Northumbrians far and wide, reaching the royal town which is called after Bebbe, a former queen; and since he could take it neither by assault nor by siege, he tried to burn it down. Having pulled down the villages he came across in the neighbourhood of the town, he brought there an immense quantity of planks, beams, partition-walls, wattles and thatch, and with these he surrounded the town to a great height on the side next the land; and when he saw that the wind was favourable, he set fire to it and tried to burn the town.

At that time the most reverend Bishop Aidan was living on the island of Farne, which is almost two miles away from the town; for he often used to retire there for private prayer and silence; indeed the site of his solitary dwelling on the same island is shown to this day. When he saw the flames of the fire and the smoke, borne by the winds, rising above the walls of the town, he is reported to have said with tears, raising his eyes and his hands towards heaven: "See, O Lord, what great evil Penda is doing." When he had spoken, immediately the winds turned from the town and drove back the flames on those who had kindled them, so that some being hurt, and all afraid, they ceased to attack the town which they perceived to be protected by divine help.

[1] See pp. 638, 697.
[2] A further panegyric on Oswine follows, with an anecdote to illustrate his humility, and his friendship with Aidan, who survived him only twelve days. Chap. xv tells how holy oil given by Aidan calmed a storm when Eanflæd, the daughter of King Edwin, was being brought by sea from Kent to be married to King Oswiu.

CHAPTER XVII. *A prop of the church, on which Bishop Aidan was leaning when he died, could not be consumed by the flames when the rest of the building was burnt; and concerning his inward life.*

When the day of his death made him quit the body, sixteen[1] years of his episcopate being completed, Bishop Aidan was in the king's residence not far from the town of which we have spoken above. For he had in this a church and a chamber, and would often turn aside and stay there, and make journeys from it to preach all round about; he used to do the same at other residences of the king, seeing that he had no possessions of his own, except his church and the fields adjoining it. When he became ill they set up a tent for him at the western end of the church, so that the tent touched the wall of the church. Hence it happened that he breathed his last, leaning on a prop placed outside the church to strengthen it. He died in the 17th year of his episcopate, on 31 August, and his body was immediately translated from there to the island of Lindisfarne and buried in the cemetery of the brothers. And after some time had passed, when a bigger church was built there and dedicated in honour of the most blessed Prince of the Apostles, his bones were translated to it and buried to the right of the altar with the veneration due to so great a bishop.

Finan succeeded him in his bishopric, who also had been sent from Iona, the island and monastery of the Scots, and he remained no little time in the bishopric. It happened after some years that Penda, king of the Mercians, came into these parts with a hostile army, destroying all that he could with sword and flame, and the village in which the bishop had died, along with the afore-mentioned church, was burnt down also. But, in a wonderful manner, that prop alone, on which he was leaning when he died, could not be consumed by the flames that were devouring everything round it. . . .[2]

I have written these things concerning the character and works of the aforesaid man, in no way commending or approving that he understood imperfectly the observance of Easter; nay, very much detesting this, as I have most clearly proved in the book which I composed about the seasons;[3] but, as a truthful historian, simply relating the things which were done by him or through him, and praising what in his acts is worthy of praise, and preserving the memory thereof for the benefit of my readers; namely his love of peace and charity, of continence and humility, his mind superior to anger and avarice, and contemptuous of pride and vainglory, his zeal in keeping and teaching the heavenly commands, his alertness in reading and vigils, his authority, befitting a priest, in reproving the proud and mighty, and likewise his clemency in consoling the weak, and relieving or defending the poor. To speak briefly, as far as I have learnt from those who knew him, he took care to neglect none of all the precepts which he found in the gospels or the apostolic or prophetic writings, but to put them all into practice to the utmost of his power. These things I greatly admire and love in the aforesaid bishop, because I doubt not that they were pleasing to God. . . .[4]

---

[1] Some MSS. have 17.
[2] A similar miracle occurred when the village was burnt a second time, accidentally.
[3] Bede's *De Temporibus*.
[4] Bede then reaffirms his hatred of the error regarding Easter, and explains in what it lay.

CHAPTER XVIII. *Concerning the life and death of the religious king, Sigeberht.*

In these times, after Eorpwold, Rædwald's successor, his brother Sigeberht, a good and religious man, ruled over the kingdom of the East Angles. He had received the laver of baptism a little while before, in Gaul, when he was in exile fleeing the enmity of Rædwald; and coming home, as soon as he possessed the kingdom, he wished to imitate the things which he had seen well ordered in Gaul, and established a school, where boys could be instructed in letters, and he was assisted by Bishop Felix, whom he had received from Kent, and who supplied them with teachers and masters after the manner of the people of Kent.

And this king became so great a lover of the heavenly kingdom, that finally he relinquished the affairs of the kingdom, committing them to his kinsman Ecgric, who before held a part of that kingdom, and entered a monastery which he had himself founded, and receiving the tonsure, applied himself rather to fight for an eternal kingdom. When he had done this for a long time, it happened that the nation of the Mercians, led by King Penda, made war on the East Angles, who, when they saw that they were inferior to the enemy in battle, asked Sigeberht to come into the battle with them to encourage the soldiers. And when he was unwilling and refused, they dragged him from the monastery against his will and led him with them into the fight, hoping that the hearts of the soldiers would be less afraid, and less inclined to think of flight in the presence of a former active and distinguished leader. But he was not forgetful of his profession, and though he was surrounded by a noble army, would have nothing in his hand except a rod alone; and he was killed together with King Ecgric, and the pagans pressed on and slaughtered or dispersed all their army.

Anna succeeded to their kingdom, the son of Eni, of royal race, an excellent man and father of an excellent offspring, of whom we shall speak in due place further on.[1] He also was afterwards killed by that same pagan leader of the Mercians by whom his predecessors had been slain.

CHAPTER XIX. *Fursa built a monastery among the East Angles; and concerning his visions and his sanctity, to which his uncorrupt flesh after his death bore witness.*

Whilst Sigeberht still governed the kingdom, there arrived from Ireland a holy man called Fursa, renowned for his words and actions, and remarkable for singular virtues, desiring to live as a foreigner for the Lord's sake, wherever he should find an opportunity. When he came to the province of the East Angles, he was received with honour by the aforesaid king, and performing his usual employment of preaching the gospel, he converted many unbelievers to Christ and confirmed further in the faith and love of Christ those who already believed, both by the example of his virtue and the incitement of his words.

Here he was attacked by some infirmity of the body, and was thought worthy to see an angelic vision, in which he was admonished diligently to proceed in the ministry of the word which he had begun, and to exert himself indefatigably in his accustomed vigils and prayers; inasmuch as his end was certain, but the hour of this same end would be uncertain, as the Lord says: "Watch ye therefore, because ye

[1] pp. 658f.

know not the day nor the hour."[1] Being confirmed by this vision, he applied himself with all speed to build a monastery on ground given him by the aforesaid King Sigeberht, and to establish regular discipline there. The monastery was pleasantly situated near the woods and the sea, built inside a certain fort, which is called in the English language *Cnobheresburg*, that is, 'the town of Cnobhere'.[2] Afterwards, Anna, king of that province, and certain nobles, adorned it with more stately buildings and with gifts. . . .[3]

CHAPTER XXI. *The province of the Middle Angles became Christian under King Peada.*

At this time the Middle Angles[4] under their prince, Peada, son of King Penda, received the faith and sacraments of the truth. As he was an excellent youth, and most worthy of the name and office of a king, he was elevated by his father to rule over that nation; and he came to Oswiu, king of the Northumbrians, asking to have his daughter Alhflæd given to him as his wife. But he could not obtain what he sought except by receiving the faith of Christ and baptism along with the nation which he ruled. When he heard the preaching of the truth, the promise of the heavenly kingdom, and the hope of resurrection and future immortality, he declared that he would willingly become a Christian, even without receiving the maiden; being chiefly prevailed on to receive the faith by King Oswiu's son Alhfrith, who was his brother-in-law and friend, having married his sister, Cyneburh by name, the daughter of King Penda.

Accordingly he was baptized by Bishop Finan, with all who had come with him, *gesiths* and thegns, and all of their followers, in the famous royal estate which is called 'At the wall'.[5] And receiving four priests who by their learning and way of life seemed fit to teach and baptize his nation, he returned home with great joy. The priests were Cedd, Adda, Betti and Diuma, of whom the last was a Scot by race, the others English. Adda was brother of Utta, a noted priest and abbot of the monastery which is called Gateshead, of whom we spoke above.[6] The aforesaid priests, arriving in the province with the prince, preached the word, and were willingly heard, and daily many, as well of the nobility as of the lower folk, renounced the filth of idolatry, and were washed in the fountain of the faith.

Nor did King Penda forbid the word to be preached even in his own nation, that of the Mercians, if any wished to hear it. But on the contrary, he hated and despised those whom he perceived not to do the works of faith when they had been admitted to the faith of Christ, saying that those were contemptible and wretched who scorned to obey their God, in whom they believed. These things were begun two years before the death of King Penda. But after his slaying, when the Christian King Oswiu obtained his kingdom, as we shall tell later,[7] Diuma, one of the four priests above

---

[1] Matthew xxv. 13.   [2] Probably Burgh Castle in Suffolk, where there was a Roman fort.
[3] Here Bede gives Fursa's vision of the next world. He had heard it from an ancient brother of his own monastery, who had it from a very truthful man who had himself heard Fursa relate it. But he also uses a written Life of St. Fursa. Chap. xx consists of episcopal successions, Thomas succeeding Felix in East Anglia, to be followed after five years by Brihtgils, also called Boniface; Deusdedit the West Saxon succeeding Honorius at Canterbury; Damian the South Saxon succeeding Ithamar at Rochester.
[4] Bede gives this name in its English form, and then translates it into Latin, *Mediterranei Angli* 'Midland Angles'.   [5] Probably Wallbottle, Northumberland, which means 'the residence by the wall'.
[6] Utta escorted Oswiu's bride from Kent when Aidan's oil quieted the storm. See p. 631, n. 2.
[7] pp. 637f.

mentioned, was made bishop of the Middle Angles as well as of the Mercians, being consecrated by Bishop Finan. For the scarcity of priests forced one bishop to be over two peoples. When in a short time he had gained many people to the Lord, he died among the Middle Angles, in the region which is called 'among the Feppingas'.[1] Ceollach received the bishopric in his place, being like him from the nation of the Scots, but not long after he abandoned the bishopric and went back to the island of Iona, where the Scots held the head and mother-house of many monasteries, Trumhere succeeding him in the bishopric, a religious man and trained in the monastic life, of the race of the English, but ordained bishop by the Scots. This was done in the time of King Wulfhere, of whom we shall speak later.[2]

CHAPTER XXII. *The East Saxons received under King Sigeberht, by the preaching of Cedd, the faith which they had formerly renounced.*

At that time, also, the East Saxons received at the instance of King Oswiu the faith which they had formerly cast off when they expelled Bishop Mellitus. For Sigeberht, who reigned after Sigeberht surnamed the Little, was king of this same nation and a friend of this same King Oswiu, who, when he came frequently to visit him in the province of the Northumbrians, used to try to make him understand that those could not be gods who had been made by men's hands; that wood or stone could not be material for making a god, when the pieces remaining were either burned in the fire or formed into any vessels for human use, or were held in contempt and thrown out, trampled on and bruised to dust; that rather God is to be conceived incomprehensible in majesty, invisible to human eyes, omnipotent, eternal, who created the heaven and the earth and the human race, who rules and will judge the world with justice; whose eternal abode must be believed to be in heaven, not in vile and perishable metal; and that it ought by reason to be understood that all who learn and do the will of him by whom they were created shall receive from him eternal rewards. When King Oswiu had frequently impressed this and much more to a like effect on King Sigeberht with friendly and as it were brotherly advice, at length, aided by his friends' consent, he believed; and having taken counsel with his followers, and exhorting them, when they all approved and assented to the faith, he was baptized with them by Bishop Finan in the royal residence which we have mentioned above, which is called 'At the wall'.[3] For it is by the wall with which the Romans once invested the island of Britain, at a distance of twelve miles from the eastern sea.

And thus, having now become a citizen of the eternal kingdom; King Sigeberht returned to the seat of his temporal kingdom, requesting King Oswiu to give him some teachers to convert his people to the faith of Christ, and wash them in the font of salvation. And Oswiu sent to the province of the Middle Angles to summon to him the man of God, Cedd, and, giving him as a companion another priest, sent him to preach the word to the nation of the East Saxons. When they, travelling all over,

---

[1] This tribe does not seem to have left any trace in Middle Anglia, but it is probably its name which forms the first element of the Worcestershire place-name Phepson, which seems to mean 'settlement of the Feppingas' and was perhaps colonized by this tribe. Since the tenth-century text on the resting-places of saints says Diuma lies at Charlbury, the Feppingas are probably, as Sir Frank Stenton suggests (V.C.H., Oxon., I, p. 378), to be located in this area.

[2] pp. 638, 645, 648, 654.   [3] See p. 634, n. 5.

had collected a great Church to the Lord, it happened once that Cedd returned home and came to the church of Lindisfarne to confer with Bishop Finan; and when he found that his preaching of the gospel had been successful, he made him bishop for the nation of the East Saxons, having summoned to him two other bishops to assist at the consecration. Cedd returned to the province when he had received episcopal orders, and, completing with greater authority the work he had begun, he built churches in various places, ordained priests and deacons to help him in preaching the faith and administering baptism, especially in the city which is called *Ythancæstir*[1] in the Saxon language, but also in that which is named Tilbury; the first of these is on the bank of the River Pant, the second on the bank of the Thames. He collected in these a company of the servants of Christ, and taught them to observe the discipline of the regular life, in as far as those rude people were then capable of receiving it.

Whilst the teaching of the heavenly life was increasing daily in the aforesaid province for no short time, amid the rejoicing of the king and all the people, it happened by the instigation of the enemy of all good men that the king was killed by the hand of his own kinsmen. They were two brothers who did this wicked deed; and when they were asked what moved them to it, they had nothing else to reply but that they were incensed and hostile to the king because he was too inclined to spare his enemies, and calmly forgave the wrongs done by them as soon as they asked him. Such was the offence for which the king was killed, that he kept the evangelical precept with a devout heart. Yet, in this his undeserved death, his true offence was punished, according to the prediction of the man of God. For one of those *gesiths* who killed him was unlawfully married, and when the bishop could not prevent or correct it, he excommunicated him and ordered all who would obey him not to enter his house nor to eat his meat. The king, however, made light of this command, and when invited by the *gesith* entered his house to a banquet. And when he was coming away, the bishop met him. When the king saw him, he at once dismounted, trembling, from his horse, and fell at his feet, asking pardon for his offence; for the bishop, who was likewise on horseback, had also dismounted. Being much incensed, he touched the prostrate king with the rod which he held in his hand, and pronounced by his episcopal authority: "I tell you", he said, "because you would not keep away from the house of that sinful and condemned man, you will meet your death in his house." Yet it is to be believed that such a death of a religious man not only blotted out his offence, but even increased his merit; for truly it happened on account of his piety and his observance of the commands of Christ.

Swithhelm, the son of Seaxbald, succeeded Sigeberht in the kingdom; he had been baptized by the same Cedd in the province of the East Angles, in the royal estate which is called Rendlesham, that is, "the residence of Rendil"; and Æthelwold, king of that same nation of the East Angles, brother of their king, Anna, received him as he came forth from the holy font.[2]

---

[1] The Roman station of Othona. It is to be identified with St. Peter's Chapel at Bradwell-on-Sea, and most of Cedd's church is still standing. The River Pant is called Blackwater in the reaches below Bocking.

[2] Chap. XXIII contains an account of the founding of Lastingham, Yorks, by Œthelwald, the son of King Oswald, who was reigning in Deira, as a resting place for Cedd, and then tells of the latter's life there and his death, when he left the monastery to his brother Chad.

CHAPTER XXIV. *The province of the Mercians, when King Penda had been killed, received the faith of Christ; and Oswiu gave possessions and estates to God for the construction of a monastery, in gratitude for the victory he had obtained.*

At this time, when King Oswiu was exposed to the fierce and intolerable incursions of the oft-mentioned king of the Mercians, who had killed his brother, he finally, forced by necessity, promised to give him innumerable royal treasures and gifts, greater than can be believed, as the price of peace, provided he would return home, and cease from wasting and bringing to utter ruin the provinces of his kingdom. And when the heathen king absolutely refused to grant his request, having resolved to blot out and exterminate his whole nation from the highest to the lowest, Oswiu looked for help to the divine pity, to deliver him from the pitilessness of the barbarian; and binding himself by a vow, said: "If the pagan will not accept our gifts, let us offer them to him who will, the Lord our God." He therefore vowed that if he were victorious, he would offer his daughter to the Lord, to be dedicated in holy virginity, and would give twelve estates for the founding of monasteries; and thus he gave battle with a very small army. In fact, it is reported that the pagans had an army thirty times as great; for they had thirty legions, drawn up under most noted leaders. King Oswiu with his son Alhfrith met them, having, as I have said, a very small army, but trusting fully in Christ as their leader. His other son, Ecgfrith, was at that time held as a hostage in the province of the Mercians with Queen Cynewise; but Œthelwald, the son of King Oswald, who should have been helping them, was on the side of their adversaries, and led them on to fight against his country and his uncle, although at the actual time of the fighting he withdrew from the battle and awaited the result of the conflict in a safe place. When, therefore, the engagement began, the pagans were put to flight or killed, and thirty royal leaders[1] who had come to his help were nearly all killed; among whom Æthelhere, brother of Anna, king of the East Angles, who reigned after him and was himself the originator of that war, perished after losing his soldiers and auxiliaries.[2] And because the fight took place near the River *Winwæd*,[3] which owing to the heavy rains had overflowed its channel and all its banks, it happened that the water destroyed far more in flight than the sword in battle.

Then, as he had vowed to the Lord, King Oswiu in thanksgiving for the victory granted to him by God gave his daughter Ælfflæd, who was scarcely a year old, to be dedicated to him in perpetual virginity, granting in addition twelve small estates, on which, since they were set free from concern with earthly military service, a place and means might be provided for monks of zealous devotion to practise celestial military service and to pray for the eternal peace of his nation. He gave six of these small estates in the province of the Deirans, six in that of the Bernicians; and each of the estates was of ten hides, making 120 in all. The aforesaid daughter of King Oswiu

---

[1] Or should this be 'king's ealdormen'? There is precedent for a king of a subject province, such as East Anglia under Penda's overlordship, being considered an ealdorman by the overlord. The Old English translator chose to play for safety, when unsure whether the *duces* of his text was used technically or not, and translated 30 *ealdormanna and heretogena* '30 ealdormen and commanders', ignoring 'royal'.

[2] Or does the distinction *militibus sive auxiliis* apply to the personal following as opposed to the rest of his force, parallel to the distinction in the poem on Maldon between the *heorðwerod* and the *folc*?

[3] This river cannot be identified, but Bede places it in the district of Leeds.

who was to be dedicated to God, entered the monastery which is called *Heruteu*,[1] that is, 'island of the hart', which Abbess Hilda then presided over; who two years later bought an estate of ten hides in the place which is called *Streoneshealh*,[2] and there built a monastery, in which the aforesaid daughter of the king became first a learner of the regular life and afterwards abbess,[3] until, having reached the age of fifty-nine, the blessed virgin entered to the union and marriage with the Heavenly Bridegroom. In this monastery both she herself, and her father, Oswiu, and her mother, Eanflæd, and her mother's father, Edwin, and many other noble persons were buried in the church of the holy Apostle Peter. King Oswiu concluded this war in the district of Leeds in the thirteenth year of his reign, on 15 November, to the great benefit of both nations. For he freed his own nation from the hostile depredations of the pagans and converted that nation of the Mercians and the adjoining provinces to the grace of the faith of Christ, having cut off their heathen chief.

Diuma was made the first bishop in the province of the Mercians, as in that of the people of Lindsey and of the Middle Angles, as we have said above; and he died and was buried among the Middle Angles. The second was Ceollach, who left the episcopal office in his lifetime to return to Scotland; both of these were of the race of the Scots. The third was Trumhere, by race indeed an Englishman, but educated and ordained by the Scots. He was abbot in the monastery which is called Gilling.[4] That is, the place where King Oswine was killed, as we mentioned above. For his kinswoman Queen Eanflæd, in expiation for his unjust slaying, begged King Oswiu to grant a place for the founding of a monastery there to Trumhere, the aforesaid servant of God, because he also was a kinsman of the slain king; in which monastery continual prayers should be made for the eternal welfare of both kings, him who was slain, and him who ordered the slaying. For three years after the killing of King Penda, the same King Oswiu ruled the nation of the Mercians and also the other peoples of the southern provinces. He likewise subdued under English rule the greater part of the nation of the Picts.

At that time he granted to the aforesaid Peada, son of King Penda, because he was his son-in-law, the kingdom of the South Mercians, consisting, it is reported, of 5,000 hides, separated by the River Trent from the Northern Mercians, whose land is of 7,000 hides; but in the following spring the same Peada was very wickedly slain, it is said by the treachery of his wife, at the very time of the Easter festival. Three years after the death of King Penda, the ealdormen of the nation of the Mercians, Immin, Eafa and Eadberht, revolted against King Oswiu, setting up as king Penda's son Wulfhere, a youth whom they had kept hidden; and, expelling the ealdormen of the foreign king, they bravely recovered at the same time their territories and their liberty; and thus free, with their own king, they rejoiced to serve Christ the true King for the sake of an everlasting kingdom in heaven. This king ruled the nation of the Mercians for seventeen years, and had as his first bishop Trumhere, of whom we

---

[1] Hartlepool, Durham.

[2] Though it has sometimes been questioned, there can be no doubt nowadays that early tradition was correct in identifying this with Whitby, for it has been corroborated by excavation. The name was ousted by the present one, Scandinavian in origin, after the Danish settlement. It is only coincidence that Strensall, near York, should preserve the old name of Whitby. This also occurred in Worcestershire in Anglo-Saxon times. Its meaning is uncertain.

[3] See Nos. 152, 154.   [4] See No. 155, pp. 697 f.

spoke above, the second, Jaruman, the third, Chad, the fourth, Wynfrith. All these, succeeding one another in turn under King Wulfhere, discharged the office of bishop for the nation of the Mercians.

CHAPTER XXV. *The question was raised about the time of Easter against those who had come from the land of the Scots.*

Meanwhile, Bishop Aidan being taken from this life, Finan, who had been ordained and sent here by the Scots, received the bishopric in his stead. He built a church on the island of Lindisfarne fit for an episcopal see, yet, after the custom of the Scots, not of stone, but entirely of hewn oak, and thatched with reeds; and afterwards the most reverend Archbishop Theodore dedicated it in honour of the blessed Apostle Peter. But Eadberht, bishop of that place, removed the reeds and had it entirely covered – the roof, and also the walls themselves – with sheets of lead.

At this time there arose a frequent and important controversy about the observance of Easter, those that came from Kent or from Gaul affirming that the Scots were celebrating Easter Sunday contrary to the custom of the universal Church. Among them was a most ardent defender of the true Easter, Ronan by name, a Scot indeed by race, but instructed in the rule of ecclesiastical truth in the regions of Gaul or Italy. Disputing with Finan, he corrected many people, or inspired them to a more strict inquiry into the truth, but he could by no means prevail on Finan; on the contrary, since he was a man of a fierce temper, he made him more bitter by his reproofs and an open adversary of the truth. But James, formerly, as we said before, deacon to the venerable Archbishop Paulinus, observed the true and catholic Easter with all whom he could instruct in the more correct way. And Queen Eanflæd kept it with her followers, according to what she had seen done in Kent, having with her a priest of the catholic observance from Kent, Romanus by name. Thus it is said to have some-times happened in those times that Easter was celebrated twice in one year, and while the king, having ended his fast, was keeping Easter, the queen and her followers were still fasting, and celebrating Palm Sunday. But this discrepancy in the observance of Easter was during Aidan's lifetime patiently borne by all, for they understood that, although he could not keep Easter contrary to the custom of those who sent him, he took care to practise diligently the works of faith, piety and love, according to the custom of all holy men. Hence he was deservedly loved by all, even by those who thought differently about Easter; and was held in veneration, not only by ordinary people, but also by the bishops themselves, Honorius of the people of Kent, and Felix of the East Angles.

But when Finan, who succeeded him, was dead, and Colman, who also was sent by the Scots, succeeded to the bishopric, a more serious controversy arose concerning the observance of Easter and other rules of ecclesiastical life. Hence this question rightly disturbed the thoughts and hearts of many, who were afraid lest haply, having received the name of Christians, they "should run or had run in vain".[1] This reached the ears of the princes, King Oswiu and his son Alhfrith. For Oswiu, to be sure, having been educated and baptized by the Scots, and being perfectly skilled in their

---

[1] Galatians ii. 2.

language, thought nothing better than what they taught; whereas Alhfrith, having for his master in Christian instruction Wilfrid, a most learned man, who had formerly gone to Rome to study ecclesiastical doctrine and spent a long time at Lyons with Dalfinus,[1] archbishop of Gaul, from whom also he received the crown of ecclesiastical tonsure, knew that his teaching was rightly to be preferred to all the traditions of the Scots. Therefore he had given him a monastery of 40 hides in the place which is called Ripon,[2] which place he had given a little while before to those who were followers of the Scots for a monastery. But because afterwards when the choice was given them these preferred to leave the place rather than change their usage, he gave it to him whose life and doctrine were worthy of it.

At that time Agilbert, bishop of the West Saxons, of whom we spoke above, a friend of King Alhfrith and of Abbot Wilfrid, had come to the province of the Northumbrians, and was staying with them some time. He also at Alhfrith's request made Wilfrid a priest in his aforesaid monastery. He had with him also a priest called Agatho. The question being raised there about Easter and the tonsure and other ecclesiastical matters, it was arranged that a synod should be held in the monastery which is called *Streoneshealh*,[3] which is interpreted 'the corner of generation',[4] over which at that time Abbess Hilda, a woman devoted to the service of God, presided, and this question resolved. To it came both kings, that is, the father and the son, the bishops, Colman with his clerics from the land of the Scots, Agilbert with the priests Agatho and Wilfrid. James and Romanus were on their side, Abbess Hilda with her followers on the side of the Scots, on which also was the venerable Bishop Cedd, ordained long before by the Scots, as we said above, and he also acted as a most careful interpreter for both sides at that council.

And first King Oswiu made an opening speech, saying that it behoved those who served one God to observe one rule of life, and not to be at variance in the celebration of the heavenly sacraments, when all were looking for one kingdom in heaven; but rather to inquire which was the truer tradition, and all to follow this in unison. He ordered first his Bishop Colman to say what was the practice he followed and whence it derived its origin. Then Colman said: "This Easter which I keep, I received from my elders who sent me hither as bishop, and all our fathers, men beloved of God, are known to have celebrated it in the same manner; and that it should not seem to anyone contemptible or worthy to be rejected, it is the same which the blessed Evangelist John, the disciple specially beloved of our Lord, is recorded to have celebrated with all the Churches over which he presided." When he had said these and similar things, the king ordered that Agilbert also should lay before the assembly his manner of observance, showing whence it took its origin, and on what authority he followed it. Agilbert answered: " I beseech you, let my disciple, the priest Wilfrid, speak instead of me, for we both think alike along with the other followers óf the ecclesiastical tradition who are here present, and he can explain better

---

[1] This, an error from Eddi's Life, should be Annemundus, archbishop of Lyons. Dalfinus was the name of his brother, Count of Lyons.

[2] See No. 155, p. 698.   [3] Whitby.

[4] Accepting Professor A. H. Smith's suggestion that *fari*, 'of the lighthouse' which does not translate the English at all, is an error for *farae*, from the Medieval Latin *fara*, which, meaning 'descent, strain, generation', is a translation of Old English *streon* in one of its meanings.

and more clearly in the English language what we think, than I can through an interpreter."

Then Wilfrid, being ordered by the king to speak, began thus: "The Easter which we keep we saw celebrated by all at Rome, where the blessed Apostles Peter and Paul lived, taught, suffered and were buried; we saw it in Italy, we saw it in Gaul, which lands we traversed for the sake of study and prayer; we have learnt that it is observed in Africa, Asia, Egypt, Greece and in the whole world, wherever the Church of Christ is spread, through divers nations and tongues, at one and the same time; except only for these and their accomplices in obstinacy, I mean the Picts and the Britons, with whom, from the two remotest islands of the ocean, and not even all of these, they strive with foolish labour against the whole world." As he spoke this, Colman replied: "It is strange that you should choose to call our labour foolish, in which we follow the example of so great an Apostle who was worthy to recline on our Lord's bosom; when all the world knows him to have lived most wisely." But Wilfrid said: "God forbid that we should charge John with foolishness, when he kept literally the decrees of the Mosaic law, while still the Church acted in many respects as did the Jews, and the Apostles could not suddenly cast off all the observance of the law which had been established by God—in the same way as it is necessary for those who come to the faith to renounce idols, which were invented by devils—lest they should give offence to those who were Jews among the nations. . . .[1]

"But as regards your father Columba and his followers, whose sanctity you say you imitate, and whose rule and precepts confirmed by heavenly signs you say you follow, I could reply that when many will say at the Judgment to the Lord that in his name they prophesied and cast out devils and did many miracles, the Lord will reply that he never knew them.[2] But God forbid, that I should say this of your fathers, for it is far more just to believe good than evil of those unknown to us. Hence I do not deny them also to be servants of God and beloved of God, who loved God with rude simplicity but pious intention. Nor do I think that such observance of Easter counted much against them as long as no one had come to show them decrees of a more perfect disposition to follow; for I certainly believe that if any catholic computator had then come to them they would have followed his advice just as they are known to have followed those commands of God which they knew and had learnt. But you and your fellows, if, having heard the decrees of the apostolic see, nay, of the universal Church, confirmed as they are by the sacred Scriptures, you scorn to follow them, without any doubt you sin. For although your fathers were holy, is their small number in one corner of a remote island to be preferred to the universal Church of Christ which is throughout the world? And if he was holy and mighty in working miracles, this Columba of yours—and indeed ours, if he was a man of Christ—could he be preferred to the most blessed Prince of the Apostles, to whom

[1] Space does not permit the inclusion of the whole of Wilfrid's long and technical speech, in which he explains the difference between the Easter observance traditionally derived from St. John and that of the Celtic Churches. Colman replies by citing the authority of Anatolius, and the sanctity of St. Columba and his successors, but Wilfrid points out that the Celtic usage does not agree entirely with that of Anatolius. I give the rest of his speech. It may be noted that it is much more offensive than anything in the parallel account of this synod in Eddi (No. 154, p. 692).

[2] Cf. Matthew vii. 22, 23.

the Lord said: 'Thou art Peter, and upon this rock I will build my Church, and the gates of hell shall not prevail against it, and I will give thee the keys of the kingdom of heaven.' : "[1]

And when Wilfrid had concluded thus, the king said: "Is it true, Colman, that these words were spoken to Peter by our Lord?" He said: "It is true, king." And he said: "Can you show any such power given to your Columba?" And he said: "None." Then the king spoke again: "Do you both agree in this, without any controversy, that these words were spoken principally to Peter and that the keys of the kingdom of heaven were given to him by the Lord?" They both replied: "Yes." And thus he concluded: "And I say to you, that he is the door-keeper, and I will not oppose him; but, as far as I know and am able, I wish to obey his decrees in all things; lest perchance, when I come to the gates of the kingdom of heaven, there should be none to unlock them, he being my enemy who is proved to hold the keys."

When the king said these words, those who were sitting or standing round, both great and small, gave their assent, and renouncing the less perfect institution, hastened to conform to that which they had found to be better.

CHAPTER XXVI. *Colman, being worsted, returned home; and Tuda discharged the episcopal office in his place; and of the state of the Church under those teachers.*

When the dispute was ended and the meeting dissolved, Agilbert returned home. Colman, seeing his doctrine spurned and his party despised, gathered to him those who wished to follow him, that is, those who would not accept the catholic Easter and the crown-shaped tonsure—for there was also no small dispute about this—and went back to the land of the Scots to confer with his own people what should be done about these matters. Cedd forsook the practices of the Scots and returned to his see, having acknowledged the observance of the catholic Easter. This dispute took place in the year of our Lord's incarnation 664,[2] which was the 22nd year of King Oswiu, and the 30th year of the episcopate of the Scots which they discharged in the province of the English; for Aidan held the episcopate seventeen years, Finan ten, Colman three.

And when Colman had gone back to his own country, the servant of Christ, Tuda, received the bishopric of the Northumbrians in his place. He had been educated among the southern Scots, and ordained bishop, having according to the custom of his province the ecclesiastical crown-shaped tonsure, and observing the catholic rule regarding the time of Easter. He was indeed a good and religious man, but he ruled the Church for a very short time. He had come from the land of the Scots while Colman was still holding the bishopric, and taught diligently to all, both by word and deed, those things which belong to the faith and to truth. Moreover, Eata, who was abbot in the monastery which is called Melrose, a most reverend and gentle man, was placed with an abbot's authority over the brothers who preferred to remain in the church of Lindisfarne when the Scots left. They say that Colman when about to leave

---

[1] Matthew xvi. 18, 19.
[2] Probably the autumn of 663. See F. M. Stenton, *Anglo-Saxon England*, p. 129.

asked and obtained this from King Oswiu, because this same Eata had been one of Aidan's twelve boys of English race, whom at the beginning of his episcopate he had received to be instructed in Christ. For the king greatly loved this same Bishop Colman on account of his innate discretion. This is that Eata who not long afterwards was made bishop of that same church of Lindisfarne. When returning home, Colman took with him part of the bones of the most reverend Father Aidan; but part he left in the church over which he had presided, and ordered them to be buried in the sacristy.

The place which they ruled proves also how frugal and temperate he and his predecessors were, for when they went away, there were very few houses found there, except the church, only those, that is, without which no civilized way of living could exist. They had no money, but only cattle. For if they received any money from the rich, they gave it immediately to the poor. For there was no need either to collect money or to provide houses for the entertainment of the great men of the world, for these never came to the church except only to pray and to hear the word of God. The king himself, when occasion required, used to come with only five or six thegns, and to depart when he had performed his devotions in church. But if by chance it happened that they took a repast there, they were content with the simple and daily food of the brothers, and demanded nothing more. For at that time the whole care of those teachers was to serve God, not the world; their whole care was to feed the soul, and not the belly.

For this reason the religious habit was at that time held in great veneration, so that, wherever any cleric or monk came, he was joyfully received by all as a servant of God; and even if they met him journeying on the way, they ran to him, and with bowed head were glad to be signed with his hand, or blessed by his lips; they gave diligent heed also to their words of exhortation. And on Sundays they flocked eagerly to the church or to the monasteries, not to feed the body, but to hear the word of God; and if any priest happened to come into a village, the villagers immediately gathered together and sought from him the word of life. For those priests and clerics went into the villages for no other reason than to preach, baptize, visit the sick, and, in short, take care of souls; and they were so free from any taint of avarice, that no one received lands and possessions for the founding of monasteries, unless forced by the temporal authorities. This usage was universally maintained for some time after this in the churches of the Northumbrians. But enough has been said on these matters.

CHAPTER XXVII. *Egbert, a holy man of the English nation, led a monastic life in Ireland.*

In the same year of the incarnation of our Lord 664, there was an eclipse of the sun on the third day of the month of May, about the tenth hour of the day; and also in that year a sudden pestilence depopulated first the southern parts of Britain, attacked also the province of the Northumbrians, and, raging with grievous destruction for a long time far and wide, struck down a great multitude of men. By this plague the aforesaid priest of the Lord, Tuda, was taken from the world, and buried with honour in the monastery which is called *Pægnalaech.*[1] This plague pressed with equal

---

[1] This place has never been satisfactorily identified.

destruction on the island of Ireland. There were there at that time many of the nobles and also of ordinary people of the English nation who had left their native island in the time of the bishops Finan and Colman, and retired there for the sake either of sacred studies or of a more continent life. And some of them soon subjected themselves faithfully to the monastic life, others chose rather to apply themselves to study, going about from one master's cell to another. The Scots received them all most willingly, and took care to supply them gratis with their daily food, and books for reading, and free teaching.[1]

CHAPTER XXVIII. *When Tuda was dead, Wilfrid was ordained in Gaul, and Chad among the West Saxons, as bishops of the province of the Northumbrians.*

Meanwhile King-Alhfrith sent the priest Wilfrid to the king of Gaul, to be consecrated bishop for himself and his people. And that king sent him for ordination to Agilbert, of whom we spoke before, who, when he left Britain, had been made bishop of the city of Paris; and Wilfrid was consecrated with great honour by him himself, when many bishops had assembled in the royal village which is called Compiègne. As he still delayed in the parts beyond the sea for his ordination, King Oswiu, emulating his son's zeal, sent to Kent a holy man, of modest behaviour, well instructed in the Scriptures, and one who wisely practised the things which he learnt in them, to be ordained bishop of the church of York. This was a priest called Chad, brother of the most reverend Bishop Cedd, whom we have often mentioned, and abbot of the monastery which is called Lastingham. The king sent with him his priest called Eadhæd, who afterwards in Ecgfrith's reign was made bishop of the church of Ripon. But when they reached Kent, they found that Archbishop Deusdedit had already departed from this world, and as yet no other had been appointed bishop in his place. They therefore proceeded to the province of the West Saxons, where Wine was bishop, and the aforesaid man was consecrated bishop by him, two bishops of the nation of the Britons, who, as has often been said, celebrated Easter Sunday contrary to canonical custom from the 14th to the 20th moon, being associated with him in the ordination; for there was no bishop at that time, except that Wine, in the whole of Britain, canonically ordained.

So Chad, when consecrated bishop, at once began to devote great care to ecclesiastical truth and purity; to apply himself to humility, continence, and study; to travel, not riding, but after the custom of the Apostles, on foot, through the towns, country places, cottages, villages, great houses,[2] to preach the gospel. For he was a disciple of Aidan, and strove to instruct his hearers in the same actions and habits, according to his example and that of his brother Cedd. And Wilfrid, now made bishop, came to Britain and he also brought to the churches of the English many rules of catholic observance by his teaching. Hence it came about that, with the catholic institutions

---

[1] Here Bede gives a sketch of the life of an Englishman of noble birth, Egbert, who was the brother of Æthelwine, later bishop of Lindsey, and who, when stricken by the plague, vowed to live his life as a stranger in a foreign land if he recovered. He became a bishop in Ireland, and died in 729. We learn later that he tried to go as a missionary to the Continent, and when prevented, inspired others. It was he who persuaded the monks of Iona to accept the catholic Easter (Book III. iv).

[2] I imagine that by *castella* Bede is rendering Old English *byrig*, literally 'strongholds', but often used simply to denote a nobleman's residence, which would normally be fortified.

increasing from day to day, all the Scots who dwelt among the English either conformed to them, or returned to their own country.[1]

CHAPTER XXX. *The East Saxons reverted to idolatry in the time of the plague, but were immediately brought back from error at the instance of Bishop Jaruman.*

At the same time, the kings Sigehere and Sebbi ruled the province of the East Saxons after Swithhelm, of whom we spoke above,[2] although they were subject to Wulfhere, king of the Mercians. When that province was labouring under the aforesaid mortality, Sigehere, with his part of the people, abandoned the sacraments of the Christian faith and turned to apostasy. For that king himself and many of the common people and the nobles, loving this life and not seeking for a future life, or even not believing there to be any, began to restore the temples which were derelict and to worship idols, as if they could be defended from the mortality by these means. But Sebbi, his associate and co-heir of the kingdom, preserved with great devotion with all his people the faith he had received, and, as we shall relate later, ended a faithful life with great felicity.

When King Wulfhere discovered this, that the faith of the province was in part profaned, he sent to correct that error and recall the province to the true faith Bishop Jaruman, who was Trumhere's successor. He acted with much discretion, according to what I was told by a priest who was his companion in that journey and fellow-worker in preaching the word, for he was a religious and good man, and travelling through all the country far and near, he brought back both the people and the aforesaid king to the way of righteousness; so that, abandoning or destroying the temples and the altars which they had made, they opened the churches and joyfully confessed the name of Christ, which they had opposed, choosing rather to die with faith in the resurrection in him, than to live in the filth of apostasy among their idols. When these things were done, those priests and teachers returned home rejoicing.

BOOK IV

CHAPTER I. *Deusdedit being dead, Wigheard was sent to Rome to receive the episcopate; but as he died there, Theodore was ordained archbishop, and was sent to Britain with Abbot Hadrian.*

In the above-mentioned year of the said eclipse and the immediately following pestilence, when also Bishop Colman, overcome by the unanimous efforts of the catholics, returned to his own people, Deusdedit, the sixth bishop of the church of Canterbury, died on 14 July;[3] and Eorcenberht, king of the people of Kent, dying the

---

[1] Chap. XXIX mainly gives information repeated in Book IV, Chap. I, about Wigheard's death in Rome when sent by the kings Oswiu and Egbert for consecration as archbishop. Bede includes the pope's letter, promising to find a suitable person for the archbishopric, in which he refers to Wigheard merely as the bearer of gifts and not as the archbishop elect. This suggests that he is claiming a papal right to appoint.

[2] p. 636.

[3] On the discrepancy between this date and the recorded length of his episcopate, see F. M. Stenton, *Anglo-Saxon England*, p. 129, where it is suggested that Deusdedit died 28 October 663.

same month and day, left the throne to his son Egbert, who held it for nine years. When the see had then been vacant for some considerable time, the priest Wigheard, a man of English race, most learned in ecclesiastical knowledge, was sent to Rome by this king and by the king of the Northumbrians, Oswiu, as we related briefly in the preceding book,[1] with a request that he should be ordained archbishop of the English Church; and at the same time gifts were sent to the apostolic pope, and no small number of gold and silver vessels. When he reached Rome, where Vitalian at that time presided over the apostolic see, and he had made known to the aforesaid apostolic pope the reason for his journey, he and almost all his companions who had come with him were soon afterwards carried off by a pestilence which attacked them.

But the apostolic pope, having consulted about these affairs, made diligent inquiry for someone to send as archbishop for the churches of the English. There was in the monastery of *Niridanum*,[2] which is not far from Naples in Campania, an Abbot Hadrian, by nation an African, well learned in Holy Scripture, trained in monastic and also ecclesiastical learning, highly skilled both in the Greek and Latin languages. The pope summoned him to him and ordered him to receive the bishopric and go to Britain. He replied that he was unworthy of so great a dignity, but said that he could name another, whose learning and age made him more fit to receive a bishopric. And when he proposed to the pope a certain monk named Andrew, of a neighbouring monastery of virgins, he was adjudged by all who knew him to be worthy of a bishopric. But the weight of bodily infirmity prevented him from being made a bishop. And again Hadrian was pressed to accept the bishopric, but he asked for a respite, to see if perchance he could find in the time another who might be ordained bishop.

There was at that time in Rome a monk known to Hadrian, called Theodore, born at Tarsus in Cicilia, a man trained both in secular and religious literature, in Greek and in Latin, upright in character and of venerable age, being sixty-six years old. Hadrian proposed him to the pope, to be ordained bishop, and obtained this; these conditions, however, being laid down, that he should himself bring him to Britain, because he had twice travelled through Gaul for various reasons, and was therefore better acquainted with the way, and was sufficiently provided with men of his own; and also in order that he, being a fellow-worker with him in teaching, might take special care that he should introduce nothing according to the Greek custom, contrary to the truth of the faith, into the Church over which he presided. Theodore was ordained subdeacon and waited four months for his hair to grow so that he could receive the tonsure in the shape of a crown; for he had the tonsure of the holy Apostle Paul in the manner of the Eastern people. He was ordained by Pope Vitalian in the year of the incarnation of our Lord 668, on Sunday 26 March. And thus he was sent with Hadrian to Britain on 27 May.

When they had travelled together by sea to Marseilles, and then by land to Arles, and had delivered to John, archbishop of that city, the letters of commendation of Pope Vitalian, they were detained by him, until Ebroin, the mayor of the palace, gave

[1] See p. 645, n. 1.
[2] Probably the island of Nisida in the Bay of Naples. See R. L. Poole, in *Eng. Hist. Rev.*, xxxvi, pp. 540–545.

them leave to travel where they wished. Having received it, Theodore proceeded to Agilbert, bishop of Paris, of whom we spoke above,[1] and was kindly received by him, and entertained for a long time. Hadrian went first to Emmo, bishop of Sens, and then to Faro, bishop of Meaux, and was well entertained by them for a considerable time; for the approaching winter had forced them to rest wherever they could. When trustworthy messengers related this to King Egbert, namely that the bishop they had asked for from the Roman prelate was in the kingdom of the Franks, he instantly sent to him his reeve[2] Rædfrith to escort him; and when he arrived there, he took Theodore with Ebroin's permission and brought him to the port which is called Quentavic;[3] where he delayed some time, afflicted with sickness, and when he began to recover, he sailed to Britain. But Ebroin detained Hadrian, because he suspected that he was going on some mission from the emperor to the kings of Britain, to the prejudice of the kingdom of which at that time he had the chief control. But when he found out that he had no such mission, and never had had, he released him and allowed him to follow Theodore. And immediately he came to him, Theodore gave him the monastery of the blessed Apostle Peter, where, as I have said, the archbishops of Canterbury are wont to be buried. For the apostolic lord had enjoined on Theodore, as he was about to start, that he was to provide for him in his diocese, and to give him a place in which he and his followers could live suitably.

CHAPTER II. *As Theodore visited all parts, the churches of the English began to be imbued with catholic truth and with the study of the holy writings; Putta was made bishop of the church of Rochester in place of Damian.*

Theodore arrived at his church the second year after his consecration, on Sunday, 27 May, and spent in it 21 years, 3 months and 26 days. And soon he travelled over the whole island, wherever the peoples of the English dwelt, for he was most willingly received by them all and also heard, and, everywhere accompanied and assisted by Hadrian, he spread the right rule of life and the canonical custom of celebrating Easter. And this was the first among the archbishops whom the whole Church of the English agreed to obey. And because, as we have said, they both were amply instructed in sacred as well as secular literature, they gathered a crowd of disciples, and rivers of wholesome knowledge daily flowed to water the hearts of their hearers; and, together with the books of the sacred writings, they delivered to them also the knowledge of the metrical art, of astronomy, and of ecclesiastical computation. It is a testimony of this that until today some of their disciples are still living who know the Latin and Greek languages even as their own, in which they were born. And certainly there were never happier times since the English sought Britain; for, having very powerful and Christian kings, they were a terror to all barbarous nations, and the desires of all were bent on the joys of the heavenly kingdom of which they had recently heard, and whoever wished to be instructed in sacred studies had masters at hand to teach them.

---

[1] See pp. 627f., 640, 644.   [2] *prefectus.*
[3] At the mouth of the Canche, near Étaples, the main port for Channel traffic at that time.

From that time also they began to learn through all the churches of the English the mode of chanting which hitherto had been known only in Kent; and except for James, of whom we spoke above,[1] the first singing master in the churches of the Northumbrians was Eddi, surnamed Stephen,[2] who was invited from Kent by the most reverend man Wilfrid, the first of the bishops who were of English race to learn to deliver to the churches of the English the catholic manner of life.

And thus Theodore, journeying through all parts, ordained bishops in convenient places, and corrected with their help such things as he found faulty. Among the rest, when he charged Bishop Chad also with not having been duly consecrated, he made a most humble answer: "If you know that I have not duly received episcopal ordination, I willingly resign the office, for I have never thought myself worthy of it; but, though unworthy, I consented for obedience sake, when ordered to undertake it." And Theodore, hearing the humility of his reply, said that he ought not to give up the episcopal office; but he himself completed his ordination afresh after the catholic manner. But at the time when Deusdedit died, and a bishop for the church of Canterbury was sought, ordained and sent, Wilfrid also was sent from Britain to Gaul to be ordained; and since he returned before Theodore, he also ordained priests and deacons in Kent, until the archbishop should come to his see. But when Theodore soon came to the city of Rochester, where after the death of Damian the see had long been vacant, he ordained a man trained in ecclesiastical learning and addicted to simplicity of life rather than active in worldly concerns, whose name was Putta; he was especially expert in Church music in the Roman manner, which he had learnt from the disciples of the blessed Pope Gregory.

CHAPTER III. *Chad, of whom we have spoken above, was given as bishop to the province of the Mercians; and concerning his life, death, and burial.*

At that time King Wulfhere ruled the province of the Mercians, and when on the death of Jaruman he asked for a bishop to be given to him and his people by Theodore, the latter did not wish to ordain a new bishop for them; but he requested King Oswiu that Bishop Chad should be given to them. He was then leading a quiet life in his monastery, which is in Lastingham, while Wilfrid administered the bishopric of the church of York, and of all the Northumbrians, and likewise of the Picts, as far as King Oswiu could extend his dominion. And because it was the custom of that most reverend prelate to go about the work of the gospel everywhere on foot, rather than to ride, Theodore ordered him to ride whenever a long journey was involved; and as he was very reluctant, in his zeal and love of pious labour, he himself lifted him on to his horse with his own hands; for he found him to be truly a holy man, and compelled him to go on horseback, wherever he had need to go. Chad, having thus received the bishopric of the nation of the Mercians and also of the people of Lindsey, took care to administer it with great perfection of life, according to the example of the ancient fathers. King Wulfhere also gave him land of 50 hides to found a monastery in the place which is called Barrow, that is, 'at the grove', in the province of Lindsey, in which until this day traces of the regular life instituted by him remain. He had his

---

[1] See pp. 620, 622, 639.   [2] See No. 154.

episcopal see, however, in the place which is called Lichfield, in which he both died and was buried; where is also the see of the following bishops of that province until this day. . . .[1]

In his place Theodore ordained Wynfrith, a good and modest man, to preside, like his predecessors, in the office of bishop for the provinces of the Mercians, the Middle Angles and the people of Lindsey, of all of which Wulfhere, who was still alive, held the government. Wynfrith was one of the clergy of the prelate whom he succeeded, and had discharged the office of deacon under him for no small time.

CHAPTER IV. *When Bishop Colman had left Britain, he built two monasteries in the land of the Scots, one for the Scots, the other for the English, whom he had taken with him.*

Meanwhile Colman, who was the bishop from the land of the Scots, leaving Britain, took with him all the Scots whom he had gathered together in the island of Lindisfarne, and also about thirty men of the race of the English, both parties having been trained in the duties of the monastic life. And leaving some brothers in his church, he first came to the island of Iona, from which he had been sent to preach the word to the nation of the English. Afterwards, he retired to a small island, which is far removed, off the west coast of Ireland, and is called in the Scottish tongue Inishboffin, that is, 'the island of the white heifer'. Arriving there, he built a monastery, and placed in it the monks whom he had brought of both nations. But they could not agree among themselves, for the reason that the Scots, in the summer season when the harvest had to be gathered, left the monastery and wandered through places known to them, but returned the following winter and wished to use in common what the English had provided. Colman sought a remedy for this dissension, and travelling everywhere, far and near, he found a place in the island of Ireland suitable for the construction of a monastery, which is called Mayo in the language of the Scots; and he bought a small part of it from the chief[2] to whom it belonged, to found a monastery there; this condition being added, that the monks dwelling there were to offer prayers to the Lord also for him who let them have the place. He immediately constructed a monastery, with the help also of that chief and all the neighbours, and placed there the English, leaving the Scots on the aforesaid island. That monastery is to this day held by the English inhabitants; and it is the same which, having now grown large from a small beginning, is usually called Mayo; and, as all were long ago converted to better customs, it contains an excellent band of monks, who are gathered there from the province of the English, and according to the example of the venerable fathers live by labour of their hands under a rule and a canonical abbot in great continence and sincerity.

---

[1] A detailed account is given of Chad's end, two and a half years later, which was accompanied by a vision witnessed by Owine, who had been chief thegn, governor of the household, to Queen Æthelthryth, with whom he had come from East Anglia when she married Ecgfrith. A summary of Chad's character is given, partly on the authority of Trumberht, one of the brothers who instructed Bede in the Scriptures, who had been educated in Chad's monastery. Egbert, the English voluntary exile in Ireland, told Higebald, an abbot from Lindsey, of a vision of the reception of Chad's soul in heaven.

[2] *Comes*, the term by which Bede, when referring to English affairs, is probably translating Old English *gesith*.

CHAPTER V. *Concerning the death of the kings Oswiu and Egbert and the synod held at Hertford, over which Archbishop Theodore presided.*

In the year of the incarnation of our Lord 670, which was the second from the time when Theodore came to Britain, Oswiu, king of the Northumbrians, was afflicted by illness, of which he died in the 58th year of his reign. He at that time was filled with so great affection for the Roman and apostolic institution, that, if he had recovered from that illness, he had decided to go to Rome and end his life there at the holy places, and had asked Bishop Wilfrid to be his guide on the journey, with a promise of no small gift of money. When he died on 15 February, he left his son Ecgfrith heir to the kingdom; in the third year of whose reign Theodore assembled a council of bishops, along with many other teachers of the Church, who both loved and knew the canonical decrees of the fathers. When they were met together, he began, in a spirit which became a bishop, to enjoin the observance of such things as were in accordance with the unity and peace of the Church. The terms of these synodal proceedings are as follows:

In the name of our Lord God and Saviour Jesus Christ, that same Lord Jesus Christ reigning for ever and governing his Church, it was thought meet that we should assemble according to the custom of the venerable canons, to treat about the necessary affairs of the Church. We met on the 24th day of the month of September, the first indiction, in the place which is called Hertford; I, Theodore, although unworthy, appointed by the apostolic see bishop of the church of Canterbury, and our fellow priest and brother, the most reverend Bisi, bishop of the East Angles; and with us also our brother and fellow priest, Wilfrid, bishop of the nation of the Northumbrians, was represented by his own deputies. There were present also our brothers and fellow priests, Putta, bishop of the fortress of the people of Kent which is called Rochester, Leuthere, bishop of the West Saxons, and Wynfrith, bishop of the province of the Mercians. And when, all coming together, we had sat down each according to his degree, I said: "I beseech you, my dearest brothers, for the fear and love of our Redeemer, that we may all treat in common for the good of our faith; that whatever has been decreed and defined by holy and approved fathers may be kept inviolate by us all." This and much more I spoke, which belonged to charity and to the preserving of the unity of the Church. And when I had finished my preface, I asked each one of them in turn, if they consented to observe those things which were canonically decreed by the fathers of old. To which all our fellow priests replying, said: "It pleases us all very well, that we keep willingly with a ready heart whatever the canons of the holy fathers lay down." I immediately produced the same book of canons,[1] and showed in the presence of them all ten chapters from that book, which I had marked in various places, because I knew them to be especially necessary for us, and I asked that these should be the more carefully received by all.

Chapter I. "That we all in common keep the holy day of Easter on the Sunday after the 14th moon of the first month."

---

[1] Probably the collection of canons made by Dionysius Exiguus.

II. "That no bishop intrude into the diocese of another, but be content with governing the people entrusted to him."

III. "That it shall not be lawful for any bishop to disturb in any matter any monasteries dedicated to God, nor to remove by force any of their possessions."

IIII. "That the monks themselves shall not move from place to place, that is, from monastery to monastery, unless sent forth by their own abbot; but they are to continue in the obedience which they promised at the time of their profession."

V. "That no cleric, forsaking his own bishop, shall wander about anywhere, nor be received anywhere without commendatory letters from his own prelate. But if he is once received, and will not return when summoned, both the receiver, and he who is received, shall be under excommunication."

VI. "That bishops and clerics, when travelling, are to be content with the hospitality offered them; and it shall not be lawful for any one of them to perform any priestly functions without the permission of the bishop in whose diocese he is known to be."

VII. "That a synod shall be held twice a year." But because various causes hindered this, it was approved by all that we should meet once a year, on 1 August, at the place which is called *Clofesho*.

VIII. "That no bishop, through ambition, shall set himself above another, but all are to observe the time and order of their consecration."

VIIII. The ninth chapter was discussed in common: "That more bishops should be made as the number of the faithful increased"; but we passed over this matter for the present.

X. Relating to marriages: "That nothing but lawful wedlock be allowed to anyone. No one shall commit incest, no one shall leave his own wife, unless on account of fornication, as the holy gospel teaches. And if anyone divorces his own wife, joined to him by lawful wedlock, he shall take no other, if he wishes truly to be a Christian; but remain as he is, or be reconciled with his own wife."

And when these chapters had been thus discussed and defined in common, in order that henceforth there should arise no stumbling-block of contention from any one of us, and that nothing should be falsely substituted, it was thought fit that each one of us should confirm the things so defined with the subscription of his own hand. Which judgment, as defined by us, I dictated to be written by Titillus our notary. Done in the month and indiction above written. Whoever, therefore, shall attempt in any way to contravene and infringe this decision, confirmed according to the decrees of the canons by our consent and the subscription of our hands, shall know that he is excluded from every priestly function and from our fellowship. May the divine grace keep us safe, living in the unity of his Holy Church.

This synod was held in the year of the incarnation of our Lord 673, in which year Egbert, king of the people of Kent, died in the month of July, his brother Hlothhere succeeding him in the kingdom, which he held eleven years and seven months. And Bisi, bishop of the East Angles, who is shown to have been at the aforesaid synod, a man of great sanctity and piety, was the successor of Boniface, whom we mentioned above.[1] For when Boniface died after an episcopate of seventeen years, he was made bishop in his place, Theodore ordaining him. While he was still alive, but prevented from administering his bishopric by most serious infirmity, two bishops, Æcci and Baduwine, were elected and consecrated in his place; and from that time until today that province has had two bishops.

CHAPTER VI. *After Wynfrith was deposed, Seaxwulf received his bishopric, and Eorcenwold was given as bishop to the East Saxons.*

Not long after these events, Archbishop Theodore, taking offence at Wynfrith, bishop of the Mercians, as a result of some act of disobedience, deposed him from his bishopric after he had held it for only a few years, and ordained as bishop in his place Seaxwulf, who was the founder and abbot of the monastery in the region of the Gyrwe,[2] which is called *Medeshamstede*.[3] Wynfrith, when deposed, returned to his monastery which is called Barrow, and there ended his days in an excellent mode of life.

Then also Theodore appointed Eorcenwold bishop in the city of London, for the East Saxons, over whom at that time Sebbi and Sigehere were ruling, whom we mentioned above.[4] The life and conversation of this man, both while he was a bishop and before, are said to have been most holy, as is even now testified by heavenly miracles. For to this day his horse-litter, in which he was accustomed to be carried when sick, is kept by his disciples, and continues to heal many suffering from fevers or enfeebled with other ailments; and not only are sick persons healed if placed under or beside that litter, but even splinters cut off from it and borne to sick men are wont immediately to bring them healing.

This man in truth, before he was made bishop, had founded two famous monasteries, one for himself, the other for his sister Æthelburh, and established them both in regular discipline of the best kind; that for himself in the district of Surrey, by the River Thames, at a place which is called Chertsey,[5] that is, 'the island of Cerot'; and that for his sister in the province of the East Saxons, in the place which is called Barking,[6] in which she might be a mother and nurse of women dedicated to God. Having received the government of that monastery, she showed herself worthy in all respects of the bishop, her brother, both by living rightly herself and by caring duly and piously for those under her, as also celestial miracles testify.[7]

CHAPTER XI. *Sebbi, the king of that same province, ended his life in the monastic persuasion.*

At that time, as the same little book[8] tells us, a man very devoted to God, Sebbi by name, of whom we spoke above,[9] ruled the kingdom of the East Saxons. He was

---

[1] p. 634, n. 3.
[2] A people living in and by the Fenlands. They are mentioned in the Tribal Hidage, and were divided into a northern and southern division, each of 600 families (or hides).
[3] This place was later called Peterborough.   [4] p. 645.   [5] Cf. No. 54.   [6] Cf. No. 60.
[7] Chaps. VII–X are concerned with the miracles of St. Æthelburh of Barking, for which Bede mentions a written source. They speak of the ravages of pestilence, but do not say that Æthelburh's own death was from this cause, but on the contrary, that she suffered for nine years from the disease which killed her. On the date of her death, see p. 447. Her successor, Hildelith, is mentioned, to whom among others Aldhelm dedicated the poetic version of his treatise on *Virginity*.
[8] At the beginning of chap. VII Bede has mentioned that there were written sources for miracles performed at Barking. He probably had a Life of St. Æthelburh and refers to it here as a *libellus*.   [9] p. 645.

intent on religious deeds, frequent prayers, and the pious fruits of almsgiving; preferring a private and monastic life to all the riches and honours of the kingdom. He would have adopted this life long before, abandoning his kingdom, if his wife had not firmly refused to be divorced from him; for which reason many thought and often said that a man of such a disposition was better fitted to be ordained a bishop than a king. And when he had spent thirty years in his kingdom as a soldier of the heavenly kingdom, he was seized with a very great bodily sickness, in which he afterwards died, and he admonished his wife that they should then at least together devote themselves to the divine service, since they could no longer together enjoy, or rather serve, the world. When he had obtained this from her with difficulty, he went to the bishop of the city of London, called Wealdhere,[1] who had succeeded Eorcenwold, and with his blessing he received the religious habit which he had long desired. He also took to him a large sum of money to be distributed to the poor, keeping nothing at all for himself, but rather desiring to remain poor in spirit for the sake of the kingdom of heaven. . . .[2]

CHAPTER XII. *Hædde received the bishopric of the West Saxons in place of Leuthere, Cwichelm the bishopric of the church of Rochester in place of Putta, and was himself succeeded by Gefmund; and who were at that time bishops of the Northumbrians.*

The fourth bishop of the West Saxons was Leuthere. For the first was Birinus, the second Agilbert, the third Wine. And when Cenwealh died, in whose reign Leuthere had been made bishop, sub-kings[3] received the rule of the people, and held it divided among them for about ten years; and during their rule, Leuthere died, and Hædde held the bishopric in his place, being consecrated by Theodore in the city of London. During his episcopate, Ceadwalla conquered and removed the sub-kings and received the supreme power; and when he had held it for two years, and while the same bishop still governed the Church, he was at length inspired by love of the heavenly kingdom, and relinquished his rule, and going to Rome he ended his life there, as shall be told more fully later on.[4]

In the year of the incarnation of our Lord 676, when Ethelred, king of the Mercians, brought a hostile army and was ravaging Kent and profaning churches and monasteries without regard for religion or the fear of God, he included in the general destruction the city of Rochester also, in which Putta was bishop, although he was away at the time. When he learnt that his church was despoiled and all its goods carried off, he went to Seaxwulf, bishop of the Mercians, and, accepting from him the possession of a certain church with an estate of no great size, he ended his life in peace there, doing nothing at all about the restoration of his bishopric, because, as we said above, he was more industrious in ecclesiastical than in worldly affairs; serving God in that church alone, and going wherever he was asked to teach church music.

---

[1] Cf. No. 164.
[2] The king's death, the vision he saw before it, and the miraculous conformation of the stone coffin to the shape of his body, are then related. He was succeeded by his sons Sigeheard and Swæfred, who reigned jointly.
[3] Bede is here out of agreement with the Chronicle, in which Cenwealh is succeeded for a year by his queen, then by Æscwine, followed by Centwine, called king of the West Saxons by Eddi and Aldhelm.
[4] pp. 669 f.

Theodore consecrated Cwichelm bishop of the city of Rochester in his place; but as he, not long after, departed from his bishopric for want of necessities, and withdrew to other parts, Theodore put Gefmund as bishop in his place.

In the year of the incarnation of the Lord 678, which was the eighth year of the rule of King Ecgfrith, there appeared in the month of August the star which is called a comet; and continuing for three months, it rose in the morning, sending out, as it were, a tall pillar of shining flame. In that year also, a dissension arose between King Ecgfrith and the most reverend Bishop Wilfrid, and this prelate was expelled from his episcopal see, and two bishops substituted for him, to be over the nation of the Northumbrians: namely Bosa, who was to govern the province of the Deirans, and Eata, for that of the Bernicians; the former having his episcopal see in the city of York, the latter in the church of Hexham or of Lindisfarne; both of them promoted to the episcopal dignity from a community of monks. Along with them Eadhæd was ordained bishop for the province of Lindsey, which King Ecgfrith had recently acquired, after defeating Wulfhere in battle and putting him to flight. And this was the first bishop of its own that that province received, the second being Æthelwine, the third Edgar, the fourth Cyneberht,[1] who is there at present. For before Eadhæd it had Seaxwulf as bishop, who was at the same time bishop of the Mercians and Middle Angles; and when expelled from Lindsey, he continued in the government of those provinces. Eadhæd, Bosa and Eata were ordained at York by Archbishop Theodore; and three years after the departure of Wilfrid, he also added to their number two bishops, Tunberht for the church of Hexham–Eata remaining at Lindisfarne–and Trumwine for the province of the Picts, which was at that time subject to the dominion of the English. When Eadhæd returned from Lindsey, because Ethelred had recovered that province, Theodore placed him over the church of Ripon.

CHAPTER XIII. *Bishop Wilfrid converted the province of the South Saxons to Christ.*

But Wilfrid was expelled from his bishopric, and wandering for a long time through many places, he went to Rome,[2] and returned to Britain. Although he could not be received into his country or his diocese on account of the enmity of the above-mentioned king, he could not be restrained from preaching the gospel; for, making his way into the province of the South Saxons, which extends from Kent south-west to the West Saxons, and contains 7,000 hides of land, and which at that time still observed pagan rites, he administered to it the word of the faith and the baptism of salvation. The king of that race was Æthelwealh, baptized not long before in the province of the Mercians, in the presence and by the persuasion of King Wulfhere, who also received him as a son as he came forth from the font, and as a sign of his adoption gave him two provinces, namely the Isle of Wight and the province of the *Meonware*[3] among the nation of the West Saxons. And thus the bishop, with the king's consent, or rather to his great delight, washed in the sacred font the foremost

[1] See p. 589. [2] Wilfrid's first appeal to Rome was in 677, and he returned in 680.
[3] The name survives in the River Meon, Hants, with East and West Meon, and Meonstoke, on it. The 'people of the Meon' probably formed part of the Jutish settlement which Bede places on the mainland opposite the Isle of Wight. In chap. xvi he says that the Hamble, a neighbouring river, flows through the territory of the Jutes.

ealdormen and thegns of the province; and the priests, Eappa, Padda, Burghelm and Eddi, baptized the rest of the people, either then or later. The queen, however, Eafe by name, had been baptized in her own province, that of the Hwicce. For she was the daughter of Eanfrith, the brother of Eanhere, both of whom were Christians with their people. Otherwise, the whole province of the South Saxons was ignorant of the divine name and faith.

There was, however, a certain monk of the nation of the Scots, called Dicul, who had a very small monastery in the place which is called Bosham, surrounded by woods and sea, and in it five or six brothers, serving the Lord in a humble and poor way of living. But none of the people of the province cared either to imitate their life or to listen to their preaching.

But Bishop Wilfrid, preaching the gospel to this nation, not only delivered it from the misery of eternal damnation, but also from an indescribable calamity of temporal death. For no rain had fallen in those parts for three years before his coming into the province, and hence a grievous famine fell upon the people and destroyed them by a pitiless death. In fact, it is said that often forty or fifty men together, spent with hunger, would go to some precipice, or the sea-shore, and joining hands would miserably cast themselves down all together, either to perish by the fall, or to be swallowed up by the waves. But the very day on which that nation received baptism in the faith, there fell a soft but plentiful rain, the earth revived, the season was pleasant and fruitful, the fields growing green again. And thus, their former superstition cast away, their idolatry extinguished, the hearts and bodies of all rejoiced in the living God; understanding that he, who is the true God, had enriched them by his heavenly grace both with inward and outward blessings. For the bishop, when he came into the province and saw there such great misery from famine, also taught them to procure food by fishing. For their sea and rivers abounded in fish, but the people had no skill in fishing except only for eels. The bishop's men, accordingly, collected eel-nets everywhere, and cast them into the sea, and, with the help of the divine grace, soon caught 300 fish of various kinds. They divided these into three parts, giving 100 to the poor, 100 to those from whom they had received nets, keeping 100 for their own use. By this benefit the bishop greatly gained the affection of them all, and they began more readily at his preaching to hope for heavenly benefits, when they received by his help those that are temporal.

At that time King Æthelwealh gave to the most reverend Bishop Wilfrid land of 87 hides, where he could maintain his men, who were wandering as exiles; it is called Selsey, which means 'island of the seal'. That place is surrounded by the sea on all sides except on the west, where there is an entrance about the cast of a sling in breadth; such a place is called in Latin a peninsula, in Greek a cherronesos. When, therefore, Bishop Wilfrid had received this place, he founded a monastery there, and established regular life, chiefly of the brothers he had brought with him; and his successors are known to hold this place until today. He himself both in word and deed discharged the office of bishop, justly honoured by all, in those parts for five years, that is, until the death of King Ecgfrith. And since the king gave him with the aforesaid estate all the goods that were there, with the fields and the men, he instructed all in the faith of

Christ, and cleansed them in the water of baptism; among whom there were 250 slaves and bondwomen, all of whom, giving them liberty, he released from the yoke of human servitude just as he saved them by baptism from servitude to devils.[1]

CHAPTER [XV].[2] *Ceadwalla, king of the Gewisse, having killed King Æthelwealh, laid waste that province with a savage slaughter and devastation.*

Meanwhile, Ceadwalla, a most vigorous youth of the royal race of the Gewisse, when exiled from his own country, arrived with an army and killed King Æthelwealh, and wasted that province with a savage slaughter and devastation; but he was soon driven out by the king's ealdormen, Brihthun and Andhun, who afterwards held the government of the province. The first of them was later killed by the same Ceadwalla, when he was king of the Gewisse, and the province was reduced to more grievous servitude. And also Ine, who reigned after Ceadwalla, subjected that province to like affliction for a space of several years. For this reason it came about that all that time they could have no bishop of their own; but when their first bishop, Wilfrid, had been recalled home, they were subject to the bishop of the Gewisse, that is, the West Saxons, who were in the city of Winchester.

CHAPTER XIV [XVI].[3] *The Isle of Wight received Christian inhabitants, and two royal youths of that island were killed immediately after they had received baptism.*

After Ceadwalla had obtained possession of the kingdom of the Gewisse, he seized also the Isle of Wight, which till then was entirely given over to idolatry, and strove to exterminate all the inhabitants with a cruel slaughter, and to put in their place men of his own province; binding himself by a vow, although it is said that he was not yet regenerated in Christ, that he would, if he captured the island, give a quarter of it and of his booty to the Lord. He fulfilled it by offering it to Bishop Wilfrid, who by chance had come from his own people and was there at that time, to be used for the service of the Lord. The size of that island, according to the computation of the English, is of 1,200 hides; hence a holding of 300 hides was given to the bishop. And he entrusted the part which he had received to a certain of his clerics whose name was Beornwine, who was also his sister's son, giving him a priest named Hiddila, to administer the word and laver of life to all who wished to be saved.

I think it should not be omitted here that, as the first fruits of those who were saved by believing, two athelings, brothers namely of Arwold, king of the island, were crowned by the special grace of God. For when the enemy was approaching, they escaped from the island by flight, and crossed over into the neighbouring province of the Jutes, where they were brought to the place which is called Stone,

---

[1] Chap. XIV, which is missing from one branch of MSS., and in others forms, along with chap. XV, one chapter with XIII, and which, in still other MSS., forms a single chapter with XV, distinct from XIII. relates a miracle of St. Oswald, on the authority of Bishop Acca, who had it from a brother of the monastery of Selsey where it occurred. A vision seen by a boy dying of the plague spoke of the intercession of Oswald, since it was the anniversary of his death. Its main interest is the mention of 'codices in which the burial of the dead is noted down'; presumably the same is meant by the term *annalis* 'annal' a little further on.

[2] On the numbering, see next note.

[3] From here to the end of this book, following Plummer, I give the chapter numbering of the Moore MS., which, since it includes chaps. XIV and XV as part of XIII, is two behind the MSS. which have these two chapters separately. The numbering of MSS. of the latter type is given in brackets.

believing that they would be concealed from the victorious king; but they were betrayed and ordered to be killed. When a certain priest and abbot called Cyneberht, who had a monastery not far from there in the place which is called *Hreutford*,[1] that is, 'the ford of reeds', heard this, he came to the king, who was then in those parts in concealment, to be cured of the wounds which he had received when fighting in the Isle of Wight, and begged of him, that, if the boys must needs be killed, he might first be allowed to instruct them in the sacraments of the Christian faith. The king consented, and the abbot, having instructed them in the word of the truth and cleansed them in the font of the Saviour, assured for them an entry into the eternal kingdom. When soon the executioner approached, they joyfully underwent the temporal death, through which they did not doubt they were to pass to the everlasting life of the soul. Thus in this manner, after all the provinces of Britain had received the faith of Christ, the Isle of Wight received it also; yet as it was under the affliction of foreign subjection, no one received the office or see of a bishop before Daniel, who now is bishop of the West Saxons.[2]

This island is situated opposite the frontier between the South Saxons and the Gewisse, separated from it by a sea three miles wide, which is called the Solent. In this sea the two tides of the ocean, which break all round Britain from the boundless northern ocean, daily meet in conflict beyond the mouth of the River Hamble, which runs into the aforesaid sea through the lands of the Jutes which belong to the district of the Gewisse; after this conflict the tides return into the ocean from which they came.[3]

CHAPTER XVI [XVIII]. *Concerning John, the precentor of the apostolic see, who came to teach in Britain.*

Among those who were present at this synod and confirmed together the decrees of the catholic faith was the venerable man John, the archchanter of the church of the holy Apostle Peter, and abbot of the monastery of the blessed Martin,[4] who had lately come from Rome at the command of Pope Agatho, conducted by the most reverend abbot, Bishop, surnamed Benedict, of whom we spoke above.[5] For when this same Benedict had built a monastery in Britain in honour of the blessed Prince of the Apostles, by the mouth of the River Wear, he with his fellow-worker and companion in this work, Ceolfrith, who was abbot after him in the same monastery, went to Rome, as he had often done before, and was honourably received by Pope Agatho of blessed memory. He asked and obtained from him, in defence of the liberty of the monastery which he had built, a letter of privilege confirmed with the apostolic authority; according to what he knew King Ecgfrith had desired and permitted, by whose consent and grant of land he had founded that monastery. He obtained also the aforesaid Abbot John, to bring him with him to Britain, that

---

[1] Now Redbridge.   [2] See Nos. 167, 175.
[3] Chap. XV [XVII] tells how Theodore, hearing of the heresy of Eutyches at Constantinople, called a synod at Hatfield on 17 September 680, in which the orthodoxy of the English Church was set forth.
[4] One of the small monasteries close by and attached to St. Peter's in Rome. This is the earliest reference to its existence, the next, referring to 732, being in the *Liber Pontificalis*.
[5] Not in his *Ecclesiastical History*. Bede is probably thinking of his *History of the Abbots*, an earlier work. On Benedict and Ceolfrith see No. 155.

he might teach in his monastery the method of singing throughout the year, just as it was done in St. Peter's at Rome. Abbot John did as he had been commanded by the pope, teaching the singers of the aforesaid monastery the order and manner of singing and reading aloud, and also committing to writing all that was requisite throughout the whole year for the celebration of festivals; which writings are still preserved in that monastery, and have already been copied by many others round about. But John did not only teach the brothers of that monastery, but those who were skilled in singing flocked to hear him from almost all the monasteries of that province; and many invited him to teach in various places.

Besides his task of singing and reading, he had received another in the mandates of the apostolic pope, that he was diligently to inform himself concerning the faith of the Church of the English, and give an account of it when he returned to Rome. For when he came, he also brought with him the decision of the synod of the blessed Pope Martin, held not long before at Rome, with the consent of 105 bishops, mainly against those who taught that there is only one operation and will in Christ; and he gave it to be transcribed in the aforesaid monastery of the most religious Abbot Benedict. For at that time men holding such an opinion greatly perplexed the faith of the Church of Constantinople, but by the gift of the Lord they were then discovered and vanquished. Wherefore, Pope Agatho, wishing to be informed of the state of the Church in Britain, as in other provinces, and to know to what extent it was free from the contagion of heretics, gave this matter in charge to the most reverend Abbot John, then appointed to go to Britain. When a synod had been assembled for this purpose in Britain, as we have said,[1] the catholic faith was found to be untainted in them all; and a copy of its acts was given for him to take back to Rome.

But as he was returning to his own land, he was attacked soon after he had crossed the ocean by a malady, and died; and for love of St. Martin, over whose monastery he had presided, his body was borne by his friends to Tours[2] and honourably buried there. For he had also received kind entertainment at that church on his way to Britain, and had been greatly pressed by the brothers that when he returned to Rome he would take that road and turn aside to that church; and moreover he received there some men to help him on his journey and in the work laid upon him. Though he died on the way, the testimony of the catholic faith of the English nevertheless was taken to Rome, and received with the greatest joy by the apostolic pope and all who heard or read it.

CHAPTER XVII [XIX]. *Queen Æthelthryth always preserved her virginity, and her body suffered no corruption in the tomb.*

King Ecgfrith married a wife called Æthelthryth, daughter of Anna, king of the East Angles, of whom we have often made mention,[3] a very religious man, and excellent in every respect in mind and deeds. Another man had had her to wife before him, namely a prince[4] of the South Gyrwe[5] called Tondberht. But as he died soon after he had married her, she was given to the aforesaid king. Although she lived with him for twelve years, she yet remained in the glorious integrity of perpetual virginity,

---

[1] In chap. xv [xvii].　[2] St. Martin's church at Tours.　[3] *e.g.* pp. 627f., 633.　[4] princeps.　[5] See p. 652, n. 2.

as Bishop Wilfrid of blessed memory informed me, when I questioned him, since some doubted whether this was so; and he said that he was an undoubted witness of her virginity, in that Ecgfrith promised to give him many lands and much money if he could persuade the queen to fulfil her marriage duty, for he knew that she loved no man more than him. Nor is it to be doubted that that could happen in our age also which reliable histories relate to have happened several times in former ages, by the gift of one and the same Lord, who promises to abide with us even until the end of the world.[1] For also the token of a divine miracle, by which the flesh of this woman when buried could not suffer corruption, is a sign that she had not been defiled by familiarity with man.

After she had long asked of the king to allow her to leave worldly cares and serve only the true King, Christ, in a monastery, she at length obtained this with difficulty, and entered the monastery of Abbess Æbbe, who was King Ecgfrith's aunt, which is situated in the place which they call Coldingham, having received the veil of the religious habit from the aforesaid Bishop Wilfrid. But after a year she was herself made abbess in the region which is called Ely, where she built a monastery, and began to be the virgin mother of very many virgins devoted to God, by the example of a heavenly life and by her teaching. . . .[2]

She was succeeded in the office of abbess by her sister Seaxburh, whom Eorconberht, king of the people of Kent, had married. And when she had been buried sixteen years, the same abbess thought fit to take up her bones, put them into a new coffin, and translate them into the church; and she ordered some of the brothers to find stone from which they could make a coffin for this purpose. They went on board ship, for the region of Ely is surrounded on every side with waters and marshes, and has no large stones, and they came to a certain small deserted city not far away which is called *Grantacæstir*[3] in the language of the English; and presently they found near the walls of the city a coffin of white marble, most beautifully made, and fittingly covered with a lid also of the same sort of stone. Perceiving, therefore, that their journey had been prospered by the Lord, they gave him thanks and carried it back to the monastery. . . .[4]

Ely is in the province of the East Angles, and is a region of about 600 hides, of the nature of an island, surrounded, as we have said, with marshes and waters, and therefore it takes its name from the great plenty of eels which are taken in those marshes. The afore-mentioned handmaid of God wished to have a monastery there, since she came from that same province of the East Angles, as we have said.[5]

CHAPTER XIX [XXI]. *Bishop Theodore made peace between the kings Ecgfrith and Ethelred.*

In the ninth year of the reign of King Ecgfrith, a great battle was fought between him and Ethelred, king of the Mercians, by the River Trent, and there was killed Ælfwine, King Ecgfrith's brother, a youth of about eighteen years, much beloved by both provinces; for King Ethelred had married his sister, who was called Osthryth.

[1] See Matthew xxviii. 20.   [2] Here occurs a passage dealing with her austerities and her death.
[3] Cambridge.
[4] An account of the translation of the uncorrupt body is given, and it leads to a longer account of her death given by her physician Cynefrith.
[5] Chap. XVIII [XX] is occupied by Bede's Latin poem on St. Æthelthryth.

Though occasion seemed to have been given for a more violent war and more lasting enmity between the kings and their fierce peoples, Theodore, the prelate beloved of God, relying on divine aid, completely extinguished by his wholesome admonitions the dangerous fire that was flaring up; with the result that the kings and peoples on both sides were pacified, and no man's life was given for the killing of the king's brother, but only the due compensation in money to the avenging king. And this peace treaty lasted for a long time after between those kings and their kingdoms.

CHAPTER XX [XXII]. *The chains of a certain captive were loosed when Masses were being sung for him.*

In the aforesaid battle, in which King Ælfwine was killed, a memorable incident is known to have occurred, which I think ought by no means to be passed over in silence, for if it is related I think it will be conducive to the salvation of many. Among other of the king's thegns, a young man called Imma was struck down there, and when he had lain as if dead among the corpses of the slain all that day and the following night, at length he came to himself and revived, and sitting up bound his wounds as best he could. Then having rested a while, he stood up and began to go away, to see if he could find friends anywhere who would look after him. But as he did so, he was discovered and taken captive by men of the hostile army, and brought to their lord, a *gesith* of King Ethelred. When asked by him who he was, he was afraid to confess that he was a thegn; he replied rather that he was a peasant and a poor man, and married; and declared that he had come on that campaign with others of his kind to bring provisions to the troops. The other received him, and ordered his wounds to be cared for, and when he began to get well, he ordered him to be bound at night, so that he should not escape. But yet he could not be bound; for as soon as they that had bound him were gone, his bonds were loosed.

Now he had a brother whose name was Tunna, a priest and abbot of a monastery in the city which is still called by his name *Tunnacæstir*.[1] When this man heard that he had been killed in battle, he went to see if by chance he could find his body, and finding another very like him in all respects, he thought it was he. He brought this body to his monastery, and buried it honourably, and took care often to say Masses for the absolution of his soul. And by the celebration of these it came about, as I have said, that no one could bind him without his being immediately loosed. Meanwhile the *gesith* who kept him began to wonder and to inquire why he could not be bound, whether perchance he had about him letters capable of releasing,[2] as are spoken of in fables, by means of which he could not be bound. He replied that he knew nothing of such arts: "But I have a brother," he said, "a priest in my province, and I know that he, thinking me dead, is saying frequent Masses on my behalf; and if I were now in the other life, my soul would be released from pains there through his intercession."

While he was held captive for some time with the *gesith*, those who observed him more attentively, noticed from his face and bearing and speech that he was not of the meaner sort, as he had said, but of the noble class. Then the *gesith* summoned him

[1] This has not been identified.
[2] *i.e.* runes, the letters of the Germanic alphabet, which it was believed could, if properly arranged, produce various magical results, such as to unbind fetters.

privately to him, and questioned him more closely, whence he was, promising that he would do him no injury if he would frankly tell him who he was. When he did so, showing that he had been a king's thegn, the other replied: "I realized by all your replies that you were not a peasant, and now indeed you deserve death, for all my brothers and kinsmen were killed in that battle; yet I will not kill you, that I may not break my promise."

Accordingly, as soon as he had recovered, he sold him in London to a certain Frisian; but neither by him, nor as he was being taken there, could he be bound in any way. But when his enemies placed on him all manner of fetters, and he who had bought him saw that he could not be kept in bonds, he gave him the chance of redeeming himself, if he could. Now it was at the third hour, when Masses were wont to be said, that his bonds were generally loosed. And having given an oath to return, or to send money for himself, he went to Kent to King Hlothhere, who was the son of the sister of Queen Æthelthryth, of whom we spoke above,[1] because he had once been that queen's thegn. He sought and obtained from him the price of his ransom, and as he had promised sent it to his master.

Returning afterwards to his own country, and coming to his brother, he revealed to him in order all the misfortunes, and the consolations in misfortune, which had befallen him; and from what the brother told him, he understood that his bonds were most often loosed at those times when the solemnities of the Mass had been celebrated for him; and he perceived that also other advantages and favours which had happened to him in his danger, had been granted to him from heaven through the intercession of his brother and the oblation of the saving sacrifice. And many who heard these things from the aforesaid man were stirred up in faith and pious devotion to pray or to give alms, or to offer up to God the sacrifice of the holy oblation, for the deliverance of their friends who had departed this world; for they perceived that the saving sacrifice availed for the eternal redemption both of soul and body.

This story was told me by some of those who heard it from the man himself to whom it happened; hence, because I have clearly ascertained it, I have thought it should undoubtedly be inserted into my *Ecclesiastical History*.

CHAPTER XXI [XXIII]. *Concerning the life and death of the Abbess Hilda.*

In the following year, that is, the year of our Lord's incarnation 680, the most religious handmaid of Christ, Hilda, abbess of the monastery which is called *Streoneshealh*,[2] as we mentioned above, after many heavenly deeds which she did on earth, passed from earth to receive the rewards of the heavenly life, on 17 November, when she was sixty-six years old. These being divided into two equal parts, she spent the first thirty-three living most nobly in the secular habit; and still more nobly dedicated the same number of following years to the Lord in the monastic life. For she was of noble birth, that is, the daughter of King Edwin's nephew, Hereric by name, and with that king at the preaching of Paulinus of blessed memory, the first bishop of the Northumbrians, she received the faith and sacraments of Christ, and preserved the same undefiled until she deserved to attain to his sight.

[1] pp. 658 f.   [2] Whitby.

When she had resolved to give up the secular habit and serve him alone, she withdrew into the province of the East Angles, for she was a relation of its king; wishing, if she could by any means, to go from there to Gaul, leaving her country and everything she had, and so lead the life of a stranger for the Lord's sake in the monastery of Chelles, that she might the more easily deserve an everlasting country in heaven. For in that same monastery her sister Hereswith, the mother of Ealdwulf, king of the East Angles, living under regular discipline, was at that time waiting for an eternal crown; and, led by her example, she also continued a whole year in the aforesaid province with the design of going abroad. Afterwards she was recalled home by Bishop Aidan, and received a place of one hide on the north bank of the River Wear, where likewise for a year she led a monastic life with very few companions.

After this she was made abbess of the monastery which is called Hartlepool, which monastery had been founded not long before by the religious handmaid of Christ, Heiu, who is said to have been the first woman in the province of the Northumbrians who took upon her the life and habit of a nun, being consecrated by Bishop Aidan. But not long after she had founded that monastery, she went away to the city of *Calcaria*, which is called *Kælcacæstir*[1] by the nation of the English, and there fixed her dwelling. When Hilda, the handmaid of Christ, was set over that monastery, she immediately tried to order it in all things under a regular life, as she had been able to learn it from learned men; for Bishop Aidan, and such religious men who knew her, were wont because of her innate wisdom and love of the divine service frequently to visit, heartily love, and diligently instruct her.

When she had for some years governed this monastery, very intent on establishing a regular life, it happened that she also undertook to build or set in order a monastery in the place which is called *Streoneshealh*,[2] and she industriously fulfilled the work enjoined on her; for she established this with the same rules of regular life as her earlier monastery, and indeed taught there strict observance of justice, piety, chastity and other virtues, but especially of peace and charity; so that, after the example of the primitive Church, no one there was rich, no one poor, all things were common to all, and no one had private possessions. Her prudence was so great, that not only ordinary people in their need, but sometimes also kings and ealdormen sought and obtained counsel from her. She made those under her charge apply themselves so much to the study of the divine Scriptures, and exercise themselves so much in works of righteousness, that many could very easily be found there who might fitly discharge the ecclesiastical order, that is, the service at the altar.

In fact, we have seen five bishops from that monastery afterwards, and all of them men of singular merit and sanctity, whose names are Bosa, Ætla, Oftfor, John and Wilfrid. Of the first we have said above[3] that he was consecrated bishop of York; of the second it is to be stated briefly that he was ordained to the bishopric of Dorchester; of the last two we must speak hereafter, that the first of them was ordained bishop of Hexham, the second of the church of York.[4] Of the middle one, we may say here that when he had applied himself to the reading and observance of the Scriptures in both of Abbess Hilda's monasteries, desiring greater perfection, he at length went to

---

[1] Usually identified with Tadcaster.   [2] Whitby.   [3] p. 654.   [4] pp. 669, n. 4, 685 f.

Kent to Archbishop Theodore of blessed memory, and after he had spent some time there in sacred studies, he resolved to go also to Rome, which at that time was reckoned very beneficial. Returning from there to Britain, he took his way into the province of the Hwicce, which King Osric was then ruling, and stayed there a long time, preaching the word of the faith, and at the same time giving an example of good living to those who saw and heard him. At that time, the bishop of that province, Bosel, was weighed down with so great infirmity of body that he could not himself perform the duties of the bishop's office; on this account, by the judgment of all, the aforesaid man was elected to the bishopric in his place, and by King Ethelred's orders was ordained by Bishop Wilfrid of blessed memory, who was at that time administering the bishopric of the Middle Angles; because Archbishop Theodore was now dead, and as yet no other had been ordained bishop in his place. In that province a little while before, that is, before Bosel, the aforesaid man of God, a most vigorous and most learned man, of excellent ability, Tatfrith by name, from this same abbess's monastery, had been elected bishop, but was snatched away by an untimely death before he could be ordained.

Thus this handmaid of Christ, Abbess Hilda, whom all who knew her used to call mother, for her singular piety and grace, was not only an example of life to those living in her own monastery, but also afforded opportunity of salvation and amendment to many living at a distance, to whom the blessed fame of her zeal and virtue was brought. For it was necessary that the dream should be fulfilled which in her infancy was seen by her mother, Bregoswith. When her husband, Hereric, lived in exile under Cerdic,[1] king of the Britons, where also he perished from poison, she fancied in a dream that he was suddenly taken away from her and she was seeking him with all diligence, but there was no trace of him anywhere. But when she was seeking him most carefully, she all at once found a very precious necklace under her garment, and as she looked at it more closely, it seemed to shine with such a blaze of light that it filled all the ends of Britain with the beauty of its brilliance. This dream was certainly fulfilled in the daughter of whom we are speaking, whose life set an example of the works of light, not only to herself, but to many wishing to live rightly.[2]

CHAPTER XXII [XXIV]. *That there was in her monastery a brother who was divinely granted the gift of song.*

In the monastery of this abbess there was a certain brother specially distinguished by the divine grace, in that he used to compose songs suited to religion and piety; so that whatever he learnt by translators from the divine Scriptures, he soon after put into poetic words with the greatest sweetness and humility, and brought it forth in his own language, that is, English. By his songs the minds of many were often fired with contempt of the world and with desire for the heavenly life. And indeed others after him in the English nation attempted to compose religious poems, but no one

[1] Probably Ceretic, whose death is entered in *Annales Cambriæ* 616. From Nennius we learn that he was king of the British kingdom of Elmet, in the West Riding. See No. 2, p. 237.
[2] The chapter concludes with an account of her death, and two visions announcing it, one to a nun of Hackness.

could equal him. For he did not learn that art of singing from men, nor taught by man, but he received freely by divine aid the gift of singing. For this reason he could never compose any trivial or vain poem, but only those which belonged to religion suited his religious tongue. For he had lived in the secular habit until he was well advanced in years, and had never learnt anything of versifying; and for this reason sometimes at an entertainment, when it was resolved for the sake of merriment that all should sing in turn, if he saw the harp approaching him, he would rise from the feast and go out and return home.

When he did this on one occasion, and having left the house where the entertainment was, had gone to the stable of the cattle which had been committed to his charge that night, and there at the proper time had composed himself to rest, there appeared to him someone in his sleep, and greeting him and calling him by his name, he said: "Cædmon, sing me something." But he replied: "I cannot sing; and for this reason I left the entertainment and came away here, because I could not sing." Then he who was speaking to him replied: "Nevertheless, you must sing to me." "What", he said, "must I sing?" And the other said: "Sing of the beginning of creation." On receiving this answer, he at once began to sing in praise of God the Creator, verses which he had never heard, of which this is the sense: "Now must we praise the Maker of the heavenly kingdom, the power of the Creator and his counsel, the deeds of the Father of glory; how he, since he is eternal God, became the Author of all wondrous works, who, as the almighty Guardian of the human race, first created the heaven as a roof for the sons of men, and next the earth."[1] This is the sense, but not the order of the words as he sang them in his sleep; for verses, though never so well composed, cannot be translated word for word from one language to another without loss of their beauty and grandeur. Awaking from his sleep, he remembered all that he had sung when sleeping, and soon added more words in the same manner in song worthy of God.

In the morning he came to the reeve,[2] who was over him, and told him of the gift he had received; and he was conducted to the abbess and ordered to tell his dream and sing the song in the presence of many learned men, that it might be tested by the judgment of them all what this which he related was, and whence it came. And it seemed to them all that heavenly grace had been conferred on him by the Lord. They expounded to him a passage of sacred history or doctrine, enjoining him, if he could, to put it into verse. And having undertaken this task he went away, and returning the next morning, he rendered what they had ordered composed in most excellent verse. Whereupon the abbess, joyfully esteeming the grace of God in the man, advised him to give up the secular habit and take upon him the monastic way of life, and she received him into the monastery, and with all her people she joined him to the company of the brothers and ordered that he should be taught the course of sacred history. And remembering all that he could learn by listening, and like, as it

---

[1] The Old English lines which Bede is translating are preserved, both in an Old Northumbrian version, found already in the two oldest MSS. of Bede's *Ecclesiastical History*, and also transposed into West Saxon in the Old English Bede of Alfred's time, where the translator substitutes the actual poem for Bede's Latin summary. See E. van K. Dobbie, *The Manuscripts of Cædmon's Hymn and Bede's Death Song*, pp. 10-48.

[2] *vilicus.*

were, a clean animal chewing the cud, he turned it into most harmonious song, and, sweetly singing it, he made his teachers in their turn his hearers. He sang of the creation of the world and the origin of mankind, and all the history of Genesis, of the exodus of Israel from Egypt and the entry into the land of promise, of very many other stories of Holy Scripture, of the incarnation of the Lord, his passion, resurrection, and ascension into heaven, of the coming of the Holy Spirit, and of the teaching of the Apostles. Also he made many songs about the terror of the future judgment, and the horror of the pains of hell, and the sweetness of the heavenly kingdom; besides very many others about the divine blessings and judgments, in all of which he endeavoured to draw men away from the love of vice and to incite them to the love and practice of well-doing. For he was a very religious man, and humbly submissive to the discipline of the rule; but against those who wished to do otherwise, he burned with the zeal of great fervour; for which reason he finished his life with a beautiful death.

For when the time of his departure drew near, he laboured for fourteen days preceding it under bodily infirmity, yet so moderately that all that time he could both speak and walk. There was in the neighbourhood a house to which those who were sick and who seemed near to death were wont to be carried. He therefore asked his attendant as evening approached on the night when he was to depart from this world, to prepare in it for him a place to rest. And the man wondered why he should ask this, for he by no means seemed yet about to die, but yet he did what he had asked. And when they had moved there and with a joyful heart were conversing and jesting with those who were already there, and it was already past midnight, he asked if they had the Eucharist within. They replied: "What need is there of the Eucharist? For you are not likely to die yet, when you talk so cheerfully with us, as if in health." He replied: "Yet bring me the Eucharist." And, receiving it in his hand, he asked if they were all in charity with him, and had no complaint against him, nor quarrel nor grudge. They replied that they were all in perfect charity with him, and free from all anger, and in their turn they asked him to be in charity with them. He replied instantly: "I am in charity, my children, with all the servants of God." And thus, fortifying himself with the heavenly viaticum, he prepared for entry into another life; and he asked how near was the hour when the brothers should be aroused to sing the nocturnal praises to the Lord. They replied: "It is not far off." And he said: "It is well, let us then await that hour." And signing himself with the sign of the Holy Cross, he laid his head on the pillow, and falling asleep for a little while, thus ended his life in silence.

And thus it came about, that, as he had served the Lord with a simple and pure mind and quiet devotion, he also left the world by a quiet death, and came to his sight; and with the tongue which had composed so many salutary words in praise of the Creator, he uttered also his last words in his praise, signing himself and commending his spirit into his hands; and by what we have related, he seems to have had foreknowledge of his death.[1]

[1] Chap. XXIII (XXV) tells how the Scot Adamnan had a vision that the monastery of Coldingham, where discipline had become slack, would be burnt down, and how after the death of its abbess, Æbbe, the vision was fulfilled.

CHAPTER XXIV [XXVI]. *Concerning the death of the kings Ecgfrith and Hlothhere.*

In the year of the incarnation of our Lord 684, Ecgfrith, king of the Northumbrians, sent Ealdorman Briht with an army to Ireland, and miserably laid waste that unoffending people, always most friendly to the English nation, to such an extent that the hostile force spared not even churches or monasteries. But the islanders both repelled force with force, as far as they were able, and, invoking the help of the divine goodness, called down the vengeance of heaven with constant imprecations. And though such as curse cannot possess the kingdom of God,[1] yet it was believed that those who were justly cursed for their impiety, soon suffered the penalty of their guilt by the vengeance of God. For the very next year, when that same king had rashly led his army to devastate the province of the Picts, though many of his friends opposed it, and especially Cuthbert of blessed memory, who had lately been ordained bishop, the enemy pretended to flee, and the king was drawn on into a narrow pass in inaccessible mountains, and destroyed with the greater part of the forces he had led there, in the 40th year of his age, and the 15th of his reign, on 20 May. And indeed, as I have said, his friends had advised him not to undertake this war; but since in the preceding year he had refused to listen to the most reverend Father Egbert, who advised him not to attack Ireland which was doing him no harm, it was laid on him as a punishment for his sin that he now should not listen to those who wished to hold him back from death.

From that time the hope and strength of the kingdom of the English began "to ebb and slide backwards away".[2] For the Picts recovered their own land which the English had held, and the Scots who were in Britain, and also some part of the Britons, recovered their liberty, which they have now enjoyed for about forty-six years. Among many of the race of the English who were either killed by the sword there, or given up to slavery, or escaped from the land of the Picts by flight, the most reverend man of God, Trumwine, who had received the bishopric among them, withdrew with his people that were in the monastery of Abercorn, situated it is true in the country of the English, but near to the arm of the sea which separates the lands of the English from those of the Picts. Commending his followers to his friends in the monasteries, wherever he could, he himself chose his place of abode in the often mentioned monastery of the servants and handmaids of God, which is called *Streoneshealh*;[3] and there with a few of his followers he led a life of monastic austerity for many years, beneficial not to himself alone, but to many. There also he died, and was buried in the church of the blessed Apostle Peter, with the honour due to his life and order. At that time the royal virgin, Ælfflæd, was presiding over that monastery, along with her mother, Eanflæd, both of whom we have mentioned above.[4] But when the bishop came there, that devout teacher found him a very great help in governing, and a comfort in her own life. Aldfrith succeeded Ecgfrith in the kingdom, being a man most learned in the Scriptures, who was said to be his brother, and a son of King Oswiu; and he nobly restored the ruined state of the kingdom, though within narrower bounds.

[1] I Corinthians vi. 10.   [2] Virgil, *Aeneid* ii. 169.
[3] Whitby.   [4] See pp. 614, 622, 637f., 639.

The same year, which was 685 from the incarnation of our Lord, Hlothhere, king of the people of Kent, when he had reigned twelve years after his brother Egbert, who had reigned nine years, died on 6 February. For he was wounded in a battle against the South Saxons whom Eadric,[1] the son of Egbert, had gathered against him, and died while the wound was being dressed. This same Eadric reigned one and a half years after him, and on his death, kings of doubtful title and foreigners wasted that kingdom for some time, until the legitimate king, Wihtred,[2] the son of Egbert, becoming secure in the kingdom, delivered his people from foreign invasion by his piety and zeal.

CHAPTER XXV [XXVII].[3] *The man of God, Cuthbert, was made a bishop; and how he lived and taught while still in the monastic life.*

In the same year in which King Ecgfrith departed from life, he had the holy and venerable man Cuthbert ordained bishop of the church of Lindisfarne, as we have said. He had led for many years a solitary life in great continence of body and mind in a very small island, which is called Farne,[4] in the ocean, distant about nine miles from that same church. Indeed, from his earliest childhood he had always been inflamed with zeal for the religious life, and he adopted the name and habit of a monk when quite a young man. He first entered the monastery of Melrose, which is on the bank of the River Tweed, and which was then ruled by Abbot Eata, the most gentle and simple of men, who afterwards was made bishop of the church of Hexham or of Lindisfarne, as we have said above.[5] The prior of the monastery was at that time Boisil, a priest of great virtue and prophetic spirit. Cuthbert, humbly submitting himself to this man's direction, received from him both a knowledge of the Scriptures and an example of good works.

After he had departed to the Lord, Cuthbert was made prior of the same monastery, and instructed many in the regular life by his authority as a master and by the example of his behaviour. Nor did he bestow advice concerning life under the rule and his example on his own monastery only, but also endeavoured to convert the people round about far and wide from a life of foolish habits to a love of the heavenly joys. For many profaned with wicked deeds the faith they held; and some also in the time of the plague neglected the sacraments of the faith in which they were trained, and had recourse to the false remedies of idolatry, as if they could stop the plague sent by God the Creator with incantations or amulets or any other secrets of devilish art. Therefore to correct the error of both sorts, he often went out of the monastery, sometimes riding on a horse, but more often going on foot, and came to the surrounding villages and preached the way of truth to those going astray; which also Boisil had been wont to do in his time. It was then the custom of the English people, that when a cleric or priest came into a village, all flocked at his command ready to hear the word, willingly listened to what was said, and still more willingly followed up with deeds the things which they could hear and understand. Moreover, Cuthbert had such great skill in speaking, such great desire to convince of what he

---

[1] See No. 30.   [2] See No. 31.
[3] In this and the following chapters Bede draws largely on his separate Life of this saint. I have curtailed still further, giving only those parts important for ecclesiastical and political history.
[4] See p. 631.   [5] See pp. 642 f.

had begun to teach, such light in his angelic face, that no one present presumed to conceal from him the secrets of his heart; but all openly revealed in confession the things they had done, because they certainly thought that these could by no means be hidden from him; and they wiped out the sins they had confessed by "fruits worthy of repentance"[1] as he commanded. He was wont especially to visit those places, to preach in those villages, which were far away among steep and wild mountains, which others were afraid to visit, and whose poverty and ignorance prevented the approach of teachers. But he, willingly devoting himself to that pious work, tended them with such industry in his skilful teaching, that when he went out of the monastery he often did not return for a whole week, sometimes for two or three, and occasionally even for a full month; but he stayed among the mountains, to call that rustic people to the things of heaven by his preaching of the word as well as by virtuous deeds.

When this venerable servant of the Lord had spent many years in the monastery of Melrose, and distinguished himself by many miracles, his most reverend abbot, Eata, transferred him to the island of Lindisfarne, that there also he might instruct the brothers in the observance of regular discipline both by a prior's authority and his own behaviour. For the same most reverend father then governed that place also as abbot. For from ancient times there, the bishop lived with his clergy and the abbot with his monks, who yet belonged likewise to the bishop's charge as part of his household; because Aidan, who was the first bishop of the place, coming with monks and being himself a monk, established the monastic way of life there; as the blessed Father Augustine is known to have done earlier in Kent. . . .[2]

CHAPTER XXVI [XXVIII]. *St. Cuthbert, living the life of an anchorite, by his prayer brought forth a spring in the dry land, and obtained a crop by labour of his hands from seed sown out of season.*[3]

. . . When he had served God there[4] in solitude for many years, the mound which encompassed his dwelling being so high that he could see from it but the heavens, which he thirsted to enter, it happened that a great synod was assembled in the presence of King Ecgfrith by the River Aln at a place which is called 'Twyford', which signifies 'at the double ford', over which Archbishop Theodore of blessed memory presided, and Cuthbert was by the unanimous consent of all elected to the bishopric of the church of Lindisfarne. When he could not, however, by any means be drawn from his monastery by many messengers and letters sent to him, at length the aforesaid king himself, with the most holy Bishop Trumwine, and also other religious and powerful men, sailed to the island. Also many of the brothers of the island of Lindisfarne came together for this same purpose; and all knelt, conjured him by the Lord, poured out their tears, implored; until they drew him, also in tears, from his beloved retreat, and brought him to the synod. When he arrived there, he was overcome, though greatly resisting, by the unanimous wish of them all, and forced to submit his neck to the yoke of the bishopric; being especially prevailed on by the words of Boisil, the servant of the Lord, who had predicted that he would become

---

[1] Luke iii. 8. [2] Bede then quotes part of Gregory's letter on this subject (see p. 599).
[3] This rubric describes only the first half of the chapter, which I have omitted, retaining only the part of more historical interest, which the rubric ignores. [4] On Farne island.

a bishop when he revealed to him with prophetical sight all things that would befall him. Yet the consecration was not decreed immediately; but after the winter, which was then approaching, it was performed at the festival of Easter at York in the presence of the aforesaid King Ecgfrith, seven bishops having assembled for his consecration, among whom Theodore of blessed memory held the primacy. He was first elected to the bishopric of the church of Hexham in place of Tunberht, who had been deposed from the episcopate; but since he preferred to be set over the church of Lindisfarne, in which he had lived, it was thought fit that Eata should return to the see of the church of Hexham, to which charge he had first been ordained, and Cuthbert should take upon him the government of the church of Lindisfarne. . . .[1]

CHAPTER XXVII [XXIX]. *Cuthbert, now bishop, foretold that his death was at hand to the anchorite Herbert.*[2]

. . . The most reverend father died in the island of Farne, earnestly entreating the brothers that he might also be buried there, where for no short time he had been a soldier for the Lord. But at length won over by their prayers, he gave his consent that he should be taken back to the island of Lindisfarne and buried in the church. When this was done, the venerable Bishop Wilfrid held the bishopric of that church for one year, until a bishop should be chosen to be ordained in Cuthbert's place. And after this Eadberht was appointed, a man distinguished for knowledge of the divine Scriptures, and for his observance of the heavenly precepts, and especially for alms-giving; so that he gave every year according to the law the tithe not only of four-footed beasts, but also of all corn and fruits, as also of garments, to the poor.[3]

BOOK V

CHAPTER VII.[4] *Ceadwalla, king of the West Saxons, went to Rome to be baptized; and his successor Ine also devoutly approached the same threshold of the holy Apostles.*

In the third year of Aldfrith's reign, Ceadwalla, king of the West Saxons, when he had ruled his people most vigorously for two years, relinquished his rule for the sake of the Lord and an everlasting kingdom, and went to Rome; desiring to obtain for

[1] Here follows a panegyric of his behaviour as bishop, in general terms.

[2] Here again, the rubric refers only to part of the chapter. The chapter tells how Herbert, who lived on an island in Derwentwater, was granted by Cuthbert's intercession his desire not to outlive him, and of their both dying on the same day, 20 March 687.

[3] Chap. XXVIII [XXX], from the Life, treats of the finding of Cuthbert's body uncorrupt at his translation on 20 March 698. In chaps. XXIX [XXXI] and XXX [XXXII] Bede adds some miracles not in the Life, the healing of a palsied man, and of a youth with a diseased eye. This took place at Swithberht's monastery at Dacre, the existence of which we should not otherwise have known.

[4] Chap. I tells of the miraculous calming of a storm by Œthelwald, Cuthbert's successor as hermit on Farne, for many years a priest in the monastery of Ripon. Bede learnt it from Guthfrith, abbot of Lindisfarne. Chaps. II–VI are occupied with the miracles of John, Eata's successor at Hexham, and later, when Wilfrid was restored to Hexham, Bosa's successor at York. Some are told on the authority of Brihthun, abbot of the monastery founded in 'the wood of the Deirans' (*i.e.* at Beverley) by John. One took place near a chapel on the Tyne, near to Hexham, dedicated to St. Michael. Another, at a nunnery at Watton, Yorkshire, where Abbess Hereburh presided, is of interest in that John quotes a statement of his teacher Archbishop Theodore, that bloodletting on the fourth day of the moon was dangerous. We learn also that John was asked to dedicate two churches founded by men with the title *comes* 'gesith' on their estates.

himself the singular glory of being cleansed in the baptismal font at the threshold of the blessed Apostles, for he had learnt that in baptism alone the entrance into the heavenly life is opened to mankind; and he hoped at the same time that when baptized he would soon pass, pure and freed from the flesh, to the eternal joys; both which things, by the help of the Lord, came to pass as he had planned. For when he arrived there, in the pontificate of Sergius, he was baptized on the Holy Saturday before Easter Day in the year of our Lord's incarnation 689, and was seized by sickness while still in his white robes, and released from the flesh on 20 April and admitted to the kingdom of the blessed in heaven. At his baptism the aforesaid pope had given him the name of Peter, that he might be also united in name to the most blessed Prince of the Apostles, to whose most holy body he had come from the ends of the earth, led by pious love; and he was likewise buried in his church, and by the order of the pope an epitaph was written on his tomb, in which both the memory of his devotion might be preserved for ever, and the example of what he had done might kindle those reading or hearing it to zeal for religion. . . .[1]

When Ceadwalla went to Rome, Ine succeeded to the kingdom, being of royal race; and when he had held rule over that nation thirty-seven years, he in like manner relinquished the kingdom and committed it to younger men, and himself set out for the threshold of the blessed Apostles when Gregory was holding the pontificate, desiring to live as a stranger for a time on earth in the neighbourhood of the holy places, that he might deserve to be received with greater friendship by the saints in heaven. Many of the nation of the English, nobles and commons, laymen and clerics, men and women, were wont eagerly to do this at that time.

CHAPTER VIII. *When Theodore was dead Brihtwold received the dignity of the archiepiscopate; and among many whom he ordained he made Tobias, a most learned man, bishop of the church of Rochester.*

The year after that in which Ceadwalla died at Rome, that is, 690 from the incarnation of our Lord, Archbishop Theodore of blessed memory, an old man and full of days, for he was eighty-eight, died; and he had been wont long before to predict to his followers that he would live to that age, having had it revealed to him in a dream. He held the bishopric twenty-two years, and was buried in the church of St. Peter, where the bodies of all bishops of Canterbury are buried; of whom, as well as of his fellows of the same degree, it may rightly and truly be said that "their bodies are buried in peace, and their name liveth unto generation and generation".[2] For, to speak briefly, the churches of the English received more spiritual advantage in the time of his episcopate than they ever could before. His character, life, age and death are plainly and lucidly unfolded to all comers by the epitaph in thirty-four heroic lines on his tomb. . . .[3]

Brihtwold succeeded Theodore in the episcopate, being abbot in the monastery which lies near the northern mouth of the River Yantlet, and is called Reculver; he

---

[1] Bede gives this epitaph, which adds to our factual knowledge that the pope stood sponsor to Ceadwalla, and that the latter was about 30 when he died.
[2] Ecclesiasticus xliv. 14.
[3] Bede quotes the first four and the last four lines. They tell us that Theodore died on 19 September.

also was a man trained in knowledge of the Scriptures and deeply learned in ecclesiastical as well as monastic discipline, yet not to be compared with his predecessor. He
was elected to the bishopric in the year of our Lord's incarnation 692, on the first day
of July, when Wihtred and Swæfheard were reigning in Kent, but he was consecrated
in the following year on Sunday, 29 June, by Godwine, metropolitan bishop of Gaul,[1]
and was enthroned on Sunday, 31 August. Among the many bishops whom he
ordained, when Gefmund, bishop of the church of Rochester died, he consecrated in
his place Tobias, a man skilled in the Latin, Greek and Saxon languages, and of much
erudition otherwise.

CHAPTER IX. *The holy man Egbert wished to go to preach in Germany, but could not; then
Wihtberht went, but because he could not succeed at all, he came back to Ireland, whence he
had come.*

At that time the venerable servant of Christ, the Bishop[2] Egbert, who is to be
named with all honour and who, as we related before,[3] spent his life as a stranger[4] in
the island of Ireland to acquire a country in heaven, planned in his mind to profit
many; namely to take up the apostolic work, and by preaching the gospel, to bring
the word of God to some of those races who had not yet heard of it; many of such
nations he knew to be in Germany, from whom the Angles or Saxons who now
inhabit Britain are known to have derived their race and origin; for which reason they
are still corruptly called *Garmani* by the neighbouring nation of the Britons. There are
the Frisians, Rugini,[5] Danes, Huns, Old Saxons and the Boructvari;[6] there are very
many other peoples in the same parts still following pagan rites, to whom the aforesaid soldier of Christ intended to come, sailing round Britain, to try if perchance he
could deliver any of them from Satan and bring them over to Christ; or, if this could
not be done, to go to Rome to see and adore the thresholds of the blessed Apostles
and martyrs of Christ. . . .[7]

However, one of his companions, Wihtberht by name, since he was noted for his
contempt of the world and for his learning, for he had lived the life of an anchorite
in great perfection for many years as a stranger in Ireland, took ship, and arriving in
Friesland preached the word of salvation for two whole years to that nation and its
king, Radbod,[8] but gained no fruit for so great labour among the barbarous hearers.
Then returning to the place of his loved pilgrimage, he gave himself up to the Lord
in his accustomed silence; and seeing that he could not profit foreigners by leading
them to the faith, he took care to profit more fully his own people by the example
of his virtue.

---

[1] He was archbishop of Lyons.
[2] Bede sometimes uses *sacerdos* in its older sense of bishop, not merely priest, and as there is adequate
evidence that Egbert was a bishop, it probably has that meaning here.
[3] p. 644, n. 1.
[4] The word *peregrinus* combines the meaning of 'foreigner' and 'pilgrim'.
[5] This people gave its name to the island of Rügen, but later moved south, occupying the present
Austria in the fifth century.
[6] A people living in Westphalia.
[7] But visions seen by one of his followers, a disciple of Boisil, and a storm at sea, convinced him that it
was his duty to remain in Ireland and to bring the Columban monasteries to the catholic Easter.
[8] See No. 157.

CHAPTER X. *Willibrord, preaching in Friesland, converted many to Christ; and his fellows the Hewalds suffered martyrdom.*

When the man of God, Egbert, perceived that he himself was not permitted to go to preach to the nations, being withheld for the sake of some other advantage of the Holy Church, of which he had been forewarned by a revelation, and that Wihtberht when he went into those parts had had no success, he still attempted to send holy and zealous men to the work of preaching the word, among whom the most illustrious was Willibrord, eminent for his rank of priest and his merit. When they arrived there, twelve in number, and turned aside to Pippin, ruler[1] of the Franks, they were gladly received by him; and as he had lately subdued the nearer part of Friesland, expelling King Radbod, he sent them to preach there; supporting them at the same time with his sovereign authority, that none might molest them in their preaching, and advancing with many benefits those who were willing to accept the faith. Thus it came to pass, with the help of the divine grace, that in a short time they converted many from idolatry to the faith of Christ.

Following their example, two priests of the nation of the English, who had lived in exile in Ireland for a long time for the sake of the eternal country, came to the province of the Old Saxons, to see if perchance they could acquire there any for Christ by their preaching. They were both alike in name, as in devotion; for each of them was called Hewald, but with this distinction, that on account of the difference in their hair one was called Black Hewald, the other White Hewald. Both were full of religious piety, but Black Hewald was the better educated in the Holy Scriptures. On entering that province they came into the guest-house of a certain reeve,[2] and besought him to conduct them to the magnate[3] who was over him, because they had a message to his advantage which they must communicate to him. For those Old Saxons have no king, but several magnates set over their nation, and if war breaks out they cast lots impartially, and all follow as commander and obey in time of war whomsoever the lot indicates; but when the war is over, all the magnates again become equal in power. Accordingly the reeve received them, and promising that he would send them to the magnate who was over him, kept them for some days with him as they asked.

But when the barbarians perceived that they were of another religion—for they devoted themselves continually to psalms and prayers, and offered daily to God the sacrifice of the saving oblation, having with them sacred vessels and a consecrated table for an altar—they grew suspicious of them, that if they came to the magnate, and spoke with him, they might turn him from their gods, and convert him to the new religion of the Christian faith, and thus gradually all their province should be forced to change its old religion for a new. So they suddenly laid hold of them, and put them to death, White Hewald with a quick death by the sword, but Black Hewald with long torture, tearing him horribly limb from limb. They threw the dead bodies into the Rhine. But when the magnate whom they had wished to see heard this, he

---

[1] Pippin was Mayor of the Palace, and real ruler of the Franks. Bede uses the same Latin term as for the English official called an *ealdorman*, the highest secular authority under the king.
[2] *vilicus.*   [3] *satraps.*

was greatly enraged, that strangers wishing to come to him had not been allowed; and he sent and killed all those villagers and burned the village with fire. The aforesaid priests and servants of Christ suffered on 3 October. . . .[1]

CHAPTER XI. *The venerable men are ordained bishops of Friesland, Swithberht in Britain, Willibrord in Rome.*

At the time of their first coming into Friesland, as soon as Willibrord found that he had leave given him by the prince to preach, he hastened to go to Rome, where Pope Sergius then presided over the apostolic see, that he might undertake the desired work of preaching the gospel to the nations with his licence and blessing; also hoping to obtain from him some relics of the blessed apostles and martyrs of Christ, so that when he destroyed the idols and erected churches in the nation to which he preached, he might have the relics of saints at hand to put into them; and having deposited them there, might accordingly dedicate each of those places to the honour of the saint whose relics they were. He desired also to learn there or receive from there many other things which so great a work required. And when he had obtained his wish in all these matters, he returned to preach.

At that time, the brothers who were committed to the ministry of the word in Friesland chose out of their own number a man of modest behaviour and meek of heart, Swithberht, to be ordained bishop for them. He, being sent into Britain, was consecrated at their request by the most reverend Bishop Wilfrid, who at that time had been driven from his own country and happened to be living in exile in the districts of the Mercians. For Kent had no bishop at that time; Theodore was dead, and Brihtwold, his successor, who had gone across the sea to be ordained, had not yet returned to the see of his bishopric.

When the said Swithberht had been made bishop and had returned from Britain, he not long afterwards departed to the Boructvari and brought many of them to the way of truth by his preaching. But not long after, the Boructvari were conquered by the nation of the Old Saxons, and those who had received the word were dispersed abroad, and the bishop himself with certain others came to Pippin, who at the intercession of his wife, Bliththryth,[2] gave him a dwelling-place on an island in the Rhine, which is called in their language 'On the shore';[3] on which he built a monastery, which his heirs still possess, and for a time led a most continent life in it, and ended his days there.

After those who had come thither had taught for some years in Friesland, Pippin, with the consent of them all, sent the venerable Willibrord to Rome, where Sergius still held the pontificate, requesting that he might be ordained archbishop for the Frisian nation. And thus it was done as he asked, in the year of the incarnation of the Lord 696.[4] He was consecrated in the church of the holy martyr Cecilia, on her

---

[1] Their bodies floated upstream, and were revealed by a ray of light and by a vision to one of their comrades, Tilmon. Pippin had them buried with honour in Cologne.

[2] *i.e.* Plectrudis in Frankish sources.   [3] Now Kaiserswerth.

[4] The note written in Willibrord's calendar, doubtless by himself, gives the date as 695. If Bede is commencing his year on 24 September, St. Cecilia's day, 22 November 695, would fall in his 696. The calendar shows that the consecration was on the eve of this festival, not on the day itself. The 23 November is St. Clement's day, hence Willibrord's name.

festival, and he was given the name of Clement by the said pope, and sent at once back to his bishopric, 14 days after he had arrived in the city.

Pippin gave to him a site for his episcopal see in his famous fortress which is called in the ancient language of those races *Wiltaburg*, that is, the town of the Wilti, but in the language of the Gauls *Trajectum*;[1] in this the most reverend bishop built a church, and, preaching the word of the faith far and wide, and recalling many people from error, he erected several churches through those regions, and some monasteries. For not long afterwards he himself appointed also other bishops in those regions out of the number of the brothers who came to preach there, either with him, or after him; some of whom have now fallen asleep in the Lord. But Willibrord himself, surnamed Clement, is still alive, venerable for his great age, being in his 36th year as a bishop, and longing with all his heart for the rewards of the heavenly recompense after the manifold conflicts of heavenly warfare.[2]

CHAPTER XV. *Several churches of the Scots, at the instance of Adamnan, accepted the catholic Easter; and the same Adamnan wrote a book about the holy places.*

At this time a great part of the Scots in Ireland, and also some of the Britons in Britain, adopted by the grace of God the reasonable and catholic time of observing Easter. For when Adamnan,[3] priest and abbot of the monks who were in the island of Iona, was sent by his own nation on an embassy, and came to Aldfrith, king of the English, he stayed for some time in that province and observed the canonical rites of the Church. He was earnestly admonished by many of the more learned men, not to presume to live contrary to the universal custom of the Church, either in the observance of Easter or in any other decrees whatever, with his very few followers dwelling in the farthest corner of the world; and changed his views, so that he readily preferred the things which he had seen and heard in the churches of the English to the customs of himself and his followers. For he was a good and wise man, and excellently instructed in the knowledge of the Scriptures.[4]

CHAPTER XVIII. *The South Saxons received Eadberht and Ealla, the West Saxons Daniel and Aldhelm, as their bishops; and concerning the writings of the same Aldhelm.*

In the year of the incarnation of our Lord 705, Aldfrith, king of the Northumbrians, died, before the end of the twentieth year of his reign; and his son Osred, a boy of about eight years, succeeded him in his dominion and reigned eleven years. At the beginning of his reign, Hædde, bishop of the West Saxons,[5] departed to the heavenly

---

[1] Utrecht.

[2] Chaps. XII–XIV contain accounts of visions of the other world, a type of literature that obtained great popularity. The first was granted to a man called Dryhthelm, of the district of Cunningham in Northumbria, who came back from the dead to relate a horrific tale, and entered the monastery of Melrose, in the abbacy of Æthelwold, later bishop of Lindisfarne. King Aldfrith was deeply impressed by his vision. The second was revealed to a worldly king's thegn of King Cenred of Mercia. Bede learnt the story from Bishop Pehthelm of Whithorn. The third came to a brother Bede had himself known, whose name and monastery he deliberately conceals. [3] See No. 153.

[4] The rest of the chapter deals with Adamnan's unsuccessful attempt to make Iona adopt the catholic Easter, with his death, and with his book on the holy places, written on the authority of a Gaulish bishop Arculf who had been to Jerusalem and was shipwrecked in Britain. Adamnan presented this book to King Aldfrith, and Bede wrote on the same subject, inserting passages from his own work in chaps. XVI and XVII.

[5] See pp. 627, 653.

life, for he was a good and just man, and his life and teaching as a bishop were actuated more by his innate love of virtue than by what he had learned from books. In fact, the most reverend Bishop Pehthelm, of whom we must speak further on in the proper place,[1] who for a long time while still a deacon or monk was with his successor Aldhelm, used to say that many miraculous cures were wrought in the place where he died, through the merits of his sanctity, and that the men of that province used to put dust brought from there into water for sick men, and the drinking or sprinkling of it restored health to many sick, both men and animals; so that by the frequent removal of the sacred dust a large hole was made there.

Upon his death, the bishopric of that province was divided into two dioceses. One was given to Daniel, which he governs to this day; the other to Aldhelm, which he presided over most vigorously for four years; both were fully instructed as well in ecclesiastical matters as in knowledge of the Scriptures. In truth Aldhelm, when he was still priest and abbot of the monastery which is called Malmesbury, wrote at the command of a synod of his nation a notable book against the error of the Britons, in not celebrating Easter at the proper time, and in doing many other things contrary to the orthodoxy and peace of the Church, and through the reading of the book many of the Britons who were subject to the West Saxons were led by him to the catholic celebration of the Lord's Easter. He wrote also an excellent book on virginity, which, after the example of Sedulius, he composed in two-fold form, in hexameter verse, and in prose. He wrote also some other things, being a man most learned in all respects, for he had an elegant style, and was, as I have said, remarkable for learning both in liberal and ecclesiastical writings. On his death, Forthhere received the bishopric in his place, and is still alive today, he also being very learned in the Holy Scriptures.

While they were administering the bishopric, it was decided by a synodal decree that the province of the South Saxons, which hitherto belonged to the diocese of the city of Winchester, over which Daniel presided, should have an episcopal see of its own, and its own bishop; and Eadberht was consecrated as their first bishop; he was abbot of the monastery of Bishop Wilfrid of blessed memory, which is called Selsey. On his death, Ealla received the episcopal office. But since he was taken from this world some years ago, the bishopric has been void until this day.

CHAPTER XIX. *Cenred, king of the Mercians, and Offa, king of the East Saxons, ended their lives in the monastic habit at Rome; and concerning the life and death of Bishop Wilfrid.*

In the fourth year of the reign of Osred, Cenred, who had governed most nobly the kingdom of the Mercians for some time, still more nobly relinquished the sceptre of his kingdom. For he went to Rome, and was tonsured there when Constantine held the pontificate, and became a monk, remaining at the threshold of the Apostles in prayers, fasts and almsgiving, until his last day. He was succeeded in the kingdom by Ceolred, son of Ethelred, who had held the same kingdom before Cenred. With Cenred went the son of Sigehere, king of the East Saxons, of whom we spoke above,[2] Offa by name, a youth of most pleasing age and comeliness, and most eagerly desired by his whole people to hold and keep the sceptre of the kingdom. Led by like devotion of mind, he left wife, lands, kinsfolk and country for Christ and for the gospel, that he might in this life receive an hundredfold, and in the world to come, life everlasting.[1] When they came to the holy places at Rome, he also received the tonsure and, ending his life in the monastic habit, attained to the long-desired sight of the blessed Apostles in heaven.

In the same year in which they left Britain, the celebrated bishop, Wilfrid, ended his days in the province which is called Oundle, after he had been bishop for forty-five years; and his body was laid in a coffin and brought to his monastery, which is called Ripon, and buried with the honour due to so great a bishop in the church of the blessed Apostle Peter. Concerning the manner of whose life, let us turn back, and speak of a few of the things which took place.[2] Being a boy of good disposition, and virtuous beyond his years, he behaved so modestly and discreetly in all things, that he was deservedly loved, honoured and cherished by his elders as one of themselves. When he reached fourteen years, he preferred the monastic to the secular life. When he told this to his father, for his mother was already dead, he readily assented to his heavenly wishes and desires, and advised him to persist in his wholesome resolve. He came, therefore, to the island of Lindisfarne, and giving himself up to the service of the monks there, tried diligently to learn and practise the things which belong to monastic chastity and piety. And since he was of keen intelligence, he very quickly learnt the psalms and some other books; indeed, while yet untonsured, he was in no small measure remarkable for those virtues of humility and obedience, which are greater than the tonsure; on which account he was deservedly loved both by his seniors and those of his own age. And when he had served God for some years in that monastery, being a youth of keen mind, he gradually noticed that the way of virtue which was taught by the Scots was not perfect, and he resolved to go to Rome, and see what ecclesiastic or monastic rites were observed at the apostolic see. When he told this to the brethren, they praised his design, and encouraged him to carry out what he had planned. He immediately went to Queen Eanflæd, because he was known to her, and had been admitted into the afore-mentioned monastery by her advice and help, and told her that it was his wish to visit the thresholds of the blessed Apostles. She was delighted at the youth's good purpose, and sent him to Kent to King Eorcenberht, who was the son of her uncle, requesting that he would send him to Rome in an honourable manner. At that time, Honorius, one of the disciples of the blessed Pope Gregory, a man eminently instructed in ecclesiastical matters, held the archbishopric. While he stayed there some time, and, being a youth of an active mind, diligently applied himself to learn the things which he observed there, another youth arrived there, Biscop by name, surnamed Benedict, of the English nobility, also desiring to go to Rome. We have spoken of him above.[3]

---

[1] Matthew xix. 29, 30; Luke xviii. 29, 30; Mark x. 29, 30.

[2] Bede draws considerably from the Life of Wilfrid by Eddi, sometimes verbally. He leaves out much in the interests of brevity, but probably sometimes for other motives; for Bede was not dependent on Eddi alone for his knowledge of Wilfrid, most of whose troubled career took place in Bede's own lifetime. He had himself met Wilfrid, and his great friend Acca had been brought up in his household and accompanied him to Rome. Bede's omission of Wilfrid's miracles has occasioned comment.

[3] pp. 657f.

The king joined Wilfrid to his company, and ordered him to take him with him to Rome. When they reached Lyons, Wilfrid was detained there by Dalfinus, bishop of that city,[1] but Benedict eagerly completed the journey he had begun as far as Rome. For the bishop was delighted with the youth's prudent discourse, with the grace of his handsome face, with his alacrity in action, and with the constancy and maturity of his thought; therefore he supplied him and his companions with all things they needed in abundance, as long as they were with him; and moreover offered that. if he wished, he would commit to him the government of a considerable part of Gaul, and would give him a maiden, the daughter of his brother, as his wife, and would always regard him as an adopted son. But Wilfrid, thanking him for the kindness which he was pleased to show towards him, though he was a stranger, replied that he had rather resolved upon another mode of life, and for that reason had left his country and undertaken the journey to Rome.

Hearing this, the bishop sent him to Rome, giving him a guide and generously furnishing all the things necessary for the journey; and earnestly requested that when he was returning to his own land, he would remember to come that way. When he arrived in Rome, and constantly applied himself daily to prayers[2] and to the study of ecclesiastical matters, as he had planned, he gained the friendship of a most holy and learned man, the Archdeacon Boniface, who was also counsellor to the apostolic pope, by whose instruction he learned in their order the four gospels; and from the teaching of the same master he understood the correct computation of Easter, and many others things, which he could not learn in his own country, appertaining to ecclesiastical discipline. And when he had spent some months there, engaged in these happy studies, he returned to Dalfinus in Gaul, and stayed with him for three years, and was tonsured by him,[3] and held in such affection by him that he intended to make him his heir. But, that this should not happen, the bishop was cruelly killed, and Wilfrid reserved for the episcopate of his own people, that is, of the English. For Queen Balthild sent soldiers and ordered the bishop to be killed; and Wilfrid attended him, as his cleric, to the place where he was to be beheaded, desiring likewise to die with him, though he himself greatly opposed it. But the executioners, understanding that he was a foreigner, sprung from the nation of the English, spared him, and would not put him to death with his bishop.

Returning to Britain, he became a friend of King Alhfrith, who had learnt always to follow and love the catholic rules of the Church. Therefore, since he found him to be catholic, he at once gave him land of 10 hides in the place which is called *Stanford*, and not long afterwards the monastery of 30 hides in the place which is called Ripon, which place he had formerly given to those who followed the Scots, for the construction of a monastery there. But because they afterwards preferred to leave the place, when given the option, rather than accept the catholic Easter and the other canonical rites according to the use of the Roman and Apostolic Church,[4]

---

[1] See p. 640, n. 1.

[2] Eddi tells of his praying in the oratory of St. Andrew, before the gospels on the altar, that he might be granted a ready mind to read the gospels and teach them to the nations.

[3] Thus receiving the Roman, not the Celtic tonsure.

[4] Eddi says nothing about this earlier monastery at Ripon.

he gave it to him, whom he saw to be instructed in better rules and customs.

At that time by the order of the aforesaid king, he was ordained priest in the same monastery by Agilbert, bishop of the Gewisse, of whom we spoke above,[1] as the king desired that a man of so great learning and piety should be specially his priest and teacher in inseparable companionship. . . .[2]

Afterwards, in the reign of Ecgfrith, he was expelled from his bishopric,[3] and others consecrated bishops in his place, whom we have mentioned above;[4] and when, intending to go to Rome to plead his cause before the apostolic pope, he took ship, he was driven by a west wind to Friesland,[5] and honourably received by the barbarians and their king, Aldgisl. He preached to them of Christ and instructed many thousands of them in the word of truth, and cleansed them from the filth of their sins in the font of the Saviour. Thus he first began there the work of the gospel which afterwards Willibrord, the most reverend bishop of Christ, completed with great devotion. After a winter spent there happily with this new people of God, he set out again on his way to Rome;[6] and when his case was brought forward in the presence of Pope Agatho and many bishops, he was found by the judgment of all to have been wrongly accused, and to be worthy of the episcopate.

At that time, when Pope Agatho assembled at Rome a synod of 125 bishops, against those who asserted that there was one will and operation in our Lord and Saviour,[7] he ordered Wilfrid to be called also, and to declare, sitting among the bishops, his own faith, and that as well of the province, or island, from which he had come. And when he and his people were found to be catholic in faith, it was thought fit to record the same among the other acts of this same synod, and it was written in this way: "Wilfrid, beloved of God, bishop of the city of York, appealing to the apostolic see about his cause, and being acquitted by that authority from all charges specified or unspecified, and having been appointed to the seat of judgment with the other 125 fellow-bishops in the synod, confessed the true and catholic faith on behalf of all the northern part of Britain and Ireland, and the islands which are inhabited by the nations of the English and Britons, as well as the Scots and the Picts, and confirmed it with his own subscription."[8]

[1] *e.g.* pp. 627f. 640, 644, 647.
[2] Bede reports the account of Wilfrid's consecration as bishop in Gaul, and the consecration of Chad to York while he delayed abroad. See pp. 644, 648. Wilfrid received the whole province of the Northumbrians three years later when Chad retired.
[3] Bede throws no light on the reason for this expulsion. He omits Eddi's claim that it was owing to the queen's enmity towards Wilfrid, and also the long account of the proceedings in Rome, including Wilfrid's petition that, if his see must be divided, the bishops appointed should be persons with whom he could work in unity. Nor does he tell us that Agatho's pronouncement was that Wilfrid should be restored and choose his fellow-bishops with the consent of a council. He has also left out all Eddi's account of Wilfrid's activities in his episcopate, *e.g.* his restoration of York, and his buildings at Ripon and Hexham (see No. 154); also Ecgfrith's victories against the Picts (671–674) and the Mercians (673–674) while he was on good terms with Wilfrid. See No. 154.
[4] p. 654.   [5] According to Eddi, Wilfrid's landing in Friesland was intentional.
[6] Eddi describes his journey at some length, and includes an interesting conversation with the Lombard king, Perctarit, who had been bribed to hinder him, but refused, remembering how a pagan king of the Huns had refused to betray him when he himself was an exile.
[7] The Monothelite heresy.
[8] Bede puts this attestation in its chronological place. Eddi, chap. LIII, mentions it only because it was quoted when Wilfrid's last appeal was considered in Rome in 704 (see p. 679).

After this, he returned to Britain,[1] and converted the province of the South Saxons from the rites of idolatry to the faith of Christ.[2] And he also sent ministers of the word to the Isle of Wight;[3] and in the second year of Aldfrith, who reigned after Ecgfrith, he received his see and his bishopric at that same king's invitation.[4] But five years later, accused afresh, he was driven out of his bishopric by the same king and several bishops; and coming to Rome.[5] he was given the opportunity to defend himself in the presence of his accusers, before a session of many bishops with the apostolic Pope John, and it was shown by the judgment of them all that his accusers had in fact devised false accusations against him; and a letter was written by the aforesaid pope to the kings of the English, Ethelred and Aldfrith, that they should cause him to be restored to his bishopric, because he had been unjustly condemned.

His acquittal was much aided by the reading of the acts of the synod of Pope Agatho of blessed memory, which was, as we said before, formerly held when Wilfrid was in Rome and sat among the bishops at that same council. For when the acts of that synod were, as the case required, read by the orders of the apostolic pope before the nobles and a concourse of the people for some days, the place was reached where it was written: "Wilfrid . . . and the rest", as we stated above.[6] When this was read, the hearers were filled with amazement, and when the reader ceased, they began to ask one another, who that Bishop Wilfrid was. Then Boniface, the counsellor of the apostolic pope, and many others, who had seen him there in the days of Pope Agatho, said that it was that bishop who lately came to Rome, accused by his own people, to be judged by the apostolic see; "who", they said, "long ago came here upon a like accusation, and as soon as the cause and controversy of both parties had been heard and examined, was shown by Pope Agatho of blessed memory to have been wrongfully expelled from his bishopric; and was held in such honour by him, that he commanded him to sit in the council of bishops which he had assembled, as a man of incorrupt faith and upright mind". When they heard this, all pronounced, along with the pontiff himself, that a man of so great authority, who had discharged the office of bishop for nearly forty years, ought by no means to be condemned, but being cleared completely of all the faults of which he was accused should return to his own land with honour. . . .[7]

When the letters, which he had brought from the apostolic pope, were read, Archbishop Brihtwold and Ethelred, formerly king, but then abbot, readily took his part; for Ethelred called to him Cenred, whom he had made king in his place, and

---

[1] Bede is silent about Ecgfrith's refusal to accept the papal mandate, and his imprisonment of Wilfrid. It was only some nine months later that he was released and went eventually to Sussex.

[2] See pp. 654–656.   [3] See p. 656.

[4] Probably in 686. It was preceded by a reconciliation between Wildrid and Archbishop Theodore, when Wilfrid had taken refuge with Ceadwalla of Wessex. But Wilfrid seems only to have recovered Ripon. For, though Eddi says he received Hexham and York, according to Bede, Eata was immediately followed at Hexham in 686 by John, while Bosa retained York until 705.

[5] Here Bede omits the events of many years. Wilfrid spent eleven years under the protection of Ethelred of Mercia, administering his diocese. He brought his case before Sergius I by proxy in 699 or 700, and it was not until after his claims had been rejected by an English synod at Austerfield about 703 that he again went to Rome. Eddi also seems unaware of the time that elapsed between the visits.

[6] Bede repeats the opening words of the passage he has already quoted.

[7] On his way home Wilfrid fell ill, and saw a vision of the Archangel Michael, who prophesied that he would have four years to live, and would recover most of his possessions. This is the only miraculous occurrence that Bede retains in connexion with Wilfrid.

asked him to be a friend to the bishop, and prevailed. But Aldfrith, king of the Northumbrians, refused to receive him, and did not live long afterwards. So it came about that in the reign of his son Osred a synod was soon held by the River Nidd, and after some contention on both sides, at length he was admitted into the bishopric of his church with the consent of all.[1] And thus for four years, that is, until the day of his death, he lived in peace. He died in his monastery, which he possessed in the province of Oundle, under the government of Abbot Cuthwold; and was carried by the ministry of the brothers to his first monastery, which is called Ripon, and placed in the church of the blessed Apostle Peter by the altar to the south, as we mentioned above.[2]

CHAPTER XX. *Albinus succeeded to the religious Abbot Hadrian, Acca to Wilfrid in his bishopric.*

The next year after the death of the aforesaid father, that is, the fifth of King Osred, the most reverend father, Abbot Hadrian, the fellow-worker in the word of God with Bishop Theodore of blessed memory, died, and was buried in his monastery in the church of the blessed Mother of God; this was the 41st year after he was sent with Theodore by Pope Vitalian, and the 39th after he reached Britain. Of whose learning, as of Theodore's, it is one testimony among others, that his pupil Albinus, who succeeded to the government of his monastery, was so well instructed in the study of the Scriptures that he had no slight knowledge of Greek, and knew Latin no less than English, which was his native tongue.

Acca, his priest, succeeded Wilfrid in the bishopric of the church of Hexham, being likewise a most vigorous man, and eminent in the sight of God and man. He ennobled the structure of his church, which is dedicated in honour of the blessed Apostle Andrew, with multifarious adornments and marvellous works. For he took care, and he does to this day, to procure from all parts relics of the blessed apostles and martyrs of Christ, and to put up altars in veneration of them, in separate side-chapels for this purpose within the walls of the same church. He collected with the greatest industry the histories of their passions, along with other ecclesiastical books, and made there a most ample and noble library, and also he most zealously provided holy vessels, and lamps, and other such things which belong to the adornment of the house of God. He also invited to him a distinguished singer, called Maban, who had been trained in singing by the successors of the disciples of the blessed Pope Gregory in Kent, to instruct himself and his clergy, and retained him for twelve years, that he might both teach those chants of the Church which they did not know, and by his teaching restore to their former state those which had once been known, but had begun to be corrupted by long use or neglect. For Bishop Acca himself was a most skilled singer, just as he also was most learned in Holy Writ, and most orthodox in confession of the catholic faith, and well versed in the rules of ecclesiastical practice; nor does he cease to be so, until he shall receive the rewards of his pious devotion.

---

[1] He seems merely to have been restored to his churches of Ripon and Hexham. See No. 154.

[2] Bede then gives the verse epitaph, which summarizes his activities: his founding of Ripon, his gifts of gold and purple hangings, of a gold cross, of the gospels written in gold and a gold case for them, his correction of the error in observing Easter.

For he was brought up and educated from boyhood among the clergy of the most holy Bosa, beloved of God, bishop of York; and then coming to Bishop Wilfrid in the hope of a better way of life, he spent the rest of his life in his service until the bishop's death, and going with him to Rome, learnt there many profitable things about the ordinances of the Holy Church, which he could not have learnt in his own country.[1]

CHAPTER XXIII. *The present state of the English nation or of all Britain.*

In the year of the incarnation of our Lord 725, which was the seventh year of Osric, king of the Northumbrians, who succeeded Cenred, Wihtred, son of Egbert, king of the people of Kent, died on 23 April, and left as heirs to the kingdom which he had held for 34 years and a half, three sons, Ethelbert, Eadberht and Alric. The next year, Tobias, bishop of the church of Rochester, died, a most learned man, as we have said above.[2] For he was a pupil of those masters of blessed memory, Archbishop Theodore and Abbot Hadrian; hence, as has been said, besides his deep knowledge of both ecclesiastical and general literature, he so learnt both the Greek and Latin tongues that they were as well known and familiar to him as his native speech. He was buried in the chapel of St. Paul the Apostle, which he had himself built within the church of St. Andrew as his own place of burial. After him Ealdwulf received the office of bishop, and was consecrated by Archbishop Brihtwold.

In the year of the incarnation of our Lord 729, two comets appeared about the sun, to the great terror of the beholders. One of them went before the sun in the morning at its rising; the other followed it in the evening at its setting, as if presaging dire destruction both to the east and to the west; or assuredly one was the forerunner of the day, the other of the night, to signify that mortals were threatened with calamities at both times. They carried their torch of flame towards the north, as if it were ready to kindle a fire; they appeared in the month of January, and continued for nearly two weeks. At that time a dreadful plague of Saracens wasted Gaul with miserable slaughter, but themselves not long after suffered in that same province the punishment due to their unbelief.[3] In this year the holy man of God, Egbert,[4] departed to the Lord, as we have said above, on Easter Day itself; and immediately after Easter, namely on 9 May, Osric, king of the Northumbrians, departed this life, when he had decreed that his successor to the kingdom, which he had governed for eleven years, should be Ceolwulf, the brother of that King Cenred who had ruled before him; the beginning and course of whose reign have been filled with so many and great disturbances from opponents, that it cannot yet be known what ought to be written about them, or what end they will have.

[1] Chap. XXI tells of the request of the Pictish king, Naiton, to Abbot Ceolfrith for a letter to confute those who opposed the Roman Easter, and for builders to build a stone church. The long letter sent by Ceolfrith is certainly Bede's. It shows that Adamnan had visited Ceolfrith's monastery. Chap. XXII tells how Iona was persuaded to adopt the Roman Easter by Egbert (see p. 671), in 716, when Osred of Northumbria had been slain, and Cenred had succeeded.

[2] p. 671.

[3] If, as is generally assumed and seems probable, Bede is referring to the victory of Charles Martel at Tours in 732, he must have added this passage after he had, as he says, finished the work in 731.

[4] See pp. 644, n. 1, 671.

In the year of the incarnation of our Lord 731, Archbishop Brihtwold, consumed with old age, died on 13 January; he had occupied his see 37 years, 6 months and 14 days. An archbishop was appointed in his place in the same year, Tatwine by name, from the province of the Mercians, who had been a priest in the monastery which is called Breedon.[1] He was consecrated in the city of Canterbury by the venerable men, the bishops Daniel of Winchester, Ingwold of London, Ealdwine of Lichfield, and Ealdwulf of Rochester, on the tenth day of the month of June, a Sunday; he is a man renowned for piety and wisdom and notably learned in sacred Scriptures.

And thus at present the bishops Tatwine and Ealdwulf preside over the churches of the people of Kent;[2] Bishop Ingwold over the province of the East Saxons,[3] Bishops Ealdberht and Hathulac over the province of the East Angles,[4] Bishops Daniel and Forthhere over the province of the West Saxons,[5] Bishop Ealdwine over the province of the Mercians,[6] and Bishop Wealhstod over those people who dwell beyond the River Severn to the west,[7] Bishop Wilfrid over the province of the Hwicce;[8] Bishop Cyneberht over the province of the people of Lindsey. The bishopric of the Isle of Wight belongs to Daniel, bishop of Winchester. The province of the South Saxons, having now for some years remained without a bishop, seeks its episcopal ministrations from the prelate of the West Saxons. All these provinces, and the other southern provinces as far as the boundary formed by the River Humber, with their kings, are subject to Æthelbald, king of the Mercians.

But in the province of the Northumbrians, where King Ceolwulf reigns, four bishops now preside: Wilfrid[9] in the church of York, Æthelwold in that of Lindisfarne, Acca in that of Hexham, Pehthelm in that which is called *Candida Casa*,[10] which, as the number of the faithful has increased, has lately been made into an episcopal see and has him as its first bishop.

The nation of the Picts also at this time both keeps a treaty of peace with the race of the English, and rejoices in having its part with the universal Church in catholic peace and truth. The Scots who live in Britain, content with their own territories, meditate no attacks or plots against the English people. The Britons, though for the most part they oppose the race of the English from their personal hatred, and the appointed Easter of the whole Catholic Church in error, with their wicked customs, can yet, as both divine and human strength resists them, in neither case attain their purpose as they wish; for though in part they are their own masters, yet part of them are brought under subjection to the English.

In times of such happy peace and serenity, many in the race of the Northumbrians, nobles as well as private persons, laying aside their weapons and receiving the tonsure, are eager to devote themselves and their children to monastic vows rather than to engage in military pursuits. What will be the end of it, a later age will see.

This is for the present the state of all Britain, in the year since the coming of the English to Britain about 285, and in the year of the incarnation of our Lord 731; in whose perpetual reign "let the earth rejoice", and while Britain exults with them

---

[1] Breedon-on-the-Hill, Leics.	[2] Canterbury and Rochester.	[3] London.
[4] Dunwich and Elmham.	[5] Winchester and Sherborne.	[6] Lichfield.
[7] Hereford.	[8] Worcester.　　　[9] Wilfrid II.	[10] Whithorn.

in his faith, "let many islands be glad",[1] and "give praise to the memory of his holiness".[2]

CHAPTER XXIV. *Chronological recapitulation of the whole work;*[3] *and concerning the author himself.*

I have thought fit briefly to recapitulate the things which have been considered more at length in the division of periods, for preserving them in memory.

In the sixtieth year before the incarnation of our Lord, Gaius Julius Caesar, first of the Romans, invaded Britain and was victorious but yet could not obtain the rule there. [I. II.]

In the year of the incarnation of our Lord 46, Claudius, second of the Romans to come to Britain, received the surrender of the greater part of the island, and also added the Orkney islands to the Roman empire. [I. III.]

In the year of the incarnation of our Lord 167, Eleutherius, being made bishop of Rome, ruled the Church gloriously for fifteen years. Lucius, king of Britain, sending a letter to him, asked to be made a Christian, and obtained his request. [I. IV.]

In the year of the incarnation of our Lord 189, Severus, being made emperor, reigned for seventeen years, and enclosed Britain with a rampart from sea to sea. [I. V.]

In the year 381, Maximus, created emperor in Britain, crossed to Gaul, and killed Gratian. [I. IX.]

In the year 409, Rome was stormed by the Goths, from which time the Romans ceased to rule in Britain. [I. XI.]

In the year 430, Palladius was sent by Pope Celestinus to the Scots who believed in Christ, as their first bishop. [I. XIII.]

In the year 449, Marcian receiving the empire along with Valentinian held it seven years, in whose time the English, invited by the Britons, came to Britain. [I. XV.]

In the year 538, there was an eclipse of the sun on 16 February, from the first hour until the third.

In the year 540, there was an eclipse of the sun on 20 June, and the stars appeared for almost half an hour, after the third hour of the day.[4]

In the year 547, Ida began to reign, from whom the royal family of the Northumbrians derives its origin, and he continued twelve years on the throne.[5]

In the year 565, the priest Columba came from the land of the Scots to Britain, to teach the Picts, and built a monastery on the island of Iona. [III. IV.]

In the year 596, Pope Gregory sent Augustine with his monks to Britain, to preach the word of God to the nation of the English. [I. XXIII.]

In the year 597, the aforesaid teachers arrived in Britain; this was 150 years, more or less, from the coming of the English into Britain. [I. XXV.]

In the year 601, Pope Gregory sent the *pallium* to Britain to Augustine, who was already made bishop; also several ministers of the word, among whom was Paulinus. [I. XXIX.]

---

[1] Psalm xcvi, 1.   [2] Psalm xxix, 5.
[3] This chronological summary is of interest for its influence on the Anglo-Saxon Chronicle.
[4] There is nothing about these eclipses in the narrative part of the work.
[5] This is not in the narrative portion.

In the year 603, a battle was fought at *Degsastan*. [I. xxxiv.]

In the year 604, the East Saxons under King Sæberht and Bishop Mellitus adopted the faith of Christ. [II. iii.]

In the year 605, Gregory died. [II. i.]

In the year 616, Ethelbert, king of the people of Kent, died. [II. v.]

In the year 625, Paulinus was ordained bishop for the people of Northumbria, by Archbishop Justus. [II. ix.]

In the year 626, Eanflæd, daughter of King Edwin, was baptized with twelve companions on Whit-Saturday. [II. ix.]

In the year 627, King Edwin, with his people, was baptized at Easter. [II. xiv.]

In the year 633, King Edwin being killed, Paulinus returned to Kent. [II. xx.]

In the year 640, Eadbald, king of the people of Kent, died. [III. viii.]

In the year 642, King Oswald was killed. [III. ix.]

In the year 644, Paulinus, formerly bishop of York, but then of the city of Rochester, departed to the Lord. [III. xiv.]

In the year 651, King Oswine was killed and Bishop Aidan died. [III. xiv.]

In the year 653, the Middle Angles under their Prince Peada were instructed in the mysteries of the faith. [III. xxi.]

In the year 655, Penda perished and the Mercians became Christian.[1] [III. xxiv.]

In the year 664, there was an eclipse. Eorcenberht, king of the people of Kent, died, and Colman went back to his people with his Scots; and a pestilence arose; and Chad and Wilfrid were ordained bishops of the Northumbrians.[2] [III. xxvi–xxviii; IV. i.]

In the year 668, Theodore was ordained bishop. [IV. i.]

In the year 670, Oswiu, king of the Northumbrians, died. [IV. v.]

In the year 673, Egbert, king of the people of Kent, died; and a synod was held at Hertford, in the presence of King Ecgfrith, Archbishop Theodore presiding; [it was] most profitable, [and issued] ten chapters. [IV. v.]

In the year 675, Wulfhere, king of the Mercians, dying after he had reigned seventeen years,[3] left the dominion to his brother Ethelred.

In the year 676, Ethelred ravaged Kent. [IV. xii.]

In the year 678, a comet appeared; Bishop Wilfrid was driven from his see by King Ecgfrith, and Bosa, Eata and Eadhæd were consecrated bishops instead of him. [IV. xii; V. xix.]

In the year 679, Ælfwine was killed. [IV. xxi.]

In the year 680, a synod was held in the plain of Hatfield, concerning the catholic faith, Archbishop Theodore presiding; at which the Roman abbot, John, was present. In this year Abbess Hilda died in *Streoneshealh*.[4] [IV. xvii, xviii, xxiii.]

In the year 685, Ecgfrith, king of the Northumbrians, was killed. In the same year Hlothhere, king of the people of Kent, died.[5] [IV. xxvi.]

---

[1] Several MSS., of what Plummer calls the Durham and Winchester groups, add here: "In the year 658 Wulfhere was set up as king."

[2] These same MSS. add here: "In the year 667, our abbot wrote."

[3] The date of Wulfhere's death is not given in the narrative.   [4] Whitby.

[5] The above-mentioned MSS. add a reference to Wilfrid's reception by King Aldfrith under the year 686, and to his expulsion by Ecgfrith [*sic*] under 687.

In the year 688, Ceadwalla, king of the West Saxons, went from Britain to Rome. [V. vii.]

In the year 690, Archbishop Theodore died.[1] [V. viii.]

In the year 697, Queen Osthryth was killed by her own—that is, the Mercian—nobles.

In the year 698, Brihtred, ealdorman of the king of the Northumbrians, was killed by the Picts.[2]

In the year 704,[3] Ethelred, after he had ruled the nation of the Mercians for thirty-one[4] years, became a monk and gave the kingdom to Cenred. [V. xix.]

In the year 705, Aldfrith, king of the Northumbrians, died.[5] [V. xviii.]

In the year 709, Cenred, king of the Mercians, after he had reigned five years, went to Rome.[6] [V. xix.]

In the year 711, the 'prefect' Brihtfrith fought with the Picts.[7]

In the year 716, Osred, king of the Northumbrians, was killed, and Ceolred, king of the Mercians, died; and the man of God, Egbert, brought the monks of Iona to observe the catholic Easter and the ecclesiastical tonsure. [V. xxii.]

In the year 725, Wihtred, king of the people of Kent, died. [V. xxiii.]

In the year 729, comets appeared, the holy Egbert passed away, and Osric died. [V. xxiii.]

In the year 731, Archbishop Brihtwold died. In the same year Tatwine was consecrated the ninth archbishop of the church of Canterbury, in the fifteenth year of the rule of Æthelbald, king of the Mercians.[8] [V. xxiii.]

[In the year 731, King Ceolwulf was taken prisoner, tonsured and sent back to his kingdom; Bishop Acca was driven from his see.

In the year 732, Egbert was made bishop of York in place of Wilfrid.[9]

In the year 733, there was an eclipse of the sun on 14 August, about the third hour of the day, so that almost the whole orb of the sun seemed as if it were covered by a very black and dreadful shield.[10]

In the year 734, the moon was suffused with a blood-red colour, for about a whole hour, on 31 January, about cockcrow, after which a blackness followed, and then it returned to its own light.][10]

These things concerning the ecclesiastical history of Britain and especially of the English nation, as far as I could learn them from the writings of the ancients, or from the tradition of our forefathers, or from my own knowledge, with the help of the

---

[1] The same MSS. add a long entry on the career of Wilfrid, his expulsion by Aldfrith, his long exile etc., under year 692.

[2] These entries for 697 and 698, which have nothing corresponding in the narrative, are omitted in the eighth-century Brit. Mus. Cott. Tiber. C. ii, (C) and in others.

[3] 703 in the Durham and Winchester MSS.   [4] Thirty in the eighth-century MS. C.

[5] MS. C adds: 'and Osred received the kingdom; and Bishop Wilfrid was received into his see'. The Durham and Winchester MSS. have this with a further addition about Wilfrid.

[6] This annal is omitted by MS. C and several others.

[7] This is not mentioned in Bede's narrative. See No. 154, p. 696, and p. 14.

[8] A number of MSS., including the early MS. C, omit the latter part of this annal, after archbishop, and then add the annals for 733 and 734, but not 731 and 732. The Moore MS. has the whole group 731–734, which cannot have belonged to the first recension of the work, but may be an addition of Bede's own.

[9] These two entries, for 731 and 732, are in the Moore MS., but not in MS. C and many later manuscripts.

[10] Not only the Moore MS., but also C and several other MSS., contain these entries, which refer to events later than the date at which Bede says he wrote his work.

Lord, I, Bede, a servant of Christ, and priest of the monastery of the blessed Apostles Peter and Paul, which is in Wearmouth and Jarrow, have set forth.

I was born on the estates of the same monastery, and when I was seven years old I was given by the care of my kinsmen to be educated by the most reverend Abbot Benedict, and afterwards by Ceolfrith; and spending all the time of my life from then dwelling in that same monastery, I have wholly applied myself to the study of the Scriptures; and amidst the observance of the monastic rule, and the daily charge of singing in the church, I have always taken delight in learning, in teaching, or in writing.

And in the nineteenth year of my life I received deacon's orders, in the thirtieth, the degree of the priesthood, both of them through the ministry of the most reverend Bishop John, at the order of Abbot Ceolfrith.

From the time of receiving priest's orders until the fifty-ninth year of my age, I have been at pains for my own needs and those of my brethren to compile from the works of the venerable fathers brief notes on Holy Writ, and also to make additions according to the manner of their meaning and interpretation. . . .[1]

Likewise concerning the histories of saints: I translated a book of the Life and Passion of St. Felix, Confessor, into prose, from the metrical work of Paulinus; I have corrected according to the sense, as far as I could, the Life and Passion of St. Anastasius, which had been badly translated from the Greek, and worse emended by some unskilled person; I have written the Life of the holy Father Cuthbert, who was both monk and bishop, first in heroic metre, and afterwards in prose.

The History of the Abbots of this monastery, in which I rejoice to serve the Divine Goodness, Benedict, Ceolfrith, Hwætberht, in two books.

The Ecclesiastical History of our Island and Nation, in five books.

The Martyrology of the festivals of the Holy Martyrs, in which I have endeavoured diligently to note down all whom I could discover, and not only on what day, but also by what sort of combat, and under what judge they overcame the world.

A Book of Hymns, in various sorts of metre or rhythm.

A Book of Epigrams in heroic or elegiac metre.

Concerning the Nature of Things, and concerning Times, one book of each; likewise one larger book concerning Times.[2]

A book on Orthography, arranged in alphabetical order.

Likewise a book on the Metrical Art, and added to it another little book concerning Figures of Speech or Tropes, that is, of the figures and modes of speech in which the Holy Scriptures are composed.

And I beseech thee, good Jesus, that to him whom thou hast graciously granted to drink sweetly of the words of thy knowledge, thou wilt grant also in thy kindness that he may some day come to thee, the fountain of all wisdom, and appear before thy face for ever.

---

[1] Bede first lists his commentaries and theological writings, under 25 different titles, making 61 'books' He then proceeds to his historical and miscellaneous writings.

[2] To these two books are attached Bede's shorter and greater chronicles.

(b) EARLY SAINTS' LIVES

152. Extracts from the Life of Saint Gregory by a Whitby monk

This work was written after the death of Eanflæd, who had retired to Whitby after her husband, King Oswiu, died in 670, and during the abbacy of her daughter, Ælfflæd, from 680 to 713 or 714. It is obvious that the author was a monk of Whitby, but nothing else is known of him. There is only one manuscript of this work, St. Gall MS. 567, of the first half of the ninth century. I have selected the section dealing with the conversion of the English. It gives the first version of Gregory's famous meeting with English youths in Rome, and it records some traditions of the conversion of Northumbria which Bede did not use. On the other hand, it shows how little was known in Northumbria of the Gregorian mission until Bede undertook his researches. It is of interest to compare the two authors where they relate the same incident. See No. 151, pp. 606, 613–616.

P. Ewald edited chaps. IX–XXII of this work in *Historische Aufsätze dem andenken an Georg Waitz gewidmet* (Hanover, 1886), and these, with further curtailment, are printed as an appendix to the second volume of Plummer's Bede. They have been translated by Dom T. L. Almond, in *Downside Review*, XXIII (1904), pp. 15–29. The full text is given by F. A. Gasquet, *A Life of Pope Gregory the Great, written by a monk of the Monastery of Whitby* (Westminster, 1904), but with many inaccuracies. It is translated by C. W. Jones, *Saints' Lives and Chronicles in Early England*, but until a better edition of the text is available, any translation can only be tentative.

IX. We ought by no means to pass over in silence how devoutly and with what incomparable discernment of the eyes of the heart he furthered our conversion to God by his foresight. The faithful narrate that before his aforesaid pontificate certain of our nation, beautiful in form and fair-haired, came to Rome.[1] When he heard of their coming, he was at once eager to see them; and, receiving them with the vision of a pure heart, and hesitating over their new and unfamiliar appearance, and, most important, God prompting him inwardly, he asked of what race they were. And when they replied: "Those from whom we are sprung are called Angles", he said: "Angels of God." Then he said: "What is the name of the king of that people?" And they said: "Ælle"; and he said: "Alleluia, for the praise of God ought to be there." He also inquired the name of the tribe from which they specially came, and they said: "The Deire." And he said: "Fleeing together from the wrath[2] of God to the faith."

X. Thus kindled by the spiritual opportunity, he so eagerly begged Pope Benedict,[3] his predecessor in the pontificate, to give him permission to journey hither that he could not refuse the urgency of his prayer, since he said: "It were a wretched thing that hell should be filled with such beautiful vessels." As he said these and other like sayings, the pope gave him permission to make his way hither. Now by this permission he greatly distressed the Roman people. Hence they are said to have formed a plan of dividing themselves into three companies along the road which the same pontiff took to the church of St. Peter; and as he passed, each company thus cried out to him: "You have offended Peter; you have destroyed Rome; you have sent away Gregory." And so, hearing so dreadful a cry for the third time, he quickly sent messengers after him and made him turn back. Gregory knew beforehand the manner of this return, since God spoke to him with holy intent by means of a locust. For when they had completed a three-day journey, and were resting after the manner of travellers, a locust came to him as he was reading. Immediately he understood by its

---

[1] A sentence placed later on must either follow here, or be a misplaced gloss. It runs: "Some say they were beautiful boys, some that they were curled and elegant youths."

[2] *i.e. de ira.*   [3] Benedict I.

name as if it were saying to him: "Stay in this place";[1] yet he quickly exhorted his companions to prepare to go on. While he was continuing with them, he was prevented by the messengers and brought back to Rome.

XI. Not long afterwards, when the pope was dead, he was elected to the pontificate, as we have written above. He sent hither with as much haste as he could the men of revered memory, Augustine, Mellitus, and Laurence and the rest; ordaining Augustine bishop, by whom Mellitus is said to have been ordained and Laurence by Mellitus.

XII. Accordingly, Ethelbert, king of the people of Kent, having been converted by them to the faith of Christ—the first of all the kings of England to be converted —purified by his baptism, shone forth with his nation. After him in our race, which is called the Humbrians, King Edwin, son of the aforesaid Ælle, whom we rightly mentioned above in connexion with the alleluia prophecy of divine praise, excelled all kings in matchless wisdom as also in the authority of royal dominion, since the time when the race of the English came into this island. . . .[2]

XIV. Verily Edwin, whose name, consisting of three syllables,[3] truly symbolizes the mystery of the Holy Trinity, was fore-ordained the vessel of God's mercy, though perchance still in his father's loins at the time when this prophecy was made; this he taught who calls to him all who are baptized in the name of the Father, Son and Holy Ghost. The father in baptism of this Edwin was the venerable Bishop Paulinus, one of those whom Gregory sent among us, as we have said. He is said to have given very readily a sign of his knowledge of God, on a certain Sunday, I believe.

XV. When the aforesaid king, with his attendants, was hastening with him to the church, to the catechizing of those who hitherto were in the bonds not only of heathendom, but of illegal wedlock also, from the hall in which they had urged them to amend both these things, a crow with a strident voice sang with an evil omen. Then the whole of the royal company, which was still in the public street, hearing the bird, turned towards it in amazement, and halted, as though the "new canticle" were not in truth to be "a song to our God"[4] in the Church, but false and profitless. Then, with God seeing and ordering all things from his throne, the venerable bishop said to one of his servants: "Shoot an arrow carefully into the bird." And when this had been done in haste, he ordered the bird and the arrows to be kept until it could be brought into the hall after the catechizing of those who were to be catechized was over. When all were assembled there, he fully explained the matter to the recent and as yet uninstructed people of God, and proved that they should know by so clear a sign that the ancient evil of idolatry was worthless to anybody; saying also that since that foolish bird did not know that it sang of death for itself, it could by no means foretell anything profitable to men entirely reborn, baptized to the image of God, who have "rule over the fishes of the sea, and the fowls of the air, and all living creatures upon the earth . . ."[5]

XVI. As we have mentioned our most Christian King Edwin, it is also worth while to mention his conversion, how it is reported to have been foretold to him in

---

[1] *Sta in loco*, playing on *locusta*. [2] Paragraph XIII merely elaborates the puns on Angles and Ælle.
[3] The name (*Eadwine*) is trisyllabic in Old English. [4] Psalm xxxix. 4. [5] Genesis i. 28.

former times. We may repeat briefly, but not so concisely as we heard it, yet striving after the truth, what we believe to have happened, though we have not heard it from the report of those who knew more than others about him. Yet we do not consider it right that what is so piously reported by the faithful should be passed over in total silence; for the report of any event when transmitted through many periods and great distances may reach the ears of divers persons in divers ways. This, then, took place long before the days of all who are now alive.[1] But we all know that it is true that the same king was an exile with Rædwald, king of the East Angles.[2] His rival, the tyrant Æthelfrith, who drove him from his country, so persecuted him everywhere that he even sought to purchase his death with his money. They say that at one time, when he was fearing for his life, there appeared to him one day someone of beautiful appearance, crowned with the Cross of Christ, and began to comfort him, promising him a happy life and future reign over his people, if he would obey him. And when he promised that he would, if he proved what he promised to be true, he replied: "You shall prove it true, and you ought to obey him who shall first appear to you with this form and sign. And he shall teach you to obey the one true and living God, who created all things, the God who shall give you the things which I promise, and who shall show by means of him all that you ought to do." And thus, they say, the aforesaid Bishop Paulinus first appeared to him in this likeness.

XVII. O most merciful Father, Lord God Almighty, although we were not worthy of the afore-mentioned presence of the blessed Gregory, yet let thanks ever be given to thee through him for our teacher Paulinus, whom, at his death, thou didst manifest faithful to thee. For it is said by those who saw it that the soul of this man migrated to the heavens when he died in the form of a white bird, great like a swan, and very beautiful.

XVIII. But to continue with my subject, I tell how the lamp of Christ began to glow with the blossoms of wonders through this King Edwin, that his merits may shine more clearly. Thus it is worth setting on record how the relics of the bones of this royal man were in truth discovered by God's revelation. There was a certain brother of our race called Trimma, discharging the office of priest in a monastery of the South English[3] in the days of their King Ethelred, while Eanflæd, daughter of the aforesaid religious King Edwin, was still alive, leading a monastic life. A certain man appeared to this priest as he slept, saying to him: "Go to a place I will tell you of, which is in the district which is called Hatfield,[4] where King Edwin was slain; for you must take up his bones there and bring them with you to Streoneshealh'[5]–which is the most famous monastery of Ælfflæd,[6] daughter of the above-mentioned Queen Eanflæd, the daughter, as we said above, of Edwin, now a very religious woman. The priest answered him, saying: "I do not know that place. How can I set out when I do not know where to go?" But he said: "Go to this village in Lindsey"–our brother, a relative of this priest, who related this story to me, could not remember its name–"and in it inquire for a certain ceorl[7] called Teoful. Ask him about that

[1] Compare the same story in No. 151, pp. 614–616.   [2] The text has wrongly 'West Angles'.
[3] See No. 67.   [4] See No. 151, p. 621.   [5] Whitby.   [6] See No. 151, pp. 637 f., 666; 154, p. 695.
[7] The term used, *maritus*, means 'married man', but as this is one of the meanings of *ceorl* (in fact, *maritus* in Aldhelm is glossed *ceorl*) I suspect that the word this author is rendering is his native *ceorl*, a peasant proprietor.

place; he can show you where it is." The priest, knowing that the deception of dreams is manifold, of which, to be sure, it is written "Dreams have deceived many",[1] paid no heed to the matter thus revealed. When he was therefore admonished more forcibly by the same man, he recounted it exactly as it was revealed to him to another of his brethren; but he accounted it a dream, in the way we have described, and made him disregard it.

xix. After these events, his man appeared still a third time to the same priest [and chastised him with great reproof with a whip][2] and said threateningly: "Have I not twice shown you what you should do and you have neglected it? Show now whether you choose still to be disobedient, or obedient, to me." Then indeed he journeyed in haste to the aforesaid ceorl, and speedily seeking where it was, he found it as he had been directed. Inquiring very diligently of him, he learnt clearly by given signs where he should look for the king's relics. Immediately it was disclosed he went to the place indicated to him; and still he did not find what he sought at the first digging, but only by digging more strenuously a second time, as often happens. He brought away with him the desirable treasure which he found to this our monastery, in which these same holy bones are now honourably laid with other of our kings in the church of St. Peter, Prince of the Apostles, to the south of the altar which is dedicated in the name of the most blessed Apostle Peter, and to the east of that which is dedicated to St. Gregory in the same church. It is said also that this same priest, who afterwards dwelt for a time at the previous holy place of burial, declared that he often saw the spirits of four of the slain, and certainly baptized, persons coming in splendour to visit their bodies, and he added that if he could, he would build a monastery there.

153. A passage from Adamnan's Life of St. Columba

Bede knew about Adamnan and used his work on the Holy Places (see No. 151, p. 674), but he appears to have had no access to his Life of Columba. It seems desirable, therefore, to include the following passage as an independent account of Oswald's victory over Cadwallon, derived, at a remove, from Oswald himself.

Adamnan wrote this Life at Iona, at the request of the brethren, some time between his accession as abbot in 679 and his death in 704. He cannot have finished it before about 688, for at the end of Book II he tells of two visits made to King Aldfrith of Northumbria at an interval of two years, and the last took place in 688–689. He speaks of the immunity of himself and his companions from the plague that was devastating England at that time. Bede gives an account of a visit of Adamnan to Aldfrith in Book V, chap. xv (No. 151, p. 674). Adamnan's espousing of the cause of the Roman Easter led to his being absent from Iona from 697 to 704, and the Life probably antedates this period.

Adamnan refers to an earlier book on St. Columba by Cummeneus Albus (Cuimene Ailbe, abbot of Iona, 657–669), and if an extant work printed by Mabillon, Acta Sanctorum ordinis S. Benedicti and by Pinkerton, Vitae antiquae sanctorum, and translated in Metcalfe's book cited below, actually represents this work, Adamnan has borrowed from it its brief account of this particular vision. Even so, his own fuller account may be indebted, as he claims, to Failbhe's recital. But there is some doubt whether the work that passes as Cuimene's is not in fact a later work extracted from that of Adamnan.

The best editions of this work are W. Reeves, The Life of St. Columba, founder of Hy, written by Adamnan, ninth abbot of that monastery (Dublin and Edinburgh, 1857) also reproduced, with some re-arrangement, and translation, in Historians of the Church of Scotland, VI (Edinburgh, 1874); Adamnani Vita S. Columba, ed. J. T. Fowler (Oxford, 2nd ed., 1920); W. M. Metcalfe, Pinkerton's Lives of the Scottish Saints, I (Paisley, 1889). It is translated by W. Huyshe, The Life of St. Columba (London, 1906).

---

[1] Ecclesiasticus xxxiv. 7.   [2] This clause is in the margin of the manuscript.

Book I, chapter 1. . . . We will cite one example of so great an honour[1] conferred from on high by the Almighty on this honourable man, which was revealed to the Saxon ruler Oswald the day before he joined battle with Catlon,[2] the very brave king of the Britons. For when this same King Oswald had pitched his camp in readiness for the battle, and was sleeping one day on his pillow in his tent, he saw in a vision St. Columba, shining with angelic beauty; and his majestic figure seemed to touch the clouds with the crown of his head. And the blessed man revealed his own name to the king, and, as he stood in the middle of the camp, he covered with his glittering raiment that same camp except one small corner. And he uttered these encouraging words, the same, in fact, which the Lord spoke to Joshua, the son of Nun, after the death of Moses before the passage of the Jordan, saying: "Take thou courage and do manfully; behold, I shall be with thee, etc."[3] And St. Columba, speaking these words to the king in the vision, then added: "This coming night go forth from the camp to battle; for on this occasion the Lord has granted me that your foes shall be put to flight and your enemy Catlon given into your hands, and that after the battle you shall return a victor and rule in prosperity." After these words the king arose and related this vision to his assembled council; and, all being encouraged by it, the whole people promised that they would believe and receive baptism after their return from the battle; for until that time all the Saxon land had been wrapped in the darkness of heathenism and ignorance, except for King Oswald himself and twelve men who had been baptized with him when he was an exile among the Scots. What more need I say? The ensuing night, just as he had been instructed in the vision, King Oswald advanced from the camp to battle against many thousands with a much smaller army, and, as had been promised him, he was granted by the Lord a happy and easy victory. And when King Catlon had been killed, Oswald returned from the battle a victor, and he was afterwards established by God as overlord of the whole of Britain.[4] This account my predecessor, our Abbot Failbhe,[5] nothing doubting, told to me, Adamnan, and he solemnly declared that he had heard it from the lips of King Oswald himself, as he related this same vision to Abbot Seghine.[6]

154. From the Life of Bishop Wilfrid, by Eddius Stephanus

The Fell manuscript of this Life, in the Bodleian library, declares it to be the work of a priest called Stephen, as also does William of Malmesbury in his *De Gestis Pontificum*,[7] and at any rate from the sixteenth century this Stephen has been assumed to be the 'Eddi, surnamed Stephen' whom Bede mentions as being invited from Kent by Wilfrid as a singing master.[8] The Life itself refers to this Eddi as one of two singers taken back to Northumbria by Wilfrid, probably in 669. He would have plenty of personal knowledge of Wilfrid, and he also learnt from Wilfrid's kinsman Tatberht what Wilfrid had told him of his history on the ride to Oundle on his last journey. He presumably wrote the Life not long after Wilfrid's death in 709.

It is to be regretted that space does not permit the inclusion of this work in full. For, though Eddi writes as a partisan, and can sometimes be shown wrong on matters of fact as well as of opinion, the whole not only gives a vivid picture of the saint, but is full of information on many aspects of life in England in the late seventh and early eighth centuries; moreover, it contains an account of

---

[1] The gift of prophecy.　　　　[2] Cadwallon, king of Gwynedd.　　　[3] Joshua i. 6, 18.
[4] The office which is called that of *Bretwalda* in the Anglo-Saxon Chronicle (No. 1, p. 171). Adamnan uses the word *imperator* 'emperor', and his statement supports Bede's remarks (No. 151, p. 610), on the *imperium* held by various kings, including Oswald.　　　　　　　　　[5] Abbot of Iona, 669–679.
[6] Abbot of Iona, 623–652.　　　[7] Ed. Hamilton, p. 210.　　　[8] No. 151, p. 648.

the conduct of an appeal to Rome, the first known appeal from an English ecclesiastic. But as the main events of Wilfrid's career are given in Bede, who used this Life, but had also other sources of information, I have selected only those chapters which add most significantly to our knowledge of Northumbrian history. The extracts consist of the account of the Synod of Whitby, for comparison with that given by Bede, since it is desirable to have both contemporary accounts of so all important a council; the building and dedication of the church of Ripon; the references to Ecgfrith's wars, which have material not in Bede; the description of the church of Hexham; and the synod of the Nidd, where in the course of the discussion we learn something of the troubles after Aldfrith's death, and where agreement was reached after the long controversy.

There is an excellent edition of this work, with introduction, translation and commentary, by B. Colgrave, *The Life of Bishop Wilfrid by Eddius Stephanus* (Cambridge, 1927), from which, with his permission, I have taken the translation here given. It is also edited by W. Levison, in *Mon. Germ. Hist., Script. Rer. Merov.* VI.

CHAPTER X. *Of the strife of St. Wilfrid the priest with Bishop Colman about the keeping of Easter (664).*[1]

On a certain occasion in the days of Colman, bishop of York and metropolitan, while Oswiu and Alhfrith his son were reigning, the abbots and priests and men of all ranks in the orders of the Church gathered together in a monastery called Whitby, in the presence of the holy mother and most pious nun Hilda, as well as of the kings and two bishops, namely Colman and Agilbert, to consider the question of the proper date for the keeping of Easter—whether in accordance with the British and Scottish manner and that of the whole of the northern district, Easter should be kept on the Sunday between the fourteenth day of the moon and the twenty-second, or whether the plan of the apostolic see was better, namely to celebrate Easter Sunday between the fifteenth day of the moon and the twenty-first. The opportunity was granted first of all to Bishop Colman, as was proper, to state his case in the presence of all. He boldly spoke in reply as follows: "Our fathers and their predecessors, plainly inspired by the Holy Spirit as was Columba, ordained the celebration of Easter on the fourteenth day of the moon, if it was a Sunday, following the example of the Apostle and Evangelist John 'who leaned on the breast of the Lord at supper'[2] and was called the friend of the Lord. He celebrated Easter on the fourteenth day of the moon and we, like his disciples Polycarp and others, celebrate it on his authority; we dare not change it, for our fathers' sake, nor do we wish to do so. I have expressed the opinion of our party, do you state yours."

Agilbert the foreign bishop and Agatho his priest bade St. Wilfrid, priest and abbot, with his persuasive eloquence explain in his own tongue the system of the Roman Church and of the apostolic see. With his customary humility he answered in these words: "This question has already been admirably investigated by the three hundred and eighteen most holy and learned fathers gathered together in Nicaea, a city of Bithynia. They fixed amongst other decisions upon a lunar cycle which recurs every nineteen years. This cycle never shows that Easter is to be kept on the fourteenth day of the moon. This is the fixed rule of the apostolic see and of almost the whole world, and our fathers, after many decrees had been made, uttered these words: 'he who condemns any one of these let him be accursed'."

Then, after St. Wilfrid the priest had finished his speech, King Oswiu smilingly asked them all: "Tell me which is greater in the kingdom of heaven, Columba or the Apostle Peter?" The whole synod answered with one voice and one consent: "The

---

[1] See No. 151, pp. 639–642.   [2] John xxi. 20.

Lord settled this when he declared: 'Thou art Peter and upon this rock I will build my Church and the gates of hell shall not prevail against it. And I will give thee the keys of the kingdom of heaven; and whatsoever thou shalt bind on earth shall be bound in heaven; and whatsoever thou shalt loose on earth shall be loosed in heaven.'"[1]

The king wisely replied: "He is the porter and keeps the keys. With him I will have no differences nor will I agree with those who have such, nor in any single particular will I gainsay his decisions so long as I live."

So Bishop Colman was told what he must do, should he reject the tonsure and the Easter rule for fear of his fellow-countrymen, namely he must retire and leave his see to be taken by another and a better man. Thus indeed he did.

CHAPTER XVII. *Concerning the building of the church at Ripon and its dedication (671–678).*

So, amid the worldly prosperity which God gave him, there grew up in our bishop, the friend of the eternal Bridegroom, a love which ever increased in ardour for the virgin Bride espoused to one husband and born of charity the mother of all goodness. He adorned her fairly with the rules of discipline as with the flowers of virtue, making her chaste and modest, continent, temperate and submissive, and clothed her in garments of many hues. In the words of the prophet: "The king's daughter is all glorious within."[2] For as Moses built an earthly tabernacle made with hands, of divers varied colours according to the pattern shown by God in the mount, to stir up the faith of the people of Israel for the worship of God, so the blessed Bishop Wilfrid wondrously adorned the bridal chamber of the true Bridegroom and Bride with gold and silver and varied purples, in the sight of the multitudes who believed in their hearts and made confession of their faith. For in Ripon he built and completed from the foundations in the earth up to the roof, a church of dressed stone, supported by various columns and side aisles.

Afterwards, when the building had been finished, he invited to the day of its dedication the two most Christian kings and brothers, Ecgfrith and Ælfwine, together with the abbots, the reeves and the sub-kings; dignitaries of every kind gathered together; like Solomon the wise, they consecrated the house and dedicated it to the Lord in honour of St. Peter the chief of the Apostles, to assist the prayers of the people in it. The altar also with its bases they dedicated to the Lord and vested it in purple woven with gold; the people shared in the work, and thus all was completed in a canonical manner.

Then St. Wilfrid the bishop stood in front of the altar, and, turning to the people, in the presence of the kings, read out clearly a list of the lands which the kings, for the good of their souls, had previously, and on that very day as well, presented to him, with the agreement and over the signatures of the bishops and all the chief men, and also a list of the consecrated places in various parts which the British clergy had deserted when fleeing from the hostile sword wielded by the warriors of our own nation. It was truly a gift well pleasing to God that the pious kings had assigned so many lands to our bishop for the service of God; these are the names of the regions:

---

[1] Matthew xvi. 18, 19.   [2] Psalm xliv. 14.

round Ribble and Yeadon and the region of Dent and Catlow and other places. Then, when the sermon was over, the kings started upon a great feast lasting for three days and three nights, rejoicing amid all their people, showing magnanimity towards their enemies and humility towards the servants of God. Our holy bishop also provided for the adornment of the house of God, among other treasures, a marvel of beauty hitherto unheard of in our times. For he had ordered, for the good of his soul, the four gospels to be written out in letters of purest gold on purpled parchment and illuminated. He also ordered jewellers to construct for the books a case all made of purest gold and set with most precious gems; all these things and others besides are preserved in our church until these times as a witness to his blessed memory; here too his remains rest, and daily, without any intermission, his name is remembered in prayer.

CHAPTER XIX. *Of the king's victory over the warlike Picts (671–673).*

Now in those days, the pious King Ecgfrith, and his most blessed Queen Æthelthryth (whose body, still remaining uncorrupted after death, shows that it was unstained before, while alive) were both obedient to Bishop Wilfrid in all things, and there ensued, by the aid of God, peace and joy among the people, fruitful years and victory over their foes. For as when Joash, the king of Judah, was young, so long as Jehoiada the great high priest was alive, he pleased God and triumphed over his enemies; but when the priest was dead, he displeased God and diminished his kingdom; so when King Ecgfrith lived in peace with our bishop, the kingdom, as many bear witness, was increased on every hand by his glorious victories; but when the agreement between them was destroyed, and his queen had separated from him and dedicated herself to God, the king's triumph came to an end during his own lifetime. For in his early years, while the kingdom was still weak, the bestial tribes of the Picts had a fierce contempt for subjection to the Saxon and threatened to throw off from themselves the yoke of slavery; they gathered together innumerable tribes from every nook and corner in the north, and as a swarm of ants in the summer sweeping from their hills heap up a mound to protect their tottering house. When King Ecgfrith heard this, lowly as he was among his own people and magnanimous towards his enemies, he forthwith got together a troop of horsemen, for he was no lover of belated operations; and trusting in God like Judas Maccabaeus and assisted by the brave sub-king Beornhæth he attacked with his little band of God's people an enemy host which was vast and moreover concealed. He slew an enormous number of the people, filling two rivers with corpses, so that, marvellous to relate, the slayers, passing over the rivers dry foot, pursued and slew the crowd of fugitives; the tribes were reduced to slavery and remained subject under the yoke of captivity until the time when the king was slain.

CHAPTER XX. *Of his victory over the king of the Mercians (673–674).*

Thereupon after this victory King Ecgfrith, ruling the people with the bishop of God, in righteousness and holiness, strong like David in crushing his enemies yet lowly in the sight of God, breaking the necks of the tumultuous tribes and their warlike kings, emboldened as he was by the help of God, in all things always gave thanks to God. Now Wulfhere, king of the Mercians, proud of heart and insatiable in spirit, roused all the southern nations against our kingdom, intent not merely on fighting but on compelling them to pay tribute in a slavish spirit. But he was not guided by God. So Ecgfrith, king of Deira and Bernicia, unwavering in spirit and true-hearted, on the advice of his counsellors trusted God, like Barak and Deborah, to guard his land and defend the churches of God even as the bishop taught him to do, and with a band of men no greater than theirs attacked a proud enemy, and by the help of God overthrew them with his tiny force. Countless numbers were slain, the king was put to flight and his kingdom laid under tribute, and afterwards, when Wulfhere died through some cause, Ecgfrith ruled in peace over a wider realm.

CHAPTER XXII. *Concerning the building of the house of God at Hexham (672–677).*

So continually, in the words of the Psalmist, he drew near to God,[1] placing in him his hope and rendering to the Lord who had given him all things, his dearest vows. For in Hexham, having obtained an estate from the queen, St. Æthelthryth, the dedicated to God, he founded and built a house to the Lord in honour of St. Andrew the Apostle. My feeble tongue will not permit me to enlarge here upon the depth of the foundations in the earth, and its crypts of wonderfully dressed stone, and the manifold building above ground supported by various columns and many side aisles, and adorned with walls of notable length and height, surrounded by various winding passages with spiral stairs leading up and down; for our holy bishop, being taught by the Spirit of God, thought out how to construct these buildings; nor have we heard of any other house on this side of the Alps built on such a scale. Further, Bishop Acca of blessed memory, who by the grace of God is still alive, provided for this manifold building splendid ornaments of gold, silver and precious stones; but of these and of the way he decorated the altars with purple and silk, who is sufficient to tell?

CHAPTER LX. [*The Synod on the Nidd (706).*]

In the first year of King Osred, Brihtwold, archbishop of the Church of the Kentish people and of nearly all Britain, came from the south, having, in accordance with the precept of the apostolic see, earnestly to invite the king of the northern regions with all his bishops and abbots and the chief men of his whole kingdom to the place of synod to consider the case of the blessed Bishop Wilfrid; and he carried out the command. The king and his chief men, three of his bishops and their abbots, as well as the blessed Abbess Ælfflæd,[2] always the comforter and best counsellor of the whole province, all gathered together in one place near the River Nidd and on its eastern side. Archbishop Brihtwold also and Bishop Wilfrid arrived together on the same day. The king and the bishops and their chief men took their seats in the place of synod and the archbishop began to speak in these words: "Let us pray our Lord Jesus Christ to grant us concord and peace in our hearts by the Holy Spirit. Both I and the blessed Bishop Wilfrid have writings from the apostolic see, for some have

---

[1] Cf. Psalm lxxii. 28.   [2] See No. 151, pp. 637f., 666; No. 152, p. 689.

been sent by messengers to my unworthy self, and others likewise have been brought by him. We humbly ask that these may be read in your revered presence." The venerable lords gave them permission and the documents of both were read before the synod for all to hear from beginning to end.

After the reading all were silent and Brihtfrith,[1] a chief man next in rank to the king, said to the archbishop: "We who need a translation should be glad to hear what the apostolic authority says." The archbishop answered him: "The judgments of the apostolic see are expressed in roundabout and enigmatic language, but nevertheless both documents show the same meaning in the matter. I will explain the bare sense in brief. The apostolic power to bind and to loose, which was first given to Peter, has decided of its own authority in the matter of the blessed Bishop Wilfrid that, in the presence of myself, though unworthy, and of the whole assembly, the prelates of the churches in this province, leaving the old enmity, for the salvation of their souls, be reconciled for good with the blessed Bishop Wilfrid. For to these my fellow-bishops a choice is offered out of two decrees made by the apostolic see: let them choose which of the two they will, either to make a complete and perfect peace with Bishop Wilfrid and to restore to him such parts of the churches he formerly ruled as wise counsellors and myself shall settle, or if they are unwilling to take this, the best course, to go all together to the apostolic see, and there be judged in a greater council. If anyone show his contempt (which God forbid!) and will do neither of these, let him know that, whether he be king or layman, he is excommunicated from the body and blood of Christ; but if he be bishop or priest who acts thus—which is more horrible still and dreadful to speak of—he is to be degraded from all holy orders. These in brief are the decrees of the apostolic see."

The bishops, however, resisted and said: "Who can anywise alter that which was once decided by our predecessors, Archbishop Theodore who was sent forth from the apostolic see, and King Ecgfrith; and what we and the bishops of almost the whole of Britain and in your most excellent presence, archbishop, afterwards decreed with King Aldfrith in the place called *Eostrefeld*?"[2]

Meanwhile the most blessed Ælfflæd spoke with holy words: "I tell you truly in Christ the testament of King Aldfrith in the illness which brought his life to a close. He vowed a vow to God and to St. Peter, saying, 'if I live, I will fulfil all the decrees of the apostolic see concerning the blessed Bishop Wilfrid which I once refused to obey. But, if I die, bid my heir, my son, in the name of the Lord, that he fulfil for the good of my soul the apostolic judgment concerning Bishop Wilfrid.'"

When she had finished her speech, Brihtfrith the aforesaid chief man of the king made answer: "This is the will of the king and of his chief men, that we obey the mandates of the apostolic see and the commands of King Aldfrith in all things. For when we were besieged in the city called Bamburgh and surrounded on every hand by a hostile force and were sheltering in a narrow place in the stony rock, taking counsel amongst ourselves, we vowed that if God granted our royal boy his father's kingdom,[3] we would fulfil the apostolic commands concerning Bishop Wilfrid. As

---

[1] See No. 151, p. 685.   [2] Probably Austerfield, near Bawtry, Yorks.
[3] In chap. LIX Eddi has told us that on Aldfrith's death a certain Eadwulf reigned for two months, and was then driven out.

soon as our vow was made, the minds of our enemies were changed; with all haste they all plighted their friendship to us with an oath; the gates were opened, we were freed from our narrow quarters, our enemies were put to flight, and the kingdom became ours."

After these words were finished, the bishops separated from the rest and began to take counsel together; sometimes the archbishop consulted with them and sometimes the prudent virgin Ælfflæd. The end of this holy council was that all the bishops and the king with his counsellors made a complete peace with Bishop Wilfrid, which they kept until the end of their lives; they returned him the two best monasteries, Ripon and Hexham, with all the revenues belonging to them; and on that day all the bishops kissed and embraced one another and communicated in the breaking of bread. They gave thanks to God for all this holy blessedness, and went to their homes in the peace of Christ.

155. The anonymous Life of Ceolfrith, abbot of Jarrow

Beyond that he was a monk of Jarrow or Monkwearmouth, nothing is known of the author of this important and attractive work. It was written after 716, probably soon after, and was used by Bede when he came to write his *History of the Abbots of Monkwearmouth and Jarrow*. It gives a vivid picture of religious life in early Northumbria, including some concrete details omitted by Bede. For example, we learn from it that the abbot in Gaul from whom Benedict Biscop obtained architects for his buildings had an English name, and thus was probably an English *peregrinus*; its information that Botwulf's monastery was in East Anglia disproves the identification of *Icanho* as Boston; its account of the bible which Ceolfrith intended to present to the pope allows us to identify this quite definitely with the surviving Codex Amiatinus now in Florence.

This Life has come down in two manuscripts, the tenth-century Brit. Mus. Harley MS. 3020, and the twelfth-century Digby 112, in the Bodleian Library. The Digby version is a copy of the Harley text, with some passages from Bede's work interpolated. The work was first edited by J. Stevenson, *Venerabilis Bedae Opera Historica Minora* (1841), but the best edition is that of C. Plummer, *Venerabilis Baedae Opera Historica* (1896), I, pp. 388–404, with commentary in II, pp. 371–377. There is a translation by D. S. Boutflower, *The Life of Ceolfrid* (Sunderland, 1912).

Here begins the life of the most holy Abbot Ceolfrith, under whom the blessed Bede received the habit of holy religion, and who after his death received for his merits the palm of eternal felicity.

1.[1] The Apostle Paul, writing to the Hebrews, enjoins: "Remember your superiors who have spoken the word of God to you; whose faith follow, considering the end of their conversation."[2] From this it is plainly seen that you do excellently, dearest brethren, in ordering a discourse to be made in commemoration of our most reverend father and superior Ceolfrith, who spoke to us the word of God. For in truth he was such, that not only his egress from a life devoted to God, but also his entry and his progress in it ought duly to be traced, and the constancy of his unfeigned faith imitated.

2. For, begotten by noble and religious parents and himself devoted from the first years of boyhood to the pursuit of virtues, he preferred, when he had almost reached the eighteenth year of his age, to lay aside the secular habit and become a monk; and he entered the monastery situated in the place which is called Gilling, which his brother Cynefrith, a devout man and pleasing to God, had ruled, but had

---

[1] The paragraphs are numbered as in Plummer.　　　　[2] Hebrews xiii. 7.

committed shortly before to the rule of their kinsman Tunberht, who was afterwards consecrated bishop of the church of Hexham,[1] Cynefrith himself withdrawing to Ireland in his zeal for the study of the Scriptures, combined with his desire to serve the Lord more freely in tears and prayers.

3. So Ceolfrith, being devoutly received by his kinsman aforementioned, conducted himself more devoutly, being diligent in every way about reading, labouring, and the discipline of the rule. And not long afterwards, when the pestilence was raging far and wide, that same Cynefrith, along with other English nobles who had gone there before him to study the Scriptures, departed by a transitory death to the eternal life, and Tunberht, with Ceolfrith and several of the brethren of his monastery, withdrew at the invitation of Bishop Wilfrid to the monastery of Ripon,[2] where in due course Ceolfrith, subjecting himself to the regular way of life according to custom, was elected and ordained to the priesthood by the aforesaid bishop, at about 27 years of age. Soon after he was ordained, he visited Kent, from a desire to learn fully the practices of the monastic life and of the order which he had undertaken.

4. He came also to East Anglia to see the monastic practices of Abbot Botwulf,[3] whom report had proclaimed on all sides to be a man of unparalleled life and learning, and full of the grace of the Holy Spirit; and he returned home abundantly instructed, as far as he could be in a short time, so much so that no one could be found at that time more learned than he either in the ecclesiastical or the monastic rule. Yet, in consideration neither of his order, nor of his erudition, nor even of his noble birth, could he like some people be drawn away from his attitude of humility; rather he was at pains to subject himself in all things to the discipline of the rule. Indeed, for no short time, while he held the office of baker, he was careful in the midst of sieving the flour, lighting and cleansing the oven and baking in it the loaves, not to omit to learn and also to practise the ceremonies of the priesthood. At this time also he was ordered to take under his charge the instruction of the brethren in the observance of the rule, that by virtue of his innate learning as well as the fervour of his divine zeal, he should teach the ignorant and restrain the stubborn.

5. As the time drew near at which the heavenly Judge had resolved to make him more eminently a ruler over faithful souls, Benedict, our pastor and abbot of blessed memory, learnt of the grace of his learning, godliness and diligence, and when he had planned to found this monastery in which the goodness of heaven has gathered us together, contrived for this man to be given to him by his bishop aforementioned, as his helper and fellow-worker in the establishment of the monastery; not that a man of such experience required his teaching for his own instruction, when, since he had crossed the sea many times and travelled in the regions of Gaul and Italy, and even of the islands, he was already most fully acquainted with the statutes of ancient monasteries.

6. In fact, he was accustomed to say that he had learnt in 17 ancient monasteries the rule which he taught, and whatever things he had seen most valuable anywhere, these he had brought to Britain as if hidden in the coffer of his breast and delivered

---

[1] See No. 151, pp. 654, 669.   [2] See No. 151, pp. 640, 677; No. 154, p. 693.
[3] See No. 1, p. 152.

them for us to follow. But just as the Apostle Barnabus, though he was a good man and full of the Holy Ghost and of faith, when about to teach in Antioch, came first to Tarsus, where he knew Saul to be, whom he remembered to have shown great signs of virtue already in his first steps in the faith he had accepted, in order that by using this helper he might fulfil the ministry of the word as he had resolved;[1] or just as Moses, who was elected and trained by the Lord himself for the leadership of the people of Israel, was attended by the help of his brother Aaron, lest by himself he should fear to sustain the weight of so great a command, in order that, aided by him as priest and prophet, he might discharge the office he had undertaken;[2] so, to be sure, the famous Abbot Benedict, though he was most learned in all monastic practices, sought in founding his monastery the help of Ceolfrith, who might both strengthen the observance of the regular life by a zeal for learning equal to his own, and also, being in priest's orders, discharge the service at the altar.

7. They began then to build a monastery by the mouth of the River Wear, in the year of our Lord's incarnation 674, the second indiction, and in the fourth year of King Ecgfrith, having received land from him, at first of 50 hides; for afterwards it was increased either by his gift or that of other kings and nobles. In the year following the foundation of the monastery Benedict crossed the sea and sought from Abbot Torhthelm, who had once been united with him in friendship, builders by whose superintendence and labour he might build a church of stone. When he had obtained them he brought them from Gaul to Britain.

8. Meanwhile his position of prior began to be irksome to Ceolfrith, and the freedom of monastic quiet to appeal to him more than the responsibility of governing others; for he suffered from the jealousies and most violent attacks of certain nobles, who could not endure his regular discipline. Returning to his own monastery, he hastened to subject himself to the accustomed lowly service of his former way of life; but when Benedict followed him and begged him to return, he was at length won over by his loving entreaties, and returned and diligently carried out the regulations for establishing the monastery and setting it in order, which he had begun with him.

9. When a church of excellent workmanship had been built with great speed, and dedicated in honour of the blessed Apostle Peter, the most reverend Abbot Benedict arranged to go to Rome to bring back home a great supply of holy books, some sweet memorial of the relics of the blessed martyrs, paintings, worthy of reverence, of the canonical stories, but also other things, gifts from foreign parts, as he was accustomed; especially teachers to teach in the church he had recently founded the order of chants and services according to the rite of the Roman use.

10. Ceolfrith accompanied him on his journey, desiring to study in Rome the duties of his order more thoroughly than he could in Britain; and Eastorwine, a priest and a kinsman of Abbot Benedict, was left in charge of the monastery until they should return. And, with God's assistance, their plan was put into effect, and they learnt there many statutes of the Church, and they brought back with them to Britain John, archchanter of the Roman Church and abbot of the monastery of the blessed

---

[1] Acts xi. 24, 25.   [2] Exodus iv. 14–16.

Martin, who amply taught us the regular order of chanting, both personally and by his writings.[1]

11. Eight years after they had begun to found the aforesaid monastery, it pleased King Ecgfrith also to grant for the redemption of his soul to the most reverend Abbot Benedict other land of 40 hides on which a church and monastery might be raised to the blessed Paul; not, indeed, separated from the community of the former monastery, but united to it in all things in harmonious brotherhood. Ceolfrith most vigorously carried out this work enjoined on him; for, taking with him 22 brothers, ten tonsured, twelve, however, still awaiting the grace of tonsure, he came to the place when all the buildings especially required by the needs of a monastery had first been erected there, and there also began the observance of the very same discipline of obedience to the rule and all the same canonical method of chanting and reading, which they observed in the earlier monastery; at a time when by no means all of those who had come with him knew how to chant psalms, still less how to read in church or to say the antiphons or responses. But their love of the religious life helped them, and the example of their zealous ruler and his wise persistence; for, until he might plant a deep root of monastic observance, it was his practice often to frequent the church with the brethren at the canonical hours, and to eat and rest with them, so that if there should be anything to be corrected, or to be taught to the novices, he might be present to perform it himself.

12. Now in the third year from the foundation of the monastery, he began to build the church which was to be consecrated in the name of the blessed Paul, where Ecgfrith himself had marked out the place of the altar; and this work grew so fast day by day, that, though the workmen were few, it reached dedication in the second year from its commencement. At the time when the most reverend Abbot Benedict had sent Abbot Ceolfrith thither, he also appointed Eastorwine, whom I have mentioned, a priest and his kinsman, to be ruler of the older monastery; not because one and the same monastery can have or ought to have two abbots, but, since he himself was wont often to be summoned to the king on account of his innate wisdom and the ripeness of his counsels, and had not always leisure to be involved in managing and arranging the affairs of the monastery, he sought a colleague for himself, with whose help he might more lightly and more serenely bear the requisite burden of government. Moreover, he was hastening to go to Rome, to bring home from abroad those goods which were necessary to the monasteries which he had founded.

13. And while he was tarrying in places beyond the sea, behold, a sudden storm of pestilence swept Britain and laid it waste with widespread destruction, and in it were snatched to the Lord many men from each of his monasteries, including the abbot, venerable and beloved of God, Eastorwine himself, in the fourth year from when he became abbot. The brethren, with the counsel of Abbot Ceolfrith, appointed as abbot in his place Sigefrith, a deacon of the same monastery, a man of wondrous sanctity, amply learned in the Scriptures and singularly devoted to their study.

14. Further, in the monastery over which Ceolfrith presided, all who could read or preach, or say the antiphons and responses, were carried off, except the abbot

[1] See No. 151, pp. 657f.

himself and one little boy, who had been brought up and taught by him, and who now at this day, being in priest's orders in the same monastery, duly commends the abbot's praiseworthy acts both by his writings and his discourse to all desiring to know them.[1] He–the abbot that is–being very sorrowful by reason of the aforesaid pestilence, ordered that the former use should be suspended, and that they should conduct all the psalm singing without antiphons, except at vespers and matins. When this had been put into practice for the space of a week, with many tears and laments on his part, he could not bear it any longer, and resolved to restore again the course of the psalmody with the antiphons according to custom; and, all exerting themselves, he fulfilled what he had resolved, with no small labour, by himself and the boy whom I have mentioned, until he could either himself train, or gather from elsewhere, sufficient associates in the divine work.

15. But when Benedict came home from Rome, laden, as always, with foreign wares, he was grieved indeed at the disaster which had befallen, but very glad that Sigefrith, a man loved of God, had been elected abbot in Eastorwine's place; and he enjoined him to conduct vigorously the charge of the monastery which he had received, himself helping him in teaching and prayers. But not long afterwards both of them fell sick, and the affliction gradually increased until both were bed-ridden, without being able even to rise to a sitting position.

16. Therefore when Benedict had taken counsel with the brethren, he summoned Ceolfrith and appointed him abbot of both monasteries, enjoining that it should be one monastery in all things, although situated in two places, governed always by one abbot, protected by the same security of privilege; and, in accordance with the contents of the same privilege which he had obtained from Pope Agatho, and with the rule of the holy Father Benedict, no abbot was ever to be sought for the same monastery by reason of hereditary succession, but for his manner of life and his diligence in teaching; according to which principle he had himself now appointed Ceolfrith, who was united to him more by spiritual than carnal relationship, although he had a brother in the flesh, very near to him by relationship indeed, but very far distant from him by lack of heart.

17. Ceolfrith, then, was appointed abbot there in the third year of King Aldfrith, the first indiction, on 12 May, which was the eighth year from his foundation of the monastery of the blessed Paul. And in the same year the venerable abbot and deacon, Sigefrith, purified by long sickness, migrated to the heavenly kingdom on 22 August, in the third year from when he became abbot. Furthermore, at the beginning of the following year, that is, on 12 January, Abbot Benedict, beloved of God, himself also after the furnace of long infirmity, in which he ever continued to give thanks to God, went to the rest and light of the heavenly life, having passed 16 years in monastic government.

18. He had, in fact, himself ruled the monastery of the blessed Apostle Peter for eight years, and devoted just as many also to the care of the monastery of the blessed Paul through the medium of Ceolfrith; and during the first four of these latter years he governed the monastery of St. Peter, as has been set out above, with Eastorwine as

---

[1] The boy is presumably Bede.

his assistant; for the next three he had Sigefrith, for the last Ceolfrith, as his colleagues in authority. Benedict was buried in the chapel of the blessed Peter, east of the altar, where afterwards the bones of the most reverend abbots Eastorwine and Sigefrith were translated also.

19. And when he had been taken from death into life, Ceolfrith took charge of both monasteries, or rather of the one monastery situated in two places, and maintained it with watchful skill for 27 years. For he was a man of keen intelligence, energetic in action, burning with zeal for righteousness, glowing at once with love and fear of God, stern in reproving sinners, gentle in cherishing penitents, assiduous in upholding and teaching the statutes of the regular life, kind in relieving the poor and in almsgiving, generous also with money, whether in giving the things which were asked from him, or in recompensing the things which were given to him, and he paid attention to prayers and psalmody with pious regularity.

20. Thus he enriched the monasteries over which he presided, both externally with abundant wealth, and no less within; and in order that he might make them more secure from molestation by impious men, he sent envoys to Rome and sought and obtained a letter of privilege from Pope Sergius of blessed memory, after the manner of that which his predecessor Benedict had received from Agatho. And also he enriched them most copiously with vessels which belong to the service of the church or the altar; and he nobly increased the library which either he himself or Benedict had brought from Rome, so that among other things he caused to be transcribed three bibles, two of which he placed in the churches of his two monasteries, so that it should be easy for all who wished to read any chapter of either testament to find what they wanted; while the third he resolved to offer as a gift to Peter, Prince of the Apostles, when he was about to go to Rome.

21. For indeed, when he saw that, worn out as he was with old age, he could no longer set an example of his former vigour to his pupils, he thought of a profitable plan, that he should relinquish the monastic government to younger men, and himself make a pilgrimage to the thresholds of the Apostles; and there, set free from earthly cares, await his last day in unhindered application to prayer, imitating the example of his brother Cynefrith, who, as we have related above, gave up the charge of his monastery in his zeal for the contemplative life, and exchanged his own land for voluntary exile for the sake of the Lord.

22. He therefore prepared a ship, drew up a list of envoys whom he intended for Rome, decided on the gifts which were to be rendered to the blessed Peter, and procured a sufficiency of the things which might be necessary for so great a journey. But for the time being, he purposely kept secret the fact that he was himself to go with them, for fear that if what he intended should be published openly, either he would be forbidden or retarded by his friends, or else, at least, that many would grant him money whom he would have neither time nor power to repay; for, indeed, he always maintained the habit of a bountiful mind, that if any gift were given to him by anyone, of high rank or low, he on no account let him depart unrepaid, but often presented his benefactor with a more ample favour.

23. When everything was ready and the day of departure at hand, he called

together into the church the brethren who were in the monastery of the blessed Peter, and revealed what he intended. All wept, falling on their faces, and laid hold of his feet, beseeching him with copious tears not to depart thus suddenly, but to stay among them for one day at least. He acceded to their prayers, and remained with them that day and night–it was the Tuesday before Whit Sunday–and in the morning set out with many companions to the brethren living in the monastery of the blessed Paul; and speaking with them, informed them that he had now planned to go away. And since they wept greatly, and were dismayed at his sudden departure, he addressed them all gently and kindly, asking them to observe the rule which he had taught, to persevere in the fear of the Lord, and not to hinder with their entreaties and weeping the journey which he had planned; and, if he had done anything more intemperately than was right, to pardon him, because he himself now forgave from his whole heart all who had offended against him in any way, and desired that the Lord should be merciful to them all, both then and for ever.

24. But after they had resisted for no little time, at length, himself also weeping greatly, he prevailed on them to give him permission to go with their blessing and favour, as was proper, and they besought him urgently, if he arrived at the sacred shrines of the blessed Apostles, to commend them to the Lord in frequent prayers; if he should die before, ever to be mindful to intercede for their salvation.

25. He set out the same day, whether burning with desire to journey, or driven by weariness at the distress of the brethren, after enjoining that they should appoint as abbot for them whomsoever among themselves they judged most worthy, with the grace of his blessing, and according to the rule of the holy Father Benedict and the injunctions of their own privilege. And returning to the monastery of the blessed Peter as soon as day dawned, after Mass had been sung at St. Peter's and St. Mary's and those present had received the communion, he, being quickly prepared, called all the brethren into the church of the blessed Peter, asked them to pray for him, said also a prayer himself, kindled the incense, and, holding the censer in his hand, took his stand on the steps where he had been wont to read, and gave the kiss to many of them, for he was prevented by his grief and theirs from giving it to all. He went out with the censer to the oratory of the blessed martyr Laurence, which is in the dormitory of the brethren, and they followed singing the antiphon from the prophet: "The way of the just is made straight, and the way of the saints is prepared"[1] and "going from strength to strength",[2] adding also the 66th psalm: "May God have mercy on us and bless us; may he cause the light of his countenance to shine on us; and may he have mercy on us."[3] And leaving there with the incense kindled, he again addressed them all, that they should keep peace one with another, and beware of enmities, disparagements and causes of offence; and according to the precept of the gospel they should first singly, then two or three together, admonish all sinners, and endeavour to recall them to the way of truth; and if fruit should come of their diligence, let them rejoice, but if otherwise, then at length bring forward their faults in public;[4] that they should preserve concord and brotherly unity with the brethren who were at St. Paul's, and

---

[1] Isaiah xxvi. 7, but not the Vulgate text.   [2] Psalm lxxxiii. 8.
[3] Psalm lxvi. 1, from the Old Latin text.   [4] Cf. Matthew xviii. 15–17.

remember that they were both one monastery, ever to be ruled by one abbot, lest when the bond of fraternity had been broken within, the door should be opened to harmful invasion from without, as in the case of the Hebrew people, which, when it was divided against itself through the folly of the son of Solomon, never had respite from external disaster.

26. When the address was ended, they resumed the antiphon with the above-mentioned psalm, and went out to the river, leading forth their father with a mournful song as one already on the point of departure, and as before, he gave to each in turn the kiss of peace, while their chant was often interrupted by their tears; and having said a prayer on the shore, he entered the ship and seated himself in the prow. Deacons seated themselves beside him, one holding a cross of gold which he had made, the other lighted candles.

27. As the ship hastened across the river, he looked towards the brethren mourning his departure, and heard the glorious music of the song mingled with grief, and could by no means restrain himself from sobbing and tears. But this alone he repeated with frequent utterance: "O Christ, have pity on that band. O Lord Almighty, protect that company. For I know most truly that I have found none better than they or more inclined to obedience. O Christ, O God, defend them." Thus, leaving the ship, he did reverence to the cross, mounted his horse and departed, his secular cares laid aside, hastening also from the English people, his kindred, to be a stranger in foreign lands, that he might with greater freedom and purity of mind devote himself to the contemplation of the companies of the angels in heaven.

28. The brethren returned to the church, and when prayers were ended took counsel what to do, and it seemed right that amid prayer and fasting they should inquire of the Lord whom they were to appoint as abbot over them. But since the venerable father when leaving had enjoined that none of them were to fast on the day of his departure, but rather that all were to hold a greater feast, and had even enjoined that some of those accompanying him were on that account to wait with them until the end of the midday meal—it was the Thursday before Whit Sunday—it seemed proper to fast the following day and night, and to refresh themselves on the Saturday only at the ninth hour, for they could not prolong the fast beyond then by reason of the vigils of the Sunday solemnity; and also to add several psalms throughout the fitting hours of canonical prayer, and all to beseech the heavenly goodness that, on the day when he deigned to hallow the beginnings of his Church through the coming of the Holy Spirit, he should also indicate to them, who were in truth a portion of that Church through the grace of that same Spirit, a worthy superior.

29. These matters thus concluded, there came from the monastery of St. Paul several of the brethren on the day of Pentecost, and by unanimous consent they chose Hwætberht to be ordained in the abbot's place; he had passed his life from an early age in the same monastery, and had been trained in ecclesiastic as well as monastic learning, and at that time was already effective in priest's orders. Immediately he was elected abbot, he wrote a letter in which he commended to the apostolic pope his father and predecessor, and at the same time he made ready presents to send, and following Ceolfrith's steps with certain of the brethren, he read the letter to him and

brought forth the gifts which he was to deliver, having found him in Ælfberht's monastery, which is situated in the place which is called *Cornu Vallis*.[1]

30. Ceolfrith accepted gladly the brethren's choice and confirmed it with his blessing, and gave him full instruction in many matters as to how he ought to preside over the management of the monastery. And the beginning of the letter is as follows:

"To the lord most beloved in the Lord of Lords and thrice-blessed Pope Gregory, Hwætberht, your humble servant, abbot of the monastery of the most blessed Prince of the Apostles, Peter, in the Saxon land, sends perpetual greeting in the Lord.

"I do not cease to give thanks for the dispensation of the heavenly Judge, along with the holy brethren who in these places desire with me to bear the most sweet yoke of Christ to earn rest for their souls, that it has deigned to appoint you, so glorious a vessel of election, to the government of the whole Church in our times; to the end that through this light both of truth and faith with which you are yourself filled from heaven, it may abundantly besprinkle all of lower degree with the radiance of its goodness. We commend to your holy benignity, O father and lord most beloved in Christ, the venerable grey hairs of our most beloved father, Ceolfrith, abbot and nourisher and guardian of our spiritual liberty and peace in our monastic quiet. And first, indeed, we give thanks to the Holy and Indivisible Trinity, that although it was not without our intense sorrow, groaning, grief and accompaniment of tears that he went from us, he has yet arrived at the holy joys of his long-desired rest; now, even worn out with age, he has devotedly sought afresh those thresholds of the holy Apostles, which, as he continually recalled them, he rejoiced to have approached, seen, and adored in his youth; and, after the long labours and the continual cares of more than forty years, in which he presided with an abbot's authority over the government of monasteries with an unparalleled love of virtue, he once more begins, as if[2] newly summoned to the society of the heavenly life, though worn out with extreme age and already at the point of death, to live an exile for Christ, that the glowing fire of repentance may more freely consume the old thorns of secular cares in the spiritual furnace. Finally, we beseech your Paternity that–what we have not been worthy to do– you diligently fulfil for him the last act of kindness; knowing for certain that although you have his body, yet we as well as you have his spirit devoted to God, whether remaining in the body, or freed from bodily chains, as a great intercessor for our transgressions with the heavenly goodness and as a protector."

31. Ceolfrith set out from his monastery on 4 June, the fifth day of the week, intending to put out to sea by the mouth of the River Humber. On 4 July, a Saturday, he embarked in a ship, which, before it touched the coast of Gaul, was brought to land in three provinces, in each of which he was honourably received by all and held

---

[1] No place-name has been found of which this is a likely translation. The place was probably near the mouth of the Humber, and has been tentatively identified with the cell founded by Wilgils, St. Willebrord's father, which afterwards came into Alcuin's possession by inheritance. See No. 157.

[2] Reading *quasi* for *quas*.

in veneration, because he had determined to crown the grace of his former perfection by an example of incomparable virtue.

32. The voyage ended, he reached Gaul on 12 August, the fourth day of the week, and in those parts also he was magnificently honoured by all, especially by King Hilperic himself, who, in addition to the gifts which he offered, gave him also letters through all the provinces of his kingdom, that he might everywhere be received in peace and that no one might presume to cause him delay on his journey. Moreover, he recommended him and also all his followers to the kind treatment of Liutprand, king of the Lombards. He arrived at Langres, a city of Burgundy, on 25 September, the sixth day of the week, where, tired out equally by great age and sickness – yes indeed, according to what the Scriptures are wont to say "decaying in a good old age – he was gathered to his fathers".[1] For he was 74 years old, and had served in the priest's orders for 47 years, holding the position of independent abbot for 35 years.

33. He left in the monasteries a company of soldiers of Christ of more than six hundred; and furthermore, land of nearly 150 hides, by the computation customary among the English. From when he departed from his monastery until he ended his last day, he chanted the psalter of David right through three times a day, besides the canonical psalmody, thus increasing his former practice, by which for several years he was in the habit of going through the whole psalter twice a day; and on no day did he omit to offer to the Lord the sacrifice of the sacred oblation for himself and his friends, not even when, unable to ride because of excessive weakness, he was carried in a horse-drawn litter, except only on that one day when he was tossed all day at sea, with storms beating on the ship, and except on the four days before his death.

34. In his company there were about 80 men, gathered from various parts, who all followed and cherished him like a father. For he had ordered his attendants that if they should find that any one of those accompanying him was without provisions of his own, they were to give him immediately either food or money. For, indeed, he was very kindhearted by nature, and a very great supporter of the poor. Consequently, when he was about to depart, and was setting out, the unanimous lamentation of the poor and homeless bore witness that they were deprived, as it were, of a father and sustainer. He was anxious to practise diligently this kind of virtue, not only as commended by fear and love of God, but also as acquired from his parent as if by hereditary right. For his father, when he held a most noble office in the king's personal retinue, always took such great pleasure in works of mercy for the benefit of the poor, that when on one occasion he had prepared a very magnificent banquet for the king's entertainment, and the unexpected exigency of war intervened to prevent him from coming, he gave thanks to the divine providence and immediately caused all the poor, the strangers and the sick to be summoned from all sides to the feast; and with the things which he had intended for the entertainment of an earthly king and his thegns, he entertained the highest king in the person of his lowly followers, for the sake of eternal reward; himself, indeed, discharging all the service of the male guests while enjoining his wife herself to undertake in all things the office of the lowliest of handmaidens to the women.

[1] Genesis xxv. 8.

35. Now Ceolfrith reached Langres about the third hour of the day, on 25 September, as we have said, at the beginning of the fifteenth indiction;[1] and arriving in the meadows round that same city was gladly received by Gangulf, the lord of those regions, who had, indeed, met him previously on the way and had bidden him to come to him, and to be kindly received even if he himself should not be present; urgently beseeching him not to go away until he was well, but rather, if God should so will it, to await there, at the tombs of the holy martyrs, the entrance to the heavenly life.

36. It happened that on the very day on which he arrived, he departed to the Lord about.the tenth hour; and on the next day, with a great company both of his own followers and of the inhabitants of the city, his body was brought for about three miles to Gangulf's monastery, which was on the southern side of the city, at a distance of about a mile and a half. It was buried in the church of the holy martyred brothers, whose names are Speusippus, Eleosippus and Meliosippus, who, being born of one mother at one birth, were crowned with martyrdom there in ancient days and buried in that same place, where also their grandmother, Leonella by name, was buried, who also had left the body with a martyr's confession.

37. So when the father had been buried, certain of the brethren who had escorted him returned home, to relate in his own monastery where and when he had died; some, however, completed the proposed journey to Rome, to deliver the presents which he had sent. Among which presents was the bible, as we have said, translated from the Hebrew and Greek originals by the interpretation of the blessed priest Jerome, which had written at its beginning verses in this wise:

"To the body of the sublime Peter, justly to be revered, whom ancient faith declares head of the Church, I, Ceolfrith, abbot from the farthest ends of England, send pledges of my devoted affection; desiring that I and mine may ever have a place amidst the joys of so great a father, a memorial in the heavens."[2]

38. Moreover, some preferred to reside in that same city of Langres, through love of their father buried there; yet afterwards these fulfilled their resolve and desire to visit Rome. And the companions of the most reverend abbot found so great favour with Gangulf, that he entertained them all to a magnificent feast after the funeral and also furnished guides to those departing in various directions, as well as supplies for the journey; and in addition he arranged for means of subsistence for those who stayed on, for as long as they wished to remain.

39. What indeed the apostolic pope thought of him and of his gifts, the letter witnesses which he sent in reply, which begins:

' Bishop Gregory, servant of the servants of God, to the religious abbot Hwætberht.

"We have perused the tenor of the writings of your estimable piety, which

---

[1] The year of the indiction was reckoned to commence on 24 September.

[2] This bible survives, being the *Codex Amiatinus* at Florence, and still contains these lines, except that parts have been erased to make room for alterations to make them suitable to a later gift of the manuscript by Peter, an abbot in Lombardy, to the Church of the Saviour. The inscription is facsimiled by the Palaeographical Society, 2nd. Series, part IV, pl. 66.

show that you rejoice in the truth by whose grace 'those things which are not' are called 'as those that are'[1] as regards our promotion, and that you profess yourself willingly subject to the authority of the apostolic law, whose office we, although unworthy, discharge. For which reasons, know that you ought, collaborating in prayers with him whose supremacy you welcome, to pray the more earnestly that he may be of profit to himself, and to you, and to many; further, that he whose venerable grey hairs, dedicated to God, you were anxious to commend, was by God's summons translated from things temporal to things eternal, before he was received by us; after he had sent as an everlasting memorial a gift to our lord and common patron the blessed Peter, highest lord of the Apostles. Approving his faith in the bestowal of this gift, we have adjudged him worthy of constant commemoration; and we pray that this most approved preceptor of the holy institutions of the rule may before God show the way to worthy disciples; that the heavenly grace which has taken him away may, perfecting his merits, liken him to Aaron and Moses, the holy leaders of the divine people, called forth when on their way to the promised land, and to the holy Elias, suddenly snatched away into the heavens; and may adorn his pupil, who survives and succeeds him, along with the followers he is to govern, with the spiritual gifts and dignities of Joshua, that most choice leader, and of Phineas and Elisha. Farewell."

The companions of our father, loved of God, who returned to us, used to tell us that in the night after his venerable body had been committed to the tomb, while three guards of the same church were keeping the night watches, according to custom, the fragrance of a wonderful odour filled the whole church; and it was followed by a light, which remained no little time, and finally rose to the roof of the church. They went out quickly, and gazing they saw the same light rapidly rise to the skies, so that all places round about seemed to be illumined by its glow, as if it were day-time; so that it was clearly given them to understand that ministers of eternal light and perpetual sweetness had been present and had consecrated by their visitation the resting-place of the holy body. Hence a custom spread among the natives of that place that throughout the various hours of daily and nightly prayer, when the canonical rite of psalmody was ended, all the men should bend their knees in supplication at his tomb. And also report spread abroad that other signs and cures were done there, by the grace of him who is wont both to aid his saints as they strive in this present life and to crown them victors in the future life. Amen.

156. Extracts from the Life of St. Guthlac, by Felix

This work supplies some information about early Mercian history, a subject on which we know far too little. It was written before 749, for Ælfwold, king of the East Angles, to whom it is dedicated, died in this year. From the author's confidence that the prophecies of future greatness, made to Æthelbald of Mercia by Guthlac in a vision, were fulfilled, it seems probable that we should not date the Life much before 730, when Æthelbald's power was speading over all England south of the Humber. He claims to have his information from Abbot Wilfrid, the priest Cissa, and

---

[1] Romans iv. 17.

others who had known Guthlac, who died 11 April 714. The work had some popularity: two Anglo-Saxon poems of the second part of the eighth or the early ninth century make use of it, and it was translated into vernacular prose towards the end of the tenth century, or a little later. Birch in his edition refers to seven manuscripts, the earliest being a fragment in Brit. Mus., Royal MS. 4 A xiv, of the late eighth or early ninth century, and a full text in the ninth-century C.C.C.C., MS. 307. For a detailed description of the manuscripts, including some not known to Birch, as well as a much needed critical text, the reader is referred to a forthcoming edition by B. Colgrave, who has generously placed his knowledge at my disposal in my dealing with this difficult text. The selection I have given helps us to form some idea of an important and interesting Mercian king, the recipient of Boniface's letter of remonstrance (No. 177), gives a picture of the life of a young man of rank, and shows how severely Mercia could be threatened by Welsh hostility. It reveals that Repton was a double monastery, and that the diocese of Headda of Lichfield included Crowland.

Until Mr. Colgrave's edition appears, one is dependent on that of W. de G. Birch, *Memorials of St. Guthlac of Crowland* (Wisbech, 1881). The Anglo-Saxon translation is edited by C. W. Goodwin (London, 1848), and by P. Gonser, *Das angelsächsische Prosa-Leben des hl. Guthlac* (Heidelberg, 1909), which includes passages from the Latin Life.

[Guthlac's father]

p. 9, § i.[1] In the days of Ethelred, the illustrious king of the English,[2] there was a certain man of a distinguished family of the Mercians, called Penwealh, whose dwelling was in the regions of the Middle Angles and was enriched with an abundance of diverse goods.

§ ii. The descent of this man came through the most noble names of illustrious kings in direct line back to Icel from whom it began.[3]

[Guthlac's early career]

p. 12, § xii. When therefore his strength had increased in his adolescence, and a noble love of command began to glow in his young breast, remembering the strong deeds of former heroes, he gathered round him bands of followers, and with a changed disposition, as if awakened from sleep, gave himself up to arms; and when he laid waste the towns and residences, villages and fortresses, of his opponents with fire and sword, and brought together comrades from diverse races on all sides and collected immense booty, he used to give back to the owners the third part of the assembled treasures, as if taught by the divine counsel.

p. 13, § xiii. Therefore when about nine years had gone by, during which he brought about the notorious downfall of his persecutors and opponents by frequent blows and devastations,[4] their strength being at last exhausted after so many raids, slaughters and plunderings which their arms had wrought, they desisted in weariness. And thus, when the aforesaid man, Guthlac, of blessed memory, was tossed among the whirlpools of the fluctuating world, in the midst of the doubtful issue of revolving time and the mists of dark life, one night after he had composed his tired limbs for his accustomed rest, and was in his usual manner anxiously pondering on human cares with a roving mind in earnest contemplation, suddenly, wondrous to relate, a spiritual flame began to kindle all the heart of the renowned man, as if he were struck in the breast. For when he contemplated the miserable deaths and shameful end to life of the ancient kings of his stock in past ages, and also considered with a wakeful mind

---

[1] I follow Birch's pagination.   [2] King of the Mercians, 674–704.

[3] Icel appears in the genealogy of the Mercian royal family, five generations above Penda.

[4] The rest of this sentence is omitted in the Royal MS. on which Birch based his text. I have given the reading of the Harley MS.

the fleeting riches of the world and the contemptible glory of the temporal life, he then imagined to himself the manner of his own death; and, shuddering in his anxious heart at the inevitable end of this short life, he pondered on its course day by day and to the end. Moreover, he recollected that he had heard "may your flight be not in the winter or on the sabbath".[1] Reflecting on these and similar things, lo, he suddenly by the prompting of the divine will vowed that he would become a servant of Christ if he preserved his life until the morrow.

p. 14, § xiiii. Accordingly, when the mists of the shadowy night were dispersed and the sun had put forth its fiery dawn for troubled mortals, and the birds of morning chirped, he raised his mail-clad limbs and got up from his rustic couch, and having crossed himself with the sign of salvation, he ordered those accompanying him to choose another leader for their expedition; for he said that he had devoted himself to the divine service. When they heard this his companions were struck with immense amazement, and prayed him with importunate entreaties not to undertake what he said. He scorned their prayers and persisted unmoved in what he had undertaken. And thus the flame of the divine grace so blazed in him that not only did he despise the reverence due to royal descent, but scorned his parents and his country and the companions of his youth. [§ xv.] For when he reached the twenty-fourth year of his age, he renounced the pomps of the world[2] and had a firm and certain faith in Christ.

Then, beginning his course and leaving everything, he came to the monastery at Repton, in which he received the mystic tonsure of St. Peter, Prince of the Apostles, under the abbess, Ælfthryth by name; and having received the clerical habit, he strove to expiate his past sins. For, from the time when he received the symbol of the apostolic tonsure, he did not taste one draught of intoxicating liquor or of any kind of pleasing drink except at the time of communion.

p. 15, § xvii. For when, having been taught to read, he liked best to learn the singing of the psalms, the divine grace abundantly watered the fertile heart of the above-mentioned man with the moist showers of heavenly dew; and under the care of the best masters, by the help of the divine grace he was instructed in the Holy Scriptures and the monastic rules.

p. 16, § xviii. Being therefore trained for two years in canticles, psalms, hymns, prayers, and ecclesiastical customs, he was eager to imitate the special virtues of the individual brethren of the monastery; for he imitated this one's obedience, that one's humility, this man's patience, another's forbearance, the abstinence of these, the purity of each, the temperance of all, the sweetness of everyone, and, to be brief, the virtues of all in everything.[3]

---

[1] Matthew xxiv. 20.
[2] This clause is not in Birch's text, but in the other MSS. (Colgrave).
[3] After two years in the monastery, Guthlac was inspired by what he read of the hermit life of monks in the past to desire it for himself. With the permission of his elders he left the monastery and came to the fens, where a certain Tatwine directed him to an island called Crowland where no one dared live because of evil spirits. He began to live there on St. Bartholomew's day (25 August), having first returned to Repton and brought two youths back with him. He built his hut over a rifled tumulus. His ascetic life and the terrible attacks of demons are described, and the appearance of St. Bartholomew to comfort him. His next vision has historic importance.

How he put to flight by his prayers visionary crowds of demons who were simulating a British army.[1]

p. 29, l. 17. Thus it happened in the days of Cenred, king of the Mercians,[2] when the Britons, the dangerous enemies of the Saxon race, were oppressing the nation of the English[3] with war, pillage and devastation of the people, that on a certain night at the time of cockcrow, as the man of blessed memory, Guthlac, was devoting himself according to his wont to vigils and prayers, he was suddenly, as he supposed, overcome by sleep, and seemed to hear the shouts of a raging crowd. Then, in less time than it takes to tell it, roused from a light sleep, he went outside the little cell in which he was sitting, and standing, pricking up his ears, he recognized the words that the crowd were saying and that British hosts were approaching his cell. For in former vicissitudes of other times, he had been an exile among them, long enough to be able to understand their sibilant speech. They strove without delay to enter the house across the swamp, and almost at the same moment he saw all his buildings on fire, with the flame rising above them; him too they caught, and began to lift him up aloft on the sharp points of their spears. Then truly the man of God at length plainly perceived the thousand-fold shapes of the deceitful enemy with his thousand-fold wiles, and chanted as if with prophetic mouth the first verse of the 67th psalm: "Let God arise." When they heard this, all the hosts of demons, in less time than it takes to tell it, vanished at that same moment like smoke from his sight.[4]

[Æthelbald of Mercia visits Guthlac during his exile]

p. 51, l. 12. Neither am I reluctant to relate an example of the above-mentioned Guthlac's spiritual foresight, by his prophetical spirit. For at a certain time, when that exile, Æthelbald,[5] whom we have mentioned above, was driven by the persecution of King Ceolred hither and thither among divers nations, one day when his own strength and that of his followers was failing in the midst of hazardous perils, and his exhausted powers had at length given out, he came to confer with the holy man Guthlac, as he was wont, that when human aid had failed he might approach divine aid. And as he was speaking with the blessed man Guthlac, the man of God, like an interpreter of a divine oracle, began to expound in order the things which were to happen to him,[6] saying: "O my child, I am not without knowledge of your hardships, I am not ignorant of the miseries that have been yours from the beginning of

---

[1] This rubric in four MSS. (Colgrave).   [2] 704–709.

[3] Does Felix use this word as a synonym of Saxon, or to apply to the Angles in a narrow sense? By Saxon he seems to mean the Germanic inhabitants of Britain, not only of the Saxon districts.

[4] Various miracle stories follow: Guthlac's foreknowledge of the future frustrates an attempt on his life by his envious servant Beccel, whom he forgives; he prevails against demons in animal forms; a page of writing stolen by a crow from Wilfrid, when Guthlac's guest, is miraculously found; wild creatures are subservient to him, etc. The story of the restoration to the same Wilfrid of his gloves which crows have stolen is of interest for its mention that an exile called Æthelbald, of a noble Mercian family, had come with him, for this is the future king, often mentioned later on. Two of his companions, Ecga and Ofa, are miraculously healed when visiting Guthlac with their exiled lord, and one of them, Ofa, survived into Æthelbald's prosperous days, for he witnesses his charters (Nos. 64, 66 f.). Other visitors include Headda, bishop of Lichfield, with his secretary Wigfrith, who had lived among the Scots. Headda consecrated the church, and ordained Guthlac priest. Abbess Ecgburh, daughter of King Ealdwulf of East Anglia, came and was told by Guthlac that the man who would succeed him was still a heathen, which proved true, for Cissa was not baptised until later.

[5] See pp. 21 f.   [6] All after 'expound' is from the Harley MS.

your life. Pitying your distress therefore, I have prayed the Lord to help you in his compassion, and he has heard me; and he has given you domination over your people, and he has set you as a ruler of nations, and will subdue the necks of your enemies under your heel. And you shall have their possessions and they that hate you shall flee from before your face,[1] and you shall see their backs, and your sword shall conquer your enemies. And thus take courage, because the Lord is your helper; be patient, lest you turn aside to a counsel which you cannot establish.[2] Not as pillage nor as spoil will a kingdom be given to you, but you will be given it from the hand of the Lord. Wait for him, whose days are spent,[3] for the hand of the Lord oppresses the man whose hope is seated in wickedness,[4] and his days will pass away like a shadow."[5] As Guthlac said these and similar things, Æthelbald from that time placed his hope in the Lord; nor did vain hope deceive him, for all that the man of God had told him happened exactly in the same way, order and connexion; as the actual outcome of present events shows.[6]

p. 60. Accordingly, after the aforesaid exile Æthelbald, who was dwelling in distant regions, heard of the death of the blessed Father Guthlac, who alone had been his refuge and his consolation in his troubles, he came, stricken with sudden grief, to his body, hoping in the Lord, that he would give him some refreshment in his trouble through the intercession of so great a man as Guthlac. And when he reached his tomb, weeping, he said: "My father, you know my miseries; you have ever been my helper. While you were alive, I did not despair in afflictions; you were with me in great dangers; through you, I called on the Lord and he delivered me. Whither now may I turn my face? Whence will help come to me, or who will counsel me, excellent father, if you desert me? Who will console me? In you did I hope, nor did the hope deceive me." Speaking these and many other things, he stretched himself on the ground, and humbly praying he bedewed all his face with frequent floods of tears. But when, as the shades of night drew near, he was passing the night in a certain chamber where he had been wont to lodge when Guthlac was alive, and impelling his sad mind hither and thither, in a short while, after his nightly prayers were over, he closed his eyes in a light sleep; and being suddenly wakened, he saw the whole cell in which he was lying, shining all round with a glory of immense light. And when he was struck with fear by the unknown vision, forthwith he saw the blessed Guthlac standing before him, clothed in angelic splendour, saying: "Fear not. Be valiant, for God is your helper. For this reason have I come to you, that the Lord through my intercession has heard your prayers. Be not saddened, for the days of your misery are passed and the end of your trouble is at hand. For, before the sun has revolved round its annual orbit with twice six monthly changes, you will be granted the sceptre of the kingdom." But not only, it is said, did he prophesy a kingdom for him, but also

---

[1] Cf. Numbers x. 35.   [2] Cf. Psalm xx. 12.   [3] Ceolred of Mercia. Cf. Psalm lxxxix. 9.
[4] Cf. I John v. 19.   [5] Cf. Psalm cxliii. 4.
[6] There follows a long account of Guthlac's last illness and death, most of it borrowed verbally from Bede's Life of St. Cuthbert, though Felix gives some of it on the authority of Beccel, Guthlac's attendant, who was with him when he died. Guthlac ordered the news to be taken to his sister Pega. He died on the Wednesday of Easter week (11 April), 714, and was buried in his chapel. A year later the body was translated and found incorrupt; the sarcophagus was placed in a richly ornamented monument given by King Æthelbald, to whose career Felix returns after a few sentences in Guthlac's praise.

revealed to him in order the length of his days and the end of his life.[1] Æthelbald said:
"Lord, what sign shall I have that all will happen thus?" Guthlac replied: "You shall
have this sign: when tomorrow arrives, before it is the third hour, gifts of provisions
will be granted to those who dwell in this place, from an unexpected source." When
he had said this, the light which had appeared receded from Æthelbald's eyes. Quickly
the words were followed by results. For before the third hour of the day approached,
they heard a signal sounded at the landing-place, and saw men bringing thither
unexpected gifts. Then, remembering all the things which had been said to him, he
believed with sure faith that they would come to pass, and fixed immovable faith in
the prophecies of the man of God. Nor did his faith deceive him, for from that time
until this very day, the glorious happiness of the reign increased from day to day in
the times that followed.[2]

157. From Alcuin's Life of St. Willibrord

This Life, which was written some time between 785 and 797, deals more with the miracles than
with the history of the saint. Its most interesting parts are the beginning, for the light thrown on
early Northumbrian conditions, and the account of Willibrord's abortive attempt to convert the
Danes. The Life is addressed to Beornred, archbishop of Sens, an Anglo-Saxon and a relative of
Willibrord, over whose foundation of Echternach he had been abbot. It survives only in manuscripts of continental origin. It is edited by W. Levison, *Mon. Germ. Hist., Script. rer. Merov.* VII,
pt. I, pp. 81–141, and translated by A. Grieve, *Willibrord, Missionary in the Netherlands, 691–739*
(London, 1923).

Chap. 1. In the island of Britain, in the province of the Northumbrians, there was
a certain head of a household,[3] a Saxon by race and Wilgils by name, leading with
his wife and all his household a religious life in Christ, as was afterwards made
manifest by signs. For, relinquishing the lay habit, he chose the monastic way of life,
and not much later, as the fervour of spiritual life increased in him, he gave himself
over to stricter religious practices in solitary austerity on the headland which is
surrounded by the ocean and the River Humber, serving God there for a long time
in fasts and prayers and vigils in a little oratory dedicated in the name of St. Andrew,
the Apostle of Christ, so that he was also distinguished by miraculous signs and his
name became famous. Nor did he cease to exhort the crowds who flocked to him
with most sweet instruction in the word of God, and he came also to be so honoured
by the king and nobles of that people that they bestowed on him as a perpetual gift
some small estates adjacent to that headland, to build a church to God. In this the
pious father collected a congregation of the servants of God, small indeed, but
virtuous, and in this also, after manifold conflicts in holy labour, he rests in the body,
crowned by God, and his descendants to this day possess it by the gift of his sanctity.
I, the last of these in merit and order, have received the governance of the same little
cell by legitimate succession, and have written this history of the most holy father and

[1] If he had foretold that he should be murdered by his own guards Æthelbald would have found it poor
comfort. See No. 1, p. 163; No. 3, p. 241.
[2] The Life ends with an account of the healing by Guthlac's relics of a blind boy from the province
of the *Wisse*, probably a tribe dwelling on the banks of the Wissey and Great Ouse.
[3] *paterfamilias*. No claim is made for noble rank, so it is probable that Wilgils was an ordinary freeman,
a *ceorl*.

highest teacher Willibrord, at your orders, most blessed pontiff Beornred, who by the grace given you by God, have become the most worthy heir to so great a father, both by the dignity of the highest priesthood, and by lineal descent, and by your care of the holy places which were founded by him in honour of God.[1]

Chap. 9. Also the same man of God [Willibrord] tried to make the rivers of celestial teaching flow beyond the bounds of the Frankish kingdom. For he did not fear to approach Radbod, king of the Frisians, a heathen at that time with his people, and wherever he arrived, he preached the word of God with all confidence. But the aforesaid king of the Frisians, though he received the man of God kindly with the grace of humility, could not soften his stony heart with the consolations of eternal life. And when the man of God realized that he could win no harvest with him, he went to preach the gospel to the most savage peoples of the Danes. There, it is reported, reigned Ongendus, a man more cruel than any beast and harder than any stone, who nevertheless, by God's command, treated the herald of truth with honour. When the latter found [the country][2] obdurate in its customs and given up to idolatry, with no hope of a better life, he took there thirty boys of that country, and hastened to return to the peoples of the kingdom of the Franks whom God had chosen. On that journey he washed in the fount of life the boys who were being instructed in the faith, for fear that he should suffer any loss of them from the perils of the very long voyage or from the attacks of the savage inhabitants of the land, for he wished to anticipate the cunning of the ancient enemy, and to fortify with the sacraments of the Lord the souls he had gained.

Chap. 10. While the pious preacher of the word of God was making this journey, he arrived on the boundaries of the Frisians and Danes at an island which was called by the inhabitants of the land *Fositesland*[3] after a certain god called Fosite, because sanctuaries of that god had been constructed on it. This place was held in such great veneration by the pagans that none of the heathens dared to touch anything on it, whether animals grazing there or anything else whatever, or even presumed to draw water from the spring which bubbled up there, except in silence. When the man of God was cast up there by a storm, he remained there some days, until the storm should abate and a fit time for sailing arrive. But scorning the foolish sanctity of this place and the very savage disposition of the king, who used to condemn to a very cruel death the violators of his sanctuaries, he baptized three men in that spring by the invocation of the Holy Trinity, and moreover he ordered animals grazing on the island to be slaughtered as food for his party. The pagans who saw this, thought that they would either go mad or even perish by a swift death. When they saw that they suffered no ill, they were terrified and astounded, yet told King Radbod what they had seen done.

---

[1] The birth of Wilgils's son Willibrord, with the usual prophetic vision before it, is then given, followed by an account of his education at Ripon, his departure to Ireland, the commencement of the mission to Friesland, his obtaining of the support of Pippin, who controlled the western parts of Friesland, and his visit to Rome. Cf. No. 151, pp. 672–674.

[2] Some word has dropped from the text.

[3] Usually identified with Heligoland. This sanctuary was destroyed by St. Liudger, the missionary of the Old Saxons, in 790.

Chap. 11. And inflamed with great anger, he planned to avenge on the priest of the living God the injuries to his own gods, and according to his custom, he cast lots three times a day for three days, and, with God defending his own, the lot of the condemned could never fall on the servant of God or any of his men, except that one of his comrades alone was singled out by lot and crowned by martyrdom. The holy man of God was called to the king and greatly upbraided by him, and asked why he had violated his holy things and done injury to his god. The herald of truth replied to him with steadfast mind: "It is not God whom you worship, but the devil, who has deceived you, king, with the worst error, that he may give your soul to the eternal flames. For there is no God but one, who created heaven and earth, the sea and all that in them is;[1] whoever worships him with true faith shall have everlasting life. I, his servant, today testify to you, that you may at length turn from the vanity of ancient error which your fathers worshipped, and, believing in one Almighty God, our Lord Jesus Christ, and baptized in the font of life, you may wash away all your sins, and having thus cast off all iniquity and unrighteousness, may henceforth live as a new man in all sobriety, righteousness and holiness. If you do thus, you will possess eternal glory with God and his saints. If, however, you scorn me who am showing you the way of salvation, know for certain that you will suffer eternal punishments and infernal flames with the devil whom you obey." The king, amazed, replied to these words: "I see that you have not feared our threats, and your words are just like your deeds." Though he would not believe the teacher of the truth he yet sent him back with honour to Pippin, ruler of the Franks.

158. Two extracts from Willibald's Life of St. Boniface

This Life was written before 769, the year in which Megingoz, bishop of Würzburg, to whom, along with Lul, it is dedicated, died. According to an early eleventh-century Life of Boniface, written at Mainz, Willibald wrote it on wax tablets and had it approved by these two bishops before copying it on parchment. One may therefore agree with Levison (*England and the Continent in the Eighth Century*, p. 54) that, though it is "incomplete and inadequate", it "gives parts of a coherent narrative based on contemporary information". Space does not allow of a large selection, giving the history of Boniface's mission, which belongs to continental rather than to English history, but the account of the sending of the young Wynfrith (Boniface) to Canterbury is of great interest as containing the oldest record of a West Saxon synod. It seems right also to include the account of the martyrdom of the saint and his companions at Dokkum in 754, which is recorded in No. 3, p. 241 and No. 5, and which called forth Archbishop Cuthbert's letter, No. 183.

The best edition is by W. Levison, *Vitae Sancti Bonifatii Archiepiscopi Moguntini* (*Script. rer. Germ. in usum Schol.*, 1905). There is an English translation by G. W. Robinson, *The Life of St. Boniface by Willibald* (Cambridge, Mass., 1916).

[*Wynfrith is sent as an envoy to Canterbury*][2]

And when he was subduing his heart to the above-mentioned virtues for a long time and in priest's orders advancing from day to day to higher proofs of good qualities, a sudden and urgent situation arose in the reign of Ine, king of the West Saxons,[3] for a new dissension had sprung up; and immediately, by the counsel of the aforesaid king, a synodal council of the servants of God was held by the primates of

---

[1] Cf. Revelations x. 6.
[2] Ed. Levison, pp. 13-15. Wynfrith (Boniface) is now at Nursling, Hants, having come there from the monastery of Exeter which he entered in boyhood.
[3] 688-726.

the churches. And as soon as all were assembled, there took place among the priestly grades of the ecclesiastical order a most wholesome inquiry and deliberation about this recent dissension. And forming the more prudent resolution, they decided that envoys, faithful in the Lord, should be sent to the archbishop of the city of Canterbury, Brihtwold by name,[1] lest if they were to act without the advice of so great a pontiff it should be attributed to presumption or temerity on their part. And when this prudent discussion was concluded and all the council and the whole order of clerics assented, the king at once addressed all the servants of Christ and asked to whom they would entrust the performance of this legation. Then quickly the abbot highest in Christ, Wynberht by name, who ruled over the aforesaid monastery,[2] and Wintra, who presided over the monastery which is called Tisbury,[3] and Beorwold,[4] who governed by the divine ordinance the monastery which is called by the name given of old, Glastonbury, and also many other fathers of this holy way of life, summoned this holy man and brought him to the king. And the king charged him with the message and business of this legation, appointed companions for him, and sent him off in peace. And when this legation had been committed to him, he arrived, according to the command of the elders, in Kent after a prosperous journey, and skilfully disclosed to the archbishop, who was endowed with the badge of the highest pontificate,[5] everything in due order, just as the king had instructed him. And when he had received a favourable answer, he returned not many days later to his country, and wisely reported to the aforesaid king and the afore-mentioned servants of God present with him the favourable reply from the venerable archbishop, and gave great joy to all. Thus, by the wonderful benevolence of God's dispensation, his name was henceforth spread abroad and held in honour among all, secular dignitaries as well as men in ecclesiastical orders, with the result that he advanced from this time on and very often took part in their synods.

[*The martyrdom of St. Boniface*][6]

When the Lord wished to snatch his servant from the trial of this world and to raise him from the tribulations of the temporal life, it was then determined by the Lord's dispensation, that along with the servants of God who accompanied him he should come to Friesland, which he had once deserted in body, but never, indeed, in his heart; so that there, where first entering on the task of preaching he had begun to heap up rewards, he should, leaving the world, receive the payment of his remuneration.

But by a marvellous and in some measure prophetical prediction he foretold to the aforesaid bishop[7] the ensuing day of his death, and told him by what kind of death he should at length leave the world, and gave him instructions concerning the building of churches and the teaching of the people, saying: "I indeed wish to carry out my proposed expedition; I shall not be able to turn back from that wished-for journey. For now the time of my dissolution is at hand,[8] and the day of my death approaches; for now, laying aside the prison-house of the body, I return to the prize of eternal remuneration. But you, dearest son, bring to full completion the building of churches

---

[1] 692–731.   [2] Nursling.   [3] Wilts. On Wintra, see No. 55.   [4] See No. 166.
[5] The *pallium*.   [6] Levison, pp. 45–51.   [7] Lul.   [8] II Timothy iv. 6.

I have begun in Thuringia; most constantly call back the people from the by-paths of error; finish the erection of the church already begun at Fulda, and bring thither my body, aged with the passage of many years." And when this speech was ended, he added further words of this kind, and speaking thus, said: "My son, provide by your most prudent counsel all the things which must be gathered for use on this our journey, and also place in the chest with my books a linen cloth to enwrap my decrepit body." When indeed the aforesaid bishop could not restrain the sobs of his great lamentation, but burst into tears, St. Boniface closed the conversation and turned to other matters; and a few days later he did not draw back from the journey he had undertaken.

But having selected his fellow-travellers, he went on board ship, and journeying by the channel of the River Rhine he sought harbours for the nights, until, entering the watery fields of the Frisians, he arrived safely across the swamp which in their tongue is called *Aelmere*,[1] and went round to inspect the shores barren of the divine seed. And when he had escaped the perilous passage of the rivers, sea and immense waters, he now advanced without danger into danger, and visited the pagan race of the Frisians, which is divided into many cantons by the intervening waters, in such a way that, though they are called by various names, they yet denote the property of one race. . . .

Travelling therefore through all Friesland, he earnestly preached the word of God, overthrowing the pagan worship and destroying the erroneous rites of heathenism; and when he had broken the power of the temples, he built churches with great zeal. And he baptized many thousands of persons, men, women and children, with the help of his fellow-soldier the assistant bishop Eofa, whom he had appointed for the Frisians, to assist his own feebleness in old age, assigning to him the bishopric in the city which is called Utrecht, and also with the priests and deacons whose names are as follows: Wintrung and Walthere, and also Æthelhere, all endowed with the sacerdotal office of the priesthood; Hamund, Scirbald and Bosa, assigned to the deacons' service; Wacchar and Gundaecer, Illehere and Hathowulf, elevated to the monastic order. These with St. Boniface broadcast widely through the people the seed of eternal life and, with the support of the Lord God, spread it abroad so greatly that for those to whom, by the example of the apostolic institution, "there was but one heart and one soul",[2] there should be one and the same palm of martyrdom and remuneration of victory.

Therefore, after the splendour of the faith shone through Friesland, as we have said, and the happy end of this saint's life drew near, he now pitched his tents by the banks of a river which is called Borne, which is within the borders of those who are called in the native language *Ostor-* and *Wester-aeche*, surrounded only by a number of his followers. Since he had announced to the people, now scattered far and wide, a solemn day for the confirmation of the neophytes, and for the laying on of hands by the bishop and the confirmation of those lately baptized, everyone had returned to his own house,[3] that they might all present themselves on the day fixed for their confirmation according to the express command of the holy bishop.

But when the aforesaid day grew light, and, the sun having arisen, the dawn broke

---

[1] The Zuider Zee.   [2] Acts iv. 32.   [3] John vii. 53.

forth, there arrived, on the contrary, enemies in place of friends, and, in fact, new executioners in place of fresh practitioners of the faith; and an immense crowd of enemies, with glittering weapons, armed with spears and shields, rushed on the camp. Then suddenly his young followers sprang from the camp against them and rushed to arms on both sides, longing to defend the saints–the martyrs to be–against the insensate host of the raging people. But immediately the man of God heard the assault of the storming crowd, he summoned to him his band of clerics, took the relics of saints which he was wont to have constantly with him, and came out of the tent. And he hastily reproved the young men and forbade them to do battle, saying: "Cease, boys, from fighting and leave off strife, for we are truly taught by the testimony of the Scriptures not to render evil for evil, but even good for evil. For now approaches the day long hoped for, and the desired time of our dissolution is at hand.[1] Be strengthened therefore in the Lord, and bear gladly what his grace allows; hope in him, and he will set free your souls." And to those standing by, priests and also deacons, and men in lower orders as well, given up to the service of God, he said, admonishing them with fatherly words: "Men and brothers, be of good courage, and fear not them that kill the body, since they cannot kill the soul[2] which remains for ever; but rejoice in the Lord and fix the anchor of your hope on God, for he will straightway give you the reward of eternal salvation and will grant you a seat in the celestial hall with the angelic hosts of the heavenly city. Do not give yourselves up to the vain delight of this world, do not take joy in the fleeting adulation of the gentiles; but undergo with constancy the sudden moment of death here, that you may reign with Christ for ever." And while he was urging on his disciples to the crown of martyrdom with such encouragement and teaching, suddenly a mob of pagans raging over them attacked with swords and all martial equipment, and covered in blood the bodies of the saints by a happy death.

And when they had mutilated the mortal bodies of the righteous, the crowd of heathens in exultation seized the victors' spoils to their damnation, and pillaging the camp, tore apart and shared out the booty. They carried off the chests in which there were many volumes of books, and the boxes of relics; believing that they had enriched themselves with a great supply of gold and silver, they bore them, just as they were with the bolts of the chests locked, to the ships in which were the daily provisions of the clerics and their followers, and still a little wine remaining from that same allowance. Suddenly, when they discovered the dearly loved drink of wine, they began to appease the gluttonous voraciousness of their bellies and to inebriate their sodden stomachs with wine, and eventually, by the wonderful dispensation of Almighty God, to hold a council and discuss the spoils and booty which they had taken, and to consult how the gold and silver–unseen, indeed–should be divided among them. And when they had disputed at some length about so great an estimated sum of money, angry strife broke out again and again, and such great enmity and discord arose, that the crowd, raving even with insane fury, was divided into two factions; and finally, cruelly fighting, they turned on themselves the weapons with which they had just before murdered the holy martyrs.

<hr />

[1] II Timothy iv. 6.   [2] Cf. Matthew x. 28.

When the greater part of the raving crowd had been thus destroyed, those who survived ran joyously to the wealth acquired at the cost of their souls and lives, since the opponents were dead who h1d resisted them about the treasure their cupidity desired; and when they had broken open the containers of the books, they found, indeed, books instead of gold, Scriptures of the divine knowledge instead of silver. And deprived thus of their precious prize of gold and silver, they scattered some of the volumes they found over the surface of the field, and threw away others, casting some into the reed-beds of the marshes, and hiding others in various places; but by the grace of Almighty God, and also by the prayers of St. Boniface, archbishop and martyr, they were found unharmed and unstained after the passage of a great space of time, and were sent back by all the various finders to the house[1] in which they advance the salvation of souls to this day.

159. From the Life of Leofgyth, abbess of Tauberbischofsheim, by Rudolf of Fulda

Rudolf's Life of Leoba, or Leofgyth, Boniface's chief woman helper in his mission, was written in 836, largely from information obtained from four of her pupils and written down by a priest called Mago; but it is adorned in places with extracts from other Saints' Lives (see Levison, *England and the Continent*, p. 76, n. 2). Its most interesting part for our purpose is its account of Leofgyth in England, including as it does some information on the double monastery of Wimborne. I have selected also the sections describing her administration of her own monastery, and Boniface's farewell visit on his way to his death in Friesland. On Leofgyth see also No. 169.

The Life is edited by G. Waitz in *Mon. Germ. Hist., Script.* xv, pt. I (1887), pp. 118–131.

§ 2. In the island of Britain, which is inhabited by the nation of the English, is a place called among that people by the ancient name Wimborne, which, interpreted, can be rendered 'fountain of wine';[2] it received this name because of its great clarity and excellent flavour, in which it surpassed the other waters of that land. Here two monasteries were of old founded by kings of that race, surrounded with high and stout walls, and supplied with a sufficiency of income by a reasonable provision; one a monastery of clerics, and the other of women. From the beginning of their foundation, each of them was regulated by that rule of conduct, that neither of them was entered by the opposite sex. For a woman was never permitted to enter the congregation of men, or any man the house of the nuns, except priests only, who used to enter the churches solely to perform the office of Mass, and when the service was solemnly concluded, immediately to return to their own dwelling. Truly, any woman who renounced the world and wished to be associated with their community, entered it never to go out again, unless a good reason or matter of great expediency sent her out by the advice [of the abbess]. Moreover, the mother of the congregation herself, when she had need to make arrangements or give orders about any outside affairs for the profit of the monastery, spoke through the window, and from there decided whatever expediency required to be arranged or commanded.

§ 3. To this place, after some abbesses and spiritual mothers, there was preferred a religious virgin, Tette by name, noble certainly by the dignity of secular family—she was, in fact, the king's sister[3]—but much more noble by the goodness of her behaviour

---

[1] Fulda.   [2] This is a false etymology. The name means 'meadow stream'.   [3] Of Ine of Wessex.

and tokens of holy virtues. She ruled both monasteries with great skill and discretion. For she showed all good and holy things more by example than by words, and whatever things she taught to be contrary to the welfare of the soul, she demonstrated by her deeds how to avoid them. Also she maintained strict discipline – for which that place was always esteemed before others – with such care that entry to the women was never open to the clerics. Indeed, she so wished the maidens, with whom she herself continuously remained, to be immune from consort with men, that she refused entry into their congregation not only to laymen and clerics, but even to the bishops themselves. Very many tokens of virtue are related of her, which the venerable maiden Leoba, her pupil, used delightfully to recount from memory. Of these I have troubled to record two[1] only, as from these the rest can be inferred.

§ 4. In that nunnery there was a certain nun who was often made prioress and frequently appointed dean by custom, on account of her zeal for discipline and for observance of a more strict life, in which she seemed to excel the others. And in maintaining discipline imprudently and without discretion over those subject to her, she aroused the hatred of most of them, and especially of the young, against her. With an obstinate heart she despised their unhappiness and the maledictions uttered against her, which she could meanwhile have mollified by gentleness, and remained so unyielding against them that she took no steps to calm their hearts by any amends in the last hour of her life. In this unyieldingness, therefore, she died, and was given to the tomb, and a mound was raised over her grave with the earth piled up according to custom. However, the anger of the young who hated her was not stilled, but on the contrary, as soon as they saw the place where she was buried, they cursed her cruelty, nay more, they mounted the mound and, trampling it as if it were the dead corpse, they reproached the dead woman with most bitter insults to relieve their mortification. When Tette, the venerable mother of the community, discovered this, she restrained the temerarious presumption of the young with strong reproof, and went to the grave and saw that in a wonderful manner the earth which had lately been heaped up had subsided and sunk to the distance of half a foot below the top of the grave. Seeing this, she was violently afraid. For she realized from the disappearance of the earth the punishment of the woman buried there, and measured the severity of the just judgment of God by the damage to the tomb. Therefore, calling together all the sisters, she began to upbraid them for their cruelty and hardness of heart, because they were implacable about the injury done to them and, on account of the momentary bitterness of correction, maintained perpetual rancour; and, though it belongs to Christian perfection to be at peace even with the enemies of peace, they on the contrary not only did not love their enemies, but even impiously cursed the sister when dead whom in her lifetime they had hated against the Lord's command. She admonished them moreover to abstain from enmities, accept injuries willingly, be ready to pardon, and, as they wished their offences to be forgiven them by the Lord, so in return forgive offences from the heart. She implored them, on behalf of the dead sister, that dismissing from the mind whatever sin she seemed to have done against any of them before her death, they should fall together with

---

[1] I have included only one of these.

her in prayer, and invoke the divine clemency for her absolution. And when all unanimously agreed to her exhortations, she enjoined on them a three days' fast, advising that each should zealously persist in psalms, vigils and holy prayers for her. On the third day, when the fast was ended, she entered the church with all the congregation of nuns, and while they chanted litanies and invoked the name of the Saviour and the help of his saints, she prostrated herself with tears before the altar, to pray for the soul of the dead sister. And when she persisted in prayer, the hole in the grave, which before seemed almost empty, gradually began to fill with the rising soil, so that in one and the same moment she arose from prayer and the earth made level the grave. Hence it is plainly shown that, when the monument visibly returned to its former state, the divine virtue invisibly absolved the soul of the dead woman through the prayers of the holy nun . . .

§ 6. Leoba's parents, English by race, were indeed of noble family and both were zealous in religion and in the observance of the mandates of God. Her father was called Dynna, her mother Æbbe. But as they were sterile and unfruitful, they remained long without children. When a long time had passed; and already old and advanced in years they had no hope of generating offspring, her mother saw herself in a dream as if she had in her bosom a bell of the church, which in the vulgar tongue they call *clocca*, and putting in her hand, she drew it out ringing. And thus awakened, she called her now aged nurse to her, and revealed to her the dream she had seen. She said with prophetic spirit: "Now you will see a daughter from your womb whom it behoves you already now to vow to God. And just as Hannah offered Samuel to serve in the temple of God all the days of his life,[1] so you must grant this child, reared from infancy in sacred learning, to serve him in holy virginity as long as she lives." When the woman had made this vow, she conceived not many days later, and she bore a daughter whom she called Thrutgeba,[2] surnamed Leoba, because she was beloved;[3] for this is the interpretation of the nickname. She consecrated her to God when grown up, and entrusted her to the aforesaid mother Tette to be educated in divine studies; she rewarded truly her nurse with the gift of liberty, because she had predicted there such future joys. . . .

§ 9. At the time when the blessed maiden Leoba flourished in the monastery in the pursuits of the celestial life, the holy martyr Boniface was ordained bishop by Gregory, bishop of the Roman see (who succeeded Constantine in the pontificate), and was sent to preach the word of God to the people of Germany. And there, since he found the harvest indeed great and the people inclined to the faith, but had few labourers to work with him in the Lord's field,[4] he sent messengers and letters into the land of the English, from which he was himself sprung, and summoned some from the divers orders of the clergy, versed in the divine law and suitable by due probity of life and habits for preaching the word, with whose support he vigorously discharged the mission enjoined on him. . . .

§ 10. . . . Likewise[5] also he sent messengers into his own country with letters to Abbess Tette, who has been mentioned above, begging her to send to him for the

---

[1] Cf. I Samuel i. 27 f.   [2] This would represent an Old English *þryþgifu*, which is unrecorded.
[3] The name means 'the dear one'.   [4] Cf. Matthew ix. 37 f.; Luke x. 2.
[5] The paragraph begins with an account of the training of Sturmi, for his appointment over Fulda.

solace of his exile and the support of the mission which had been enjoined on him the maiden Leoba, the fame of whose sanctity and virtuous teaching had been spread abroad through distant lands, and filled the mouths of many with repeated praises. The mother of the community indeed felt her departure very grievously, but yet, since she could not resist the divine dispensation, she sent her with honour to the blessed man just as he had asked, that the interpretation of the dream she had once seen might be proved true.[1] The man of God received her with great respect when she came, loving her not so much for their kinship, in that she was related to him on the maternal side, as for her holiness of life and wise teaching, with which he knew that she would profit many by word and example.

§ 11. Therefore he regulated the charge of the monasteries and the pattern of life according to the rule, just as he had desired; and he put Abbot Sturmi over the monks and decided that the religious maiden Leoba should be the mother of virgins, and established a monastery for her in a place called Bischofsheim, where was collected no small number of handmaids of God, who were set to the study of celestial learning after the example of their blessed mistress, and profited so much by her teaching that many of them were afterwards made mistresses over others; so that there were either very few, or no monasteries of women in those districts which did not desire teachers from her pupils. For she was a woman of great virtues, and so confirmed in the strength of the purpose she had undertaken that she remembered neither her country nor her relations, but employed all her zeal on what she had begun, that she might show herself blameless before God and be to all subject to her a model of salvation in word and way of life. She always took care not to teach other than as she herself acted. No arrogance, no pride influenced her behaviour, but she showed herself affable and kind to all, without regard to persons. For she was of angelic aspect, of pleasant speech, of clear intelligence, great in counsel, orthodox in faith, most patient in hope, most generous in charity; and though she always showed a glad countenance, she never gave way to laughter with too great hilarity. No one ever heard a curse from her mouth, "the sun never went down on her anger".[2] She herself practised very sparingly the use of food and drink, though she showed the greatest kindness to others. There-fore the little cup from which she used to drink was called by the sisters, because of its size, "the little one of the loved one". She applied herself to the pursuit of reading with such diligence that, unless she were occupied in prayer or refreshing the body with food or sleep, the divine Scripture was never out of her hands. For, since she had been educated from early infancy in grammar and in the study of the other liberal arts, she tried to attain to the perfection of spiritual knowledge with such great earnestness in meditation that, as natural gifts combined with diligence, she became most erudite by the double gift of nature and industry. For with a keen mind she went through the volumes of the Old and New Testaments, and committed divine precepts to memory. And she added also the sayings of the holy fathers and the decrees of the canons, as well as the laws of the whole ecclesiastical system in full perfection. Especially she observed discretion in every act and instruction, and always

[1] In § 8 a dream of Leofgyth's was interpreted by one of the sisters with prophetic insight to foretell that she would benefit others by teaching and example in distant nations.
[2] Ephesians iv. 26.

gave attention to the end of any undertaking, lest perchance things unadvisedly begun
might afterwards by their incompleteness cause her regret. And as she knew that
attention of mind was necessary for the pursuit of prayer and diligence in reading, she
used to uphold moderation in vigils as in other exercise of virtues. For always, though
for a short time, yet through the whole summer, both she herself and all the sisters
subject to her rested for a while after dinner, and she did not give leave to any of them
who wished to watch indiscreetly; for she said that by loss of sleep understanding was
lost, especially in reading. And also it was her custom when sleeping, whether at
night or midday, for the Holy Scriptures to be read by her bed. Junior nuns discharged
this office in turn ungrudgingly. And, marvellous to relate, they could not omit one
word, or even one syllable, in their reading, without immediately being corrected by her
although she slept. For, as those to whom the duty had been allotted themselves said
afterwards, when they saw her to be sleeping deeply, they often deliberately made a
mistake in reading to test her, but never could they escape detection. Nor, indeed, is
it wonderful that she could not be deceived when sleeping, whose heart he possesssed
who "slumbers not, neither sleeps, keeping Israel";[1] and who could say with the
bride in the Song of Songs: "I sleep and my heart watcheth."[2] She truly practised the
virtue of humility with so great zeal, that, though she was set above the others by
merit of holiness and her position of mistress, she believed in her heart that she was
the last of all, and revealed it in her speech and showed it in her bearing. She set
particular store by hospitality; for to all, without any exception of person, she opened
her house, and produced a feast, the mother herself fasting, and with her own hands
washed the feet of all, being guardian and servant of the teaching of our Lord. . . .

§ 17. Meanwhile the blessed Archbishop Boniface prepared to go to Friesland and
resolved to visit with celestial medicine the people who were given over to pagan
rites and lay sick with the disease of heathenism. He called his disciple Lul, who
afterwards succeeded him in the bishopric, and entrusted to him various matters as he
wished, and in particular charged him with the care of the believers and with persistence in preaching and in constructing the churches begun by himself in diverse places.
But concerning the monastery of Fulda, which he had founded in the wilderness of
the vast Boconian forest, by the authority of Pope Zacharias and the favour of
Carloman, king of Austrasia, he gave special commands; that, because the monks
inhabiting that place were poor, and as yet had no other help, but supported themselves by the labour of their hands alone, he was to bring to completion the building
of the church already founded there, and transfer his body after his death for burial
there. And when he had given him these and other like charges, he exhorted the
maiden Leoba, who had been summoned to him, not to desert the land of her
pilgrimage, nor to grow weary in performance of the course she had undertaken, but
daily to increase with all zeal the good she had begun, saying to her that she should
not consider the weakness of the body, nor reckon the long space of time, nor think
the end of virtue arduous or the labour of attainment heavy, especially since the
periods of this time are brief compared to eternity, and the sufferings of the present
world not worthy to be compared with the glory to come that shall be revealed in

---

[1] Psalm cxx. 3, 4.   [2] Song of Songs v. 2.

the saints.[1] He commended her to Bishop Lul and to the senior monks of the aforesaid monastery who were present, admonishing them to care for her with honour and reverence, and affirming it to be his wish that after death her body should be laid next to his bones in the same grave, so that they might await together the day of resurrection, since in their lives they had served Christ with like vow and zeal. When he had said these things, he gave her his cowl, exhorting her again and adjuring her not to abandon the place of her pilgrimage. And thus, when all things necessary for the journey had been prepared, he journeyed to Friesland, where he ended his labours by a glorious martyrdom, after he had acquired to Christ no small portion of that people. And his body was translated to Fulda, and, as he had previously ordered, buried there with due honour.

160. From the Life of St. Liudger, by Altfrid

The two extracts I have chosen from this Life of a Frisian saint, composed before 849, throw light on Northumbrian affairs in the eighth century, revealing the existence of a Frisian trading community at York, illustrating the working of the blood-feud, and demonstrating the important part played by Northumbria in the conversion of Friesland. The Life is edited by G. H. Pertz, *Mon. Germ. Hist., Script.* II (1829), pp. 403–419.

Chap. 9. Endowed with greater grace after this, Liudger asked his parents to entrust him to some man of God for instruction. And since they were good people, they glorified God when they saw the young man's intention, and entrusted him to the venerable man Gregory, disciple and successor of St. Boniface the martyr, to be reared for the Lord. He received him gladly, and discovering the boy's intelligence educated him carefully. And thus Liudger grew up, advancing in the fear of God, and laying aside the lay habit, gave himself up entirely to the study of the spiritual state in the monastery of Utrecht. And in that school of Gregory's there were also other noble and wise fellow-pupils, some of whom afterwards became bishops, while others in lower orders became teachers in churches. Liudger was held with great affection among them, for he was a man of wondrous gentleness, of cheerful countenance yet not easily moved to laughter, and in all his actions combined prudence with temperance. For he was an assiduous meditator on divine Scripture, and especially on those parts of it which belonged to the praise of God and to the catholic doctrine. For these things he was loved by the venerable master like an only son.

Chap. 10. Meanwhile there came to Abbot Gregory a man from the land of the English, Aluberht by name, desiring, with the help of God, to be of use in teaching the people of that district, for they were ignorant in faith. Abbot Gregory gladly received him, and discovering that he was a good and learned man persuaded him to become a bishop for him. For Gregory was not ordained to the degree of bishop, but remained in priest's orders. Therefore the prudent man replied: "That you may know that I have come over here with the permission and advice of my bishop, send faithful brothers with me to the land from which I have come, to my bishop, that I and they may be ordained by him; for on such terms I give my consent." Abbot Gregory heard this gladly, and sent him, and with him Liudger and another brother

[1] Cf. Romans viii. 18.

of maturer age, Sigibod by name, to the bishop of whom Aluberht had spoken. He ordained the same Aluberht bishop,[1] Sigibod priest, and Liudger deacon, and they stayed there a year. And in that place Alcuin was master, who afterwards in the times of Charles was in charge of the teaching at Tours and in the Frankish kingdom. Liudger at once eagerly attached himself to him, imbibing from him spiritual doctrines. When those who had been sent returned after the passage of a year, they came by the guidance of God to Abbot Gregory, who received them kindly and was very delighted at their coming; and Aluberht remained with him, collaborating in the Lord's work.

Chap. 11. St. Liudger, desiring to saturate himself in the sweetness of the honey-comb of which he had had a foretaste, asked leave from Abbot Gregory to return to the master Alcuin. He, taking this ill, refused to allow it, yet he did not wish to sadden the petitioner, but began to restrain him with gentle words. And when he perceived that he could not withhold him from his intention by any objections, he summoned his father and asked that he should try to withhold him from the journey he desired; but the studious deacon persevered earnestly in his desire. Then Liudger's parents and Gregory, at length overcome by entreaties, sent him to the aforesaid master at York, a city of the English, bestowing the things needful for him on the journey; and the illustrious master Alcuin received him with great joy. And received thus, Liudger was dear to all in his accustomed fashion, because he was distinguished by good habits and holy studies, and there he remained for three years and six months, advancing in the pursuit of learning. For he wished to remain there longer in holy study, but he was not given the chance. For, when the citizens went out to fight against their enemies, it happened that in the strife the son of a certain noble[2] of that province was killed by a Frisian merchant, and therefore the Frisians hastened to leave the land of the English, fearing the wrath of the kindred of the slain young man.

Chap. 12. Then, compelled by necessity, Alcuin sent Liudger with the aforesaid merchants, and with him his deacon, Pyttel by name,[3] for he was afraid that Liudger in his love of learning would go to another city of that region and suffer some attack in vengeance for the aforesaid young man. For he said that he would rather die, than that his beloved son should suffer any deadly hurt. And Liudger, thus sent off, reached his native land by a prosperous course, well educated and having with him a supply of books, and he was then as much more worthy and acceptable to Father Gregory and the rest as he was the more distinguished in monastic learning. The deacon who had accompanied him went on to Rome according to Alcuin's instructions, later to return; and he also came afterwards in priest's orders with Alcuin to Gaul.

Chap. 13. While these things were happening, a holy and learned priest, of the race of the English, Leofwine by name,[4] came to Abbot Gregory, saying that he had

[1] Cf. No. 3, p. 243.
[2] comes 'companion', used in early Anglo-Latin sources of a (veteran) member of a king's household, and later as a term for an ealdorman. It is not easy to know its precise significance in a foreign writer at this date.
[3] Cf. No. 191.
[4] Lives of this saint are extant, of which the oldest (ed. A. Hofmeister, Mon. Hist. Germ., Script. xxx, pt. II, pp. 789 ff.) belongs to the mid-ninth century, and has been claimed as a product of Werden, the monastery founded by Liudger. It includes an account of Leofwine's bold intrusion into the meeting of Saxon deputies at Marklo.

been commanded in fearful fashion by the Lord with a three-fold admonition that he must render service in teaching the people on the borders of the Franks and the Saxons by the River Yssel, and he asked that Gregory would have him conducted to that place and to the river named to him by the Lord. Then, because the place belonged to his diocese, Gregory kindly took care to send him there, giving thanks to the Supreme Pastor because he visited his people. He sent with him also the servant of God, Marchelm,[1] of the race of the English, who had been from his boyhood educated in holy customs by St. Willibrord the bishop, that he might set him over the people. Accordingly the priest Leofwine, when he had been received by a certain woman called Averhild and the rest of the believers, sowed the teaching of salvation and watered the meadows of their minds. And they made an oratory for him on the west side of the aforesaid river, in a place which is called *Hwilpa*; and after this they also built him a church on the eastern bank of the same river, at a place whose name is Deventer. And when the people flocked to it on account of the holy man's teaching, the Saxons, who at that time were darkened with pagan rites, were infuriated, and collected an army and put the Christians to flight from those places and burnt the church with fire. Then the man of God, Leofwine, returned to Abbot Gregory and waited for the consolation of the Lord. Therefore, when the revolt had been settled and the plunderers had returned home, the man of God rebuilt the church which had been burnt, and did not cease to preach the teaching of salvation to his flock in his wonted manner, until he rendered his precious soul to the Supreme Pastor, and, dying, was buried in the same church.

[1] Not apparently the same as the Marchelm mentioned in another chapter, an Anglo-Saxon, who with his brother Marcwine, was assigned to Gregory of Utrecht by Boniface, and brought with him from Rome.

(c) EARLY CORRESPONDENCE

161. Letter of Pope Gregory I to Candidus (September 595)

This is perhaps the most interesting of those letters relating to the English mission that are not in Bede. It survives in the register of this pope (see p. 572). It gives evidence of the export of slaves from England in the sixth-century. It is possible that Gregory's wish to purchase English slaves to be trained as missionaries was what gave rise to the story of his encounter with the English youths in Rome. (See No. 151, p. 606; No. 152 p. 687.) The text is edited by P. Ewald, *Mon. Germ. Hist., Epist.* I, pp. 388 f. and by Haddan and Stubbs, III, p. 5. It is translated by A. J. Mason, *The Mission of St. Augustine to England* (Cambridge, 1897), pp. 17 f.

Gregory to the priest Candidus, setting out for the patrimony of Gaul.

We desire that, when you proceed with the help of our Lord Jesus Christ to the management of the patrimony which is in Gaul, you would be so good as to buy with the money which you will receive clothes for the poor and English boys who are seventeen or eighteen years old, that they may be given to God and educated in the monasteries; to the end that the money of the Gauls, which cannot be spent in our land, may be usefully spent in the place where it belongs. If indeed you are able to recover any of the money which is said to have been taken away, with this also we desire you to buy clothes for the poor, and as we have said above, boys who may make progress in the service of the Almighty God. But because those who are to be had there are pagans, I desire that a priest be sent with them, lest any sort of sickness befall on the way, so that he may duly baptize those whom he perceives to be dying; be so good, therefore, as to act thus, and to be prompt in carrying out these things diligently.

162. Letter of Pope Gregory I to Theoderic and Theodebert, kings of the Franks (July 596)

After Augustine had returned to Rome, as recorded by Bede (No. 151, p. 596), Gregory sent him back on the mission with a whole series of commendatory letters to the rulers and bishops of Gaul. Bede gives the one addressed to Etherius, bishop of Lyons (wrongly given as Arles by Bede. See No. 151, p. 597). Others, including the one I have selected, are preserved in the papal register. The kings to whom it is addressed were sons of Childebert II, Theoderic holding Burgundy and Alsace, Theudebert Austrasia and Germany, but at this date they were children and the real power was held by their grandmother Brunhild, to whom Gregory sent a separate letter. An interesting feature of this present letter is the statement that the English were desirous of conversion. The text is edited by P. Ewald, *Mon. Germ. Hist., Epist.* I, pp. 423 f.; by Haddan and Stubbs, III, p. 10. It is translated by Mason, *op. cit.* pp. 31–33.

Gregory, to the brothers Theoderic and Theudebert, joint kings of the Franks.

Ever since Almighty God has adorned your kingdom with the orthodoxy of the faith, and has made it outstanding among other races by its integrity in the Christian religion, we have seen in you much to make us suppose that you desire those subject to you to be completely converted to that faith in which indeed you, their kings and lords, are yourselves. And thus it has reached us that the English nation, by the compassion of God, eagerly desires to be converted to the Christian faith, but that the priests in the neighbourhood neglect it and refrain from kindling by their exhortation the desires of the English. On this account, therefore, we have arranged to send thither Augustine, the servant of God, the bearer of these presents, whose zeal and steadfastness are well known to us, along with other servants of God. We have also enjoined them to take with them some priests from the neighbourhood, by means of whom they may be able to get to know the intentions of the English, and, as far as God may allow, assist them to their desires by their admonition. In order that they may show themselves effective and capable in this affair, we beseech your Excellencies, greeting you with paternal love, that those whom we have sent may deserve to meet with your gracious favour. And because it is for the sake of souls, may your power protect and aid them, so that Almighty God, who knows that you give support in his cause with devout mind and all eagerness, may direct your affairs by his protection, and lead you after your earthly sovereignty into the celestial realms.

In addition, we request that your Excellencies should regard with favour our most dear son the priest Candidus, and the small patrimony of our church which is situated in those parts; to the end that the blessed Peter, Prince of the Apostles, may answer with his intercession for you who in consideration of this reward give protection to the things of his poor.

163. Extract from a letter of Pope Gregory I to Eulogius, bishop of Alexandria (July 598)

The letter containing this report on the spectacular initial progress of the Augustinian mission is preserved in the papal register. The text is edited by P. Ewald, *Mon. Germ. Hist., Epist.* II, pp. 30 f.; by Haddan and Stubbs, III, p. 12. It is translated by Mason, *op. cit.*, pp. 44 f.

But since in addition to the good deeds that you do yourself it is known that you rejoice along with others, I repay you for your favour in kind, and announce things not unlike yours;[1] that, while the people of the English, placed in a corner of the world, remained until now in the false worship of stocks and stones, I resolved, with the aid of your prayers, to send by God's instigation a monk of my monastery to preach to that people. And he, having received my permission, was made bishop by the bishops of the Germans, and brought, also with their support, to the aforesaid race at the end of the world. And even now letters have reached us telling of his safety and of his work, that both he and those that were sent with him shine amongst that race with such miracles that the miracles of the Apostles seem to be imitated in the signs which they exhibit. And on the feast of our Lord's Nativity which occurred this first indiction, more than ten thousand of the English are reported to have been baptized by this our brother and fellow-bishop. I have related this that you may know what you perform both among the people of Alexandria by preaching and in the ends of the world by praying. For your prayers are where you are not; your holy works are evident where you are.

[1] Eulogius has reported the conversion of heretics in Alexandria.

164. Letter of Wealdhere, bishop of London, to Brihtwold, archbishop of Canterbury (704–705)

This letter survives in its original form, and is also of great interest in the light it throws on the relations between the kingdoms of the Heptarchy and the difficulties of a Church that superseded national boundaries. As to date, it is long enough after the accession of Cenred of Mercia in 704 for a meeting to have been convened and held, and before the division of the West Saxon see in 705. On Brihtwold, see No. 151, p. 670. There is a facsimile of this letter, Brit. Mus., Cott. Augustus II, 18, in *Brit. Mus. Facs.*, I, pl. 6. It is No. 115 in Birch, and in Haddan and Stubbs, III, pp. 274–275.

To the most reverend lord, to be blessed by the proclamations of the catholic fathers, Brihtwold, ruling the government of all Britain, Wealdhere, the humble servant of your Grace, sends greeting.

Truly, when things were going well, my mind was always ready to seek the advice of your Holiness and to attend to your most wise commands; how much more in adverse and difficult circumstances does voluntary necessity urge my ignorant insignificance to consult your diligent and prudent consideration. Therefore, now that a matter of necessity is threatening, I think it worth while to inquire with entreaty of your Grace's sagacity what ought to be done. Indeed, I do not think it can have been hidden from your notice how many and what sort of disputes and discords have meanwhile arisen between the king of the West Saxons and the rulers of our country, and, what is still more unfortunate, also the ecclesiastics on both sides who share the direction of the government under them, have willy-nilly been involved in this same dissension. Yet often they established peace in meetings of both parties, and made a treaty that we were to drive out exiles and they were to undertake not to inflict on us such evil as they threatened in their words—all of which hitherto was not fulfilled. But a few days ago they assented to this decision by common consent, that all the kings of both parties, bishops and abbots and other councillors, should assemble on 15 October at the place which is called Brentford; and having summoned a council there, should determine the causes of all dissensions, and in as far as each shall be proved to have offended, he shall make amends to the other with legal compensation. It is fitting that I should be present at this council, as they request and as our own people advocate and the peculiar needs of our church urge; especially since both sides promised to observe the conditions of the pact which I and their bishop peacefully and unanimously agreed on. Hence I implore your Holiness's authority, by the Almighty Creator of all things, that you deign to inform me what I ought to do in this matter, because I can by no means reconcile them, and become as it were a hostage of peace, unless a very great amount of intercourse takes place between us, and this I will not and dare not do unless you wish it and give permission. For I remember how in last year's synod it was decided that we ought to have no intercourse with them if they did not hasten to fulfil your decree about the ordination of bishops, which up till now they have neglected and failed to carry out. On that account, therefore, although they invite me and our own people beseech me, I am ready rather to obey the command from your mouth. And you, excellent father, give wise counsel, that I may either consent to the voice of the suppliants, if this should please you, or shun and absent myself from the discussion at this council, if you consider this right; if only I may in any case remain ever of the same opinion as you. I did not go, though summoned, to the meeting of King Cenred and his bishops and his other leaders, which lately they held about the reconciliation of Ælfthryth, because I was ignorant what your Holiness's prerogative might wish to decide in this matter; so that when I had learnt this I might consent more freely if I had not previously taken part in the contrivance of others. What more need be said? I choose what you may choose, refuse what you may refuse, and hold the same view as you in all things. I have been at pains to intimate this to you by letter so that it may not be divulged and known to many.

May the Divine Trinity deign constantly to protect your Grace, praying for us.

165. From a letter of Aldhelm to the clergy of Bishop Wilfrid

We owe the preservation of this letter to William of Malmesbury (see p. 575), though he only gives parts of it. Unfortunately he omits the superscription, which might have helped to date the letter. Ehwald would date it 705–706 (= 704–705 by indictional dating), when Wilfrid went to Rome for his final appeal; but he had been exiled from Northumbria already in 691, and the letter could have been sent at that time. William of Malmesbury says the letter was addressed to Wilfrid's abbots, and he may have got this from its superscription. In that case it is addressed to the heads of the many religious communities placed under Wilfrid's control. The views expressed in this letter are of very great importance, for they re-echo the sentiments of the vernacular heroic poetry, and prove that this was not merely using an outworn poetic convention in the great demands it made on the loyalty of a man to his lord. On Aldhelm see No. 151, p. 675, and on Wilfrid, No. 151, pp. 640–642, 654–656, 676–680, and No. 154.

The text is in William of Malmesbury's *De Gestis Pontificum* (ed. Hamilton, pp. 337–339), and is edited also by R. Ehwald in *Mon. Germ. Hist., Auct. Ant.*, xv, pp. 500 ff., by J. A. Giles, in *Patres Ecclesiae Anglicanae, Aldhelm*, i, pp. 334 ff., and in Migne, *Patrologia Latina*, lxxxix, col. 100.

Recently, as you have learnt by experience, the raging disturbance of a storm has shaken the foundations of the Church like a great earthquake, and its noise has resounded far and wide through the various parts of the earth like the crash of thunder. And therefore with humble prayer, on my knees, I implore you, my deeply loved fellow-countrymen, not to be made to stumble by the ruse of this disturbance, that no one of you in sluggish inaction may grow dull in faith, even if necessity require you to be driven from your native land with the prelate who is deprived of his episcopal dignity, and you have to go to any parts of the broad realms across the sea. For what toil, I ask, is so hard and cruel as to divide and shut you off from the bishop who, nourishing, teaching, reproving, raised you in fatherly love from the very beginning of your first studies and from the early infancy of tender years to the flower of adult manhood; and like a nurse bearing and reviving her loved fosterlings in her warm embrace, mercifully clasped and cherished you in the bosom of his love? . . .[1]

If therefore a creature lacking reason, whom the innate rules of nature govern without written laws, obeys in this way the command of its leader in alternating seasons, tell me, I ask, whether those are to be charged with the infamy of a horrible and detestable act who, though endowed with the seven-fold grace of the Holy Spirit, break the curb of devoted submission in a frenzied fashion? But listen, why I, assembling arguments from diverse things, run on with strident pen to stir up the hearts in your breasts! Behold, if laymen, ignorant of the divine knowledge, abandon the

[1] Aldhelm adds here one of his long similes, comparing the way a swarm of bees follows the movements of the leader. It is very lengthy, but may even have been longer, or have been followed by others, for William of Malmesbury curtails, going on "And after other things . . .".

faithful lord whom they have loved during his prosperity, when his good fortune has come to an end and adversity befallen him, and prefer the safe ease of their sweet native land to the afflictions of their exiled lord, are they not regarded by all as deserving of ridicule and hateful jeering, and of the clamour of execration? What then will be said of you if you should let the pontiff who has fostered you and raised you go into exile alone?[1]

166. Letter of Brihtwold, archbishop of Canterbury, to Forthhere, bishop of Sherborne, on the redemption of a captive (709-731)

The date of this interesting letter could be narrowed to no later than 712, if we could accept the evidence of Birch No. 128, which purports to be a grant to Ealdberht, the successor of the Abbot Beorwold here mentioned, and is dated 712. One should note that the ransom offered is the same as the wergild of a person of the highest rank in Kent. The letter is Tangl, No. 7, and Haddan and Stubbs, III, p. 284. Part is translated by R. W. Chambers, *England before the Norman Conquest*, pp. 183 f.

To his most reverend and holy fellow-bishop Forthhere, Brihtwold, servant of the servants of God, sends greeting in the Lord.

Since my petition, which I made in your presence to the venerable Abbot Beorwold[2] about the ransoming of a captive girl, who has kinsmen among us, has, contrary to my expectation, proved in vain, and I am importuned afresh by their entreaties, I have considered it best to send this letter to you by the brother of the girl, Eppa by name. By it I implore you to obtain from the aforesaid abbot that he will accept 300 shillings for that girl by the hand of the bearer of these presents; and give her over to him to be conducted hither, that she can pass the remainder of her life with her relations, not in the sadness of servitude, but in the joy of liberty. When your kindness brings this about, you will have both a reward from God and thanks from me. Also, in my opinion, our brother Beorwold loses nothing of what rights he had in her. I beseech you, as I should have done before, that, when you are mindful of yourself in frequent prayers, you will deign none the less to remember me. May Jesus Christ our Lord preserve your Reverence unharmed to an advanced age.

167. Letter of Daniel, bishop of Winchester, to Boniface (722-732)

Daniel, who was bishop from 705 to 744, wrote a letter of recommendation for Wynfrith (Boniface) in 718, at the beginning of his mission (Tangl, No. 11), and Boniface kept in touch with him and valued his advice. (See No. 175.) It is a pity that no reply is extant to this letter, so we do not know whether Boniface tried this approach to the heathen or not. It apparently does not occur to Daniel that the pagans may have their own accounts of the origin of the universe.
The letter is No. 23 in Tangl, and is in Haddan and Stubbs, III, pp. 304-306. It is translated by Kylie, pp. 51-55; by Emerton, pp. 48-50.

To the revered and beloved bishop, Boniface, Daniel, servant of the people of God. Although, my brother and dearest fellow-bishop, I may rejoice that you deserve the chief prize of virtue, who, trusting in the magnitude of the faith, confidently assail the stony and hitherto barren hearts of the heathen, and, untiringly working with the ploughshare of the gospel-preaching, strive by daily labour to turn them into fruitful fields, so that to you truly can be applied the saying of the prophet and the evangelist:

[1] There was more of this letter, for William has 'etc.' here.
[2] Of Glastonbury. See No. 158, p. 716.

"A voice of one crying in the wilderness, etc.";[1] nevertheless a portion of a second prize will not unfittingly be given to those also who rejoice to further so religious and beneficial a work with what aid they can, and supply their needs with suitable support, that they may endeavour to carry on the glad work of preaching thus begun and to bring forth for Christ a succession of sons.

Hence, in devoted friendship, I have been at pains to make a few suggestions to your prudence, that you may better perceive by what means you can in my opinion best overcome the stubbornness of the barbarians. For you ought not to offer opposition to them concerning the genealogy of their gods, false though they are, but allow them to assert according to their belief that some were begotten of others through the intercourse of male and female, so that you may then at any rate show gods and goddesses born after the manner of men to have been men, not gods, and, since they did not exist before, to have had a beginning.

When they have perforce learnt that the gods had a beginning, seeing that some were begotten by others, they should then be asked whether they think this world had a beginning, or has always existed without a beginning. If it had a beginning, who created it? For certainly they can in nowise find a place of subsistence or habitation for their begotten gods before the establishment of the universe; for, by universe, I mean not only this visible sky and earth, but also the whole extent of space, which even the pagans can conceive in their thoughts. But if they contend that the world always existed without beginning, strive to refute and overcome this with many proofs and arguments. Ask the disputants: Who controlled the world before the birth of their gods? Who ruled it? And how could they bring under their domination or establish in their possession a world that had always existed before them? And whence and by whom and when was the first god or goddess appointed or begotten? And do they believe that the gods and goddesses still beget other gods and goddesses? Or, if they do not procreate now, when and why have they ceased from copulation and child-bearing? If, however, they still procreate, the number of gods must by now have become infinite. And it is unknown to mortals who among so many and great beings is the most powerful, and great care must be taken not to offend a mightier one. And ask whether they think the gods are to be worshipped for temporal and present, or for eternal and future blessings. If for temporal ones, let them say in what respect the pagans are now happier than the Christians. And what do the pagans believe that they confer by offerings of wealth to gods who have all things in their power? Or why do these same gods leave it in the power of those subject to them to decide what they shall give to them? If they are in need of such things, why not rather choose better things for themselves? And if they are not in need of them, it is futile for people to think that they can please the gods with such offering of sacrifices.

These, and many like questions, which would take too long to enumerate now, you ought to put to them, not in a way to insult or irritate them, but calmly and with much moderation. And from time to time their superstitions should be compared with our, that is, the Christian, dogmas of this kind and touched on as if by the way, so that the pagans more from confusion than from exasperation may blush for such

[1] Isaiah xl. 3; Matthew iii. 3.

absurd opinions, and not think that their abominable rites and fables are hidden from us.

This also is to be inferred: If the gods are almighty and beneficent and just, they not only reward worshippers, but also punish those who scorn them. If they do both in the temporal world, why then do they spare the Christians who are turning almost the whole globe away from their worship and overthrowing their idols? And while they, that is, the Christians, possess fertile lands, and provinces fruitful in wine and oil and abounding in other riches, they have left to them, the pagans that is, with their gods, lands always frozen with cold, in which these, now driven from the whole globe, are falsely thought to reign.

There must also often be brought before them the might of the Christian world, in comparison with which those who still continue in the ancient false faith are few.

And in order that they may not boast of the rule of the gods over these races as legitimate and in existence from the beginning, they must be told that once all the world was given up to the worship of idols, until by the grace of Christ it was illumined with the knowledge of the true, almighty Creator, Ruler and One God, restored to life and reconciled to God. For, when among the Christians children of the faithful are baptized daily, what do they do other than purify them singly from the filth and guilt of heathenism, in which once the whole world was involved?

Out of love, my brother, I wished to mention these things to you briefly; although I, heavily weighed down with bodily sickness, suffer so that I may fitly say with the psalmist: "I know, O Lord, that thy judgment is just, and truly thou hast afflicted me.[1] Wherefore I entreat the more earnestly your Reverence that, with those who with you serve Christ in spirit, you may deign to pour out prayers of supplication for me, that the Lord, who "has made me drink the wine of sorrow",[2] may also hasten with his compassion; that he who justly chastised may mercifully forgive, and of his goodness cause me also to sing with joy the words of the prophet: "According to the multitude of my sorrows in my heart, thy comforts, Lord, have given joy to my soul."[3]

I desire that you may be well in Christ and remember me, dearest fellow-bishop.

168. Letter of Boniface to Abbess Bucge (before 738)

This is included as a pleasant example of Boniface's correspondence with English ladies. We see from Tangl, No. 105, that Bucge did eventually reach Rome and met Boniface there in 738. Between 761 and 765, Archbishop Bregowine of Canterbury writes to Lul that they celebrate the day of her death, 27 December, in words that suggest that her death has recently occurred (Tangl, No. 117).

This letter is No. 27 in Tangl, and is translated by Kylie, pp. 68–70, by Emerton, pp. 56 f.

To Abbess Bucge, his most loved lady and sister, to be set before all other women in the love of Christ, Boniface, a poor and unworthy bishop, sends eternal greeting in Christ.

Be it known to you, dearest sister, as regards the advice which you asked of me, unworthy as I am, by letter, that I do not presume either myself to forbid you a

[1] Psalm cxviii. 75, but Tangl points out that it is not the Vulgate text but Jerome's version from the Hebrew.   [2] Psalm lix. 5.   [3] Psalm xciii. 19.

journey abroad or strongly to urge it. But I will tell you how it strikes me. If, indeed, you gave up the anxious charge you had over the servants and handmaids of God and over the monastic life, to obtain quiet and contemplation of God, why should you now with toil and tedious anxiety be a slave to the words and wishes of worldly men? For it seems better to me, if you can by no means have quiet freedom of mind in your own country because of worldly cares, that you should acquire freedom for contemplation, if you wish and can, by pilgrimage; just as our sister Wihtburh did, who has told me in her letters that she has discovered by the thresholds of St. Peter the quiet life which she desired and sought for a long time. But she advised me concerning your wish–for I wrote to her about you–that you should wait until the revolts and attacks and threats of the Saracens, which have lately manifested themselves among the Romans, have quieted down, and until she, God willing, sends letters of invitation to you. And this seems to me best. You may prepare for yourself the things necessary for your journey, and wait for word from her, and do afterwards what the goodness of the Lord shall command.

Concerning the copying of the passages for which you asked, you must pardon my shortcomings, for owing to pressing labours and continual journeys I have not yet finished copying what you asked for; but when I have finished it, I shall be sure to send it to you.

And thanking you for the gifts and vestments which you sent, we ask Almighty God to repay you with the gift of an eternal reward with the angels and archangels in the holy summit of the heavens. I beseech you therefore through God, my dearest sister, nay rather, my mother and most sweet lady, to deign to pray for me assiduously, because for my sins I am wearied by many tribulations, and disturbed far more by tribulation and anxiety of mind than by bodily affliction.

May you know that the long-established trust between us never fails. Farewell in Christ.

169. Letter of Leofgyth to Boniface (soon after 732)

This letter should be compared with No. 159. Leofgyth's biographer, Rudolf, was apparently unaware that she began her education under Abbess Eadburh, at Minster in Thanet. Two letters of Boniface to Leofgyth are extant. One (Tangl, No. 67) is addressed to her and Tecla, Cynehild and the other nuns, and is a request for their prayers; the other (Tangl, No. 96), is a brief business letter. One letter from Lul to her has survived (Tangl, No. 100).

Some of the phraseology in the present letter is identical with that favoured by Lul. See, for example, No. 176 and also Tangl, Nos. 49 and 140. It betrays the influence of Aldhelm's writings The letter is No. 29 in Tangl, and is translated by Kylie, pp. 110f., and by Emerton, pp. 59f

To Boniface, the most reverend lord, endowed with the badge of the highest dignity, and most dear in Christ and bound to me by the ties of kinship, Leofgyth the lowest handmaid of those who bear the light yoke of Christ, sends greeting of everlasting health.

I ask your clemency to deign to remember the former friendship which you formed long ago in the western regions with my father, whose name was Dynna, who was withdrawn from this light eight years ago, that you may not fail to offer prayers to God for his soul. And I also commend to you the memory of my mother, who is called Æbbe, who, as you well know, is joined to you by the bonds of consanguinity, and who still lives in suffering, having long been greatly oppressed by infirmity. I am the only daughter of both my parents; would that I, although I am unworthy, might deserve to have you in place of a brother, for in none of the men of my race have I placed so much faith and hope as in you. I have troubled to send this small gift, not as if it were worthy that your Grace should look on it, but in order that you may hold me, insignificant as I am, in your memory, and not through the great distance separating us let me pass into oblivion, but rather that the bond of true love may be knotted firmly for ever. This, beloved brother, I implore you most earnestly, that I may be defended by the shield of your prayers against the poisonous darts of the secret enemy. I ask this also, that you may deign to correct the rude style of this letter and not fail to send me of your kindness some words as a model, which I eagerly long to hear.

I tried also to compose the little verses written below according to the rules of the poetic tradition, not trusting in my own boldness, but desiring to practise the first steps of a meagre and feeble talent, and wanting your help. I learnt this art from the teaching of Eadburh,[1] who continues unceasingly to search into the divine law.

Farewell, being ever the happier in life as the older in years, interceding for me.[2]

170. Letter of Bede to Egbert, archbishop of York (5 November 734)

This letter is a most important document for the history of the organisation of the early Church in England and of the holding of land by title-deed, and I have therefore given it in full. The amount of repetition it contains is a sign of the writer's sense of the urgency of the reform he suggests. It is particularly interesting to compare it with No. 184, for this shows that the archbishop, and his brother King Eadberht, tried to put at least one of its recommendations into force, and in so doing earned the papal displeasure. The present letter shows how far removed Bede was from later monastic opinion on episcopal interference, and it is not surprising that it was not so frequently copied as his other works. Only two manuscripts were known to Plummer, the twelfth-century Brit. Mus. Harley MS. 4688, which he dated too early, as tenth-century, and the fifteenth-century Merton College MS. 40. Laistner refers to an early tenth-century manuscript at the Hague (Koningklijke Bibliotheek, 70 H 7). The letter was first edited by Sir James Ware, *Venerabilis Bedae epistolae duae* (Dublin, 1664). The most accessible editions are Haddan and Stubbs, III, pp. 314–326; C. Plummer, *Venerabilis Baedae Opera Historica*, I, pp. 405–423, with commentary, II, pp. 378–388. It is translated by J. A. Giles, *The Historical Works of Venerable Bede* (London, 1845), II, pp. 138–155.

To the most loved and reverend Bishop Egbert, Bede the servant of Christ sends greeting.

I remember that you said last year when I stayed with you some days in your minster[3] for the sake of study, that this year also when you came to that same place you would like to converse with me in our common zeal for learning. If, God willing, it had been possible to accomplish this, there would have been no need to send these things to you by letter, since speaking face to face I could more freely suggest in private talk whatever I wished or considered necessary. But, since the state of my health, as you know, has become such as to prevent this taking place, I have tried to

[1] Abbess of Minster in Thanet. See Nos. 172, 173.
[2] Four lines of verse, closely dependent on Aldhelm, follow, commending him to the protection of God.
[3] Anglo-Saxon usage employed the word 'monastery' in a wider sense than ours, and Bede could mean York, which is not a community of monks. But the reference seems rather to be to some other house which Egbert visited occasionally.

do what I could, in return for your love and for the sake of brotherly devotion, by sending by letter what I could not, coming to you in person, say in conversation. And I pray you, by the Lord, not to suppose the words of this letter to be the pride of arrogance, but rather recognize them truly to be the submission of humility and duty.

Therefore, bishop most beloved in Christ, I exhort your Holiness to be mindful to strengthen both with holy works and with teaching that sacred dignity which the Author of dignities and Giver of spiritual gifts has deigned to entrust to you. For neither virtue can be duly completed without the other: if either he who lives a good life neglects the duty of teaching, or a bishop who teaches rightly disdains to practise right behaviour. But he who truly does both, such a servant assuredly awaits with joy the coming of his Lord, hoping soon to hear: "Well done, good and faithful servant, because thou hast been faithful over a few things, I will place thee over many things; enter thou into the joy of thy Lord."[1] If, however – which God forbid – anyone who has accepted the dignity of the episcopate takes no pains to correct either himself from evil acts by good living, or the people subject to him by chastening and admonishing, what, when the Lord comes at an hour that he hopeth not,[2] shall happen to him, the gospel sentence declares clearly, by which it is said concerning the unprofitable servant: "Cast ye him out into the outer darkness. There shall be weeping and gnashing of teeth."[3]

Before all, I urge you, holy father, to restrain yourself with pontifical dignity from idle conversations, disparagement, and the other polutions of an unbridled tongue, and to occupy your tongue and your mind as well with the divine words and with meditations on the Scriptures, and especially with reading the letters of the Apostle Paul to Timothy and Titus, and also the words of the most holy Pope Gregory, in which he discoursed very skilfully concerning the life and vices of rulers, whether in the *Book of the Pastoral Care* or in the homilies on the gospels; that your speech may always be seasoned with the salt of wisdom, more elevated than common diction, and may shine forth more worthy of the divine hearing. For just as it is unbecoming if the sacred vessels of the altar be ever profaned for common uses and vile offices, so it is in every way improper and lamentable if he who was ordained to consecrate the Lord's sacraments at the altar shall at one moment stand ready to serve the Lord by performing these sacraments, at the next begin suddenly on leaving the church to say paltry things and to do what will offend the Lord with the same mouth and hands with which a little before he handled sacred things.

For preserving purity of speech and conduct, the society of those who serve Christ with faithful devotion is, along with divine study, a great help. So that, if at any time either my tongue begins to run wild, or vicious behaviour to steal upon me, I may be soon upheld by the hands of faithful companions, and prevented from falling. Since it is most useful for all servants of God thus to provide for themselves, how much more for that order which has not only to take care for its own salvation, but also to devote necessary attention to the welfare of the Church committed to it; according to him who says: "Besides those things that are without; my daily instance, the solicitude

---

[1] Matthew xxv. 21.　　　　　[2] Matthew xxiv. 50.　　　　　[3] Matthew xxv. 30.

for all the churches. Who is weak, and I am not weak? Who is scandalized, and I am not on fire?"[1] I do not speak thus as if I knew you to do otherwise, but because it is rumoured abroad about certain bishops that they serve Christ in such a fashion that they have with them no men of any religion or continence, but rather those who are given to laughter, jests, tales, feasting and drunkenness, and the other attractions of a lax life, and who daily feed the stomach with feasts more than the soul on the heavenly sacrifice. I should like you to correct such, if you find them anywhere, by your holy authority, and warn them to have witnesses of their manner of life by day and night, who may be competent both to benefit the people by conduct worthy of God and by suitable exhortation, and to assist the spiritual labours of the bishops themselves. Read indeed the Acts of the Apostles, and you will see, as the blessed Luke reports, what kind of companions the Apostles Paul and Barnabas had with them, also what they themselves did by their labours wherever they went. For immediately they entered cities or synagogues they took care to preach the word of God and to spread it everywhere. I desire that you also, my most loved friend, carry this out wisely, wherever you can. For to this office you were chosen by the Lord and to this you were consecrated, that you might preach the word with great virtue, the King of Virtues himself, our Lord Jesus Christ, granting you his help. And you will accomplish it aright if, wherever you come, you soon collect to you the inhabitants of the place and reveal to them the word of exhortation, and at the same time, as if the leader of a heavenly troop, set an example of living, along with all who come with you.

And because the distances between the places belonging under the rule of your diocese are too great for you alone to be able to traverse them all and preach the word of God in the several hamlets and homesteads even in the full course of a whole year, it is very necessary that you appoint several assistants for yourself in the sacred work, by ordaining priests and instituting teachers, who may devote themselves to preaching the word of God in the various villages and to celebrating the heavenly mysteries, and especially to performing the rites of holy baptism, wherever opportunity arises. In expounding this preaching to the people, I think that you ought before everything else to see to it with all urgency that you endeavour to impress deeply on the memory of all under your rule the catholic faith which is contained in the Apostles' Creed, and the Lord's Prayer which the text of the holy gospel teaches us. Indeed it is most certain that all who have studied the Latin language have also learnt these well; but make the ignorant people—that is, those who are acquainted with no language but their own—say them in their own language and repeat them assiduously. This ought to be done, not only in the case of laymen, that is, those still leading a secular life, but also of those clerics or monks who are ignorant of the Latin language. For thus is it brought to pass that every band of the faithful may learn how to be faithful, by what steadfastness they ought to fortify and arm themselves against the assaults of the unclean spirits; and that every choir of suppliants to God may understand what especially should be sought from the divine clemency. On this account I have myself often given to many ignorant priests both of these, the Creed and the Lord's Prayer,

---

[1] II Corinthians xi. 28, 29.

translated into the English language. For the holy Bishop Ambrose, when speaking of faith, advises each of the faithful to repeat the words of the Creed in the morning, and by it, as if by a spiritual antidote, to fortify themselves against the poisons of the devil which he can cast at them by day or night with malignant craft. Also the custom of assiduous prayer and genuflexion has taught us that the Lord's Prayer should often be repeated.

For if your pastoral authority achieve these things, as we suggest, in ruling and feeding Christ's sheep, it cannot be told how great a heavenly reward you will prepare for yourself with the Shepherd of shepherds in the future. For the rarer the examples of this most sacred work you find among the bishops of our race, the higher the reward you will receive for your singular merit; inasmuch as you, inspired by paternal pity and solicitude, will have kindled the people of God through frequent repetition of the Creed and the sacred prayer to understanding, love, hope, faith, and inquiry about those same celestial gifts which are there enumerated. Just as, on the contrary, if you perform the business entrusted to you by the Lord less diligently, you will in the future receive your portion along with the wicked and slothful servant, for keeping back the talent;[1] especially if you presume to demand and receive temporal advantages from those whom you will be found not to have repaid with gifts of celestial benefit. For when the Lord, sending disciples to preach the gospels, had said: "And going, preach, saying 'The kingdom of heaven is at hand',"[2] he added shortly afterwards: "Freely have you received; freely give. Do not possess gold, nor silver."[3] If therefore he ordered them to preach the gospel freely, and allowed them to receive neither gold nor silver nor any temporal goods from those to whom they preached; what peril, I ask, may threaten those who do the contrary?

Pay heed what a very heavy crime those will have committed who strive to demand most diligently earthly rewards from their hearers and expend no labour at all for their salvation by preaching, exhorting, or reproving. Ponder it anxiously and with careful attention, most beloved bishop. For we have heard, and it is rumoured, that many villages and hamlets of our people are situated in inaccessible mountains and dense woodlands, where there is never seen for many years at a time a bishop to exhibit any ministry or celestial grace; not one man of which, however, is immune from rendering dues to the bishop. Nor is it only a bishop who is lacking in such places to confirm the baptized by the laying on of hands; there is not even a teacher to teach the truth of the faith and the difference between good and evil conduct. And thus it comes about that some of the bishops fail not only to preach the gospel freely, and lay their hands on the faithful, but even, which is more serious, after accepting money from their hearers, which was forbidden by our Lord, they despise the ministry of the word which the Lord ordered them to perform; whereas it may be read that Samuel, the high-priest loved of God, did very differently, by the testimony of all the people. He says: "'Having then conversed with you from my youth unto this day, behold, here I am. Speak of me before the Lord, and before his anointed, whether I have taken any man's ox, or ass; if I have wronged any man; if I have oppressed any man; if I have taken a bribe at any man's hand. And I will despise it

---

[1] Matthew xxv. 26, 30; Luke xix. 22. [2] Matthew x. 7. [3] Matthew x. 8, 9.

this day, and will restore it to you.' And they said: 'Thou hast not wronged us, nor oppressed us, nor taken ought at any man's hand.'"[1] And by the merit of his innocence and justice he deserved to be numbered among the first leaders and priests of the people of God, and to be worthy in his prayers to be heard by God and to talk with him, as the psalmist says: "Moses and Aaron among his priests; and Samuel among them that call upon his name. They called upon the Lord, and he heard them. He spoke to them in the pillar of the cloud."[2]

If we believe and confess that any advantage is conferred on the faithful by the laying on of hands, by which the Holy Spirit is received, it follows, on the contrary, that this same advantage is absent from those who have lacked the laying on of hands. On whom does their privation of good reflect more than on those bishops who promise to be the 'protectors'[3] of those for whom they either neglect to perform the office of spiritual 'protection', or else are unable to do so? There is no greater cause of this whole crime than avarice. Arguing against this, the Apostle, through whom Christ was speaking, said: "The desire of money is the root of all evils."[4] And again: "The covetous", he says, "shall not possess the kingdom of God."[5] For when a bishop, at the dictates of love of money, undertakes in the name of his office the charge of a greater portion of the people than he can by any means reach by his preaching and visit in the whole space of a year, it clearly results in deadly peril both for himself and for those over whom he is preferred by the false name of 'protector'.

In making a few recommendations with regard to the sad state in which our nation miserably labours, I sedulously implore your Holiness, most beloved bishop, to contend as much as you can to bring back to a right rule of life the things which you perceive to be done most amiss. For you have, as I believe, a very ready helper in so just a work, namely King Ceolwulf, who will both take care through his inborn love of religion constantly and with a firm intent to assist whatever belongs to the rule of godliness, and will especially help you, since you are his most beloved kinsman, to perfect those good things which you shall undertake. Therefore I would like you to admonish him prudently to attend to the restoration in your days of the ecclesiastical condition of our race, better than it has been hitherto. And this, as it seems to me, cannot be carried out better by any other arrangement than by consecrating more bishops for our people, and by following the example of the lawgiver, who, when he could not alone sustain the disputes and burden of the Israelite people, chose for himself, by the help of divine counsel, and consecrated, seventy elders with whose support and counsel he could carry more lightly the burden placed on him.[6] For who, indeed, cannot see how much better it would be to divide such a great weight of ecclesiastical government among several, who could bear their share more easily, than to weigh down one under a load which he cannot carry? For also the holy Pope Gregory, when he treated in a letter sent to the most blessed Archbishop Augustine of the faith of our race,[7] which was still in the future and needed to be preserved in Christ, decreed that twelve bishops were to be ordained there, after the faith had been

---

[1] I Samuel xii. 2–4.   [2] Psalm xcviii. 6, 7.
[3] Bede plays on the literal sense of *præsul*, which is often used as a term for bishop.
[4] I Timothy vi. 10.   [5] I Corinthians vi. 10.
[6] Numbers xi. 16ff.   [7] Bede means the Northumbrians alone.

accepted, among whom the bishop of York should receive the *pallium* and be metropolitan.[1] I should now like you, holy father, supported by the help of the aforesaid king, most pious and beloved of God, wisely to endeavour to complete that number of bishops, so that in the abundant number of leaders the Church of Christ may be more perfectly established in those things which belong to the practice of holy religion. But indeed we know that through the carelessness of preceding kings and through most foolish donations it has come about that it is not easy to find a vacant place where a new episcopal see should be made.

Therefore I would consider it expedient that after a great council has been held a site among the monasteries should be procured, both by pontifical consent and also royal edict, where an episcopal see may be made. And in case the abbot or monks should try to oppose or resist this decree, permission is to be given them to choose for themselves from their own number someone who may be ordained bishop and take episcopal charge of as many of the adjacent places as belong to the same diocese, along with that monastery; or if perchance no one can be found in that monastery who should be ordained bishop, yet it is to depend on their investigation according to the statutes of the canons, who is to be ordained bishop of their diocese. If you perform this as we suggest, with the Lord's help, you will, we think, also easily obtain that the church of York may have a metropolitan pontiff according to the decrees of the apostolic see. And if it appears necessary that a more ample provision of lands and possessions should be added to such a monastery on account of its receiving a bishop, there are innumerable places, as we all know, allowed the name of monasteries by a most foolish manner of speaking, but having nothing at all of a monastic way of life; some of which I would wish to be transformed by synodal authority from wanton living to chastity, from vanity to truth, from over-indulgence of the belly and from gluttony to continence and piety of heart, and to be taken over in support of the episcopal see which ought newly to be ordained.

And because there are many and large places of this kind, which, as is commonly said, are useful neither to God nor man, in that neither is there kept there a regular life according to God's will, nor are they owned by thegns or *gesiths*[2] of the secular power, who defend our people from the barbarians; if anyone should establish an episcopal see in those same places on account of the necessities of the times, he will be proved to incur no guilt of violation of duty, but rather to be doing an act of virtue. For how can it be considered a sin if the unjust judgments of princes be corrected by the scrutiny of better princes, and the lying pen of wicked scribes be deleted and made void by the discreet pronouncements of prudent priests; according to the example of sacred history, which, when describing the times of the kings of Judah from David and Solomon to the last of them, Hezekiah, shows that some among them indeed were religious, but more of them wicked, and that in alternation, now the impious rejected the deeds of the good men who went before them, now on the contrary the just corrected with all urgency the harmful acts of their impious predecessors, as was right, the spirit of God aiding them through holy prophets and priests; according to

[1] See No. 151, p. 601.

[2] Bede is probably translating the Old English *gesith* when he uses the Latin *comes*. A gesith 'companion' was a veteran member of the king's following, with a household of his own.

what the blessed Isaiah says, commanding and saying: "Loose the bands of forced covenants. Let them that are broken go free and break every unjust document."[1] By this example, it also behoves your Holiness, with the religious king of our people, to annul the irreligious and unjust acts and writings of our predecessors, and to provide for those things which may be useful to our province, whether in matters of Church or State; lest in our times by the ceasing of religion, love and fear of him who sees into the heart be abandoned, or else, by the dwindling of the supply of secular troops, there arise a lack of men to defend our territories from barbarian invasion. For–what indeed is disgraceful to tell–those who are totally ignorant of the monastic life have received under their control so many places in the name of monasteries, as you yourself know better than I, that there is a complete lack of places where the sons of nobles or of veteran thegns can receive an estate; and thus, unoccupied and unmarried, though the time of puberty is over, they persist in no intention of continence, and on this account they either leave the country for which they ought to fight and go across the sea, or else with greater guilt and shamelessness devote themselves to loose living and fornication, seeing they have no intention of chastity, and do not even abstain from virgins consecrated to God.

But others by a still heavier crime, since they are laymen and not experienced in the usages of the life according to the rule or possessed by love of it, give money to kings, and under the pretext of founding monasteries buy lands on which they may more freely devote themselves to lust, and in addition cause them to be ascribed to them in hereditary right by royal edicts, and even get those same documents of their privileges confirmed, as if in truth worthy of God, by the subscription of bishops, abbots and secular persons. And thus, having usurped for themselves estates and villages, and being henceforward free from divine as well as from human service, they gratify their own desires alone, laymen in charge of monks; nay, rather, it is not monks that they collect there, but whomsoever they may perchance find wandering anywhere, expelled from true monasteries for the fault of disobedience, or whom they can allure out of the monasteries, or, indeed, those of their own followers whom they can persuade to promise to them the obedience of a monk and receive the tonsure. With the unseemly companies of these persons they fill the monasteries which they have built, and–a very ugly and unheard-of spectacle–the very same men now are occupied with wives and the procreation of children, now rising from their beds perform with assiduous attention what should be done within the precincts of monasteries. Moreover, with like shamelessness they procure for their wives places for constructing monasteries–as they say–and these with equal foolishness, seeing that they are lay-women, allow themselves to be mistresses of the handmaids of Christ. To them fits aptly the popular proverb, that wasps can indeed make honeycomb, but they store in it not honey, but poison.

---

[1] Isaiah lviii. 6, but neither the Vulgate nor the Old Latin text. Plummer points out that Bede's version agrees exactly with that in Ambrose, *De Elia*, chap. 10, col. 545. The Vulgate text, which is translated: "Undo the bundles (*fasciculos*) that oppress. Let them that are broken go free: and break asunder every burden (*onus*)", would not suit his purpose. The Old Latin is very similar to the text as he gives it, but where, instead of *fasciculos deprimentes* of the Vulgate, Ambrose and Bede have *obligationes violentarum commutationum*, it has *cautionum* for the last word; and it has *scripturam* for the *onus* of the Vulgate, instead of the *conscriptionem* of Ambrose and Bede.

Thus for about thirty years, that is, from when King Aldfrith was removed from earthly things, our province has been demented with that mad error, so that there has hardly been one of the reeves[1] since then who has not procured for himself during his time of office a monastery of this kind and involved his wife with him in the guilt of this hateful traffic; and with the prevalence of this worst of customs, the king's thegns and servants also have exerted themselves to do the same; and thus by a perverse state of affairs, numberless people have been found who call themselves abbots and at the same time reeves or thegns or servants of the king, and who, although as laymen they could have learnt something of the monastic life, not by experience but by hearsay, are yet absolutely without the character and profession which should teach it. And indeed, as you know, such persons suddenly receive the tonsure at their pleasure, and at their own judgment are made from laymen not into monks, but abbots. But since they are found to have neither the knowledge nor love of the aforesaid virtue, what is more applicable to them than the evangelical malediction, by which it is said: "If the blind lead the blind, both fall into the pit?"[2] This blindness could now at last surely be ended and be restrained by regular discipline and expelled far beyond all the limits of Holy Church by pontifical and synodal authority, if the very bishops did not themselves prove rather to give help and to pledge themselves to crimes of this kind; for not only do they not trouble to annul unjust decrees of this kind by just decrees, but rather are eager to confirm them, as we have said above, with their signatures; driven at the dictates of avarice to confirm the same wicked documents, as were the buyers to procure monasteries of this kind.

I could indeed tell you many more things by letter about these and such like abuses by which our province is miserably harassed, if I did not know that you yourself are certainly aware of these matters. For I have not written thus as if to inform you of things which you did not already know, but in order to admonish you with friendly exhortation to correct with urgent diligence as far as you can the things which you best know to be at fault.

And at this moment I earnestly beg and implore you by the Lord to protect assiduously the flock committed to you from the audacity of the attacking wolves, and to remember that you have been appointed, not a hireling, but a shepherd, to show love of the Chief Shepherd by the careful feeding of his sheep; and to be ready with the blessed Prince of the Apostles to lay down your life for these sheep, if occasion demand it. I pray that you pay careful heed lest, when that same Prince of the Apostles and the rest of the leaders of the flocks of the faithful offer to Christ on the Day of Judgment the greatest fruits of their pastoral care, any part of your sheep deserve to be set apart among the goats to the left of the Judge and to depart with a curse into eternal punishment; but rather that you yourself may then deserve to be entered among the number of those of whom Isaiah says: "The least shall become a thousand, and a little one a most strong nation."[3] For it is your duty to look most diligently into what is done right in the various monasteries of your diocese, what wrong; so that neither an abbot ignorant or scornful of the rule nor an unworthy abbess may be set over a society of servants or handmaids of God; nor on the other

---

[1] The term used is *prefectus*. See pp. 63 f.　　　[2] Matthew xv. 14.　　　[3] Isaiah lx. 22.

hand a contemptuous and undisciplined crowd of contumacious disciples rebel against the supervision of their spiritual masters; especially since it is commonly reported that you (bishops)[1] are in the habit of saying that what is done in the various monasteries does not belong to the charge of kings, nor to the jurisdiction of any secular rulers, but solely to your episcopal inquiry and investigation, unless it happen that anyone in the monasteries is shown to have offended against those very rulers. It is, I say, your duty to provide that the devil may not usurp a kingdom for himself in places consecrated to God, and that discord may not take the place of peace, quarrels that of godliness, drunkenness that of sobriety, fornications and homicide that of love and chastity; and that none be found among you of whom it may justly be complained and said: "I saw the wicked buried, who also when they were yet living were in the holy place, and were praised in the city as men of just works."[2]

It is also necessary for you to take solicitous care of those who yet continue in the secular life, so that, as we advised at the beginning of this letter, you remember to employ for them adequate teachers of the salutary life, and cause them to learn among other things by what works they may chiefly please God, from what sins those who wish to please God ought to abstain, with what sincerity of heart they ought to believe in God, with what devotion to pray in supplication to the divine clemency, how they have need to fortify themselves and all their possessions frequently and diligently by the sign of the Lord's Cross against the continual snares of unclean spirits, how salutary for every class of Christian is the daily partaking of the body and blood of our Lord, according to what you know is wisely done by the Church of Christ throughout Italy, Gaul, Africa, Greece and the whole East. This kind of observance and devout sanctification to God has been so long absent from nearly all the laymen of our province, through the carelessness of teachers, as to be almost foreign to it, so that those among them who are more religious do not presume to participate in the sacred mysteries unless at the Lord's Nativity, Epiphany and Easter, though there are innumerable blameless people of chaste conduct, boys and girls, young men and maidens, old men and women,[3] who could without a grain of doubt participate in the celestial mysteries every Sunday, or also on the nativities of the holy apostles or martyrs, in the way you have yourself seen it done in the holy Roman and Apostolic Church. And the married also, if anyone puts before himself a due standard of continence, and attains to the virtue of chastity, can freely, and will gladly, do the same.

I have been at pains, most holy bishop, briefly to write down these things for you, both in consideration of your love and for the sake of the common good, greatly desiring and greatly exhorting you to take care to rescue our race from its old errors and endeavour to bring it back to a safer and straighter way of life; and, if there are some men, of whatever rank or order, who try to retard and impede your good undertakings, nevertheless to strive to carry through the holy and virtuous plan to a safe conclusion, mindful of the heavenly reward. For I know that some will greatly oppose this our exhortation, and especially those who feel that they are themselves involved in the crimes from which we restrain you; but it behoves you to remember

---

[1] As Plummer points out, Bede's change from the singular to the plural pronoun here shows that he does not mean Egbert alone.

[2] Ecclesiastes viii. 10.   [3] Cf. Psalm cxlviii. 12.

the apostolic reply: "We ought to obey God rather than men."[1] Surely the command of God is: "Sell what you possess, and give alms";[2] and "Unless a man forsaketh all that he hath, he cannot be my disciple."[3] But it is a practice of certain persons in these times, who profess themselves to be servants of God, not merely not to sell what they have, but also to procure what they have not. For with what countenance dare anyone about to approach the service of the Lord either retain the riches which he had in the secular life, or amass those which he had not, under pretext of a holier life; when also the apostolic rebuke is well known, which hastened, not to correct Ananias and Sapphira by any penance or payment of compensation, when they were endeavouring to do this crime, but to punish them immediately with the sentence of avenging death?[4] And yet they did not choose to amass the goods of others but merely to retain their own unfittingly. Hence it is clearly manifest how far removed was the mind of the Apostles from receiving acquisitions of money, who properly served God under the rule: "Blessed are ye poor, for yours is the kingdom of God";[5] and on the other hand were none the less instructed by the warning displayed to the other side: "Woe to you that are rich, for you have your consolation."[6] Do we perchance imagine that the Apostle erred and wrote a lie when admonishing us he said: "Brethren, do not err", and immediately added: "Neither the covetous, nor drunkards, nor extortioners shall possess the kingdom of God."[7] And again: "But know you this, that no fornicator, nor unclean, covetous or rapacious man—which is a serving of idols—hath inheritance in the kingdom of Christ and of God."[8] Since the Apostle thus clearly calls avarice and rapacity idolatry, how can we suppose them to have erred who have either withheld their hand from subscribing to avaricious traffic, although the king commanded it, or have set their hand to the cancelling of hurtful documents and their subscriptions?

Indeed, one must marvel at the temerity of fools, or rather weep over the misery of the blind, who are shown everywhere and every day without regard for the fear of God to rescind and hold of no account what the apostles and prophets have written by the inspiration of the Holy Spirit; yet, on the contrary, are afraid to erase and emend what they, or others like them, instigated by avarice or wantonness, have written, as if it were holy and secured by heaven itself; in the manner, unless I am mistaken, of the heathens, who despise the worship of the true God and venerate, fear, honour, adore and entreat as gods the things which they have themselves formed and invented in their hearts, meriting indeed that rebuke of our Lord's, who refuted the Pharisees when they put their traditions[9] before the law of God, saying: "Why do you also transgress the commandment of God for your tradition?"[10] Even if they also produce charters drawn up in defence of their covetous acts, and confirmed with the subscription of noble persons, never you forget, I pray, the decree of our Lord, in which it is said: "Every plant which my heavenly Father hath not planted, shall be rooted up."[11] And truly I would like to learn of you, most holy bishop, seeing that the Lord protests and says that "wide is the gate and broad is the way that leadeth

---

[1] Acts v. 29.   [2] Luke xii. 33.   [3] Luke xiv. 33.   [4] See Acts v. 1-11.
[5] Luke vi. 20.   [6] Luke vi. 24.   [7] I Corinthians vi. 9, 10.   [8] Ephesians v. 5.
[9] *deuteroses*, the word applied to the scribal tradition of interpretation of the law.
[10] Matthew xv. 3.   [11] Matthew xv. 13.

to destruction, and many there are who go in thereat. How narrow is the gate and strait is the way which leadeth to life and few there are that find it"; [1] what you believe about the life and eternal salvation of those who are known to go through the wide gate and the broad way during their whole lifetime and trouble not to withstand or resist for the sake of heavenly reward their desires either of body or of mind even in the smallest matters—unless perchance we are to believe that they can be absolved from guilt through alms, which they were seen to give to the poor amid their daily covetousness and pleasures, when the very hand, as well as conscience, which shall offer a gift to God ought to be clean and free from sin; or else unless we are to hope that they can be redeemed by others, when they are dead, through the mysteries of the sacred oblation, of which they were unworthy while they lived. Does perhaps the sin of avarice seem to them trifling? Of this I may treat a little more fully. It made Balaam, a man most full of the spirit of prophecy, to be exiled from the lot of the saints; defiled Achan, son of Carmi, by his share in the accursed thing, and destroyed him; stripped Saul of the insignia of kingship; deprived Gihazi of the merits of prophecy and soiled him and his seed with the plague of perpetual leprosy; deposed Judas Ischariot from the glory of the apostolate; injured even with death of the body Ananias and Sapphira, of whom we spoke above, as unworthy of the society of monks; [2] and, to come to higher things, cast out the angels from heaven, and expelled the first created beings from a paradise of perpetual delight. And, if you wish to know, this is that three-headed dog of hell, to whom the fables gave the name of Cerberus, from whose savage teeth the Apostle John would keep us, saying: "Beloved, love not the world, nor the things which are in the world. If any man love the world, the love of the Father is not in him. For all that is in the world is the lust of the flesh, and the lust of the eyes, and the pride of life, which is not of the Father, but is of the world."[3] These things I have said briefly against the venom of avarice. For the rest, if we should wish to deal in like manner with drunkenness, feasting, loose living, and the other pollutions of this kind, the length of this letter would be immoderately extended.

May the grace of the Highest Shepherd keep you safe for the wholesome feeding of his sheep, bishop most beloved in Christ. Written on 5 November, in the third indiction.[4]

171. Letter of Boniface to Nothhelm, archbishop of Canterbury (736)

This is a letter of particular interest on the matter of the authenticity of Gregory's responses to Augustine, and should be compared with Bede's statements (No. 151, p. 599). It sheds a little light on the keeping of archives at Rome, and it should be noted that Nothhelm, when in Rome before he became archbishop, had obtained for Bede the documents on the Gregorian mission to England, and so it is easy to see why it was to him that Boniface should apply. Something of Boniface's own strength of character and independence of judgment is seen in this letter, which is No. 33 in Tangl, and in Haddan and Stubbs, III. pp. 335 f. It is translated by Kylie, pp. 71–73, by Emerton, pp. 62 f.

To his lord most beloved, endowed with the highest badge of the pontificate,[5] Archbishop Nothhelm, Boniface, a poor servant of the servants of God, sends greeting of eternal love in Christ.

[1] Matthew vii. 13, 14.
[2] Plummer points out that this shows "that Bede regards the communism of the early Jerusalem Church as marking the foundation of a monastic institution".   [3] I John ii. 15, 16.
[4] November in the third indiction falls in 734.   [5] The reference is to the *pallium*.

I beseech your Grace's clemency with most profound entreaties that you may deign to remember me in your holy prayers; and may endeavour by your prayers to make secure in a harbour of firm rock the ship of my mind, which is tossed about by the waves of various storms among the German nations; and that I may be united with you in brotherly fellowship with a spiritual bond, just as your predecessor, Archbishop Brihtwold of venerable memory, granted to me when I was departing from my native land; and that, bound by the tie of love, together with my brethren the companions of my pilgrimage, I may deserve to be ever associated with you in the unity of the catholic faith and the sweetness of spiritual love.

Likewise I earnestly beseech that you will take care to send me a copy of that letter in which are contained, as they say, the questions of Augustine, the bishop and first preacher to the English, and the replies of the holy Pope Gregory; in which among other chapters it is stated that the faithful are permitted to marry in the third degree of relationship; and that you will diligently try to investigate with minute care whether or not that document can be proved to be by our above-mentioned father, St. Gregory. For when it was looked for in the archives of the Roman Church, it could not, the custodians[1] assert, be found with the other transcripts of the aforesaid pontiff's writings.

Moreover, I wish to hear your advice concerning the commission of a sin which I have committed in ignorance by yielding to a certain man in a question of matrimony. It happened in this way: a certain man, as many are wont to do, raised the son of another from the holy font of baptism and adopted him as his son; and afterwards he took to wife the boy's mother when she was left a widow. This the Romans assert to be a sin, even a capital sin; so that they require a divorce to be made in such cases. And they affirm that in the reigns of the Christian emperors the crime of such a marriage was to be punished by sentence of death or to be expunged by perpetual banishment. If you find this reckoned so great a sin in the decrees of the catholic fathers or in the canons, or indeed in Holy Writ, will you take care to inform me; that I also may understand and know whose is the authority for that judgment. For I can by no means understand why in that one case spiritual affinity should be so grave a sin in the joining of carnal union, when we all, being in holy baptism sons and daughters of Christ and the Church, can be shown to be brothers and sisters.

Likewise I ask that you take care to inform me in what year from the incarnation of Christ the first preachers, sent by St. Gregory, came to the nation of the English. Farewell.

172. Letter of Boniface to Abbess Eadburh, asking for the Epistles of St. Peter in letters of gold (735–736)

Eadburh, on whom see also Nos. 169, 173, was abbess of Minster, Thanet. This letter affords evidence that manuscript illumination was practised in nunneries. It is No. 35 in Tangl, and is translated by Kylie, pp. 90 f., Emerton, pp. 64 f.

To his most reverend and beloved sister, Abbess Eadburh, Boniface, a poor servant of the servants of God, sends greetings of love in Christ.

[1] scriniarii. R. L. Poole, Lectures on the History of the Papal Chancery, pp. 15 f. shows that these officials not only kept the records but also wrote the papal letters.

I pray Almighty God, the requiter and rewarder of all good works, that he may grant you in the celestial mansions and the eternal tabernacles, and in the heavenly court of the holy angels, an eternal reward for all the kindnesses which you have rendered to me, because in your goodness you have often comforted my sadness both with the solace of books and assistance with clothing. So I now pray you to add to what you have begun, namely to write for me in gold the epistles of my lord, St. Peter the Apostle, to secure honour and reverence for the Holy Scriptures when they are preached from before the eyes of the heathen; and because I particularly wish to have always with me the words of him who guided me to this course. And by the priest Eofa I send [the gold][1] for writing this which I ask.

Therefore, dearest sister, do in regard to this our petition as your kindness has ever been wont to do in all my requests, that here also your works may shine forth with letters of gold to the glory of the heavenly Father.

I wish that you may be well in Christ, and advance in holy virtues, mounting to still higher things.

173. Letter of Boniface to Abbess Eadburh, thanking her for sending books asked for in the preceding letter (735–736)

This is No. 30 in Tangl, and is translated by Kylie, p. 92, by Emerton, pp. 60f.

To his most beloved sister, Abbess Eadburh, from long since joined to him by the kinship of spiritual alliance, Boniface, servant of the servants of God, sends everlasting greeting in Christ.

May the eternal rewarder of just works make you joyful, dearest sister, in the heavenly court of the angels, since by sending gifts of sacred books you have consoled with spiritual light an exile among the Germans; because he who must shed light in the gloomy recesses of the Germanic nations will fall into the snare of death[2] unless he have the word of God "as a lamp to his feet and a light to his paths".[3] Besides this, trusting constantly in your love, I beseech you to deign to pray for me, because for my sins I am tossed by the tempests of a perilous sea; and to ask that he "who dwelleth on high and looketh down on the low things",[4] pardoning our offences may grant me "speech, that I may open my mouth",[5] that the gospel of the glory of Christ "may run and be glorified"[6] among the nations.

174. Letter of Boniface to the whole English race, appealing for the conversion of the Saxons (738)

This letter was probably occasioned by Charles Martel's victory over the Saxons of Westphalia, which made their conversion seem possible. Pope Gregory issued an appeal to the Old Saxons about this time. But Charles's success was only temporary, and the Saxons were not converted until a generation later. Of special interest is the consciousness revealed in this letter of bonds of kinship between the English and the continental Saxons. The letter is No. 46 in Tangl, and Haddan and Stubbs, III, p. 313. It is translated by Kylie, pp. 194f., by Emerton, pp. 74f.

---

[1] Tangl suggests that it is the gold that is implied here, though the letter does not say what he is sending.
[2] Cf. Psalm xvii. 6. [3] Psalm cxviii. 105. [4] Psalm cxii. 5.
[5] Ephesians vi. 19. [6] II Thessalonians iii. 1.

To all most reverend fellow-bishops, to venerable men in the white robes of the priesthood, to deacons, canons, clerics, abbots and abbesses set over the true flock of Christ, to monks, humble and submissive before God, to virgins consecrated and vowed to God and all the consecrated handmaids of Christ, nay more, to all God-fearing catholics in common, sprung from the stock and race of the English, a native of that same race, Boniface, also called Wynfrith, legate of the universal Church to the Germans and servant of the apostolic see, appointed archbishop without the claim of merit, sends greetings of humble fellowship and most sincere love in Christ.

We beseech with most profound entreaties your fraternal clemency to deign to remember our insignificance in your prayers, that we may be delivered from the snare of the hunter Satan and from "importunate and evil men",[1] and "that the word of the Lord may run and may be glorified";[2] and to be eager to obtain by your holy prayers that our God and Lord Jesus Christ, "who will have all men to be saved and to come to the knowledge of God",[3] may turn to the catholic faith the hearts of the pagan Saxons; and that they may escape from the snares of the devil by which they are held bound, and be joined to the sons of Mother Church. Have pity on them, for even they themselves are wont to say; "We are of one blood and one bone"; remembering that the way of all the earth[4] draws near, and no one shall confess to the Lord in hell, nor shall death praise him;[5] and the way of all the earth draws near. And know that for this request I have received the assent and approval and blessing of two pontiffs of the Roman Church. Act now on this our supplication, that your reward may shine and increase in the heavenly court of the angels.

May the omnipotent Creator preserve eternally the unity and fellowship of your love strong and advancing in Christ.

175. Letter of Boniface to Daniel, bishop of Winchester (742–744)

This letter is a good example of how Boniface turned to his countrymen for advice and consolation. Partly under his influence, Frankish synods, the first for a very long time, were held in 742 and 743, and reforms inaugurated in the Frankish Church. Boniface had to face much opposition from many members of the higher Frankish clergy who lived much like laymen and were opposed to reform, and he was also harassed by 'false prophets', priests who taught contrary to the doctrine of the Roman Church. Daniel's reply to the present letter is extant (Tangl, No. 64; Kylie, pp. 121–129), and he tries to reassure Boniface with many scriptural texts in support of his continued intercourse with such men at the Frankish court. But the memory of his oath still worried Boniface; he laid the matter before Pope Zacharias in 751 (Tangl, No. 86; Emerton, pp. 157–159), and was absolved of guilt in the Pope's reply (Tangl, No. 87; Emerton, pp. 159–164), for he had mixed with the false clergy only for the good of the Church. On Daniel, see No. 151, pp. 589, 675, and No. 167.

This letter is No. 63 in Tangl, and in Haddan and Stubbs, III, pp. 343–346. It is translated by Kylie, pp. 115–120, by Emerton, pp. 114–117.

To his most beloved master, Bishop Daniel, Boniface, servant of the servants of God, sends greeting in the love of Christ.

It is known to be a custom among men, when to any there happens some sad or burdensome thing, for them to seek comfort for an anxious mind and counsel from those in whose friendship and wisdom and loyalty they chiefly trust. In the same way I also, my father, trusting in your proved wisdom and friendship, reveal to you the

---

[1] II Thessalonians iii. 2.   [2] *ibid*. iii. 1.   [3] I Timothy ii. 4.
[4] Joshua xxiii. 14.   [5] Cf. Isaiah xxxviii. 18.

troubles of a weary heart and seek your Holiness's counsel and comfort. For we have not only, in the Apostle's words, "combats without, fears within",[1] but also fights within as well as fear, especially through false priests and hypocrites, who both oppose God and ruin themselves and lead astray the people by many stumbling-blocks and various errors, saying to the people in the words of the prophet: "'Peace, peace, and there is no peace.'"[2] And the seed of the word, which, taken from the bosom of the Catholic and Apostolic Church and entrusted to us, we are eager to sow, they try to sow over with tares and to suffocate, or to pervert into a plant of a poisonous kind. And what we plant, they do not water to make it grow, but strive to root it out that it may wither; offering and teaching to the people new doctrines and errors of various kinds. Some abstain "from meats which God hath created to be received";[3] some, feeding themselves on honey and milk alone, reject bread and other foods; and some affirm–which harms the people exceedingly–that homicides or adulterers, persisting in these crimes, can nevertheless become priests of God. And the people, according to the saying of the Apostle: "will not endure sound doctrine, but according to their own desires they will heap up to themselves teachers", etc.[4]

When we seek help and support in the palace of the Franks, we indeed cannot abstain from personal contact with such and keep ourselves apart according to the precept of the canons, except only in this, that we do not have communion with them by the sacred solemnities of the Mass in the sacred mysteries of the body and blood of our Lord. And also we avoid taking counsel and agreeing with them. For to such men our labours and battles both with the heathens and with the disorderly and lowly multitude seem alien. In truth, when anyone, priest or deacon, cleric or monk, departs from faith and truth out of the bosom of Mother Church, he then at once together with the heathens bursts into abuse of the sons of the Church. And this will be a dreadful hindrance to the gospel of the glory of Christ.

In all these concerns, in order that we may without detriment to our souls fulfil the course of our ministry, we chiefly ask for your fatherly intercession with God, and beseech you by God with heartfelt prayers to deign to intercede for us; that God, the faithful consoler of those that labour, may deign to keep our souls unharmed and safe from sin amid such storms from various causes.

I am very eager to hear and obey your wholesome counsel regarding the aforesaid intercourse with the said priests. Without the protection of the ruler of the Franks, I can neither govern the people of the Church nor defend priests and clerics, monks and handmaids of God; nor am I able to prevent the rites of the heathens and the worship of idols in Germany without his mandate and the fear of him. But when seeking help in these matters I come to him, I cannot possibly abstain, in accordance with the canons, from personal intercourse with such persons, but only from agreement with them. Now I fear guilt in that intercourse, because I recall that at the time of my consecration I swore on the body of St. Peter, at Pope Gregory's command, that I would shun intercourse with such, if I could not convert them to the canonical path. I fear still more the loss to the teaching which I am bound to give to the people, if I do not come to the ruler of the Franks. Deign to tell me, my father, what you

---

[1] II Corinthians vii. 5.   [2] Jeremiah vi. 14.   [3] I Timothy iv. 3.   [4] II Timothy iv. 3.

choose to decide and judge and recommend in these matters to a son sad and in doubt. For it seems to me I have mainly separated myself from them if I abstain from consultation and agreement with them and from sharing in the ministry of the Church, where they are not canonical.

Moreover, if I may presume, I should like earnestly to ask your paternal clemency with my heartfelt prayers for a consolation in my exile, that is, to send me the book of the prophets which Abbot Wynberht,[1] of revered memory, formerly my master, left when he departed from this life to the Lord, in which the six prophets are contained in one volume, written with clear and detached letters. And if God inspire your heart to do this, you cannot send a greater comfort to my old age, and a greater pledge of reward for yourself. For I cannot procure in this land a book of the prophets such as I desire; and as my eyes grow dim, I cannot clearly distinguish small and connected letters. I ask for the above-mentioned book for the reason that it is written so clearly with distinct and detached letters.

Meanwhile I send to you by the priest Forthhere letters and small gifts as a token of pure love; namely a cloak, not of pure silk but mixed with goat's wool, and a towel for drying your feet.

Also, by the report of a priest who came straight from you to Germany, I lately learnt that blindness had befallen you.[2] But you know better than I by whom and through whom it was said: "Whom the Lord loveth, he chastiseth, etc."[3] And the Apostle Paul says: "When I am weak, then am I powerful" and "Power is made perfect in infirmity."[4] And the psalmist: "Many are the tribulations of the just, etc."[5] You have, my father—as Anthony is reported to have said concerning Didymus—eyes with which God and his angels can be seen, and the glorious joys of the heavenly Jerusalem discried. And therefore, trusting in your wisdom and patience, I believe that God has given this to you for the advancement of your virtues and the increase of your merits, and in order that you may see and desire the better with the eyes of the spirit the things which God orders and loves, and may regard and covet the less those things which God loves not, but has forbidden. For what, indeed, are bodily eyes in this perilous time except, if I may say so, mainly in truth windows of sin, through which either we look on sins and sinners, or, what is worse, considering and desiring shameful things, we draw them to ourselves.

I earnestly wish that your Holiness may be well and pray for me in Christ.

176. Letter of Lul to his former master, Dealwine (745–746)

An interesting feature of this letter is the request for Aldhelm's works to be sent abroad (see p. 575). Lul's style was greatly influenced by this author. This letter is No. 71 in Tangl, and is translated by Kylie, p. 103.

To his most reverend brother Dealwine, long ago his master, Lul, an unworthy deacon, discharging without the claim of merit the office of deacon, sends greeting in the Lord.

---

[1] Of Nursling. See Nos. 55, 158.

[2] There was an opinion in some quarters that Daniel did not adequately discharge his functions, for a fragment of a letter (Tangl, No. 115) tells of a vision in which the souls of children who had died without baptism in Daniel's time were seen in hell.

[3] Proverbs iii. 12.　　　　　[4] II Corinthians xii. 10, 9.　　　　　[5] Psalm xxxiii. 20.

I beseech your Grace's clemency with my deepest entreaties that you may deign to support the ship of my insignificance with your kind prayers, so that, protected with a shield by your intercessions and prayers, I may deserve to reach the harbour of salvation and to obtain pardon for my sins in this earthly prison-house; just as I already requested during the past year through our brother Denewold, the bearer of my letters. Accordingly some poor little gifts are sent with this letter, not worthy of you but sent with a devoted heart. Likewise I beg that you will deign to send me some works of Bishop Aldhelm, whether in prose or in verse, to console my exile and in memory of that same blessed bishop. And inform me in some of your kind words what your brotherly love can accomplish concerning these requests, which I eagerly long to hear.

I deeply desire that you may be in health and advancing in prosperity and interceding for me for a long time.

177. Letter of Boniface and seven other missionary bishops to Æthelbald, king of Mercia, urging him to reform (746–747)

Besides the continental version of this letter, there are traces of one in England. William of Malmesbury gives part of this letter (*De Gestis Regum*, ed. Stubbs, I, pp. 80–82), and its address and valedictory conclusion are quoted in the earliest Life of St. Ecgwine. William's version is very much briefer than that in the continental manuscripts, and it is to be regretted that we cannot tell how far this is due to William's re-writing and abbreviating of his copy, or how far the version actually sent to King Æthelbald was modified from the first draft, from which the continental version may descend. In my translation I have accepted the additions in the portion in the Life of St. Ecgwine, and have referred in notes to the new matter found in William of Malmesbury. It is hardly necessary to draw attention to the historical interest of this letter, both for Mercian history and for knowledge of Boniface's character. On Æthelbald see especially No. 156, and pp. 21f.

The letter is No. 73 in Tangl, and in Haddan and Stubbs, III, pp. 350–356. It is translated by Kylie, pp. 160–172; by Emerton, pp. 124–130.

To the most dear lord, to be preferred in the love of Christ to all other kings, King Æthelbald, wielding the glorious sceptre of imperial rule over the English, Archbishop Boniface, legate of the Roman Church to the Germans, and Bishop Wera, and Bishop Burgheard, and Bishop Werberht, and Bishop Abel, and Bishop Willibald, and Bishop Hwita, and Bishop Leofwine,[1] send eternal greetings of love in Christ.

We avow before God and the holy angels, that, whenever we hear through faithful messengers of your prosperity and faith in God and your good works in the eyes of God and men, we give glad thanks for it to God, rejoicing in it and praying for you; begging and beseeching the Saviour of the world to preserve you for a long time in the rule of a Christian people, in health and stable in faith and upright before God in your deeds. When, however, there comes to our ears any injuries to you, beloved king, done against the condition of your kingdom or in the chance of war, or, what is worse, any harm committed that imperils the safety of your soul, we are tormented by sadness and grief; for we rejoice with you in your joy in the will of God, and mourn with you in adversity.

[1] The last two names are only in the Life of St. Ecgwine. The sees of two of the bishops in this list have not been identified. The others are Burgheard of Würzburg, Abel of Reims, Willibald of Eichstätt, Hwita (Witta) of Buraburg, and, probably, Wera of Utrecht.

We have heard, indeed, that you give very many alms. And we rejoice greatly in this; because those who bestow alms on the least and needy brethren, will according to the evangelical truth hear from the Lord on the Day of Judgment the merciful sentence, which says: "As long as you did it to one of these my least brethren, you did it to me. Come, ye blessed of my Father, possess you the kingdom prepared for you from the foundation of the world."[1] We have heard also that you strongly prohibit theft and iniquities, perjury and rapine, and that you are known to be a defender of widows and the poor, and that you maintain firm peace in your kingdom. And in this also, praising God, we have rejoiced; for the Truth itself, and our Peace, which is Christ, said: "Blessed are the peacemakers, for they shall be called the children of God."[2]

But among these things there has reached our ears a report of an evil kind concerning your Excellency's way of life, and we were greatly grieved when we heard it. And we wish that it were not true. For it has been disclosed to us from the account of many persons that you have never taken in matrimony a lawful wife. This was ordained by the Lord God from the very beginning of the world, as is also enjoined and repeated by Paul, God's Apostle, who teaches and says: "But for fear of fornication, let every man have his own wife; and let every woman have her own husband."[3] Now, if you desired to do this for the sake of chastity and abstinence, so that out of fear and love of God you abstained from union with a wife, and you prove it true and undertaken for God's sake, in this also we rejoice; for this is not reprehensible, but, on the contrary, laudable. If, however—which God forbid—you have, as many say, neither taken a lawful wife nor maintained chaste abstinence for God's sake, but governed by lust, have stained the fame of your glory before God and men by the sin of lasciviousness and adultery, we are extremely grieved by this; for it is regarded both as a disgrace in the sight of God and the ruin of your reputation among men.

And yet, what is worse, those who tell us this, add that this shameful crime is especially committed in the monasteries with holy nuns and virgins consecrated to God. For there is no doubt that this is doubly a sin. To give an illustration, to what punishment is a servant liable from his master if he violates his master's wife in adultery? How much more he who defiles with the filth of his lust the bride of Christ, the Creator of heaven and earth; as the blessed Apostle Paul says: "Know you not that your members are the temple of the Holy Ghost?"[4] And elsewhere: "Know you not that you are the temple of God and that the spirit of God dwelleth in you? But if any man violate the temple of God, him shall God destroy. For the temple of God is holy, which you are."[5] And again in his account and numbering of the sins he joins adulterers and fornicators to the servitude of idolatry, saying: "Know you not that the unjust shall not possess the kingdom of God? Do not err: Neither fornicators nor idolaters nor adulterers; not the effeminate nor liers with mankind nor thieves nor covetous nor drunkards nor railers nor extortioners shall possess the kingdom of God."[6] Indeed among the Greeks and the Romans—as if the man guilty of this crime had committed blasphemy against God—[we find] that if a candidate

---

[1] Matthew xxv. 34, 40.   [2] Matthew v. 9.   [3] I Corinthians vii. 2.
[4] I Corinthians vi. 19.   [5] ibid. iii. 16 f.   [6] ibid. vi. 9 f.

before ordination, being specially asked about this sin, were discovered guilty of intercourse with a nun veiled and consecrated to God, he was debarred from all orders of God's priesthood. On this account, most dear son, one should most carefully consider how heavy this sin is judged to be in the eyes of the eternal Judge, when it places the doer among the slaves of idolatry and prohibits him from the divine service at the altar, although he may have previously done penance and been reconciled with God. For bodies, consecrated to God through the vow of our own response and through the words of the priest, are said by Holy Scripture to be temples of God. And thus violators of them are regarded according to the Apostle as the sons of perdition. But Peter, the Prince of the Apostles, forbidding lust to the voluptuous said: "For the time past is sufficient, etc."[1] Then [it is said]: "For the price of a harlot is scarce one loaf; but the woman catcheth the precious soul of a man."[2] And elsewhere: "The fault is not so great when a man hath stolen; for he stealeth to fill his hungry soul. And if he be taken, he shall restore seven-fold. But he that is an adulterer, for the folly of his heart shall destroy his own soul."[3] It would indeed take long to enumerate how many spiritual physicians have denounced the fearful poison of this sin and laid a terrible ban on it. For almost is fornication graver and lower than all sins; and it can truthfully be called the snare of death and the pit of hell and the whirlpool of perdition.

On that account we beseech and adjure your clemency, most dear son, by Christ the Son of God and by his coming and by his kingdom, that, if it be true that you practise this crime, you correct your life by repentance and amend it by purification, and remember that it is proved to be indecent that you should transform the image of God, which is created in you, into the image and likeness of the malignant devil through wanton living, and that you—whom not your own merit but the abundant goodness of God appointed king and ruler over many—should appoint yourself through wanton living a slave of the evil spirit; for according to the saying of the Apostle, whatever sin a man commits, he is the servant of it.[4]

Not only by Christians, but even by the pagans it is held as a reproach and a shame. For the pagans themselves, ignorant of the true God, observe by nature in this matter what is lawful and what God ordained from the beginning; since they preserve the bonds of marriage with their own wives, and punish fornicators and adulterers.[5] For in Old Saxony, if a maiden stains with adultery her paternal home, or if a married woman breaks the bond of matrimony and commits adultery, they sometimes force her to end her life by her own hand, hanging herself by a noose; and when she has been burnt and cremated, they hang her violator over her pyre. Sometimes a crowd of women is gathered, and the matrons scourge her and lead her all over the district, striking her with rods and cutting off her garments to the girdle; and cutting and pricking all her body with wounds with their knives, they send her from village to

---

[1] I Peter iv. 3. The verse continues: "to have fulfilled the will of the Gentiles, for them who have walked in riotousness, lusts, etc."

[2] Proverbs vi. 26.   [3] ibid. vi. 30–32.   [4] Cf. John viii. 34.

[5] This passage, from the beginning of the paragraph, is replaced in William of Malmesbury by: "Moreover we have heard that almost all the nobles of the race of the Mercians, following your example, desert their lawful wives and lie with adulteresses and nuns. How far this departs from decency, the institutions of a foreign race teach us."

village bloody and lacerated. And new scourgers are always joining them, prompted by their zeal for chastity, until they leave her dead, or barely alive; that others may be afraid of adultery and lasciviousness. And the Wends, who are a most foul and depraved race of men, preserve mutual love of the married state with so great zeal that a woman refuses to live after her husband is dead. Among them a woman is considered praiseworthy if she kills herself with her own hand and burns on one and the same pyre with her husband.

Since, therefore, the Gentiles, who according to the Apostle know not God and "have not the law, do by nature those things that are of the law", and "show the work of the law written in their hearts";[1] since, moreover, you, most dear son, bear the name of Christian and worshipper of the true God; if in the youthful age of your adolescence you were befouled with the filth of debauchery and rolled in the mire of adultery and immersed in the whirlpool of lust as if in the pit of hell, it is now time that you remember your Lord and turn from the snares of the devil and wash your soul which is stained with the foulness of lasciviousness. It is now time that for fear of your Creator you do not presume to repeat such a sin and to defile yourself further. It is time that you should spare the multitude of perishing people, who, following the example of their sinning ruler, fell into the pit of death. Because, for as many as we either by good examples bring to the life in the heavenly fatherland or by bad examples lead to perdition, for so many, without a doubt, we shall receive from the eternal Judge either punishments or rewards.

For if the race of the English–as it is noised abroad throughout those provinces and is cast up against us in France and in Italy, and is used as a reproach by the pagans themselves–spurning lawful marriage, lives a foul life in adultery and lasciviousness after the pattern of the people of Sodom, it is to be expected that from such intercourse with harlots there will be born a degenerate people, ignoble, raging with lust; and in the end the whole people, sinking to lower and baser things, will finally neither be strong in secular warfare nor stable in faith, neither honoured by men nor loved by God. Just as it has happened to other races of Spain and Provence, and to the Burgundian peoples; who thus, turning from God, committed fornication, until the omnipotent Judge allowed avenging punishments for such crimes to come and destroy them, through ignorance of the law of God, and through the Saracens.

And it should be noted, that under that crime there lurks another monstrous evil, namely homicide; because, when those harlots, whether nuns or laywomen, bring forth in sin offspring conceived in evil, they for the most part kill them; not filling the churches of Christ with adopted sons, but crowding graves with bodies and hell with unhappy souls.

Moreover, it has been told us that you have violated many privileges of churches and monasteries, and have stolen from them certain revenues. And this, if it is true, is regarded as a heavy sin, by the witness of Holy Scripture, which says: "He that stealeth any thing from his father, or from his mother, and saith: 'This is no sin', is the partner of a murderer."[2] Our Father without doubt is God, who created us, our Mother the Church which gave us spiritual regeneration in baptism. Therefore he

---

[1] Romans ii. 14, 15.   [2] Proverbs xxviii. 24.

who steals or plunders the possessions of Christ and the Church, will be adjudged to be a homicide in the sight of the just Judge. Concerning whom one of the wise said: "He who seizes the money of his neighbour, commits iniquity; but he who takes away the money of the Church, commits sacrilege."[1]

And it is said that your ealdormen and companions offer greater violence and oppression to monks and priests, than other Christian kings have done before. Now, ever since the apostolic pope, St. Gregory, sending preachers of the catholic faith from the apostolic see, converted the race of the English to the true God, the privileges of the churches in the kingdom of the English remained untouched and unviolated until the times of Ceolred, king of the Mercians, and Osred, king of the Deirans and Bernicians.

These two kings by the prompting of the devil showed by their wicked example an open display of these two greatest of sins in the provinces of the English, in defiance of the evangelical and apostolic commands of our Saviour. And lingering in these sins, that is, in debauchery and adultery with nuns and violation of monasteries, condemned by the just judgment of God, thrown down from the regal summit of this life and overtaken by an early and terrible death, they were deprived of the light eternal and plunged into the depths of hell and the abyss of Tartarus. For Ceolred, your venerable Highness's predecessor,[2] feasting in splendour amid his companions, was—as those who were present have testified—suddenly in his sin sent mad by a malign spirit, who had enticed him by his persuasion to the audacity of breaking the law of God; so that without repentance and confession, raging and distracted, conversing with devils and cursing the priests of God, he departed from this light without a doubt to the torments of hell. Osred also was driven by the spirit of wantonness, fornicating, and in his frenzy debauching throughout the nunneries virgins consecrated to God; until with a contemptible and despicable death he lost his glorious kingdom, his young life and his lascivious soul.[3]

Wherefore, most dear son, beware of the pit, into which you have seen others fall before you. Beware of the darts of the ancient enemy, by which you have seen your own relations fall wounded in front of you. Guard yourself from the snare of the waylayer, in which you saw your friends and fellow-soldiers entrapped and deprived of both the present and the future life. Do not follow the examples of such to perdition. For such, according to the prophecy of Holy Scripture, are those who have afflicted the just and who have stolen their labours.[4] In the Day of Judgment they will say: "We have erred from the way of truth, and the light of justice hath not shined unto us, and the sun hath not risen upon us";[5] and, "The way of the Lord we have not known",[6] and, "What hath pride profited us or what advantage hath the boasting of riches brought us? All those things are passed away like a shadow, and like a post that runneth on, and as a ship that passeth through the waves; whereof the trace cannot be found, or as when a bird flieth through the air."[7] And a little

[1] Tangl notes a very similar passage in Jerome's Letter 52, *ad Nepotianum*.

[2] The version of William of Malmesbury adds: "a violator of nuns and infringer of ecclesiastical privileges".

[3] *ibid.* "Also Charles, ruler of the Franks, the destroyer of many monasteries and the converter of ecclesiastical property into his own use, perished in long torment and fearful death."

[4] Wisdom v. 1.   [5] *ibid.* v. 6 f.   [6] *ibid.* v. 7.   [7] *ibid.* v. 8–11.

further on: "So we also being born, forthwith ceased to be; we are consumed in our wickedness. Such things the sinners said in hell; for the hope of the wicked is as dust which is blown away with the wind; and as a thin froth which is dispersed by the storm, and a smoke that is scattered abroad by the wind; and as the remembrance of a guest of one day that passeth by."[1] And elsewhere: "The number of the days of men at the most are a hundred years. As a drop of water of the sea are they esteemed."[2] For all these things are by the authority of Holy Scripture most like by analogy. Thus also James, the brother of our Lord and an Apostle, discussing the impious rich man, has said: "As the flower of the grass shall he pass away. For the sun rose with a burning heat and parched the grass; and the flower thereof fell off, and the beauty of the shape thereof perished. So also shall the rich man fade away in his ways."[3] And the Truth itself has set forth and said in the gospel: "For what doth it profit a man, if he gain the whole world, and suffer the loss of his own soul?"[4] For earthly riches shall profit nothing on the day of vengeance,[5] if a man ends this present life using them evilly; since after the death of the body he falls into the eternal punishment of the soul. Therefore, I beg, most dear son, that instructed by these admonitions, you assent to the wholesome words of the law of God and amend your life. Abandon vices, and be zealous in the practice of holy virtues; and thus you will live prosperously in this world and will attain an everlasting reward in the future. Farewell. May the Almighty God amend your life into a better state, that you may deserve of the Lord himself to obtain his eternal grace.

178. Letter of Boniface to the priest Herefrith, asking him to deliver the preceding letter to King Æthelbald (746–747)

The recipient of this letter is presumable the 'man of God' of this name whose death in 747 is entered in the *Continuation of Bede*. See No. 5. The text is No. 74 in Tangl, and Haddan and Stubbs, III, pp. 357 ff. It is translated by Kylie, pp. 173–175, and by Emerton, pp. 130 f.

To his most beloved and reverend brother Herefrith the priest, Boniface, servant of the servants of God, sends eternal greeting in the love of Christ.

I beseech your Grace's clemency with most heartfelt entreaties to deign to remember me in your holy prayers, even though I do not doubt–and those who have come from you tell me–that you, my brother, have already done and will do this; that the saying of St. James the Apostle may be fulfilled in us, where he says: "Pray one for

---

[1] *ibid.* v. 13–15. [2] Ecclesiasticus xviii. 8. [3] James i. 10 f.

[4] Matthew xvi. 26. The rest of this letter is not in William of Malmesbury's version, which continues instead: "Wherefore, most dear son, we implore you with fatherly and humble prayers, not to despise the counsel of your fathers, who for the love of God strive to appeal to thy Highness. For nothing is more beneficial to a good king than that such deeds, when they are shown him, should be willingly corrected, for it is said by Solomon: 'He that loveth correction, loveth knowledge' (Proverbs xii. 1). Therefore, most dear son, showing good counsel, we enjoin and implore you by the living God and by his Son Jesus Christ and by the Holy Spirit, to remember how fleeting is the present life and how brief, and how momentary is the delight of the impure flesh, and how shameful it is that a man of a short life should leave a bad example to posterity for ever. Begin therefore to regulate your life with better habits and correct the past errors of youth, that you may have praise here among men, and may rejoice in eternal glory in the future. We wish your Highness health and advancement in good morals." The valediction is almost in complete agreement with that in the Life of St. Ecgwine, and the style reads like Boniface, so that it is likely that this was the original last paragraph of the letter as it was sent.

[5] Cf. Ecclesiasticus v. 1.

another, that you may be saved," and "The continual prayer of a just man availeth much."[1]

Moreover, we eight bishops who assembled at a synod, and whose names are noted below,[2] in common implore you, dearest brother, to make known the words of our admonition to Æthelbald, king of the Mercians, interpreting and reading them out, and to show them to him, carefully relating and announcing them in the way and order in which we send them written to you. For we have heard that in your fear of God you fear not "the person of men";[3] and that the afore-mentioned king condescends on some occasions to listen to your advice to some extent. And be it known to your love that we have sent these words of admonition to that king from no other motive than pure friendship and love, and because, born and reared in that same race of the English, we live in exile by the command of the apostolic see. We are glad and rejoice at the praise of our race, but we are distressed and saddened by its sins and the reproaches cast on it. We suffer, indeed, the reproach of our race both by Christians and by pagans, who say that the race of the English, spurning the custom of other nations and despising the apostolic command, nay, more, the ordinance of God, refuses to have lawful wives, and, following the practice of neighing horses and the manner of braying asses, by wanton living and adultery wickedly brings everything to disgrace and confusion.

Therefore, dearest brother, if this greatest of crimes really does exist, let us all in common urge the afore-mentioned king to reform himself with his people; that the whole nation, with its prince, may not perish here and in the future life, but that, by amending and reforming his own life, he may by his example guide his own people back to the way of salvation, and, where before he committed sin, deserve there eternal reward.

Moreover, we have sent some incense and a linen cloth, as a gift and token of our sincere love for you.

May the Holy Trinity eternally keep you, loved brother, flourishing in holy works and advancing in laudable habits, and in good health.

179. Letter of Boniface to Egbert, archbishop of York, with reference to the letter to King Æthelbald (746–747)

The recipient of this letter is the man to whom Bede wrote his long letter (No. 170) on Church government. See No. 184, and p. 89. Besides its interest in connexion with the letter to Æthelbald, the present letter contains Boniface's first reference to Bede, and a statement that he has obtained letters of Gregory I from the papal archives. It is No. 75 in Tangl, and in Haddan and Stubbs, III, pp. 358–360. It is translated by Kylie, pp. 138–140, and by Emerton, pp. 132 f.

To his most beloved and reverend brother Archbishop Egbert, Boniface, servant of the servants of God, legate from the apostolic see to the Germans, sends sincere greetings of spiritual brotherhood in Christ.

Having received the gifts of your love, and the books, I gave great thanks, raising my hands to heaven, to Almighty God who has allowed me in my long exile to find such a friend, who has sent to me both help in earthly things and divine solace in

[1] James v. 16.   [2] They are not preserved in this letter, but known from that to Æthelbald.
[3] Matthew xxii. 16 ; Mark xii. 14.

things spiritual, in prayer and in unity of communion. But now I beseech your Grace's clemency with the deepest entreaties from my heart, that I along with the servants of God who labour with me may deserve to be united to the company of your brotherhood, and that you may be to me a counsellor and helper in searching out and investigating the ecclesiastical rules according with the judgments of God; and that you may understand that I am not asking and speaking in joking words, but in earnest, and not consider me arrogant or proud or unduly satisfied with my own judgment. For the Catholic and Apostolic Roman Church, when it sent me an unworthy and poor preacher to preach to the erring or pagan nations of Germany, ordered me, if going among the Christians I anywhere saw people going astray or the rules of the Church depraved by evil habits, or men led into by-paths away from the catholic faith, to strive with all my strength to summon and recall them to the way of salvation with the authority of the Roman pontiff.

Desiring to obey this command, I have sent a letter of admonition or entreaty to Æthelbald, king of the Mercians, with the counsel and consent of the bishops who are with us. I gave orders that this should be shown to you, my brother, that, if any things in it are badly put, you may amend them, and may season with the salt of your wisdom those things that are right and confirm them with your authority; and that, if you see any shoot of the crimes which are treated of in that letter against the king of the Mercians, trying to sprout forth in your people, you may cut it off like a prudent and wise husbandman, with the sickle of our Lord's authority and uproot it in time, lest, if it flourish, "their vine should become of the vineyard of Sodom, and their stock from Gomorra, and the fury of dragons be their wine and the fury of asps, which is deadly".[1] For it is an evil unheard of in past ages, and, as the servants of God here, who are learned in the Scriptures, say, one surpassing three-fold or four-fold the licence of the Sodomites, that a Christian people should, against the custom of the whole world, nay, more, against the precept of God, despise lawful matrimony and cleave to incest, licence and adultery, and commit abominable violation of women who are consecrated and have taken the veil.

Moreover, I beseech you to copy and send to me some treatises from the work of the teacher, Bede, whom lately, as we have heard, the divine grace endowed with spiritual understanding and allowed to shine in your province, so that we also may benefit from that candle which the Lord bestowed on you.

Meanwhile I have sent to you, my brother, as a token of love, copies of the letters of St. Gregory which I have obtained from the archives of the Roman Church, and which I did not think had reached Britain; and I shall send more, if you require them, for I obtained many from there; also a corporal-cloth[2] and a towel for drying the feet of the servants of God when you wash them.

We wish your Holiness to be well and to advance in holy virtues in Christ.

---

[1] Deuteronomy xxxii. 32 f., but not the Vulgate text. This part of Deuteronomy was used as a canticle sung at lauds on Saturdays, and the text used was often the Old Latin. The reading here is exactly that in the canticles placed after the psalms in the eighth-century Vespasian Psalter. In another letter (Tangl, No. 78) Boniface uses the Old Latin when quoting Habakkuk iii. 17, part of another canticle, also contained in the same manuscript.

[2] A cloth on which the sacred elements were placed and with which they were covered after the celebration of Mass.

180. Letter of Boniface to Hwætberht, abbot of Wearmouth (746–747)

This is one of several requests by the missionaries to have the works of Bede sent out to them. Cf. Nos. 179, 185, 188, 216. For Hwætberht, see No. 155, pp. 704 f. It is No. 76 in Tangl, and is translated by Kylie, pp. 141 f.; by Emerton, pp. 133 f.

To his most beloved and reverend brother, Abbot Hwætberht, and to all the brethren of his holy congregation, Boniface, a poor servant of the servants of God, sends greeting of brotherly love in Christ.

We beseech your brotherly goodness with most heartfelt entreaties to assist with your holy prayers us who are toiling among the wild and ignorant peoples of Germany and planting the seeds of the gospel, that by your Holiness's prayers the fierce heat of the Babylonian fire may be extinguished in us, and the seed scattered in the furrows may spring up and be multiplied to a harvest. For, according to the saying of the Apostle: "Neither he that planteth nor he that watereth is anything, but God that giveth the increase;[1] that speech may be given to me that I may open my mouth[2] and the word of the Lord may run and may be glorified."[3]

Meanwhile we ask that you will deign to have copied and sent to us certain of the works of that most skilful investigator of the Scriptures, the monk Bede, who, we have heard, has lately shone in the house of God among you with knowledge of the Scriptures like a candle of the Church. And if it is not a trouble to you, send us a bell, as a great comfort in our exile. And as a token also of our deepest love, we have sent you some goats' hair bed-clothes,[4] as they are called here; which we beseech you to accept for memory's sake, although they are not worthy.

May the gracious Trinity and one Divinity strengthen you and keep you well, my brother, advancing here in holy virtues, and glorify and reward you in future blessedness among the glorious companies of rejoicing angels.

181. Letter of Boniface to Fulrad, abbot of St. Denis, concerning the future of his helpers in Germany (752)

This is perhaps one of the most poignant letters that Boniface wrote, and in the light it sheds on his character, and on the conditions in which Englishmen worked abroad, seems to deserve a place in this volume. It is No. 93 in Tangl, and is translated by Emerton, pp. 169 f.

Boniface, servant of the servants of God, by the grace of Christ, bishop, to his most dear fellow-ecclesiastic Fulrad the priest, sends everlasting greeting in the love of Christ.

I cannot render adequate thanks, as you have deserved, for the spiritual friendship of your brotherly love, which you often for the sake of God showed to me in my necessities; but I pray Almighty God, that he may recompense you in the high summit of the heavens with the reward of his favour eternally in the joy of the angels. Now in the name of Christ I pray, that what you have begun with a good beginning, you may complete with a good end; that is, that you will greet for me the most glorious and gracious Pippin our king, and give him great thanks for all the acts of kindness which he has done for me; and that you will tell him what to me and my friends seems

---

[1] I Corinthians iii. 7.   [2] Ephesians vi. 19.   [3] II Thessalonians iii. 1.   [4] *lectisternia caprina.*

very likely to take place. It seems that I must soon finish this temporal life and the course of my days through these infirmities. Therefore I pray our king's Highness in the name of Christ the Son of God that he will deign to send me word and inform me while I am yet alive, about my disciples, what favours he will do to them afterwards. For they are almost all foreigners. Some are priests appointed in many places to minister to the Church and to the people; some are monks throughout our monasteries, and children set to learn to read; and some are growing old, who have toiled and helped me, living with me for a long time. I am anxious about all these, that they may not be scattered after my death, but may have the favour of your counsels and your Highness's support, and not be scattered like sheep that have no shepherd; and that the people near the frontier of the pagans may not lose the law of Christ. Therefore I pray your Grace's clemency urgently in the name of God, to make my son and suffragan bishop Lul–if God will and it pleases your Grace–to be appointed and constituted to the ministry of the peoples and churches as a preacher and teacher of the priests and people. And I hope, if God wishes, that the priests may have in him a master, the monks a teacher of the rule, and the Christian people a faithful preacher and shepherd. I beg most especially that this be done, because my priests near the frontier of the pagans have a poor livelihood. They can get bread to eat, but cannot obtain clothing there, unless they have a counsellor and supporter elsewhere, to sustain and strengthen them in those places for the service of the people, in the same way as I have helped them. If the goodness of Christ inspires you to this, and you will consent to do what I ask, deign to send word and inform me by these my present messengers or by your Holiness's letters, so that I may either live or die the happier for your favour.

182. Letter of the priest Wihtberht to the abbot and monks of Glastonbury (732–754)

This little letter from a new recruit to the mission field, with its reference to the hardships, and the slight glimpse it affords of Boniface, seems worthy of inclusion. It is No. 101 in Tangl, and is translated by Kylie, pp. 113 f.; by Emerton, p. 174.

To the holy lords, most worthy of love in Christ, the fathers and brothers placed in the monastery of Glastonbury, Wihtberht the priest and assuredly your servant, and suppliant of the servants of God, sends greeting in the Lord.

Blessed be God, "who will have all men to be saved and to come to the knowledge of the truth",[1] and who directed our prosperous course by his will into these provinces, that is, the borders of the heathen Hessians and Saxons, across the sea and through the dangers of this world, without any merit of ours, but by your permission and prayers, and his mercy. You know, brothers, that no earthly distance of land divides us whom the love of Christ unites. Therefore I am ever filled with brotherly love and reverence and with prayers for you to God. I wish you also to know, beloved brothers, that when our Archbishop Boniface heard of our arrival, he deigned to come himself a long way to meet us and receive us with great kindness. And now, most beloved, believe that our labour is not vain in the Lord, but that you will share the reward. For Almighty

[1] Timothy ii. 4.

God through his mercy and your merits completes the good result of our work, though living here is very perilous and full of hardship in almost every way, in hunger and thirst, in cold and the attacks of the pagans. Therefore I ask earnestly: pray for us "that speech may be given us in the opening of our mouths"[1] and permanence and success in our work.

Farewell in the Lord. Greet the brothers round about, first Abbot Ingild and our community, and send word to my mother Tette[2] and her community of our safe journey. I beseech you all in common, with earnest entreaties, to grant us a return for our constant prayers, and I desire that your Holiness, praying for us, may be protected by the divine clemency.

183. Part of a letter of Cuthbert, archbishop of Canterbury, to Lul, after St. Boniface's martyrdom (754)

This letter illustrates the attitude of the English at home to the continental missions, and the relations of the latter with the see of Canterbury. Boniface himself corresponded with Cuthbert, and in 747 had written to inform him of the decisions taken at a Frankish synod (Tangl, No. 78), many of which were incorporated by the synod of *Clofesho* of 747 (Haddan and Stubbs, III, pp. 360–383). Another of the letters of condolence written to Lul on Boniface's death has survived, that of Bishop Mildred of Worcester (Tangl, No. 112).

The letter here given is No. 111 in Tangl, and is in Haddan and Stubbs, III, pp. 390–394. It is translated by Kylie, pp. 198–205, and by Emerton, pp. 183–187.

To Lul, his most reverend brother, and fellow-bishop most dear in the love of Christ, and also to those bishops and priests of God who work with you, whose names should be preserved and written in the book of life, Cuthbert, servant of the servants of God, with other fellow-bishops of Christ, and priests and abbots, sends greeting of eternal prosperity and peace in the Lord.

We avow, dearest brothers, with most sincere hearts before God and his chosen angels, that, whenever we hear bearers of tidings report that you, beloved, have advanced in peace and prosperity, progressed in holy religion in Christ, and reaped in the conversion of others a more abundant harvest of your holy preaching, we gladly give thanks to God the granter of all good things, rejoicing greatly and earnestly praying for you. But when we are told of any injury done to your Holiness, or of any loss inflicted on you, we are wracked by grief and sadness; since, in truth, as we rejoice with you in your joy in Christ, so also we suffer with you in your adversity for Christ's sake. For never can be obliterated from our memory the distress of the various and unceasing tribulations which we in our hearts, you in person with our father beloved of God, the martyr Boniface of blessed memory, have borne for a long time among pagan persecutors and heretical and schismatical seducers in so dangerous and savage an exile for the love of the heavenly country; nor that, now that he has departed with many of his household gloriously and blessedly by a martyr's death to the eternal rest of the heavenly country, you who live on after such men move perchance among divers trials with greater danger and difficulty in that you are deprived of so great a father and teacher.

---

[1] Ephesians vi. 19.   [2] Abbess of Wimborne. See No. 159.

Although for this some bitterness of grief mightily torments our hearts, yet often a certain gladness of a new and great exultation comes into our minds and cheers and quietens the groans of this sorrow; the more frequently we reflect on it, we exult and give thanks to the admirable, or rather, the ineffable goodness of God, that the race of the English, a foreign race from Britain, deserved to send out afar, laudably before the eyes of all, so distinguished a searcher of the heavenly Scriptures, so famous a soldier of Christ, with many well-trained and well-instructed disciples, to spiritual conflicts, and, by the grace of Almighty God, to the salvation of many souls; so that by the influence of his holy exhortations and the example of his piety and goodness, he as leader and standard-bearer, going before and stoutly resisting all opposition with the help of God, might happily lead the most savage nations from far and wide, who were long wandering through by-paths, back from the broad and spacious abyss of everlasting perdition to the shining streets of the heavenly country. What has truly been accomplished thus, is shown more gloriously by the results than by words; it is seen even in places which no teacher before him tried to reach for the sake of spreading the gospel. Wherefore, after the mystery, unequalled in the whole world, of the election and number of the Apostles, and the ministry of the other disciples of Christ preaching the gospel at that time, we both lovingly regard and venerate with praise this man among the foremost and best teachers of the orthodox faith.

Accordingly, in our general synod–where we also conferred more fully on the other matters, which we disclose to your Highness only in brief–we made known the festival day of him and of his band who were martyred with him and decided to celebrate it solemnly with an annual observance; seeing that we both seek and certainly believe to have him, with the blessed Gregory and Augustine, as our especial patron before Christ the Lord, whom in his life he ever loved, and in his death nobly glorified, as by Christ's grace he deserved. . . .[1]

For we deem that this[2] should be done the more zealously, with watchful skill, because according to the prophecy of the Apostle "perilous times" now threaten, and the other things which he continues with in the same epistle.[3] And because there is no need to write to you of the external attacks and misfortunes, which, I think, you have frequently suffered, namely persecutions, pillaging, hatred, scandals and similar things, yet behold how in most places the condition of the Christian religion greatly totters, while almost on all sides, outside and in, the right course of ecclesiastical affairs is disturbed, and almost everywhere wicked sects with new ways of life spring up. Nor is it to be wondered at, when the decrees of the ancient fathers have been disregarded and the ecclesiastical laws abandoned, and many think, declare and act, according to their own invention, wicked things harmful to the safety of many, as, in fact, is well known to have been said and done in the past year by a certain man of great authority. Faced with these things, what ought we–timid, I fear, and too little kindled by zeal for righteousness–chiefly to do, other than unceasingly to demand the help of the holy apostles and martyrs of Christ and of the venerable bishops of

---

[1] At some length, and with much scriptural quotation, the archbishop promises to advise and comfort Lul and his followers.

[2] The renewal of the community of prayer established by Boniface with the church of Canterbury.

[3] Cf. II Timothy iii. 1.

the churches of God; that in this office to which we were called and appointed, the grace of Christ may make us to persevere with continual watchfulness; and that we be not false, but accepted, not indolent, but active, not dispersing, but gathering whomsoever we can to the unanimity of the Christian religion and the unity of the ecclesiastical mode of life; to the end that the performance of our stewardship and the skill of our labour may redound to the praise and glory of Almighty God, so that we may deserve at length to hear with those serving God well and pleasing him: "Blessed is that servant, whom when his lord shall come, he shall find watching. Amen, I say to you, he shall place him over all his goods."[1]

Therefore let us very frequently call to memory, for the sake of the example, in what manner and with how great skill the illustrious master and martyr, blessed Boniface of revered memory, laboured in the knowledge of God, what great dangers and difficulties he bore willingly for the love of Christ and for the gain of souls even until his very death. And because he has now become a companion[2] of the Almighty, let your prudence carefully consider if it behoves you to accord with his sacred admonitions and to follow the example of his piety with all your might. For he, in as much as he has become one of the household of him whom he loved before all things, will be able to obtain from him the greater favours. Hence, if any of those subject to him, over whom the divine dispensation once set him as a master, dissent from his spiritual teachings or withdraw into an evil way of life, he who could at the eternal Judgment be their defender, becomes rather their accuser, and along with the Judge himself will the more sternly demand an account from them. But, on the other hand, whoever duly follow the rules of his holy instruction and teaching, may certainly know that they have both in life and after death perpetual communion in prayers, and celebration of Masses, as we said above, with the Roman and Apostolic Church by which he was sent as legate and teacher to them, and likewise with us all; provided they do not disdain to obey you, henceforth their teacher and director of their salvation, humbly and lovingly to the end for the sake of God and an eternal reward; never falling away, like faithless or deceitful folk, but always progressing like disciples of good disposition, and faithfully clinging to the leader of their service in Christ, to the reward of the heavenly summons of God and the glory of the kingdom of heaven.

We have written these words of greeting to your Holiness, not as if you were ignorant or required the guidance of our ignorance, but for the sake of charity and mutual intercourse; adjuring and beseeching you by the Almighty God and his Son Jesus Christ and his coming and his kingdom, that you all, dearest brothers, in common with those subject to you in Christ, may in all things ever be faithful helpers of one another and unanimous fellow-workers against all enemies of the orthodox faith, heretics and schismatics and men of most wicked way of life. For by this you will be worthy of the love and praise of good men, and acceptable and dear to Almighty God. And thus, with your aforesaid blessed father and predecessor, you may each deserve to hear in the future from Christ the Judge of all men the glad

---

[1] Matthew xxiv. 46, 47.

[2] *familiaris* literally means a member of a family, or household, and a few lines later Cuthbert varies it with *domesticus*. The first of these terms is used by Anglo-Saxon writers of the members of a lord's comitatus or following, and Cuthbert may have a secular parallel in mind in this passage.

words: "Well done, good and faithful servant; because thou hast been faithful over a few things, I will place thee over many things. Enter thou into the joy of thy Lord."[1] Amen.

✠ May the Almighty God long deign to keep you all safe in his holy love and fear, most beloved brothers and sons.

✠ Archbishop Cuthbert,
✠ to his fellow-bishop Lul.[2]

184. Letter of Pope Paul I to Eadberht, king of Northumbria, and his brother Egbert, archbishop of York (757–758)

This letter should be read in connexion with Bede's letter to this archbishop (see No. 170), for it would seem that he and his brother the king have been carrying out Bede's advice on the suppression of spurious monasteries to recover their lands for the reward of the king's secular followers. Though the archbishop is named in the superscription, the pope addresses himself to the king.

Only part of this letter was entered in Brit. Mus. Cott. Vespas. A xiv, though a modern hand has completed it in the margins. The full letter is in Brit. Mus. Cott. Tiber. A xv, though it is now barely legible in this much scorched manuscript. The printed texts, Birch, No. 184 and Haddan and Stubbs, iii, pp. 394–396, go back to Wilkins, *Concilia*, i, p. 144, who used a manuscript belonging to Ussher.

To his most dearly loved brother Archbishop Egbert and also to his most excellent son King Eadberht, Pope Paul sends greeting.

The Judge and Maker of all things, who, fashioning all from nothing by his word alone, created mankind from dust, our Triune and One Lord our God, whom the framework of the heavens and the matter of the earth serve by perennial law, to this end appointed that your most prudent nobility should undertake the charge of the people under his sway, that you might strive to perform eagerly with diligent care those things which concern the worship of his divine majesty; that by the help of your diligence the welfare of those who are [not] free from the snares of this dark world might be protected. For, most beloved, we have abundantly learnt from the report of many that you are well endowed with competence and skill. And because you strive very assiduously to ponder with devout mind on that blossoming life which is followed by no end, we have most readily considered it fitting to demand of your love and excellence through our apostolic admonition the performance of the things which concern the salvation of your soul. The religious Abbot Forthred, arriving at the thresholds of your protectors the blessed chiefs of the Apostles, Peter and Paul, at once reported to us that three monasteries had been granted to him by a certain abbess, namely the monasteries which are called Stonegrave and Coxwold and *Donaemuthe*;[3] and that your Excellency took these monasteries from him by force and gave them to a certain 'patrician',[4] his brother, Moll by name. We were

[1] Matthew xxv. 21.

[2] This was probably copied into the manuscript from the address on the back of the original letter.

[3] This cannot be the place of this name mentioned in the Chronicle 794 D, E, if this is correctly identified as Jarrow, for the latter place seems never to have been a double monastery, nor was it in lay hands in the mid-eighth century. Sir Frank Stenton has suggested to me that there may have been a monastery at the mouth of the Yorkshire Don.

[4] See p. 244, n. 6.

greatly saddened by this affair, O most excellent son, since you have done this entirely against the precept of God. And surely it is obvious that it pertains to the ruin of your soul, to have taken away the said monasteries from him who discharges the office of the divine worship, and to have been eager to grant them to him who toils in the cares of the world. For it is not proper, most excellent son, to have greater regard to human favour than to the fear of God. Your most excellent prudence ought from your own wealth, lands and amenities, to bestow privileged support and help on these venerable men; for it is written: "Honour the Lord with thy substance."[1] Therefore we exhort you by your good sense and warn you by the admonition of the apostolic see, that with true obedience, as becomes you, for the love of your protector, you restore to the aforesaid Abbot Forthred those three monasteries; that he may be allowed to enjoy them without any uncertainty or troublesome molestation just as they were granted to him by the aforesaid abbess; and in accordance with the innate intelligence with which you are endowed, hasten to cherish all venerable places with pious regard, and to protect them in all things. And let it be your care by all means to restore to the same holy man what has been taken away from them; so that when this wrongful and vicious seizure has been rescinded, permission may never again be granted to any layman or any person whatsoever to invade the possessions of religious places; but rather, that the things which are concerned with the purpose of the religious life may by your zeal be more abundantly increased. For from this, O most excellent son, you will receive the divine help and remuneration and will prevail against the cunning of the fierce enemy, and will without doubt deserve to obtain the life eternal.

185. Letter of Cuthbert, abbot of Wearmouth, to Lul (764)

Cuthbert is probably the disciple of Bede who wrote the account of his death. His letter shows the veneration felt for Bede and the demand for his writings abroad. (Cf. Nos. 179, 180, 188.) It has a reference to the great winter of 763–764, recorded in the Chronicle, and of interest too is the abbot's request for a man to make glass vessels and another to play a kind of harp.

Cuthbert wrote another letter to Lul (Tangl, No. 127), in reply to one (Tangl, No. 126) in which Lul had asked for Bede's works on *The Building of the Temple* and the *Song of Songs*.

This text is No. 116 in Tangl.

To the most desired and sweetest friend in the love of Christ, and dearest of all prelates, Bishop Lul, Cuthbert, disciple of the priest Bede, sends greeting.

I have gratefully received the gifts of your love, and the more gratefully, in that I know you send them with the deepest affection and devotion; you have sent, namely an all silk robe for the relics of Bede, our master of blessed memory, in remembrance and veneration of him. And it indeed seems right to me, that the whole race of the English in all provinces wherever they are found, should give thanks to God, that he has granted to them so wonderful a man in their nation, endowed with diverse gifts, and so assiduous in the exercise of those gifts, and likewise living a good life; for I, reared at his feet, have learnt by experience this which I relate. And also you have sent to me for myself a multi-coloured coverlet to protect my body from the cold. This I have given with great joy to Almighty God and the blessed Apostle

---

[1] Proverbs iii. 9.

Paul, to clothe the altar which is consecrated to God in his church, because I have lived in this monastery under his protection for forty-six years.

Now truly, since you have asked for some of the works of the blessed father, for your love I have prepared what I could, with my pupils, according to our capacity. I have sent in accordance with your wishes the books about the man of God, Cuthbert, composed in verse and prose. And if I could have done more, I would gladly have done so. For the conditions of the past winter oppressed the island of our race very horribly with cold and ice and long and widespread storms of wind and rain, so that the hand of the scribe was hindered from producing a great number of books.

And six years ago I sent to you, my brother, some small gifts, namely twenty knives and a robe made of otter-skins, by my priest Hunwine, when he was travelling to your districts and anxious to see Rome; but this priest Hunwine, arriving at the city called Beneventum, migrated from this light there. Therefore neither through him nor any of your people has any reply ever been given me whether those things reached you. We took care to send to you, Father, two palls of subtle workmanship, one white, the other coloured, along with the books, and a bell such as I had by me.

And I pray that you will not spurn my petition and my need; if there is any man in your diocese who can make vessels of glass well, that you will deign to send him to me when time is favourable. But if perhaps he is beyond your boundaries outside your diocese in the power of some other, I ask your brotherly kindness to urge him to come here to us, because we are ignorant and destitute of that art. And if perchance it happen that one of the makers of glass is permitted, God willing, by your good offices to come to us, I will treat him with kind indulgence as long as I live. It would delight me also to have a harpist who could play on the harp which we call 'rottae';[1] for I have a harp and am without a player. If it be not a trouble, send one also to my disposal. I beg that you will not scorn my request nor think it laughable.

Concerning the works of Bede of blessed memory, of which you have no copies, I promise to assist your wishes, if we live.

Abbot Cuthbert greets you again and again. May Almighty God keep you safe for ever.

186. Letter of Abbot Eanwulf to Charles the Great (25 May 773)

The occasion for this letter was doubtless the victories over the Old Saxons and the destruction of their sacred 'irminsul' in 772, which caused men to hope that the conversion of the Old Saxons would soon be accomplished. Nothing is known about this abbot, but it is probable that the letter was sent along with No. 187. If so, it illustrates the continued interest taken in the continental missions by the Northumbrians, and shows that their Church was in contact with Charles the Great before Alcuin entered his service. The letter, most of which is identical with Gregory I's letter to Ethelbert of Kent (No. 151, p. 603), is No. 120 in Tangl.

To Charles, the most glorious lord and most excellent king of the Franks, Eanwulf, a humble abbot, sends wishes for his desired good health.

For this reason does Almighty God advance good men to the government of nations, that he may impart by means of them the gifts of his mercy to all over whom

[1] The precise nature of this instrument is not known.

they are placed. We know this to have taken place in the nation of the Franks, over whom your glory has been raised in order that, through the blessings granted to you, heavenly benefits may also be conferred on the nation subject to you. And therefore, illustrious king, guard with careful heart that grace which you have received from heaven, hasten to spread the Christian faith among the peoples subject to you, increase your righteous zeal for their conversion, suppress the worship of idols, cast down the buildings of their temples, build up the morals of your subjects by great purity of life, exhorting, terrifying, persuading, correcting, and setting an example of good works; that you may find a rewarder in heaven in him whose name and knowledge you will have spread on earth. For he, whose honour you seek and maintain among the nations, will also render the fame of your glory more glorious even to posterity. In addition, glorious king, we wish you to know that we will strongly and incessantly intercede with the heavenly goodness for the safety of you and of your race; humbly beseeching your Majesty to deign to be mindful of us and to receive us as friends, that we, who urgently commend you to the Lord in frequent prayers, may have you as a protector and patron.

And thus may the Almighty God make perfect in you his grace which he has begun, and prolong your life here through the course of many years, and after a long time receive you into the congregation of the heavenly country.

May the heavenly grace keep your Excellency safe, O most loved lord.

Written in the eleventh indiction, on 25 May.

187. Letter of Alhred, king of Northumbria, and his wife Osgifu to Lul (773)

For the occasion of this letter, see introduction to the previous letter. The interest taken by this king in the continental missions is shown also by the sending of Willehad as missionary to the Frisians and Old Saxons by a synod called by King Alhred (Life of St. Anskar, chapter 1). Moreover in his reign an Englishman called Aluberht was consecrated bishop of the Old Saxons at York in 767. (No. 3, p. 243; No. 160.) This letter is of interest as evidence of intercourse between the Northumbrian court and that of Charles the Great. It is No. 121 in Tangl, and in Haddan and Stubbs, III, p. 434.

King Alhred and Queen Osgifu to the venerable Bishop Lul, bound to us in perpetual friendship, send greeting in Christ.

We have received your Holiness's letters with due and grateful reverence, along with the gifts conferred with the letters, and have given special thanks to Almighty God, that he has preserved you with the desired good health, toiling in so long an exile and contending in the contests of Christ. And thus, when the venerable men are returning, we indicate our joy by the attestation of sacred letters, and we ask that your episcopal dignity may deign to devote care and prayers for our welfare with daily petitions, and that you will cause us, with the names of our friends and relations which are written below[1] to be included in the safe-keeping of writing; and that we may be commended to the perpetual protection of God in prayers and celebrations of the Mass. And in the same way we have been careful to do as you asked about yourself and about the names sent to us. In all the monasteries subject to our authority they are commended with the everlasting memorial of writing and offered daily to

[1] They were not copied into the register, however.

God with the help of prayers. And know that it has greatly pleased us that your Holiness concerned yourself about the disturbance in our churches and people; we believe it to be foreseen that such things happen, by some plan of God's dispensation.

Also, most loved brother, we beseech that you will help and care for our embassies to your lord the most glorious King Charles, that you may make peace and amity, which are proper to all, to be firmly strengthened between us.

May the Divine Majesty deign to preserve you, toiling with unwearied struggle for the Church of Christ.

We have sent to your episcopal dignity some small presents, namely twelve cloaks, along with a gold ring, a substantial gift for an endowment.

188. Letter of Lul to Coena (Ethelbert), archbishop of York, asking for prayers and the works of Bede (767–778)

Lul wrote at least one other letter to Coena asking for books, for an extant letter from Coena (Tangl, No. 124; Haddan and Stubbs, II, p. 437) is a reply to a lost letter in which Lul has asked for books about the earth and tides, and other works of cosmography. Coena says he only has some very difficult ones, and has so far been unable to procure copyists.

This letter is No. 125 in Tangl, and in Haddan and Stubbs, III, pp. 435 f.

To his brother and fellow-bishop Coena, most dear to the Lord for his merits, and endowed with the highest badge of the pontificate, Lul, a poor servant of the servants of God, sends everlasting greeting in Christ.

I humbly beseech the reverence of your Holiness, that you deign to remember the friendship formerly joined between us in Christ and begun once for ever, lest what we concluded before God by faithful vows grow old and be given to oblivion. Truly, for the sake of Christ's name it behoves us to glory in insults and tribulations[1] and in the exaltation of his Church, which is daily afflicted, burdened and harassed, because the rulers of our time make new customs and new laws at their pleasure. Therefore I importune your Excellency with humble prayer to be a continual intercessor for the safety of my soul. For I am driven by incessant sickness of body and anxiety of mind to leave this wretched and most perilous life, to render account to the faithful and stern Judge.

I have sent a few small gifts to your love; that is, a pall all of silk of the best quality, by the bearer of these letters.

I beseech that you acquire and deign to send us any of those books which Bede the priest, of blessed memory, composed, for our consolation in our exile; namely four books on the first part of Samuel as far as the death of Saul, and three books on Ezra and Nehemiah, and four books on the gospel of St. Mark. Perhaps I make heavy demands; but I enjoin nothing heavy to true love.

We hope that your holy Excellency may ever advance to the profit of the Holy Church of God.

Commending to your Holiness the names of our brothers and friends departing this life. They are . . .[2]

---

[1] Cf. Romans v. 3.   [2] The names were not copied into the manuscript.

189. Letter of an anonymous monk to Lul (754–786)

There is so little trustworthy evidence about the monasteries of Wessex in early times that it seems worth while to include this little document. The writer's name is not given, but both Hahn and Tangl think that he should on stylistic grounds be identified with the writer of another anonymous letter (Tangl, No. 79) addressed to a certain Andhun, apparently in Friesland, which asks him if he knows how Boniface will act in the situation caused by the abdication of Carloman (747–748), and which incidentally shows that Carloman's abdication was not in favour of his brother Pippin but of his own son. This writer appears to be a member of the continental mission, but from the present letter it would seem that he has returned to England. He writes a very ungrammatical Latin. The letter is No. 135 in Tangl.

To the most holy and venerable Bishop Lul . . . servant of the servants of God, sends heartfelt greeting in the Lord.

I ask you, dearest brother, as I have strong trust in you, not to be forgetful, but always to recall to memory with most acute mind our old friendship which we had in the city of Malmesbury when Abbot Eafa reared you in loving charity. And I record this epithet, that he called you by name "Little". Abbot Hereca[1] therefore greets you in holy salutation, and all the community which are in his monastery, that you may duly hold us in your memory. "He that shall persevere in peace to the end, he shall be saved."[2]

Be well, beloved, in happiness for ever, my dear one, chosen of God, for love is without price.

Abbot Hereca made this mark.

190. Letter of Cynewulf, king of Wessex, to Lul (757–786)

This is the king whose death in 786 is reported with such circumstantial detail in annal 755 of the Anglo-Saxon Chronicle, and who was a generous donor to religious foundations. (See Nos. 70, 71.) The tone of the letter suggests that it was not very long after Boniface's death, and we should probably date it early in the reign. It is No. 139 in Tangl, No. 249 in Birch and is in Haddan and Stubbs, III, pp. 439 f.

To the most blessed lord, to be venerated with special love, Bishop Lul, I, Cynewulf, king of the West Saxons, along with my bishops and also with the company of my leading men, send eternal greeting of good health in the Lord.

We testify to you that we are ready to perform gladly according to the measure of our ability whatever your Holiness shall desire or command, just as we arranged with the most reverend and holy man of God, your predecessor Boniface, whether in prayers devoted to God or in any other things whatsoever, in which by God's ordinance human frailty is found to need mutual consolations. Likewise we beseech you that with those who with you invoke the name of the Lord Jesus you may remember to make supplication to the Lord for our insignificance and for the peace of our Church. We commend to your kindness the bearer of these letters, who was previously sent by you, for he will endeavour to obey us faithfully in all things.

May Almighty God, who gathers together what is scattered and preserves what is gathered, himself protect you by his grace and allow us to see the fruit of your labour in the eternal country.

---

[1] An abbot of this name witnesses Birch, Nos. 181, 185, in 757 and 758.   [2] Matthew x. 22.

191. From the report of the Legates to Pope Hadrian (786)

Until a discovery of a manuscript of this text at Wolfenbüttel, it was known only in the incomplete form printed by the Magdeburg Centuriators, and reprinted by Wilkins, *Concilia*, I, pp. 145–151, and others. Although no English manuscript seems to have survived, the report was known to Archbishop Wulfstan of York (1002–1023), who makes use of it. It sheds valuable light on the holding of synods in England, and on the position of Offa of Mercia. As several of the twenty decrees laid before the councils consist only of the ordinary general injunctions of the Church, I have given only a summary of these, but have translated in full those which have a specific application to English conditions.

This document is No. 3 in Dümmler. Haddan and Stubbs, III, pp. 447–462, has it without the rubrics and first paragraph. Birch, No. 250, omits in addition the statutes themselves.

The synod which was held in English Saxony in the days of the thrice-blessed and co-angelical Lord Hadrian, supreme pontifex and universal pope, in the reign of the most glorious Charles, most excellent king of the Franks and Lombards and patrician of the Romans, in the eighteenth year of his reign, when George, bishop of Ostia, and Theophylact, venerable bishop of the church of Todi, had been sent by the apostolic see–our Lord Jesus Christ reigning for ever–in the year of the incarnation of this same Lord 786, the tenth indiction.

By the inspiration of the divine clemency, O illustrious, highest, holy, glorious pastor, honourable, gracious pontifex Hadrian, you sent to us by Theophylact, venerable bishop of the holy church of Todi, letters containing most salutary statutes and things necessary to all Holy Church, at the same time urging with paternal goodness our insignificance to travel across the sea to the people of the English, in order that, if any tares had spoilt those crops, sown with the best seed, which the blessed Pope Gregory had planted through the mouth of St. Augustine, we might be zealous with our highest endeavour to uproot completely anything harmful and to secure most wholesome fruit.

Your holy prayers favouring us, we indeed set out complying with your orders with a glad countenance, but the tempter hindered us with a contrary wind; but he who calms the waters, hearing your prayer, stilled the blue straits, brought us across to a safe haven, and led us to the shores of the English, afflicted with many dangers, yet unharmed.

We were first received by Jænberht, archbishop of the holy church of *Dorovernia*,[1] which is called by another name, Kent, where St. Augustine rests in the body, and residing there we advised him of those things which were necessary. Journeying from there, we arrived at the court of Offa, king of the Mercians. And he received both us and the sacred letters sent from the highest see with immense joy and honour on account of his reverence for the blessed Peter and your apostolate. Then Offa, king of the Mercians, and Cynewulf, king of the West Saxons, met together in a council; and to him also we delivered your holy writings; and they promised forthwith that they would reform these vices. Then, when counsel had been taken with the aforesaid kings, bishops and elders of the land, we, considering that that corner of the world extends far and wide, allowed Theophylact, the venerable bishop, to visit the king of the Mercians and the parts of Britain.[2]

Myself, however, taking with me a helper whom your most excellent son, King Charles, sent with us out of reverence for your apostolate, a man of approved

---

[1] Canterbury.   [2] *i.e.* Wales.

faith, Wigbod, abbot and priest, I went on into the region of the Northumbrians, to King Ælfwold and Eanbald, archbishop of the holy church of the city of York. But, since the aforesaid king was dwelling far to the north, the above-mentioned archbishop sent his messengers to the king, who forthwith with all joy fixed a day for a council, at which assembled all the chief men of the region, both ecclesiastical and secular. But it was related in our hearing that there were other, no less serious vices requiring correction there; for, as you know, since the time of the holy pontiff, Augustine, no Roman priest has been sent there except ourselves. We wrote a capitulary concerning the various matters and produced them in their hearing, treating of them all in order. And they honoured with all humble subjection and clear will both your admonition and our insignificance, and pledged themselves to obey in all things. Then we gave them your letters to read, warning them to observe the holy decrees both for themselves and for those subject to them.

These are the chapters which we brought forward for them to observe . . .[1]

Chap. 10. . . . We saw there also that bishops gave judgment in secular councils, and we forbade them with the apostolic saying: "No man, being a soldier of God entangleth himself with secular business, that he may serve him to whom he hath engaged himself."[2]

Chap. 12. In the twelfth chapter we decreed that in the ordination of kings no one shall permit the assent of evil men to prevail, but kings are to be lawfully chosen by the priests and elders of the people, and are not to be those begotten in adultery or incest; for just as in our times according to the canons a bastard cannot attain to the priesthood, so neither can he who was not born of a legitimate marriage be the Lord's anointed and king of the whole kingdom and inheritor of the land. . . .[3] Let no one dare to conspire to kill a king, for he is the Lord's anointed, and if anyone take part in such a crime, if he be a bishop or anyone of the priestly order, let him be expelled from it and cast out from the holy heritage, just as Judas was ejected from the apostolic order; and everyone who has consented to such sacrilege shall perish in the eternal fetters of anathema, and, associated with Judas the betrayer, be burnt in the eternal fires; as it is written: "Not only they that do such things, but they also that consent to them that do them"[4] escape not the judgment of God. . . .[5] For it has often been proved by examples among you, that those who have been the cause of the slaying of sovereigns ended their lives in a brief space, and were cut off from divine and secular rights.[6]

---

[1] The first ten chapters deal with the following topics: the observation of the Nicene creed and the six universal synods; baptism; the holding of synods and episcopal visitations; the life and habit of canons; the election of heads of monasteries; the ordination of priests and deacons; the observation of the canonical hours; the respecting of papal privileges; the prohibition against ecclesiastics taking food in secret; details about the celebration of Mass.

[2] II Timothy ii. 4. The eleventh chapter of the decrees deals with the functions of kings and the pre-eminence of priests.   [3] A number of texts follow to stress the obedience due to kings.

[4] Romans i. 32.   [5] Some biblical examples follow.

[6] Conditions in England may well account for the long section on this theme; Æthelbald of Mercia in 757 and Oswulf of Northumbria in 758 were killed by their own thegns. The murder of Cynewulf of Wessex later in 786, of Ælfwold and Ethelred of Northumbria in 788 and 796 respectively, suggests that the legates made little impression.

Chaps. 13-18 deal with just judgments; the suppression of fraud, robbery and impositions on churches; breaches of the marriage laws; the cutting off of illegitimate children from inheritance; the payment of tithe and prohibition of usury; the keeping of vows.

19. The nineteenth section. We have added that each faithful Christian must take example from catholic men; and if anything has remained of the rites of the pagans, it is to be plucked out, despised, cast away. For God made man fair in beauty and comeliness, but the pagans have by diabolical prompting added most hideous scars, as Prudentius says: "He painted also the harmless earth with unclean spots";[1] for he clearly does injury to the Lord who defiles and disfigures his creature. Certainly if anyone were to undergo this injury of staining for God's sake, he would receive for it a great reward; but whoever does it from the superstition of the Gentiles, it does not tend to his good, any more than does circumcision of the body to the Jews without belief of heart.

Also, you wear your garments according to the fashion of the Gentiles whom by the help of God your fathers expelled by arms from the country. It is a marvellous and dumbfounding thing, that you imitate the example of those whose life you have always detested. You also by an evil custom mutilate your horses, slit their nostrils, fasten their ears together and make them deaf, dock their tails; and though you can have them unblemished, you do not desire this but make them hateful to everybody.

We have heard also that when a lawsuit arises among you, you cast lots in the manner of the Gentiles, which in these times is reckoned altogether as sacrilege. Also many among you eat horses, which no Christian does in the East. Give this up also. Strive that all your acts be done decently and according to the Lord.[2]

These decrees, most blessed Pope Hadrian, we propounded in the public council before King Ælfwold and Archbishop Eanbald and all the bishops and abbots of that region and also the councillors, ealdormen and people of the land; and they, as we have said above, vowed with all devotion of mind that, the divine clemency helping them, they would keep them in all things to the utmost of their ability; and they confirmed them in our hand in your stead with the sign of the Holy Cross, and afterwards inscribed with a careful pen on the paper of this page, affixing thus the sign of the Holy Cross.

> I, Eanbald, by the grace of God archbishop of the holy church of York, have subscribed to the pious and catholic validity of this document with the sign of the Holy Cross.
>
> I, Ælfwold, king of the people across the Humber, consenting have subscribed with the sign of the Holy Cross.
>
> I, Tilberht, prelate of the church of Hexham, rejoicing have subscribed with the sign of the Holy Cross.
>
> I, Higbald, bishop of the church of Lindisfarne, obeying have subscribed with the sign of the Holy Cross.
>
> I, Ethelbert, bishop of Candida Casa,[3] suppliant, have subscribed with the sign of the Holy Cross.
>
> I, Ealdwulf, bishop of the church of Mayo, have subscribed with devout will.

[1] Prudentius, *Dittochaeon* .. 3, has Adam, not *humum* 'earth'.
[2] The 20th chapter deals with conversion, penance and confession.   [3] Whithorn.

I, Æthelwine, bishop, have subscribed through delegates.

I, Sicga, 'patrician',[1] have subscribed with serene mind with the sign of the Holy Cross.

To these most salutary admonitions we too, priests, deacons of the Church and abbots of the monasteries, judges, chief men and nobles, unanimously consent and have subscribed:

I, Alric, ealdorman, have subscribed with the sign of the Holy Cross.

I, Sigewulf, ealdorman, have subscribed with the sign of the Holy Cross.

I, Ealdberht, abbot,[2] have subscribed with the sign of the Holy Cross.

I, Ecgheard, abbot, have subscribed with the sign of the Holy Cross.

When these things had been enacted and benediction given, we set out, taking with us the illustrious men, the representatives of the king and archbishop, to wit the readers Alcuin and Pyttel.[3] They travelled with us and brought the same decrees with them to the council of the Mercians, where the glorious King Offa had come together with the senators of the land, along with Jænberht, archbishop of the holy church of Canterbury and the other bishops of those parts. And in the presence of the council the separate chapters were read in a clear voice and lucidly expounded both in Latin and in the vernacular,[4] in order that all might understand. And they all, giving thanks with a ready mind for the admonitions of your apostolate, promised with one voice that they, the divine favour supporting them, would observe these statutes in all things with a most prompt will according to their ability. They, too, just as we set out above, both the king and his chief men, the archbishop and his colleagues, confirmed in our hand in your lordship's stead the sign of the Holy Cross, and again ratified the present document with the sacred sign.

I, Jænberht, archbishop of the holy church of Canterbury, suppliant, have subscribed with the sign of the Holy Cross.

I, Offa, king of the Mercians, consenting to these statutes, have subscribed with ready will with the sign of the Cross.

I, Hygeberht, bishop of the church of Lichfield, have subscribed with the sign of the sacred Cross.

I, Ceolwulf, bishop of the people of Lindsey, have subscribed.

I, Unwona, bishop of Leicester, have subscribed.

I, Ealhheard, bishop,[5] have subscribed.

I, Eadberht, bishop,[6] have subscribed.

I, Cyneberht, bishop,[7] have subscribed.

I, Heardred, bishop,[8] have subscribed.

I, Esne, bishop,[9] have subscribed.

I, Totta, bishop,[10] have subscribed.

I, Wærmund, bishop,[11] have subscribed.

---

[1] See p. 244, n. 6. On Sicga, see No. 3, pp. 246 f.   [2] Of Ripon. See No. 1, p. 166; No. 3, p. 245.
[3] See No. 160.   [4] theodisce.   [5] Of Elmham.   [6] Of London.   [7] Of Winchester.
[8] Of Dunwich.   [9] Of Hereford.   [10] Of Selsey.   [11] Of Rochester.

I, Æthelmod, bishop,[1] have subscribed.

I, Hathored, bishop,[2] have subscribed.

Æthelheard, abbot.[3]

Ealhmund, abbot.

Botwine, abbot.[4]

Utel, abbot.[5]

I, Brorda,[6] ealdorman, have subscribed with the sign of the Holy Cross.

I, Eadbald, ealdorman, have subscribed.

I, Brihtwold, ealdorman, have subscribed.

I, Eadbald, ealdorman, have subscribed.

192. Letter of Alcuin to Colcu (early in 790)

This letter, with its reference to a dissension between Charles and Offa, should be compared with No. 20. Colcu is an Irish name. Kenney (*Sources for the Early History of Ireland*, I, p. 534) doubts the identification of Alcuin's correspondent with the abbot of Clonmacnoise. See also p. 84. Colcu appears from Dümmler No. 8 to have been for a time at York. It is uncertain where he was when this letter was sent, or where Bealdhun's monastery, mentioned in the letter, was situated. It is probably only coincidence that there should have been about this time a priest Bealdhun, trained at Worcester, who is called abbot of Kempsey in a charter in the Worcester cartulary, Brit. Mus. Cott. Tiber. A XIII, which seems based on genuine material. (See Birch, Nos. 295, 304.) The letter is No. 7 in Dümmler.

To the blessed master and pious father, Colcu, Alcuin, a humble deacon, sends greeting.

Having heard of your health and prosperity, my father, I am delighted, I avow, in my innermost heart. And since I thought you anxious to know about our journey and about the things recently done in the world, I have taken care to inform your prudent mind through these letters in my unpolished style of the things which I have heard and seen.

First, be it known to your love that by the mercy of God his Holy Church in the regions of Europe is at peace, progresses and increases. For the Old Saxons and all the tribes of the Frisians have been converted to the faith of Christ, with King Charles urging and inciting some by rewards, and others by threats.

Last year the same king attacked with an army the Slavs whom we call Wends, and subjected them to his rule.

And two years ago the Greeks came with a fleet to Italy, and were defeated by the generals of the aforesaid king and fled to the ships. Four thousand of them were slain and one thousand taken prisoner.

Likewise the Avars, whom we call Huns, broke out against Italy, and, overcome by the Christians, returned home with shame. They also attacked Bavaria, and here also were overcome by a Christian army and dispersed.

Moreover, the generals and officers of this same most Christian king captured a great part of Spain from the Saracens, some three hundred miles along the coast. But—alas the pity of it—the same accursed Saracens, also called Aggareni, are dominant

---

[1] Of Sherborne. [2] Of Worcester. [3] Probably the future archbishop, abbot of Louth.
[4] Of Peterborough. [5] Later bishop of Hereford. [6] See No. 3, p. 250.

over all Africa and the most part of greater Asia. I have, I think, written before to your venerable prudence about their invasion.

For the rest, most holy father, let your Reverence know that I, your son, and Joseph your disciple, are well, by the mercy of God; and all your friends who are with us serve God in prosperity. But I do not know what is going to happen to us. For a certain dissension, fomented by the devil, has lately arisen between King Charles and King Offa, so that on both sides the passage of ships has been forbidden to merchants and is ceasing. There are some who say that we are to be sent to those parts to make peace. But I implore you that we may be protected by your holy prayers, whether we stay or come.

I know not in what I have sinned, that I have not deserved for a long time to see your most sweet letters, my father; yet I believe I am daily aware of the very necessary prayers of your Holiness. I have sent to your love some oil, which is now scarcely met with in Britain, for you to dispense where the bishops require it for the utility and honour of God. I have sent also 50 shekels[1] to the brothers out of the alms of King Charles – I beseech you to pray for him – and 50 shekels from my alms; and 30 shekels from the alms of the king and 30 from my alms to the southern brothers of Bealdhun's community;[2] and 20 shekels from the alms of the *pater familias* Arieda and 20 from my alms; and 3 shekels of pure silver to each of the anchorites; that they may all pray for me and for the lord, King Charles, that God may preserve him for the protection of his Holy Church and for the praise and glory of his name.

May Almighty God hear you, as you intercede for his Holy Church, and make you to advance in the prosperity of eternal life.

193. Letter of Alcuin to Ethelred, king of Northumbria (793, after 8 June)

This letter and the next are among those called forth by the viking raid on Lindisfarne, which Alcuin saw as a sign of the divine wrath. In its account of portents before the raid it should be compared with No. 1, p. 167 and No. 3, p. 247. It is No. 16 in Dümmler, and in Haddan and Stubbs, III, pp. 492–495. It was known to William of Malmesbury, who quotes part of it in his *De Gestis Regum*, ed. Stubbs, I, p. 73. Part of it is translated by G. F. Browne, *Alcuin of York*, pp. 128–132.

To the most beloved lord King Ethelred and all his chief men, Alcuin the humble deacon, sends greeting.

Mindful of your most sweet love, O men my brothers and fathers, also esteemed in Christ the Lord; desiring the divine mercy to conserve for us in long-lasting prosperity our land, which it once with its grace conferred on us with free generosity; I do not cease to warn you very often, my dearest fellow-soldiers, either with words, when present, if God should grant it, or by letters when absent, by the inspiration of the divine spirit, and by frequent iteration to pour forth to your ears, as we are citizens of the same country, the things known to belong to the welfare of an earthly kingdom

---

[1] A *siclus* was a quarter of a Roman ounce (about 105 grains). H. M. Chadwick (*Studies in Anglo-Saxon Institutions*, p. 44) pointed out that in ninth-century charters it is equated with the West Saxon shilling, and that the five silver pennies of which this shilling consisted would reach approximately to the required weight. Only four pence were reckoned to the shilling elsewhere, but it is possible that Alcuin was using the term loosely as a translation of the native word shilling.

[2] Literally 'of the Bealdhunings', *i.e.* 'of the descendants, or dependants, of Bealdhun'.

and to the beatitude of an eternal kingdom; that the things often heard may be implanted in your minds for your good. For what is love in a friend, if it is silent on matters profitable to the friend? To what does a man owe fidelity, if not to his fatherland? To whom does he owe prosperity, if not to its citizens? We are fellow-citizens by a two-fold relationship: sons of one city in Christ, that is, of Mother Church, and natives of one country. Thus let not your kindness shrink from accepting benignly what my devotion is eager to offer for the welfare of our country. Do not think that I impute faults to you; but understand that I wish to avert penalties.

Lo, it is nearly 350 years that we and our fathers have inhabited this most lovely land, and never before has such terror appeared in Britain as we have now suffered from a pagan race, nor was it thought that such an inroad from the sea could be made. Behold, the church of St. Cuthbert spattered with the blood of the priests of God, despoiled of all its ornaments; a place more venerable than all in Britain is given as a prey to pagan peoples. And where first, after the departure of St. Paulinus from York, the Christian religion in our race took its rise, there misery and calamity have begun. Who does not fear this? Who does not lament this as if his country were captured? Foxes pillage the chosen vine, the heritage of the Lord has been given to a people not his own; and where there was the praise of God, are now the games of the Gentiles; the holy festivity has been turned to mourning.[1]

Consider carefully, brothers, and examine diligently, lest perchance this unaccustomed and unheard-of evil was merited by some unheard-of evil practice. I do not say that formerly there were no sins of fornication among the people. But from the days of King Ælfwold fornications, adulteries and incest have poured over the land, so that these sins have been committed without any shame and even against the handmaids dedicated to God. What may I say about avarice, robbery, violent judgments?—when it is clearer than day how much these crimes have increased everywhere, and a despoiled people testifies to it. Whoever reads the Holy Scriptures and ponders ancient histories and considers the fortune of the world will find that for sins of this kind kings lost kingdoms and peoples their country; and while the strong unjustly seized the goods of others, they justly lost their own.

Truly signs of this misery preceded it, some through unaccustomed things, some through unwonted practices. What portends the bloody rain, which in the time of Lent in the church of St. Peter, Prince of the Apostles, in the city of York, which is the head of the whole kingdom, we saw fall menacingly on the north side from the summit of the roof, though the sky was serene? Can it not be expected that from the north there will come upon our nation retribution of blood, which can be seen to have started with this attack which has lately befallen the house of God?

Consider the dress, the way of wearing the hair, the luxurious habits of the princes and people. Look at your trimming of beard and hair, in which you have wished to resemble the pagans.[2] Are you not menaced by terror of them whose fashion you wished to follow? What also of the immoderate use of clothing beyond the needs of human nature, beyond the custom of our predecessors? The princes' superfluity is poverty for the people. Such customs once injured the people of God, and made it

---

[1] Cf. Amos viii. 10.   [2] Cf. No. 232.

a reproach to the pagan races, as the prophet says: "Woe to you, who have sold the poor for a pair of shoes",[1] that is, the souls of men for ornaments for the feet. Some labour under an enormity of clothes, others perish with cold; some are inundated with delicacies and feastings like Dives clothed in purple, and Lazarus dies of hunger at the gate.[2] Where is brotherly love? Where the pity which we are admonished to have for the wretched? The satiety of the rich is the hunger of the poor. That saying of our Lord is to be feared: "For judgment without mercy to him that hath not done mercy."[3] Also we read in the words of the blessed Peter: "The time is that judgment should begin at the house of God."[4]

Behold, judgment has begun, with great terror, at the house of God, in which rest such lights of the whole of Britain. What should be expected for other places, when the divine judgment has not spared this holy place? I do not think this sin is theirs alone who dwell in that place. Would that their correction would be the amendment of others, and that many would fear what a few have suffered, and each say in his heart, groaning and trembling: "If such great men and fathers so holy did not defend their habitation and the place of their repose, who will defend mine?" Defend your country by assiduous prayers to God, by acts of justice and mercy to men. Let your use of clothes and food be moderate. Nothing defends a country better than the equity and godliness of princes and the intercessions of the servants of God. Remember that Hezekiah, that just and pious king, procured from God by a single prayer that a hundred and eighty-five thousand of the enemy were destroyed by an angel in one night.[5] Likewise with profuse tears he averted from him death when it threatened him, and deserved of God that fifteen years were added to his life by this prayer.[6]

Have decent habits, pleasing to God and laudable to men. Be rulers of the people, not robbers; shepherds, not plunderers. You have received honours by God's gift; give heed to the keeping of his commands, that you may have him as a preserver whom you had as a benefactor. Obey the priests of God; for they have an account to make to God, how they admonish you; and you, how you obey them. Let one peace and love be between you; they as interceders for you, you as defenders of them. But, above all, have the love of God in your hearts, and show that love by keeping his commandments. Love him as a father, that he may defend you as sons. Whether you will or not, you will have him as a judge. Pay heed to good works, that he may be propitious to you. "For the fashion of this world passeth away";[7] and all things are fleeting which are seen or possessed here. This alone from his labour can a man take with him, what he did in alms-giving and good works. We must all stand before the judgment-seat of Christ, and each must show all that he did, whether good or evil. Beware of the torments of hell, while they can be avoided; and acquire for yourselves the kingdom of God and eternal beatitude with Christ and his saints in eternal ages.

May God both make you happy in this earthly kingdom and grant to you an eternal country with his saints, O lords, my dearest fathers, brothers and sons.

[1] Cf. Amos ii. 6.   [2] Cf. Luke xvi. 19 ff.   [3] James ii. 13.   [4] I Peter iv. 17.
[5] Isaiah xxxvii. 36; II Kings xix. 35.   [6] II Kings xx. 3 ff.; Isaiah xxxviii. 1 ff.   [7] I Corinthians vii. 31.

194. Letter of Alcuin to Higbald, bishop of Lindisfarne, and his monks, condoling with them for the sack of Lindisfarne (793, after 8 June)

In his horror at this calamity, Alcuin wrote many letters. Cf. No. 193. He wrote also to the monks of Wearmouth and Jarrow, whose exposed situation laid them open to similar attack (Dümmler, No. 19), and his fears were fulfilled the following year; and to Æthelheard, archbishop of Canterbury (Dümmler, No. 17). The present letter is No. 20 in Dümmler, and is in Haddan and Stubbs, III, pp. 472–473. It is translated in G. F. Browne, *Alcuin of York*, pp. 132–135.

To the best sons in Christ of the most blessed father, St. Cuthbert the bishop, Bishop Higbald and all the congregation of the church of Lindisfarne, Alcuin the deacon sends greeting with celestial benediction in Christ.

The intimacy of your love used to rejoice me greatly when I was with you; but conversely, the calamity of your tribulation saddens me greatly every day, though I am absent; when the pagans desecrated the sanctuaries of God, and poured out the blood of saints around the altar, laid waste the house of our hope, trampled on the bodies of saints in the temple of God, like dung in the street.[1] What can we say except lament in our soul with you before Christ's altar, and say: "Spare, O Lord, spare thy people, and give not thine inheritance to the Gentiles, lest the pagan say, 'Where is the God of the Christians?'"[2] What assurance is there for the churches of Britain, if St. Cuthbert, with so great a number of saints, defends not his own? Either this is the beginning of greater tribulation, or else the sins of the inhabitants have called it upon them. Truly it has not happened by chance, but is a sign that it was well merited by someone. But now, you who are left, stand manfully, fight bravely, defend the camp of God. Remember Judas Maccabaeus, how he cleansed the temple of God, and set free the people from foreign servitude.[3] If anything ought to be corrected in your Grace's habits, correct it quickly. Call back to you your patrons who have left you for a time. They lacked not power with God's mercy; but, we know not why, they kept silence. Do not glory in the vanity of raiment; this is not a glory to priests and servants of God, but a disgrace. Do not in drunkenness blot out the words of your prayers. Do not go out after luxuries of the flesh and worldly avarice, but continue steadfastly in the service of God and in the discipline of the regular life, that the most holy fathers, who begot you, may not cease to be your protectors. Treading in their footsteps, you may remain secure by their prayers. Be not degenerate sons of such great fathers. In nowise will they cease from defending you if they see you follow their example.

Yet be not dismayed in mind by this calamity. God chastiseth every son whom he receiveth;[4] and thus he perhaps chastised you more harshly, because he loved you more. Jerusalem, the city loved by God, perished with the temple of God in the flames of the Chaldeans. Rome, encircled by a crown of holy apostles and innumerable martyrs, was shattered by the ravages of pagans, but by the pity of God soon recovered. Almost the whole of Europe was laid desolate by the fire and sword of the Goths and Huns; but now, by God's mercy, it shines adorned with churches, as the sky with stars, and in them the offices of the Christian religion flourish and increase. Exhort

---

[1] Cf. Isaiah v. 25.   [2] Cf. Joel ii. 17.
[3] II Maccabees x. 2–4.   [4] Cf. Hebrews xii. 6.

yourselves in turn, saying: "Let us return to the Lord Our God, for he is bountiful to forgive,[1] and never deserts them that hope in him."[2]

And you, holy father, leader of the people of God, shepherd of the holy flock, physician of souls, light set upon a candlestick, be the pattern of all goodness to all who see you; be the herald of salvation to all who hear you. Let your company be of decent behaviour, an example to others unto life, not unto perdition. Let your banquets be in soberness, not in drunkenness. Let your garments be suitable to your order. Do not adapt yourself to the men of the world in any vain thing. Empty adornment of clothing, and useless elegance, is to you a reproach before men and a sin before God. It is better to adorn with good habits the soul which will live for ever, than to deck in choice garments the body which will soon decay in the dust. Let Christ be clothed and fed in the person of the poor man, that doing this you may reign with Christ. The redemption of man is true riches.[3] If we love gold, let us send it before us to heaven, where it will be kept for us, and we have that which we love. Let us love what is eternal, and not what is perishable. Let us esteem true riches, not fleeting ones, eternal, not transitory. Let us acquire praise from God, and not from men. Let us do what the saints did whom we praise. Let us follow their footsteps on earth, that we may deserve to be partakers of their glory in the heavens. May the protection of the divine pity guard you from all adversity, and set you with your fathers in the glory of the celestial kingdom, O dearest brothers.

When our lord King Charles returns home, having by the mercy of God subdued his enemies, we plan, God helping us, to go to him; and if we can then be of any profit to your Holiness, regarding either the youths who have been led into captivity by the pagans or any other of your needs, we will take diligent care to bring it about. Farewell in Christ, most beloved, and ever advancing, be strengthened.

195. Letter of Alcuin to Offa, king of Mercia (787–796)

As little has come down to us to shed light on the character of Offa, it is worth including this little letter which shows him taking an interest in learning. It is No. 64 in Dümmler. Part of it is translated in G. F. Browne, *Alcuin of York*, pp. 93 f.

To the most excellent lord, King Offa, Alcuin, a humble deacon, sends greeting. Desiring always to comply faithfully with your wishes, I have sent back to you, as you asked, this my most dear son; beseeching you to maintain him with honour, until, God willing, I come to you. Do not let him wander in idleness or take to drink, but provide him with pupils, and strictly charge him to teach diligently. I know that he has learnt well; I hope that he may do well. For the success of my pupils is my reward with God.

And it greatly pleases me that you are so intent on education, that the light of wisdom, which is now extinguished in many places, may shine in your kingdom. You are the glory of Britain, the trumpet of proclamation, the sword against foes, the shield against enemies. Have God ever before your eyes, do justice, love mercy, for

---

[1] Isaiah lv. 7.   [2] Cf. Judith xiii. 17.   [3] Cf. Proverbs xiii. 8.

he who forgives will be forgiven. Learn and love the commandments of Christ, that his blessing may follow you and your descendants in all goodness and prosperity for ever.

May the divine grace attend you and your kingdom with heavenly benediction, most excellent lord.

196. Letter of Charles the Great to Æthelheard, archbishop of Canterbury, and Ceolwulf, bishop of Lindsey (793–796)

This letter concerns the relations between Charles and Offa, and it also affords an instance of followers sharing their lord's exile. It is No. 85 in Dümmler, and is in Haddan and Stubbs, III, pp. 487 f. Part is translated in G. F. Browne, *Alcuin of York*, pp. 120 f.

Charles, by the grace of God, king of the Franks and Lombards and patrician of the Romans, to Archbishop Æthelheard and his fellow-bishop Ceolwulf, sends greeting of eternal beatitude.

By no means do we think it right that the vast distance by land and the breadth of the stormy sea should sever the bonds of a friendship joined in Christ. But the longer the distance dividing human intercourse, with so much firmer faith should be maintained the pact of loyalty between friends. Since in his presence fear or shame often reveals outwardly in a man's face what he does not hold in his heart, holy fidelity is laudable in those absent and admirable in those present.

Hence, relying on that friendship which once, when we were together, we established in loyal words, we have sent to your kindness these miserable exiles from their country, praying that you may deign to intercede for them with my dearest brother King Offa, that they may be allowed to return to their native land in peace and without unjust oppression of any kind, and to serve anyone whatever. For their lord, Hringstan,[1] has died. It seemed to us that he would have been faithful to his lord, if he had been allowed to remain in his own country. But to shun the danger of death, as he was wont to say, he fled to us; and was ever ready to purge himself with oath from all disloyalty. We kept him with us for some little time, for the sake of reconciliation, not out of enmity.

If indeed you can obtain peace by your prayer for these fellow-countrymen of his, let them remain in their own land. But if my brother reply more harshly concerning them, send them back to us uninjured. It is better to live in exile than to perish, to serve in a foreign land than to die in one's own. I have confidence in my brother's goodness, if you intercede earnestly for them, that he will receive them kindly, for our affection and still more for the love of Christ, who said: "Forgive, and you shall be forgiven."[2]

May the divine goodness keep your Holiness, interceding for us, safe into eternity.

---

[1] The manuscript has *Umhringstan*, an impossible name. I suspect that *um-* has been repeated in error from the previous word, *illorum*.

[2] Luke vi. 37.

197. Letter of Charles the Great to Offa, king of Mercia (796)

This document, so important for our knowledge of the relations of Offa with Charles, and of English trade, was known to William of Malmesbury, who quotes excerpts from it in *De Gestis Regum* (ed. Stubbs, I, p. 93). It is No. 100 in Dümmler, and in Haddan and Stubbs, III, pp. 496-498. It is translated in G. F. Browne, *Alcuin of York*, pp. 99-103.

Charles, by the grace of God, king of the Franks and Lombards and patrician of the Romans, to the revered man his dearest brother, Offa, king of the Mercians, sends greeting of present prosperity and eternal blessedness in Christ.

Between royal dignities and exalted personages of the world, the keeping of the laws of friendship joined in the unity of peace, and of the concord of holy love, with the deepest affection of heart, is wont to be of profit to many. And if we are commanded by our Lord's precept to untie the knots of enmity, how much more ought we to take care to secure the links of love? Hence, most beloved brother, mindful of the ancient pact between us, we have sent these letters to your Reverence, that the treaty established in the root of faith may flourish in the fruit of love. Having perused your brotherly letters, which have at divers times been brought to us by the hands of your messengers, and endeavouring to reply adequately to the several suggestions of your authority, we first give thanks to the Almighty God for the sincerity of the catholic faith which we found laudably set down in your pages; recognizing you to be not only a most strong protector of your earthly country, but also a most devout defender of the holy faith.

Concerning pilgrims, who for the love of God and the salvation of their souls desire to reach the thresholds of the blessed Apostles, as we granted formerly, they may go in peace free from all molestation, bearing with them the necessities for their journey. But we have discovered that certain persons fraudulently mingle with them for the sake of commerce, seeking gain, not serving religion. If such are found among them, they are to pay the established toll at the proper places; the others may go in peace, immune from toll.

You have written to us also about merchants, and by our mandate we allow that they shall have protection and support in our kingdom, lawfully, according to the ancient custom of trading. And if in any place they are afflicted by wrongful oppression, they may appeal to us or to our judges, and we will then order true justice to be done. Similarly our men, if they suffer any injustice in your dominion, are to appeal to the judgment of your equity, lest any disturbance should arise anywhere between our men.

Regarding the priest Odberht,[1] who desires on his return from Rome to live abroad for the love of God, as he often says, and did not come to accuse you, I inform you, dear brother, that we have sent him to Rome with the other exiles who in fear of death have taken refuge under the wings of our protection; so that in the presence of the apostolic lord and your archbishop–since, as your letters have informed us, they had bound themselves by a vow–their cause may be heard and judged, that equitable judgment may be effective where pious intercession failed. What could be safer for us than that the opinion of the apostolic authority should determine a case in which the views of others disagree?

[1] This name is the continental form of Old English Eadberht.

As for the black stones which your Reverence begged to be sent to you, let a messenger come and consider what kind you have in mind, and we will willingly order them to be given, wherever they are to be found, and will help with their transport. But as you have intimated your wishes concerning the length of the stones, so our people make a demand about the size of the cloaks, that you may order them to be such as used to come to us in former times.   •

Moreover, we make known to your love that we have sent a gift from our dalmatics and palls to the various episcopal sees of your kingdom and of Ethelred's, in alms for the apostolic lord, Hadrian, our father and your friend; beseeching you to order diligent intercession for his soul, not having any doubt that his blessed soul is at rest, but to show our trust and love towards a friend most dear to us. So, also, the blessed Augustine has taught, that intercessions of ecclesiastical piety ought to be made for all; asserting that to intercede for a good man profits him who does it. Also from the treasure of earthly riches, which the Lord Jesus Christ has granted us with freely bestowed kindness, we have sent something to each of the metropolitan cities; also to your love, for joy and thanksgiving to Almighty God, we have sent a belt, and a Hunnish sword and two silk palls.

To the end that everywhere among Christian people the divine clemency may be preached and the name of our Lord Jesus Christ be glorified in eternity, we pray that you cause assiduous intercessions to be made for us and for our faithful subjects, nay more, for all Christian people; that the most merciful goodness of the heavenly King may deign to protect, exalt and extend the kingdom of the Holy Church. May Almighty God deign to preserve in long-lasting prosperity the excellence of your dignity unimpaired for the protection of his Holy Church, most longed-for brother.

198. Letter of Alcuin to Offa, king of Mercia (796, after 18 April)

This letter was written soon after Charles's letter to Offa (No. 197) and should be compared with it. Its chief interest is in its account of the reception of the news of King Ethelred's murder. It is No. 101 in Dümmler, and the first part is in Haddan and Stubbs, III, p. 498. Part is translated in G. F. Browne, *Alcuin of York*, pp. 103–105.

To the most excellent man and to us most dear, Offa, king of the Mercians, his humble friend Alcuin sends greeting.

Be it known to your reverend love that the lord king, Charles, has often spoken to me of you in a most loving and loyal way, and in him you certainly have a most faithful friend. Thus he is sending envoys to Rome for the judgment of the apostolic pope and of Archbishop Æthelheard. He is also sending fitting gifts to you. Moreover, he is sending presents to all the episcopal sees in alms for himself and for the apostolic pope, that you should order prayers to be offered for them. Do you act faithfully, as you are always wont to act towards your friends.

Similarly, he had sent gifts both to King Ethelred and to his episcopal sees. But alas, the pity! When the gifts and letters had been given into the messengers' hands, the sad news came to us by the messengers who had returned from Ireland by way of you, of the treachery of the people and of his murder. King Charles withdrew his generous gifts, and was so greatly enraged against that nation, holding "that perfidious and perverse race, murderers of their lords", as he called them, worse than pagans, that whatever benefit he could have taken away from them, or whatever evil he could have contrived, he would have put into effect, if I had not interceded for them.

I was prepared to come to you with the gifts of King Charles and return to my country. But it seemed better, for the sake of the peace of my people, for me to remain abroad; for I do not know what I could do among them, where no one can be safe or prevail with any wholesome counsel. Look at the most holy places laid waste by the pagans, altars defiled by perjuries, monasteries profaned by adulteries, the earth polluted with the blood of kings and princes. What can I do other than groan with the prophet: "Woe to the sinful nation, a people laden with iniquity, a wicked seed, ungracious children; they have forsaken the Lord; they have blasphemed the holy Saviour of the world in their wickedness."[1] And if what was read in your Highness's letter be true, that the iniquity started from the elders of the people, where then is safety and fidelity to be hoped for, if the turbulent torrent of iniquity flowed from the place where the purest fountain of truth and faith was wont to spring?

You, most wise ruler of the people of God, correct very diligently your people from perverse habits and instruct it in the precepts of God, that the land given to us by God may not be destroyed for the sins of the people. Be a father to the Church of Christ, a brother to the priests of God, and kind and just to all the people, moderate and peaceful in all your bearing and speech, and ever devout in the praise of God; that the divine clemency may preserve you in long-lasting prosperity, and may deign by the grace of his goodness to exalt, enlarge and crown in eternity with the benefits of everlasting piety, your kingdom, nay more, that of all the English.

I implore you that you order the several churches of your Reverence to intercede for me, your servant and fellow-worker for your honour. The charge of the church of St. Martin has come into my keeping, all unworthy as I am, not by my wishes but to a certain measure by necessity and from the advice of many. Yet know that I am free faithfully to offer prayers for you there, and wherever I can.

Be with all love and care a friend of God and fill your days with his commands. Endeavour that an eternal reward may follow you and the heavenly blessing your descendants. Again and again I implore you for the love of God to take thought for the country, lest it perish; and for the churches of God, lest they be destroyed; and that truth with mercy may increase in it. For by the true saying of Solomon, the throne of the kingdom shall be strengthened in truth and mercy;[2] these things may confirm you and your throne for ever, that you may rule happily in this world and live in glory with Christ in the heavenly kingdom.

May you flourish, by the favour of the Lord Christ, in all felicity, and may you advance in all goodness, for the consolation of the Holy Church of God, and the joy of Christian people, O Lord most excellent and to us most dear.

I pray you, greet with my love that most noble youth[3] and instruct him diligently in the fear of God; and may the hope of many not come to naught in him. Remember

---

[1] Isaiah i. 4.   [2] Cf. Proverbs xx. 28.   [3] Ecgferth, Offa's son.

the proverb of Solomon: "For in what way a boy is reared, when he is old he will not depart from it."[1] Greet also the queen[2] and lady of the royal household. May she live happy, rejoicing in an offspring of a happy father. And also I pray that you greet in my name all your Highness's children. May the right hand of Almighty God ever protect, direct and guard you all.

I pray you to receive with your accustomed goodness the pupils we have trained and taught, and the messengers of the royal dignity. They indeed bear a peaceful message in their mouth and hands. Through them you can demand of me what you wish.

199. Letter of Alcuin to Eardwulf, king of Northumbria (796, after May)

This is the Eardwulf who survived his execution at Ripon in 790 (see No. 3, p. 246), an event referred to in this letter. Twenty-seven days after the murder of King Ethelred of Northumbria on 18 April 796, Osbald was driven out and Eardwulf raised to the throne. On the events of his reign see No. 3, and on his expulsion in 808 and return the following year with Charles the Great's help, see No. 21. This letter is No. 108 in Dümmler. It is translated by G. F. Browne, *Alcuin of York*, pp. 141–143.

To the illustrious King Eardwulf, Alcuin the deacon sends greeting. Mindful of the old friendship agreed between us, and also rejoicing greatly in your revered salutation, I have been at pains to write a few words to advise your laudable person concerning the prosperity of the kingdom conferred on you by God and concerning the salvation of your soul, and by what means the honour given to you may by the grace of God remain stable.

You know very well from what perils the divine mercy has freed you, and how easily it promoted you, when it chose, to the kingdom. Be ever mindful of and grateful for such great gifts from God to you; and especially that, as far as you can understand it, you may carry out his will with your whole heart and be obedient to the servants of God, who admonish you concerning his commandments. Know most certainly, that none other can preserve your life than he who has freed you from present death, and none other can protect and keep you in that honour than he who with freely bestowed goodness conceded that dignity to you. Keep diligently in your mind mercy and justice; because, as Solomon says, and, what is more, God concedes: "The throne of the kingdom shall be established in mercy and justice."[3]

Consider most intently, for what sins your predecessors lost life and kingdom, and watch most carefully that you do not the like; lest a similar judgment befall you. God condemned the perjury of some; he punished the adultery of others; he avenged the avarice and the frauds of others; the unjust deeds of others displeased him. God is no respecter of persons;[4] but those who do such things shall not possess the kingdom of God. Instruct first yourself in all goodness and sobriety; afterwards the people, whom you govern, in all modesty of life and apparel, in all truth of faith and of judgments, in keeping the commandments of God and in probity of morals. Thus you will both establish the kingdom for yourself and preserve the nation and free it from the wrath of God, which by certain signs has long been threatening it.

[1] Cf. Proverbs xxii. 6.   [2] Cynethryth.   [3] Cf. Proverbs xvi. 12; xx. 28; xxv. 5.   [4] Acts x. 34.

Never would so much blood of nobles and rulers be shed in this nation, and never would pagans thus devastate the holy places, nor so much injustice and arrogance prevail among the people, if the manifest vengeance of God did not threaten the inhabitants of the land. Do you, being, as I believe, preserved for better times and reserved for the correction of your country, with the help of God's grace, labour with full intent in the will of God for the salvation of your soul and the prosperity of the country and the people committed to your charge; to the end that from the correction of those subject to your authority, the present kingdom may happily be made secure to you and your descendants, and the glory of the future kingdom be granted for ever.

May this letter, I beseech you, be kept by you and often read as a reminder of your welfare and our love; that Almighty God may deign to keep you in the increase of his Holy Church for the prosperity of our race, flourishing for a long time in your kingdom and advancing in every good thing. Live and fare well, by the gift of God, in eternal ages.

200. Letter of Alcuin to Osbald (796, after May)

On the recipient of this letter, see p. 17 and No. 3, pp. 248, 250. After the murder of King Ethelred of Northumbria, he held the throne for under a month, and was in exile among the Picts when Alcuin wrote this letter. He evidently took Alcuin's advice, for Simeon notes that he was an abbot when he died in 799. The letter is No. 109 in Dümmler. It is translated in G. F. Browne, *Alcuin of York*, pp. 143–145.

To his beloved friend Osbald, Alcuin the deacon sends greeting.

I am displeased with you, because you did not obey me when two years ago I advised you in my letters to abandon lay life and serve God according to your vow. Behold now, a worse reputation and an unhappier cause has disordered your life. Turn again, however, turn again and fulfil what you vowed.

Seek out an opportunity to enter the service of God, lest you perish with the wicked men, if you are innocent of the blood of your lord. If, indeed, you are guilty in consent or in design, confess your sin and be reconciled with God and flee the society of criminals. Better for you is the friendship of God and the saints than of evildoers.

Do not pile sin upon sin by ravaging the land, by shedding blood. Consider how much blood of kings, princes and people has been shed through you or through your kinsfolk. An unhappy line, through which such great evils have befallen the country! Free yourself, I implore you by God, lest your soul perish in eternity. While you have light, run, hasten, hurry to the mercy of God, who is ready to receive the penitent and to console those that turn to him; lest there come to you a day when you would, and cannot. Do not allege to yourself the shame of abandoning what you have begun; it is a greater shame that your soul should perish for ever than that you desert impious men in the present. But, better still, if you can convert any of them from the evil they have perpetrated, do this diligently; that you may have the reward of your own repentance from evil and likewise that of another's. And this is the love which covers a multitude of sins;[1] and doing this, live happily and farewell in peace.

[1] I Peter iv. 8.

I beseech you, that this letter be very often read in your presence; that you may be mindful of yourself in God and may know how much care I, though now far removed, have for your welfare.

If you can at all exhort the race[1] among whom you are exiled concerning its salvation, do not neglect to do so; that you may the more quickly by the gift of God's grace attain also to your own salvation.

201. Extract from a letter of Alcuin to Charles the Great (796–797)

After some paragraphs of elaborate compliments, Alcuin describes his activities as a teacher at Tours, and asks for books to be sent for to York. This letter is No. 121 in Dümmler, and part is translated in G. F. Browne, *Alcuin of York*, pp. 202–204.

I, your Flaccus,[2] according to your exhortation and encouragement, am occupied in supplying to some under the roof of St. Martin the honey of the sacred Scriptures; am eager to inebriate others with the old wine of ancient learning; begin to nourish others on the fruits of grammatical subtlety; long to illumine some with the order of the stars, like the painted ceiling of a great man's house; becoming many things to many men,[3] that I may instruct many to the profit of the Holy Church of God and to the adornment of your imperial kingdom, that the grace of the Almighty be not void in me,[4] nor the bestowal of your bounty in vain.

But I, your servant, miss to some extent the rarer books of scholastic learning which I had in my own country through the excellent and devoted zeal of my master[5] and also through some toil of my own. I tell these things to your Excellency, in case it may perchance be agreeable to your counsel, which is most eager for the whole of knowledge, that I send some of our pupils to choose there what we need, and to bring into France the flowers of Britain; that not in York only there may be a "garden enclosed", but in Tours the "plants of Paradise with the fruit of the orchard", that the south wind may come and blow through the gardens by the River Loire, and the aromatical spices thereof may flow;[6] and finally, that there may come to pass what follows in the Canticle from which I have taken this metaphor: "Let my beloved come into his garden and eat the fruit of his apple-trees"; and he may say to his young men: "'Eat, friends, and drink and be inebriated, my dearly beloved.' I sleep, and my heart watcheth";[7] or that admonitory utterance of the prophet Isaiah on the teaching of wisdom: "All you that thirst, come to the waters. And you that have no money, make haste, buy and eat. Come ye: buy wine and milk without money and without any price."[8]

202: Letter of Alcuin to the Mercian Ealdorman Osbert (797)

The importance of this letter in which Alcuin expresses his views on Offa's rule and on contemporary events in Northumbria needs no demonstration. It is from William of Malmesbury (*De Gestis Regum*, ed. Stubbs, I, p. 73) that we know the name of the recipient, as the surviving versions have no name. The letter is No. 122 in Dümmler.

---

[1] The Picts.   [2] One of Alcuin's names for himself.   [3] Cf. I Corinthians ix. 22.
[4] Cf. I Corinthians xv. 10.   [5] Ethelbert, afterwards archbishop of York.
[6] Alcuin is borrowing the language of the Song of Songs, iv. 12 f.
[7] Song of Songs, iv. 16; v. 1 f.   [8] Isaiah lv. 1.

To the most venerable man, [Osbert] the 'patrician',[1] Albinus,[2] a humble deacon, sends greeting.

Mindful of your praiseworthy fidelity and of the friendship formerly agreed on between us, I was eager to send you this letter to remind you of my sentiments and my welfare; for being now at a distance, we have ceased to have the pleasure of personal intercourse and the intimacy of mutual discourse, because of the great distance and the raging storms of the sea.

I have heard that many things have befallen you which your heart may not endure without great grief. Nor has it been a special tribulation to you alone, but also to all the kingdom whose counsellor you should be, by the wisdom which God has granted you; as also very great misfortunes have befallen my people[3] from the treachery of evil men. Therefore, with the help of God, you ought to consider with much counsel and prudent foresight what can profit not only yourself, but also all the peoples of the English.

For times of tribulation are everywhere in our land, loyalty declining, truth silent, malice increasing, and arrogance adding to our miseries. Indeed, it is not now enough to follow the tracks of our forefathers either in dress, in feasts and in decent behaviour; but he who is more foolish than others contrives something new and unsuited to human nature and hateful to God, and soon almost the whole people strives with the utmost eagerness to follow it.

No wonder, when you see these evils, if your mind is dismayed and consumed with continuous grief. Yet put your hope in God, who till this day has brought you to many honours. And while you can profit the kingdom, peoples and races of the English with wise counsel, I by no means think it right for you to hide your talent in the earth or conceal the light of knowledge under a bushel;[4] but with careful consideration, distribute your alms and prayers through the places conferred on you by God, that you may have fruit in both ways, in brotherly compassion and ecclesiastical intercession.

For truly, as I think, that most noble young man[5] has not died for his own sins; but the vengeance for the blood shed by the father has reached the son. For you know very well how much blood his father shed to secure the kingdom on his son. This was not a strengthening of his kingdom, but its ruin. The wise man errs more than the fool, not regarding the goodness of the highest God, that he, who had granted him a son by the prayer of the saints, would preserve him also through works of piety.

Therefore admonish the more diligently your king,[6] and also the king of my country,[7] that they hold themselves in godliness, avoiding adulteries; and do not despise their former wives in order to commit adultery with women of the nobility; but under the fear of God either keep their own wives or with their consent hold themselves in chastity. I am afraid that our king, Eardwulf, must quickly lose the kingdom on account of the insult he did to God, dismissing his own wife, and publicly taking a concubine, as it is reported. Let your dearest king beware of this, that the

---

[1] See p. 244, n. 6.   [2] Alcuin.   [3] The Northumbrians.   [4] Matthew xxv. 25; v. 15.
[5] Ecgfrith, Offa's son who survived him only a few months.   [6] Cenwulf.
[7] Eardwulf of Northumbria.

divine clemency and protection may follow him and may grant him and his people long-lasting prosperity.

It partly seems that the happiness of the English is nearly at an end, unless perchance by assiduous prayers and decent ways and humility of life and chastity of behaviour and observance of faith they deserve to win from God the country which God conceded by his free gift to our forefathers. It is good that you should be in his counsels, if he is one who will obey you. But if not, correct your life and turn yourself the sooner to the service of God, that you may make safe your own soul, if you cannot those of many, because of the sins of the people. Let there be in you an example of all probity and moderation and sobriety and nobility of morals, so that those who see and hear you may ever be strengthened in good actions and in regard for the welfare of their souls. Little time remains to you in this life; work so that you may have eternal blessed days with Christ and his saints in everlasting ages.

Also admonish all the race of the Mercians diligently to observe the good, moderate and chaste customs, which Offa of blessed memory established for them; that they may have blessing from the Lord their God, and stability and strength for their kingdom against their enemies; and the bishops and servants of God to serve Christ in integrity and humility, and to preach to the people in the piety of the holy religion, and to set an example for good; that they may deserve to be heard by the Lord God Almighty in holy prayers for their people. And require the lay magnates to make just judgments for the people and lawful marriages, and to be faithful to their lord, and in agreement and unity among themselves.

For our kingdom, that is, that of the Northumbrians, almost perished from intestine dissensions and false oaths. And it seems to me that the end of their evil is not yet.

You, indeed, guard yourself, lest such things come about as you have seen already to have happened to them. But love the Lord God and keep his commands, that his blessing may be upon you, and you may be the protector of the country which the Lord God gave to our fathers. I had more to write to you from love of our country, but these few things suffice for your wisdom.

Greet the lord king peaceably with my words, if it can be done; and urge him to please God and adorn himself with good habits; and let him be zealous to prepare for himself out of an earthly kingdom the glory of the eternal kingdom.

Live happily and fare well in Christ, my dearest friend.

203. Letter of Alcuin to Æthelheard, archbishop of Canterbury (797)

Apart from the mention in the Anglo-Saxon Chronicle of a contentious synod in which Archbishop Jænberht lost part of his province (No. 1, p. 166), this is the first document in this volume to relate to the temporary elevation of Lichfield to an archiepiscopal see. On this matter, see General Introduction, pp. 91 f. Other documents concerned with this matter are Nos. 204, 205, 206, 209, 210. From this letter of Alcuin's, we see that the question of abolishing this third archbishopric was already under consideration and the question of the treatment of Hygeberht, its archbishop, was being discussed. Soon after Offa's death in 796 Kent had revolted against Cenwulf of Mercia, and Archbishop Æthelheard, whose Mercian sympathies had made him disliked by the men of Kent, had fled. Alcuin here censures him for this flight, and he had earlier in 797 written to the clergy and people of Kent exhorting them to recall their archbishop and warning them of the danger of viking attack in the midst of their internal dissensions (Dümmler, No. 129; Haddan and Stubbs, III, pp. 509–511). The present letter is No. 128 in Dümmler, and in Haddan and Stubbs, III, pp. 518–520.

To the man of supreme dignity and father of ecclesiastical excellence, Archbishop Æthelheard, his faithful son Alcuin sends greetings of perpetual affection in Christ.

Our son, returning by way of you, has delivered most sweet words of love, and had at the same time the gifts of your liberality in his hands. Delighted with these, I perceived that you held in memory the friendship we once agreed on, just as tested loyalty always shines clear in a perfect man. Wherefore I give thanks to your Excellency, wishing with all the desire of my heart that you may preside over the Christian people in long-lasting prosperity and exalt with fitting honours the holy see which for a time you deserted because of the impious usurpers of the kingdom, by the advice of the priests of Christ,[1] as the aforesaid pupil has told me.

Your venerable authority has thought fit to ask me by him about what I felt in this matter. What other is there for my insignificance to say than to agree with the counsel of the holy priests of Christ? Yet, if they have so great authority for the suggestion that the shepherd should flee when the wolf comes, as great is the superiority of the gospel, which calls him a hireling, not a shepherd, who timidly flees the fury of the wolf.[2] Perhaps they protest, since the Truth says: "If they shall persecute you in this city, flee into another."[3] But one ought to discern of what time of flight and of what persecution this was said, and that of these things the same Truth says again: "The good shepherd giveth his life for his sheep, but the hireling fleeth."[4] You will best understand this by reading for yourself in the homilies of the blessed Pope Gregory, our preacher. You are yourself aware for what cause you left your see; whether for fear of death or for the cruelty of torments or for the abomination of idolatry; as we read the most holy pontiff of the same see, Laurence, once wished to do, but being chastened by apostolic authority, repented of the plan he had begun.[5]

Yet, whatever was the cause, it seems good, to my loving consideration, that penance be done for it. And this, it seems, can be done fittingly, if by the common consent of the whole people a fast is declared—for you on account of the deserted see, for them on account of the error they have accepted—that God may be propitious to you all. Prayers also, and alms-giving and the celebration of Masses are to be zealously performed everywhere, that God may blot out whatever may have been done by any of you in this affair.

Also let your reverend wisdom especially bring into the house of God the zeal for reading, that there may be there young men reading, and a choir of singers, and the study of books, that the dignity of that holy church may be renewed by your diligence, that they may have among their own number him whom they can elect as their pontiff. And also let your preaching be done in all places, and before all the bishops in the general synod, concerning just ordinations and perseverence in preaching, and the ecclesiastical offices, and the sanctity of baptism, and the bestowal of alms, and the care of the poor throughout the various churches and parishes, especially among the venerable race over which God has chosen you to preside as pastor. Often

---

[1] The community of Christ Church, Canterbury.   [2] John x. 12 f.
[3] Matthew x. 23.   [4] John x. 11, 13.   [5] See No. 151, pp. 611 f.

the wounded soldier fights more bravely, just as the tired ox more surely plants its hooves.[1]

As the devil has been gladdened by your flight, act so that Christ may rejoice in the manifold progress of souls through you, and your reward may increase; that same Truth saying: "Even so there shall be joy in heaven before the angels of God over one sinner that doth penance more than over ninety-nine who need not penance."[2] Weighing all these things altogether most diligently, may you always advance in the love of Christ; loving him from your whole heart, with all your strength and with all your mind, who has exalted, honoured and preserved you in the day of your prosperity.

May you be zealous to do away with the most vain style of dress and the immoderate habit of feasting, as much as you can, from yourself, and your fellow-bishops, or, rather, from all the clergy and all grades of ecclesiastical orders. Blessed Peter, the Prince of the Apostles, washed away the triple stain of his denial with the three-fold truth of his confession;[3] wash you away your flight, done in simple error, by the multiple good of your preaching; that especially the study of the Holy Scriptures may be renewed through your most holy care, and the ecclesiastical dignity be exalted everywhere, and that the holy see which was the first in the faith may be the first in all wisdom and sanctity and honour, so that there the inquirer may discover and the ignorant learn what he desires, the learned see what he may praise.

And in order that the unity of the Church—which is in part torn asunder, not, as it seems, by reasonable consideration but by a certain desire for power—may, if it can be done, be peacefully united and the rent repaired, it seems right to take counsel of all the priests of Christ and of your fellow-bishop of the church of York; in such a way, however, that the pious father[4] be not deprived of the *pallium* in his lifetime, although the ordination of bishops is to revert to the holy and original see. May your holy wisdom weigh all these matters, that loving concord may result between the chief pastors of the churches of Christ.

If I have declared anything superfluously in these letters of mine, may your holy patience, I pray, receive it kindly, and not lay the blame on me, who write, but on yourself, who command. Nor have I acted with presumptuous boldness, but with humble obedience, weighing—what could profit many—whether there were, or were not, any blame in flight. However, as far as my devotion could decide, it is better to do what I suggest than to neglect it. Entirely in loving charity I advise you to preach constantly the word of God; this is your office, this your reward, this the fruits of your labour, this the dignity, praise and honour of a priest; to the end that you may appear in the sight of the Lord God by the multiple fruit of your labour, and be made worthy to hear the desirable words: "Well done, good and faithful servant, because thou hast been faithful over a few things, I will place thee over many things. Enter thou into the joy of thy Lord."[5]

May the Almighty God make you to prosper manifoldly in every perfect work for the exaltation of his Holy Church, most holy father.

---

[1] Dümmler points out that this proverb, which Alcuin also used in a letter of 791–792, occurs in the letters of St. Jerome. [2] Luke xv. 7.
[3] John xxi. 15–17. [4] Hygeberht, archbishop of Lichfield. [5] Matthew xxv. 21.

204. Letter of Cenwulf, king of Mercia, to Pope Leo III about the archiepiscopate of Lichfield (798)

Since none of the correspondence between England and Rome, before Offa took the step of creating a new archbishopric, has survived, it is only from the letters dealing with its abolition that we learn what led up to its foundation. (See pp. 91 f.) We learn from this letter that Offa was actuated by dislike of Jænberht, archbishop of Canterbury, and of the people of Kent. Cenwulf, in asking for the abolition of this archbishopric, clearly hints that London, not Canterbury, should be the seat of the southern metropolitan. He had tried in the previous year to raise the matter at Rome, but his messenger had been incompetent. He refers also to letters sent by Archbishop Æthelheard. These have not survived. Other documents dealing with this matter are Nos. 203, 205, 206, 209, 210. This letter is preserved only in William of Malmesbury, *De Gestis Regum* (ed. Stubbs, I, pp. 86-89). It is No. 287 in Birch, and in Haddan and Stubbs, III, pp. 521-523.

To the most blessed and truly most loving lord Leo, pontiff of the holy and apostolic Roman see, Cenwulf, by the grace of God king of the Mercians, with the bishops, ealdormen and every degree of dignity under our authority, sends greeting of sincerest love in Christ.

We ever give thanks to the Almighty God, who is wont to guide the Church, bought with his precious blood, ever with new leaders – the former leaders having been taken to eternal life – amidst the diverse storms of this world to the haven of safety, and to infuse it with new light that it may be darkened with no error of darkness, but may without stumbling tread the way of truth; hence the whole Church throughout the world justly rejoices, that, when the true Rewarder of all good men had led the most glorious shepherd of his flock, Hadrian, to be rewarded for ever above the skies, his kind providence yet raised up a leader for his sheep, no less skilled to lead the flock of the Lord to the fold of life. Also we, who dwell at the end of the world, in the same way justly glory beyond all others, that its sublimity is our safety its prosperity a perpetual source of exultation for us; because whence apostolic dignity came to you, thence came to us the truth of the faith. Therefore I think it fitting humbly to turn an obedient ear to your holy commands, and to fulfil with all endeavour what things seem to your Holiness to be incumbent on us; but to avoid and sometimes utterly renounce, those things which shall be found contrary to reason.

Now I, Cenwulf, king by the grace of God, humbly entreat your Excellency, that I may speak to you without offence to your mind, as I wish, about our progress, that you may receive me into the bosom of your goodness with tranquil peace, and the generous bounty of your benediction may enrich one, who is encouraged by no store of merits, in the ruling of his people; that the Almighty may uphold together with me my people, whom your apostolic authority has imbued with the rudiments of the faith, by your intercession, against the attacks of foreigners, and may deign to extend the kingdom which God himself gave us. This benediction all who before me were advanced to the sceptre of the Mercians deserved to receive from your predecessors; this I myself humbly beg, and from you, O most holy man, I desire to obtain, that you will especially receive me as your son by adoption, just as I love you in the person of a father, and always honour you with obedience with all my strength. For it is meet that holy faith be kept among such great persons, and inviolate love be guarded; for paternal piety is to be believed to be filial happiness in God, according to the saying of Hezekiah: "The father shall make thy truth known to the children,

O Lord."[1] In which words I implore you, loved father, that you will not refuse to make known to your son, although unworthy, the Lord's truth by your sacred words, that by your sound instruction, with the help of God, I may deserve to attain to a better way of life.

Moreover, most sweet father, I pray, with all our bishops and persons of whatever rank among us, that you will kindly reply to us concerning the inquiries of many kinds on which we deemed it fitting to consult your very great penetration; lest the traditions of the holy fathers, and the rules handed down by them to us, be corrupted in anything among us, as if unknown; but let your words come to us, sent in love and kindness, that by the mercy of God they may bring forth profitable fruit in us. And first is that our bishops and certain most learned men among us say that against the canons and apostolic decrees which were established for us by the direction of the most blessed Father Gregory, as you know, the authority of the metropolitan of Canterbury has been divided into two provinces, though twelve bishops ought by that same father's command to be subject to its rule, as is read throughout our churches in the letter which he sent to his brother and fellow-bishop Augustine, concerning the two metropolitan bishops of London and York, which I do not doubt you also possess.[2] But first that same highest pontifical dignity, which was then appointed for London with the honour and ornament of the *pallium*, was for his sake conferred and bestowed on Canterbury. For because Augustine, of blessed memory, who by Gregory's order preached the word of God to the nation of the English, and presided most gloriously over the churches of the Saxon land, died in that same city, and his body was buried in the church of the blessed Peter, Prince of the Apostles, which his successor Laurence consecrated, it seemed to all the wise men of our race that the metropolitan dignity should remain in that city where rests in the body he who planted in these parts the truth of the faith. The prime honour of this dignity, as you know, King Offa tried to remove and to disperse into two provinces, on account of the enmity he had formed against the venerable Jænberht and the people of Kent; and your most godly fellow-bishop and predecessor Hadrian at the request of the aforesaid king began to do what no one had presumed before and exalted the bishop of the Mercians with the *pallium*. But we blame neither of these, whom Christ, as we believe, honours with eternal victory. But yet we humbly implore your Excellency, on whom has been justly conferred the key of wisdom by God, to inquire into this matter with your wise men, and to deign to reply to us whatever it may seem to you that we ought to observe henceforth; that the coat of Christ, woven without seam,[3] may not suffer the rent of any dissension among us, but may as we wish be brought to the unity of true peace by your sound teaching. We have written this to you with great humility as well as affection, most blessed pope, entreating earnestly your clemency to reply kindly and justly to the things which we have of necessity displayed to you; and to deign to examine with pious love the letter in which Archbishop Æthelheard wrote to you in the presence of all our provincial bishops more fully about his own affairs and needs and those of all Britain; and to remember to make clear to us with the page of truth whatever the rule of faith requires concerning the

---

[1] Isaiah xxxviii. 19.   [2] No. 151, p. 601.   [3] John xix. 23.

matters which are written in that letter. Therefore I sent last year my embassy and that of my bishops by Abbot Wada; but though he accepted that embassy, he performed it lazily, nay foolishly. But now I send to you as a token of love a small gift by Byrne the priest and Cildas and Ceolberht my thegns, loved father, namely 120 mancuses, with my letter, praying you to accept them graciously and to deign to grant us your blessing.

May the Almighty God keep you safe for a long time to the praise of his Holy Church.

205. Pope Leo's reply to Cenwulf's letter (798)

This letter, which survives in Brit. Mus. Cott. Vespas. A xiv, is in reply to No. 204. We learn from it that in spite of the contentious synod on the matter, Offa told the pope that the English were unanimous in wishing for the Lichfield archbishopric. The pope shows here that he has grasped Cenwulf's implication about removing the metropolitan dignity from Canterbury to London, but refuses to consent. Offa's payment to Rome mentioned in this letter has sometimes been regarded as the origin of Peter's Pence; but see F. M. Stenton, *Anglo-Saxon England*, p. 215, n. The text of this letter is bad and its rendering uncertain in places. It is No. 288 in Birch, No. 127 in Dümmler, and in Haddan and Stubbs, III, pp. 523–525.

To the most excellent lord his son Cenwulf, king of the Mercians, and all the most beloved bishops and most glorious ealdormen, Pope Leo.

We have received your writings through the bearers of these letters of your renowned Excellency, namely Byrne the priest and Cildas and Ceolberht the thegns; and reading them, we have found them full of faith and strengthened by the ancient tradition regarding the blessed Peter, Prince of the Apostles and his vicar. And as the most Christian kings your predecessors always drank the fount of truth and the irreproachable and orthodox faith from that same Church of the blessed Peter, so also your Excellency, truly possessing it as a protectress and instructress, must honour and maintain it to the end. Since you have inquired whence it happened that Pope Hadrian, of blessed memory, our predecessor, diminished contrary to custom the authority of the bishop of Canterbury,[1] and by his authority confirmed the division into two archiepiscopal sees, to that we truly reply that he did this for no other reason than because your most excellent king, Offa, testified in his letter that it was the united wish and unanimous petition of you all, both on account of the vast size of your lands and the extension of your kingdom, and also for many more reasons and advantages. For these reasons chiefly did the lord apostolic Hadrian send the dignity of the *pallium* to the bishop of the Mercians. As for what was said in your letter asking us if the authority of the supreme pontificate could by canonical consent be situated in the city of London, where Augustine received the dignity of the *pallium* sent by St. Gregory, we by no means dare to give to them the authority of the supreme pontificate; but as that primacy was established at Canterbury, we concede and pronounce it by our decree the first see; because our holy and venerable predecessor Pope Celestinus instructed us, saying: "Let there be no vainglory; let those who are bishops obey by episcopal custom those who have the *pallium*."[2] And therefore according to the canons it is right that it should be, and be called, the primacy, and in the order that was arranged by our predecessors, thus be venerated

---

[1] Jænberht.   [2] Mansi, *Sacrorum Conciliorum . . . collectio*, iv. 467, c. 6.

and honoured as the archiepiscopal see in all things. And concerning that letter which the most reverend and holy Æthelheard sent to us, just as your Excellency requested, perusing it more plainly, as was fitting, we have sent a reply more clearly to his Holiness: that as regards that apostate cleric who mounted to the throne,[1] we, accounting him like Julian the Apostate, excommunicate and reject him, having regard to the safety of his soul. For if he still should persist in that wicked behaviour, be sure to inform us quickly, that we may send the apostolic reminder to all in general, both to princes and to all people dwelling in the island of Britain, exhorting them to expel him from his most wicked rule and procure the safety of his soul. For on account of a king of this kind,[2] we have very greatly blessed and praised our brother the aforesaid archbishop, because he endangered his life for the orthodox faith.

Knowing you to be fruitful in all good works, we recall to your mind with full knowledge how King Offa of blessed memory, for the victories of the kingdom which he held by the support of St. Peter, possessing and honouring him as his standard-bearer and comrade in that same kingdom, made a vow before a synod of all the bishops and ealdormen and chief men and all the people dwelling in the island of Britain, and also of our most faithful legates the most holy bishops George and Theophylact,[3] to that same Apostle of God, the blessed Peter, keeper of the keys of the Kingdom of Heaven, that he would send every year as many mancuses as the year had days, that is, 365, to that same Apostle of the Church of God, for the support of the poor and the provision of lights; which he did, both for himself and for his successors who continue in that kingdom, for ever in perpetuity, on account of the victory of that same kingdom, since the blessed Peter conceded it by his gracious favours. And if your Excellency wishes to have ampler victories and honours in that same kingdom, paying the same contribution, let it remain likewise confirmed more amply by your Excellency in perpetuity, that that Apostle of God may always grant victory through you in that kingdom, and may cause you to reign in eternal life with his saints for ever.

206. Letter of Alcuin to Charles the Great (801)

This letter shows Alcuin's continued concern with the affairs of his native land. Among the English-men it recommends to the king on their way to Rome is Archbishop Æthelheard, whose visit was connected with the suppression of the Mercian archbishopric of Lichfield, on which see pp. 91 f., and Nos. 203–205, 209, 210. The Torhtmund who accompanies him is the Northumbrian nobleman who had avenged the murder of King Ethelred of Northumbria in 796, on which see No. 3, p. 248, No. 198. Alcuin expresses approval of his act, for the vendetta was the only means recognized by Anglo-Saxon law of punishing homicide. This letter is No. 231 in Dümmler, and is in Haddan and Stubbs, III, p. 533.

To the most beloved lord, King David,[4] Flaccus[5] your pensioner sends eternal greeting in Christ.

The sweetness of your love and trust in your well-proved kindness often encourage me to send letters to your Highness, and to perform by means of writing what the

---

[1] Eadberht Præn. Cf. No. 1, pp. 167f.; No. 3, p. 249.
[2] The manuscript reads *regi* corrected to *rege*. Stubbs suggested amending to *re* or *negotio*.
[3] See No. 191.
[4] The name by which Charles the Great was known in the circle of the Palace School.
[5] Alcuin uses two Latin nicknames, this and Albinus.

frailty of my body prevents my will from fulfilling. But recent matters which have arisen force me again to produce new letters, that this document may express my heartfelt affection and pour out to your Grace's ears entreaties, which never, I truly own, were made in vain in your merciful sight. Nor do I believe that my entreaties for your security and safety are made in vain in the sight of God; for the divine grace willingly accepts the tears which flow from the fount of love.

I have been told that some friends of your Flaccus wish to approach your Grace: namely Æthelheard, metropolitan of the church of Canterbury and pontiff of the first see in Britain; and a former thegn of King Offa, Ceolmund by name, from the king-dom of the Mercians; and also Torhtmund, the faithful servant of King Ethelred, a man proved in loyalty, strenuous in arms, who has boldly avenged the blood of his lord. They were all very true friends to me and were my helpers on my journey and protectors of my pupils as they hastened hither and thither. On their behalf I implore your great clemency to receive them with your accustomed kindness, for they were very close friends to me, each in his place.

I have often noticed that religious priests, devoted to the service of Christ, and brave and loyal men in the secular ranks, are held in esteem by your just mind. For there is no doubt that every good man, approved by his own conscience, loves the good, taught by the example of Almighty God, who is the highest good. And it is most certain that every rational creature, in as far as it has good, has it illumined by his goodness, the same Truth saying: "I am the light of the world. He that followeth me walketh not in darkness, but shall have the light of life."[1]

May the grace of Christ grant you perpetual light, together with the saints, David beloved of God.

207. Letter of Alcuin to Eanbald II, archbishop of York (801)

This letter should be compared with No. 206. It includes also some interesting references to Northumbrian affairs. It is No. 232 in Dümmler, and in Haddan and Stubbs, III, pp. 534–536.

To the son of his desires, Simeon[2] the bishop, Albinus sends greeting.

When that religious man, your fellow-bishop Æthelheard, was on his way to Rome, my messenger met him at St. Judoc's.[3] As he asked me previously in his letter, and again there, he was kindly received according to his wish, having with him two other bishops[4] and our friends Ceolmund and Torhtmund. I sent letters to my lord, King David, for their comfort.

Among other things which the aforesaid venerable father had informed me in his letters, he made known to me your troubles. For which reason I was eager to send to your love these letters of consolation, praying you to act valiantly in the sight of God and be of good courage. It is not always night nor always day, but they take their turns; so also the adversity and prosperity of this world. Today the tempest threatens, but tomorrow fair weather smiles. Let the anchor of hope be fixed in Christ. He who rejoices in prosperity, let him fear adversity; and he who is fatigued

---

[1] John viii. 12.   [2] Alcuin's name for Eanbald.   [3] Saint-Josse-sur-mer.
[4] The Anglo-Saxon Chronicle, 799 (for 801), says that Cyneberht, bishop of the West Saxons, accom-panied Æthelheard.

with adversity, let him hope that prosperity will come quickly. Gold will not be of perfect beauty until it is tried in the furnace of the fire.

I think that part of your trouble arises from your own fault. You perhaps receive the king's enemies or protect the possessions of his enemies. If indeed you suffer justly, why are you disturbed? If, however, unjustly, why not remember the saints? "You have heard of the tribulations of Job", says James the Apostle, "and you have seen the end of the Lord."[1] He who shares in the tribulation of the saints, will also share in the glory.

Do not think of flight, but hope for the crown. Stand bravely in the front line like a standard-bearer of the army of Christ. If he who bears the standard flees, what does the army do? If the trumpet is silent in the camp, who prepares himself for battle? If the leader is afraid, how shall the soldier be saved? The Apostle says: "You have not yet resisted unto blood, and you have forgotten the consolation. God chastiseth every son whom he receiveth."[2] The son ought not to be saddened by the chastisement of paternal kindness. "The sinner shall gnash upon the just man", says the Scripture, "but the Lord shall break in pieces their teeth",[3] and he brings to nothing their attack. Read diligently, how the old man Mathathias, in the very hour of his death, exhorted his sons to act valiantly and fight strongly against the adversaries of God;[4] and how the saints were crowned through tribulations; and–I will not say how small–but how null is the glory of a sinner. He said among other things: "Fear not the words of a sinful man; for his glory is dung and worms; today he is lifted up and tomorrow he shall not be found; because he is returned into his earth and his thought is come to nothing."[5]

Nor is it necessary to look for examples from far distant times, when you have present ones in plenty. You yourself have seen how kings perished, princes who were opposed to your predecessors and the Church of Christ. Does God sleep in their crimes, because they think they can rage with impunity, and think not that the eye of God watches over their madness? They became fools in their wisdom,[6] not fearing the judgment of God. Your patience and goodwill is indeed to pray for them, in case by chance God may give them penitence, and they may from enemies become friends of God. But if their perdition is determined, your Holiness will by no means be without the reward of eternal happiness. Like smoke their pride vanishes, and your patience shines like light in perfect day.

I implore that the reading of this letter may strengthen your mind to act valiantly and stand stoutly in the front rank of the army of Christ. Who should fear, when Christ is leading and going before the troops of his battle? He carried before his Cross to the Passion, ready to suffer for the salvation of the world; calling to all: "If any man will come after me, let him deny himself and take up his cross and follow me."[7] "I am the light of the world; he that followeth me walketh not in darkness, but shall have the light of life."[8] "I am the way, the truth and the life."[9] Strengthened by these testimonies, run with intrepid foot after Christ, that you may deserve to have his mercy in eternity.

---

[1] James v. 11.   [2] Hebrews xii. 4–6.   [3] Psalm xxxvi. 12: lvii. 7.   [4] I Maccabees ii. 49 ff.
[5] I Maccabees ii. 62 f.   [6] Cf. Romans i. 22.   [7] Matthew xvi. 24.   [8] John viii. 12.   [9] John xiv. 6.

I know that my day has approached, and I rejoice to have you surviving me. Do you truly for my soul as a faithful son for a father.

And as I told Cuculus[1] to tell your Holiness, so have I done:[2] desiring by the mercy of God, to live quiet in Christ, who says: "learn of me, because I am meek and humble of heart, and you shall find rest to your souls".[3]

May the highest grace of God accompany you in all your way, defend, rule and govern you, my son, my most loved son.

208. Letter of Alcuin to his pupils Calvinus and Cuculus (801)

This letter should be compared with No. 207. It throws some interesting light on conditions in Northumbria. Calvinus is called elsewhere (Dümmler, No. 209) 'priest and monk of St. Stephen's', but the location of this house is unknown; Cuculus 'cuckoo' received a letter of admonition (Dümmler, No. 66) and a poem against over-indulgence in wine (*Mon. Germ. Hist., Poet. Lat. Carol. Ævi*, I, p. 269). This nickname may refer to Alcuin's pupil Dodo. This letter is No. 233 in Dümmler; most of it is translated in G. F. Browne, *Alcuin of York*, pp. 168 f.

Albinus sends greeting to Calvinus and Cuculus, his dearest sons. I have heard of the tribulations of our dear son, Simeon.[4] Exhort him to act faithfully and not be faint-hearted in trials. Such were his predecessors accustomed to suffer; not they only, but indeed all the saints. John the Baptist, we read, was killed for testifying the truth. Let him take care that there be in him no other cause of trial than his preaching of the truth.

I am afraid that he is suffering to some extent for his landed possessions or for harbouring the king's enemies. Let his own possessions suffice him; let him not strive after those of others, which often result in peril for their possessors. While he may think he is benefiting a few, he is injuring many for whom he ought daily to intercede, and he may harm the flock which he ought to govern.

And what does he want with such a number of thegns in his retinue? He seems to maintain them out of pity. He is harming the monastic folk who receive him with his following. He has, as I hear, far more than his predecessors had. Moreover, they too have more of the common sort, that is, low-born soldiers, than is fitting, under them. Our master[5] allowed no one of his followers to have more than one such, except for the heads of his household, who had two only. That pity is imprudent that benefits a few—and those perhaps criminals—and harms many—and those good men. Let him not reproach me, who suggest such things, but amend himself, who does them.

As I have said to Cuculus, I have laid down the burden of the pastoral care and sit quiet at St. Martin's, watching for when the voice shall come: "Open to him who knocks, follow him who commands, hearken to him who judges." May your holy solicitude by the grace of God aid me that day to escape. And admonish all our friends to remember us in their holy prayers; and most of all, in whom I especially trust, our son, Archbishop Simeon. May God be gracious to him in this life, that he may deserve to receive future beatitude with the saints of God.

Live happily, dearest sons, into eternity.

Greet Credulus and our other friends with kindness in our name.

[1] See No. 208.   [2] *i.e.* given up the charge of his abbey at Tours.
[3] Matthew xi. 29.   [4] Archbishop Eanbald II of York.   [5] Archbishop Ethelbert of York.

209. Letter of Pope Leo III to Æthelheard, archbishop of Canterbury (18 Jan. 802)

In this letter, preserved only by William of Malmesbury, the pope finally acknowledges the right of Canterbury to the whole of its former province, thus abolishing the archbishopric of Lichfield, on which see pp. 91 f. and Nos. 203–206, 210. It is in William of Malmesbury, De Gestis Pontificum, ed. Hamilton, p. 57, and is No. 305 in Birch, and in Haddan and Stubbs, III, pp. 536f.

Leo, bishop, servant of the servants of God, to Æthelheard, archbishop of Canterbury, for ever.[1]

It eminently accords with the pontifical discretion to give a hearing to the prelates of the Churches according to their irreproachable faith, and to allow the performance of the things which they have desired to accomplish, through the blessed Peter, Prince of the Apostles, and through us, and which are not opposed to canonical decrees; that, when they obtain what they desire, they may become more ardent in their love of religion. And thus we ought to advise and instruct your brotherly goodness, for the sake of the dioceses of England committed to you, that is, of the bishops and monasteries, whether of monks, canons, or nuns; just as your church held them in ancient times, as we have learnt from investigations in our sacred archives, so we confirm that they should be held by you and your successors.

The holy and noble preacher Gregory ordained and confirmed according to orthodoxy, that all the churches of the English were to be subject for ever to blessed Archbishop Augustine, his chaplain,[2] by the sacred use of the *pallium*. And, therefore, by the authority of the blessed Peter, Prince of the Apostles–to whom was granted by the Lord God the power of binding and loosing, when he said: "That thou art Peter, and upon this rock I will build my church. And the gates of hell shall not prevail against it. And I will give thee the keys of the kingdom of heaven. And whatsoever thou shalt bind upon earth it shall be bound also in heaven; and whatsoever thou shalt loose on earth, it shall be loosed also in heaven"[3]–and moreover according to the established judgment of the holy canons, we, holding though witnout merit the office of the same Peter, keeper of the keys of heaven, concede to you Æthelheard and to your successors all the churches of the English just as they were from former times, to be held for ever in your same metropolitan see by inviolable right, with due acknowledgment of subjection.

If indeed anyone–which we do not wish–shall attempt to contravene the authority of our decision and apostolic privilege, we have decided by apostolic authority that, if he is an archbishop or bishop, he is to be cast out from the order of the episcopate. Likewise if it be a priest or deacon or other minister whatever of the sacred ministry, he is to be deposed from his order. And if it is one of the number of laymen, whether king or prince, or any person of high rank or low, he is to know himself separated from participation in the sacred communion. We grant by the authority of the blessed Peter, Prince of the Apostles, whose ministry we discharge, the document of this privilege to you, Æthelheard, and to your successors to be held for ever.

[1] This phrase often replaces a greeting in solemn papal documents.
[2] *sincellus*, the sharer of his private room, a sort of confidential secretary.
[3] Matthew xvi. 18, 19.

For its security we have subscribed with our own hand and ordered it to be signed with our name. We also order it to be written by our notary[1] Sergius in the month of January.

Given on 18 January by the hand of Eustace, chief of the notaries[2] of the holy apostolic see, in the reign of the lord, Charles, the most pious consul, crowned Augustus by God, great and peaceable emperor, in the second year after the consulate of the same lord, the tenth indiction.

210. Decree of the synod of "Clofesho" of 803, abolishing the archbishopric of Lichfield

This is the conclusion of the negotiations described on pp. 91 f. (See also Nos. 203–206, 209.) It has come down on a ninth-century parchment, Brit. Mus. Cott. Augustus II. 61, which is facsimiled *Brit. Mus. Facs.* II, pl. 6. It is No. 185 in Kemble, No. 310 in Birch, and in Haddan and Stubbs, III, pp. 542–544.

Glory to God in the highest, and on earth peace to men of goodwill. ✠ We know indeed that it is known and manifest to many who faithfully trust in God, and yet nothing in it seems pleasing to those who belong to the English peoples, that Offa, king of the Mercians, presumed in the days of Archbishop Jænberht with very great fraud to divide and cut asunder the honour and unity of the see of St. Augustine our father in the city of Canterbury; and how, after the death of the aforesaid pontiff, his successor, Archbishop Æthelheard, by the gift of the grace of God, happened after the passage of years to visit the thresholds of the Apostles and Leo, the most blessed pope of the apostolic see, about many of the rights of the churches of God. Among other necessary matters of business he related also the division that had wrongfully been made of the archiepiscopal see; and the apostolic pope, as he heard and understood that it had been done wrongfully, immediately made a decree by the privilege of his authority, and sent to Britain and ordered that the honour of the see of St. Augustine should be completely restored with all its dioceses, according as St. Gregory, the apostle and teacher of our race, had arranged, and should be given back in all things to the honourable Archbishop Æthelheard when he returned to his country; and Cenwulf, the pious king of the Mercians, carried this out along with his councillors, in the year of our Lord's incarnation 803, the eleventh indiction, on 12 October.

I, Archbishop Æthelheard, with all the twelve bishops subordinate to the holy see of the blessed Augustine, command by the apostolic injunctions of the lord Pope Leo, in the synod held in the famous place which is called *Clofesho*, with the unanimous advice of all the holy synod, in the name of the Almighty God and of all his saints, and by his fearful judgment, that never shall kings or bishops or ealdormen or men of any tyrannical power presume to diminish the honour of St. Augustine and his holy see, or to divide it in the slightest extent, but it shall always remain most fully in

---

[1] *scriniarius*, literally keeper of the archives, but these officials also acted as secretaries and wrote the papal letters.
[2] *primicerius*. On this important official, whose full title was *primicerius notariorum*, see R. L. Poole, *Studies in the Papal Chancery*, pp. 14–17, 55–57.

all things in that honour and dignity in which it certainly is held in the constitution of
the blessed Gregory and in the privileges of his apostolic successors, and also as is
considered right in the decrees of the holy canons. Now also, with the co-operation
of God and the lord apostolic, Pope Leo, I, Archbishop Æthelheard, and the others
our fellow-bishops and with us all the dignitaries of the synod, unanimously confirm
with the sign of the Cross of Christ the primacy of the holy see; commanding this also
and writing with the sign of the Holy Cross: that an archiepiscopal see shall never be
placed from this time in the church of Lichfield, nor in any place anywhere except
only in the city of Canterbury, where is the church of Christ, and where first the
catholic faith shone forth in this island, and holy baptism was celebrated by St.
Augustine. Moreover, we pronounce, with the consent and permission of the lord
apostolic, Pope Leo, that the charter sent from the Roman see by Pope Hadrian about
the *pallium* and the archiepiscopal see in the church of Lichfield is invalid, because it
was obtained by deception and misleading suggestion; and therefore by the manifest
tokens of the heavenly king we have decreed that the supremacy of archiepiscopal rule
is to remain, with canonical and apostolic support, where the holy gospel of Christ
was first preached in the province of the English by the blessed Father Augustine, and
was then by the grace of the Holy Spirit spread widely abroad. If, indeed, anyone in
defiance of the apostolic injunctions and those of us all dare to cut the coat of Christ
and divide the unity of the Holy Church of God, let him know that he is damned
eternally unless he makes fitting amends for what he wickedly did against the holy
canons.

Here are the names of the holy bishops and abbots who confirmed the afore-
written chirograph in the synod which was held at *Clofesho*, in the year from the
coming of the Lord 803, with the sign of the Holy Cross of Christ.

✠ Æthelheard, archbishop.

✠ Ealdwulf, bishop.[1]

✠ Werenberht, bishop.[2]

✠ Ealhheard, bishop.[3]

✠ Wigberht, bishop.[4]

✠ Ealhmund, bishop.[5]

✠ Osmund, bishop.[6]

✠ Eadwulf, bishop.[7]

✠ Deneberht, bishop.[8]

✠ Wihthun, bishop.[9]

✠ Tidferth, bishop.[10]

✠ Wulfheard, bishop.[11]

✠ Ealhmund, priest and abbot.

✠ Beonna, priest and abbot.

✠ Forthred, priest and abbot.

✠ Wigmund, priest and abbot.

[1] Of Lichfield.   [2] Of Leicester.   [3] Of Elmham.   [4] Of Sherborne.   [5] Of Winchester.
[6] Of London   [7] Of Lindsey.   [8] Of Worcester.   [9] Of Selsey.   [10] Of Dunwich.
[11] Of Hereford.

(d) VERNACULAR VERSE

211. "The Wanderer"

This is one of the best known of Old English poems, and has been variously regarded. Some scholars have seen in it a heathen poem to which a perfunctory Christian colouring has been given by additions at the beginning and end; others, with whom I associate myself, see in the Christian message the purpose of the poem. To those who hold the second view, the title, which goes back to Thorpe, seems inadequate: 'Mutability' has been suggested as an alternative, though I might prefer something like 'True Security'. The poet considers first the lot of a lordless man, for whom all earthly security and happiness is ended by his lord's death, and then ponders on the vanishing of older and mightier civilizations, brought home to the English by the presence of majestic ruins of the Roman period. He concludes, after an *ubi sunt* passage similar to many in the homilies, that all earthly ties are fleeting, and only by the man who puts his trust in God is security to be found. It is not only at the beginning and end that Christian references occur. It is 'the Creator of men' who has brought to ruin a mighty residence, and so the decay of older empires must be regarded as part of the divine scheme of things. Whichever way one regards the poem, its value as an emotional expression of the loyalty of a man to his lord remains unimpaired. Like most Old English poetry, the poem cannot be exactly dated.

Innumerable readers and books of selections include this poem, and there are also editions of the whole manuscript, the Exeter Book, which contains it, *e.g.* by I. Gollancz, for the Early Eng. Text Soc., 1895, by G. P. Krapp and E. van K. Dobbie, *The Anglo-Saxon Poetic Records*, III (1936). Among readers may be mentioned Sweet's *Anglo-Saxon Reader*, 12th edit. rev. C. T. Onions (1952), A. J. Wyatt, *An Anglo-Saxon Reader* (1919), and N. Kershaw, *Anglo-Saxon and Norse Poems* (1922). This includes a translation, as does Gollancz's edition mentioned above, and A. S. Cook and C. B. Tinker, *Select Translations from Old English Poetry* (Boston, 1902).

Often a solitary man experiences the mercy of the Lord, though sad at heart he must long row over the rime-cold sea and traverse the paths of exile. Fate is inexorable [?].

Thus spoke a wanderer, mindful of hardships, of cruel slaughters, the fall of kinsmen:

"Oft, alone, I had to lament my sorrow every dawn. There is now no one living to whom I dare reveal openly my thoughts. In truth, I know that it is a noble virtue in a man to bind fast the locks of his heart, to guard the treasure-chamber of his heart, think as he will. The weary-hearted cannot oppose fate, nor can the troubled mind afford help. Therefore those eager for good repute often bind fast sad thoughts in their breast. Thus, distraught with care, deprived of my country, far from my noble kinsmen, I often had to bind my heart with fetters, since years ago the darkness of earth covered my generous lord, and abject and with a wintry heart I went thence over the expanse of the waves, sadly seeking the hall of a giver of treasure, where, far or near, I could find someone to show favour to me in the mead-hall, to comfort me in my friendlessness, and draw me to him with delights."[1]

He who experiences it knows how dire a comrade is grief to the man who has few beloved confidants. The track of exile holds him, not twisted gold, a frozen heart, not the riches of the earth. He recalls the retainers and the receiving of treasure, how in his youth his generous lord entertained him with feasting; joy has all passed away. For this he knows who must long forgo the counsel of his dear lord, when sorrow and sleep together lay hold on the wretched solitary man, that it seems in his mind

[1] It is by no means obvious where the wanderer's speech is meant to end, and many editors take the next two paragraphs as part of it.

that he is embracing and kissing his liege lord, and laying hands and head on his knee, as sometimes in days of yore he enjoyed the bounty from the throne. Then the friendless man awakens; he sees before him the dark waves, the seabirds dipping, and spreading their wings, frost and snow falling, mingled with hail. Then the wounds of his heart are the heavier, in grief for his loved one. Sorrow is renewed when the memory of his kinsmen passes through his mind; he greets them joyously and scans them eagerly. The companions of men vanish away; the troop of sailors does not bring back there many familiar speeches.[1] Care is renewed to the man who must repeatedly send over the waves a weary heart.

Therefore I can think of no reason in this world why my heart should not be darkened, when I consider all the life of men, and how the proud retainers suddenly left the hall. Thus this world, each and every day, droops and declines.

Therefore a man cannot become wise before he has a share of years in the earthly kingdom. A wise man is patient, he is not too passionate nor too hasty in speech, neither too feeble a warrior nor too rash, not too timid nor too jubilant nor too avaricious, and never too ready to boast ere he has full knowledge. A high-spirited man must wait when making a boast, until he knows well whither the thoughts of his heart will turn. A prudent man perceives how terrible it will be when all the wealth of this world shall stand desolate, just as now there stand in various places throughout this world walls beaten on by the winds, covered with frost, dwellings in ruins.[2] The banqueting halls crumble, the rulers lie bereft of revelry; the host has all fallen, proudly by the wall. Some war destroyed, bore them on their way hence; the bird bore off one over the high sea; one the grey wolf tore when dead;[3] one a sad-faced warrior hid in a grave. Thus the Creator of men laid waste this habitation, until, bereft of the revelry of the citizens, the old works of the giants[4] stood empty.

He who pondered wisely on this ruined site, and meditates deeply on this dark life, wise in spirit, remembers many slaughters afar back, and speaks these words:

"What has become of the steed? What has become of the warrior? What has become of the seats of banquet? Where are the joys of the hall? O for the bright cup! O for the mailclad warrior! O for the glory of the prince! How that time has passed away and grown dark under the cover of night, as if it had never been. All that stands on the track of the beloved host is a wall wondrous high, marked with serpent-forms.[5] The might of spears, these weapons eager for slaughter, and the glorious fate, have carried off the nobles; and storms beat on these heaps of stone, a falling snowstorm binds the earth; and the terror of winter, when the dark shadow of night comes lowering, sends the fierce hailstorm from the north in hostility to men. All the kingdom of earth is full of hardship; the decree of the fates changes the world beneath the heavens. Here wealth is transitory, here a

[1] This part of the poem is very obscure and the translation doubtful.
[2] Or perhaps, 'storm-beaten'.
[3] This passage probably is a version of the convention by which birds of prey and wolves form part of any battle-piece.
[4] This term is used in verse of works of the Roman or pre-Roman period.
[5] Variously interpreted, as referring to carved or painted patterns on the walls of the ruin, or, taking the first element as *wurma*, *wyrma*, a red or purple dye, as parallel to the *readfah* 'red-stained' in a poem called *The Ruin*.

friend is transitory, here a liegeman[1] is transitory, here a kinsman is transitory. The whole structure of this earth will become empty."

So spoke the wise in heart; he sat apart in meditation. Good is he who keeps his faith. A man must never too readily reveal the grief of his heart, unless he knows beforehand how to remedy it bravely. Well will it be with him who seeks grace and consolation from the Father in heaven, where for us all that security lies.

212. From "The Seafarer"

This popular poem has been variously interpreted. Some have seen it as a dialogue between an old and a young sailor, contrasting the hardship of seafaring with its irresistible appeal, others as a monologue of a man who is moved by the latter in spite of sufferings at sea. To holders of either view the latter part of the poem seems to be an irrelevant didactic addition. It has also been suggested that the poem is an allegory, in which the voyage represents both "the life of the pious on earth" and "life on the road to Eternity, and in this sense also death" (O. S. Anderson, *The Seafarer: An Interpretation*). In my opinion the poem is a unity, but not an allegory. The speaker represents the point of view of the hundreds of men and women who felt impelled "for the love of God" or "for the sake of the heavenly country" to undertake again and again pilgrimages and exile across the sea, renouncing the pleasures of ease and security in their native land. (See D. Whitelock, in *The Early Cultures of North-Western Europe*, H. M. Chadwick Memorial Studies, pp. 259–272.) In this case the second part, dealing with the transitory nature of human glory, is a closely connected theme.

The authorities are the same as for *The Wanderer*, except that the second volume of the Exeter Book is edited for the Early Eng. Text Soc., by W. S. Mackie, and that there is a translation in Anderson, *op. cit.*

I can utter a true lay about myself, relating my journeys, how I often endured days of toil and a time of hardship, and have felt bitter care at heart, explored in my ship many abodes of distress, the dire tossing of the waves. There the anxious night-watch often found me at the prow of my ship when it was dashing against the cliffs. My feet were nipped with cold and numbed by the icy bonds of frost; passionate care sighed in my heart; hunger within tore the spirit of one weary of the sea. The man whose lot is cast most pleasantly on land cannot conceive how I dwelt in winter on the ice-cold sea, distraught with care on the paths of exile, deprived of my friendly kinsmen, and hung with icicles. The hail flew in showers. There I heard nothing but the roar of the sea, the ice-cold waves, and sometimes the song of the swan. For my entertainment I had the cry of the gannet, and the sound of the godwit instead of the laughter of men, the singing seamew instead of mead-drinking. Storms beat on the rocky cliffs, and the icy-feathered tern gave answer; full often shrieked the dewy feathered eagle. No protecting kinsman could comfort my desolate heart. Hence he who has experienced the joy of life in great houses, and few calamities, proud and flushed with wine, scarcely believes how wearily I must often linger on the ocean-path. The shadow of night lowered, snow came from the north, and frost bound the earth; hail, coldest of grains, fell on the ground.

My heart's thoughts constrain me to venture on the deep seas, on the tumult of the salt waves; at all times my heart's desire urges my spirit to travel, that I may seek the land of foreigners afar off; because there is no man on earth so high-hearted, nor so liberal with his gifts, nor so bold in his youth, nor so daring in his deeds, nor having so gracious a lord, that he will not always feel anxiety over his voyage, as to what is

[1] Assuming that 'man' in this context refers to the tie between a man and his lord.

the Lord's purpose for him. He will have no mind for the harp, nor for the receiving of rings, no pleasure in woman nor delight in the world, nor mind for anything else, except the tossing of the waves, but he who puts out to sea has always yearning.

The groves blossom, cities grow fair, the fields become beautiful, the world's astir. All these things urge on to his journey the man eager of heart, urge on the spirit of him who thus intends to depart far on the paths of the sea. Likewise the cuckoo with its mournful note urges him, the herald of summer sings, forebodes bitter sorrow in his heart. The man living happily in luxury does not know what some endure, those who journey furthest on the paths of exile.

My thoughts are now roaming beyond the confines of my breast; with the ocean flood my spirit roams widely over the surface of the earth, over the whale's domain, and comes back to me eager and hungry; in its solitary flight it calls urgently, irresistibly impels my heart on the whale's path across the expanse of the seas; because dearer to me are the joys of the Lord than this dead life, transitory on earth: I do not believe that earthly happiness will endure for ever.

Ever one of three things brings uncertainty to each before his lifetime is done; sickness or age or the sword's hate will take life from the man doomed to depart. Therefore for every man the best of epitaphs, the praise of those who live on and speak of him afterwards, is that by kind acts[1] on earth against the enmity of fiends, by brave deeds against the devil, he bring it to pass before he must go on his way, that the sons of men will praise him afterwards, and his praise shall live for ever among the angels, the glory of eternal life, joy among the hosts of heaven.

Gone are the days of old, and all the glory of the earthly kingdom. There are now no kings or emperors, or treasure-givers, as once there were, when they performed among themselves the greatest of glorious deeds and lived in the most lordly splendour. All this noble company is fallen, its joys have vanished; weaker men now live and hold this earth, enjoy it by toil.

Glory is brought low; the grandeur of the earth grows old and withers, just as does each man now throughout the world. Age comes on him, his face grows pale; the grey-haired one grieves, knowing his former friends, sons of nobles, given to the earth. Nor, when his life fails, can his body swallow delicacies, nor feel pain, nor move a hand, nor think with the brain. Although a brother will strew the grave with gold for his brother born, bury him beside the dead with various treasures, that will not[2] go with him; nor can gold be a help to the soul which is full of sins against the dread [judgment] of God, when he hides it beforehand, while he lives here [on earth].

Great is the dread of the Lord, for the world changes. He established the immovable depths, the surface of the earth and the heavens above. Foolish is the man who does not fear his Lord; death will take him unprepared. Blessed is he who lives humbly; to him comes mercy from heaven. The Lord will make his heart steadfast, because he trusts in his power.[3]

---

[1] Emending *fremman* to *fremum* (Sisam).

[2] This negative is supplied, in agreement with K. Sisam's rendering of this passage, which I have followed. See *Rev. Eng. Stud.*, XXI, pp. 316 f., where it is pointed out that the passage is based on Psalm xlviii. 7–9.

[3] A passage of moral instruction follows, which is partly illegible. The poem ends with a homiletic conclusion, that we should strive to attain to the heavenly home.

213. "The Endowments of Men"

After several lines of introduction on the divine wisdom in distributing his gifts among men, the poet gives a catalogue of various types of personality and profession that go to make up Anglo-Saxon society.

The poem is in the Exeter Book, which is edited by I. Gollancz for the Early Eng. Text Soc., and also by G. P. Krapp and E. van K. Dobbie. There are translations in Gollancz's edition and in R.K. Gordon, *Anglo-Saxon Poetry* (Everyman's Library, 1926).

. . . He who has the power of doom distributes variously throughout this world men's bodily powers to the dwellers on earth. To one he grants possessions and worldly treasures here on earth. One is poor, an unfortunate man, yet he is skilled in the arts of the mind. One receives physical strength in greater measure. One is noble, beautiful in form. One is a poet, endowed with songs. One is eloquent. One is more successful in hunting, a pursuer of beasts. One is a favourite with a man of power. One is bold in battle, a warrior skilled in war where shields clash. One can in the assembly of wise men determine the custom of the people, where there is a gathering of councillors together. One can wondrously plan the building of every kind of lofty structure. As befits a craftsman, his hand, skilled and powerful, is taught to set up a hall. He knows how to secure firmly the spacious building against sudden fall. One can pluck the harp with his hands; he has cunning in deft playing of the instrument. One is a runner, one a straight shooter, one skilled in songs, one swift on the land, fleet of foot. One can steer the prow on the dark wave, knows the currents, the pilot of the company over the wide ocean, when bold seamen ply the oars with quick strength by the ship's side. One is a swimmer, one a cunning craftsman in gold and gems, when a leader of men bids him prepare a jewel for his honour. One, a skilled smith, can make many weapons for the use of men, when for men's battles he works a helmet or a dagger or a coat of mail, a bright sword or a shield-boss, firmly fitted to repel the flying javelin. One is pious and generous in alms-giving, virtuous in his behaviour. One is an active servant in the mead-hall. One is well versed in horses, wise in the manage of a steed. One, self-controlled, accepts in patience what he must. One knows the laws, where men deliberate. One is quick at the dice. One is witty at the wine-drinking, a good dispenser of beer.[1] One is a builder, capable of raising a dwelling. One is a general, a strong leader of an army. One is a councillor. One is at the service of bold men, a thegn with his prince. One possesses patience, a steadfast soul. One is a fowler, skilled with the hawk. One is bold on horseback. One is agile, he has a skilful art, the gift of giving entertainment before the retainers by his actions, light and flexible. One is lovable, his mind and speech are pleasant to men. One eagerly revolves in his mind the needs of the soul here on earth, and chooses the favour of the Lord before all earthly wealth. One is fearless in strife against the devil, he is ever ready in the battle against sins. One has skill in many functions of the Church, he can loudly glorify the Ruler of life in many songs of praise, he has a noble clear voice. One is versed in books, able in learning. One is deft of hand in writing mysteries of words.[2]

[1] *i.e.* if the unique word, literally 'beer-keeper', is an analogous formation to *hlaford*, 'lord', literally 'loaf-guardian'. But perhaps it means 'cellarer'.

[2] The poem ends, as it began, with an explanation that the Lord scatters his gifts lest one individual should become proud.

B. THE CHURCH IN AND AFTER THE VIKING AGE

(a) LATER CORRESPONDENCE

214. Letter of Ecgred, bishop of Lindisfarne, to Wulfsige, archbishop of York (830–837)

This letter, which we owe to the collection in Brit. Mus. Cott. Tiber. A xv, is one of the last surviving records of the Church of Northumbria before the devastations of the viking invasions of the second half of the ninth century. It shows the episcopate active in protecting their flock from heresy, and the writer appears as a man of moderation and good sense. The wild story of a letter from heaven, enforcing under dire threats the rigid observance of Sunday, was old before it was used by Nial and Pehtred. It is heard of in the late sixth century, and it was condemned at a Frankish synod in 789. Nevertheless, there are six vernacular homilies in eleventh-century English manuscripts that accept its truth. Of these two are of special importance (Nos. XLIII and XLIV in Napier's *Wulfstan*), for they include also some account of the deacon Nial in similar terms to those in this letter (except that they say he was dead for five weeks) and have also the reference to Pope Florentius. It is very probable, therefore, that they are based on Pehtred's book. We cannot wonder that the episcopate found it impossible to stamp out such legends, when we see how impressed King Æthelwulf was with a vision of this kind. (See No. 23.) On the whole question one should consult R. Priebsch, "The Chief Sources of Some Anglo-Saxon Homilies" (*Otia Merseiana*, I, pp. 129 f.), and K. Jost, *Wulfstanstudien*, pp. 221–236. The letter is edited by Haddan and Stubbs, III, pp. 615 f.

To the highest and reverend pontiff, to be named by us with all honour, Archbishop Wulfsige, Ecgred, humble servant of the servants of God, sends greeting in the love of Christ.

I have received with devoted mind the letters of your authority, in which I have recognized your zeal for the defence of the holy Mother Church, on whose behalf we ought to persist with firm stability of faith and give our aid, lest it be endangered in any of its members.

I indeed speak for myself that I by no means will give assent to those errors which you have claimed to be written in Pehtred's book and which you have formerly shown to us; neither will I allow it by my wish to any of those subject to God and me; but if anywhere I hear that any glimmer of them arise from anyone, I will immediately extinguish it as far as I can, and I endeavour myself to preserve completely the catholic faith and yours, which we have learnt to observe in the gospel of Christ and from his Apostles and the apostolic doctors of the universal Church, and to urge with diligent care whatever others I can to this same end. And we believe it right, and know it true, to observe in every way the honour of the Lord's Day on account of the glory of the resurrection of the same Son of God, and not the sabbath with the Jews; but to obey the commands of our Saviour, who fasted forty days and nights for the salvation of the world, and rested three days and as many nights according to the Scriptures in the heart of the earth; and not to comply with the assertions of Pehtred, who says with foolish falsehood that Nial[1] the deacon was dead for seven weeks and came to life again, and partook of no food afterwards, and many other things which the same Pehtred, whether through himself or through Nial or

---
[1] Nial's death is recorded in Irish annals, 859.

other liars, has given out with mendacious raving concerning the Old and New Testaments, all of which are to be rejected and by no means followed by any orthodox person. And if such letters written in gold by the hand of God had arrived upon the tomb of the blessed Peter in the days of Pope Florentius, why was not such a message divulged throughout the Christian peoples by the apostolic see? Or what should be done about it, if it were true? For in our documents where we have the names of the pontiffs of the apostolic see, we have not found the name of Pope Florentius. Concerning the Day of Judgment and the hour, who, by the attestation of the Lord, knows but he alone? The devil was not created devil by God, but, puffed up with pride against his Creator, depraved by his vice, and deprived of the glory of God, he was turned from an angel of light to the prince of darkness. Prompted by his malignity, the aforesaid Pehtred has scattered new and sundry tares in the Lord's field, whereas the Apostle ordered us to avoid the profane novelties of words.[1] Concerning all these things, your prudence knows far better than our littleness can know; yet I dared not do other than send certain–though very unpolished–letters in reply to yours; and if it thus please your Grace, it seems good to me that you order through letters or messenger the bishop in whose diocese Pehtred dwells, and the other servants of God dwelling in his neighbourhood, to admonish and instruct him out of brotherly charity, that he may come to his senses out of the errors in which he was deceived, and correct as far as he can the others whom he deceived; and if he pay heed to you, you will save his soul from death. If, however, in the stupidity of an obstinate mind he should wish to persist in his wickedness and cannot be acquired for God with brotherly admonition or correction once or more often, let him be as a despiser of the Church, as our Lord says: "as the heathen and publican";[2] and the Apostle says: "A man that is a heretic, after the first and second admonition, avoid; knowing that he that is such an one is subverted and sinneth, being condemned by his own judgment."[3]

215. Letter of Lupus, abbot of Ferrières, to Wigmund, archbishop of York (852)

This letter and the next have a peculiar interest in being the last evidence of learned intercourse between Northumbria and the Continent before the Danish settlement. It is natural that there should have been a close bond between Ferrières and York, for the former was one of the monasteries given to Alcuin, and his friend and scholar Sigulf had succeeded him there as abbot. Lupus had been a pupil at Ferrières in his youth, and then studied under Alcuin's pupil Hrabanus Maurus at Fulda. He was elected abbot of Ferrières in 840. He was not only a theologian, widely read in patristic and other theological works, but also a keen student of classical literature, and although he was called upon to play a practical part in the politics of his time, he found time to copy, collate and correct manuscripts of classical authors, e.g. Cicero, Virgil, Livy, Symmachus. Finding his own monastic library inadequate, he tried to borrow what he needed, from his friend Einhard, from Tours, from Prüm, from Fulda, and, as we see in No. 216, from York.

Levillain considers that all the four letters to English recipients were sent at the same time, and interprets the reference to the peace to belong to the agreement between the kings in May, 851, and the agreement with the Bretons in August, 851. The congratulations expressed in the letter to King Æthelwulf would then refer to his victory over the Danes at Aclea in 851. (See No. 1, p. 173.)

This letter is edited by E. Dümmler, Mon. Germ. Hist., Epist. Karol. Aevi, IV, p. 61; by Haddan and Stubbs, III, pp. 634–635; and, with French translation, by L. Levillain, Loup de Ferrières: Correspondance (Les Classiques de l'Histoire de France au Moyen Age), vol. II (Paris, 1935), pp. 74–77.

---

[1] I Timothy vi. 20.   [2] Matthew xviii. 17.   [3] Titus iii. 10, 11.

To Wigmund, most reverend and to be acknowledged with great veneration, archbishop of the church of York, and to all serving the Lord God under him, Abbot Lupus and the whole congregation of the monastery of Ferrières send greeting in the Lord.

A great space of time has passed in which, as various disorders increased, the alliance which was begun at the Lord's instigation by our predecessors has produced no tokens of love except prayers. But now that the grace of peace is beginning and we have recovered the cell of St. Judoc,[1] from which we are writing these letters, we have been anxious, as was fitting, to emulate in kindness our predecessors and to incite you to renew and manifest your friendship. First, and above all, we humbly ask that both in private and in public prayers you may deign to remember us. Next, it is our wish that we endeavour mutually to carry out whatever is shown to be welcome by the interchange of letters, and what our means will permit. Hasten therefore to set forth your wishes to us, that we may prepare to gratify you at once, and also that our Lord God may be glorified and made glad by the fruits of love. I wish you to be well and happy, most loved fathers.

216. Letter of Lupus, abbot of Ferrières, to Ealdsige, abbot of York (852)

On the author and date of this letter, see introduction to No. 215. Lupus seems to have been unsuccessful in procuring Jerome's Commentaries on Jeremiah and the Quintillian from this quarter, for we find him asking Pope Benedict III for them between 855 and 859 (see Dümmler, *op. cit.*, No. 103; Levillain, *op. cit.*, II, pp. 120–125). This letter is edited by Dümmler, *op. cit.*, p. 62; Haddan and Stubbs, III, pp. 635f.; Levillain, *op. cit.*, II, pp. 78–81.

To the venerable Abbot Ealdsige, Lupus of the Bethlehemite monastery, otherwise Ferrières, sends eternal greeting in the Lord.

Now that by the great clemency of our God the pestilential discord, which hitherto cruelly vexed all Gaul and Germany, has been assuaged, I have been eager among the first fruits of this peace to renew the compact which once existed between your Church and ours by a letter sent to the most reverend Bishop Wigmund. Since I have learnt that you are inflamed with the love of knowledge, for which I also am eager, and that according to what Cicero says: "like flock easily to like",[2] or by the statement of received Scripture: "Every beast loveth its like, and so every man";[3] I offer my friendship by this epistle and aspire to yours, that we may be zealous to profit each other not only in sacred prayers but also in other benefits of any kind whatever. And in order that you may be the first to give effect to what I suggest, I beg earnestly that you send to me by most reliable messengers to the cell of St. Judoc, which has at long last been given back to us, the 'Questions' of the blessed Jerome, which according to Cassiodorus he composed on the Old and New Testaments, and likewise the 'Questions' of your Bede on both Testaments; also the books of the aforesaid Jerome in explanation of Jeremiah, those that follow the first six, which we have here; in addition, the twelve books of Quintilian's *Concerning the Training of an Orator*; to be given there to Lantramn, who is well known to you, for them to be copied there, and returned to you as quickly as it can be managed. If you cannot send all, but are

---

[1] Saint-Josse-sur-mer.   [2] *De senectute*, chap. 7.   [3] Ecclesiasticus xiii. 19.

not reluctant to send some, you will receive from God the recompense for the charity you have discharged, and from us whatever return we can make for so great a service, if only you ask.

Farewell, and as soon as opportunity offers, gladden us with the reply we hope for.

217. Letter of Lupus, abbot of Ferrières, to Æthelwulf, king of Wessex (852)

On the author and date of this letter, see introduction to No. 215. It is important in affording evidence for intercourse of the West Saxon court with Frankish churchmen and in showing that Æthelwulf had a Frankish secretary. It is edited by Dümmler, *op. cit.*, pp. 22 f.; by Haddan and Stubbs, III, pp. 648 f.; Levillain, *op. cit.*, pp. 70 ff.

To King Æthelwulf, to be proclaimed with great praises to the praise and honour of God, Lupus, the least of all the servants of God, abbot of the monastery of St. Judoc,[1] sends greeting of felicity in the present time and the salvation of eternal beatitude.

As we have received a good report of your rule and heard of the strength conferred on you by God against the foes of Christ,[2] we entreat Almighty God who has bestowed this same strength, that he, who by his incomprehensible, but nevertheless just power always orders all things, may make you invincible against all the enemies of the Christian name. Truly, since a vast distance separates my insignificance from your Excellency, I desire to be known to you by my service; especially since I have heard of your zeal in the worship of God from Felix, who discharged the office of your secretary. Command me therefore whatever you think possible for me, and you will find me ready to serve in all things.

But in order to urge you to deserve well of God, we show you first an occasion for vying with us, and a hope in the present age and doubtless a reward to be granted in the future. We are striving to cover with lead the church in our monastery which lies inland, and is called Ferrières, and bears also the name of Bethlehem, bestowed on it by its founder, and is consecrated in honour, after God, of the blessed Peter and all the other Apostles; and, if you condescend, we pray you to share in this work. Help, therefore, to complete this in God's honour, not for our merit, but in consideration of the divine reward. For we, who intercede for you without your generosity, will be the more eager if we receive a gift which will so greatly profit you and us, regarding only the remedy of the soul. We shall, however, as we have already signified, be ready in anything possible that you may enjoin on us.

May Almighty God cause you and your posterity to be princes of your land for a very long time, for the propagation and conservation of his faith, and finally the heirs of eternal beatitude.

218. Letter of Lupus, abbot of Ferrières, to Felix, King Æthelwulf's secretary (852)

This letter is addressed to the secretary mentioned in No. 217. On the author and date, see introduction to No. 215. It is edited by Dümmler, *op. cit.*, p. 23; by Haddan and Stubbs, III, pp. 649 f.; by Levillain, *op. cit.*, p. 73 ff.

---

[1] Saint-Josse-sur-mer. See previous letter.
[2] Possibly a reference to the victory at *Aclea*. See No. 1, p. 173.

To his most loved friend Felix, Lupus, abbot of the monastery of Ferrières and St. Judoc, sends greeting.

Although some years have passed since the time when we first became acquainted, by the generous grace of God, in the monastery of Faremoûtiers, and opportunity for intimate talk has not since occurred, as I hoped it would, yet, since in neither of us the fervour of love has grown cold, I pray that my petition to your laudable lord, Æthelwulf, may have effect through your diligence. For calling to mind how very generous you proclaimed him, I importune him by a letter, seeing that I have decided to cover the church of St. Peter, Prince of the Apostles, in the monastery of Ferrières with lead for the durability of the roof, to condescend to grant us some of the lead for the said work, as much as God should inspire him, for the increase of his good deeds. If I obtain this by the abundant clemency of God and your zealous co-operation, it will again be your care to see that his generous benefaction is conveyed to the village of Étaples. And for our part, as we have also stated in the letter sent to the aforesaid king, we are ready both to pray for him always, and, if he should enjoin anything within our powers, to carry it out with speed. I desire you to be well and happy.

219. Extract from a letter of Pope Leo IV to Æthelwulf, king of Wessex (853)

Quotations from the register of Leo IV are contained in the British collection of canons mentioned above (p. 572), but only two relate to England. Of these, one is a brief passage of a letter to Ceolnoth, archbishop of Canterbury, and Brihtwulf, king of Mercia, consisting of a general statement that those made pastors of men should not depart from the institutions of their fathers either in canon or secular law; it tells us nothing of the circumstances that called forth this ruling. But the other, from a letter to King Æthelwulf, though again only a brief extract, is important, for from it we see what the ceremony actually was that caused some of Alfred's contemporaries to imagine that the pope had consecrated him king in 853. (See No. 1, p. 174.) The passage is given in W. H. Stevenson, *Asser's Life of King Alfred*, p. 180, and by A. de Hirsch-Gereuth in *Mon. Germ. Hist.*, *Epist. Karol. Aevi*, III, p. 602, along with the other fragments from the register of the pope.

To Æthelwulf, king of the English.

We have now graciously received your son Alfred, whom you were anxious to send at this time to the thresholds of the Holy Apostles, and we have decorated him, as a spiritual son, with the dignity of the belt and the vestments of the consulate, as is customary with Roman consuls, because he gave himself into our hands.

220. Extract from a letter of Pope John VIII to Burgred, king of Mercia (874)

This passage is contained in the manuscript of canons discussed on p. 572. In Birch it is wrongly attributed to John IV, but the *Bulcredo* of the rubric is clearly an error for Burgred, and it is correctly assigned by E. Caspar. The evidence it affords that the papal see was dissatisfied with conditions in England in the later part of the ninth century is in agreement with that in Nos. 222, 227. The text is best edited by E. Caspar, *Mon. Germ. Hist.*, *Epist. Karol. Aevi*, V, p. 293. It is No. 21 in Birch, and in Migne, *Patrologia Latina*, LXXX, p. 607.

Since, as we have heard, the sin of fornication is especially rife among you, in that many men of your kingdom presume to marry nuns and women dedicated to God, and women of their own kindred, disregarding the statute of St. Gregory, which of necessity was decreed for the newly converted people, we advise, exhort and command by this letter from our apostolic dignity all those who are under your rule, whether laymen or clerics, to avoid from now on what is certainly a crime and serious offence, and to do proper and fitting penance for their deeds, and never to commit any further deeds of this kind. But if it perchance seems difficult to you to amend this wickedness, for which you sustain such adversities,[1] inform us, your father, by your letter, that we may censure those who in their weakness are slaves to such abominable behaviour, and reprove them in every way with the decrees of the apostolic see.

221. Extract from a letter of Pope John VIII to Ethelred, archbishop of Canterbury, and Wulfred, archbishop of York (873–875)

This passage "from the register of John VIII" is included in the collection of canons made by Cardinal Deusdedit; it is not contained in the surviving portion of that register. (See p. 572.) It is of special interest in showing that the papacy tried to keep up contact with the see of York, in spite of the Danish invasion. The best text is in V. W. von Glanvell, *Die Kanonenssammlung des Kardinals Deusdedit* (Paderborn, 1905, I, p. 225), and E. Caspar, *Mon. Germ. Hist., Epist. Karol. Aevi*, v, p. 293 f. That in Birch, No. 119, and Haddan and Stubbs, III, p. 264, lacks the names in the address, and so was wrongly attributed to John VI or VII.

Bishop John to our most reverend and holy fellow-bishops Ethelred of Canterbury and Wulfred of York, archbishops, and all the bishops, priests and deacons and all the clergy appointed throughout the land of England.

Among other things, all the leading men of England who were then living near the blessed Apostle Peter having thus been assembled, the opinion of the apostolic see so far prevailed after due discussion on both sides, that all the English clerics voluntarily gave up the lay habit, voluminous but also short, on the vigil of St. Gregory,[2] and clothed themselves in tunics reaching to the ankle after the Roman fashion. On this account, we by the apostolic authority advise you also to put off lay garments and, in like manner as we in the body of our Holy Church enfold our own limbs, resume the clerical vestments according to the custom of the Roman Church.

222. Letter of Pope John VIII to Ethelred, archbishop of Canterbury (end of 877 or early in 878)

This letter is preserved in the register of John VIII copied at Monte Cassino. (See p. 572.) It was written either shortly before or else during the Danish invasion which almost succeeded in conquering Wessex. One may well wonder whether the letter the pope says he has written to the king ever reached him. It has not survived, so we can only guess at what action of Alfred's caused the pope to reprove him for impairing the rights of Canterbury. It might be that the Church claimed rights of exemption from public services beyond what the king was prepared to acknowledge. As in No. 220 the pope is concerned at the failure of the English to obey the teaching of the Church regarding marriage. Compare also No. 178. The best text is in E. Caspar, *Mon. Germ. Hist., Epist. Karol. Aevi*, v, pp. 71 f. It is also in J. D. Mansi, *Sacrorum Conciliorum nova et amplissima collectio*, XVII, cols. 54 f., and Migne, *Patrologia Latina*, CXXVI, col. 745.

To our most reverend and holy brother Ethelred, archbishop of the race of the English.

Having perused your letter, we observe with clear understanding how great is the loyalty of true love and sincerity with which you love Christ, your God, and your

---

[1] The viking invasions. King Alfred also regarded these as punishment for sins. See No. 226.
[2] 11 March.

neighbour; and how it burns with faithful devotion to the apostolic see. For, in accordance with the custom of your predecessors, you seek both to refer the necessary concerns of your Church to our episcopate as to its teacher, and to receive from the apostolic see, in which God Almighty has established the foundation of the whole Church, the advice and support of authority concerning certain adversities which it is suffering. And because you, being placed in the life of the present age, which truly is a trial upon earth, daily sustain certain hardships, we not only weep for our own, which we likewise suffer, but we also sorrow with you, suffering, alas, such things. As "the whole world is seated in wickedness",[1] and many adversaries against the servants of God are everywhere, we ought to be so much the stronger, being supported by the comfort of Christ, the greater and beyond measure more frequent the trials which daily threaten us. For our Holy Writ declares: "Blessed is the man that endureth temptation; for when he hath been proved, he shall receive the crown of life which God hath promised to them that love him";[2] and the same God is blessed for ever "who will not suffer you to be tempted above that which you are able: but will", as the Apostle says, "make also with temptation issue, that you may be able to bear it".[3] We, however, exhort and warn you, my brother, on account of the necessity of the present time, that you station yourself as a wall for the house of the Lord,[4] laying aside every worldly fear, as a proper servant of God, and, kindled by zeal for him, do not cease to resist strenuously not only the king, but all who wish to do any wrong against it, making your service honourable, as long as you are permitted by the divine will to discharge the supreme episcopate; and feed the people of the Lord committed to you with the food of holy doctrine, namely strive with willing heart to rule and protect the priests and men and women of the Church, and also widows and nuns, according to their order, with all your strength, that you may appear a fit pastor before God. For we have been at pains to admonish and exhort your king with a letter from the apostolic see, not to neglect to be obedient to you and a devoted helper for the love of Jesus Christ our Lord in all things which are beneficial to the holy church committed to you—as we remember, as history tells us, his predecessors, the most godly kings of the English, to have been—if he wish to keep safe the kingdom committed to him in this world, and afterwards to receive the life of the eternal kingdom.

Those whom you affirm to leave their own wives, against the precept of the Lord, we command, that no man leave his wife, nor wife her husband, "excepting for the cause of fornication".[5] If anyone separates for this cause, he, or she, is to remain unmarried, or they are to be mutually reconciled; since, as our Lord says, "what God hath joined together, let no man put asunder".[6] Thus, as no one can leave a previous wife joined to him in legal matrimony, by no reason is it allowed him on any account to marry another while the former wife is alive. If he does it, and is not eager to make amends by due penance, let him remain separated from the fellowship of the Church. Neither are you to permit anyone to marry within his own kindred, by the established decree of our holy predecessor Gregory, the teacher of your race.

---

[1] I John v. 19. [2] James i. 12. [3] I Corinthians x. 13.
[4] Cf. Ezekiel xiii. 5. [5] Matthew v. 32; xix. 9. [6] Matthew xix. 6.

We indeed wish to preserve for you unimpaired and beyond doubt the privilege of your see, in the manner of the blessed Augustine, sent there by St. Gregory for the salvation of many and the conversion of the king, and we enact and command that it is to be observed for ever by all orders, whether ecclesiastical or lay, according to the [statute] of the same St. Gregory, our predecessor, the ray of whose wisdom illumines the Church of Christ dispersed throughout the globe. And whatever adverse thing may be related to us concerning you by any man whatever, we will by no means believe it before true investigation; nay, rather, we have admonished your king to show due honour to you for the love of Jesus Christ the Lord, and be anxious to preserve all the rights of your privilege in everlasting security and to keep them undiminished, if he wishes to have the grace and benediction of the apostolic see as his predecessors deserved to have by their well-doing.

223. Abstract of a letter of Fulk, archbishop of Reims, to King Alfred (890 or soon after)

Flodoard, the historian of Reims, refers to two letters written by Fulk to England, as well as mentioning briefly one written to Pope Stephen "about the reception of certain Englishmen". The abbey of Reims must have kept copies, or drafts, of outgoing letters. The two letters to England chime in with the other correspondence of Alfred's reign in their expression of discontent with the state of the English Church. This passage is in Flodoard, *Historia Remensis Ecclesiae, Mon. Germ. Hist., Script.* XIII, p. 566.

To Alfred, a king across the sea, he sent friendly letters, thanking him that he had appointed a man so good and devout and suitable according to the rules of the Church as bishop in the city called Canterbury. For he had heard that he was concerned to cut down with the sword of the word that most perverse opinion, arisen from pagan errors, until then surviving among that people. This opinion seemed to permit bishops and priests to have women living near them, and anyone, who wished, to approach kinswomen of his own stock, and, moreover, to defile women consecrated to God, and, although married, to have at the same time a concubine. How contrary all these things are to sound faith he shows by most convincing examples and cites in support the authority of the holy fathers.

224. Abstract of a letter from Fulk, archbishop of Reims, to Plegmund, archbishop of Canterbury (890 or soon after)

It seems likely that Fulk wrote this letter soon after Plegmund's appointment to Canterbury, which occurred in 890. It is from Flodoard, *op. cit.,* p. 568.

[Fulk wrote] to Plegmund,[1] an archbishop across the sea, congratulating him on his good exertions, by which, he had learnt, he was working to cut off and extirpate the incestuous heats of lasciviousness, mentioned above in the letter which he had written to King Alfred, which would seem to have sprung up in that race; instructing and arming him with the sacred authorities of canonical censure, and desiring truly to be sharer in his pious labours.

[1] *Pleonico.*

225. Letter of Fulk, archbishop of Reims, to King Alfred (883–about 890)

This letter is now usually accepted as genuine; it has come down in a tenth-century evangeliary, probably from the west of England (see *2nd Report Hist. MSS. Comm.*, 1871, App. pp. 74–76), as well as in the fourteenth-century *Liber Monasterii de Hyda*, and it is difficult to see to whose interest in England it would be to fabricate it. Its problems, and the career of Grimbald in general, are ably discussed by P. Grierson in *Eng. Hist. Rev.*, LV, pp. 529–561, who is inclined to attribute the fact that Grimbald never received a bishopric to his own reluctance. Winchester tradition claimed that he was offered Canterbury, but refused it in Plegmund's favour. The same source says he was given a 'little monastery' at Winchester, and that he encouraged Edward the Elder to found the New Minster. In its arrogant and patronizing tone Fulk's letter is in striking contrast to earlier letters from the Continent.

The letter was edited by Francis Wise, *Annales rerum gestarum Ælfredi Magni auctore Asserio Menevensi* (Oxford, 1722), pp. 123–129, and is No. 555 (for 556) in Birch. The later copy is edited by E. Edwards, *Liber Monasterii de Hyda*, pp. 31–35.

To the most glorious and Christian king of the English, Alfred, Fulk, by the grace of God archbishop of Reims and servant of the servants of God, wishes ever victorious rule of a temporal kingdom and eternal joy of celestial dominion.

First, truly, we give thanks to the Lord our God, "the Father of lights" and the Author of all good things, from whom is "every best gift and every perfect gift";[1] who has not only wished the light of his knowledge to shine in your heart through the grace of the Holy Spirit, but has also deigned to kindle the fire of his love; that illumined and likewise kindled by this, you administer strenuously the profit of the kingdom committed to you from above, both by striving for and defending its peace with warlike weapons, with the divine assistance, and by earnestly desiring with a religious heart to raise the dignity of the ecclesiastical order with spiritual weapons. Hence we beseech the heavenly clemency with unwearied prayers, that he who has directed and kindled your heart to this, may cause you to have that wish by satisfying your desire with good things;[2] in order that peace may increase for your kingdom and your people in your days, and also that the ecclesiastical order – which, as you say, has fallen in ruins in many respects, whether by the frequent invasion and attack of pagans, whether by the great passage of time or the carelessness of prelates or the ignorance of those subject to them – may be reformed, improved and extended by your diligence and zeal as quickly as possible.

Since you desire that it may chiefly be done through our help, and on this account seek counsel and support from our see, over which the blessed Remigius, truly the Apostle of the Franks, presides, we believe that this is not done without divine prompting; that, just as once the people of the Franks deserved to be freed by the same blessed Remigius from manifold error and to know the worship of the one true God, so the people of the English may beg to receive such a man from his see and teaching, through whom it may learn how to guard against superstitions, to cut off superfluities, and to extirpate any things harmful, springing from ancient use and barbarian custom; and, walking through the Lord's field, may learn to pluck the flowers and avoid the snake.

Certainly St. Augustine, the first bishop of your people, sent to you by the blessed Gregory, your Apostle, neither could demonstrate in a short time all the decrees of the apostolic ordinances, nor wished suddenly to burden a rude and barbarous race

---

[1] James i. 17.   [2] Psalm cii. 5.

with new and unknown laws; for he knew how to have regard to their weakness, and to say with the Apostle, as it were to little ones in Christ: "I gave you milk to drink, not meat."[1] And just as Peter and James "who seemed to be pillars",[2] with Barnabas and Paul and the rest of the assembled elders, did not wish to burden with a heavy yoke the primitive Church flocking from the nations to the faith of Christ, except to enjoin them to "abstain from things sacrificed to idols, from fornication, from things strangled and from blood";[3] thus also we know was done with you in the beginning.

But indeed, the rearing from barbaric and savage beginnings to the divine knowledge required this alone; and faithful and wise servants, set over the Lord's family, knew well to give to their fellow servants their measure of wheat in due season,[4] that is, for the capture of hearers. As time passed and the Christian religion grew, Holy Church would not and had no right to be content with these things, but only with the model received from those Apostles, their masters and founders, who after the propagation and diffusion of the evangelical teaching by the celestial master himself, accounted it not superfluous and useless, but necessary and beneficial, to establish the faithful more perfectly with the frequent admonitions of their letters, and to strengthen them more firmly in the true faith, and to deliver to them more abundantly a way of living and a pattern of religion.

Nevertheless, whether disturbed by adversities or nourished by good fortune, the Church has never ceased to seek the advantage of its sons whom daily it begets to Christ, and to further their progress either in private or in public, inflamed by the fire of the Holy Spirit. Hence councils were assembled not only from neighbouring cities and provinces, but just as often from regions across the sea; hence synodal decrees were often issued; hence sacred canons were often established and consecrated by the Holy Spirit, by which the catholic faith is greatly strengthened and the unity of the peace of the Church kept inviolate, and also its order befittingly arranged. Indeed, as it is not allowed to any Christian to transgress these canons, for clerics and priests not to know them is especially and utterly abominable. Since for the reasons mentioned above the salutary observance of these canons and of the religious and ever to be honoured tradition either never became fully known among your people, or else has now for the most part grown cold, it seemed right and pleasing to your authority and royal prudence, with the best–and, we believe, divinely inspired–counsel, to consult our insignificance on this matter and to seek the see of the blessed Remigius, by whose merits and teaching that same see, the church over all the churches of the Gauls, from his times ever flourished and excelled with all religion and doctrine.

And since, when about to seek and beg such things from us, you did not choose to appear illiberal and with an empty hand, your royal lordship deigned to honour us with a very great gift, very necessary and timely, and sufficiently suited to the matter in question; on which account we have both given praises, admiring greatly the heavenly providence, and also have returned no small thanks to your royal generosity.

---

[1] I Corinthians iii. 2.   [2] Galatians ii. 9.   [3] Acts xv. 29.   [4] Cf. Luke xii. 42.

You indeed have sent us dogs, of noble stock and excellent, nevertheless corporeal and mortal, for driving away the fury of visible wolves, with which our country, among other scourges inflicted on us by the just judgment of God, greatly abounds; yourself also seeking from us dogs, not corporeal, but spiritual, not such, to wit, as the prophet upbraids, saying: "Dumb dogs, not able to bark",[1] but such as the psalmist speaks of: "The tongue of thy dogs may be red with the same [blood] of thy enemies";[2] who surely shall know how and be fit to bark loudly for their master, and continually guard his flock with the most vigilant and sagacious watch, and keep afar off the bloodthirsty wolves of the unclean spirits, who are the betrayers and devourers of souls. Of this number you ask us for one in particular, by name Grimbald,[3] priest and monk, to be chosen for this office and appointed to the charge of pastoral authority; to whom truly the universal Church, which nourished him from an early age in true faith and holy religion, and which advanced him by ecclesiastical custom through the various grades to the priestly dignity, testifies, proclaiming him to be most worthy of pontifical honour and capable also of teaching others. But as we wished rather that this should be done in our kingdom, and planned at one time to perform it with Christ's consent at an opportune season, so that we might have him, whom we had as a faithful son, also as a colleague in our ministry and a most trusty helper in every ecclesiastical service, it is not without immense grief— as we might say—that we suffer him to be torn from us, and to be separated from our sight by such a distance of land and sea.

But, on the other hand, because love counts no cost, nor faith any loss, and no distance between lands separates those whom the chain of true love binds, we have most willingly granted the request of you to whom we can deny nothing, nor do we grudge him to you, at whose advancement we rejoice as at our own, and whose gains we consider ours. For we know that in every place the same God is served, and that the Catholic and Apostolic Church is one, whether Roman or across the sea. Therefore it is for us to concede him to you canonically, but for you to receive him honourably; he is to be sent to you on conditions and terms which are both for the glory of your kingdom and for the honour of our church and episcopate, with his electors, and with some of the magnates and chief men of your kingdom, that is, both bishops, priests and deacons, and also religious laymen. They shall by word of mouth avow and promise in the presence of all our church that they will hold him in due honour all the time of his life; and also that they will observe inviolably all their days the canonical decrees and the ecclesiastical injunctions handed down by the Apostles and the apostolic men of the Church, which they can then hear and see from us, and afterwards learn from this their pastor and teacher according to the form handed on by us. When they have done this with divine benediction, receiving him duly consecrated according to ecclesiastical custom by the authority of the blessed Remigius through our ministry and the laying on of hands, and most fully instructed in all things, they are to escort him with due honour to his own see, eager and glad that they will always enjoy his support and be constantly instructed by his teaching and example.

Because truly "the members have care one for another, and either rejoice if one

---

[1] Isaiah lvi. 10.   [2] Psalm lxvii. 24.   [3] See No. 7, p. 269; No. 226.

member rejoice, or if one member suffer all the members suffer with it",[1] we commend him more carefully and particularly to your royal highness and most far-seeing clemency, that he may always teach with free authority without opposition from anyone, and put into effect whatever he can find consonant with the integrity of the Church and the instruction of your people, and useful according to canonical authority and the custom of our church; lest perchance, which God forbid, anyone led by diabolical prompting shall set on foot controversy or stir up sedition against him with the zeal of malice and ill-will.

Thus it will be your care to foresee this and restrain in every way with the royal censure such persons if by chance they should appear, and to subdue barbaric ferocity with the bridle of your governance; but it will be his care to consult always with pastoral skill the welfare of those committed to him and rather to draw all to him with love than to drive them with fear.

May your most noble dignity, your most holy piety, and also most unconquered fortitude, ever rejoice and flourish in Christ the King of Kings and Lord of Lords.

226. The Old English prose and verse prefaces to King Alfred's translation of Gregory's "Pastoral Care"

In the prose preface, couched in the form of a letter to each of the bishops to whom a copy of the work was sent, Alfred discusses the decline of scholarship in England in his time, and outlines his programme: all free young men of means are to learn to read English, and those destined for the Church to study Latin. Since there are already many who can read English—a most interesting statement—the king proposes that translations be made of the most necessary books, and himself has translated Gregory's *Pastoralis* with the help of certain scholars. The choice of this as one of the first books is natural, for it had long been a text-book much used by English ecclesiastics. The verse preface records the tradition that the original Latin work was brought to England by St. Augustine, and also gives information on the production of copies for circulation. Copies were to be sent all over to centres where others could be made from them, and these were then to be sent back to the king; they were then supplied with the preface before they were sent to the individual recipients. Hatton MS. 20, in the Bodleian Library, is the copy that went to Bishop Wærferth of Worcester; the two pages which contain the prefaces are separate from the rest of the volume, and the prose preface is considered by Mr. N. R. Ker to be in the same hand as Brit. Mus. Cott. Tiber. B xi, a manuscript so damaged in the Cottonian fire that only a few fragments, and an odd leaf at Kassel, now remain, though fortunately it was transcribed by Junius before the fire. Since this manuscript leaves a blank for the bishop's name, and once contained the note: "Archbishop Plegmund has been given his book, and Bishop Swithwulf, and Bishop Wærferth", it would seem that this was a copy kept at headquarters. A very clear account of the probable method of production and circulation of the work is contained in K. Sisam, "The Publication of Alfred's *Pastoral Care*" in *Studies in the History of Old English Literature*, pp. 140–147.

There are also fragments of an early tenth-century manuscript, Brit. Mus. Cott. Otho B ii, where the bishop named in the preface is Heahstan (of London); the eleventh-century Camb. Univ. Lib. MS. Ii.2.4. has the name of Bishop Wulfsige (of Sherborne) in this position. Another Worcester manuscript, the eleventh-century C.C.C.C. MS. 12, omits the address to a specific bishop, but has importance as an independent copy of the Tiberius manuscript, while there is a manuscript at Trinity College, Cambridge (R. 5. 22) believed to come from Salisbury, which omits the preface. Putting together the names of these persons and those named in the preface as Alfred's helpers, we can date the preface between 890, when Plegmund became archbishop, and 896, the latest possible date for the death of Swithwulf of Rochester. If this work is the first of Alfred's translations, a date close to the earlier limit would be desirable to allow time for his other works, the *Orosius*, the *Boethius*, the *Soliloquies of St. Augustine*, before his death in 899. Asser does not mention the work, and this is sometimes held to suggest a date after 893, when Asser was writing; but it is not altogether safe to argue from the silences of Asser, whose Life of Alfred was probably unfinished. His account of Alfred's educational reforms has verbal parallels with the phrasing of this preface. (See No. 7, pp. 267f.) Asser could have helped with the drafting of it.

---

[1] I Corinthians xii. 25, 26.

Both prefaces are edited by H. Sweet, *King Alfred's West-Saxon Version of Gregory's Pastoral Care* (Early Eng. Text Soc., 1871), from both the Hatton text, and the Junius transcript of the Tiberius MS., and with readings from the Otho fragments; the prose preface is included in innumerable Anglo-Saxon readers, of which the most accessible are those of H. Sweet, and A. J. Wyatt (see p. 801); the versions in C.C.C.C. MS. 12 and Camb. Univ. Lib. MS. Ii. 2. 4. are edited by F. P. Magoun, Jr. "King Alfred's Letter on Educational Policy according to the Cambridge Manuscripts", *Mediaeval Studies*, XI. The verse preface is edited by E. van K. Dobbie, *The Anglo-Saxon Minor Poems*, p. 110. Sweet's edition has a translation of both prefaces. Among translations of the prose preface may be mentioned that by R. W. Chambers, *England before the Norman Conquest*, pp. 222–225. There is a translation of the verse preface in Dr. Sisam's article cited above. My translation is based on the Junius transcript of the Tiberius MS.

A. *The Prose Preface*

 K ing Alfred sends greeting to   [1] in loving and friendly words.
And I would have you informed that it has very often come into my mind what wise men there were in former times throughout England, both of spiritual and lay orders; and how happy times then were throughout England; and how the kings who had rule over the people were obedient to God and his messengers; and how they both upheld peace and morals and authority at home, and also extended their territory abroad; and how they prospered both in warfare and in wisdom; and also how zealous the spiritual orders were both about teaching and learning and all the services which they should do for God; and how foreigners came hither to this land in search of knowledge and instruction, and we now would have to get them from abroad, if we were to have them. So completely had learning decayed in England that there were very few men on this side the Humber who could apprehend their services in English or even translate a letter from Latin into English, and I think that there were not many beyond the Humber. There were so few of them that I cannot even recollect a single one south of the Thames when I succeeded to the kingdom. Thanks be to God Almighty that we now have any provision of teachers. And therefore I charge you to do, as I believe you are willing, detach yourself as often as you can from the affairs of this world, to the end that you may apply that wisdom which God has granted you wherever you may be able to apply it. Remember what temporal punishments[2] came upon us, when we neither loved wisdom ourselves nor allowed it to other men; we possessed only the name of Christians, and very few possessed the virtues.

When I remembered all this, I also remembered how, before everything was ravaged and burnt, the churches throughout all England stood filled with treasures and books, and likewise there was a great multitude of the servants of God. And they had very little benefit from those books, for they could not understand anything in them, because they were not written in their own language. As if they had said: "Our forefathers who formerly held these monasteries loved wisdom, and through it they obtained wealth and left it to us. Their track can still be seen, but we cannot follow it up, and we have now lost both the wealth and the wisdom, because we were unwilling to incline our mind to that track."

When I remembered all this, I wondered exceedingly at those good and wise men who were in former times throughout England, and had fully studied all those books,

[1] This blank was then filled with the name of the person for whom the copy was destined.
[2] The viking invasions.

that they would not turn any part of them into their own language. But then at once I answered myself, and said: "They did not think that men would ever become so careless and learning so decayed; they abstained intentionally, wishing that here in the land there should be the greater wisdom, the more languages we knew."

Then I remembered also how the divine law was first composed in the Hebrew language, and afterwards, when the Greeks learnt it, they turned it all into their own language, and also all other books. And the Romans likewise, when they had learnt them, turned them all through learned interpreters into their own language. And also all other Christian nations turned some part of them into their own language. Therefore it seems better to me, if it seems so to you, that we also should turn into the language that we can all understand some books, which may be most necessary for all men to know; and bring it to pass, as we can very easily with God's help, if we have the peace, that all the youth now in England, born of free men who have the means that they can apply to it, may be devoted to learning as long as they cannot be of use in any other employment, until such time as they can read well what is written in English. One may then teach further in the Latin language those whom one wishes to teach further and to bring to holy orders.

When I remembered how the knowledge of the Latin language had previously decayed throughout England, and yet many could read things written in English, I began in the midst of the other various and manifold cares of this kingdom to turn into English the book which is called in Latin *Pastoralis* and in English 'Shepherd-book', sometimes word for word, sometimes by a paraphrase; as I had learnt it from my Archbishop Plegmund, and my Bishop Asser, and my priest Grimbald and my priest John. When I had learnt it, I turned it into English according as I understood it and as I could render it most intelligibly; and I will send one to every see in my kingdom; and in each will be a book-marker[1] [?] worth 50 mancuses.

And I command in God's name, that no one take that book-marker from the book, nor the book from the church. It is unknown how long there may be such learned bishops, as now, thanks be to God, are almost everywhere; therefore I would like them always to be at that place, unless the bishop wish to have it with him, or it is anywhere on loan, or someone is copying it.

B. *The Verse Preface*

This message Augustine brought to the islanders from the south across the salt sea, as the Lord's champion, the pope of Rome, had formerly composed it. The wise-minded Gregory considered many true doctrines, through the wisdom of his heart, his treasury of cunning thoughts. For he acquired for the Guardian of the skies the greatest number of mankind, he the best of the Romans, wisest of men, most famous for deeds of glory.

[1] It seems most probable that an *æstel* (from *hastula* 'a little spear', 'a thin piece of wood') was a pointer to keep the reader's eyes on the line he was reading. It is once glossed *indicatorium*, which suggests something of the kind. Its very great value – 50 mancuses being the price of 300 sheep or 50 oxen – is not incongruous with this interpretation, for we find mention elsewhere of small objects of very great value, *e.g.* armlets of 80 or even 120 mancuses. We may assume that it was of precious metal and jewels, and that the king wished to stress the importance he attached to his project by letting so valuable an object accompany each of his gift-copies. An alternative view takes it to be the binding of the book.

Afterwards King Alfred translated every word of me into English, and sent me south and north to his scribes; ordered more to be brought to him according to the example, that he could send them to his bishops, for some of them, those who knew least Latin, needed it.

227. Letter of Pope Formosus to the bishops of England (891–896)

Though this letter survives only in post-Conquest sources, William of Malmesbury and a Canterbury register, and has been tampered with to support the claim of Canterbury against York, it is highly probable that the first part of it is genuine. It is in a similar tone to other papal letters to England in the late ninth century, and the severity of the rebuke for neglect in missionary work is understandable from a pope who had himself been a missionary (see F. M. Stenton, *Anglo-Saxon England*, p. 429). Letters of his survive in which he stresses the importance of the missionary work in Denmark carried out from Hamburg (*Mon. Germ. Hist., Epist. Karol. Aevi*, v, pp. 366 ff.). The presence in England of a letter from this pope to the English bishops would help to explain how the erroneous belief set out in No. 229 arose, that Formosus had written to King Edward the Elder, who did not ascend the throne until some three and a half years after Formosus's death.

It is possible that the original letter spoke of the privileges of Canterbury in terms similar to those used by John VIII in No. 222; in that case all that the Canterbury forgers had to do would be to expand the text in front of them.

This letter is No. 573 in Birch, and in William of Malmesbury, *De Gestis Pontificum*, ed. Hamilton, pp. 59–61, and Migne, *Patrologia Latina*, cxxix, col. 846 f.

To his brothers and sons in Christ, all the bishops of England, Formosus.

Having heard that the abominable rites of the pagans have sprouted again in your parts, and that you kept silent "like dogs unable to bark",[1] we have considered thrusting you from the body of the Church of God with the sword of separation. But since, as our beloved brother Plegmund has informed us, you have at length awakened, and have begun to renew the seed of the word of God once admirably sown in the land of the English, we withdraw the sword of anathema, and send to you the blessing of Almighty God and of the blessed Peter, Prince of the Apostles, praying that you may persevere in what has been well begun. For you, brothers, are they speaking of whom the Lord says among others things: "You are the salt of the earth, but if the salt lose its savour, wherewith shall it be salted?"[2] And again: "You are the light of the world";[3] wishing to signify that the minds of men ought to be seasoned by you through the wisdom of the word, and that zeal for well-doing ought to appear in your habits and your life as a light of faith, through which those proceeding to life may see how they may walk with caution; that running without stumbling[4] they may be able to attain the promise of eternal beatitude. Now, therefore, gird yourselves and watch against the lion who "goeth about seeking whom he may devour",[5] and do not any longer in your country suffer the Christian faith to be violated, the flock of God to wander and be scattered and dispersed, for the lack of pastors; but when one dies, another who is suitable is to be canonically substituted forthwith. For according to the law, many priests were made because death prevented them from continuing. David, considering this, and foreseeing in spirit that the Church of Christ would remain to the end of time, says: "Instead of thy fathers, sons are born to thee; thou shalt make them princes over all the earth."[6] And thus when any of the priests departs from this life, another ought to be substituted without

---

[1] Isaiah lvi. 10.   [2] Matthew v. 13.   [3] Matthew v. 14.
[4] Cf. John xi. 9, 10.   [5] I Peter v. 8.   [6] Psalm xliv. 17.

delay. As soon as the death of the brother is announced to him, who, bearing the rule of the chief see, is set over the rest of the bishops among you, a canonical election is to be made and another to be consecrated and to succeed. And it is well known from ancient times who among you ought to hold the authority, and which episcopal see is superior to the others and holds first rank. For, as we understand from the writings of the blessed Gregory and his successors, it is agreed that the metropolis and first episcopal see of the kingdom of the English is in the city of *Dorobernia*,[1] over which now our venerable brother Plegmund is set, the honour of whose dignity we do not permit to be diminished on any consideration, but we order him to have charge of the apostolic duties in all things. And just as the blessed Father Gregory appointed all the bishops of the English to be subject to the first bishop to your people, Augustine, we confirm the same dignity to the aforenamed brother, archbishop of *Dorobernia* or Canterbury, and to his legitimate successors; enjoining and commanding with the authority of God and of the blessed Peter, Prince of the Apostles, that all are to obey his canonical directions, and no one is to violate those things which have been granted to him and his successors by apostolic authority.

If, however, any man attempts to contend against this at any time, and to diminish it, let him know that without doubt he will be punished with a heavy anathema, and be separated for ever from the body of the Holy Church which he tries to disturb, unless he comes to his senses.

228. Letter of Radbod, prior of St. Samson's at Dol, to King Athelstan (924-6)

This is the only letter surviving from Athelstan's time. It fits with other evidence such as relic-lists, that show Athelstan as a great collector of relics. (Cf. No. 8, p. 282, No. 140, and J. Armitage Robinson, *The Times of St. Dunstan*, pp. 71-80.) It is interesting to find not only Athelstan, but also his father Edward, in contact with continental religious houses. The letter was found by William of Malmesbury at Milton Abbas, in a shrine. It is printed in William of Malmesbury, *De Gestis Pontificum*, ed. Hamilton, pp. 399-400.

To King Athelstan, most glorious and munificent by the honouring of the supreme and indivisible Trinity and by the excellent intercession of all the saints, I, Radbod, prior of the supreme bishop, Samson, wish glory in this world and blessedness in the eternal world.

In your piety, benevolence and greatness, surpassing in renown and praise all earthly kings of this age, you, King Athelstan, will know well that, while our country was still at peace, your father King Edward commended himself by letters to the confraternity of St. Samson, supreme confessor, and of Archbishop Jovenian my superior, and my cousin, and his clerics. Hence till now we pour out to Christ the King unwearied prayers for his soul and your welfare, and day and night, seeing your great compassion on us, we promise to pray to the merciful God on your behalf, in psalms and Masses and prayers, as if I, with my twelve canons, were prostrate before you. And now I send to you relics, which we know to be dearer to you than all earthly substance, namely bones of St. Senator, and of St. Paternus, and of St.

[1] Canterbury.

Scabillion, master of the same Paternus, who likewise departed to Christ on the same day and hour as the aforesaid Paternus. Most certainly these two saints lay with St. Paternus in the sepulchre, on his right and left, and their solemnities like his are celebrated on 23 September. Therefore, most glorious king, exalter of Holy Church, subduer of wicked barbarism, mirror of your kingdom, example of all goodness, disperser of enemies, father of clerics, helper of the poor, lover of all the saints, invoker of the angels, we, who for our deserts and sins dwell in France in exile and captivity, pray and humbly implore that you with your blessed liberality and great compassion will not forget us. And now and henceforth you can command without delay whatever you will deign to entrust to me.

229. Old English letter concerning some estates of the diocese of Cornwall (late tenth century)

The following document was accepted by the editors of the Crawford Charters as a genuine letter of Archbishop Dunstan, and dated 980–988, whereas J. Armitage Robinson (*The Saxon Bishops of Wells*, pp. 27f.) offers the alternative suggestion that it may have been "composed by a Cornish ecclesiastic to counter the claim of a papal sanction for the assignment of the properties to the see of Crediton", comparing a document (Birch, Nos. 614, 615) in several manuscripts (the earliest being a parchment strip of the tenth century included in Brit. Mus. Addit. MS. 7138), which tells a story of the division of the West Saxon dioceses very similar to that in this letter, only with additions such as a visit of Plegmund to Rome to appease the pope's anger, his consecration of seven bishops on one day in Canterbury on his return (to the five West Saxon sees and also for Selsey and Dorchester), and with the significant difference that the three estates are left in the possession of Crediton, and a papal anathema is pronounced on anyone who alters the arrangements as set out in the document. The present letter, if forged, cannot be dated precisely, but its hand shows it would have to have been an early forgery. There are no suspicious features in the document itself, however, and it would be rash to reject it merely because it is in someone's favour. Whether it is what it purports to be or not, the letter has historical interest, for it is likely that the statements about the sees of Crediton and Cornwall in the later tenth century are to be relied on; these events were too recent for it to be safe to make false statements, nor does there seem any obvious motive for so doing. While the account of the division of the West Saxon dioceses contains impossible features, since Formosus was dead before Edward became king, and Wessex was never without bishops, the central fact, that it was divided into five sees in Edward's reign (probably after the death of Denewulf of Winchester in 908 and Asser of Sherborne in 909), is true. Nevertheless, this letter, along with the Latin statement above mentioned, affords a good example of how an erroneous account could become widely believed at no very great date from the event in question. For a possible reason why Formosus should have been associated with this division, see No. 227. ee also R. R. Darlington, *Eng. Hist. Rev.*, LI, pp. 423–425.

The letter is No. 7 in *The Crawford Collection of Early Charters*, ed. A. S. Napier and W. H. Stevenson.

This letter the archbishop sends to his lord, King Ethelred. It happened that the West Welsh[1] rose against King Egbert. Then the king went thither and subdued them, and gave a tenth of the land [to God] and disposed of it as seemed fit to him. He then gave to Sherborne three estates, Pawton, Callington and Lawhitton, and that lasted thus for a long term of years, until heathen armies overran and occupied this country. Then there followed another period after that, when teachers fell off and left England because of the unbelief that then assailed it, and the whole West Saxon kingdom was without a bishop for seven years. Then Pope Formosus sent from Rome and admonished King Edward and Archbishop Plegmund to amend this, and they did so with the advice of the pope and of all the councillors of the English nation:

[1] The Cornish.

they appointed five bishops where there were two before, one, namely Frithestan, at Winchester, the second, namely Athelstan, for Ramsbury, the third, namely Wærstan, for Sherborne, the fourth, namely Æthelhelm, for Wells, the fifth, namely Eadwulf, for Crediton; and to him were assigned the three estates in Cornwall into the authority of Devon, because its people had previously been disobedient, without awe of the West Saxons.[1] And Bishop Eadwulf enjoyed these estates for his lifetime, and also Bishop Æthelgar after him. Then it happened that King Athelstan gave to Conan the bishopric as far as the Tamar flowed.[2] Then it happened that King Eadred ordered Daniel to be consecrated and he assigned those estates as the councillors advised him to St. Germans to the bishopric. After that when King Edgar ordered me to consecrate Wulfsige, he and all our bishops said that they did not know who might own the estates with greater right than the bishop of the diocese, when he was thoroughly loyal and preached God's faith rightly and loved his lord. If then this bishop now does so, I do not know why he should not be entitled to those estates, if God and our lord grant them to him.[3] For it does not seem to us that any man may own them with greater right than he. And if any man seizes them for himself, may he hold them without God's blessing or ours.

230. Letter of Pope John XV to all the faithful, concerning the reconciliation of Ethelred, king of England, and Richard, duke of Normandy (991)

But for this letter, which survives in an early eleventh-century manuscript (Brit. Mus. Cott. Tiber. A xv), and in William of Malmesbury (*De Gestis Regum*, ed. Stubbs, I, pp. 191–193), we should not have known of the strained relations between these rulers. It is edited by Stubbs, *Memorials of St. Dunstan*, pp. 397 f.

John the fifteenth, pope of the holy Roman Church, to all the faithful.

All faithful members of holy Mother Church, and our sons of either order spread throughout the regions of the world, should know how we have been informed by many of the enmity between Ethelred, king of the West Saxons, and Richard the marquis. Greatly saddened by this, seeing that it concerns our spiritual sons, I at length took wholesome counsel and summoned a certain legate of ours, namely Leo, bishop of the holy church of Trèves, and sent him thither with our letters of exhortation, that they should recover from this violence. Traversing the great intervening space of land, he at length crossed the boundaries of the sea, and arrived in the presence of the aforesaid king on the day of our Lord's Nativity; and after greeting him on our behalf, gave the letter which we had sent to him. The king summoned all the loyal men of his kingdom and the councillors of both orders, and for the love and fear of Almighty God, and also of St. Peter, Prince of the Apostles, and through our paternal admonition he granted a most firm peace, with all his sons and daughters, present and future, and with all his loyal people, without deceit. Therefore he sent Æthelsige, bishop of the holy church of Sherborne, and Leofstan, son of Ælfwold, and Æthelnoth,

[1] The Latin document gives a more convincing motive, to enable the bishop to visit the Cornish people annually to correct their errors.
[2] This sentence is added in another hand.
[3] The rest is added in the same hand which made the previous insertion.

son of Wigstan,[1] and they crossed the boundaries of the sea and came to Richard, the aforesaid marquis. After peacefully receiving our warning and at the same time hearing the decision of the above-mentioned king, he confirmed the same peace with a willing heart, along with his sons and daughters, present and future, and with all his faithful people, on the following terms: that if any of their people, or they themselves, were to commit any wrong against the other, it should be atoned for with a fitting compensation; and the peace should remain for ever unshaken, and confirmed by the mark of the oaths of both parties, namely on the part of King Ethelred, Æthelsige, bishop of the holy church of Sherborne, and Leofstan, son of Ælfwold, and Æthelnoth, son of Wigstan; on the part of Richard, Bishop Roger, Rodulf, son of Hugh, Tursten, son of Turgeis.

Done at Rouen on the first of March, in the year of our Lord's incarnation 991, the fourth indiction. And Richard is to receive none of the king's men, or of his enemies, nor the king any of his, without their seal.

231. Letter of Pope John to Ealdorman Ælfric (983–1009)

There were two ealdormen of this name, one who was ealdorman of Mercia from 983 to 985, and another, who was ealdorman of Hampshire, whose signatures first appear in 983 and who were killed in 1016. The pope concerned could therefore be John XIV (about 983–984), John XV (985–996) John XVI (about 997–998), John XVII, who was pope for a few months in 1003, or John XVIII (1004–1009). Papal letters to English laymen are rare. This one supplies supporting evidence for the lawlessness of the reign of Ethelred the Unready. It survives in Brit. Mus. Cott. Tiber. A xv, and there is another version in William of Malmesbury (*De Gestis Regum*, ed. Stubbs, 1, pp. 172 f.), but this has been interpolated in the interests of Glastonbury. The letter in its original form is edited by Stubbs, *Memorials of St. Dunstan*, pp. 396 f.

Bishop John, servant of the servants of God, to Ælfric the famous ealdorman, our most dearly loved spiritual son, wishes perpetual health and apostolic benediction.

We have learnt from the report of certain faithful people that you commit many injuries against the church of Mary the holy Mother of God, which is called Glastonbury, and in your greedy cupidity have seized estates and villages from its rightful ownership, and you are constantly harmful to it because you cling to a dwelling close to the same place. It would have been fitting, when you became its neighbour, that the holy church of God might have greatly benefited by your support, and have been enriched in possessions by means of your help; but, what is abominable, it is impoverished by your opposition and humiliated by your oppression. And because we do not doubt that we, though unworthy, have received from the blessed Apostle Peter the charge of all churches and the care of all the faithful, we therefore admonish your love to cease pillaging that place, for fear of the Apostles Peter and Paul and out of respect to us, usurping nothing of its rights, villages and possessions. If you do not do this, may you know that you are excommunicated by our authority in place of the Prince of the Apostles, and cast out from the company of the faithful, subjected to a perpetual anathema, and delivered for ever with Judas the betrayer to the eternal flame.

[1] This Æthelnoth attended a council in London in 989 or 990. See No. 120.

232. Fragment of an Old English letter

Letters in the vernacular have rarely survived (see p. 577), and this one has the additional value of showing the attitude of the English to the Danish invaders. Cf. Nos. 191, 193. It was copied into a Worcester manuscript, Junius 22, after some injunctions about abstention from blood. Nothing is known of the recipient, and the writer is anonymous. After the passage I quote, he goes on to ask Edward to try to stop a disgusting habit among women in rural districts, since he more often goes among these than does the writer. The fragment is edited by F. Kluge, *Englische Studien*, viii, pp. 62 f.

I tell thee also, brother Edward, now that thou hast asked me, that you[1] do wrong in abandoning the English practices which your fathers followed, and in loving the practices of heathen men who begrudge you life, and in so doing show by such evil habits that you despise your race and your ancestors, since in insult to them you dress in Danish fashion with bared necks and blinded eyes. I will say no more about that shameful mode of dress except what books tell us, that he will be accursed who follows heathen practices in his life and in so doing dishonours his own race.

233. Letter of Fulbert, bishop of Chartres, to King Cnut (1020?)

This letter is usually dated 1020 or soon after, on the assumption that the most likely reason for Cnut's gift was the appeal for contributions to the rebuilding of the church of Chartres after it was burnt down in 1020. William, duke of Aquitaine, is thanked by Fulbert in another letter for a payment for this purpose. Larson, however, suggests that Cnut sent this gift on his way from Denmark to Rome in 1026 (*Canute the Great*, p. 227). A peculiar feature of the letter is that Cnut should simply be addressed as king of Denmark. Fulbert must have known that he was also king of England. One wonders if the continental prelates were loath to admit his right to a throne to which there were legitimate heirs in exile in Normandy.

The letter is in Migne, *Patrologia Latina*, cxli, col. 235 and in part in M. Bouquet, *Recueil des historiens des Gaules et de la France*, x, p. 466.

To the most noble king of Denmark, Cnut, Fulbert, by the grace of God bishop of Chartres, with his clerics and monks, sends support of prayer.

When we saw the gift you conferred on us, we were amazed at your wisdom, and equally at your piety: wisdom, indeed, that you, a man ignorant of our language, separated from us by a long stretch of land and sea, not only vigorously administer the concerns which are round about you, but also diligently inquire into those round about us; piety, truly, when we perceive that you, whom I had heard to be a ruler of pagans, not only of Christians, are also a most gracious benefactor to the churches and servants of God. Giving thanks therefore to the King of Kings, from whose dispensation such things descend, we ask that he may cause your kingdom to be prosperous under you, and may absolve your soul from sins, through the eternal Christ our Lord, only begotten of one substance with him, in the unity of the Holy Spirit. Amen. Farewell, remembering us, and be not unmindful of yourself.

[1] The change of number here shows that the author means the English people in general.

234. Extracts from the oldest Life of St. Dunstan

This Life is dedicated to Ælfric, archbishop of Canterbury, 995–1005, and it had been copied and a revised version sent to Abbo of Fleury before 1004. The author, who twice claims to have been a witness of events he relates, is referred to merely by his initial, 'B'. He tells us he was a priest and a Saxon. Older attempts, beginning with Mabillon, to identify him with the Ramsey writer, Byrhtferth, have been discredited on stylistic grounds; these support Stubbs's suggested identification (*Memorials of St. Dunstan*, pp. xxii–xxv) of him with the author of three anonymous letters, who in one of them is called 'B'. If this identification is accepted, it follows that the author was from the Continent, for in the letter in question the writer tells Archbishop Æthelgar, Dunstan's successor, that he has spent his youth under the patronage of the bishop of Liége, since whose death he has been in exile (*op. cit.*, pp. 385–388). Another of the letters attributed to him is addressed to Dunstan himself, and speaks of his having placed himself under his protection (*op. cit.*, pp. 374–376). But even if the author of the Life has some personal knowledge of his subject, it must be remembered that he is writing at least seventeen years after Dunstan's death; moreover he is much more concerned with his claims to sanctity than with his actions in the world; and he writes in a very inflated and sometimes obscure style. This feature caused the Life to be revised at St. Augustine's, Canterbury, and their version, sent to Abbo with a request that he should turn it into verse, is represented by the St. Gall MS. 337, which corrects some of the grammar and replaces some of the strange words, as they occur in the Arras MS. 812. The Brit. Mus. Cott. MS. Cleo. A xiii also gives a revised text.

For all its shortcomings, the Life is of great importance. The second early Life, by Adelard, a monk of Ghent, written between 1005 and 1012, expands the miraculous element, but adds little factual information. I have chosen from 'B's' Life the account of studies at Glastonbury before the days of the monastic revival, the passages which tell us most about his attainments and practices, and those of chief importance for political history.

My text is translated from the edition by W. Stubbs, *Memorials of St. Dunstan*, pp. 3–52, which is from the Arras MS.

5. The aforesaid parents, seeing so great excellence in their son,[1] put on him the proper tonsure of the clerical office and associated him to the famous monastery of the church of Glastonbury, that he might by day and night continually serve God and Mary, Mother of God, in that place. And now, his youth overcome, he passed the blooming years of his adolescence bound to sacred studies; and like the cedar of Lebanon, just in the house of his God, he flourished in the strength of his virtues,[2] and planted in the divine courts he daily stretched forth to the stars the strength of his increase. Meanwhile the report of his great constancy was manifest in the king's palace, so that it was spread far and wide with glorious signs of praiseworthy virtues. Yet he did not strive after the vain favours of this world, but, protected by an abundance of virtues, bore within him the glory of the Eternal King, which great wisdom, with the learned finger of spiritual gifts, pointed out to him, with the variety of studies also, and not with the glittering splendour of gold adornments. For, like a clever bee, he darted through many fields of sacred and religious volumes, with the rapid course of an able mind, to refresh the mind rather than the body with divine studies, and devoutly to fill with the taste of nectar his soul, the retreat of his chaste heart, suffused with the breath of the Holy Spirit. Moreover, Irish pilgrims, as well as other crowds of the faithful, cherished that place of Glastonbury, which I have mentioned, with great affection, especially in honour of the blessed Patrick the younger, who is said to rest there happily in the Lord. Dunstan diligently studied their books also, meditating on the path of the true faith, and always explored with critical

---

[1] Dunstan. [2] Cf. Psalm xci. 13.

scrutiny the books of other wise men which he perceived from the deep vision of his heart to be confirmed by the assertions of the holy fathers. Thus he controlled his way of life so that, as often as he examined the books of divine Scripture, God spoke with him; as often, however, as he was released from secular cares and delighted with leisure for prayer, he seemed himself to speak with God.[1]

12. Among his sacred studies of literature he also diligently cultivated the art of writing, that he might be sufficient in all things; and the art of harp-playing, and skill in painting likewise; and, so to speak, he excelled as a keen investigator of all useful things. On this account a certain noble woman named Æthelwynn called him to her on one occasion with a friendly request to design her a stole for the divine service, with divers figures, which she could afterwards diversify and adorn with gold and gems. When he came to her for this work, he usually brought with him his *cythera*, which in the native language we call 'harp', that he might at times delight himself and the hearts of his listeners in it. Then one day after dinner, when he and the aforesaid woman returned with her workwomen to the said work, it happened by a marvellous event that this same harp of the blessed champion, hanging on the wall of the chamber, rang out a melody of jubiliation of its own accord, without anyone touching it, with a clear sound in the hearing of all. For it rang out and played the melody of this anthem, and continued chanting the melody right through to the end: "Let the souls of the saints who followed the steps of Christ rejoice in the heavens; and because they shed their blood for his love, they shall reign with Christ for ever." And when they heard it, he and the aforesaid woman and all her work-women were terrified, and completely forgetting the work in their hands, gazed at one another in astonishment, marvelling greatly what new warning that miraculous act might prefigure.

13. At length, when King Athelstan was dead, and the condition of the kingdom changed, the authority of the succeeding king, namely Edmund, ordered the blessed Dunstan, who was of approved way of life and erudite conversation, to appear before him, that he might be chosen and numbered among the royal courtiers and chief men of the palace. Not rashly resisting these orders, but rather remembering the Lord's command, he hastened to render to the king the things that were the king's, and to God the things that were God's.[2] Likewise, admonished by the order of the blessed Apostle James,[3] he did not cease "to be subject to every human creature" and especially to the mighty, "whether to the king as excelling, or to governors as sent by him for the punishment of evil-doers and for the praise of the good . . ."[4] For thus, though wearisomely, he dwelt a long time among the nobles in the royal palace, holding in holy governance a pair of reins, namely of the contemplative rule and of the practical life. Some of the thegns living with him began to love him with un-matched sweetness of charity and brotherly love when they saw the constancy of his way of life. But on the other hand very many, blinded by their dark minds, began to

---

[1] The Life then tells how other young men of the court became envious and got him expelled from the court; how he was tempted to marry, but was persuaded by a serious illness and by Ælfheah, bishop of Winchester, to become a monk. After relating a few miracles, it includes one which reveals Dunstan's artistic talents.
[2] Matthew xxii. 21.   [3] Yet his text is I Peter ii. 13.   [4] Further texts to the same effect are quoted.

detest the man of God with most bitter and foolish hatred, and to envy his prosperity even to wishing him dead. Indeed, to add to their malice, these execrators begged any others they could to persecute the servant of God also. For they twisted about him the rope of their iniquity for so long, though destined to entangle themselves in it rather than him, that they infected the king himself with their vices and made him believe their deceptions. And at once, as he had been directed by the wicked men, being moved with great anger, he ordered him to be stripped of every office and also deprived of every honour, and to procure for himself patronage where he chose, away from him and his followers. There were at Cheddar, where these things took place, some venerable men, namely messengers of the eastern kingdom,[1] staying at that time with the king. Dunstan, as if already destined to exile, knowing no other course for himself, approached these, praying that they would not desert him, abandoned as he was by the king, but would take him with them to any country to dwell there. They took pity on his unhappiness and promised him all the advantages of their kingdom if he went there in their company.[2]

15. Therefore after this the servant of God, Dunstan, undertook at the king's command the management of the aforesaid office;[3] and following the most wholesome institution of St. Benedict in the afore-mentioned way, he shone as the first abbot of the English nation; and thus from the affection of his heart he vowed to render willing service to God. Then, as a very prudent shepherd, he first fortified firmly the fences of the precincts on every side with monastic buildings and other defences, as had already been revealed to him a long time before by an old man in a vision.[4] There he enclosed the Lord's sheep, gathered in flocks from far and wide, that they might not be torn to pieces by the invisible wolf. Next, the same teacher of God's doctrine began to nourish the community assembled and committed to him there with the consolation of the divine word, and to give them to drink from the heavenly fountain, namely the mellifluous teaching of Holy Scripture; showing that one should pass through the troublesome pathways of this life to the eternal delights of the celestial banquets. For it is manifest to almost all the faithful on all sides that after an interval of a few years the tender disciples whom by his toil he ingrafted into the vine of the true faith, that is, Christ, throve abundantly, and bore fruit of good work in pleasing beauty; and that after this many pastors of churches, instructed by his teaching and example, were sought for divers cities or other places of the saints, to be there elected as instructors in sacred government and the pattern of righteousness, as priors, deans, abbots, bishops, even archbishops, pre-eminent over the other orders. Whosoever among his disciples was finally freed from the bodily coils in these times and underwent inevitable death, attained without doubt the high joys of the heavens.[5]

19. When King Edmund had been killed by a wicked robber,[6] the next heir, namely Eadred, at once received the kingdom in succession to his brother. And when

---

[1] It is clear that a foreign land is meant, presumably the eastern part of the Frankish empire, which is called *eastrice* 'eastern kingdom' in the Anglo-Saxon Chronicle.

[2] The next chapter relates the king's repentance when in danger of death at the brink of a cliff, when stag-hunting. Dunstan is made abbot of Glastonbury.   [3] Of abbot of Glastonbury.

[4] This refers to a vision of new buildings, which Dunstan had had when taken to Glastonbury as a boy by his father. It is told in chap. 3 of the Life.

[5] Chaps. 16–18 are occupied with miracles.   [6] See No. 1, p. 203.

thus confirmed on the throne, he loved the blessed Father Dunstan with such great warmth of love that he preferred hardly anyone of his chief men to him. And the man of God on his side was accustomed to acclaim the king dearest of all to him, in order to make a return of love from the deepest affection of his heart to him who loved him. Indeed, out of this loving trust, the king committed to him all the best of his goods, namely many title-deeds and also the ancient treasures of preceding kings, as well as various precious things he had acquired himself, to be faithfully kept in the security of his monastery . . .[1]

20. . . . Being then anxious about his life by reason of his long sickness, he[2] sent on all sides to collect his goods, to distribute them, while he could, to his followers with a willing and free disposition in his lifetime.[3] The man of God, Dunstan, went for this purpose, just as did the other keepers of the royal treasures, to bring back to the king what he had in his custody. When some days later he was returning with this treasure in packs, the way he had come, a voice was heard coming from heaven which said to him: "Behold, now King Eadred has departed in peace." The horse which the man of God was riding was suddenly struck dead at this voice, because it could not endure the presence of the angel's sublimity. When he arrived, he discovered that the king had ended his life at the very time when the angel announced it to him on that journey. The bands of his faithful followers who were present commended his departed soul to the Lord its maker, to peaceful repose, and likewise his lifeless limbs to be buried according to the custom of mortals.

21. After him succeeded Eadwig, the son of King Edmund, a youth indeed in age and endowed with little wisdom in government, though, when elected, he ruled in due succession and with royal title over both peoples.[4] A certain woman, foolish, though she was of noble birth, with her daughter, a girl of ripe age, attached herself to him, pursuing him and wickedly enticing him to intimacy, obviously in order to join and ally herself or else her daughter to him in lawful marriage. Shameful to relate, people say that in his turn he acted wantonly with them, with disgraceful caresses, without any decency on the part of either. And when at the time appointed by all the leading men of the English he was anointed and consecrated king by popular election, on that day after the kingly anointing at the holy ceremony, the lustful man suddenly jumped up and left the happy banquet and the fitting company of his nobles, for the aforesaid caresses of loose women. When Archbishop Oda saw that the king's wilfulness, especially on the day of his coronation, displeased all the councillors sitting around, he said to his fellow-bishops and other leading men: "Let some of you go, I pray, to bring back the king, so that he may, as is fitting, be a pleasant companion to his followers in the royal banquet." But one by one, fearing to incur the king's annoyance or the women's complaint, they withdrew themselves and began to refuse. Finally they chose from them all two whom they knew to be most firm of spirit, namely Abbot Dunstan and Bishop Cynesige,[5] Dunstan's kinsman,

---

[1] Eadred wished to make Dunstan bishop of Crediton on Æthelgar's death, but, in spite of the queen-mother's intercession, he refused.

[2] Eadred.   [3] Eadred's will is extant, No. 107.

[4] Literally "he filled up the numbers and the names of kings among both peoples", i.e. among those who afterwards rejected him as well as in Wessex.

[5] Of Lichfield.

that they should in obedience to the command of all bring the king, willing or un-willing, back to his deserted seat. When in accordance with their superiors' orders they had entered, they found the royal crown, which was bound with wondrous metal, gold and silver and gems, and shone with many-coloured lustre, carelessly thrown down on the floor, far from his head, and he himself repeatedly wallowing between the two of them in evil fashion, as if in a vile sty. They said: "Our nobles sent us to you to ask you to come as quickly as possible to your proper seat, and not to scorn to be present at the joyful banquet of your chief men." But when he did not wish to rise, Dunstan, after first rebuking the folly of the women, drew him by his hand from his licentious reclining by the women, replaced the crown, and brought him with him to the royal assembly, though dragged from the women by force.[1]

24. It came about that the aforesaid king in the passage of years was wholly deserted by the northern people, being despised because he acted foolishly in the government committed to him, ruining with vain hatred the shrewd and wise, and admitting with loving zeal the ignorant and those like himself. When he had been thus deserted by the agreement of them all, they chose as king for themselves by God's guidance the brother of the same Eadwig, Edgar, who struck down the wicked with the imperial rod, but peacefully guarded the good under the same rod of equity. And thus in the witness of the whole people the state was divided between the kings as determined by wise men, so that the famous River Thames separated the realms of both.[2] Then Edgar, being thus assigned to the kingdom by the aforesaid people, by God's will sent to recall the reverend abbot from the hateful exile in which he was dwelling, remembering how much he had been revered by his predecessors, to whom he rendered untiring service and loyal obedience with wholesome counsel. When he had brought him back from his place of stay, he maintained him with every honour and dignity as was due to such a father.

Meanwhile the brother of this same Edgar, because he turned from and deserted the just judgments of his God, breathed his last by a miserable death, and Edgar received his kingdom, being elected by both peoples as true heir and united the divided rule of the kingdoms, subjecting them to himself under one sceptre. He once more restored the blessed Dunstan to the honour of the former office of which he had been deprived; and also his grandmother[3] and some others whom his brother had caused to be plundered by an unjust judgment when he held that same eminence.

25. Afterwards a great assembly of councillors was held in the place which is called Bradford, and there by the choice of all Dunstan was ordained bishop, especially that he might constantly be in the royal presence on account of his farseeing and prudent counsels. And as soon as the king had been fittingly instructed in royal usage and sacred customs by the blessed Dunstan and other wise men, he began to suppress evil-doers everywhere, to love with a pure heart the just and virtuous, to subdue kings and tyrants on all sides, to restore or enrich the destroyed churches of God, and to

---

[1] Not unnaturally, this action roused the king's anger and the women's enmity, and Dunstan was exiled. He went to Gaul (to St. Peter's at Blandinum, Ghent).

[2] See No. 1, p. 205.

[3] Eadgifu, widow of Edward the Elder. An extant charter (Birch, No. 1064; Harmer, No. 23) speaks of the confiscation of her property under Eadwig.

collect together communities serving in praise of the Supreme Godhead, and to preserve in kingly fashion his whole country with peaceful protection.[1]

37. . . . While Dunstan toilfully inhabited the wearisome dwelling of this life, it was his chief care to occupy himself constantly and frequently in sacred prayers and in the ten-stringed[2] psalmody of David; or to pass the night in continuous vigils, overcoming sweet sleep; or to sweat and labour in the concerns of the Church; or also, when he could see the first light of daybreak, to correct faulty books, erasing the errors of the scribes; or, giving judgment with a keen intelligence between man and man, to distinguish the true from the false; or by calm words to bring to harmony and peace all who were at enmity or quarrelling; or to benefit with his kind support widows, orphans, pilgrims and strangers in their necessities; or to dissolve by just separation foolish or wrongful marriages;[3] or to strengthen by the word of life or by example the whole human order, triply divided in its proper and stable design;[4] or with serene probity to support and enrich the churches of God by just contribution of his own procuring or from other sources; or to season with the celestial salt, that is, with the teaching of wholesome knowledge, the ignorant of both sexes, men and women, whoever he could, by day and night. And therefore all this English land was filled with his holy teaching, shining before God and men like the sun and moon; and also when he resolved to render to Christ the Lord the due hours of his service and celebrations of Masses, he so performed and recited them with his whole soul that he seemed to speak face to face with the Lord himself, even though he had been much vexed before by the agitated disputes of the people; with eyes and hands directed to heaven after the custom of the blessed Martin, never relaxing his spirit from prayer. And as often as he fitly and splendidly[5] discharged any other work of perfection, as in the holy ordination of priests, or the consecration of churches or altars, or in the institution of any divine matters whatever, he always performed it with a great flow of tears, which the invisible indweller, the Holy Spirit, who constantly dwelt in him, mightily drew forth from the rivers of his eyes.[6]

235. Ælfric's Life of St. Æthelwold

Two Lives of this important prelate, who was one of the three leading figures of the tenth-century monastic revival, are extant, this by Ælfric, the preface of which was written 1005–1006, and one (printed in Mabillon, *Acta Sanct. ordinis S. Bened.*, Saec. v, pp. 608–624; *Acta Sanct.* 1 August, pp. 88–98; Migne, *Patrologia Latina*, cxxxvii, col. 81–108) which J. Armitage Robinson (*The Times of St. Dunstan*, pp. 106–108) claimed to be a post-Conquest elaboration of Ælfric's Life. Recently, however, D. J. V. Fisher ("The Early Biographers of St. Ethelwold", *Eng. Hist. Rev.*, LXVII, pp. 381–391) has discussed his arguments and made a good case for reverting to the older belief that it is in fact the work of a contemporary, Wulfstan, the precentor of Winchester, as stated by William of Malmesbury. Mr. Fisher believes that it was earlier than Ælfric's work, since there is evidence that a Life of

---

[1] Dunstan's appointment to the sees of Worcester, London, and eventually Canterbury is then described, and his journey to Rome for his *pallium*. His behaviour as archbishop on his return is related in general and conventional terms, and certain visions are related. In one (chap. 34) occurs the interesting statement: "For the venerable man was ever, as we have said, kindled in the love of God, and therefore was careful to go round the places of holy communities for the edification of souls." A more personal picture is given in chap. 37, which I include.   [2] Psalm xxxii. 2.

[3] In the Life by Adelard (ed. Stubbs, p. 67), Dunstan refused to obey a papal mandate permitting the illicit marriage of a certain nobleman.   [4] Cf. No. 239 (H).

[5] Accepting the reading of the St. Gall MS.   [6] The work ends with an account of Dunstan's death.

Æthelwold was known to the writer of the Life of St. Oswald, before the death of Archbishop Ælfric in 1005, whereas he holds that Ælfric did not write until after this archbishop's death. This argument does not seem entirely convincing, for Ælfric may have written the work before the preface, and it could thus have been his work, and not Wulfstan's, of which the author of the Life of St. Oswald was aware. At least it seems odd that Ælfric should have written to the brothers of Winchester in the terms he did, if they already possessed a Life of the saint and all he had done had been to curtail it. It still seems possible to hold that Wulfstan added to Ælfric's Life various details and elaborations from the tradition current at Winchester. Even so, these additions may be important, and so I have referred to the more important of them in the footnotes. Moreover, the longer Life enables us to correct some of the errors of the only surviving manuscript of Ælfric's Life (Paris, Bibl. Nat. Lat. 5362). On Ælfric see No. 239.

This work is edited by J. Stevenson, *Chronicon Monasterii de Abingdon*, R. S., II, pp. 253–266. It has been translated by S. H. Gem, *An Anglo-Saxon Abbot: Ælfric of Eynsham* (Edinburgh, 1912), pp. 166–180.

Here begins the prologue to the Life of St. Æthelwold.

1. Abbot Ælfric, a pupil of Winchester, to the honourable Bishop Cenwulf and the brothers of Winchester, sends greeting in Christ.

Considering it fitting, now that twenty years have passed since his death, to commend to memory some things concerning the acts of our father and eminent teacher, Æthelwold, I have set down in writing what I have learnt from reliable persons among you or others, in a brief narrative, even if in an unpolished one, after my manner;[1] lest perchance they should wholly be given to oblivion because of the scarcity of writers. Farewell.

Here ends the prologue and the Life begins.

2. The parents of St. Æthelwold were inhabitants of the city of Winchester, flourishing in the time of Edward, king of the English, honoured with a remarkable gift from God in that they deserved to give birth to such a son, by whose example not only the people of the present age, but also of the future, might be freed from the darkness of error. Accordingly his happy mother, while she bore him in her womb, saw a dream of this kind, a presage of future results. For it seemed to her that she was sitting before the door of her house and that there appeared before her eyes a lofty standard, whose top seemed to touch the sky, and bowing reverently it surrounded the pregnant women with its fringes. Again in like manner the woman when oppressed with sleep the same night saw as it were a golden eagle come out of her mouth and fly away, so immense that the whole city seemed to be shadowed by its gilded wings. But we can easily interpret these dreams, as the event has proved, and recognize in the lofty standard that the son whom she was carrying in her womb was to be a standard-bearer of the soldiers of God, as he truly became; and in the golden eagle the celebrated man, as the Lord says in the gospel: "Wheresoever the body shall be, thither will the eagles also be gathered together."[2]

3. Another time, the mother was standing one day in the church crowded with citizens to hear the holy Mass, when she felt that the soul had come to the boy she was carrying in her womb and had entered into him, as afterwards the saint himself, who was to be born, told us with rejoicing when he had become a bishop. From this it is mâde manifest that he was chosen of God even before he was born; and that the soul of man comes not from the father nor from the mother, but is given to each by the Creator alone.

[1] Reading *meatim*.   [2] Luke xvii. 37.

4. When the child was born, his parents called him Æthelwold when he was washed with the sacred baptism. It happened on a certain feast day when his mother was sitting at home and holding the child on her lap, that a stormy wind arose, so strong that she could not go to the church as she had resolved; but when she had given herself up to prayer with groans, she was suddenly found sitting with the infant in church where the priest was celebrating Mass.

5. The boy grew and was set in his very boyhood to the study of the sacred writings. When he was a young man and his fame had spread, he was made known to King Athelstan, son of Edward, and he belonged to his following for a long time, where he learnt from the king's councillors many things useful to him, for he was of keen intelligence; and at length by the king's orders he was tonsured and consecrated into the priestly orders by Ælfheah, bishop of Winchester. This Ælfheah was strong in the spirit of prophecy, and it happened that he ordained at the same time Dunstan and Æthelwold and a certain Athelstan, who afterwards abandoned the monastic habit and remained an apostate to the end. But after Mass, Bishop Ælfheah said to those following him: "I have consecrated three priests today, two of whom will attain to the episcopal dignity, one in my see, the other in another diocese." Then Athelstan said: "Am I one of the two who will reach the episcopal dignity?" "No," said Ælfheah, "nor will you continue in the holy life in which you began"; as indeed he did not.

6. Æthelwold greatly benefited by the teaching and example of Ælfheah, who had ordained him, and whom he zealously served for some time by the king's orders, and afterwards, going to Glastonbury, he placed himself under the instruction of the glorious man, Dunstan, abbot of that monastery. Profiting much from his supervision, he at length received from him the habit of the monastic order, giving himself up with humble devotion to his rule. For he learnt there the art of grammar and metrics, and the sacred books and authors, devoting himself exceedingly to vigils and prayers, subduing himself by abstinence, and always exhorting the brothers to higher things.

7.[1] At length, when a long time had passed after he had received monastic orders, he determined to go to lands across the sea, to train himself more perfectly in sacred books and monastic discipline; but the venerable Queen Eadgifu, King Eadred's mother, prevented his attempts, advising the king not to let such a man depart from his kingdom. It then pleased King Eadred by his mother's persuasion to give to the venerable Æthelwold a certain place, Abingdon by name, in which a little monastery was situated in ancient days; but it was then waste and deserted, consisting of poor buildings and possessing only 40 hides. The rest of the land of this place, namely 100 hides, the aforesaid king was holding by royal right. It was brought about with Dunstan's permission and according to the king's wish, that Æthelwold took charge of the aforesaid place, in order that he might ordain monks serving God according to rule. The afore-mentioned servant of God therefore came to the place committed to him, and at once certain clerics from Glastonbury followed him, namely Osgar, Foldberht, Frithegar, and from Winchester Ordberht, and from London Eadric,

---

[1] This and the next few paragraphs should be compared with No. 238.

submitting themselves to his instruction; and in a short space of time he collected to him a flock of monks, over whom he was ordained abbot by the king's orders.

8. The king also gave to the abbot and the brethren the royal property which he had owned in Abingdon, namely 100 hides, with excellent buildings, to augment the daily provisions, and he assisted them greatly with money, but his mother did so even more generously. Then the king came one day to the monastery to plan himself the structure of the buildings, and he measured out all the foundations of the monastery with his own hand, exactly as he had determined to erect the walls; and the abbot invited him to dine in the refectory with his men. The king assented on the spot, and there happened to be with him several men from the race of the Northumbrians, and they all came with the king to the feast. The king was merry and ordered mead to be supplied in abundance to the guests, when the doors had been closed so that no one might hurry away and leave the drinking at the royal[1] banquet. To be brief, the servers drew drink for the feasters the whole day in full measure, but the drink in the vessel could not be used up, except to a span's depth, until the Northumbrians were swinishly[2] intoxicated and withdrew in the evening.

9. Nevertheless, the abbot did not begin to construct the building assigned to him in the days of King Eadred, for he soon died, but in the reign of Edgar he built and completed in that place a noble temple in honour of St. Mary, Mother of God and ever Virgin, which can better be shown than described. About this time Dunstan was elected to the bishopric of the church of Worcester; and after the passage of years he was made archbishop and remained in Kent 37 years, like an immovable pillar, pre-eminent in doctrine, alms-giving and prophecy. We have heard also that frequent miracles are performed at his tomb.

10. Æthelwold sent the monk Osgar across the sea to the monastery of St. Benedict at Fleury, there to learn the customs of the rule and then expound them by his teaching to the brethren at home, to the end that Æthelwold might follow the regular way of life together with those subject to him, and, avoiding every false path, might guide the flock committed to him to the promised land. In that congregation there was a certain brother, a guileless and very obedient man, Ælfstan by name, who was ordered by the abbot to provide food for the builders of the monastery. He applied himself most zealously to this service, and daily cooked meat and served the workmen, kindling the hearth and fetching water and again cleansing the vessels, while the abbot thought that he performed this with the help of a servant. It happened one day while the abbot was wandering about the monastery according to his habit, that he caught sight of that brother standing by a boiling cauldron, preparing food for the workmen; and, entering the kitchen, he saw all the vessels spotless and the floor swept, and he said to him with a glad countenance: "My brother, you have robbed me of this obedience which you practise without my knowledge; but if you are such a soldier of Christ as you show yourself, put your hand in the boiling water and draw out for me a morsel of food from the bottom." At once, without delay, he put his hand to the bottom of the cauldron and drew out a hot morsel, feeling no heat from the boiling water. When the abbot saw this, he ordered him to put down the morsel

---

[1] The longer Life has *regalis*, not *regulis*.   [2] *suatim*, alternatively 'after their fashion'.

and to reveal this to no one alive. We have heard that that brother was afterwards made an abbot, and in truth we have seen him later as bishop of the church of Wilton.[1]

11. Æthelwold was indeed a great builder, both while he was abbot and after he became a bishop; hence the common enemy laid his snares for him, so that one day while he was working on the building, a huge post fell on him and threw him down into a pit and broke nearly all his ribs on one side; and if the pit had not received him, he would have been completely crushed. However, he recovered from this affliction by the help of God, and Edgar, the most blessed king of the English, chose him for the bishopric of the church of Winchester, before the above-mentioned church was dedicated, and Dunstan, archbishop of the church of Canterbury, consecrated him by the king's orders.[2]

12. Now at that time in the Old Minster, where the episcopal seat is situated, there were evil-living clerics, possessed by pride, insolence and wanton behaviour, to such an extent that several of them scorned to celebrate Mass in their turn; they repudiated wives whom they had married unlawfully, and took others, and were continually given over to gluttony and drunkenness. The holy man Æthelwold by no means put up with this, but when King Edgar's permission had been given, he very quickly expelled the impious blasphemers of God from the minster, and bringing monks from Abingdon, placed them there, being himself both their abbot and bishop.

13. Now it happened that while the monks who had come from Abingdon were standing at the entrance of the church, the clerics inside were finishing Mass, singing for the communion: "Serve ye the Lord with fear, and rejoice unto him with trembling; embrace discipline, lest you perish from the just way."[3] As if they were saying: "We would not serve God, nor observe his discipline; do you at least act so that you may not perish like us." And the monks, hearing their singing, said one to another: "Why do we linger outside? Behold, we are exhorted to enter."

14. The king also sent a certain very celebrated thegn of his, Wulfstan by name,[4] with the bishop, and he commanded the clerics by the royal authority speedily to give place to the monks or to accept the monastic habit. But they, detesting the monastic life, instantly departed from the church; nevertheless three of them were afterwards converted to the regular way of life, namely Eadsige, Wulfsige and Wilstan. For hitherto there were at that time no monks in the English nation except in Glastonbury and in Abingdon.

15. Hence at length, by the ill-will of the clerics, the bishop was given poison to drink, in his hall in which he was dining with the guests, in order that they could freely enjoy their former deeds of shame after he was dead. For it was his custom on account of infirmity to drink a little after taking three or four morsels; and he drank all that the cup held not knowing that what was brought to him was poison. And immediately his face turned pale, and his bowels were greatly racked by the strength of the poison. He then arose, going with difficulty from the table to his couch, and the

---

[1] Thus, correctly, Wulfstan, instead of the erroneous 'Winchester' of the surviving MS. of Ælfric's version.

[2] Wulfstan's Life gives the date of his consecration, 29 November 963, the first Sunday in Advent.

[3] Psalm ii. 11, 12.

[4] Wulfstan says that he was Wulfstan of Dalham. This man appears in other records as a powerful land-owner in the eastern counties.

poison spread through all his limbs, threatening him with death. But at length he began to reproach himself, saying to his soul: "Where now is thy faith? Where are the words of Christ, in which he said: 'and if they shall drink any deadly thing, it shall not hurt them'?"[1] The faith kindled in him by these and like words quenched the deadly draught which he had drunk, and he soon arose, and went to the hall cheerful enough, and did not repay his poisoner with any ill.

16. After that, Æthelwold spread his wings, and expelled the clerics from the New Minster, with King Edgar's consent, ordaining his pupil Æthelgar abbot there, with monks under him leading a life according to the rule. Æthelgar was afterwards made archbishop in Kent.

17. He made Osgar abbot of Abingdon, and that place was enriched with 600 hides and more. And he placed religious women in a nunnery, over whom he set Æthelthryth as mother superior. There is moreover a place in the region called Ely, greatly ennobled by the relics and miracles of St. Æthelthryth,[2] the virgin, and her sisters; but it was then deserted and given up to the royal treasury. Æthelwold bought this from the king and stationed in it many monks, over whom he placed as father his pupil, Brihtnoth by name; and he endowed the place most richly with buildings and lands. He acquired another place from the king and the nobles of the land, situated on the banks of the River Nene, which of old was called *Medeshamestede* in the English tongue, now usually *Burh*,[3] where in like manner he assembled monks, placing over them as abbot Ealdwulf, who afterwards obtained the archbishopric of the city of York. Also he acquired by purchase a third place, close to the aforesaid river, named Thorney in English, which he committed to monks under the same conditions; and when he had constructed a monastery, he appointed an abbot to it, Godeman by name, and enriched it abundantly with possessions.

18. Æthelwold was in King Edgar's confidence, prevailing nobly in word and deed, preaching everywhere the gospel of Christ according to the admonition of the prophet Isaiah, who says: "Cry, cease not, lift up thy voice like a trumpet, and show my people their wicked doings, and the house of Jacob their sins."[4] His preaching was greatly assisted by St. Swithin, who was translated at that same time; because what Æthelwold taught by words, Swithin wonderfully adorned by miracles. And thus it was brought to pass with the king's consent that monasteries were founded everywhere among the English people, partly by the counsel and action of Dunstan and partly by that of Æthelwold, some with monks and some with nuns, living according to the rule under abbots and abbesses.

19. And Æthelwold went round the individual monasteries, establishing good usages by admonishing the obedient and correcting the foolish with rods. He was terrible as a lion to the disobedient or undisciplined, but gentler than a dove to the gentle and humble. He was a father of the monks and nuns, a comforter of widows and a restorer of the poor, a defender of churches, a corrector of those going astray, for he performed more by his work than we can relate in words.

20. He was often afflicted with illness in his bowels and legs, spending sleepless nights from pain, and nevertheless going about by day as if well, though pale. Yet

---

[1] Mark xvi. 18.   [2] See No. 151, pp. 658f.   [3] Peterborough.   [4] Isaiah lviii. 1.

he did not indulge in the flesh of animals or birds except once for three months, when forced by great infirmity—and this, moreover, he did at the command of Archbishop Dunstan—and again during the sickness from which he died. It was always a pleasure to him to teach young men and boys, and to explain books to them in English, and with kindly exhortations to encourage them to better things. From this it came about that several of his pupils were made abbots and bishops[1] in the English people.

21. It happened once that his clerk, who had been appointed to carry his ampulla, took less oil than was required, and even this he lost on the way. When the bishop came to their destination, and wished to have the chrism, he had none. Very troubled, the clerk then retraced the road he had come, and discovered the ampulla, which before had not been half full, lying full of oil.

22. A monk serving under him, Edwin by name, stole the purse of a guest, by the instigation of the devil. The bishop spoke to the whole congregation in chapter about this matter, saying that if anyone had taken it he should return it with his blessing, or throw it down in a place where it might be found. When three days had passed without the money being discovered, the bishop spoke again to all the brethren, saying: "Our thief would not return the stolen goods with our blessing, as we ordered; let him now return it with our curse; and let him be bound, not only in soul, but also in body, by our authority." What more need be said? The brethren said "Amen", and, behold, the thief sitting there was bound wretchedly with his arms stuck to him beneath his cope, and he remained thus confounded until the third hour, pondering what he ought to do. Yet he had power to move all his limbs except his arms, which the bishop had rendered useless by the power conferred on him by God. However, the wretched man arose thus bound, and going after the bishop, was constrained to confess that he had the thing secretly, saying nothing about his binding. Then the bishop said to him gently, as was his habit: "At least you have done well in confessing your crime now, although late; have then our blessing." And immediately his arms were loosed without the bishop knowing. But he went away gladdened by this and told everything about his binding and his release to a certain brother, Wulfgar by name, who advised that this should rather be kept hidden in silence.

23. When the bishop wished to restore the old church with great effort, and ordered the brethren frequently to work alongside the workmen, it happened one day that while the monks were standing with the masons on the top of the roof of the church a monk named Goda fell from the top to the bottom. And immediately he touched the ground he got up without having suffered any injury from such a fall, and mounted to the work where he had stood before and seizing a trowel completed what he had begun. To whom therefore ought this miracle to be ascribed unless to him by whose order he went out to this work?

24. Also a certain monk, Theodric by name, went to the bishop in the nocturnal interval wishing to inform him by signs about a certain necessary matter, and discovered him reading with a candle, and sharpening his aged eyes by unremittingly blinking his eyelids; and he stood a long time marvelling at how diligently he kept his

[1] Wulfstan adds "and some even archbishops".

eyes fixed on the page. Then the bishop rose from his reading and that brother took the candle and began to read, trying if he could sharpen his sound eyes to the reading as diligently as the bishop had done his failing eyes. But that temerity did not go unpunished, for the following night, when he had given himself to sleep, there appeared to him someone of unknown countenance, saying to him with terrible threatening: "How dared you reproach the bishop in his reading last night?" And, saying this, he struck him a blow in the eyes with his finger, and there immediately followed a violent pain in the eyes which afflicted him greatly for many days, until he obliterated by amends the fault which he had heedlessly committed against the holy man.

25. Again, it happened that when the bishop was reading by night he fell asleep from too many vigils, and the burning candle fell on the page and continued to burn on the leaf until a brother[1] arrived and took the flaming candle from the book, and saw the glowing pieces of the candle lying on many lines inside, and when he blew them out he found the page undamaged.

26. Lo, I confess openly that it does not seem easy to me to write how many and what sort of things St. Æthelwold endured for monks and with monks; and how kind he was towards the zealous and obedient; and how much he laboured in the construction of the monastery, restoring the church and building the other houses; and how watchful he was in prayers; and how kindly he exhorted the brethen to confession. But from these few things more can be understood which cannot be told by us. He died in the twenty-second year of his episcopate, on 1 August, in the reign of Ethelred, king of the English, and was buried in the church of the blessed Peter and Paul at his episcopal see. We have heard that miracles were performed at his shrine, both before his bones were elevated from the tomb, and after. I insert only two of these in this brief account.

27. There was a certain citizen of Oxford,[2] Ælfhelm by name, afflicted by blindness for several years, who was warned in dreams to go to the shrine of St. Æthelwold, and was told the name of a monk of Winchester of whom up till then he had never heard, who would lead him to the tomb of the holy bishop. In short, he went to Winchester and summoned the monk by name just as he had learnt it in dreams –namely Wulfstan, the precentor–and asked him to be his guide to the saint's shrine, and related to him the course of his vision. The monk then led the blind man to the saint's grave, but he returned with his sight, requiring no guide.

28. Also Ælfheah, St. Æthelwold's successor, related to us that he had sent to prison a thief who had been flogged, and when the man had thus lain some time in punishment, St. Æthelwold came to him in a vision, saying to him: "Why do you lie thus wretchedly, stretched out in the dungeon [?] for so long?" But, recognizing the saint whom he had often seen in his mortal life, he replied: "My lord, I suffer merited punishment and am tormented thus by the just sentence of the bishop, because I did not stop thieving." Then said the saint: "Stop even now, wretch, stop, and may you be released from the bonds of this prison." The thief arose, set free on the

---

[1] Leofred, according to Wulfstan.
[2] Wulfstan says he was a citizen of Wallingford.

spot, and came to Bishop Ælfheah, and told him in detail what had been done for him, and he released him, letting him go away uninjured.

29. Therefore the faith of the Holy Trinity and the true Unity shines with such wonderful signs for the merits of his saints. To him is honour and dominion throughout eternal ages. Amen.

236. Extracts from the anonymous Life of St. Oswald, archbishop of York

The author of this work was a monk of Ramsey Abbey, writing between 995 and 1005. A strong case has been made by S. J. Crawford in "Byrhtferth and the anonymous Life of St. Oswald" (*Speculum Religionis, Essays . . . presented to C. G. Montefiore*, 1929) for identifying him with Byrhtferth of Ramsey, the author of a scientific *Manual*. D. J. V. Fisher, who discusses this text in "The Anti-Monastic Reaction in the Reign of Edward the Martyr" (*Camb. Hist. Journ.*, x, Part III, 1952), answers an objection of J. Armitage Robinson (*Journ. Theol. Stud.*, xxxi, pp. 35–42) to this identification, that the Life contains certain usages foreign to Byrhtferth's work, by suggesting that a Life by Byrhtferth received some additions at a Mercian monastery. He bases this opinion on certain errors in the Life that are strange in a Ramsey writer of so early a date, *e.g.* the placing of Dunstan's death later than the battle at Maldon, and the confusion which gives Ordmær instead of Ordgar as the name of the father of Ælfthryth, wife of Æthelwold of East Anglia and later of Edgar, and which makes her mother, instead of step-mother, of Edward the Martyr. One may note also that the author lets Edgar survive his delayed coronation several years, instead of two only.

The Life gives an account of the career of one of the three chief leaders of the monastic revival, and tells us something about ecclesiastical affairs in the times just before that revival. It has also important information on political history, especially on the confusion after the death of Edgar and on the murder of Edward, being probably the oldest surviving account of this crime. It should be compared with No. 1, p. 210. I have given this passage, and also the account of two battles in Ethelred's reign, one in Devonshire which is probably that entered in the Anglo-Saxon Chronicle, 988, the other the famous fight at Maldon, which should be compared with the poem. (See No. 10.) Unfortunately the style of this author is verbose and florid, often with vague generalizations and scriptural quotations where precise detail would have been welcome. It may be that the vagueness is sometimes intentional, for reasons of policy.

The work survives only in Brit. Mus. Cott. Nero. E I, and is edited by J. Raine, *The Historians of the Church of York and its Archbishops*, I, pp. 399–475. The text is corrupt in places, and scholars will welcome the new edition which Mr. Fisher has in hand.

P. 443. [The troubles after Edgar's death]

When several years had passed after his consecration, and after he had accomplished everything in kingly fashion, he was suddenly taken from this world, while there were with him a few men and thegns. Yet we can say of him what the Book of Wisdom says: "The just man, if he be prevented with death, shall be in rest."[1] Fittingly do faithful monks and especially pastors of the people pray for him, since he was not only their lord but their father. O ruler Benedict, succour with gracious prayer this the defender of your servants, and make him worthy to be crowned on the right hand, who showed himself your friend worthy of veneration. The illustrious king died on 8 July, and by his death the state of the whole kingdom was thrown into confusion, the bishops were agitated, the noblemen stirred up, the monks shaken with fear, the people terrified; the clerics were made glad, for their time had come. Abbots, with their monks, were expelled; clerics, with their wives, were introduced; and the last error was worse than the first.[2] Abbot Germanus[3] also was expelled along with the others – and fittingly, that he who shared in the injustice, should share in the transmigration. For we know that the just man often perishes with the wicked, not in spirit, but in body. These words which I utter are not extravagant, but well known, because before the holy churches of God were laid waste by our countrymen, when

---

[1] Wisdom iv. 7.   [2] Matthew xxvii. 64.   [3] Of Winchcombe, formerly prior of Ramsey.

28

the servants of the Lord, who ceased not day and night from the divine praises, were expelled, though some did not act rightly, yet many did well. Indeed it is written: "Not only those who do, but also those who consent"[1] are guilty. Thus also the ealdorman of the Mercian people, Ælfhere by name, appropriating enormous revenues, which blind the eyes of many, ejected, as we have said, with the advice of the people and the outcry of the crowd, not only the sheep but the shepherds also. Those who before were wont to ride on caparisoned horses, and to join with their fellows in singing the mellifluous song of King David, you could then see bearing their burden, not borne, as the patriarch of old, by a chariot into Egypt; or else walking with companions or friends, without a scrip, without shoes, and thus involuntarily fulfilling the words of the holy gospel.[2]

In those days, if the common crowd discried a man of our habit, an outcry was raised as if it saw a wolf among the sheep, for they put their trust in the above-mentioned ealdorman, being unmindful of the words of the psalmist who says: "Put no trust in princes, nor in the children of men, in whom there is no salvation."[3] It came to pass after the course of a few years that those who were then especially violent against the monks had neither their own nor others' goods. Indeed, it is a scandal how the common folk and many—one cannot say nobles, but ignobles, since they can more rightly be called thus—perished, defiling themselves with filth. When the fickle opinion and hostile madness of the enemy wished to reach with its polution the eastern peoples of the Mercians, and to root out the glory of the people and the monasteries, God-fearing men stood firm against the blast of the mad wind which came from the western territories, driven from its proper course by the pleasures which withdraw the hearts of many from the right way and incite their minds to evil desires. The warlike thegn Ælfwold[4] opposed the iniquity which the will of Ælfhere, prospering according to the world's grandeur, was supporting, along with the people gathered to him. The wicked said among themselves, not rightly considering: "Let us encompass the monks and oppress them, 'and the inheritance shall be ours'.[5] May there be none to pity them, but let them be expelled, hurled down, derided, suppressed, bound, beaten, that not one may remain in all the land of the Mercians." O the evil threats of wicked men! O the deceit of the ancient enemy! O the ancient pretexts of battle, which thou inspirest in the limbs of weak men! But he who once suppressed the force of the winds and immediately granted tranquillity to his followers, is mighty to resist thy venomous machinations. Very many assented to these unhappy counsels and did not truly resist in their hearts what they heard; wherefore many departed shamefully from this life and lament eternally because they consented to iniquity. Such frenzy surged forth among the Christian people as once in Judea when they persecuted the Lord, in which crime the feeble head of Caiphas was raised, and the apostolic man was made a base apostate, not to speak of the villainous Pilate. The disciples were timid with fear, as in these days the monks with affliction. But the holy mind of the righteous man Æthelwine[6] was by no means ready to tolerate this, but assembling a noble army he, whom the prince of angels protected

---

[1] Romans i. 32. [2] Matthew x. 9; Luke x. 4, xxii. 35. [3] Psalm cxlv. 3.
[4] Brother of Æthelwine, ealdorman of East Anglia. [5] Mark xii. 7. [6] Ealdorman of East Anglia.

and strengthened, himself became the leader of the forces. After the death of the glorious King Edgar all the more noble thegns and the illustrious sons of leading men came to him with devoted heart, knowing for certain that in him was "wisdom to do judgment".[1] In synod, he said he could in nowise suffer, while he lived, that the monks, who by the help of God[2] maintained all the Christianity in the kingdom, should be expelled from the kingdom. And when the unworthy crowd wished to oppose him, there arose the intrepid thegn Ælfwold, his brother, tall of stature, pleasant in speech, dignified in aspect, but his face then burning with anger, and, like another Judas incited to war, said to all who could hear: "If my life is preserved unharmed by Christ, I wish to preserve the things that are mine, and give them willingly to whoever pleases me and is obedient to my authority. If indeed Christ is prince of all things, shall he not have the portion which religious men gave to him for the redemption of their souls, but be driven far from us? How", he said, "can we guard our own without his great help? By him who caused me to be re-born, I may not tolerate that such men be ejected from our territories, by whose prayers we can be snatched from our enemies." Then Ealdorman Brihtnoth[3] got up, "a religious man and fearing God",[4] and demanded silence and said to the army: "Listen to me, veterans and young men, we all wish and desire that you should desire what the excellent thegn has now said."[5]

p. 448. And when the glory of rulers, and emperor of the whole of Albion, had been snatched from the whirlpool of this inconstant world, and saved from the wrecking deep of the raging sea, after the time of joy that had peacefully lasted in his time there began to approach on all sides dissension and tribulation, which neither bishops nor leaders in ecclesiastical and secular affairs could allay. . . .[6] Certain of the chief men of this land wished to elect as king the king's elder son, Edward by name; some of the nobles wanted the younger, because he appeared to all gentler in speech and deeds. The elder, in fact, inspired in all not only fear but even terror, for [he scourged them][7] not only with words but truly with dire blows, and especially his own men dwelling with him. Meanwhile nine and five months had run out and the tenth moon was shining for mortals,[8] after he had been elected; the zealous thegns of his brother rose up against him when he was hastening to come to talk with his beloved brother. Treacherous and evil, they sought the life of the innocent youth, whom Christ predestined and fore-ordained to share a martyr's dignity. When a certain day was nearing evening, the illustrious and elected king came as we have said to the house where his much loved brother dwelt with the queen, desiring the consolation of brotherly love; there came out to meet him, as was fitting, nobles and chief men, who stayed with the queen, his[9] mother. They formed among them a wicked plan, for they possessed minds so accursed and such dark diabolical blindness

---

[1] I Kings iii. 28.   [2] Reading *deo* for *eo*.

[3] Ealdorman of Essex, and hero of the Battle of Maldon. See No. 10.   [4] Acts x. 2.

[5] The author then relates how Ælfwold killed a man who wished to seize land from the abbey of Peterborough. A couple of pages are then devoted to an account of the completion of Ramsey and of visits to it, after which we return to the troubles after Edgar's death.   [6] Here a long diatribe against sedition occurs.

[7] Some such words must be supplied to complete the sense here.

[8] This roundabout phraseology apparently means 'almost two years later'. If it is correct, it must mean that Edward's coronation did not take place until about March, 976; but this author is weak on chronology.

[9] Ethelred's. But in an earlier passage, p. 429, both Edward and Ethelred are said to be Ælfthryth's sons.

that they did not fear to lay hands on the Lord's anointed. Armed men surrounded him on all sides, and with them also stood the cupbearer to perform his humble office. The revered king indeed had with him very few thegns, for he feared no one, trusting "in the Lord and in the might of his power".[1]

He was versed in divine law, by the teaching of Bishop Sidemann,[2] and he was also strong and vigorous in body. And when his betrayers encircled him, just as the Jews once surrounded Christ, he sat undaunted on his horse. Certainly a single frenzy was in them, and a like insanity. Then the worst of villainies and the fierce madness of the devilish enemy was inflamed in the hearts of the venomous thegns; then the poisoned arrows of the crime of Pilate rose up very cruelly against the Lord and against his anointed, who had been elected to defend the kingdom and empire of this most sweet race on his father's death. The thegns then holding him, one drew him on the right towards him as if he wished to give him a kiss, but another seized roughly his left hand and also wounded him. And he shouted, so far as he could: "What are you doing—breaking my right arm?" And suddenly leapt from his horse and died. The martyr of God was carried by the servants and brought to the house of a certain unimportant person; where no Gregorian harmony nor funeral dirge was heard, but so glorious a king of the whole land lay covered with a mean covering, waiting the light of day. Discerning such wicked deeds of wretched men, the King of Kings would not desert for ever his soldier and pre-elected and appointed vice-regent in the land, and leave him as if shameful and vicious, but allowed him to be buried, not so worthily at that time as he deigned to permit him to be later. When twice six months had passed of the days of the solar and lunar year, the renowned Ealdorman Ælfhere came with a multitude of people, and ordered his body to be lifted up from the earth; and when this was done and the body uncovered, they found and saw him as whole from every stain or pollution as he was in the beginning. Seeing this, all were amazed, rejoicing with exultation in the Lord, "who alone doth wonderful things"[3] in the world. The servants then washed the body of the reverend king, and placed it, clothed in new vestments, in a coffin or shrine, and noble thegns with the bier placed on their shoulders carried him to the place in which they buried him honourably, where Masses and sacred oblations were celebrated for the redemption of his soul, by the ealdorman's orders.

When these things were ended, the madmen who did these things imagined that the King of the heavenly city did not see them from the high throne of his glorious majesty, or that, seeing, he forgot the blood of his soldier which in his innocence was shed; but it happened as follows—for I conceal neither the punishments of those men, nor the garlands of the king: he who required the blood of the son of the first man from the hand of his brother, the same demanded the blood of their king from the hands of those men. A space of life was granted to them, but not for repentance, since their mouths spoke vain things, and "their right hands were the right hands of iniquity".[4] Not to them were given the lamentations of King David, nor the holy weeping of the door-keeper of the wonderful glory of heaven; but they flourished, they passed away; they drank, they lived in wantonness, because they were corrupted

---

[1] Ephesians vi. 10.   [2] Of Crediton.   [3] Psalm lxxi. 18.   [4] Psalm cxliii. 8.

and abominable to God.[1] Their foolish hearts were hardened, lest they should do penance, just as once was that of the king of Egypt, lest he should set free the people of the Israelites. One of them, however, received such an analogous punishment, in that, losing both eyes, he sustained the indescribable loss of both lights–the light, I mean, of this life, and likewise of the future life. He lost the light of this world, when he could not see the sight of the sun and the day, nor dear servants ministering to him; he took from himself that of the other life, since he had not the mercy of our Saviour. But, as is right, he suffered punishments; not the punishments which mortals inflict on mortals, but such as mercilessly afflict the souls of the wretched, as it is read: the souls will "pass from the snow waters to excessive heat".[2] Many things could be said in this place about the calamities of those who killed him, but because we move on to other matters, we believe that what has been said is sufficient. . . .

[The renewal of the Danish attacks]

p. 455. King Ethelred, the illustrious atheling, was consecrated to the supreme dignity of the kingdom by the apostolic man Dunstan and his co-apostle Oswald, and there was great rejoicing at his consecration. For he was young in years, graceful in manners, beautiful in face and comely in appearance. Soon indeed, before he had passed the age of adolescence, the Prince Behemoth rose against him, with all his preparation and his satellites, having with him *caelethi*,[3] that is, slayers. During his reign the abominable Danes came to the kingdom of the English, and laying waste and burning everything, did not spare men, but, glorying in flashing blades and poisoned arrows, armed themselves in bronze helmets, in which they fought and were wont to terrify beholders. A very severe battle took place in the west, in which our countrymen, who are called Devonshiremen, strongly resisted and obtained the victory of a holy triumph, thus gaining glory. Many of our side fell, more of theirs. For of our men, a most brave thegn, Streonwold by name, was killed, with some others, who preferred to end their lives by a warlike death than to live in shame.

When not many months had passed, another very violent battle took place in the east of this famous country, in which the glorious Ealdorman Brihtnoth held the front rank, with his fellow-soldiers. How gloriously, how manfully, how boldly he urged his leaders to the front of the battle, who, relying on an elegant style, can make known? He himself, tall in stature, stood conspicuous above the rest; his hand was not sustained by Aaron and Hur, but supported by the manifold faithfulness of the Lord, since he was worthy. He smote also on his right hand, unmindful of the swan-like whiteness of his head, for alms-deeds and holy Masses strengthened him. He protected himself on his left hand, forgetful of the weakness of his body, for prayers and good deeds sustained him. And when the beloved leader in the field saw his enemies fall, and his own men fight bravely and cut them down in many ways, he began to fight with all his might for his country. An infinite number, indeed, of them and of our side perished, and Brihtnoth fell, and the rest fled. The Danes also were wondrously wounded, and could scarcely man their ships.

[1] Cf. Psalm lii. 2.   [2] Job xxiv. 19.
[3] Possibly this is a corrupt reading for *cerethi*, which is interpreted *interficientes* by Jerome, *De nominibus Hebraicis*.

(c) VERNACULAR PROSE LITERATURE

237. Extracts from King Alfred's works

It was Alfred's habit to expand his original, often with the addition of a concrete simile to make clearer an abstract argument. As he drew these similes from his own experience, they sometimes have great value for the historian. This present selection of passages not in the sources shows among other things the nature of bookland, the existence of the sealed letter a century before the earliest surviving example, and the king's views on royal expenditure.

Alfred's translation of St. Augustine's *Soliloquies*, which apart from a small fragment has come down in one twelfth-century manuscript only, is edited by H. L. Hargrove, *Yale Studies in English*, XIII (1902) and translated by him in *ibid.*, XXII (1904), and by S. Potter in *Philologus*, XCVIII (1949). Alfred's translation of Boethius, *De Consolatione Philosophiae*, is edited by W. J. Sedgefield (Oxford, 1899) and translated by him in 1900.

A. From Alfred's version of St. Augustine's Soliloquies

FROM THE PREFACE

Then I gathered for myself staves and props and bars, and handles for all the tools I knew how to use, and crossbars and beams for all the structures which I knew how to build, the fairest pieces of timber, as many as I could carry. I neither came home with a single load, nor did it suit me to bring home all the wood, even if I could have carried it. In each tree I saw something that I required at home. For I advise each of those who is strong and has many wagons, to plan to go to the same wood where I cut these props, and fetch for himself more there, and load his wagons with fair rods, so that he can plait many a fine wall, and put up many a peerless building, and build a fair enclosure with them; and may dwell therein pleasantly and at his ease winter and summer, as I have not yet done. But he who advised me, to whom the wood was pleasing, may bring it to pass that I shall dwell at greater ease both in this transitory habitation by this road while I am in this world, and also in the eternal home which he has promised us through St. Augustine and St. Gregory and St. Jerome and through many other holy fathers; as also I believe he will, for the merits of them all, both make this road more convenient than it has hitherto been, and also enlighten the eyes of my mind so that I can find out the straight road to the eternal home, and to the eternal mercy, and to the eternal rest which is promised to us by the holy fathers. So be it.

It is not to be marvelled at that one expends labour on such material both in the carriage and in the building; but every man, when he has built a village on land leased to him by his lord, with his help, likes to stay in it sometimes, and to go hunting and fowling and fishing, and to support himself in every way on that leased land, both on sea and land, until the time when through his lord's mercy he may acquire bookland and a perpetual inheritance. So shall the rich giver act, who rules both these transitory habitations and the eternal mansions. May he who created both, and rules both, grant me that it may be in my power both to be useful here and to attain thither.

BOOK I, p. 23, l. 13.[1]

Reason. . . . Consider now, if your lord's letter and his seal comes to you, whether you can say that you are not able to recognize him by it, and not able to understand

[1] References are to Hargrove's edition.

his will in it. If, however, you say that you can understand his will in it, say then which seems to you more right, to follow his will or to follow after the wealth which he previously gave you in addition to his friendship?

Augustine. Whether I will or not, I must needs speak the truth, unless I wish to lie. If then I lie, God knows it. Therefore I dare not say other than the truth, according as I can perceive it. It seems better to me to abandon the gift and follow the giver, who is steward for me both of the wealth and of his friendship, if I cannot have both. Yet I would like to have both, if I could follow both the wealth and also his will.

Reason. You have answered me full rightly, but I would ask you whether you think that you can have all that you now have without your lord's friendship.

Augustine. I do not imagine that any man is so foolish as to think that.

Book I, p. 44, l. 1.

Reason. . . . Consider now whether many men ever come to the king's estate when he is in residence there, or to his assembly, or to his army, and whether it seems to you that they all come thither by the same road. I think, however, that they come by very many different roads: some come from a great distance and have a very long, very bad, and very difficult road; some have a very long and very straight and very good road; some have a very short, yet crooked, narrow and miry road; some have a short and smooth and straight one; and yet they all come to one and the same lord, some more easily, some with greater difficulty; they neither all come thither with equal ease, nor are they all equally at ease there. Some are in greater honour and greater comfort than others, some in less, some almost without any, except only what has the lord's approval. So it is also with wisdom. Each of those who desire it and pray zealously for it can come thither and dwell in its court and live by it, though some may be nearer it, some farther off. Just so all kings' residences: some men are in his chamber, some in the hall, some on the threshing-floor, some in prison; and yet they all live by the mercy of one and the same lord, just as all men live under one sun and by its light see what they see.

Book III, p. 69, l. 7.

And again, the righteous, when they are out of this world, very often remember both the good and the evil which they had in this world, and rejoice very greatly that they did not desert their lord's will either in easy or in hidden matters, while they were in this world. Just as if some mighty man in this world has driven one of his favourites from him, or he has been forced from him against the will of both of them, and he then has many sufferings and misfortunes in his exile, and yet he comes back to the same lord with whom he was formerly, and is there in much greater honour than he was before. Then he remembers the misfortunes which he had here in his exile, and yet is none the sadder.

B. *From Alfred's version of Boethius*

Chapter xvii.[1] . . . You know that covetousness and greed for worldly dominion never pleased me over much, and that I did not all too greatly desire this earthly rule,

[1] The reference is to Sedgefield's edition.

but yet I desired tools and material for the work that I was charged to perform, namely that I might worthily and fittingly steer and rule the dominion that was entrusted to me. You know that no man can reveal any talent or rule and steer any dominion without tools and material. That without which one cannot carry on that craft is the material of every craft. This, then, is a king's material and his tools for ruling with, that he have his land fully manned. He must have men who pray, and soldiers and workmen.[1] Lo, you know that without these tools no king can reveal his skill. Also, this is his material, which he must have for those tools—sustenance for those three orders; and their sustenance consists in land to live on, and gifts, and weapons, and food, and ale, and clothes, and whatever else those three orders require. And without these things he cannot hold those tools, nor without these tools do any of the things that he is charged to do. For that reason I desired material to rule that dominion with, that my powers and dominion would not be forgotten and concealed. For every talent and every dominion is soon worn out and silently passed over, if it is without wisdom; because no man can bring forth any craft without wisdom, for whatever is done in folly can never be accounted as a craft. In brief, I desired to live worthily as long as I lived, and to leave after my life, to the men who should come after, my memory in good works.

238. An Old English account of King Edgar's establishment of monasteries

This text survives only in Brit. Mus. Cott. Faust. A x, where it follows the Old English version of the Rule of St. Benedict. It is generally agreed that the latter was translated by Æthelwold, bishop of Winchester, on the evidence of the twelfth-century author of the *Historia Eliensis* (Book II, chap. 37), who no doubt had an older source before him when he informs us that Edgar and Ælfthryth gave Sudbourne, Suffolk, to Æthelwold on condition that he would translate the Rule. Agreements in style between the translation and this account of the monastic revival, and the absence of any terms of praise in reference to the abbot (clearly Æthelwold) mentioned in the treatise, make it probable that this too is a work of his pen, though J. Armitage Robinson (*The Times of St. Dunstan*, pp. 159–168) rejects this view, mainly because it does not mention Eadred's part in the foundation, and in his opinion implies that all was done by Edgar. But it must be remembered that there is a lacuna where Eadred's work would be in place, and the completion and dedication of the church was in Edgar's reign. (See No. 235, p. 834.) It does not follow, however, even if we accept Æthelwold's authorship, that the treatise formed the preface to the translation of the rule as first issued. Already in 1885 Schröer (*Bibl. der angels. Prosa*, II, pp. xviii–xxviii) pointed out that all extant versions betray by their pronouns that they come from a version originally made for the use of women. In that case this treatise, which does not suggest that the work was primarily intended for this end, may have been written to accompany a version modified from the first translation, for general use.

The interest of this work to historians is not dependent on whether Æthelwold wrote it. It gives an early, if partisan, view of Edgar's government, and, though it is only repeating the preface to the *Regularis Concordia* in its account of the relation of this king and his queen to monastic foundations, its final remarks illustrate the danger arising to church property from its being treated as the private estate of the abbot or abbess, whether by the royal officials or the heads of the monastery themselves.

The text is edited, with translation, by O. Cockayne, *Leechdoms, Wortcunning and Starcraft of Early England* (Rolls Series), III, pp. 432–444.

p. 434.[2] . . . understood and knew him[3] a true steward of his holy churches before he was revealed to men. For that reason he gave to him manifold and plentiful possessions

---

[1] Cf. No. 239 (H).

[2] As the fragmentary text has come down, it begins with the conversion of the English, and refers to Gregory's instruction to Augustine to build monasteries. Then at least a folio is missing.

[3] Edgar? It has hitherto been assumed that this refers to Dunstan, and that the subject of the sentence is Edgar. It makes an equally good sense, if not better, to take the subject to be God, and the object Edgar.

and power. Neither did he delay long, nor withhold power. It was not long before his brother[1] ended the time of this transitory life, who had through the ignorance of childhood dispersed his kingdom and divided its unity, and also distributed the lands of the holy churches to rapacious strangers. After his death, Edgar, the aforesaid king, obtained by God's grace the whole dominion of England, and brought back to unity the divisions of the kingdom, and ruled everything so prosperously that those who had lived in former times and remembered his ancestors and knew their deeds of old, wondered very greatly and said in amazement: "It is indeed a very great miracle of God that all things in his royal dominion are thus prosperously subjected to this youthful king; his predecessors, who were mature in age and very prudent and far-seeing in wisdom and hard to overcome in any strife, never could maintain this dominion in so great peace and tranquillity, neither by battle nor by tribute." But it is not to be wondered at as if it were an unusual thing when God Almighty rewards gloriously each of those who promise him good service, and afterwards fully carry it out; the Lord Christ is very greatly to be praised in these things with all gladness of heart. Truly the Almighty God, who is cognizant of all things, who knows before-hand all that is to come, and who knew how beneficial he would be, was ever very gracious to him, and ever had in store for him all good things to his profit; as if the righteous and faithful Rewarder preached not with words but with deeds, and said thus: "Now that you zealously protect and advance my name and dominion–that is, my Church which I rightly have in my special dominion–as a recompense to you I will glorify your name and increase and advance in prosperity your kingdom which you hold under my dominion."

What man is there dwelling in England who does not know how he advanced and protected God's kingdom, that is, God's Church, with benefits both spiritual and worldly, with all his strength? Certainly, as soon as he was elected to his kingdom, he was very mindful of the promise which he had made as an atheling in his childhood, to God and St. Mary, when the abbot[2] had invited him to the monastery.[3] As we have said above, admonished by that promise he began in the beginning of his reign to be very intent on advancing that place just as he had promised in his childhood, and he endowed it so greatly with all things that it was no different from or inferior to many of those which his ancestors had advanced over a long period. He imme-diately ordered to be built there within three years' time a glorious minster. That will seem unbelievable to all men who see that place in later times and do not remember this. He ordered that same minster thus speedily built to be consecrated to St. Mary for the praise and honour of God, and assembled there a great company of monks to the end that they should serve God according to the teaching of the holy rule.

Before that there were only a few monks in a few places in so large a kingdom who lived by the right rule. This was in no more places than one, which is called Glastonbury, where his father, King Edmund, first established monks. The afore-mentioned abbot was brought from that place and consecrated to the aforesaid monastery which King Edgar established and set with monks. Edgar was greatly

---

[1] Eadwig, 955–959. In 957 the Mercians and Northumbrians chose Edgar in his place.
[2] Æthelwold.
[3] *munuclif*. Cockayne renders 'monastic life' but the word is also used in Old English as 'monastery'.

gladdened by that spiritual beginning with monks, and began eagerly to inquire first of all how he could rectify his own life with true piety. It is also written in books: "He who plans to begin a good work, let him make a beginning with himself." After he had been amended himself, he began zealously to set monasteries in order widely throughout his kingdom, and to set up the service of God. By the supporting grace of God, it was performed thus: he availed himself continually of the counsel of his archbishop, Dunstan; through his admonition he constantly inquired about the salvation of his soul, and not that only, but likewise about all the religion and welfare of his dominion. He cleansed holy places from all men's foulnesses, not only in the kingdom of the West Saxons, but in the land of the Mercians also. Assuredly he drove out canons who abounded beyond measure[1] in the aforesaid sins, and he established monks in the foremost places of all his dominion for the glorious service of the Saviour Christ. In some places also he established nuns and entrusted them to his consort, Ælfthryth, that she might help them in every necessity. He was himself ever inquiring about the welfare of the monks, and he kindly exhorted her to take thought for the nuns in the same way, following his example.

With earnest scrutiny he began to investigate and inquire about the precepts of the holy rule, and wished to know the teaching of that same rule, by which is laid down the practice of a right life and honourable vocation, and the regulations which attract men to holy virtues. He wished also to know from the rule the wise disposition which is prudently appointed concerning the ordering of unfamiliar matters. Out of a wish for this knowledge he commanded this rule to be translated from the Latin into the English language.

Although keen-witted scholars who understand clearly the two-fold wisdom (that is, the wisdom of things actual and spiritual – and each of those again consists admittedly of three divisions) do not require this English translation, it is nevertheless necessary for unlearned laymen who for fear of hell-torment and for love of Christ abandon this wretched life and turn to their Lord and choose the holy service of this rule; lest any unconverted layman should in ignorance and stupidity break the precepts of the rule and employ the excuse that he erred on that day because he knew no better. I therefore considered this translation a very sensible thing. It certainly does not matter by what language a man is acquired and drawn to the true faith, as long only as he come to God. Therefore let the unlearned natives have the knowledge of this holy rule by the exposition of their own language, that they may the more zealously serve God and have no excuse that they were driven by ignorance to err.

Therefore, then, I pray my successors with all devotion and implore in the Lord's name, that they ever increase the observance of this holy rule through the grace of Christ, and may, improving it, bring it to full perfection. Nor is any one of them to presume through the devil's prompting or through any avarice to diminish God's patrimony or with any ill-will to seek how it may be diminished, either in estates or in any other possessions, lest through poverty and penury the fire of holy religion should become lukewarm and grow completely cold. May that never come to pass! In my opinion, the observance of this holy rule was impaired in former times through

---

[1] Conjecturing that the partly illegible *ofer . . . de* of the text is for *oferflede* 'in flood'.

the robbery of evil men, and through the consent of the kings who had little fear of God. We should all very greatly take warning and pray to our Lord, that that miserable state may never come back to our religion.

We also instruct abbesses to be deeply loyal and to serve the precepts of the holy rule with all their hearts, and to enjoin the commands of God Almighty, so that none of them shall presume senselessly to give God's estates either to their kinsmen or to secular great persons, neither for money nor for flattery. Let them consider that they are set as shepherds on God's behalf, and not as robbers. If any one of them, led astray by the temptation of the devil, be convicted of crime against the Church or the State, let neither king nor secular lord[1] be glad at it, as if the way were cleared and a reason given for him to rob God, who owns those possessions, and who never committed any crime; nor indeed let any earthly king be so greatly undermined with avarice that he will not let the heavenly king who created him be entitled to the same rights as he is himself. If any of the king's reeves is convicted of crime against God or man, what man is so foolish or senseless as to deprive the king of his property because his reeve is convicted? Therefore in the same way let whatever among the possessions of the churches is given to the eternal Christ stand for ever. If anyone is so presumptuous that he perverts this, he shall be miserably tormented in eternal torments. May it not come to pass that any of my successors shall deserve such wretchedness!

239. Extracts from the Old English works of Abbot Ælfric

Ælfric was a pupil of St. Æthelwold, bishop of Winchester, and was sent about 987 to take charge of the teaching at the newly founded abbey of Cerne Abbas, Dorset. Its founder was Æthelmær, son of Ealdorman Æthelweard (the chronicler), and when he also founded the abbey of Eynsham in 1005, he moved Ælfric to it as its abbot. That is about all we know of the events of Ælfric's life; both the date of his birth and that of his death are uncertain. But he had a prolific literary career, and his great learning earned for him the respect of his ecclesiastical contemporaries, two of whom, Bishop Wulfsige of Sherborne and Archbishop Wulfstan of York, employed him to write pastoral letters. He brought out his work known as the *Catholic Homilies* in two volumes, the first in 990, the second the following year. Each volume contained 40 homilies for the chief feast days. A few years later, he wrote his series of Saints' Lives for those festivals which were observed more by the monastic clergy than the secular. Meanwhile he had had the novel idea of writing a Latin-English grammar, accompanied by a 'colloquy' for the practice of conversation in Latin. Probably while he was still at Cerne, certainly before he became abbot, he translated, but only under pressure from his patron Ealdorman Æthelweard, some parts of Genesis and other portions of the Pentateuch, Joshua and Judges. After he became abbot of Eynsham he produced a treatise on the Old and New Testament for an Oxfordshire thegn called Sigeweard of Asthall, as well as one on chastity; and for a Warwickshire thegn, Wulfgeat of Ilmington, one about the Trinity and the Atonement. To this period belong his pastoral letters for Archbishop Wulfstan, and a few scattered homilies, his Latin Life of St. Æthelwold (see No. 235) and a set of excerpts from the latter's *Regularis Concordia* for the use of his Eynsham monks.

Though much of Ælfric's work is of theological content, it is full of small passages of interest for the historian, for he often uses concrete parallels to illustrate his points, and these sometimes afford a welcome insight into contemporary customs or opinions. I have selected what seem to me the most valuable.

The following are the best editions of the works from which the passages here given have been taken: *The Homilies of the Anglo-Saxon Church*, part I, *The Sermones Catholici*, ed. B. Thorpe, 1844–1846 (normally cited as *Catholic Homilies*): *Aelfric's Lives of Saints*, ed. W. W. Skeat, 1881–1900 (Early Eng. Text Soc., vols. 76, 82, 94, 114); *The Old English Version of the Heptateuch, Aelfric's Treatise on the Old and New Testament and his Preface to Genesis*, ed. S. J. Crawford, 1922 (Early Eng. Text Soc., vol. 160). The editors supply translation to the first two of these works, and W. L'Isle's translation of the *Treatise on the Old and New Testament* is included in the third.

---

[1] *woruldrica* 'secular ruler'. The owner of private jurisdiction is meant, who would benefit by the fines and forfeitures incurred.

A. Ælfric's English Preface to the first volume of his "Catholic Homilies"

I, Ælfric, monk and priest, though meaner than is fitting for that order, was sent in the reign of King Ethelred by Bishop Ælfheah, Æthelwold's successor, to a monastery which is called Cerne, at the request of the thegn Æthelmær–his rank and virtue are known everywhere. It then entered my mind, by the grace of God, I trust, to turn this book from the Latin language into the English tongue, not from confidence of great learning, but because I saw and heard much error in many English books, which unlearned men in their simplicity accounted great wisdom; and I was sorry that they did not know nor possess the evangelical teaching among their books, except for those men alone who knew Latin, and except for the books which King Alfred wisely translated from Latin into English, which are obtainable. For this reason, trusting in God, I presumed to undertake this work, and also because men particularly require good teaching in this age which is the end of this world; and there will be many perils among mankind before the end comes, as our Lord in his gospel said to his disciples: "Then shall be tribulations such as never were before from the beginning of the world. Many false Christs shall come in my name, saying 'I am Christ', and shall work many signs and wonders, to deceive mankind and likewise the elect, if it is possible; and unless the Almighty God were to shorten those days, all men would perish; but for the elect's sake he shall shorten those days."[1] Everyone can the more easily sustain the future temptation, through God's help, if he is strengthened by scholarly teaching, because those shall be preserved who continue in the faith until the end.

Many tribulations and hardships shall arise in this world before its end, and they are heralds of the eternal perdition to evil men, who shall afterwards suffer eternally in the black hell for their sins. Then shall the Antichrist come, who is human man and true devil, just as our Saviour is truly man and God in one person. And the visible devil will then work innumerable marvels, and will say that he himself is God, and will wish to compel mankind to his error; but his time will not be long; for the wrath of God will destroy him, and afterwards this world will be ended.

Christ our Lord healed the infirm and the sick, and this devil who is called Antichrist, which, interpreted, is 'adverse Christ', will injure and enfeeble the hale, and will not heal anyone from infirmities, except him alone whom he himself has injured. He and his disciples will secretly injure men's bodies by the devil's art, and openly heal them in men's sight; but he cannot heal anyone whom God himself has enfeebled. By cruelty he will force men to turn from their Creator's faith to the lies of him who is the origin of all lying and wickedness. The Almighty God will allow the impious Antichrist to work signs and wonders and persecutions for three and a half years; for at that time there will be so much evil and depravity among men that they will well deserve the diabolical persecution, to the eternal perdition of those who yield to him, and to the eternal bliss of those who through faith oppose him. God also permits his chosen servants to be cleansed from all sins through the immense persecution, as gold is tested in the fire. Then the devil will slay those who withstand him, and they will go

---

[1] The speech is made up from Matthew xxiv. 21, 5, 24, 22.

by holy martyrdom to the kingdom of heaven. Those who believe his lies, he will honour; and afterwards they will have the eternal torment as a reward for their error.

The impious one will make fire to come down as if from heaven in the sight of men, as if he were God Almighty, who has rule over heaven and earth. But Christians must be mindful how the devil behaved when he asked of God that he might be allowed to test Job. He then made fire to come down as if from heaven, and burnt up all his sheep in the field and the herdsmen with them, except for one who should announce it to him. The devil did not send fire from heaven then, although it came from above; for he was not himself in heaven after he had been cast out for his pride. Neither has the cruel Antichrist power to send heavenly fire, although by the devil's art he can pretend to do so.

It will now be wiser that everyone pay heed to this and know his faith, whoever must endure the great misery. Our Lord charged his disciples to instruct and teach all peoples the things which he himself taught; but now there are too few who will teach well and set a good example. The same Lord spoke through his prophet Ezekiel: "If thou stayest not the wicked and warnest him not that he turn from his wickedness and live, the wicked man shall then die in his iniquity and I will require of thee his blood"—that is, his destruction. "But if thou give warning to the wicked, and he will not turn from his wickedness, thou hast delivered thy soul with that warning, and the wicked shall die in his iniquity."[1] Again, the Almighty spoke to the prophet Isaiah: "Cry, and cease not, lift up thy voice like a trumpet, and show my people their wicked doings and the house of Jacob their sins."[2] Because of such commands, it seemed to me that I should not be guiltless before God if I would not manifest to other men either in speech or by writings that evangelical truth which he himself spoke and afterwards revealed to holy teachers. For well do I know many in this country more learned than I am, but God reveals his wonders through whom he will. As an Almighty Artificer, he performs his work through his chosen, not as if he requires our help, but that we may gain eternal life through doing his work. The Apostle Paul said: "We are God's helpers";[3] and nevertheless we do nothing for God without God's help.

Now I pray and entreat in God's name, that if anyone wishes to make a copy of this book, he correct it zealously according to the exemplar, lest we are blamed through careless scribes. He who writes falsely does much evil, unless he corrects it; it is as if he brings the true teaching to false error. Therefore each must correct what he previously rendered incorrectly, if he wishes to be guiltless in God's judgment.

B. *From the homily for Palm Sunday* ("*Catholic Homilies*" I. p. 212)

We will give you an illustration. No man can make himself king, but the people has the choice to choose as king whom they please; but after he is consecrated as king, he then has dominion over the people, and they cannot shake his yoke from their necks. So also has each man his own choice, before he commits a sin, whether he

---

[1] Ezekiel iii. 18, 19.   [2] Isaiah lviii. 1.   [3] I Corinthians iii. 9.

wishes to follow the devil's will or to resist it. If then he binds himself fast with the devil's works, he cannot unbind himself by his own power, unless the Almighty God unbinds him with the strong hand of his mercy.

C. *From the homily on the Nativity of John the Baptist ("Catholic Homilies" I. p. 358)*

It is known to all wise men that the old law was easier than Christ's ordinance is, because in the former there was no great continence, nor the spiritual ways of life which Christ established afterwards, and his Apostles. The ordinance which the king commands through his ealdormen and reeves is one thing; quite another is his own decree in his presence.

D. *From the homily on the dedication of a church ("Catholic Homilies" II. pp. 592ff.)*

Every Christian man is to know that no one shall accept money for the Church of God; and that, if anyone so acts that he gives for money the bride of God, that is, the Church, he is like Judas who received from the Jews money for Christ, and he shall suffer with Judas in eternity, unless he has previously made amends for it with God in his lifetime. No layman is to presume to have direction or authority over the servants of God. How can, and how dare, any layman take on himself with arrogance the functions of Christ? Not even a man in orders shall take it on himself to represent Christ over his holy household, unless the office is entrusted to him by God's teachers. If the layman wishes to found or endow some monastery, he is to entrust to God whatever he does for it, and to establish the community by the counsel of illustrious teachers; and the layman is never to hold authority over the ordained servants of God. If anyone does so, let him know that he is acting against the ordinance of Christ and of all his saints. He may help the servants of God in worldly concerns, and leave them to live according to the direction of their books, and the teaching of their spiritual superior.

E. *From the homily for Ash Wednesday ("Saints' Lives" I. pp. 264ff.)*

There was in the household of Ælfstan, bishop of Wiltshire, a certain foolish man who would not go to the ashes on the Wednesday as did the other men who then attended Mass. Then his companions begged him to go to the priest and receive the mysteries which they had received. He said: "I will not." They still begged him; he said that he would not, and spoke impudent words, and said that he would use his wife in the forbidden time. They then desisted. And it happened that the misguided man rode on some errand during that week. Then dogs attacked him very violently, and he defended himself until his spear-shaft got fixed in front of him, and his horse bore him on so that the spear went right through him and he fell dying. He was then buried, and many loads of earth lay upon him within a week of the time when he refused those few ashes.

In that same week there came a certain buffoon to the bishop's household, who paid no heed to the Lenten fast, but betook him to the kitchen while the bishop was saying Mass, and began to eat. He then fell at the first morsel, backwards in a swoon, and spat blood; however, his life was with difficulty granted to him. Also the holy Bishop Æthelwold,[1] who now works miracles through God, very often told us that he knew a man with Bishop Ælfheah who in Lent would drink when he liked. Then one day he asked Bishop Ælfheah to bless his cup. He would not, and the fool drank without the blessing and went out. By chance a bull was being baited outside, and the bull ran towards him and crushed him so that he lost his life, and thus paid for that untimely drink.

F. *From the homily on the Prayer of Moses ("Saints' Lives" I. pp. 292ff.)*

If men in orders observe the service of God at the appointed times, and live soberly, and if laymen live in accordance with what is right, we know then for certain that God will provide prosperity for us and peace among ourselves, and in addition give us eternal joy with himself. If, however, the leaders and the ordained teachers pay no heed to this, but think about worldly matters and heed not God's commands nor his worship, God will manifest to them their contempt of him either by famine or by pestilence, so that they may acknowledge that the Almighty Ruler thus avenges contempt of him; and in addition they shall suffer in the other life, for a long time or for ever, for their heedlessness in this life. We can well reflect how well it went with us when this island was dwelling in peace, and monasteries were held in reverence, and laymen were ready against their enemies, so that our reputation spread widely throughout the earth. How was it then afterwards when men overthrew monasteries and held God's services in scorn, but that pestilence and famine came to us, and afterwards a heathen army held us to scorn?

G. *From the Life of St. Swithin ("Saints' Lives" I. p. 468)*

We have now spoken thus briefly about Swithin, and we say in truth that that time was happy and joyful in England when King Edgar advanced Christianity and founded many monasteries, and his kingdom continued ever at peace, so that no fleet was ever heard of except of our own people who held this land. And all the kings who were in this island, Cumbrians and Scots, came to Edgar, once eight kings on one day, and they all submitted to Edgar's direction. Moreover, such miracles as we have related were performed by the holy Swithin, and as long as we lived there,[2] miracles were frequent. At that time also there were worthy bishops, the resolute Dunstan in the archiepiscopal see, and the venerable Æthelwold, and all the others. But Dunstan and Æthelwold were chosen of the Lord, and they most of all exhorted men to do the will of God, and established every good thing to the satisfaction of God. That is shown by the miracles which God works through them.

H. *From the Treatise on the Old and New Testament (Crawford. pp. 71f.)*

When there is too much evil in mankind, councillors should investigate with wise deliberation, which of the supports of the throne has been broken, and repair it at once. The throne stands on these three supports: *labourers, soldiers, beadsmen*.[3] *Labourers*

---

[1] See No. 235.   [2] In Winchester.
[3] Ælfric used the Latin terms *laboratores, bellatores, oratores*. Cf. No. 237 (B).

are they who provide us with sustenance, ploughmen and husbandmen devoted to that alone. *Beadsmen* are they who intercede for us to God and promote Christianity among Christian peoples in the service of God, as spiritual toil, devoted to that alone for the benefit of us all. *Soldiers* are they who guard our boroughs and also our land, fighting with weapons against the oncoming army; as St. Paul, the teacher of the nations, said in his teaching: "The soldier[1] beareth not the sword without cause. He is God's minister to thy profit, appointed for vengeance on him that doth evil."[2] On these three supports the throne stands, and if one is broken down, it falls at once, certainly to the detriment of the other supports. But what does it concern us to investigate into this? This those shall investigate who ought to care for it.

The righteous God loves just judgments; but bribes too often pervert the just judgments against the Lord's will, and evil befalls the whole people wherever that abuse securely reigns. He who is God's servant should judge rightly with fairness without any payment; then he would be honouring God with that good practice and his reward would be great with God, who lives and reigns for ever and ever. Amen.

I. From "Judges" (Crawford. pp. 416f.)

In England also kings were often victorious through God, as we have heard say; just as King Alfred was, who often fought against the Danes, until he won the victory and protected his people; similarly Athelstan, who fought against Olaf and slew his army and put him himself to flight, and afterwards lived in peace with his people. Edgar, the noble and resolute king, exalted the praise of God everywhere among his people, the strongest of all kings over the English nation; and God subdued for him his adversaries, kings and earls, so that they came to him without any fighting, desiring peace, subjected to him for whatever he wished, and he was honoured widely throughout the land.

240. "The Sermon of the Wolf to the English"

Lupus, 'the Wolf', was the literary alias of Wulfstan, who was bishop of London from 996 to 1002, archbishop of York 1002–1023, holding this see in plurality with that of Worcester until 1016. His political importance, and the great extent of his writings, have only been recognized within recent years. Besides homilies, he composed much of the legislation of the reigns of Ethelred and Cnut. (See Nos. 44–47, 50.) His authorship of the so-called *Canons of Edgar* was demonstrated by K. Jost in "Einige Wulfstantexte und ihre Quellen" (*Anglia*, LVI, 1932), and the same writer points out his connexion with the 'poems' in the Anglo–Saxon Chronicle, 959 D E, 975 D. (See No. 1, pp. 205, 209.) A general account of Wulfstan's career and writings, and of the present state of Wulfstan studies is given by D. Whitelock, *Sermo Lupi ad Anglos* (Methuen's Old English Library, 2nd ed., 1952), which contains a bibliography. Specially important are K. Jost, *Wulfstanstudien* (Swiss Studies in English 23, Berne, 1950), D. Bethurum, "Archbishop Wulfstan's Commonplace Book" (*Publ. Mod. Lang. Assoc. Amer.*, LVII, 1942); D. Whitelock, "Archbishop Wulfstan, Homilist and Statesman" (*Trans. Royal Hist. Soc.*, 4th Series, XXIV, 1942).

Wulfstan's most famous work, this *Sermon to the English*, survives in five manuscripts, representing three recensions of a homily probably first preached in 1014, certainly between Ethelred's expulsion late in 1013 and his death in 1016. The manuscript chosen as the basis of this translation is Brit. Mus. Cott. Nero A 1, one of the longer versions. This is in a contemporary hand, and has close connexions with Wulfstan. But as he was in the habit of using his work again and again, it

---

[1] The Vulgate text has no reference to a soldier here. It is to be noted that Ælfric translates the Latin *miles* as *cniht*, showing what a military connotation this word (originally *servant*) now had.

[2] Cf. Romans xiii. 4.

is possible that many of the variant readings and additions in the other manuscripts issue from him, and the more important of these are therefore added in notes. Many editions give a composite text, but I prefer to keep to a form in which we know that the homily existed in, or soon after, Wulfstan's lifetime.

As the homily gives a striking picture of England in Ethelred's reign, it has been edited many times, first by William Elstob in 1701, whose text is in G. Hickes, *Dissertatio Epistolaris*, pp. 98 ff., and most recently by D. Whitelock, *op. cit.*, where other editions are cited. There are translations in A. S. Cook and C. B. Tinker, *Select Translations from Old English Prose* (Boston, 1908), G. Sampson, *The Cambridge Book of Prose and Verse* (Cambridge, 1924), and R. W. Chambers, *England before the Norman Conquest* (London, 1926).

The sermon of the Wolf to the English when the Danes persecuted them most, which was in the year 1014 from the incarnation of our Lord Jesus Christ.[1]

Beloved men, realize what is true: this world is in haste and the end approaches; and therefore in the world things go from bad to worse, and so it must of necessity deteriorate greatly on account of the people's sins before the coming of Antichrist, and indeed it will then be dreadful and terrible far and wide throughout the world.[2]

Understand well also that now for many years the devil has led astray this people too greatly and there has been little loyalty among men, though they spoke fair enough; and too many wrongs prevailed in the land, and there were never many men who sought after a remedy as zealously as one should; but daily evil was piled on evil and wrongs and many lawless acts committed far too widely throughout all this people; also we have on that account suffered many losses and insults, and, if we are to experience any improvement, we must then deserve better of God than we have previously done. For with great deserts have we merited the miseries which oppress us, and with very great deserts must we obtain relief from God if henceforward things are to start to improve. For lo! we know full well that a great breach will require much repair, and a great fire no little water, if the fire is to be quenched at all; and great is the necessity for every man that he keep henceforward God's laws eagerly and pay God's dues rightly.

Among heathen peoples one dare not withhold little or much of what is appointed to the worship of false gods; and we everywhere withhold God's dues all too often. And one dare not among heathen peoples curtail within the sanctuary or outside any of the things which are brought to the false gods and delivered for sacrifices, and we have entirely despoiled God's houses inside and out. And the servants of God[3] are everywhere deprived of respect and protection; while among heathen peoples one dare not in any way ill-use the servants of false gods as one now does the servants of God too widely, where Christians ought to keep God's law and protect God's servants.

But it is true what I say, there is need of that relief, for God's dues have dwindled too long in every district within this nation, and the laws of the people have deteriorated all too much,[4] and sanctuaries are violated far and wide, and the houses of God

[1] This rubric is in Latin.

[2] MS. C (C.C.C.C., 201) incorporates what was probably a marginal note: "This was composed in the days of King Ethelred, four years before he died. Let him who will, pay heed how it then was and what happened afterwards." As this gives an impossible date for the text as it has come down, it seems possible that the scribe of C wrote "four years" for "few years".

[3] Wulfstan defines this expression elsewhere as covering "bishops and abbots, monks and nuns, priests and women under religious vows".

[4] MS. E (Bodleian MS. Hatton 113) adds: "since Edgar died". Wulfstan's writings often refer to the happier conditions of this king's reign.

are entirely despoiled of ancient privileges and stripped inside of all that is seemly.[1] And widows are wrongfully forced into marriage, and too many are reduced to poverty and greatly humiliated. And poor men are sorely deceived and cruelly defrauded[2] and sold far and wide out of this country into the power of foreigners, although quite innocent; and children in the cradle are enslaved for petty theft[3] by cruel injustice widely throughout this people. And the rights of freemen are withdrawn and the rights of slaves are restricted and charitable obligations are curtailed;[4] and, in short, God's laws are hated and his precepts despised. And therefore we all through God's anger are frequently disgraced, let him perceive it who can; and this injury will become common to all this people, though one may not think so, unless God protect us.

For it is clear and manifest in us all that we have previously transgressed more than we have amended, and therefore much is assailing this people. Things have not gone well now for a long time at home or abroad, but there has been devastation and famine, burning and bloodshed in every district again and again; and stealing and killing, sedition and pestilence, murrain and disease, malice and hate and spoliation by robbers have harmed us very grievously, and monstrous taxes have afflicted us greatly, and bad seasons have very often caused us failure of crops. For now for many years, as it may seem, there have been in this country many injustices and wavering loyalties among men everywhere.

Now too often a kinsman does not protect a kinsman any more than a stranger, neither a father his son, nor sometimes a son his own father, nor one brother another; nor has any one of us ordered his life as he should, neither ecclesiastics according to rule nor laymen according to law. But we have made desire a law unto us all too often, and have kept neither the precepts nor laws of God or man as we should. Nor has anyone had loyal intentions towards another as justly as he should, but almost everyone has deceived and injured another by word or deed; and in particular almost everyone wrongly stabs another in the back with shameful attack[5]–let him do more, if he can.

For here in the country there are great disloyalties both in matters of Church and State, and also here in the country there are many who are traitors in various ways. And it is the greatest of all treachery in the world that a man betray his lord's soul;[6] and a full great treachery it is also in the world that a man should betray his lord to

---

[1] Three MSS., C, B (C.C.C.C. 419) and H (Bodleian MS. 343), add: "and ecclesiastical orders have now for a long time been greatly despised".

[2] MSS. B and H add: "both of reputation (?) and of sustenance and of money and all too often of life". See p. 396, n. 4.

[3] The laws of Ine state that if a man steal with the knowledge of his household, all are liable to penal slavery. See No. 32, p. 365. Cnut's laws, drawn up by Wulfstan, legislate against the application of this to young children. See No. 50, p. 430.

[4] MS. C has an important addition here: "Free men are not allowed to keep their independence, nor go where they wish, nor to deal with their own property as they wish; and slaves are not allowed to keep what they have gained by toil in their own free time, or what good men have granted them in God's favour, and given them in charity for the love of God. But every charitable obligation which ought by rights to be paid eagerly in God's favour every man decreases or withholds, for injustice is too widely common to men and lawlessness dear to them."

[5] MS. E adds: "and with accusations".

[6] i.e. by persuading him to do evil, or by failing to carry out religious benefactions for his soul after his death.

death, or drive him in his lifetime from the land; and both have happened in this country: Edward was betrayed and then killed, and afterwards burnt,[1] [and Ethelred was driven out of his country].[2] And too many sponsors and godchildren have killed one another far and wide throughout this people.[3] And far too many holy foundations far and wide have come to grief because some men have previously been placed in them, who should not have been, if one wished to show respect to God's sanctuary. And too many Christian people have been sold out of this country now all the time; and all this is hateful to God, let him believe it who will. And it is shameful to speak of what has happened too widely, and it is terrible to know what too many do often, who commit that miserable deed that they contribute together and buy a woman between them as a joint purchase, and practise foul sin with that one woman, one after another, just like dogs, who do not care about filth; and then sell for a price out of the land into the power of strangers God's creature and his own purchase, that he dearly bought. Also we know well where that miserable deed has occurred that a father has sold his son for a price, and a son his mother, and one brother has sold another, into the power of strangers. And all these are grave and terrible deeds, let him understand who will. And yet, what is injuring this people is still greater and even more manifold: many are forsworn and greatly perjured, and pledges are broken again and again; and it is obvious in this people that God's anger violently oppresses us, let him perceive it who can.

And lo! how can greater shame befall men through God's anger than often does us for our own deserts? Though any slave runs away from his master and, deserting Christianity, becomes a viking, and after that it comes about that a conflict takes place between thegn and slave, if the slave slays the thegn, no wergild is paid to any of his kindred; but if the thegn slays the slave whom he owned before, he shall pay the price of a thegn.[4] Very base laws and shameful tributes are common among us, through God's anger, let him understand it who can; and many misfortunes befall this people again and again. Things have not gone well now for a long time at home or abroad, but there has been devastation and persecution in every district again and again, and the English have been for a long time now completely defeated and too greatly disheartened through God's anger; and the pirates so strong with God's consent that often in battle one puts to flight ten,[5] and sometimes less, sometimes more, all because of our sins. And often ten or a dozen, one after another, insult disgracefully the thegn's wife, and sometimes his daughter or near kinswoman, whilst he looks on, who considered himself brave and mighty and stout enough before that

---

[1] Edward the Martyr, murdered in 978. See No. 1, p. 210; No. 236, pp. 841 f. No other authority mentions the burning of the body, but strictly contemporary records are reticent about the whole business, and this categorical statement by a man who must have been at least a youth at the time, and who later had opportunity of learning the facts, deserves attention.

[2] Three MSS., including Nero A 1, omit the reference to Ethelred, possibly from motives of policy, for the reason for Ethelred's flight to Normandy late in 1013 was that Swegn, King Cnut's father, had been accepted as king by the English. It is clear, however, that the clause is necessary to complete the sentence, and I have added it from MSS. B and H.

[3] MS. E adds: "in addition to far too many other innocent people who have been destroyed all too widely"; and this is added in the margin of the Nero text.

[4] The Danish freeman was equated for purposes of the wergild with the English thegn, and presumably the Danes claimed this for any member of their forces, even English run-aways.

[5] MS. C adds: "and two often twenty".

happened. And often a slave binds very fast the thegn who previously was his master and makes him into a slave through God's anger. Alas for the misery, and alas for the public shame which the English now have, all through God's anger. Often two seamen, or maybe three, drive the droves of Christian men from sea to sea, out through this people, huddled together, as a public shame to us all, if we could seriously and rightly feel any shame. But all the insult which we often suffer we repay with honouring those who insult us; we pay them continually and they humiliate us daily; they ravage and they burn,[1] plunder and rob and carry on board; and lo, what else is there in all these events except God's anger clear and visible over this people?

It is no wonder that things go wrong with us, for we know full well that now for many years men have too often not cared what they did by word or deed; but this people, as it may seem, has become very corrupt through manifold sins and many misdeeds: through murders and crimes, through avarice and through greed, through theft and robbery, through the selling of men and through heathen vices, through betrayals and frauds, through breaches of law and through deceit, through attacks on kinsmen and through slayings, through injury of men in holy orders and through adultery, through incest and through various fornications. And also, far and wide, as we said before, more than should be are lost and perjured through the breaking of oaths and of pledges and through various falsehoods; and failure to observe fasts and festivals widely occurs again and again. And also there are here in the country degenerate apostates[2] and fierce persecutors of the Church and cruel tyrants all too many, and widespread scorners of divine laws and Christian virtues, and foolish deriders everywhere among the people, most often of those things which God's messengers command, and especially of those things which always belong to God's law by rights. And therefore things have now come far and wide to that full evil pass that men are more ashamed now of good deeds than of misdeeds, for too often good deeds are reviled with derision and godfearing people are blamed all too greatly, and especially are those reproached and all too often treated with contempt who love right and possess the fear of God in any extent. And because people behave thus, blaming all that they should praise, and loathing too much what they should love, they bring all too many to evil intentions and wicked acts, so that they are not ashamed, although they sin greatly and commit wrongs even against God himself, but because of idle calumny they are ashamed to atone for their misdeeds as the books teach,[3] like those fools who because of their pride will not protect themselves from injury until they cannot, although they much wish it.

Here, in the country as it may seem, too many are sorely blemished with the stains of sin. Here there are manslayers and slayers of their kinsmen, and slayers of priests and persecutors of monasteries,[4] and here there are perjurers and murderers,[5] and here there are harlots and infanticides and many foul adulterous fornicators, and

---

[1] MS. C has instead of "burn": "cut down, bind and insult".

[2] MS. C explains this foreign term by adding 'God's adversaries', and MSS. B and H replace apostates by this gloss.

[3] *i.e.* the penitentials used in the Anglo-Saxon Church, some of which have survived.

[4] MS. E adds: "and traitors and open apostates".

[5] MS. E adds: "and here there are injurers of men in orders and adulterers and people greatly corrupt through incest and various fornications".

here there are wizards and sorceresses,[1] and here there are plunderers and robbers and spoliators,[2] and, in short, a countless number of all crimes and misdeeds. And we are not ashamed of it, but we are greatly ashamed to begin the atonement as the books teach, and that is evident in this wretched corrupt people. Alas, many can easily call to mind much besides this which a single man could not quickly investigate, showing how wretchedly things have gone all the time now widely throughout this people. And, indeed, let each examine himself eagerly and not put it off all too long. But lo! in God's name, let us do as is needful for us, save ourselves as we best can, lest we all perish together.

There was a historian in the times of the Britons, called Gildas,[3] who wrote about their misdeeds, how with their sins they angered God so excessively that finally he allowed the army of the English to conquer their land and to destroy the host of the Britons entirely. And that came about, according to what he said,[4] through robbery by the powerful, and through the coveting of ill-gotten gains, through the lawlessness of the people and through unjust judgments, through the sloth[5] of the bishops and the wicked cowardice of God's messengers, who mumbled with their jaws where they should have cried aloud; also through the foul wantonness of the people and through gluttony and manifold sins they destroyed their country and themselves they perished. But let us do as is necessary for us, take warning from such; and it is true what I say, we know worse deeds among the English than we have heard of anywhere among the Britons; and therefore it is very necessary for us to take thought for ourselves and to intercede eagerly with God himself. And let us do as is necessary for us, turn to the right and in some measure leave wrong-doing, and atone very zealously for what we have done amiss;[6] and let us love God and follow God's laws and perform very eagerly what we promised when we received baptism, or those who were our advocates at our baptism; and let us order our words and deeds rightly, and eagerly cleanse our thoughts, and keep carefully oath and pledge, and have some loyalty between us without deceit. And let us often consider the great Judgment to which we all must come, and save ourselves from the surging fire of hell torment, and earn for ourselves the glories and the joys which God has prepared for those who do his will in the world. God help us. Amen.

[1] Wulfstan used the word 'valkyries', but it is clear from the context that it does not here refer to a goddess or supernatural being. It originally meant 'choosers of the slain'. It is used in Old English to gloss classical names, e.g. the Furies, a Gorgon, Bellona and even Venus.

[2] MS. E adds: "and thieves and injurers of the people and breakers of pledges and treaties".

[3] See No. 151, pp. 590–595. Much of this paragraph is translated literally from a passage in one of Alcuin's letters written after the sack of Lindisfarne by the Danes in 793 (Dümmler, No. 17).

[4] MS. E adds: "through breach of rule by the clergy and breach of law by the laity".

[5] MS. E adds: "and folly".

[6] MS.C adds: "Let us kneel to Christ and with a trembling heart invoke him frequently and gain his mercy."

INDEX

INDEX TO TEXTS

The figures refer to the numbered documents. In the few cases when, for the sake of clarity, it has been found necessary to add a page reference, this has been placed within parentheses.

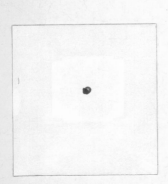